FORD MADOX FORD

FORD MADOX FORD

A DUAL LIFE

VOLUME II
THE AFTER-WAR WORLD

Adult lives were cut sharply into three sections—pre-war, war,
and post-war. It is curious—perhaps not so curious—but many
people will tell you that whole areas of their pre-war lives have
become obliterated from their memories. Pre-war seems like pre-
history.

(Richard Aldington, *Death of a Hero*)

The world before the war is one thing and must be written about
in one manner; the after-war world is quite another and calls for
quite different treatment.

(Ford to T. R. Smith, 27 July 1931)

Max Saunders

Oxford   New York
OXFORD UNIVERSITY PRESS
1996

Oxford University Press, Walton Street, Oxford OX2 6DP

Oxford New York
Athens Auckland Bangkok Bogota Bombay
Buenos Aires Calcutta Cape Town Dar es Salaam
Delhi Florence Hong Kong Istanbul Karachi
Kuala Lumpur Madras Madrid Melbourne
Mexico City Nairobi Paris Singapore
Taipei Tokyo Toronto
and associated companies in
Berlin Ibadan

Oxford is a trade mark of Oxford University Press

British Library Cataloguing in Publication Data
Data available

Library of Congress Cataloging in Publication Data
Data available
ISBN 0-19-212608-3

1 3 5 7 9 10 8 6 4 2

Typeset by Best-set Typesetter Ltd., Hong Kong
Printed in Great Britain
on acid-free paper by
Biddles Ltd.
Guildford and King's Lynn

To Janice Biala

ACKNOWLEDGEMENTS

Once again I am happy to record my gratitude to Janice Biala, both for allowing me to quote freely from Ford's published and unpublished writing, and also for the conversations and letters in which she has given such a vivid sense of Ford's life in the 1930s. As the most important witness to his last years, her help was particularly valuable for this volume, which is duly dedicated to her.

The indispensable collection of Ford's papers at Cornell University has now been relocated in the new Carl A. Kroch Library. Mark Dimunation and his staff have again been extremely helpful, and I should once again like to record my gratitude to the Division of Rare and Manuscript Collections of Cornell University Library for permission to quote from its collection, and to Lucy B. Burgess for all her friendly assistance.

Princeton University Library and the Beinecke Rare Book and Manuscript Library of Yale University hold the other major collections. I am again grateful to the librarians of both for copying material for me, and for allowing me to quote from it.

Most of the other individuals and institutions thanked in the preceding volume also helped with this one. The acknowledgements in Volume I should thus be taken to cover this volume too. Most of those named here helped specifically with this volume. I am very grateful for information and assistance from: W. T. Bandy; Martin Beisly of Christie's, London; C. M. Brain; Montagu Bream; Cleanth Brooks; Dr Andrew Brown, Cambridge University Press; Dr Iain G. Brown, National Library of Scotland; Tom Carter; Sir Tobias and Lady Clarke; Alfred Cohen; Clare Crankshaw; Carla Davidson; Oliver Davies; Nick Dennys; Monroe Engel; Charles Fenn; Hugh Ford; Vita Fortunati; Raymond Gadke; Richard Garnett; Graham Greene; Robert Hampson; Areta Hautman of King Alfred School; Christopher Hawtree; Dr Anton Willhelm Hüffer; Philip Horne; Bruce Hunter; Neville Jason; Martien Kappers; Mrs P. Karet of University College School; Louise Kennelly; Jerry Kuehl; Robert Langenfeld; Robie Macauley; Warren Magnussen; Paul Metcalf; Naomi Mitchison; Ray Monk; Francesca Oakley; Leonée Ormond; John Postgate; Sita Schutt; Willis A. Selden; Tiggy Sharland; Oliver Soskice; Virgil Thomson; Nora Tomlinson; Ulysses Bookshop; Laura Verplank; Janet Wallace; Fred Wegener; Joan Winterkorn; J. Joseph Wisdom, Librarian of St Paul's Cathedral; and Francis Wyndham.

I am also grateful to the following libraries and institutions for their help: Joseph Regenstein Library, University of Chicago; the Librarian of St Joseph's Church, Avenue Hoche, Paris; the Mansell Collection; the National Library of Scotland; the New York Public Library; New York University; the Library, University of Reading; and the Witt Library, Courtauld Institute of Art.

To the following I am grateful not only for assistance but for permission to quote unpublished material: Diana Athill, for permission to quote from a letter to Arthur Mizener; the estate of W. H. Auden, for a quotation from a letter; Janice Biala, for permission to quote from some of her own letters and manuscripts; The British Library, for quotations from unpublished Conrad letters; Rare Book and Manuscript Library, Joseph Regenstein Library, the University of Chicago; James

Brown Associates Archives, Rare Book and Manuscript Library, Columbia University; the Trustees of the Estate of Joseph Conrad; Clare Crankshaw, for quotations from letters by Edward Crankshaw; the estate of Theodore Dreiser; the Trustees of the Thomas Hardy Memorial Collection in the Dorset County Museum, Dorchester, Dorset; Mrs Valerie Eliot, for quotations from T. S. Eliot; Charles Fenn; The Society of Authors as the Literary Representative of the Estate of John Galsworthy; Richard Garnett, for a quotation from Edward Garnett; the estate of Caroline Gordon; the estate of Graham Greene; David Higham Associates; The House of Lords Record Office; The Huntington Library; The Harry Ransom Humanities Research Center, Austin, Texas; Rare Book and Special Collections Library, University of Illinois at Urbana-Champaign; Alexander James, Esq., for quotations from Henry James; John Lamb, for quotations from Katherine Lamb, Elsie Hueffer, and Dr William Martindale; the estate of Paul Nash; the McCormick Library of Special Collections, Northwestern University; Oxford University Press, Inc., New York, for quotations from its files; Olivet College Library; University Research Library, UCLA; A. P. Watt Ltd. on behalf of the Literary Executors of the Estate of H. G. Wells; Mrs Caroline White, for permission to quote from Olive Garnett's diary; the estate of William Carlos Williams; Francis Wyndham, for quotations from Jean Rhys; and Theodora Zavin.

For permission to reproduce photographs I am grateful to: Janice Biala; Tom Carter; the Division of Rare and Manuscript Collection, Cornell University Library; Culver Pictures; John Quinn Memorial Collection, Rare Books and Manuscripts Division, The New York Public Library, Astor, Lenox, and Tilden Foundations; Princeton University Library; Oliver Soskice; and the Beinecke Rare Book and Manuscript Library, Yale University.

Earlier versions of parts of this book have appeared as part of the introduction to the Everyman library edition of *The Good Soldier*, 'A Life in Writing: Ford Madox Ford's Dispersed Autobiographies', *Antæus*, 56 (Spring, 1986), 47–69, and 'Duality, Reading, and Art in Ford's Last Novels', *Contemporary Literature*, 30/2 (Summer, 1989), 299–320 (published by the University of Wisconsin Press). I am grateful to the editors and publishers for permission to include considerably revised versions here.

For permission to quote I should also like to thank the following publishers and copyright holders: the Wyndham Lewis Estate and the Calder Educational Trust, London, for excerpts from Wyndham Lewis's *Blasting and Bombardiering*, copyright © The Wyndham Lewis Estate 1937, 1967 and 1982; Carcanet Press Ltd., for excerpts from *The Ford Madox Ford Reader*, ed. Sondra J. Stang; Robert Secor and Marie Secor, and *English Literary Studies*, for excerpts from the Secors' *The Return of the Good Soldier: Ford Madox Ford and Violet Hunt's 1917 Diary*; Faber and Faber (Publishers) Ltd., for excerpts from *Pound/Ford: The Story of a Literary Friendship*, ed. Brita Lindberg-Seyersted; and Robert Lowell, 'Ford Madox Ford' (from *History*); HarperCollins Publishers, for excerpts from Stella Bowen's *Drawn from Life*, and Arthur Mizener's *The Saddest Story*; Louisiana State University Press, for excerpts from *The Southern Mandarins: Letters of Caroline Gordon to Sally Wood, 1924–1937*, ed. Sally Wood; New Directions Pub. Corp., for excerpts from William Carlos Williams's *Collected Poems 1939–62*. Copyright by William Carlos Williams; Penguin Books Ltd., for excerpts from Jean Rhys, *Quartet*; University of Pennsylvania Press, for excerpts from *The Presence of Ford Madox Ford*, ed. Sondra J. Stang; Laurence Pollinger Ltd., for excerpts from Arthur Mizener, *The Saddest Story*. Laurence Pollinger Ltd. and the Estate of Frieda Lawrence Ravagli, for permission to quote from *The Letters of D. H. Lawrence*, ed. James T. Boulton. Princeton University Press, for excerpts from *Letters of Ford Madox Ford*, ed. Richard M. Ludwig. Copyright © 1965 by Princeton University Press, renewed 1993.

CONTENTS

LIST OF ILLUSTRATIONS

Between pages 290 and 291

I

1916: THE SOMME AND SHELL-SHOCK

The imaginative artist like every other proper man owes a twofold duty—to his art, his craft, his vocation, and then to his State.

(Ford, 'Hands Off the Arts', *American Mercury*, April 1935)

Second Lieutenant Ford Madox Hueffer arrived in France that summer of 1916, the artist expecting soon to become the stuff to fill graveyards. The Welsh soldiers sang on the river-boat that took them up the Seine to Rouen. Ford later recalled the vision of the local bourgeois turned out in their Sunday best to watch them from the river banks as the most moving of the war, because the majority of the soldiers would be dead in six days time in Mametz Wood. When the boat reached Croisset, the captain or pilot astounded Ford by his knowledge of Flaubert, pointing out his house, and saying that he too had hoped for English help during the Franco-Prussian War. At the base camp in Rouen Ford and his fellow members of the Welch Regiment were attached to the 9th Battalion, and left Rouen on 18 July to join their units. Ford still had not heard where he would be sent, though he thought it would be 'presumably in the front line'. He wrote to his daughters at the convent, St Leonards-on-Sea, what he probably imagined would be his last letter (squeezed on to an army letter-card), hoping to regain their sympathy:

My dear Kids
I am just going up to the firing line—so that seems a proper moment to write to you both—though I do not seem to have much to say—Or rather, I have so much that it w^d be no use beginning. So take it all as said. I was looking thro' the dedication of the book called Ancient Lights that I wrote for you, the other day. I don't think I want to change it or add to it. Read it again yourselves if anything happens to me. You know I have always loved you both very, very dearly—but I c^d not wrangle for you. I took the Commun[ion] this morning & prayed for you both. Pray for me.[1]

When Christina sent the original to Katharine in 1969 she did not remember having seen it before. If she had, perhaps she would not have felt so strongly that Ford was indifferent to her ('I have always had such an inferiority complex myself that it never occurred to me that anything I did mattered to him at all').

Ford's friend and fellow officer Timothy Sugrue described him as 'a big, florid, heavy, unhealthy looking man of about 40 and in 1916 rather old for a junior infantry officer': 'He was most anxious to obtain front line experience (and no doubt inspiration) but Colonel Cooke, the then C.O., would not allow him, on account of his age, to go up to the front with the men much to H's disappointment.'[2] Instead he was stationed with the battalion transport, near Bécourt Wood, just behind the front line near Albert. This was at the bottom of 'Sausage Valley' (named after the German observation balloons hanging over it) in which the 9th Welch had seen heavy losses during the grisly battle of Mametz Wood, and the Allied attempts to advance up the valley to La Boisselle. The battle of the Somme had begun on 1 July. The heaviest fighting took place on the first day, when the British Army suffered the blackest day in its history: almost 60,000 casualties, over 21,000 of whom were killed in battle or died of wounds. By the time the battle ended on 14 November the Allied casualties exceeded 600,000, of whom over 400,000 were British. The German losses were as heavy. The shelling was still intense by the end of July, as Ford wrote to Lucy Masterman on the 28th:

We are right up in the middle of the strafe, but only with the 1st line transport. We get shelled two or three times a day, otherwise it is fairly dull—indeed, being shelled is fairly dull, after the first once or twice. Otherwise it is all very interesting—filling in patches of one's knowledge [. . .] The noise of the bombardment is continuous—so continuous that one gets used to it, as one gets used to the noise in a train and the ear picks out the singing of the innumerable larks. . . .[3]

Being out of the front-line trenches didn't mean being out of danger. The battalion transport was generally two or three miles behind the Front, within range of the big guns. As Alan Judd explains, the view that Ford spent all his time 'behind the line' and afterwards 'grossly inflated his own role' is misleading; and also ignorant: 'being behind the line did not mean that one was not involved in the action. The great majority of troops at any time were behind the front line and many never saw it at all.' Whereas a transport officer would have had to make regular supply runs up to the Front, 'often along routes that were singled out for shelling'. Ford wrote of 'the process of the eternal waiting that is War'; and, as Judd remarks, the routines and the waiting were many men's 'predominant experience of war'. Later Ford said he began translating *The Good Soldier* into French 'in Bécourt-Bécordel wood in July 1916'.[4]

Either later on in the day he described the bombardment to Lucy Masterman, or the next day, he was 'blown into the air by something'—a high-explosive shell—and landed on his face, concussed and with a damaged mouth and loosened teeth. The concussion erased whole patches of his knowledge: 'I had completely lost my memory so that [. . .] three weeks of my life are completely dead to me.' He even forgot his own name for thirty-six hours. His teeth became 'very bad', affecting his 'whole condition'. When the battalion went into rest camp he applied to the medical officer for treatment. 'He sent me in an ambulance to a Field Ambulance', Ford told Masterman: 'the F.A. sent me to C.[asualty] C.[learing] S.[tation] 36; C.C.S. 36 had no appliances for treating me & sent me back to the F.A.; the F.A. sent me to C.C.S. wh. had no appliances for treating me, & ordered me to report to H.Q. of the 4th Army.'[5] In one of his last books he remembered the harrowing fears and confusions of the aftermath:

after I was blown up at Bécourt-Bécordel in '16 and, having lost my memory, lay in the Casualty Clearing Station in Corbie, with the enemy planes dropping bombs all over it and the dead Red Cross nurses being carried past my bed, I used to worry agonizedly about what my name could be—and have a day-nightmare [. . .] I thought I had been taken prisoner by the enemy forces and was lying on the ground, manacled hand and foot . . . and with the enemy, ignoring me for the time, doing dreadful stunts—God knows what—all around me. . . . Immense shapes in grey-white *cagoules* and shrouds, miching and mowing and whispering horrible plans to one another!

As Arthur Mizener rightly notes of this passage: 'Out of these horrors he made Christopher Tietjens' nightmare of forgetting.' Ford combines the forgetting of his name with another incident that occurred at Corbie: 'When I was in hospital a man three beds from me died *very* hard, blood pouring thro' bandages & he himself crying perpetually, "Faith! Faith! Faith!" It was very disagreeable as long as he had a chance of life—but one lost all interest and forgot him when one heard he had none.'[6] In *Some Do Not . . .* the wounded man rolls out of his bed, comes over to Tietjens and tries to strangle him:

He let out a number of ear-piercing shrieks and lots of orderlies came and pulled him off me and sat all over him. Then he began to shout '*Faith!*' He shouted: 'Faith! . . . Faith! . . . Faith! . . .' at intervals of two seconds, as far as I could tell by my pulse, until four in the morning, when he died. . . . I don't know whether it was a religious exhortation or a woman's name, but I disliked him a good deal because he started my tortures, such as they were. . . . There had been a girl I knew called Faith. Oh, not a love affair: the daughter of my father's head gardener, a Scotsman. The point is that every time he said Faith I asked myself 'Faith . . . Faith what?' I couldn't remember the name [. . .]. (p. 212)

The orderlies save Tietjens from strangulation, but they cannot restore the stability, the identity, of his orderly world of country house hierarchy. The doubling of the forgotten names conveys how it is not only Tietjens who will not be the same, but also his whole society. The version in the novel—and it is typical of Ford's gift for seizing on the given and elaborating its significances—adds to the scene the melodramatic menace and violence of nightmare. In its context it is the entirely appropriate image for otherwise incommunicable shocks to the physical and moral senses. The unobtrusive detail of the pulse suggests that it is also Tietjens's life which is being threatened, challenged by the cry of humanity delivered with mechanical regularity. The shouting makes Tietjens ask himself 'Faith what?' But for Tietjens, wondering what his life has amounted to, and what it will be like after the war, the question is also 'Faith *in* what?' Should he govern his life by religious values, or the exhortations of desire? These are Ford's questions too, and they take us back to *The Good Soldier* as well as forwards into Ford's post-war life.

The later reminiscence of the hospital (in *Mightier Than the Sword*) goes back still earlier. Not only does the horror of the experience go into the making of *Parade's End*, but, as Ford later came to recognize, the form that experience took itself came out of his childhood fears. Once again, at its most charged moments his writing reaches back to his formative experiences, and to his earlier writings about them:

It has only just occurred to me that that Corbie-phobia of my middle years must have taken at least its shape from my childhood's dreads. I might well, I mean, have had as my chief dread in those white huts surmounted with the Red Cross, the fear of being taken prisoner by the Germans—but I doubt if my imagined Germans would have taken just that gigantic miching and mowing shape if it hadn't been for the nature of my childhood's ambience. I was then horribly imbued by those people with a sense of my Original Sin so that I used to have innumerable fears when the candle was put out. . . . But that was the worst of all . . . the dread that Mr. Ruskin or Mr. Carlyle or Mr. Holman Hunt—or even Herr Richard Wagner!—should with their dreadful eyes come into a room where I was alone and where there was no other exit . . . and, fixing me with their dreadful, shining eyes . . . God knows what then. . . . (pp. 265–6)

That 'God knows' suggests that the transfixing eyes are the sight of God, passing judgement on the sinful child. 'Faith!' has a more than merely figurative significance for Ford at Corbie.

It was Charlotte the housemaid who allayed his fears of 'the awful, monumental, minatorily bearded tumultuous and moral Great of those days' with narrative, humanizing them through tales of their foibles and exploits: 'The great seen from the linen room were thus diminished for me [. . .] Insupportably moral they were, and I imagine the sense of original sin that in those days possessed me in their presences would have overwhelmed me altogether but for the moral support that the anecdotes in the linen room afforded me.'[7] The stories give Ford moral support against the insupportably moral; and in telling the story about the stories, he is contemplating a possible source of his own anecdotal energies; registering how narrative can master fear and menace, offering psychological protection. In an unpublished essay on 'Great Writers', written soon after the war, he suggests that his childhood sense of sin came from his failure to enjoy the writings of the moral Great. Thus he is also analysing the origins of the kind of writer he has become: someone who opposes moral intimidation by humanizing anecdote.[8]

So, at Corbie when the candle of his intellect and sanity seemed to have all but gone out—indeed when his life had nearly ended—his mind prevented itself from being overwhelmed by going back over his past life. Unable to remember himself, can he have faith in his own identity? With three weeks simply erased from his life, can he believe in himself as a continuous person? His shell-shock duplicated the question of dual identity that had already been his subject in books like *The Young Lovell* and *The Good Soldier*.

When Dowell in *The Good Soldier* amazes himself by saying, without being conscious of it, that Florence's suicide leaves him free to marry Nancy, he comments: 'It is as if one had a dual personality, the one I being entirely unconscious of the other' (p. 123). This dual personality makes Dowell Edward's double too, for earlier the same evening Ashburnham also recognizes and expresses his unconscious passion for Nancy as he speaks to her in the 'dark park' outside the Casino. The manuscript originally emphasized the doubling of the two passions, but even with the explicit connection deleted, the similarity is unmistakable. The deleted passage is restored in italics:

And then, it appears, something happened to Edward Ashburnham—*something very similar to what happened to me a little[?] later in the same evening. As far as I can make it out the other half of his dual personality spoke—to the girl.* He assured me—and I see no reason for disbelieving him—that until that moment he had had no idea whatever of caring for the girl. He said that he had regarded her exactly as he would have regarded a daughter. He certainly loved her, but with a very deep, very tender and very tranquil love [. . .] But of more than that he had been totally unconscious.[9]

The sudden realization that he too loves Nancy is only one example of how Dowell comes to see himself as following Edward: 'In my fainter sort of way I seem to perceive myself following the lines of Edward Ashburnham. I suppose that I should really like to be a polygamist; with Nancy, and with Leonora, and with Maisie Maidan and possibly even with Florence. I am no doubt like every other man; only, probably because of my American origin I am fainter' (p. 272). However, when he shifts from saying he is 'like' Ashburnham, to his culminating declaration that he *is* the other man ('I can't conceal from myself the fact that I loved Edward Ashburnham—and that I love him because he was just myself' (p. 291)), his exaggeration provokes a dual response: a sceptical assent. Dowell's words seem to reveal his passion for Edward to him rather as Edward's speech brings his feelings for Nancy into consciousness. And yet in most other ways he is so unlike Edward (not least in not being loved by any of the book's women) that his claim to identity sounds risible—or ironic—at the same time as it sounds plausible and heartfelt.

The problem of identity and identification dominates Ford's writing from *A Call* onwards: notably in the series of autobiographies, and in the late novels of doubles and mistaken identities. The increasing importance of Arthur Marwood has also been recognized. Marwood's death impressed him more profoundly than any since those of his father and grandfather. Ford started writing elegiacally about him immediately after the war, and implicitly acknowledged him as the most significant source for the character of Tietjens when he wrote in the prefatory letter to *No More Parades*: 'Even then—it must have been in September, 1916, when I was in a region called the Salient, and I remember the very spot where the idea came to me—I said to myself: How would all this look in the eyes of X . . .—already dead, along with all English Tories?' (p. 7). This was soon enough after his discharge from hospital to indicate that he was probably thinking about Marwood at Corbie too. Thomas Moser argues that 'Marwood, in dying, would save Ford's life by making possible Ford's mad and detailed imitation of the man'.[10] But the implications that Ford could not have lived if Marwood hadn't died, that he wasn't already imitating him before his death, and that Ford ever stopped being an artist rather than a convalescent country gentleman are themselves absurd. There is a difference between the pious wishfulness of imagining a close friend as still alive, and the pathology of thinking you have become them. There is evidence that his thoughts about identity and exchange have an even more significant source in Ford's own narrow escape from death, when he was almost hit by a shell only two-and-a-half months after Marwood's death. It is not just that the near coincidence of dates may have prompted thoughts about why it was that he had been reprieved and Marwood had not. The first prose he wrote after the war, which has been neglected by his critics and biographers, indicates that the concussion and resulting 'shell-shock' radically disturbed Ford's sense of identity.

An unpublished fragment, 'True Love & a G.C.M.', sheds revealing light on how the experience of shell-shock forced Ford back to his childhood memories. It was written between September 1918 and March 1919, and shows how he was connecting overwhelming dread with bearded and looming Germanic figures soon after his experiences at Corbie. This intriguing work describes Gabriel Morton's partial recuperation from shell-shock, his fears for his fragile sanity, and his post-war alienation from both the army and society. One reason for its abandonment is probably that the

105 pages of manuscript make little progress towards describing either the 'True Love'—Morton's affair with a married woman, Hilda Cohen—or the 'G.C.M.'—General Court Martial.[11]

The other reason why Ford may not have wanted to complete and publish the novel is precisely the reason why it is of such biographic interest. It is an extremely candid, largely autobiographical work. It is not only his most immediate effort to render the anxieties of war, but it also promises to become one of his more successful treatments of a relationship between father and son. His little contact with his own father gets reflected in the way fathers tend to be marginal, or replaced by surrogates, in his novels. (Henry Martin, driven partly by his father to attempt suicide in *The Rash Act*, is a rare exception.) However, it is as if once the book reached a point at which it could only become more revelatory, more self-analytic, and more intensely filial, Ford broke off. What he was able to salvage from it re-surfaces in Jethro Croyd's wartime experiences in another unpublished (though complete) novel, 'Mr Croyd'; as Tietjens's shell-shock; and in the psychological explorations of hauntingly significant memories in *No Enemy*.[12]

After he had written most of *Parade's End* he recalled: 'As soon as the war was over I wrote a novel. But when I came to read it over I found that I had been writing like a madman. The book was not readable. I suppressed it.' If Ford is referring to 'True Love & a G.C.M.' here, there is one passage in particular which suggests what he might have later found it necessary to suppress: 'He would wonder if his mind differed in its action from that of other men—but he never had the courage to ask other men. He never had the courage because he suspected that it might mean that he was a little mad—it might be a symptom of brain disease; so that if he revealed it by questions to others it might be put about that he had queer brain symptoms.'[13] One of the mental actions he is worrying about here is the panic that results from military action—and more disconcertingly, from periods of inaction in the line. As he was discovering, it was 'that eternal "waiting to report" that takes up 112/113ths of one's time during war'. (Compare the refrain of Wilfred Owen's poem 'Exposure': 'But nothing happens'; much of the writing about the Front is perplexed by the different ways in which 'nothing' can happen.) 'There will be no man who survives of His Majesty's Armed Forces', Ford wrote later, 'that shall not remember those eternal hours when Time itself stayed still as the true image of bloody War! . . .' The emphasis on 'courage' stresses the related, but more shaming fear that the other men would think him cowardly. In all his war prose Ford writes penetratingly about the battle to square the conventional image of stiff-upper-lip resilience and nonchalance with the overwhelming eruptions of uncontrollable panic. He is acutely sensitive to the war's undermining of conventional assumptions about what made for courage, manliness, or cowardice: 'The most you could afford to say as to your mental state was that you had got the wind up like Hell. You could say that to any extent; indeed it was an assertion of courage to be able to say with extravagant emphasis that you *had* got the wind frightfully up on occasions. It meant you had been in the devil of a tight place.'[14]

No Enemy recounts—with extravagant emphasis—a moment when Gringoire, Ford's *alter ego*, got the wind frightfully up by mistake. 'He thought the bottom of Hell had dropped out. It was his worst shock of the war. I shouldn't wonder if it were not the worst shock any one ever had between the 4/8/14 and the 28/6/19.' An extravagant claim indeed about that multitudinously shocking war. What caused the shock? While Gringoire is dozing in a dug-out, a gun-wheel caught its spokes in the corrugated iron roof, lifted it, and dropped it again. Something like this probably happened to Ford; and the extravagant emphasis is battling against the knowledge that no form of words can reproduce that terror of crashing awake to what you think must be your death. Gringoire tells the story 'because it probably accounted for his imme-diately subsequent exultation; it was, I suppose, so good to be just alive after that'. The subsequent exultation almost certainly happened to Ford too before he was blown up at Bécourt, and is another example of the strange mental states that constant fear can produce. Gringoire walks downhill through the thistles 'with immense, joyful strides':

And an innumerable company of swallows flew round him, waist high, just brushing the thistledown. 'They were so near,' Gringoire said, 'that they brushed my hands, and they extended so far that I could see nothing else. It is one of the five things of the war that I really see, for it was like walking, buoyantly, in the pellucid sunlight, waist-high through a sea of unsurpassed and unsurpassable azure. I felt as if I were a Greek god. It was like a miracle.[15]

No Enemy's impressionist psychology of war is organized around these five visions of landscapes and people. Characteristically, Ford's feelings are refracted through litera-ture, and combine his reading of W. H. Hudson watching thistledown, Gilbert White watching birds, and St Francis communing with them. It was, perhaps, the first of several intimations that he had escaped the death he expected and dreaded. That exultation is the sign of a reincarnation. 'It would be interesting to know what that class of feeling comes from', speculates the narrator: 'possibly from some sort of atavistic throwback to the days when the gods were nearer.' It also became a focal moment in *Parade's End*, when Marwood's reincarnation, Christopher Tietjens, has a similar vision of the blue of swallows' backs: an omen of his ability to assert his own powers in the world. In a later novel, *The Rash Act*, Ford's hero takes a boat out to sea intending to commit suicide; but he is caught in a storm, and instinctively saves himself from death. Ford himself may have been surprised on the Western Front by how much stronger was his unconscious desire for self-preservation than his desire for death.[16]

Much of his war fiction has at its heart the experience and survival of fear, including fear of fear and fear of cowardice. Samuel Putnam reported one of Ford's war remin-iscences of the late 1920s as an example of how the 'born story-teller' 'carried his fictionizing over into real life':

'I remember,' he is saying. 'It was in No Man's Land. We were making a night attack. I had gone ahead to reconnoiter. I was crawling along on my—er—stomach when suddenly, above the roar of battle, I heard a sound—it was larks singing. Then I looked up and saw that it was light as day. From the bursting shells, y'know. The larks had seen the light and thought it was morning.'[17]

When Putnam told Aldington the story, they thought they saw the light of Ford's larks. 'Richard bellowed. "Just imagine!" he exclaimed. "Just imagine Ford crawling anywhere on that stomach of his!"' Ford's written stories are all so much subtler than his conversational ones (usually reported in order to satirize him), so one must be wary here. Ford isn't likely to have been sent on a night attack. He was responsible for bringing new drafts up to the line, and helping with administrative duties such as billeting and supplies. If he was on a night raid, he is unlikely to have been sent ahead. The 'y'know' doesn't sound very authentic; Putnam may have exaggerated details himself when recalling the story twenty years after he heard it. Ford's stomach had become more exaggerated than his reminiscence here. Even if he did reshape his war-experiences into this kind of conventional front-line heroics—and the evidence of *No Enemy* suggests he didn't—it's significant that even such a story as this has its basis in an eerier story in 'True Love & a G.C.M.' that probably does have a basis in fact. Gabriel Morton has been sent with three men to take a sample of the German wire in No Man's Land. He is apprehensive that he might 'put his hand, when he was creeping, into something nasty':

Once, on the high land behind La Boisselle he had dropped on his hands and knees amongst the six-foot high, dusty thistles, to avoid the burst of a shrapnel shell—and he had stuck his hand right into a dead, putrid, Hun's ribs. He didn't want to do it again—in the dark. It was very dark the rain stopped; it was extraordinarily still. There did not seem to have been a sound for hours since a machine gun, to the right, had stopped some slumberous ejaculations like snores. But when he looked at the watch on his wrist only two minutes had gone by since then. He jumped to his feet and said 'Hell! Oh Hell!' and his heart beat fifty to the minute and he felt sick. It was because there had been a loud rustle just under his invisible left hand. A bird had got up from a tuft in the darkness and fluttered away. He caught a glimpse of it against the pale sky—for there were some Very lights going up sleepily away towards Messines and in consequence there was a pale glow on the sky in that direction [. . .] What the devil was a skylark doing there; frightening you out of your wits.

Though the psychological truths of 'True Love & a G.C.M.' sound autobiographical, it was to be a novel, and the wire-gathering party may not have included Ford. The other experiences could easily have been his: corpses, bombardments, and larks were all common elements of trench life; the detail of being more frightened by the bird than the guns is a typically plausible Fordian paradox. The story he told Putnam is an only slightly reimagined version of this episode. It isn't just that the surprise and fear are rendered so convincingly, but that the episode is exactly the kind of haunting impression that Ford tried to unperplex himself by writing out, and that he had been reliving as he wrote *Parade's End* and revised *No Enemy*. Who is to say that something like it did not happen? Certainly not Aldington, or whoever told Putnam that Ford's wartime duties had been 'largely confined to the liaison service in Paris'. His manner often provoked people to want to deflate him, cut him down to size: but their pur-ported 'corrections' were often further from the truth than Ford's improbable stories. And who is to say whether he had become deluded into believing the truth of his own fiction; or whether, having reimagined the episode again in *Parade's End*, he wanted to test out the plausibility of his fiction on a live listener?[18]

The hero of a later story tells his wife: 'I do not conceal from you that I was an arrant coward'; to which she replies: 'Oh, *Douglas*! . . . But you've got decorations and things, haven't you?'[19] The war brought volunteers and civilians to recognize what good soldiers have always known: bravery—conduct deserving decoration—is more a question of understanding fear than of denying it. Ford is rendering his own time in terms of his own time; but he is simultaneously exploring the impact made by the war on his understanding of himself, his imagination, and his being as a writer. In *Mightier Than the Sword*, for example, he shifts straight from the ordeal of his Corbie-phobia to thinking about writers and madness, recalling what Cocteau said about Victor Hugo: 'That man's mad. He thinks he's Victor Hugo.' It is a remark intended to shock us all into thinking we might be mad not to realize the duality of our own identities, and to believe that we are who we are said to be. This is the other mental idiosyncrasy that the war makes Ford reassess—one that is fundamental to his writing. It is the basis of his Impressionism: his sense of mental duality—that 'we are almost always in one place with our minds somewhere quite other'.[20]

The disorientating intensity of his reveries during the war made the psychological implications more pressing. In 'True Love & a G.C.M.' Gabriel is perplexed by the force of his visions of his past:

It was sometimes startling—it was sometimes, indeed, even a little alarming to him—to notice how much these things were the real things to him, whilst what was actually going on round him was hardly even apparent. Indeed, in Red Cross Hospital No II, he asked himself once or twice if he wasn't a little mad—if he hadn't been a little mad all his life. He lay there, for long periods, sometimes quite alone—and he thought a great deal, and generally about his own past.

His past came back to him in waves. It came back to him in waves of an extraordinary intensity; it was as if they took hold of him and overwhelmed him [. . .]

The realization that his life is continuous—continuously imaginative—is also a realization that it is continuously present. For in his books of reminiscence, Ford's remembering becomes this type of vivid imagining: more real than the things around him, and more real than even the things remembered, which get reimagined as he recalls them. This movement of mind, looking back from a present predicament to its past prefiguration, is entirely characteristic. The psychological effects of war trigger off meditations about the history of Morton's mental life. Ford comments on Gabriel's mental doubleness: 'His mind—which always worked in double pictures—gave him at once a double picture.'[21] His experiences don't have the playfulness of Ford's own childhood imaginings; they are more like immobilizing or depersonalizing trances. Such visionary seizures are not entirely attributable to the effects of war, as Morton realizes. Their precursors in Ford's fiction are Sorrell's hallucinatory impressions of the fourteenth century, or the Young Lovell's visions of the White Lady. But the war not only gave him different kinds of visions, but made it possible for him to approach them less through historical fantasy, myth, and romance, and more through psychological realism. Ford had always thought a great deal about his own past, and had written about it before the war. But after the war his writing was to become increasingly, and more searchingly, autobiographical.

Rather than transporting Gabriel to other worlds, letting him escape from himself, his visions take him back to formative and revelatory moments of his past. One scene in particular recurs: 'And then, suddenly, and more clearly than had ever happened to him before, he found himself again in the Library' (pp. 18–19). The library, for Ford as well as for Gabriel, is indeed the place where he discovers his identity: finds his self.

Gabriel is given the run of his father's library from an early age, but his mother is anxious about the possible consequences: 'there are books—and books!' (p. 11). The manuscript is explicit about the influence of his reading upon him. Also in the library is a painting by Burne-Jones which haunts both father and son, of a woman in an olive tree, holding a mysterious fruit—an apple, perhaps, or a lemon or shaddock; 'or even a pomegranate' (p. 14). This Eve or Persephone figure is doubled by another vision of Gabriel's, this time of his father transfixed by the sight of a different woman, described in even more highly sexualized language—a Pre-Raphaelite Pandora, complete with ominous box:

One day he saw him leaning a little back on his feet, looking with half closed eyes at a very beautiful woman, with frizzy black hair parted in the middle, with red lips and a great throat, standing against an immense black lacquer cabinet on which the scarlet of conventionalised peacocks showed like the dripping of blood. Then he knew his father for the dreamer that he really was [. . .] He seemed to see into his father's mind [. . .] (pp. 21–2)

What he sees is how much he has *not* seen in his visions. 'For it certainly didn't till long after come into his mind [. . .] to imagine that his father coveted the beautiful lady' (pp. 22–3). Once he does realize this, he is able to see into his own mind; and prompted by the thought that he might not survive the war, he recognizes the nature of his own desire: '*He wanted to have a healthy, gay, son by Hilda Cohen . . .*' (p. 88). He is worrying whether he isn't just 'repeating his father—the dreamer who never stretched out his hand to grasp what he wanted' (p. 99). But the recognition marks the beginning of his—and Ford's—ability to liberate himself from his earlier denial of his sexuality. It is a quintessentially Fordian moment: not just because Morton sounds close to the Ford who wrote to Masterman: 'I wish I had a son'; but also because it is the kind of psychological moment on which all his major fiction turns: the coming to the surface of a repressed desire; the thinking the thought which had until then been 'unthinkable'.[22] Ashburnham realizing as he speaks that he is in love with Nancy; Dowell surprising himself by saying that he too wants her; Tietjens allowing himself to recognize that he wants Valentine: these are the turning-points towards which the respective plots have been inching. 'True Love & a G.C.M.' is itself a turning-point in Ford's attitude to sexuality. Before the war desires are recognized in order to be renounced. Max Webb has written well of the centrality of this Jamesian aspect of Ford's earlier art, in which the central character demonstrates a moral superiority, an altruistic nobility, by an act of sacrifice: 'Edward abandons Nancy, and the Fifth Queen "chose" to die rather than compromise herself or her faith.'[23] He argues that *Some Do Not . . .* is 'a Jamesian novel of renunciation', whereas *Parade's End*, the tetralogy as a whole 'modifies the pattern by allowing Christopher to realize that renunciation is sometimes an evasion of life'. Ford had realized this earlier, and so arguably had Ashburnham and Dowell; but the realization cannot save them, either because (like Ashburnham) they cannot live with it, or (as in Dowell's case) it comes too late to be of any good. The tragic impasse of *The Good Soldier* is that both renunciation and enunciation are worse than evasions of life: they are destructions of life. In the post-war writing the heroes live through an unleashed destruction which has a moral and theological as well as a historical significance—'Armageddon'—but they *do* live through it, as through a purgation by fire. Ford had always been interested in the predicament of being 'On the Edge', as he entitled an early story about a man on the verge of running off with another man's wife until he finds that the hypochondriac husband is in fact on the verge of death. Dowell feels on the edge of life in the 'catalepsy' precipitated by Florence's death. The narrator of *The Marsden Case*, Ernest Jessop, has a similar feeling after the war, having emerged from a nerve-cure marking 'the last stage of a mental pilgrimage begun among beastly horrors, lasting for horrible years'. He describes himself as 'one nearly come back into active life'. Like the Young Lovell on the edge of this world's reality, Ashburnham fighting for his life against his desire, Tietjens struggling to retain his sanity, the Fordian hero is 'on the edge': of death, suicide, madness, time.[24] In 'True Love & a G.C.M.' and *Parade's End* the realization of polygamous desire, of repressed sexuality, becomes profoundly ambiguous: something which can incapacitate a man, drive him to the edge of sanity, but also make him want to live again.

In *Parade's End* Morton's self-recognition is rewritten into Tietjens's realization that he loves Valentine Wannop (who is not married, although he, unlike Gabriel, is). But the two elements that Ford abandons (suppresses?) are the coming to terms with the father's sexuality, and—the most characteristically Fordian detail—the curious way this very sexuality is mediated by art: by the books and paintings in the library. Gabriel's original attempts to understand his father are made by reading: 'the first book he had looked at had been a large copy of Men of the Time, to see who his father really was' (p. 20). Both Francis Hueffer and Ford Madox Brown figured in the 1887 edition of *Men of the Time*—a *Who's Who* of its day.[25] After his father's death in 1889 Ford may well have looked into this book to find out who his father really had been. After the death of Gabriel's father in Venice, two trains of thought obsess him. One is a phrase he had read in J. A. Symonds's *Renaissance in Italy* in the library: 'Before committing yourself to any action reflect deeply upon the affair in all its aspects and act along the lines of your most generous impulse!' (p. 102). The other is a phrase of his father's about the 'little village of Apperley', and again Gabriel remembers reading something about the place in *Men of the Time*:

his father's first employment had been the restoration of the Early English Church in the village of Apperley—in either Yorkshire or Durham. No doubt the job had been secured for Gabriel's father by his own father who had been Dean of several dioces[es] is succession but had never risen to the episcopal bench. His mother, of course, had been the daughter of a bishop. No doubt, then, the Dean had insisted on his son's marrying the bishop's daughter, so that he should get more and yet more jobs of restoration . . . And possibly the vicar of Apperley had had a daughter . . . Or perhaps . . . He remembered suddenly how his father had said to him, three months before: 'It's a good thing to keep your eyes in your own boat.' (p. 102)

The fragment does not resolve what actually happened at Apperley, although an affair with the putative vicar's daughter is implied. Presumably he failed to keep his eyes in his own boat, suggesting adultery, or at least polygamous desire once more. It certainly has a bearing on Gabriel's birth, though it is uncertain whether the implication is that he is illegitimate, or that he simply would not have been born if his father had married his 'True Love':

[Gabriel] gathered that, in his father's view, his grandparents had behaved wrongly at some crisis of Morton's father's life [. . .] 'You're sitting there', he had gone on, 'Reading. What? Forming your character. And what ought I to do . . . If things had been different at Apperley . . .' And then he had said, after a long, brooding pause during which his glance seemed to pour over Gabriel like a long caress. 'But then, you wouldn't have been there . . .' And then: 'And I shouldn't have liked you not to be there, my dear!'

These were the last words Gabriel had heard from his father [. . .] (p. 101)

Similarly, the relationship between the two remembered phrases is uncertain. Did the father fail to act along the lines of his most generous impulse, or did he not reflect deeply enough before acting? The point at which the completed first part ends (and Ford only wrote two pages of the remainder) suggests that he did not act at all, but remained transfixed in an aesthetic rapture. It is the strangest part of this work, and a moment which has profound implications for Ford's impressionism. At the moment his father gives the advice about keeping your eyes in your own boat, Gabriel's mind gives him one of its startling double pictures, through someone else's eyes (and, even more enigmatically, of yet another person's eyes):

And all of a sudden, looking deeply into the folds of the heavy maroon window curtains, seated as he was before the great mirror with the gambolling, gilt cupids, Gabriel was going out of the door of a small manor house or a large farm . . . in Apperley in the North. He did not know if it was he or his father [. . .] In front of the door was a stretch of garden, then a little stream running level with the turf on each side; what they call in the North a bank,— a low, long hill, rose up against the sky & on it were silver birch trees, their foliage thin & delicate against the sky. And, in among the birches were a grey dress, a large grey felt hat & two enigmatic, dark eyes. He was standing looking—with hardly any impulse, with hardly any resolution. (pp. 102–3)

As so often in Ford, the double picture is itself something double: both a picture of dual mental processes, and also a picture of the doubleness of the act of imagining— in particular of the action of the imagination which is reading. As Gabriel thinks of the two phrases from the reading which has helped to form his character, he sits in front of window curtains and a mirror. Ford's writing is superbly economical, all of the details being at once precisely specified and intensely suggestive—as it were, double pictures. He is interested in the way experiences—including the experience of read-ing—give the double pictures that the impressionist sees in the window. Like a curtain they can conceal or reveal a view outwards, of 'somewhere quite other', the point of view of another person. Or, like a mirror, they can reflect back a picture of the observer. It is the perfect image of how Ford's prose is both autobiographic and fictional. What needs emphasizing, however, is that although the material Ford treats of in this work is highly charged, bringing together feelings about his father, sexuality, psychology, identity, art, and reading, he never loses his objectivity about them (his 'sense of proportion'). For the investigations are consistently secured to the compel-ling autobiographical questions of who he really is, and, equally important, of how he came to be the writer he really is. Who else would stage a primal scene in a library? The passage about his father and grandfather making careerist marriages considers how family pressures and family history help to form the self. Like Ford, named after his artist-grandfather, Gabriel has been named after Rossetti. But what he remembers best about Rossetti is how he gave his young namesake a book—the volume of picaresque novels Rossetti gave young Ford (p. 28). The familial influence is supplemented by the literary. Heredity is augmented and retraced in imagination.

The two pages of the next part are explicit about the way the war has forced a revaluation of the past. Gabriel, who must be the first chartered accountant as a fictional hero, uses the important Fordian image of 'stocktaking', with its connotations of summing up at the end of a phase. As it might also soon be the end of his life, there are also connotations of the Final Reckoning.

That was how his past life came back to him, in those scenes of strong colours, remembered with strong emotions, though they seemed to be memories of no emotions whatever. And if [. . .] he had as it were indulged in a stocktaking of his individuality, he would have said that that was all he was & that was all he possessed. He was a record—as it were a Gramophone pot-pourri record—of coloured & connected scenes; & all he possessed were just those memories of scenes, highly enough coloured since he recollected with an extreme vividness alike the gilt amorini of the Venetian hotel & the seven, blue, momentarily immobilised stars of Very lights over Kemmel hill & the stretched, slightly agonised eyebrows of Hilda Cohen & the lady in the olive tree holding rather than picking a shaddock—yes, scenes highly enough coloured & vividly remembered, yet connected so very slightly,—since the only connection between them was his almost unknown self. For indeed he felt that *he* hardly existed. . . .

It was almost as if he were invisible—as if he were just a point, a theoretic spot in space; the centre for the things that he saw all round him. If it hadn't been that he had to return salutes he might just as well not have been in existence at all, &, if he had ceased to exist no-one in the wide world would have missed him. He might have gone out then & there, like an extinguished candle &, it seemed to him no-one would have missed him—except, for a minute or so, the limping officer. And the limping officer would merely have thought that Morton had turned suddenly down a side-street.

He had nothing; he was almost nobody. His only possessions, apart from remembrances, seemed to him to be, in a tent in a camp, a disreputable bed, some dirty army blankets which he w^d. have to return to store, a washstand made of a sugar box that supported someone else's tin basin & that contained an old pot of vaseline, some damp army papers &, possibly, a field pocket book or two & an old razor strap.[26]

The self-pity which irrupts here is poignantly evocative of Ford's post-war condition, and suggests a further reason why he felt, during and after the war, that he could not go on. The emotions he was not able to master in 1919 return under magnificent control in *A Man Could Stand Up*— (1926), with Tietjens, bereft of memory and furniture alike; and in *It Was the Nightingale* (1934), when Ford describes himself after demobilization with scarcely more to his name than Morton.

However, Morton's putative 'stocktaking of his individuality' is a crucial moment in Ford's impressionism. All he has—all, psychologically, he *is*—is these disparate clairvoyant memories, loosely connected by 'his almost unknown self'. This comes from a real ontological anxiety brought on by Ford's amnesia: what is the self that holds together the self's memories? The novel becomes a court martial of the self. But Morton's analysis of his identity could also stand as a definition of an impressionist novel, which juxtaposes significant but enigmatic moments ('remembered with strong emotions, though they seemed to be memories of no emotions whatever'), without explicit authorial comment or obtrusive plotting. This is certainly what critics of Fordian impressionism had regularly attacked his books for being. Morton's feeling of near-invisibility strains for pathos (note how the image of the extinguished candle recalls Ford's childhood fears of the dark), but it also makes him the type of the impressionist author, who should be 'sedulous to avoid letting his personality appear in the course of his book. One the other hand, his whole book, his whole poem is merely an expression of his personality.' The 'almost unknown self' that connects the impressions corresponds to the unobtrusive style Ford strives to achieve. The style is the incarnation of the invisible but omnipresent author. Like him, it is paradoxical: you should only be aware of it in an oblique, dual way. Like the image of the window, it is what enables the reader to see the created world, but it superimposes upon that vision a glimpse of your own face, and also of the author's personality: 'a face of a person behind you'.[27]

As the impressionist tries to imagine the lives of others, or even to remember in an objectified form his own past life, his identity begins to fuse with that of the other. The first part of 'True Love & a G.C.M.' ended with Gabriel not knowing whether the subject of his memories 'was he or his father'. When the second part picks up the story by saying 'That was how his past life came back to him', the confusion is continued. His father's life (if it was a memory of his) is now *his* life. The idea is baffling at first sight, but one way of making sense out of it is to turn to one of Ford's descriptions of how reading influenced his own life. He wrote of W. H. Hudson:

He shared with Turgenev the quality that makes you unable to find out how he got his effects [. . .] When you read them you forget the lines and the print. It is as if a remotely smiling face looked up at you out of the page and told you things. And those things become part of your own experience. It is years since I first read *Nature in Downland*. Yet [. . .] the first words that I there read have become a part of my own life. They describe how, lying on the turf of the high sunlit downs above Lewes in Sussex, Hudson looked up into the perfect, limpid blue of the sky and saw, going to infinite distances one behind the other [. . .] little shining globes, like soap bubbles. They were thistledown floating in an almost windless heaven.

Now that is part of my life. I have never had the patience—the contemplative tranquil-lity—to lie looking up into the heavens. I have never in my life done it. Yet that is I, not Hudson, looking up into the heavens [. . .][28]

The anxiety expressed in 'True Love & a G.C.M.' about whether one's mental processes are eccentric or pathological is thus an aesthetic as well as a psychological matter. The impressionist, who aims to record 'Your actual mental processes', must continually take the risk that Morton fears of exposing his own psychology.[29] That Ford knows this, and takes the risk, is what makes this work something much saner, despite the volatility of the material, than he feared. It is a humane and honest recording of how his brief exposure to battle forced him to live on the verge of sanity. The experience provided much of what is most compelling about all his best post-war prose. When Ezra Pound heard about Ford's concussion, he told John Quinn that Ford was suffering from 'shell shock, or nerve shock or something due to shell bursting too close for detached and placid literary contemplation of the precise "im-pression and the mot juste required to render it".' It sounds callous to imply that literature is still the most important consideration even at such a time—though Pound probably needed to imply it to justify his own detachment from the war. But on another level it is a penetrating remark. The war became—as it did for most combatants—the crucial event in Ford's life. It not only summoned back spectres of childhood dreads, but added new and unforeseen terrors which haunted him until his death. But it also presented new *aesthetic* problems. The question of how to *render* his impressions of war—and how to transform them into narrative—did become Ford's predominant concern throughout the next decade.[30]

2

1916: KEMMEL HILL AND AFTER

I was personally happier when I was somewhere in France between August,
1914, and November 11, 1918, than I ever was previously [. . .]

(Ford, 'Preparedness', *New York Herald Tribune Magazine*, 6 Nov. 1927)

Ford was still extremely tense when he left Corbie to rejoin the 9th Battalion of the
Welch Regiment, which was now stationed in the Ypres salient near Kemmel Hill.
The hero of the unpublished novel 'Mr Croyd' is described as being 'desperately
excitable—so excitable that when one of his fits [was] on him he had terrible desires to
strangle'. Anger is both the impulse and the subject of these two unpublished works,
and it lours large in *Parade's End* too. Ford told an interviewer for *Time* magazine in
1927 that, 'Returning from the war with health impaired, he wrote two novels in anger
which were not published. He intended to write no more. He changed his mind,
however [. . .]'[1] Writers such as Siegfried Sassoon or Wilfred Owen were able to
recognize and express their anger immediately. But Ford's sense of his altruism, and
his feeling that it was essential for himself as a man and an artist to sustain indifference
to his fate, made this impossible. Danger and fear of battle stir feelings of aggression,
but Ford needed to deny his own aggression. For all his admiration for the British
Army, he was no conventional militarist. There is a point at which his 'Indifferentism'
shades off into seeing himself or his characters as Christ-like in their infinite gentle
suffering; their refusal to kick against the pricks. 'Mr Croyd' and 'True Love & a
G.C.M.' are turning-points in this respect too, for they show Ford's heroes transforming themselves, as Ford did, from passive victims to men who can take decisive action
to save themselves.

At Kemmel Hill Ford found it 'quiet here at its most violent compared with the
Somme'—even during the 'strafe that the artillery got up for George V', whom Ford
said he'd seen 'strolling about among the Cheshires' on a royal visit to the Front,
where he 'really was in some danger': 'At least', said Ford, 'he was in an O.[bservation]
P.[ost] that was being shelled fairly heavily when I was in it "for instruction".' He saw
the Prince of Wales too, even though he was 'quite unrecognizable', and 'perfectly
businesslike'. In a later reminiscence he describes waiting in a mess-hut, and sitting
down to play 'a defective piano'. He was 'getting away with a brilliant execution of the
finale of TRISTAN UND ISOLDE' when a 'little, shining, staff-captain', decorated with
some ribbons Ford didn't recognize, stepped in, saying 'Don't get up . . . Go on
playing'. Later he is told it was 'The Prince of Wales of course. Running around
without even an orderly' on a tour of inspection. Ford wrote to Lucy Masterman that
he was 'fairly cheerful again', but there were danger-signals: 'I do not get on with the

C.O., & the Adjt. overworks me because I talk Flemish. So I have to buy straw and pacify infuriated farmers as well as attending all parades & fatigues.' He hoped to get a staff job where his talents might be better used, 'but the C.O.—an ex-Eastbourne Town Councillor & the adj[utan]t., an ex-P.O. clerk—annoy me', he told her; 'the C.O. says I am too old & the adjt. thanks me all day long for saving the H.Q. Mess 2 frs. 22 on turnips & the like. I don't know which I dislike most.' They can't have come across anyone like Ford in their civilian lives. Relations with his CO, Lieutenant-Colonel Cooke, deteriorated. Ford wrote again to Lucy Masterman to vindicate himself from Cooke's objections to his age:

With the labour of 184 men I have today drained a considerable portion of this country & I have also marched 12 miles to bring up a draft. So I have not been idle. But the C.O. continues to impress on me that I am too old for this job. I think he wants to force me to relinquish my commission. I suppose you do not know anybody who cd. impress on Gen[l] Bridges the desirability of having me in his In[tgce] [Intelligence] Dept? It wd. be a good action—because I am sure I deserve better—even in a military sense—than to be harassed by a rather doting Lt. Col. [. . .] who cherishes a special dislike for the Special Reserve.

I suppose I am a bore: I am terribly afraid of becoming a bore with a grievance.[2]

As the antagonism worsened, it became clear that Ford's being 'terribly afraid' was of more concern to Cooke than his age. The Colonel sent for him and read a letter that he had sent soon after his concussion, which read:

I consider that he is quite unsuitable to perform the duties required of an officer in this campaign. He would not inspire his men with confidence and his power as a leader is nil [. . .] I recommend that he be sent home as early as possible as there is no use to which I can put him.

I could not place him in command of men in the field.

I cannot recommend him for employment at home.

Ford objected that none of the officers had seen him 'in contact with the men' because he had been 'only in the 1st Line Transport wh. is composed mostly of mules'.[3] But even if Cooke's pragmatic verdict was right about Ford's unlikeliness to inspire confidence in the field, his service when he was back in England from the spring of 1917 proved the injustice of the last sentence.

Meanwhile, his hopes of a staff job did not materialize (because his record was so bad, he told Masterman), and he was sent back to the first line transport. He wrote to Masterman to protest that Cooke had only seen him once before writing his damning report. It was, as Mizener said, a plea for help, though even under such stress (or perhaps because of it) Ford presented himself as the dispassionate novelist: 'I thought you ought to know these details wh. I present to you without comment, simply asking you to believe that I have certainly committed no military offence of any kind [. . .]' Through the forced manic jollity of a letter to his mother one can hear him finding the war as exhilarating as it was nerve-wracking: 'it is very hot here & things are enormously exciting & the firing all day keeps me a little too much on the jump to write composedly. However it is jolly to have been in the two greatest strafes of history—& I am perfectly well & in good spirits, except for money worries wh. are breaking me up a good deal—& for the time, perfectly safe. / God bless you.'[4] The firing didn't keep

him too much on the jump to write, though. In the first week of September 1916 he
wrote three extraordinary letters to Joseph Conrad. He had written earlier in the
summer too, but only Conrad's replies have survived: the first, saying they were glad
to hear his news. 'Whatever happens you would have put up a jolly good try', Conrad
told him: 'Everybody who knows you can appreciate the inner value of your action.—
All luck to you.' (The double-edged tone is familiar: did he suspect it was a Fordian
delusion that he was going to manage the Western Front?) This was probably responding to a letter written before Ford was shell-shocked, since Conrad wrote again on the
following day, having just heard about it: 'We are very much distressed at your news
[. . .] Believe in our warmest sympathy and our earnest wishes for your speedy
recovery.' Ford later said that Conrad had sent him £5 while he was in France, after
Chance had sold the 14,000 copies Ford had bet him it would.[5]

Ford's letters to Conrad of late 1916 detail his impressions of the war—particularly
'notes upon sound'. They bear out his reminiscence that it had been while returning
to the Front in late 1916 that the thought had occurred to him that he was the only
novelist of his age to be in the fighting. This made it all the more necessary that he
should bear witness; and he recalled: 'I began to take a literary view of the war from
that time.' The first of the letters describes suddenly finding himself under a table
during an artillery barrage:

Well I was under the table & frightened out of my life—so indeed was the other man with
me. There was shelling just overhead—apparently thousands of shells bursting for miles
around & overhead. I was convinced that it was up with the XIX Div^n because the Huns had
got note of a new & absolutely devilish shell or gun.
    It was of course thunder. It completely extinguished the sound of the heavy art[iller]y, &
even the how[itzer] about 50 yds. away was inaudible during the actual peals & sounded like
stage thunder in the intervals.[6]

It matters to readers of *Parade's End* who have not experienced an artillery barrage to
know that the fanciful image with which Ford focuses Tietjens's response to the
shellfire preceding the German attack—'The orchestra was bringing in *all* the brass,
all the strings, *all* the wood-wind, all the percussion instruments. The performers
threw about biscuit tins filled with horse-shoes; they emptied sacks of coal on cracked
gongs, they threw down forty-storey iron houses'—it matters to know that that conceit
of the guns sounding like stage thunder was one which occurred to Ford in Flanders.
'I thought this might interest you as a constatation of some exactness', he explained to
Conrad. The surface tone is that of the fellow-craftsman passing on some vivid
glimpses of experience that might be useful. But the prose expresses how hard-won is
its detachment—as the image of Ford under the table and frightened out of his life
shows. It is a form in which he can both imagine his own death, and dramatize his
mastery over the fear and self-pity. He tells Conrad: 'I have lain down wet in the wet
for the last three nights & do not seem to have taken any harm except for a touch of
toothache.' Or: 'I have been for six weeks—with the exception of only 24 hours—
continuously within reach of German missiles &, altho' one gets absolutely to ignore
them, consciously, I imagine that subconsciously one is suffering.' The second letter
describes his attempt to buy fly-papers in a shop while a shell lands nearby, and the

Tommies joke as if the noise was made by the flies. 'No interruption, emotion, vexed at getting no flypapers', writes Ford: 'Subconscious emotion, "thank God the damn thing's burst".' Despite all this, he could say with strangely detached irony: 'It is curious—but, in the evenings here, I always feel myself happier than I have ever felt in my life.—Indeed, except for worries, I am really very happy [. . .]' It is indeed curious that he can say this in a letter beginning 'I wrote these rather hurried notes yesterday because we were being shelled to hell & I did not expect to get thro' the night'. It is a piece of characteristically theatrical stiff-upper-lip bravado that puts into devastating perspective just how unhappy he had been over the last few years. The new forms of camaraderie that struck many volunteers; the escape from Elsie and Violet and legal actions; the escape from literary jealousies and the need to write for money: these may have all contributed to that feeling of release. But the thought that he might not get through the night seems also to have cheered his evenings; the thought that soon, perhaps, he would no longer need to keep all on going.[7] It sounds like the moment of calm that might precede a suicide. Yet the need to cling to life is obliquely present: he did feel the need to go on writing; a paradox he addresses in the third letter (in a passage Graham Greene marked in his copy of Ford's *Letters*):

I wonder if it is just vanity that in these cataclysmic moments makes one desire to *record*. I hope it is, rather, the annalist's wish to help the historian—or, in a humble sort of way, my desire to help you, cher maître!—if you ever wanted to do anything in '*this line*.' Of course you wd. not ever want to do anything in this line—but a pocketful of coins in a foreign country may sometimes come in handy. You might want to put a phrase into the mouth of someone in Bangkok who had been, say, to Bécourt. There you wd. be! And I, to that extent, shd. once more have collaborated.

As ever, that desire for a spiritual communion—collaboration, a sympathetic listener—is precipitated out of the imagining of impending death, and the hope that his literary personality will survive it, even if disguised as a Conradian cameo. In saying 'There you wd. be!' he is also saying 'There I wd. be!' He has been accused (most vehemently of all by Conrad) of a hypersensitive and self-destructive vanity; but the humility with which yet again he tried to rekindle their friendship despite Conrad's coolness is touching. Conrad was to be less than three months dead when Ford began *No More Parades*, one of his most Conradian performances (together with *The Good Soldier* and *A Man Could Stand Up*—), and the first he published to use these perceptual details about his war experiences. At the same time as he was working on the novel, he was writing his memoir *Joseph Conrad*. It was as if, even after Conrad's death, Ford wanted to continue their collaboration.[8]

Violet Hunt had sent Ford the proofs of her novel *Their Lives*. He wrote a brief preface, signed with a bitter, ironic anonymity 'Miles Ignotus' ('Unknown Soldier'), in which he described reading the proofs on a hillside. The 'very great view' included the sight of the Germans shelling the Belgian civilians in Poperinghe. It seemed an example of senseless Prussian cruelty, and is described as such in the passage in *No More Parades* where Tietjens recalls having watched the same sight. There, as in Ford's other description of the scene—in *No Enemy*—what he records as disturbing is a conflict between on the one hand a kind of aesthetic pleasure in the 'new forms' of the shell-clouds ('he saw, suddenly unfolding in the air above the towers, two great white swans. They extended laterally, dazzling, very slow.'); and on the other hand the thought of the human suffering they represented. There was also a feeling of joy at the sight of Allied shells bursting ('the little white balls went on coming into existence') over the German trenches. The point is less the vengefulness of the exultation but the emotional volatility that could produce it: 'at any rate, there the emotions came, crowding and irrepressible.' This cluster of feelings—a kind of baffling hysteria at the conflict between awe, pity, and outrage—is, as we shall see, at the heart of the most significant piece he wrote while on the Western Front: the essay 'A Day of Battle', dated 15 September 1916, and also signed 'Miles Ignotus'. And that essay is significant not least for the way it illuminates how the same cluster of feelings is at the heart of *Parade's End*. There is a note of hysteria in the other main point Ford relates to his view of the shelling in his preface to *Their Lives*. He argues impressionistically that Hunt's characters—'these remorselessly rendered people who were without remorse or pity—these people were Prussians'. He explains:

For that horrible family of this author's recording explains to me why to-day, millions of us, as it were, on a raft of far-reaching land, are enduring torture it is not fit that human beings should endure, in order that—outside that raft—other eloquent human beings should proclaim that they will go on fighting to the last drop of *our* blood.

This may sound a little obscure; but if the somnolescent reader will awaken to the fact that selfishness does create misery he may make a further effort of the imagination, and see that the selfishness of the Eighties—of the Victorian and Albert era—is the direct Ancestor of . . . Armageddon.[9]

It would have sounded less obscure in 1916, when the eloquent human being particularly being alluded to would have been recognized as Lloyd George: Ford had complained to Lucy Masterman just before his concussion that he had seen from a newspaper 'that the Rt. Hon. D[avid] L[loyd] G[eorge] still has his back to the wall & will fight to the last drop of our blood. I wonder what he wd. say if he were out here for a week.' Ford is doing more than voicing the widespread fear that the soldiers were being betrayed by their leaders. He is also generalizing the connection he had made at Corbie between his childhood dread of the Pre-Raphaelite great, and the horrors of the war, and of war-cant. (Hunt cannot have been particularly pleased with the line of argument, since the three daughters of what he calls 'that horrible family' are evidently portraits of herself and her sisters.) The feeling that pre-war hypocrisy was culpable for wartime excesses was also a widespread one. Richard Aldington, for example, wrote that: 'It was the régime of Cant *before* the War which made the Cant *during* the War so damnably possible and easy.' There is another way in which Ford's outburst of anger against the oppressive adults of his childhood is more than a mere personal grouse. The pseudonymity of the piece enables him to express much more directly than he could in his letters or even the work published under his own name his vision of the war as an immense, ceaseless, tragic human sacrifice. This comes across not just in the pathetic vision of millions on a raft, 'enduring torture'; but also in the ending, in which he describes the futile shelling of a nearby church as he is writing: 'Truly, Our Lord and Saviour Christ dies every day—as he does on every page of this book, and in every second of this 7-9-16.' This seems to me more a matter of seeking a divine sanction for the more effective expression of human misery, than testifying to a particularly religious view of the war. As in the letter to Conrad, he explains how 'whilst you are saying "Thank God!" because it has not hit you, you hear the thin, sifting sound of the stained glass dropping down into the aisles'. Besides that reflex of relief at survival, the effect comes from the suggestion of the author saying his prayers because of the omnipresence of death. *Parade's End* is not a Christian work in any orthodox sense. But that image of the man-god dying on every page could scarcely be bettered as an impression of its effects of pathos.[10]

Ford managed to spend some of war's waiting by reading. He said he wrote to London for the books he had always championed: Flaubert's *Éducation sentimentale* and *Trois contes*; Turgenev's *Fathers and Children, The House of Gentlefolk*, and *A Sportsman's Sketches*; several volumes of Anatole France; Hudson's *Nature in Downland, Green Mansions*, and *The Purple Land*; Maupassant's *Fort comme la mort* and *Yvette*; Conrad's *Lord Jim, The Nigger of the 'Narcissus'*, and the orginal *Youth* volume; and James's *The Portrait of a Lady, The Spoils of Poynton*, and *What Maisie Knew*. It was his rereading of Crane's *The Red Badge of Courage* which made the greatest impression on him: 'having to put the book down and go out of my tent at dawn', remembered Ford, 'I could not understand why the men I saw about were in khaki', rather than the blue or grey of the American Civil War; 'the impression was so strong that its visualization of war completely superimposed itself for long hours over the concrete objects of the war I was in'. Rereading James gave him the same disorientating feeling of duality, of double vision.[11]

He applied for leave to be in Paris for the publication by Payot of the French translation of his second 'propaganda' book, *Entre Saint Denis et Saint Georges*. He also wrote to the Medical Orderly asking to see a dentist: 'I only know that I am beastly bad—with rheumatism & agoraphobia—wh. w^{d.} all go if my (literally) bleeding teeth c^{d.} be pumped out.'[12] He was in Paris for the weekend of 9 to 11 September, and was thanked by the Minister of Instruction, who asked if he could be of help to Ford. But he was discomposed when Ford, his mind characteristically somewhere quite other, asked if the minister could find some ferrets: the regimental ones used for rat-catching had all died, and he was preoccupied about how to replace them.[13] The weekend was enervating. He 'spent 36 hours in strenuous work' making alterations to the translation, but: 'The writing rather exhausted me—& indeed I collapsed & was made to see the M.O. who said I was suffering from specific shell-shock & ought to go to hospital.' But he wouldn't go. He was back in the Salient by the 13th.[14]

Soon after this he was sent back to the 3rd Battalion's home base in North Wales, at Kinmel Park, near Rhyl. It was probably during the following six weeks or so he spent in Britain that he was walking down New Oxford Street and suddenly realized he had walked past his brother without recognizing him:

My companion on that day said that I exclaimed—it was during the period when my memory was still very weak:

'Good God! that was my brother Oliver. I have cut my brother Oliver. . . . One should not cut one's brother. . . . Certainly one should not cut one's brother! It isn't *done*.'[15]

He said he ran back along the street, but Oliver had gone down the Tube lift before he caught him up. According to Ford they were not to meet again until 1923, in another chance encounter on the street, this time in Paris. Oliver had got his commission in the

3rd Battalion of the East Surrey Regiment, was also in the trenches that summer, and had had as close a shave as Ford's. He had been wounded by a shot from a German sniper while he was on a reconnaissance: 'Oliver fell wounded into a shell crater and the German was unwise enough to look over the edge of it, whereupon Oliver shot him through the head. Later [. . .] he was very upset because letters found on the German showed his family were looking forward to his coming back at Christmas.'[16] Ford found his new posting a new waste of his abilities, and—without overseas pay—a strain on his financial resources. He asked Masterman to help him get sent back to France, but when he heard nothing from the War Office he began to despair: 'As things are I see nothing for it but to relinquish my comm^n [. . .] & to disappear into a decent obscurity. I am doing no good here, either to myself or to anyone else—& the training we give the men here seems ridiculously ineffective—so I can't even console myself with the idea that I am doing useful work.' Masterman commissioned some 'useful work' in the form of a propaganda article for Wellington House, but Ford's despair made even that seem difficult: 'No: I am not doing any writing', Ford told him: 'to write one must have some purpose in life—& I simply haven't any.'[17] His depression was not only the aftermath of punishing stress, but was compounded by the domestic anxieties from which battle had at least partially distracted him. What he described as Violet Hunt's 'campaign of vilification' only exacerbated matters.[18]

The plan to relinquish his commission, though he assured Lucy Masterman it was not due to 'depression, or pique, but just common sense', was a desperate device. By 'a decent obscurity' he meant not dropping silently out of the army, but transferring to the ranks so as to be sent back to France as soon as possible. The thinly veiled threat of a legitimate suicide testifies to how intensely Ford craved anonymity, or annihilation. 'You see', he told Masterman (recalling the phrase his Kentish peasant friend Meary Walker would use), 'one has phases of misfortune that get too heavy for one as one gradually loses resiliency & I am too tired now to keep "all on gooing".' When the War Office did eventually order him back to France at the end of November, one set of dreads was knocked out by another: the prospect of being sent back to Lieutenant-Colonel Cooke. When once again he enlisted Masterman's help, he writes as one making what he hopes will be a last request: 'All I am really anxious about is that I sh. not go back to the IX Welch. Wd. it be too much to ask you to ask Genl. Braid to suggest to Col. Dickinson at the Base camp at Rouen that this wd. be inconsiderate. I don't at all want not to be killed—but I don't want to be strafed unjustly as well.'[19] Saying he doesn't want not to be killed is in part a way of saying that he is not trying to evade danger, but wants to face it unhindered by prejudiced superiors. But saying he doesn't *at all* want not to be killed comes dangerously close to saying that he actively wants to die. With characteristic duality, intense self-pity is turned into a gesture of ultimate self-sacrifice, as Ford lives the role of the soldier as tragic altruist.

When he reached the base camp at Rouen he discovered that his strategy had failed, and that he had indeed been re-attached to the 9th Welch, and was given 'various polyglot jobs' such as 'writing proclamations in French about thefts of rations issued to H.[is] B.[ritannic] M.[ajesty]'s forces & mounting guards over German sick'. While he was 'wet thro' and coughing [his] head off', he was interviewing one of them absent-mindedly about where he was from, and what he did. 'Herr Offizier,

Geisenhirt!', was the reply. He wrote to Conrad to share the joke: 'So there was our: "Excellency, a few goats!"' Ford himself fell ill during mid-December. 'As for me, c'est fini de moi, I believe, at least as far as fighting is concerned', he told Conrad: 'my lungs are all charred up and gone.' The Medical Board wanted to send him home, but he protested that he 'didn't in the least want to see Blighty ever again'. Nevertheless he wanted to stay in touch with his children: he wrote to Katharine to let her know about his and Oliver's injuries, and encouraged her to take up some war-work. She went 'on the land' in the spring, working for a farmer below Kitcat Cottages. Christina had entered Mayfield Convent in East Sussex as a novice.[20]

Ford was 'marked R.B.' (Reserve Battalion), which meant staying in Rouen. But then he became worse, and had to be sent to Rouen's No. II Red Cross Hospital, 'in the old priests' seminary that the Prussians had used as a hospital in 1870'. He wrote to Masterman: 'my lungs were found to be in a devil of a way, with extensions at the bases & solidifications & all sorts of things—partly due to a slight touch of gas I got in the summer & partly to sheer weather.'[21] Mizener asserts that Ford was never gassed, though his only evidence is Sugrue's cautious recollection of fifty years later: 'I do not think [. . .] that he was ever in the way of being accused of cowardice, or, for that matter of being shell shocked, or gassed, or wounded.'[22] 'Shell-shock' is an imprecise term, but there is no doubt that Ford was seriously shaken by his concussion. Sugrue may not be more reliable about the gassing. There is no reason to doubt that Ford experienced gas attacks. He varied the story later, telling a marvellous tale about how his lungs were ruined by gas inadvertently released from his portmanteau in a hotel bedroom while on leave in Paris (he had been packing when the gas attack began!) It may have been true: he certainly collapsed while in Paris in September. Perhaps a whiff of gas from his case brought back memories of the Front which overpowered him. Or perhaps it was the way he explained to himself the familiar phenomenon of the breakdown occurring not at the time of maximum strain, but as soon as the strain is relaxed.[23] Although in retrospect the desire to invent a more military—or more entertaining—account must have been powerful, his letters from Rouen are remarkable in the way they play down the exposure to gas. Writing to his mother he describes himself 'wheezing all the time like a machine gun', and attributes it to 'the touch of gas I got at Nieppe'. He told Masterman his lung trouble was 'partly due to a slight touch of gas I got in the summer & partly to sheer weather'. That is probably the truth.[24] If there is a striving for a tone of heroic stoicism in that way of making the most feared weapon sound trivial (like a touch of bronchitis), there is also a literal honesty: for someone of Ford's age, living in the damp cold of the support lines, it would only take a touch of gas to aggravate lungs that were already weak.

The despair returned with the illness. Since he has been accused of 'improving' his war experiences and sufferings, it is important to realize that he knew exactly what the main problem was: not the physical damage to his teeth and his lungs, but the psychological after-effects of concussion. 'I wasn't so much wounded as blown up by a 4.2 [inch artillery shell] and shaken into a nervous breakdown', he wrote to Katharine from Rouen, adding that it had made him 'unbearable to myself & my kind'. The letter to his mother ends, with plangent morbidity, on his inability to end: 'It w^d. be really very preferable to be dead—but one isn't dead—so that is all there is to it.' His companion in the priests' cell did not make for cheerfulness. He was another shell-shock case: a Black Watch second lieutenant—about 20, wild-eyed, black haired:

He talked with the vainglory and madness of the Highland chieftain that he was, continuously all day. Towards ten at night he would pretend to sleep.

As soon as the last visit of the V.A.D.'s was over he would jump out of bed and rush to a wall-press with sliding doors. He took out a kilt and a single shoe. His face assumed a look of infinite cunning. He would fix his black, shining, maniacal eyes on me and, stealthily stretching out an arm, would extract from the press a *skene dhu*. A *skene dhu* is the long, double-edged dagger that Highlanders carry in their socks. From the creasing of his lips you could tell when he had put a sufficient edge on that instrument. He would be sharpening it on the sole of his single shoe. He never removed his eyes from mine. He would run his thumb along the edge of the blade and with a leering, gloating look he would whisper:

'*We* know who this is meant for.'

I never ascertained. Delirium would then come on. I was delirious most nights.

When he had a relapse on Christmas Eve, the full horror of the 'Corbie-phobia' returned:

all night I lie awake & perceive the ward full of Huns of forbidding aspect—except when they give me a sleeping draft.

I am in short rather ill still & sometimes doubt my own sanity—indeed, quite frequently I do. I suppose that, really, the Somme was a pretty severe ordeal, though I wasn't conscious of it at the time. Now, however, I find myself suddenly waking up in a hell of a funk—& going on being in a hell of a funk till morning. And that is pretty well the condition of a number of men here. I wonder what the effect of it will be on us all, after the war—& on national life and the like.[25]

Doubting his own sanity, discussing the way his mind is overrun by fears of dangers that he wasn't conscious of at the time: Ford is able to voice to Masterman, his most loyal friend at this time, exactly those doubts that Gabriel Morton did not have the courage to discuss. In doing so, he first states what were to become his great post-war subjects: the curious effects of war on the mind, and in particular the delayed action of fear (a form of time-shift of the emotions); and the after-effects of war on soldiers and society alike. Everything he wrote afterwards is part of a twenty-year attempt to render and to understand the changes wrought by the war in the world and in himself.

One immediate effect the war had on him was that he began to speak as if he were already dead, or should be dead. He wrote to his mother from Rouen: 'It is very quiet here: I don't hear anything either of or from anybody nowadays wh. makes one feel rather like a ghost.' The image began to haunt him. Not only did he use it in other letters, but it became a leitmotiv of his reminiscences (and supplied the title for his first post-war book, *Thus to Revisit*), in which the Ford who had been pronounced 'Exploded!' and 'Finished!' by *les jeunes* returns as a ghost to take stock of literature, and to remember his pre-war haunts.[26] Contemplating your own death can incite self-pity. It allowed Ford to invoke the elegiac pathos about himself that he had previously only created around fictional characters like Edward Ashburnham. Before condemning him for inviting pity, though one must remember that he was in a pitiful state. But primarily, he was expressing a survivor's guilt in feeling that he had outlived the span allotted to friends and comrades—most of them younger: this was one reason why the phrase 'the lost generation' applied first to those lost in battle, and later to those who were lost because they had survived. While in the Red Cross Hospital at Rouen Ford wrote the poem 'One Day's List', commemorating the four second lieutenants and '270 other ranks' who died on one day of action. He told Katharine that of the fourteen officers who came out with him he was the only one left at the base, and he was 'pretty well a shattered wreck': 'And I sit in the hut here wh is full of Welsh officers all going up—& all my best friends—& think that very likely not one of them will be alive in a fortnight. I tell you, my dear, it is rather awful.' Goldring was right to say the poem was written 'in an agony of compassion for "the little boys"'. In 'A Day of Battle' Ford had written that 'there is no emotion so terrific and so overwhelming as the feeling that comes over you when your own men are dead. It is a feeling of anger . . . an anger . . . a deep anger! It shakes you like a force that is beyond all other forces in the world: unimaginable, irresistible.' The poem is simultaneously an agony of self-pity, but curiously the effect is not to diminish the compassion for the others, but to take the war-poetry cliché of the dead being happy in their glory, and exact its truth by imagining the survivor's fate they have escaped. Somehow the pathos of that fate—the one Ford was remembering from his past, and imagining in his future—transfers itself to the young dead too, making the idea of their eternal spring something much more moving than the blithe denials of their anguish that characterize the war poetry of a writer like Rupert Brooke:

> But we who remain shall grow old,
> We shall know the cold
> Of cheerless
> Winter and the rain of Autumn and the sting
> Of poverty, of love despised and of disgraces,
> And mirrors showing stained and ageing faces,
> And the long ranges of comfortless years
> And the long gamut of human fears. . . .
> But, for you, it shall be forever spring [. . .].[27]

Ford's talking of himself as a ghost is also an understandable, salutary reaction to having narrowly escaped death—which he had now done at least twice. After being concussed by the shell which had consigned him to a premature psychological hell, he had also nearly been hit by a bullet:

I remember riding, rather sleepily, along such a sleepy road behind the lines at Kemmel, in Belgium [. . .] I was about a mile behind our front line: I didn't imagine I was in any danger: indeed I wasn't thinking of danger altho' I knew that the road was visible from the Hun lines [. . .].

And then: [']Zi . . . ipp!' a single rifle bullet as nearly as possible got me. I would swear that it passed between me & my horse's neck! At any rate it can't have missed me by more than two feet. I found my self saying: 'Four seconds! Four seconds!' & I got over the hill skyline very quickly indeed. 'Four seconds' presented itself to my mind like that, because it would take a sniper about four seconds to load, aim & fire again. And that bit of information seemed to pop up from nowhere & to remain isolated. . . .

It was a pretty long shot: over 2,000 yards. But I suppose the chap had telescopic sights [. . .]

Curiously enough that sniper—if it was a sniper—is the most present in my mind of all the thousands of blue grey beasts that, in one capacity or another, one saw out there. . . . And yet I, naturally, never saw him. I *do* see him. He has a black moustache, a jovial, but intent expression: he lies beside a bit of ruined wall, one dark eye cocked against his telescopic sight, the other closed. And through the circle of the sight he sees me riding slowly over the down: a small, unknown figure of a man upon a sleepy roan mare. And his finger is just curling tenderly round the trigger. He is a Bavarian. And so he lies, & so he will continue to lie, in my mind, for ever.

I daresay that really, he was a lean Prussian—it was the celebrated Brandenbergers that we had opposite us there—who let his rifle off at a venture.

But, otherwise, the Huns always seemed to me to be impersonal—blue-grey beasts, as I have called them—except when they had their helmets on, when they became, for me, blue grey hob-goblins. But beasts: never human.[28]

In the playful concession that it perhaps was not so near a miss as Ford 'would swear', he recognizes that his imagination is too vivid *not* to keep imagining ways he might be killed. Like Hemingway, injured in an explosion near Fossalta in 1918, 'He died in imagination'.[29] What is remarkable in this piece, written soon after the event and long before he had fully recovered, is its novelistic combination of detachment from himself and sympathetic imagination of his enemy's point of view. It goes beyond psychological dissociation, into novelistic introspection. Unhindered by self-pity he is able to analyse the psychological effects of sudden danger, seeing himself from outside, through the eyes of his would-be killer at the moment of firing. Furthermore, he is able to disavow for a moment the propagandist view of the Germans, and humanize this particular enemy as a jovial individual. Finally, Ford's imagining of his death has a symbolic value which goes beyond any desire to arouse pity for his suffering. For it is also a liberation from the shackles of his old self and life. Aldington said that 'Adult lives were cut sharply into three sections—pre-war, war, and post-war. It is curious—perhaps not so curious—but many people will tell you that whole areas of the pre-war lives have become obliterated from their memories.'[30] The war certainly became the decisive break in Ford's life, making him feel perhaps that he had 'taken what he got' for his involvements with Elsie Martindale and Violet Hunt, and that he had suffered enough. Paradoxically, as he wrote of himself as a haunter, he became a less haunted man: the post-war Ford was a more robust, balanced person. Postulating the death of Ford Madox Hueffer was a necessary stage in the rebirth of Ford Madox Ford.

3

1917: THE EDGE OF UNREASON

> There were many who went over the edge of unreason—but there were many
> and many who stayed, by the grace of God, just on this side of the edge.
>
> (Ford, 'The Colonel's Shoes')

When he was well enough, he was sent to Lady Michelham's convalescent hospital at Menton:

A peeress of untellable wealth and of inexhaustible benevolence had taken, for us chest sufferers of H.M. Army . . . for us alone all the Hôtel Cap Martin. . . . One of those great gilded caravanserais that of my own motion I should never have entered [. . .] We slept in royal suites; the most lovely ladies and the most nobly titled, elderly seigneurs walked with us on the terraces over the sea. . . . Sometimes one looked round and remembered for a second that we were all being fattened for slaughter.[1]

On 2 February he left Menton, and took a train to the frozen, snow-covered north. He remembered the journey as a 'turning point' of his career: 'it is not just a subway ride going back to the line after a period in a particularly luxurious hospital on the Riviera.' At Hazebrouck station in Flanders he was 'rendered particularly moody by the fact that on the dimmed bookstall of the dimmed station I had seen a dim copy of one of my own books'. 'It seemed to me amazing that I had ever written books at all', he said later. In the version of this reminiscence worked into *The Marsden Case*, the Fordian narrator Jessop gives a more expressive account of his despair at the sight: 'I saw the back of someone's translation of one of my own books. Dusty! No human soul would ever assimilate it. And no human soul, I thought, would ever think of me again. . . .' His nearness to oblivion was brought home when German aeroplanes bombed the line in front of his train out of Hazebrouck, and he had to spend the night waiting in the windowless and doorless carriage.[2]

When he returned to Rouen he was assigned to a Canadian casual battalion for three weeks. 'I could tell a story about the accretion of blankets in a Canadian Regiment that I had the honour to command', he wrote. He didn't tell it, but the comment gives an indication of his duties. A letter to F. S. Flint draws out the dismal contrast between the south and the north—a contrast which was to become the basis of his later cultural fictions opposing the 'Great Trade Route' of the Mediterranean to its Nordic invaders:

But this is the bare, cold & trampled North, with nothing but khaki for miles & miles . . . Bare downs . . . & tents . . . & wet valleys [. . .] and mud . . . and bare downs.

And I am promoted to Adj[utant]—& run a B[attalio]n. much as I used to run the *Eng[lish] Rev[iew]*—It's the same frame of mind, you know, & much, much easier—or more difficult, according to one's mood. . . .[3]

At the end of February he was put in charge of a hospital tent of German prisoners at Abbeville. As Alan Judd says, it was 'a task to which he was probably well-suited, having their language, a sense of fairness and decency and a belief in the necessity for discipline', and an ability to feel compassion even for the enemy. Yet on the evidence of *Parade's End* he found the idea of the task appalling. His revulsion from prisoners perhaps came from his own fear of becoming one: as his persona 'Gringoire' says in *No Enemy*: 'one was damned afraid of being taken prisoner' (p. 64). What is curious, however, about Tietjens's thoughts on prisoners is that, while ostensibly about control of captured enemies, they suggest a radical ambivalence about *all* forms of control. For all the abandonment of personal responsibility that joining the army may have meant to him, there is a hint here of a deep unease about surrendering his volition to his superiors, which perhaps sheds light on his rows with them. It is here that Ford's Toryism reveals its radical, anarchic side:

It was detestable to him to be in control of the person of another human being—as detestable as it would have been to be himself a prisoner . . . that thing that he dreaded most in the world. It was indeed almost more detestable, since to be taken prisoner was at least a thing outside your own volition, whereas to control a prisoner, even under the compulsion of discipline on yourself, implies a certain free-will of your own [. . .] It was not sensible; but he knew that if he had had to touch a prisoner he would have felt nausea. It was no doubt the product of his passionate Tory sense of freedom. What distinguished man from the brutes was his freedom.[4]

Early in March 1917 Ford was invalided home. It was snowing in London. Instead of going to South Lodge, he stayed in the YMCA at Grosvenor Gardens. F. S. Flint had a telephone call on 8 March. A voice said: 'Is that you Flint. I'm Ford Madox Hueffer!' Ford asked him to dine. They met outside the barber's in Coventry Street; they walked to his lodgings in the YMCA bungalow at Victoria, then to the nearby Roman Catholic cathedral, then to the Authors' Club for sherry, and on to the Rendezvous in Soho, where Ford bought him a dinner of salmon and turkey, washed down with Chambertin, for 16s.6d. He had asked Flint to organize a volume of his poems to be published 'before the war ends or I am killed'. When they got back to the Authors' Club Ford dictated a list of the poems he wanted included. He wanted to get back to France, and made several attempts; as it happened, he was to spend the rest of the war in England, and was able to see *On Heaven and Poems Written on Active Service* through the press himself. Flint found him 'very quiet': 'some great change has come over him [. . .] He is no longer the fat man he was, and he is uglier, and there is another look in his eyes. He still invents his life rather, but I felt that he was rather down and out.'[5]

He wrote to Violet Hunt to tell her he was in town. Neither of them were sure whether their relationship still had any future. When Ford had told her, 'I am tired of fighting', he suggests the analogy between the war of the sexes and the war of the nations upon which *Parade's End* is founded.[6] He is demoralized by the war, as well as tired of fighting with Hunt. What is less clear is whether he wants to live with her in peace, or to make his peace with her by leaving. He stayed at her Selsey cottage for a week at the end of March. In July she had (through her solicitor) withdrawn her financial guarantee. The last time he had written, from the hospital in Rouen, he had told her that he couldn't bear to think of life without her, but then added:

That may seem to you ironic, in face of the fact that I have so obstinately refused to break with another woman—but pray take the statement as sincere, tho' it is no doubt of no great value to you. Still, there it is.

I don't suppose we shall meet again in this life [. . .] But at the same time, do believe that I am absolutely loyal to you and shall be as long as I live. I mean that you have only to ask me to come to you and I will come [. . .].[7]

The other woman was Brigit Patmore, who had written to Ford from what she thought was her death-bed to what she supposed was his, at the hospital at Menton. Ford had created once again the familiar predicament of the man torn between two passions— or was it three? Not only had Violet somehow managed to get hold of the love letter Ford had written to Miss Ross in Wales. She had also heard that Sextus Masterman (C.F.G.'s brother) had said that 'F was disliked by his fellow officers because he patronises & lectures them & then is seen coming out of the house of ill fame (at Rouen) himself'. She thought that 'Miss Ross (the girl in Wales he has I am told) might have something to say to that. Not I—any more.' She appears not to have taken this story very seriously. Ford recognized a kindred fabulator in Sextus Masterman, who was one of his superiors in the battalion, talking of 'Sixtian nonsense' on an earlier occasion, and calling him 'uproarious'. Only two months later, when she wrote that Ford had been 'unfaithful twice in 2 years', if the lovers in question are Patmore and Miss Ross (the only two Hunt names) then she was forgetting about whatever happened at Rouen.[8]

Hunt tried not asking him to come to her for as long as she could, which was less than two days. 'No word from F—my death warrant. I must do it!' she wrote. But then the next day she said she '*Could* not stand it'. Lucy Masterman told her she ought to let him know she was willing to see him if she didn't want to lose her hold over him. She got drunk at dinner and telephoned the YMCA. When she said she would see him, he said 'It is in your hands', and Hunt said she replied: 'I know.' They made an appointment to meet in the London Library; had lunch; called on friends; saw a revue. He took her home, and gave her the bafflingly evasive and unconsoling 'explanation' that 'if he wrote a love letter to Miss Ross it was in delirium & intended for Brigit with whom he is still infatuated'. He told her that 'he must go to her if she sends for him but that she won't'. The conversation Hunt recorded in her diary is so extraordinary (with Ford sounding extraordinarily like Ashburnham) that it's hard to imagine the tones in which it could actually have been said—not least because after this dismaying revelation he asked if he could stay at South Lodge, and Hunt agreed.[9]

After a week at Selsey she confronted him: ' "Well let us settle it . . . are you in love with Brigit?" "Of course I am!" he retorted.' As a lover, too, Ford's mind was somewhere quite other. (Did Rebecca West have Ford and Hunt in mind in her novel of the following year, *The Return of the Soldier*, in which a shell-shocked soldier returns to his passion for a previous lover, and is amnesiac about his present wife and their dead son?) A week later he volunteered an Ashburnhamesque explanation of his explanation. Now it is Brigit who is the distant object of his sustaining passion: 'I would not be here if I didn't care for you. . . . but I shld be at Brighton (where she was) . . . I do love you, I dare say, with the reservation that in a still small room B is sitting waiting for me & if she sends for me, I will go to her. I must.'[10]

Hunt's diary is a highly novelistic one, with speeches recalled just too fluently to carry full conviction. She used to go over the entries at later dates, commenting, adding, sometimes even typing them out as if for publication. However—as with Ford's own reminiscences—though the details may have been 'improved', the diary gives some memorable vignettes from a frustrating series of estrangements and reconciliations during March, when Ford was on duty and on leave in London and at Selsey. His view of himself was as dual as his love at this time, oscillating between the depressive and the decisive in a very similar manner to Mr Fleight's in his novel of 1913, or to Ford's dual response to the war in his *Outlook* articles. 'You know dear, I am not the sort of animal that makes love to women', Hunt recorded him as saying to her: '"I never shall, again. I don't care about women, really. I am cold and I have one passion now, the Army & that England should win . . . I believe I wld sacrifice *even* Brigit to the army! I am a broken down man." *Next breath* "I am a man, fit, strong— gallant, not the shivering pill-taking valetudinarian you took. . . ."'[11] The following day they returned to London. 'To town. Very cold', Hunt wrote in her diary. The following sentence suggests she didn't only mean the weather. 'He came & lay in my bed & I left it.'

Edgar Jepson recalled Ford coming in uniform with Hunt to the Soho restaurant, Bellotti's, where what he oddly called the 'Neo-Georgians' met. T. S. Eliot, Aldington, and H.D. used to come to these dinners, along with Pound and his wife Dorothy Shakespear, Wyndham Lewis, Arthur Waley (the translator of Chinese poetry), May Sinclair, Mary Butts, and her husband John Rodker. Iris Barry, a poetess whom Pound encouraged to leave Birmingham for London in 1917, recalled Ford vividly as: 'Semi-monstrous, bulging out his uniform, china-blue eyes peering from an expanse of pink face, pendulous lower lip drooping under sandy moustache as he boomed through endless anecdotes of Great Victorians, Great Pre-Raphaelites, Henry James [. . .].'[12]

On 30 March Ford took the train to Liverpool, on his way back to Kinmel Park. His old friend, the writer and editor Ferris Greenslet, got into a first-class compartment at Euston Station, to find 'a single large British officer exuding an incredible hauteur'; 'a fine figure of a fighting man'. Ford altered the story in his later reminiscences, and said he had a special compartment reserved for him in order to write a report about German prisoners who had been killed while in his care by German Zeppelins trying to raid an ammunition dump behind the lines. Greenslet remembered a more mundane subject: 'he prepared an elaborate report for his regimental adjutant concerning four blankets missing from his company's quota.' This sounds typical of the mundane paperwork he was being given to do; though the Zeppelin story may none the less be true, even if Ford misremembered the conversation with Greenslet. Ford gives a marvellous self-parody of his grand manner before he recognized Greenslet: 'Guard, remove this civilian'; but then the hauteur dissolved into friendly surprise: 'By God, it's F.G.!'[13] This anecdote is typical of Ford's reminiscential impressionism. He teased Greenslet by telling him he was reading the proofs of 'an erotic novel he had written in French'. He says he was returning from Belgium: in fact he had been in London for at least three weeks; and his last known location on the continent was Abbeville, in the Somme. Yet he was still suffering from the after-effects of his shell-shock. Though most of his memory had come back, it is not surprising that—like Tietjens—he was still finding it hard to remember details. He had been in Belgium in 1916, so could in 1931 quite easily have confused which of his periods of service in France he was returning from. Or perhaps he *was* in Belgium again for a short while, for which we have no records, between Abbeville and London. Most important, however, is that despite such quibbles (which are typical of the objections made by critics alleging Ford's inaccuracy), the essential details of the story are true. He did travel with Greenslet in the train, after meeting by chance. Greenslet even confirms Ford's change of tone. Ford had been in charge of prisoners of war. He did have to write army reports. The essential *effect* of the story is true too: it is a vivid vignette, showing how differently people act according to who they assume their audience to be, and catching Ford suddenly breaking out of an assumed persona to greet an unexpected friend.

As Mizener says, the worst of his habit of exaggeration was that 'it led people to think that there was no truth at all in Ford's stories, till they came to believe that his rather brave, if not very glorious, war service itself was entirely an invention'. Yet Mizener himself tended to exaggerate Ford's exaggerations, and was himself too much influenced by H. G. Wells's novel, *The Bulpington of Blup*, which he took as Wells's portrait of Ford, rather than as a work of the imagination which extrapolates—with Fordian gusto and fantasy—on Wells's view of Ford. Wells said that Ford's 'extraordinary drift towards self-dramatization—when he even changed his name to Captain Ford—became conspicuous only later, after the stresses of the war'. The implication here is that his promotion to captain was, like Theodore Bulpington's, pure self-promotion. But Ford was a captain by the end of the war (from 14 March to 1 August he was even given the temporary rank of brevet major). Wells wrote to Goldring that: 'In the 1914–18 war he was a bad case of shell-shock from which he never recovered. The pre-war F.M.H. was tortuous but understandable, the post-war F.M.H. was incurably *crazy*.' But Wells saw little of Ford after the war, and that little was before Ford moved to France in 1922—before he recovered, which he did, gradually, throughout the early 1920s. As Mizener recognizes, Wells was responding mainly to Ford's *Thus to Revisit*, his first post-war book of prose, which parodied Wells as the 'Eminent Novelist' whom Ford had to instruct about musical form in the novel. He also countered Ford's story in *Joseph Conrad* that he had cycled over to try to stop Ford collaborating with Conrad. Wells always liked to have the last word in his amicable sparring with Ford, and was perhaps taking his revenge for Ford's using some of his traits in Horatio Gubb in *The Simple Life Limited*, and less forgivably in Herbert Pett in *The New Humpty-Dumpty*. Bulpington is a fantasist of the kind Ford never was: he is 'a brain-storm in narrative and literary form' out of neurotic self-protectiveness. When he can't accept a reality, such as a rejection from the woman he loves, 'after his habit of mind he dramatized it and told himself stories about it', and then he begins to believe in his own stories. He has none of Ford's conscious relish of the fictive; he is a product of Wells's feeling that Ford and Conrad bothered themselves excessively over questions of narrative and literary form. Bulpington's shell-shock is a fiction, used to cover the fact that he turned around and ran away out of fear during a battle. Whereas Ford's shell-shock was frighteningly real; and rather than concealing his fear with fictions, his writing about the war is a supremely candid rendering of fear. As Mizener says: 'In any realistic sense he was behaving with some heroism when he continued on active duty after his first breakdown in July.' We have seen how, after his second collapse, in September, he was able to admit that he frequently doubted his own sanity. But Mizener goes on to claim that Ford 'could not live very long with a self that was heroic only in this way', and that he 'quickly improved his war experience' in order 'to see himself, and to believe others saw him, as the conventional upper-class officer-hero', and thus 'obscured the very real if homelier heroism of his actual conduct'. Yet there is something extraordinarily perverse in taking another novelist's fiction, which (as he admits) only very generally parallels Ford's life, as a more direct insight into Ford's reality than his own writings. Ford's writings after the war show that he lived long with the fear and insanity of the war, and never pretended otherwise. The insult to Ford's imaginative integrity is perhaps worse than that to his honesty, since his most penetrating study of fear and madness, *Parade's End*, may have an upper-class officer as its hero, but it would be hard to find a *less* conventional military hero than Christopher Tietjens.[14] What Mizener misses in *The Bulpington of Blup* is Wells's suggestion that Theodore is somehow representative despite his eccentricity. The novel's subtitle is: 'Adventures, Poses, Stresses, Conflict and Disaster in a Contemporary Brain.' A passage discussing shell-shock, probably influenced by the passage from *The Marsden Case* on how 'the eyes, the ears, the brain and the fibres of every soul to-day adult have been profoundly seared by those dreadful wickednesses of embattled humanity', asserts the universality of the psychological effects of war:

every human brain that is thrust into modern warfare is thrust towards something that, full face, is too unnatural, too incoherently, aimlessly and stupidly cruel, to endure. The individual is carried into it, upon a stream of usages, loyalties, sentimentalities, conceptions of honour and courage, confidences in governments and in leadership, only to encounter a shattering incompatibility in that vast destructive futility. Everyone who got to that completeness of encounter did not cry out or run or fall flat; only a proportion of the war neurotics came to hospital; but all without exception were damaged, distorted and crippled.[15]

Wells is less concerned with guying Ford, and more with using insights from his knowledge of Ford, and his cultural and aesthetic traditions, to explore the inadequacies of these traditions to withstand the forces of war and passion. It is Ford's own subject.

According to Stella Bowen, Ford 'could show you two sides simultaneously of any human affair, and the double picture made the subject come alive, and stand out in a third dimensional way that was very exciting'. He has been criticized for using his fictions to present flattering images of himself; but it has not adequately been recognized how he shows both sides even of himself; how his fiction explores his doubts as much as his wishes or fantasies about himself. None of his war prose presents its heroes as conventionally heroic. Ford knew he was not a 'good soldier' in that conventional sense. On the other hand, his sense of his military value was shaken by his struggles with Colonel Cooke. In 'True Love & a G.C.M.', as in *Parade's End*, the central character eventually surmounts sustained persecution ('strafing') by those who are his military superiors but his moral inferiors. Morton's colonel cannot forgive him for successfully defending the men he wanted to get rid of. But, as Morton discovers later, the Colonel's resentment is also due to the fact that he erroneously believes Morton to be the ringleader of all the other officers who are trying to get rid of the Colonel. The Colonel's nickname is 'Old Judas', but the conspiracy of mistrust among the officers shows that the treachery cuts both ways. This turn stops the story sounding like a paranoiac's vindication, and instead gives an insight into how the pressures of war can induce feelings of helplessness and paranoia. When Morton hears of the plot to complain about the Colonel, his access of pity for his enemy demonstrates the Christian comprehension and forgiveness also exemplified by Tietjens:

He was suddenly sorry for old Judas—the nervous, worrying, worried, lean old man with a too difficult job. For it is a terrible job for an ageing man—to command a desperately pushing B[attalio]n in the line—there are all the papers and papers and papers, and the responsibility—and the considerable danger. It was really, too much, Morton knew, for any one man.[16]

The effect of Morton's compassion on his story is to exonerate him—somewhat too facilely—from the suspicions about his personality and his sanity that Ford has been so patiently accumulating. The only accusation against him that the Colonel can make is that of cowardice, on the grounds that when, while on patrol, he saw a group of six Germans, he did not kill them. But to do so would have jeopardized the patrol. The accusation is too preposterous to be convincing, too palpably a foil to enable Morton to stand unjustly accused. In this work the Colonel's view—in which we can recognize Colonel Cooke's view of Ford—can only be given as long as it is labelled as deranged and unjust.

However, Ford does also present that much more disturbing and unflattering view of himself in another important but neglected work of the same period: the short story 'The Colonel's Shoes'.[17] Like most of his post-war fiction, this story gauges the pressures pushing men to the 'edge' of sanity during the war: 'There were many who went over the edge of unreason—but there were many and many who stayed, by the grace of God, just on this side of the edge [. . .] It was like that with Lieut.-Colonel Leslie Arkwright—and it was very nearly like it with his nephew, Lieut. Hugh, both of my Battalion.' The story has been told to the narrator by an army medical officer, which gives it this diagnostic tone—and is also designed to check our incredulity at its later paranormal occurrences.

The uncle and nephew are so close that 'they thought alike'—until they encounter the dubious figure of Captain Gotch:

(that isn't his name. He is alive still. He would be.) This was one of those men as to whom there is a black mark against their names in the High Books. There are such men and there are such books in the world. (I don't mean the Confidential Records of a Battalion Orderly Room—but books kept higher still.) They are men who appear foursquare, able, intelligent, they generally have flashing teeth—and they are unsound. They get on—but they don't get on as well as you expect them to. The inexperienced like them enormously; the experienced hold their tongues about them.

Hugh is one of the younger men who 'liked Captain Gotch immensely'; and he finds it unjust that every time Gotch applies for staff jobs, the Colonel 'holds his tongue' by not recommending him. The Colonel is near the edge of exhaustion from the protracted strain, and keeps dropping off in uncontrollable narcoleptic naps. This psychological idiosyncrasy (like Morton's—and Ford's—panics) manifests itself only after the event, once the battalion is out of the trenches. When Gotch accuses some of his men of disobeying orders, the Colonel, who has had one of his momentary sleeping fits, wakes up to hear himself saying 'Case explained'—despite the severity of the charge. Hugh feels that his uncle has again been unjust.

The story characteristically disperses its author throughout the personae. If 'Lieut. Hugh' sounds like Lieut. Hueffer, and the worn out Colonel sounds like the Ford who wrote to Hunt from Rouen, 'I am tired of fighting', it is Gotch who embodies many of Ford's concerns about what he might be like. He shares Ford's ability to gain the admiration of the young—*les jeunes*—together with the distrust of the old. Ford had written to Lucy Masterman from the Somme: 'the off'rs here are a terrible lot, without a soul that one can really talk to except the little boys.' The Arkwrights are eventually reunited in suggesting that Gotch should apply for a job with the Divisional Follies. The Colonel is prepared to recommend him for a job as an artist! In a central scene Hugh overhears him working off his frustration playing the piano in the large French house occupied by the Battalion Headquarters—rather as in Ford's later story about the Prince of Wales telling him to 'Go on playing'. He certainly felt that 'black mark' against his name: not just in his service record—Colonel Cooke had read to him the communication from GHQ turning down his application for a staff job because his record was so bad—but also in the putative 'book, kept in a holy of holies, in which bad marks are set down against men of family and position in England'.[18] As an artist, he was not quite 'sound'; not quite a gentleman. He was not quite English. Later in the story Gotch hears his own name, whereas the Company Sergeant-Major swears he was talking about the 'Boche'. The confusion, which is not resolved, mixes together Ford's sensitivity about his double nationality with a paranoiac feeling that things are being said about him. There is a more ominous hint that the higher books are those of Fate, or of the Recording Angel, inscribed with a possible character flaw: unsoundness of mind, or cowardliness. Gotch's nickname conjoins Ford's own, and also his approximate age (which Colonel Cooke, at least, held against him), with the charge of cowardice. He is known as 'Old Forty': ' "Forty foot down and still digging," the men called him, because he never left the bottom of the deepest dug-out.'

The character whose 'foursquare' appearance is at odds with his deeds is familiar from *The Good Soldier*. In *Parade's End* Christopher Tietjens's moral four-squareness is at odds with the slanders and rumours which circulate about him. The typescript of 'The Colonel's Shoes' contains examples of the rumours about Gotch, which echo the rumours about Ford and women, and his possibly German sympathies: 'things were said about him—they were probably untrue. They ranged from nasty—very nasty things about him and women and the Colonel of his Reserve Battalion, to the allegation that a firm, in which he had been a junior partner before the war, had been fined heavily for trading with the enemy.'[19] But in the published version even this was omitted. Gotch appears to make his elders feel he is 'unsound'. We are told that his men hold him in contempt; that many of them are going sick; and also that (like Ford) he has 'debts'. But we are given no sound reasons *why*: nothing to substantiate the distrust. The only hint is made in connection with his musical performances, and possibly (though not necessarily) suggests a *sexual* unsoundness: 'He would sing the popular sentimental songs of the day, and put in nasty meanings and raise one brown eyebrow when he came to them. It made him popular with the men of the Battalion who were not in his Company when he sang to them at smoking concerts improvised in old barns and tents and pigsties. But his own Company was nasty.' This last cryptic comment is not explained either. (Does it mean that they had reason to be hostile to Gotch? That they were themselves too inured to 'nasty meanings' to find them entertaining? That he was unlucky to be in such an unsympathetic unit?) If there is an implication that pigsties are the appropriate setting for his work, whether such a verdict is just or not is simply not justified. Gotch is a characteristically Fordian enigma. We know what responses he provokes, but not why. He is significant, but it is hard to define what he signifies. The picture becomes dual in the way the narrator keeps disavowing the judgements he is reporting ('I daresay I am unjust to him; but then I didn't like him'). It may be an unjust picture, but it is all we have to go on.

It is in this way that Ford's genius for showing two sides of an affair enables him to face both sides of the imbroglio with Colonel Cooke: to acknowledge that, like Gotch, he may have plagued his Colonel, as well as having been plagued by him, as both Gotch and Morton are by theirs. Without any attempt at self-justification or self-pity, the story is an attempt to understand how he might appear to others—to someone *in* 'the Colonel's shoes'; and why. The main sense of the title, however, is one which returns us to the questioning and fusing of identities in 'True Love & a G.C.M.' The climax of the story comes when Hugh goes, rationally speaking, over the edge, and begins to have 'illusions'. Sitting in an engrossed reverie as Gotch plays the piano, he suddenly realizes 'that it was his uncle's worries he was feeling'. As his uncle falls asleep again, Hugh's mind as it were relieves him, and becomes him. It is thus Hugh who finds himself in 'The Colonel's Shoes', at the moment when Gotch's second charge is being heard—this time against the Sergeant-Major who would not back Gotch up in his previous charge of insubordination by the men. In his uncle's shoes, Hugh makes the same decision, dismissing this case too. After the Flaubertian realism of *The Good Soldier* such a story sounds fanciful. Indeed, it is introduced as the sort of tall story the MO (who 'happened to be an Irishman') would tell to while away a long train journey. But—as his remarks about psychological extremity indicate—it has its place in a thriving wartime genre of trench-myths and supernatural tales.[20] The strains of prolonged exposure to danger and familiarity with death fostered a profusion of tales of ghosts, the supernatural, the bizarre.

The sympathies of the story seem to be with the uncle and nephew. The MO recounts conversations with both of them, but none with Gotch, which tends to alienate him. But there is a strength in the strange connection in the story between the total mental sympathy between these two, which enables Hugh to assume his uncle's identity (as Gabriel had assumed his father's), and the act of imaginative sympathy with which Ford is able to penetrate the identities of the very kinds of people who found him least sympathetic. It is Gotch's art that enables the mental communion. The theme of the con-fusion of identities, which Ford begins to sound in these two works, and the complex forces of sympathy it marshals, becomes increasingly important in Ford's last phase. 'True Love & a G.C.M.' and 'The Colonel's Shoes' suggest the impact of Ford's war experience on the notion of exchanged and mistaken identity which governs *The Rash Act* and *Henry for Hugh*. The *donnée* of those books seems much more plausible than many critics have found it once it is seen as deriving from Ford's confusion about his identity after his shell-concussion, and from the questions that made him ask about himself. Ford's conception of the novelist's sympathetic insight gave him a strong propensity towards the feelings of alienation from the self produced by shell-shock. The feeling that you are inside another mind, trying improvisatorily to find your way around a new identity, is familiar from his pre-war fiction too. To some extent Mr Sorrell's need to maintain the fiction that he is the medieval pilgrim he is believed to be in *Ladies Whose Bright Eyes* anticipates the theme of exchanged identities. More surprisingly, his con-fusion is also triggered by concussion: the shock of the train-crash. Rather than a mysterious coincidence, it is an example of Ford's tendency to respond most directly to those experiences to which his fictional experiments had already sensitized him. It is for this reason that his life sometimes seems to act out scenes from his previous fiction. What the pre-war versions lack is the penetrating combination of the themes of exchanged identity and incipient insanity.

The Medical Board would not pass Ford as fit to return to France, so he was given command of a company of the 23rd King's Liverpool Regiment, stationed at Kinmel Park. The duties were light, and he was officially under medical treatment until mid-May. Here, in contrast to Lieutenant-Colonel Cooke, he found a friendly command-ing officer who had confidence in him. Lieutenant-Colonel G. R. Powell commended Ford in his service record in terms which vindicated him from at least some of Cooke's strictures: 'Has shown marked aptitude for grasping any intricate subject and pos-sesses great powers of organization—a lecturer of the first water on several military subjects—conducted the duties of housing officer to the unit (average strength 2800) with great ability.'[21] The change that Flint had noticed in Ford had become apparent to Hunt too. Her 1917 diary—the main source of evidence we have for his life during the rest of the year—makes painful reading. He was still feeling emotionally unstable, and her own erratic attempts first to repossess and then to relinquish him only made matters worse. When she describes the 'sexual rage' that overcame her when he was with her at Selsey in March, one can see elements that would be fused into the compound that would be Sylvia Tietjens. Hunt's accounts of her visits during the summer to Redcar, by the Tees bay on the Yorkshire coast, where Ford had been transferred to a training command, almost read like notes for Sylvia's following Tietjens into France in *No More Parades*: the emotional frenzy, the disconcerting *voltes-faces*, the adultering of the military and the marital, even some of Hunt's turns of phrase, all get into the novel.[22] Their life seems uncannily to re-enact the hysterical convulsions of *The Good Soldier*. Hunt felt that 'Something changed' when on 22 March they started talking frankly about Patmore. When Hunt threatened vengeance, he congratulated her: 'that is the first human—natural thing you have said! I suppose it will all settle itself. You & Brigit will claw each other & either she will get me—or you. That's life. Take what you can get.' It is, approximately, Ashburnham's predica-ment, uttered with Dowell's resignation.

Hunt became convinced that Ford was acting coldly because she had withdrawn her financial guarantee. But her tendency to pay his bills after each reconciliation proved self-destructive, confirming her sense that he had only stayed with her while she could give him 'pleasurable sensations of opulence of flattery of consequence'. She did lasting damage to Ford's reputation by telling her friends that Ford only stayed with her for her money. Moral double standards ensured that once it was known that Ford accepted a woman's money (which he did), it was assumed that he was immoral, a sponger or cad, lazy, and indulgent—which he wasn't. Few people can have tried harder to live by their writings than Ford, averaging three major books per year (in addition to the poetry and the prolific journalism) from 1910 to 1915. But the army left him neither the time nor the strength to write much, and he soon found himself more than usually hard up. He told his mother: 'I cannot afford to keep going in the Regt. in England—tho' I can manage well enough in France.' Since the doctors would not pass him as fit enough to go out again, he was again considering resigning his commission and enlisting as a private: 'It wd. be disagreeable; but not, really, as disagreeable as the perpetual struggle to make both ends meet that I have had ever since I have been in the army.'[23]

He was trying to extricate himself from his relationship with Violet. By 1926 she was able to say (rather as Elsie later came to see) 'F.M.H. would have done very well without me; perhaps better, as I have come to see now.' But for the rest of the war she fought not to let him go: 'I told him when he left me that he was no longer free like other men that if he found he couldn't bear to live with me, his only remedy before having let me into such an impasse was to cut his throat.'[24] Ford's instinctive chivalry made him susceptible to such arguments. Hunt heard from her friends that 'He says he is to stick to me whatever I do, since the circumstances in which we came together make it impossible for him to leave me'. This left them in an impossible position—an Ashburnhamesque façade of marriage. There was much private bitterness, perhaps exacerbated when Ford found he had become more dependent upon her—emotionally as well as financially—than he had realized. After he had been to their friends the Haseldens for bridge on 28 March they had a row. She told him to leave South Lodge, '& not sleep here if he didn't love me': 'He said he cared for me but he wouldn't be bound—the feeling of the moment. He explained—that I was a most irritating person to live with—that he couldn't love me in this house with these old servants . . . that domesticity had killed the feeling.' He agreed to go, but reluctantly, and in the afternoon. Hunt said 'no—*now*, before lunch—for good. He said "All right" & went & then came back.' When he asked her to send his things on or make a parcel of them, she became blind with silent rage. Then Ford began to fulminate wildly that Hunt, 'by insulting a servant of the King had insulted the British Army'. She shrewdly—and rather generously—noted: 'The 3 days at the YMCA still rankled and I had to give in.' He wanted to leave, but he couldn't quite stay away.

On 2 May Hunt recorded her own 'first infidelity to F'. There is no evidence that Ford ever knew of it, but Hunt wrote that the memory of it bore her up when, at Redcar on 2 June, she berated him about his infidelities, asking him if he had loved her or Miss Ross when he had been in hospital at Christmas. He didn't say, but when she persisted, asking 'If you were very ill then and the doctor had said that someone shld be sent for would you have sent for me?', she says he was 'on his ear' in a moment, teasing her: 'It depends—one can't tell at supreme moments. I might have sent for you or Jane [Wells?] or Nora [Haselden] or Brigit [Patmore]', and added with novelistic curiosity: 'it is interesting to speculate.' 'I had asked for it & got it', mused Hunt: 'But how can one be devoted to a cruel jester like that! Later he said: "You see I *can not* care for people with any constancy." ' She oscillated between, on the one hand, capitulating to Ford ('it is a matter of personal liking & I want F in the house so much that I will be his housekeeper in it & nothing more'), and on the other, struggling *not* to be devoted to him, by trying to adopt a detached attitude, and by encouraging an admirer of her own, Arthur Watts. But she could not forget Ford, and could not help writing to him. 'I long to be able to tell him that I have not love for him enough and not even respect only an unholy passion that will last till I die', she wrote in May; and later: 'Ford dominates me to such an extent I *can't* keep up an attitude.'[25] She referred to Nora Haselden as a 'Dear sad complacent commonplace rival!' Then she suspected that Ford was infatuated with Mrs Powell ('a terrible, plain, flirt—the worst'), the wife of his new colonel. Ford had given manuscripts of poems from *On Heaven* to Jane Wells, Mrs Jackson, and Lucy Masterman. To Hunt's chagrin, he asked Mrs Powell to help arrange the poems for the volume.[26]

There were other signs of Ford's mental strain, which often manifested itself in feelings of persecution. He had consulted a Dr Head—almost certainly Henry Head, the leading neurologist, shell-shock specialist, and amateur poet, who had treated Virginia Woolf before the war (he is thought to be a character source for Sir William Bradshaw in *Mrs Dalloway*), befriended Robert Graves and Siegfried Sassoon during it, and Thomas Hardy afterwards. When Hunt had been to tea with Mrs Head, she noted: 'I heard Ford did threaten in a club to prosecute Dr Head for abusing him & divulging professional secrets. It makes my path easier. He is not responsible.' The army disagreed, promoting Ford to lieutenant on 1 July.[27] Hunt found him 'a stranger on Redcar platform' when she visited him in August. They rowed throughout the month. When he denied writing the letter to Miss Ross, which Hunt said she had got hold of, she wrote in her diary: 'That settled it all. I hit him & then took him to bed. He is not sane.' Taking him to bed only made her more frustrated and angry. After one particularly fierce night, his face 'all scratched' by her, he told her he was impotent. She didn't believe him.[28] When he was on leave at Selsey he told her on 23 October: 'I suppose I want adventure'; 'If I could have another woman I might desire *you*.' 'It seemed perverted,' said Hunt, 'but F is so queer', and added: 'I took it calm.' She should not have done. When he told her he could have her 'through another woman', the other woman had just left the room. Like Leonora Ashburnham, Hunt appears to have decided that if she couldn't stop her partner's affairs she could manage them. She had invited Stella Bowen, a 24-year-old Australian painter, and her friend and flat-mate Phyllis Reid, to stay at Selsey, because Ford had 'asked for "something young" ' while he was there. Hunt had met Bowen when Ezra Pound brought her to a party in July; when Bowen danced with Arthur Watts she admitted to feeling a little jealous. Phyllis Reid she described as a 'great beauty'. Nevertheless, she invited these two young temptations to meet Ford. He had told her that he wanted 'to end letters'; so it was probably a desperate attempt on her part to attract vicariously the man who was now 'nor husband nor lover'. She was re-creating the scenario of two (or more) passions, in which Leonora acquires Maisie Maidan for Edward, and tries to persuade Nancy to become his mistress in *The Good Soldier*, which in turn drew on Hunt's complicity in the flirtations between Ford and her niece Rosamond or her friend Brigit. Ford must have met Stella Bowen on 22 October 1917, when he turned up at Selsey. He and Violet were soon quarrelling:

All was lost when Stella B going out of the room he threw his arms round me & kissed me. I *could* not respond. He turned sour. At night, after she had gone, he said coldly 'Well, I'm going to bed'—(I had given him the big double bed & stayed in my own small bedroom). Then I made my first mistake. I exclaimed 'And is this all—you have come all this way for—after all this time!'

No more amenity. Yet he makes me go to his bed & lie in his arms for a time. I hate it. He says he is *not* impotent, but he can't have *me*—'I could have you through another woman.' That is simply to say he is tired of me. I realised it & had the sense not to say anything. I just went. He kissed me. I said 'Don't be rough because of my nose bleeding again' & he said with pride 'I *am* rough!'[29]

Ford and Stella did not begin an affair while he was still living with Violet—some do not . . . But this first meeting transformed him. When, back in Yorkshire, he wrote to Stella to thank her for the trouble she had taken over some arrangements for a Mrs Mitchell to visit Redcar, it was 'Dear Miss Bowen'; but the note of flirtation is unmistakable: 'It seems very remote & cold here & the pale gleams from a luminary that might be a dim sun or a bright moon do little to make up for the sunshine of y^r. smile!' Hunt found him more than usually protean. Iris Barry had told her that Ford was 'an elemental . . . a male Undine, compact mostly of water'. (Undine is the seductive water-nymph who needs to marry in order to get a soul, but who eventually returns to the water.) In December, undecided herself about how to behave towards Ford, Hunt elaborated the idea:

Still wondering. I shall call Ford Kühleborn for he is like Undine's Uncle, who when the Knight struck at him dissolved into foam. F is like him. One can neither depend on him or fight him.

Then I come home & find a lyric he has sent me that if it was written to her, any woman would forgive a man anything![30]

With hindsight she realized that the poems testified to the stirrings of a new love, and she added, as an afterthought: 'To Stella.' It is true that he was writing some of his most beautiful lyrics this December; though the ones that have survived are not *about* Stella. The three 'Regimental Records' are dramatized monologues, imagining the loves of some of the men; such as 'Pte. Barnes':

> He said: 'I love her for her sense
> And for her quiet innocence,
> And since she bears without complaint
> An anxious life of toil and care
> As if she were a fireside saint. . . .
>
> 'And so her quiet eyes ensnare
> My eyes all day and fill my sense

> And take
> My thoughts all day away from other things; and keep
> Me, when I should be fast asleep,
> Awake!'

For all the sentimentality of the female stereotype, this is moving in its picture of intimacy subduing anxiety. The bold lineation of the second stanza brings out the musicality of the structure—and the feeling. The transition from musing to song-like reverie is all the more effective for the slight incoherence, as the syntax of the first stanza trails away into a vision of love: a vision in which that strategically placed word 'sense', which already sounded slightly unstable in its rhyme with 'innocence' (which almost makes 'sense' sound like its opposite!), returns, its meaning transformed from 'common sense' to a broader notion which includes perceptual senses. The wonderful unfolding of the final clause, surprising but inevitable, leaves us with that effective juxtaposition of 'asleep, | Awake!', suggesting that the quiet power of his love has taken him out of his senses. If there is any autobiographical reference here, it is to the kind of domestic security Ford *couldn't* have with Violet, rather than to any experience he had yet had with Stella. Another poem, which he sent to Hunt on his birthday, 17 December, is less oblique. 'One Last Prayer' is in his best Christina Rossetti mode: breathless, subdued, dying cadences:

> Let me wait, my dear,
> One more day,
> Let me linger near,
> Let me stay.
> Do not bar the gate or draw the blind
> Or lock the door that yields,
> Dear, be kind!
>
> I have only you beneath the skies
> To rest my eyes
> [. . .][31]

Hunt had prepared a 'letter that Ford will call an ultimatum'. She doesn't say exactly what its terms were—presumably that he could only live with her as her husband or lover, not as her lodger. 'It is the end of the world', she felt: '—that world at least but I shall feel better, not in a false position.' She thought, with less than usual self-knowledge, she would be 'F's friend', and added: 'Nothing is changed. I have only legalised our separation as it were.'[32] The poem reads more as a plea to Violet not to banish him, rather than an address to a new lover. Its effectiveness is a matter of tone. Ostensibly pleading for love, its images are all of coldness. '*One* more day' acknowledges that any rapprochement can only be temporary; 'One *Last* Prayer' intimates that the end is near—the end of the relationship, or perhaps even the end of his life. The short lines following the long enact a resignation, a settling for less. It is a plea which expects the answer 'No'; another of Ford's exact evocations of half-heartedness.

'No' was evidently the answer Ford got, since he wrote to Lucy Masterman in January asking her if she knew of any cheap lodgings he could take for his leave in London, since 'South Lodge does not seem to be available'.[33] He wrote to Hunt: 'I

suppose then our relations are at an end. I am very sorry, but I suppose it had to be.'
Yet part of him seemed to want it not to be. When she replied 'I am very sorry too',
he answered: 'If you sorry & I sorry cannot we come together?' But her verdict was: 'If
he isn't ravenous for me, then there is no need to try & come together.' In the event
Hunt let him stay at South Lodge while she herself stayed the nights with Ford's
mother in Brook Green. She wrote that she was 'otherwise friends' with him. They
were still appearing together in public this winter. Grace Lovat Fraser described an
air-raid party to which Hunt brought Ford when he was on leave: 'Violet, with
inspired sartorial genius, arrived wearing Ford's "tin hat" firmly anchored to her head
by a broad pink satin ribbon tied in a bow under her chin. Her entrance was hilariously
greeted and she took this very well; but I have never been quite sure whether she wore
the helmet as a joke or as a serious attempt at protection.'[34] But during this leave she
must have taunted him with having failed what she saw as a test of his love: 'that he was
willing to accept board & lodging without me'; for he left annoyed with her, and Hunt
wrote that 'He said "De Lorge—the man who was sent into the lion's den by the lady
for her glove. He got her glove, but never forgave!"' Froissart's legendary character
De Lorge (written about by Schiller, Leigh Hunt, and Browning too) was dared by his
lady to recover the glove she had tossed into an arena of wild beasts to test his love. 'He
accepted the challenge, but on his return flung the glove into her face, his love turned
to contempt at this revelation of the lady's character.'[35] Ford resented this further
challenge to his integrity. Hunt wrote, on 24 January, in her last entry for this 1917/
18 diary: 'F never forgave me for going to Mrs H's while he was on leave. That did it,
finally.' Though she added as an afterthought: 'Did it? It was Stella . . . the new
passion.'

4

1918: A TALE OF RECONSTRUCTION:
STELLA BOWEN

He had known everyone, and was full of stories . . .
(Stella Bowen, *Drawn from Life*)

Ford was probably at Redcar over Christmas. Hunt spent the day alone in London, and dined with the Soskices. Ford invited her to the New Year's Eve ball at Redcar, but she didn't go. Between Christmas Eve and New Year's he wrote 'a patriotic poem [. . .] with nothing about "Britannia" & the Lion & so on, in it'. He called it 'Footsloggers'—a tribute to the infantry—and dedicated it to 'C.F.G.M.[asterman]'. The poem didn't only draw on his war experience—'For me, going out to France | Is like the exhaustion of dawn | After a dance'—it shows him preparing himself to go out to France again, soon after the festivities. On 7 January he was promoted to captain. He told Lucy Masterman that the colonel of the 14th Battalion had asked for him, but Redcar wanted to keep him; and that afterwards he asked to resign the Redcar job, but the doctors would not pass him fit enough to fight, so he had had to apply to be attached to a Labour Battalion. 'It is annoying because a Labour Bn is just as danger-ous & uncomfortable as a Service one, yet the credit is less', he wrote, adding—not quite convincingly?—'However, I don't mind that.' In the event he didn't get sent out again. Instead, he was given a new job attached to the staff, to go 'all over the N.[orth] of England inspecting training & lecturing'. He began to feel his luck had changed: 'It is in many ways lucky for me', he wrote to Katharine, 'as I was passed fit & should have gone out to my B^n again just the day after I got the order to join the Staff'; though contemplating his escape made him feel more than ever a ghost: 'my B^n has been pretty well wiped out since then, so I suppose I sh^d have gone West with it.' He offered to send her a copy of *On Heaven*, thinking of which made him feel ghostlier: 'most of the poems were written in Albert & just in front of Bailleul where the Germans now are again. It is rather an eerie feeling because, having had to pay so much attention to the nature of the ground, I seem to know say Armentières & Plugstreet better than any other place in the world—& now it is all gone again, or worse than gone, for itself, poor dear.'[1]

His Staff job lasted until the end of the war, and he was even offered 'an after the war post as Educational Advisor to the Northern Command, permanently', with the rank of lieutenant colonel. (He thought about it seriously, but realized it would have stopped him writing.) From 14 March to 1 August he was given the temporary rank of brevet major (meaning that he got the extra status but not the extra pay). He lectured on the Ross rifle, 'which was a gimcrack concern at the best, with aperture

sights and fittings like watch springs and innumerable ways of being put out of order';
and on 'the Causes of the War or on any other department of the rag-bag of knowledge
that we had to inflict on the unfortunates committed to our charge'. His other topics
included 'Censorship', 'War Aims', 'Attacks on Strong Points', 'Salvage', 'Military
Law', 'Harmonising Rifle Fire', 'Cyphers', 'Geography and Strategy', 'Hospitals',
and—of course—'French Civilisation'—'So I must be some sort of Encyclopaedia',
he told Bowen. He always remembered the lessons he learned about narrative from his
own lecturing experiments: that a strategic digression—about 'the best way those
troops could spend their money when next on leave in Rouen', or about his 'first ride
in an automobile'—could actually intensify the audience's expectations about the
main topic. By way of digression in one of his post-war books, *A Mirror to France*, he
recalled asking the audiences: 'If you had lashings of money: all the money you could
ask for, and if you had lashings of leave: all the leave in the world! what would you do?'
The novelist may have been looking for plots, but Ford said he 'never but once got an
answer beyond a usual gasp of agony' at the image he had raised. The exception was
'the licensed humorist' in his own regiment, who called out 'bravely but with immense
feeling [. . .] *"Go mad!"* ' 'It gave me the chance to answer myself better than usual',
says Ford, 'for after many orderly rooms I knew og Evans as well as I knew any man.'
'Oh no, you would not', Ford answered:

'[. . .] With a white waistcoat and a Panama hat, with a fat cigar in your lips, three dozen of
Veuve Clicquot in the rumble, a tart in your arms, and a gramophone braying beside the
chauffeur, you'd be running down through the South of France to make a hog of yourself in
a white-and-gilt hotel at Monte Carlo.'
   And a dozen awestruck voices whispered:
'Gawd! Old 'Oof's struck it!'
They called me 'Old 'Oof' in that unit.[2]

Characteristically, he catches himself sounding too self-congratulatory—perhaps
claiming too much for his rapport with the men, or his psychological acumen—so he
jokes deflatingly: 'But whether they were disclosing their own secret thoughts or
merely referring to the known proclivities of og Evans, I don't know.' Yet—equally
characteristically—what sounds provocatively implausible was based on fact. Ford
was popular in the regiment, and was known as 'old Hoof'. Violet Hunt was struck
with Ford's ability to tell her what she would have said to another man. No doubt he
could also surprise his regiment with his sharp renderings of their desires and expressions. *A Mirror to France* was written between *No More Parades* and *A Man Could
Stand Up—*, and one can hear Ford inhabiting his character of Christopher Tietjens.
What is remarkable here is the intensity with which he has identified himself and
Tietjens, novelist and soldier. The knowledge of his men—a quality Ford particularly
prizes in Tietjens—is more than a pseudo-feudal superiority: it is a novelist's imaginative involvement. The technically aware speaker, sensitive to the responses of his
audience, is a figure for the novelist getting his effects.[3]
   In May Ford came back from lecturing in Leeds to find that his Commanding
Officer got hold of the pre-war *Daily Mirror* interview in which Ford had claimed to
be a German citizen. He asked Ford why he had not revealed this when he applied for

his commission, but Ford told him that he had been assured by Masterman on the outbreak of the war that his nationality was not in question, and anyway he had shown allegiance to the king. He wrote to Hunt to assure her: 'I take it that these questions do not affect our marriage as that took place in France', but suggested that she shouldn't come to visit him because the marriage might be questioned. But the marriage was by now only an empty form: a fiction to preserve Hunt's 'reputation'. Ford was beginning a new romance—by letter—with Stella Bowen. By the end of June he was replying to a 'triple letter' from her: 'Dear Miss Bowen: / Of course you may call me Ford if you like—& shall I not proudly wag my tail like any large Newfoundland when its mistress calls it Parto?' With a fine piece of Fordian dis-avowal, he added: '(That is not *meant* to be an insult—but a compliment.)' Bowen was not as shocked as other young colonial ladies might have been at the notion of being Ford's 'mistress'. She found the flirtatious proud pathos of his letters irresistible. 'I am going to lecture to 3,000 WAC's and VAD's [the Women's Army Corps and the Voluntary Aid Detachment] this week. Imagine it! It is a job for Yeats or Ezra rather than for poor old me.' Yeats and Pound are not merely examples of self-possessed and self-projecting lecturers. Ford is also contrasting himself with them as poets. His wartime habit of talking of himself as a ghost became his way of talking about his literary persona too. He had said his farewell to Literature. But with *On Heaven: and Poems Written on Active Service*, published in April and dedicated to Lt.-Col. Powell, he had visibly come through the war as a writer. Now, when he considered his return, it was as a strange survival of the pre-war literary scene, one elbowed aside by the energetic *jeunes*. 'But how you gifted people with all the talents frighten me!', he told Bowen. And when Pound's friend, the young poet Iris Barry, asked him for criticism of her work, he wrote revealingly about how his own work was animated by self-pity at his own—imaginary—extinction:

Dear Miss Barry:
   I have been reading yr. poems & the adventures of Bridget with a great deal of attention—& pleasure. Of course I like them—& admire them. There is a certain—I was going to say ferocity—but let us say determination of attack on visible objects that I have always tried to get at myself—without much success—but that you seem to get in your stride. I have always been preaching to people not to write 'about' things but to write *things*—& you really do it—so I like to flatter myself that you are an indirect product of my preachings—a child of my poor old age. Now that I am an extinct volcano you shall continue eruptions [. . .]⁴

That talk of his 'poor old age' is partly ironic. Yet, aged only 44, 'old Hoof' had decided he was going to act the part. As Alan Judd says, Ford seemed more at ease with himself as he grew older. It also transformed his relations with other writers. Criticism from the young was what was to be expected if you were an extinct volcano: 'Of course you will say, with the proud assurance of youth, that you have never read any of my work', he told Barry, 'But that is not necessary'. After his experiences in the war, and his proximity to death there, Ford had the proud assurance of age that enabled him to give criticism as unruffledly as he took it. With the characteristic magisterial cadence—'Of course, you will say [. . .]'—he modulates from the novelist (who knows how cruelly the young genius behaves) to the poet-critic. Iris Barry's poems were not quite 'the real right thing', he told her in Jamesese, because they didn't convey 'the sort of joy in words as such that is the province of the authentic poet':

You seem to be looking at the reader and saying: 'See what I can do with seven silver balls!' Forget yourself, mon amie—forget yourself & the admiring reader. At least—that is how I feel it. A poem—a volume of poems—isn't a set of cubes for mosaics exhibited in the black velvet of museum cases. It is a quiet monologue during a summer walk in which one seeks to render oneself beloved to someone one loves. It is a revelation of a personality that wants sympathy from men of goodwill—not a bludgeoning of Times Literary Supplements or a display of dexterity. That is what, for the time being, is wrong with yr Imagiste & Cubist Associates. They are too much 'out' for the purpose of expressing scorn, & try to be loveable in original media—too little. Of course that is a phase that will pass with youth—which eventually sees that clubbing one's grandfathers is only a means to an end.

Ford never forgave himself for having clubbed his own grandfather with his clumsy adolescent wit, and it is characteristic of him to imagine himself as both the clubber and the clubbed. His critical position here is dual in another way. The familiar criticism that *les jeunes* are circus performers of the ego is qualified by the way he is also recognizing the role of the ego in his own mode. The impressionist paradox puts the self back into the heart of the work which was founded on self-forgetting: it reveals the personality of the impersonal artist. To 'render oneself beloved' one must first 'render oneself', his language hints, even while he is telling Iris Barry to forget herself. His envisaging of the reader is dual too. She should forget the 'admiring reader'—because performing *for* admiration can become a narcissistic parade of self-admiration. Yet the reimagining of the reader as lover makes it impossible to forget the reader. Ford himself never did forget his reader—which is why he was so aware of the dangers of histrionic self-consciousness (when the writer winks at the reader instead of getting on with the story). There is, then, a form of modesty in his hauteur, since he knows he needs his lecture as much as his neophyte—possibly even more, since she can succeed where he knows he usually fails.

On Heaven was not a volcanic publication, but it proved Ford not to be extinct. He inscribed a copy to Stella Bowen on 23 July; and he was proud enough to tell her when he heard that the *British Weekly* had noted that his 'literary power does not fall short of genius', and that there were 'fine, appealing, piercing things on every page'. (When he came into breakfast everyone at his mess table exclaimed 'Genius!', he told her.) The faithful *Outlook* praised 'a power of sensation extending beyond the normal and the knowledge of handling his material that comes of long experience', and made a point about the poetry that could also stand as one of the truest values of his prose: 'Mr. Hueffer has one faculty to an unusual degree, that of portraying the several parallel levels of feeling at any given moment.' Even the *Times Literary Supplement* did not exactly bludgeon: after carping about the self-deprecating preface, it conceded grudgingly: 'His war poems do achieve an emotional effect, but by no means always the harmonious beauty born of the magic of word and cadence.' Well, no: but 'harmonious beauty' isn't what the Western Front usually conjures to mind. The reviewer would presumably have preferred Rupert Brooke to Wilfred Owen, but he (or she; or they) could recognize that Ford's rendering of unhistrionic patriotism was truer than Brooke's elegant pose of self-sacrifice: ' "Footsloggers" [. . .] contains one of the finest celebrations we have seen of the pathetic beauty of the English countryside as a thing worth dying for.' And that is the point of Ford's sermon to Iris Barry: if you are too preoccupied with how you appear to your audience, your expressions will be falsified. His image of the reader as the lover is beautifully apt, not (or not only) because Ford's seductive intimacy is part of the effect he is always trying to achieve; but because lovers' talk is a paradoxical blend of heightened self-awareness (near the verge of self-consciousness) and yet unparalleled naturalness and selflessness.[5]

Stella Bowen's father, an estate agent in Adelaide, had died when she was 3. When her mother also died, in 1914, Stella persuaded her guardian uncle to let her visit England. She sailed in April 1914, a few weeks before her twenty-first birthday, to study painting for a year at the Westminster School of Art, where she was a pupil of Sickert's. She never went back. She and her striking flat-mate Phyllis Reid knew Ford very well by reputation, wrote Bowen, 'because he was one of the writers whom Ezra allowed us to admire. *Ladies Whose Bright Eyes* and *The Good Soldier* were two of the best-thumbed books on our shelves, and Ford's war poems [. . .] were being discussed and admired at Harold Monro's Poetry Bookshop, whose weekly poetry readings we frequented.' Hunt, too, encouraged their interest in Ford's writing; she appears not to have realized what other interests were developing when she gave them a copy of *Mr. Fleight* in June, inscribed to them jointly as 'Stillis'. 'Ford was an innovation in our circle', wrote Bowen:

because not only was he in khaki, but he actually liked it. He was the only intellectual I had met to whom army discipline provided a conscious release from the torments and indecisions of a super-sensitive brain. To obey orders was, for him, a positive holiday, and the pleasure he took in recounting rather bucolic anecdotes of the army was the measure of his need for escape from the intrigues and sophistications of literary London.

It was also the measure of his need for, his existence through and within, narrative. 'He had known everyone, and was full of stories', said Bowen: he was 'considerably older than the rest of our friends, and much more impressive. He was very large, with a pink face, yellow hair, and drooping, bright blue eyes. His movements were gentle and deliberate and his quiet and mellow voice spoke, to an Australian ear, with ineffable authority.'[6]

By August 1918 his passion for her had become explicit. 'My dear', he wrote, '[. . .] I only know that nothing but you can interest me for ten minutes together—but perhaps you do not want to hear from me.' He was rendering himself beloved to someone he had fallen in love with, sensing her responsiveness to his claims for pity. 'I ought not to write: I ought to be dead, I think—for you said, truly, that I was a harassed personality. I wonder how you knew?' 'I belong to you altogether—& to you only', he told her—she must have wondered whether Hunt wasn't going to claim a stake in him—'for good, and all. That is the truth.' Something he had said or done had upset her, and he tried to explain it as 'a sort of irritation—and I did not expect to see you again'. Perhaps she didn't think she ought to see him (the husband of her friend, an older woman) again, and kept away. 'There are such a lot of things I sh[d.] like to say to you', he wrote, '—because, you know, you are practically the only person I have to talk to—or care to talk to—I wonder if we shall ever meet again.' He imagined having 'remembrance now' of their present life, implicitly imagining himself dead, or at least gone: 'In years away from this, when I am quite forgotten, maybe you will turn up some of these old letters & feel a little like saying: "Ronsard m'a célebrée Du temps que j'étais jeune!". But then I am not Ronsard!' She did. After the Second World War, when most art had been quite forgotten, she wrote of how having 'the run of a mind of that calibre, with all its inconsistencies, its generosity, its blind spots, its spaciousness, and vision, and its great sense of form and style, was a privilege for which I am still trying to say "thank you"'.[7]

It filled her with pride to have him 'confiding all his troubles and weaknesses'. She found him irresistible:

The stiff, rather alarming exterior, and the conventional, omniscient manner, concealed a highly complicated emotional machinery. It produced an effect of tragic vulnerability; tragic because the scope of his understanding and the breadth of his imagination had produced a great edifice which was plainly in need of more support than was inherent in the structure itself. A walking temptation to any woman, had I but known it!

To me he was quite simply the most enthralling person I had ever met. Worth all of Phyllis's young men put together, and he never even looked at her!

He began to tell me about himself [. . .] The most monumental of authors—the fount, apparently of all wisdom, who appeared already to have lived a dozen lives now—amazingly—announced that he wished to place his person, his fortune, his future in my hands. Revealed himself as a lonely and very tired person who wanted to dig potatoes and raise pigs and never write another book. Wanted to start a new home. Wanted a child.

I said yes, of course. I accepted him as the wise man whom I had come across the world to find.[8]

'You ask me how I live & what I do', Ford wrote, casting himself as the 'aged, aged man' from *Through the Looking-Glass*: 'well: I live in a tent & wash in a bucket &, since the floor of my tent is dust, or in the alternative, mud, I have seldom lily white feet.' He told her how he had an 'exhausting and worrying time' after he was given the task of defending someone in a court martial (an experience which would presumably have gone into 'True Love & a G.C.M.' had Ford completed it): 'the wretched man [. . .] began to go mad last Sunday', he wrote: 'was certified yesterday, & the Court Martial washed out. This morning he rushed into my tent, having escaped from his escort: tried to strangle his father, bit me, & has just been carried off to an asylum.' He added: 'If there is anything of that sort going I am generally in it!' Ford was not a well man himself (which was why he could identify with 'the wretched man'); he had been 'in bed with neuritis' in July. Even so, he could not help himself from wanting to write another book. Even before this incident, he was thinking of using the General Court Martial in fiction. When the publisher Martin Secker (who had reprinted the *Henry James* he had published for Ford in 1914, and brought out a second edition of the *Collected Poems* in 1916) asked Ford for a new novel, he suggested 'a new one called "G.C.M."', and began it in the second half of September. (In the same letter Ford mentioned what was to become his driving ambition to find a publisher for a collected edition. He wanted to include *Ladies Whose Bright Eyes*, *Mr. Apollo*, and *The Fifth Queen*.) As we have seen, the fragment stems from the imaginative juxtaposition of war and love: the trials and madnesses of the war which have all but destroyed the protagonist, followed by the regenerative madness of the passion which restores him, gives him new life. It was to be the emotional and formal basis of his *Parade's End* sequence; and shows how early he tried to write out his war experiences, and how early that basis was formed.[9]

Bowen had 'reacted violently against him at first on the grounds that he was a militarist'. But his militarism, like most of his interests, was subordinate to his aesthetics. 'You see', he told her: 'soldiering is interesting—even peace-time soldiering because—in civil life you live alongside people & see their poor little scandals & divine their poor little intimacies. But, in this show, you actually mould their poor lives. It is writing novels in fleshly plasticine!' It was a feeling of responsibility, combining ideas of omnipotence and impotence, that was worked into Tietjens's feeling of responsibility for his men in *Parade's End*. Even when the army was this congenial to Ford, he never lost his sense of the superiority of good writing. When he told Bowen that he thought Turgenev's *Letters of a Sportsman* 'the finest things that were ever written', he added: 'I would rather have written "Bielshin Prairie" than have done anything else in the realm of human achievements—even military achievements! So there, my dear Pacifist.' She soon found that if he was any kind of militarist, 'he was at the same time the exact opposite'—as she discovered when he confided to her the dream that was to become the reality of their life together after the war:

You see, my dear Pacifica, I am not so eaten up by militarism dans mon fort intérieur—tho' it behoves one to keep a bristling front to a silly world!—No, I really want the little cottage, in a valley, five miles from a market town—& you! more than anything in the world.

As it is I am going to breakfast in a marquee where the rain drips down upon my thinning chevelure—& after that a long parade in which I shall teach little, dark, foreign speaking Welch devils, the mechanism of the Lewis gun—first stoppage, second stoppage, third stoppage & so on.

I am going to York to lecture to the Staff on Thursday. I wish you c^d. be there—but that will be in the station Hotel, an immense & gilded caravanserai. What fun if you c^d. just come popping out of the lift!

Anyhow, think of—& pray for

Your FMH

What are you painting—& why? Tell me—& all about the next door neighbour.[10]

He had had an impressionist vision of that rural sanctuary—'the inviolable corner of the earth'—during the battle of the Somme, when the landscape, like humanity, was being so brutally violated:

It came like one of these visions that one's eyes, when tired, will see just before one falls asleep. There was a rhomboid of deeper, brighter green, of a green that was really alive, beyond the gray-green of the field they were in. It existed in front of the purple of scabrous flowers on the great shoulder that masked the battlefield. It wavered, precisely as you will see the colored image cast on a sheet by a magic lantern, then slowly, it hardened and brightened, took shape as a recumbent oval, like eighteenth century vignettes. Gringoire said that it became perfectly definite—'The little view that I shall see at this moment if I raise my eyes. And it didn't connote any locality [. . .] It was just country—but perfectly definite [. . .].'

Possibly that little vision of English country, coming then, was really a prayer, as if the depths of one's mind were murmuring: 'Blessed Mary, ask your kind Son that we may have the peace of God that passes all understanding, one day, for a little while in a little nook, all green, with silver birches, and a trickle of a stream through a meadow, and the chimneys of a gingerbread cottage out of Grimm just peeping over the fruit trees.'[11]

Mizener said 'Ford was convinced that this longing had developed during the strain' of the Somme (as if the biographer were unconvinced), and that 'When he found himself again in London, poor, forgotten, persecuted—he believed—for having fought for his country in the war, he became the simple gentleman philosophically committed to the pastoral life, "Captain Ford," "Gallophile, Veteran, Gardener, and, above all, Economist, if not above all Poet," [. . .]' But Ford remained above all a writer. 'He had a real, consuming passion for letters, and this was the mainspring of his life.' The 'simple gentleman' smallholder was an ideal Ford lived up to for the rest of his life. He turned it into something more than a pose: prose. He never stopped writing. He knew that the inescapable duality of being the kind of artist he was necessitated living out other roles, and that all these were at odds with his true vocation. His alter-egotist in *No Enemy*, Gringoire (from whom Mizener takes Ford's psychological likeness) knows this too—hence the raised eyebrow of the phrase 'if not above all Poet'. But Mizener needed to suppress this ironic self-recognition to make Ford fit his diagram of the self-deluding fantasist. Yet when Ford is revealing the mental turmoil that actually caused him to see visions, he is—dually—exploring those very mechanisms of delusion, and at the same time explaining how intimately the artist is impelled by the mystic. So in this case he poses the vision first as a hypnagogic state, but then likens it to a religious experience—but one which, in turn, might be explained psychologically. It is an ontologically disturbing experience. 'It existed': the strange phrase makes the experience strange, the foreignness characteristically suggested with a phrase that sounds more French than English. There is an uncanniness in the way the green colour looks 'really alive', an idea developed in the strange hints of animation in the landscape: it has a 'shoulder', covered with 'scabrous' flowers. But the superstition that animates matter is inseparable from the magic which animates artistic form: hence the image of the magic lantern casting the colour on a sheet (as the words on a sheet of paper summon up colours to the mind's eye). That detail, the oval vignettes, and the mention of Grimm remind us that we are considering not only psychology and geography, but art; art which can 'make you see' definite visions, which none the less need not correspond to factual localities—which are, in short, fiction.[12]

Ford told Stella he had liked her at once, but he conceded that he may have sounded 'rather a PIG at Selsey on first acquaintance—very likely because I liked you at the first moment. That is often the case: if one likes a person one tries to make one's little impression, à soi, & one forces a note of one sort or another &, just as often, it's a jarring note.' He made love to her in letters (there is no evidence that they met more than twice in 1918)—sincere self-revelations meant to let her know him better than that first acquaintance. Some of his most intimate self-portraits can be found in this wonderful correspondence:

My dear:

I think we think along such curiously dissimilar lines! I daresay that is why you interest me—when no one any longer does, as a sustained interest. I don't believe that I have any settled—or even unsettled—scheme of ethics, like you. I don't believe I *could* have—because I never had any 'Views'—I have only had sympathies in this life. I don't think I even 'presumed' to form, much less to formulate, any general scheme of life.

As I look at morality—my own private morality—I feel 'good' when I can take an interest (& be kind) to the people & animals & things of daily & accidental contacts: I feel I am 'bad' when I can't. After all, kindness of personal contacts & tentativeness in framing judgements are the real essentials of life—at any rate for me [. . .]

No: I'm not indifferent to human suffering—but I have had my share of it, & it matters extremely little you know. It folds up into a lot of withered leaves—just as human joys do. —And one can make so much too much of them—because of the spoken word. Humanity pegs along, stolidly, in all sorts of circumstances until the appointed day. Then something cracks—but even the cracking is only a part of the pegging along, if you understand me.

The great thing is to have some soul one can believe in—as I—perhaps—delude myself into thinking that I can rely on you. Given that one can stand the oppressions of militarisms, the lash of the weather & the chances of hunger, death & injustice with great equanimity.[13]

The great thing was also to have another soul who could believe in him. The shadow of Conrad falls across his words there—the Conrad who quoted Novalis saying 'It is certain any conviction gains infinitely the moment another soul will believe in it'. Ford reconstructs his identity, spelling it out letter by letter, getting Bowen to believe in him so that he could believe in himself. It was a reciprocal rather than an egotistical affair, however. He helped her to believe in herself too, and her own art. 'Don't be discouraged about your painting because you don't like what you are doing or do it against the grain', he told her:

The only work that one does that is any good is always the work one does against the grain— because then one is working advisedly and consciously. When one likes what one is doing & it all goes easily—then one may begin to suspect oneself.

I feel a great belief in you, my dear—but I am rather worried when you say you don't know any painters. Get to know some—because one must live in the milieu & be as deep as possible in the atmosphere of one's own art [. . .] Art, you know, is a contagious thing—or rather a thing of contacts.

Intimate communication was more important to Ford than sexual intimacy. Tietjens says 'You seduced a young woman in order to be able to finish your talks with her'. Ford's and Bowen's correspondence keeps starting conversations that could only be finished by living together. Like Dowell, he talks of his love as a longing for imaginative penetration of the other: 'He wants to get, as it were, behind those eyebrows with the peculiar turn, as if he desired to see the world with the eyes that they overshadow.' 'I thought you might like to know what I was looking at', he wrote to Bowen after describing the sand 'rushing along like cold flame' on the beaches near Redcar, and the sight of an immense convoy 'creeping up towards Newcastle': 'I wonder what you can see at this moment—the studio, or the woodshed at the cottage. You made me so happy there, my darling. But you make me happy every where. When you smile I want to cry with happiness.' His letters frequently dramatize his suffering to heighten its pathos, and draw forth her sympathy; but their dominant note is of this unexpected invigorating happiness.[14]

They had managed to meet at Stella's cottage at Bottom Farm, Berkhamstead, while Ford was on leave at the end of September. On 1 October he made what he called 'a painful scene' with her, letting his turbulent feeling disrupt his placid surface, and he wrote the next day to apologize: 'I am very ashamed of myself & mortified.' He worked himself 'into a state of panic' at not hearing from her for four days. 'Y^r. little letter made all the difference in the world to me', he told her when she did write: 'You don't know how much moral support the large creature you have taken in tow needs & will clamour for. I wonder if you like that—it is rather like looking after a baby!' He was soon true to his word, in bed with 'flu, and asking Bowen to come and see him. In the second week of October she came to Redcar, where he was based for the rest of the war. They appear to have been keeping their affair discreetly concealed from Hunt. Bowen cabled her from Redcar saying: 'shall stay till you come or he leaves as doctor says he must have nursing'—as if she were only visiting as a concerned friend. But 'My dear' had already given way to 'Darling', and Ford teased her by affecting jealousy: 'It is all very well your running about with "Bertram" all day & not writing to me—but you will have to choose, you know, between him & me one day—So I suppose you had better have y^r. good time now. . . .':

Of course there is no reason why you should not be free—as long as you let me pretend to tyrannise now & then . . . just to make believe. But I'm not really tyrannous—only I like to pretend every now & then that I'm the arrogant male of the Prussian Officer type—just as, every now & then, you like to appear the elusive female of Gyp's novels.

('Gyp' was the pseudonym of the French humorous novelist the Comtesse de Mirabeau de Martel, 1849–1932.) Imagining their amorous role-play was bound up with imagining living once more by his writing: 'I can always make 5 or 600 [pounds] a year by writing articles', he explained: '& the old novel will get itself written when I haven't any other bothers. Of course it's a fairy tale written to please you. I suppose I have always been writing fairy tales to please you—waiting for the person whose Favourite Author I sh^d. one day be. But there isn't any *money* in novels [. . .].' He could imagine their finances as a form of fairy tale too: 'I don't mind being like a tramp for months if, for a week or so, now & then we can appear—& be—Dukes & Duchesses— that sort of thing.' It was the fairy tale their life together was to prove. His envisioning of it was in part to prove to Bowen that their plan wasn't only make-believe, and that he could be realistic about money: 'I really think about these things too. I am not the incapable visionary that Violet so delights to represent me as being.'[15]

Ford must have known that at Redcar he was only a few miles from Arthur Marwood's family seat (since 1587) of Busby Hall, near Stokesley—that he would reinvent as Groby Hall in *Parade's End*. His army life in Yorkshire helped him to combine in Christopher Tietjens his own experiences with characteristics of Marwood's. He was kept busy with the engrossing chores of army logistics—getting billets cleaned up, checking the quartermaster's stores, even organizing a 'Peace demonstration'. The young Captain Herbert Read was surprised and delighted to meet Ford at the end of August 1918 when he joined the staff at the Tees Garrison.

'Yesterday I had a very interesting if not even a very momentous day', he wrote after Ford had invited him over. Read proved an irresistibly reverent listener, and elicited some reminiscential romancing from Ford which shows how his wartime version of himself as unjustly eclipsed by the very writers he had fostered was causing him to reinvent his past, projecting his *English Review* (and Madox Brown) persona of the discoverer of genius back into the 1890s:

What a day I had! He talked to me for a solid eight hours. Just imagine the joy of walking along the cliffs from Redcar to Saltburn with a man who knew Henry James *intimately*. I did 'pump' him, as you can guess. He is, I should say, about 45, a man of charming manners and immense knowledge. Quite a sportsman too, for he has been to the front and been wounded. I can't quite see *why* he is in the Army since he could so easily be out of it if he wanted. It must be some ideal within him. He is married and his wife (Violet Hunt, the novelist) is taking a house (or rooms) at Runswick of all places. But he has stayed there before and loves it and Whitby dearly [. . .] Hueffer discovered Wells [. . .] He came into the *Saturday Review* office and asked for reviewing work (scientific) and Hueffer, rather attracted by him, walked home with him and Wells confided to him that he was penniless and must have that reviewing work, so Hueffer went back to the office and arranged for some, but advised Wells to write scientific short stories, which Wells didn't want to do but was persuaded to try and with such success [. . .] I had read one or two of Hueffer's books—the one on James and his latest volume of poems particularly and these two, together with one called *The Good Soldier* which I am going to get, are the only ones that he considers really matter. But he rather prides himself on being one of the few stylists in the English language. I guess—I don't know *yet*— that he is little but a stylist. But we shall see.

Two weeks later he saw. 'I've been reading Hueffer's novel *The Good Soldier*. It is very grim and tragic but I rather think a great book.' The two men soon became friends— despite the fact that Read, twenty years Ford's junior, had (as Ford put it later) 'mopped up that staff job over my head'. Ford was 'not unwilling to adopt the rôle of mentor', said Read, who had hopes then of becoming a novelist. But he was less secure about Ford's other forms of role-playing. 'Ford was, beyond any doubt', says Read, 'the most superb liar of our time. He was not a malicious liar; I do not think he ever lied in a bad cause. But he carried over into life the imaginative faculty which gave him such facility in writing fiction.' By way of example he says that 'Most people who knew him would be told sooner or later a fantastic story of the part he played in the Great War. It varied from commanding a brigade of Canadian Pioneers in the battle of the Somme to being called to Paris to advise the French General Staff.' But—as Read says—Ford didn't tell him these stories himself: 'because it was in the Army that I first met him, towards the end of the war, and the position he then occupied, at a training camp in England, was Brigade Sanitary Officer. His duties consisted mainly of the daily inspection of latrines, and I believe the only time he went to France was as officer conducting a draft of men to the Base.' But if Ford didn't tell him the stories, who did? The distortions involved might come from others' gossip rather than Ford's fantasies, but either way, the two main points seem to be that both stories have a germ of truth, and that Ford didn't boast of them to Read. If he had, Read would have known that Ford *had* been in the battle of the Somme; that he *had*—later—commanded Canadians (a Casual Battalion, not a Pioneer brigade); that he had been called to Paris to be thanked by the Minister of Instruction; that he had been out to France *twice*; and that he had been doing much more than inspecting latrines in Yorkshire. Read says that he tells the story not to score a point off a man he liked and respected, but 'only because it is the kind of thing, multiplied hundreds of times during the course of his life, which led to people not taking him seriously, either as a man or an artist'. True, though he missed how it was often Ford's self-deprecations (rather than his boastings) which misled people. The story that the only use the army could find for him was as an inspector of latrines is just as likely to be Fordian impressionism—a way of resigning himself to the army's not having taken him seriously. In fact, he was given tasks such as accompanying 'an inspecting Brigadier going round cookhouses & dining halls'—an experience that was to go into the ending of *No More Parades*, when Tietjens accompanies General Campion, descending upon the awestruck cookhouse like a godhead in a mystery ceremony. The battalion, Ford said, had 'got into the habit of sending me to outlying detachments to tidy them up before the Generals arrive. It is flattering but tiring.' And he had just returned from York, where he had been lecturing to the Staff, when Read met him.[16]

5

1918: ARMISTICE

In November Ford heard that he had been due to go with a large draft of troops that was to be sent to France on the 7th, but that his name had been struck off because he was 'indispensable to the B[attalio]n'. 'I suppose I am', he wrote to Bowen, 'but it is rather annoying as it is the last chance, probably. However I am going over to the Orderly Room as soon as I have finished this to make myself as unpleasant as I can.' His other indispensable services included going up in a 'blimp', and composing notices about such things as 'Salvage' (urging the men to save for recycling 'valuable material that used to be regarded as rubbish'). He sent one to Bowen as 'a specimen of my prose—for, tho' the signature be that of Alexander [Lieutenant-Colonel Alexander Pope, his CO], the voice is y^r F.M.H's'. He was right about having missed his last chance to return to the Front: the Armistice was declared four days later. Bowen dragged Pound out of his flat in Kensington Church Street, and they took an open-topped bus towards Trafalgar Square, 'Ezra with his hair on end, smacking the bus-front with his stick and shouting to the other people packed on the top of other buses jammed, alongside ours, which were nosing a cautious route through the surging streets'. Pound recalled seeing King George's open carriage only a few feet away in Piccadilly: 'Poor devil was looking happy, I should think, for the first time in his life', he wrote to John Quinn. Ford was at Redcar that day. 'I remember Armistice Day very well', he wrote later, 'because I was kept so busy with military duties that I was on my feet all day until I fell into bed stone sober at 4 next morning.' 'Darling,' he wrote to Bowen, 'Just a note to say I love you more than ever. Peace has come, & for some reason I feel inexpressibly sad. I suppose it is the breaking of [sic] after the old strain!' He wrote a poem, 'Peace', to express this emotion. There is no explicit reference to the Armistice. The war is present only as a pressing absence—an unfamiliar noiselessness. Ford takes 'Peace' in the sense of 'rest' too: 'die Ruhe', which the beloved promises to be, but which desire destroys:

> The black and nearly noiseless, moving, sea:
> The immobile black houses of the town,
> Pressing us out towards the noiseless sea
> No sounds. . . .
> And, Thou of the Stars! beneath the moving stars
> Warm yellow lights upon the moving sea . . .
> Moving. . . .[1]

That insistent punning wonders at the unfathomable connection between the sea's motion and the seer's emotion. Ford was doubtless right that the after-effects of long strain contributed to his sadness: but the poem hints at another reason. The 'black houses of the town' are 'Pressing' the lovers out towards the sea. There is a desperate, perhaps even suicidal current, under the quiet scene; and it is a response to other people. The army had granted Ford some financial security, and a certain independence from Hunt. With the prospect of peace, Ford once again felt like 'a poor lion in a den of savage Daniels'. He began rowing with people. First with Lieutenant-Colonel Pope. Ford told Bowen: 'after a frightful row with the C.O. in wh. we told each other several home truths, I have been given command of a tiny detachment well out in the country', at Eston (between Redcar and Middlesbrough):

My rows with the C.O. are only funny—not worrying, because he is desperately afraid of me & only speaks to me as it were with his cap in his hand. The last one arose just after he had said to me at a dance: 'Well, H., I suppose now peace is here you are the great man & I am only a worm at your feet.' And I cordially agreed. The dance, however, lasted to 0400 hours & I had taken over the daughter of the Q.[uarter] M.[aster]—the girl I talked to with her mother, on the steps of the Royal Hotel—&, as far as I c^d· see, the R.A.F. had provided no transport. So, seeing in the darkness, a car whose invisible driver said he was going to Redcar & had two seats vacant, I just popped Miss Hill into it & sat on the step myself. Then it turned out that the invisible driver of the car was the brigadier & the two other seats were for the C.O. & M^rs· Pope. We drove to Redcar in great amity—but two days afterwards the Adjutant turned up & said he was the bearer of a terrific strafe from the general & the C.O. because I had put a Q.M.'s daughter into M^rs· Pope's car. I then delivered an oration to the Adjt, such as I hope you will never hear me deliver to anyone else. I said that if the strafe was disciplinary and on behalf of the Brigadier & the C.O. I wd. take the matter straight to the Commander in chief. So then he turned pale & said it was really only on behalf of M^rs· P. who thought herself above Miss Hill. Then I flew off to the C.O.'s house & delivered another oration on the subject of the social equality of all officers & that anyhow, Hill is a regular & he is only a militiaman. So then Poor old Pope said he didn't know anything about it only the Brigadier was angry because M^rs· Pope had not ridden beside him. So then I insisted on seeing the Brigadier for the purpose of apologising. Pope begged me not to, but I insisted & the Brigadier said it was the first he had heard of it & that he had been delighted to be of service. So then I told Pope that I applied to be transferred to another unit as I certainly w^d· not stop in the same town as M^rs· P. and himself. Then the Q.M. came into it & raised Hell & three other officers applied for transfer & the Asst. Adjutant resigned—& then Pope agreed to give me this Det. till my transfer shd. go through. I don't know where they will send me—possibly to my own Bn.—the IXth—in Flanders wh. w^d· be all right. Do you know the IX Welch is the only Bn. that has ever been mentioned by name in Haig's despatches, of all H.M. Army!

I tell you all this because it strikes me as comic—I mean my bothering my head & getting into the most frightful tempers on the surface, over such matters. But still it *is* a serious thing for the Army, wh. is the only thing I much care about, when Colonel's wives won't ride with Q.M.'s daughters.[2]

He spent a few days at Eston, but was back at Redcar by 22 November, where he stayed until he was gazetted out of the army. Wisely, he turned down the offer to stay on with a peace-time commission. 'You ask what I am like when I am in a rage', he wrote to Bowen, who may have begun to wonder whether life with him wouldn't be one sustained 'strafe': 'no, I don't shout, I go cold & speak very slowly & distinctly & say wickedly cruel things.' But the army provided the necessary duality—between the creature of rank and regulations on duty, and the human being of personality and prejudices off duty—to enable him to get over his disputes:

I have been having a most frightful strafe all this morning & afternoon with the Quarter Master—not a quarrel but an endless argument before the C.O.; the Adjutant and the P.[resident of the] R.[egimental] I[nstitute] as to where 'postings' are to go on arrival—&, as no one at H.Q. knows anything about it we both invented A.[rmy] C.[ouncil] I[nstruction]'s & authorities as hard as we could go & roared at each other & grew purple in the faces with rage—& then went off arm in arm to the mess & had drinks.

It is funny how you can get into the most violent rages over duty & yet be the best of friends in the mess two seconds later, without a syllable about what went on over the road. I wonder if it wouldn't be possible to conduct married life on that sort of line: it w^d. be a tremendous solution.[3]

It was also, approximately, his solution when dealing with other temperamental artists. The argument about the Colonel's wife and the Quartermaster's daughter was about more than just 'the social equality of officers'. As Ford's letter to Bowen shows—not by making the point explicitly, but simply with a deft transition—it was about social equality in general, and his dislike of envy and pretension. It is another of the marvellously candid letters in which he reveals himself to her:

I wish I had y^r. gift for writing letters that made me see things—for y^r. letters are the best I have ever read & tell me enormously of what is going on. As for politics I never did or could take any interest in them. The one glorious fact in the world is that the Rhine is going to be in French hands. If only you knew how, all my life, I have suffered from the dull, stupid, arrogant pedantry of the Hun Professor you w^d. realise it. It is like a fairy tale & to have had only the remotest hand in getting rid of Germandom from the Rhine & France there instead is more than I ever asked of life. You see, both my grandfathers were French subjects, although Violet loves to rub into people the fact that I am a Prussian. My father was of course a Prussian subject by conquest, but he left Westphalia when he was sixteen being unable to stand Prussian rule, & never went back [. . .].

As for Bolshevism it is nothing to me. I never had or wanted great possessions—only I hate people to want other people's goods—or rather to grudge other people what they have. In the matter of Capital & Labour I am for Labour every time—as I always sh^d. be for the physical worker against the administrator—for the Infantry Orfcer agst. the B——y Staff & so on. But I hate envy & the commercial spirit—so I don't want to see Bolshevism in this country [. . .] because I sh^d. not like to see ces messieurs succeed.

A country ought to be ruled by Kings who are poets—that is the only thing that matters— that the poets of the country should rule—& no doubt also, the I[nfantr]y Orfcers because they are good & disciplined & accept responsibilities & take little pay & are content with simple pleasures. Outside that let the workman get *all* the profits of his labours, by all means & damn the manufacturer, who is always a sweating beast. Amen.[4]

As when he wrote to Iris Barry, or discussed art with other *jeunes*, the self he reveals is one that aspires to the ideal of Madox Brown's 'reverence for youth'; the Madox Brown who late in life could say: 'how cleverly these young men sketch. I never remember to have seen such work. If only I could do anything so good.'[5]

Ford said he had another row with Arnold Bennett just before the Armistice, when he was summoned from his battalion to the Ministry of Information. Bennett had been directing British propaganda in France since May for Lord Beaverbrook, the Minister of Information. In September he was made head of the whole ministry. He was now Masterman's superior, and subordinate only to Beaverbrook himself. 'Imagine a way-ward novelist, with no experience of bureaucratic methods, having dominion over hundreds of exalted persons', he wrote, relishing his authority over bank-directors, heads of trusts, and even generals. Ford said Bennett ordered him to write about 'terms of peace', and that they then 'disagreed very violently. *Very* violently!' about what the peace treaty would secure for France. Three of Ford's versions of the meeting agree closely on essentials: that the ministry summoned him and told him to write the article; that Sir William Tyrell of the Foreign Office exasperated him by arguing that the German empire should be preserved, whereas Ford advocated its dismemberment, and the creation of neutral buffer states to separate France and Germany; that he wrote the article anyway, but the ministry suppressed it by saying that it must have got lost in the post; and that soon afterwards a military superior reminded him that as an army officer he was forbidden to write for the press. The story is not improbable (though the fourth version—that someone connected with the ministry asked him to write the article for a periodical, but the periodical refused to publish it—may be more likely). Bennett was indeed concerned with circulating propaganda about peace terms in the weeks before the Armistice. H. G. Wells had a similar experience with Tyrell when he was trying to get the Foreign Office to endorse a statement about war aims at about the same time. (He said Tyrell lectured him on the 'characters' of France and Germany, sounding like 'a bright but patriotic school-boy' who had 'learnt that stuff for gospel from his governess'.) Ford thought Bennett had played a trick on him, giving him an 'Enigmatic' smile as he ordered Ford to write the article he had already decided he would officially lose. The episode left no other trace, so it's impossible to know how justified Ford's suspicion is; but it may be explained by the fact that Bennett resigned his post two days after the signing of the Armistice, and the ministry was soon closed down. Ford certainly told Bowen he was writing a 'silly French article' in October; that the Ministry of Information had asked for more French articles; and that he then wrote a 'very silly article about Alsace Lorraine'; but only the first has been traced, a propagandistic reminiscence about his journey towards the Front with the Welch Regiment.[6]

After the Armistice war-games gave way to more peace-games. Ford had time for violent hockey matches ('I am a battered wreck today, with my left hand smashed & an ankle as large as a tomato & a black eye'), and also billiards, bridge, and golf. 'No: the billiards, hockey, Bridge side of my life isn't essential to my happiness', he reassured a surprised Bowen: 'only I like to think I can do *any*thing fairly well [. . .]' He told her how he was pleased one night when he heard three of the younger officers discussing who was 'the coolest person on a certain night in J[ul]y. 16 when we were suddenly shelled behind Bécourt Wood'. They agreed that 'old Hoof was by a long chalk & that old Hoof ought to have had the M.C. only the C.O. didn't like him'; one of them added: 'But then, one expected it of Hoof!' The rest of the letter is quintessential Ford: ironizing the very egotism it risks; attending to the art of the novelist; and unobtrusively shaping a vignette of lethal comedy:

I remember the occasion quite well: I was so busy looking after an officer who had got very drunk & was trying to expose himself, that I never really noticed the shelling at all except that I was covered with tins of sardines & things that had been put out for our dinner.

That was really the worst of the Front from the novelist's point of view. One was always so busy with one's immediate job that one had no time to notice one's sensations or anything else that went on round one. H. G. [Wells] w^d· no doubt do it very much better!

Goodbye darling: this is egotism—[bu]t it is also love too![7]

Ford turned his perplexity about the rendering of war to advantage when he made this displacement of sensation the cardinal principle of *Parade's End*. The novelist of duality was particularly suited to presenting this psychology of battle, in which the obtuseness and subliminal noticings of the protagonist become an index to the mental strain he is under.

He was still feeling that strain, despite the engrossments of battalion routine. When he went to benediction at Eston on 17 November, the priest announced that the *De Profundis* would be sung for the German as well as the British dead. 'I couldn't stand it', Ford told Bowen:

I tried to, but I *could* not stand in my place & wish that the dead Huns sh^d· go where our dead go. It was as if an irresistible power forced me out of my seat. I seemed to see our dead—I mean particularly the Welch dead, rising up like a cloud of darkness from a great stretch of territory and I cd.n't pray that the Huns sh^d· rise with them. After, if you like, or before, but not at *our* Last Post.

I suppose you will think I am barbaric—& I was astonished at myself. I just jumped up, shivering, & ordered the men out of the church & marched them home.[8]

The 'irresistible power' which forced Ford out of his seat is an uncanny epiphany. The religious occasion modulates into a macabre secular resurrection (which reveals how seriously Ford felt the war as 'Armageddon'—the last battle which precedes the eschatological resurrection). The vision of the dead rising from their unhallowed graves is attended by the 'shivering' which betokens the uncanny. Yet his seeming to see is also his novelistic vision. He had been haunted by that vision of the Welch dead since the Ypres Salient, and, as we shall see, the writing of *Parade's End* is impelled by the need to exorcise it, to stop that shivering; and by another vision—of the 'great stretch of territory' that was the entire Western Front. Even in his self-astonishment Ford is beginning to work his feelings of awe and fear (common to soldiers who had been thrust into such unaccustomed and appalling proximity with unburied corpses) into the subject of his war-prose, which turns repeatedly on the way mental strain issues in such unpredictable impulses.

'I love you too much, you know', he told Stella. When he went to London to see Hunt on his birthday (17 December) Bowen stayed in town to see him the evening before, and probably went to a party for him at South Lodge. '[W]e can behave quite "nicely", can't we?', Ford asked enigmatically before the meeting. Afterwards he wasn't sure he had, when the post delayed two of her letters, and he feared she'd been offended, or found another lover. 'I suppose it is comic,' he wrote to her from Redcar, 'but it is very painful: I have been going about like a sick cow—last night I caught sight of my face in the glass & I thought I looked like a dying man! Darling: if you ever didn't love me I sh^d· go out of my mind. I don't think it is really right & sanitary of

Provvy [Providence] to construct one so that one loves so much.' He was not able to
get to London for Christmas, he told her, because he had to 'arrange the festivities and
be father Xtmas for the children'. But he was in London between Christmas and New
Year's Eve, when he went to a party given by the French Embassy to thank writers
who had supported France. Bennett was there, though Ford did not want to speak to
him after their row about the Armistice. 'It was seven years since I had written a word',
says Ford, exaggerating to convey his sense of being an extinct volcano since writing
The Good Soldier four years before. The occasion only sharpened his sense of alienation from the worlds of letters and of the living:

A long black figure detached itself from Mr. Bennett's side and approached me. It had the
aspect of an undertaker coming to measure a corpse. . . . The eyes behind enormous lenses
were like black pennies and appeared to weep dimly; the dank hair was plastered in flattened
curls all over the head. I decided that I did not know the gentleman. His spectacles swam
almost against my face. His hollow tones were those of a funeral mute:
  'You used to write,' it intoned, 'didn't you?'
  I made the noise that the French render by '!?!?!'[9]

His confidence in his own creative abilities was returning, and he was generalizing
with authority to Bowen. 'All "styles" are in the end, conventions, & as such are
justifiable', he told her: 'but *oneself* isn't adapted to like all styles.' Yet he still saw
himself as a literary pariah, and the idea dominates 'Mr Croyd' and *Thus to Revisit*. But
he was not really forgotten. His war poems had been praised. 'Women and Men'—
which *was* seven years old, and which Pound had announced as 'the best book Ford
Madox Hueffer has written'—had been appearing in the *Little Review*, where it had
attracted favourable attention. And he could still command the admiration of *les jeunes*
such as Read, who asked him in December for poems for a new review. But he needed
to imagine his own literary death, in order to stage his rebirth as Ford Madox Ford.[10]

  Ford said later that when he was demobilized he found his name in category 18 of
the discharge lists, which included, 'along with authors, gypsies, travelling-showmen
and unemployables. We were all non-productive and consequently to be discharged
last!' It became an emblem for him of how the British treat their artists, and how their
artists consequently try to pretend that they are gentlemen rather than artists. When
he was gazetted out of the army on 7 January 1919, he made an ambiguous move. He
took a single-room 'studio' in a small London house, making clear his separation from
Hunt; yet the house was in the next street to hers—at 20a, Campden Hill Gardens. He
was re-creating the situation he had been in with Elsie, still living with her or near her
while loving someone else. His conscious motives were of the most honourable: to save
Hunt's reputation (such as it now was) by not appearing publicly to have deserted her.
Yet it is hard not to suspect that, unconsciously, he was also provoking Hunt to
persecute him, as (he already knew from Selsey and Redcar) she would be unable to
resist doing. On her part, she knew he would not resist an appeal to his chivalry, and
used it, getting him to promise to make regular appearances at South Lodge. She
could not relinquish the object of her love-hate. She even got Ford to Selsey, by
persuading his mother to come and stay. She wrote an account of the three-hour
discussion she had there with Ford in a letter to their mutual friend Edgar Jepson,

which explains that she told Ford she knew she had been 'rather horrid to him in the last year', but that she had wanted to see him to clear the air. 'Then he walked about and said you can see yourself we never can live together [. . .] You don't realise how you hurt me. How you drove me out of the house by insults—saying I only lived with you for the sake of your money. I will not, I will not sleep in the house again.' He was too agitated to sit still, but paced breathlessly and nervously, saying that 'the doctor had said that he could not *live* a fortnight in London and he meant to live in the country all his life'. At this point she admits she began calling him names. Bowen wrote to him: 'You know, you're very brave about saying you don't really mind V's rows & it gives her satisfaction, when you're not the middle of them. But you know they kill you really.'[11]

Ford came to Hunt's dinners and parties from time to time for eighteen months. He had his mail sent to South Lodge for her benefit, but she (or Annie Child, her housekeeper) would open it. 'I am just going to SL for the usual Sat. Afternoon Causerie', Ford wrote to Bowen in March. When Alec Waugh (the brother of Evelyn) dined there with them and W. L. George in January 1919, he had no idea that Ford and Hunt had parted. But more-intimate friends realized there had been a change. Scott-James noticed 'a sort of forced gaiety in Ford's manner' when he saw him at a party at South Lodge before the end of the war. He didn't then understand what it meant; but after the war he went to other functions there and 'realized that something was wrong'. Ford was living in poverty, sleeping on an army camp-bed, probably wearing his military clothes, and, like his character Mr Croyd, using his army overcoat as a dressing-gown. But he was soon making sorties back into the literary world. He called on Pound on 27 January; on 13 February he gave a Poetry Bookshop reading of the newer poems from *On Heaven* at the Queen's Square Art Workers' Guild; and on 20 March he gave a lecture, which he described to Bowen as his 'farewell to Highbrow London'. Mizener said that one day he also went 'on impulse' down to Charing, where Elsie lived with Katharine; but he was only able to speak to their landlord, Hickman. Occasionally he would spend the day with Bowen at Berkhamstead. 'It was a lovely day', he wrote to her after one visit: 'one of the loveliest I have ever had.'[12]

1919: RED FORD

Hunt dined at Ford's studio on 16 March. Her diary entry registers the tensions. 'I insulted him about forging my name', she wrote. (Later he was to accuse her of forging his. The claims are poignant given her legal struggle to use his name.) On 29 March he saw her off to Selsey, telling her that he too was going into the country for a spell. What he didn't tell her was that Stella Bowen had found a cottage for the two of them—'built of old red brick and old red tiles, all greened over with mossy stains, and it was tucked under a little red sandstone cliff, and faced over a lush meadow which sloped downwards to a little stream, and upwards to a wood on the opposite side.' It was damp, had a big hole in the red-tiled roof, and a 'dip-hole' down the garden from which water had to be fetched in a pail. But, said Bowen, 'It *looked* all right, and that was the main thing'. It looked like the gingerbread cottage of Ford's post-war fairy-tale imaginings of their life together. It cost five shillings a week, and had the auspicious name of 'Red Ford' ('from an iron spring that ran down the dingle'). On 3 April Ford went there alone. Bowen's brother Tom, who had been in the army in France, was now in England, and she didn't want him to hear about her affair. Though he was three years her junior, he felt responsible for her; and besides, the rest of the family in Australia would be scandalized. Ford was dismayed at the cottage's dilapidation when he first saw it: falling ceilings, rotten laths, rats, damp. Panes had fallen from the windows; mud had washed under the door. Fifteen years later he re-created his despair: 'Naked came I from my mother's womb. On that day I was nearly as denuded of possessions. My heavier chattels were in a green, bolster-shaped sack. All the rest I had on me—a worn uniform with gilt dragons on the revers of the tunic.' He was 'the ruined author, in a bare room that shadows were beginning to invade from every corner', and with just the army camp-bed and broken canvas table for furniture (Gringoire, in the earlier version in *No Enemy*, also had a paraffin stove). Humping his kit-bag, he thought of himself as the dung-beetle he had watched on a Corsican hillside before the war: an insect Sisyphus, alternately climbing, then rolling backwards cling-ing on to his pellet of dung. (Was he thinking later of Kafka's 'The Metamorphosis'?) In Corsica Ford had considered playing Providence to the beetle. Now he wished he had, because he could not see how, 'without the intervention of an immense and august finger and thumb' that should lift him out of his depression, he would ever reach Parnassus—or the Mediterranean. He hadn't intervened in the beetle's fate, he explains, because W. H. Hudson had told him that if an animal was too weak to survive unaided, to preserve its life would be 'to give to a world of fear and cruelty a being that, after a short span of dreads and pains, must incur a fearful death'. The thought leads him to consider how he had 'always been, not so much a believer in, as subject to omens'. The 'ridiculous omen' at Red Ford was his first meal. Too weary to peel the shallots for the stew, he closes his eyes and tips them in 'skins and all'—'a thing that I have never done before or since'. He makes a pact with himself: 'I would try once more to push that dung up the long hill if those onions came unstuck in the course of boiling.' They did, of course, or we would not be reading this wonderfully intricate mental musing (which loses so much of its flavour in paraphrase). Ford's pact is ambiguously posed. As a ruined *author*, to continue pushing would be to continue writing. The beetle is introduced with a comment of Henry James's, that 'the best goods are not done up in the most fashionable-looking parcels'. At once the literary reference suggests that the parcels could include books (that ruined authors may console themselves that best-sellers are rarely best-writers). The mention of Hudson, too, makes a literary as much as an ethical point. Ford as an author tries to avoid playing Providence in his plots, preferring a Hudsonian aloofness of natural observation. 'Cooking is an art', he tells us before describing the auspicious stew, reminding us of his greater art, and how its artistry depends on a willingness to drop characters in predicaments, and see if they will sink or surface without the author imposing the outcome. On the other hand, the ominous setting makes Ford imagine himself as Red Ford's ghost: it is 'a space filled with shadows. The house had been unoccupied for many years: if one had spoken one would have whispered.' 'I have said that the word despair is not to be found in my vocabulary', he disavows, showing that it *can* be found in his vocabulary, and *may* have been found in his mind: the despair, that is, of the potential suicide, since the other suggestion in his pact is that if the shallots hadn't floated, this *ruined* author would not have kept all on going with the uphill struggle of living:

If the skins came off the shallots I was to make a further effort. If not I was to let go.
　　To where? [. . .] I don't know. But by that time I was already in the peasant frame of mind. [. . .] the peasant has the final gift of the really Happy Dispatch [. . .] He can say: 'Enough' and fade—and fade further, and lie down in the shadow of a rick, under a date palm or in his bed and so pass away.

Ford keeps the word suicide out of the vocabulary of this story; but the duality by which he is able to suggest and master the thought is important not just because it expresses his mood at the time—he wrote to Bowen the evening he arrived at Red Ford that his initial dismay had 'given way to comparative complacency' after the meal—but also because it is characteristic of his general mental duality. By another paradoxical pose, he disavows this too, saying: 'I am one of those fortunate—or unfortunate—beings who can think of only one thing at once.' He claims that 'whilst you are doing anything concrete your powers of observation desert you', and gives examples from army life, saying that 'as long then as I had any duty to perform I would be almost completely dead to my surroundings'. It is true that if your mind is 'somewhere quite other', then it is not quite on your surroundings. Yet you are only *almost* completely dead to your surroundings. The story of the first meal at Red Ford shows him engrossed in his cooking (too engrossed, that is, to brood); yet that very concentration is at the same time shown to involve thinking of many things at the same time, and to express the despair he is trying to suppress with his single-minded activity. The structure of the prose doubles the movements of his mind, concocting a subtle blend of memories, aspirations, literary acquaintances, and personal impressions. Not only does the writing *express* the very duality he disavows, but it explores it, showing how it is only through such dual forms that he can understand his own literary personality. That is, only by dropping his mental ingredients into the vessel of story can he muse upon what exactly his states of mind were. His literary autobiography is always refracted through other stories in precisely this way; so that to understand his state of mind on 3 April 1919, he must recall James, Hudson, the visit to Corsica (probably with Violet Hunt in 1913, just after the *Throne* débâcle, at another of his darkest moments), the Somme (the landscape of which in turn reminded him of 'the downlands behind the Pent'), and his thoughts about superstition, Providence, and Catholicism.[1]

There are three further—related—points to make about this story. First, that it is emotionally dual. The letter to Bowen about his 'comparative complacency' after dinner doesn't detract from the reality of his depression beforehand. The parallel moment in *No Enemy*, when Gringoire enters his 'Gingerbread Cottage' to find 'the wave-marks of inundations and half-inches of mud on the brick floors', evokes his sense of embattlement: 'He had come down with his valise contents, his camp-bed, a knife and fork, a paraffin stove, and a gallon of oil, determined, as he puts it, to dig himself in in the face of destiny.' Alan Judd, juxtaposing three of the versions, argues that in *It Was the Nightingale* Ford 'used the incident to create an impression of how he felt, if not at that time then at others'. But one has only to recall Ford's image of Gabriel Morton, depersonalized in his destitution, to see how accurate *No Enemy* and *It Was the Nightingale* are about his feelings at precisely that time. However, though a story about despair, its outcome is the surviving of despair. The waiting for the stew 'constituted the most depressed period of my life', he wrote in a fourth version, entitled 'Rough Cookery'. And 'when you are rather down and out, when there remains to you nothing in the world, the merest little nod from august, inscrutable and usually, blind Destiny will be of more heartening effect than all the treasure of the Indies at other times'. Whereas even by 1920–1, in *Thus to Revisit*, Ford's primary feeling about coming back (to England, to peace, to sanity, to sexual happiness) was that he was revisiting as a ghost, by 1928 he was recalling Red Ford as where he 're-began life'; and by 1933 he was reimagining his re-beginning as a rebirth, saying that on the day of his 'release from service in His Britannic Majesty's army' he was 'nearly as denuded of possessions' as on the day of his birth. The self pity here, which sees the demobilized 45-year-old as a helpless infant, or as the pathetic dung-beetle, is braced against the 45-ness of hope for the new life, and heroism in the beetle's perseverance; just as the vision of himself as minuscule insect at the mercy of Providence is braced against his imagining himself as the Providence too. This is one of the hardest things to grasp about Ford—his duality of self-pity and self-aggrandizement, which is never just the false modesty or arrogance his detractors have sometimes claimed. The 1933 reminiscence is accurate about his 1919 feeling of rebirth too. Ford wrote to his mother in June that he was 'starting a new life'. Secondly, this coming back is also his literary come-back. *It Was the Nightingale* is the story of how his resolve to keep on going was also a resolve to keep on writing; how the experiment in the art of cooking became emblematic for his renewed commitment to the experimental art of writing. Finally, it is, exactly, a *story*—as the fairy-tale references remind us. Does the retrospective autobiographic pattern of *It Was the Nightingale* mean that truth to the actual moment has been lost? Well, in facts, perhaps. He didn't go to Red Ford the day he was demobbed, but three months later (excising that tangled period from the book protected Hunt and Bowen, while also making the transition from army to garden clearer than life). The letter he wrote to Bowen the same evening gives the menu as 'fried chicken and beans and oranges—but *no* drink'. (He was anxious to show Stella he was 'quite cheerful', and keeping away from alcohol.) Admittedly, even on significant evenings one can't always remember exactly what was for dinner. Yet the discrepancy might mean that the story of the floating shallots, and the superstitious significance attached to them, is a retrospective invention. The patterning of the autobiography is so intricately ambiguous that even its exaggerations don't seem forced into untruth. It's true, that is to say, as an impression of Ford's emotions, doubled between the depression at what he had seen and suffered in the war, and in his rows with Hunt, and his excitement at the opening of his new life with his new love. It's a good example of how the essential structure of feeling not only survives a change of factual detail, but can be more incisively expressed. Its impressionistic energy in reimagining the meal, and cooking up an entire story from the new ingredients, is the proof of his having come back, renewed, as a writer of fiction. It might, though, also be true too. 'Rough Cookery' gives a third recipe, describing the dish as a 'soup' made from beef bones, rather than the 'mutton-neck' of *It Was the Nightingale*. Even a depressed Ford could probably have cooked himself a soup and then some chicken.[2]

Stella was only able to visit him there twice before she came to live with him early in June: once for a long weekend at Easter with Phyllis and one of her prospective suitors, providing complex chaperoning alibis; and again in the middle of May, for her birthday on the 16th. Otherwise they wrote their love and their loneliness almost every day. 'I like to write to you just before going to bed', he intimated. When he didn't hear from her he frustratedly accused the postman, only to find that the 'suspected postman' was 'a good looking young woman to whom I had several times expressed—in the Post Office—my doubts as to the postman's honesty, reliability & sense of duty!' (That parenthesis is a touch defensive, as if expressing things to a good-looking young woman made him doubt his own honesty and reliability.) They had been keeping their affair secret from everyone except Phyllis; but her boyfriend Peter had realized at once when he saw them together. Now Bowen wanted to tell her friend Margaret Postgate too. Ford demurred, wondering: 'even if all about us came out & it snowed all the black snow that it c^d.—we sh^d. be oceans happier than either of us is now [. . .].' Once she was able to visit, they were. Bowen had worried that Phyllis was going mad: she was involved with two men, one of whom was involved with two women, and the emotional tensions and uncertainties meant she was constantly snapping at Stella. 'P. says she's on the edge of a breakdown & certainly behaves like it', she told Ford: 'I don't know where she gets her adjectives from—nor her facial expressions!' At the same time, Bowen's brother Tom had also got himself involved with two women. One of them, Kitty, was possibly consumptive, and appeared to be using her illness to manipulate Tom into a marriage. Stella had also feared that Kitty might be about to commit suicide. But the weekend at Red Ford made her feel, as Ford had encouraged her to feel, that her real life was with him, not amidst her London problems. (He was also able to give some practical advice which reflected his wishes about Hunt: 'You ought to impress on K[itty]. that she ought not to claw on to Tom if he wants to go to another woman, just because of her health.') He wrote to tell Bowen how he had begun to repair the house, and to turn 'the living room into a bower for ladies; the entresol into a gent's room & the kitchen into a kitchen'; and he planted onions and peas. 'Darling', he added:

you made me wonderfully happy here. I have never before in my life had a period that was *all* happiness—& I have never remembered or imagined such happiness. Do you remember when we opened the door & looked out at the stars. That was the happiest moment I have ever known in all my life.

Goodbye, my own, own darling: I love you so much more, now.

Yr. own

FMH

I have got some sweet pea plants to climb up by the door for you. Don't say I don't spoil you![3]

She agreed: 'that moment when we looked at the stars was *my* happiest moment in life, too,—I think. And the evening before that, when we talked by the fire, you made me happier than I had ever been before [. . .].' With Ford she had found a family and a home as well as a lover: 'To have you really belong to me & to belong, really, to you, is like coming home after a long exile. You don't know what it's like to be as detached a thing as I've been, not belonging anywhere. You don't know what having a home means to me—let alone everything else.'[4] They were preoccupied with domestic details as well as expressions of love; indeed, the discussions about the house became expressions of love, as their love was the centre of their domestic arrangements. 'It is funny mixing up these things with a love letter, isn't it?' asked Ford: 'But they are part of the atmosphere of our love—woodfires & digging & funny little windows & the cottage out of Grimm.' He would try to write 'a real love letter—not one about "things"', experimenting to capture in prose the effect of his love; and sounding like both Dowell and Tietjens in the process:

[. . .] I do want to be able to tell you in what way I do love you & what you are to me. But I don't seem able to catch hold of anything significant to say. I go about for hours thinking of nothing but digging or seeding or hoeing.—And then, suddenly, without thinking anything at all, I find myself saying: 'I shall put the parsley here, for my darling!' It comes in a wave, just like that. I suppose there is some sort of rhythm to it;—there must be waves going all the time underneath, until some sort of seventh wave shews itself, breaking & foaming.[5]

'[. . .] I wish I could tell you what you mean to me', he told her in another letter: 'But it is one of the things, like music, that once can never tell. I suppose one is meant to *live* how one feels—and I almost believe I do. Because every moment I just live my love for you.' And he went on to reassure her: 'When I make fun of you, you know it is just the sort of overtone of gladness.' She bought a puppy—a Selyham, that Ford wanted to call 'Brigadier, after my late Brig. Brig Seely!' (though later he calls it 'Dai Bach', the Welsh nickname for Lloyd George). But there were strict regulations which stopped her getting it to Ford, and its howling drove Phyllis and the neighbours mad if she left it alone. So with the puppy, and then visits from Tom and Kitty, Bowen found it impossible to join Ford, who was busy renovating the cottage. He already had a cat, Sidney, and had hired a boy, Joseph Burton, to help him. 'Darling', he wrote:

You now possess a white cat, seven more eggs than you did yesterday & twenty four lordly tomato trees rear their proud heads in your garden. The white cat is Sidney her new garb being due to the active rather than intelligent interest she displayed in the whitewashing of the kitchen. This is now an accomplished fact, Joseph and I having spent the afternoon on the job. As the work is my own I will not dilate on its success. I will only say that I wish the whitewash did not trickle down one's arm whilst one was doing the ceiling. An armpit full of whitewash is less agreeable than almost anything I know—except a visit to S.L.![6]

He was in pain from a growth on his neck, eventually diagnosed as 'a carbuncle on top of a sebaceous cist'; and a bad leg made it difficult to walk far. Yet he bought 'a job-lot of old oak boards of which he was inordinately proud', said Bowen, and with them he built 'a cock-eyed lean-to outside the kitchen door to accommodate the oil stove' on which they cooked, and which belched its smuts into the kitchen:

In a slip of a room between the kitchen and the living-room, Ford used some more of his oak boards to construct a rough dining-table fastened for support to the side of the tiny staircase which led to the floor above. With two brass candlesticks and a pot of flowers, this table was also a great source of pride, and soon got so loaded with beeswax that its roughness became quite soft and gentle to the touch [. . .]

But if Ford was inexpert in the use of tools, he was extraordinarily skilful with his hands when it was a question of making things grow, or concocting some of his famous dishes. Then his movements were easy and sure, and everything he touched succeeded and came right. The garden, which had been neglected for years, soon began to blossom under his hands, and to supply our needs at table.[7]

Within a month he had planted a formidable range of fruits and vegetables—lettuces, beans, peas, carrots, onions, haricots, spinach, radishes, mustard, cress, salsify, beet-root, kohl rabi, melons, marrows, sunflowers, and plenty of herbs. The garden was not only a source of food, but of impressions. Ford was soon the Gilbert White of Pulborough. It is not surprising that in thinking of Red Ford he remembered W. H. Hudson, or the Corsican dung-beetle, for he spent much of his solitude observing nature, and recording his impressions:

This morning I got up early to see who pulled up the lettuces. I watched at the window for close on an hour; I suspected a pheasant & had borrowed a gun from the keeper for him. But, for the whole hour, nothing happened. A pair of chaffinches that are always hopping about my legs went quietly about; then a strange chaffinch cock, very brilliant, paid attentions to the lady & was driven off by the annoyed husband. There was also a robin & a hedgesparrow, very quiet & engrossed with invisible insects.

And then, all of a sudden, gloriously, a jay was on the ground where I had planted the sunflowers—just under my nose.—I had never seen one so close & it was extraordinarily exciting. He tried a sunflower seed with great deliberation, with his head on one side, just like a connoisseur of old port. He didn't like it & dropped it. I reached the gun towards him—but I couldn't shoot him. I had rather he ate $\frac{1}{2}$ the seeds in the garden; the other $\frac{1}{2}$ wd. be enough for us.

Do you think I am sillily sentimental? I'm not really. He was such a beautiful bird in his full, new spring uniform—ruby coloured mostly, with bright blue & white wings & blue & white over the eyes. And the downward flight is extraordinary; it's really like the way a trained acrobat drops from a trapeze—no checking the flight with the wings, as the pigeon does, or any other bird—No, it's suddenly just there—as sh^d. be the case with such a rogue & thief & brigand as the jay is!

Goodnight, my own dear love. I found my first orchid to-day. Here it is, little Horsetrilian, who didn't know orchids grew in Hingland.[8]

It is a novelist's nature, teeming with anthropomorphic drama (the adulterous triangle of chaffinches; the jay as port connoisseur or trapeze artist)—though the projections of plots and characters on to the birds is done to bring out, rather than obliterate, their natures. His pride in his work let him think of himself as the garden's creator: 'Darling, walking in the garden in the cool of the evening—like God!—it suddenly seemed as if there was nothing left to do but just to wait for you', he told Bowen. But as always, such an imagination of his novelistic aloofness from his creation was doubled by his sense of the earth's indifference to him. 'Indeed, before you can approach any work of art and expect to derive anything from it you must realise that you are a matter of profound indifference to everything', he was to write three years later in Sussex: 'The Art of Literature no more exists in order to benefit you than the Earth exists in order to grow your cabbages.' Returning to the soil returned him to his past: 'Yesterday was, by the way, a curious anniversary for me', he told Bowen: '25 years from the day I was first married. So the wheel comes round.' And he added: 'At any rate I am a better gardener than I was then [. . .].' His previous period as a 'small producer' had left him feeling (as in 'The Small Farmer Soliloquizes') that the earth mocked man's toil; that he was 'buried' in the countryside. This time, the earth could provide a sanctuary rather than a grave. 'None the less the Earth *does* grow your cabbage if you treat it properly or even only reasonably well.' Gardening was putting him back in touch with his own creative fertility, which was in turn bound up with his desire to create more children. Soon he was naming the animals in his modest paradise, recalling not only his last life in the countryside, but also the literary associations of those years, and his earlier enjoyment of the comedy of naming animals after literary friends. He could even turn gardening into fictionalized literary reminiscence:

Darling:

I have been sitting in the failing light watching an immense old Sacky Toad burgle my marrow frame. It was most imposing & he was so exactly like the late H.[enry] J.[ames] that I hadn't the heart to interfere. He first got on top of the frame & burrowed into the sacking of which he managed to work a fold right over his shoulders so that only his eyes looked out & rolled—just like Henry's. Then, apparently not satisfied with the warmth, he moved majestically to the edge of the frame & somersaulted over—looking exactly Henry James in a pair of bathing drawers! Then—I daresay with a great deal of wheezing—he deliberately pushed up the lid of the frame—y^r. bedroom window—& squashed between that and the tile-wall. How his poor dear Tummy could stand it I can't imagine. So he dived & struggled in. As it was quite dark I went & got a candle & there he was, ensconced under the root of my largest marrow, his golden-rimmed eyes cocking up at me for all the world as if he were saying: 'My dear H. Can you, at your, if I may say so, advanced age, be so inconceivably childish as to imagine that I am going to move since [?] here, in a manner of speaking, we all are?' And there he still is. I must introduce you to Henry when you come.

And you are coming on Friday. Hurray! Tell Mop I like her very much—& as for her views, I don't mind *any* views; it is only people I dislike, if I suspect them of being self-seeking & having 'views' wh. will grind their own axes.—& I don't suspect her a bit—or Coles.[9]

'Coles' was G. D. H. (Douglas) Cole, who was to become one of the leading labour movement theorists of his time, Professor of Social and Political Theory at Oxford, and president of the Fabian Society. Mop was Margaret Postgate, whom he had married in 1918. Ford was to combine aspects of her and Bowen to create the heroine of *Parade's End*, Valentine Wannop. Margaret was the daughter of the Classicist scholar J. P. Postgate, author of the standard Latin grammar. Her brother Raymond collaborated with Cole on a history of *The Common People*, married Daisy Lansbury (the daughter of the Labour MP and suffragette supporter, and founder of the *Daily Herald* George Lansbury), then went on to become a co-founder of the British Communist Party and to write *The Good Food Guide*. Ray recalled formidable Sunday dinners at home, when conversation had to be in Latin: once when Margaret said '*Da mihi bovem, sis*', her father took her literally ('Give me the ox please') and pushed the whole sirloin in front of her. She burst into tears and ran out of the room, until her mother explained the Latin for 'give me some ox', whereupon she got her slice, and her younger siblings could stop watching their Yorkshire puddings grow cold. Just before the war Margaret had left Girton College, Cambridge, to become junior classics mistress at St Paul's Girls' School in London (Ford makes Valentine a physical instructress at a girls' school during the war at the start of *A Man Could Stand Up* —). 'As a young woman she had been extremely shy which was offset on many occasions by a notable fierceness', says the *DNB*. Stella Bowen called her 'brilliant and forthright'. (Valentine shares all these qualities.) Margaret Cole too later became honorary secretary of the Fabian Society, and a leading figure in the labour movement.[10]

Before long Ford had 'a goat, called Penny, because it had a certain facial resemblance to Mr. Pound, and a drake that someone called Fordie, because it lived at Red Ford and was good to look at. These beasts had a great dislike of being left alone', he recalled in *It Was the Nightingale*: 'so that when I went out I was followed by dog, drake and goat—sometimes for great distances. A little later I acquired a black pig. This animal was also companionable, but I thought my procession would look too noticeable if she were added to it. I built her a sty in part of a sort of natural cave in the bank at the back of the house. So she died.' He was particularly proud of his pigs. Later he told Allen Tate he enjoyed raising them for the 'romance' of it. As he had metamorphosed himself into the man about town after his 1904 breakdown, his post-war reincarnation as anti-social 'lonely buffalo' was also a return to his earlier ideal of living off the land as a small producer. In his discussion of the paranoiac Schreber, Freud wrote: 'The delusional formation, which we take to be the pathological product, is in reality an attempt at recovery, a process of reconstruction.' After the war the world-reconstruction fantasies that psychoanalysis recognizes in paranoiacs was much more widespread. 'That was the era of reconstruction', wrote Ford in *It Was the Nightingale*, 'and each human being had his own plan for the salvation of humanity.' As he explains later in the book, the writing of *Parade's End* was such a plan: it was 'a work that should have for its purpose the obviating of all future wars'. All his post-war work is in some sense a fantasy of reconstruction. More facetiously, he recalled earlier, earthier, fantasies: the dream of discovering 'a method of wastelessly administering nutriment to plants'; and 'of evolving a disease-proof potato'. Even his potatoes would be named after writers, so that Ford's man Joseph (chosen perhaps as a nominal reminder of Conrad?) would 'dash in with startling pieces of literary information': 'Mr. 'Enry James have picked up proper in the night, but Mr. Conrad do peek and pine and is yallowin'. Mr. Galsworthy's beetles 'ave spread all over Miss Austin. . . .' He distinguished between his own literary way of looking, and Bowen's pictorial one: '[. . .] you see with the eye & not with the mind. It's funny, that. I remember y^r speaking, as if with contempt, of people who saw with the mind. And yet beauty, if it's anything, must be an affair of association. I like things if they seem to remind me of you—'. Beauty's 'affair of association' reminds him of their affair; but, typically, his example all but disavows the theory it purports to illustrate; 'thus I picked these two white pansies this afternoon—because they reminded me of you—tho' heaven knows why they sh^d, because you are not at all like a white pansy.' He was, of course, also writing, and sending instalments of a novel—probably 'True Love & a G.C.M.'—to Bowen in May. When she read the sentence '*He wanted to have a healthy, gay, son by Hilda Cohen* . . .', she can't have missed the echo of her own name in the character's.[11]

She evidently couldn't join him that Friday at the end of May as they had planned. Instead, he visited her in London on 29 May, and was worried by her 'careworn expression'. She was depressed, not only by the waiting, but by arguments with Phyllis about what Violet Hunt should be told. He didn't want her to know he was in love with Bowen, arguing that it would be 'the basest form of betrayal of a trust' if Phyllis were to reveal their secret. Phyllis 'has always seemed evil & dangerous to me', he told her—a remark which suggests that her beauty, promiscuity, and fraught nerves may have contributed to the character of Sylvia Tietjens. He wanted to wait until Tom was 'as it were, out of earshot'; then he would get Ethel Colburn Mayne to break the news to Hunt. He hated talking about his private affairs, or having them talked about: his patrician attitude of 'never apologize, never explain' precluded his justifying or excusing his conduct to others. But they were now resigned to the fact that she could not be kept in the dark indefinitely: 'I suppose V. will track us down in time', Bowen wrote to him: 'We must just live thro' it. After all, she can't separate us.' 'God knows I'm desperately sorry for her', Bowen told Ford: 'but I *can't* understand her lack of pride.' Hunt had by now guessed that there was another woman, and probably suspected it was Stella Bowen. Back in London, she tried to 'cadge pity & sympathy' from Bowen, being 'dreadfully pathetic, of course, about being deserted'. 'I believe she wants to force me into the most devilish hypocrisies', Bowen told Ford, 'or to embarrass me very badly by making great demands on my pity.' All of which may have been true, but must have been subsidiary to wanting to find out what Ford was up to. Ford's advice was not to let Hunt manipulate her sympathy: 'The best line to take w^d be to say that you think it rather fine of me to start a new life at my age & to stick out for independence. If it leads to a quarrel or a coldness so much the better, because it is

rather unnatural y^{r.} being friendly with her.'[12] He explained (with sardonic disavowal)
how he had broken the news of their broken relationship to Hunt: 'short of kicking
Violet in the face or saying that she was a superannuated Hecate (of both of wh.
proceedings I am incapable) I have told her definitely that things are at an end between
us, at bed & at board, every way & for ever.' 'I am very sorry this has happened', Hunt
said, 'but I am not out to stop you doing what you want.' She too knew she couldn't
separate them. But neither could she let go. In March she had told Ford: 'we *must* have
an interview soon', because 'things have been said to me by Stella and Phillis [Phyllis
Reid] that you must either contradict or endorse.' Now she rang up Bowen, and
'plunged straight into a passionate appeal' to her to help in another attempt to get Ford
to see her. She said she knew Ford didn't want to live with her, but had no idea he
didn't want to *see* her. She threatened suicide if he wouldn't meet her. Then, as Bowen
explained to Ford:

she said she *must* know why you were leaving her—that if you belonged to another woman,
then she had no right to you & no right to try & get you back, but that if it was only for
financial reasons etc., then there was still hope & she would fight on. She said she did think
she might be allowed to know how she stood—and lots more in the same vein. And I *could
not* tell her a direct lie because I thought she *had* a right to know how she stood, & there was
an awful pause, & then I said 'I don't think it's only for financial reasons', and she said 'thank
you for telling me' & I said 'goodbye', & so did she, & we rang off.—So now she knows. And
God knows what she'll do.[13]

Thus far, Ford's characters couldn't have behaved with more decorum, understatement, and veiled inference.

When Ford had written to South Lodge, he hadn't given his address; Hunt said
Bowen confessed to her that she had posted his letters in London, to prevent his being
traced from the postmark. Though Hunt assured him: 'we need not be enemies', her
way of getting her friends and Ford's family enmeshed in the tangle only humiliated
and outraged him. Juliet Soskice was perhaps thinking of this period as well as the days
of the *Throne* case when she later parried her talk of her sufferings: 'As regards
suffering my dear Violet, I think that few people of any dignity can have suffered from
a greater sense of shame and degradation than I, and if I may say my poor mother too
at various times have felt through the results of Ford's most unhappy connection with
you.' Hunt even asked Bowen to get Ford to visit her—Bowen said she would not stop
Ford trying to 'make matters easier' for Hunt, but that Ford's reply was 'that his
decision never to see you again was *no* concern' of Bowen's, and that she should stop
talking about it. 'You begged me to protect him from the evil consequences of a public
scandal', continued Bowen to Hunt: 'But indeed, this rests in your hands, rather than
in mine.' Ford began to feel himself at the centre of a new scandal—more private than
the *Throne* case, but potentially damaging. He was still particularly upset by the
thought of Hunt saying that he had lived with her for her money. It was the kind of
betrayal that made him feel most persecuted, though (as so often with persecutory
feelings) there is reason to believe that some of his feeling was justified. Hunt herself
wrote to his mother to apologize for one outburst. 'Dear Mother', she wrote (tenacious
of her connection with his family), 'You have written me a very angry letter and I am

sure I deserve it. I *do* talk in a very wrong way about your son whenever you come to see me [. . .].' After this meeting, she explained, she broke down—'I have been in bed since Friday, and I believe I have broken a small blood vessel'—though one of her biographers claims she feigned illness to inveigle Ford to visit. 'Ford has come up at another woman's petition', she explained to Cathy Hueffer: 'He saw me. And we have agreed to stay together without love. It is a very trying proposition for me and we had been arguing it out by my bedside all Monday morning [. . .].' Either she wanted everyone—even Ford's mother—to be told only this official version; or she could not herself face the fact of separation.[14]

It was early June, once Tom had left, that Bowen went to live at Red Ford. Ford changed his name at once. This was partly from apprehension about what Hunt's 'histrionic impulse' might lead her to if Bowen got referred to as 'Mrs Hueffer' ('So I am not now even the wife of his pen!' she wrote to H. G. Wells when she heard). But though Ford was uncertain about the wisdom of the change, there were other reasons. He didn't want publishers to hear that he owed Hunt money. He also wanted to stop her 'depleting' his bank account, which she did by sending a blank cheque to at least one tradesman, and by signing his name on other cheques. ('No: I don't know that V had any *right* to sign my name; she just did it', he told Bowen stoically.) He was also anxious to keep his third major affair out of the newspapers. He considered calling himself 'Heffer'; but decided to change his surname to his grandpaternal first name. It was a symbol for himself of how he had created his new life (in his new, eponymous home).[15]

Ford stuck to the official version of his separation from Hunt for their close friends and family. When he explained his move to his mother and Masterman (who were both close to Hunt as well), he didn't yet mention Bowen. The two main reasons he gave for leaving South Lodge were that he could not 'stand not being, or appearing, independent'; and that Hunt's stories about his living on her (which was what made him appear dependent) had become intolerable. He told his mother that his nerves were 'a bit jumpy'. When he wrote to her again in July he still didn't want to give her his address lest it 'embarrass' her, since she was still seeing Hunt 'pretty frequently'; he was writing from the Authors' Club, where letters could reach him. But this time he did mention Bowen (perhaps because he knew by then that Hunt had already told her as much); and his defensiveness about his new love, and about his relations with Hunt and with his family suggest that Bowen had been right about how much Hunt's rows upset him. 'Dear Ma!', he wrote: 'I gather from Soskice & Juliet that they feel themselves slighted at not hearing from me—but they seldom write to me or I to them, so it is not unusual.' (David Soskice had returned to Russia in June 1917 as Petrograd correspondent for the *Manchester Guardian*. He also became one of Kerensky's private secretaries from mid-August until the October Revolution. He thought he wouldn't get out of the Winter Palace alive; but his journalistic credentials helped him escape in November.) 'I may as well, however, explain', continued Ford to Cathy Hueffer:

in clearing various matters up, that some time ago—I think in the spring of last year—Violet told me that Juliet had uttered various strictures on my conduct & I rather resented them. I never comment on anybody myself: I do not suppose you have ever heard me say a word against anybody & I do not see why people should comment upon me. Of course it is possible that Juliet did not utter all the remarks that Violet said she did—but I may say that it was these remarks which have induced me to leave London for good. They were, amongst other things, to the effect that I lived on Violet & victimised her & so on. A man cannot, you know, go on in Society if that sort of thing, true or untrue is said about him—especially if they are said by his sister & his wife.

I told Violet then, perfectly distinctly, that if I heard that sort of thing again either from her or from other people I should leave South Lodge & only return to attend her parties to save her face, in the vulgar phrase. In January of this year I heard that a gentleman, an intimate friend of Violet's, had said in a drawing room, to a friend of mine, on Violet's authority that I was living on Violet. I also heard that Violet was constantly associating with two people who during the war denounced me to the police as a German spy. When I heard the first statement I gave Violet an opportunity of contradicting it; she refused to & I left South Lodge for the studio. When I heard the second I told Violet that if she did not give up altogether the acquaintance of these three gentlemen & two others whom I regard as my bitter enemies I should break with her for good. I gave her, in fact, the choice between myself & these people. She chose them: I daresay she thought I was joking. I was not. I therefore left London; it seemed to me that it was up to me to prove that I could support myself & I have done so. It seemed to me also that no man could be expected to stand treachery of that particular nature [. . .]

In June I set up house with another lady. I am not going to comment upon this or excuse myself. It is simply done. We are in pretty poor circumstances but not starving & at any rate none can say that I am being kept—tho' I suppose they will. I appeared at Violet's party at this lady's request & I shall continue to do so, though it is against my own judgment. However, she wishes to save Violet the mortification of appearing officially deserted, so let it go at that. Only it does not make things easier that Violet turned up & made a scene at my Club on the afternoon of her party. Of course she is at liberty to make scenes at my Club, but it makes it rather difficult for me to explain it away afterwards. Still, I have done my best.

I sh^d· like you to believe that I sh^d· not have left Violet if she had not acted as she did. I daresay you won't—but if you come to consider how I did stick to her during all the years when I knew perfectly well how she was calling me drunken & dirty & parasitic to everyone in London & the ruin it has caused me professionally & personally, you must see that it had got pretty well past bearing. I know Violet can't help saying that sort of thing of her dearest & best & that was why I stood it as long as I did. But I am getting on in years & it was getting late to make another start in life & I am not as patient as I was.

At any rate that is why I have disappeared & why I am determined to remain hidden.[16]

Some would reprehend the disingenuousness with which he blames Hunt for his decision to leave her, and even presents it as her choice, meanwhile giving the impression that his liaison with Bowen was an effect rather than an additional cause of Hunt's vindictiveness (rather as he had presented himself as driven by Elsie, Marwood, and his depression over the *English Review*, into Hunt's arms). It could also be objected that the lofty claim never to comment on anybody himself is belied by his censure of Juliet's disloyalty, Hunt's treachery, and his insinuation that she had been lying. His comment about his jumpy nerves shows that he knew he was reacting neurotically; but this isn't surprising given his sensitivity to 'scenes', 'treachery', gossip, and scandal. And though in part he may have been projecting on to her his own guilt for his betrayal of her (for which his accusations become his alibi), his falling out of love was catalysed by his knowledge that she was discussing him with their mutual friends. Like Sylvia Tietjens, suffering herself from her man's disenchantment with her, Hunt knew how to make him suffer. His notion of his own gentlemanly honour seems at best anachronistic, at worst perverse here, when preserving the appearance of their marriage becomes more important than preserving the good character of the woman he still calls his 'wife'. One can only say that Hunt too seems to have felt that the most important thing was to be able to say they were still 'together'—that at her age it would indeed have been mortifying to be publicly deserted by the man on whom she had staked all her social credibility. Though Ford was still prepared to maintain this façade to protect her, he was no longer prepared to let her humiliate him. When he told his mother: 'I sh^d. like you to believe that I sh^d. not have left Violet if she had not acted as she did', it's not (or not only) that he needs to put a better construction on his actions. He would like her to believe it because he knows Hunt would want her to believe it. The version he wants believed is also partly designed to protect Bowen. It's not just that he didn't want to get her talked about; though that motive, together with the fact he was also a friend of Hunt's, stopped him mentioning her to Masterman: he certainly didn't want them talked about to Hunt; and he wanted to spare their mutual friends the awkwardness of having to keep secrets from Hunt. It was also that when she was talked about, he didn't want it said that she had broken up her friend's marriage. If this was Fordian impressionism (it was true that Hunt had befriended Bowen first, before introducing them), it was, as always, founded on a truth—that the 'marriage' had already been a crumbling form when Bowen and Ford met; and that he *had* given Hunt the ultimatum about the three men before he met Bowen, and even earlier than he remembered: on 11 March 1917. They had a more immediate reason to play down Bowen's role: while Ford was still appearing at Violet's parties—such as her annual garden party on the last day of June, the one he mentioned to his mother—he could hardly give the impression of still being with her if he was widely known to be living with someone else. He wasn't able to give a very good impression of still being with Hunt anyway. Alec Waugh said of one such occasion:

It was one of the biggest parties I have ever been to—champagne, white ties, etc. I got there a little early and Violet kept saying 'I wonder what's keeping Ford. I wish he'd hurry'. When eventually he did arrive it was to moon around looking very lost. He did not seem to know if he was a guest or host. He appeared surprised when I went up to say 'good-bye' and 'thank you'. I suppose it was their last public bow. It certainly was a party.

Waugh thought this party was in July 1919, but it may well have been the one on 30 June, in which case Ford would have been suppressing his anger at the scene Hunt had made at his club that day—perhaps the occasion when she turned up with a bundle of his clothes and demanded to know his whereabouts. After the guests had left, they started arguing. First about money—some time before she had signed his name to withdraw £15 from his account. Then she said:

Ford: Why need we be this hostile? I am not interfering or troubling you It hurts me more than all the rest! . . . He walked into the little room & with his back to me said [']It is obvious I can't talk about things with you' I said Why not. . . . My future must some time be settled. . . . Am I not still your wife? He sat down opened his hands & sneered & said 'I came here on the condition that there was no discussion' I said 'There *is* no discussion[.] Go—go now' and I went up & sat in the dark.[17]

There was, probably, in the letter to his mother, also a chivalrous motive behind Ford's appearing to shift the blame to Hunt, since it presents it as *her* decision to reject *him* (rather as a man might begin adultery, but then hire a co-respondent to enable his wife to begin the divorce proceedings). The official version for more general consumption—that Ford was not at South Lodge because he was 'buried in the country writing a novel', appears to have been accepted for a while. But Ford was perfectly open with friends such as Herbert Read, who were not also Hunt's friends, telling him when he was due to visit later in the year: 'My Establishment (including of course, H.Q. Staff, Maltese Cart for use of M.O., cats, dogs, ducks, etc) includes a Mrs. Ford whom you don't know but who, besides ministering to my, really, declining years, paints portraits of—generally ugly—people.'[18]

Ford's letter to his mother is significant in another way. His wanting her to believe his story—though suspecting she won't—is characteristically dual and characteristically provocative. It intimates a further connection between his psychology and his impressionism. His refusal to comment upon his characters (his determination to 'remain hidden' in his writing too) is bound up with the wish that people shouldn't comment upon him, and with the feeling (as he and Hunt expressed it during the *Throne* case) that one's friends ought to be given the benefit of the doubt. 'As you may have observed', he told Masterman, 'I dislike talking about my feelings or affairs & I only do so to you because I am really grateful to you for all your backing in the past four years so that I think I owe it to you to keep you posted as to my motives & movements. If it is a nuisance to you, forgive it for that reason.' Working up impressionistic versions of his experiences was a way of expressing himself without talking about himself (his explanation of Hunt's scene at the Authors' Club must have been quite a story!). What is also surprising about the letter is how close its sense of persecution and disgrace is to Tietjens's state of mind in *Parade's End*.[19]

The only person he would discuss the situation with more directly was Bowen. She had voiced doubts about whether Ford's official version would convince either Hunt or their friends:

There is *no one* in the world I would rather not have know my private affairs—I quail when I think of her power of vulgarising everything she touches,—& I know that the sort of thing she would say would go much against us in the future. But I want to act honestly. And I don't wonder that the reason you give for leaving S. L.—namely, that she won't give up some of her friends—doesn't carry conviction as the *real* reason. It's all right as a technical reason tho' even so it won't sound a very good one when repeated. Doesn't she *know* it's because you can't stand the way she torments you & the way she vulgarises your intimate life in public? Because that is the real reason isn't it? And it would have parted you anyhow, some time, even without me, wouldn't it? [. . .]

One wonderful sentence of V's I treasured, remembering how you took nothing but your own few things.—'He's taken his bed—he's taken my sheets—he's taken all my things—he's taken my best . . . you see how awful he is!' Which just shows what she *can* do with *no* material to work on!

They were giving Ford material to work on in another sense, since out of this report he would imagine Sylvia Tietjens's accusations that her husband had stolen her sheets. Ford himself evidently did believe his own official version, and replied that Hunt's refusal to give up 'certain men' *was* the real reason:

I sh^d. never have left her but for that. I sh^d. just have sat on my love for you, probably at the very beginning & have got through somehow.

I hope my saying that does not hurt you—but I did have a very strong sense of my duty to V. &, if she had any where near—within a thousand miles!—done her duty by me I w^d. have killed myself rather than leave her.[20]

This could be made to seem self-deceiving and self-glorifying, making himself out a martyr rather than a philanderer. It is the world of his fiction, where an Ashburnham does suppress his passion for Nancy, to the point where he kills himself. But it is also the world of Ford's life: he had, after all, 'sat on' his infatuation with Brigit Patmore, leaving Hunt not for her, but for the war, which was nearly a way of killing himself. If he seems to be denying his sexual motive for infidelity, it is because we find it hard to believe in the ethical code of his age, which valued duty and honour more highly than pleasure. That he knew exactly what he was doing, and why, is shown by an extraordinary letter he had written to explain his motives to Bowen. It is, as he says, one of his most revealing pieces of prose. He said of Hunt: 'for the life of me, I cannot see why she will not adopt that line & say that she kicked me out of the house because of my evil habits. It w^d. save her face & there w^d. be an end of it.' But of course Hunt didn't want an end of it:

But, you see, she believes so firmly that I am just a gross feeder & that the meat & wine & olive oil from Provence & all the rest of the things in the Cloaca of S.L. will lure me back in the end—that she banks on that & on that alone. I am to return contrite & writhing all over the body as Beau [Ford's half-crown mongrel] does after he has chased a forbidden rabbit & she will lead me on the leash thro' all the drawing rooms of the West End. It is an ambition like another—not particularly culpable or mean—but you who have seen me as I really am & have really listened to what are my desires & my ideals, know how little attraction for me there w^d. be in the programme.

I say all this because I want you to realise that tho' Violet has lived with me for nearly ten years she has never *once* listened to a word I said. Because she cannot listen [. . .]

As for 'telling' people: it is the one point on wh. we differ—because I suppose it is the one point on wh. I am thoroughly un-English. I *never* want to talk about myself, really. I do, as you have told me, swank a bit about inessentials. But I was brought up to think it—& I feel it to be—an impertinence, to inflict my views, ambitions, wishes or wisdom on other people. You can see that in the impersonality of my books.

Per contra: I do resent most frightfully being asked questions about myself. You are the only person I have ever allowed to do that *twice*—& that is the greatest proof of love I have ever given you. All such questions as: 'What are you doing now?' & so on—wh. one hears every day in English life, seem to me to be as gross an outrage as if one were to be asked to strip off one's clothes for the common amusement of a room. You will find every Frenchman thinks like that—because the French have the duel.

In England they carry it to such an opposite extreme—probably because there is no confessional—that a perpetual intrusion of personality is taken to be almost a saving grace.

I believe you think you will be a little nearer heaven if you give V. the chance to earn eternal damnation by revealing the secrets of y^r & my hearts to Mrs Reeve Wallas, Mrs Byles, Mrs Sieveking & the rest of the pack. But you won't really—you will only harm that unfortunate creature &, just a little, lower yourself. Believe me, as in the Arts, so in life, Reticence is the first of all qualities.

That is why I don't want you to defend me—ever. Friends who don't feel instinctively that lies about one are lies, are friends better lost. Real friends will condone all one's actions for the sake of one's personality. I shouldn't care what you had *done*; it is what you *are* that matters to me.

Still, believe me, I am not trying to dissuade you from telling any friend to whom you think you owe it to tell them all about our relationships. But I do hope you will be able to do it without blackening the character of the unfortunate Violet. She may deserve it, or she may not. But it is hateful to me, beyond anything, to say anything against one's enemies. It is perhaps a mania with me. [. . .] Tell y^r friends I mean that you love me & that I love you— as I do my own darling, so very tenderly—& just let it go at that. As for plans, ethics, justifications, ambitions & the like—leave them, if you can, alone. You will never, while I live, make y^r friends or mine know what nature of man I am; it can't be done; simply because I haven't got the motives that the rest of humanity have. I don't want money, power, influence, authority or any of the things that most people want. I have always wanted to find in the world just one person I c^d trust—& that I have in you—& a number to whom I c^d feel kindly; that I have in the fowls of the air & in young writers. Otherwise I want nothing— except to do my job well.

This, dear, is the fullest confession I ever made to anyone—& I make it to you because I love you, finally & irrevocably! It is the greatest compliment I have ever paid you—& the greatest I have ever paid to any human being.

Goodnight, darling. I am *so* tired.[21]

'The foregoing is rather a lecture', he added, when he continued the letter the following afternoon: 'but I wanted to say something like it, because it is all matter that I feel rather deeply.'

The horror of exposure has a pathological edge here, inevitably so given the horrors to which he had been exposed in the war. (His memory of getting 'covered with tins of sardine' while the drunken officer tried to expose himself during a bombardment explicitly connects the two kinds of vulnerability.) Ford had always valued privacy. But he was still haunted by the war's nightmare in which there was no sanctuary from violence and destruction. Now more than ever he needed to secure his defences against the outside world. He had always had the fear that domesticity was itself insecure: that a mother-dove could devour her young, or a father could die without warning. Life with Hunt, and life at the Front, made him feel that violence could erupt anywhere, at any time, amidst civilized life. *Parade's End* is founded on that duality: its structure implies that domestic-sexual violence and military destruction are fundamentally related: two faces of the world's rage.

The dualities run deep in this letter. Ford is both Bengel, who 'cannot do anything at all without being most severely punished', and whom 'the rest of humanity' will never understand; and also Bingel, who can do anything he likes because his heart is in the right place. The plea to be accepted for what he is recalls his childhood feelings that his parents were indifferent to him, or rejected him as the stupid donkey compared to his Bingel-brother Oliver. The letter is as revealing about his art as about his personality. In one sense it seems paradoxical to adopt a reticence which you say is like the impersonality of your books, and on the other that your friends should forgive your deeds because of your personality. But in another sense it isn't, simply reflecting a dual sense of audience. To those who will never understand or accept you, you present an aloof indifference; but disclose your personality to the readers you can trust. This sense of writing for intimate, sympathetic individuals within the general readership is deeply characteristic (perhaps he got the readership he defined, of passionate advocates defining themselves against the general misjudgement of him). His telling Bowen that she was the reader for whom he had always been writing fairy tales is itself a fairy-tale version of the yearning for communion with a sympathetic soul that impels Dowell to tell his story. It is perhaps a necessary tactic for a reticent person who wants to express a personality. Or, conversely, the difficulty of self-revelation might be what incites a reticent person to become an artist, and find oblique and displaced modes of self-expression. Ford's comment about the confession is suggestive about this need, and therapeutic value, of self-disclosure. The idea in the letter about personality mattering more than deeds shows how far Ford is from a truly theological view (though this too bears on his aesthetic: impressionism is a domain where perception matters more than action; where personality—of characters or authors—overshadows deeds). Dowell's monologue reads with the force of a secular confession; as does Ford's letter to Bowen. 'Confession' as a metaphor has several implications: it exalts the listener; it poses the moral *need* to be listened to; but it also involves a duality of intimacy and impersonality. There is an isolated intimacy—the priest is the only (human) listener; but he is listening in an impersonal role, and invisibly, behind a screen. It could also be a metaphor for Ford's relation to his readers. The letter, like his art, is at once a humble plea for acceptance and love, and, in its sardonic bitterness, a demonstration of superiority. Another passage from it shows how well Ford understood this duality at the heart of love and art: 'I am absolutely yours' he told Bowen: 'either as a big baby to be a responsibility all the days of y^r life, or a "quiet me" on wh. to rely—or, probably, just a mixture of both, wh. is the best way of all [. . .].'

He didn't want to lose friends like the Mastermans. In the letter he wrote to Charles on the day the Versailles peace treaty was signed, he made a gesture of support that casts as much light on his politics as on his gratitude:

Dear C.F.G.,

The guns are going—so thank God it's over. I am pretty well satisfied with the results: for me they have not gone far enough in splitting up L'Infame [the Rhineland was not given to France as he had hoped it would be; instead, the Versailles Treaty stated that the territory to the left of the Rhine was to be occupied for fifteen years]. Still it's like a fairy world. I daresay they go too far for you—still it can't be unsatisfactory to you.

I should like to say one thing, for what I am worth & that is that I believe after long consideration & some knowledge of the war that the greatest credit of all is due to the Asquithian Liberals; that the winning of the war was altogether due to you people & that the behaviour of the country at the last election was a piece of dastardly ingratitude. I don't suppose either my pen or my voice are much good—but if you care to make use of either they wd. be as wholeheartedly at your disposal on these lines as they were at the disposal of the country during the war. I will speak for you anywhere you like & write for you anywhere you like & at any time. I don't suppose the offer is worth very much, but it is very sincerely made.

Although Lloyd George remained prime minister of the Coalition government after the December 1918 election, the Conservatives and Unionists had gained over a hundred seats from the Liberals. Asquith himself, prime minister from 1910 to 1916, had lost his seat. Ford's support for Irish Home Rule had always distanced him from orthodox Toryism. But now he had more personal reasons for identifying with the old-style Liberals: they too seemed betrayed and ruined—the kind of lost cause that always appealed to his imagination (and that his support for them would itself have been). Masterman, who had lost his seat in 1914 due to his support for National Insurance, didn't take up Ford's offer; and for no evident reason other than Ford's leaving London, then later England, their friendship cooled as it evaporated.[22]

That 'fairy world' feeling had been enhanced when Ford left his 'cottage out of Grimm' to go up to London on 4 June and sign the petition which would allow him to change his surname. He decided he couldn't afford 'even a sherry and bitters at Short's', so he 'drifted, more desultorily than ever, in on his agent, Pinker, whose office was just around the corner'. 'You've just got ten minutes!', panted Pinker by way of greeting. A Hollywood studio had offered $5,000 for the cinema rights to *Romance*: Ford had till four o'clock to get to the American Embassy before the option expired. If he had stopped for that sherry and bitters he would have missed his chance. 'But I had resisted temptation', he said, 'at the dictates of Economy. For the first and last time in my life!' It seemed like the magical reward of a fairy world. With the £429 that was left of his share after his debt to Pinker was deducted, together with some of Bowen's capital, they were able to buy a new home: Coopers Cottage in the small village of Bedham, about three miles from Petworth.[23]

The money meant he could rest, buy the Sussex Large Black Pigs he wanted, and regain the strength of mind he needed to return to novel-writing. He had been translating Euripides' *Alcestis* in the spring for the actor-manager and producer Nigel Playfair, and said that in working on it he had 'recovered some shadow of power over words. But not much.' Recovery and power are at the heart of the play, and Hercules' descent into the underworld to recover Alcestis from the land of shadows might well have figured to Ford his own brushes with death, and chimed with the post-war mood of having come through. When Hercules says 'They are a very turbulent and oppressive breed, the sons of Mars, and it is well that I should rid the earth of them', he could speak for Ford's wartime antagonism towards Prussians. Ford later wrote that the serving-maid's speech reporting Alcestis' sentimental farewell to her marriage-bed was his 'favorite passage of all Greek drama' (he was to recall it in *Parade's End*, when Tietjens's camp-bed has to suffice as 'nuptial couch', and Ford writes: 'What an Alcestis!'); but it was not only that celebration of marriage through anticipating her own death that appealed to him. The omnipotence of the demigod-figure always attracted him. And Euripides presents extreme acts of altruism in all three main characters: Alcestis' offer to sacrifice her own life, and die in her husband's place; her husband Admetus' suppression of his grief over her death in order to observe the codes of hospitality, and entertain Hercules; and Hercules' willingness to brave the underworld in order to give the couple a new life together. *Alcestis* was to provide a paradigm for all Ford's major post-war fictions, in which the hero (like Hercules) faces death (in battle, or by attempted suicide), but survives, to be (re-)united (like Admetus) with his love. Euripides provides a model for more than just the plot. Ford's elusive dual tone, in which irony and romance is won from the brink of tragedy, has its precursor too in the *Alcestis*. In telling the story of what happened to the translation, Ford brings out how close he (like Alcestis) was to ruin. Just after calling on Pinker he drew two small cheques on his bank account, but both bounced. He said he had had £72 at the time, which was to have lasted him until the play was performed. But 'A friend'—presumably Violet Hunt, if Sylvia Tietjens's similar actions are a clue—'had drawn out the whole of my £72 on two forged cheques!' Then, 'By the next post', he had a letter to say that the manuscript of the play had been lost, and could he send a copy. He couldn't, he explained, because 'for economy's sake' he had not had a copy typed. 'Think of what my position would have been if Destiny had made me put off my call on Mr. Pinker!', ends the first part of *It Was the Nightingale*.[24]

He was determined to end the rumours of his dependence on Hunt, and got his sister to write to her explaining: 'He wants it definitely settled whether he does or does not owe you £4000. You have sometimes, he says, declared that he does; and then again declared that you have taken pictures, book, furniture, and autographs under a Bill of Sale against the debt. This he wants settled *once for all, in one way or the other* [. . .].' He would only come to South Lodge to 'preserve appearances' 'if this question of the debts is finally and definitely settled' in whichever way Hunt chose. Since he was broke, and all his possessions of any value were already at South Lodge, he couldn't have hoped to raise one thousand pounds, let alone four. He may have banked on her wanting to keep his belongings if she couldn't keep him; but even so, the Madox Brown paintings, water-colours by George Boyce and Frederick Sandys, the family furniture, and autograph manuscripts and letters would not have been worth £2,000 in 1919 (the Madox Brown painting of Ford as Tell's son didn't reach its reserve of £100 when Hunt tried to auction it years later). It isn't known whether, or how, they settled the matter. Hunt later told him that the debt was £2,000, but that she would count his belongings at South Lodge (which he had ceded to her in lieu of debts) as cancelling only £500 of it. He can't have ever paid back the remainder: the *Romance* film money was under a third of the sum, and he needed it desperately to let him find his form again as a writer, and to find somewhere more salubrious to live (Red Ford's charms wore thin in the winter damp and mud). He was struggling for money for the rest of his life, and even in his one brief period of relative prosperity in the late 1920s he wouldn't have been able to spare £1,500.[25]

7

THE POST-WAR WRITER

Nay, it had been revealed to you that beneath Ordered Life itself was stretched,
the merest film with, beneath it, the abysses of Chaos [. . .]

(Ford, *It Was the Nightingale*)

Coopers Cottage had a sitting tenant who refused to move, and then died. Ford and
Bowen only took possession of it in March 1920, and they weren't able to move in until
September. Meanwhile, visitors streamed to Red Ford, undeterred by the austerity:
the Herbert Reads, Francis Meynell, Phyllis Reid, Mary Butts and John Rodker,
Margaret and Douglas Cole, and Ray and Daisy Postgate. Inviting F. S. Flint down for
a weekend, he warned him: 'George Lansbury's daughter is here too as a guest, but I
suppose you are not afraid of Bolshevists. . . .' The guests found dinner 'an ever-
retreating mirage', said Bowen, with Ford writing upstairs, and calling down 'Oh, give
me another twenty minutes', the food put on the table, then taken away to reheat.
When they were alone, the two of them would work on the house and garden in the
morning, then go for long walks in the afternoon. Living in the 'green nook' that he
had envisioned during the war, he could now let his mind wander over quite other
landscapes. He began writing 'English Country'—essays published that August and
September in the *New Statesman*, then worked into *No Enemy: A Tale of Reconstruction*: a book which registers the psychological effects of Ford's war by exploring his
relationship to landscape—the way crucial moments of his wartime experience come
back to him as visions of the landscape. He thought of it as a ' "piece of writing", like
the *Soul of London*', not only because its mode of topographical impressionism is
similar, but because it also maps Ford's recovery from mental breakdown. He wanted
it published by Duckworth, who had reprinted the English trilogy; but John Lane had
the option on Ford's next novel after *The Good Soldier*.

You speak of it as a 'novel' [Ford told Pinker] & that rather troubles me. If it is a novel it
simply has to go to Lane. I regard it as what is called a 'serious book'—I suppose it is really
betwixt & between.

Can you approach Lane about it? Or should I? I do so dislike being in false positions about
books—yet I always seem to get into them, with the best intentions in the world. I wish you
could get over your antipathy to J.[ohn] L.[ane]—at any rate for the occasion—& put the
matter to him. I would—but then I might seem to be going behind *your* back & there we
should be again.

I meant *English Country* to be a 'piece of writing', like the *Soul of London* and to go,
eventually, to Duckworth.

I wish you wd. send me that Northern Newspapers money. My pigs have been sick—and that is ruinous as well as distracting.

I suppose you wd. not care to buy a pig—not a sick one—about 20 st.[1]

Ford understood his knack of getting into false positions, even if he was not conscious of the need that fomented them. He had got into yet another one with Hunt, his whole relationship with whom went through a sequence of false positions: a secret affair; an affair screened by a fictitious(?) affair with Gertrud Schablowsky; a fictitious marriage; the double passions that included Rosamond and Brigit Patmore and now Stella Bowen; and the fictitious fidelity to protect Hunt's reputation. In this letter he even begins to get into exactly the false position about books that he dislikes. The critic who had fiercely opposed the dominance amongst English readers of the 'serious book' over the novel, now claims that his latest is just that. Or does he? If the inverted commas insinuate a disavowal, so, doubly, does the complete sentence: 'I regard it as what is called a "serious book"—I suppose it is really betwixt & between.' He regards it as one thing, but supposes it between two things. There is more to this than classifying his books to suit his plans of consolidating his publishing (feeling that his idiosyncratic genre of social and psychological impressionism would be recognized more clearly if *No Enemy* were published alongside the English trilogy). It is also indicative of his ability to hold contrasting views about his own writing, even by returning upon the stated positions of his own criticism. The 'serious book', he wrote, 'is produced by gentlemen more distinguished for their industry than for their gifts, insight, or love of their subjects. That a serious book should possess form, imaginative insight, or interest for anyone not a specialist, would, generally speaking, be considered a very unsound proposition.' For Ford, the serious book is antagonistic to the novel; and his inverted commas show how he enjoys provoking the hostility of the 'serious', while insisting that it is art which is the serious pursuit. The 'serious book' is associated with death and decay: 'It is a purveyor above all of Views', and 'The moment they are expressed they begin to decay'. 'Views in fact are like those bones that are found in ancient coffins or in niches in dry hillsides: the moment they are uncovered they begin to decay, to crumble beneath the eye until there is nothing left but a little dust that would not fill a cup.' Clearly Ford is not telling Pinker he has written *this* sort of book; but his hesitation reveals an uncertainty about how far *No Enemy* could be said to be a novel—which for him is inseparable from the question of whether it is crafted and styled enough to achieve immortality. The letter is, finally, an example of Ford's habit of getting himself into false positions in order to extricate himself with a characteristic combination of self-pity and wit. He imagines getting into rows not only with Lane, but even Pinker. But the phrase '& there we should be again!', with its tonal up-turn, and reminiscence of Ford's parodying of James (and of how he used to wind Pinker up by pretending to joke about James) transforms ire to irony. The comic offer of the pig pulls him back together after having contemplated the animals' death and his own ruin. '*I suppose* you wd. not care to buy a pig': the ironic mastery of tone here (of course Pinker had no use for a whole pig!) is very different from the creative uncertainty about his book's genre—'I suppose it is really betwixt & between'. And yet the habit of supposition—of not exactly *holding* a view, but *supposing* it—posing it, and throw-

ing himself imaginatively into the mentality of someone who did hold it—this habit is
central to his art of fiction, in which the quality of the rendering is paramount, and the
subjects themselves are means to that end. As a writer, Ford's duality sharpened his
vision (whereas as a serious bookman it would merely have blurred his arguments).
Like Tietjens, 'He got into appalling messes, unending and unravellable [. . .]'; yet he
also had Tietjens's 'positive genius for getting all sorts of things out of the most beastly
muddles'—not just by extricating things from their muddles, but creating other
things—novels—out of those muddles. But then all creators need a chaos in their
beginning.[2]

When Violet Hunt wrote to Scott James in the spring of 1921 enlisting him to
persuade Ford to come and see her, she told him (with an impressionistic vividness
and perhaps inventiveness) that Ford had visited her in the autumn of 1919, while he
was writing for the short-lived *Piccadilly Review*, but that the visits ceased when the
review collapsed in late November. Then she asked him to come in February, and said
that he did, and kissed her, saying that he would see her the next week; but that he
didn't, and that they didn't meet again until they 'went to the Anglo-French dinner to
meet Berthelot together in May'. This was probably actually in March, since Ford
arranged to pick her up then, writing: 'If—as seems likely—Davray's party is a swell
affair I ought to have a tail-coat, opera hat & Inverness.' (Davray was the co-editor of
the *Anglo-French Review*.) After that, she said, they corresponded about 'the long O in
Virgil', and the death of their friend, the agent and publisher René Byles. But Ford
contested this version, saying that he arranged to go with her to Durham for the
funeral of her sister in April, who died only twenty days after the death (from measles
and pneumonia) of her daughter, Violet's 29-year-old niece Rosamond. There are
certainly two telegrams saying Ford would accompany Hunt to Durham. And there is
also a correspondence from May 1920 between Ford and her solicitors, who tried to
get him to sign a statement that his pictures and furniture at South Lodge were her
'absolute property'. Ostensibly she was worried that if Ford predeceased her, Elsie or
her children might claim them. But it was also another convenient alibi to keep herself
entangled in Ford's affairs.[3]

His new stability and happiness with Bowen enabled him to throw himself into his
work with gusto. A new typewriter eased his writer's cramp. Harold Monro, who had
always admired his verse, asked him for a poem for his *Chapbook*. 'Of course I am a
poet', replied Ford: 'I have just written two poems & feel a third bubbling near the
surface—which has not happened for years.' The first poem was 'Immortality: An
Elegy on a Great Poet Dying Abroad', published in the *Chapbook* in July 1920. Ford
never collected it, perhaps because it is too raw and bitter—too powerful—to satisfy
his desire for the subdued and unobtrusive in verse. Parts of it sound as if they would
support Mizener's reading of it as an expression of 'his fantasy that he was a great
writer shockingly neglected' (though Ford always said you never knew whether you
were a great artist or not):

> Heaven knows, you may well prove Immortal
> So consummate, consummately handled your prose is,
> And your poems the summit of Poetry [. . .][4]

It gains its energy of pathos, certainly, from being—to some extent—another of Ford's elegies for himself: 'here, at home, you could not find one hearth | To crave your shadow falling from the ingle | Towards the curtains. This is your own land | And your face forgotten.' Violet Hunt read it as autobiographical: 'Of course the One who died Abroad is yourself. I can never stay away from you if you go on making appeals like that', she wrote, and continued by making her own appeal: 'I think I am the most miserable of loving women. And Byles died on Sunday—my last friend.' (An autograph draft of this letter survives amongst her papers; if she sent a version of it to Ford, his reply is not known.)[5] It was an appeal to his English readership rather than to her, of course. The angry satire of the literary establishment in 'Mr Croyd', or even the better-humoured version in *Thus to Revisit*, are unequivocal about Ford's feeling that his *books* had been forgotten, and his reputation with them. He knew that in Stella he had found precisely the sympathetic soul craving his presence. It is at this point that the poem turns into something other, something more complexly poised. For against his neglect—which was very real: a public fact, not a private fantasy—Ford tenses the idea of the human cost of literary immortality:

> Did you have a face,
> Eyes, heart to beat and circulate warm blood
> Through chilly limbs? Or, did you have a voice
> To make one hearer thrill with joy; a palate
> For meats or the juice of the grape? Could you rejoice
> Over a little money; did you ever know
> The ups and downs of fortune quicken your pulse,
> Engage in a wager; yearn for pleasant sin
> Live lecherously or contrive delights
> From human passions?

From this point of view, Ford is not the writer of chilly aloofness and dispassionate renunciation: not George Moore, say (who lived until 1933, but about whom Ford later wrote in a similar vein), nor Henry James (d. 1916). Instead, he is gauging the compensations of mortality, which he knew; the human pleasures which, for the Jamesian artist, appear predators upon the life and energies of art. As the poem goes on to suggest that there is a calculating ambitiousness in the dead poet's obsession with immortality, it becomes an elegy for the kind of artist Ford does not want to be; a 'great' figure like the Victorians that terrorized his childhood; someone who takes impersonality to the point of inhumanity:

> I know you aimed at Fame
> Consummately. Once I lived with you
> Five years, day in day out; and once could gather
> So much from your unrevealing eyes and lips.
> And whilst you sucked the last few pence from our purses
> We know you made towards Immortality
> Consummately, by means of unstirred prose
> And stirless verses. . . . You may get it yet!
> Only!
> Will there be a face to look up from your page

Kindly and smiling into young men's eyes?
Or a form that any woman would recognise
And deem it like her lover's. . . . As for us,
We crave to be remembered, warm, in the flesh [. . .]

Here the details point to Conrad. If Ford had had any hopes of renewing their friendship after the war, he must have realized by now how distant Conrad was determined to remain. (In the same month Conrad was telling Hugh Walpole that 'Hueffer belittled everything he touched because he had a *small* soul').[6] Conrad did not die until four years later; and of course he was not a poet. It may be that Ford wanted to express his feelings of hurt and betrayal, but that his strict code of not attacking other living writers required some protective disguising—even killing Conrad off in imagination, responding to a former friend's stonewalling by writing the epitaph of their friendship. In saying this we have come a long way from arguing that the dead poet is Ford himself. But it is the duality of perspective which makes the poem a truly dramatized monologue, and not the direct transcription of self-pity Mizener assumes. Ford can imagine his way into the minds of both the dead poet and his elegist, and he does so to dramatize a critical debate that mattered to him: the question of how much artists should embrace life, or how much they should renounce it. There is a deathliness about the Great Poet's immortality; his art is at once Ford's ideal—'consummately handled'—and its opposite—an egocentric denial of the self, an extinction of the personality that smiles from the page: immortality at the expense of humanity. This is brought out (consummately . . .) in the dual attitude towards the word 'consummately', suggesting an art at once fulfilled and empty. The poem shows Ford once again questioning his own aesthetic grounds, and shifting towards more inclusive principles. This was not simply a matter of acknowledging the Falstaff in himself ('bulbous, veined-nosed, | Cut-pursey Falstaffs. . . . I had rather that | Than immortality of your frozen kind'); but also of turning towards a more vitalist literary ideal which celebrates the sensual. It was a development that made possible the shift from the styptic formalism of *The Good Soldier* to the looser but broader *Parade's End*.

Certainly Ford could give a playful impersonation of the 'Great Figure'. 'It is true I am a great Writer', he told F. S. Flint, giving his fictive last will and critical testament in the process of apologizing for offending Flint by attacking Amy Lowell in his essay about Gaudier-Brzeska:

My dear Flint: will you take this as the settled basis for our future intercourse. I, Ford Madox Ford, being of sound mind depose that: I believe there are two exquisite poets in England, yourself and Hilda [Doolittle]. I believe that there is one exquisite poet in the U.S.A.—Miss Lowell. I believe that there are two other poets in this country, myself and Ezra who are vital because of a certain large carelessness, generosity—and scrupulous attention to words as means of intercommunication between man and man. . . . All the others are just wearinesses on the make . . .[7]

But when Herbert Read approached him with the deference reserved for the Great Figure, Ford bit his head off, stylistically, with a parody of elevated disdain:

Sir;
    You appear to labour under a misapprehension. I can neither recall your identity nor imagine what motive can have prompted you to address to me your obscene and even

blasphemous volume, 'Eclogues'! I should have thought that mere consideration for the great Shades of Milton, Mr. Rudyard Kipling, Sir Henry Newbolt [. . .] would have induced you to stay your hand [. . .] In other words, 'Come Off It!'

It is unnecessary to address me as if I were an obliviscent Panjandrum with head a mile above all clouds. Of course I should be pleased to hear from you and to get your volume.

Though he enjoyed being, and being treated as, someone whose judgement deserved respect, he didn't demand an obsequious subservience. He liked being *cher maître* to *les jeunes*, but eschewed the hierarchic aloofness of the Official Personage—eschewed it by sometimes becoming the parody of such persons, as when he told Monro: 'I think that at my time of life it is time I turned my attention to becoming really Tol-Loll, enveloping myself in clouds of mystery and the like.' His self-importance and self-deprecation were always held in dramatic, creative tension.[8]

He particularly enjoyed the company of the rebellious, innovative young artists, not only because their attacks on him ministered to his need to be (like his grandfather) betrayed and neglected, but also because he wanted once again to be in the avant-garde—especially the poetic avant-garde. This, too, guaranteed a certain amount of the persecution needed to sustain his energies of indignation and self-pity. (He told Read he remembered one of his periodicals, which had caused him 'quite an insulting time with a fierce young poetess of the Aesthetic type who said it made her gorge rise. Go on making them rise', he counselled: 'I think you are on the right road.') Pound, Read, and Flint each visited Sussex to discuss literature with Ford. He was in the avant-garde, but not exactly of it: he was stimulated by the radical polemics to write verse which still looked 'extinct' besides the allusive intensity of *The Cantos* or the compacted disillusion of Eliot's 'Gerontion'. When the *Athenæum*'s reviewer was dismissive of Flint's *Otherworld: Cadences*, Ford wrote an impassioned defence of *vers libre*, saying: 'when human beings are undergoing fears, joys, passions or emotions they do not really retire to studies and compose in words jigsaw puzzles: they relieve their minds by rhythmical utterances. These, if rendered by an artist, make up the utterances of passion that are endurable or overwhelming' ['make up' in what sense?]. One of the poems in *Otherworld*, 'Dusk', is probably the one Ford wrote about to Flint asking him to remove the superscription if he ever published it 'because—though I don't know why one should—one dislikes having one's psychology presented to the world'. The poem includes the stanza:

> You spoke of your art and life,
> Of men you had known who betrayed you,
> Men who fell short of friendship
> And women who fell short of love;
> But, abiding beyond them, your art
> Held you to life, transformed it, became it,
> And so you were free.

On 3 August 1920 he and Bowen moved to Scammells Farm in Bedham, where they stayed for a month while Coopers Cottage was being made ready. Just before leaving Red Ford he wrote to Pound: 'I think it important that we should agree upon a formula for vers libre, non-representationalism and other things before I go any further. We want some manifestoes.' Pound obliged: 'Dante: "A poem is a composition of words set to music." / That bloody well differentiates prose and verse [. . .] All one can claim is the right to use the musical component with a musicians [*sic*] freedom."[9]

The second poem Ford had mentioned to Harold Monro was *A House*, a spacious and leisurely dramatic poem celebrating their life at Red Ford, which was published as a single issue of the *Chapbook* in March 1921. The 'third bubbling near the surface' is a third *poem* (it may have been *Mister Bosphorus and the Muses*, which wasn't finished until late 1922); but there was also a third *person* bubbling near the surface of their lives. Stella was four months pregnant, and Ford's imaginative fertility was stirred by the prospect of that new life, his third child. An earlier version of *A House* called 'Serenada (Your Poet & Some Nightingales)' was written for Stella's birthday on 16 May. But Ford simplified the poem, toning down the literary associations: the nightingale becomes more an observed bird, and less a symbol of the inspiration of 'Your Poet': he wanted to remove the sexual associations between the married poet and the birds of the night, because they threatened the stability of the domestic idyll he wanted to prepare for their unborn child. The implied aesthetic—that it is the lure of sexuality that incites creativity—had to wait for another inventive dramatic poem—*Mister Bosphorus and the Muses*—to be fully worked out.[10]

A House is subtitled '(A Modern Morality)', its morality being that of *No Enemy*. Both voice the need for a rural 'sanctuary' in which to recuperate from the war, and to reconstruct both the self and its faith in society. 'The Country is good when one has discovered for oneself various hollownesses', Ford wrote to Herbert Read: '—those of the plaster Pillars of the State and the papier maché hearts of men.' The poem is written in the mode he found most congenial: a paradoxical verse form neither stanzaic nor 'free', but developing coherently, against the odds, out of lines of unpredictable length rhymed at unpredictable intervals. In the poems of this kind about the war their very facility renders them facile: their sleight-of-hand improvisatory polish gives them the air of blasé party-pieces, uncomfortably close to the *bouts rimés* at which Ford was proud to excel at parties. *Antwerp*, for example, written immediately after the city surrendered to the Germans on 9 October 1914, intermittently achieves a plangency which can support its constated pathos:

> These are the women of Flanders.
> They await the lost.
> They await the lost that shall never leave the dock;
> They await the lost that shall never again come by the train
> To the embraces of all these women with dead faces;
> They await the lost who lie dead in trench and barrier and foss,
> In the dark of the night.
> This is Charing Cross; it is past one of the clock.
> There is very little light.
>
> There is so much pain.[11]

The liturgical accumulations ('await . . . again . . . train . . . await . . . pain') create the protracted anguish of lost hopes. There are other strengths to admire. The poem's clock-watching tolls the knell for the Belgian dead. 'This is Charing Cross; it is past one of the clock' summons up the spectre of Christ's agony. The clock of the station suggests to Ford as it were 'the stations of the clock'—the ritualized suffering measured out over the hour the narrator witnesses at this Station of the (Charing) Cross. But as even here, where the word 'foss' sounds as if it is only there for the rhyme with 'Charing Cross', the playing of rhyme against the studied conversational phrasing is poised on the brink of doggerel.

For a poem published the year after Pound's *Hugh Selwyn Mauberley*, and a year before *The Waste Land*, *A House* sounds dated and slack, subsiding into bathos and *faux-naïveté*. It is voiced by the house itself, its occupants ('Himself' and 'Herself'), the cat and dog of the house, the rooster and milch-goat, even the tree and the nightingale in it:

> THE HOUSE: I am the House!
> I resemble
> The drawing of a child
> That draws 'just a house.' Two windows and two doors,
> Two chimney pots;
> Only two floors.
> Three windows on the upper one; a fourth
> Looks towards the north.
> I am very simple and mild;
> I am very gentle and sad and old.
> I have stood too long.

It is certainly minor poetry, as unambitiously derivative as Ford suggested by describing it as: 'a long poem [. . .] of a Fairy Tale type. Beautiful! A sort of (relatively) Jazz Patmore, Angle in the House Affair.' It is indeed a relaxed modernizing of Coventry Patmore's 'The Angel in the House'. Nevertheless it is, in its own terms, successful; and after being published in Harriet Monroe's Chicago-based *Poetry* in March 1921, in October it was awarded the magazine's prize of $100 for the best poem of the year.[12] What is striking about it is how Ford for the first time finds the ideal scenario for his particular verse skills. *A House* turns the danger of doggerel into a poetic resource. Ford's 'Angel in the House' is 'THE UNBORN SON OF THE HOUSE'. It is not just that this spirit speaks in the poem, but the scene is framed around him: it is a domestic nativity, and it is presented in terms of a child's perception. The Tree echoes the House in describing itself as a child's drawing:

> I am the great Tree over above this House!
> I resemble
> The drawing of a child. Drawing 'just a tree'
> The child draws Me!

The delighted self-recognition in the 'Me!' evokes the child Ford hopes will draw his experiences (he too would have to be a genius); and the language testifies to Ford's fine ear for children's speech: he was always very good with children.

A House shows Ford discovering how to make art by capitalizing on potential weaknesses. One of its other strengths points to something at the centre of all his work, but something which became more pressing after the war: the aesthetics of suppression. Whereas in *A Call* or *The Good Soldier* it is generally passion that gets suppressed, the war presented a vast store of agonizing experiences, and these brought with them the associated technical problems for the writer. Conventional heroism enjoined a stiff upper lip; but not only would the participants not want to talk about their experiences, but their listeners might not want to hear—because they had shared them at the time, and were also trying to forget; or because of their own losses, of which they did not want to be reminded; or perhaps because they had not been involved, and did not want to be reminded.

Ford's own response to the war was profoundly dual: a sense of release and exhilaration at having miraculously come through, coexisting with a sense of grief at the universal suffering through which he too had gone and come. The tonal problem for the post-war prose was how to render justice to one without subverting the other. Concentration on the dead and damaged can only bring out the tragedy of the war; but to the Ford who returned to live anew, in a fairy-tale cottage with a new young lover, there is also the sense of the absurdity of the hazard which can blast and bless so indiscriminately. What then holds *A House* back from the banal rural sentimentality it might seem, is that the idyll is held against the ordeal. The rendered domesticity achieves its value against the wartime past that is only briefly mentioned when the poem sets the perils of being a small producer against the fears of battle:

> All the sows that died,
> And the cows all going off milk [. . .]
> It used to be something—cold feet going over
> The front of a trench after Stand-to at four!
> But these other things—God, how they make you blench!
> Aye, these are the pip-squeaks that call for
> Four-in-the-morning courage . . .
> May you never know, my wench,
> That's asleep up the stair!

The male protectiveness is wishful here. According to Bowen's reminiscences, it was Ford who needed protecting from domestic and financial anxieties.[13] When the same experiences were re-worked into *Last Post*, Ford was able to be more objective about Valentine Wannop's share of anxiety. But it was not merely autobiographic honesty that it took Ford time and distance to attain. After all, *A House* is *not* exactly an autobiography. If Red Ford is recognizable in its rudimentary outlines, the poem is emphatically a fairy tale: a world in which animals and spirits speak, and romance triumphs over anxiety. (Though there is some autobiographical justification for such wish fulfilment. The poem ends with the postman bringing a letter staving off financial disaster, which corresponds to the arrival of the unexpected cheque for the film rights of *Romance*.) What also goes wrong with the poem is its treatment of the war. We cannot believe that the agricultural setbacks, however dispiriting, could be worse than going over the top into battle (and knowing that Ford was spared that grim experience doesn't make the comparison any more convincing). He takes the protective attitude to his readers too, by effectively shielding them from the realities of war (as if to say it was not as bad as more mundane catastrophes). The danger is that instead of seeming composed about the war, he sounds hysterical about the house—as if he had temporarily lost all sense of proportion. *The Good Soldier* works marvels with the same trope in the remark of Dowell's which we have already scrutinized from other perspectives: 'Some one has said that the death of a mouse from cancer is the whole sack of Rome by the Goths, and I swear to you that the breaking up of our little four-square coterie was such another unthinkable event.' The exaggeration of the saying immediately arouses scepticism; when Dowell says that the breaking up of his coterie was 'such another' event, we then ask: 'such as the death of the mouse, or such as the sack of Rome?' Whether Dowell is in control of his irony is something the book leaves magnificently uncertain. Both the saying, and Ford's narrative frame for it, elicit a dual response. There is an important truth about death levelling all, including us, so that in the death of the mouse, as in the sacking of Rome, we contemplate our own ends. But there is also an excess in denying us any discrimination between different kinds of tragedies. Does it not matter whether the story of the Ashburnhams and Dowells is as sad as the death of a mouse, or as sad as the end of an empire? Even if it does not matter to Dowell, should it not matter to us? In *The Good Soldier* one of the possibilities left open for us is that Dowell is emotionally so involved with Edward and Nancy that he has lost all proportion. What hysteria we detect is then explicable by the plot. In the example from *A House*, we are meant to feel that the man's exaggeration is a result of the war experiences he is trying to play down. Thus his very attempt to suppress and overcome them becomes expressive of his suffering, registering the radical effects of the war (which has in turn made him excessively susceptible to despairs over other—more mundane—disasters). It is an effect which Ford begins to perfect in his prose fiction, but he only masters it by *Parade's End*. In *A House* the relation between the war and the house remains shadowy and uneasy; it is not integral to the poem.

Even Ford's unsure performances have their interest. He was incapable of writing a soporific sentence. These works are all vivid documents of his state of mind, and, his mind being one of the more capacious and perceptive of the age, they are also renderings of a crucial phase of history—one which is often overshadowed by the war. As he put it in *No Enemy*: 'it struck the writer that you hear of the men that went, and you hear of what they did when they were There. But you never hear how It left them. You hear how things were destroyed, but seldom of the painful processes of Reconstruction' (p. 9). The works of this period all take 'Reconstruction' in its broadest sense, covering not only the restoration of damaged landscapes and buildings, but also the resuscitation of damaged bodies, the reorientation of deranged psyches, the recreation of domestic happiness, the reconstitution of 'ordered life'. This phrase appears in *A House*, when the woman longs for 'an ordered life in a household'. But an unforgettable vision of London in *It Was the Nightingale* shows how the envisaged 'order' is something more ontological than a matter of domestic arrangements:

One had had [in the London of 1919] little sense of the values of life if indeed one had the sense that life had any values at all.

Now it was as if some of the darkness of nights of air-raids still hung in the shadows of the enormous city. Standing on the Hill that is high above that world of streets one had the sense that vast disaster stretched into those caverns of blackness. A social system had crumbled. Recklessness had taken the place of insouciance. In the old days we had seemed to have ourselves and our destinies well in hand. Now we were drifting towards a weir. . . .

You may say that everyone who had taken physical part in the war was then mad. No one could have come through that shattering experience and still view life and mankind with any normal vision. In those days you saw objects that the earlier mind labelled as *houses*. They had been used to seem cubic and solid permanences. But we had seen Ploegsteert where it had been revealed that men's dwellings were thin shells that could be crushed as walnuts are crushed. Man and even Beast . . . all things that lived and moved and had volition and life might at any moment be resolved into a scarlet viscosity seeping into the earth of torn fields [. . .] Nay, it had been revealed to you that beneath Ordered Life itself was stretched, the merest film with, beneath it, the abysses of Chaos. One had come from the frail shelters of the Line to a world that was more frail than any canvas hut. (pp. 48–9)

After such knowledge, what forgiveness? This eloquent passage sounds some of Ford's central post-war themes and preoccupations, and we shall return to it. It also recalls his pre-war abodes of crisis, since Airlie Gardens, where the 1904 breakdown began, is just off Campden Hill Road; and South Lodge is on it. The third novel of *Parade's End*, *A Man Could Stand Up—*, is his fullest account of experience in the Line, and it is dominated by the phrase in the title—the longing to be able to stand up 'on a hill'. The need to duck behind parapets, crouch in trenches, produced the need to be able to stand erect, and survey the scene in which one had been trying to efface oneself. But here (writing in 1933), Ford pictures himself doing just that: 'Standing on the Hill.' Instead of the anticipated release, however, the great view of civilized normality is overshadowed by the psychological effects of the war.

What is also striking is how Ford characteristically confronts psychological and social questions through ideas about art. That Fordian sceptical plural in 'the values of life' suggests at once that 'value' will be complex and multiple—the old single-minded certainty about 'our destinies' has been fragmented in the war—and it also suggests that life's values are best registered through the values of art: it is the shadow over London that obscures its 'values', both pictorial and moral.

Ford's reconstruction is finally also a matter of artistic reconstruction. Primarily this means reconstructing a sense of perspective and proportion—a 'normal vision' which can present a sane view of 'Ordered Life', even if the renewed vision must do justice to the new doubts about the solidity and permanence of that ordering. 'Ordered Life' is, of course, a way of describing fiction (or the form of fictionalized autobiography Ford is writing in *It Was the Nightingale*). The phrase intricates the social order of life, and the artistic ordering with which the life can be represented. Both are reconstructionary for Ford, since during this period he was continually reconstructing not only himself, his life, and his view of the world, but also his writing. All of the works between 1917 and 1924 are reconstructed into *Parade's End* and subsequent books. Some of them, particularly *No Enemy*, *Thus to Revisit*, and the poems, stand as independent (if uneven) works. But major elements from even these books are re-examined in the later writing. Even *Thus to Revisit* (1921), which elides the war altogether, returning to remember Ford's pre-war literary contacts with James, Conrad, and Hudson, was later recast into *Return to Yesterday* (1931).

A House performed the necessary post-war work of trying to reconstitute the solidity and permanence of *houses*. It is fraught with the fear of 'sinking': the house is like a ship, at the mercy of the elements, and dependent upon the efforts of its crew. It is a new image for Ford's sense of the precariousness of civilized life. Writing about the 1920s in *It Was the Nightingale* he takes the motto of the City of Paris, *Fluctuat Nec Mergitur*, describing the boat on the emblem which 'is borne up and down on the waves and does not sink', as the motto for his own life and morale during that decade (pp. 135, 237).

8

1920–1921: BEDHAM: LA VIE LITTÉRAIRE ('MR CROYD', *THUS TO REVISIT, THE MARSDEN CASE*)

His house was the house of fiction, open to new friends as to new forms. Ford's letters to Herbert Read during the summer of 1920 reveal what good practical advice he could give to his literary friends. He encouraged Read to visit because:

If you want to talk about and scheme out a novel it is—so I have found by long, long, long experience—better to begin it early. If you talk with a bloke to whose judgement you feel inclined to pay some deference the less you have actually written the better; because, if there is a lot put down it is apt to make one obstinate in its defence; the natural law of laziness comes in. Whereas if one talks of a project one sees it crystallise in various shapes as the conference proceeds and one has a more open choice. . . . I mean to say: there is the whole open question of Impersonalism to discuss. And then: the house is open to you: You can come and talk about it at practically every stage, if you want to.[1]

'No', he had reassured Read: 'not a bit have I grown tired of talk about books.' Once Read had begun a novel, Ford encouraged him, stressing the importance of finding a 'formula' to guide the construction:

there is one very great material advantage in having the line really planned out: it means one can sit down after interruptions—which in your case are diurnal—and just carry straight on because the work has been done in one's head. Whereas, if one has neither formula nor Form, when one comes to the Pen one spends immeasurable time in the effort to catch on or to invent.[2]

This advice came from experience too. Ford was having to relearn the habit of making that effort to catch on or to invent, despite interruptions. Though he had told Monro that he was 'rather thinking of going for the laurels of de la Mare or Masefield', he had not given up prose. He was just feeling overwhelmed by it: 'I have begun two immense Novels that look like being seven million words long each, and I am sick and tired of writing immense novels and, anyhow, I don't seem to get well enough to write much.' Nevertheless, he produced his first completed post-war novel, 'Mr Croyd', that summer and autumn. 'I am just finishing a novel about La Vie Litteraire', he told Pound in July: 'It is turning out rather finely macabre.' He had hoped to finish it before leaving Red Ford, but—as he told Pound three days later—'It is turning into an Immensity—a sort of Literary Via Dolorosa. . . . I viewed it with suspicion at first; but it comes on.' It was September before he got it off to the typist, and 21 October when he sent the manuscript to Pinker: it had taken him an unprecedented eighteen months to write. He realized he had been right to view it with suspicion, and chose not to publish it as it stood. When he revised it in 1928, he couldn't find a publisher for it.[3]

It is a raw, disturbed book, powerful in its expression—always on the borderline of paranoia—of wartime hysteria and terror, and of post-war feelings of ingratitude and betrayal. Jethro Croyd (who shares his initials with Conrad as well as Christ) is one of Ford's most obviously autobiographical characters in a novel. He has edited a literary magazine; been in an army hospital at Rouen after being wounded; he was a successful author before the war (as Ford had been with *The Fifth Queen* and *Ladies Whose Bright Eyes*), who was forgotten after he had risked his life for his country, and took the blame for his friend Snowdon's discredit. His experiences during the war have left him in mental tumoil, which he is struggling to repress; combatants '*had* to see vivid pictures' of the war, even if, like Croyd, they have been told not to by their doctors. Like Ford (and George Heimann in *The Marsden Case*) he has visited a 'mind specialist'. (The novel even plays on names to suggest that 'Freud' is somewhere between 'Ford' and 'Croyd': 'young nerve doctors were eaten up with the ideas of a man named Froyd'—note the anagram.) Croyd is a projection of Ford's ideal of himself. He is an embodiment of 'Charity—the Christian virtue'; someone perhaps strong enough to set charity 'before all instincts, passions, desires'; someone who reduplicates Ford's and Madox Brown's 'life-long aim of helping along, at whatever cost to himself, any Younger Schools'. Like Ford, he had 'a great store of what they call "instances" from the war. . . . Insight into men's lives. He might still write a masterpiece.' Ford would: *Parade's End*. But the ideal occasionally slides into the fantasy that charges it, as when Croyd is called 'the man who saved Europe'—a literary redeemer. . . . Or when, like Ford (and like Tietjens) he undergoes a symbolic death and rebirth: he is believed dead, but the romance ending of this 'Romance of Reconstruction' proclaims him alive after all, 'having left for an unnamed destination'—like Ford seeking sanctuary in Sussex. Yet, as in all Ford's dealings with fantasy, escapism gets refracted back into self-reflection. Like Ford, 'Croyd had always associated himself with lost or suspect causes'—of which writing is one: 'It's what the writer does. You must give your whole life—and be scorned'; 'Around Croyd there hung always an aroma of disreputability, unsoundness,—the French point of view in fact' (Croyd is half-French to Ford's half-German). Croyd focuses Ford's feelings about the 'greatness' he did and did not feel he possessed. He seems 'a friendly omnipotent deity'; he has 'achieved such greatness'; 'But in what did it consist?' Greatness, that is, is posed as a problem. Two answers the manuscript offers are typically Fordian. First, sympathetic insight: 'you can't be a damn great writer unless you enter into the hearts of others'—as Croyd's war instances will enable him to do. Secondly, it is a matter of expressing personality: 'he will at times hope that, in the general body of [his work], enough of his personality will come through and that that personality will be good enough [. . .] to let him escape damnation.' Though not yet sufficiently in command of his war material, Ford produces fine images for how writing effects this duality of repression and expression, revelation and evasion, catching on to the self by re-inventing and transforming it. 'He heard himself go on talking—but he was talking mechanically. His mind, shaken by the thought of his old school-fellow, raced backwards and forwards across his own past.' In 'Mr

Croyd' one can hear Ford hearing himself going on talking—sometimes it is mechanically—whilst his mind races across his own past.[4]

When Ford and Bowen got to Scammells Farm Ford told Flint they would be there for a month:

we are going to paperhang, paint, plaster—and perhaps poetise! I did not answer your last letter because it overwhelmed with its phrase 'the peace of Bedham!'—and by the suggestion that I might yet do great things. Thank you; I am really touched.

By one post, yesterday morning I recei[v]ed the following information: Ezra considers me gaga; H. G. Wells ditto me a parasite, presumably on him; Ethel Colburn Mayne ditto me apparently a blackmailer—Or I can't quite make that out! See the English and the Little Reviews . . . In the Athenaeum a Mr Engelherz suggests that I am unacquainted with the principles of phonetic syzygy and a Mrs or Miss Someone that I do not feel the delirious calling of the Jazz! All this fell on my chest in one morning's post. And all because I support you young things with slim figures against gentlemen whose waists, like my own, are near 42″! Yet, I shall continue, for what it is worth, my poor old support!

All these criticisms had been published, but none was as persecutory or as personal as he needed to feel them: some were even appreciative. Pound said he 'must not be forgotten', though his suggestion that Ford's best work 'is possibly ten years old' rankled. Mayne and Wells were both correcting Ford's stories about them in the first instalment of 'Thus to Revisit', which had begun running as a serial in the *English Review*; Ford told Pound they were 'dancing over [his] corpse'. Mayne said his flattering claim she had influenced *The Yellow Book* was 'simply *persiflage*'. He found Wells's counterblast the most hurtful, for all his acknowledgement that Ford had 'written some delightful romances' and was 'a very great poet' (so much for *A Call*, *Mr. Fleight*, and *The Good Soldier*). 'I have long had an uneasy feeling about my old neighbour in Kent, Mr. Ford Madox Hueffer', Wells said: 'I knew that he was capable of imaginative reminiscences, and that in a small way he had been busy with my name.' Now, according to Wells, he was making 'capital of the friendliness and hospitalities of the past to tell stupid and belittling stories of another man who is, by his own showing, a very inferior and insignificant person'. Lecturing Ford on how not to write reminiscences, he denied ever having lectured him on how to write a novel, suggesting—disingenuously—that he kept himself sedulously 'out of that talk' between Ford, Conrad, and James about the technique of fiction. On *his* own showing, in *Boon*, in his correspondence with James, in *Tono-Bungay*, he was taking a very forcible part in the debate, even if he was defining his position against theirs. Ford wrote Wells a long private letter, defending anything he had said about him in terms of the friendship that Wells was accusing him of exploiting. He recalled a scene that recurs in his reminiscences—however 'imaginative' it may be, it refers to an event that made a profound impression on him:

You may remember—or you may not remember—a number of years ago you took me to the zoo. Afterwards you walked with me round and round the Inner Circle of Regents Park. You told me your life; you said that that was your official biography and requested me to repeat it exactly whenever certain matters connected with your life were mentioned in my presence. I thought at the time that it was a good deal—and a dangerous service—to ask of anyone. It has proved dangerous. I can only assure you that, since that date, whenever that seemed necessary in your interest, I have repeated exactly what you asked me to say and no more and no less. In commenting on it, if I did comment, I have backed you through thick and thin—indeed with a violence that has made me several lasting enemies.[5]

The disavowals here (if he did talk of Wells, it was under Wells's instructions; if he did comment, it was to support him) touch interestingly on the relationship of fiction to biography. Ford thought that the 'official biography' could never reveal the 'true truth' about a writer. But here Wells tells him a fiction (an 'imaginative' autobiography), and Ford, as fellow-writer, is prepared to repeat it however impressionistic it may be, so that it might become his 'official biography'—a lost cause given the imminent scandal (perhaps of Wells's 1908–9 affair with Amber Reeves). When he reworked his reminiscence of this episode in the 1930s, Ford brought out the significance of the setting. Wells, he said, lectured him on that occasion 'on the protective colouring of small birds'. Wells too was engaged in a bit of protective colouring; and Ford understood this himself, but recognized that the habit of covering one's tracks came easily to novelists, whose stories are at once the metamorphoses of their lives, and the cocoons which protect their real lives, giving them imaginative space to effect those transformations. Ford knew that his literary criticisms of Wells must have been irksome—not least because they were right. 'I have said over and over again that I thought you a genius who wasted too much of his time on journalism—by journalism I mean social speculations', he continued, adding a comment that clarifies his persistent objection to journalism, propaganda: 'Social conditions seem to me to be temporary matters which change and then what is written of them dies.' For the artist (as opposed to the Historical Figure) what guarantees immortality is not the subject-matter (as Wells had argued it was, in his 'lecture'), but style and technique.

Ford's feeling of literary embattlement was strong, and colours all of his work until *The Marsden Case*. The third section of *Thus to Revisit* is called 'The Battle of the Poets'. 'Mr Croyd' speaks of 'the desperate Armageddon that is English Literary life', and some of its unbalance comes from its attempt to present the internecine proceedings of a literary society (modelled on Gosse's Academic Committee of English Letters) as if they were as serious a threat to civilization as the Great War. Ford had responded to the war in literary terms. Even his desire to die is not extricable from his feeling that *The Good Soldier*—his 'great auk's egg'—would make him immortal, establish his progeny. He never lost that sense of the literariness of his war, but with books like *The Marsden Case* and *Parade's End* he develops the line pursued in *No Enemy*, absorbing his technical intelligence into the question of how to present the war. In these later novels it is the more general condition of the 'war between the sexes' that replaces the skirmishing between authors as the primary analogy. Yet, as there is a fine comedy in those books about even the most painful accounts of persecution and mental torment (the social comedy of Sylvia Tietjens's exploits amongst the British army in France, or the music-hall absurdities of Tietjens's experiences under bombardment); so Ford's presentation of the literary world shows him beginning to master his feelings of exclusion and neglect through humour and satire: the self-mockery about his waist in the letter to Flint, or the 'finely macabre' satire of 'Mr Croyd'.[6]

Completing a new novel set Ford thinking about his publishing arrangements. He believed John Lane had agreed not only to take all his future novels, but also to republish the previous ones. When he asked Pinker to get Lane to produce a contract, Lane stalled with excuses about production costs and the difficulty of obtaining paper, though he said he would always be pleased to see whatever Ford should write. Ford had suggested the idea of a 'Collected Edition' to Lane before leaving for France in 1916: if he saw it then as a monument to his career, even when he had survived the war he thought of a Collected Edition as his guarantee of literary immortality, and devoted great energy and ingenuity in his dealing with publishers to getting one started. He knew he was never going to be a best-seller, and his expectations were not unrealistic: 'I do not want to press for an entire re-publication in six months, or anything of that sort, but I do want a definite arrangement.' Many now-unread authors had their Collected Editions—in 1915 Lane himself was publishing fifteen novels by William J. Locke and eight by F. E. Mills Young, all advertised in his list of fiction printed at the end of *The Good Soldier*. But he rejected the idea of Ford's edition, and then when Ford tried to hold him to what he thought was 'Lane's word' he got angry at the claim that Ford had let him have *The Good Soldier* at 'a very easy rate' on the understanding that he would publish the Collected Edition. He pointed out that he had none the less made a loss of £54. 10s. 0d. on the book—an argument hardly likely to mollify Ford; and he added that although he remembered discussing the Collected Edition, 'the terms were not even touched on, and those suggested in Mr. Hueffer's letter are wholly hypothetical'. (Ford wasn't lying about the terms. His point was that though he was sure 'some sort of arrangement was made between Lane and a third party' around the beginning of the war, he couldn't remember its terms, had no copy of a contract, but now wanted written confirmation.) Lane's refusal even to discuss terms for Ford's new novel until he'd seen the manuscript was the kind of response—the tradesman arrogating the right to judge the artist—that always exasperated him. His response was characteristically proud and self-destructive. He told Pinker: 'My friend Mr Daniel Chaucer whose work Mr. John Lane is so anxious to get hold of writes me that he is just as anxious to get out of the clutches of Mr. Lane.' He asked Pinker to offer the manuscript of 'Mr Croyd' to Lane as the third of the Daniel Chaucer novels he was contracted to offer, but 'as against so considerable an advance of royalty that either Mr Lane pays it—which would be agreeable to Mr. Chaucer—or Mr. Lane refuses'. If Lane saw the manuscript he must have refused it, as Ford knew he would. When Harold Monro expressed annoyance that Ford had let Lane publish *On Heaven* instead of giving it to him, Ford riposted that he *had* offered it, but one of Monro's staff had told him to send the manuscript which 'would receive consideration in due course'. 'I just hated to be written to like that [. . .]', explained Ford. Then he engaged in reconciliatory role-play: 'However, I did not write a rude letter in reply and you too refrained; so we are both gentlemen and all is well.' (Graham Greene was struck by this passage, and marked it in his copy of Ford's *Letters*.) The elegant humour makes light of something Ford took seriously: his feeling that it was undignified to defend and explain himself. Not all publishers were so wary of him this summer (though it was typical of Ford to exaggerate his persecutions and play down his recognition). Alec Waugh, whose father Arthur had published *Ancient Lights*, read 'Thus to Revisit' in the *English Review*, and wrote to ask if he could publish it as a book. Ford was self-deprecatory about the essays, telling Waugh 'they are rather occasional and more written with a purpose—to boost you young things!—than with the repose that a book should have'; but he agreed to write more into it to 'make it, possibly, a little more serene—and possibly a little more malicious, or at least teasing—to the self important'. He assured Pinker it would not libel anyone, but added: 'and as for giving offence, I live to give offence to fools [. . .].' As so often with Ford's prickly, unconventional humour, rising from self-pity to self-amusement, the literary establishment didn't much enjoy the teasing. There was praise for the 'really vivid reminiscence' in the book (which Ford had told Waugh could be considered a continuation of *Ancient Lights*). But Ford's habit of writing against the grain of his critical precepts offered hostages to self-important reviewers who complained that the champion of Hudson's unobtrusiveness was all too obtrusive on each page (as if Hudson's naturalistic obser-vations were intended as literary autobiography), or that Ford was 'in danger of becoming a busybody of literature [. . .] singularly devoid of illuminating thoughts or arresting sentences'. One can see why Ford became implacably opposed to the *Times Literary Supplement*. The book was designed (unconsciously?) to confirm the aliena-tion it expressed. Mizener called it a 'brave and foolish' book, arguing that his memory and judgement were not 'sufficiently recovered for him to control the fantasies by which [. . .] he explained the unjustified neglect from which he believed he suffered'. This would be a fair description of 'Mr Croyd'; but it misses the two essential points of *Thus to Revisit*. First, that it is about the neglect of literature, both past and present. It continues the project of Ford's *English Review* editorials and his propaganda books, arguing that 'Creative Literature—Poetry—is the sole panacea for the ills of harassed humanity [. . .] the only thing that can explain to man the nature of his fellow men; and a great, really popular Art, founded on, and expressive of a whole people, is the sole witness of the non-barbarity of a Race'. (He was fortunate not to witness the barbarity of music-loving Nazis.) Secondly, Mizener missed the book's central fantasy: the idea—that gives it its title—that Ford is dead; pronounced a defunct impressionist by Lewis and his modernist associates; treated by the literary establishment as someone whose writing days were over; and feeling still haunted by the war: 'an insubstantial ghost, revisiting the light of a moon ['the English literary world'] I had purposed never to see again.' This fantasy is less a special pleading for his own reputation, than it is deeply expressive of his post-war state of mind.[7]

Early in August Pound came to visit and argue about *vers libre*. He appeared, said Ford, 'aloft on the seat of my immense high dog-cart, like a bewildered Stuart pretender visiting a repellent portion of his realms. For Mr. Pound hated the country [. . .].' He was amused by the goat Penny, 'so-called because he facially resembled (but was not) POUND, Ezra', for he found other resemblances when he tried to define for Ford his relationship to impressionism: 'certainly one backs impressionism', he wrote—'all I think I wanted to do was to make the cloud into an animal organism. To put a vortex or concentration point inside each bunch of impression and thereby give it a sort of intensity, and goatish ability to butt.' A less welcome visitor was Violet Hunt, who had finally tracked Ford down. She had paid an impulsive visit to Elsie, using the notion that, having no children herself, she would leave Katharine a legacy, in order to form an alliance with her former enemy. (Christina's vocation meant she wouldn't need a dowry.) Elsie was frostily civil to her (though Hunt later wrote that she had 'got in several very nasty ones' about her money, 'her not unchequered past', and her age), speaking to her over the fence but not asking her inside, and not letting her see Katharine. Hunt wrote to her after the visit:

Dear Mrs. Hueffer:

   You will think it very strange of me, but I felt a great peace after I had seen you. Your wonderful attitude towards F. made me feel how strong a virtue self-control is, and your dignity, when you spoke to me, brought out the best in me—who am still storm-tossed. I hope I shall see you again [. . .] Thanking you for your reception of me—

   Yours,

   V.H.

I will be seeing Mary [Martindale] soon—but I will not tell Ford's mother I saw you, shall I?[8]

Elsie didn't reply, but Hunt wrote again at the end of the year: 'Dreadful things have been happening, and I wish I could see you with regard to the disposition of my legacy to your daughter—there needs some sort of trust, I think', and adding: 'Will you write to me, as Miss Violet Hunt, of course, now.' But Elsie returned her peace-offering of Conrad's latest book, and said she didn't see that there was anything to be gained 'by their communicating with one another'. Nothing came of the legacy; and Violet's apparent willingness to be Miss Hunt once again didn't last. As late as 1923 she was still trying to enlist her friends in the battle over Ford's abandoned name. This time it was Wells, who told her with gentle force: 'leave the whole business alone & go on being called & calling yourself *Violet Hunt*. If Ford will go on behaving like an ass there is no reason why you should follow suit.' Two years later Hunt wrote a thinly fictionalized account of the meeting, referring to Elsie as 'Number One', herself as 'Number Two', and Stella as 'Number Three', and describing her propensity for 'irregular situations'. She created another 'irregular situation' (and shattered her new-felt peace) when she paid a similar surprise visit to Bedham a few days later. She had been trying to get Ford's address ever since he left London. Ford thought she must have had Pound followed when he came down (as Sylvia Tietjens puts detectives on to Christopher and Valentine); though she later said she had been given the address by her sister's solicitors, 'who appear to be watching him in *her* interests' (lest he was getting any of Mrs Hunt's contested estate); but given the hostility between Hunt and 'Goneril' and 'Regan', the story is not very probable. Violet said she didn't see Ford when she went to Bedham towards the end of August: 'I went to see him but did not—for I saw Stella who was going to have a child.' Ford complained to Pound of 'interruptions from Violet who has planted herself in the neighbourhood & runs about interrupting my workmen & generally making things lively'. She got to know Mrs Hunt, the wife of the carpenter who was helping with Coopers Cottage, and paid her to spy on Ford and Bowen, sending her parcels as a pretext for her calling. On one visit Hunt brought May Sinclair with her, and 'the two women peered at him over a gate while he was feeding his pigs'. One day Ford and Stella, up on their high, ill-sprung dog-cart, 'had the pleasure of passing, without a flicker of recognition, a whole car-load of London busy-bodies coming to peep at Ford in his new retreat, gently rolling backwards down the hill!' No one feels persecuted without *some* cause, and the 'continuing activities & incursions of Violet and her agents—which are really bad for Stella', only exacerbated his embattlement. There is no evidence that he saw Hunt again, except for one meeting which probably took place years later.[9]

Early in September Ford and Bowen moved into Coopers Cottage, 'white plaster and oak beams with a steep tiled roof', about 300 years old, and in 'an extravagantly beautiful and quite inaccessible spot on a great wooded hill [. . .]'. They had ten acres: 'an orchard full of wild daffodils [. . .] a small wood full of bluebells lower down behind the cottage, and below that, a big rough field.' When Stella was too heavily pregnant to run errands outside, she stripped off thirteen layers of wallpaper inside, and chopped away the worm-eaten parts of the oak beams with an axe. They were exhilarated: it was 'the' cottage, she said: 'I loved everything that I did, because it was all real, immediate and useful, and had to do with living things. And I loved being with someone with the same tastes and who lived through his eyes in the same way that I did. We took such perpetual and unanimous pleasure in the *look* of everything, the sky and the weather and the view and the garden and the arrangement of our cottage.' Yet what Ford had called 'the difficult Art of Small Holding' while he was learning it at Red Ford was no easier at Coopers. There was too much hard work to combine it with careers as artists and parents: 'You can almost live upon a view', Bowen wrote: 'Almost.' But small-holding was a more expensive business than Ford had reckoned. The wages not only for Mr Hunt and his son, but for 'old Standing, who worked out-doors', and for a young woman called Lucy they had hired to help in the house, cost more than they could possibly make from their pigs, eggs, garden produce, or firewood—especially since 'Ford was not the man to pay less than the highest current wages'.[10]

In the face of his domestic difficulties, Ford considered translating—more as a distraction than as a way of making a living. 'Ref. Proust', he wrote to Pound, who had suggested the idea: 'It wd. amuse me to do *chez S[wann]*—& I would do it if yr. publishers wd. give me *plenty* of time, so that I cd. do a bit now & then when not in the mood for other work. It they wanted a complete Proust I wd. edit it: i.e: go through anyone else's translation to see that it was all right, & write an introduction: but I couldn't translate the whole: it wd. bore me to tears.' Pound sent a copy of his *Instigations* for approval, and Ford responded with a classic of constructive and suggestive criticism. Was he showing that he could lecture as well as be lectured at about the novel?

Firstly: It is a very good piece of work; full of good definitions and makings clear. The JAMES I still think is the best of it; I don't know whether it would gain or lose by being more carefully arranged; perhaps it would lose in impressionistic value [a bit sly, this suggestion that Pound's principles of organization were *impressionist* in spite of himself] . . . There are one or two points: In your appraisement of Henry's individual works you are too American (I daresay I am too European). If you look them through again you will notice that you cease to be interested in them as soon as the Transatlanticism goes out of them & only take notice again with the American Scene—after Antæus had actually touched Western Earth again.[11] You are in fact bored with civilisation here—very properly; and so you get bored with the *rendering* of that civilisation. It is not a good frame of mind to get into—this preoccupation with Subject rather than with rendering; it amounts really to your barring out of artistic treatment everything and everyone with whom you have not had personal—and agreeable—contacts. There is the same tendency in your desire for STRONG STORY and in your objection to renderings of the mania for FURNITURE. You don't, as a cadenced verse writer, like prose at all and want to be helped to read prose by being given stories written à coups de hache; and, having no taste for bric a brac you hate to have to read about this passion. . . . But it is one of the main passions of humanity [. . .] You might really, just as legitimately, object to renderings of the passion of LOVE, with which indeed the FURNITURE passion is strongly bound up . . . Still, these are only notes; but I think you might think about them—because you *might* harden into the Puritanism of the Plymouth Rock variety—which would be a disaster . . . Anyhow it is a very valuable piece of work and I am very glad you have done it; some passages give me real pleasure in the reading, I mean pleasure in the language, which is a rare thing. . . .[12]

Pound's disastrous hardening was something Ford could foretell long before Mussolini figured in Pound's imagination (the blackshirts marched on Rome in 1922). And Ford's contrasting of the puritanism of a 'preoccupation with Subject' with a 'pleasure in the language' might have shown Pound, had he heeded it, where the *Cantos* become unreadable—the sections on Chinese and American history when his passion for 'ideas' makes him impatient with 'rendering'. Ford was equally 'bored with civilisation'; but knowing how his best work explored the forces that fracture the social veneer, he couldn't be bored with rendering the contemporary world and its materialisms and spiritualisms. His comment about love and furniture is extraordinarily suggestive about his own writing; not only because the feelings of laconic characters like Ashburnham or Tietjens get articulated through *possessions*—homes, horses, dog-carts, family silver, money, clothes; but also because the unobtrusive impressionist seeks to direct pleasure in the language towards appreciation of the literary form as *object*. Ford's fiction, that is, exploits a fetishism of language to express the emotional fixes of his protagonists.

The same day he wrote a long letter to Herbert Read (he was catching up on his correspondence as soon as 'Mr Croyd' had gone to the typist). Read's decision to abandon his attempts at novel-writing elicited from Ford a defence of 'the immense advantage that the Novel has over the frivolous apparition called the Serious Book'—that 'you can ram all the metaphysics in the world into it and it can still be a fine work of art'. Read too was lectured on not letting himself undergo a 'hardening process'—but in his case it was a matter of not letting a 'Yorkshire dislike of the Arts' blinker his appreciation of literature. As with Pound, Ford's efforts were to let Read be true to his artistic self:

Of course I see you aiming at becoming another Henri Beyle: But it is a miserable ambition. . . . Learn of Stendhal all you can—and there is, if you do not happen to be Middleton Murry—an immense deal to learn in an artistic sense. . . . But don't model yourself on him. . . . I can imagine no more terrible being to himself, than a Yorkshireman, true to type, and modelling himself on Mr. Beyle!—The end would be the most horribly costive neurastheniac you could imagine, with incredible sex obsessions sedulously concealed, swaddled up to the ears in red flannel for fear of draughts, and with more hypochondrias and phobias than are to be found in all Freud, Jung, and the late Marie Bashkirtseff put together. . . . And with a yellow, furred tongue, and a morgue britannique beyond belief. . . .

No, try not to become that. . . . You may not like novel writing but it would be a good thing to stick to it so as to avoid turning your soul into a squirrel in a revolving cage. . . .

'Still,' he added, becoming wary of the influence he might himself be exerting, 'it is not for me to interfere with the destiny of others and, if you will, you will.' Thinking of novelistic influence made him think of Conrad—because both men had avowed to model themselves on the styles of Flaubert and Maupassant, but also because, reconstructing himself as a writer, Ford was gauging whether his apprenticeship to James and Conrad had distorted his own development. 'You are unjust, rather, to Conrad', he told Read, settling his account with his master in a breathtaking combination of arrogance, abasement, and fine judgement:

He has done an immense deal for the Nuvvle in England—not so much as I, no doubt, but then that was not his job, and he is of the generation before mine. I learned all I know of Literature from Conrad—and England learned all it knows of Literature from me. . . . I do not mean to say that Conrad did not learn a great deal from me when we got going; I daresay he learned more actual stuff of me than I of him. . . . But, but for him, I should have been a continuation of DANTE GABRIEL ROSSETTI—and think of the loss that would have been to you young things. . . . And think what English literature would be without Conrad and James. . . . There would be nothing![13]

'This might be read as humorous bluffing,' commented Read, 'but not by anyone who knew Ford. He did actually believe that he had been an essential link in the evolution of modern English literature [. . .].' Yet there *is* humorous bluffing here, together with the histrionic self-importance. As with the fantasy about the Yorkshire Beyliste, he was adept at exaggerating his self-revelations, appearing to disavow the self-caricature (much of his intensest writings, as well as sufferings, spring from the expressive sedulous concealment of sex-obsessions). But neither his humorous bluffing nor his exaggerated bluff should obscure the truth that Ford *was* an essential figure in the history of modern English literature. His influence on writers as influential as Pound, Read, and even Conrad and Lawrence, would earn him that role, even if he hadn't written some of the greatest books of the century.[14]

Unlike Sylvia Tietjens, who shows herself what Ford called a 'sport', and abjures her persecution of her husband when she realizes his mistress is about to have a child, Violet Hunt still could not leave Ford alone—even though she told Scott-James: 'I have never *asked* him to come back to live with me. I don't want it. But the tension lasting with aggravations for nearly five years, added to the tension of his 3½ years in the Army when I was alone—is killing me and hurting my brain. All I *want* is an *amicable* agreement to live apart, to calm me, and give me peace.' But Ford somehow got to see two letters she had written to Mrs Hunt, the carpenter's wife. They were written 'in a kind of madness'—she had been shocked by the sudden deaths that spring of Rosamond and her mother Silvia. Hunt feared she had slandered or libelled Ford: she had told her spy (who was beginning to have qualms about what she was doing) that she 'wasn't his first wife's sister in law but his wife & that his name wasn't Ford but Hueffer [. . .]'. Ford said that she also threatened to come with Cathy Hueffer when she came to visit the baby. Hunt then used the occasion of her publisher asking her to cut and tone down her latest autobiographical novel, *Their Hearts*, as a pretext to summon Ford to South Lodge. 'A great misfortune has befallen me', she wrote, and appealed to his literary altruism: 'Are you disposed to give me your advice?' He couldn't resist the appeal to his artistic judgement, but he felt she had broken the rules he made for their irregular game. He wrote to her solicitors saying that because of her appearance at Bedham he would no longer give her 'social backing' by appearing at South Lodge: 'I will no longer see your client unless she should wish to discuss matters of business and then only at your office or at the office of my own solicitor and in the presence of a partner of one or other firm', he told them, saying that he would only do this on their written assurance 'that visits from Mrs Hueffer or her agents to this place, or any further tampering with my servants or tenants or attempts to take houses or apartments in the neighbourhood by her or her agents shall cease for good'. He added with ironic understatement: 'I am aware that this is an unusual request and one difficult for you to fulfil, but the circumstances are unusual.' However, he wrote to Hunt herself saying that he would be prepared to read her manuscript (though he had told the solicitors he would 'much dislike doing so', and added with mischievous hauteur that she would be 'better advised to consult, say, Mr H. G. Wells'):

you know I have always taken a great interest in your work; it should be unnecessary to say that; and I am content to drop what is past and will read the m.s. of your novel and write to you about it as well as I can. I should not, at this juncture, do as much for anyone else as I have already missed an instalment of my book in two reviews, owing to one bother and another and it is a serious matter to fail to keep up with the press. But, if I do read it, you must give me a definite undertaking not to visit this place again and to stop any intrigues by your friends in this place. I am sorry to introduce a bargain into what should be merely a matter of art, but I do not see any other way either in your interests or mine.

On Armistice Day, fittingly enough, she apologized. But she told Scott-James that Ford's recourse to lawyers 'only rubs in the fact that if he doesn't uphold the validity of our union, I am but a cast-off mistress. It is what I am, I suppose. But I don't believe Ford wants me humiliated. He simply wants to be let alone–till he *doesn't* want to be let alone!'[15]

In November Ford and Bowen went to stay with the Coles in Bramerton Street in Chelsea. Stella went into a nursing home to give birth. The unborn son of *A House* proved another daughter. Esther Julia was born at 8.30 p.m. on 29 November 1920, after a delayed and difficult birth. Margaret Cole wrote that 'Ford was sympathetically brought to bed with some chest-trouble which according to him demanded very special dieting'. He said he had bronchitis. One day he said he could 'touch nothing but a devilled sirloin-bone (meat-rationing was still in force)'; then he made 'a pathetic request for clear soup with plenty of oysters' (she had to send Pound to buy them). It was 'very like Ford', she said: 'the great suffering, which I do not for a moment suggest he did not feel at the time, and the preposterous demand for solace according to English country-house standards.' Ford dedicated *Thus to Revisit* 'To Mrs. G. D. H. Cole | wishing she would write | more poems.' She thought it was one of his misfortunes that 'the acts which he put on, his extravagant poses and gestures, were almost all out of timing with the currents of public opinion, and so earned him unpopularity'. She felt indignant at him 'wallowing [. . .] like an obese cockatoo' in the spare bed, when everyone else was concerned about Bowen. 'None the less,' she conceded, 'he was a real artist, a passionate lover of literature as a real force [. . .] and a lover of freedom.' In one particular his unorthodoxy chimed with the Coles' socialism: 'Even at the time when he was groaning and wheezing away in the spare-room bed, he was directing, with the co-operation of ourselves and Johnny Rodker, a propaganda campaign against the Black-and-Tans and the English occupation of Ireland, which had certainly nothing phoney about it.'[16]

Harold Monro was involved; also Goldring, who had been delighted to meet Ford again at Monro's house above the Poetry Bookshop at 35 Devonshire Street, Theobald's Road. 'He certainly looked stouter and more robust than he had done when I saw him last, was more genially pontifical and evidently happier.' Goldring drafted a manifesto and got other writers to sign it. 'It had, of course, no effect,' said Goldring, 'beyond that of relieving the consciences of the signatories.' There was a misunderstanding when Monro expected Ford to organize a meeting and Ford thought he had explained why he could not. His disavowal of his efficacy shows that he was not going to make the same mistake he had made with the Fabians, when he tried to help Wells reform them in 1906:

I obviously cannot run it from here and it is impossible for me to be in Town. I have no lodging there, I cannot afford the fares up and down, I have hedging and ditching to do, animals to feed, men to superintend. And I am not a popular character with the type of person that would normally be expected to attend the MEETING. In fact I should obviously have done more harm than good.[17]

Ford and Bowen returned to Bedham with their new-born daughter Julie at the New Year. 'Ford adored her', said Bowen: 'He simply doted. His large, slow person and quiet voice were just what young things liked, and his infant gave him a big new stake in the post-war world where he still felt pretty lost.' He always called her 'ma petite princesse', and 'spun the most enchanting fairy stories for her as soon as she grew old enough to enjoy them'—as he had for his sister, and for Christina and Katharine. His third and last child had not made him forget his older daughters. He had sent Katharine a book for Christmas—it was presumably *On Heaven*, and he probably sent Christina something too. When Katharine responded with the resentment of the child who feels abandoned, Ford felt bitter: 'I was rather hurt by y[r.] letter about my book', he told her: 'One doesn't, you know, write in those terms to even the least distinguished or most unrelated of Authors on the receipt of presentation copies.'[18]

When the hard, cold winter let up, Violet Hunt began a spring offensive. Ford said he heard on 7 March from a third party that she was threatening to renew her descents upon Bedham unless he answered her letters. He said he hadn't received any letters, and sent the third party's letter on to his solicitor. She claimed he only 'pretended he didn't get the letter' that she had written when (she said) she was ill, asking him to come to her. But she understood the situation, though she couldn't 'accept' it: 'He doesn't *want* to come, & he doesn't *want* to put it on record that he refuses isn't that it? It is a horrible thought to lie in bed with, when one cares for anyone.' On 16 March Ford received 'an anonymous, abusive telegram from Notting Hill'—around the corner from South Lodge. He told Scott-James he instructed his solicitor to go to the police, but after a delay over Easter he relented, and told the solicitor to stay his hand.

Scott-James had transmitted Hunt's request that Ford should visit her, but Ford tried to make clear in his answer how categorically he considered their relationship over:

With these facts to go upon I think you will agree that your suggestion offers no way out and that I cannot and will not see Mrs Hueffer in any circumstances or for any purpose. There are bitternesses too great to be put into words and of certain such things only oneself can be the judge. But I imagine that you will now see that to continue or revive the mockery of social intercourse with South Lodge would be madness on my part and merely cruelty to Mrs Hueffer. The last time I did see her she stabbed at me with an immense knife and threatened me with a revolver. That may have been only theatrical display, but threatened as she says she is with attempts by her family to 'put her away', she endangers herself by these indulgences [. . .]

And, although I have always had the greatest contempt for prudential motives, in this matter Mrs Hueffer has cut her own throat. You know very well that, for years the lady has informed nearly every one she met that I lived only by and for the flesh-pots and wine-jars of South Lodge. That was not true; but you have only to read Miss Sinclair's story in last month's English Review to see how widely it is believed. To be rid of it I re-started life as an agricultural labourer at the reasonably mature age of 48 or so, with a camp-bed, a flea-bag and a Beatrice oil-stove for sole possessions. If I now returned, even only ostensibly, to South Lodge, what would you all say of me? Besides, it would be an indecent and abhorrent thing to do. You must see that.[19]

Six or seven years after *The Good Soldier*, their lives were acting out an even more melodramatic variation of betrayed passion, threats, and madness. Ford had to explain to Scott-James why he hadn't seen him for many years, even though they were 'once intimate and connected enough': partly because of what he called 'speeches attributed to you by Mrs Hueffer, concerning myself'; and partly because he had 'made an almost absolutely final resolve not to know any one who goes to South Lodge'. 'Almost', because he didn't want to isolate himself from his former friends more than was necessary if he were to keep Hunt at a distance. When Scott-James disclaimed any such speeches, Ford showed how his magnanimity was greater than his sensitivity to criticism:

Thanks. I am very glad of yᵣ· disclaimer which settles the matter. I never attached *much* belief to the original story: you may say that I am to blame for having attached any & that I ought to apologise to yᵣ· wife for having entertained even a slight suspicion. But these things—he saids & she saids—are apt to work very insidiously on the imagination & I am more silent than perhaps I ought to be when such situations arise. But certainly it makes the world seem a better place when chance lets one's old friends deny these horrors. Pray ask Mʳˢ· Scott James to believe that I do apologise very sincerely—& gladly.

As for the police-solicitor motif: after her stay in this place Mʳˢ· Hueffer wrote to our housekeeper, amongst other things: 'If Mʳ· Hueffer's mother goes to see the baby *I shall be with her*,' underlining the last words. I interpret this as a threat [. . .]

As for solicitors—Mʳˢ· Hueffer has employed them for several years against me: I only took advice after the letter quoted above. As for doctors: at his—& obviously at Mʳˢ· Hueffer's— request I saw her doctor, a psychoanalyst, last year. He begged me, for her sake, not to see her again.

Excuse my mentioning all this. I hate it. But you may not understand, without it, how irrevocable my determination is.[20]

In the spring Ford was preoccupied with seeing *A House* through the press. Bowen designed some illustrations for it. Bringing up her daughter, entertaining, protecting Ford from financial worry, and otherwise supporting his ego made it hard for her to paint more than intermittently; nevertheless she was later to design the dust-jackets for several of his books. Ford's need for money (doctors, taxes, the voracious but sickly pigs) made him more concerned to sell the poem than to worry about the copyright, and he sold it to Harriet Monroe (of *Poetry* Chicago) without warning Harold Monro (who had it for *The Chapbook*). English Monro was put out, but Ford mollified him with an energetic explanation, weaving flattery, patronage, the probable and the fictitious:

You see I am a bleedin nuvvelist when everything is said and done and used to mopping up all sorts of sums for all sorts of rights of which you as poetry publisher and poet may never even have heard—American, Colonial and Tauchnitz book, first, second and third English and American and Colonial serial and many others. And as you, pro tem. publisher said nothing about these I took it that, as in the case of a mere prose-producer, you did not want these. However I will take it that you as Poet have forgiven me the vexation that I, as hardened fictionist seem to have caused you and hope that the southern suns make all cares seem small [Monro was in France].[21]

'Prose-producer' by analogy with 'small-producer', perhaps. 'I pass my time mostly in the raising of pedigree pigs', he told Harriet Monroe, 'as the war has left me under the necessity of living in the open air; but sometimes I go indoors and write fabulous attacks on Academic poets and ferocious applause of Vers Libristes and the like.' ('Fabulous' is a quintessentially Fordian word, compacting the desire to be remembered, as in fable, with the recognition that his accounts of himself were fabulatory.) When Flint was due to visit in May, Ford said to him: 'I don't know why people talk about my writing well:—that sort of stuff I just write. Still, it's pleasant to be told that one wields a pen of gold (Ballad metre, accidental). | But of all these things we will discourse at just length between feeding the pigs.' And he suggested to him: 'Bring an old dinner jacket with you if it's not too much of a bore. I go about in filth all day & put on a cricket shirt & very old dress things at night—not for swank but because I have only one other respectable suit which I have to save for the metropolis.' When the American professor (of German), Lawrence Marsden Price, got in touch with him again—they had met before the war in Germany—Ford warned him that his conversation would be 'chiefly about corn and big black hogs'. Undeterred, Price accepted the invitation to Bedham. He was struck by the way Ford 'looked and spoke not like a poet but rather like a typical country squire'. 'One should not meet one's life heroes', noted Ford wryly, saying that Price had been dismayed to find him looking 'like a tramp dressed in military clothes that I had rescued from a scarecrow, and talking of hogs'. Price's memoir of this visit indicates that Ford may have been having some fun at his expense (he later gave him an autographed copy of *The Simple Life Limited*, by Daniel Chaucer, 'which he said many people attributed to him'):

I put on my working clothes and helped the master and his man with the hay, and the master tutored me as to etiquette that I might not offend the man. When I carried the cider to him at mid-day, for example, I must drink alternately with him out of the same big cup. The

English farm hand has a fine sense of propriety, and a cautioning word in German was sometimes necessary to forestall a grave social error.

He evidently encouraged Price to call him 'Captain Ford'; though two years later he was playfully rebuking A. E. Coppard: 'Why address so pacific a person as me as "Capt Ford."?' He told the linguist from Berkeley that he allowed himself three weeks to learn a new language (but that it had taken him four to master the speech of the Welch Regiment). Price had noticed the quotation from Machiavelli that Ford had used as the epigraph for *Thus to Revisit*, which had just come out in book-form: 'But when evening falls I go home and enter my writing room. On the threshold I put off my country habit, filthy with mud and mire and array myself in costly garments; thus worthily attired, and for four hours' space I feel no annoyance, forget all care; poverty cannot frighten me. . . . I am carried away.' (It is typical of Ford's attentiveness to notice such an unfamiliar concern with the private and imaginative world of literature in the writer most identified with public political cynicism.) Price was thus forewarned about the evening dress; but once the writer took over from the gentleman-farmer, he saw the real, intimate, Ford emerging:

We had goose, and cider, and the inevitable peas [. . . .] The room was lighted with candles, which were no affectation for no other light was in the house. After dinner my host began to talk about the really important things of life. From his scanty book shelf he reached down a copy of Matthew Arnold and read *Dover Beach*, which he said was quite important in the development of free-verse. It was very beautiful, he said, before he intoned it [. . . . Without this episode, would we have guessed that Ford had even read Arnold? Yet what is the vision of France at the end of his 'The Great View' (first published in 1901) if not 'Dover Beach' without the portentous allegory about the 'sea of faith'?]

Suddenly he asked me who I was anyway—I must have written something. This was just the question I had been dreading, for like his grandfather he hates the 'demned academician.' His most recent critical work, *Thus to Revisit*, had been, at least in half-part, a tirade against the academicians with their superabundance of derivative printed matter. I answered that I had never written anything he would ever have heard of. He immediately concluded that I was a modest young author and offered me some of the secrets of his trade. When I introduced a new person I should always let him say first something that revealed his personality, etc. [. . .] The technique of his occupation gives him great satisfaction and he likes to talk shop. But I believe these rules he fancies have less to do with his success than he thinks: it is rather by putting himself into a certain frame of mind that he writes.

Lyric poetry, he says, should not be something pretentious and formidable. When you write poetry you speak very simply and softly, as if to one you love [another reason why he would have admired 'Dover Beach': for its framing of a 'world-view' within a lover's speech, about an actual view 'France *seen* from the cliffs', as Pound said, quarreling once again with the impressionistic ocularity of Ford's criticism]. You pose a very little, to be sure, when you write, but you always pose a very little when you speak to one you love. His conception of good prose is much the same.[22]

If Ford was posing as the 'dean of English novelists', the old man mad about writing, he was as sincere as any intoxicated lover. Stella Bowen, too, found his initiatory encouragement of *les jeunes* extraordinary; though she put it down to his need for reassurance. Surrounding himself with disciples was a way of convincing himself he was a master ('It is certain that my conviction gains immensely as soon as another soul can be found to share it'—Ford quoted the favourite Novalis tag again when thanking Harriet Monroe for the *Poetry* prize for *A House*). Because he was 'all too ready, anyhow, to feel discouraged when things went wrong', and because 'he found so many reasons for feeling frightened', he knew how much writers valued encouragement and reliable advice:

He gave them much of himself; patient perusal and brilliant criticism of their efforts, and even when their work was mediocre, he always managed to put heart into them and make them proud of their calling and determined to screw the last ounce out of their talent. He had no professional secrets and would take any aspiring writer behind the scenes and explain exactly how he got his effects; the long, slow-moving passage heightening the effect of the subsequent quick crisis; the need for minute precision in a visual description; the different tension to be used in the short, long-short, or long story, the opening sentence which set the key for the whole work. In exchange for the help that he gave Ford received something very valuable—something that was good for him and without which he could scarcely live. He received the assurance that he was a great master of his art.[23]

'We are all so afraid, we are all so alone, we all so need from the outside the assurance of our own worthiness to exist.' When he wrote an essay arguing that Conrad was 'the only novelist now left in the Anglo-Saxon world', he paused to imagine his audience: 'I imagine that I am writing now for young novelists with the right aspirations; indeed, I seldom write for anyone else, that seeming to me the justification of criticism.' Other American visitors to Bedham included the art-critic and museum director Monroe Wheeler, and his companion, the novelist and short-story writer Glenway Westcott, 'very young, and solemn, and eager', recalled Bowen, 'in a long cape with a silver clasp, an exotic figure in our homely landscape'. When Ford invited his old friend Edgar Jepson down in July, he told him:

I could give you plenty of poker of which I have been playing a good deal with U.S.A. pilgrims to this shrine. They come in small shoals to talk highbrow; and we set them to feed the pigs—of which I have a number—or to carry the hay of which we have successfully harvested a nice little stack. And in the evenings I take their money at poker—and we have sweet corn and punkins [*sic*] growing, so they feel homesick.

'There is only one danger here', Ford warned him: 'if Stella thinks you—or anyone— sufficiently unattractive she gently but firmly makes them sit. This spring she did a portrait of the Mayoress of Edgbaston so successfully that the Mayor fainted.' Jepson braved the danger, as did David Garnett, and Edward Shanks.[24]

His earnings from poker can't have been great. 'I am as usual short of money', Ford told Pinker: 'Could you get hold of the American royalties for THUS TO REVISIT and send me them?' And he went on to tease him in the role of the gentleman farmer:

My famous pedigree pigs ANNA and ANITA, 344702 and 344704 in the herd book of the Large Black Pig Society cost a deuce of a lot to keep; but when, as they certainly will, they take prizes at the Lincoln Show I will stand you a champagne dinner. I could supply you with February hatched ducks at 96/- the dozen. You never seem to reply with any enthusiasm to my offers of farm produce. Why is this?[25]

Thus to Revisit was published around 10 May, and Ford gave Stella an inscribed copy on her birthday on the 16th. It was his first post-war book of prose. Pound took his cue from Ford's comment that 'almost everybody I have ever come across has lectured me—from Mr. Holman Hunt to Mr. Pound', and after writing one letter complimenting him on writing 'several pages of the only criticism that has been in England', wrote another criticizing that criticism:

DEER old Bean

To continue lectures begun by Holman 'Unt, despite present outrageous postal rates.

WOT you dont bloomin' see is that wot you do with ideas is just as bad for the reader's morale as wot Bridges does with langwidge.

I.E. you hang onto a lot of old tarabiscotage Sancte Foi Catholique, Tory Party, etc. [. . .]

In return for the blessings conferred upon me in 1911 by your lecture of, let us say Aug 7th of that year, these presents.

And that my ancient Feve [bean] is why Mr Conrad who writes worse, and all the bloomin others who write worse, sell more [. . .] No, mong cher, you are full of suppressed forsooths and gadzookses of ideation. For which reason some liar has just said yr. book is not a treatise on the art of writin'. etc.

AND it aint any use, not to you it aint, no more than my early clingin to 'forloyn's and swevyns.

'And so they begat each other', Pound perorated, exaggerating his reciprocal influence. His attack on Ford's way of making fetishes of social ideas had its effect, though, and must be reckoned as one of the stimuli helping Ford to reassess himself in the writing of *Parade's End*. By the following year he had 'arrived at the stage of finding the gentleman an insupportable phenomenon', he was to write later. But Pound could appreciate neither the seriousness of Ford's commitment to his agrarian activities, nor his paradoxical combination of avant-garde and traditionalism. It was a posture that was *intended* to irritate. When Herbert Read congratulated him on the book, Ford retorted with agricultural vigour: 'My good chap: Thus to Revisit *isn't* a good & inspiring book. How *could* you? It is a bad, wicked, UnXtian pitchfork stuck into the behinds of certain snobs.' But he hadn't expected Pound to get stuck up about it. He must have written resentfully of this 'lecture', for Pound was soon writing to explain: 'I wrote you a long but incomprehensible letter to say that you[r] talk of a 'ymn of 'ate was nonsense. I was only writing you because of the great love an' admiration and admiratio that I manage to bear you.' By way of atonement, he enclosed a letter he had had from the publisher Horace Liveright, saying he had been thinking a good deal about Ford, and asking Pound what of his it would be best for him to publish in America. Cordiality was restored, and they met when Pound visited London in October. 'Hueffer about as usual', Pound wrote to his mother.[26]

Another publisher had the same idea at about the same time: H. S. Latham, of the New York Macmillan Company, wrote that it would be a pleasure to consider publishing him. In August Ford sent synopses of several books, amongst them 'True Love & a G.C.M.', and the new novel he was planning, *The Marsden Case*:

As you will see I have been thinking of most of them for some years—one or two of them for several years, or indeed a great many. This does not mean that I have any doubts of them as subjects; I always do think of my books for very long periods before setting pen to paper, when I write them, usually, very rapidly. Moreover, I have not been well enough since being invalided out of the Army, to risk the strain of such prolonged indoor work as has been entailed by anything other than very desultory writing. But I think I could now begin on any one of the books foreshadowed in that fascicle and carry it to a fairly speedy conclusion. If therefore one of these subjects appealed to you and we came to terms—as I hope we may, for I do not think I am exacting—I could begin at once on hearing from you.[27]

It's true he was publishing less than before 1916, or after 1923. This was partly because, as he explained to Herbert Read, 'E[sther] J[ulia] is a flourishing monster & wastes so much of my time'. But what he called his 'desultory writing' was still prolific by most people's standards (*No Enemy*, one-and-a-half novels, a long poem, a book of criticism, and also 'Just People', the reminiscential sketches of interesting types he had met, also written at Bedham). Latham was enthusiastic about the synopses, said the first book should be a novel, and suggested—gently—that perhaps it should be 'True Love'. But the renewed interest had already spurred Ford to start *The Marsden Case*, so he replied that he would prefer to finish that one first. He hoped that Macmillan would take on the Collected Edition that Lane had rejected: 'I want to get into relations with a publisher with whom I could reasonably hope to remain for the rest of my life' (the analogy with marriage is not coincidental, given the tendency for authors to regard their books as progeny, and Ford's failure to establish a lifelong relationship with a woman). As usual, his expectations were not unreasonable, though he knew publishers would need coaxing to make such a large investment, and he characterized himself—accurately (and with a steadily accumulative syntax)—as a writer who had 'always written with a view to a steady and continuing, rather than an immediate and sensational, sale':

What I want now to find is a publisher—and I should be extremely pleased if it could be your house—who would whilst commissioning some of my future work, publish two or three of my historical and modern novels and a fairly large representative selection of my poems as coups d'essai and who would then go on to publish more if the experiment proved successful. Of course if it did not, after a fair trial, the experiment would be dropped: but if it proceeded we might proceed to a fairly complete and definitive edition.[28]

Latham agreed with the principle of a long-standing relationship, and encouraged Ford to state his terms. Pinker sent a contract late in September, and early in October Ford was counting his literary chickens, telling Herbert Read:

I have got an immense contract from New York which shd. last me all my life: *Thus to Revisit* is going into editions & I get cheques in excess of advance of royalty which never happened to me before: οἱ πολλοί not Les Hauts du Front [the masses not the highbrows]—& indeed in spite of them!—are reading me. It is all very funny & as it should be, and we pass our time speculating on whether it is to be a Rolls Royce or an Overland [. . .]

The drought has simply made me give up Agriculture: nothing will grow: but we live on our own chicken & bacon, drink our own cider & reel hoglike to bed. None of yr. cultivating the Muses on a little thin oatmeal.

But it is unlikely that Macmillan signed the contract. In January 1922 Latham said he was sure they could come to terms once he had had the manuscript read. A month later Ford sent them the novel, but they rejected it in the summer, and never published any of his work.[29]

*

'I believe that, as "treatment", it's the best thing I've done—but the subject is not a very good one, though it's one that has haunted me certainly ever since I was eighteen on and off.' Thus Ford writing about his first novel to be published after the war, *The Marsden Case*. Finishing a novel often made him feel it was his best. Posterity has confirmed his sense of a disjunction between the 'treatment' of the book and its 'subject'. Unease with the elements of fantasy and absurdity in the plot had tended to cause recent critics to judge *The Marsden Case* as a 'rehearsal' for the more successful treatment of the experiences of war and reconstruction in *Parade's End*.[30]

It says something about the disjunction of the time, split between celebrating peace and mourning loss, as well as saying something about romance's delicate joining of fantastical narrative and familiar feeling, that *The Marsden Case* seemed so much more effective to the reviewers of 1923. They could recognize the plot as 'absurd' without feeling the need to censure it or apologize for it. Were they so wrong to find it 'a brilliant and magnificent nightmare. . . . extremely clever and entertaining comedy'; 'funny and yet serious, fantastic, and painful too'; 'a romantic novel of so ingenious a fancy and such satisfying brilliance of technique'?[31]

It is *The Marsden Case*'s relation to the war that has made it problematic for later critics. The book doesn't describe the Western Front (as *No Enemy* or *Parade's End* do), but it none the less registers, obliquely, the *effects* of the Great War on the whole range of characters, partly by means of representing analogous forms of warfare: battles of will, battles in public life, war between the sexes, the struggles of (the publishing) business, litigation, the psychomachia within men's minds. As the narrator, Ernest Jessop, explains:

This is not a war novel. Heaven knows I, who saw something of that struggle, would willingly wipe out of my mind every sight that I saw, every sound that I heard, every memory in my brain. But it is impossible, though there are non-participants who demand it, to write the lives of people to-day aged thirty or so, and leave out all mention of the fact that whilst those young people were aged, say, twenty-two to twenty-eight, there existed—Armageddon. For the matter of that, it would be wicked to attempt it, since the eyes, the ears, the brain and the fibres of every soul to-day adult have been profoundly seared by those dreadful wickednesses of embattled humanity. (pp. 143–4)

In the humane light of this passage it seems wrong to say, as Ann Barr Snitow does, that *The Marsden Case* is 'a study of the mind not facing the war itself'. Rather, it is a study of the mind choosing—needing—to write about something else in order to regain sanity after such universally deranging experiences. When E. M. Forster read T. S. Eliot's first book of verse in wartime Cairo, he found its silence about the war, and the absence of 'public spiritness' in his poems, significant values:

For what, in that world of gigantic horror, was tolerable except the slighter gestures of dissent? He who measured himself against the war, who drew himself to his full height, as it were, and said to Armadillo-Armageddon 'Avaunt!' collapsed at once into a pinch of dust. But he who could turn aside to complain of ladies and drawing-rooms preserved a tiny drop of our self-respect. He carried on the human heritage.[32]

This is one reason why so much of the best writing about the war (including *Parade's End*) couldn't be written until the later 1920s or the 1930s.

The involved plot of *The Marsden Case* follows George Heimann's discovery that he is the legitimate son of Earl Marsden. But he shares Ford's fear of publicity, which he is driven to incur by his sister, Marie Elizabeth, and her friend, Miss Jeaffreson, who are selfishly determined to establish Marie Elizabeth as 'Lady Mary' (as Violet Hunt and her friend, Mary Martindale, fought to establish Hunt as Ford's legal wife). The plot complicates considerably when it turns out that the legal documents that could prove George's title are on the Continent. He embarks on a hectic search for them just as war breaks out; is imprisoned by the Germans as an English spy; then denounced as a German spy when he returns. (Here the echoes of Ford's attempted German divorce, and the consequent doubts about his British patriotism are evident.) His father commits suicide. Publicity overwhelms him. Like Ford, his divided allegiances and familial anxieties lead him to despair and breakdown. But he is rescued by love, in the guise of the young artiste Clarice Honeywill (who plays Bowen's role in Ford's life, though she owes much to her flat-mate Phyllis Reid, who gave readings at the Poetry Bookshop).[33]

The book's obliqueness about the war rings false now. *The Marsden Case* is permeated by the guilt of a 'lost generation' survivor for the loss of his dead comrades, but suppresses it in this form, transferring it instead to the contrived pathos of George Heimann's 'case'. George's sufferings are not negligible: they drive him to attempt suicide, in an exact reconstruction of his father's death. The book's characteristic tones and cadences seek to create a sense of false inevitability (by suggesting that George has died, when he hasn't—rather as Ford kept suggesting about himself), and to equate his private suffering with the larger public tragedy. But their *effect* is—now—the opposite of what was intended: George's adversity seems trivial by comparison. As Robert Green says: 'there is a strange lack of connection between the public events and the suffering hero.'[34]

The contemporary reviewers appear to have been willing to supply the connection themselves, reading George's sufferings as a sustained innuendo for the experience of war, and praising Ford's 'fine restraint' in subduing his responses. As one said: 'the way in which the war is introduced is surely incomparable.'[35] Whereas the further the war recedes into history, the less it is felt as the cardinal fact of the modern world; the less it forms the shared background which contemporary readers could not help reading *The Marsden Case* against. More-recent critics have concentrated on the explicit (but more superficial) plot, without registering the effort Ford needed to play down the war. The problem here is instructive about the achievement of *Parade's End*, for there Ford involves Tietjens in the war, compounding the private and the public anguish, and the magnificent result is to make him vividly representative of the public neurosis, rather than a private neurotic who appears to be over-reacting to vaguely specified difficulties.

The Marsden Case's double-perspective—reaching tentatively and painfully back across the devastated zones of memory to the hysteria of the war's eve, constantly superimposes the war's shadow on its social scene: 'In costume he was an exact replica of George Heimann, only he was not quite so tall. That was uniform, really, for certain dashing young men. Well, they had uniforms enough a very little later' (p. 90). This blurring of the lines between the civilian and military, between private and public, is a central feature of *Parade's End* too, where its climax is Sylvia's vindictive surprise visit to France in *No More Parades*. Sometimes the contrast is left implicit in *The Marsden Case*. The underground night-club, for example, foreshadows the underworld of trenches and dugouts. In such ways the whole novel could be said to be a complex innuendo for the war, attempting to render Ford's ambivalences about its reverberations. Forrest Reid thought that it was Ford's 'indirect method' that produced 'the most complete illusion', and made *The Marsden Case* 'a brilliant novel'.[36] Certainly, like *A Call* (though less derivatively of Henry James), it shows Ford at his most allusive and suggestive, presenting his characters living in a tissue of hints and innuendoes.

What Ford wanted to achieve in *The Marsden Case* was the feeling that George's breakdown comes about not just out of petty but enervating social quarrels and a neurasthenic aversion to publicity, but because he has somehow taken the burden not only of his family's anguish, but of Europe's suffering and violence upon himself, and, like Tietjens, is prepared to sacrifice himself for others' sakes, only to be resurrected miraculously: George when his suicide attempt fails and he is rescued; Tietjens when he is buried by mud from a shell-burst, then reborn from the earth, to save others and reinvent his own life. As in *Parade's End*, the seriousness and pathos of the protagonist's suffering is held in tension with the savage comedy of manners (whether in society or in the army), which continually hovers on the brink of farce. As in *The Good Soldier*, this combination of pathos and farce is quintessentially Fordian.[37] *The Marsden Case* is ultimately a lighter work than these. But, read with historical sensitivity, it is a subtly entertaining comedy of nerves.

It is also, characteristically, an oblique self-analysis; an account of how Ford had survived his pre-war anxieties, then the war itself; and how he had recovered enough to reconstruct himself as a writer. The Fordian narrator Ernest Jessop (whose name also echoes Edgar Jepson's, the novelist to whom the book was dedicated) is a novelist. There is a portentous German poet, Curtius, who combines aspects of Levin Schücking and Francis Hueffer. The book's other writer, the journalist Pflugschmied (who has now Anglicized his name to Plowright, as Ford had recently Anglicized his from Hueffer), is verbally savaged by the Marwoodian (and also Fordian) George— now Earl Marsden—for his irrepressible inaccuracy: 'You'd think that fellow would know his own wife's correct name' (p. 332). He goes on to correct Plowright's mistakes about Jessop, 'seeming to tick off the inaccuracies with vindictive pleasure'—as Marwood might have done. In putting Plowright right, George dictates Jessop's war record. Jessop says he is embarrassed: 'since I had not his unconcern as to displaying my personality in public [. . .]' (p. 333). This is odd, since Jessop's whole novel displays George's personality in publication. But it underlines the way George is acting as a Fordian novelist might, telling a man's story in order to express his personality (and, simultaneously, to express his own in the writing). Plowright is so terrorized by George that he no longer dares to write. Jessop has to write his 'stories' for him; an exercise which helps to rehabilitate him: 'it got me back, a little, into the habit of writing so as to be printed!' (p. 336)—which returns us to the printed word of the book's beginning. Amongst other things, the book has told the story of how

George becomes an authority on writing (almost a writer); and how Jessop becomes a writer once more.

The concern with writing goes deeper. Jessop says Plowright 'poured out a fantastic parody of my war services' (p. 332). But Plowright is himself Ford's fantastic parody of the kind of artist Ford was often accused of being: one whose defence of his 'impressionism'—'I don't really deal in facts, I have for facts a most profound contempt'—was taken to indicate a scant regard for truth. Jessop's sarcastic inverted commas around the word 'stories' when he refers to Plowright's journalism complain that Plowright can't tell the difference between fact and fiction; what he writes is unwitting fiction. (The same complaint was often made about Ford's reminiscences, in which he freely fictionalizes factual characters and events.) But Ford's irony here is that the boundary is not always so easily drawn. Jessop sneers that inaccuracies are 'the heart's blood of journalism' (p. 336). But Ford the prolific journalist knew that impressionism was its heart's blood; that the 'story'-ness of a newspaper article is what most makes for readability. What we have been reading is itself a fictional 'story'; so that all the 'facts' that George is able to marshal are themselves created within this fictional matrix. Ford valued George's accuracy; he also valued the power of Plowright's impressionism, and the humanity of his ability sympathetically to identify with his subjects (even as he garbles their predicaments); though Ford was simultaneously scrupulous about the dangers of such a method:

It was indeed as if he entered into the troubles of others with such immense dash that he never had time really to master what those troubles were. And the resulting impression would thrill New York, Chicago, Philadelphia [. . .] I have sometimes wondered if they would so have stirred those great states if the stories had had any relation to the vicissitudes of the victims. I daresay they would not have; but it does not seem to matter much. (p. 326)

The ending of *The Marsden Case*, bringing together George and Plowright (who are now brothers-in-law, since George's sister has married the journalist), and having Jessop writing Plowright's stories for him, could be read as allegorizing Ford's attempt to unite impression and accuracy. This is also the project for *Parade's End*, where Ford's virtuoso impressionism displays the personality of Christopher Tietjens, his most obsessively accurate character; and in the result Ford wants to thrill both Europe and America with a fictional story about the war which none the less does have a 'relation to the vicissitudes of the victims'.

When he told Jepson that the subject of *The Marsden Case* had haunted him ever since he was 18, Ford explained: 'It's the story of [W. R. S.] Ralston, the first translator of Turgenev—a man I liked very much. At any rate, that suggested it to me.' Ford remembered Ralston as 'an intimate friend' of the Hueffer family, and recalled sitting on his knee as a child being told fairy stories about Russia. He describes him as the physical double of Turgenev, but a spectral figure beside the Russian: 'it may have been because the shadow of his approaching suicide—for one of the most preposterous reasons of misery and shyness after a fantastic *cause célèbre*—was already upon Ralston.' Ralston's father was a merchant who made a fortune in Calcutta, but lost it when he returned and became possessed of the idea that he was the rightful heir to the

Ralston property in Ayrshire. But he used up his fortune in a vain attempt to prove himself legitimate under English law (his father had married 'without benefit of clergy', and gone to live in New York, where the union was recognized). William Ralston, a manic depressive, had to earn a living in the British Museum as a result. He died in 1889—the same year as Ford's father.[38]

In the figure of George's father, Earl Marsden, Ford combines his memories of the deaths of five father-figures, three of them suicides: his father's, Marwood's, Ralston's, and two other suicides: those of his father-in-law, and of the Frankfurt waiter (who killed his wife and children and then himself). He had recently been writing about the waiter again in 'Just People', and his story was important to the genesis of *The Marsden Case*. The last chapter shows George, now an earl, in a hotel dining-room where 'a miserable waiter had just upset a full sauceboat over his boots' (perhaps *that* was why Ford insulted the Frankfurt waiter?) (p. 323). The hotel-keeper begs him not to insist on the waiter's dismissal, because (like most of the novel's male characters), he is 'an extreme nervous subject. He might lose his nerve and be unable ever to wait again. He had so much suffered' (p. 327). He had once been the proprietor of a central European hotel, but had seen it 'sacked by Cossacks, gutted by Servians, burned by Austrians, his wife murdered by I forget whom, and his daughter carried off by Montenegrins [. . .]' (pp. 328, 336–7). He cooked for the successive conquerors, but then had 'so frightful a nervous breakdown on the declaration of peace [. . .]'. His story thus combines the history of war-torn Europe with Ford's memories of his angst-torn periods in Europe in 1904, 1910–11, 1913, and 1916–17. Jessop likes to think that 'his disaster with the sauce-boat was the beginning of his rehabilitation', because Clarice took a subscription list around the dining-room to collect money so that the waiter could buy a new hotel—by a station. 'And had that young man not been so self-possessed, so every inch an Earl, that poor little fairy tale would never have found its earthly, so fortunate close', the book ends. This chapter was originally intended to be the first; to set the note of the whole book of potential nerve-shattering disaster and suicide fortunately avoided. Like *The Good Soldier* and *Parade's End*, the novel presents a dual picture of its protagonist. Jessop says 'one of the queerest feelings' he has ever known is to have seen George as the 'magnificent young' guardsman, yet knowing that the next morning he would be utterly disgraced (p. 207). Yet—again like those other works—there is the idea that through a 'simple, sentimental benevolence' like that of the hotel-keeper who rescues the waiter, people's disgraces and flaws are to be forgiven them. As Dowell finally expresses his love of Ashburnham, Marie Elizabeth tells Miss Jeaffreson: 'My brother is a good man' (p. 298). But whereas the destructiveness and frustration caused by Ashburnham and Tietjens is confronted fully in their books, with the waiter scene, Ford appears to be rewriting a shameful episode the way he wished he had acted. Though the book is frankly 'A Romance', its reimagining of Ford's autobiography feels more like evasion than invention.[39]

George Heimann's story links the death of the father with the son's wish to commit suicide, in the book's most bizarre act of reconstruction—also an act of re-destruction: George's mimicking of his father's suicide. Thomas Moser reads this as an allegory for 'Ford's half-conscious awareness' that Marwood's death had 'saved his life' by enabling Ford increasingly to assume Marwood's persona, and thus write *Parade's End*.

This may be part of the truth, but (as in 'The Colonel's Shoes' and 'True Love & a G.C.M.') the sense of the son's life doubling the father's is central. *The Marsden Case* thus also allegorizes how the son of Franz Hüffer became Ford Madox Ford. The 'auto-suggestion specialist' he visits tells Clarice 'that George's abortive hanging of himself had saved his reason and his life. He said that nothing but that shock could have cleared up all the complexes of George's worried brain' (p. 335). Ford may have felt something like that: that his pre-war breakdown and relapses were expressions of guilt that he had survived his father; that his suicidal longings reflected an unconscious (or barely conscious) desire to imitate his father's death; and that his near-death on the Somme at almost the same age at which Francis Hueffer had died and soon after Marwood had died had exorcized both fatherly ghosts. Or that his imaginings of his own death in fiction had 'saved his reason and his life' (the phrase echoing Ford's words to Violet Hunt, after she had taken away his bottle of poison in 1909). Whereas Dudley Leicester and Nancy Rufford live the death in life of the loss of their reason, Ford's post-war fiction celebrates new life achieved after near death (the Alcestis paradigm again).[40]

In *It Was the Nightingale*, Ford's marvellous reminiscences of his own post-war reconstruction, he tells a story which again enables us to connect *The Marsden Case* with ideas about writing and death:

the life of the writer—of any artist—is the best life if only because he alone never 'retires.' His philosopher's stone—the technical discovery that will at last content him with his own work—is always just around the corner.

There was Hokusai—the Old Man Mad about painting. The following version of his life was given me by Mr. A. E. Coppard, sitting on the trunk of a felled beech above the great common where my Large Blacks roamed. . . . There are of course many versions of the sayings of Hokusai, but this one pleased me most because of the dark gipsy earnestness of the narrator who was such a great artist in words—and who so admirably lived the only life worth living.

Hokusai, then, when he was seventy, said: 'Now at last I begin to divine faintly what painting may be.' At eighty he said: 'Now I really think that after ten more years of research I shall know how to paint.' At ninety he said: 'Now it is coming. A little more research and thought! . . .' On attaining the age of a hundred years, he said: 'To-morrow I am going to begin my Work of Works. . . .' And so died. . . .

It is that that makes the following of an Art such a blessed thing [. . .] So one supports with equanimity what would make a banker commit suicide. (pp. 123–4)

The setting of that story about how art can save the artist from suicide (though the immortality it confers doesn't save him from death) is Ford's cottage in Bedham; but it is equally recognizable as the setting of the Marsdens' suicides: the beech trees with the pigs beneath. It also goes back to the days when Ford was courting Elsie Martindale in 1894, suggesting suicide pacts with her, and quoting Berlioz's last words: 'When I see the way in which certain people look on love and what they seek in artistic creation I am involuntarily reminded of hogs rooting and grunting under the grandest of trees.' He had her parents in mind, who opposed the match.[41] Was Ford reminded of these words when he was writing *The Marsden Case*? Doubtless Ford the expert breeder of Large Sussex Blacks would now have thought the comparison with philistines was insulting to the hogs. Nevertheless, the associations with Hokusai and Berlioz suggest that George's suicide attempt and salvation represented the self-sacrifice of the artist (as urged by Ford Madox Brown: 'Beggar yourself rather than refuse assistance to any one whose genius you think shows promise of being greater than your own'); and also Ford's repeated sense of the abyss between artists (or 'constructive intellects') and 'the stuff to fill graveyards', the philistine hogs. The novel fuses these ideas together with George's desire (it may have been Ford's as well) to reconcile himself to his father by dying in a similar manner. There is a diluted version of such filial guilt in *Parade's End*, where one motive for Tietjens's willingness to sacrifice himself might be his anxiety about whether his father died by suicide on hearing of his son's affair with Valentine, whom he suspects is Christopher's half-sister.[42] But *The Marsden Case*'s engagement with familial guilt makes it something stranger and more significant than a 'rehearsal' for the tetralogy.

However, the fact that we need to turn to a memoir written a decade later, and to a letter written three decades earlier, to construe the novel shows a crucial way in which *The Marsden Case* is not fully achieved. In a work so involved with dark family struggles and the impulse to suicide, Ford may well have felt that he was in danger of displaying aspects of his personality he did not wish to make public—not least because the inadvertent expression would be an instance of the unconscious action that he found alarming ('I did not rightly know what I was doing'). He covered his tracks, separating off the man (George) who suffers from the mind (Jessop's) which creates, and thus obscuring the novel's exploration of the sources of his own creativity. Something similar happens in *The Good Soldier* (where he separates the victim of passion, Ashburnham, from its narrator, Dowell), but it is not easy to explain why it doesn't seem like an evasion there. Perhaps it is because the formal tautness and the greater plausibility simply keep the reader distracted from the subliminal issues. In *Parade's End*, on the other hand, Tietjens is enough of a 'constructive intellect' to combine the figures of artist and victim. It is only in these two great works of fiction, and in his virtuoso books of reminiscence, that Ford found the right relation between formal control and courageous self-revelation. None the less, *The Marsden Case* remains an illuminating work: both for its suggestiveness about the relations between writing, reconstruction, and psychology; and for what it can tell us of the intimacy of Ford's art with ideas of sacrifice, suicide, death, elegy, and rebirth.

9

1922: THE LAST OF ENGLAND

Aye, we are quit of the North;
But the mind looks back.

(Ford, *Mister Bosphorus and the Muses*)

While he was working on *The Marsden Case* early in 1922, still under the impression
that Macmillan would take it, Ford was shocked to hear of the death of Pinker from
pneumonia, in New York on 8 February. 'I am worried out of my mind myself', Ford
told Jepson—ostensibly because Pinker was '—or was supposed to be—fixing up my
contract with Macmillans that was to have kept me in clover for the rest of my life'; but
also because Pinker's death 'without any warning at all' (he was under 60) came as a
warning to someone wondering about the rest of his life, and how long it might last.
For all Pinker's support, he had remained a puzzle to Ford to the end: 'I never could
quite know how I felt towards him. He was so good and helpful and patient with
Conrad and Crane and James and so quarrelsome to myself.'[1]

As soon as he had finished *The Marsden Case*, he turned to the manuscript Pound
had sent him in January of his latest 'Canto' (it was number VIII in the drafts, but
eventually became number II). 'I put yr. m.s. away in an exceptionally safe place while
I was finishing my novel', Ford explained,

—& have spent the fortnight or so since I finished in searching for the m.s.. Here it is at last,
however, pencilled according to yr. commands.

Pardon if the suggestions are mostly zoological. That is how it falls out. Zoological
mistakes don't matter a damn [. . .] but zoological *questionabilities* [. . .] do because they arrest
the attention of the Reader of Good Will & that arresting of the attention blurs the effect of
the poem. One says: 'Do *waves*, wirling or billowy things run in the valleys between hillocks
of beach—*beach-grooves*? I don't think they do: they are converted into surf or foam as soon
as they strike the pebbles & become wash or undertow in receding & then run.'

Per se that does not matter—but the weakening of the attention does.

It is the same with your compound words like 'spray-whited' & 'cord-welter.'—But as to
these I am not so certain: my dislike for them may be my merely personal distaste for Anglo-
Saxon locutions which always affect me with nausea & yr. purpose in using them may be the
purely aesthetic one of roughening up yr. surface. I mean that, if you shd. cut them out you
might well get too slick an effect [. . .]

I wouldn't bother you with these verbal minutiae if you hadn't asked for them; the latter
part of the poem—of the first page & a half is a very beautiful piece of impressionism, as good
as anything you have ever done & that is what really matters [. . .]

Of course, I think that, in essence, you're a mediaeval gargoyle, Idaho or no! And it's not
a bad thing to be.

Pound was grateful, despite the raillery and repeated attempt to claim him as an impressionist *après la lettre*: 'Dear Hesiod', he replied: 'Thanks orfully. It is only the minute crit. that is any good, or that prods one.' Yet it didn't stop him making his usual inadequate general criticism of Ford in print once more: 'I think Hueffer goes wrong because he bases his criticism on the eye, and almost solely on the eye'—an obtuse response to Ford's criticism based on the attention of the reader, and effects of the word. Ford had reason to be grateful to Pound too, who had been working on his behalf in Paris. First the Peruvian-born Victor Llona wrote to ask for the French rights of four of his books. Then Samuel Roth, who owned the New York magazine *Two Worlds Monthly*, asked him to act as its English editor. He approached potential young contributors, but, as he told one of them, A. E. Coppard, he soon heard 'lugubrious rumours as to [the magazine's] solvency', and wisely distanced himself— Roth turned out to be unreliable in other ways, using Pound's name without permission, and then pirating *Ulysses*. Finally, in August, Pound said he had encouraged a printer—William Bird—to publish a series of prose booklets, and suggested Ford's 'Women and Men' for one volume. It was an auspicious connection, since Bird was to be the printer of Ford's Parisian *transatlantic review*.[2]

After the isolation of the Bedham winter, Ford and Bowen had a social spring and summer. They had in the house 'a very sick colonel whose stay in consequence is indefinite and very telescopic [. . .]'. On 11 May Ford gave a reading of his poems at the Poetry Bookshop. He lunched at the Mont Blanc beforehand, and afterwards went to a party given by Mr and Mrs Henry Forman (the editor of *Collier's* who had sent Ford to Rome in 1911) to meet Sinclair Lewis and his wife. When Bowen wrote to thank Mrs Forman she said it had been the first social gathering they had been out to for three years. H. G. Wells and May Sinclair were also there, as was a 'celebrity' who, said Ford, 'was the gentleman who had said in *The Times* that I thought I was a personage, but I wasn't'. There is a vivid reminiscence of the occasion in *It Was the Nightingale*, recounting how 'the brilliant and noisy conversation turned on nothing but boxing', and how the 'celebrity' asked Wells: 'Haw. . . . H. G., who's your omniscient friend.' Wells, who, said Ford, had 'a little joke' about his omniscience, declaimed his 'name and titles'. 'It was as if the celebrity felt something disagreeing violently with him. | He said: | "Good God! Disgraceful! They told me that that fellow . . .".' Ford didn't hear the end of the sentence, but the episode confirmed his feeling that the London literati had assumed he was 'either in the workhouse or the gaol'. He and Stella spent the night at the rather grand Grosvenor Hotel, Victoria.[3]

Back in Bedham, the pigs were 'always finding new gaps in the hedges and escaping into the property of some irate neighbour'. One day the sow got on to the road to Fittleworth (where the boar lived), and since Bowen was the only person nearby, pushing Julie along in her pram, she had to give chase—there was a £50 fine for allowing animals on the road because of a foot-and-mouth epidemic. 'I expect it looked funny enough for a woman to be chasing a pig with a baby in a pram', she mused, 'but it did not seem funny to me.' They had a 'double shock' in June. Bowen had a bad bicycle accident, injuring her arm; then, just after the doctor left,

E.[sther] J.[ulia] got at the aspirin he had left for Stella and ate it all! We passed an agonising time expecting her to die [Ford told his mother:], all the local ladies came in with stomach pumps & the most alarming prophecies & Stella & I & the two young men who were stopping with us sat up all night in relays to make sure that her breathing did not become stertorous. And nothing happened at all & the doctor merely laughed![4]

Hearing that Macmillan had turned down *The Marsden Case* must have made for a triple shock. Ford then turned to Horace Liveright, whom Pound had encouraged to publish *Mr. Fleight* in America (it had only been published by an English firm in 1913), and who had approached Ford just after Macmillan in 1921. He sent off a copy of *Mr. Fleight*, but tried to interest Liveright in *The Marsden Case*, a volume of poems, and the work that was beginning to engross him, 'a HISTORY OF ENGLISH LITERATURE of a livelier description than are most such histories'. 'I *can't* write much about your stories now', Ford apologized to Anthony Bertram (art critic for the *Spectator* and *Saturday Review*, lecturer at the National Portrait Gallery, as well as aspiring writer; Bertram was probably one of the two young men who sat up to watch Julie's breathing): 'I am sick and tired of writing about writing, having suddenly determined to get a real move on with my History of British Literature.' Needless to say, he did go on to write detailed and patient comments on the stories, which he found 'too written', advising him to 'try—literally!—talking as you write for a month or so and, after that, try writing as you find you talk. I believe you would then find words have quite another savour.' Liveright rejected the proposal. Like *Mr. Fleight* (and more than ten others of his books), *The Marsden Case* was not published in America; and although T. S. Eliot admired it and considered it for the *Criterion*, Ford eventually cannibalized his intriguing 234-leaf typescript of 'Towards a History of English Literature' as a serial for his own *transatlantic review*. The approach, as in *Thus to Revisit*, is an 'attack on an Academicised universe', waged this time on behalf of the literature of the past. He tries to establish the critical standards he always found lacking in the English literary establishment, and to see how the great works of the past looked in the post-war world. (In 1919 Eliot formulated his version of the way the present transforms the past, in 'Tradition and the Individual Talent'.) Ford asks: 'How much knowledge of imaginative Literature, then does it need to make a proper man?' He stresses the axiom on which his practical advice to writers was always founded: 'Literature exists for the Reader and by the Reader.' He argues that the curse of the Anglo-Saxon literary world is the desire of writers to become socially respectable, and chooses Dr Johnson as a representative and initiatory figure, 'at once an over-neglected imaginative writer and the father of the nineteenth century Intelligentsia'; too great and untidy himself ever to become quite respectable, but 'nevertheless he was the first Literary Man to attempt that form of Frightfulness'. There is an impassioned attack on the textual critic's tendency to obscure the creativity of literature with apparatus and variora. 'The main thesis of this work', says Ford, 'is that Art can come only of the people and that the further it removes from the people the less it flourishes until, as far as the Great World is concerned, it dies as in Anglo-Saxondom it has died.' (Characteristically, he playfully disavows the exaggeration: 'There are however plants with creeping root stocks . . .') He elaborates his familiar contrast between imaginative literature and

'The Serious Book'. The published serial ends with a sensitive consideration of 'The Reader'. The typescript ends with fine essays on 'Pure Literature' (discussing religious verse, and advocating literature's indifference to moral instruction or propounded beliefs); and on 'Great Writers'. The whole is a historical counterpart to *Thus to Revisit*'s map of the literature of Ford's own time. It is not an academic historical survey, of course, but rather a gathering of notes '*Towards* a History'. The title he gave it later for the *transatlantic review*, where it appeared as another work by 'Daniel Chaucer', is the adequate description of its scope: 'Stocktaking: Towards a Revaluation of English Literature.' Like all Ford's criticism, it is a teasingly personal performance. 'I am not writing biography—or only concealedly!' he disavows, after listing some of the childhood reading he found most engrossing: *Lorna Doone, 'Hark-Away Dick, Sweeny Todd, the Demon Barber; The Scalp-Hunters; Westward Ho'*. This alerts the reader to how even Ford's critical pieces *are* concealed autobiography: partly because he had himself lived out (and lived through) the revaluation of literary estimates he discusses—he has been a driving force in the changes in literary taste this century—and he was testing books against his own critical pulse; partly because the essays are alive with glimpses of Ford, sometimes concealed as 'a friend', sometimes *in propria persona*, in prison, in the army, in a club, or reading his favourite books; but mainly because, in discussing reading, he touches on how a writer's personality is concealed in the style used at once to express and conceal it—and, reciprocally, how readers can hear aspects of their own personalities echoed in those cadences:

But I *will* delay a moment to pay a tribute to what I thought then—and I think it still—*sui generis* the most beautiful book in the world: Samuel Smiles' *Life of a Scottish Naturalist*. I found this book by chance a year ago, bought it for sixpence and recognised at once that my intimate cadence, the typical sentence that I try all my life to create, that I hear all the while in my ear and only once in a blue moon am aided to write, is to be found always in the recorded speeches of Thomas Edward. His sentences have a dying fall, a cadence of resignation. He will write of dotterels on the wet sands, of spoonbills labouring in the immense engineering feats of turning over a great dead fish, of foxes in their homes on the faces of the sea-cliffs—and it is as if you were hearing a *nunc dimittis* spoken without pomp or self-consciousness.[5]

What could be more autobiographical for a writer? The casual delivery should not stop us hearing the penetrating thought that what is most intimate in an author's style may be precisely what was found in the expression of someone else's personality. This is not to say that Ford's style is the same as Edward's; but that the hearing of another's voice can be a writer's vocation—his or her continual impulse and ideal.

Other visitors that summer included Dyneley Hussey, who followed in Francis Hueffer's footsteps, becoming music critic for *The Times* (and was probably the other young man staying up to watch over Julie); A. E. Coppard, whom Ford introduced to Monro as the 'White Hope of the Short Story—so behave prettily to him'; and Alec Waugh, whom Ford told he'd sold a potato for £400. Margaret Cole and Phyllis (*née* Reid, who had now married an architect called Harry Birnstingl) both came, bringing their new daughters. Ford told Bertram the house was 'full, full, full of babies, nurses and mothers'. 'Esther Julia flourishes', he wrote to Jepson, 'the centre of a perfect cloud of other babies whom she flaxenly dominates, like a monstrous Germania amongst the Nations'. When his mother visited (without Hunt) she wrote to her grandson Frank Soskice: 'Uncle Ford has a hut in which he writes [it was draughty and the roof leaked, but its isolation was essential when they had guests staying, and he couldn't work at his desk on the landing in front of the guest-room]—when not working on his ground as a labourer—it is a big place and they have [. . .] two *huge* pigs who to me are most hideous but your Uncle stands by them with a bland smile & a straw in his mouth & says they are "beautiful".'[6]

Despite farming, entertaining, and writing 'Towards a History', Ford also made time for his first post-war journalism to recapture the force and poise of his *English Review* and *Outlook* pieces. Answering a questionnaire in the *Chapbook*, he was axiomatic: 'The function of poetry in the Republic is still, always has been, and always will be to instil imagination—that is, sympathetic insight!—into the Human Brute. It civilises. Rhythms or broken rhythms are a necessity for humanity.' For Clifford Bax's new journal *Golden Hind* he extracted a section of 'Towards a History' elaborating the charge that Shelley was a 'third-rate poet'—a charge which Bax said Ford had made, but which he typically disavows while elaborating. It's a balanced piece, full of admiration for Shelley's passionate sincerity, and arguing that he 'deserves the love of all mankind' for opposing injustice. 'Your poet must be a Man before anything and moved to mad despairs by the viler happenings of his times'; in a work like 'The Mask of Anarchy', 'Shelley the man rose into the first rank of poets of the philippic'. 'But something further—a deeper and more painful self-negation—is demanded by the poet: he must observe with exactitude and reverence, and with reverence and exactitude he must render.' It is here that Shelley falls short of Ford's axiom. His inaccurate similes (Ford makes ornithological criticisms of Shelley's 'Skylark' reminiscent of his naturalist's comments on Pound) are 'a symptom of an inexact mind'. He asserts imagination—his own—without instilling imagination, or rendering with imagination. In a striking contrast Ford argues that a poet like Herbert can achieve an 'actually startling religious effect [. . .] by the merest use of material objects'; whereas Shelley's 'aristocratic laziness' in his 'unceasing employment of Spirits, Beings, and what used to be called operatic machinery' means that his attempts to elevate material facts into spiritual truths falters on a dated eighteenth-century sentimentalist notion of the 'sublime'. When Ford wrote to congratulate Eliot on *The Waste Land*, Eliot reciprocated by saying Ford's view of Shelley came closer to his own than any other he had read.[7]

Ford was back in the thick of contemporary literature, and was beginning to master his feelings of being cut off and neglected. His command of the new idioms was evident when he extended his revaluation of literature to discuss the contemporary British novel. Here too he wants to rank authors, but (as with all his schematic criticism) the purpose is to give us a plan to help us appreciate the particularities of each individual artist. The novelists 'of the first flight', he says, are Conrad, Hardy, George Moore, Hudson, '—and possibly Mr. Bennett. That I regard as indisputable if we may take the novel as giving us something more than the tale—as being a tale with a projection of life, a philosophy, but not an obvious moral, or propagandistic purpose. First-flight novelists, then, will be those who have perfected their methods and are resigned.' Critics might object to his definition that short stories too have their projections of life, their philosophies; a point which to Ford would probably have seemed like academic carping, since he is about to include short-story writers in his discussion. 'The second flight', he continues, 'will be, in our literature, Pushkin's "haughty and proud generation: vigorous and free in their passions and adventures".' In this group he places Norman Douglas, Wyndham Lewis, D. H. Lawrence, Frank Swinnerton, Katherine Mansfield, Clemence Dane, Dorothy Richardson, and James Joyce. Though they are not much read now, Dane and Swinnerton were well known at the time. More surprising than the fact that Ford includes them, is the sureness of his judgement. The only writers missing from this essential history of the British modernist novel are Woolf (whose best books were still to come) and—even more surprisingly for those who regard Ford as a self-advertiser—Ford himself. If it sounds odd to talk of Joyce as in the 'second flight', one must remember that Ford's terms place his sympathies (and his own performances) in the second rather than the first flight: there is something tired and defeatist about having perfected your methods and becoming resigned. It is the vigorous experimentalism that distinguishes the second flight, rather than any inferiority. To see this one need only read Ford's closing words on Joyce, whose *Ulysses* had come out in February. Ford had only read fragments of the book before its publication; he was one of the first to write about it:

One can't arrive at one's valuation of [. . .] 'Ulysses' after a week of reading and two or three weeks of thought about it. Next year, or in twenty years, one may. For it is as if a new continent with new traditions had appeared, and demanded to be run through in a month. 'Ulysses' contains the undiscovered mind of man; it is human consciousness analyzed as it has never before been analyzed. Certain books change the world. This, success or failure, 'Ulysses' does: for no novelist with serious aims can henceforth set out upon a task of writing before he has at least formed his own private estimate as to the rightness or wrongness of the methods of the author of 'Ulysses.' If it does not make an epoch—and it well may!—it will at least mark the ending of a period.[8]

This is concealed autobiography too, for someone whose main life is the life of the imagination in reading and writing. Less than a month after reading the book, Ford knew that his next fictional task would inevitably be influenced by *Ulysses*. He had always striven to render human consciousness, but the Joycean stream of consciousness had inaugurated new techniques of presentation. Later in the year Ford told Jepson: 'personally I'm quite content to leave to Joyce the leading novelist-ship of this country, think he deserves the position, and hope it will profit him.' *Ulysses* made *Parade's End* possible in another way: the 'ending of a period' that Joyce marks is not just a period of literary history, but the historical period within which that literary transformation occurred. The 'ending of a period' is also the *subject* of Ford's own inaugurative monsterpiece ('Period's End'?), which itself marks the ending of a period—the period of the historical novel, the Victorian panoramic novel, the 'Condition of England' novel.[9]

Ford's fantasy of a Grimm sanctuary began to seem like an exile, as winter approached and their outdoor duties became 'a grim trial'. 'The Londoner's horror of the country in winter meant isolation for us during the long evenings', wrote Bowen. So when Harold Monro—another visitor that summer—told them about his little villa 'on top of a rock at Cap Ferrat, and described the sun and the view and all the charm of the Mediterranean in winter, Ford was at once filled with an immense nostalgia for his beloved Provence'. Monro was prepared to let it to them cheaply (£7 per month), so they soon made plans 'to winter abroad'. Ford said that the visit of a Tory election agent (before the General Election on 15 November) predisposed him 'towards expatriation'. When Ford gave his profession as 'Writer', he said the agent 'was appalled and became almost lachrymose', and answered: 'Oh, *don't* say that, sir. Say: "Gentleman."' They expected to be away until March or April, so the animals had to be sold—the pedigree pigs at bacon prices; and Bowen had to mend Ford's battered dress-clothes: 'fortunately he looked impressive in anything', she said. Ford's preparation for leaving involved writing a magnificent poem expressing his frustrations with England, and his exhilaration at the prospect of leaving it for the south. Pound had been assuring him that 'There is the intelligent nucleus for a movement here [in Paris], which there bloody well isn't in England'. It was perhaps in this way that Pound's influence on him was strongest. He was, at any rate, now ready to leave England for good. He had even begun to think of himself as writing primarily for an American readership—an idea that was to become increasingly dominant: 'I see no prospect of publishing any more in Great Britain', he told Jepson, since no publisher would take up his work for good, and there was 'not in these islands any periodical at all that would publish me or in which I could contemplate with equanimity being published. In America there are ten or a dozen.' He was writing an 'immense poem' throughout October and November.[10]

The anger that was still unharnessed in 'Immortality' is turned to mordant satire in the much longer poem Ford referred to as his 'Dunciad'.[11] Its title page conveys the humour and invention of this unusual, experimental work: *Mister Bosphorus and the Muses or a Short History of Poetry in Britain. Variety Entertainment in Four Acts . . . with Harlequinade, Transformation Scene, Cinematograph Effects, and Many Other Novelties, as well as Old and Tried Favourites.* It was published in a handsome volume with woodcuts by Paul Nash, whom Ford visited in Dymchurch, Kent, to plan the design. Mizener reads this poem too in a single-mindedly biographical way, arguing that it expresses Ford's reasons for leaving England: 'the climate, particularly in the winter at Bedham; the insensitivity of critics to the kind of art he admired; and the middle class's stupid disapproval of real love.' But the passage he quotes reveals a force of language Ford was rarely to achieve in verse. There is real bite in the satire, the imaginative precision of which gives it a spirit more like magnanimity than petty complaint and rebuke:

> But how is it possible that men hold dear,
> In these lugubrious places,
> This dreary land; the clod-like inglorious races,
> The befogged, gin-sodden faces;
> The lewd, grim prudery; for-ever-protracted chases
> After concealëd lechery; hog-like dull embraces
> Under a grey-flannel sky; un-aired and damp
> Like poems a-stink of the lamp:
> And the learned bronchitics that vamp
> Hodden-grey thoughts all to stamp [. . .].[12]

There is great compression of thought here, as words like 'befogged' and 'grey-flannel sky' condense the argument that a dull climate propagates a dull people; or as the bronchial critics (choked by the study and the weather alike) are cut down to size as vampiric 'bronchitics'. A vigour and panache about the whole poem shows Ford regaining his gusto. There is also an energy of dramatization: Mr Bosphorus may ride some of Ford's hobby-horses, but he is no more (nor less) Ford than was the 'Great Poet' of 'Immortality'. Though he was about to leave England, the Ford who had written *A House* and was soon to write *Parade's End* knew how it was that a man could hold England dear. *Mr Bosphorus* is the dramatization of a mood; an inspired pastiche of the history of English verse, demonstrating that Ford had honed his satiric edge sharper since the pre-war novels *The Simple Life Limited* and *The New Humpty-Dumpty*. It is a cinematic presentation of a series of 'dissolving views': in short, impressionism rather than autobiography. Finally, it demonstrates a more conscious awareness of his own provocativeness. He knew the poem would 'annoy quite a number of people' ('if they can understand it'), and therefore that it would entrench the very hostility it decries.[13]

Had Ford read *The Waste Land* before writing the poem? The novel uses of working-class voices and rhythms are comparable, as are the use of parody and the disillusionment with post-war London. As usual, the chronological evidence is inconclusive. Ford was already 'struggling' with *Mister Bosphorus* by 8 October. Eliot's poem was published around the 15th. Ford had read it by 25 January (when he wrote to him about it), but we don't know exactly when. He might have heard about it from Pound, who had seen it earlier in the year. On the other hand, Ford's love of music hall, his letter to the *Athenæum* defending Flint, his use of peasant speech in his early verse, all point towards his having been able to arrive at the techniques of the poem on his own. Even if *Mister Bosphorus* was influenced by *The Waste Land* (as it was by the 'Circe' or 'night-town' section of *Ulysses*) it would not be merely derivative. Its inventiveness, deftness, use of fantasy, and celebration of the South are all quintessentially Fordian. The poem turns his near-paranoid anxiety about an orchestrated obliteration of his reputation into a celebratory fantasy of escape and regeneration. It achieves the difficult combination of bitter pathos, macabre satire, and social comedy, that not all his prose succeeds in sustaining (perhaps only *Mr. Apollo*, *Mr. Fleight*, *The Good Soldier*, *Parade's End*, and the reminiscences do so). It also demonstrates his ability creatively to return on his critical premises in order to transcend them: it is the antithesis to the thesis that poetry should be like quiet talk, and much closer to the central modernist emphases on language, form, and parody. When Conrad wrote to congratulate him and thank him for sending a copy, he said: 'Tho' knowing you well I had no idea that your versatile genius could master so well the comic spirit/both so grim and so ferociously gay.'[14]

Despite Ford's high hopes of American publishers, *The Marsden Case* was rejected by Liveright, and then by Knopf, Brentano's, Holt, Scribner's, and Dodd Mead. The manuscript had now gone to Duckworth; ironically, it was on an English publisher's response that his future depended. Ford's disdain for 'prudential motives' is evident in Bowen's account of their reckless departure: 'in our usual foolhardy fashion, we went right ahead with our plans, trusting that the Lord would provide':

The luggage was packed, the passports obtained, and we were actually piling into the dog-cart to drive to Fittleworth station, when the postman delivered the manuscript—returned! This caught us hard in the pit of the stomach. As we stood on the windy station platform, Lucy [whom they had arranged to take with them] and Julie and Ford and I, feeling that it was the height of folly to have burned our boats and to be leaving our blessed home, I managed secretly to undo a corner of the parcel, in case there was a letter inside, for Ford hated opening anything disagreeable. The letter said that Duckworth would like to publish the book if Ford would make certain minor alterations, for which purpose he was returning the manuscript![15]

Thanks to Duckworth they 'had a happy journey after all', said Bowen. Did Ford suspect that he was never to live in England again? He spoke to Violet Hunt, probably over the telephone, on 15 November just before they left for Paris, *en route* to Cap Ferrat. From Paris he wrote to her to apologize for not having rung her again before leaving, and suggested unwillingly that they could perhaps meet at Jepson's when he returned. She wrote on the envelope that it was his last letter to her (though they did meet at least once again, years later). He and Bowen arrived in Paris on 17 November 1922, and stayed for a month in the Hotel du Blois, a *hôtel meublé* in the rue Vavin: 'The lowness of the franc makes this just possible', Ford told Jepson, 'even to persons of our exiguous means!' At first they found Paris 'rather fatiguing'. 'Ford and I were both slow people,' wrote Bowen, 'and our natural slowness had been encouraged by our bucolic existence [. . .] We were tired, jumpy and overworked, and I can remember both of us almost sobbing under the nervous strain of being buffeted along the narrow pavements of the clattering and screaming streets of the Left Bank.' But what Ford called 'the rest of my small caravan'—Lucy and Julie—'trots around to Museums, parks, parties & so on with great enthusiasm & vigour, Esther Julia [now barely 2, but already acquiring some of her father's tastes] having developed such a passion for motor cars that, if one draws up on the sidewalk near her, she bolts into it before the occupants can get out'. Pound had organized a party of people to greet them. Ford found him 'going very strong', whereas Joyce, to whom Pound now introduced him, was 'going rather weak'. Joyce recommended a doctor in Nice, and asked Ford to look for a shell cameo for him if he got to Menton. Ford's brother Oliver was also living in Paris, and was now 'enormously fat & prosperous'. The event that most impressed Ford during his first few days back in Paris was the death of Proust on 18 November. John Peale Bishop remembered being presented to Ford by Eyre De Lanux, and sitting 'on the edge of the circle about him, listening and only half hearing the low pitched talk, while he sat, the bulky form bent slightly forward, with Valery Larbaud on one side and the Duchess of Clermont-Tonnerre on the other, while they discussed at long length Henry James'. A young woman came in 'with a look on her face that already spoke catastrophe', to say: 'Proust est mort.' 'Paris was a stricken city': taxi-drivers and waiters mourned the loss to France: 'the country had a sense of the subterranean and ignored strivings of that steadfast personality.' 'Proust's death has cast an extraordinary gloom on literary parties', Ford wrote to Jepson, 'tho he was pretty generally disliked personally.' Such widespread grief for a writer was—and still is—unimaginable in England. Ford had been supposed to meet him the day he died; he and Bowen went to the funeral at the church of Saint-Pierre-de-Chaillot on the 21st instead. It was 'a tremendous affair', with 'perfect stage-management'; though Bowen panicked when Ford told her the time had come to kiss the next of kin, and 'her shyness made her bolt out of a back door [. . .]'. Ford had not yet read Proust—'for a very definite professional reason', he said, probably meaning that he felt Proust's explorations of time and consciousness might overwhelm his own. (When he did later read *À la recherche* he found in it 'all the supernatural hypnosis that his most devoted followers obtain from it'. But, he added: 'I do not think I have imitated him since. . . .') 'Nevertheless,' wrote Ford in *It Was the Nightingale*, 'it was his death that made it certain that I should again take up a serious pen.' This, he is careful to explain, does not meant that he had any 'idea of occupying Proust's place': 'even at that date I still dreaded the weakness in myself that I knew I should find if I now made my prolonged effort.' Yet, with the examples of Pound's *Cantos*, Joyce's *Ulysses*, and now Proust's great sequence, he felt it was time he made that prolonged effort. 'I think I am incapable of any thoughts of rivalry', he wrote. But he wanted to see some literary work done, 'something on an immense scale': 'I wanted the Novelist in fact to appear in his really proud position as historian of his own time. Proust being dead I could see no one who was doing that.' The gestation of *Parade's End* had begun—in elegy.[16]

He remembered another encounter in Paris that heightened the urgency of writing about the war. In front of Notre Dame he met a man called Evans from his regiment. They went into the cathedral 'and looked at the little bright tablet that commemorates the death of over a million men'. Inevitably, they began to reminisce about the war. They had met when Ford was on his way to rejoin his battalion from Corbie after his shell-blast and terrifying amnesia. Evans was in the same wagon, returning from England where he had been recovering from a wound in the thigh. 'The wagon had jolted more abominably than ever,' recalled Ford, 'and I could, in Notre Dame, remember that I had felt beside my right thigh for the brake. The beginnings of panic came over me. I had forgotten whether I found the brake!' 'The memory that had chosen to return after Corbie must be forsaking me again', worried Ford. As often with him, the prospect of reliving one of his breakdowns seemed as appalling as the breakdown itself; and, as often, his fear, and the ensuing urge to write novels, was associated with thoughts of death: 'I thought Evans had been killed the day after we had got back to the line—but he obviously hadn't.' Ostensibly Ford was anxious that he would not be able to write a convincing war novel if his grasp of factual detail was weakening. The significance of such detail was more personal, however (he could, after all, have rediscovered factual details with some research). If he could not recall the matter of his past, it was as if he were becoming the stuff to fill graveyards; as if he might be mistaken for dead. The worry he experienced as a result of this meeting was decisive for *Parade's End* in another way. It wasn't just that he panicked about his memory. For *what* he remembered was, itself, chiefly—panic and anxiety; and it became an integral part of his aim for the series to convey the sensation of this anxiety: 'it seemed to me that, if I could present, not merely fear, not merely horror, not merely death, not merely even self-sacrifice . . . but just worry; that might strike a note of which the world would not so readily tire.'[17]

While in Paris Ford signed a contract with Duckworth. He told Jepson they would take over all his work, 'future, present & past' as the copyrights reverted to him: 'This is what I have been waiting for all these years, so I am rather pleased—& you will yet see my next book in an English frock.' Mizener was characteristically quick to doubt Ford's word for it, saying that 'Duckworth's records were destroyed in the war, but if they ever agreed to such an arrangement, nothing came of it'. Nothing, that is, apart from all of Ford's next eleven books published in England over the next six years (the only ones they didn't publish being *Women & Men*, which had already been arranged, and the two slim American volumes *New Poems* and *New York Essays*). Since they had also published four of his previous books (the Popular Library of Art monographs on Rossetti, Holbein, and the Pre-Raphaelite Brotherhood, and *The Critical Attitude*) and had reissued all three volumes of his English trilogy, they were in a strong position to gather together a collected edition. In most of Ford's books they published during the 1920s (all in a uniform green binding, apart from *Mister Bosphorus* and *The Nature of a Crime*—though in three different sizes for novels, art books and discursive books), they printed a table of his other works, in which they included their earlier publications as still in print. If they didn't collect works like *The Good Soldier*, it is as likely that it was due to the unwillingness of other publishers to sell at reasonable prices rights to books they thought others might profit from, than because Duckworth hadn't indicated a willingness to reissue (John Lane, for example, brought out a second edition of *The Good Soldier* in 1928, perhaps hoping to benefit from *Parade's End*'s largely favourable publicity). Unlike most of the many publishers Ford was involved with, Duckworth neither demanded nor expected high sales of one of Ford's books before taking on the next. (Stanley Unwin was to prove another generous exception a decade later.) Soon after signing, he told Goldring that he greatly admired Ford, but that: 'the trouble is, we can't sell the old boy.'[18]

Towards the end of December Ford and Bowen joined the winter 'rush to the Riviera', sitting up all night in a second–class carriage. Harold Monro's 'quite ordinary little villa' at St-Jean-Cap-Ferrat, perched between Nice and Monte Carlo, seemed 'magical' to them when they moved in on the 20th. 'You climbed to it by a rough mule-track', said Bowen, 'or alternatively by long flights of stone steps of a giddy and exhausting steepness.' There were 'three microscopic rooms in front and two behind'; cooking had to be done on what she called 'the usual peasants' charcoal contraption'; there was a hip-bath which, wrote Bowen, 'we find invaluable for washing clothes, ourselves, & the baby'; the previous tenants had left it in a disappointing state, and a storm at the end of December did more damage. But Monro was a kind landlord, willing to pay for repairs and improvements. Water and electric lights were already laid on; and the view was spectacular: 'The front windows opened on to a great luminous sky with a Saracen fortress on the skyline opposite, and the translucent blue-green water of Villefranche harbour below.' From the villa's site, up on the saddle of the isthmus leading to St-Jean, there is an equally spectacular view in the other direction, east to Beaulieu and towards Monaco, where they took Julie to see the aquarium. Their plan to return to England in the spring did not last long. In February Bowen wrote to Monro saying that they would be staying on in France 'for a whole year more'. 'This is a comic place,' Ford told Bertram:

we have the Duke of Connaught on one side of us, & the Rothschilds next door & the Louis
Mountbattens with all the wealth of Cassell just above us & all the divorcing duchesses,
Westminsters & Marlboroughs in rows along the water's edge below; & white marble & palm
trees & Ricketts' blue sea & Monte Carlo & its vices & splendours ten minutes away & Claire
de Pratz—the lady about whom your Mr. Armson was groaning—comes in & cooks om-
elettes for us & Stella is painting pictures for all the world like the posters of the P[aris]–
L[yons]–M[éditerannée Railway] & I can't write at all.[19]

Yet there are signs of how he was preparing himself to begin again. When he asked
Edgar Jepson if he could dedicate *The Marsden Case* to him, he added a postscript that
Goldring thought expressed Ford's point of view about writing exactly (not least in its
conjunction of writing, death, and immortality). 'I have just come across this To-
Day's Great Thought in Jules Renard': '*Oui. Homme de lettres! Je le serai jusquà ma
mort. . . . Et, si par hasard, je suis éternel, je ferai, durant l'éternité, de la littérature. Et
jamais je ne me fatigue d'en faire, et toujours j'en fais, et je me f . . . du reste, comme le
vigneron qui trépigne dans ma conte "Le Vigneron".*' By 1 March he had begun *A Mirror
to France*, his tribute to his new homeland. More importantly, it was at the Villa des
Oliviers that, after a final struggle with his novelistic courage, he began his largest
fiction—his only work which rivals the greatness of *The Good Soldier*—*Parade's End*.
The omens were good. They found a golden sovereign in a secret drawer of Monro's
desk—'under St. Anthony', as Ford superstitiously noted. He associated the same
image of the saint with his ability to begin *Some Do Not . . .*: 'one day I sat down at
Munro's [*sic*] grandfather's campaign-secretaire—it had been on the field of Waterloo—I took up my pen: saluted St Anthony, who looked down on me, in sheer
gratitude for his letting me find my pen at all, and I wrote my first sentence.' They
were 'really extremely happy' at Cap Ferrat. It was only during this year that he felt
he had recovered from his shell-shock. As he told Wells: 'I've got over the nerve tangle
of the war and feel able at last really to write again—which I never thought I should
do.'[20]

1923: THUS TO RE-VIEW

In March 1923 Bowen spent a fortnight in Italy. Dorothy Pound had written from
Florence to ask if she would like to join her in a tour of Assisi, Genoa, Perugia,
Cortona, Arezzo, and Siena, while Ezra went to Rimini 'to acquire a further store of
that erudition which he was in the habit of extracting from old documents' (he was
researching Sigismundo Malatesta for the *Cantos*). They had decided it was about time
she 'saw some real pictures'. She joined the Pounds in Florence, leaving Ford and Julie
for the first time. She missed them 'horribly', but her 'taste of freedom' revived all her
'old excitement about painting'. She found Catholicism disturbing, however, writing
to Ford: 'Your darn'd religion is a queer thing', and recounting her distaste for the
'peep-show' of the effigy of St Clara at Assisi, which made her feel that the church was
'a wicked, wicked place'. Ford replied firmly that after all St Clara 'founded the Poor
Clares & was the friend of St. Francis—about the two best people the world has
produced!', but adding that he understood her criticism: 'I feel just as *frightened* when
I go into a Protestant place of worship!' He also countered with some of his own
superstition, dating his letters impressionistically by saints' days (some arcane or
fictitious: Doctrorius, Euphrasius, Cyriax), or telling her: 'And it's curious: I gave
10 frs. to a Franciscan monk the other day. He came here begging. . . . & while I was
still talking to him the telegraph boy came to say Cooper's was let. Naturally, when
giving the 10 frs. it crossed my mind to hope that St. F. might straighten out our
financial affairs.' Now they could afford to stay in France for the rest of the year. He
also described some strange encounters. He had begun writing a four-act play (now
lost), probably about Madame Récamier. (Her story would have appealed to Ford for
its passion and renunciation. She was a great beauty and literary hostess, a friend of
Mme de Staël and Chateaubriand, and worshipped by Benjamin Constant. When
Prince August of Prussia wanted to marry her, her elderly husband, a ruined banker,
agreed to a divorce, but ultimately she could not desert him.) But instead of sitting
down to work at it after getting the telegram, he sat on the Beaulieu parade talking to
a general and an invalid lady playwright in a tricycle who gave him practical advice
about how to write plays. '*Isn't* the world full of queer people', he asked Bowen: '&
don't I seem to run against them?': 'I had a long conversation in the tram yesterday
with an old maid who had just come back from Florence & talked about pictures, &
when I said that I thought Giotto was more decorative than Holbein she . . . quoted
my own "Holbein" against me, without knowing my name . . . But I think she had a
shrewd suspicion that I was . . . Maurice Hewlett.' Looking after Julie had its perils:
'Baby is as well as can be & more mischievous than ever', Ford wrote. 'She got my
specaticles [*sic*] yesterday & bent the ear pieces into S's; however I have straightened

them out again. She is making progress with her reading & can—most times—identify the round O & the curly S & the elegant L. Perhaps she will be writing short stories by your return! I shall take her to see the ships this aftn.' One of his other daughters, Katharine, now a veterinary student in Dublin, wrote him a letter that March which both sought intimacy and recrimination, pointing out that he hadn't seen her since 1916, and begging him to write and tell her what he thought of her news, 'even if it is only to make me feel less than the dust, as usual—Because, that is better than complete indifference!' The tone is understandable from a neglected child; none the less, Ford told Stella he was 'a little rattled' by it. He also had some sharp observations on Wells's *The Outline of History* (1920):

I think it wickeder than I did: but it's an amazing piece of book-making. When he gets past classical & medieval times he's quite sound from a Left point of view till he gets to Napoleon! But *how* jealous he is of all great men from Pericles & J. Caesar to everyone else. You see him saying: 'No! I couldn't do what Alexander did! So I'll do for *his* reputation!' And the joke of it is that he damns every one of them—Solomon, Mahomet, Alexander, Julius Caesar & the rest for being untrustworthy with women! I've never seen Satan so splendidly reprove sin.[1]

When she got back to Cap Ferrat Bowen 'proceeded to wrestle with three or four small portraits', which were accepted for the Salon d'Automne in Paris that year. Late in April they decided to move to Tarascon, the city that Ford said he had 'always loved best in the world'; he wanted to show Bowen 'the real Provence of the Rhône valley'; they would 'drift through Provence northwards to Paris' with Julie and Lucy. Julie was 'growing like a giraffe', but learning 'no French at all'. They were well-treated at the Hotel Terminus, and would pass the time of day in the Café de Paris with the local *notaire* (solicitor) and Anglophile *avocat* (barrister). With the *avocat* Ford would 'discuss at length the proper use of the subjunctive, in elaborate French prose. Ford really knew French perfectly but he spoke it badly because he never moved his lips enough'. When the *notaire* got tickets, Ford took Bowen to Nîmes to see her first bullfight (she found the ceremony and spectacle turned brutality to unreality). Bowen spent a fortnight in Paris having painting lessons, while Ford stayed in Tarascon to finish his play. He 'wrote in a great dim old room with alcoves in a great dim old hotel [. . .] the jalousies tight-closed against the sun and the nightingales singing like furies'. It was an inexpensive way of life then, and it suited his writing: he finished the play and worked on *Some Do Not* . . . 'Besides, the French make much of me', he told Jepson, 'which at my age is inspiriting.' Bowen said the people at Cap Ferrat respected him too. She saw the Pounds in Paris; she proved less robust than Ford in the face of Pound's criticism, and Ford had to write to console her in a letter alive with analogies between the arts, and analyses of modernist modes:

Darling;

Your poor distressed letter has so distressed me that I am cutting my walk to write to you about things. I know you think I'm an old duffer & that, what applies to me & my art don't to you and yours: but they do.

Let us begin with Ezra. His *criticisms* of yourself you simply should not have listened to: they arise solely from a frantic loyalty to W.[yndham] Lewis—and no doubt to Dorothy. He is in fact singularly unintelligent on the *aesthetic* side of any art—at any rate in conversation.

It is only historically that he is sound about anything.—Of course if it doesn't depress you too much it's a good thing to listen to gramophonic records of Lewis's dicta (in wh. Lewis himself doesn't for a moment believe): but if you do get depressed by it, just don't listen.

And, as I have said to you over & over again: the prevalence of one type or other of Art— *any* Art—is merely a matter of cycles: or even of strata of society.—And again: there are certain axioms, one of which is that good drawing will always cause emotions to arise; so will good colour, good pattern. And goodness means observation rendered—in each case. (If you consider that even Ingres holds his own in Cubist circles you will understand what I mean!)

As for not going to the Old Fellows—you *must* go to them!—to the same ones, like Holbein & Cranach & Simone Martini. Even Lewis went to them all right ten years ago—but he won't say so [. . .]

Darling: I assure you that you have all the makings of an artist; the only thing you need being a certain self-confidence. If you attain to that you would see that, even in your work as it is, there is the quality of serenity—of imperturbability [. . .]

And there is another thing. You must remember that the Present School is largely a reaction against the Instantaneous photograph. It doesn't say so—but it is hypnotised & afraid of that phenomenon. (A Literary Artist might be afraid of the Daily Paper as a form!) And this leads the Dorotheans into a desire to be hyper human—to the point of producing work that is not a rendering but a comment on the inspected object. And that is a foredoomed fallacy! So don't pay *too* much attention to them . . .[2]

Bowen's morale improved after getting Ford's reassurance. Perhaps suspecting that Dorothy Pound's attack on representational art (like Bowen's portraits) was also the familiar Poundian assault on his own impressionism, carried on by other means, he wrote again to Bowen defining and defending the Fords against the Pounds, and arming her with counter-arguments:

nonrepresentational Art is the same thing as—or analogous to—'comment' in Literature. 'Rendering' is what one wants—unless the comment is per se valuable because rendering is so much more universal as a communication.

Ezra thinking of Shakespeare may see this

Or I thinking of Shakespeare may see this

= a smile. But as an *artistic* comment it has no more value than if Ezra should say: 'When I think of Shakespeare I see a kaleidoscope,' or than if I shd. say that in the same circumstances I see a smile.

I don't say that these comments have *no* value: but it is a value rather literary than aesthetic. If, that is to say aesthetic value consists in the causing of emotions. . . . whereas Holbein's portrait of Xtina of Milan or the Kranachs really make you feel at least all—& a great deal more—of the emotions one ought to feel on meeting X. of M. or the Markgraf of Hesse . . . And that is your line—at any rate for the moment—& y^r business is to continue, monastically, like the late F. Angelico! on y^r own way. God may then vouchsafe you a vision: or He may be content with what you do!

When he finished the play, and sent it to Bowen for her comments on the last act, he borrowed a bicycle from the proprietor of the Hôtel Terminus to 'bike' to Les Baux on 10 May by way of celebration. But he didn't make the ten or so miles, he explained to her, because: 'M. Goudre's bicycle caused me too much agony in an intimate portion of my anatomy. But I lounged about St. Remy in deep conversation with a bullfighter whom I picked up at that café in front of the church & learned all sorts of things about the Mañadas & capia. It was most thrilling, really, for the man was quite as contented & austere & as against modernisms as any artiste peintre could be.'[3]

Bowen was back in Tarascon for the second half of May, when the heat 'mounted higher and higher'. Ford wrote that though the nightingales had not disturbed his 'tranquil penmanship', 'twelve steam organs under my Tarascon window did drive me away at last'. The provincial fair from Beaucaire had moved across the Rhône bridge and settled by their hotel: 'the shouts and howls and mechanical music which screamed under our windows until late into the night were death to the functioning of the creative mind.' The *avoué* recommended they should move to St Agrève in the Ardèche, a little market town Ford didn't know, but which seemed to be 'on the highest point of the plateau of the Massif Central'. Bowen had sent on their winter clothes and heavy luggage separately; when their mountain train reached St Agrève in June they froze in the windswept and wintry grim town—a 'cold-climate architecture', said Bowen. 'For three weeks (it took that time for our big trunk to arrive) we shivered as I have never shivered before or since', she wrote. 'After being grilled—not to mention dusted and torn to pieces by the mistral—in the plains, we are now being cold-stored in the mountains', Ford told Jepson. He came down with severe bronchitis. Summer materialized at the same time as the trunk. Ford was struck by the rapidity of the seasons: 'Immediately the fields are covered with grass of an amazing emerald green and enamelled with blazing flowers of primary hues, so that the grass disappears.' He said he heard the voice of Hilaire Belloc, checking into the same Hôtel Poste one evening; and the next day he saw him 'at the other end of the market talking to a farmer and punching a fat bullock as if he had been a grazier all his life'. But before Ford had a chance to 'get round to him' he had left the town, and Ford was amazed that in his 'not more than ten hours, some of which must have been devoted to sleep', he managed to collect material for a newspaper article about the town: 'How did he do it?', Ford wondered, while he was struggling to dredge up from his memory his own observations about the war. 'I can't consider "subjects" quickly & write about 'em', he explained to Bertram, 'because I am in the middle of "subjects" of my own wh. exhaust all the small brain I've got'. Though the accommodation at the hotel was spartan, the food was excellent, and 'by moving into an annexe, Ford was able to have a place for writing'. Bowen painted outdoors, 'and between-whiles was being further educated by Ford on the subject of the Albigenses and the bitter religious wars that had once shaken the part of the country we were in'. They were joined by Phyllis and Harry Birnstingl, with whom they visited Le Puy, and the source of the Loire. They had decided by this time not to return to England, even though Monro, whose *Chapbook* had failed unexpectedly, had found someone to rent the villa for six months—an offer they couldn't meet. Bowen explained to Monro: 'I think we have really decided not to undertake house-keeping worries & expenses next winter. We find the French inns in unfashionable parts very pleasant and inexpensive.' When September came, and it began to grow cold again, they returned to Paris. It was there that Ford symbolically placed his decision not to return (though he impressionistically dated it as 'perhaps in August, 1923'). He was sitting outside 'the old Lavenue's, which used to be one of the best restaurants in Paris', reading an English newspaper while waiting for James Joyce. (Ford and Nina Hamnett decided to hold fortnightly gatherings there for expatriate artists.) When he read that the British government 'had abolished the post of Historical Adviser to the Foreign Office', he said, it was then that he decided: 'Perhaps I had better never go back to England!' Bowen tells a different (though not incompatible) version. One Sunday evening that autumn, 'with the level sun shining through the plane trees and under the awnings of the great cafés and with the crowds milling around more than usually *en fête* [. . .] Ford and I suddenly turned to each other and said together, "Do you want to go back to Bedham!" I don't know who spoke first. Then we said, "don't lets." It was decided just as easily as that!'[4]

Hardly had they got back to Paris when they met 'another large, pink-faced blue-eyed gentleman' on an island on the Boulevard St Michel. Ford asked Bowen 'do you know who this is?', and she guessed that it had to be brother Oliver, who was now living with the novelist Muriel Harris. The brothers hadn't met 'for many years'—there's no record of a meeting since Ford's double-take in London during the war ('one should not cut one's brother! It isn't *done*'). Yet, as he had in the past, Oliver once again drew Ford into his life warmly; and this latest manifestation was to be even more significant. 'We went home with him to his cottage', said Bowen:

which was behind a group of shabby old studios—*style rustique* in the Boulevard Arago, and met his delightful wife, a keen-faced writer with a twinkling smile and thick, wavy white hair. She was just off to America and said we could have their *rez-de-chauss[é]e* for two hundred francs a month. This was a godsend. Nothing could have been cheaper, and since Lucy was homesick and had to be sent back to England, it seemed possible to economise on domestic help as well.[5]

The cottage, in the artists' colony known as the *Cité Fleurie* at 65, Boulevard Arago, just next to the Santé prison, was extremely picturesque, and had the associations Ford relished: Rodin, Gaugin, and Modigliani were among the artists who had used the nearby studios. But it was damp (being built straight on the earth without foundations), and had no gas or electricity, only the usual charcoal cooker. 'But in those warm early autumn days', wrote Bowen, 'when we first began to feel the exhilaration of being in Paris, it was fun to lead people down [the] yellowing greenery of the little winding path behind the studios and give them tea in the tiny room with the shabby divan and the big French windows, and the sun pouring through the hanging sprays of creeper.' Ford tried to persuade his mother to come and live with them, explaining that though he had 'certainly not made more than—if as much as—£150 a year since the war', with this and Stella's income they could all live in reasonable comfort in France. Ford found it 'distressing' that she didn't come, thinking that her excuses about the journey and having to let her flat simply meant that she didn't want to. He told her: 'there ought to be greater understanding between us.' Working on *Some Do Not . . .* he could say: 'I have only quite lately got back the faculty of being able to write at all well or regularly.' Pound thought his renewed sense of his powers justified when Ford read to him from the manuscript: 'best he has done since *Good Soldier*, or *A Call*', Pound told his father. When Douglas Goldring passed through Pairs he too was 'lured' back for a reading. Ford, he said, made him lie on a couch—the only other furniture in the room besides a desk and chair—and began a rather adenoidal reading, punctuated by 'strange noises' which Goldring attributed to wartime gassing:

Various efforts were made by Ford's entourage to find an onomatopoeic word to describe these curious sounds. The best suggestions were 'whoof' and 'honk', though neither of these was quite satisfactory. Ford started off like this. 'The two young men—they were of the English public official class (honk)—sat in the perfectly appointed railway carriage (whoof). The leather straps to the windows were of a virgin newness (whoof); the mirrors beneath the new luggage racks immaculate as if they had reflected very little; the bulging upholstery in its luxuriant (honk), regulated curves was scarlet and yellow in an intricate, minute dragon pattern, the design (whoof) of a geometrician in Cologne.'

Goldring passed out during the reading—several Pernods before lunch had done little to relieve a hangover—but fortunately woke before Ford reached the end of the chapter. 'If he had noticed my inattention, he was not in the least offended.' Goldring was acting as London agent for the New York publisher Thomas Seltzer. He offered to put Ford in touch with Seltzer, and before he left Ford gave him a memorandum proposing terms for *The Marsden Case*, *Mister Bosphorus*, and *Some Do Not . . .*— merely £100 advance for all three, plus 10 per-cent royalties ('or otherwise as arranged'); and the hope that Seltzer would take all his future books, and collect together a uniform edition of these and his previous books as the copyrights reverted to him, paying as an advance on receipt of the manuscript the 'amount actually earned to date by preceding works of same class (Novels, poems in vol. form and "serious" books, essays, etc., each constituting separate class), such payments to be on account of royalty of 10 per cent. or otherwise as arranged.' Seltzer published *Some Do Not . . .* before he went bankrupt.[6]

Ford began to frequent the Dôme and the Deux Magots with Pound, and to meet new artists. So that not only Joyce, but soon also Hemingway, and two English painters called Cedric Morris and Lett Haines, 'who, in beautiful B.B.C. voices, were pleased to regale us with tales of their more lurid adventures', were brought back through the walled garden for tea. Ford's own account of his meeting with Oliver is slightly different, and brings out the event that was of most significance to him that autumn, the founding of his new magazine, the *transatlantic review*:

. . . In 1923, then, my brother stood beside me on a refuge half-way across the Boulevard St. Michel and told me that some Paris friends of his wanted me to edit a review for them. The startling nature of that coincidence with the actual train of my thoughts at the moment made me accept the idea even whilst we stood in the middle of the street. He mentioned names which were dazzling in the Paris of that day and sums the disposal of which would have made the durability of any journal absolutely certain. So we parted with the matter more than half settled, he going to the eastern pavement, I to the west.

Ten minutes after, I emerged from the rue de la Grande Chaumière on to the Boulevard Montparnasse. Ezra, with his balancing step, approached me as if he had been awaiting my approach.—He can't have been.—He said:

'I've got a wonderful contribution for your new review,' and he led me to M. Fernand Léger, who, wearing an old-fashioned cricketer's cap like that of Maître Montagnier [the *avocat*] of Tarascon, was sitting on a bench ten yards away. M. Léger produced an immense manuscript, left it in my hands and walked away. . . . Without a word.[7]

In the same hallucinatory logic of comic mild paranoia, Pound provides Ford with a hysterically anti-communist White Russian exiled colonel for a sub-editor (within five minutes he was convinced that Ford was a Soviet agent), and, as private secretary, 'also a beautiful specimen of his type', there was 'an English Conscientious Objector, an apparently mild, bespectacled student. He too was starving.' This was Basil Bunting. By the time Ford got home that evening, manuscripts had begun to arrive, as had 'a very vocal lady from Chicago and an elegant, but bewildered husband', potential subscribers if only Ford would make the magazine a vehicle 'of course, for virtue, but also for some form of dogma connected, I think, with psychiatry'. 'So there I was', he said, 'with all the machinery of a magazine—sub-editor, secretary, contributions, printers, subscribers [. . .] It was as if I had been in one of those immense deserts inhabited by savages who have unknown methods of communication over untold distances.' Pound had been fired from his well-paid job with the *Dial*, and had no outlets for work in America. The new monthly review was to be truly international, distributed in France, America, and England: an exile's magazine. In his vivid account of the intrigues leading up to its launch in January 1924, Ford says that the original plan was for him to edit a magazine that a wealthy racehorse-owner (whom Ford calls 'Mr. X——', joking about the 'Société Anonyme' that legally owned the review) had taken over 'as against advertising debts'. Another businessman ('Mr. Q——') had been lent a copy of one of Ford's novels on a boat in Egypt (Ford calls it 'The only permanently popular novel I ever wrote', thus *Ladies Whose Bright Eyes*). 'Mr. Q—— had never read a novel before or since. But he said that that was the happiest evening of his whole life. He couldn't get over it.' So he recommended to the racehorse-owner that Ford should be hired as editor. Ford went, together with Oliver, Pound, the White Russian, 'and others', to meet the owner's representative, a 'city man' ('Mr. P——') who, Ford thought, owned a firm of solicitors, and plan the company to be formed to take over the existing magazine. The company was to relieve Ford 'absolutely of all business and financial responsibilities'; and certainly Ford, who was gifted at turning the wish into the achieved reality, or turning a publishers' talk into contracts, was soon telling his friends that this had been arranged, though it is doubtful that Ford and his collaborators mastered enough of the intricacies of French company law ever to get the company incorporated and registered. Ford says the lawyer and the owner mistrusted the group of eccentrics in their offices, suspecting them of being anarchists or communists. Bowen thought that Ford was misled about what the backers were offering. His prospectus for the magazine probably didn't help—and can't have done anything to pacify the White Russian either: 'The politics will be those of its editor who has no party leanings save toward those of a Tory kind so fantastically old fashioned as to see no salvation save in the feudal system as practised in the fourteenth century—or in such Communism as may prevail a thousand years hence.' The owner then insisted that he should censor the magazine himself. Joyce said the backers offered Ford the editorship on condition that he didn't publish anything of Joyce; that Ford

declined, and that then the backers gave in. The owner also stipulated that the
magazine should contain articles each month by himself on racing form, and by the city
man on finance. This interference was intolerable; but then John Quinn stepped in.[8]

Quinn was a wealthy lawyer, patron of the arts, picture-collector, and supporter
of—amongst others—Conrad and Joyce. He had defended *Ulysses* in court, and
financed the *Little Review*. But he had rowed with Joyce over manuscripts, so at first
he too had refused to back the *transatlantic review* unless Joyce was excluded. Ford
stood up for his fellow writer, however, even reserving the first page of the January
1924 issue for him. (In return, Joyce inscribed him a copy of the second edition of
Exiles.) Ford and Joyce enjoyed each other's company. Pound had arranged a reception at his studio for Quinn on 12 October 1923. Jeanne Foster was there, 'the
ravishingly beautiful lady who bought Mr. Quinn's pictures for him', who managed
the American side of the review, and with whom Ford kept up an intimate platonic
correspondence in which he would sometimes sign himself 'Ford Ford'. Bill Bird, who
would be the printer, and Joyce were also there. Joyce told Ford the story of his
encounter with Proust (at which both denied having read the other's work, and they
ended comparing notes on their maladies). Ford said he was trying to avoid Quinn,
who had annoyed him by pretending to mistake him for George Moore. Ford got stuck
in one of the chairs Pound had made ('It was enormous, compounded of balks of white
pine, and had a slung canvas seat so large that, once you sat down, there you lay until
someone pulled you out'); Mrs Foster pulled him out. Just as business relations were
being severed with the original backers of the review, and Ford feared that they were
trying to get Frank Harris to take his place as editor, Quinn sent Mrs Foster to
extricate Ford again. Ford was summoned to the hotel where Quinn was confined—
he was terminally ill with cancer—and Quinn (perhaps at Pound's instigation) proposed to finance a completely new review for him.[9]

Ford told Wells how they hoped to buy a small house in Paris with the money from
the sale of their Sussex cottage, 'and one almost smaller in Provence. It is egotistic to
write in this strain but after many years of great anxiety and strain things have rather
suddenly gone all right together.' But he was apprehensive. Would Quinn want to
interfere with the editing? What worried him most was 'the thought of having to
manage the business affairs of the *Review*', a job that would have been Oliver's under
the previous scheme: 'I am a very good business man when it comes to other people's
affairs. I know the ins and outs of printing, publishing, and business-editing a review
as few others do. But when it comes to managing my own affairs, I am worse than
hopeless. I do not manage them at all, and if they have any chance of becoming
complicated at all they become incredibly complicated.' Ford was well aware of his
own unbusinesslike way with money. He liked to imagine he was capable of being a
'very good businessman' (and would imagine it in his later novels). There was as much
truth as self-parody in what he told Gertrude Stein about his multiple roles in Paris:
'I am a pretty good writer and a pretty good editor and a pretty good business man but
I find it very difficult to be all three at once.' What also worried him—and worried
Bowen more—was that now he *would* have financial responsibility for the project.
Quinn offered to put up a sum of 35,000 or 40,000 francs if Ford could match it: half
($1,000) in the autumn of 1923, and up to the same amount (but no more) later if

needed. Bowen had been house-hunting in the suburbs frantically, trying to find a little *pavillon* with a garden; but, she wrote, 'Ford was becoming more and more absorbed in his scheme and I could not help seeing how lovely it would be for him if he could have his review'. Expectations of the new magazine were too high in the Latin Quarter for Ford to have backed out now with impunity even if he had wanted to. They put in over £400 at first, and when the original capital ran out in May 1924, Bowen subsidized the review with some of her own money. 'We never had any arguments or difficulties about money at all', she wrote: 'When necessary, I withdrew small slices of my capital from Australia, and considered that I was investing it in a promising career.' The review ran gloriously for a year, costing them in the end probably around 120,000 francs (about $7,000, or about £1,500); 'and I never got my house', said Bowen. She 'joined that sad army of Paris wives who spent their days following up vague clues of flats to let'.[10]

At first it was to be called the 'Paris Review'. The name was changed when Ford broke with the original backers; the new title helped to secure advertising from the 'Compagnie Transatlantique' shipping line. Ford used a version of the Paris city seal as a logo: a small ship on a rough sea. 'The motto, *Fluctuat*, was for good luck: any Parisian could supply the next two words, *nec mergitur*.' The new title was printed on the letterhead and the prospectus as *The Transatlantic Review*, with capitals; but when Ford and Bird were redesigning the cover they found that they could get 'the distinguishing word TRANSATLANTIC' to fit the page exactly only if they printed it all in lower case. Ford liked the idea: he had seen a shop-front in Paris using an uncapitalized name, and it reminded him of e. e. cummings's typographical modernity. The magazine became *the transatlantic review*.[11]

Ford wrote to all the writers he admired asking for contributions. He told Coppard:

It isn't an exaggeration to say that I've started this review with you in mind as I started the *English Review* to publish stuff of Hardy's that other periodicals wouldn't publish. I've a great admiration for your work & though I hope you can serialise all you write I imagine, this sad world being what it is, that you may have some that you can't.

I may say that I *prefer* not to have sexually esoteric, psychoanalytic, mystic or officially ethical matter but don't bar any of them obstinately—& if you hadn't short stories available I'd be glad of 'essays' or any other form.

He wrote to T. S. Eliot, with whom he had been having a courteous correspondence since February 1923, when Ford had praised *The Waste Land*. 'There are *I* think about 30 *good* lines' in it, Eliot wrote to him, adding felinely: 'Can you find them?' (Ford evidently couldn't: 'As for the lines I mention, you need not scratch your head over them', wrote Eliot: 'They are the 29 lines of the water-dripping song in the last part'; thanking Ford for his 'flattering remarks', Eliot said: 'It is a great deal to find that there is one person, and that person yourself, who regards the poem as having any pretensions to coherence and unity at all.') Eliot said he would be delighted to write an open letter for Ford's magazine, though he wanted to know more of its editorial policy first. Ford asked Jepson if he could add his name to the list of contributors: 'If you'd send me something rude about literary London I'd love it.' Flint, Wells, Bertram, and Goldring were all asked to contribute. Pound was also busy soliciting material. He told

Wyndham Lewis: 'Policy of the review certainly favorable to yr activities; though I have heard you express unfavorable opinion of the editor', and assured him that his stories would be welcome. 'Stories of course the hardest thing to get; as Ford does NOT intend to dally with the Lawrence, Murry, Mansfield contingent.' Lewis was sardonically unimpressed, writing to Eliot: 'Letter from Pound saying Hueffer and he starting paper. No answer of course to that. So natural.'[12]

Ford also thought of Conrad once again, still hoping to salvage their wrecked friendship. When he had been asked to write something on Conrad in 1921 he was reluctant, saying he felt he had 'written enough about Conrad in the course of a toilsome life': 'and to tell the truth his later work appeals to me so relatively little that I don't want to write any more about it. I mean, it's difficult to do so without appearing, and for all I know, being, ungenerous'. Yet he did write a brief piece. And somehow during the autumn of 1923 he found time to review the nineteen-volume uniform edition of Conrad that Dent had just brought out. He called Conrad 'the greatest English poet of to-day because, more than any other writer, he has per-ceived—he has gradually evolved the knowledge—that poetry consists in the exact rendering of the concrete and material happenings in the lives of men'. That was the knowledge Ford had been gradually evolving—and which he was bringing to bear magnificently in the exact renderings of *Some Do Not . . .*; so he evidently still thought, or hoped, that they were working, if not living, in sympathy. He wrote to ask Conrad to contribute, and got an apparently warm reply saying how pleased he was that Ford had 'got hold of such interesting work, in conditions which will permit you to concentrate your mind on it in peace and comfort'. He sent his 'warmest wishes for its success', adding—with perhaps ironic negativity: 'I won't tell you that I am "honoured" or "flattered" by having my name included amongst your contributors, but I will tell you that I consider it a very friendly thing on your part to wish to do so.'

The early E.[nglish] R.[eview] is the only one I ever cared for. The mere fact that it was the occasion of you putting on me that gentle but persistent pressure which extracted, from the depths of my then despondency, the stuff of the Personal Record, would be enough to make its memory dear. My only grievance against the early E.R. is that it didn't last long enough. If I say that I am curious to see what you will make of this venture it isn't because I have the slightest doubts of your consistency. You have a perfect right to say that you are 'rather unchangeable'. Unlike the Serpent (which is Wise) you will die in your original skin. So I have no doubt that the Review will be thoroughly Fordian—at all costs! But it will be interesting to see what men you will find and what you will get out of them in these changed times.[13]

Ford wrote to ask if he could print that paragraph. Conrad's approval still meant much to him; and a published testimony to their friendship meant more. He probably could not, or would not, hear the double-edgedness in Conrad's insinuations that Ford's original sin was (in Conrad's eyes) his consistent inconsistency, whereby his personal-ity (which Conrad had become unchangeably convinced was a paranoiac and monoma-niacal one) would impose itself on its associations 'at all costs'. Or perhaps he did. He wasn't afraid in *Return to Yesterday* to discuss Conrad's 'abuse' of him (alluding to the letter to Garnett in which Conrad 'describes how I sat at the desk writing and reading out what I wrote whilst behind my back he stormed and raved and declared that every word I produced was the imagination of a *crétin*'). 'But', he said, 'in spite of these rubs of the game—and what a game for rubs it was!—our friendship remained unbroken and only interrupted by the exigencies of time, space, and public events.' This sounds deluded or deluding—or at least misleading: the animosities over the *English Review* and Ford's private life were to some extent 'public events', but Ford wants us to think instead of the war. Yet—entirely characteristically—his next sentence is completely candid about the impressionism of the claim: 'It is in the end better if the public will believe that version—for nearly ideal literary friendships are rare, and the literary world is ennobled by them.' If he wasn't quite able to believe himself that their friendship remained unbroken, he still felt it was a nearly ideal one, and that it had ennobled his life. Certainly his reply to Conrad is movingly free of two-facedness, while it recognizes the emotional distance between them:

I am much touched by your letter: for it makes a difference to me to know that we are working—at however great a distance—somewhat in sympathy. You are the only man I ever met with whose literary ideas I ever felt absolutely in accord: indeed I'd go as far to [sic] say that you are the only man I ever met who completely understood what literature was & what are the problems of the writer.

I write a little awkwardly because I want to come to business. i. Would you permit me to print the four or five lines from y^r letter wh. I have typed out? That w^d be a great favour. ii. Could you possibly write for me about 5,000 words—of Personal Record? [. . .]

I know what a beastly thing it is to ask—I know it fully. But if you took the line of least resistance & just wrote down—even in the form of a letter to me—a personal note as to how the original Personal Record came into being it would be all that I should ask. I am writing in great haste—I am always in great haste now—so pardon any *grossièretés* in the expression, please.

Yours always
FMF.[14]

Conrad expanded the original paragraph into a miniature reminiscence, recalling how Ford sought him out in his study at 2 a.m. to make him 'concentrate suddenly on a two-page notice of the "Ile des Pinguins [*sic*]"'. He called it 'A marvellously successful instance of editorial tyranny! I suppose you were justified', perhaps feeling that Ford's editorial pressure was tyrannically arm-twisting rather than secretarially gentle. But he wouldn't do any more, adding a note: 'I am afraid the source of the Personal Record fount is dried up. No longer the same man.' He had the grace to thank Ford for wanting his work; but was evidently irritated that Ford was still taking him for the same man—and the same writer—as twenty years ago: 'I'd like to do something for the sake of old times—but I daresay I am not worth having now.'

Ford wrote to Hardy too, hoping that a contribution from him would be another memorial to the *English Review*. His letter recalled the memory of Marwood coming over to say that a magazine had refused to print Hardy's 'A Sunday Morning Tragedy', and exclaiming: 'We must start a Review to print it in!' The letter was also a memorial to Marwood, and to his own past: 'that moment', said Ford, adding perhaps teasingly that '—it was a Sunday morning—is one of the moments of my life that I look back to with great satisfaction—there being so few.' But Hardy, like Eliot and Conrad, preferred to write a letter of support than offer a new work. 'I have received

your interesting letter,' he replied, 'and quite admire your purposed attempt to start
the publication you describe, which, as you imply, seems rather a venturesome step.'
But he said: 'There is really nothing I can find at present which would suit', and asked:
'Don't you think you should invite young men more particularly, and keep out old
men like me?' But Ford's ideal for the review was that it should represent what he
called 'the Republic of Letters', in which distinctions of age, or nationality, or literary
faction, should not bar communication; in which all that mattered was good writing.
The prospectus said that the review had two purposes: 'the major one, the purely
literary, conducing to the minor, the disinterestedly social':

The first is that of widening the field in which the younger writers of the day can find
publication, the second that of introducing into international politics a note more genial than
that which almost universally prevails. The first conduces to the second in that the best
ambassadors, the only non-secret diplomatists between nations are the books and the arts of
nations. There is no British Literature, there is no American Literature: there is English
Literature which embraces alike Mark Twain and Mr. Thomas Hardy with the figure of Mr.
Henry James to bracket them. The aim of the *Review* is to help in bringing about a state of
things in which it will be considered that there are no English, no French—for the matter of
that, no Russian, Italian, Asiatic or Teutonic—Literatures: there will be only Literature, as
today there are Music and the Plastic Arts each having Schools Russian, Persian, 16th
Century German, as the case may be. When that day arrives we shall have a league of nations
no diplomatists shall destroy, for into its comity no representatives of commercial interests
or delimitators of frontiers can break. Not even Armageddon could destroy the spell of
Grimm for Anglo-Saxondom or of Flaubert and Shakespear [*sic*] for the Central Empires.[15]

T. S. Eliot's fiercely ambivalent letter warned against the dangers of a sentimental
internationalism: 'The present age, a singularly stupid one, is the age of a mistaken
nationalism and of an equally mistaken and artificial internationalism.' He advised
Ford: 'Let us not have an indiscriminate mongrel mixture of socialist internationals, or
of capitalist cosmopolitans, but a harmony of different functions.'[16] The review managed to achieve this, printing English, American, and French literature in its own
languages. And Ford achieved its true internationalism without the eugenicist stri-
dency that creeps into Eliot's tone. The title-page of the prospectus listed Wells, Eliot,
Conrad, Hardy, Pound, Ford, Coppard, and Joyce. Also included were cummings,
Luke Ionides (an 80-year-old, friend of W. M. Rossetti: Pound as well as Ford
admired his reminiscences), 'D. Chaucer' (Ford's old pseudonym, used for his 'Stocktaking' series in the review), Jeanne Foster, Mary Butts, and Robert McAlmon. The
French contributors were listed as R.[ené] Descharmes, Philippe Soupault, Jean
Cassou, and V.[alery] Larbaud. Seltzer published the magazine in America;
Duckworths in England.

When Lincoln Steffens—known for his journalistic exposés of capitalist corruption—got back from Russia and had tea with Pound, he met Ford ('the English master
of prose') who took him home and enthused about the review. 'His idea is to use the
thing as a playground for the younger writers now working in silence and the dark. I
know some of them. He thinks an English magazine in Paris will be free and may be
fine.' A younger American writer, Carlos Drake, had befriended Oliver and Muriel,
and knocked on the door without realizing that they had left. Ford answered:

'Come in! Come in! Sit down!' he insisted. 'Tell me about yourself. Are you a painter or writer?'

'I'm trying to be a writer,' I said.

'Then stop trying. Just be one. What've you done?'

'Oh, a few stories . . . not very good ones, I'm afraid, sir.'

'Don't call me sir! That's a ghastly American habit. And don't say your things aren't any good. Let me decide that. Maybe I can use one or two. I'm starting a magazine.'[17]

Ford had also managed to get an American contract that autumn, presumably from Seltzer. 'For once in a way we're flourishing', he told Jepson: 'I have fixed up a contract in U.S.A. for all my work as in England—and though I shan't make a penny out of this thing [the review] & work myself to death on top of it—it pleases me.' He got a grim enjoyment out of that prospect of the magazine killing him. As he told Eliot when he sent him the prospectus: 'It will give you an idea of the aims of this infernal enterprise which, since it appears three times as often as The Criterion will kill me three times as fast as The Criterion kills you.' He had also, thanks to Pound, acquired an admirable secretary for the *transatlantic*, Marjorie Reid, who Bowen said became the 'backbone of the concern'. She makes her first appearance in a letter to Goldring, also remarkable in demonstrating Ford's tact in talking to writers whose work he didn't unqualifiedly admire:

My dear Goldring,

I have been a brute to you though I did manage, I believe, to find time to thank you for your services over the Seltzer affair.

But I have never thanked you for your books though I have really read both of them with interest. I don't like them, but you wouldn't have expected me to so that doesn't matter. The *roman à thèse* is a thing I have always detested. But, quite obviously, you have a way with you of putting things that, should you find the right subject ought to let you do something. Perhaps that will turn up in what you are sending me. Then we will all go to the Café de la Paix and drink the wine of the country together, for no one will be pleaseder than I am.

Alas, *The Transatlantic Review* will be the old *English Review* all over again [. . .] the editorial offices are much the same ramshackle sort of place that Holland Park Avenue used to be and, although I can't go to the Shepherd's Bush Empire—you infernal scoundrel—I do still as I used to do, do most of my editing in between violent games of tennis, as we've got a court just next door.

I never read your *Reputations* though we actually had it in the house ever since it was published. But I never read a word that is said about me. However the other day, an American lady—for sure, no English lady could have done it and lived—pinned me firmly into a corner and read to me your reminiscences of the old *English Review* days. It was a dastardly proceeding but, as the lady in question is now occupying the position that you used to occupy and typing this letter, I won't say any more about that. However, they are, your reminiscences, very kind and generous, and I am much obliged to you. Mrs. Ford sends her regards and we hope you will soon be over here again.

Yrs always

F.M.F.[18]

When Harriet Monroe, the editor of the Chicago magazine *Poetry*, visited Paris she called on Ford. 'As we had tea in his garden under a thirteenth-century wall of broken stones', she informed her readers, 'Mr. Ford elaborated his opinion that the only hope for civilization lies in France', as opposed to the American culture he dismissed contemptuously as 'a civilization of bath-tubs and telephones!'[19]

He was laid up 'with an attack of something resembling influenza' in November, he explained to Conrad, typing 'from a table across my bed'. Dent had asked him to produce a Conrad Supplement of appreciations to mark the Collected Edition, but there was not time to get them 'from anyone worth mentioning'. Instead he suggested reprinting their unfinished collaboration, 'The Nature of a Crime', that first appeared (under the pseudonym of 'Baron Ignatz von Aschendrof') in the *English Review*. 'I have looked at it again and it seems to me a pretty good piece of work', he said, but Conrad was grudging (perhaps resenting Ford's desire to appear once again as his collaborator, his equal). 'If you think it advisable to dig up this affair, well, I don't see how I can object', he objected, and continued objecting: 'it seemed to me somewhat amateurish, which is strange because that is not our failing either separately or to-gether.' Still hoping that Conrad would collaborate once again, Ford even suggested: 'if it would amuse you, a little later I would come over to a near-by pub & see if we couldn't again evolve something like the original passage of the *Mirror* [*of the Sea*].' But Conrad kept his distance, and a little later the distance widened. Ford objected that the Collected Edition had included *Romance* and *The Inheritors* without his permission, and without his name being mentioned on the catalogues, bindings, or wrappers. He had been arguing about it with Pinker, and then with Pinker's sons, for two years, and told Conrad that his complaint 'reads rather like the tangled tale of a lunatic, but I think you will agree that I have some right, considering the cumulative nature of this extreme insolence [from Eric Pinker, Dent, and Doubleday Page], to express some irritation.' Conrad vented his fury to Eric Pinker, describing Ford as 'the man who seems to be suffering from the idea that everybody in the world has insulted him. One would think it a mania if one did not suspect that there is a purpose in it.' When Ford objected to having to pay Eric Pinker, who he said had treated him with 'gross insolence', a commission on a deal Ford had made himself with Duckworth, who offered £150 for an edition of *The Nature of a Crime*; and also to having to wait for Pinker to pay him his share, Conrad told Pinker that he thought that 'a small sacrifice [of paying Pinker Ford's half of the commission out of his own share] is worth getting rid of the damnable "incubus" of that rotten "Crime" embroglio [*sic*]'; 'In fact it is cheap, and what a luxury it would be to get rid of him [emended by hand to 'his nonsense'].' *The Nature of a Crime* fragment wasn't worth republishing, and Ford's commentary on the collaboration, though indispensable to critics and biographers of either man, reads too much like padding to fill out the slim volume. It was a rare occasion when Ford's literary judgement was overwhelmed by other feelings: admira-tion for Conrad, and pride in the collaboration. (In fact the book got good reviews, probably out of respect for Conrad, who died shortly before it was published.)[20]

Ford also tried to use the review to restore his relationship with Katharine, and to show her how far from indifferent to her he was. The Irish Free State had been proclaimed less than a year before, and he was eager to have a Dublin correspondent. His suggestion that she might want to write may betray a disappointment at her choice of career:

I as you will no doubt gather, am at my old game of starting reviews and this one—barring the earthquakes that have beset my career—looks mildly like succeeding—So that in case you get tired of vetting or get pilled at an exam I might find you a job either in Paris or in the alternative in London or New York as you pleased. In the meantime, suppose you try your hand at a London—or rather a Dublin letter. I daresay you could write if you tried. Look at the copy of the Review that I will send you at the beginning of next month: you will see three separate letters representing London, Paris and New York: somewhere between the tones of the one or the other you might find a mode that would suit you, or you could cut out a path for yourself. I really want a Dublin correspondent who will inform the world as to either the political or literary activities of Dublin.[21]

1924: *the transatlantic review*

As a critic he was perhaps wrecked by his wholly unpolitic generosity. In fact, if he merits an epithet above all others, it would be 'The Unpolitic.' Despite all his own interests, despite all the hard-boiled and half-baked vanities of all the various lots of us, he kept on discovering merit with monotonous regularity.

(Pound, 'Ford Madox (Hueffer) Ford: Obit')

'The early days of the *Transatlantic Review*, before it became apparent that by no conceivable chance could it be made to pay, were great fun', said Bowen. 'The whole thing was run in conditions of the utmost confusion.' The best account is Ford's frenetic slapstick in *It Was the Nightingale*. The elegant White Russian colonel 'almost went out of his mind because he read communism into every incomprehensible English sentence'—incomprehensible because of the errors introduced by the Russian printers he had found. When he saw Lincoln Steffens's article on the Soviet Union he resigned, and disappeared with the manuscript of Ford's first editorial. Then Bunting was put in prison—the Santé. He had spent the salary advance Ford had given him getting drunk and disorderly. Pound told Ford he had to go and vouch for Bunting's character, which he didn't know much about. 'I perjured myself all right', he said. Bunting became sub-editor—a job which involved more than just sub-editing. He came to live with the Fords, sleeping in their 'damp little store-room', and helping to bathe Julie. When Coppard planned to visit Paris, Ford wrote welcomingly: 'How delightful! But of course you will stop more than a day [. . .] Paris cannot be seen in a day. Neither can the Fords [. . .] we will either meet you or have you met by Bunting—a dark youth with round spectacles, in a large Trilby hat and a blue trench coat with belt who shall hold up a copy of the TRANSATLANTIC REVIEW towards passengers arriving at the barrier and smile.' The first issue appeared in December, but was dated January 1924 (the date it was published in America). It included messages of encouragement from Thomas Hardy, H. G. Wells, and T. S. Eliot. Ford's dream had been realized again. The combination of the *review* and *Parade's End* returned him to the centre of the modernist literary world. 'The twin constellations of the English-speaking literary groups in the Paris of the twenties', said Goldring, were Joyce and Ford.[1]

Was the *transatlantic* the old *English Review* all over again? Ford's first editorial announced that its 'birth is in truth a rebirth', and recalled Marwood's desire to print Hardy's 'A Sunday Morning Tragedy'. The *transatlantic* was, amongst other things, the last phase of Ford's literary rebirth, the renewed writer again metamorphosed into editor. Its mixture of the old and young, the regional and the international, is familiar. It has been thought the less-dazzling editorial performance, partly because Ford couldn't claim he had made any discoveries as significant as Lawrence, Pound, or Lewis. Writers like Hemingway, cummings, Stein, and Carlos Williams were already known to the avant-garde expatriates. Ford's editorials tended towards the un-ashamedly personal and flippant, which gave the magazine a less serious air than the *English*. Yet a respectable number of the works it published or excerpted could be called masterpieces: not only Ford's own *Some Do Not . . .* and *Joseph Conrad*, but *Finnegans Wake*, some of Hemingway's best stories (such as 'Indian Camp'), two of Pound's Cantos (XII and part of XIII), Stein's *The Making of Americans*. Other major writers, such as Conrad, Dos Passos, Jean Rhys, Paul Valéry, and William Carlos Williams were represented by minor pieces. As with the *English Review*, what is remarkable is the catholicity of Ford's good judgement. Most of the best writers and many of the best visual artists and composers were featured: Djuna Barnes, Tristan Tzara, Dorothy Richardson, Erik Satie, cummings, Bunting, George Antheil, Juan Gris, Catherine Wells, Nathan Asch, Coppard, H.D., Flint, Bryher, Cocteau, Picasso, Braque, Brancusi, Juan Gris, Man Ray, Gwen John, and Havelock Ellis all appeared. The *transatlantic review* stands up well as a discriminating cross-section of post-war international modernism.[2]

A new printer was found—an Englishman, this time, Herbert Clarke—and William Bird found Ford a new editorial office. He had taken a great domed wine-vault at 29, quai d'Anjou, on the Île St Louis, for his Three Mountains Press. 'The ground floor was occupied by his great iron, seventeenth-century hand-press and his formes', said Ford, 'and we all took hands at pulling its immense levers about' when Bird was printing his 'Contact Editions' (the series that included *Women & Men*, Hemingway's *Three Stories and Ten Poems*, and Pound's *Indiscretions*). The review office was in 'a gallery like a bird-cage' that covered half the vault. It was not high enough for Ford to stand up: 'Miss Reid and I had permanently contused skulls', he wrote: 'Every time anybody who looked like a purchaser rang the door bell, we would spring up from our tables', and 'onlookers below trembled for the safety of the whole structure'. 'And the excitement when somebody bought a copy of a *Review*!' Their social life was 'like an avalanche' once the first number was out. They started giving what Ford called 'a modest Thursday tea' for the contributors:

But you never saw such teas as mine were at first. They would begin at nine in the morning and last for twelve hours. They began again on Friday and lasted till Saturday. On Sunday disappointed tea-drinkers hammered all day on the locked doors. They were all would-be contributors, all American and nearly all Middle Westerners. If each of them had bought a copy of the *review* we should have made a fortune. Not one did. They all considered that as would-be contributors they were entitled to free copies.

I had to shut these teas down and to admit no one except contributors to the current numbers, and instead of a Thursday tea I gave a Friday dance. I do not mind giving dances. I can think my private thoughts while they go on nearly as well as in the Underground during rush hours—and if any one is present that I like and there is a shortage of men, I dance. I would rather dance than do anything else.

It was during one of these festivals that I had my first experience of Prohibition. I was dancing with a girl of seventeen, who appeared to be enthusiastic and modest. And sud-denly—amazingly—she dropped right through my arms and lay on the floor like a corpse. I was, as it were, shattered. I thought she had died of heart disease.

No one in the room stopped dancing. They were all Americans from the Middle West [. . .] I don't believe I had ever seen a woman or even a man—in such a condition before.[3]

He and Bowen moved into one of the big studios in the Boulevard Arago *cité fleurie* at the end of the year. It was immense, had neither gas nor electricity; 'its kitchen was a black underground dungeon', said Bowen:

There was a gallery at one end, filled with stacked canvases, and here the unfortunate Bunting had his shakedown. The place was well heated by an ancient and leaky anthracite stove, the fumes from which were my constant anxiety. Huge gold frames containing gloomy, indecipherable pictures hung on the walls, which were bursting into large white pimples of damp through the grey distemper. Long serge curtains, once red, hung dustily over the gallery stairs. We liked the furniture. It consisted chiefly of heavy carved chests and antique cupboards, one of which had glass doors and contained four shelves of fragile etruscan remains. This was locked.

When the studio was lit by a couple of dozen candles, in bottles, or stuck onto saucers, it looked very dramatic.[4]

Here they began giving parties. Ford invited his friends Sisley Huddleston and his wife to one that he called 'an elementary and inexpensive sort of gramophone-hop'. One particularly eventful one—it may even be the one at which Ford's dancing partner collapsed—was described by Harold Loeb and Stella Bowen—their quite different accounts showing how reminiscing inevitably reinvents the past. Someone had kicked Mary Butts's behind, and a fight broke out, involving her partner, Cecil Maitland, 'a lovable but dilapidated Scotch "aristocrat"'. He was 'a young man who was said to be always trying to commit suicide, and Mary Butts [. . .] was usually able to prevent it'. As Maitland was given a bloody nose, Bowen roared up from the subterranean kitchen: 'Miserable man, he's spoiling my party by committing suicide.' There was blood but no body', said Loeb. He was dancing with a Swede when the photographer 'Berenice Abbot fell on her back in the middle of the floor. | Waldo Pierce looked at her tersely. Some of the guests seemed confused but Ford was quite calm.' The fight ended under the concierge's window. The next morning Bowen was 'accosted by a wild-eyed Madame Annie (recently engaged to look after Julie) [. . .] She had seen the blood and heard the concierge's story, which by then had become a legend including a duel, possibly a death, with crowds of wild women rushing out into the Boulevard.' Nevertheless, 'Everyone in the Quarter said it had been a good party', thought Loeb. The more Ford wrote, the more he needed such diversions. He was later to say that anyone revising a long novel (as he was now revising *Some Do Not . . .* for the review, and for book-publication probably in April) 'will then feel prostrate for a long time. But to cure mental prostration, one goes precisely to dances and gives teas. One desires to forget the stress and torture through which one has lately passed.' When William Carlos Williams and his wife Florence visited Paris in January 1924 Ford was one of many writers and artists Robert McAlmon invited to meet him at a big dinner at Le Trianon—Joyce (who often dined there), Man Ray, Duchamp, Aragon, Mina Loy, Sylvia Beach, Adrienne Monnier, Peggy Guggenheim, Kitty Cannell were there, as was Harold Loeb, who claimed Ford had spoken to him at length about the artist's 'divine right to existence'. Williams was impressed by his first view of Ford: 'the lumbering Britisher, opening his mouth to talk, his napkin in one hand, half-stammering but enjoying the fun, a mind wonderfully attractive to me [. . .].' Yet one can be lonely in a crowd, thinking out one's own problems while those around lose their heads or their consciousnesses. Ford combined Madox Brown's need to feel a neglected genius with the need to be recognized as a motive force. In self-imposed exile (as his father, too, had been in England), he had established himself at the centre of a fluctuating group of *émigrés*, at once their leader and a representative of the social and aesthetic traditions they were rebelling against. He had ensured a stormy passage as long as the review survived. But he relished the rejection as much as the adulation. Like his protagonist Tietjens, he lived most fully under the most extreme and contradictory pressures. Of him, as of the *transatlantic review*, it could be said '*Fluctuat nec mergitur*'.[5]

Juliet Soskice wrote to Ford at the end of January to tell him their mother was ill. A doctor had said she was dying of diabetes. Ford wrote at once to Katharine, saying 'I have just heard that y^r grandmother is dying—a matter of a month or so'. Cathy Hueffer, who was 73, had not been told how serious the family thought her condition was, so Ford maintained the fiction when he wrote to say he was coming to see her: 'I have got an unexpected chance to come over to London for a day or so.' He saw Conrad too. 'We met as if we had seen each other every day for the last ten years', Conrad told Eric Pinker: 'As we talked pleasantly of old times I was asking myself, in my cynical way, when would the kink come [. . .].' Ford wanted 'to be friendly in personal relations with me', he added: 'In fact, *entre nous*, too friendly [. . .].' Ford's meeting with his mother was more disturbing. As she wrote to her grandson Frank: 'Uncle Ford came to England on business, & looked in at Girdler's Road & brought with him a portrait of himself as a present—painted by Stella—a very clever but *hideous* as a [sic] likeness exactly like him and also looking like a Frenchman with a past.' He later told Katharine: 'after I came back from London I was too ill to do anything beyond just struggle through the business of the Review. I got rather a shock at seeing the condition of your grandmother who looked much worse than I expected and that upset me for rather a long time.' Being told that he looked exactly like a clever but hideous person with a past may not have helped. Mrs Hueffer was not on the point of death: she lived for another three years. He could ill spare the time away from the review, the second issue of which came out while he was in England for the weekend. Joyce wrote to Quinn about it: 'Between lack of funds, printers' errors, absconding secretaries and general misunderstandings, it appears to be shortening people's lives.'[6]

The American Women's Club in Paris burned the second issue of the *transatlantic* in their hall fire, alleging that Georges Pillement's story 'Ah, Que d'Amour gâché sans profit pour personne' was indecent. When Ford defended the story in an editorial, saying it merely rendered how their menfolk behaved in Parisian night-clubs, the American Women cancelled their subscription. This started Ford worrying about whether the extract from *Finnegans Wake* that he had eventually persuaded Joyce to let him publish would create legal difficulties. He called in Sisley Huddleston—'the most representative official Englishman we could find', Ford called him, because he had been Paris correspondent for *The Times*; Huddleston was not convinced, thinking of himself as a Bohemian—and Joyce read 'as only he can read'. 'I waited in vain for the obscenity and blasphemy which I was warned would be apparent', wrote Huddleston; but they were not apparent to him: 'If they were there they were carefully concealed.' Ford's anxiety was not as misplaced as Huddleston suggests. As Bernard Poli says, seizure by the British or American customs could have been fatal to the review. As Joyce realized, what Ford feared was a charge of blasphemy rather than obscenity. The only passage Joyce was ready to detach was 'the four old men, *Mamalujo*': the reference to Matthew, Mark, Luke, and John could easily have proved inflammatory. It was published in a special supplement to the April issue, entitled 'From Work in Progress', together with one of Hemingway's best stories (untitled in the review, but later called 'Indian Camp'), and a piece by Tzara, 'Monsieur Aa L'Antiphilosophe'. These, together with Stein's *The Making of Americans*, which began as a serial in the same issue, represented a considerable coup for Ford's editing.[7]

Hemingway probably met Ford early in February 1924. *It Was the Nightingale* has Hemingway at the meeting with Quinn, Joyce, and Pound in October 1923, but he was in Toronto then, and didn't get back to Paris until the end of January. Pound had written to Hemingway in Canada, before the magazine had begun to appear, inviting him 'to come home and direct its policy etc.'. Hemingway shrewdly told Gertrude Stein and Alice B. Toklas he thought 'the invitation has been exaggerated'. None the less, since Pound wanted Hemingway involved with the review, the rest of Ford's impression is probably accurate. He said he had seen Hemingway at the Dôme, and played early-morning tennis with him and Pound, and his neighbour and tennis-partner, the painter Latapie. Then he saw Hemingway in Pound's studio in 70 bis, rue Notre-Dame des Champs (Hemingway lived in the same street, on the Luxembourg Gardens side of the Boulevard du Montparnasse, at number 113). He has Hemingway shadow-boxing his way around the studio. When he threatens a Chinese work, Ford says to Pound: 'That young man [. . .] appears to have sinophobia. Why does he so dislike that. . . . ?' Pound assures him Hemingway is just 'getting rid of his superfluous energy', and recommends Ford take him on as sub-editor: 'He writes very good verse, and he's the finest prose stylist in the world.' Infinitely patient, Ford overlooks the fact that it was Pound who insisted on his engaging the Russian Colonel, and who only yesterday had called Ford the finest prose stylist in the world (' "You!" Ezra exclaimed. "You're like all English swine. . . ." '), and takes on Hemingway.[8]

Pound relished Ford as a teasing mentor he could tease; Hemingway could never reconcile Ford the grand old man, condescending to his employee as 'That young man', with Ford the writer who would sacrifice himself, his cherished magazine, his rare chance of owning his own home, for the genius of writers like Hemingway. He was always grateful for Ford's praise, but the man himself made Hemingway increasingly infuriated and aggressive. 'Ford can explain stuff i.e. Thus to Revisit or Thus to Revise-it', he explained to Pound—suggesting that he could only see the inventions in Ford's reminiscences—'but in private life he is so goddam involved in being the dregs of an English country gentleman that you get no good out of him.' This was Pound's complaint too, though Pound saw some good in him. Ford said that Americans couldn't tell whether he was in earnest or not: doubtless he teased Hemingway as he had teased young Americans before the war, and Hemingway couldn't or wouldn't hear the irony in his re-visioning. His blind spot was his *machismo* ideal, which Ford didn't match: 'He has never recovered in a literary way from the mirricale [. . .] of his having been a soldier', he told Pound: 'I'm going to start denying I was in the war for fear I will get like Ford to myself about it.' By *Last Post* Ford had recovered from the miracle of having almost died and then survived. It was Hemingway who never recovered from having been in the war, and became a worse kind of self-parody. Ford said of Hemingway: 'he comes and sits at my feet and praises me. It makes me nervous.' At one of Ford's Thursday afternoon teas he predicted to Hemingway, 'you will have a great name in no time at all'. Largely thanks to Ford, he did.[9]

Stein's *Autobiography of Alice B. Toklas* records how they had met Ford and Hunt before the war—it may have been in Paris, since Ford recalled trotting through the streets there trying to catch up with Stein driving her Ford car in 1913; or it may have been in London the following year. When they met one day for dinner, Toklas had sat next to him: 'I liked him very much and I liked his stories of Mistral and Tarascon and I liked his having been followed about in that land of the french royalist, on account of his resemblance to the Bourbon claimant.' What? Ford wanted to publish Stein in the *transatlantic*. She had already thought the review looked interesting, when Hemingway visited her, 'very excited' about it, and explained that he had suggested serializing *The Making of Americans*. He even copied out the first instalment with Toklas's help (Stein later said he learned much from it). 'Ford alleges he is delighted with the stuff and is going to call on you', Hemingway reported to Stein. 'I told him it took you 4½ years to write it and that there were 6 volumes [. . .] I made it clear it was a remarkable scoop for his magazine obtained only through my obtaining genius. He is under the impression that you get big prices when you consent to publish. I did not give him this impression but did not discourage it [. . .] Treat him high wide and handsome.' Such comments only confirmed her suspicion that Hemingway was trying to trick Ford, that there was 'some other story behind it all'. Ford said Hemingway had given him 'the impression that it was a long-short story that would run for about three numbers', but added generously: 'It was probably my fault I had that impression.' Hemingway certainly did not discourage it. 'Had I known that it was to be a long novel', Ford continued, 'I should have delayed publishing it until my own serial had run out and should then have offered you a lump sum as serials are not accounted so valuable as shorter matter. I do not get paid for my own serial at all, neither does Pound for his.' Stein was fond of Ford, whom she considered 'more or less the old guard'. Ford only discovered the mistake when the money was running out but the serial wasn't. Then Hemingway told him that Eliot's *Criterion* had offered her 'real money' for it. Ford wrote to her, saying 'I should be very sorry to lose you, but I was never the one to stand in a contributor's way'. She drafted a reply: 'I like the magazine and I like your editing. I am sincerely attached to both so suppose we go on as we are going.'[10]

The writing of *Some Do Not . . .* and the editing of the *transatlantic* had worked Ford into a coruscation of creative activity. Thanking Jeanne Foster for her praise of the essay he wrote for Eliot's *Criterion*, he boasted, with a mocking cliché: 'I am a great but neglected writer!' But as the review, and *Parade's End*, began to appear, he became less neglected. When the *Chicago Tribune* launched a Sunday Magazine in Paris they commissioned a series of 'Literary Causeries', which ran from 17 February to 11 May 1924. He probably didn't want to overload the *transatlantic* with his own work; and he needed the money (to pay Marjorie Reid's wages, as he said later). He defined the 'Causerie' as 'something self-indulgent, a little unbuttoned': 'a sort of chat that takes place over the after-dinner table-cloth, the elbows between the port glasses, the walnuts in the nutcrackers between the fingers.' There are fleeting glimpses of Ford's life at the time: 'when my young friend Mr. Robert McAlmon tells me that I shall never be able to write because I know too much he is probably in the right of it'; taking a little tour to Château-Thierry, and trying (but failing) to enjoy reading La Fontaine, who was born there; reading three French novels in as many days; walking along the Seine quays, discussing the second-hand bookstalls with his companion; getting involved in a controversy in the magazine with Marcel Pagnol, over whether H. G. Wells had plagiarized the plot of *The New Machiavelli* from a French novelist; going to see an experimental play of 'My friend M. Tzara at the Cigale Theatre in Montmartre'. Yet, as so often in Ford's writing, there are profounder explorations happening beneath the casual surface. As in the *transatlantic*, he was constantly revaluing literature; setting the work of 'The Younger American Writers' whom the magazine was involving him with more and more against the pre-war work he most admired. Under the pretext of reviewing new books on Crane or Hudson, he was conducting autobiography by other means—concealedly. As always for him, literature and memory were inextricable. The highest praise he could give Hemingway was that he had achieved just that intricacy: 'To read Mr. Hemingway is to be presented with a series of—often enough very cruel—experiences of your own that will in turn be dissolved into your own filmy remembrances' (the syntax itself dissolves Hemingway's subjects into Ford's experiences, not just with the engulfing parenthesis, but in the blurring of whether the experiences are Ford's only after he has read Hemingway, or whether Hemingway presents experiences that someone like Ford has already had.) He revisits some of the formative reading he has recalled in *Thus to Revisit*: those transporting engrossments in Conrad, *The Red Badge of Courage*, and *What Maisie Knew* during the war.[11]

An extraordinary essay about the centenary of Byron's death reveals how Fordian literary autobiography is not only to do with recalling the effects of past readings, but of seeing yourself as you read about someone else (as Ford imagines having Hemingway's experiences as he reads him); and thus avoiding the resistances produced by direct self-confrontation. (Conversely, reading about himself made him feel like someone else. He said reading Marsden Price's 1920 essay on him, which provided him with a philosophy and a religion he didn't recognize, was 'like waking up and discovering that one was really the Prince of Wales'. That feeling went into his novels of exchanged identities, *Ladies Whose Bright Eyes* and *The Rash Act*.) It is Byron's self-dramatizing and his reputation as a libertine that most disturbs Ford. His response is to 're-construct Byron as the novelist would attempt to do it'. If it becomes a fictitious novel about Ford, that doesn't make it any less true of Byron:

A man with so many transformations to him as Byron struck so many people from so many and such varied angles [. . .] Byron in short was so many things to so many men and was so innumerably more things to himself that one has as it were to go through a whole wardrobe of dissimilar fancy dresses pushing costume after costume aside before one arrives at the real Lord Byron, if even then one arrives at anything real. And one must begin by predicating what he was not.

Thus he certainly was not what the French call *cabotin* [a bad actor] for, though he did act parts to every human soul with whom he came in contact, the probability—the absolute certainty—is that for the moment he believed that part to be in very truth the whole of himself. That is not acting.

The probability—the absolute certainty—is that Ford believed in his own roles in precisely that way. It was this role-playing that Hemingway couldn't understand (or couldn't stand, because it threw into relief his own posturing). It is in Byron's works of the imagination that Ford can see that he was 'more things to himself' than he was to others: 'Just as he acted with conviction the parts of Lara, of the Corsair, of Manfred, so he aspired to the aspect of Red Republican; applauded Bonaparte, decried the Duke of Wellington and spouted endless platitudes as to Liberty and the Rights of Man.' Thus his public acts are an extension of his imaginative roles. It's not just that Ford's political statements need to be read in this way—his review editorials as footnotes to *Parade's End*—but that his actual private life needs to be detached from the haze of scandal and gossip. 'And indeed whatever Byron was he was not a Don Juan [neither is his Don Juan, of course . . .], nearly all of his *bonnes fortunes* turning out to be most unfortunate affairs which he was quite unable to treat with the cynicism of a Lara'—such as were Ford's unfortunate affairs with Mary Martindale and Violet Hunt? 'Byron, however, the necessary deductions being made, was, even in his relations with women, a goodish, puzzled sort of a fellow, and it is a misnomer to attach even to them the name of dissipation, which is the working up of coldnesses to an abandonment of the equilibrium.' Soon after writing this, Ford felt he should warn Conrad that Elsie was suing Violet over Ford's 'abandoned patronymic', fearing that Conrad would not want to be involved (as a collaborator in print) in more scandal over Ford's 'relations with women'. He wrote that, 'though I'm determined never to utter anything in the nature of an apology for my existence [. . .] when I look back on my life I can see nothing to regret except mistaken—or miscalculated, generosities'. ('These are of course as flagitious as crimes or any other form of dishonour', he added cynically.) But the Byron essay can be read as precisely an apology for Ford's conduct with women—albeit an oblique one, which dissolves Byron's experience with his own. This sympathy with Byron might seem at odds with the antipathy Ford expressed later, saying 'a more heartless being can never have lived'. The author of *The Good Soldier* could scarcely be called 'heartless'; though one of the things that novel worries at is whether there isn't a heartlessness (an egotistical insatiability) at the heart of 'heart' (in the sense of sexual desire). *The March of Literature* gives a clue to his ambivalence towards Byron, suggesting that it was the sexual scandals of Byron's life that disturbed Ford; and in particular, the question of incest. Perhaps he foresaw how, in his own case too, 'persons will be found forever to write memoirs going to prove or disprove that he committed incest [. . .]'.[12]

Byron was also, Ford speculated, 'the only Englishman who by his works and figure changed the whole mentality of the occidental world'—as perhaps he felt the modernism of Pound, Joyce, Eliot, and Hemingway was again doing. The causerie on La Fontaine modulates into thoughts about prose. Anglo-Saxondom must realize, he argues, 'that the greatest of all vehicles, the supreme vehicle, for Poetry is prose': 'And the problem—the really very great problem of the day—is precisely the evolution of a prose language that shall have a certain international validity.' This is the attempt in

Parade's End, and the aim of the *transatlantic review.* The young Americans he admired 'write a living language with a certain vigour'—what he had been advocating for years—'but without that discernment that lets a man know what words in the vernacular of his day are certain of survival and which are a mere part of a temporary provincialism'. And he took a playful swipe at the poets he most admired. If their poetry was as well-written as prose, their prose wasn't so well-written: 'American verse-poets when they handle prose regard it as the very worst vehicle for poetry, the prose even of Mr. Eliot being singularly frigid and self-conscious whilst the prose of Mr. Pound is no more nor less than a national disaster.' In a moving, meditative remembrance of Hudson, Ford concentrates on the naturalist's conversation. His complete freedom from Byronics makes Ford admire him all the more, as a reminder that some of the most effective writing comes from not trying to produce effects, make an impression. This recollection of Hudson's talk, which figures for Ford as an ideal for prose-rendering, comes when he was particularly concerned with how to render talk in novels:

The man of letters is continually troubled by the problem that,—in cold print, the inflections and the tempi of the human voice are as impossible of rendering as are scents and the tones of musical instruments. It is to be doubted if there is anyone who ever used a pen who has not from time to time tried by underlinings, capitals and queerly spacing his words to get something more on the paper than normal paper can bear. Mr Cummings with the bravery and logic of relative youth attempts cadences and surprises that we who are old, old and not brave long since abandoned and in so far as he succeeds he deserves well of all humanity who use the pen for even so little a matter as a note to go by the post.

   For ourselves we limit ourselves to the use of. . . . to indicate the pauses by which the Briton—and the American now and then—recovers himself in order to continue a sentence. The typographical device is inadequate but how in the world. . . . how in the whole world else?—is one to render the normal English conversation?[13]

He found a way of describing it, at least, in a marvellous image, saying that 'the noise that is English conversation' resembles 'the sound put forth by a slug eating lettuce'. Ford's earliest fiction had been concerned with the (Jamesian) matter of ambiguous suppression, the innuendos lurking within ejaculations like 'Oh!' and 'Ah!'. But what had changed was his technique of presentation. Soon after *Some Do Not . . .* was published in April, he sent Conrad a copy, saying: 'I'm pretty sure it's the best thing I've done. You'll notice I've abandoned attempts at indirect reporting of speech—as an experiment. How late in life does one go on experimenting?'[14]

   In May Ford visited London again. He saw Eric Pinker and had what was to be his last meetings with Conrad on the 9th and 10th, when (as he later told his solicitor) they promised not to let any more editions of the collaborations appear without his name on the covers, wrappers, and catalogues. Jessie Conrad wrote maliciously to Pinker: 'That odious Hueffer has just turned up. J.C. wanted to bring him up here for tea but I declined as what is the use of letting him get very friendly again. I dislike him profoundly.' This suggests that Conrad's politeness may not have been beguilingly hypocritical as Najder assumes; and also that there was some substance to Ford's feeling that it was Conrad's entourage that prevented a *rapprochement.* He almost certainly saw his mother again, since he called on the Soskices. In one of the 'Stocktaking' essays in the *transatlantic* later in the year he recounted talking to one of his nephews, who was sitting in a window-seat reading Goldsmith ('there is no reading like that of a boy in the long dusks: it is the deepest abandonment of the soul that we know on this earth'). When David Soskice came home he began to chide the boy for wasting time when he should be reading for a scholarship examination, and then began to upbraid Ford 'for writing disrespectfully of Shelley, an English Classic'; 'He said he had been told that I was hurting my reputation' rather than challenging Shelley's. In fact Ford's standing in England hadn't been higher since the *Throne* case; *Some Do Not . . .* was his greatest critical success since his Edwardian historical fiction. The *Daily Mail* called it 'one of his cleverest and grimmest studies of mankind' (but paused to complain: 'why is it that the post-war novelist must always covertly discredit the marriage tie?'). 'There is no need to worry about the state of the English novel while books like this are being produced', said the *Manchester Guardian*. The *Bystander* reviewer found it 'one of the most stimulating works of fiction' he had read in some time—perhaps because 'In places it is amazingly, almost shockingly, outspoken'. The *English Review* called it 'the biggest novel of the century [. . .] the twentieth century *Vanity Fair*'. Even the *Times Literary Supplement*, which had doubts about whether the methods of *The Marsden Case* were as suitable to a serious story like Tietjens's, recognized 'a novel of unusual power and art', commenting shrewdly: 'Mr. Ford manages, with quite extraordinary ingenuity, to dovetail into his admirable dialogue long passages of reflection which reveal the essentials of an extremely complicated tissue of events.' The few dissentient voices worried about the inconclusiveness of the structure; the fact that 'it points no noteworthy moral'; and the book's strangeness. But even these praised the gifts they thought Ford was wasting.[15]

Ford stayed with Dyneley Hussey in London, and it was from Hussey's flat in Lincoln's Inn that he wrote the editorial (dated 'May') for the June issue of the review. The 'English atmosphere' of the panelled room made him 'wonder depressedly' about the condition of England and of 'the English world of letters'. 'You have on the one hand four or five serious novelists who build up a world looking more or less as the world looked before the war and who have hardly had time to so much as guess at the riddle of an after-war world. They are serious and engrossed.' 'You have half a dozen ladies of some seriousness'; but, he says, 'we are dealing for the moment only with men and of course not at all with the novelist of British commerce'. On the other hand there were 'the more or less bright, more or less young things', who appeared lacking in vitality: 'With gentle anaemia they fumble with placket strings.' The relevance of this diagram to his own novelistic predicament is evident. *Some Do Not . . .* had plunged him into the imagining of the pre-war and wartime world, and its sequels would force him to guess at the riddle of an after-war world. But his own practice is rooted in a broader literary and social context. Though in his editorial role of encouraging new talent he prophesied that 'A more vital generation will come [. . .]', his own experience in Paris had convinced him that he had been right to think that it would come not from England but America. (When, a decade later, he came to write his memoirs of this period, this is the shape he gave them—and it is the novelistic shaping that most distinguishes his autobiographies from the displays of name-dropping, the ramblings of anecdotage in too many memoirs: the shape of his own leaving England for Paris, then trying to span the Atlantic, seen against the background of the literary avant-garde's similar shifts.) The writing of Stein, Hemingway, and Carlos Williams had particularly impressed him for its 'historic sense'. Yet, with characteristic duality he was also able to say that if the (particularly Middle-Western) young disliked his work, 'it is because, most of it being based on historic contemplations and comparisons, it reveals an equanimity that is properly repulsive to the eager'. Ford's preface to *Transatlantic Stories* shows how important was his growing awareness of contemporary American literature both to the *transatlantic review* and to his conception of twentieth-century writing—including the writing of *Parade's End* (in the same piece he writes of the 'pomps and parades that used to sway us'). He said the 'clearness of vision' of the stories 'comes very definitely from the fact that the writers' minds are definitely not lumbered up by all the bric-a-brac of monumental ideals that we used to have'. *Parade's End* is a more thorough inventory of bric-à-brac—both people's material and mental furniture—than any of his writing since *The Fifth Queen*. But it is also (like all Ford's impressionism) an *analysis* of how humanity puts its trust in matter and habits of mind: which is what Pound couldn't see when he kept berating Ford for inhabiting the concepts 'Tory', 'gentleman', and 'Catholic'—what he called the 'suppressed forsooths and gadzookses of ideation'.[16]

Ford's political editorials in the *transatlantic* explain why he felt the historic sense to be disappearing in England. '[T]wo things are abhorred by the Left of to-day, the Historic Sense and peasant populations; one and the other they must at all costs root out, oblivious of the fact that historic crimes ensure a certain Nemesis.' And the Left were in government in England, if not in power: the first Labour government, under Ramsay Macdonald, was formed after the inconclusive election of 1923. The strength of Ford's tone against the Left sounds hard to reconcile with his aim of seeking to define an intellectual Toryism beyond the embattlements of party politics. Yet seen in context his criticisms express the independence of his political thought, rather than a covert Conservatism. First, he is criticizing the programme of the Left because it was the programme of the government (as he had criticized the governments of the Liberals Asquith and Lloyd George (over women's suffrage and Ireland), and would criticize that of Conservative Chamberlain (over appeasement with Nazi Germany, and the policy on Jewish refugees). Secondly, he was particularly concerned about Macdonald's foreign policy, which effected a compromise between France and Germany over war reparations and the re-establishing of borders. Historians have praised the skill of Macdonald's diplomacy: as A. J. P. Taylor said, it set the pattern of British foreign policy for several years. But Ford was right about the anti-French feeling in British governmental circles. Any attempt to regenerate German industry smacked of Prussianism to Ford, and seemed to him to make another European war more likely. It did. He felt that the British Left's initial objection to the declaration of war on Germany in 1914 had only encouraged the Germans to invade Belgium and France. Thirdly, he argued that far from liberating the working class, a commitment to industrial progress ('rooting out peasant populations') would only further degrade and alienate humanity. Closer to the spirit of the Victorian Great than he might have acknowledged, he gives a Ruskinian or Carlylean sketch of the industrial heartland from mid-Yorkshire to west Lancashire: 'There is no district in the world more horrible than is this city of thirteen million slaves. Yet it is to preserve intact this city and its system that the British Left labours.' Ford's commitment to agrarian frugality has its feudal affinities; but the sentiment here is radical, and is a clairvoyant glimpse of the criticism, that has dogged the Labour Party ever since, of being a Labourite rather than truly socialist organization. It may, finally, seem self-contradictory to take the Inns of Court as a symbol for a stultifying traditionalism, while at the same time complaining that the country is losing the 'historic sense'; but it is meant for a thought-provoking paradox. Ford's interest in Toryism was always paradoxical. Its paternalism and disinterestedness may conduce to the clear-thinking scepticism that Ford admired in Marwood. But conversely it is antipathetic to the Fordian novelist. The Tory, said Ford, 'was intolerant, impractical; he was forcible of speech, contemptuous of opposition; without any apparent power of introspection; with no respect for the arts'. But, by a further paradox—one that can be recognized in Marwood, Mr Blood, and Tietjens—'he was so skeptical that he was almost completely self-contradictory'. It is these paradoxes that best define what Ford meant when he called himself a Tory—together with 'a sense of the responsibility of his class that at times would reach up towards becoming a loving kindness for his dependants that can have seldom been surpassed', and that Ford said he had witnessed on the fields of Flanders. Like Eliot, Ford thought that Tory scepticism was 'a necessity for the world if the world is to be kept from rushing down mad slopes at the urging of one craze after another'. So, paradoxically again, if Toryism had no respect for art, it could none the less save the world for art. Thus Ford justified the central paradox in his aesthetics of a classicizing modernism. Herbert Gorman was struck by Ford's ability to call himself a Tory and yet champion Pound; or to call himself a Catholic but to recognize Joyce's genius. Apart from Marwood, it wasn't Tories he sought out, but young revolutionaries: 'when any young people with whiskers and sombreros are kicking up any sort of row, anywhere, about anything I will—if they permit it!—be with them.' What Ford objected to in England was a tradition of vagueness, 'too ancestral, too heavy, too dim-minded'. Like Pound, Eliot, and Joyce, he wanted to abandon the nineteenth-century Anglo–Saxon tradition, and 'make it new', asserting a counter-tradition which looked back to Classical and Romance literatures, and forward to the avant-garde. France was for Ford the realization of this ideal. In *A Mirror to France*, his paean to his new homeland, written between 1923 and 1926, he wrote an essay on the 'Rive Gauche', celebrating the Quartier Latin as the ideal environment for the arts. He also drew on his experience of taking Julie to play in the Jardin de Luxembourg, and pondering on the impression the atmosphere would make on a young mind. In a curious passage in which he addresses the reader as a putative child, he describes the statues, the trimmed trees, the vista towards the Observatoire: 'So your earliest impressions will be of serenities, austerenesses of placidity, of order and perspective, of History, of Classic Lore; of Pure Literature or Applied Science as things to be honoured.' When the Coles visited Paris in 1923 and 1924, Margaret was made to feel 'the philistine from across the water, representative of the smug and commercial civilisation whose unappreciative dust Ford had shaken from his feet'. This must have been irksome to such dedicatedly anti-commercialist thinkers, but she said she listened rather than talked, and 'generally got much pleasure out of Ford, even at his most perverse'.[17]

The *transatlantic review* made Ford feel personally overwhelmed by literary America. After Bunting had left in early January, his place was taken by Ivan Beede, 'who wore large, myopic spectacles, in front of immense dark eyes, wrote very good short stories about farming in the Middle West, and boasted of his Indian blood and the severe vastnesses that had enveloped his childhood'. Ford felt he was living in a western, imperilled by tonguefights at the Quai d'Anjou:

the eyes of Middle Westerners during discussion look exactly like the eyes of men looking down their gun barrels. Or else it is like lassooing. . . . I used, in my office, to feel like a poor Sheriff. . . . I would try, about once an afternoon, to get out some sort of remark or another and at once. . . . Bang. . . . Whizz! Some fellow would whirl forth a rope of words that would coil round my legs and bring me down breathless. I do not suppose that I ever finished a sentence in that establishment: I am getting a little bit of my own back now.[18]

Certainly Hemingway was getting gruffer about Ford and Bowen, whose relationship seemed to him less serene than it appears in Bowen's *Drawn from Life*. He guyed them when he wrote *The Sun Also Rises* the following year. Bowen appears as Mrs Braddocks, 'who in the excitement of talking French was liable to have no idea what she was saying'; Ford as Braddocks, imperious, so anxious to seem the connoisseur that he claims to have known the narrator's *poule* 'for a very long time'. Hemingway kept Pound (who was in Italy recovering from appendix trouble) abreast of the Latin Quarter gossip:

Ford recently in England. Mrs. Ford, i.e. Stella, confided to Hadley [i.e. Mrs. Hemingway] twice in same evening that she had, 'you know I caught Ford too late to train him.' [. . .] On the slightest encouragement when dining out she will start on the tale of her 50 hour confinement that produced Julie [. . .]

Every few days Madam F—— comes over here in her best Australian manner and while complaining in a high voice of her troubles, all her troubles, sneezes and coughs on our baby. He recovers from these attacks and is doing well. [. . .]

I suspect Ford of writing in praise of his own work under various pseudonyms in Transatlantic Review [. . .]

The thing to do with Ford is to kill him. Actually, the thing to do with Mrs. Ford is crucify her.

I am fond of Ford. This aint personal. It's literary.

You see Ford's running whole damn thing as compromise [. . .]

[. . .] Don't let any of this get back to Ford because then it would just mean a row with me and no good done. We're on the friendliest basis now and I'm going to do what I can for him right straight along. I dont want any rows.

(He was wrong to suspect Ford of praising his own work: the pseudonym in question belonged to Ford's old friend Edgar Jepson.) It was Ford's ideal of 'strict impartiality'—of being 'determined to give equal space to all schools'—that was compromise for Hemingway: the wish that 'Cubism shall in your columns lie down amongst the work of the Futurists; photographic realism and the absolutely non-representational in your pages shall kiss each other'. Yet Ford knew the avant-garde well enough to know that to expect the warring factions to take each other lying down was a lost cause—but then it was lost causes that most appealed to his imagination. He imagined the review as a lone voice speaking against the Anglo-Saxon mistrust of the arts: 'a just man in

Sodom', as he put it in one of his editorials, 'if possible to redress the balance'. And he went on to quote a favourite image from one of his own early poems, which best expressed his sense of the violences that militate against communication: '"When other birds", as the poet said of the robin, "sing mortal loud and swearing; when the wind lulls we try to get a hearing".' Pound appreciated what Ford was trying to do, however, and wrote a weirdly disjointed letter from Assisi. 'April number good. Especially Hem. & Djuna', he said, and threatened to 'come back to worry you at close range before you bring out many more numbers.' Ignoring Pound's block capitals, 'NOT FER PUBLIKATION', Ford published an edited version in the June number, signed 'Old Glory', with a note appended to assure readers: 'The above—by the bye, is a real letter.' Ford didn't print the passage that might have sounded too much like log-rolling: 'April number. best argument yet—for continuing the review—Damn good number—better, if I remember rightly than Eng. Rev. was in the "ole days".'[19]

The review was soon beginning to look like a lost financial cause, however. It had sailed close to the wind from the start. In February Ford told Conrad he was being maddened by French company law and by Quinn being slow in sending money. Pound tried to raise what he called 'capertal', but couldn't. In April Ford told Jeanne Foster: 'A small syndicate here is negotiating taking over the Review and putting more money into it.' It's not clear whether this happened or not. He feared that he would lose control of it, as he had the *English Review*, and wanted to raise a further 115,000 frs. of capital (about $6,000 or £1,400 at the time). A month later he was writing to offer shares to subscribers, in the hope that they 'would prefer the Review to maintain as nearly as possible its present character; for any large influx of capital from outside would give the eventual control of the Review to persons who might be quite out of sympathy with its present objects'. The review did eventually acquire shareholders (who may or may not have made up the 'syndicate')—apart from Quinn, Ford, Bowen, and Pound, money was put in by Gertrude Stein, William Bird, Robert Rodes (who was soon to marry Marjorie Reid), Nancy Cunard, Mrs Romaine Brookes, William Bullitt, and Natalie Barney (the 'Amazon of Letters'). The largest contribution came from an old friend of Hemingway's, called Friend. But if Ford did sell any shares in May, they can't have been enough to guarantee the future of the review. He told Conrad he planned to 'give up editing this thing after the next number', and compared himself to the dung-beetle he had seen in Corsica, rolling its pellet of goat's droppings 'nearly up to the castle gate' before it rolled down the entire slope and had to start again. He added laconically: 'I do not know whether it ever got to the top.' At the end of May he determined to take a month's trip to America to try to raise more money from Quinn, who had not been answering Ford's letters, and to extract money (or at least accounts) from Seltzer. He borrowed one of Bill Bird's large suitcases 'in order to carry as many copies of the Review as he could'. Pound wrote to his father: 'Ef yew see Ford; feed him; but dont fer Gawd's sake put any money into the Transatlantic Review.'[20]

Ford took the *Paris* from Cherbourg. As it approached Plymouth he thought of Conrad again, who had acknowledged *Some Do Not . . .* by saying: 'between us two, if I tell you that I consider it tout a fait chic you will understand perfectly how much that "phrase d'atelier" means to the initiated.' Ford later said he was 'seized with an overwhelming conviction' that he would never see Conrad again: 'I got up and desperately scrawled him a last letter assuring him of my forever unchanging affection and admiration for his almost miraculous gifts.' His memory is impressionistic here, fusing the actual letter he indeed wrote from the boat, with other letters he had written in previous months, in which he had indeed assured Conrad that he was the only man he knew 'who completely understood what literature was', and said: 'you know that my admiration for your work has always been so great'. He had just seen Conrad, and may have had a premonition that he hadn't long to live. The actual last letter is eloquent in its baffled knowledge of how difficult it is to express these things— particularly to someone whose affection is less unchanging:

Dear Conrad:

I have been so dreadfully rushed all this week that my memory has completely gone. I *know* there is something I ought to write to you about—in answer to some letter I think, but I have been searching my mind for an hour & can't remember what it is &, as we are nearing Plymouth I let it go at that & forgive.

I am going to go through the Fr. translation of *Romance* on board: It seems to be pretty good. The captain has promised to depute one of his officers to go through the nautical phrases, so they may come right—Will you, in any case look at the proofs? Or not?

I've also got the proofs of the Good Soldier to get thro' before I return but I shall come back by a slow boat.

By the bye: at a shareholders meeting of the T.R. last week I was unanimously requested not to resign the editorship, so I shall not. It will be run while I'm away by young Hemingway who's the best boy that I know—with tastes astonishingly like my own. . . .

I started writing this morning at 5.30 & had written 2,000 words by 9.0.: so I've still some vigour left—or I had this morning.

No—I can't remember what it was. We are just running into Plymouth.

    Yr^s always

    F.M.F.

Let me know how Jessie fares. My address will be the Columbia University Club, New York till the 21st.

Why—in a perfect hurricane of rain should a hand forward on the deck be spraying the deck & the paintwork from a hose?[21]

Ford also wrote the next editorial for the review off Plymouth. He continued his analysis of the English malaise, fusing his own experiences as novelist and army officer to argue that the national characteristic of 'muddling through' meant that English men remained immature; whereas 'our females and our army officers develop intelligence because their lives are passed in the study of the psychology of others'. When he disembarked at New York he had to pay import duty on the dozen presentation copies of his own books he had brought with him. But although he was disturbed by the increasing puritanism of the American government, expressed in 'Anti-Drink Legis- lation, Anti-Realist Literature Legislation, Anti-Emigration and all the Anti- Legislation whose end would seem to be to enforce on the American citizen what we will call the Old German virtues'—in other words, Prussianism by other means—he was impressed with the New Yorkers' 'lavish hospitality', saying he only had to pay for two meals while he was there. At the National Arts Club he took tea 'between Mr. William Allen White and Miss Mary Austin, who told me, the one, all about the

Democratic Convention, and the other all about the American Indian'. White was an influential Republican editor and commentator, who was reporting on the Convention; one day he took Ford along. (Besides writing about Indians, Mary Austin had published a novel called *The Ford* in 1917.)[22]

When he saw Quinn Ford found him too ill to attend to the review's business. Another appointment was made, but broken because of a misunderstanding about the date. Quinn was too ill for a later meeting. Ford spent a day with the editor and critic Burton Rascoe, who took him to a publicity-stunt lunch organized by the dancer, Gilda Gray (who invented the 'shimmy'), in honour of an albino monkey. 'He sat between Miss Gray and Ada Patterson, the interviewer', said Rascoe, 'and seemed to enjoy himself greatly, though at times he looked a little bewildered.' Ten days later, when Rascoe went to a tea with his publisher, Horace Liveright, Ford was there, with Hendrik Van Loon and Carl Van Vechten. 'I am amazed at Ford's mental resiliency and receptivity', wrote Rascoe, 'by which he keeps abreast of his time in three countries and brings a sympathetic appreciation to new work of merit among the younger experimenters.' When Ford sailed back on the RMS *Majestic* at the end of June, 'He was fatigued, he was short of funds, and his vaguely momentous, transatlantic affairs appeared to be in a chronic muddle'. On the boat he befriended an Episcopalian cleric called Harris, whose odd accent (hybridized by elocution lessons) had caught his ear. Like everyone else, Harris and his schoolboy son Markham weren't quite sure what to make of Ford's stories:

And this business of spending whole nights on deck [. . .] because his cabin-mates were insupportable! Did one of them really insist, as Mr. Ford claimed, upon fingering the stuff of his odds and ends of jackets and trousers? Did another actually slide himself fully clothed between the sheets, there to peel item by item in gasping and encumbered modesty? Then there were the point-blank literary claims. The greatest living this! The greatest that in English! Certain of Conrad's novels were not by Conrad alone; they were by Conrad-Ford.

'Let me tell you something, my boy,' said Harris senior: 'Your Mr. Ford is either very much of a somebody or very much of a nobody.'[23]

He was back in Paris on 4 July, just as the August number of the review, put together by Hemingway, was about to go to press. Hemingway told Pound he had 'tried to run his paper the way he would have liked to have it run, except for not printing J. J. Adams and such poets'. But he had also not printed the final instalment of Luke Ionides's memoir, nor the instalments of Ford's 'Stocktaking' and the serialization of *Some Do Not . . .*. As Poli says, it was a slap in the face to the editor. It was guaranteed to annoy Ford in other ways. 'Hemingway assisted me', he wrote wryly, 'by trying to insert as a serial the complete works of Baroness Elsa Von Freytag Loringhofen. I generally turned round in time to take them out of the contents table.' This time he was too late. The Baroness was a 'fascinating and grotesque' figure, who pursued Carlos Williams 'with a bold and shameless passion'. Ford said she was often at the review office, and that he thought 'the stories of her eccentricities were exaggerated' until he agreed to help her get her *permis de séjour* extended. He made a date to meet her at the Paris Consulate-General, waited there for two hours, then went home:

I found the telephone bell ringing and a furious friend at the British Embassy at the end of it. He wanted to know what the hell I meant by sending them a Prussian lady simply dressed in a brassière of milktins connected by dog chains, and wearing on her head a plum-cake! So attired, she that afternoon repaired from the Embassy to a café, where she laid out an amiable and quite inoffensive lady, and so became the second poet of my acquaintance to be expelled from France. The Embassy discontinued its subscription of the *review*.[24]

Most importantly, Hemingway had also violated the internationalist principle of the review, by making the August number a predominantly American one. It was too late to change the contents. Ford could only add a paragraph at the end of his editorial headed 'An Americanisation':

During our absence on those other pavements this Review has been ably edited by Mr. Ernest Hemingway, the admirable Young American prose writer [. . .] It must prove an agreeable change for the Reader and it provides him with an unusually large sample of the work of that Young America whose claims we have so insistently—but not with such efficiency—forced upon our readers [. . .]

For the rest, with its next number the Review will re-assume its international aspect, the final instalments of Mr. Chaucer and Mr. Ionides being to appear, and, should any large body of readers so demand, some more of *Some Do Not*. Other works of English and French writers will also be again allowed to creep in.

Mild enough under the circumstances, but Hemingway was enraged, feeling that his own writing had suffered while he had been helping Ford. Predictably, a large body did not demand Ford's continuation. 'Two readers have made that request,' Ford reported in September with grim humour: 'We therefore continue.'[25]

Despite the financial and factional pressures, Ford was still an exemplary editor, writing detailed advice to the writers whose work he was rejecting. 'As *machining* this story is wrong, though it's attractive', he told Llewelyn Powys, who had submitted a story which turned on a woman taking offence at a note she found: 'a psychological story sh^d. not have a material turning point'—excellent advice, doubtless sharpened by his having thought about how to keep the material turning-point at the end of Part I of *Some Do Not* . . . —when Campion's car smashes into Valentine's and Tietjens's dog-cart—from overwhelming the psychological turning-point as they fall in love. Characteristically, even Ford's rejections were encouragements: 'Send me something else, will you?' he asked Powys. 'Try to be a little more vulgar', he advised another would-be contributor whose work he thought 'all too literary': 'read, say, the worst passages of *Ulysses* a great many times over. In that case The Adelphi, Life and Letters, the Weekly Westminster and the rest will never print you again and you will probably be arrested for smashing windows in Tiger Bay. But you will feel a different man.'[26] It's hard to imagine any other editor giving such bizarrely comic advice. This extraordinary letter is a good example of why Ford's generous, omniscient cynicism can provoke divided responses: is it tactless arrogance, a 'nerve', to be funny at the expense of someone's ambitions; or is it the best kind of criticism an aspiring writer could get?

Ford and Bowen gave a dinner for the Harrises, and William Aspenwall Bradley and his French wife Jenny, at the Pavillon du Lac at the Parc Montsouris. Stella greatly admired Jenny Bradley, the best conversationalist she had met, and wise and courageous as well as witty. William Bradley was 'an extremely cultivated and sensitive person with a kind of whimsical gaiety that could create the party spirit at any dinner-table where he sat'. Markham Harris was being the awkward teenager, leaving 'a finely qualitative progression of wines all but untasted'. When Ford noticed that he wasn't trying the finale either—a Cinq Fruits liqueur—he called the boy to the head of the table: 'The Master, seizing a lump of sugar, dipped it into his own diminutive portion and advanced it towards the boy's lips. The eucharistic morsel dissolved mildly and unforgettably on his tongue.' Ford gave Pound a sketch of his routine this summer in Paris: 'I am generally here [in the Boulevard Arago studio] of a morning till 11; reach my office about 11.30 and stay there till lunch. We dine practically every evening at the Nègre de Toulouse, next the Closerie de Lilas and almost as invariably go to drink coffee at the Closerie de Lilas itself.' They colonized the back room with only tables at the Negre de Toulouse, where they 'had the fun of eating in company without having to entertain', becoming friendly with the owner and his wife (Bowen painted their portraits). They held a Bastille Day party at the Dôme. Markham Harris called it Ford's 'literary levee', and was struck by the number of well-known writers who attended, and by being introduced to 'the two most beautiful women in Paris'— William Bullitt's wife, and a Mrs Murphy. Later they moved on to a street dance. Yet despite the festivities, Ford had written to Pound on the same day saying that he was calling a meeting of the directors' to wind up the review'. It didn't take place, because the lawyer was out of town. On 28 July John Quinn died. The future of the review was looking bleak. Hemingway said Ford was 'threatening to bring out a quarterly which was pretty vaporous as he had about decided to use the death of Quinn as an excuse to kill off the magazine'. But it was then that Hemingway produced Krebs Friend as a backer. Nathan Asch, one of the review's contributors, described Friend as a 'confused war veteran' who looked like 'what later came to be known as *death warmed over*', and who had married an heiress forty years older than himself. They lived in one of the few rooms rented by La Tour d'Argent, and ordered their meals from the restaurant. Her hope was that the review would 'focus his attention sufficiently to want to become a writer or an editor or something that was not a melancholy specter, as he was, who wanted more than anything to die'.[27]

'Well the news is that the transatlantic is going on', wrote Hemingway to Stein and Toklas:

I have a friend in town who (or whom) I got to guarantee Ford $200 a month for six months with the first check written out and the others the first of each month with an option at the end of 6 mos. of buying Ford out and keeping him on as Editor or continuing the 200 a month for another six months.

That of course was not good enough for Ford, who had hitherto stayed up all night writing pneumatiques and spent 100s of francs on taxis to get 500 francs out of Natalie Barney and that sort of business. Once the grandeur started working Ford insisted on 25,000 francs down in addition and then as the grandeur increased he declared he wanted no money at all till October if Krebs, this guy, could guarantee him 15,000 francs then! It is a type of reasoning that I cannot follow with any degree of sympathy.

I got Krebs to back the magazine purely on the basis that a good mag. printing yourself and edited by old Ford, a veteran of the world war, etc. should not be allowed to go haywired.

Now Ford's attitude is that he is selling Krebs an excellent business proposition and that Krebs is consequently a business man and the foe of all artists of which he—Ford—is the only living example and in duty bound as a representative of the dying race to grind he—Krebs, the natural Foe—into the ground. He's sure to quarrel with Krebs between now and Oct. on that basis and Krebs was ready with the ft. [fountain] pen and check book. I hope that Bumbie [the Hemingways' baby son] will not grow up and get the megalomania.[28]

The Fordian grand manner with businessmen sounds all too accurate; Ford referred to Friend privately as 'the capitalist'. But according to Marjorie Reid, the Friends 'expected it to be profitable and also to attain a status in the publishing field'. At first things went smoothly. Krebs was made president of the review at a meeting on 15 August, and had breakfast every morning with Ford. But according to Hemingway, 'Ford of course refused to take a definite sum from Krebs and would accept nothing except Krebs taking over the debts and running it as a business proposition, i.e. a money making proposition, filling him up on fake figures to feed his own ego and kidding himself that it was a money making proposition'. When they found debts that Ford 'neglected to mention', Henrietta Friend became suspicious; the cheques weren't sent to contributors. 'I'm sick of Ford and his megalomaniac blundering at the way he spoiled the chance he had with the review that it takes a great effort not to row, but I won't', said Hemingway, unconvincingly. When Ford discovered that *The Making of Americans* was not the novella Hemingway had let him believe, he wrote a confidential letter to Stein to apologize for the mistake. But when Hemingway saw it, he couldn't keep up his pretence of separating the personal and the literary any longer. He wrote furiously to Stein and Toklas denouncing Ford as 'an absolute liar and crook always motivated by the finest synthetic English gentility'. The Friends tried to reduce expenditure by suggesting that the younger writers should contribute without being paid 'and show their loyalty to the magazine by chasing ads during the daylight hours'. Hemingway was plotting to oust Ford: 'I am getting young Bus [Barklie M.] Henry that married Barbara Whitney into shape so that if anything ever happens to Krebs we can throw out Ford and the whole lot of them and make a real magazine out of it.' No wonder Ford described himself as 'a sort of half-way house between nonpublishable youth and real money—a sort of green baize swing door that everyone kicks both on entering and leaving' (this was another passage that Graham Greene annotated as representing Ford's 'Quixotism'). Only a year later, he could see—with equanimity—that 'It is the duty of the young to hate the old'. The review 'went out as it were to drift until some pirates or other took possession of it': 'That is how the periodical you think to administer takes charge [. . .].' If business elicited a bluffing that looked like mega-lomania to Hemingway (as it had to Conrad in the days of the *English Review*), editing, like writing, elicited the opposite: an extraordinary responsiveness.[29]

1924: THE LAST OF CONRAD AND OF THE *transatlantic*

Sleep after toyle, port after stormie seas,
Ease after warre, death after life, does greatly please

(Edmund Spenser, quoted by Conrad as epigraph to *The Rover*)

When the tenancy of the Boulevard Arago studio was coming to an end Gertrude Stein told Ford of an attractive house at Guermantes, a tiny village of about eight cottages, three miles from Lagny, and hour's train-ride east of Paris. Bowen went to look. The house was too big, but nearby she found 'an old stone labourer's cottage with four rooms and a small orchard, to let at five hundred francs a year'. 'We took it as a kind of insurance against complete homelessness', she said. When she had decorated it ('with the help of an aged villager'), Julie was installed, together with 'an un-co[o]perative and suspicious Madame Annie'. Madame Annie, 'a lively little widow of forty with a formidable temper', was getting possessive of her charge, and began to resent Ford's and Bowen's presence at the weekends, and Julie's pleasure in seeing them. Nevertheless, they kept the cottage for nearly three years. It became 'something of a home'. It was 'pleasant country of an insignificant sort', said Ford: 'not far from Paris and just this side of the devastated zone'. It was probably from Guermantes that Ford drove, from 'a ramshackle, commonplace farm-building in an undistinguished country over slight hills on a flinty by-road and suddenly heard Conrad saying to him: "Well, Ford, mon vieux, how would you render that field of wheat?"' The similarity of the landscape to the 'country of commonplace downlands' over which he and Conrad used to drive ('say between 1898 and 1905') made him imagine he was hearing Conrad's voice again. He went on thinking about how to describe the landscape as he and 'his companion' (Stella?) bought tickets and an English paper at the 'dilapidated station':

The writer exclaimed: Look! *Look!* . . . His companion unfolded the paper. The announcement went across two columns in black, leaded caps. . . . *SUDDEN DEATH OF JOSEPH CONRAD.*
They were demolishing an antiquated waiting-room on the opposite platform, three white-
dusty men with pickaxes: a wall was all in broken zigzags. The writer said to himself: 'C'est
le mur d'un silence éternel qui descend devant vous!' There descended across the dusty wall
a curtain of moonlight, thrown across by the black shadows of oak trees. We were on a
verandah that had a glass roof. Under the glass roof climbed passion flowers, and vine
tendrils strangled them. We were sitting in deck chairs. It was one o'clock in the morning.
Conrad was standing in front of us, talking. Talking on and on in the patches of moonlight
and patches of shadow from the passion flowers and vines! The little town in which we were

dominated the English channel from a low hill-top. He was wearing a dark reefer coat and white trousers.

He was talking of Malaysia, palm trees, the little wives of rajahs in coloured sarongs [. . .]

That then was Conrad on the occasions when he talked as he did on that first evening after dinner. His voice was then usually low, rather intimate and caressing. He began by speaking slowly but later on he spoke very fast.[1]

James had died in 1916, Hudson in 1922. Conrad was the last of his three great mentors, and (since Marwood's death in 1916) the last intimate friend of his Winchelsea days. So there was personal force in Ford's critical assessment that it was 'the end of a whole literary phase'.[2] The double-displacement in this passage—from the French station to Winchelsea, then from Winchelsea to Malaysia (and even that is hesitant, disavowed: 'it might have been Palembang, but of course it was not Palembang')—registers the disorientation of Ford's shock of grief. 'Unless you have these details you cannot know how immensely strong an impression this beautiful genius made on a mind not vastly impressionable or prone to forming affections. . . .' So, unless we have the details of the precise moment when Ford found out Conrad was dead, we cannot know the force of that impression. The cubistic, slightly surreal images—the dilapidation, the three 'white-dusty men with pickaxes', the broken zigzags of the wall—evoke the pathos of decay. The passion flowers strangled by vine leaves present an extraordinarily expressive image for friendship and grief (it says the plot of *The Good Soldier* with flowers). But the vertiginous shift in which the broken wall becomes 'le mur d'un silence éternel', the descent of this wall becomes the descent of a curtain (a paradoxically immaterial 'curtain of moonlight', like the invisible curtains and tents of Ford's visionary fables), and day becomes night—this shift evokes the force of Conrad's presence in his mind (as he had been present, in Ford's mind's ear at least) on the journey to the station.

As always for Ford, biography is concealed autobiography. When the *Yale Review* had asked him for a personal piece about Conrad in 1920 he had apologized that the essay he wrote was 'not of a very personal character':

When you live in terms of close intimacy with a person it is difficult, or indeed impossible to write of them personally—at any rate whilst they are alive. Had it been Henry James whom I knew quite as well as I know Mr Conrad, it would have been a different matter—because, I do not know why, the dead seem to offer themselves more freely, as persons, to the pen than the living.[3]

Because they don't answer back? A hostile critic might say that death granted him a poetic licence. But his rendering of hearing about the death of Conrad is reaching towards a subtler understanding of what released his most potent reminiscential energies. The *mise en abyme* of memories takes us from Ford writing his memoir, to the scene three weeks before when he was remembering Conrad, just before hearing of his death; the news takes him back to the days of their collaboration; but what he remembers as most characteristic is Conrad doing the same thing: reminiscing about his own past. This doesn't just pose Ford as Conrad's double, with an affinity for reminiscence. In recording his impression of Conrad's death, he is also expressing how death elicits his most intimate reminiscences, bringing down a curtain of moonlight by which he can (like old Hamlet's ghost) revisit the past; how reading the news while thinking Conradianly about how to render the circumstances leads him to render the circumstances in which he heard the death, and those about which he was thinking when he heard the news—the collaboration, and what it meant to him. In other words, he is also explaining what it is that impelled him to write his superb memoir, *Joseph Conrad*. Ford had expressed anxiety that he could no longer write about Conrad with generosity (and lack of generosity was for him a mortal sin). But now, Conrad's death empowered another of Ford's finest books; rather as Marwood's ghost was presiding over the writing of *Parade's End*. Samuel Putnam, (who met Ford in America and knew him in Paris in the later 1920s) said he was often laughingly known as 'the great Reminiscer': 'he had an indubitable gift for bringing to life any sector of the literary past that, in the course of his long years, he had chanced to touch.' Ford described his reminiscences in similar terms, saying that the 'Official Biography' has killed off great writers until 'the time comes, years after, for some creative artist to have a try at re-breathing life into their dead bones'. Yet, as always in Ford, the power of animation is predicated on the sense of mortality. It was more than two years later that Ford wrote about the impact of the deaths of Conrad, Crane, and James, saying: 'it is only at this moment that for the first time in my life I have actually realized that they are all three dead, so vividly do I still see them and still feel their wonderful presences.' Now he felt that his 'intimate contact with artistic life is completely at an end with the death of the last of them. To realize that is like dying oneself [. . .].'[4]

His idea that 'the purpose of the novel today seems to me to be purely historic' turns on a similar duality of pastness and presence. He thought the novel 'has to form the history of our own times brick as it were by brick, simply because our life is so varied in aspect and so overwhelmingly peopled'. The paradoxical notion of the 'history of our own times', rather than the history of time past, tells a truth about narrative. Whatever tense a novel is narrated in, the fact that we hold the finished product in our hands shows us that the events are finished before the narrative has begun. It tells a truth about consciousness—one particularly important to Ford—that the moment we have *perceived* something, and grasped what it is, what it means, then that perception is already in the past. (The perplexed dialogue in his novels is the best example of this, where comprehension continually lags behind listening or reading.) But it is also a way of staving off, and mastering, anxieties about your own death. Becoming the historian of your own times, you become in effect your own historian, bringing yourself back to the life you imagine as having taken place in the past. The advantage of becoming your own ghost is that you have put even death behind you. When Ford praised novelists for the 'historic sense' he meant to distinguish timeless art from ephemeral journalism. (But, again, the criterion is immortality: if the writing is good enough it will survive.) One feature that distinguishes fiction from journalism is that it is free from the fiction that it is 'news'—about the present. (Christine Brooke-Rose has pointed out—on television—that the solution found by television news to combat this instant death of reportage is to frame much of its comment in the future tense.) Ford wanted the novel to minister to the bewilderment of a varied and overwhelming life; and he found the most effective way to do that was to imagine having 'remembrance now' of that life, through the imagined displacement of memory.[5]

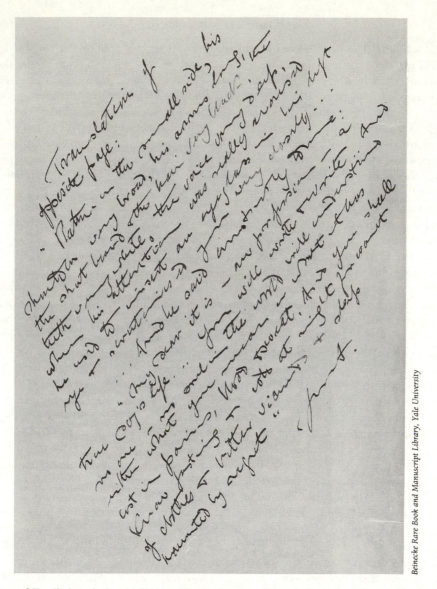

Part of Ford's inscription in George Keating's copy of *Joseph Conrad: A Personal Remembrance*, translating his own French inscription, taken from pp. 253–6 of the book:

Translation of opposite page:

'Rather on the small side, his shoulders very broad, his arms long, the short beard & the hair very black, the teeth very white, the voice very deep, when his attention was really aroused he used to insert an eyeglass in his left eye & scrutinised you very closely . . .

. . . And he said insistently to me:

'My dear it is—our profession—a true dog's life . . . You will write & write. And no one—no soul in the world will understand either what you mean or what it has cost in pains, blood & sweat. And you shall know fasting and cold at night for want of clothes & bitter viands & sleep haunted by regret'

Ford wrote a brief tribute to Conrad in French—the language that Conrad had told him, once again when they had met in May, was the language he thought in—less than a week after learning of his death. It was published in the Paris *Journal Littéraire* on 16 August. 'Aujourd'hui il est mort: le plus grand maître, le plus grand dompteur de ces choses sauvages que sont les mots, les rythmes, les phrases et les cadences de la langue anglaise—le plus grand que nos îles aient vu . . .' In another attempt to convey the strength of his feelings, he reprinted the article as an appendix to the book on Conrad he wrote—'at fever heat', he said, 'in an extraordinarily short time for I had, as it were, to get it out of my system'—over the next two months. He said he was appending the article 'For those not dreading more emotion than the English language will bear', and that he 'could not face its translation'—a disavowing expression of what he is suppressing. In it he describes Conrad, driving his long-eared mare that people mistook for a mule, as the last Don Quixote of the *mot juste* in England; which made Ford, as he ironically acknowledged, surely his Sancho Panza. The nondescript cornfields were his windmills. Several years later, when he gave a copy of the book to George Keating, he did translate a couple of paragraphs as an autograph inscription. One is probably the most emotional passage in the essay:

And he said insistently to me:
'My dear it is—our profession—a true dog's life . . . You will write and write. And no one—no soul in the world will understand either what you mean or what it has cost in pains, blood & sweat. And you shall know fasting and cold at night for want of clothes & bitter viands & sleep haunted by regret'[6]

The French continues: 'Et vous trouverez jamais, jamais pendant toute votre vie, une âme pour vous dire si à la fin vous êtes le plus grand génie du monde . . . Ni non plus si vous êtes le dernier, le plus infecte descendant de . . . Ponson du Terrail . . .' That was certainly Ford's anguish too: that he could never be sure whether he was a genius or a hack (Ponson was a best-selling nineteenth-century roman-feuilletonist, who could produce up to forty volumes a year). Ford became the person who could tell Conrad that he was the greatest genius; and why the fact of having collaborated mattered so much to him was that it showed Conrad's belief in his—Ford's—powers: the reassurance was implicit and reciprocal; for 'It is certain any conviction gains infinitely the moment another soul will believe in it'. Ford's memoir is also an attempt to persuade other souls to believe in his conviction that Conrad's *presence* survives his death. This, more than any desire to enshrine himself with Conrad for posterity, impels the book: a sense of how thoroughly Conrad's influence has pervaded Ford's life and writing.

Joseph Conrad is remarkable for the courage with which it does face the more disturbing aspects of their relationship, especially Conrad's aggression towards Ford. This comes out most strongly in the vignette describing how they went to London to deliver some of the proofs of *Romance*. Conrad remembered a phrase he wanted to correct, and, because of the jolting of the train, had to lie on his stomach on the floor of the carriage to write. They were alone. 'Naturally when the one phrase was corrected twenty other necessities for correction stuck out of the page.' Conrad became completely engrossed:

The final shadow of Charing Cross was over us. It must have been very difficult to see down there. He never moved. . . . Mildly shocked at the idea that a porter might open the carriage door and think us peculiar the writer touched Conrad on the shoulder and said: 'We're there!' Conrad's face was most extraordinary—suffused and madly vicious. He sprang to his feet and straight at the writer's throat. . . .

The writing gives a powerful impression of the powerful impression the scene made on Ford, which made him repeat the story several times. Its power comes partly from the surprise: the scenes in Ford's novels of train journeys terminated with explosive crashes (*Ladies Whose Bright Eyes*; *The Marsden Case*) owe much to the way this routine trip suddenly erupts into murderous passion. The episode occurs under the 'final shadow' of death, of course: the prophetic glimpse of Conrad as dead—lying on the floor, in an underworld of darkness, unmoving; and Ford's own, strangled by his closest friend of those days. Conrad here acts like one of the dead or absent fathers in Ford's fiction who haunt their offspring, driving them to death. Which suggests that Ford's feelings of guilt towards his father are invoked here by his feelings for Conrad as a father-figure. The rage of the prostrate figure may be related to the homoeroticism that is also touched on in the idea that they might be thought 'peculiar', a thought that makes Ford touch Conrad's shoulder. The scene captures all the uncertainty about Conrad's true feelings that his nervous irritability made Ford feel. There are two ways in which Ford struggles to evade that wrath. First, he tries to account for it as an occupational hazard: 'The practice of expressing your thoughts with exactitude in words is one demanding a great tenseness of the brain, is an operation at times almost agonising, always engrossing, frequently it causes exasperation with the outer world, beyond reason, moderation or decency.' 'To be suddenly disturbed is apt to cause a second's real madness', especially when the *homo duplex* is in another world. So if you don't want to get bitten, avoid the *métier de chien*. Secondly, Ford uses to describe the attack the very idea that he and Conrad used to describe the subject's hold on its author ('certain subjects will grip you with a force almost supernatural, as if something came from behind the printed, the written or the spoken word [. . .] and caught you by the throat, really saying: *Treat me*'); the author's hold on his subject ('gripping it by the throat, extract from it every drop of blood and glamour'); and the work's hold on its reader ('the reader's attention must be gripped'; Ford liked to think it was half-sentences of his—like 'Excellency, a few goats. . . .'—that 'jumped out of the prose and caught Conrad by the throat'). Ford is trying to recuperate Conrad's rage as technique; as something that united rather than antagonized them. To that extent he seems to be denying his anxieties about betrayal and neurotic anger, rather as Dowell tries to deny his, saying he was relieved by Leonora's explanation of the 'Protest' scene. But of course like that episode it is another of Ford's magnificent dual effects. His *context* works to neutralize the outburst, saying that even though Conrad hurt him 'a good deal' (as he puts it in the unpublished version), he is easily forgiven because it was an expression of Conrad's commitment to their collaboration rather than a sign of hatred. But the *image* isn't so easily pacified, and stays in the mind as the episode did in Ford's (its echoing through the book being an element of its deft technique). Though much of Ford's writing about Conrad attempts to deny their rupture—which to Ford was as unbelievable as Conrad's death—it is, as here, haunted by the signs of the ambivalences that heralded Conrad's eventual rejection of him.[7]

When Ford heard that the Harrises were going to visit Canterbury, he asked them to put flowers on Conrad's grave. He sent them money by *pneumatique*, together with a card almost certainly carrying the message: 'C'est toi qui dors dans l'ombre'—part of the last line of Hugo's 'Tristesse d'Olympio' that they had used as epigraph to Ford's poem that was itself epigraph to *Romance*. He used the same words as the title for the serial on Conrad he also began that August (since the first section appeared in the September *transatlantic*)—the serial that became most of the first part of his book *Joseph Conrad*. The complete line is 'C'est toi qui dors dans l'ombre, o sacré souvenir'. ('It's you who sleep in the shadow, sacred memory'.) Ending it with *ombre* makes it more sombre: the sleep a euphemism for death. Restoring the ending makes it more ambiguous. Is the *souvenir* the act of recollection (by which memory can restore the past), or the thing recollected (whose pastness is irrevocable)? The point is not just Ford's tact in recalling the phrase which sets the tone of their major collaboration as the aptest expression of mourning, and of the hope that Conrad should rest in peace. It is also that the line stands for the power of the shadow of death to stir Ford's reminiscence, and to arouse his romancing about the past.[8]

Now he would produce a Conrad Supplement to the review. But there was little time if it were to appear in September. According to Robert McAlmon, Ford wired several writers asking for appraisals of Conrad. Then McAlmon spoke to Hemingway and Mary Butts amongst them: 'Each of us thought that his article was to be the sole article, and, if I remember rightly, not any of us had ever been Conrad enthusiasts.' But then if McAlmon had ever been a Ford enthusiast, it didn't last after Ford, unimpressed by Pound's enthusiasm for him, and returning McAlmon's lecture on how he (Ford) would never be able to write, made him the target of one of his rare denigrations of writers (especially living writers). 'The two worst writers I have met in Paris (I don't, of course, meet any banal ones!) are Waldo Frank and Robert McAlmon', he wrote the following year. After that, McAlmon took his revenge by adopting Hemingway's version of Ford as the bungling mythomaniac. In August he wasn't too offended to contribute a rambling essay on Conrad. None of the essays were the tribute Ford (rightly) felt Conrad deserved. But it was Hemingway's that upset him, as it was meant to. He began with a parody of what the 'editorial writers' would say about Conrad; compared the critics writing about Conrad to prairie dogs; and ended with a further dig at his review's own editorial writer and Conrad critic, saying that he wished to God that 'some great, acknowledged technician of a literary figure'— read Ford—had been taken instead of Conrad. He said that people told him Conrad was a bad writer and T. S. Eliot a good one, but that Conrad had taught him something that he'd got 'from nothing else' he had read, and that if he knew 'that by grinding Mr. Eliot into a fine dry powder and sprinkling that powder over Mr. Conrad's grave Mr. Conrad would shortly appear, looking very annoyed at the forced return and commence writing', then he would 'leave for London early tomorrow morning with a sausage grinder'.[9]

Hemingway's onslaught on Ford was visible in his own 'editorial' for the same issue.

He said Ford had asked him to write a 'Pamplona Letter', to make amends for having published the writer 'X' (probably the Baroness Elsa Von Freytag-Loringhofen). But instead he wrote about the argument they almost certainly had then. He wouldn't write 'journalism' unless he were better paid for it: 'when you destroy the valuable things you have by writing about them you want to get big money for it [. . .] It is only by never writing the way I write in a newspaper office, though, that I make you believe that I can write.' 'It is only when you can no longer believe in your exploits that you write your memoirs', he said. If this is shrewd about the motivations of autobiography, it scarcely disguises his contempt for Ford's story-telling; though, as Poli suggests, readers of Hemingway's own reminiscences in *A Moveable Feast* might wonder what doubt it casts on that book's fidelity. Hemingway had Ford cornered. While his friend was financing the review it was impossible for Ford to sack him, even if he had wanted to rid himself of an attacker. The future of the review, and his own editorial scrupulousness about not wishing to censor, made it impossible for him to edit Hemingway's insults out of the magazine. He returned to the 'sausage grinder' remark in his November editorial, saying: 'We had invited that writer to write, we had indicated no limits to his blood thirstyness: our hands fell powerless to our sides. We were besides convinced that Mr Eliot would not mind. He does not. We take the opportunity of expressing for the tenth time our admiration for Mr Eliot's poetry.' But passive resistance did not pacify Hemingway, and Ford's joshing attempts to make peace seemed to him a treacherous apology (Ford's implication that the editorial 'We' didn't include his sub-editor must have rankled too). He continued boxing at his shadow-Ford. When Burton Rascoe and his wife came to Paris Ford sent them a *pneumatique* inviting them to dinner. Afterwards, he took them to a *bal musette*:

Ford introduced us to Nancy Cunard, E. E. Cummings, Robert McAlmon [. . .] and to Mrs. Ernest Hemingway. Hemingway was there, but he and Ford were not speaking. Hemingway came up to me and introduced himself. After Ford had asked my wife and me and Mrs. Hemingway to sit at a table with him, Hemingway said to Mrs. Hemingway, 'Pay for your own drinks, do you hear! Don't let him [nodding toward Ford] buy you anything.'[10]

This was the Bal du Printemps in the rue du Cardinal Lemoine, behind the Panthéon. It was a simple cafe that doubled as a working-class dance-hall. It was usually closed on Fridays, but in the summer Ford had got the owner to open it so that he and Bowen could entertain there. 'The music was dispensed by a gloomy, collarless accordion-player, with a perpetual half-smoked cigarette dangling from his lips', said Goldring, 'who sat in a sort of pulpit above the dance floor.' Bowen described how 'the rough tables and wooden benches were painted scarlet and the walls around the dance floor were set with mirrors and painted pink, with garlands, all done by hand!' There was a long zinc bar. It made for volatile social gatherings. Strangers might drift in. 'You would find yourself dancing with someone', said Bowen:

Nothing but the coat sleeve to indicate whether he should be addressed in French or English. You decide to try English:
   'I love an accordion,' you say.
   He, 'So do I. I have a beauty at home, in carved ivory and pink silk. My wife gave it to me the first time she was unfaithful to me.' Dare you ask if he got a piano the second time?

'Perhaps not', she added—she had never lost that trace of middle-class propriety and restraint. Jean Rhys, who had, described it (in fiction) as 'a family ball. If you want something *louche* you walk further on [. . .].' The British were the life and soul of the party, said Bowen: the painters Lett Haines and Cedric Morris, Mary Butts, Lady Duff Twysden (the model for Lady Brett Ashley in *The Sun Also Rises*), and her companion Pat Guthrie ('a well-known Montparnasse play-boy whose services to the arts have not been recorded', said Goldring, but didn't record them; 'a tall, dissipated Scot with narrow shoulders and a wide-ranging thirst', said Carlos Baker). The *transatlantic* crew were regulars. But these groups were disapproved of as 'decadent artists' by what Bowen called '100 per cent efficient and clean living Americans who wanted to organise the whole thing as a club', with subscriptions and an attendance register:

Then journalists began to drop in who wanted to write us up, which made Ford very angry, especially when one of them asked if he was 'making a good thing out of it!' And the journalists would bring Englishwomen in evening dress, who thought it fun to go slumming in Paris, to see how the artists amused themselves in their lairs. So eventually the whole thing died.[11]

Rhys (her mind perhaps running on Ford's partiality to grand cars), sketched a proprietorial-sounding Ford as 'Mr Rolls, the author', who hired the Bal du Printemps for his weekly parties:

the quality of the brandy left a great deal to be desired. Imagining that it was very weak, people drank a good deal of it, and it generally had a very bad effect on their tempers.
    Midnight. The band struck up *Valencia* for the sixth time.
    Somebody said to somebody else: 'It's all very well to talk about Jew noses, but have you ever tried to paint your own mouth?'
    The artist addressed burst into tears.
    'He's only trying to be modern and brutal and all that, poor dear,' said her friend . . . 'Don't mind him.'
    '*Fine à l'eau*,' bawled a tall dark gentleman immediately in Mr Rolls's ear.
    'Don't shout in my ear,' said Mr Rolls irritably.
    'Well, get out of the way,' said the tall dark gentleman. 'Always blocking up the bar.'
    'It's my bar,' remarked Mr Rolls with majesty.
    'Then you ought to give your clients a chance,' said the other.
    Mr Rolls wandered about, asking: 'Who brought that chap? How did that chap get in here? Who on earth is that chap?' Nobody knew. It did not matter.[12]

When Pound left Paris in October it was for good, to settle in Rapallo. Ford said that he too was out of France, finishing *Joseph Conrad* in Bruges on 5 October. The book describes the Hueffer–Conrad trip to Bruges in 1900, so doubtless Ford wanted to end it by recalling the scene of that collaboration which had been its main theme. Which is not to say that he wasn't there. He was finding it harder to write in Paris, and may have had to leave for a few days to get the book finished. He dropped in on Huddleston, living nearby in the Boulevard Raspail, to read to him from the proofs of *Joseph Conrad*: of all his books, this must have been the one he most needed to read aloud, with its evocation of the two collaborators reading to each other. In his preface to *The Nature of a Crime* Ford said: 'We wrote and read aloud the one to the other.

Possibly in the end we even wrote *to* read aloud the one to the other.' Ford had lost his imagined sympathetic listener; the man with whom he would have imaginary conversations about composition. From his high roof-garden, Huddleston looked over the 'myriad lights of Paris sprinkled among the stars of an autumn night' as Ford read, and he was 'touched to tears by the magic of words'.[13]

Just as the November issue of the magazine was going to press, Ford heard of the death of Anatole France (whose 'charitable irony' Conrad had praised in the review Ford had badgered him to write in the *English Review*). He wrote another elegiac editorial, praising France's 'clearness of expression', carried 'to a point beyond which no man will perhaps ever go'. He probably knew this would only confirm the young Americans' impression of him as *passé*; he may even have intended a gentle rebuke that Hemingwayesque sparseness and bluntness wasn't the only form of clarity, and wasn't necessarily the most effective. For he also acknowledged the war amongst the editors, saying: 'If our sub-editors permit it the end of the first part of *Some do Not* will appear in this number'—the serial was then to be discontinued now that the book had also been published in America in October. He also published some poems by 'the gentle poet' Ralph Cheever Dunning, which Hemingway said didn't look 'very solid': 'There is one about "Then put a lily in my hand And float me out to sea" or something like that that's pretty near the goddamdest poem I've ever read.'

It's hard to know what exactly to make of Ford's next, and final editorial. Poli calls it a transparent allegory, assuming it to describe an 'imaginary episode'. But in those carefree and alcoholic days it's not impossible that something of the sort took place.

On a windy night last week any traveller blown along the Parnassian heights of Paris might have observed, setting out from a flaring hostelry, a Band bearing ropes and illuminated by their own torches. The names of their leaders will be found on our covers; from their upraised voices you would have known that they were about to burn down this Office and that from those ropes, suspended sixty feet above the Seine and the conflagration, should dangle . . . Ourselves. That was because last month we dared to print certain Regular Poems . . . What became of that band we do not know. From the other side of the street we watched them until they became entangled with a band of openmouthed British tourists: it was also Guy Fawkes day! . . . Or the reflection may have occurred to the leaders that if they then burned this building and hanged ourselves their names probably would not—as they do—this month adorn our covers. At any rate the Seine still flows before our grey doors and our necks feel normal.

That is how the course of Literature makes its way. When we are gathered to Anatole France the happy band who are now the crew of this periodical shall issue a pamphlet called *A Rotten Corpse* and so dance upon our remains. That is proper.[14]

Ford referred to this as 'what we will as irritatingly as possible style a Children's Number, with Mr. Havelock Ellis, Miss Stein and ourselves parentally to gaze upon the firelit revels'. The *enfants terribles* included Rhys, and the Americans Hemingway, McAlmon, Evan Shipman, Nathan Asch, and Ivan Beede. For all the burlesque of the pompous editorial 'we', there are earnest undertones. Imagining *les jeunes* dancing on his remains is more than just a self-mocking staging of his own death. *A Rotten Corpse* alludes to the pamphlet the French Surrealists published about Anatole France's death: *Un Cadavre*. (Though Ford had imagined himself as a 'Mouldering Corpse' in one of his 'Tristia' sequence of wartime poems.) Ford dated his editorial 'Armistice Day', signifying not only his remembrance of the war, but the fact that there would have to be a cease-fire in the battle of the poets and *prosateurs* of the *transatlantic*. For he had other reasons to talk of his demise. At the end of November he had to call a meeting to explain to the directors and shareholders that the review could not continue unless they could find 'anyone else to carry it on'. They couldn't. The disarray amongst the editorial team didn't help. Ford was refusing to have anything more to do with Seltzer, who had still not sent any money either for the American copies of the review or for *Some Do Not . . .*. He told Monroe Wheeler: 'I will not continue to edit the review if Mr. Seltzer goes on publishing it. Absolutely not [. . .] I pay for the review out of the earnings of my books, the money paid by other people being a mere flea-bite compared with what I have spent on it. If then Mr. Seltzer does not pay for my books and does not pay for the review, I cannot continue it.' Yet he still hoped he could continue it with another New York publisher, and in the same letter asked Wheeler to investigate an offer of American backing: 'We need exactly £1,000 to go on here for another six months. If your people can find two thirds of this I am ready to go on and find the other third [. . .] I have already found nearly frs 120,000 personally and as it has mostly gone to boosting American writers it is time your side took a hand.' He ended his last editorial saying that he was forced 'to suspend the appearance of this review for a short period', but that 'a—really very hard faced!—member of our staff' would go to America to try to make other arrangements; and that meanwhile 'we shall occupy ourselves with the study of French Company Law. Then once more, towards the spring, the *transatlantic review* will resume its tranquil voyagings.'[15]

It never did, and its place in Paris was soon filled by more consistently avant-garde magazines like Ernest Walsh's *This Quarter* and Eugene Jolas's *transition*. But Ford remained convinced that what was needed was a truly international and unpartisan review, and later tried to relaunch it. Writers like Hemingway and McAlmon thought the ideal was a lost cause, and that Ford had misjudged his audience. Some critics have felt that both aspects of his inclusiveness were self-defeating: that the *transatlantic* was too international to sell well in any one nation; and that it represented too many literary schools to be esteemed by any one. The praise from reviewers indicates that Ford's ideal appealed to some discerning readers, though they were probably too few for commercial success. The comprehensiveness of the magazine expressed Ford's literary personality and sense of his own imaginative domicile—as a writer born in England, taught how to write by the French (Flaubert, Maupassant) and the Americans (James, Crane), living amongst young Americans in Paris, and becoming more interested in Literary America. There are signs that Ford expected it to fail—needed to martyr and beggar himself for ungrateful geniuses. There were three symptoms of his altruism addiction in the review. First, an offer to supply free copies 'to such practising artists as are really unable to afford francs 7.50' (the money provided by 'One of our subscribers'—probably Ford). Secondly, a proposal to run a 'Book Service' for readers having trouble getting foreign books (the suggestion that the choice of titles could be left to the review staff seems to guarantee complaint). This caused a row with Sylvia Beach, who took the comment about the 'notorious' cost of foreign books to be a criticism of the prices asked at her bookshop, Shakespeare & Company. She removed Ford's photograph from her wall, and his books from her window, and buried the *transatlantic*, so that her sales of it dried up. Thirdly, an offer to readers disappointed by the cessation of the *Some Do Not . . .* serial that if they confirmed their subscriptions for the following year Ford would furnish them with copies of the book at his own expense, and would leave it 'to the applicant's conscience to decide whether they really do want to read it': an offer which imagines people deceiving him for profit. But even so, the magazine remains remarkably far-sighted. This is not just because so many of the writers he backed have proved central to our conception of modernism; nor just because his understanding of writing as an international process has become ours; it is also because he edited, as he wrote, as the historian of his own times. Though individual readers may have balked at particular styles, the historian of modernism is stimulated by the sheer variety of styles, from Conrad to Ford to Stein to Joyce to Hemingway to Rhys. Ford's claim in the December editorial is acceptable now in a way that it probably wasn't to its contemporaries. He argued that the review had helped to define a 'Movement. And with a very definite complexion.' If this movement was predominantly American, that was because the American contributors demonstrated the greatest 'curiosity as to form'. This was what he most valued in writing—he praised Rhys too for her 'instinct for form'; and he found it throughout that development of modernism from James to Pound and Joyce that he had played such a central role in defining.[16]

As he has been portrayed as quick to quarrel, it is worth noting that Ford was remarkably sanguine about the American *putsch* on the magazine. He portrayed it as a historical inevitability—one which he had foreseen at Bedham: the result simply of the quality and vigour of American writing, rather than of a predisposition to violence on the part of American writers (though he joked about the personal violences of Pound and Hemingway). What did upset him was when he felt other writers were being petty, valuing money above art. He took a dour pride in the thought that he had to go on paying the review's debts to contributors after the capital ran out (the point of forming a limited company had been so that he wouldn't have been responsible; but even if the company had achieved legal status he would have paid anyway out of a sense of honour and altruism). One day Nathan Asch (who hadn't been paid 200 francs for a story) and Evan Shipman (who had once promised to finance the review when he inherited money) decided to go to Ford to collect the debt. Asch pretended to collapse from hunger in Ford's flat, claiming that he hadn't eaten for a week. Asch thought Ford didn't notice the deception (though it's hard to see how he didn't notice the furious glances from Bowen, that told Asch she had noticed); he made them some beef broth and wrote them a cheque. Ford didn't object: he admired Asch's writing and knew he needed the money. But he ends his account of the review in *It Was the Nightingale* with a different kind of story about a contributor asking for money. He said he bought some work from a writer he admired. Because the man was poor, Ford paid more than the review's standard rate, paying the extra himself. Then, after Ford had sent a cheque, the writer asked to be paid. Ford discovered that someone else had endorsed the cheque, from which Ford deduced that the writer 'was in domestic difficulties, he had left home and a member of his family without his knowledge must have taken the money'. Ford didn't wish 'to make mischief for Mr. X——' —he means us to understand that he was too tactful to discuss the man's marital difficulties with him. When he could afford it, he sent a second cheque. Soon after that he was asked to write a review of Mr X——. By the same post he got a letter from Mr X——:

I have never received such a letter. Mr. X—— began by saying that he had denounced me to every literary paper and to every author's society in England and America.

I was a thief, a rogue, a swindler. I got writers to write for me and robbed them. He had been persuaded to write for my filthy *review* because people said it would do him good in America. What good had it done him? From the first he had been against writing for a fat, capitalist brute like me [. . .]

My secretary—there *are* fatalities!—in making out that cheque had dated it a year ahead, and I had not noticed!

I got dollar bills, registered them to his address, and marked the envelope: 'To be delivered into addressee's hands and to no other.' I never heard that he got it, but I suppose he did. I never heard either whether he actually sent out his denunciation of me. I daresay he did.

I sat down and wrote my article about him. In it I expressed my great admiration for his marvellous power of language and his great genius. . . . There *is* a pride which apes humility . . .

But I asked myself, naturally: What price glory! Then I went back to writing my long book.[17]

This is quintessentially Fordian. It sounds improbable, self-serving, too 'written' not to provoke scepticism. Yet, characteristically, it has considerable basis in fact; though, winding up his story of the *transatlantic*, Ford makes the row sound as if it was solely about payment for inclusion in the review in 1924, whereas it was also about the publication of *Transatlantic Stories* in 1926. Ford said he was 'Right in the middle of writing a eulogy' of A. E. Coppard's *The Field of Mustard* when he was visited by Jonathan Cape who told him that Coppard was 'enraged' with Ford because his story 'The Higgler' had been republished without his permission. Ford wrote to apologize, saying that 'of course the office of the T.R. was a rag-time affair and a great many letters and things did go astray'; enclosing a cheque; assuring him that 'there are few writers for whom I have more esteem and few persons I like more personally'; and suggesting that they should meet a few weeks later when he was to be in London. But either Coppard didn't receive the cheque, or it bounced. Coppard was a socialist (which is why Ford has him denouncing him as a capitalist), and had lived very simply. But *The Field of Mustard* was doing well—partly thanks to the eulogy that Ford had indeed written. If Coppard did write the menacing letter Ford describes, it hasn't survived amongst his papers (perhaps Ford destroyed it?). Ford then wrote again, sympathizing ('you have been badly used indeed'), sending Coppard not dollar bills, but a dollar cheque from his personal account, and pointing out that if Coppard carried out his threat to have the sales of the book stopped in England, he would inflict hardship on the other contributors.[18]

Why didn't Ford name 'Mr. X——' as Coppard? So that he wouldn't answer back? As a gesture of superiority ('he may have denounced me, but I won't stoop to denounce him—however great the provocation')? To avoid libel? Or in the not very realistic hope that he could tell the story and yet avoid alienating or hurting Coppard, about whom he speaks with fondness (and by name) elsewhere in *It Was the Nightingale*? To rebuke Coppard privately with an example of magnanimity, since only he would recognize the dual attitude the book was expressing towards him? Or simply because the exchange in fact ended with Coppard's handsome acknowledgement of gratitude and friendship, whereas Ford wanted his story to end with ingratitude and uncertainty? None of these motives may be completely absent. But to read the story in this way is to be deaf to it *as* a story, and to ignore Ford's claims for his reminiscential impressionism. What, then, can the story itself tell us?

First, that 'Mr. X——' is what he sounds: a mysterious cipher; a fiction made out of a reminiscence. Coppard had been (as Ford said in his review) the first writer he wrote to for contributions for the review. There was a symmetry (of a kind to appeal to Ford the fatalist) in the idea that the very writer Ford had felt he was launching the review to help was the one who turned upon him after another attempt to help him—in this case a project which symbolized the ending of the review: the collection of its best stories into a volume. Where Ford departs most significantly from the facts of this episode is in saying that he had no response after sending the second payment. Doubtless he was angered by the legal threats, but he must have been gratified by Coppard's friendly reply:

Dear Ford
Thank you immensely for your letter & cheque, it is very handsome of you.

I did not have anything to do with stopping the sale of TS in England, it was Cape's own retort to the infringement of *his* rights. I was only concerned to get a financial recognition.

You have said such nice things about me that this is hardly the moment to tell you of my very great love for your trilogy, yet I may say that those books have to my mind (& surely not mine alone) put you easily at the head of English novelists, & they certainly leave me
    Your admiring disciple
    A. E. Coppard

If Coppard had then come to symbolize for Ford the type of writer he wanted to help, and the way such writers had treated him, 'Mr. X——' is a compound character, combining feelings about Coppard with feelings about the way other writers (equally representative, but this time of the new American writing) treated him at the actual time of the review's demise: writers like Asch, who also asked for payment; Hemingway, who was actually denouncing Ford as dishonest, and, like Rhys, was soon afterwards to create scathing portraits of him in fictional characters; McAlmon, who told him he couldn't write—all these, plus the other, no-longer identifiable, writers from the internecine milieu of the Left Bank who Ford felt wanted, figuratively speaking, to lynch him. 'Mr. X——' is an emblem of why the review failed, and how its failure shows Ford something about his own fate to be the green baize door kicked from both sides. Thus the story tells another form of truth about Ford: about his feeling that, in the *métier de chien* that is writing, the lame dogs he helped over styles turned to bite the hand that gave them their cheques. The more one of his protégés attacked him, the more he supported them. Even Hemingway, who later claimed he had 'Learned nothing from old Ford except mistakes not to make that he had made', had to add that Ford 'was damned generous about writing things about what I wrote'. Yet he treated Ford like a mentor, sending him inscribed first editions of his books.

This trait of Ford's was also apparent in his writings about Conrad. Whenever Ford's statements about their intimacy were doubted, his response was to write all the more effusively about Conrad, as a man and as a writer.[19]

That idea of the 'pride which apes humility' seemed to Ford to be saying something important about him. When Janice Biala asked him about the way he 'convinced these young writers that they were more important than he was, and they believed him', he said: 'Did you ever hear of the pride that apes humility?' Was this another Fordian paradox? Or did he really think that his apparent self-abasement before younger 'genius' was in fact an inverted vanity? His thoughts about Coppard are revealing here too. In the 'eulogy' of *The Field of Mustard* he writes frankly about envy—a feeling he generally disavowed. In a characteristic move of critical reminiscence, he recalls the experience of first reading Coppard—first encountering his literary personality: 'I experienced at once a distinctly disagreeable sensation'—it's an unorthodox mode of eulogism—'I was reading a sentence—a queer sentence about bananas—and I found myself saying to myself: "Damn it all, this fellow writes better than I do." Or rather [he disavows] it was perhaps that I thought I should have to extend myself if I wanted to write as well as that. I was, in short, instantly jealous of the talent of Mr. Coppard.' 'Writing is,' the essay continues, 'alas, a jealous occupation. I suppose one is lucky if one can live the sensation down.' One way of living it down was to project it on to the very people he felt it for, and to represent himself as the victim of their aggression. He also understood that his extravagant praise could work as a way to stave off envy of good, perhaps better, writers. He as it were catches himself out feeling something he hoped he could live down: 'I found myself saying to myself [. . .].' But the phrase is typically dual. In this moment of self-awareness, he found himself.[20]

A similar self-awareness is playing across the story about the end of the review at the end of *It Was the Nightingale*. The phrase about the pride which apes humility is from Coleridge's poem 'The Devil's Thoughts'. Its context helps us to recover the complexity of Ford's conclusion:

> He pass'd a cottage with a double coach-house,
>   A cottage of gentility;
> And the Devil did grin, for his darling sin
>   Is pride that apes humility.

Ford's sitting down to eulogize 'Mr. X——' after being denounced by him shows him that there *is* such a thing. Coleridge defines it in terms of the English upper-class dread of ostentation; and certainly Ford's fascination with the codes of class got him criticized by Pound and Hemingway. But something stranger is happening in the allusion, since Ford identifies both with the Devil, and the sinner. It is *his* favourite sin not so much because its insidiousness catches up the unwary (though his novels are interested in the ways class cuts across individual desire); but because he indulged in it himself, concealing a sense of superiority behind an altruistic front.[21]

The sense of superiority itself springs from a feeling of inferiority: 'I wish people would not write better than I do', he says. Ford's vanity was the *alter ego* of this true humility: recognizing the excellence of another writer made him feel that he would have to extend himself to match them, and this sometimes involved distending his achievements, his past. He needs to live down envy by turning it to fictional pride; but this in turn gets expressed by aping humility. The passage burns with an awareness that his eulogies of others are generous recognitions of real talent, and yet that they have something suspect about them; that they incite their beneficiaries to denounce him as a thief, a rogue, a swindler. What is also apparent in the book is that he knows why he does it; and that, as always in his literary autobiography, the point of the analysis is to discover what it reveals about his *literary* personality. He knows that it's necessary to 'live the sensation [of envy] down' in order to write even if it gives others the pretext, possibly even the right, to denounce you as a liar. The way he tells the story about 'Mr. X——' expresses these things; which is why it's important that there seems to be something about it that it not quite straight. Aren't we supposed to have our flicker of doubt as to the coincidences, the patient altruism, the meticulous and equally patient detective work, coupled with an extraordinary generosity? Here too there's a deep disavowal: since if we don't believe him, he *is* a cheat; a fictionist. He always relished keeping his readers uncertain as to his earnestness; so here he keeps us guessing about the identity of 'Mr. X——', the truth of the story, his attitude to it.

He knows these things, and they help him to get on writing. 'Then I went back to writing my long book'—that is the point of the story, and the climax of *It Was the Nightingale*, the main story of which is the story of the story of *Parade's End* (about Tietjens, whose pride also apes humility), and whose humility apes pride. This, for him, is what the ending of the *transatlantic review* signifies, including the wondering about whether his humility in ostensibly founding the review to help others were not a covert pride; and his using it to guarantee getting slaughtered by his protégés were not an oblique form of self-sanctification. Of course the irony in the offbeat end, just clinched with the amusing quotation fixes the tone—all important as ever—stops it being simply self-pitying or simply blasé. Instead, from such unpromising materials Ford achieves a rare poise of humane self-knowledge—by telling a tall story. As with most of his literary reminiscence, the story tells not only of his (literary) personality, but also about how and why he writes the *kind* of story he does: it moves from a probing of his motives for running the review, praising *les jeunes*, performing altruisms, and so on, to an understanding of how these things get turned into narrative. How actual people (such as Mr Coppard) get turned into fictions (such as 'Mr. X——').

Ford's fiction is more secure than his discursive prose and his conversation from the charge that he did not distinguish fantasy from reality. There is a social consensus that works of fiction suspend the writer's responsibility to be true to the facts of actual lives. But few are willing to allow the same latitude in talk, or autobiography. Whereas Ford consistently denied the distinction, famously (and infamously) calling his memoir of Conrad 'a novel'; partly to draw attention to his own modifications of fact; and partly to proclaim the importance of the novel-form as he was transforming it:

here, to the measure of the ability vouchsafed, you have a projection of Joseph Conrad as, little by little, he revealed himself to a human being during many years of close intimacy. It is so that, by degrees, Lord Jim appeared to Marlowe, or that every human soul by degrees appears to every other human soul. For, according to our view of the thing, a novel should be the biography of a man or of an affair, and a biography whether of a man or of an affair should be a novel, both being, if they are efficiently performed, renderings of such affairs as are our human lives.

This then is a novel [. . .] It is the writer's impression of a writer who avowed himself impressionist. (pp. 5–6)

He continues by casting doubt on the book's factual accuracy, not only by conceding that his memory occasionally 'proved to be at fault over a detail', but by saying that even when he has checked details and found them faulty he has left them on the page, because: 'as to the truth of the impression as a whole the writer believes that no man would care—or dare—to impugn it.' Most did not. *Joseph Conrad* was reviewed widely, and generally with admiration—as 'a moving tribute'; creating an effect of 'remarkable intimacy'; a work that seemed 'to break new ground in the art of biography'. Even those reviewers who scented egotism were prepared to forgive it on the strength of Ford's insight into Conrad; of its contributions to Ford's reminiscences (which he had begun 'many years ago and which are among the most witty and entertaining memoirs of our time'); and of his illuminating discussions (in Part III, 'It is Above All to Make You See. . . .') of the fictional techniques hammered out with Conrad. One said Ford had 'given to writers of the English language the best text book and treatise on composition that I have ever seen'. There were, however, two predictably dissenting voices: Edward Garnett's and Jessie Conrad's.[22]

Garnett reviewed the book twice. First, he objected that 'In the magic name of "impressionism" a man can magnify, distort, or suppress facts and aspects to his own glorification [. . .] and then, on being brought to book, he can turn round reprovingly and protest, "But this is a work of art!"'; though he added that Ford 'conveys excellently the atmosphere of The Pent, and Conrad's love for Kent and England, and that he hits off in a lifelike way many of Conrad's personal ways and mannerisms'. Two months later he wasn't sure 'whether to be more amused or irritated', saying that the book was just what he had expected of Ford: 'something between romance and record, fact and fable'; though this time he doubted Ford's accuracy in presenting Conrad's conversation. Garnett's critique of Fordian impressionism is telling. Ford's transgressions of the frontier between memoir and fiction could not but be provocative, and can only perplex critics preoccupied with accuracy of 'record' and 'fact'. Garnett may have had personal reasons for his severity: Ford's claim to intimacy with Conrad may have offended him, and he may have thought that he knew better, having that letter from Conrad in which the barbed comments about collaboration ('And poor *H* was dead in earnest!') intimated that Garnett was a closer friend than Ford, and one in whose judgement he had more faith. Garnett may have felt the critic's inferiority to the creative writer, and resented Ford's implication that only another creative writer could really understand Conrad. Nevertheless, his uncertainty about how accurately Ford had 'caught' Conrad's manner is telling too. His principled worry about impressionism's untruth needs to be met by a contrary principle: a scepticism about whether any 'truth' other than rhetorical, fictional ('impressionist') truth *can* be achieved in matters as subjective as biography and reminiscence. Ford's impressionism is finely attuned to the different impressions we make on different people. His writing about Conrad knows how differently writers appear in and out of their work, and Ford knew as much about Conrad in his work as he knew about

Conrad working—in both cases more than anyone else. How could Garnett be so sure that Conrad didn't talk to Ford in 'the nebulous, sensational, highly coloured anecdotes' he felt Ford was putting into Conrad's mouth? It might be objected that Garnett meant that Ford caught Conrad's mannerisms (gestures, accent, habitual expressions) but not the content of his talk. But this wouldn't be very plausible: with a good conversationalist the two are harder to separate. Besides, Garnett travesties Ford's book in saying that these anecdotes are 'retailed by Mr. Ford as droppings from Conrad's lips'. The book isn't an anthology of Conrad's table-talk. Most of the stories Ford retails he retells, placing them not in inverted commas but in impressionistic narrative, in which (as he said he and Conrad designed their novels to do) one ceases to be conscious of the story-teller (Conrad), who is replaced by Ford as a Marlow-like narrator who tries to make you see Conrad himself. Surely Garnett's description ('nebulous, sensational, highly coloured') is truer of itself than of Conrad's speeches in Ford's book. Though it could describe Conradian or Fordian impressionism as a method. *Heart of Darkness*, for instance, could be called a nebulous, sensational, highly coloured anecdote.[23]

Garnett missed the minor point that, as collaborating novelists, Conrad and Ford spoke novelese: not just exchanging technical terms (as their letters demonstrate), but speaking novels and anecdotes to each other: writing so as to read aloud to each other; reciting passages of Flaubert or Maupassant to each other; or speaking their memoirs, as Conrad did when Ford took down *A Personal Record* from dictation. In such a literary friendship, anecdotes become more than retailed information: they become examples of narrative method; or pastiches, parodies, illuminative exaggerations. But Garnett also missed the major point that Ford's calling his memoir 'a novel' instead of a biography is more than an irresponsible defence (though it mobilizes concerns about irresponsibility). It is meant with full seriousness. *Joseph Conrad* is a novel about the novelist: not just Conrad, but Ford too; and not just their double-act, but about any novelist. This is the point of one of Ford's mannerisms that one reviewer objected to: his habit of calling himself 'the writer'. Ford is writing not as the private individual 'Ford Madox Ford', author or subject of biographies. He writes as 'the writer'. His experience as writer is what enables him to understand Conrad as writer (as opposed to Conrad the conversationalist, or Conrad the husband). It is in this sense that *Joseph Conrad* is one of Ford's most autobiographical books, in his most intimate mode of oblique or displaced autobiography, in which the deepest insights are refracted through other people, his doubles. In fact Ford claimed too little in his preface. The book is more than a rendering of Conrad according to the Conrad–Ford canons of impressionism. Besides being an *example* of impressionism, it is a study of it: a discussion of its methods, and also an investigation into the mind of an impressionist writer—the fragmentary, hallucinatory quality of his memory; his reticence about his own past; his fascination with the power of the written word. Impressionistic licence is very much a subject of the book, rather than being its surreptitious procedure. 'For, like every inspired raconteur Conrad modified his stories subtly, so as to get in sympathy with his listener.' This is as subtle about the inspired raconteur who is an impressionist novelist or reminiscer as it is about conversation. Ford not only modifies his stories but shows himself doing so. 'I am in truth an Impressionist', he said. Really an impressionist? Or an impressionist with the truth? The fictional status of his impressions is always foregrounded. What is more, his examples of counter-factual impressionism are usually framed within stories about being, or becoming, an artist. They function not as examples of sleight of hand, but as allegories or insights into the writer's life.[24]

Jessie Conrad's attack on the book was a vitriolic letter published in the *Times Literary Supplement*. She begged to 'correct a few of the most fantastic statements' regarding Conrad, denying—falsely—that Conrad had used plots of Ford's; protesting that between 1898 and 1909 Ford 'never spent more than three consecutive weeks under our roof'; and saying that after 1909 Conrad never sought Ford out, which was true. She complained that Ford presented their friendship to his own advantage—an odd claim, since Ford's awe of Conrad's talent infuses every page. What seems particularly to have riled her was Ford's handling of the story that it was a copy of Ford's first novel (*The Shifting of the Fire*) seen by Conrad 'on the bookstall of Geneva railway station, that had first turned his thoughts to writing English as a career'. Jessie Conrad singled out Ford's comment that 'nothing would have pleased Conrad's generous and effusive moods better than to claim the writer as his literary godfather', commenting: 'That claim is, like nearly everything else in that detestable book, quite untrue.' But Ford is quite explicit about how it couldn't have been true: Conrad had been wrong about the colour of the bindings, ' "So it couldn't be me," as the old mare said'. It is Jessie Conrad's claim that Ford claimed to be Conrad's literary godfather that is quite untrue. Ford's point is that it is the kind of distortion Conrad enjoyed; and that the relishing of such fabulation is the novelist's passion. The controversy stirred up by this attack continued into 1926, and did Ford's reputation damage both in America, where he was becoming well known, and in England, where it revived the animosity caused by the *Throne* case. It fostered the impression—still harboured by some Conradians—that Ford was parasitic on Conrad's prestige. His Madox Brownian altruism was in fact the opposite: an extraordinary willingness to become the attendant to a talent he thought greater than his own. He wrote a reply to the *TLS* saying that though it was 'absolutely impossible to enter into any discussion with the wife of the man I knew and loved so well as to the precise degree of our comradeship, collaboration and mutual esteem', 'Certainly no suggestion that I have belittled the memory of Conrad can withstand a reading of the book which is my tribute to his genius and his character.' If he ever sent the letter, it was not published.[25]

Ford narrates *Joseph Conrad* rather as Dowell tells *The Good Soldier*, shuttling backwards and forwards in time, giving characteristic dual impressions of its subject, as impressions are at once pressed and suppressed, cast into doubt or parody:

With a hypersensitiveness to impressions the writer, too, remembers Conrad throwing teacups into the fireplace during a discussion over the divine right of kings—a discussion with a lady who alleged light-heartedly that Marie Antoinette had been guilty of treason to France. The whole of the discussion the writer did not hear because he was discoursing to a very deaf gentleman on the genealogical tree of the Dering family. Nor indeed can Conrad have thrown the tea-cups into the fire since on going away the lady said: 'What a *charming* man Mr. Conrad is! I must see him often.' (p. 19)

Tea-cups? More than one? How many? When we first meet the story, our response is probably going to be one of incredulity. Surely Conrad, described on the previous page as a man of 'Oriental' politeness, would not demolish his way through the crockery during an English tea? The scene appears as insane as it is improbable, and is designed to arouse a form of attentive mistrust. He makes us listen very carefully, to make sure we have heard him aright, and that we know what to believe. As he continues, though, the scene becomes oddly convincing. Ford is not really listening, as, he explains to apprentice-novelists later in the book, people do not really listen to much of each other's conversation.[26] So Conrad's behaviour was half-caught in one ear over the sound of his own voice shouting, presumably, into the ear of his unideal listener, the very deaf gentleman. Ford got the 'impression' of Conrad's imaginative sympathy, remembering Marie Antoinette 'in the Conciergerie, so ill-clad, so deprived of her children, so pallid and unkempt that to him she was real and he remembered her' (p. 20). As Conrad creates for himself the 'impression' of Marie Antoinette, or rather as Ford creates Conrad's novelistic impression for us, Ford gets the impression of Conrad's response, which strikes him as a kind of passionate explosion. What Ford actually heard, according to Violet Hunt (for the lady was none other, being taken to visit Conrad at the end of 1911) was 'a noise and a clatter' as 'Conrad brought his fist down on the tin tea-tray, and the cups danced horribly, but not one was broken'. One can see where Ford got the idea to connect tea-trays in *Parade's End* with violence. But what he really wants to convey here, and what his inventive, dual method is designed to render, is Conrad's self-control: 'It was the want of imagination in all humanity, thus in little summed up and presented to him, that aroused in him such passion and called for such self-control. For it is to be hoped that it is apparent that it was only to the writer that the impression remained of tea-cups thrown into the fireplace.'[27] First he shows us what would have been the adequate expression of Conrad's exasperation; then he shows us Conrad courteously suppressing his passion. But the suppression means much more to a reader who knows what it costs Conrad— the force of feeling he is holding back (as opposed to the anger he forgot to suppress when he sprang at Ford's throat). The vignette of provocation illustrates a provocative method. It is a method which gives a three-dimensionality to its characters, since we are shown more than one side. And this is why, for all its idiosyncrasies, unreliabilities as literary history, glossings over aspects of Conrad's actual life (such as Jessie Conrad, who for Ford figures very small in Conrad's life as a writer), this book remains one of the best studies of Conrad.

Ford's impression of an emotional storm in the tea-cups is fundamental to an understanding of his impressionism, and should be taken as a paradigm of all his fabulations about real people and events. (Curiously, the scene echoes one written the year before, in which Sylvia Tietjens drops some sugar, then drops the whole tea-tray down on to a table, when vexed by Father Consett's criticisms of her marriage.)[28] With his 'hypersensitiveness to impressions the writer, too, remembers' Conrad throwing tea-cups, rather as Conrad is imagined as hypersensitively 'remembering' a Marie Antoinette he had only read about. It is characteristic of the kind of writer he and Conrad are, to visualize, experience, and then 'remember', 'impressions' of events which are not necessarily the same as the events themselves. The stumbling-block for most critics of Fordian impressionism is that—as Ford himself often argues—an impression is thought of as the effect, the impress, of a fact on the mind. But the causal link here is so close that if the impression is at odds with the fact, it is hard to see what accuracy it can claim. One type of answer is manifest in Ford's impression of Conrad's non-existent ballistic tea-cups. Ford's mind is divided, preoccupied, under the strain of trying to make someone hear while he himself is trying to hear someone else. So the waywardness of his impression becomes an index to his perplexity, to the intermittence of his concentration. Ford was accustomed to sudden outbursts from Conrad. So, feeling that he was likely to react passionately to the facile moralizing, Ford may for a moment have actually believed that Conrad had actually thrown something, as a bewildering noise suggested one possible explanation. According to this phenomenological type of answer, Ford does not really think the tea-cups were thrown, but because the idea crossed his mind at the time he reproduces the misapprehension. The justification for doing so is not a self-indulgent desire to record his own emotions at the expense of Conrad's actions, but the claim that what he imagined happening actually expressed an important truth about Conrad: his furious interiority; his extreme combination of passion and politeness.

13

TALL STORIES

In all great deceivers a remarkable process is at work, to which they owe their power. In the very act of deception with all its preparations, the dreadful voice and face and gestures, amid the whole effective scenario they are overcome by *their belief* in themselves; and it is this belief which then speaks so miraculously, so persuasively, to their audience . . . For men believe in the truth of all that is seen to be firmly believed.

(Nietzsche, *Human, All Too Human*, § 52)

I like that old story-teller Ford Madox Ford.

(Lewis Gannett)

The story about Conrad and the tea-cups is true, since Ford's illuminative exaggeration is perfectly candid. However, some of his 'impressions' cannot be understood as (acknowledged) misapprehensions; and these are the ones that chiefly earned him his reputation as a liar. They are often impressions about himself, in which he cannot simply have been mistaken about what happened. A typical example occurs in Brian Lunn's autobiography, describing an evening in Paris in 1930:

Alan Duncan asked me to meet Ford Madox Ford the evening I arrived. We talked of the war, and Kitchener being mentioned Alan said that Kitchener wanted to number the battalions of the new army from one to four or five thousand instead of tacking them on to existing regiments. I said this was a good instance of Kitchener's practical imagination; a number acquired sentiment as readily as a name [. . .]

Alan and Ford disagreed with me, and Ford told us that he had led a new army battalion in an attack with a battalion of regulars on his right. He said that the superior discipline of the regular battalion had saved the morale of the men under his own command and this he attributed to the regimental tradition, a story which, although I did not see it at the time, only went to shew that to call their units by the names of the regular army did not make better soldiers of the duration men.[1]

Even the bewilderment of shell-shock does not account for Ford's impression that he led a battalion in an attack. This is the Ford satirized by Wells in *The Bulpington of Blup*. Like all effective satire, *Bulpington* has an element of truth; and of course there is self-aggrandizement in Ford's presentation of himself to Lunn and Duncan as a leader of men. But it is unjust to let this aspect dominate the entire picture. For self-glorification is only one of the things to be heard in Ford's stories. And the fact that he generally kept such conversational exaggerations out of his published work suggests that it was something he could control. There is an almost malicious comedy in the way Lunn, for all his striving for retrospective wisdom ('although I did not see it at the time'), was so preoccupied with his hobby-horse—a topic he tells us he would try out regularly—that he could not see how *he* was the one being led by Ford, up the garden path of fiction. One can see where the animus against Ford came from, for no one likes to be taken in so completely, and those who were later disabused found it easier to abuse than to forgive him.

The question remains of why Ford told such stories. If his motive is not pathological self-protectiveness, is there not something odd, perhaps pathological, in his desire to deceive? Before answering this, one should investigate the difference between the 'desire to deceive' in a story like this purportedly about the life of an actual person—himself—and the 'desire to deceive' with a work of fiction. It is mostly a matter of narrative conventions: if Defoe writes a fictional autobiography published as if it were Moll Flanders's or Robinson Crusoe's own true story, it is not (or not any longer) seen as a hoax; whereas to practise tricks of confidence in conversation is to risk being treated as a confidence trickster. Ford goes even further than this, however, radically transgressing the boundaries of autobiography and fiction. He takes autobiography, a genre which rests on the convention of veracity, self-knowledge, and tact towards acquaintances; and he writes fiction, including fiction about himself, and also about people he knew, who duly became outraged by the liberties taken with the facts of their lives. His medium was fiction, and everything he said or wrote partakes of fictionality, even when it was true, which it usually was. It would not be an exaggeration to say, with Janice Biala, that his life was a fiction. 'I am a painter,' she said, 'and as I look at you I'm continually painting a portrait of you'; 'Picasso was painting his life every day, but nobody accused him of lying'; 'Ford's life was a novel'; he 'was constantly writing and rewriting that novel'. He did it because it gave pleasure: 'he found spontaneous fiction vastly entertaining, both to himself and others', wrote Kenneth Rexroth. The epitaph of the Roman dancer used in *The Rash Act* is Ford's justification for any artist's life, including his own: 'He danced. He gave pleasure. He is dead.' Ford romanced and gave pleasure, knowing that he would be dead.[2]

The reason his stories are not lies, and not pathological—though they are 'odd', marvellously distinctive—is that they are not meant simply to deceive. Lunn is an unfortunate casualty of Ford's habitual dual mode. One of the main things that can be heard in this war-story is Ford's delight in narrative illusion. The story is impeccable as a story: completely poised, selecting just the right details to sound plausible, such as saying that the regular battalion was on the right; and even including the hint that appears self-deprecatory even in the midst of the self-aggrandizing, that the low morale of his men just might have something to do with his limitations as a commanding officer. It is not a particularly impressive story in Lunn's version, but in the telling it evidently achieved its effect, which was to make the impression of battle vivid enough to make Lunn forget for a time his preoccupation with names and numbers.

Ford relished conversational fabulation. Frank Swinnerton called him 'a good talker, with a considerable sense of his audience'. This included a sense of what they would believe. Compton Mackenzie referred affectionately to Ford as one of the 'greater' liars: 'some people incapable of speaking the truth have been able to write it. Ford Madox Ford is an example of that.' In a passage Ford deleted from the preface of 'Towards a History of English Literature' he shows he could write with humorous

self-awareness about his romancing: 'The Present writer [. . .] does however claim to
be an ordinary man', he said:

If you tickle him he will laugh, if you offer him a spin in your automobile, ten to one he will
accept [. . .] *if you boast of your prowess on the golf-course, during the late war, in the rearing of
prize cattle or after the hounds or in the prediction of political events or in any other field of human
activity—why he will boast of his and as likely as not out-talk you. Ten to one you would call him
a liar* [. . .][3]

Thus 'Ford romanticized—but in an extremely candid way', as Janice Biala has said.
'He said once that some relative of his was called Hill, and since Shakespeare too had
a direct something or other called Hill, he felt he was probably descended from
Shakespeare. Then he added, "*Someone* has to be."' Biala says 'no one was fooled'.
Obviously some like Lunn were, but it was a very harmless kind of fooling, not done
to rob or to hurt. You would have needed a good ear and eye to notice the candour; but
then he chose as his friends those with the best ears for language, and the best eyes for
personality; and his tallest stories were part of his selection process. 'It is true that his
stories were generally better than the facts', said Kitty Cannell: 'But often he was just
seeing whether he could get away with something.' His stories were at once a technical
challenge for him, and a challenge to his audience: decide whether I'm in earnest or
not. He had constructed this uncertainty about his earnestness long before Garnett
published the letter in which Conrad said 'Poor *H* was dead in earnest'. But afterwards
he became more obsessive about the idea, as if to be in earnest would be a kind of
death, and as if he were trying to exorcize his anxiety about himself, and about what
others thought about him, by showing that they had been wrong to think him in
earnest. 'His comments just hover on the edge of seriousness, are so delicately exaggerated that one both accepts them and sees past them to the engaging, slightly comic,
larger than life figure they disclose.'[4]

Virginia Woolf, who had met Ford and Hunt through the Cambridge historian
G. W. Prothero, said she found the reminiscences she was reading 'fascinating, and
even endearing'. But she longed 'to know the truth about him'. His conversation was
equally tantalizing. 'He had a vague yet positive manner of speech', said Brigit
Patmore, 'and could maintain the most controversial assertions'—those Marwoodian
'sweeping dicta'. 'For instance, that to avoid catching cold one must expose oneself to
raining torrents, omit changing one's clothes, and especially avoid hot drinks. Or he
could prove that only half of *Don Quixote* was written by Cervantes.' The other half
was, as it were, written by Ford, trying to deny Cervantes's disturbing ridicule of the
altruistic, chivalrous, Fordian Don. When Sherwood Anderson met Ford in Paris he
was told 'You are just the man I have been wanting to see', and led into a corner:

He began speaking of a house he had in the hills of Pennsylvania. There it was. He described
the house, the view from a terrace at the front, the garden, the apple trees that grew on a nearby hillside. The house was beautifully furnished and there was a retinue of servants. The pity
was that he had built the house, intending to go there to work but had never been able to do
so.
    And what was a man to do? He could not bear the thought of discharging the servants and
closing the house. And why should I not take the place, go there to live, Ford wanted to
know. It would cost me nothing.

'Please,' said Ford: 'you take it.' He tried to get Anderson to promise at least to spend a summer there. 'His voice was rich with fervor. There was an eager light in his eyes.' Anderson said he didn't know Ford well then. 'He is a rich man who has houses scattered about the world', he thought. During the course of the evening Ford offered him two other houses, in Florida and California. ('Of course, only a Quixote gives what he does not possess', said Edward Dahlberg when Anderson told him the story, 'because of a goodly, savoury, free nature.') Given Ford's usual poverty, the fantasy about the number of houses and of servants, the Tory concern for the dependants, the largess with which he is all but giving the house away to someone he doesn't even know very well, is either demented or funny. The extraordinary thing is that Anderson believed it all at the time (because he was nearly broke, he said later). 'Only those who knew Ford well will understand how sincere the offer was, how real and tangible the house had become to him', he claimed. Certainly Ford's conviction gained immensely from finding another soul to share it. But someone to whom the glint in Ford's eye signified only fervour and sincerity never got to know Ford as well as he thought. Instead, he proved Ford's point that Americans often had trouble knowing whether or not he was in earnest. 'Most of the stories he told to delighted audiences were as much "fairy stories" as those he related to his daughters at bed-time', said Goldring. The trouble was that some of his adult listeners were more naïve than children. John Peale Bishop was an astute exception, remembering the pleasure Ford gave by his anecdotes, 'and the after taste which they left, which was so often one of doubt, while one wondered whether these little tales Ford made up for his pleasure and ours would not in time impose upon history and what was an admirable fiction be accepted as accurate fact'. The opposite happened, of course. Once Ford's reputation as a romancer spread, the less admirable fictions of others got accepted as accurate fact wherever they differed from Ford's often true stories. And where his obviously untrue stories are concerned, this vision of the consummate and pleasurable artist has been usurped by the travesty of him as someone who had lost his grip on the real. 'And you *might* consider that Ford had a sense of humour—and sometimes had a twinkle in his eye as he made some wild statement or other', Janice Biala told Mizener, shocked at how wrong his portrait was: 'And after all he used to say "I'm a *bit of* a liar myself".'[5]

Several of Ford's descriptions of the effects he wants writing to achieve use images of hypnotic illusion. The classic statement is in *Thus to Revisit*:

Is the Reader, then, conversant with the Theory of Podmore's Brother? ... Podmore's Brother was accustomed to perform certain tricks on members of the public whilst so holding their attentions that they were quite unconscious of his actions. He talked so brilliantly that whilst his tongue moved his hands attracted no attention. It is not a very difficult trick to perform ... If the Reader will give a box of matches to a friend and then begin to talk really enthrallingly, he will be able to take the box of matches from his friend's hands without his friend being in the least conscious that the matches have gone. Closing his discourse, he will be able to say to his friend: 'Where are the matches?'—and the friend will not have any idea of their whereabouts ... It is a trick worth performing—the tongue deceiving the eye ... (pp. 138–9)

In his post-war criticism this idea of the writer as an illusionist, verging on the charlatan, begins to overshadow the earlier view of the artist as passive recorder of impressions. He frequently suggests both views at the same time, such as in *A Mirror to France*, in which the tarnished conceit of art as like a mirror is given a new sparkle when Ford discourses on the idiosyncrasies of individual mirrors:

It has always been my humble ambition to be a mirror to my time [. . .]

Mirrors are of all shapes and sizes and conformations; one will differ in the qualities of its reflections from all other mirrors as much as one man differs from all other men, or as one witness of an event from all other witnesses. Go into any looking-glass shop such as one of a mysterious wizard's aspect that I lately visited in a mediæval-Georgian, utterly Parisian street, with innumerable signs of handicrafts and small commerces protruding all over the footways or carved in stone on the house-fronts, with dates from 1535 to 1792; or go into any big departmental store in whose furnishing department mirrors are displayed side by side, poor things, like slaves in the market. And then look at yourself in mirror after mirror. You will see that, not only do mirrors differ, but that you are capable of being so oddly viewed that you may well have misgivings as to your real self. (pp. 7–8)

If this brilliant prose is a mirror, it is the kind of looking-glass that invites you through, into its magical world, presided over by that image of the mysterious wizard. The diversity of critical metaphors—is art a mirror, magic, a slave of society and commerce; do we view it, or does it view us? How much does it flatter, and how much disturb and cause misgivings about one's self?—is at the service of Ford's view of the diversity of human life: different men, innumerable signs, various trades, networks of footways, a range of houses and dates. One reason why he was such a good critic is that although he had established a critical canon for himself, and often recited it in print, he would never impose it on new talent: a writer did not have to write in the school of Turgenev, Flaubert, Maupassant, James, and Conrad to gain his appreciation.

The writers whose work excited his admiration most after these, his masters, were the modernists—Pound, Lewis, Lawrence, Hemingway, Joyce, Stein, Carlos Williams; the young whose talent he fostered as an editor. All of these writers had great personal affection for Ford apart from Lewis and Hemingway, and even they were not without a grudging fondness. But their aesthetic ideas were often hostile to Ford's, and it was seeing his own art reflected in theirs, and their responses to his which gave him creative misgivings about his real artistic self: creative misgivings because their aesthetic onslaughts changed the way he wrote. One of the stories he tells most often is about this confrontation of impressionism and modernism; and it helps to explain why the figure of the performer, the illusionist, the visible presence of the artist, becomes more important in both his criticism and his novels after the war. It is the story of Wyndham Lewis's 1914 death-sentence on him. In most versions of the story Pound is present, talking 'incessantly' in 'his incomprehensible Philadelphian'. But in the fullest, most polished version he has been removed from the composition:

Mr. Wyndham Lewis (Percy) caught me mysteriously by the elbow, willed me out into Holland Street and, in his almost inaudible voice . . . said it. . . .

'You and Mr. Conrad and Mr. James and all those old fellows are done. . . . Exploded! . . . *Fichus!* . . . *Vieux jeu!* . . . No good! . . . Finished! . . . Look here! . . . You old fellows are merely nonsensical. You go to infinite pains to get in your conventions. . . . *Progression d'effets*. . . . *Charpentes*. . . . Time-shift. . . . God knows what. . . . And what for? What in Heaven's name for? You want to kid people into believing that, when they read your ingenious projections, they're actually going through the experiences of your characters. Verisimilitude—that's what you want to get with all your wheezy efforts. . . . But that isn't what people want. They don't want vicarious experience; they don't want to be educated. They want to be amused. . . . By brilliant fellows like me. Letting off brilliant fireworks. Performing like dogs on tightropes. Something to give them the idea they're at a performance. You fellows try to efface yourselves; to make people think that there isn't any author and that they're living in the affairs you . . . adumbrate, isn't that your word? . . . What balls! What rot! . . . What's the good of being an author if you don't get any fun out of it? . . . Efface yourself! . . . Bilge!"[6]

Ford casts himself as the doomed Old Guard, about to expire in the European catastrophe along with his social and aesthetic ideals of tact and unostentatiousness. But it is a searchingly ambivalent scene. Under attack from Lewis's percussive denunciations, Fordian impressionism appears benignly tolerant. It also gets a fuller investigation here than in the other versions, since Lewis's contemptuous catalogue lists all the technical means Ford valued most highly. The Ford 'willed' out for a walk by Lewis is the personification of 'will-less impressionism'. In the other versions he is virtually being kidnapped, Pound at one arm and Lewis at the other, enforcing an opportunity to inflict manifestos upon him, bewildering him by both speaking relentlessly at the same time. As in the other versions, it is Lewis who domineers. Ford does not get a word in. The monologue dramatizes the triumph of the new forms over the old, the young over those who are about to die. And yet. It is not just that, through Lewis's blast, Ford manages to make heard the voiceless and will-less principles he respects. Described like this there is nothing ambiguous about the scene. Ford would be satirizing an uncongenial movement in order to defend his own aesthetic position. But the ambiguity enters in the field of aesthetics itself. For, above all, the episode is a bravura performance. In part it is Lewis's performance, and one cannot but admire the vigour and concision of his assault. But it is also Ford's performance, a stunning impersonation of being stunned by an explosive character. As such, it is not 'impressionism' by the canons blown up by Lewis. Hugh Kenner calls Lewis's analysis of Joyce 'the most brilliant misreading in modern criticism'.[7] His assassination of Ford is just as brilliantly wrong-headed. He couldn't see that Ford was already doing unobtrusively what he advocated blatantly. The overall effect is not, as in Turgenev or Conrad, of having heard an entirely convincing piece of characterization, a speech that might actually have been witnessed in real life. Instead, Ford had become the kind of impressionist who does 'impressions' of people. With mimicry, the intention is not to fool the audience into thinking they are actually hearing a famous politician, but to produce an intensely pleasurable dual response from recognizing the tricks of speech of the real person as being a trick of the mimic's art. Whereas poor Garnett thought F was dead in earnest.

Ford's doubters, however, judge as straightforward realism something that is quite other: a form of affectionately mocking mimicry which is akin to spinning someone a yarn and then tipping them the wink, or at least letting a twinkle in your eye make them wonder. Charles Williams, one of the few critics to understand what Ford was doing in his later reminiscences, wrote finely in a review of *Mightier Than the Sword*:

Mr. Ford has never been without what, in any one else, would have been a touch of malice. There is a suggestion of malice without tears here, a faint flicker of something that might, elsewhere, be malice, and is no more than the extra sharpness of the pencil [. . .] By love and by brilliant intelligence the book is full of the most thrilling things—Henry James talking to the housemaid, Lawrence appearing in the drawing room which was the office of the *English Review* [. . .][8]

By impersonating Lewis rather than rendering him, by doing rather than giving an impression of him, Ford himself gets a lot of fun out of being an author. He adopts some of Lewis's modern techniques to show Lewis consigning him to anachronism. In his impersonation of Lewis, we are half aware of Ford, not effacing himself according to the letter of impressionism, but giving an entertaining, pyrotechnic performance. The vigour and bravado of Ford's portrait gives it as much to do with showmanship ('like dogs on tightropes') as with patient psychological presentation. But this description makes it sound too much like a put-down; whereas the love and brilliant imagination that Williams warms to are indeed there, and bound up with the scene's aesthetic ambiguity. Ford is not picking up Lewis's methods in order to put him down. In the act of parodying him, he is also finding a sympathy with the man and his methods: seeing Lewis as a kind of double of his artistic self, someone who is continuing his lifelong campaigns for new forms, only by other, more belligerent, means; and, most importantly, recognizing that the kind of art Lewis is advocating should not be seen as in uncompromising opposition to his own work, since he has been practising something like it all along, perhaps without realizing it. That is, the importance of the encounter reveals to him that his 'impressionism' involves both senses of the word— both a will-less immersion in phenomena, and at the same time a display of personality. When T. S. Eliot argued that poetry was 'not a turning loose of emotion, but an escape from emotion; it is not the expression of personality, but an escape from personality', he added: 'But, of course, only those who have personality and emotions know what it means to want to escape from these things.' Ford's dual effect was to express the emotions and personality from which he was escaping. The charlatan's performance hypnotizes the audience in order to efface the writer.[9]

The very fact that Lewis's speech—like so many of Ford's crucial memories— exists in so many versions, points up the prime paradox of Fordian impressionism. Like the Conradian tea-cups, first described and then retracted, Lewis's words both are and are not true representations. The more Ford rewrites the story, the clearer becomes the point, and the more polished the performance. But at the same time it becomes less probable that we are getting the actual words. What is important about a Fordian impression is not that it is the record of an actual fact; but that it should strike us, as it perhaps struck him, as dubious, disturbing, equivocal. It turns the sceptical impasse of a Dowell, to whom 'It is all a darkness', into a *method* of doubt and dubiety. There is a form of realist motive for Ford here, because for him life is like that: we can never be sure if we have seen, or heard, or understood aright; and his literary method reproduces such uncertainties, everywhere causing misgivings about real selves—whether his, his characters', or our own. It is another aspect of his method of creating a sense of reality through intimations of unreality. Ford's impressions are of what *might* have been (as when he subtitles *Mr. Apollo* 'A Just Possible Story'); or of what did not actually happen, but could, or should have done (such as Conrad throwing china; or a novel about the fifth queen of Henry VIII which has its heroine behave differently from the historical original).

Brian Lunn's story does not give us enough evidence to be sure that Ford was pulling his leg, or even that he was impersonating a heroic leader for other reasons—such as living his way into a fictional role, like the Tietjens he had created, and the Hugh Monckton he would invent in *The Rash Act* a year or so later. It is not even a matter of arguing that one should rule out the possibility that part of the desire to convince others came from a need to convince himself that the record of his actions was not as bad as he sometimes feared. What is crucial is to recognize that, possibly even while partly trying to convince himself, Ford none the less retained an awareness that he was dealing in fictions; practising his narrative arts, always pursuing technical investigations into just what people will believe. (Podmore, whose brother talked people out of their matchboxes, was presumably Frank Podmore, of the Society of Psychical Research.)[10]

A true charlatan, or trickster, actually wants to convince the audience. The better listeners to Ford's conversation let one hear enough to know that this was not how his stories worked. Curtis Brown, one of the first literary agents along with Pinker, met Ford occasionally, and in his memoirs reproduces a speech in which, like Tietjens, Ford considers the mechanics of golf:

[Ford] told us why he had given up playing golf on the lovely wind-swept course at Littlestone, or anywhere else.

'You know what that third hole is like,' he said. 'You tee up on a lovely plateau, drive across a sandy valley and over a distant sand-hill that looks like a mountain. Some distance beyond that is the green. Most people drive into the bunker on the hither side of the sand-hill, but a good player such as I was would carry the ridge and find the green below. I recently did so, but my ball was lost. After a prolonged search for it by all concerned, I was on the point of giving it up when I happened to look in the hole, and there it was.

'I said to myself: When one can play as well as that, golf ceases to be a sport and becomes a mere matter of mechanics. With play of such excellence and accuracy one might as well pick up the ball and walk over to the hole and drop it in [. . .]'.[11]

Liar, or entertainer? The finesse and absurdity of that clinching image gives the game away. The ball may or may not have been his, and he may or may not have hit the hole in one. But he knows perfectly well that it cannot be done at will—especially not when, as the geography implies, you can't even see the green from the tee. It is a pose, and he is completely aware of its preposterousness, and that is all part of the joke. The image of dropping the ball in the hole is curiously like the flourish with which the illusionist ends his performance. It is then that his style shows the twinkle in the eye, whether his eye did or not. What vanity there is in the boast is not about golf, but about story-telling; and it is conscious and witty.

This story shows that Wells was wrong in seeing Ford's romancing as a post-war craziness. It had always been at the heart of his way with words. Mizener told Ann Snitow that he thought 'healthy Ford had a sense of the absurdity in both his fictional world and his moral views'. I don't believe he ever lost this sense, though it became shaky for a year or two after the war. His mental health manifested itself in an

enjoyment of the fictionality of fiction. His 'air of pained surprise when taxed with
some especially flagrant distortion indicated that he wished [his anecdotes] rather to be
enjoyed than believed'. He cultivated the enjoyment of disbelief, the savouring of the
sceptical after-taste. He was the great twentieth-century writer about the great nineteenth-century topic: doubt. His method of approaching the problem of how writers
'poetize' about the self was to foreground doubt: to dramatize excess, exaggeration,
unreliability. Some whom he misled into believing his fictions resented his plausibility; but others, who want fiction to feign vicarious experience, object that he is too
implausible; that his manner spoils even his best novels. The objections cancel each
other out (an implausible liar's career would be short); they are both based on a failure
to understand the nature of his wit, in which 'there was neither cruelty nor malice'.[12]

The malice in Ernest Hemingway's sketch of Ford in *A Moveable Feast* is well
documented. But it needs to be read alongside *The Torrents of Spring*, Hemingway's
strange parodic squib, aimed mainly at Sherwood Anderson's latest novel *Dark
Laughter*, but with ambivalent swipes at Ford's *transatlantic* editorial notes and his
pride about the time-shift. ('Would it be any violation of confidence if we told the
reader that we get the best of these anecdotes from Mr. Ford Madox Ford? We owe
him our thanks, and we hope the reader does, too [. . .]. It is very hard to write this
way, beginning things backward, and the author hopes the reader will realize this and
not grudge this little word of explanation.') The anecdotes themselves are entertainingly tantalizing. David Garnett in his introduction to the English edition said they
were indeed Ford's: 'Ford is as fertile with stories as Boccaccio and these are as good
and as characteristic as any which I can remember.'[13]

Hemingway admired Ford's improvisatory panache, though in *A Moveable Feast* he
is primarily exasperated by a Ford he presents as speaking self-importantly while
being wrong about everything. None the less, though he was not prepared to be
amused by Ford, he was a good enough listener to be able to record the entertainer in
the poseur. The chapter on 'Ford Madox Ford and the Devil's Disciple', makes Ford
sound diabolically annoying. Hemingway is sitting at a table outside one of Ford's
favourite cafés, the Closerie des Lilas. Ford comes out and joins him, to Hemingway's
distaste. A man walks past. Ford asks Hemingway if he saw him 'cut' Belloc. To the
American this sounds like something out of a novel by Ouida, so he teases Ford by
feigning naïveté about English social codes. This enables Ford to pontificate on his
favourite subject:

'A gentleman,' Ford explained, 'will always cut a cad.' [. . .]
   'What is a cad?' I asked. 'Isn't he someone that one has to thrash within an inch of his life?'
   'Not necessarily', Ford said.
   'Is Ezra a gentleman?' I asked.
   'Of course not,' Ford said. 'He's an American.'
   'Can't an American be a gentleman?'
   'Perhaps John Quinn,' Ford explained. 'Certain of your ambassadors.' [. . .]
   'It's very complicated,' I said. 'Am I a gentleman?'
   'Absolutely not,' Ford said.
   'Then why are you drinking with me?'
   'I'm drinking with you as a promising young writer. As a fellow writer, in fact.'

'Good of you,' I said.
'You might be considered a gentleman in Italy,' Ford said magnanimously.[14]

Ford knows he is being mocked (as he knew Hemingway was parodying him in print),
and rises magnificently to the occasion, caricaturing the type that Hemingway is taking
him for. He invents a posture of authoritativeness, then superimposes disbelief over it
as he reduces his definition to a scholastic absurdity. Hemingway's antagonism has
been seen as a resentment of how much he owed to Ford, who consistently praised,
publicized, and encouraged his work. Though of the multitude of writers Ford supported, many, such as Pound, William Carlos Williams, and Robert Lowell, remained
loyal champions, others felt, with Hemingway, that they were being patronized in
earnest, and that this had more to do with supporting Ford's *soi-disant* role as the 'dean
of English novelists' than with supporting art for its own sake. But what really
disturbed Hemingway was that he didn't know how much to believe of what Ford told
him. A stylistic puritan, he mistrusted Fordian elaboration and fantasy. When Derek
Patmore visited Paris in 1925, he heard Hemingway ask Pound and Dos Passos: 'How
much is one to believe of Ford's anecdotes? How much of them is true? If he feels
you're not convinced, Ford always puts in some small detail, such as an observant
onlooker might notice . . .' Fine criticism of Ford's aesthetics of intimate affective
conversation; but it reveals Hemingway as one of the young Americans who couldn't
tell when Ford was in earnest. Pound always defended Ford, said Patmore. He
exclaimed: 'Well, he has a prodigious memory—he can quote pages from all the books
he's read. Of course, he can't help it always if the memory is embroidered a bit.'[15]
    In *A Moveable Feast* Hemingway is trying to master his unease about Ford's
veracity; and giving an untrue impression that he was never taken in. (His later
grumble that he had known Ford 'too bloody well' is similarly half-untrue.) He
presents the encounter as a battle of styles. Ford, living in a world that never was of
sentimental fiction, is opposed by his own disabused, cynical immediacy. At face
value, Ford's self-parodic, theatrical persona is the antithesis of everything
Hemingway strove for. And yet, when Hemingway wrote *A Moveable Feast* over thirty
years later, his style of authenticity had become a pose of laconic *machismo*; and his
critics were beginning to accuse him of becoming a self-parody himself. His description of Ford is redolent of an uncomfortable proximity: 'I always held my breath when
I was near him.' Ford's friends denied Hemingway's charge that Ford smelled.[16] But
it is a tribute to Hemingway's genius that, mixed up with the childish animus, is an
intelligent recognition that he might be nearer to Ford than he had thought; and that,
just as he plays a role in order to spar with Ford's English Gentleman role, so his own
writing involves the play of roles and personae. There is a kind of affection in this
recognition, behind the gut-aversion; and it makes the sketch less vindictive than it has
generally been taken to be. The dialogue, which has the ring of a more important kind
of authenticity, suggests instead a playful contest of equals—something which Ford
even says. The episode ends with a Fordian *coup de canon*. Hemingway is told that the
man Ford thought he had cut was not Belloc, but Aleister Crowley (the Satanist, hence
'the Devil's Disciple'). But this is unlikely, since Ford knew Belloc well from the Mont
Blanc days before the war; and Kitty Cannell said he knew *both* men well.[17]

Hemingway suggests that Ford has confused the writer and the magician; the artist and the charlatan. Why the mistake matters so much to him is that he was wondering whether he was not making the same mistake: confusing a performance of authenticity with authenticity itself.

Ford's preoccupation with the English Gentleman, and his living the part of one, has always been controversial, not least because of the way it is bound up with ideas of impersonation and imposture. Pound, writing to him about *Return to Yesterday* in 1931, could not see how Ford, who could see so much, could not see how entangled he was in the very social system he was rendering:

Dear Fordie
    Wall, yew ave got a funny kind ov'a mind [. . .]
    Thank god I was born ten years later than you were. Escaped a lot of god damnd nonsense. Not sure the beastly word gentleman hasn't caused more trouble in yr/ bright l'il life than all the rest to the lang. (lang. = langwidg) [. . .]
I was about to remove the paragraph about the 'gent' or at any rate rewrite it// thinking it wd. prob. make you pewk over the floor/
    First idea of softening it was: Fordie, you AVE got a rummy job lot of 'idees recues'.

and I come back to it that you HAVE bitched about 80% of yr/ work through hanging onto a set of idees recues.

    parenthesis / not as to *fact* but to language)[18]

But what Pound could never see was how a great strength of art like Ford's and Conrad's is its principled refusal to allow itself the illusion of a superior diagnostic stance. Ford never succumbs to the callousness that Pound's surgical pretensions lead him into. He writes too well about what it is like to live with and through received ideas to be able to think that one can do entirely without them. It is this that makes him like Flaubert, and it is this that Pound, with his inappropriately Imagist emphasis on the direct treatment of 'things', could not see in either Flaubert or Ford. Flaubert uses the language of Emma Bovary's received ideas about romantic heroines, just as Ford works within the language of the English class system. Class has always been absurdly rigid and strangulating in England, and rarely more so than in the first half of this century. But to Americans, who generally think they do not really have it, it seems merely an irrelevance, a joke.

    Certainly Ford was obsessed by class. But good writing often comes out of a compulsive fascination; a need to understand, assimilate, master, and overcome—or just to come to terms with—a perplexing involvement. (Think of Joyce and religion, or Ireland; Conrad and the sea.) We shall return to the question of Ford's role-playing in a later discussion of his autobiographical explorations of self. What concerns us here is whether his writing is damaged by his preoccupation with the Gentleman. There are three main points to be made. First, that an *idée reçue* need not become an *idée fixe*. Not only is Tietjens's relation to the class system always problematic—he is more gentle-manly than the conventional gentlemen, who therefore shun him; his embodiment of the gentlemanly ideal shows up the hypocrisy and fictionality of conformists such as Campion and Macmaster. But also the way in which he acts the gentleman changes through the tetralogy, as society and individuals change through the war. So Ford is showing how a code of conduct is transformed by circumstance, rather than delivering reflex class-responses. Secondly, *Parade's End* is one of the greatest books in English about class—specifically about the upper-middle class: about how class works; what it is; what it feels like; how it was changing. Amongst a multitude of other things, it is a study of the psychology of class: an interior presentation of how social codes shape our behaviour and our sense of self. It is about how class contributes substantially to the roles we play; and nowhere does this come across so powerfully as in the scenes in which Tietjens self-consciously composes himself into the picture of the gentleman he feels he ought to be. Thirdly, Ford was himself well aware of the dangers of making a fetish out of class. He argued—in a cancelled passage from *Return to Yesterday* about the very craft of writing that Pound thought Ford's obsession impeded—that 'it is more commonsensible to study the technical details of your pursuit than not to do so out of want of intellectual curiosity or to refuse to do so because of an obsession of gentlemanliness'. It would be absurdly obsessive for a writer to shun technique as the literary equivalent of being 'in trade'. It would be equally absurd for a writer about England to lack intellectual curiosity about class.[19]

14

PARADE'S END

That is just how I was affected by my war experiences. I thought I had experienced them clearly and vividly, I was almost bursting with images of them; the roll of film in my head seemed miles long. But when I sat at my writing-desk, on a chair, by a table, the razed villages and woods, the earth tremors caused by heavy bombardment, the conglomeration of filth and greatness, of fear and heroism, of mangled stomachs and heads, of fear of death and grim humour, were all immeasurably remote, only a dream, not related to anything and could not really be conceived [. . .] Even those who took part in it did not for a long time experience it. And if many really did so—they forgot about it again. Next to the hunger to experience a thing, men have perhaps no stronger hunger than to forget.

(Hermann Hesse, *The Journey to the East*)

Impressionism and Authority

Introduction: A Vision Of The Line: War, Repression, Will

It had taken a series of fictional approaches to get his tale of passion into the proportions of *The Good Soldier*. Just as *A Call*, *Ladies Whose Bright Eyes*, and *The Young Lovell* can be seen as tentative investigations into disturbed sexuality, so most of Ford's prose between *The Good Soldier* and *Parade's End* forms a series of oblique, many-minded approaches to the turmoil of war. So devastating and disrupting an experience takes time to assimilate, master, and reconstruct. Not only *Parade's End*, but most of the classic prose about the war was not written until the late 1920s: Edmund Blunden's *Undertones of War* (1928), Robert Graves's *Goodbye to All That* (1929), Erich Maria Remarque's *All Quiet on the Western Front* (1929), and Siegfried Sassoon's *Memoirs of an Infantry Officer* (1930).

In Ford's case the difficulty of mastering the experience was technical as well as psychological. The war presented a formidable challenge to literary impressionism, since it subjected humanity *en masse* to unprecedented extremes of experience, shocks to the nervous system. Impressionism's foregrounding of sensation offered a way of presenting a war which soon made traditional narrative frameworks seem inadequate to make sense of it—frameworks of 'victory', 'campaigns', 'heroic sacrifice', 'patriotism'—even Christianity, which Ford later said he thought the war had finished. It made him feel even more like Dowell: 'I don't know anything any more', he wrote:

If, before the War, one had any function it was that of historian. Basing, as it were, one's mentality on the Europe of Charlemagne as modified by the Europe of Napoleon I, one had something to go upon. One could approach with composure the Lex Allemannica, the Feudal System, problems of Aerial Flight, the price of wheat or the relations of the Sexes. But now, it seems to me, we have no method of approach to any of these problems.[1]

Instead of trying to locate the meanings of their experiences within familiar military or political contexts, participants attached significance to their sensations, often made strange by the very disjunction from, or uncertain connection with, the received contexts. The front line became a kind of anthropological demarcation: going over the top was an initiation, a 'baptism of fire', which separated the soldier from the civilian whom he tries to convince of its horrors, while remaining sceptical that he can ever succeed.

Thus far war ought to have been the ideal impressionist subject: experience overwhelming plot; rendering rather than comment. But Ford realized with astounding prescience that the mind's repression of war-suffering made it difficult to exorcise the suffering, and by the same token difficult to convey it in prose. About a month after the outbreak he found himself 'absolutely and helplessly unable—to write poems about the present war', and attributed it to 'the hazy remoteness of the war-grounds; the impossibility of visualizing anything, because of a total incapacity to believe any single thing that I read in the daily papers'. But being in the war-grounds didn't make the experience much easier to visualize in words. While still in the Ypres Salient he wrote the essay 'A Day of Battle' (the first half of a two-part piece called 'War and the Mind'), which is one of the key documents in the genesis of *Parade's End*.[2] It is a deeply paradoxical piece, vividly re-creating the predicament of someone who feels he can no longer create vivid representations: 'As far as I am concerned an invisible barrier in my brain seems to lie between the profession of Arms and the mind that put things into words' (p. 457). As in his letters to Conrad about the sounds and psychological phenomena of bombardment, the sensations described are primarily to do with what the mind doesn't perceive—or at least not quite consciously:

I used to think that being out in France would be like being in a magic ring that would cut me off from all private troubles: but nothing is further from the truth. I have gone down to the front line at night, worried, worried, worried beyond belief about happenings at home in a Blighty that I did not much expect to see again—so worried that all sense of personal danger disappeared and I forgot to duck when shells went close overhead. (p. 460)

This is the first voicing of his three central and related themes concerning war. First, that the war might have seemed like an escape from private entanglements, but it was not. Secondly, it follows from this that the soldier, like the impressionist (or a reader), is in one place with his mind somewhere quite other: 'he is indeed *homo duplex*: a poor fellow whose body is tied in one place, but whose mind and personality brood eternally over another distant locality'. Thirdly, that this 'never-ending sense of worry' produced 'mental distresses' that were as significant as the 'physical horrors': 'The heavy strain of the trenches came from the waiting for long periods of inaction, in great—in mortal—danger every minute of the day and night.'[3]

One paradox is that although the war does not provide a magic screen against domestic worries, the worries can screen the soldier from the war. The invisible barrier in the brain, the 'magic ring'—or 'invisible tent' in *The Marsden Case*; 'inviolable sphere' in *Parade's End*—are all vivid images of psychological repression.[4] The mind is aware of something being repressed ('cut off'), but the mechanism of repression is invisible, 'magic'. When panic and weakness were taboo, the fear was probably transferred from the war to the other preoccupations with which the soldier tried to take his mind off the war. The trope of saying that domestic worry is worse than fear of battle also figured in *A House*. But it works better in describing the mind while under stress than while recovering from it. In the war suppression was necessary to protect the self from being overwhelmed by fear; and fear of danger was supposed to be suppressed, but could not be mastered: it gets expressed obliquely. Ford's combination of suppressed blankness about his surroundings together with enervating anxiety about other people ('the men', the French, the dead, their relations) effectively conveys his and Tietjens's suppression of fear, together with a sense of the power of that fear. Whereas the trope can seem indulgent when used to describe experiences after the war. We find it easier to empathize with someone in the grip of terror, than someone still upset by past terrors.

When Ford discusses psychological repression in 'A Day of Battle' he does so in visual terms. The essay is also important for what it says about vision, bringing together some of his persistent preoccupations: hallucination, insight, 'impressionism', and the concern about where the 'visions' of the writer and reader shade off into delusions. It begins by asking why it is that he cannot write about the war:

With the pen, I used to be able to 'visualize things'—as it used to be called [. . .] Now I could not make you see Messines, Wijtschate, St Eloi; or La Boiselle, the Bois de Bécourt or de Mametz—although I have sat looking at them for hours, for days, for weeks on end. Today, when I look at a mere coarse map of the Line, simply to read 'Ploegsteert' or 'Armentières' seems to bring up extraordinarily coloured and exact pictures behind my eyeballs—little pictures having all the brilliant minuteness that medieval illuminations had—of towers, and roofs, and belts of trees and sunlight; or, for the matter of these, of men, burst into mere showers of blood and dissolving into muddy ooze; or of aeroplanes and shells against the translucent blue.—But, as for putting them—into words! No: the mind stops dead, and something in the brain stops and shuts down: precisely as the left foot stops dead and the right foot comes up to it with a stamp upon the hard asphalt—upon the 'square', after the word of command 'Halt', at Chelsea! (p. 456)

That word 'visualize' encapsulates the technical problem, punning between the artist visualizing for himself, and making things visual for others: making us see. Ford's own visions are 'extraordinary' (remarkable, or abnormal?); but he cannot translate them into words that would make us see them. Anyone trying to stop thinking of that image of men, 'burst into mere showers of blood and dissolving into muddy ooze' might doubt the crisis in Ford's impressionism. But although the essay does convey with great power a series of such images, as with the essay 'Nice People', the sense of perplexing elusive significance remains with him, leaving him unsatisfied by the presentation. As in *The Good Soldier*, tantalizingly significant pictures are not settled into a stated meaning. And, again like the earlier essay, most of the images recur in later work, until they are given contexts which can harness the significances, and exhaust their aspects—even when their significance is a strange blankness. One such image, which (like the images of maps, towns, casualties, and aeroplanes) is reworked in both *No Enemy* and *Parade's End*, is of a vision of the front line. If it wasn't suggested by the opening vision of Henri Barbusse's *Le feu* (*Under Fire*, 1916)—the only great novel of the war to be written before 1918—it is strikingly similar in effect:

And it came into my head to think that here was the most amazing fact of history. For in the territory beneath the eye, or not hidden by folds in the ground, there must have been—on the two sides—a million men, moving one against the other and impelled by an invisible moral force into a Hell of fear that surely cannot have had a parallel in this world. It was an extraordinary feeling to have in a wide landscape.

But there it stopped. As for explanation I hadn't any: as for significant or valuable pronouncement of a psychological kind I could not make any—nor any generalization. There we were: those million men, forlorn, upon a raft in space. But as to what had assembled us upon that landscape: I had just to fall back upon the formula: it is the Will of God. Nothing else would take it all in. I myself seemed to have drifted there at the bidding of indifferently written characters on small scraps of paper. W.O. telegram A/R 2572/26: a yellow railway warrant; a white embarkation order; a pink movement order; a check like a cloakroom ticket ordering the C.O. of one's Battalion to receive one. But the Will that had brought me there did not seem to be, much, one's own Will. No doubt what had put in action the rather weary, stiff limbs beneath one's heavy pack had its actual origin in one's own brain. But it didn't feel like it. (pp. 457–8)

It wasn't just the unimaginably large numbers of the living that made this vision of the line so haunting: as that phrase 'a Hell of fear' intimates, they were sharing the terrain with the twentieth century's equivalent of a Hieronymus Bosch vision of the dead:

We *don't know how many men have been killed*. . . . One is always too close or too remote. On the Somme in July 1916, or under Vimy Ridge in February 1917 one saw [. . .] such an infinite number of dead—& frequently mouldering—Huns [. . .] when you see the dead lie in heaps, in thousands, half buried[?], intact, reposeful as if they had fallen asleep, contorted as if they were still in agony, the heaps of men following the lines of hillocks, of shell holes, like so much rubbish spread before an incinerator in the quarter of a town where refuse is disposed of. . . . Well, you think of Armageddon and on any hill of that Line, as I have seen it, from the Somme up to the Belgian Coast where you see, & can feel, the operations of [. . .] millions of men moving million against million—you think again of Armageddon. And the War seems of infinite importance.[5]

We have seen how Ford already knew, when returning to the Front in late 1916, that he would write about the war. In the dedicatory letter to *No More Parades* he said: 'Few writers can have engaged themselves as combatants in what, please God, will yet prove to be the war that ended war, without the intention of aiding with their writings, if they survived, in bringing about such a state of mind as should end wars as possibilities' (p. 6). But in 'A Day of Battle' he can only *tell* of the psychological effects: the vision of the whole impresses upon him 'the most amazing fact of history', and produces 'an extraordinary feeling'. It is only in *Parade's End* that he was able to *show* his amazed response.

This chapter will discuss the ways in which the tetralogy confronts and attempts to objectify and substantiate the feelings expressed in his vision of the line. In particular, it will explore two dualities: that of trying to visualize the whole of a war which figures in the mind as vivid fragments, disparate scenes; and that of the will—of trying to convey the sense in which the whole war seems animated by 'wills' which cannot be accounted for by the volitions of the individuals taking part. The discussion concentrates on three related areas. First, how Ford's impressionism involves a political and historical understanding; a penetrating analysis of authority, seen in terms of social power, individual self-control, and aesthetic ordering. Second, psychological extremity: terror, intense worry, persecutory anxiety; and their relation to ideas of the father, God, and death. Third, questions of representation: reality, unreality, metaphor; of the tetralogy's use of tropes and time-shifts, of autobiographical material, of visions.

The conjunction of the two ideas of visualization and volition in 'A Day of Battle' is characteristic (though the feeling of being 'borne up by an exterior volition' during an attack was something another writer, David Jones, corroborated). Christopher Tietjens is similar to Young Lovell as his chivalric and military ideals are first jeopardized then realized when he is rapt in his visions of the other woman, the White Lady. What is also characteristic is Ford's tendency to articulate his responses in terms of literature. This is partly because for him, to wonder about the effects of the war is necessarily to wonder about how to convey them by literary effects, and to worry that one psychological effect is to inhibit his ability to make others see. It is also because his responses come already structured in terms of the aesthetic, the literary (hence the ironic glance at the texts—'indifferently written characters on small scraps of paper'—which have transported him to France). One of the most striking episodes in *No Enemy* recounts how a young girl of eight has been kidnapped from her mother by her father, who has left her in 'Gringoire''s charge and disappeared. She is on Gringoire's mind when (like Ford) he visits a government minister in Paris. Ford calls the girl Maisie, and writes: 'You see: it was almost a drop too much in my cup—to be plunged straight into "What Maisie Knew" [. . .] It was too much bewilderment.'[6] It would be specious to say that he responded to the war as if it were a novel—the novel he would go on to create out of it. But there is a sense in which his particular responses are those of someone who does think predominantly in aesthetic terms. The apprehension of 'a million men, moving one against the other and impelled by an invisible moral force' shares its structure with the apprehension of a work of art, expressing a moral vision through its amassing of scintillating detail. Although it is *felt*, the 'Will of God' that has 'assembled us upon that landscape' is as inscrutable as the moral purpose of a true impressionist artist ought to be. Ford's response to the war is paradoxical in the way that someone's response to a novel can be: one is aware of a vision, a personality, controlling, shaping, impelling; but that presence is also an absence: a self-effacement, a restraint from imposing the will upon intractable humanity which is necessary if the characters are to have room to live: in short, what Ford called (while he was still at work on *Parade's End*) 'will-less impressionism'.[7] Thus his thoughts about 'the most amazing fact of history' 'came into' his head rather than being willed by him; rather as what had put in action his weary limbs 'had its actual origin in one's own brain. But it didn't feel like it.' (So, when we read, amazing facts come into our head, but don't feel as if we have originated them.)

It is not altogether surprising that he was unable to write immediately about the war. His deepest narrative impulse, the retrospective and elegiac, militated against an immediate journalistic *reportage* of events. The novelist of spatial dualities, one of whose great subjects was how the mind is usually somewhere quite other, was not likely to produce his most compelling accounts of the war while he was there. In *Joseph Conrad* (also contemporary with *Parade's End*) he wrote of how being in the war exacerbated that feeling of mental doubleness:

had you taken part actually in those hostilities, you would know how infinitely little part the actual fighting itself took in your mentality. You would be lying on your stomach, in a beast of a funk, with an immense, horrid German barrage going on all over and round you and with hell and all let loose. But [. . .] your thoughts were really concentrated on something quite distant [. . .] You were there, but great shafts of thought from the outside, distant and unattainable world infinitely for the greater part occupied your mind. (p. 192)

To be able to *see* the war, and to make us see it, Ford needed to be somewhere quite other, as a strange passage about redoubled doubleness in *No Enemy* symmetrically puts it: 'though I had listened with all my ears to the Staff Officer at Penhally, my eyes, even then had been playing the trick of showing me Pont-de-Nieppe—just as at Nieppe in France they insisted on showing me Penhally in Wales' (pp. 247–8). The war left him dually alienated: physically he had escaped from England, but then he escaped mentally back. *Parade's End* is Ford's fullest, most searching treatment of mental division; of what he later called 'duplicate cerebration'. 'A Day of Battle' sees this duality as a necessity of all human perception, since our perceptual apparatus and anxious engrossments impede our understanding of what we do, or of what happens to us. 'Lookers-on see most of the Game'; but he knew that the peculiar battle-numbness that beset him was due to more than an awkward perspective: 'it is carrying the reverse to a queer extreme to say that one of the players should carry away, mentally, nothing of the Game at all.'[8]

Point of View: Arthur Marwood

Since Ford pointed it out in *Return to Yesterday* and *It Was the Nightingale*, it has been well known that the central character of *Parade's End*, Christopher Tietjens, was broadly based on Arthur Marwood; though like all Ford's characters he is compounded from many acquaintances, and also Ford himself. The way Ford presents the decision to involve Marwood reveals much about his conception of the tetralogy, and the importance of his stories about its genesis has not been recognized.

The first thing to say about them is that they are—characteristically—quite different. We have seen how (in the dedication to *No More Parades*) he places the crucial moment in the Salient in 1916, when he asked himself: 'How would all this look in the eyes of X . . .—already dead, along with all English Tories?' By 1931 Ford identified 'X' as Marwood, but, surprisingly considering his memory of 'the very spot where the idea came' to him, the scene is now set in Menton, during Ford's convalescence in the spring of 1917. He tells how he had been experimenting with Marwood's 'system' for gambling at Monte Carlo:

It was whilst I was thus passing my time that it occurred to me to wonder what Marwood would have thought about the War and the way it was conducted. In the attempt to realise that problem for myself I wrote several novels with a projection of him as a central character.

Of course they were no sort of biography of Marwood. He died several years before the War, though, as I have said, that is a fact that I never realise.[9]

He always found it hard to accept the fact of death. So much of his writing tries to realize it; though paradoxically it does so by reincarnating people, fantasizing about them still being alive. Though such fantasies are 'impressions' rather than delusions, the imagination of still being able to *hear* Marwood *through* the persona of Tietjens mattered to Ford. The third version occurs in *It Was the Nightingale* (1934). Ford recalls a conversation in a railway carriage in 1908 or 1909:

I said to Marwood:
  'What really became of Waring?'
  He said:
  'The poor devil, he picked up a bitch on a train between Calais and Paris. She persuaded him that he had got her with child. . . . He felt he had to marry her. . . . Then he found out that the child might be another man's, just as well as his. . . . There was no real knowing. . . . It was the hardest luck I ever heard of. . . . She was as unfaithful to him as a street-walker. . . .'
  I said:
  'Couldn't he divorce?'
  —But he couldn't divorce. He held that a decent man could never divorce a woman. The woman, on the other hand, would not divorce him because she was a Roman Catholic.[10]

This provides the story-line of Tietjens's marriage to Sylvia. (It also suggests how in both *The Good Soldier* and *Parade's End* he came to reverse the religious contrast between himself as the Catholic and Elsie Hueffer or Violet Hunt as nominal protestants.) But it includes nothing yet of the complications ensuing from Tietjens's adulterous love for Valentine Wannop. This second stage comes when Ford is staying in Harold Monro's villa at St-Jean-Cap-Ferrat during the winter of 1922–3. Nearby lives 'a poor fellow who had had almost Waring's fate'. He does not name the man; but one reason why his story must have stuck in Ford's mind is its similarities to the stories of Dowell and Ashburnham:

He was a wealthy American who had married a wrong 'un. She had been unfaithful to him before and after marriage. He had supported these wrongs because of his passion for the woman. At last she had eloped with a ship steward and had gone sailing around the world. The husband being an American of good tradition considered himself precluded from himself taking proceedings for divorce, but he would gladly have let the woman divorce him and would have provided liberally for her. She, however, was sailing around the world and he had no means of communicating with her. Almost simultaneously, after a year or so, he had conceived an overwhelming passion for another woman and the wife had returned. . . . What passed between them one had no means of knowing. Presumably she had announced her intention of settling down again with him and had flatly refused to divorce him. So he committed suicide. . . .
  The dim sight of the roof of his villa below me over the bay gave me then another stage of my intrigue [. . .] It suddenly occurred to me to wonder what Marwood himself would have thought of the story—and then what he would have thought of the war [. . .] I imagined his mind going all over the misty and torrential happenings of the Western Front [. . .] I seemed, even as I walked in that garden, to see him stand in some high place in France during the

period of hostilities taking in not only what was visible, but all the causes and all the motive powers of distant places. And I seemed to hear his infinitely scornful comment on those places. It was as if he lived again. (pp. 200–2)

Waring's life, like the Ashburnhams', is a perplexing enigma. 'There was no knowing' for Waring whether his wife's child was his; 'one had no means of knowing' what passed between the wealthy American and his 'wrong 'un' wife. In the version of this man's story sketched briefly in the dedication to *No More Parades* even the husband's suicide is uncertain: 'he drank himself to death, it was said deliberately, after he had taken his wife back' (p. 9). The preoccupation with *knowing* (in the carnal as well as the intellectual sense) which impels most of Ford's fiction is as dominant as in *The Good Soldier*. But the emphasis falls differently in *Parade's End*. Rather than mesmerizing us with the obscurity of human motive, it attempts to reconstruct what *can* be known: to imagine what passes between people.

Seeing the American's villa reminds Ford of Waring, which reminds him of Marwood. Seeing one view makes him see the view of the Front, though now the consciousness of Marwood provides the critical attitude, the astute comments and generalizations that Ford himself could not make in the Salient. These three versions are not inconsistent or contradictory: although he stresses the suddenness of each thought (which gives it the freshness of an entirely new idea), he does not claim that the idea to use Marwood *first* came to him at Menton or at Cap Ferrat. On the contrary, the superimposition of scenes is important. Standing in one high place in the South of France enables him to recall the wartime view from a high place in the Salient (as he saw Pont de Nieppe from Penhally). It is as if he can only present his experience by distancing it from himself, forming it through remembered views and persons; seeing himself from outside. (Compare Tietjens: 'He viewed his case from outside. It was like looking at the smooth running of a mechanical model.') Just as he sees one landscape *through* another, he sees the Front through the eyes of another. This enables him to comprehend—and therefore to make us see—the perplexing experiences of 1916. *Return to Yesterday* is explicit about how Ford turned to Marwood, in person when he was alive, as well as in fiction after his death, in order to see himself:

I do not know that I ever consulted him over any of my personal difficulties as I invariably consulted Conrad—and indeed, rather often, Mrs. Wells. It was much more as if I 'set' my mind by his. If I had personal problems I would go and talk to him about anything else. Then the clarity of the working of his mind had an effect on mine that *made me see*, if not what was best to do then what would be most true to *myself*.[11]

This idea of the value of contact with another personality is central to Ford's aesthetic. It is the same effect that contact with literature has upon us: the novelist's clarity can help us in an oblique way to see ourselves. We shall return to this principle in later chapters (on doubles and on autobiography). The relevance to *Parade's End* of these versions of a man *standing up* and looking out over the panorama of the war is obvious. (We have already seen one transposition of it, as Ford surveys London from Campden Hill in 1919). The idea to base Tietjens on Marwood is a double resurrection: it is not just that it makes Marwood live again in Ford's (and his reader's) mind; it also brings Ford's own past back to life—his past life that paradoxically dragged him back to his childhood terrors and nervous breakdown just when his life seemed to have ended in 1916 (and again in 1919). Like all his best work, *Parade's End* is a vast time-shift of the creative mind, plumbing his deepest feelings about this past.[12]

The decision to model the novel's central consciousness on Marwood is more than simply the solution to a problem of fictional technique, though it is the means by which Ford faces and masters his bafflement at the Front. A further reason why he keeps returning to the decisive moment(s) is that it provides a governing image for the entire tetralogy. The vision of Marwood's mind 'going all over the mist and torrential happenings of the Western Front' is a fine one for the genesis of *Parade's End* (and one which, as we shall see, is echoed in different transformations throughout the tetralogy). It is a curiously theological image, the disembodied mind perhaps suggesting the words of Genesis about the Spirit of God moving over the face of the waters. The image also condenses the creation of the world of a novel (the misty and torrential surface of the Front) and the creation of the novel itself. For in one sense it is an image for the technique of writing; more precisely, of 'point of view'. Ford looking out over the Salient tries to synthesize his personal experiences of the war (images of casualties, aeroplanes, and maps) into the kind of 'great view' he sees before him; but it still seems incomprehensible; like the ending of *The Good Soldier*, 'a picture without a meaning': 'it all seemed to signify nothing.'[13] Seeing through Marwood's eyes, he can synthesize his own intractable impressions with a generalizing, totalizing consciousness. He can objectify his war experiences as he had not been able to before *Parade's End*. Having explored the sceptical implications of first-person narration almost to the limit in *The Good Soldier* (perhaps only Nabokov has gone further), he experiments in *Parade's End* with a form of omniscient narration, figured in Marwood's God-like mind moving over the created and destroyed earth, which will do justice to the subjective experience it transcends, as *Parade's End* seeks a form which can do justice to Ford's disturbing visions and memories of the war (such as the scenes recalled in *No Enemy* of the view of the line, the sight of shells exploding in the distance, the blue of swallows' backs, and so on), and interpret his place in the post-war world.[14] The vision of Marwood is, in short, another image of Fordian dual perspective. It superimposes Ford's vision of the Line upon a vision of the Line (with Ford/Tietjens in it) seen from outside, from above.

Political Views

Ford thought of Tietjens, as he thought of Marwood, as the incarnation of Toryism. *Parade's End* is, in one respect, an elegy—Ford's finest—for an England that was no more. Carl Van Doren thought it 'The best record of the political and social shift' which caused the 'disappearance of the nineteenth-century conception and presentation of the governing class in fiction'. It is Ford's *The Last of England*; another of his acts of homage to his grandfather. He described Madox Brown's move to Manchester as if he were leaving the country: 'A certain bravery is required to enact the tragedy of the *Last of England*, when the hero is at the age of sixty.' A quarter-of-a-century later, he was re-enacting that emigration, aged almost 50, and taking stock of the homeland he was leaving, writing his farewell to it as the kind of panorama of social history that

Madox Brown's paintings of contemporary life were. *Parade's End* is a *Paradise Lost*; but it would be as rash to accuse Ford of reactionary nostalgia as it would Milton. Discussions of Tietjens as 'the last Tory' have dominated the criticism of the series, tending to imply that the novels conceal an anachronistic politics.[15] But Ford's laments for codes of behaviour which were being transformed, for the atomization of social responsibilities into a frenetic materialism and individualism, do not mean that he identified himself with the political platform of Edwardian Conservatism. As ever, his politics were too paradoxical and flexible to be partisan. He understood politics, as he constructed novels, by moving amongst opposing viewpoints. He felt his sympathies lay 'towards the Right', but that 'The literary man in England is usually predestined to the left'.[16] It is a sociology of the missing middle: a sympathy with the traditional landowners and the working classes, but an aversion to the middle-classes, and to political moderates, and to *arrivistes* like Tietjens's friend Vincent Macmaster. Ford's support of the suffragettes and his championing of Irish Home Rule would both have been anathema to the Conservatives. Instead, he is rendering the pervasive anxiety of the pre-war years that traditional values and the traditional order were being shaken.

His comments on Madox Brown's dual allegiances show that it was once again his grandfather who sat as the model for Ford's paradoxical politics, and provocative pronouncements. Tietjens is, like Marwood, and also like Ford himself, exactly Madox Brown's type of romantic Tory revolutionary. Someone whose Tory paternalism is so extensive that he would reorganize society in a radical manner in order to improve conditions for the working class. In such arguments 'feudalism' is more a metaphorical entity than a historical actuality (though Ford's novels of medieval life offer a comprehensive picture of feudal existence which is far less romanticized than the Victorian medievalisms of the Pre-Raphaelites and socialist Arts-and-Craftists). Calling himself a Tory was also a form of self-protective camouflage: a way 'to avoid the imbecilities of politicians', he explained, rather as Shelley 'styled himself atheist not because he was an Atheist but to avoid theological discussions'. For the Tory party, being 'the Stupid Party' 'never employs writers of any talent to support it'. (Some traditions survive.) Whereas 'If you announce yourself as belonging to one or other parties of the Left you will eventually succumb to the temptation of prostituting your pen'.[17]

The basis of Fordian 'feudalism' is a distrust of the liberal insistence on 'rights'.[18] For Ford, liberal individualism is a form of egotism; rights are generally alibis for exploiting those with fewer rights. His ideal of political conduct is the Tory altruist, who, rather than asserting his will and his 'rights', effaces himself in his 'responsibilities'. In this utopian view it becomes difficult to distinguish between my responsibility for someone else's well-being, and their *right* to well-being. This is where Toryism becomes radical and revolutionary. If it be argued that such an ideal is morally unrealistic—an impossible idealization of self-less conduct—one must recognize how, in Ford's writing, it becomes a standard against which he can see actual conduct with remorseless clarity. Ford's politics, like all his attitudes, are impressionist: 'illuminative exaggerations', unrealistic renderings of unrealistic positions, which make us *see* political realities. There is nothing sentimental or unrealistic about his perceptions of the moral blind-spots of the liberal position. Immediately after positing that 'Presumably you cannot better the feudal system', he turns to one way in which we might have worsened it:

So I was always a sentimental Tory. But inasmuch as the Tories stood in the way of Home Rule for Ireland, I never voted or wrote for that Party. The Liberals of the 'nineties on the other hand were mostly great employers of labour. Their aim was to have always fringes of pauperised and parasitic working people so that wages might be kept low. It was perhaps an unconscious aim. My Tory view was that every workman should first be assured of four hundred a year. Let the employer of labour assure that before he started his factory—or clear out. So, though the Liberals supported Irish Home Rule I could not support them.[19]

This shows how untrue is Robert Green's claim that Ford 'championed the traditional pieties of the Conservative Party, "individualism and property as against collectivism and labour legislation"'. Even in the pre-war work he is discussing, the materialist individualist characters (like Leonora Ashburnham) are shown in a highly critical light. As early as 1905 Ford knew how reductive such distinctions were: 'There is in each man of us an Individualist strain more or less strong, and in each, a more or less strong flavour of the Theorist who sees mankind only in the bulk.' Fordian 'Toryism' precisely cuts across party lines, posing feudalism (rather as Ruskin had posed it) as an ideal form of collective life. Ford was no individualist in the sense of a champion of *laissez-faire* capitalism. For him, as for Conrad, the artist needed to be an individualist in so far as art is a 'single-minded attempt to render the highest kind of justice to the visible universe'. Yet of course Ford's collaboration with Conrad testifies to a hope that art could come out of the union of two minds. And Ford knew that human minds, and especially those of artists, were complex. When (in January 1914) he asked how it was that 'any man who can read at all [could] hold the vast number of contradictory opinions that are necessary to a "Progressive" of to-day', we sense that the Fordian artist might be better able to hold them.[20] The difference is in the *way* in which the artist holds them: not tendentiously, with the zeal of the progressive reformer or the complacence of the conservative, but tentatively, self-questioningly. A creative artist, he writes, 'is an observer and a recorder. He may have passions but he must mistrust them.' If his writings on social questions account for his politics in terms of his 'temperament', the converse is also true: his emotions were themselves already politicized. Questions of sexuality were still as intensely political after the war as they had been just before. And Ford's feelings for Marwood are inseparable from his political understanding.[21] It is striking how Ford's shrewd insights into liberalism's contradictions did not lure him to single-minded totalitarianism (as it did with Pound and Lewis, and partly did with Yeats and Eliot). Like Joyce, Ford delighted in plurality (in politics as well as in art); and accepted that his Tory views themselves involved 'a vast number of contradictory opinions'—the prime contradiction of which was perhaps over whether Toryism could still be said to exist. For, ultimately, Ford's 'Toryism' is an impression rather than a political manifesto. And one reason why it so suited his temperament was that it was a lost cause. 'Feudalism was finished', Tietjens thinks on Armistice Day: 'to-day the world changed.' *Parade's End* is feudalism's elegy rather than its symptom. It is the story of how 'the last Tory' can re-create himself as a small producer after the war, as Ford had re-created himself as both small producer and writer.[22]

Ford continually distinguished between 'propaganda' and art. (Characteristically, his own writing of propaganda brings off the dual act of being both.) His own interest in politics was that of an artist rather than a propagandist: a fascination with political machinations. A dense passage from *Return to Yesterday* is suggestive about the complex ways his political—and aesthetic—ideas are embodied in his fiction:

I never took any stock in politics. But political movements have always interested me. I have only once voted. It is one of my most passionate convictions that no one individual can be sufficiently intelligent to be entrusted with the fortune or life of any other individual. Far less can he be morally capable of influencing to the extent merely of a single vote the destinies of millions of his fellows. I at any rate never could feel myself so entitled. I don't believe a creative artist can have any intellect: he is an observer and a recorder [. . .].[23]

That last remark is provocative in Ford's familiar dual mode, suggesting how an opposition can be resolved (surely exact observation and just recording *is* an exercise of the intellect?), but crucially preferring not to resolve. The provocation also comes from the derogatory sense of implying that artists are devoid of intellect. One's desire to say that Ford does not mean that artists are stupid is checked by the possibility that this might be exactly what he does mean. When he calls the Tory party 'the stupid party', the denigration in the phrase is countered by the nuance of moral superiority.[24] When political 'cleverness' involves manipulating 'the destinies of millions', often for the vested interests of those who have precisely taken 'stock' in politics (the metaphor contracts the contradictions he identifies in liberalism), then stupidity takes on the aura of innocence. Again he's recalling his father's judgement. In the Fordian lexicon, 'patience' signifies more than merely waiting. It is passivity, certainly, but it is also cognate with 'passion': feeling and suffering. Four days after England's declaration of war upon Germany, Ford wrote about the national conflict words which also stand for the artist's response to all conflict, whether between nations, classes, or individuals: 'because for my sins I am a cosmopolitan, and also, I suppose, a poet so apt to identify myself with anyone's sufferings as to be unable to take sides very violently, I have probably thought more about these things, and certainly suffer more over them, than most people.'[25] (The note of superior self-pity is not heard in the context: the point is that he suffers more primarily because, as a Germanic-Englishman with a devotion to France, he internalizes the hostilities.) The donkey is ridiculed for its stupidity, but it is a creature of receptivity and endurance. It is the type, that is, of the will-less impressionist: the artist on whom life impresses itself as felt experience, rather than one who, like the Poundian totalitarian, exults in imposing his will on his material. This is why Ford talks of the artist as observer, recorder, rather than in Pound's terms of sculptor or politician.[26] As suggested, he redeems the notion of 'stupidity' into an aesthetic value: the basis of true art. Ford's creative artist, that is, has no intellect in the sense that he receives impressions passively from the world, rather than projecting his active intelligence into the world. Put in these terms, the mental leap from politics to art becomes easier to follow. Ford observes political movements with fascination, but feels it is important not to act in them, as he feels a novelist should not obtrude and 'comment' within his fictions, but should (in Malcolm Bradbury's fine words) 'stand above and allow the logic of the material, the heart of the affair, to unfold'.[27] Only thus can the novelist be entrusted with the fortunes and lives of his characters.

The idea that the Tory stance involves a 'patience' which the world calls stupidity suggests the figure of Tietjens, a man who refuses to ingratiate himself with his superiors, or to defend his reputation against Sylvia's damaging fictions about how he has seduced Valentine; how he is a communist, and models himself upon Christ. But the passage from *Return to Yesterday* (about voting) touches crucially on other aspects of *Parade's End*; in particular, questions of responsibility and authority, and of the relation between the individual and history. Tietjens's revulsion at the thought of being in control of the destinies of his prisoners of war takes up Ford's disavowal of the right electorally to influence the destiny of millions. It is of course paradoxical that someone who argues that we have no rights, but only privileges and responsibilities, should then show himself mistrustful of assuming the responsibility for others. It is typical of the way Ford's fictions dramatize the conflicts of his emotional and moral attitudes. He puts Tietjens, an exaggerated Tory, into extreme situations in order to test the values of Toryism. The army is just such an extreme situation, exaggerating and codifying the feudal order: an officer is entirely responsible for his men; both have duties and privileges, though few 'rights'. Tietjens's worrying over his responsibility for his men of the Welch Regiment recalls the classic dramatization of military responsibility: Act IV, scene 1, of *Henry V*, in which Harry, in disguise, argues with some of his soldiers about the king's moral responsibility for the deaths of his troops. At his most Mr Blood-minded, Ford wrote: 'it is obvious that those members of the ruling classes who will not say, "We are the ruling classes and we'll govern all the rest of you how we think best and hang the consequences!" are the very meanest of individuals.' *Parade's End* shows both sides of this idea. On the one hand, as the consequences of the war made this arrogation of the right to command even less defensible, Ford questions the wisdom of the politicians and generals controlling (or failing to control) the war. On the other hand, Tietjens's story is of a member of the ruling class who is thought a mean individual before the war, when he evades his responsibilities to command, but who redeems his manhood through his military command.[28] Most important, however, is that vision of the individual enmeshed in, and trying to apprehend, the vast movements of history. Ford's interest in political movements—groups of individuals which seem greater than the sum of their human constituents—is essentially congruent with his fascination with the movements of military strategy. Whether he imagines the voter setting his will and destiny against those of 'millions of his fellows', or the soldier wondering over the transformation of fearful and multifarious troops into a co-ordinated military action, he is everywhere possessed by the question of history in this broad sense.

It is a quintessentially aesthetic view of politics; one that tries to comprehend the meaning of events as we perceive the form of a novel. A concatenation of multitudinous details produces an ineluctable conclusion. History, in this version, is a *progression d'effet*. But it is—paradoxically, given Ford's politics—a liberal aesthetic by contrast with those of other writers who have sought to aestheticize politics. Walter

Benjamin's aphorism, that fascism aestheticizes politics, while communism politicizes aesthetics, gives a telling insight into writers like Wyndham Lewis and Ezra Pound, whose visions of the politician as an artist in the medium of the human are inseparable from their tendency to view humanity as a mere medium. 'Humanity is malleable mud', Pound wrote chillingly.[29] Even before Ford had seen the Somme and Flanders, where humanity was not only forced to live in lethal mud, but also to die in it and dissolve 'into muddy ooze', his aesthetic was a more tolerant and receptive one. Where the Poundian artist is the hammer of humanity, or the moulder of the other into an acceptable form, Ford's impressionism lets the world impress itself upon artists and upon their art. Though he shared the widespread feeling that the soldiers had suffered at the hands of a political conspiracy, he wasn't seduced by the totalitarian alternatives to liberalism posed by either the Right or the Left.

Madox Brown's Manchester frescoes stood for Ford as an effort 'of merging individual effort entirely beneath the tide of national movements'. Ford sought this effect in his sociological impressionism (as in *England and the English*). Tietjens and Valentine are too individual to be entirely merged beneath the tide of the war. But more than any other of Ford's novels since *The Fifth Queen*, *Parade's End* imagines its individuals in history. '[O]ur own times are our own property in a sense that nothing else is or can be', he wrote: 'for our own times are made up of the most intimate and most inviolable portion of a man—of his memories.' *Parade's End*, a historical novel of Ford's own times, works as all impressionist fiction must, presenting its world by rendering the most intimate and inviolable portions of its characters: their memories and impressions. What Ford said of history is equally true of early twentieth-century history as it is imagined in *Parade's End*: 'for us these immense movements are alive and our own because of minute contacts with immense happenings.'[30]

It isn't just that Ford talks about history in terms that could equally apply to aesthetics. (*Progression d'effet* is a sense that the minute contacts of words—the stylistic elements—are forming into an immense movement—the artistic design, fate. Sometimes our minute contacts with the printed page develop into an experience the immensity of which seems overwhelming: the death of a mouse from cancer seems as significant as the sack of Rome; a mere book becomes a revelation.) It is also that the scale of *Parade's End* enables him to use our sense of this dual form of a novel as a sustained correlative for our sense of the experience of history. It is in this way that the tetralogy most significantly engages with history. Much of the criticism of the series praises its panoramic scope on one hand, but negates that praise on the other by cavilling about the representativeness of the characters, the accuracy of Ford's picture of England, the realism of its fantasy. But his aim is obviously not to portray the average soldier, but to wonder what sense an unusually intelligent mind can make of the 'immense movements'. That term 'movement' and its cognates becomes a central pun in *Parade's End*, where it brings together ideas of motion, emotion, and progression through temporal aesthetic forms (as we speak of the 'movement' of verse or prose; or the movement of a symphony). Ford is moved by the thought of the millions of men moving in his vision of the line. That reaction is telling. He was subject to overwhelming emotions in the face of crowds; whether the joy he felt in the crowd at Cologne Cathedral, or the feeling that he described as 'the very strongest emotion—

at any rate of this class—that I have ever had', when he 'first went to the Shepherd's Bush Exhibition and came out on a great square of white buildings all outlined with lights':

There was such a lot of light—and I think that what I hope for in Heaven is an infinite clear radiance of pure light! There were crowds and crowds of people—or no, there was, spread out beneath the lights, an infinite moving mass of black, with white faces turned up to the light, moving slowly, quickly, not moving at all, being obscured, reappearing [. . .] It must have been the feeling—not the thought—of all these good, kind, nice people, this immense Crowd suddenly let loose [. . .] to pick up the glittering splinters of glass that are Romance, hesitant but certain of vistas of adventure, if no more than the adventures of their own souls—like cattle in a herd suddenly let into a very rich field and hesitant before the enamel of daisies, the long herbage, the rushes fringing the stream at the end.[31]

If there is a class-feeling here, patronizing the lower classes who are 'let loose' on the meretricious displays that are peddled as culture, it is overwhelmed by the feeling that what the crowd makes Ford aware of is human animality, and thus mortality, and thus his own death. It immediately makes him imagine himself in heaven; and that cadence that ends on the word 'end' intimates the ending of more than just a field. If a London crowd in 1913 overwhelmed Ford with a suppressed sense of his own mortality, how much stronger must the feeling have been when he contemplated crowds of troops in the line![32] This is where the oddity of Tietjens, Sylvia, or Valentine becomes so effective. Using them as the central intelligences, Ford keeps us constantly aware of the individuality of human lives, while presenting the immense movements of mass slaughter. In this respect Tietjens becomes a figure for the artist: a *homo duplex* (not least for being Marwood-Ford) whose imagination must combine life's minute contacts into 'immense movements', intelligible wholes; and thereby leave the impress of his personality unobtrusively on the work. Ford's tribute to Marwood, his strategy of seeing through someone else's eyes, has too often been discussed as if it were an easy thing to do. It is a self-effacing device, which can be confused with a mere appropriation of the *déjà vu* and the *déjà dit*. Ford has not yet received the credit he deserves for the extraordinary act of imagination needed to imagine a Marwood figure at the war. We shouldn't forget that it is *Ford* who does the imagining—not Marwood, who died before Ford went to the Somme, and thus Ford wasn't even able talk to him about his experiences there. And that act of sympathetic imagination produced one of the most unusual works to come out of the war.

The structure and texture of *Parade's End* are thoroughly informed by these political concerns. The sequence has the coherence which lets us read it as the story of the last Tory; but it also has the multi-vocality which makes it susceptible of (makes it *demand*) other readings. It has also been seen as a *Bildungsroman*; an account of the rehabilitation of the isolated Tory; a critique of the ruling class; a novel of social change; a resurrection myth; or even a Christmas pantomime.[33] If some of these interpretations trim and cramp the work to fit their thesis, they are all intelligent responses to significant aspects. The plurality of interpretations tells us something important about the experience of reading *Parade's End*. We know that literature is, by definition, multiply intelligible. But it would be hard for someone who had not read Ford's tetralogy to imagine how a single work could successfully be all those particular things simultaneously. That is the point: though the series explores Toryism, it could only be called a 'Tory novel' in the sense that Ford's Toryism is more romantic and radical than radicalism; more liberal and less manipulative than liberalism.

Parade's End gives a dual portrait of the Tory, as *The Good Soldier* gave a dual portrait of the sentimental philanderer. Tietjens is a more complex, stronger character than Ashburnham (he has none of Dudley Leicester's vacuity). One technical challenge was to represent this duality without the eccentric perspective of a Dowell. It has to be done with free indirect discourse and dialogue rather than with a narratorial monologue, in order to make us see Tietjens from the inside and the outside. As with most of Ford's books, paraphrase has been dangerously trivializing. Accounts of 'the last Tory', Tietjens's social superiority, his knowledge of men and horses, his stringent code of honour, tend to make *Parade's End* sound like a nostalgic fantasy. It isn't; for the reason that what gives these things meaning is what gets lost in paraphrase: the painstaking building up of the complex thought processes of the mind for which these traits are only an inadequate and crumbling disguise. The sequence is, as Malcolm Bradbury says, both 'a central Modernist novel of the 1920s, in which it is exemplary', and 'the most important and complex British novel to deal with the overwhelming subject of the Great War'.[34]

Ford responds to the complexity of war-torn Europe not by impressing his own designs upon his material, but by rendering the complexity. His fiction does not work to subordinate everything to his voice (as Dowell tried to, but failed); it re-creates the play of conflicting voices, volitions, attitudes and viewpoints. His writing exemplifies what the great Russian critic, Mikhail Bakhtin, called 'dialogic' prose.[35] That is, it not only represents the social world by an interplay between different discourses and idioms, but it also investigates how that interplay gets internalized. A novel—especially a novel which re-creates a whole society or a historical phase—will, like that society, be an arena across which echo the voices of the characters, and the discourses of the groupings they represent. But in a profound sense so is the individual subject, who also finds himself or herself in that arena. It is precisely Ford's ear for the multivocal that makes it rash to impose political schemes on his fictions. Just as one is not born a Tory or a socialist, but becomes one through being immersed in continual debates, so a character as capacious as Tietjens is not a Tory *ex nihilo*: he becomes one in the ways he takes up positions against other beliefs. His Toryism, that is, internalizes the contradictions and polemics of his society, which is what enables such an idiosyncratic character to be none the less representative. In Malcolm Bradbury's words again, 'Tietjens is not just the embodiment of a class, he is also at odds with it, living out the contradictions of an older code'; he 'wants just causes and true wars in the wrong age, the age of National Efficiency, bureaucracy and materialism'.[36] It is because we are still in that age that he can still be such a challenging figure.

Control

One of the novel's traditional concerns has been with the way questions that are more broadly political—questions of power, authority, order, and control—touch every aspect of our lives. *Parade's End* is a masterly imagining of the inwardness of political life. It traces how the notion of 'control' affects the totality of our being. For example, Ford's vision of the front line in 'A Day of Battle' focuses a spectrum of instances. It is, first, his attempt to master a perplexing experience. This is also (as we have seen) an aesthetic impasse: his responses are not coherent enough for him to be able to render them. The third aspect is his wondering how others, equally at the mercy of terror, are able to control themselves; to overmaster their fear, and control their instincts to the point where their obedience to their commanders takes priority over their will to survive. Military control is, of course, yet another aspect. He also wonders at the way so many ambivalent and contrary volitions can be organized into a single-minded military machine. This in turn touches on another aspect of patriotism. One of Tietjens's preoccupations is with the need for a 'Single Command' for the Allies.[37] Instead of the English and French rivalling each other and working at odds with each other, they must co-ordinate their actions if they are to win the war. Finally, the strategic control of the destinies of millions of men suggests not only the political question of how the state controls the destinies of its citizens, but also (as we have touched on) the theological one of how the 'Will of God' might move the world, and the aesthetic one of how the artist controls the matter of his creations.

This moment in the Salient made a lasting impression on Ford; one way it lasts in his *oeuvre* is by being strikingly transformed. *No More Parades* finds a way out of the psychological impasse by dramatizing his ambivalence in a dialogue between Tietjens and Levin about the emotional and moral significance of, precisely, a *view* of the war. Levin's Jewishness invokes Ford's dual anxieties about being not really English (because half-German; because an artist).[38] As a timid staff officer he also embodies Ford's fears for his own reliability, his own self-control, under pressure. Like Captain Gotch in 'The Colonel's Shoes', his 'soundness' is in question. Tietjens tells him later: 'You betray your non-Anglo-Saxon origin by being so vocal. . . . And by your illumi-native exaggerations!' Here Levin's vocal despondency about the deranging and brutalizing effects of the war elicits Tietjens's vindicating vision, in a dialogue that echoes with many of the central terms of Ford's aesthetics and psychology (given here in bold type; the italics are Ford's):

Levin said, with a pathetic appeal to Tietjens' omniscience:
    'But doesn't it mean [. . .] that if you **talk in your sleep** . . . you're . . . in fact a bit **dotty**?'
Tietjens said without passion:
    'Not necessarily. It means that one has been under **mental pressure**, but all mental pressure does not drive you over the edge. Not by any means. . . . Besides, what does it matter?'
Levin said:
    'You mean you **don't care**. . . . Good God!' He remained looking at the view, drooping, in intense dejection. He said: 'This *beastly* war! This beastly war! . . . Look at all that view. . . .'
Tietjens said:
    'It's an encouraging spectacle, really. The **beastliness** of human nature is always pretty normal. We lie and betray and are **wanting in imagination** and deceive ourselves, always, at about the same rate. In peace and in war! But, somewhere in that view there are enormous bodies of men. . . . If you got a still more extended

range of view over this whole front you'd have still more enormous bodies of men. . . . Seven to ten million. . . . All moving towards places towards which they desperately don't want to go. Desperately! Every one of them is desperately afraid. But they go on. An immense blind will forces them in the effort to consummate the one decent action that humanity has to its credit in the whole of recorded history. The one we are engaged in. That effort is the one certain creditable fact in all their lives. . . . But the *other* lives of all those men are dirty, potty and discreditable little affairs. . . . Like yours. . . . Like mine. . . .'

Levin exclaimed:

'Just heavens! *What* a pessimist you are'

Tietjens said. 'Can't you see that that is optimism!'

Tietjens's view is certainly a Tory one. It was also a view Ford expressed, as when he wrote to his mother from the Salient that 'it is jolly to have been in the two greatest strafes of history'.[39]

It is a short leap from his notion of 'An immense blind will' which animates and ennobles human action, to a faith of a Catholic complexion that it is only through the authority of an Immense All-seeing Will that anything decent will be got out of humanity. However, the presence of Levin, also Fordian, shows that Tietjens's view is only one aspect of Ford's comprehension of the war. Although Tietjens is the novel's central intelligence, and despite the Fordian capaciousness and contra-dictoriness of his intelligence, his view is not the same as the novel's views. The novel does not discredit Valentine's pacifism, any more than Ford found Stella Bowen's pacifism discreditable.[40] On the contrary, it is partly through accommodating and respecting her views that Tietjens is able to turn from the discreditable affair of his disintegrating marriage to Sylvia to his creditable affair with Valentine. His Toryism is challenged and transformed by Valentine's views, as was Ford's by Hunt's suffragism and Bowen's pacifism.

Ford uses dialogue to build up a pattern of conflicting views: an exploratory, multivocal form. His dialogical accretion of antagonisms and reconciliations enacts an answer to the totalitarian artist's insistence that it is only by subjecting your material to your act of will and imposing a form that anything decent can be got out of your art. In the greatest art the act of will is simultaneously an act of humility; an ontological passivity in the face of the perceived world—of which W. H. Hudson's attentiveness to natural minutiae was one of Ford's favourite examples. Tietjens's comments on the front line represent this form of awe when confronted with something larger, more bafflingly impressive, than individual volition, rather than a political assertion that an individual volition *should* be imposed upon the mass of humanity.

Form Ford never abandoned his Flaubertian advocacy of 'technique'. Although *Parade's End* is a less recognizably Flaubertian performance than *The Good Soldier*, Ford's mastery of the architectonics of the novel ensures that, even where the material is more diverse and overwhelming than in anything else he wrote, he retains formal command. The danger of a method which even approaches to the stream of a charac-ter's consciousness—as does *Parade's End*'s Flaubertian-Jamesian technique of *style indirect libre*: of a third-person narration inflected by the verbal and psychological traits of the central character—is that of diffuseness: when the character's mind rambles, so might the novel. After the panics and hysterias of their story, the books of *Parade's End* have a formal clarity, a monumental simplicity, which makes them more expressive than they could otherwise be.

A Man Could Stand Up—, for example, is the climax of the sequence. In it the tension is wrought to the highest pitch. Tietjens has to face a German attack, and is momentarily buried by the mud churned up by a high-explosive shell. In *Some Do Not . . .* he had already suffered shell-shock during an earlier tour of duty in France. Whereas Ford used the earlier incident to focus his experience of concussion and amnesia, Tietjens's second 'near miss' is developed into a vivid image of death and rebirth (through which Ford is able to imagine his own death and rebirth). Like the Titan suggested by his name, Tietjens is imprisoned under a mound of earth. The death of his lance-corporal, Duckett (whose face reminds him of Valentine's), who is buried with him, only points up the miraculousness of Tietjens's escape. There but for the grace of God he would be. Like Heracles in the *Alcestis*, he braves the underworld trying to save others. This third volume describes his eventual union with Valentine, which also takes place against the odds. Not only do Sylvia, Edith Ethel Macmaster (*née* Duchemin), the headmistress under whom Valentine is working as a teacher, and Mrs Wannop (Valentine's mother) all try to prevent it, but the hesitancy and tact of the two lovers almost precludes it, when they both fear that the other's reserve might mean their indifference.[41] Their meeting, which releases the tension of their principled restraint from adultery, and which ends their heroic endurance of self-denial, takes place on Armistice Day.

We have seen how in fact Ford and Bowen were not together on Armistice Day. *Parade's End* draws on Ford's experiences, but it is not autobiographic. A complex fiction cannot be said to reflect only one thing: only one attitude, feeling about the author's past, or view of the world. Just as *Parade's End* neither whole-heartedly endorses nor categorically condemns the war, Tietjens's conduct, or 'Englishness', so Tietjens's relation to Ford is complex, shifting. Tietjens is both an 'improvement' of Ford—a self-portrait superimposed upon the features he admired in Marwood—and also the creation of someone quite other. What is crucial is the combination of these moments of identification and objectification. Ford's dual form, practised in his own prose, and discovered in his criticism of other writers, combines fantasy and recognition, in mutually strengthening relation. Transforming his own experience, Ford can create the character of another. In exploring the other, he can recognize himself: can convince himself (for example) that the end of the war is also the end of his war with Violet Hunt. Christopher's reunion with Valentine on Armistice Day offers a clear example of Ford's reimagining of his actual experience. But this is not to say that the fictionalizing force of Ford's mind turns his actual experience into a fantasy-version of his life. *Parade's End* is emphatically *not* primarily a version of his life. The dedicatory letters to the second and third volumes are careful to disclaim Tietjens's opinions. Nor is it primarily a work of fantasy: its dense actuality distracts most readers from worrying about its relation to biography. What is at stake in his reimaginings is not which life he wants us to believe he led, or which life he might have led, but what makes a good story, a good novel. His conviction that fiction is the most responsible form is not merely the provocative paradox it might appear (although it is doubtless intended to provoke!) It implies a subtle argument about how fiction, by suspending the mind's responsibility to literal fact, liberates it, producing a clairvoyant concentration in which the mind can see more than it would otherwise be able to see. Fabulation becomes a means of self-realization.

The parallels between the course of Christopher's and Valentine's thwarted love and the duration of the war are clear without being so obvious as to seem forced by the novelist. Instead, Ford shows their minds being drawn along by the 'immense movements' of public events into a realization of where their personal 'minute contacts' have been leading. (In a characteristically subtle touch, it is Valentine's mother's slightly hysterical protectiveness that makes her inadvertently reveal to Tietjens that Valentine wants him.) One thing that has happened during the tetralogy is that the direction of the analogy between sex and war has been reversed: Sylvia made war on Tietjens, but Valentine's passion is the love to end all wars. However, many novelists might have contrived to unite their lovers on Armistice Day. What saves *A Man Could Stand Up*— from the charge of contrivance is what Ford called 'justification'.[42] The coincidence is shown to come from the characters' desires, not the novelist's convenience. The mass euphoria over the Armistice conduces to celebrations, release, romance. It is, for everyone, an ending which is also a new beginning. What, besides his attention to psychological 'justification', also distinguishes Ford is the formal use he makes of the symbolic coincidence. This volume is structured around one massive time-shift, which is also a shift in viewpoint. The first part is told from Valentine's point of view, as she is taking a class in PE on the morning of the Armistice. The third and final part, told partly from her point of view and partly from Tietjens's, takes place later that day. But the middle part flashes back to Tietjens facing the German attack in the line. The effects of dislocating the chronology in this way are profound. First, as Ambrose Gordon has pointed out, the sudden shift brings out concurrences between the predicaments of heroine and hero. Both are in claustrophobic circumstances (girls' school, trenches); both are temporarily in command (of a class of agitated girls, of a regiment of anxious men); and both are waiting for a crisis—a turning-point in their affairs.[43]

The parallels in their situations imply an affinity. And the merging in the final section of the lovers' viewpoints, kept separate up to that point, is the formal enactment of their union of true minds. But the shifting back in time in the central section has other effects, more characteristically Fordian. Smaller-scale time-shifts abound throughout the series. In *Parade's End* the time shifts generally follow a simple 'ABA' pattern, in which a train of association takes the mind back for a moment; it then returns to the present. (The beginning and end of *Some Do Not . . .* complicate this scheme, miming first of all Tietjens's disorientation due to Sylvia's scandals, then the mental strain of his passionate restraint towards Valentine.) The time-scheme of *A Man Could Stand Up*— is this fundamental time-shift writ large; like a musical rondo, the effect is of a satisfying reprise of the tonic; a return to home.

It is also a structure of suspense. Ford often teased the Fabian H. G. Wells for reducing literary technique to a banal matter of fictional economics: 'Never introduce your hero and heroine together in the first chapter.' 'I don't know why this should be so', writes Ford: 'For the sake of economy, I dare say.'[44] *A Man Could Stand Up*— keeps them apart for the majority of the novel. From the beginning, when Valentine hears someone hissing news of Tietjens over the telephone, we expect the plot to bring them together. The flash back to Tietjens at the Front before the day of the Armistice means that, for the whole of that long central section, suspenseful in itself, we are kept in suspense over the outcome of the romance. The suspense is heightened by an unusual form of duality. The novels lead us to believe contradictory things about Tietjens's fate. Although we (like Valentine) presume Edith Ethel is talking of Tietjens as having survived, he is not named, and the scene is so confused by the carnival of victory that Valentine can hardly hear, is not sure who is talking, and cannot stop her mind leaping from past to future and back during the conversation. So although it becomes clear later that Edith Ethel was indeed warning her that Tietjens had returned, deranged, we share in the confusion. (The device is much more effective than the false pathos with which Ford tries to mislead us into thinking George Heimann has died in *The Marsden Case*.) On the other hand, in *No More Parades*, the tension and pathos of the enervating waiting for the attack was heightened by Tietjens's conviction that his regiment would not survive. This is the other crucial import of his interview with Levin. As a staff officer, Levin has access to intelligence about strategy. He makes the depressive's claim to a superior vision of their military plight: 'You don't know how desperate things are.' Tietjens's stoic determination is again his tactful rebuke:

'Oh, I know pretty well. As soon as this weather really breaks we're probably done.'
   'We can't,' Levin said, 'possibly hold them. Not possibly.'
   'But success or failure,' Tietjens said, 'have nothing to do with the credit of a story [. . .] the thing is to be able to stick to the integrity of your character, whatever earthquake sets the house tumbling over your head. . . .'[45]

Some causes must be fought for even if they are known to be lost. In *A Man Could Stand Up*— it is the high-explosive shell which makes the earth quake, setting the world tumbling over Tietjens's head. The tetralogy shows him sticking to the integrity of his character despite all the forces that make for disintegration (again more effectively than *The Marsden Case*'s attempt to prove its hero a 'good man', since both Tietjens's ordeals and his provocativeness are more real). One question it worries at from many angles is what this integrity means in a world chaotically disturbed: in which 'there was nothing straightforward'. Levin thought that Tietjens's talking in his sleep meant he might be 'a bit dotty'.[46] If the terror and stress of battle puts men at the mercy of overwhelming emotions out of conscious control, the novels ask, does this mean they have become mad? Ford's own feeling that he had taken five years to recover from war's derangement lies behind this passage, of course. But more importantly, Ford is using his own experiences and feelings to explore a more momentous historical question: 'all proper men', he wrote in 1919, 'for the last five years have been shaken, earthquaked, and disturbed, to the lowest depths of their beings.' As we shall see, one of the war's profound changes was that it altered the ways people thought about the mind and morality. For the first time, 'shell shock' was recognized as a psychological state distinguishable from cowardice. Notions of gender are also at stake. In her study of 'Women, Madness and English Culture', Elaine Showalter quotes Tietjens's remark—'Why isn't one a beastly girl and privileged to shriek?'—to illustrate an argument that 'shell shock' was a term, acceptable to the world of male authority, for what was in fact 'male hysteria'. The war showed unignorably that hysteria and neurosis were not exclusively female complaints, but could be experienced by 'proper men'.[47] *Parade's End* is a highly individual work. Its unmistakable style is the consummation of Ford's attention to mental processes—the composite pictures the mind makes superimposing reminiscence upon perception. Its hero and heroine are both superlative beings: he, the last Tory and a brilliant mathematician; she, the best Latinist. But the singularities of subject and handling should not obscure the ways in which the novel is peculiarly sensitive to the important social issues and changes. Too much has been made of the idiosyncrasies, without seeing how they reveal the pervasive. The criticism that although the novels create a convincing picture of a world, it is the world of Ford's imagination rather than one which ever existed, misses this essential dynamic of all Ford's prose. When Tietjens criticizes Levin's 'illuminative exaggerations' as un-English, Ford indicates that his own prose works in the same way. Certainly its tones and values may be exaggerated, but such exaggeration as there is is always subordinated to the main purpose, which is to illuminate. *Parade's End* presents a massively concentrated picture of hysteria and confusion; a military historian might object that in fact most units performed their orders in rational and controlled ways. But as with so many of the novelists and memoirists of the war, Ford renders his times in different modes from the categories and generalities of historical narrative, telling instead the story of how soldiers often didn't feel rational and under control. Whereas in *The Good Soldier* it was the question of sexuality that was mainly scrutinized, here the emphasis falls predominantly upon the questions of perception, sanity, order, and control.

The opening of the first novel, *Some Do Not . . .* , is too familiar to need quoting in full. Tietjens and his friend and colleague Vincent Macmaster are on the train to Rye, in Kent. It is probably 1912, an idyll of pre-war orderliness. The railway carriage is 'perfectly appointed'; the 'regulated curves' of the upholstery and the regulated curves of the railway line bespeak a world of security and certainty. Tietjens thinks that the train ran as smoothly 'as British gilt-edged securities'; if it hadn't, he would have complained. He and Macmaster, who both work for the 'Imperial Department of Statistics', are members of 'the English public official class': they 'administered the world'. The scene is significant in the lives of the two characters: Tietjens is under great mental strain as he contemplates the disintegration of his marriage to Sylvia. At Rye he will meet Valentine Wannop, and his passion for her will be the great complicating fact of his life. Macmaster, too, will begin a romance with Edith Ethel Duchemin, the wife of an insane, scatological cleric. But Ford gives the scene a broader frame. For these two men are not only participating in an ordered world of design, communication, service, and authority. They are the source of that authority; they are the law unto the forces of law and order: 'If they saw policemen misbehave, railway porters lack civility [. . .] they saw to it' (p. 9). Tietjens may be brilliant and eccentric, but he is also representative of the fundamental principles according to which his society operates.

By the opening of the third volume, the centrality to *Parade's End* of ideas of order and control could not be more evident:

Slowly, amidst intolerable noises from, on the one hand the street and, on the other, from the large and voluminously echoing playground, the depths of the telephone began, for Valentine, to assume an aspect that, years ago, it had used to have—of being a part of the supernatural paraphernalia of inscrutable Destiny.

The telephone, for some ingeniously torturing reason was in a corner of the great schoolroom without any protection and, called imperatively, at a moment of considerable suspense, out of the asphalte playground where, under her command ranks of girls had stood electrically only just within the margin of control, Valentine with the receiver at her ear was plunged immediately into incomprehensible news uttered by a voice that she seemed half to remember. Right in the middle of a sentence it hit her:

'. . . that he ought presumably to be under control, which you mightn't like!'; after that the noise burst out again and rendered the voice inaudible.

It occurred to her that probably at that minute the whole population of the world needed to be under control; she knew she herself did. But she had no male relative that the verdict could apply to in especial [. . .]

She said into the mouthpiece:

'Valentine Wannop speaking. . . . Physical Instructress at this school, you know!'

She had to present an appearance of sanity . . . a sane voice at the very least!

As so often with Ford's prose, the drama of sentence-style tells us more about his major concerns than can critical paraphrase. This highly condensed notation of rapid thinking and responding is difficult to paraphrase without heavy-handedness. One strikingly Fordian feature is the fleeting uncertainty (about who is talking, whom they are talking about, and what they are saying). Because these queries are soon resolved, spelling them out seems unnecessarily explicit. What needs emphasizing is Ford's genius for reproducing the slight mental confusions and gradual clarifications which our vanity makes us ignore in our own lives. Like Tietjens, and like most Ford characters, Valentine under stress is always one perplexing jump behind her racing perceptions. In Ford's world—the world of his life as well as of his novels—one is not secure in the knowledge of one's selfhood, but, on the contrary, always being surprised by what that self does, or what it is becoming. In his later novels, as we shall see, this perception of the self as strange and unexpected—as, precisely, 'Other'—becomes crucial. But whereas in those novels the narrative often approaches interior monologue, and sometimes even stream of consciousness, here the elaborately unfolding sentences each represent a struggle to order mental experience amidst social chaos.

'Slowly, amidst': it is a syntax of controlled interruption, which fights for its own poise and pace, deliberately notating precise relationships. It is the syntax of the mind presenting the appearance of sanity—of painstaking rationality—in the face of the intolerable. 'Right in the middle of a sentence it hit her.' So the point of each sentence hits us, only after we have been insinuated some way into it: in the masterly opening sentence it only fully materializes in the last word. 'Slowly, amidst intolerable noises from, on the one hand [even the interrupting prepositional phrase gets interrupted here] the street and, on the other [the well-balanced antithesis tries to sustain sanity amidst the intolerable noise], from the large and voluminously echoing playground, the depths of the telephone began [at last, a main verb: but what are the depths of the telephone beginning to do?], for Valentine, to assume an aspect that [so we will not know *what* aspect they assumed for at least another clause], years ago, it had used to have—of being a part of the supernatural paraphernalia of inscrutable [even this far into the sentence Valentine's feeling is still undefined: only with the next and final word do we grasp that the disembodied voice seems to her like a 'daemon' or oracle: the voice, which has *control* over her fate, of:] Destiny.'

There is a voluminous echo of James in the labyrinthine syntax; and 'inscrutable Destiny' is part of the Conradian 'paraphernalia'. But the effects of the passage do not depend on these echoes, and are something quite other than the effects of those writers. As so often, Ford is fascinated by the transparencies and reflectivities of his medium. He works his own effects *through* those of others. He contemplates authority and communication by re-calling his literary influences. Distracting the reader with the sounds of literary allusion helps him create for the reader Valentine's distraction. The fine psychological effect of meaning gradually emerging from the welter of noise and noticing is a unique Fordian gift.

Confusion   Like E. M. Forster, Ford is a great novelist of 'muddle'. But whereas in Forster 'muddle' is the world's recalcitrance to man's good intentions (the rocks which force Fielding and Aziz to part company at the end of *A Passage to India* are only the most graphic instance of this intransigent materiality), Fordian muddle is more anarchic. Forsterian muddle jeopardizes friendships; it rarely endangers life and sanity, as Fordian muddle does. Tietjens, as the other characters observe, has 'a positive genius for getting into the most disgusting messes'. Through him Ford wonders at his own propensity to bring houses tumbling around his ears. And, in reply to those critics who have convicted Ford of exculpating himself in his fiction, one can say that, through the other characters (Sylvia, Valentine, General Campion), he sees how he bears much of the responsibility for the messes.[48] They aren't foisted upon him; he gets into them. Tietjens's passivity is what most actively irritates others. One perceptive reviewer saw how the 'bitter absurdity' of opening *A Man Could Stand Up*— with a telephone call 'exactly at the instant of the wild and furious armistice celebration' sets the tone for the whole work: 'whatever there may be of human tragedy develops out of those impertinences of life and character which obscure nobler and subtler values [. . .].' Ford keeps the tetralogy shivering on the brink between tragedy and absurdity, order and confusion. As Melvin Seiden argues, he 'allows the comic and the tragic to exist side by side in a state of constant disharmony and friction'.[49]

The tetralogy negotiates a progress through the world's moral confusion, offering a morally dual portrait of Tietjens:

we are not forced to choose between two incompatible judgements of Tietjens's character: he is not either a long-suffering and saintly man or a fool. For clearly he is both. It is one of Ford's greatest achievements to have made us feel, as Sylvia does, that Tietjens's paradoxical virtue *is* intolerable, and yet to have done this without in the least mitigating her viciousness or suggesting that Tietjens deserves the calumny he receives from her or the world.[50]

Ford sustains this moral duality—as in *The Good Soldier* it is also perforce a tonal duality—against all the odds. As Seiden shows, it owes much to the nineteenth century's master of moral confusion, Dostoevsky. The central attitude towards Tietjens is a reimagining of 'Dostoievsky's religious parable of the "idiot"-saint,

Prince Myshkin, among the vice- and guilt-ridden'. When Ford wrote about Constance Garnett's translation of *The Idiot* before the war, he said he regarded Dostoevsky's work 'with envy, with fear, with admiration'. He expressed his objection largely in terms of form: 'His characters are extraordinarily vivid; but they are too vivid for the Realist School. They are too much always in one note; they develop little; they are static. His strong scenes are strong to the point of frenzy, but they are too full-dress: everybody has to be in them at once. And they are entirely unprepared [. . .].' But here, and also in his objection to the subject—'I am tired of variations on the Christ legend'—one senses that the technical objection doubles an emotional aversion. The figure of the unjustly persecuted Christ-like Prince, his two passions, his visionary epileptic seizures, his agonies of social and sexual embarrassment, may just have been too close to the brain. So soon after his breakdowns and humiliations, Ford must have found the tendency to identify himself with Myshkin irresistible, and frightening. After the war, and after he had written *Parade's End*, he finally discussed the Russian in a way that acknowledged his debt. It is an extraordinary revelation, coming after 850 pages of *The March of Literature* in which Dostoevsky has not been mentioned once. Then, on the last page of his last book, almost as an afterthought (rather as Dowell tells us of Ashburnham's death), Ford writes what is virtually his own literary epitaph:

Let us finally say a word about Dostoievsky, who is the man who, man of letters though he was, must be considered to be the greatest single influence on the world of today [. . .] It would be absurd to claim him as a realist because his literary equipment is that of the romantics; but it would be absurd not to call him a realist, because the images he calls up are more real than life, and as visions have outlasted the lives of generations of men. The multitude of his characters is that of the crowds you will see pulsing into and out of vast industrial works; as a psychologist he surpasses anyone who has ever delved into the human mind.

We might prophesy, then, that the 'great' work of art of the future will come from the fusion of the genius of Dostoievsky with the art of the impressionists [. . .] We may imagine it, that 'great' work, psychologized as only Dostoievsky could psychologize; with a crowd form that only the genius and patience of a Flaubert could supply; with the mental subtlety of a James; the kindliness of a Turgenev; a touch of the panache of a Conrad and the minute observation of the author of the *Shepherd's Life* [W. H. Hudson]. . . .[51]

This is doubly modest. First, for ending his *summa*, which is also the summation of his career as a writer, critic, and reader, with a recollection of his father's analysis of the *music* of the future. Secondly, for writing as if this great 'fusion' of the qualities and writers Ford most admired hadn't already occurred in *Parade's End*, of which his words here give the best analysis. His involvement in the 'immense movements' of the war enabled him to make something new of that Dostoevskian influence he had earlier rejected.

Parade's End describes a period of complex muddle and confusion. In V. S. Pritchett's elegant paradox, 'Confusion was the mainspring of his art as a novelist. He confused to make clear.' Part of the great achievement of *Parade's End* is to let order from confusion spring. Its palimpsest of plots and motives is always on the verge of incoherence; it perpetually appears about to repeat, to contradict itself, or to digress.

Yet, as in the magisterial command of syntax, there is always an architectonic intelligence at work, holding together the glinting and jarring details, fusing clarities of detail into clarity of design. One of the things Ford's method makes clear *is* confusion: what Tietjens thinks of, for example, as 'The extraordinary complications of even the simplest lives!'.[52] But this is not to say that he succumbs to the mimetic fallacy of rendering confusion by writing confusedly. What he strives for is the paradoxical, dual effect of presenting simultaneously the maximum chaos and the maximum control. It is a narrative strategy which ministers to, and negotiates between, opposing impulses: the feeling that one is at the mercy of unforeseeable yet inevitable consequences, which will derange even the most prudent orderings; and conversely, the feeling that what seems most chaotic might none the less be intelligible, perhaps even subject to human design and control. The style is comparably dual. As with the paradoxical realism of Flaubert or Conrad, stylistic beauty makes you see moral horror (from which you would normally wince).

Values   Tietjens seeing the chaos of the battle of the Somme as one action (and Ford seeing himself seeing it through Tietjens's seeing) is a central Fordian moment. It not only reveals the dialectic of confusion and clarity central to all his sustained prose, and reveals it as central to his understanding of the war. It also offers another key instance of how Ford's visions of history and aesthetics are locked together. In the influential preface to his 1913 *Collected Poems*, he had written that: 'Modern life is so extraordinary, so hazy, so tenuous with, still, such definite and concrete spots in it that I am for ever on the look out for some poet who shall render it with all its values' (p. 15). The 'Preface' has a dated air now, largely because the phrase 'modern life' had been too urgent for the Victorians not to seem old-fashioned when reused by the Edwardians; but also because the conjunction of haze and glare is a special effect of the Pre-Raphaelite and 'Nineties' artists. By *The Fifth Queen*, *The Good Soldier*, and *Parade's End* Ford had learned that such 'extraordinary' double-effects were better produced by reproducing complexity and confusion, than by being emphatic about haziness and tenuity. However, the 'Preface' brings out an essential continuity throughout Ford's work: his intense attention to the double-effects of particular and general. The word 'values', for example, shimmers here, as in *It Was the Nightingale*, between the senses of painterly tones and ethical principles; between particular technique and general effect; between aesthetics and the history of culture.

'Values' also figure importantly throughout *Parade's End*, also in both senses of the rendering of life, and the morality of what's rendered. Tietjens's job at the beginning of the tetralogy with the Department of Statistics represents one possible mode of trying to assign values to human activities: numerical values. Ford was always profoundly sceptical of the value of treating people as numbers; and it is a scepticism that is merely hinted at by Tietjens's scorn for the deceitful uses to which his calculations are put. None the less, Ford found the idea of 'statistics' a powerful metaphor, and one about which he remained ambivalent. It can stand for the merciless reduction of the human and particular to the rudimentary, unimaginative, and general. But, as with the visions of battle, it can also register the imagination of impressive generality. The character of Tietjens embodies much of this ambivalence. From one perspective he appears as the infuriatingly unresponsive companion who, for all his mathematical brilliance, is unable to solve his prime 'problem'—though he can pose it with a mathematician's elegance: 'my problem will remain the same whether I'm here or not. For it's insoluble. It's the whole problem of the relations of the sexes.'[53] At the same time his exactness of observation, his responsiveness to impressions, gives him an affinity with the artist. One can glimpse the doubleness when, as here, the language puns between the mathematical and the psychologically descriptive ('problem', 'relations').

The tetralogy traces how 'values', in their broadest sense of what a society deems important and desirable, were affected by the war. Arthur Marwick has written how, 'When society settled down again in the early Twenties, important alterations in the social structure became apparent'.[54] *Parade's End* is a crucial document in this process of perception and representation. The challenges to sexual, religious, and social ortho-doxies which had been articulated by novels like *A Call* and *The Good Soldier* had developed further while the national imagination had, for the most part, been captured by the war.

Literature and criticism for Ford always involved a taking stock; a confrontation of 'where we stand'. For the generations returning from the war, which had been for them in effect a form of time-shift—a derangement of the ordering of normal life—it was particularly necessary to undertake this revaluing. For the 'lost generation', the question of 'where we stand' was also one of 'how do we stand up?': both how did they stand up to the pressures of battle, and how do they live with the psychological scarring. *No Enemy* takes the question a characteristic stage further, to ask how literature stood up to the war, which was 'a good opportunity to see what books really would [. . .] stand up against the facts of a life that was engrossing and perilous' (p. 176). The commanding metaphor of *A Man Could Stand Up—*, which gives it its title, conjoins this sense of heroic endurance with the senses of sexual potency and panor-amic envisioning. After the fighting, a man will be able to stand up and look over the landscape in which he has had to lead a buried life.

Heroism is only one of the values which is tested in *Parade's End*, though one of the central ones. In a war of attrition, virtually the only available form of heroism left *is* endurance: an ironic stoical passivity in the face of relentless persecution and mental stress. Ford's war prose shares the received idea of the poetry of Wilfred Owen, Siegfried Sassoon, Isaac Rosenberg, and Ivor Gurney, that the war demolished the conventional stances of military heroics, and denounced 'the old lie' about the exhil-aration and glory of patriotic self-sacrifice. What Ford's writing also gives (which Owen's and Sassoon's generally doesn't) is a sense of how it was possible for some people to volunteer not because they were deceived, or were pressured by their peers, but because they felt the war was an ordeal that had to be endured. In *Antwerp* Ford had asked of the Belgian dead: 'And what in the world did they bear it for?' Having himself borne life in the trenches, he offered an answer in *Parade's End* which gives an essential complement to the Owen–Sassoon–Graves view of the war as futile and mindless waste. This is another component of the force of Tietjens's unillusioned exchange with Levin.

Parade's End has an unusual ability to convey intense feelings of patriotism and awe at the scale of the fighting (widespread feelings which usually only get into the inferior poetry) without glorifying war. Ford shares with the best writers of the First World War a sense of the way courage and honour were not obliterated but transformed. For Tietjens *does* act *in extremis*, when facing the German attack in *A Man Could Stand Up*—. Although he is left in command, his authority does not issue in a display of bloodthirsty bravado, but in a characteristically Tory expression of consideration for his men. He tries to save not only the lance-corporal buried alongside him after an explosion, but also Lieutenant Aranjuez, risking his own life to carry the hysterical subordinate to safety.

Critics have made much of the religious symbolism of the series—usually too much, rather than what the novels will support.[55] If the name *Christ*opher Tie*tjens* suggests 'Christians', before we press the identification too far we should remember that it also occurs to Sylvia, who spreads the malicious rumour that Christopher 'wants to play the part of Jesus Christ'.[56] Typically, we can neither wholeheartedly affirm the parallel, nor can we wholeheartedly deny it. (One paradox of their religion is that good Christians are exhorted to model themselves on their Lord, and condemned if they think they have succeeded.) If Tietjens's heroism takes the form of salvation, his attempts to save are themselves ambiguous. Lance-Corporal Duckett is already dead. Aranjuez gets shot in the eye while Tietjens is carrying him, which causes Tietjens to feel that far from saving him he has actually been responsible for injuring him. (The case of O Nine Morgan, killed by a shell after Tietjens had refused him leave, offers another case in point. Tietjens thought Morgan would have been killed at home by the boxer with whom his wife was committing adultery. Another attempted salvation may actually have caused the death it sought to avoid.) It would be more accurate to say that Ford is testing his view that 'Christianity as a faith died a few days after the 4th August, 1914 . . .' Readings of the tetralogy that see it as Ford's self-exculpation for his affair with Stella Bowen, a self-glorification which attempts to rewrite his war experiences as heroic fantasy, as 'an ecstasy of self-pity', underestimate the ethical intricacy and subtlety of the work.[57] It is, amongst other things, a massive exploration of the nature of virtue. The theological virtues of faith, hope, and charity all make their appearance, in their sacred and profane senses. The novels explore and discuss chastity, monogamy, altruism, honour, honesty, forgiveness, kindness. Virtue and goodness themselves are explicitly invoked.[58] But *Parade's End* does not flinch from the confrontation with Tietjens's weaknesses and provocations.

While he was still in the army, Ford sensed war's transformation of values:

But, mostly, the tired brain refuses to generalise: so that, just as the cataclysm has swept over Europe, blotting out alike the Europe of Charlemagne & the Europe of Napoleon I, so a cataclysm of the author's intelligence has swept over this book. The sense of values has changed completely. . . . One has grown sentimental incredibly, coarse in a great measure, hungry, thirsty, loud voiced. The pleasures of the drawing room are unknown & not at all valued. . . . A comfortable billet or a dry tent—that's what one is on the lookout for—& a good long sleep [. . .].

He had been contemplating the ramifications of these changes for a decade before he had finished *Parade's End*, in which, as Granville Hicks wrote: 'With a brilliance that was at times almost too dazzling, Ford portrayed a revolution in manners, but what he saw underneath was a fundamental change in human values.' As Ford was later to put it, recalling the effect Dreiser's *The Titan* had had on him:

But, back in the second decade of this century while the Big Words were still alive, the *Titan* very naturally made one's gorge rise. The Big Words . . . Loyalty, Heroism, Chivalry, Conscience, Self-Sacrifice, Probity, Patriotism, Soldierly Piety, Democracy even, and even Charity which some translate as Love . . . those big words and the golden *naïvetés* that they stood for were probably in that year going stronger than they ever before had gone . . .

Whereas with the war he felt: 'Bluff has got its death blow.' When the Big Words were used as alibis for imperialism they were bluff. Though *Parade's End* charts bluff's death blow, it doesn't kill off the *values* those Big Words name. As *The Good Soldier* lacks a hero and heroine in any conventional sense, yet one can see Ashburnham's suicide as a heroic self-sacrifice, performed out of chivalry, probity, and conscience; so *Parade's End* charts how the war has redefined such values. Literary form is intricated with ethical questions here too. *Parade's End* tests the possibility of heroic action in a post-Bluff world through its testing of the feasibility of heroic actions and heroic characters in a modern novel. The sequence has a tentative, exploratory relation to Romance, neither eschewing the happy ending of uniting Tietjens with Valentine, nor relying uncritically upon it. While discussing the tetralogy in *It Was the Nightingale*, Ford writes: 'I carefully avoid the word "hero"' (p. 197). In the tetralogy, however, although he carefully avoids making his characters into anything as simple as a romance 'hero' and 'heroine', he carefully involves the terms and ideas. Valentine insists, twice: 'I'm not a heroine'; Tietjens observes 'the incidental degeneration of the heroic impulse'; and Ford characteristically uses Valentine's naïve academicism— 'You've got to define the term brave'—to hint how his art attempts just that (re)definition.[59]

Order   This detailed attentiveness to the ethical orderings of society should be seen as part of the tetralogy's panoramic scanning of social assumptions and processes: in short, of ideology. How, the novels ask, is ordered life ordered? How has it reordered itself after war's disorder? If one suggests that here too the imagination at work is an essentially novelistic one, investigating how the multitudinousness of a complex society can be perceived as a single work(ing), this is not to imply any narrowing aestheticism of attitude. *Parade's End* investigates most of the ways in which a society orders life. Its intense class consciousness—like Ford's own—is not snobbery: it is too much a dual response of fascination with the élite and scepticism about its qualities. As with Dudley Leicester in *A Call*, or Ashburnham, the exemplary 'good people' in the novel have a disconcerting habit of appearing vacuous nonentities. At the same time, Ford often likes to suggest that it is the very 'stupidity' of men like General Campion or the banker Lord Port Scatho that somehow guarantees their social 'soundness'. In a society that so prizes self-suppression, intractably evident selfhood can appear dangerous, as it does in the case of Tietjens.

The novels trace the institutions of authority and legitimacy: government, the civil service, the law, the police, and the army. They also know of the subtler controls and coercions of ideology: in particular, the way knowledge is never a neutral commodity, but a national or imperial one. There is much play in the tetralogy with the way Tietjens, a subordinate in the Imperial Department of Statistics, has internalized the *Encyclopaedia Britannica*. Statistics represent one way a government can interpret and influence the lives of its citizens. Finance is a comparable institution. Although governments or banks do not directly control an individual's life, they can influence it in a whole range of ways: by offering or denying credit, changing interest rates, adjusting taxes and wages. Tietjens's interview with Port Scatho in *Some Do Not . . .* unearths more details of Sylvia's resourceful betrayals, adding another turn to the screw of Tietjens's persecution. Port Scatho's nephew, Brownlie, has become infatuated with Sylvia, and has abused his position in the bank to disgrace Tietjens, by causing one of his cheques to his club to bounce. The interview is narrated mainly from Tietjens's point of view, which foregrounds his mental strain. While brilliantly capturing the hallucinatory perceptions of a man at breaking point, Ford's hand is sure enough also to show the complex ramifications of Tietjens's anxieties. For he is not just suffering from marital problems, but also being tormented by Sylvia's publicizing of them. The interview scene also captures the way society—in the form of clubs, friends, social circles of 'good people', the aristocracy, families—impinges on the individual psychology. It is the fact of the bank intervening in his emotional life that exasperates and enervates the intensely private Tietjens—as Ford was himself so profoundly affected by the public scandal of his affair with Hunt. *The Good Soldier* too had voiced the jeopardy of the social and sexual politics of knowledge: in one aspect it reads as Dowell's protracted agonizing over who knows what about who 'knows' whom. Through the character of the child-lover Nancy, who does not know what she is saying (says Dowell) when she offers herself to Ashburnham, or the innocent Maisie Maidan who dies *knowing* the sexual motivation of the Ashburnhams' financial kindness to her, and finally, through the comically germane fragments of guidebook history with which Leonora and Florence unobtrusively taunt each other, the theme of knowledge and education makes itself felt in the earlier novel. In *Parade's End* it is more emphatic, as the opening of *A Man Could Stand Up*— makes clear. Ford stresses the *authority* of the educator. The analogy between Valentine's PE class and (Tietjens's or Ford's) army drilling points up how society educates to command and control, legitimizing its power structures in the very act of imparting knowledge.

The terminology here is not intended to suggest that Ford is offering a Marxist critique of society. As a novelist he is concerned to represent society, not to change it. Anyway, his novels are mostly about how it has already changed. *Parade's End* is an elegy rather than a manifesto. However, Ford's 'critical attitude' towards his subjects demonstrates how his Toryism is anything but a supine acquiescence in, and glorification of, received ideas. As ever, his attitude is a dual one: his critical insight is less a rejection of the existing ordering than a historian's fascination with *how* its order works. He does not demystify class and power; but where he might be accused of *re*mystifying them, he is, rather, looking as a novelist at how characters are affected by the mystique of 'the gentleman', or 'good people'. His Toryism is radical in that he sees to the roots of social order. His more radical pronouncements are Tory when he likes what he sees—such as when he writes: 'the British regular army is one of the two most perfect institutions.'[60] Similarly with education, the regulation of sexuality, mental and physical control of oneself, Ford accepts order as a necessity. The personality, like a novel, needs order and convention—including the regulated disorder of game—if only to elude and transform them. Tietjens shares Ford's dual attitude to orthodoxy: Sylvia calls him 'so formal he can't do without all the conventions there are and so truthful he can't use half of them'. Ford's attitude to literary form is comparably dual: he's so formal he can't do without the conventions of romance, the historical novel, impressionism; but too aware of their falsities to use them single-mindedly.[61] This attitude to literary form is perhaps best thought of in the way he thought of religion—presumably the other of the 'two most perfect institutions'. He wanted his daughters brought up as Catholics so that they would have something definite to break from. Just as in *The Good Soldier* he presents the force of a passion which overruns most restraint, so in *Parade's End* he can express the powerful euphoria of a hypnotic communal outburst such as the Armistice. Yet, with Valentine, who feels that not much more remains to restrain her from becoming Christopher's mistress, he can also see that 'probably at that moment the whole population of the world needed to be under control'. And yet—again the attitude is intricately dual—the novel ends with precisely her decision to go and live with him, and defy the conventions of respectability. Despite the offbeat ending (in mid-sentence; suggestively inconclusive) of *A Man Could Stand Up*—, and the information given retrospectively in *Last Post* that Sylvia's arrival (alleging she has cancer) once again deferred the lovers' consummation, there is no sense that the union is to be condemned rather than blessed. Ford is careful *not* to preach a moral message here. He wants to show how characters act and decide; how their choices are negotiated between desires for abandonment and ecstasy on the one hand, and a need for self-control and sanity on the other. Valentine's musing on the implications of the Armistice bring out the centrality to the novels of these ideas of authority, its strength and weakness:

And Valentine wondered why, for a mutinous moment, she had wanted to feel triumph . . . had wanted *someone* to feel triumph. [In part the mutiny here is against her own pacifism.] Well, he . . . they . . . had wanted it so much. Couldn't they have it just for a moment—for the space of one Benkollerdy![62] Even if it were wrong? or vulgar? Something human, someone had once said, is dearer than a wilderness of decalogues!

But at the Mistress's Conference that morning, Valentine had realized that what was really frightening them was the other note. A quite definite fear. If, at this parting of the ways, at this crack across the table of History, the School—the World, the future mothers of Europe—got out of hand, would they ever come back? The Authorities—Authority all over the world—was afraid of that; more afraid of that than of any other thing. Wasn't it a possibility that there was to be no more Respect? None for constituted Authority and consecrated Experience? (pp. 12–13)

That fear of things getting out of hand is fundamental to Ford's most powerful work. As I have suggested, it springs from a fear of the self which he knew well, whether it is the fear that the sexual threatens to get out of 'proportion', or the fear of losing control of the mind, ceasing to be yourself, going mad. Ford wasn't alone to feel these things about the Armistice. Arnold Bennett noted that the rain the following day was 'An excellent thing to damp hysteria and Bolshevism'. Later in the week, recording the lighting of a great bonfire at Piccadilly Circus, fed by the advertising boards on theatres and buses, he said: 'Girls are still very prominent in the "doings". Swinnerton told me that the staidest girl they had suddenly put on a soldier's hat and overcoat and went promenading.' He was told that the scene at the staunchly Tory Carlton Club on the night of the Armistice was 'remarkable': 'Any quantity of broken glasses, tables overturned, and people standing on tables, and fashionable females with their hair down.' If the mandarins were behaving thus, what was to stop the working classes and the 'girls' from turning the tables too?[63] It is indicative of Ford's imaginative breadth that he sees how, although these fears are most pronounced under the tensions of war, they also operate (perhaps even particularly operate) when that tension is released. It is also deeply characteristic, as we have seen, that the novelist, who has a professional interest in what happens when things get out of hand, and in the business of imagining being someone other than yourself, frames Valentine's fears in terms which echo the terms of the novelist's art. For a novelist who aspires to be, like Flaubert, the historian of his own times, the prospect of a 'crack across the table of History' is at once his subject, and his fear that he may be unredeemably alienated from his subject—the immediate past—or from his readers in the immediate future. If the 'table of History' is imagined here as like the stone tables on which the finger of God wrote the Ten Commandments (the decalogue), then it is the type of the authoritative text. If the authority of History, Culture, of all textuality, is thus fractured, how can the novelist who sees himself as a stage in that cultural history sustain his faith in his activity? (Virginia Woolf felt that 'the history of the war is not and never will be written from our point of view'; and that 'No one who has taken stock of his own impressions since 4 August 1914, can possibly believe that history as it is written closely resembles history as it is lived'.[64]) How, Ford can be heard asking *sotto voce* in this dialogue of the novelist's mind with itself, can the Author so constitute his material, order his fictional life, so as to consecrate his Experience as Art? If there will be no more parades, no more respect for consecrated experience, will there be no more art? Does not art also result from wars between authority and desire? Also characteristic is the way that, just as the novel countenances such scepticism about literature, it simultaneously affirms the value of literature to save us from the abysses of Chaos. The someone who once said what Valentine creatively misremembers as 'Something human [. . .] is dearer than a wilderness of decalogues' was another novelist, Conrad, himself quoting another pair of collaborators, the brothers Grimm, in the epigraph of *Youth*: '. . . but the Dwarf answered: "No, something human is dearer to me than the wealth of the world".' As Ford, worrying about the fate of literature, thinks of Conrad, so Valentine, at the moment she is worrying that she will lose self-control, imagines with a novelist's sympathy the fears of her colleagues. For Ford her act of human sympathy *in extremis*, and the art which is predicated on sympathetic imagination, are what constitute the meaning of civilization, and guarantee the survival of humanity.

The war inevitably re-formed and reformulated the novelist's position. Mary McCarthy has written of 'the faith in History, which was shattered by an historical event—the impact of the First World War'. The war is both the break that divided modern people from their usable past, and the experience which most constituted their modernity. Ford's immediate reaction to the war was like Conrad's comment that 'our world of 15 years ago is gone to pieces': a sense that his world had been swept away by Armageddon, leaving him a ghost from the other side of the crack in the table of history. There is a strong continuity with his trilogy on England, and his propaganda books on European culture. The war had accelerated the industrialization which threatened agrarian traditions; Prussia had submerged the Germany he loved, and devastated much of the Belgium and France he knew best. Materially he was stripped of his pre-war luxury—like Gabriel Morton and Tietjens bereft of all but their army belongings. By *Parade's End* he had found a new 'method of approach' by which he could consider questions like 'the Feudal system' or 'the relations of the Sexes' 'with composure'.[65] And by then the changes didn't only seem like losses. The stripping away of the old layers of self didn't leave him with nothing, like Peer Gynt's onion. It was a sloughing off of dead past phases of the self; a paring down to essentials, which enabled him to see more clearly what he really was. It clarified his sense of himself as *homo duplex*, remaking him as his own double twice over: first when in France but preoccupied with England; then, after the fighting, always returning in his memory to his time in the army (he was temperamentally suited to being one of the 'Lost Generation'). The war also redefined what he wanted: a new life (for himself, with Bowen, through Julie); renewed contact with nature in his rural sanctuary; and a new phase of the old quest for the new literary forms that could make sense of the cataclysm. His use of the Armistice is essential to the form of *Parade's End*. It is the counterpart not only to the 4th of August date in *The Good Soldier*, but to Tietjens's vision of the line: an awesome spectacle of millions of people, moving, with a unison of feeling underlying the carnivalesque chaos. ('I think the GOOD SOLDIER is my best book technically unless you read the Tietjens books as one novel in which case the whole design appears', said Ford—interestingly leaving open the *possibility* of a less ordered, coercive reading.) Like the war, it is another gigantic human outburst seen from both outside and inside. Yet whereas the vision of the line represented an order based on tragic compulsion, people moving to their destiny against their will, the Armistice represents a comic celebration, its disorders coming from people expressing their desires. If it doesn't see Christopher and Valentine consummating their love, it makes that consummation possible, setting against Ford's elegy for the vanished forms that regulated conduct his celebration of the desires that their disappearance had liberated.[66]

Psychology

Fear and Death

Parade's End is one of the great fictional studies of fear.[67] It develops the Conradian hint in *The Marsden Case* that 'Every human soul has a secret dread of weakness', presenting different forms such dread can take. Ford's writing from 1916 onwards—especially his letters to Conrad from the war, 'True Love & a G.C.M.', 'Mr Croyd', *No Enemy* (on being a 'creature of dreads'), and *Parade's End*—bears the impress of that blind terror he later characterized as his 'Corbie-phobia': above all, terror of losing control of his mind. It weighed on his mind to the end of his life. (In his deathbed delirium he imagined himself back in the war.) And not just his writing. Even in conversation he can be heard experimenting with constatations of fear. When Edward Shanks walked across the Sussex fields with him (probably to Red Ford, in 1919: they had gone to the village to buy beer), he picked a button mushroom and was about to eat it when Ford suddenly knocked it out of his hand, saying it might give him anthrax. 'There is only one thing I am more afraid of than anthrax', he explained, 'and that is being savaged by a stallion.' Shanks was 'completely dumbfounded'. But he gives a context that perhaps explains what Ford was doing. They had been discussing Shanks's poems, which were evidently too artificially literary for Ford's taste. When the lights of the cottage appeared, Ford said: 'If you could write a poem about something like this [. . .] using just the same sort of words we have been using . . . but I don't suppose you ever will.' Did he mean to use the mushroom as a literary example? If the outburst over it sounds too theatrical to be a true expression of Ford's own fears, it does give an example of how an ordinary situation can become obliquely expressive of someone's deepest anxieties. Which is how *Parade's End* often works.[68]

What is so striking about the kinds of fear registered in Ford's post-war fiction, though, is the effect they don't have on him or his art. Peter Ackroyd's acute comment on Eliot's *Ash-Wednesday* could be taken to describe the kind of artist someone in the grip of such fears might have become: 'A language of order and belief is being used to stabilize an insistent sense of loss and emptiness, perhaps suggesting also the nature of Eliot's own faith.' It is no denigration of Eliot's poetry to say that this is persuasive about the origins of his authoritarianism. For all his romanticism about the army, and his feeling (also voiced by Tietjens) that the war was as 'glorious' as it was 'atrocious' an undertaking, Ford never succumbed to the lure of the totalitarian. Like Eliot, he is a master at setting the desire for order and control at odds with the chaos of uncontrolled desire. But the encyclopaedic panache of his fiction is able to do so while sustaining a magnanimity only intermittent in Eliot.[69]

He ended 'A Day of Battle'—the piece written in the Ypres Salient about the difficulty of visualizing and writing about the war—with another image which was to dominate his post-war fiction:

Yes, I have just one War Picture in my mind: it is a hurrying black cloud, like the dark cloud of the Hun shrapnel. It sweeps down at any moment. Over Mametz Wood: over the Veryd Range, over the grey level of the North Sea; over the parade ground in the sunlight, with the band, and the goat shining like silver and the R.S.M. shouting: 'Right Markers! Stead a . . . ye!' A darkness out of which shine—like swiftly obscured fragments of pallid moons—white faces of the little, dark, raven-voiced, Evanses, and Lewises, and Joneses and Thomases . . . Our dead![70]

It would not be adequate to observe that Ford imaged the valley of the Somme as the valley of the shadow of death; for on the one hand the image of the cloud is suggestively linked to a personal network of responses; and on the other, though the cloud pre-eminently mourns for the dead of the Welch Regiment, its very omnipresence connects it (as here) with other locations. Sweeping across the face of the waters and the earth, the cloud is disconcertingly reminiscent of Ford's vision of Marwood's aloof intellect surveying the war: reminiscent enough to suggest that, for Ford, the death that meant most to him since those of his father and grandfather had given a form to his feelings for the deaths in his regiment. His decision fictively to bring Marwood, as Tietjens, to the war, conjoins these powerful emotions, heightening the tetralogy's power and pathos. In *Parade's End* Ford is pre-eminently the artist *of* the stuff to fill graveyards.

These feelings are concentrated in the moments when Tietjens experiences uncanny, disturbing Fordian visions of the dead soldier O Nine Morgan ('O Nine' for the year he joined the army: Ford's batman was O Nine Evans). In the first one, Tietjens is reading over his own attempt to take stock, in writing, of his disintegrating marriage. His mind superimposes the image of the landscape on the page. When he hears the doctor's batman mention 'Poor —— O Nine Morgan' (it is presumably the word 'bloody' that the dashes suppress) it is the dead man's blood which he pictures overshadowing the imagined landscape; like Ford's own vision of a red shadow on the snow as he was returning to the war from Menton in February 1917: 'over the whitish sheet of paper on a level with his nose Tietjens perceived thin films of reddish purple to be wavering, then a glutinous surface of gummy scarlet pigment. Moving! It was once more an effect of fatigue, operating on the retina, that was perfectly familiar to Tietjens. But it filled him with indignation against his own weakness.' 'Moving!' is a nervily effective *mot juste* here. The wavering (bloodshot?) eyes present an image which wavers. But it is also an emotive image, expressing the pity and grief which move Tietjens's conscious mind, and which he is perpetually struggling to hold back. In the next vision Morgan is a shadow; but the description suggests another human sacrifice: the crucifixion: 'The valley of the Seine was blue-grey, like a Gobelins tapestry. Over it all hung the shadow of a deceased Welsh soldier.'[71]

In *The Marsden Case* Ford had registered the effects of the war by creating a world in which substance and shadow are transposed. Its mode of trying to articulate the grief and terror of the war indirectly, through suppressions and innuendos, means that central experiences are presented as obscure, shadowy, whereas the peripheral and insubstantial acquires an uncanny substantiality. The post-war memories of the pre-war 'Shadow Play' in the underground night-club shade off into the memories of the war as itself 'the shadow of death falling right across the land' (p. 197). But the war, the Armageddon-like abyss of chaos that fractures the table of History, cutting the present off from the past, turns memories of the pre-war era into unreal phantoms. People too are shadows in *The Marsden Case*. In the subterranean club in the evening-dress uniform of the day they appear as shades of the underworld; their talk is 'like shadow talk—unreal' (p. 146). The shadow is also (like the cloud) conceived as an image of anxiety. In this case, it suggests the Londoners' fear of the Zeppelins: the narrator says he shared the universal 'sense that black shapes hung over' their lives (p. 196). The shadow or cloud works so well as an image because its obscurity of meaning intimates the feeling of overwhelming but inexpressible depression: it doubles as both the deaths for which he is grieving (for the fact of mortality itself), and for the anxiety with which he feels grief.

Tietjens's sense of films of blood interposed in his vision causes an intermittent de-realization of his world (the passage wavers momentarily between placing the effect in his mind or in his eye). The moment is characteristically Fordian in its preoccupation with sensory effects (as well as the literary *effects* which can convey them); and also with shifting, overlayering and interfusing senses of temporal and visual perceptions. The ocular film here is one of many such images. In his vision of London from Campden Hill, Ford saw 'Ordered Life' as itself a film, separating civilized humanity from the abysses of chaos. There is thus a duality about such films: are they hostile irruptions of repressed pain, or protective screens from fear and madness? A crucial passage in *The Marsden Case* (recalling Ford's fantasy in 'A Day of Battle' of a protective 'magic ring') adumbrates the ambivalence of these mental operations: 'I used to think that, once out there, we should be surrounded by a magic and invisible tent that would keep from us all temporal cares. But we are not so surrounded, and it is not like that [. . .] round your transparent tent, the old evils, the old heartbreaks and the old cruelties are unceasingly at work' (p. 305). The temporal cares here are not only fears of mortal danger in war, but the domestic anxieties the soldier brings with him to the Front. Tietjens suffers from this in a particularly acute form, because his wife actually follows him out to France, irresistibly drawn to go on tormenting him at close range. Her presence behind the lines appears Ford's most striking invention in the series (there's no evidence that Hunt went to France during the war). Tietjens is not only plagued by his own problems but, as in the case of O Nine Morgan, he has (like the novelist) to assume responsibility for the domestic anxieties of his men. Instead of offering defences against former anxieties, the long periods of tense waiting in trench warfare leave the soldier doubly vulnerable: a prey to the worries from which he was trying to escape, as well as a prey to artillery and snipers. When not surrounded by the enemy, the Fordian soldier is surrounded not by any protection from anxiety, but by anxiety itself. Ford thought the psychological effects of war such as fear could not be fully presented by a direct method: it was only by concentrating on the longer-term psychological attrition of worry that the stronger emotions could be conveyed without the readers forming their own protective calluses, anaesthetizing them to the raw panics and *Angst*.[72]

Tietjens's relation with Valentine only intensifies his inner conflicts. Mizener describes how interior dialogue is deployed to represent 'the consciousness at war with itself'. This sense of inner chaos and conflict is brought to a head during moments of extreme stress—notably the bombardment in *A Man Could Stand Up*—. Tietjens finds himself—or rather, begins to lose himself—at the mercy of 'solid noise that swept you off your feet. . . . Swept your brain off its feet. Something else took control of it. You became second-in-command of your own soul.' '[H]alf the time I don't know what I'm doing', muses Sylvia, when she feels herself under the spell of her confessor, Father Consett: a figure who overshadows her mind as O Nine Morgan's overshadows her husband's.[73]

Ford described how it was a growing panic about forgetting the details of his war experiences that impelled him to write *Parade's End*.[74] That panic, an experience like the shadow of his earlier shell-shock which had temporarily de-personalized him, dematerialized his memory and identity, makes him desperate to write: to turn the stuff of the stuff to fill graveyards into the stuff of literature. (This is another way in which Tietjens's experience parallels the artist's: his need to reconstruct his obliterated memory corresponds to Ford's need to record his experiences. Tietjens's fear is an oblique expression of the artist's creative anxiety.) These fears—of losing control of one's actions, of one's mind, of one's memory—are all heard telegraphically in Valentine's thoughts on Armistice Day. They are feelings fundamental to all Ford's work following his breakdown of 1904; but they attain a peculiar prominence in the post-war fiction. The crucial question here for critical biography is what the writing can tell us of Ford's mental state; of his structures of thinking and feeling.

Paranoia

In 1924, while Ford was plotting *No More Parades*, he wrote:

With the novel you can do anything: you can inquire into every department of life, you can explore every department of thought. The one thing you can not do is to propagandise, as author, for any cause. You must not, as author, utter any views: above all you must not fake any events. You must not, however humanitarian you may be, over-elaborate the fear felt by a coursed rabbit.

'Christopher Tietjens is Ford's coursed rabbit', comments Melvin Seiden shrewdly, in one of the most penetrating essays on the tetralogy. He argues that it is ultimately to represent states of fear that Tietjens's persecutory anxiety is elaborated: 'Ford makes us feel the fear felt by his coursed rabbit, however much his cool prose seeks or pretends to seek to put us off.'[75] Analysing the theme of persecution, Seiden argues that we must confront 'the problem of paranoia in *Parade's End*'. 'Clearly Ford is not dealing with Tietjens as a kind of case study in paranoia', he says, because the novels do not give us the vantage-point we would need (such as narratorial irony or the insights of others) to diagnose Tietjens's feelings of persecution as fantasies. On the contrary:

There is no question that the malevolent persecutions of Tietjens are 'real'; the tetralogy documents them in great detail.
 Point by point, incident by incident, explanation by explanation, these persecutions are plausible. But it is just this plausibility that arouses our suspicions. The web of conspiracy against Tietjens has the excessively logical, almost mathematical coherence that we have been taught by psychoanalysis to recognize as another symptom of paranoia: the irrationality of pseudo-rationality. (pp. 160–1)

Whereas Tietjens himself does not fit the clinical description of the paranoiac (because the sinister motives he imputes to others are real; and because he does not harm himself psychically by his hatred of these others), Seiden suggests that the 'almost mathematical coherence' of conspiracy does: 'since the explanations have a persistent and strong authorial sanction, the charge of paranoia is primarily against Ford's vision of the human condition' (p. 161). It is a weakness of the essay that it does not know whether it is pressing the charge or refuting it, nor is it clear about the relevance of its clinical terminology to literary criticism. Trying to psychoanalyse an author from consciously elaborated prose, rather than from dreams or free association, and without the possibility of dialogue, is as limited as it is a limiting activity. The clinical method founders on the lack of required information and responses; the critical method is vitiated from the start by its equation of creative work with neurotic symptom. Freud's great study of paranoia based on Schreber's *Memoirs* might appear to justify psychoanalysing authors from texts. But Schreber was a judge, not an artist; and he wrote his own case history explicitly as a record of his symptoms, not as a novel.[76]

None the less, taken as a metaphor for patterns of imagination rather than as a clinical diagnosis, paranoia offers a powerful critical term. Biographically it is suggestive too, in the less rigorous sense in which biographers and critics have sometimes invoked it to describe aspects of Ford's life: the sense, that is, of delusions about persecution. Mizener, for example, repeatedly suggests that Ford's dealings with publishers were bedevilled by his conviction that they conspired against him, denying him his just recognition, profiting out of his work then cheating him out of his share, betraying him by going back on what he (according to Mizener) fantasized about as their 'word'.[77]

The real 'problem' in discussing Ford in relation to paranoia turns on six judgements. First, what exactly are the persecutions or conspiracies under consideration? Secondly, are they real or imagined? Thirdly, to what extent is the victim responsible for inciting persecution? Fourthly, does he recognize the mental condition he is in— whether it is a tendency to imagine conspiracies and persecutions, or a tendency to precipitate them? Fifthly, are the persecutory anxieties an individual aberration, or socially legitimized? And lastly, is there not a sense in which literature requires such feelings? (All thrillers, and many good plots, minister to paranoid fantasies of pursuit, persecution, and surveillance.) When Seiden writes that 'neither Christopher nor Ford understands that imputing a vast conspiracy to society is a kind of paranoia' (p. 165), he seems not to understand that it is the critical coherence he is imposing on the novel that interprets all that happens to Tietjens as one 'vast conspiracy'. The imputation is the critic's. It is perhaps the slander-mongering of 'society' that, of all Tietjens's persecutions, appears most like a conspiracy. But even here, the novels have no delusions about an actual 'plot' to do anything specific to Tietjens. They merely render the way society scapegoats someone it cannot assimilate. (In this sense persecution is the stigma of genius; 'society can only exist if the normal, if the virtuous, and the slightly-deceitful flourish, and if the passionate, the headstrong, and the too-truthful are condemned to suicide and to madness'; and it is at this level that Ford's invocation of the Christian myth is most profound and challenging.) Ford's point is that, to someone at the receiving end of social snubs and exclusions (as he and Hunt were), they *appear* concerted, intentional. Ford could do what the paranoid cannot: see paranoia dually, from the outside as well as the inside. Edward Shanks quotes from 'Süssmund's Address to an Unknown God' ('There's not one trick they've not brought off on me' . . .) as an example of 'persecution mania'. It's true that such feelings of concerted social ostracism get into novels like *The Marsden Case* and *Parade's End*. But, as Shanks concedes, it makes little sense to talk of persecution *mania* if the persecution was real, as Ford's was at the time of the *Throne* scandal. Nor does such a label take account of the way he uses a persona like Süssmund to objectify anxieties about persecution, and thus to begin to assuage them. In other words, it is a study of paranoia rather than its symptom. He knew how Madox Brown's exacting 'rule of life' (to give not only your possessions but your thoughts, endeavours, and opportunities to others) 'will expose you to innumerable miseries, to efforts almost superhuman and to innumerable betrayals—or to transactions in which you will consider yourself to have been betrayed'. The disavowal is characteristic. It demonstrates him catching himself sliding towards a paranoid feeling, but being sane enough to resist it. Brown's 'suspicions', said Ford, 'led him to discover "plots" where it is certain that none existed'.[78] The *ad hominem* argument also misses how widely the feeling of betrayal was shared by the troops in France. Yet here too Ford is explicit about how what *seemed* like conspiracy was in fact incompetence, as can be seen from a passage from *It Was the Nightingale* quoted by Seiden to support his imputed paranoia. The central character in *Parade's End* was to be 'too essentially critical to initiate any daring sorties':

Indeed his activities were most markedly to be in the realm of criticism. He was to be aware that in all places where they managed things from Whitehall down to brigade headquarters a number of things would be badly managed—the difference being that in Whitehall the mismanagement would be so much the result of jealousies that it would have the aspect of the most repellent treachery: in brigade headquarters, within a stone's throw of the enemy, it would be the result of stupidities, shortage of instruments or men, damage by enemy activities, or, as was more often the case, on account of nearly imbecile orders percolating from Whitehall itself. (pp. 197–8)

This is clear evidence that both Ford and Tietjens know that any vast conspiracy would be their imputation: things may 'have the aspect', to them, 'of the most repellent treachery', and Ford often portrays in minute detail how that aspect strikes the soldier, the spouse, the neglected and impoverished artist. But the prose knows that however, under mental stress, they may give that *impression* they are *not* necessarily treacherous conspiracies. Even a bitter passage from Ford's unpublished 'Epilogue' (probably written for *Women & Men*) about the attitude of the civilians to the war stops short of making accusations of conspiracy:

In these long days' journeys you realise that the actual theatre of war is very tiny. But there, in the Somme, or in Belgium, you & your fighting comrades seem to be the whole world. . . . But go to London or to Birmingham or to Manchester—& you hear no talk but of the sufferings, composures, heroisms & endurances—of the Civilian Population. But one does not discern that the Civilian Population has at all a bad time. There is plenty to talk about[:] plenty of excitement in the papers, plenty of junketing. [deleted sentence] In one's capacity of returned & crocked up warrior one is pushed off buses, swindled by shopkeepers who take advantage of one's necessity for specialised clothes & accoutrements; one is used as a pawn in one woman's social game or another's love affair; one is sweated and swindled by the authorities in the interests of the taxpayer, till the sinister thought crops [surges?] up in the mind that all these people would *like* the war to go on—& other wars [to?] supervene, for the sake of the fun & the talk & the moneymaking & all the rest of it. . . .

The soldier can't help having that sinister thought; but Ford isn't asserting its truth: only his truth to the soldier's impressions; and his truth to the general human limitation that makes one's own world seem the whole world, whether soldier or civilian— a limitation his art transcends while it expresses it, since *Parade's End* very effectively juxtaposes the two worlds, bringing the disoriented soldier back home in *Some Do Not . . .*, then bringing his civilian wife to the war in *No More Parades*. Seiden is right to emphasize Ford's emphasis of betrayal, treachery, and persecution: they are indeed major themes in his imaginative world—and themes that have been at the heart of the greatest writing since Homer and the Greek tragedians. Ford treats them with a subtle recognition of the difficulty of distinguishing actual treachery from feelings of betrayal; actual conspiracy and persecution from coincidental (or arbitrarily concerted) antagonisms. He also knew that this difficulty of distinguishing arises because, like impressions, feelings of persecution usually have some basis in fact (as when paranoiacs' families and psychiatrists conspire over their treatment). Perhaps the fiercest instance of Tietjens's paranoid feelings comes in *No More Parades*:

Intense dejection: endless muddles: endless follies: endless villainies. All these men given into the hands of the most cynically care-free intriguers in long corridors who made plots that harrowed the hearts of the world. All these men toys: all these agonies mere occasions for picturesque phrases to be put into politicians' speeches without heart or even intelligence. Hundreds of thousands of men tossed here and there in that sordid and gigantic mud-brownness of mid-winter . . . by God, exactly as if they were nuts wilfully picked up and thrown over the shoulder by magpies. . . . But men.[79]

Out of context this sounds paranoid. But its context is a bombardment, which is literally tossing men here and there in that mud-brownness. Tietjens is agonizing not only over his own fears, but over the men's agonies. In his rage and compassion he is asking *why* there is so much suffering. His slide from seeing it as the result of politicians' treacheries to seeing it as the work of God shows how he doesn't linger on the paranoid thought that every turn of the war is being constantly plotted by those in power—a thought that reveals the intimate connection between ideas of control and ideas of paranoia. He is crying out against fate. As in Ford's vision of the line, the thought of the movements and emotions of the multitudes of men evokes a feeling of awe about the force that could possibly compel them all to act in ways that must violate their individual volitions. For all its invocations of gods, priests, and religious ideas, *Parade's End* is not a theological work. It neither asserts nor denies that the war exemplifies God's justice, or could have been intended by him. But it does represent its characters having such questions wrung out of them *in extremis*. What this passage also shows is how Ford's renderings of paranoid reactions are, dually, a pondering on the ethics of art. As with his vision of the line, the imagining of the war raises questions of how that vision can be ordered and expressed. What I think shows Ford very much in control of his expression of the feeling here (even though the feeling itself is being shown as out of control) is the way the terms of paranoia are also the terms of his art. Intrigue is the novelist's business as well as the politician's; and it could as well be said of the effective novelist that he or she 'made plots that harrowed the hearts of the world'. The ethics of fiction are considered obliquely in the idea of making 'All these men toys'; something irresponsible artists might do for their own enjoyment, over-looking the humanity of the creatures being manipulated. For such artists, it could also be said that they make 'all these agonies mere occasions for picturesque phrases to be put into [their] speeches without heart or even intelligence'. These are the antitheses of Ford's aims in *Parade's End*. He wants to make plots that will harrow people's hearts by doing justice to suffering humanity; not to make mere picturesque phrases, but to make us visualize the war with heart and with intelligence.

The works that it makes more sense to describe as 'paranoid', are the unfinished

'True Love & a G.C.M.' and the unpublished 'Mr Croyd'. The difference between these and the tetralogy is not one of distance between author and character, since, psychologically, Tietjens is not substantially more distant from the Ford of 1923–6 than are Gabriel Morton or Jethro Croyd from the Ford of 1919–20. Rather, it is that the earlier works endorse their heroes' imputations of universal victimization, whereas the hero of *Parade's End* himself achieves enough detachment from his anxieties—his gut feelings of persecution and victimization—not to impute conspiracies. By doubling of himself with Marwood in the writing of *The Marsden Case* and then *Parade's End*, Ford himself was able to objectify his wartime experiences as he had not been able to in the earlier post-war writing. The mental distortion is most evident in 'Mr Croyd' in the way Ford's war-anxiety is transferred to his own literary career: Jethro Croyd's martyrdom by the treacherous and combative literary world is intended to take up the pathos of the war-dead, as an earlier J—— C—— assumed the burden of the world's guilt.

By the time he was writing *Parade's End*, then, Ford had recognized how his war experiences had made him again subject to overwhelming feelings of victimization, and he had mastered them to the extent that he could render them critically. He was always quite frank about his mental disturbance after the war, and shrewd in his generalizing from it. As late as 1938, an interviewer from the *New York Post* described Ford's musings on England and the after-effects of the war: 'The battlefields of France, and not the playing fields of Eton, bred the figures that dominate today's English life and letters. Roots violently torn up, hastily transplanted in blood-soaked soil, produced as their fruit not the clear-eyed, keen-minded youth of other generations but a race of spiritually stunted neurotics.'[80] This half-sounds like concealed autobiography—hiding a feeling that that was how the war had affected *him* in the claim that that was how it affected everyone. But as so often, rather than a denial of peculiarity, it is Ford's seizing on the particularity of his own experience to let it show him a general truth. The interview was subtitled: 'How Neurotics Brood on the Playing Fields While a German Corporal Wins the Last War'. Hitler, the German Corporal was beginning to fight the last war over again; the appeasers had a fatal dread of another war.

The question of paranoia, however, is not only raised by the post-war writing. Despite Seiden's attempt to contrast *Parade's End* and *The Good Soldier* to bring out the ways the tetralogy refuses to ironize Tietjens's suffering (the opposite of what he had said in his earlier essay on *Parade's End*), the earlier novel is itself fraught with actual conspiracies and betrayals, such as Florence's adulteries, Ashburnham's, his and Leonora's conspiracy to conceal his affair with Florence from Dowell. The betrayed and self-betrayed abound in his earlier novels too, from *The Inheritors* through *The Fifth Queen*.

The psychoanalytic definitions of the term 'paranoia' have a complex history. In its chronic form, however, it is generally taken to mean a psychosis 'characterised by more or less systematised delusion'. 'As well as delusions of persecution, Freud places erotomania, delusional jealousy and delusions of grandeur under the heading of paranoia.'[81] One need only read Freud's analysis of Schreber to realize that the sheer scale of delusion wildly exceeds anything demonstrated by Ford, or even imputed by his critics. Schreber's belief that he had a favoured, erotic relationship with God, who had transformed him into a woman, the surreal and bizarrely coherent system he elaborated to justify and articulate this relationship, are clearly of a different order from Ford's beliefs that his wife, or his publishers were not treating him as he deserved.

Ford was thus never a fully qualified paranoiac in the psychoanalytic sense. There is, however, a striking congruence between the clinical grouping of origins and symptoms, and some of the patterns in Ford's life and writing. To say this is to say no more than that the Ford of 1912–13 and 1919–20 was on the edge of paranoia—which revealed to him how the artist's imagination conspires with that of the paranoiac. (Psychiatrists with a mania for labelling would speak of a 'personality disorder of a paranoid type' or susceptibility.) It was probably the act of writing books such as *The New Humpty-Dumpty* and 'Mr Croyd' that therapeutically saved him. D. H. Lawrence's celebrated comment on the therapeutic value of writing—'One sheds one's sicknesses in books—repeats and presents again one's emotions to be master of them'—warns us of the dangers of working back from the books to the patient.[82] If the books are sicknesses that have been shed, then the author is cured: a near-paranoid novel cannot be taken as evidence that the author is still near-paranoiac. Of course Ford's experience of shell-shock had pathological effects. But what is astonishing about *Parade's End* is not that it still bears the impress of that trauma, but that despite Ford's suffering he was able to produce a work so generous, humane, and sane.

When Ford writes: 'You may say that everyone who had taken physical part in the war was then mad', he both is and is not exaggerating. It is an 'impression' (and one consonant with others' experience: Aldington, for example, describes his George Winterbourne as 'a bit off his head, as nearly all the troops were after six months in the line').[83] There is something disconcertingly at odds: the impassive, casual 'You may say', set against the nightmare vision of mass insanity. And the point *is* to disconcert, to make us hear how we are listening to one who took part, and was deeply shaken. *The Marsden Case* and *Parade's End* present, precisely, views of worlds gone mad; not only in the lacerating surreal exchanges between Tietjens, fearing he is on the point of losing control of his mind, with his deranged classical-scholar companion Captain McKechnie; but in all the characters, who are all shown suffering under intolerable stress, and many of whom are 'on the edge' of breaking down. The brilliant scene in the hotel in *No More Parades* is only conceivable when not only Tietjens and Sylvia, but also Perowne (her ex-lover), and the generals themselves are all on manic edge. War legitimizes forms of behaviour that in peacetime would be classed as insane— living outside in muddy holes in the ground, trying to kill, risking one's own life, waiving social rules of conduct. Its extremity cannot but disturb the mental life of its participants. *Parade's End* shows how the conditions of the First World War could produce paranoid states of mind. If someone of Tietjens's mental resilience can be reduced to amnesia and hysteria, the implication is that no one of any sensitivity could survive unscathed. There *are* real enemies, and they do plot to attack, and intend to destroy. They are likely literally to undermine you at any moment—as Tietjens fears when he hears (or dreams?) the German voice asking for a light, apparently coming from the ground underneath him. Like the Dreyfus affair, to which Ford often returned as a touchstone of true conspiracy and persecution, the war itself could seem like a real conspiracy, plotted by Chiefs of Staff and civilian governments. 'Prolonged trench warfare, whether enacted or remembered, fosters paranoid melodrama', writes Paul Fussell.[84] *Parade's End* isn't that, though it knows how perilously close it comes to both paranoia and melodrama. But the remark is suggestive about what unleashed Ford's imaginative power: when forced into a paranoid reality, he no longer needed to suppress or displace his fears about paranoia, but could confront them with devastating directness.

Ford's candour in writing about having felt insane is itself a form of courage. His experience with *The Good Soldier* and *Zeppelin Nights* had warned him that he would risk being denounced as a coward or a whiner. The difficulty of writing sanely about derangement in *Parade's End*, as well as his awareness of the risks, can be gauged from his comments about the shattering effect of the war on the mind (after the initial numbness he described in 'A Day of Battle' had worn off):

There can have been hardly an Englishman who ever expected to engage in actual warfare, so that when he did so his entire moral balance called for readjustments; his entire view of life, if he had one, was smashed to fragments; and, if he survived the war, his reaction against all its circumstances resulted in a very terrible mental fatigue from which he has not yet recovered [. . .] The results in the case of myself, with literary training enough in all conscience, were such that for several years after the armistice I was unable to write a word that had not about it at least, let us say, a touch of queerness.[85]

His psychological candour has misled critics into describing the world of *Parade's End* as a private one, seen through the distorting lenses of a disturbed subjectivity. Robie Macauley has written well of how Ford's 'is different from any other battlefield of literature. The landscape is a visual focal point for the memory and imagination'. Ford was interested in his own responses in the line less for their idiosyncrasy than for their revelation of the ways the human mind actually behaves under such duress; ways of responding that were rarely described in war literature. War is traditionally thought of as a field of action; but it forces Tietjens's mind back on itself, as the waiting, sheltering, sleeplessness, and physical hardship must have done to anyone with imagination. Even when the primacy of the psychological has been recognized in Ford's work, it has usually not been seen for what it is. Charles Hoffmann writes that '*Parade's End* is not a war novel in the sense of being concerned with the historical causes of war or with the reconstruction of actual battles; it is essentially a psychological novel in which the causes of war are traced back to psychological causes for conflict in man'.[86] But few war novels would meet his stringent, ultimately historical, criteria. There is something distorting, too, in the way he describes the psychological interest of *Parade's End*. It *is* a war novel in the sense that it is concerned with the reconstruction of what actual battle was *like*. There is, certainly, a continual exploration of the linkages and parallels between sexuality and aggression: between the world war and the sex war. But Ford does not reduce human behaviour to animal behaviour, even when he is writing about mass irrationality and inhumanity. He renders the individual's psychological crises in their historical and social contexts, and shows how the crises precipitate new visions both of the characters' individual fates and of their larger significance. (Thus the turning-point in Tietjens's marriage, when he begins to fall in love with Valentine, is set during the summer solstice.) The triumph of *Parade's End* is its rendering of Tietjens's mental torments as they are entangled in military life, the social structure of the army, the history of the era. Richard Aldington's *Death of a Hero* attempts a similar complexity, describing the war as a 'double nightmare' of his protagonist's private and public lives; seeing the military conflict doubled by the individual's 'inner conflict'; and seeing battle as 'a timeless confusion, a chaos of noise, fatigue, anxiety, and horror'. But Aldington's discursive book tells what Ford renders dramatically.[87]

Paranoia is understood as a defence against homosexuality. There is no evidence whatsoever that Ford had any sexual experience with men. But most of his fiction has intimate male friendships at or close to its centre. Mizener comments on his tendency to 'double' his heroes, and cites this as evidence for his theory of a 'fundamental division' in Ford's nature (p. xv). Another way of putting it would be to say that Henry VIII and Thomas Cromwell, Dudley Leicester and Robert Grimshaw, Ashburnham and Dowell, Gringoire and his 'Compiler', George Heimann and Ernest Jessop, Tietjens and Vincent Macmaster, Henry and Hugh (in *The Rash Act* and *Henry for Hugh*)—even Ford himself and Conrad (as portrayed by Ford in his memoir *Joseph Conrad*) are all studies of extreme male intimacy. And, as suggested, one reason why Dowell's protestation that he loved Ashburnham (and that 'I love him because he was just myself') is disturbing is that the novel doesn't let us know what to make of the possible implication that even this friendship, presented as a solidarity immune from the corruption of the sexual, might itself have a sexual (or narcissistic) element. In this case, the magnanimity with which Dowell forgives Ashburnham's cuckolding him could look starkly different. Could Dowell be offering his wife to Ashburnham in lieu of himself? The terms in which Fordian heterosexuals conceive of love—as desiring to merge their identity with their lovers'—are close to Dowell's identification with Ashburnham. By following in Ashburnham's footsteps—loving Leonora, then Nancy; buying his house—Dowell could also be said to be pursuing Ashburnham's identity as if he were a lover.[88] As everywhere in the novel, the myriad hints and suppressions foil any 'black and white' answers. The point is that the high emotional charge with which Dowell expresses his feelings makes us wonder whether they aren't in excess of their occasion (though again, the fact that the occasion is the recounting of his best friend's death immediately makes us think they might not be).

Ford's thinking about relationships between men brings together two related anxieties. First, that his male friendships might be—or might appear—homosexual. And secondly, that an artist is not a 'proper man'—that his sensitivity and impressionability might be—or be considered to be—effeminate. When he wrote about Oscar Wilde's trial he recalled Dr Richard Garnett's comment that the result meant the death of English poetry for at least fifty years. Wilde enabled the 'great public' to equate literature with perversion, and say 'Thank Heavens, we need not read any more poetry!' But it sounds like more than a betrayal of the literary profession is at stake when Ford says: 'Wilde I can never forgive.' There is an unfamiliar vehemence in his *ad hominem* remarks: 'I always intensely disliked Wilde, faintly as a writer and intensely as a human being.' Ford was never at ease with homosexuals, and told Janice Biala that he disliked Stella Bowen's gay male friends—especially artist-friends.[89]

This should not be over-emphasized. Repressed auto-eroticism need not lead to neurosis (Freud argued that even such axiomatically normal behaviour as a parent's love for a child is a form of narcissism). There is certainly no necessary connection with paranoia. But there are indications of emotional turbulence when Ford considers his intimacy with men. It is a turbulence which may have contributed to his 1904 breakdown—soon after the period of intensest involvement with Conrad during the collaboration on *Romance*, which collaboration was itself carried out as a kind of romance between its partners. It reappears in his ambivalence towards Marwood. And it may have been a factor in the army (influencing both his happiness among men, and the severity of his shell-shock collapses). This turbulence is certainly felt in the fiction and reminiscences. On the other hand, his later 'Memories of Oscar Wilde' show that Ford was not too defensive about homosexuality to be able to discuss it with wit and poise.[90] The essay is particularly amusing—and amused—by the very question of violent revulsion: by the way sexual disturbance can transform the peaceable citizen into a latent murderer:

In December of the year before the trial of Oscar Wilde the writer's uncle called the male children of his family together and solemnly informed them that if any older man made to us 'proposals or advances of a certain nature', we were morally and legally at liberty to kill him 'with any weapon that offered itself'. The person speaking thus was not merely the brother of Dante Gabriel Rossetti, the Pre-Raphaelite poet, but also Her Majesty's Secretary of the Inland Revenue; one of the most weighty and responsible of Great Britain's permanent officials, and the most reasonable human being ever sent on this earth.[91]

It is not only the case of Wilde which involves both feelings about homosexuality and feelings about the artist and homosexuality. Ford's views of writing and reading themselves invoke the idea of intimacy, sexualizing the relations between author and character.

Flaubert, with whose stylistic identity Ford tried to merge, by writing paragraphs in English which had the same cadences of passages from the *Trois contes*, famously identified himself with his creation: 'Madame Bovary, c'est moi!'[92] Ford followed Flaubert in believing that a writer's creative work was his adequate autobiography. But he also recognized the masterly equivocation: *Madame Bovary* or 'Madame Bovary'? The book, or the character? He wrote that *Madame Bovary*, *L'Éducation sentimentale*, and *Vanity Fair* are the great novels they are 'just because their authors were both in love with, and passionately intrigued by, their respective heroines'. This means one thing with a male novelist and a female character. But what if novelist and protagonist are the same sex? Does Dowell's Fordian-Flaubertian exclamation at the end of his novelistic pursuit of Ashburnham stand for Ford? Are we to understand that Ford too loves Edward, because he *is* him, or has become him through the novelist's sympathetic identification?[93]

To say this is not to offer a crass diagnosis of latent homosexuality. One cannot say that Ford's attitude to homosexuality was abnormal, nor that any refusal to accept his interest in it led to delusions, paranoid or other. Strong antipathy to—or fear of—homosexuality is, after all, common in stable, heterosexual men. One can only say that the displacement of fiction (or imaginative autobiography) allowed Ford to explore and present complex attitudes that could not otherwise have been voiced. The attitudes *are* complex, as for example when Dowell says that Edward and Nancy were 'the only two persons that I have ever really loved'.[94] So despite his apparent sexual and emotional frigidity towards Florence, it is not just the man he loves; though Nancy is not quite a woman, either, but referred to as 'the girl'; and Dowell does not say he *is* her; though that may only be because his love for her is unrequited; but wasn't Ashburnham's? . . .

What is clear, however, is that Ford's relationship with his father was a powerful influence over his own closest friendships with other men. To older writers he could be—as a man as well as a writer—manifestly, and sometimes desperately, filial. In a lecture on 'The Literary Life' given soon after the war to a female audience at University College, London, he urged that an aspiring writer 'must have a Master'. His terms fuse artistic with familial authority: 'You must have your master; you must study your master: you must pore over his every word and weigh every utterance of his that is at all characteristic. Your purpose must be to discover how he gets his effects. If you possibly can you must somehow introduce yourself into his family or at least into his study. Act, if you can, as his secretary [. . .].'[95] Ford had certainly pored over every word (read or heard) of James's and Conrad's. His generosity to Conrad, offering the older man his house, sharing a roof while taking down Conrad's dictation, meant that for a time he had indeed introduced himself into Conrad's family (to Jessie Conrad's exasperation) as well as having become something not unlike a secretary. His treasuring of James's references to him as a '*jeune homme modeste*' suggests that he might have liked to play similar roles for the man he usually referred to as 'The Master'.[96] However, his language of apprenticeship here resists any facile argument that his literary masters were surrogate parents. Rather, the suggestion is that the artist, like a craftsman, has a dual allegiance to a guild as well as to a family.

Ford would often act in ways that went beyond conventional friendship as he acted out Madox Brown's precepts. Sometimes avuncularity would become paternal protectiveness, particularly with the younger writers with whom he was so generous of his help, advice, and hospitality. (With attractive young women his feelings often exceeded the paternal.) To some—like Hemingway—the paternal manner appeared patronizing. Stephen Crane was less resentful of Ford's patronage. Ford's frequent quotation of his letter saying Ford would even patronize God ('but God will get used to it') shows that he was aware of his patronizing manner.[97] There are two ways in which his attitude to younger artists engages his feelings about paternity. Through his mockery of the Pre-Raphaelite insistence that all the children should become geniuses, one can hear a fondness for a milieu which *did* foster so much talent. With his conviction that art is the most worthwhile, and the most rewarding, vocation, Ford must have cherished a hope that his children would themselves be geniuses. (Christina and Katharine were intelligent, but neither of them were artists. Only Julie showed artistic flair, and she studied theatrical design.) His young writers could be the literary sons and daughters he never had.

The Father

Solicitude for children often has its roots in a desire for a solicitous parent. Ford's generosity to the young is utterly genuine, and an expression of many of his central concerns (altruism, the republic of the arts, the claim of true genius). It needn't detract from the nobility of his actions towards aspiring artists to suggest that it might originate in a feeling that his father did not recognize his own gifts. Was he writing of himself when he has his character Henry Martin think: 'Father was the only one that mattered.'[98] The agoraphobia which dominated the breakdown also bears the impress of Ford's feelings about fathers. For, as Freud argued: 'In the case of the man with agoraphobia the only explanation that we can reach is that he is behaving like a small child [. . .] our agoraphobic will in fact be saved from his anxiety if we accompany him across the square.'[99] This was exactly the case with Ford. Many facets of his work reflect this need for the other: the desire for a sympathetic listener or reader; the willingness to collaborate; the fascination with doubles. As with any art of complexity, such features are complexly over-determined. So it would be inadequate to suggest that, for example, *Parade's End*'s probing of 'authority', and its relation to fear and suppression, simply expressed Ford's ambivalence towards his own 'author'. After all, attitudes towards social, religious, and familial authority had rarely been in such a condition of upheaval. It would be similarly reductive to argue that his concern for 'the reader' was simply an expression of anxiety for an absent father. Many of his contemporaries too were becoming more interested in the psychology and sociology of reading, and such an interest is a response to quite other kinds of literary anxiety: anxieties about the challenge to literature represented by alternative systems of value and discourse such as science; or the challenge presented by other media such as film.

Freud writes about agoraphobia as a symptom of what he called 'anxiety neurosis'—rather than of a psychotic state such as paranoia. Many of the symptoms he associated with anxiety neurosis were displayed by Ford (though few of us are free of some combination of them): not just the general feeling of anxiety itself, but also irritability, hypersensitiveness to noise, hypochondria, doubting mania (Dowell's affliction), disturbances of the heart, the respiration, the intestines (Ford's 'dyspepsia'?), agoraphobia, even hallucinations.[100] Even during his 1904 breakdown, or his 1916 shell-shock, Ford could not be called paranoid in any other than a wildly metaphorical sense. His being 'a creature of dreads' is better explained as an expression of an anxiety neurosis. However, there is evidence that Ford himself may have accounted for his childhood fearfulness by a feeling of persecution.[101] Paranoia remains a useful concept in discussing his fiction, because of the sense in his work of what paranoia might be like. I have suggested how Ford's agoraphobia condenses his feelings about his father with his feelings about God, connecting anxiety and authority. This connection is one which most clearly brings out a tendency towards paranoia.

Like the father of Freud's Schreber, Francis Hueffer was a learned and authoritative figure, and, as Freud writes of Schreber, 'Such a father as this was by no means unsuitable for transfiguration into a God in the affectionate memory of the son from whom he had been so early separated by death'. Schreber was 19 when his father died; Ford 15. Ford's reminiscences of his father as the lawgiver ('as large as Rhadamanthus and much more terrible'), or surrounded by the bearded Victorian Great suggest that something approaching this transformation had occurred. It is hard not to see Ford's creation of fictional worlds, presided over by an omniscient novelist, but in which judgements are suspended and deferred, as in one aspect a response to this sense of overwhelming parental judgement. There is, as John Bayley has observed, a relationship between omniscient narration and agoraphobia. It is perhaps that by taking up a position of omniscient surveillance over a fictional world, an author can master anxiety about being the object of an authority-figure's omniscient surveillance, and thus take refuge from what Ford called (in one of his most poignant expressions of agoraphobia) 'the great gaze of the sky'. One function of Ford's writing (and his talking too) is to convince others and himself that he *knows* things. What the ex-sergeant-major, now Lieutenant, Cowley tells Sylvia about Tietjens is what Ford wanted said of himself: 'It's real solid knowledge of men and things he has'—like Odysseus, who knew men and cities.[102] In *Parade's End* 'omniscience' is tested in the central character as well as in the novelist. Ford's life bespeaks a need to go on talking: a pressure of narration. *The Good Soldier* dramatizes this predicament. A man who fears he knows nothing has to sustain himself by telling his story.

We saw how 'True Love & a G.C.M.' sought to explore the father–son relationship. The conjunction there of the father, agoraphobia, and the war is a suggestive one for *Parade's End*. For Gabriel Morton provides Ford's closest parallel with Schreber. He experiences curious shifts from feeling the war as pressing down unbearably upon him, to feeling a god-like and demented responsibility for it: 'He imagined that if he moved his fingers it would cause a disaster to those out there, in the Line'; 'It was one of the great, one of the terrible moments in his life, for it was one of the days on which he seemed to see himself very clearly.' Would Ford have been able to write about this instant of terrible demented self-revelation if he had not himself felt something like it? It is, anyway, a more deranged version of his own feelings in 'A Day of Battle' that, from the sense of oppressive blankness in the face of the war, 'The force of one's sense of responsibility is in fact wonderfully hypnotic and drives one wonderfully in on oneself'; or of his anxiety that his vote might interfere with the destiny of nations. It is comparable to Croyd's feeling that he has saved Europe.[103] *A Man Could Stand Up—* shows the relevance of agoraphobic anxiety to life in the trenches; and the analogies drawn throughout *Parade's End* between Christopher and Christ show how Ford grasped the way agoraphobic feelings of victimization could tend towards a defensive and more paranoid delusion of grandeur: a sense of a special relationship with God. To say 'There but for the grace of God go I', as Ford did when contemplating madness or judgement, is dually humble and egotistical: it is to have looked into the abyss of chaos and realized the precariousness of your life and sanity; but it is also to imply that God has graced you with the preservation of both.[104] It is a short step from visualizing God as an eighteenth-century-style Tory landowner, as Tietjens does, to thinking of the Tory figure of Tietjens as himself a god.

God-like attributes or delusions recur throughout Ford's fiction. From the altruist-meddler figure of George Moffat in *The Benefactor* and Robert Grimshaw in *A Call*, through the figure of the omnipotent king Henry VIII in *The Fifth Queen*, Mr Blood (who, when accused that he talks 'like God Almighty', replies coolly: 'That is rather my attitude'), to the omniscient Tietjens and the 'demigod' Napoleon in *A Little Less Than Gods*, there is a fascination with those who transgress the norms of human control and responsibility. Besides Tietjens's memory of feeling like a Greek god amongst the swallows, there are two episodes where—albeit ironically—he fantasizes about the men looking up to him as a god. He has a vision of O Nine Morgan looking at him as he had when Tietjens refused him leave (and was thus responsible for his death). The man looks at him 'As you might look at a God [. . .] Probably not blessed, but queer, be the name of God-Tietjens!' Later, Aranjuez 'had clung to Tietjens as a child clings to an omnipotent father. Tietjens, all-wise, could direct the awful courses of war and decree safety for the frightened! Tietjens needed that sort of worship.'[105] One reason why someone as diversely talented as Ford might be drawn to writing novels is that, in the Flaubertian tradition, the novelist is analogous to a god. His status is expressed in a series of ineffable paradoxes. An omniscient creator, he is invisible but omnipresent; remorseless but merciful; he produces the sense of inevitability, without explicit judgmental commentary. Thus in exploring characters who presume upon god-like activities (such as trying to order the lives of others), or who seem to themselves or others as god-like, Ford is simultaneously reflecting upon the novelist's presumption to create and order life.[106] Such characters are not simply studies of what Ford might be, or what he feared he might be, as a man; they also focus concerns about what it is to be a novelist. The subtext of *Mr. Apollo*, in which Ford depicts a real god who simply transcends human norms, seems to be that the artist (and thus himself) needs worship, but is fated to be an unrecognized god. Ford was writing at a time when, after Conrad and Joyce, the theological categories of the novel, as indeed of knowledge itself (omniscience, coherence, the authoritative point of view) were disintegrating. Eliot thought Joyce's mythic method was: 'simply a way of controlling, of ordering, of giving a shape and a significance to the immense panorama of futility and anarchy which is contemporary history.'[107] Eliot's conservatism demands that the anarchy be ordered by art. But, as in Joyce's great novel (and indeed Eliot's own poetry rather than his criticism), the narrative modes of *Parade's End* struggle to make the immense and disparate movements of the times cohere; but their sheer diversity signals the impossibility of the task, leaving us with a dual, paradoxical sense of both the ordering imagination and the world's recalcitrant chaos.

One event that might have given these questions a greater salience in *Parade's End* is the publication in 1923 of an essay by the psychoanalyst Ernest Jones on what he labelled 'The God Complex'. Ford probably didn't read Jones's book. But he is likely to have seen a review of it, which followed (on the same page) a review he wrote of Conrad's 'Uniform Edition'. The reviewer comments on 'the wide range of themes, political, artistic, literary and the like' in Jones's book; and if, as is possible, this caught his attention, Ford would not have missed the possible application to himself of the description of Jones's essay: 'He has also composed a brilliant and searching character-study of the first importance, under the title of "The God-complex," showing how unconscious self-identification with God will lead to a fantasy of omnipotence and yet an excess of modesty, insistence upon candour and yet an inability to speak straightforwardly, and a contempt for time and persons.'[108] Ford did not have a 'contempt for persons', though his sometimes haughty and indifferent manner was sometimes taken for contempt or megalomania. 'Contempt for time' would be one way of describing Ford's investigations into narrative orderings: his use of the 'time-shift' (though here too the contempt is only apparent). The other paradoxes—fantasies of omnipotence combined with excess of modesty; insistence on candour combined with a swerving from straightforwardness—both capture very accurately aspects of Ford's characters as well as of his own character. These ideas are particularly relevant to Tietjens, who (according to Sylvia, at least) desires 'to model himself upon our Lord. . . .'[109]

The 'God-complex' has not been adopted by mainstream psychoanalysis, perhaps because of the unflattering allegories it offers, not only of the unconscious but of the analyst and analysand as well. The traits discussed by Jones seem slightly too disparate to constitute a convincing single character type. It is hard not to read it now as a manifestation of Jones's discipleship of Freud (of whom he wrote a synoptic biography); and as a sublimated grudge against a powerful intellectual master. Jones discusses a tendency to resist new ideas, while assimilating and adapting them, and then recirculating them as your own: this captures Freud's jealous domination of psychoanalysis. But, like so much in this essay, it also could describe a trait of Ford's: his desire to have younger writers who would be his disciples, and address him as *cher maître* (as he, the *jeune homme modeste*, might have addressed James). Jones's essay abounds with terms which are relevant to Ford as a personality, or a novelist, or both: self-effacement combined with a desire to exhibit the self, aloofness, shrouding oneself in a cloud of mystery, reticence about the family, the desire to be 'the man behind the throne' (compare Cromwell in *The Fifth Queen*, or Assheton Smith in *A Little Less Than Gods*), 'the pleasure in visual curiosity', an 'interest in psychology', 'omnipotence phantasies', 'omniscience', regarding one's memory as 'infallible', having a great interest in the subject of language, being an authority on literary style, displaying alternating attitudes about 'judgement', an 'exaggerated desire to be loved', a belief in self-creation and in 'rebirth phantasies'.[110]

Fantasies of the self as god-like are clearly not the same as fantasies of the father as god-like. But the two might be related, as if, for example, fantasies of omnipotence were to compensate for a feeling of victimization before a powerful father. Ford's concept of impressionism manages to incorporate both of the opposing feelings: the artist is a passive sufferer in the face of the world's passions, which are *impressed upon* him; and yet he is also the active creator of new forms, through the exercise of imaginative power: 'with the novel', he says, 'you can do everything.'[111] His writings about the war are characterized by similar disconcerting oscillations between opposing views: the war as a chaos of suffering, or the expression of a single ordering intention.

Ford's agoraphobia also conjoins the images of creator and victim, God and father. It is relevant to a discussion of *Parade's End* because the anxieties of battle treated there took Ford back to the agoraphobic episode of 1904. Fear of open spaces is of course rational when there are snipers and high-explosive shells about. But the way Ford expresses the fear, especially in *A Man Could Stand Up*—, emphasizes the threat to the individual's sense of self and sanity. Conrad's moral sentence—'a man should stand up to his bad luck, to his mistakes, to his conscience [. . .]'—must have struck a chord with Ford, who had during the war stood up to these things and survived.[112] But Ford is interested in more than the pragmatic or the moral. The terrors of being under fire are seen as having profound and overwhelming effects on the mind. Ford's Virgilian imperial epic sings not so much of arms and the man, but 'War and the Mind'. Not being able to stand up is a psychological and an ontological matter. The connection with the earlier breakdown is established not merely by the degree of anxiety attached to Tietjens's trench-experiences, but also by the fact that his imagining of a time when he will once again be able to stand up takes him to Salisbury: 'He imagined himself standing up on a little hill, a lean contemplative parson, looking at the land sloping down to Salisbury spire.' It was upon Salisbury plain that Ford had his worst agoraphobic moments. The vision of a great plain recurs in Ford's writing. It is often associated with his love of a 'Great View'. But this is itself often associated with feelings of anxiety, disorientation, and God. A decade before the war he had written that:

the high places of the green earth seem for a time to communicate [to 'poor humanity'] a feeling of having the height of a giant and the powers of a godhead. In one of the infinite variations to which human thought lends itself this feeling of oversight, of control over one's own destiny, or over the destinies of an immense number—whether of human beings or of blades of grass—some species of supernatural endowment is the 'note' of the promise that the country makes to us [. . .].[113]

As with Wordsworth and Coleridge, the sublime in landscape evokes in Ford feelings of menace and pathos; though unlike them, the menace tends towards persecution rather than nurture. Fordian views are never simply visual spectacles; they are instances of a 'view of the world'; a way of understanding. In 'Epilogue', discussing his inability to theorize about the war and the post-war world he said he didn't 'dislike or despise the theorists, Heaven help me [. . .] But I don't see upon what hill they can stand in order to get their bird's eye views. Of course there are remote persons who stand aloof from humanity—but if you stand aloof from humanity how can you know about us poor people?'[114] Tietjens standing on a hill becomes a figure for the novelist's attempt to express a panoramic vision of our own times without losing touch with us poor people.

   To see how these ideas of views, judgements, and art come together, we need to return to a powerful vision from *The Good Soldier* that again draws on Ford's anguish at Salisbury, but is also eerily prophetic of the First World War battlefields:

But what were they? The just? The unjust? God knows! I think that the pair of them were only poor wretches, creeping over this earth in the shadow of an eternal wrath. It is very terrible. . . .
   It is almost too terrible, the picture of that judgement, as it appears to me sometimes, at nights. It is probably the suggestion of some picture that I have seen somewhere. But upon an immense plain, suspended in mid-air, I seem to see three figures, two of them clasped close in an intense embrace, and one intolerably solitary. It is in black and white, my picture of that judgement, an etching, perhaps; only I cannot tell an etching from a photographic reproduction. And the immense plain is the hand of God, stretching out for miles and miles, with great spaces above it and below it. And they are in the sight of God, and it is Florence that is alone. . . .[115]

The vision comes to him, both a torment and a privilege. The abject figures are 'in the sight of God', and yet it is to Dowell's sight that the picture appears. The familiar density of art-terms ('picture', 'etching', 'photographic reproduction') invokes an implicit analogy between the hand of God, which has framed the mind of man, and the mind of the artist who has framed this picture of 'that judgement'—a phrase which is tantalizingly close to the idea of the Last Judgement, although Dowell's indeterminacy would preclude such finality. More strikingly, the immense plain *is* the hand of God: the scene of judgement is also the instrument of that judgement. This is what makes the vision an agoraphobic one: the open space itself produces the guilt and anxiety about 'an eternal wrath'. There are moments in *Parade's End* when the plain of Flanders and the valley of the Somme appear as the possible arena of divine power and retribution. While Tietjens is waiting for the German attack he sees a 'slightly disordered pile of wet sacks':

The resemblance to prostrate men was appalling. The enemy creeping up . . . Christ! Within two hundred yards. So his stomach said. Each time, in spite of the preparation.

Otherwise the ground had been so smashed that it was flat: went down into holes but did not rise up into mounds. That made it look gentle [. . .] Collections of tubular shapes in field-grey or mud-colour they were. Chucked about by Almighty God! As if He had dropped them from on high to make them flatten into the earth.[116]

In Ford's writing about the war, men become, as in Dowell's vision, 'poor wretches, creeping over this earth in the shadow of an eternal wrath', whether it is the wrath of God, fear of destruction and death, or the oppressiveness of guilt. To return to the vision in 'A Day of Battle' with which this second section began:

Yes, I have just one War Picture in my mind: it is a hurrying black cloud, like the dark cloud of the Hun shrapnel. It sweeps down at any moment. Over Mametz Wood: over the Veryd Range, over the grey level of the North Sea; over the parade ground in the sunlight, with the band, and the goat shining like silver and the R.S.M. shouting: 'Right Markers! Stead a . . . ye!' A darkness out of which shine—like swiftly obscured fragments of pallid moons—white faces of the little, dark, raven-voiced, Evanses, and Lewises, and Joneses and Thomases . . . Our dead!

Ford told Conrad that the killing 'arouses in me a rage unexpressed & not easily comprehensible—to see, or even to think about, the dead of one's own regt. [. . .]'. The raging bombardments had seemed to him an expression of a supernatural wrath: 'the immensely wide, unseen densenesses of iron missiles, coming amongst the immense reverberations, all from one direction—that appeared to be the force of a Destiny so indisputable that no human mind could have invented it, directed it, or to be able to take it in.' It was an experience, he said, that made literary attempts to simulate destiny—even *Madame Bovary*—appear 'an impotent collection of accidents'. 'I find my mind mostly dormant in the matter of inventions and my thoughts turning inwards to the recollection of real happenings [. . .].' This is why he needed to fictionalize his own war experiences. Only reimagined reminiscence could hope to render that sense of scale and significance, and could exorcize that feeling of being at the mercy of an immense rage, which summoned up a corresponding rage in him. *Parade's End* came out of Ford's love for Marwood and for Stella Bowen; but also out of that feeling of overwhelming impotent rage.[117]

In the study of Schreber, Freud mentions one of his patients who, having lost his father at an early age, 'was always seeking to recover him in what was grand and sublime in Nature'. It seems probable that the mixture of love and guilt involved in Ford's responses to great views are indications of a similar process of loss and attempted recovery. The brooding black cloud that represents for him 'Our dead!' could thus conceal not only the dead of his Welch Regiment, but also the deaths that had disturbed him first and foremost: his father's and grandfather's. His impression of the Romney Marsh conveys emotions far in excess of their topographical occasions, and suggests as far back as 1900 this sense of parental oppression felt through the land-scape: 'In the depths of the Marsh [. . .] nothing rises, nothing aspires; the sky presses one down [. . .] Silence is the characteristic of the place, a brooding silence, an inconceivably self-centred abstraction [. . .] One counts for so little.' A quarter-of-a-century later it was still against this feeling that Ford was hoping a man could stand up. Where the disturbing feelings aroused by *No Enemy*'s visions of landscapes are left unexplained, in *Parade's End* they are explicitly related to the Dead whose graveyard the landscape has become. The survivor's guilt for dead comrades is a central topos of war literature, and there is no question that the guilt Ford felt over the men for whom he felt responsible was a real guilt. But he was himself well aware that the anxieties felt by combatants was often also an expression of their earlier anxieties. Freud argued that 'shell-shock' was not the physiological effect of concussion on the nervous system (as neurologists first thought, and as it suited the military authorities to believe), but what he called 'traumatic neurosis', such as happens also during peacetime accidents, when the experience of a trauma recalls and exacerbates a pre-existing conflict in the ego.[118] Although the loss of companions induces guilt for their own sakes, such a loss is very likely to have induced guilt in Ford for the sake of his other major losses: James and Marwood, who both died while he was in the army and waiting to go to France; Conrad, who died in 1924 between the writing of *Some Do Not . . .* and *No More Parades*; but above all for Francis Hueffer and Ford Madox Brown.

Seeing the black cloud as the wrath of God the father is consonant with Ford's favourite mode of discussing the war: talking of it as 'Armageddon', the last battle before the Last Judgement. Again, the representation of war as an eschatological event is a familiar trope in the literature. Many survivors of this war believed that they had lived through 'the war to end all wars'. Ford's imagining of the war in terms of divine judgement is a normal one, as is his emphasis on the extent and extremity of the devastation. But this is another point where the circumstances are so exceptional that the normal response shares features with a paranoid episode: 'At the climax of his illness, under the influence of visions which were "partly of a terrifying character, but partly, too, of an indescribable grandeur", Schreber became convinced of the immin-ence of a great catastrophe, of the end of the world [. . .] A world-catastrophe of this kind is not infrequent during the agitated stage in other cases of paranoia.'[119] The argument, then, is that for Ford, living even for short periods *in* the landscape, rather than in the city to which he had become increasingly accustomed, and being at the same time in great danger, recalled anxieties relating to God and his father. These were precipitated by his shell-shock. The guilt induced a recurrence of agoraphobia, which confirmed his fear that his creator was angry, and would destroy him and the landscape. These metaphoric relations between God and Ford's father should not obscure the more literal one. Ford's turn to Roman Catholicism, intermittent and metaphoric though his faith was, can be seen as a more direct attempt to 'recover the father'.

A final way in which agoraphobia condenses Ford's feelings about his father can be heard in Dowell's description of the picture of a judgement. The image of 'three figures, two of them clasped close in an intense embrace, and one intolerably solitary' has the power (as well as the possible content) of a primal scene.[120] But whether or not it has anything to do with the child's anger at witnessing an 'intense embrace' between its parents (for which anger the child might feel intolerable guilt after the death of one parent), the feeling of unbearable loneliness is unequivocally explicit. The need to communicate and convince, the desire for a sympathetic lover, listener or reader which has been continual throughout Ford's creative life, can thus be seen as an attempt to stave off the feeling of intolerable loneliness. Olive Garnett, whom Ford used to tease as being a 'Superior Person', testified to how on Salisbury Plain he had needed someone to catch hold of, someone to support him, in order to stave off his agoraphobic attacks. He needed the superior person to come down to his own level ('if you stand aloof from humanity how can you know about us poor people?'). But as artist he needed to be the superior being. He told her that 'qua Artist—you ought to be above all the characters [. . .] Your greatness lies in your being above *all* the philosophies'. His dual being as an artist combined these horizontal and vertical axes.[121]

Parade's End itself addresses the idea of paternity—and of maternity—in more direct ways than those of God, landscape, battle-anxiety and agoraphobia. Uncertainty about the paternity of Sylvia's son dogs Tietjens throughout the tetralogy. The reader is made to share Christopher's perplexity, for whenever he thinks the question has been settled it crops up yet again. There is also a rumour, probably malicious, that Valentine's paternity is in doubt: that she might be Christopher's half-sister, and their love incestuous.

The contrast between Sylvia's adultery and Valentine's patient loyalty is a contrast between different kinds of mother as well as different kinds of partner; and this is echoed in the contrast between the mothers of all three major characters: Sylvia's mother, Mrs Satterthwaite, Valentine's mother, Mrs Wannop, and Christopher's mother, the saint-like Mrs Tietjens. None of the characters approaches the sexual stereotype implied by such descriptions. Part of the fascination of the sequence's complex patterning is the problem posed for Tietjens's own identity by those around him. The three main characters are thus all seen as children as well as parents. Tietjens is also dogged by the anxiety that he might be responsible for his father's death, which might have been a suicide, prompted by hearing rumours about his son's licentiousness.

Last Post: *Genealogy, Elegy, And The Sense Of The End*

The concern with parentage and generation is elaborated most fully in *Last Post*, and it is one of the central ways in which that novel is a much more apt and satisfying conclusion to the tetralogy than has usually been acknowledged. Two of the new figures introduced in this book focus the parent-child relationship. Sylvia's son, young Mark, is given a brief but vivid interior monologue in Part I, Chapter 3. The baby Valentine is expecting dominates the novel, reproducing the hopefulness and excitement which had inspired Ford to write *A House*. This version of the 'Child in the House' turns out to be the only thing which can resolve the tetralogy, because it is only the idea of the mother and child which can pacify Sylvia, and effect a truce in her war with Christopher. Bowen found it implausible that Sylvia should relent: Violet Hunt's persistent hounding even after Julie's birth still rankled. But Ford's reply shows how important Sylvia's change of heart was to Ford's sense of the work's overall design: 'Yes, I suppose the volte face in Sylvia surprised you—but I had thought of it a long time and it occurred to me that, after all she was a "sport" and it takes a pretty unsporting woman to damage an unborn child.' Mizener gives a fine account of how much more complex are her motives, and how well-prepared in the earlier novels. But his claim, based on this letter, that 'Ford himself was not always aware of all that went on in his imagination' when he was creating his major characters, is a condescending confusion of the characteristic understatement of the letter with the manifest self-awareness in the construction of the tetralogy. Charles Hoffmann has noted the analogy between Sylvia's relenting and the Allies' unwillingness to pursue the enemy relentlessly. Ford's plotting creates a dual attitude towards the idea of relenting. The Tietjens brothers share Ford's view that the German empire needed dismantling to secure France. But what sympathy this view elicits is offset by making us feel what a good thing it is that Sylvia stops pursuing her enemies so tenaciously. (By 1927 Ford had begun a new romance, and thus had particular reason to suggest obliquely to Stella the importance of being a 'sport'.) Mizener argues that Sylvia 'has run out her string and, tired, hardly cares any more. Her mind is haunted by Father Consett, brutally hanged along with Roger Casement (whom Ford had known and whose judicial murder had outraged him).' In *Last Post*:

First it comes to her, with a shock so fierce that even Gunning, her arch-enemy, pities her, that in getting Groby Great Tree cut down in order to make Christopher suffer she had really been following the will of God; 'in letting Groby Great Tree be cut down God was lifting the ban off the Tietjenses.' Then she has a vision of Father Consett. 'Up over the landscape, the hills, the sky, she felt the shadow of Father Consett, the arms extended as if on a gigantic cruciform—and then, above and behind that, an . . . an August Will!' It convinces her she must free Christopher to marry Valentine.[122]

From our first view of Sylvia at Lobscheid in the Taunus Wald, described as 'the last place in Europe to be christianised', Sylvia has been associated with occult and sinister powers. 'She's a wicked devil!' exclaims her mother. Ford wants us to take that dually: to hear the note of moral fear and the conversational archness.[123] But it is not only fitting that it should be her own superstition that finally decides her to release Christopher. Her vision of Father Consett (which is not her first) has an affinity with Christopher's visions of the dead private, O Nine Morgan, and with Ford's own image of the ominous cloud of the dead. It is thus with another vision of a dead Father that the work is able to resolve itself.

The cutting down of the Great Tree is a powerful image, which both partakes of folkloric superstition and symbolizes it. It represents a break in the family's history. But the felling of the tree lets light in upon the other kind of family tree: its genealogy. For, working through Sylvia's superstition, the end of Groby Great Tree is what enables the continuance of the Tietjens family tree: just as Mark's death is held in balance with the imminent birth of Valentine's and Christopher's son.[124]

The fairy-tale element of *Parade's End* also becomes more powerful in *Last Post*. As its title indicates, the closing novel is an elegy—an elegy for Mark Tietjens, whose death is its centre, but also a tribute (in the words of the title to one of Ford's earlier poems) 'To All the Dead'. But it is also a myth of rebirth: of the expected birth, and of the rebirth it implies for Christopher and Valentine, and for English society reconstructed after the catastrophe. The book ends with Mark's death, and Valentine pondering his last words. But because he has remained silent all through the novel (whether out of obstinate principle because he disapproves of the peace terms, or because of a stroke, or both, is left wonderfully uncertain), they are his first words actually spoken in the book, which makes his death itself strangely like a re-animation. Although he does not manage to complete his laconic joke, we know from his earlier thoughts what it would have been: 'Still, things were takking oop! . . . Do you remember the Yorkshireman who stood with his chin just out of the water on Ararat Top as Noah approached. And: "It's boon to tak oop!" said the Yorkshireman. . . . It's bound to clear up!' (p. 288). *Last Post* completes the sequence thematically. It realizes the post-war alternative to Tietjens's pre-war form of life. As an Arcadian idyll it recapitulates and fulfils his wartime desires for English pastoral. Simultaneously, instead of quite fulfilling his fantasy that a man could stand up on a hill, it displaces and transforms it into the more muted, elegiac vision of a man lying immobile on a hill: Mark Tietjens on his deathbed, not quite able to conclude his joke about the Yorkshireman standing up on a mountain.[125] The chief problem in *Parade's End*, as it had been in 'True Love & a G.C.M.' and *The Marsden Case*—is to combine pity for the dead with hope for the future. In Mark's poignant death Ford finds the perfect balance. As the tetralogy moves from catastrophe and anguish to resolution, rebirth and hope for future generations, *Parade's End* begins to sound like Lawrence's great fiction of the post-war 'Condition of England', *The Rainbow* and *Women in Love*, written in reverse.

A final way in which *Last Post* can be seen to develop and complete the entire conception is in its subtle exploration of the effects of absence. All three major characters were developed in *Some Do Not . . .*. But in *No More Parades*, when Sylvia pursues her husband into war-divided France, Valentine is largely absent. The absence partly reflects Tietjens's attempt to suppress his memory of her, because he does not want to engage in an adulterous affair. In *A Man Could Stand Up—*, when thoughts of Valentine overwhelm him at about the same time that the German attack threatens to overrun the Allied lines, the structure of the book effectively absents Sylvia. In *Last Post* it is Tietjens's turn to absent himself. There is, of course, something strange about completing a tetralogy with a novel from which the most important character is absent for all but the last few pages; and about closing a series about the war with the death of someone not in the war. But there are two major aspects which mitigate the criticism that *Last Post* is merely a coda (it would be an excessively long coda if it were only that), or tangential to the design of the first three books. First, Tietjens has not simply disappeared or been forgotten. His is a felt absence, and represents the perfection of one of Ford's most characteristic and difficult effects: the representation of the suppressed, the subliminal.[126] The novel is structured around Christopher's central absence; and yet because the thoughts of all the other characters keep referring to him, he is as it were defined in silhouette by the way he impresses himself on the consciousnesses of others, and casts his shadow over their lives. The narrative of *Last Post* is animated by three expectations: Christopher's return (like a many-minded Odysseus returning to his Penelope: certainly *Last Post* is Ford's most Joycean novel), the birth of his son, and the death of his brother. It is organized in terms of events which have not happened, but which loom and influence. Mark Tietjens, the dominant consciousness present in the novel, is himself partly absent, in the sense that his silence largely removes him from normal social contact. As Ford was Oliver Hueffer's, Mark is Christopher's double. If Ford imagines his own death vicariously in *A Man Could Stand Up—*, in *Last Post* he displaces that death onto his Marwoodian double, enabling himself to be reborn. In all these ways *Last Post* is a book about absences and subliminal presences; a book about coming to terms with absence, with expectation, with death.

No More Parades takes its title from Tietjens's speech about having heard someone at the War Office devising a ceremonial to disband battalions (pp. 33–4). The whole rendering of the war is thus seen with, at the back of the mind, the thought of this passing away, not only of so many soldiers, but of their battalions and traditions. It is a characteristic dual temporal perspective: a kind of time-shift, making us see the events as they appear at the time, but also conscious of how they will seem when memorialized later on. Biographically, Ford was thinking of the passing away not only of parades, but also of parents or parent-figures. His mother was ill; he had a premonition of Conrad's death. As soon as he had finished his memoir of Conrad, Ford began *No More Parades*. And, as we shall see, *Last Post* was begun days after his mother's funeral.

The other reason why *Last Post* is more than simply a coda is because this trope of felt absence is congruent with a pair of related ideas that run through Ford's *œuvre*, but which become more central and more explicit after the war: the Flaubertian conception of the novelist as an immanent god-like being, invisible but omnipresent; and the more Fordian notion of the way literature expresses 'personality'. We shall return to the latter in Chapter 23 on autobiography, for it implies a view of literature as radically autobiographic, which, together with a particular conception of what the 'autobiographic' should be, forms an account of Ford's own excellent autobiographic work. The form taken by this curious combination of absence and presence in *Last Post* is that Tietjens is flying over the scene of the novel's action and inaction. Whereas Mark is lying down on a hill, and surveying the view, Christopher is doing more than standing on a hill: he is flying over one, having attained a god-like (or novelist-like) omniscient perspective. This doubling of viewpoints in the Tietjens brothers is a counterpoint to the earlier vision of the line, enabling Ford to combine the views of omniscient superiority and mortal humanity.

Much of the uncertainty in the critical reception of *Last Post* comes from a feeling that the novel is not true to the spirit of the first three books. One can see why Graham Greene found the purgatorial tentativeness of the ending of *A Man Could Stand Up—* a congenial resting-place after the inferno of *No More Parades*; and also why he could not endorse the promise of paradise regained in *Last Post*. The Armistice in *A Man Could Stand Up—* was for him 'an explosion without a future'; he couldn't accept *Last Post* because it imagined a future for Christopher and Valentine, and a redemptive one at that. But there's no peace for the wicked in Greeneland. He thought it 'a story of unhappy marriage', which it is only if you marginalize Tietjens's relationship with Valentine. And he controversially omitted *Last Post* from his edition of *Parade's End*, leaving the lovers in their limbo of suspension dots at the end of *A Man Could Stand Up*—. But although *Last Post* may not accord with the spirit of such a powerfully ambivalent Catholic reader like Greene, whose objections are theological as much as aesthetic, its resolution *is* true to the spirit of the whole work, which is everywhere poised between comedy and tragedy, pathos and farce.[127] *Last Post* concludes *Parade's End* in a masterly achievement of a highly precarious tone and form, and one which is profoundly expressive of Ford's temperament. It sustains what all Ford's post-war writing attempted but only fitfully achieved: a rare generic and tonal duality. Its title is itself an instance of that duality: the last post is played at the end of a day or at the end of a life.[128] The novel weighs what can stand up against what does not; what must pass away, against what will be born or reborn; and in doing so it performs a variation on Ford's perennial theme of the contrast between the artist (to whose sensibility Christopher so often approximates) and the 'stuff to fill graveyards'.

Last Post is not, however, a static balancing act. Its form, though a development of the tetralogy's presentation of consciousness, is none the less deeply consonant with the forms of the earlier books, and with what is crucial in all Ford's greatest art. Dorothy Parker, who said she knew of 'few other novelists who can so surely capture human bewilderment and suffering, for his is a great pity', felt *Last Post* fell below the standard of its predecessors. 'Ford's style has here become so tortuous that he writes almost as if he were parodying himself. There are grave hardships for the reader in the long interior monologues [. . .].' But even after such a response to the book's problems she thought it 'worth all its difficulties', finding 'a vastly stirring quality in Ford's work'.[129]

The last minute presence of Christopher, coinciding with Mark's death, is not merely a guest appearance in someone else's novel. Instead, precisely because his absence has itself been a felt presence throughout, the ending feels like a return to the home key ('F natural descending to tonic, C major'; *Some Do Not . . .* , p. 133). The sudden acceleration, and crescendo of most of the events we have been waiting for, has a similar effect to that described in the last paragraph of *No More Parades*. There, General Campion, inspecting the cookhouses, moves from questioning Sergeant-Cook Case about 'a woman he called his sister', and whom he now intends to marry, to carrying out the ritualistic military inspection:

The general tapped with the heel of his crop on the locker-panel labelled PEPPER: the top, right-hand locker-panel. He said to the tubular, global-eyed white figure beside it: 'Open that, will you, my man? . . .'

To Tietjens this was like the sudden bursting out of the regimental quick-step, as after a funeral with military honours the band and drums march away, back to barracks.

In a digression in *It Was the Nightingale*, Ford returns to the image in a way that adumbrates its relevance to *Parade's End*: 'At a British military funeral, after the Dead March from *Saul*, after the rattling of the cords from under the coffin, the rifle-firing and the long wail of the Last Post suddenly the band and drums strike up "D'ye ken

John Peel?" or the "Lincolnshire Poacher"—the unit's quickstep. It is shocking until you see how good it is as a symbol.'[130] He does not explain what it is a symbol *for*. He is reminded of the practice by seeing Nancy Cunard flash past 'like a jewelled tropical bird', stepping quickly to rejoin George Moore, who has just made Ford feel he has seen a ghost. This memory is then followed by the recollection of the two deaths (only ten days apart in January 1933) of Galsworthy and George Moore. What seems important to him is the rapid juxtaposition of moods, and its power to snap one out of depressive grief. It is perhaps a symbol of the way grief must be regulated by social rituals if life is to keep all on going: a symbol of emotional self-restraint. It is not surprising that a writer like Ford, who specializes in involving his readers in the agonizing mental complexities of his characters, should connect this idea with brilliant novel-endings which clinch their forms and release their readers from the subject's anxieties about sexuality and death. Ford's long sentence about the 'long wail of the Last Post' suggests that after the long tension of the novel *Last Post*, the conclusion is intended as another form of aesthetic and emotional quick-step as Christopher returns towards the end of Marks's long funereal silence. A later passage in *It Was the Nightingale* picks up the idea, making the connection between forms and closures while exemplifying it:

My brain, I think, is a sort of dove-cote. The thoughts from it fly round and round, seem about to settle and circle even further than before and more and more swiftly. I try in the end to let them come home with the velocity and precision of swifts that fly at sixty miles an hour into their apertures that you would say could not let them through. I hope thus to attain to a precision of effect as startling as any Frenchman who is for ever on the make.

The image of the swifts' sudden return is itself a reprise of the idea about the salutary effect of a sudden return (to hope, to barracks) after the long wail of a plangent funeral. Like the *tour de force* ending of *The Good Soldier*, the endings of the last three novels of the tetralogy end with this breathtaking change of mood: the cookhouse inspection; the surreal party at the end of *A Man Could Stand Up—*, with the motley group dancing exaggeratedly like marionettes; Christopher returning as Mark dies joking.[131] Novels are not funerals, of course. But it is highly effective that a novel like *No More Parades*, which takes place from the start under the shadow of the passing away of parade, of empire, should end with the formal equivalent of a military funeral. The nexus of ideas here reveals the extent to which Ford's elegiac, ceremonious forms are a laying to rest of the anxieties and griefs that most touched his imagination.

   The critical argument over whether *Parade's End* should be considered a trilogy or tetralogy will continue as long as *Last Post* is read. However, we need to separate out the question of Ford's intention from the question of the novel's success. His intention alternated. 'I strongly wish to omit the *Last Post* from the edition. I do not like the book and have never liked it and always intended the series to end with *A Man Could Stand Up*', he told Eric Pinker in 1930, but then he characteristically backtracked, saying that he was 'ready to be guided' by Duckworth about it. Apart from the fact that he wrote the fourth book, which is hardly evidence of an intention that is should end with the third, there is a letter written exactly a year earlier in which Ford includes *Last Post* in the list of books he wants in his Collected Edition. His subsequent comments continue fluctuating. It was 'the TIETJENS tetralogy' in 1932. In 1934 he wanted to republish 'the three Tietjens books—not the fourth—in one volume'. In 1936 he approved a blurb which described the four books as an 'immense tetralogy'. But in 1937 he was considering republishing only the first three. As Howard Erskine-Hill puts it, 'Ford was in two minds'. This ambivalence was apparent even as Ford was publishing *Last Post*. In the 'Dedicatory Letter to Isabel Paterson' he writes that he would have preferred to end the series uncertainly on the Armistice, but Paterson and the public demanded 'an ending—if possible a happy ending' (p. [v]). Thus Ford himself initiated the debate. Yet he *did* write the fourth book, which can't simply be wished away.[132]

The critical objections to *Last Post* are based on its differences from its predecessors. John Meixner argues that it is more symbolic and more sentimental. 'Elegiac lament, not spiritual assurance, lies at the core of the trilogy', he says. Yet not only is elegiac lament at the core of *Last Post*, but the spiritual assurance that coexists with it there *is* an increasing element in *A Man Could Stand Up—*. Similarly, Mizener's objection that Marie Léonie's Frenchness is not integral to the rest of the story doesn't stand up to scrutiny. France and Belgium were after all where most of the war was fought, and where Tietjens is for most of the second and third novels. If Ford wants to turn outwards in the fourth, take the kind of pan-European perspective that was characteristic of the post-Versailles world and the founding of the League of Nations, why need this invalidate his design? Sondra Stang argued that after the publication of *A History of Our Own Times* the debate 'can now gain from looking at *Last Post* as a natural bridge between Ford's work of fiction about history and his work of history'.[133]

These turns towards reconstruction and regeneration, towards pastoral, towards France, and (the other most striking difference) towards a 'stream of consciousness' technique, are all characteristic of Ford's post-war work. The continuities with his later fiction and cultural criticism are striking. The arguments about *Last Post*'s differences seem only to prove that *Parade's End* is unlike *The Good Soldier*. The inclusion of *Last Post* makes it still more unlike. But the attempts to exclude it misread the earlier books, suppressing the qualities that are latent there but elaborated in the fourth book; qualities which are central to all Ford's writing of the 1920s and 1930s. Finally, one can see the relation of *Last Post* to the whole as a large-scale instance of the tonal shift ('like the sudden bursting out of the regimental quick-step, as after a funeral') that I have argued characterizes the endings of the last three novels. *Last Post*'s ambiguous status is part of the total effect of the whole. The doubt it arouses about whether it is a continuation, coda, or reinvention, answers to Ford's sense of the uncertainty in grasping a life's pattern. 'For in this world of ours though lives may end Affairs do not' (p. vi). So in this world of his, *Last Post*, in which Mark's life ends, but that ending leaves the Tietjens Affair still as protean and alive with possibilities as ever. It also answers to his sense of not being able to accept Marwood's death: wanting *Parade's End* to be both his elegy and his immortality: 'To the best of my ability I gave him life again, and for me he lives still [. . .].'[134]

We encountered the idea of rebirth-fantasies in the 'God-complex', and their importance to Ford's view of his war experiences in *It Was the Nightingale*, and Tietjens's experiences buried alive in *A Man Could Stand Up—*. *Last Post* brings out the centrality of the rebirth myth to *Parade's End*.[135] It is a myth of the times, congruent with post-war ideas of 'reconstruction' and regeneration. With the Armistice 'the world was being reborn', said Ford soon after finishing *Last Post*. He also described a change of mentality that suggests why he turned from the Flaubertian formal tightness of *The Good Soldier* to the more capacious, anarchic form of *Parade's End*. He argues that 'the vast majority of young writers are violently seeking a reconstructive, revivifying formula', whereas to 'Post-Armageddon youth' Flaubert appeared negative; as 'erratic, violent and destructive as he seemed to his day.'[136] The idea of rebirth answers to a more private perception of Ford's. To elaborate on the earlier theological metaphor, *Last Post* can be read as an oblique fable of Ascension (Christopher in the aeroplane) followed by the Second Coming (his quick-step return). This event is prefigured by the ending of *No More Parades*, for Campion's inspection is described in comparable terms: 'The building paused, as when a godhead descends. In breathless focusing of eyes the godhead, frail and shining, walked with short steps up to a high-priest who had a walrus moustache and, with seven medals on his Sunday tunic, gazed away into eternity' (p. 318). Doubling the comic irony is a magnificent rendering of the awe inspired by the glamour of Authority. In a comparable way, one can feel the redemptive effect of the latent Christian typology of *Parade's End* without feeling that it is primarily a religious matter, or that Ford is aggrandizingly seeing Tietjens (or himself) as essentially Christ-like.[137] Rather, he echoes the familiar myth to express a feeling that he has himself returned, but in a puzzlingly transformed incarnation. The plot of absence and ghostly return is prevalent in the literature of the war. A novel such as Rebecca West's *The Return of the Soldier* illustrates how another novelist can use the idea of shell-shock to explore the psychology of war: the way the journey to France does not only alienate the soldier from his homeland, but from the land of the living, taking him into an underworld of trenches and dug-outs, or a 'No-Man's Land' with the company mainly of corpses. *Parade's End* shows how for Ford, the soldier's return and reintegration was a form of Second Coming, with Hueffer reincarnated as Ford. The near tautology of the new name suggests his recognition that this time he has fathered himself—as an author must; he has become his own author, survived the wrath of the Father, and stood up as his own man.

Writing

Unreality

With *Last Post*, the tetralogy begins to look more like a romance, in the genre of *The Marsden Case*, or even *Romance* itself, than like an aspirant towards the post-Romantic, ironic modernism of Joyce, Eliot, and Wyndham Lewis. 'The English writer is always trying to break back into romanticism', wrote Ford.[138] Each of the four novels does work through irony and experimentation; but the presence of the love-story (complete with happy ending, though without wedding-bells) is, paradoxically, disconcerting to critics who feel that literature should remorselessly and irremediably disconcert. It is typical of Ford's genius that his two masterpieces should seem critically irreconcilable. If you are moved by *The Good Soldier*'s bleak negation of the possibility of undeceived human fulfilment, must you not feel that the last two novels of *Parade's End* swerve from the logic of their conflicts into wishful make-believe? Or if you are moved by the testimony of regenerated and redefined humanity emerging at the end of the tetralogy, must you not view *The Good Soldier* as a cynical, or nihilistic cul de sac? Ford's critics have too often felt it necessary to make a choice of this kind. But what is at stake is the preference of genre, rather than the ranking of commensurable quantities. One may prefer Shakespearean tragedy to romance, for example; but few would argue that the writing of *The Tempest* somehow reneges on the insights and achievements of *King Lear*. The objections to the mixture within the tetralogy of irony and romance (its pastoral paradise after the hell of being under fire) may appear more cogent. But, again, one need only point to Shakespeare's romances to show that a generic mix does not foredoom a work to failure. One might feel (with Stella Bowen) that Ford's *desire* for reconstruction and rapprochement meant that—in *Last Post* especially—he was dissolving difficulties (such as Sylvia's aggression, or Christopher's alienation) rather than resolving conflicts. But history is on Ford's side here too, since the dominant note of the 1920s right up to the Depression was of reconstruction, and optimism about new forms of social organization, whether from the Left or the Right.

What makes *Parade's End* so much more compelling than the pre-war romances is that its particular compound of reality and fantasy—of precise social and psychological rendering together with surreal or wishful elements—is forged from a crucial aspect of Ford's war experiences: from his profound feelings of unreality. We have seen how, after his concussion, his sense of the reality of his own identity was rendered understandably precarious. In all of his war-fiction there is a fascination with the strangeness of mental operations. Because the anxieties and conflicts are so powerful, they cause the mind to behave in ways that seem uncanny, or distressing, or unreal. Besides the stories of identity-slippage, all Ford's war-fiction concerns perplexing, uncanny quirks of mind or fate. The experiences of landscape around which *No Enemy* is structured impressed him with this feeling of strangeness and unreality. Two short stories—'Pink Flannel', written 'in the line [. . .] in a tent on Kemmel Hill', and 'A Miracle', published the same year as *Last Post*, both turn on the main character performing an important action unconsciously, and invoke powerful feelings of the uncanny or supernatural.[139] Ford called 'Pink Flannel' a 'silly story'. It is introduced as 'a comedy that might have been a tragedy'. The protagonist has lost the letter from his lover that will tell him if their adulterous affair is to continue. Before falling asleep he prays to St Anthony, and then dreams that the saint hints what happened to the letter. This prompts his recollection that, running in panic to avoid a shell, he had had the presence of unconscious mind to protect the letter by putting it in his Field Service pocket-book. In the other story a young professor of biology recounts the 'miracle'. When leading a bombing party he thought he had forgotten to pack the all-important cigarettes; he prays; he opens his knapsack to reveal that the cigarettes had been packed after all. Henceforth he believes in a 'Special Providence', and this faith has made him self-confident and professionally successful. This story is less silly, though it still trivializes the war, and is vitiated by the tongue-in-cheek facility that ruins many of Ford's short stories. But it has great interest as a possible autobiographical fable. As in all of these war-tales, only more explicitly, the protagonist's outlook is changed by a quasi-mystical experience. The professor's belief in a providence is seen as being at odds with his Science, but as vital to his post-war identity. His wife, to whom he recounts the story of the bombing party, knows him well enough to realize that he must have packed the cigarettes himself, but absent-mindedly; yet she refrains from puncturing his conviction, realizing that his belief in himself, and their recently married happiness, depends upon his illusion.

The reader's point of view is the wife's, as we follow her watching him absent-mindedly finding then losing a shirt-stud. Also, like her, we are listening to his story. And the way Ford dramatizes his post-war self-confidence is precisely through the professor's story-telling, which comes across as a brilliant, masterful performance. Ford is slightly embarrassed about the science in the story. Apart from the Wellsian machinery of 'Portfolio B14', which is the problem the professor has solved on the anniversary of his providential experience, the details of his occupation are glossed over. What interests Ford about the situation is, instead, the man's story, and his ability to tell it. It is, as it were, the professor's ability to narrate which is sustained by his irrational conviction. Taking this autobiographically, it would be hinting that Ford realized his personality, and literary style, had undergone a radical transformation during the war, and had become more assured and buoyant. Certainly some of the friends who had known him before the war registered a change. Goldring, for example, said that Ford's pre-war sense of guilt 'was replaced by something like moral self-confidence'. He had paid his dues to death (his own and others') in the war, and had been able to shed the sickness of much of his intense pre-war suffering; life now seemed absurdly fortuitous. He had no more mental breakdowns after the war; and from the mid 1920s onwards he was much less prone to depression. The war-stories all pose an uncanny experience which afterwards seems implausible, or embarrassing. His descriptions of the Front as guided by a single Will are similarly touched with a quintessentially religious awe that (at least until *Parade's End*) he didn't quite know what to do with. These feelings probably stem from his own feeling of having a prayer answered: 'at night, when one had a long period of waiting, with nothing to do, in pitch blackness, in the midst of gunfire that shook the earth, I did once pray to the major Heavenly powers that my reason might be preserved. In the end, if one is a writer, one is a writer, and if one was in that hell, it was a major motive that one should be able to write of it [. . .].'[140] 'So what reason I had was preserved to me', he adds ironically. In its appalling destructiveness the war seemed indifferent to individuals. 'If you had stumbled over one of the late battlefields of France, at night, just after a great strafe you must have had moral emotions aroused in you', wrote Ford: 'but the battle did not exist for the purpose of stirring your emotions. Neither does the night, nor yet do the corpses. They are all profoundly indifferent to your existence.' Again the 'I-' word that defined his youthful 'philosophy' of Indifferentism. It was frightening for him to think of anyone being indifferent to him—whether God, his parents, or his readers; so he projected that quality into his manner and his style. His experience in the Somme, however, and the unexpected fact that he survived, appears to have reassured him that he was not a matter of indifference. He wrote of 'the Providence that has watched over my later years' after his experience of the 'dispassionate, absolutely blind Destiny' of the bombardments. 'A Miracle' also suggests that Ford felt his survival to have been providential, and that he also felt this conviction had revivified his personality and redirected his writing. His post-war work becomes more searching about the question of identity, and specifically about the Conradian question of what is necessary to sustain faith in one's selfhood. When Tietjens 'acts' during the German attack, he does so in both senses. He performs courageous actions, trying to save his men's lives; and this shows how much courage means acting—a performance which convinces oneself and others, as writing aspires to do.[141]

Parade's End is the better for eschewing the superficial *frisson* of miracles, providential dreams, and paranormal exchanges of identity. It shows Tietjens longing, as Ford longed, for safety; such as when he is pictured waiting for the German attack in a superstitious fantasy of 'extremely wishing that his head were level with a particular splash of purposeless whitewash', because then 'he would be in an inviolable sphere'— another version of the 'invisible tent' idea.[142] No novelist writes better than Ford about such subliminal tricks of mind. *Parade's End* shows Tietjens surviving, and feeling (as Ford felt) an exhilarating sense that his survival betokened some form of approval from above, from authority. Its very delicate tonal balance consists in its inviting us to participate in the exhilaration and ecstasy of survival and love, without insisting that we assent to the Romance view of the world as supernatural, providential.

In Ford's other romances the mixture of realism and fantasy seems just a *donnée* of the genre; in *Parade's End* a similar mixture becomes the expression of the shell-shocked and terror-haunted soldier's dual sense of reality and unreality. The absurdity, futility, and horror of a trench war of attrition gave cause enough for participants to retreat into wishful fantasy. But even when they did not, it often seemed inconceivable that the things they saw around them could actually be happening. This is one reason why Ford, writing at the Front in 'A Day of Battle', felt he could not describe the war. It seemed to signify nothing: he could not believe in, or comprehend, its reality. When Conrad eventually responded to Ford's 'notes upon sounds', he too despaired of impressionism's capacity to render the war: 'Methinks that to make anything of it *in our sense* one must fling the very last dregs of realism overboard. Nothing direct will do—except here and there a technical phrase than which there is nothing more suggestive.' As I hope to 'make you see', Ford was to take this advice in *Parade's End*, giving its more heightened moments a super-real or surreal hallucinatory quality that makes it one of his most compelling works. He found ingenious ways of using the technical resources of his preferred romance mode to answer to this perplexing sense of unreality coexisting with the most real facts of life and death.[143]

This dual sense of the unreality of the real, or real unreality, is central to all Ford's best work. It can be seen in the ever-tautening intrigues of *The Fifth Queen*, in which nothing is what it seems, and the more solidly Ford paints his Holbeinesque tableaux, the more evanescent becomes the political and moral outline; or in the vertiginous uncertainty of *The Good Soldier*, in which core and polished surface, heart and art become demoralizingly indistinguishable; or in the brilliant hallucinatory mental world of the late novels, in which dialogue and description blend with consciousness, memory, and reverie into an ever-dissolving and re-forming kaleidoscope of precision and indefiniteness; or in the magnificent bravura of the late discursive works such as *Great Trade Route*, in which Ford *almost*, at moments of dazzling panache, manages to convince us of the reality of his figures of speech (such as the 'frame of mind' which is 'Provence', or the notion of the Trade Route itself). In all these works the mixed mode finds its justification in the nature of the work. In *Parade's End*, the interfusion of reality and bizarrerie is powerfully justified by the psychological effects of war, the destabilizing power of fear.

In the passage from *It Was the Nightingale*, arguing that no one could have lived through the war without their sanity being affected, Ford indicates that it was partly war's ability to shake and destroy familiar conceptions of reality that made men mad: 'In those days you saw objects that the earlier mind labelled as *houses*. They had been used to seem cubic and solid permanences. But we had seen Ploegsteert where it had been revealed that men's dwellings were thin shells that could be crushed as walnuts are crushed' (p. 48). War is thus doubly de-realizing: you cannot accept the reality of the war, but having come through it, you can no longer accept the reality of peace for what it had seemed. As in *The Waste Land*, civilization seems 'Unreal' to those who have seen the underworld. Ford's techniques here are close to the literary device, particularly prevalent in Romanticism, which the Russian Formalist critics called 'defamiliarization', or 'making strange'.[144] Where Ford differs is that he poses his interest in the experience of 'defamiliarization' in relation to extreme mental stress and insanity (rather than, say, the Romantic invocation of the sublime or the supernatural). The opening of *No More Parades*, the first of the novels to introduce us to life at the Front, gives us not just one but two disconcertingly de-realizing sentences just where we would normally expect some familiarizing 'perspective' shots to give us an orientation: 'When you came in [did *we* come in?] the space was desultory [what? How can a 'space' be desultory?], rectangular, warm after the drip of the winter night, and transfused with a brown-orange dust that was light [How can dust be light?]. It was shaped like the house a child draws.'

The echo of *Genesis* ('was light') intimates that a world is being created, though a world in which light is turned to dust is a world being destroyed. The 'house a child draws' echoes *A House* ('I am the House! | I resemble | The drawing of a child | That draws "just a house"'). But here Ford has found an even better context for his image. The naïve but quintessential child's drawing captures the primitive, improvised nature of the home made out of a dug-out. But living in a dug-out makes pre-war houses seem unreal, childish fantasies, things that can at any moment be resolved into dust. It is an unreal simile, but one which evokes the feelings of unreality about both wartime and peacetime.

The appalling reiteration of death kept showing Ford how humans are, precisely, 'stuff'—matter, which a shell can instantaneously dematerialize into a 'scarlet viscosity seeping into the earth of torn fields'. War takes material reality and dematerializes it; but by disintegrating the things we had conventionally taken to be real it makes us feel their reality all the more powerfully. The reality of war in Ford's experience and his art is its feeling of unreality. The passage about 'Ordered Life' argues that the war had affected everybody's sanity, precisely because of the way it had pointed up the fragility of what we normally take as 'solid permanences'. It is in this sense that the battle-front can be read as, amongst other things, a metaphor for the separation of new forms of consciousness from the old forms.[145] *Parade's End* minutely examines the psychological effects of violent deconstructions. Even the pre-war opening of *Some Do*

Not . . . anticipates these effects. The end of the first part—just before the book's time shifts to 1916 or 1917, and Tietjens' shell-shocked return from France—describes his ride on a dog-cart with Valentine Wannop. They encounter a 'solid fog'—a magical silver mist, which dissolves the categories of material and immaterial, real and illusory. The mist acts as the glamour of romance, shedding a magical light on Christopher and Valentine, establishing a bond of intimacy between them. At the same time, it could be said to stand for the intangible but pervasive barriers of convention and fear of scandal which keep them apart at this climactic moment when 'Some do not'; or for their ethical disorientation. It is within the seemingly protective cocoon of this mist that their cart collides with the all-too-solid car of General Campion: the magic tent is ultimately protection against neither physical violence nor social scandal (Valentine is unchaperoned; Tietjens is a married man, and Campion is his godfather).

One reason why *The Good Soldier* and *Parade's End* are more effective than his other fiction is that the tone of slight hysteria and unease which makes much of his earlier work sound ineffectual is there focused by Dowell's baffled disturbance, or war's feeling of unreality. Tietjens experiences the most appalling version of this feeling when O Nine Morgan dies stoically, a wreck of blood, in his arms. Ford must have witnessed such a scene (or at least heard about it), for it haunted him as it haunts Tietjens, and his repetition of it feels like an attempt to exorcize his feelings—in Dowell's phrase, to get the sight out of his head. ('Epilogue' describes another, equally haunting description of someone dying next to him at Kemmel Hill: 'you are sitting on the firing step one day & your pal has the map & compass on his knee & the O.C. Coy is sitting on the other side of him. And he gives a little laugh & the map & compass slip off his knees into the mud. And you say: "Clumsy old b. . . .r!" & bend down to pick them up. And he will be leaning back, smiling under his dirty tin hat. . . . Just like that!') In *The Marsden Case*, Jessop recalls: 'One day, afterwards, I heard a man, half of whose chest had just been blown away, say: "Ere's another bloomin' casualty!" ' (p. 12). That phrase, with all the camaraderie and superhuman self-control it implies, recurs word for word in *No More Parades*:

A man, brown, stiff, with a haughty parade step, burst into the light. He said with a high wooden voice:
 ''Ere's another bloomin' casualty.' In the shadow he appeared to have draped half his face and the right side of his breast with crape. He gave a high, rattling laugh. He bent, as if in a stiff bow, woodenly at his thighs. He pitched, still bent, on to the iron sheet that covered the brazier, rolled off that and lay on his back across the legs of the other runner, who had been crouched beside the brazier. In the bright light it was as if a whole pail of scarlet paint had been dashed across the man's face on the left and his chest. It glistened in the firelight—just like fresh paint, moving![146]

While working on *No More Parades*, Ford wrote a review in which he remembered a bayonet instructor from the Welch Regiment, who would talk of 'the Spirit of Berlud':

He stuck imaginary Germans with the cold inches of steel. He rolled his eyes and appealed to his classes to remember the murders, rapes, and all the rest of it, of Louvain and, with exaggerated grunts, he pictured us pushing the bayonet home into the chest of a p . . . r b . . . y Hun, whilst mechanically this admirable and kind father of a family exclaimed: 'That's what yeh've gotter have, . . . The spirit of Ber*lud*.'[147]

War turns serviceable cliché into devastating reality. The spirit of blood turns a family man into a mechanical maniac, and it turns a 'poor bloody' victim into a bloody corpse. (Remember how the words 'Poor [bloody] O Nine Morgan' conjure up Tietjens's vision of blood.) To see a human being mutilated in a bombardment must be distressing enough; and seeing an 'admirable and kind' man become a professionally bloodthirsty killer could impress any sensitive observer. But the way Ford singles out the instructor's paternity might indicate that there is something more at stake here: that perhaps the thought of blood had such an overwhelming effect on him because of his feelings about his father. The essay, about the gifted young writers, mostly American, whom Ford knows in Paris, involves both his paternal stance towards protégés, and the question of nationality. For someone who has written a book of wartime propaganda called *When Blood is Their Argument*, and whose father was German, the prospect of bayoneting a 'poor bloody Hun' in the chest might easily have connoted patricide, in addition to the idea of his own German 'blood'.

Freud argues that intense feelings of unreality 'all serve the purpose of defence; they aim at keeping something away from the ego, at disavowing it'. He notes a second general characteristic: that such feelings depend 'upon the past, upon the ego's store of memories and upon earlier distressing experiences which have since perhaps fallen victim to repression'.[148] Analysing an incident of his own, which occurred while looking at the view from the Acropolis, Freud concluded that his experience of de-realization stemmed from childhood feelings of overvaluation and undervaluation of his father: of criticism and piety. Ford's connecting of his wartime nightmares about German soldiers with his childhood fears of the Victorian Great does, for all its fine malicious humour, or possibly even *because* of it, suggest that childhood distress very probably lies behind the later feelings of de-realization. The sustained terror of death in the war would perhaps be enough to produce the feelings; but in Ford's case that terror would reanimate the earlier anxiety about his father's death. Art offered him a way of denying his own death, as *Parade's End* offered a form of denial of Marwood's, distinguishing them from 'the stuff to fill graveyards'. The constant *presence* of death in the lines would have made it impossible to go on repressing the thought that he would end like his father.

Tietjens's predicament, craving inviolability, but also having to take responsible action, is thus the classic position of the Fordian romantic hero. In *Romance* itself, John Kemp muses about the start of his adventure: 'It was, I suppose, what I demanded of Fate—to be gently wafted into the position of a hero of romance, without rough hands at my throat. It is what we all ask, I suppose; and we get it sometimes in ten-minute snatches.'[149] But a few pages before, Kemp did have rough hands at his throat, trying to arrest him. So we may get what we ask in ten-minute snatches, but for the rest of the time we get what we don't ask (remember Dowell asking 'Why can't people have what they want?'). The war offered the possibility of conventional heroic exploits, together with overwhelming reasons to want to escape. Part of the greatness of *Parade's End* is to do with Ford's masterly use of the generic ambiguities of romance to present the complexities of response. It is a fiction of unreality which unerringly catches realities of fantasies and feelings.

Metaphor

In June 1925, after he had finished *No More Parades*, Ford wrote a preface to a collection of stories from the *transatlantic review* in which he said: 'the great benefit of the war was that it did make men search their hearts [. . .] you had to think what life was for—and what life was like.'[150] The ontological bafflement he felt episodically during the war made him ask such fundamental questions, and nowhere does he ask them more searchingly than in *Parade's End*, which abounds with direct and oblique questions about who Christopher and Sylvia are, and what are they. Tietjens, in particular, is an inscrutable object for the other characters, a problem that they cannot solve any more than he can solve his own 'problem of the relations of the sexes'.

For the writer, asking what life is 'like' is a particular kind of technical question: a question of metaphor. To ask what life is like is necessarily to ask what is life-like, or realistic, in the representation of life. Metaphor has long been recognized as central to modernism's reinvestigation into what life and writing are like.[151] But Ford's part in the modernist rewriting of writing has been misrepresented. Attention has been given to those aspects he drew attention to himself: notably the time-shift, the limited narrator, and 'impressionism'. The startling metaphors in *The Good Soldier* have received some notice, but in terms of conventional realism. Mark Schorer, for example, comments on 'the characteristic figures, the rather simple-minded and, at the same time, grotesquely comic metaphors: a girl in a white dress in the dark is "like a phosphorescent fish in a cupboard"; Leonora glances at the narrator, and he feels "as if for a moment a lighthouse had looked at me".'[152] Metaphor, fundamental to literature's creation of convincing perception, is equally an agent of defamiliarization, or de-realization. As here, it transforms reality into something quite other, unreal, to make us *see*. But rather than characterizing Dowell as the simple-minded object of Ford's comedy (which is how Schorer's argument runs), the metaphors are more deeply characteristic of Ford's style. For they evoke the kind of dual response that Schorer gives, as he finds them compelling yet also ('at the same time') excessive. We can laugh if we will; what has happened is that metaphor has become problematic, itself defamiliarized. In *Parade's End*, the descriptions of Tietjens as a feather-bolster or a meal-sack, the comparison of O Nine Morgan's blood to splashed paint, the image of the dug-out as like a house a child draws—most of its metaphoric resources, in fact—all work in this way, making us see an unforgettably vivid image in terms which arouse doubt about its reality: terms which make us ask what we are seeing, and what it is like.

Some of the most striking examples come where Ford is trying to make us see and hear what the war was like (passages which benefited from the kind of noting of sounds that he wrote for Conrad): 'An immense tea-tray, august, its voice filling the black circle of the horizon, thundered to the ground. Numerous pieces of sheet iron said, "Pack. Pack. Pack." In a minute the clay floor of the hut shook, the drums of ears were pressed inwards, solid noise showered about the universe, enormous echoes pushed these men [. . .].' This is the second paragraph of *No More Parades*, following on from the description of the dug-out. The effect of reading it after the picture of crude undomesticity is multiply disorientating. 'An immense tea-tray [what's a tea-tray doing here?], august [how can a tea-tray be "august"?], its voice [a tea-tray with a *voice*?] . . .' The imagined sheet-iron is also imagined speaking. It is a situation which turns men into inanimate objects, ear-drums to be pressed, bodies to be pushed 'to the right, to the left, or down'; one which is so chaotic that inanimate objects get animated, and speak. As with the incomprehensible—but all-the-more effective for being so baffling—image of 'solid noise', matter dematerializes, the immaterial materializes, and our perceptions of the real and the impossibly unreal become as confused as the brain during a bombardment. ('Solid things dissolve, and vapours ape substantiality', wrote David Jones.)[153]

The very strangeness of the tea-tray, wrenched from its context of polite society, recalls some previous appearances of this innocuously symbolic object. In retrospect we can see how this noise of bombardment has been prefigured by Sylvia's first materialization in *Some Do Not* . . . , as witnessed by Father Consett:

Walking slowly, her long arms extended to carry the tea-tray, over which her wonderfully moving face had a rapt expression of indescribable mystery, Sylvia was coming through the door.

'Oh, child,' the Father exclaimed, 'whether it's St. Martha or that Mary that made the bitter choice, not one of them ever looked more virtuous than you. Why aren't ye born to be a good man's help-meet?'

A little tinkle sounded from the tea-tray and three pieces of sugar fell on to the floor. Mrs. Tietjens hissed with vexation.

'I *knew* that damned thing would slide off the teacups,' she said. She dropped the tray from an inch or so of height on to the carpeted table. 'I'd made it a matter of luck between myself and myself,' she said. (pp. 43–4)

Our first impression of Sylvia is as problematic as that of Tietjens. It is an economic-ally dual picture, of someone at once radiant saint and hissing devil. Critics who have felt that Ford 'failed notably with Sylvia Tietjens, a monster of wantonness and perversity [. . .] she never loses a theatricality which cheapens the series', are respond-ing to Sylvia's dazzling histrionics, but failing to see how Ford has made her meretri-ciousness irresistible to everyone but her husband.[154] Like Tietjens and Ford, she too thinks about providence—hence the superstitious attentiveness to details which are taken as signs. This early suggestion that the tea-tray is associated with bad luck is summoned from the back of the reader's mind at the end of Part I of *Some Do Not* . . . , during Tietjens's surreally romantic ride in a dog-cart with Valentine through the mist and moonlight. First they run 'into a bank of solid fog': not as concussive or oppressive as 'solid noise', but proleptic of it, and of the more compromising collision to come:

Not ten yards ahead Tietjens saw a tea-tray, the underneath of a black-lacquered tea-tray, gliding towards them: mathematically straight, just rising from the mist. He shouted: mad: the blood in his head. His shout was drowned by the scream of the horse: he had swung it to the left. The cart turned up [. . .] There was a crash and scraping: like twenty tea-trays: a prolonged sound. They must be scraping along the mudguard of the invisible car. (pp. 173–4)

The car is General Campion's, only its roof visible in the mist, hence looking like the black tea-tray. But it is only at this point that we (with Tietjens) realize it. Until that moment, the reality of bewildered panic combined with the responsible action of trying to save the horse is conveyed by the unreality of the unexpected metaphor.

These interconnections form part of *Parade's End*'s own 'intricate tangle of references and cross-references': Ford's means of getting his readers as inextricably involved in the novel as his characters are tangled in their predicaments. Some have been noticed by critics, who have perceived the continuities between the pre-war tensions and hostilities and the war itself.[155] When the tea-tray returns with a vengeance in the bombardment on the first page of *No More Parades*, the bizarre connection has a dual effect. It links together pre-war civilization and the barbaric violence of warfare, compacting in the metaphor Ford's argument in the preface to *Their Lives* that the war was the legacy of Victorian conduct.

But the strangest connection here has not been remarked; perhaps because critics have been embarrassed by it, thinking it a Fordian whimsy which does not fit the picture of Ford as historian of the war. This is the connection Valentine makes between the name 'Tietjens' and the word 'tea-tray'.[156] The odd punning draws together the man and wife who share the name, and the archetypal English social object which can simultaneously be invoked at moments of disaster and destruction.

There is certainly a form of excess in such metaphors and word-play. They are Ford's illuminative exaggerations. But excess is an essential part of Ford's conception of the *mentalité* of war. Exaggerated metaphor de-realizes because, likening one thing to something else very unlike it makes it seem unlike itself. But the sheer interrelatedness of the tetralogy's metaphoric life gives it the coherence and reality of a supreme artist's vision. Ford was carrying out Conrad's advice about flinging 'the very last dregs of realism overboard'—as the best of his impressionism had almost already done. As Malcolm Bradbury says, 'Ford, moving away from realism and toward a harder modern irony, opened the way for many of his successors [. . .]'. *Parade's End* is pioneering too, along with *Ulysses* and *The Waste Land*, in its need 'to cast itself in the form of modern irony before it could begin to recover itself as myth'.[157]

Sex, War, and Unreality

War in *Parade's End* seems unreal often because it seems metaphoric, in both Tietjens's and Ford's mind. The most important way in which the novels forge one massive metaphor is by intimating that the problem of the relations between the sexes is more like a war between the sexes. We have touched on how the structure and plot of the sequence implies analogies between Tietjens's marriage and the Great War. Sylvia effectively declares war as Tietjens leaves for France, then pursues him there, combining the two antagonisms. Tietjens's affair with Valentine only becomes possible with the Armistice. The analogy is sustained throughout by individual scenes and puns, such as Sylvia's 'marksmanship' in throwing her plate of food at Christopher. Spelling it out like this, which Ford never does in *Parade's End*, makes the metaphor sound ridiculous.[158] Of course marital 'hostilities' are not the same as trench warfare; and it is to risk trivializing the suffering of the combatants even to suggest that what they underwent was somehow 'like' a domestic crisis—though the psychological critics are right to see the aggression in each case as related: Tietjens thinks Sylvia and Valentine 'the only two human beings he had met for years whom he could respect: the one for sheer efficiency in killing: the other for having the constructive desire and knowing how to set about it. Kill or cure! The two functions of man.'[159] There are two main *effects* of Ford's extended metaphor. First, it implies a connection between sexuality and violence. Immediately after Christopher feels attracted to Valentine, a car smashes into their cart, mortally wounding the horse. Immediately after they almost become lovers, Christopher has to return to the war.[160] The structure of the tetralogy makes this connection feel causal. In *A Call* Pauline Leicester quotes Grimshaw's remark back to him: 'Do what you want and take what you get for it.' Most of Ford's fiction is a meditation on this idea, usually construed in the sense of sexual desire and a punishment of either mental or physical suffering. Henry VIII does what he wants, and though it is generally others who take what they get for it, he is forced to execute the woman he still loves. Robert Grimshaw (like the Ford of 1908– 9) has a genius for *not* doing what he wants; Dudley Leicester doesn't get as far as doing what he wants before the telephone rings; but nevertheless he is punished mentally for his potential adultery. In *The Good Soldier* Ashburnham is Ford's most persistent doer of what he wants, who takes death for trying to stop himself wanting Nancy. Dowell seems not to know what he wants. Tietjens develops from a Grimshaw/Dowell figure, out of touch with his own desires, into someone prepared to act upon them. Some such combination of guilt and regeneration is characteristic of all Ford's later fiction, such as *When the Wicked Man*, in which sexual anxieties bring on visions of Nostradamus; or *The Rash Act*, in which sexual excitement causes Henry Martin a debilitating pain in the head. Desire in a Ford novel is characteristically punished by a judgement from above, as from a father or a god. Though, as the contrast between deathly Sylvia and constructive Valentine implies, not all desire is unredeemable.[161] Secondly, the entangling of marital and military conveys the mental turmoil of characters driven until they are 'on the edge' of sanity, and glimpse the abysses of chaos beneath ordered life; as in Dowell's *volte face* from describing the life of the 'four-square coterie' of friends as being like an ordered minuet, to saying that it was 'a prison full of screaming hysterics'. As so often in *Parade's End*, metaphor takes us to the edge of a paranoid vision, which, in questing after what things are 'like', sees them as something quite 'other'—something alien and threatening; persecutory. The grand metaphoric structure of *Parade's End* expresses Ford's dual sense of sexuality as something creative and destructive, romantic and tragic, erotomaniacal yet evoking restraint, beautiful and terrible. The novels de-realize sexuality itself, revealing it as stranger than literary realism generally represents it to be; as something that can itself de-realize our lives. Caroline Gordon was the first to describe the recurrence of this vision of sexuality in Ford's fiction, from the witchcraft of Anne Jeal in *The Half Moon*, through Katya Lascarides's power over men's minds in *A Call*, the Young Lovell's visions of his *belle dame sans merci*, the White Lady, the demonic energy of Sylvia, to this curious moment from *A Little Less Than Gods*:

Indeed, she did not know herself in this connection. Girls should be modest and at times take refuge in flight. But in the great glass of the mirror above the very mantelshelf that her lips had pressed she had once caught the sight of her face when he had been kneeling at her feet, clasping her knees with both arms. And her face had had the queerest expression—of ecstasy, dread, glee, cruelty, the eyes half closed, the lips rigid. And the whole attitude one of withdrawal, of forbidding—drawing herself away, setting one shoulder higher than the other to get a greater leverage, swaying to one side. Why, it had been as if something supernatural had peeped out of herself!¹⁶²

That last line spoils the effect, telling us what we have already seen, and thus making it seem less mysterious and compelling. Ford's impressionist aesthetic of suppression, apparent indirection, presentation rather than commentary, can make it hard for him to be sure whether he has achieved his effects or not. But what such an example shows is not (as it is too often asserted) that the best work is flawed in the same ways as the inferior pieces; but rather, how difficult and precarious Ford's effects are. This technical reason, as much as any biographical one, helps to explain the unevenness of his *œuvre*. It is frustrating to read books like *A Call* or *The Marsden Case* and to see how close they come to success. But such works reveal the astonishing achievements of the greater books. Graham Greene called the Tietjens books 'almost the only adult novels dealing with the sexual life that have been written in English'.¹⁶³

Biography

Sylvia Tietjens is Ford's best incarnation of that supernatural sexuality. He describes the way he conceived the character in terms of another apparition. Meeting a York-shire soldier in a French train after the war he was reminded of Marwood, and of his anecdote about 'Waring'. One of the two main female characters (Valentine) was to be based on the actress Dorothy Minto, whom he recalled seeing in a play about suffra-gettes. 'And suddenly, in Amiens station', said Ford, 'I had my other':

She stood before me in the shadows above the luggage barrack [*sic*] and the waiting passen-gers as the train ran into the station. She was in a golden sheath-gown and her golden hair was done in bandeaux, extraordinarily brilliant in the dimness. Like a goddess come in from the forest of Amiens!
    I exclaimed:
'Sylvia!' So I didn't have to cast about for a name.

This was, presumably, a complete stranger, though there is a flicker of uncertainty as he explains that 'the lady I have mentioned in a former chapter was guiltless of any of the vagaries of the character that eventually resulted from that image', this evidently being Mrs Sinclair Lewis, whom Ford had met at the dinner given by the Formans, and whom he describes as also with golden hair and wearing a golden sheath-gown.¹⁶⁴

He was of course covering his tracks, or rather the tracks of the more immediate sources, Stella Bowen and Margaret Postgate for Valentine, and Violet Hunt for Sylvia. This was partly a matter of tact: of wanting neither to rekindle controversy over his relationship with Hunt, nor to publicize the fact that Bowen (whom he had by then left) had lived with him unmarried. But there are also two critical points of significance for biographers trying to relate unreal texts to real people. First, as Hunt said, fictional characters are composites of many people rather than transcriptions of individuals. Ford goes on to make the same point, teasingly, after his reminiscence about the 'original' (or 'originals') for Sylvia: 'I may make the note that I never in my life, as far as I can remember, used a character from actual life for purposes of fiction—or never without concealing their attributes very carefully. This is not so much because I wish

to avoid hurting people's feelings as because it is, artistically, a very dangerous practice. It is even fatal.'[165] Despite talking of Tietjens as an attempt to resurrect Marwood,
Ford was explicit about the biographical multiplicity of his characters, and of Tietjens
in particular: 'My subject was the public events of a decade', he writes, and continues:
'My principal character I had compounded in the railway carriage between Calais—
where my grandfather had been born—and Paris.' The momentary digression there
plants autobiography in the middle of a sentence about imaginative germination. He
would not have written *Parade's End*, his 'Last of England', were he not Madox
Brown's grandson. Yet at the same time he reveals the distance between his own
biography and his fiction. Tietjens is 'compounded'. He is not a transcription, or even
a translation of Marwood. He is more than the dual figure of Marwood plus Ford.
Other components include Masterman (especially for his career as a public servant);
F. S. Flint, who became chief of the Overseas Section of the Ministry of Labour's
Statistics Division, was six foot two and with 'a voice which would have filled the
Garrick Theatre', and whom his son describes as 'a modern intellectual Falstaff'; and
possibly even William of Orange, with whom Tietjens ancestors are said to have come
to England: the 'Dutch William' that Madox Brown said he loved. Like Eliot's
arresting image in *Little Gidding*, in a passage which touches on ideas of literary
influence and of the sources of creativity in its haunting evocation of ageing, suffering,
and purging, an imagined character in a novel is a 'familiar compound ghost', 'Both
one and many':

> I caught the sudden look of some dead master
> Whom I had known, forgotten, half recalled
> Both one and many; in the brown baked features
> The eyes of a familiar compound ghost
> Both intimate and unidentifiable.
> So I assumed a double part, and cried
> And heard another's voice cry: 'What! are *you* here?'
> Although we were not.[166]

Biographical critics can cry 'What! are *you* here?' whenever they catch the sudden look
of a real person in a fictional character. Ford's novels continually catch such looks from
his life. This has led critics and biographers looking for the quintessential Ford to
emphasize the similarities between his books rather than the differences. Moser, for
example, states that his 'ultimate subject remains Ford's creative imagination with its
characteristic tendency to shift about, in similar but ever-changing patterns, a group
of familiar fictive counters closely connected to a few human beings'. But what he
describes is a bleakly unimaginative mode of creation, which sounds uncomfortably
like Coleridge's definition of 'fancy', as opposed to imagination, as a faculty which 'has
no other counters to play with but fixities and definites'.[167] To speak of 'counters' being
rearranged implies the fixity of characters from novel to novel. But although we can
recognize *Parade's End* as a product of the same mind as *The Good Soldier*, the
difference between the fictional worlds is far more impressive. Tietjens may share
some of Ashburnham's feudalistic principles, but it is hard to imagine that they would
have much to say to each other. Sylvia and Florence are both taken as 'based on' Hunt.
But none of the female characters in *The Good Soldier* have anything like Sylvia's

demonic passional obsessiveness, nor does Dowell's narration show us the workings of their minds with the interiority and sympathy of *Parade's End*'s omniscient presentation. It does show us how Dowell's mind works, of course, and this is what establishes the continuity of Ford's writing, rather than putative biographical sources: his delineation of how minds work, and how they do not work; how they represent things to themselves and to others; how they jump unpredictably from one time and place to another. But again, within this broad principle of Fordian psychology of *homo duplex*, variations abound. Tietjens's thoughts are so distinctive that no one would confuse them with Dowell's, or with Ashburnham's (if he has any of his own), or with Ford's own in his discursive books.

The second point is that biographical 'sourcery' is fatally reductive, crushing novels in a critical vice: on one side complaining that they are too like life (not digesting their experiences; violating tact); on the other complaining that they aren't lifelike enough, but evade realities. (The Marwood family managed to resent both Ford's inaccuracies about Arthur in his reminiscences, and his accuracy about the family in his novels.) It's not interested in the three other main elements: the novelist's engagement with history ('the public events of a decade'); the residue in the compound that can't be accounted for by real events or real people—the element of invention, imagination; and the form the artist makes out of these things. Biographical critics need also to assume a double part, and recognize that ultimately sources are as unidentifiable as they are intimate; transformed beyond recognition. In Ford's fiction there are no single 'originals' for important characters; and what sources we think we can identify shouldn't detract from what is most important in a novel like *Parade's End*: what Arthur Mizener grandly called 'the sheer creative energy' with which Ford has imagined his characters.[168] His novels are not patchworks of shreds and tatters of his families and friends and acquaintances, any more than they are *romans à clef*.

Much in *Parade's End* is not traceable to Ford, to Marwood, or to anyone else. It says something about how excessive the biographical attention to Ford's fiction has been to feel it necessary to say: it is fictional. Nowhere is this more obvious than in the crucial difference between Tietjens and Ford: Tietjens is not a writer; and he has the qualities antithetical to those of Ford's ideal writer: intellect; practical wisdom; strong opinions. Furthermore, Ford's fictions themselves show characters fantasizing, daydreaming, imagining more flattering versions of themselves and their actions: Dowell shying away from the sexual implications of Florence's touching of Ashburnham during the 'Protest' scene; Tietjens imagining himself as like George Herbert, or even Christ. These ideas aren't irrelevant, but have been applied too crudely. Because Ford was an expert role-player, and because he creates characters who play roles, and wishfully revise their roles, both his life and his fiction demonstrate too much self-awareness to be seen as symptoms of neurotic self-deception. The very fact that much of the evidence for the 'self-improvement' theory comes from the fiction makes it all the more probable that Ford had diagnosed rather than deluded himself; and not just diagnosed *himself*, but understood the common human tendencies to self-dramatization and self-elevation. That is, he is entirely un-evasive about the human need for evasion and escape; and his art is an expression of this vision, rather than the victim of self-evasion.[169]

Parade's End could nevertheless be seen as a subtle evasion of Ford's biographical problems. The tetralogy is ultimately a vindication of Tietjens, an assertion that despite his adultery, his fear, his temporary loss of mental control, his vilification and persecution, and even despite the exasperating tendencies that bring these things about, and which the novels are at pains to portray—his 'absurd principles', his provocative woodenness, his intellectually self-righteous manner, his paradoxical mixture of conventionality and defiance of convention, his 'mania for sacrificing' himself—despite all this, he is none the less a 'good man'. We have seen the power of this motive in *The New Humpty-Dumpty*, *The Good Soldier*, 'Mr Croyd', *The Marsden Case*, and *Mister Bosphorus*. And, reading *Parade's End* in conjunction with the preceding works there is indeed an element of justification and self-justification. Of course Ford wants to feel that his separations from both Elsie and Violet, or his anxieties during the war, or his lack of recognition as a writer, do not damn him, cause him to be judged as a failure as a human being. They don't. The great novels engage with his feelings about marriage and divorce, say. But whereas in fact Ford, at least nominally a Catholic, tried to persuade Elsie to give him a divorce, and when he failed he tried to get a German divorce to extricate himself, in his fictional treatments it is the women who are the Catholics—Leonora Ashburnham and Sylvia Tietjens; and the men regard it as a matter of honour not to divorce their wives. Thus, a hostile critic could say that the details that militate against a view of him as a 'good' man are precisely the ones which get whitewashed out in the fiction. But whitewashing is not what Ford does to Tietjens. Was Christopher Isherwood entirely wrong to suspect that Ford didn't really like Tietjens? He certainly registers a distance from his character. Ford knows, for example, that what Sylvia keeps calling his attempt to model himself on Christ is a problem rather than a virtue. Unlike Christ ('He saved others; himself he cannot save'), Tietjens fails to save others; but realizes: 'I've got to save myself first.' Thus, rather than simply defending his own qualities projected into Tietjens, Ford is showing Tietjens's moral change—which was also Ford's.[170] But he is not writing autobiography in *Parade's End*, so the fact that he explores the questions by transforming episodes from his own life does not mean that he cannot or will not face his own life, or that in so far as he does face it, he does so to exculpate himself. By presenting Tietjens he is not saying 'I am really like this'; he might be saying 'this is what a truly good man—a different man—might have done in similar circumstances'; in which case the very differences between Tietjens's life and his own become crucial—as they must be for any good novelist. Kundera has an ingenious metaphor for this dual relation between biography and fiction; one which chimes with Ford's exploration of persecutory feelings:

The characters in my novels are my own unrealized possibilities. That is why I am equally fond of them all and equally horrified by them. Each one has crossed a border that I myself have circumvented. It is that crossed border (the border beyond which my own 'I' ends) which attracts me most. For beyond that border begins the secret the novel asks about. The novel is not the author's confession; it is an investigation of human life in the trap the world has become.

As a critic Ford wrote penetratingly about how a work of art can penetrate the mind of the viewer or reader; how a book can ask questions of us, and make us ask questions of ourselves. So too with the writing of books, which in its very obliqueness, its doubleness in relation to the writer's life, can be more searchingly autobiographic than a servile transcription. It is a tone of description that he particularly wanted to capture in rendering Tietjens (as he had wanted to catch particular tones of narration in 'Seraphina' or in *The Good Soldier*). It was a tone he described in Villon, saying: 'it is from male suffering supported with dignity that the great poets draw the greatest of their notes—that sort of note of the iron voice of the tocsin calling to arms in the night that forms, as it were, the overtone of their charged words.' Ford heard that note in Marwood, whose illness gave him pain; and he made it the note of the mentally anguished Tietjens.[171]

Story

Two further objections to the biographical sourcery of equating characters with their alleged 'originals' are to do with a writer's interest in narrative. Tietjens's story would not have been written the way it is if Ford had not wondered about how his own life might have been different; but to say this is not to have accounted for much in the books. It is only one factor helping to shape the work; and most of the work of shaping happens *after* the preliminary wonderings. The messes and muddles of Ford's life, his inconsistencies and his tall stories, have made it too easy for his critics to ignore the conscious artistry with which his mind works, creatively transforming stories and situations from life into new fictions. As in the imaginative hyperactivity he describes during the train journey during which he 'compounded' Tietjens, or when he wonders about the narrative techniques suitable for rendering the war, thinking of Marwood and asking how it would all look in his eyes, Ford is making conscious decisions about form; altering and improving events, certainly; but more for the satisfactions of literary forms and techniques than for the self-satisfactions of moral pretence; for story, not history.

The other objection is that it is often previous fictions, as much as actual people, that are the 'sources' for a new fiction. Ford was familiar with James's prefaces, tracing the germination of novels from stories, anecdotes, and gossip. And in his own writing he stressed the importance of imitating masters, acquiring the techniques of other novelists. As *The Good Soldier* does in English what Flaubert and Maupassant do in French, so *Parade's End* is (together with *Under Western Eyes*) one of the best Russian novels in the English language. Besides reimagining *The Idiot* so as to make the central character sexually and morally realistic, it is Ford's *War and Peace*, with Tietjens combining the roles of Pierre and Andrei.

As when Ford said of *The Good Soldier* that 'the story is a true story', his stories about the story of *Parade's End* place a similar emphasis on narrative as well as acquaintances. The stories may be about his friends, or about their acquaintances. But they are presented to us as they were presented to him—as stories, complete with a point of view and a tone. He does not say 'I thought of Waring, whose wife had tricked him into marrying . . .' Instead, he dramatizes a conversation with Marwood, who tells the story of Waring in Marwood-ese: 'The poor devil, he picked up a bitch on a train between Calais and Paris.' The chosen name, evidently a pseudonym, itself asserts the literariness of the exercise, since Ford's question—'What really became of Waring?'— alludes to Browning's tale of unrequited love, unfulfilled artistic promise, and mysterious disappearance, in the poem 'Waring', which begins by asking: 'What's become of Waring?' Then, looking out over the view from Harold Monro's villa in St-Jean-Cap-Ferrat, he is struck by a doubling: 'almost before my feet as I stood in Harold Munro's [*sic*] garden was the villa of a poor fellow who had had almost Waring's fate.'[172] It is the twist of fate that brings together the two stories about twisted fates, and delivers the story of his projected novel, all tied up and at his feet, which appeals to the novelist. This story too is a true *story*. The fictional possibilities of 'Waring's' marital entangle-ments may also have appealed because of the similarities to Ford's own affairs; because he must have wondered how to render such things in a novel, and now one solution offers itself. But this is much less sweeping a claim than saying that a novel portrays an idealized version of the novelist.

It is, then, in the structures and techniques of *Parade's End* that we must look for Ford's reflecting upon his own life, as much as in the themes and characters. This is partly what is meant by the claim, to which we shall return, that it is a writer's fiction which is the truer 'autobiography': that literary form can be expressive in ways which reach beyond the superficial correspondences between real and imagined characters and episodes. The *formal* ways in which Ford takes up the question of paranoia show his vision from the front line of sanity, into the No–Man's Land of terror and carnage, to be a much more controlled, self-aware performance than its subject matter alone might lead one to believe. 'True Love & a G.C.M.' and 'Mr Croyd' are still too much at the mercy of Ford's anxieties and derangement to convince as art. And it is for precisely the same reason that they were unsuccessful as therapy. Or at least, although they helped him approach the disturbing subject of the war, they did not set his mind at rest about it. *Parade's End* is therapeutic too. It was a book Ford needed to write—before he forgot the reality of war's unreality; in order to get the sights out of his head; in order to regain the sense of proportion perturbingly lacking in his fiction between 1916 and 1924. But to say that the Tietjens novels are therapeutic is in no way to impugn their artistic success. It is because they constitute a masterpiece of writing and of form that they can be the adequate therapy and let Ford shed his sicknesses. Mizener argued that Ford's 'improved version' of events was to varying extents 'necessary to his emotional well-being' (pp. 207–8). This is true, but not in the sense he meant of Ford's fabulation being driven by an inability to face the truth (it is hard to call escapism what remains so close to what it is alleged to want to escape). It was improving the *version* that mattered to Ford's artistic well-being; wondering what details would need changing to produce a powerful effect, create a new and engrossing form.

Order and Art

It was only through the complete creative involvement and self-immersion in *Parade's End* that Ford was able to master his wartime experiences. In it, he pursues the correspondences between novel form, the idea of fiction, and the states of mind being conveyed. It brings out the element of paranoia in all plot, where, as Gillian Beer has argued, the lack of redundancy, the sense of disguised meanings behind the surface material, the drive to interpret, can make fiction seem strangely close to paranoid delusion.[173] In *The Good Soldier* Ford used the reader's complicity with Dowell in the unfolding of his story to make it impossible to distinguish a deranged subjectivity from a reliable, objective comprehension in Dowell's portraits of all the other characters. In *Parade's End* the method is quite different. He uses his prime skill at evolving an intricate tangle of references and cross-references to create, in the experience of reading the novel, an equivalent to his sense of an immense Will controlling the Destiny of the War. The use of the Wagnerian leitmotiv throughout the tetralogy does more than unify the work in the trivial sense of repetition. This occurs particularly with the title phrases, such as when, at the end of *Some Do Not . . .*, Part I, the fly-driver says: 'I wouldn't leave my wooden 'ut, nor miss my breakfast, for no beast. . . . Some do and some . . . do not' (p. 179); or when, in *A Man Could Stand Up—*, the sergeant beside Tietjens suddenly starts voicing his thoughts (just after Tietjens has been wondering about his fate, and thinking 'That's TEMPTING GOD!'): 'Then a man could stand hup on an ill' (p. 106). In both cases the effect is disorientating: how can these characters know what is going on in others' minds? There is a momentary shock of unreality, in which ideas of telepathy, or Providence, press upon the reader. In the example from *A Man Could Stand Up—* the incident is explained immediately afterwards as perhaps due to Tietjens's mental fragmentation: our uncertainty about what, psychologically, is going on, becomes an equivalent for his own momentary absence of mind: 'Presumably Tietjens had been putting heart into that acting temporary Sergeant-Major. He could not remember what he had been saying to the N.C.O. because his mind had been so deeply occupied with the image of Perowne.' But in the example from *Some Do Not . . .* there is no such explanation given. We have not been shown Christopher repeating the phrase in the man's presence, so it seems unlikely that he has just heard it. But it does not seem much more likely that he would have read the same poem that Macmaster quotes at the start of the novel (actually a rewording of the refrain running through Ford's own *Mister Bosphorus*):

> The gods to each ascribe a differing lot:
> Some enter at the portal. Some do not![174]

Is it possible that there is a hidden fate producing these echoes of the lines about fate? Macmaster had quoted them 'to himself', so it sounds as if it might be a further coincidence that Tietjens should say to Valentine: 'We're the sort that . . . *do not*!' (p. 346). Certainly here Ford wants the phrase to stand for more than a network of private allusions; it represents the rigid conventions of social morality, the pervasive obsession with what gentlemen do and what they do not do—including what they do or do not do sexually (the dots express not just resignation but also an innuendo for sexuality). He wants to elevate these into the dominant subjects of the novel. But when he has an old tramp, who has no more involvement with the story, echo the full phrase yet again, and in a position near the end of the second part which corresponds to the position of the fly-driver's speech at the end of the first, there is more at stake: ' "Some do!" He spat into the grass said "Ah!" then added: "Some do not" ' (p. 342). It is a moment of disconcerting unreality, disconcertingly dual because the phrase is also the title of the novel we are reading, so it places us dually within and without the fiction at the same time. While doing so, it gives an intimation of a controlling force operating behind the story. It represents a departure from the Conradian scruple of 'justification'—of building up a sense of inevitability by preparing each effect (such as making it seem inevitable, rather than fortuitous, that these onlookers should utter the *mots juste*). They act like the chorus in Greek tragedy (Hercules in *Mister Bosphorus* ascribes to Euripides the phrase 'The Gods ascribe to . . .'), inciting a stoic admiration for Tietjens and Valentine as heroic figures in their passion and restraint. In the case of coincidences where these two have almost identical thoughts, the effect is to create a sense of telepathic intimacy which is beyond utterance. A staunch realist would complain that Ford was contriving coincidences here too, forcing his material into trivial rather than natural patterns. But this would be to mistake the nature of the fiction, which is much more concerned to bring an awareness of its fictionality, its literariness, into the experience of reading. It is a strategy that makes *Parade's End* a much less old-fashioned, Victorian survival of a novel than it has too often been represented as being. And such a view makes Ford appear a much more innovative kind of novelist, anticipating postmodernist ideas about fabulation rather than merely harking back to a lost world of narrative omniscience.[175]

The sequence is profuse with occult as well as blatant echoes and correspondences. One major example is one which also touches again on the question of 'visions'. Freud observed that the effacement of the distinction between imagination and reality was one source of 'uncanny' feelings, and he associated the 'over-accentuation of psychical reality in comparison with material reality' with infantile and neurotic minds, where he said it was 'closely allied to the belief in the omnipotence of thoughts'. Ford's visions and interest in omnipotence may have originated in repression—of his anger towards his father; of ideas of sexuality, and particularly of the facts of death. But his *use* of them is the opposite of infantile or neurotic: rather, an attempt to stave off neurosis through the control of art. What differentiates the artist from other people is not a greater neurosis, but a greater ability to do something with thoughts and feelings. Sometimes, by an act of the very faculty Ford is discussing, visions are imagined as coming to someone other: To Oliver Madox Brown, for example, the child prodigy in both writing and dying, who Ford said 'actually saw scenes vividly with his mind's eye'.[176] There is an arresting, rapt quality about such descriptions of rapture, which would tell us—even if Ford's fiction and reminiscence did not—that he too felt the uncanny force of imagination, and saw himself to be a similar artist, and not quite like 'other men'. They are entirely characteristic of the oblique way in which Ford always wrote his most intimately autobiographic passages, refracted through descriptions of kindred personalities.

His fictional characters, too, are kindred personalities. The sympathetic imagination which creates them is grounded on a sense of kinship—of recognizing your double in someone quite other. That is to say that although Tietjens is not Ford, and much in his characterization is quite unlike his creator, some characteristics are shared; and his susceptibility to seeing visions when he is under stress is one of the most important. The two predominant ones are the vision of the dead O Nine Morgan, and the vision of the front line. One must be very careful using fiction as biographical evidence; but other evidence from other fiction as well as from autobiographical pieces makes it clear that these were both based on experiences of Ford's, and that they both acted upon him with compelling force. In *No Enemy*, a much less fictionalized book than *Parade's End*, Ford's double, Gringoire, shares the disturbing vision of the line:

And then, quite suddenly, I felt that, for thousands and thousand of miles, on the green fields and in the woodlands, stretching away under the high skies, in the August sunlight, millions, millions, millions of my fellow men were moving—like tumultuous mites in a cheese, training and training [. . .] to live a little, short space of time in an immense long ribbon of territory, where, for a mile or so the earth was scarred, macerated, beaten to a pulp, and burnt by the sun till it was all dust. . . . The thought grew, became an immense feeling, became an obsession. (p. 128)

Ford's writing about his vision of the line, and about feeling 'The Dead' of the war as a cloud-like shadow in 'A Day of Battle' and 'Epilogue'; the reiteration of the scene of O Nine Morgan's death from *The Marsden Case*; his feelings of persecution and providence—these were also obsessions, immense feelings, which it took *Parade's End* to express and to exhaust.

The different kinds of visions are connected: the single dead man, the vision of the battle-zone, the landscape turned to dust, and the creatures in the landscape many of whom will soon also be turned to dust. A stranger conjunction occurs when Sylvia has visions very similar to Christopher's. She too is almost an *halluciné*: 'Often she went into these dim trances [. . .] She seemed to be aware of the father moving about the room.' She also shares Tietjens's vision of the line, at times even reduplicating the language and images used for his vision.[177] One effect of this multiplication of visions is to imply that the stress of war pushed everyone to the edge, generating an intensity and extremity of experience: to say that 'You may say that everyone who had taken part in the war was then mad'. But Sylvia has had these experiences since childhood, like Ford; and his pre-war characters include visionaries, pre-eminently the Young Lovell.

In *Parade's End* Ford maps the line between illusion and delusion, always aware of the dizzying proximity of the fictional methods he is using to the subject-matter of war-torn psychologies. The war gave a new relevance to his constant interest in extreme states, superlative experiences, visions. As thousands suffered such experiences, they had something in common with artists, whose visionariness had traditionally alienated them. (This is the thrust of Woolf's presentation of the shell-shocked visionary Septimus Smith in *Mrs Dalloway*, for example.) If the artist can make you see too, then art can disturb your place in the social order. Just after the war Ford wrote that *les jeunes* had made progress 'in the discovery of new and individual rhythms—New Forms—with which a little to bewilder those who are growing old and slow'.[178] Art should bewilder a little; but its dual role is to do this in order to make you see: to provide a clarity of vision otherwise unattainable; an overall view, such as Tietjens hopes to attain to by standing up on a hill. Technically, Ford achieves this in part by presenting his characters' visions in a dual way too, using a free indirect style to mediate between impressionist subjectivity and omniscience; combining sympathetic imagination as we see what they see (the shadow of O Nine Morgan or Father Consett) with the critical attitude as we see them seeing (as Ford renders the attrition of exhaustion and obsession which has driven them to the edge of insanity).

Time-Shifts

One of Ford's chief resources for disturbing his readers is the time-shift. In *Ladies Whose Bright Eyes*, a work which so curiously anticipates Ford's shell-shock experi-

ence, Mr Sorrell undergoes a double displacement. He is a representative modern
man, exacerbating 'the extraordinary rush of modern life' by tipping the train driver
to get him to London faster. He is concussed when the train crashes, and he finds
himself in the fourteenth century. In the end he returns to the 'today' of 1911. We
have seen how Ford hesitates between a spiritual (fourteenth-century) and a psychological (twentieth-century) explanation. But these are both disturbing. Either 'the
fourteenth century is still here behind a curtain'; or Dionissia put the ideas into his
head in a way he was unaware of, like a form of telepathy. She too feels a disturbing
power—love—which de-realizes in order to make more real: 'Everything is different',
she tells him; 'Everything seems much more real.'[179] Because the main part of
the book, the part that seems most real to us, is the medieval part, this reunion
does read like a return to the past. With his new love of the past, and his sense
of its reality, present but invisible, Sorrell is for a second time displaced from his
century, though this time happily. At the start of the novel he is an impatient man,
frustrated by a fragmentary and hectic modernity, and cut off from history. His
traumatic time-shift back into the past acts as a therapy, returning him to the present
a whole man.

Ford's greatest fiction shares something of this form. Dowell, like Ford after the
Throne case, dismayed and exhausted amidst the ruins of all that he has loved, uses his
story to go back into his past, to try and understand what it all means, and where he
stands, and how he got there. In writing *Parade's End*, Ford went back to 1912 or 1913,
the disastrous phase in his affair with Hunt, then further back to the 1904 agoraphobic
breakdown, and then brought himself back to the present, rendering in *Last Post* the
kind of life he had reconstructed for himself. But by now his understanding of the
material was radically transformed. His worst moments with Elsie and Violet, which
had seemed like catastrophes, could now be seen as turning-points on the way to his
new life. In the war he had 'seen worse things than the social hypocrisy, unrequited
passion, and adultery that he had described in *The Good Soldier* with such an air of
desperation'; in *Parade's End* 'he was to take the romanticism and the fragile moral
conclusions of *The Good Soldier* much further'.[180] Just as *Ladies Whose Bright Eyes* also
goes back to Winterbourne Stoke and Salisbury Plain, the scene of his 1904 breakdown, and recovers Sorrell into the present, so *Parade's End* can be read as a form of
personal time-shift, enabling him fully to face his worst moments while measuring his
distance from them.

A similar idea gets into the last chapter of *Some Do Not . . .*, when Christopher and
Valentine consider the fiction of simply cutting out a passage of time from their lives—
the afternoon in which she consents to becoming his mistress, but then they think
better of it (or, in one of the novel's wonderfully disconcerting ambiguities, because
chance and Valentine's drunken brother get in the way). Tietjens, who has lost a
portion of his life in his shell-shock amnesia, insists: 'Cut it out; and join time
up. . . . It *can* be done' (p. 348). Ford's similar experience of war precipitated some of
the ideas which mattered most to him. Amnesia can be seen as a kind of oblivion, an
escape from the anxieties one does not want to remember. Romance permits the
conjuring away of the unbearable; ugliness turns to beauty, danger to happiness,
wickedness is overcome by love. Parts of Ford's life were painful enough for him to

wish to efface them, to cut them out and join time up. But amnesia is also a kind of death, a blankness of being, that threatens to turn the artist, reliant on a stock of impressions, into the stuff to fill graveyards. It is frightening and disorientating. Whereas the time-shift is a benign splicing of times in *Ladies Whose Bright Eyes*, in *The Good Soldier* it takes on the aspect of anguish. Dowell is perpetually in the wrong time, a chronological limbo, in which his vertiginous gyrating from one date to another leaves him more bewildered than ever; irrevocably exiled from his paradisal ignorance. Like this novel, *Parade's End* expresses a deep desire to escape, to efface the pain of human destructiveness. Both books oppose the wish to escape with the responsible recognition that you cannot escape your past, your history. The Fordian time-shift thus has a paradoxical, dual effect. For, though you may not be able to cut time out of your own life, artists can—must—do precisely that to their characters. But the cutting and joining of time that is Fordian impressionism cuts not in order to efface, but to face. Typically, a character is presented at a crucial, intolerable moment. The narrative then cuts back to a less tense time, seeming to flinch from pain. But the purpose of cutting is to work back towards the crucial moment, showing how it came about, what forces are at work within it. By the time we are returned to the narrative present, the issue has been faced more thoroughly than is often possible in a straightforwardly chronological treatment.

The time-shift offers a means of expressing bewilderment and a sense of fragmentation while at the same time bringing the fragments under control; or rather, like all expressive forms, it expresses *by* controlling the feelings that bewilder and threaten 'Ordered Life', reordering life for its own purposes; winning artistic form from out of psychological and emotional chaos. *Parade's End*'s massive scope and intricately tangled complexity enable it to do justice to that chaos. He renders his obsessional feeling about the war as an overwhelming movement of history by marshalling a bewildering multitude of impressions. An important aspect of *Parade's End* is its Proustian project of recovering lost time: the lost era of Edwardian innocence; the lost years of the war; the lost weeks of shell-shock. In conceiving his largest design since *The Fifth Queen*, Ford was asserting that he had not lost, or lost control of, his memory. He was countering a double threat: not only the original shell-induced amnesia, but its sequel, the fear that his memory of the war was beginning to fade.

The Power of the Word

Parade's End juxtaposes many different ways in which the mind exercises control over experience. Some examples (art, history, politics, statistics, schools, psychological repression) have already been discussed. Others include mathematics, the army, talk. Most important for a writer, however, and especially for as technically aware a writer as Ford, is the power of the written word itself both to disturb and to control. So it is not surprising that the tetralogy abounds with examples of literature, and in particular examples of different literary modes of organizing details: the observations of the naturalist Gilbert White; the novels of Mrs Wannop; Macmaster's dry monograph; even encyclopaedias, offered as an alternative to personal memory as a means of ordering knowledge. Writing which makes you see has a problematic relationship to a war the carnage and attrition of which made people stop seeing. An anecdote in

'Towards a History of English Literature' concerns this curious relationship between vision and language in the experience of war:

I was standing, then, with three other officers in the mouth of a regimental dump in a disagreeable valley during the fighting on the Somme in July 1916 [. . .] It was a quite quiet evening, and we were waiting for dinner. In front of us, fifty yards away or so were four A.S.C. men standing in a small circle, gossiping, each with the bridle reins of three mules looped through his elbows behind him. A German shell dropped and exploded in the very centre of that small circle. One man and three mules lay on the ground; the other three men after fighting for a moment with their animals let them go and bent over the man on the ground. The mules began to graze at once.

Being officers we naturally had to take charge, do what we could for the man, send to the Red Cross people whose station was in the wood just behind us, and so on. A piece of shell had gone right through that man.

Well, we went back into the dug out for our dinner and were eating and conversing very peaceably about the playing of a hand of bridge that we had lately finished. Then, the talk drifting, one of the young fellows began to talk of an operation for appendicitis he had had to undergo. We had to stop him: the mere talking of cutting flesh with a knife made us feel sick. Yet the sight of a man literally smashed into the dust had produced no emotions in us: certainly hardly more than I have put into the two paragraphs recording the affair. I know of no more striking tribute to the power of the word; at any rate I have come across none. . .[181]

One of the shocks of war was to find that ordered narrative could have more of an obvious effect upon the mind than direct experiences of battle. Such loss of affectivity is a condition found in paranoia; so one could see it as part of the paranoid state induced by being under fire; though it is also a necessity for the preservation of sanity under such conditions. This is the paradox explored in 'A Day of Battle'; that, as when Dowell hears about Florence's death, the impression can seem to make no impression. Literature could make you see what your mind was trying to stop you seeing; to illustrate which, Ford told stories of how his reading seemed more real to him than the war which surrounded him; in one example that he retold often, he got so engrossed rereading Crane's *The Red Badge of Courage* that he was surprised when he looked up to find the troops not wearing the uniforms of the American Civil War.[182] Clearly the extreme reaction to the story about appendicitis has something to do with the way the story has aroused the feelings that the officers were trying to suppress: the eating men and cut flesh bring to mind the grazing mules and smashed body. The reaction to the explosion was to de-realize it; the effect on the dinner-story is to make it seem unbearably hyper-real. In the act of retelling the stories to us Ford is again unleashing the disturbing feelings of the time; yet his controlled rendering of the emotionless responses is simultaneously a means of controlling those feelings. One of the curious features of this story is that he gives no details about the operation-story that made the officers feel sick; so that whereas for them the dinner-time story apparently made more impression than the explosion, we are given an impression of the explosion rather than the operation-story, yet from this we ought to be able to intuit their reaction to the story. The Arts, as Ford wrote elsewhere in the series, 'do not work by direct means'.[183] Part of Ford's attraction to the idea of the English Gentleman was that the discipline of the stiff upper lip, of English understatement, had much in common with the discipline of writing restrained, tonally subdued, prose. As before the war, he found the suppression of feeling its most poignant expression; and, as in this story, a refusal to be demoralized, almost a fictive cheeriness, was *de rigueur* in the army. Ford's fascination with self-suppression continues throughout—and beyond—the tetralogy. But the war gave him a further image for such mental discipline: the physical discipline of military drill. Tietjens is impressed by the effectiveness of drill:

It was a very great achievement to have got men to fire at moments of such stress with such complete tranquillity. For discipline works in two ways: In the first place it enables the soldier in action to get through his *movements* in the shortest possible time; and then the *engrossment* in the *exact performance* begets a great *indifference* to danger. When, with various sized pieces of metal flying all round you, you go *composedly* through efficient bodily movements, you are not only wrapped up in your task, you have the knowledge that that *exact performance* is every minute decreasing your personal danger. In addition you have the feeling that *Providence* ought to—and very frequently does—specially protect you.[184]

Ford too found it fascinating as a psychological phenomenon; but he went further, finding the psychology of military discipline an unexpected analogy for the psychology of art:

During the late war, for instance, the aggressive and Intellectual classes used to ask unceasingly what purpose was served in 'trench' warfare by jumping to it on parade at home. The effect is psychological [. . .]
    And the effect of imaginative culture on the natural mind engaged in human affairs is much that of drill on troops afterwards to be engaged in warfare. It affords and inspires confidence; it furnishes you with illustration in argument, knowledge of human nature, vicarious experience. It makes of the intelligent savage—a proper man![185]

The language here is provocative of the dual response: there is a provocative posture of Colonel Blimp in the crescendo saying that war will make a man of you, which would have sounded anachronistic to the Lost Generation reading this in 1924, or would sound preposterous to subsequent generations who read the war through the poetry of Owen and Sassoon, where the received military wisdom is at best an incompetent charade and at worst blind murderous inhumanity. But we do a double-take as we realize that rather than saying it is war that makes a 'proper man' out of you, Ford is actually saying that art does. Furthermore, what interests him about the parallel with army drill is not its totalitarian subordination of the individual will, but the individual and oblique psychological effects it produces, which help to save individual lives.

One of the changes we can register between *The Good Soldier* and *Parade's End* is that Dowell's corrosive self-doubt about whether he—or even Ashburnham—is a proper man or not has been replaced by the tetralogy's vindication of Tietjens's proper manhood. There is less self-pity in Ford's writing from *Parade's End* onwards—perhaps because feeling he had been saved by Providence persuaded him that he wasn't pitiable; where it does loom large in his later novels (especially *When the Wicked Man* and *The Rash Act*) it is as something the protagonist learns to escape. In the figure of Tietjens Ford manages to allay most of his uncertainties about the possible effeminacy or insanity of the artist. And in the image of army drill he has shifted from the position of *The Young Lovell*, where the artist-like vision of the White Lady threatens destruction, to a position where art is seen rather as a discipline which fortifies the mind against destruction. I think Ford felt that the war *had* made a proper man of him, though not in the sense of the *macho* rhetoric of the recruiting officer. It was, rather, because the war had almost destroyed him, but had given him the psychological experiences and insights needed to reconstruct himself, and then make us see what he had seen. The idea that art inspires self-confidence is elaborated in the story discussed earlier, 'The Miracle', written soon after he had finished *Parade's End*. By narrating his 'impressions', however bizarre or dubious they might be, the Professor sustains his new-found belief in himself. Ford was reflecting upon what he had been doing in *Parade's End*. The implication is that it is not merely the baptism of fire that transformed him, but its confirmation in novels. It is in this sense that *Parade's End* was therapeutic, since it was in the writing of it that he convinced himself that he was a whole man, purged and regenerated by the war, and now healed of his scars. His conviction was no delusion. William Carlos Williams has not been alone in thinking that the four Tietjens books 'constitute the English prose masterpiece of their time'.[186]

1924–1926: JEAN RHYS

The loss of the *transatlantic* and the controversy about *Joseph Conrad* weighed upon Ford. On Christmas Eve he told Sisley Huddleston they had 'been rather under the cloud of a house full of grippe & coughs' for nearly a month, but were 'making efforts to celebrate Xtmas with a tree for Esther Julia, rather lastminuteish'. Friends were invited to come and sample some of his great-uncle Tristram Madox's punch ('the delight of Brummell and the Regent': 'Jamaica rum, one bottle; French brandy, one-half bottle; port wine, one bottle; hock, six bottles; hard cider, six bottles; soda water, six syphons; maraschino, one-quarter bottle; the peel of fresh limes, one dozen small; the juice of fresh lemons, one dozen small'; served warm). He was feeling vulnerable. Jean Rhys reappeared.[1]

She had probably met Ford around October, when her journalist friend Mrs (H. Pearl) Adam recommended she should submit her manuscripts to the *transatlantic*. Rhys had shown Mrs Adam a long piece in diary-form. Mrs Adam rearranged it into parts and gave it the *faux-naif* title *Suzy Tells*. Ford printed the episode 'Vienne' in the last issue of the review, saying that it was 'from the novel called Triple Sec'. Not only had he changed the name of the fiction, but he also changed the name of the author, from Ella Lenglet to Jean Rhys. She rapidly became a member of Ford's entourage, drinking at the Dôme, the Closerie des Lilas, and the Deux Magots, dining in the back room of the Nègre de Toulouse, and coming to the *bal musette*. Ford had recognized her natural talent at once, but he showed her how to improve her writing, and encouraged her to write stories. At first they had melodramatic endings, she said; but 'Ford stopped that and told me to write about what I knew'. He also told her to put away stories that were giving her trouble, and to work on others.

'I can't think of any,' I said sulkily.
'Then try to translate one of my books into French. It will be very good practice for you.'
'I don't know French well enough to translate one of your books,' I said.
'Then try *La Maison Claudine*. Bring me the first chapter tomorrow.'[2]

He advised her how to cut and polish. 'One of the tricks he taught me', she explained: 'if you aren't sure of something you've written, translate it into French. If it doesn't seem right then, it's wrong.' As Carole Angier says, 'He was the first man since her father who told her that she was good at something. And unlike her father he showed her, at last, what it really was.'[3]

He was 51 that December. She was 34, but looked more like 20: one of *les jeunes*, with whom he could console himself for the loss of the review. She was attractive; her past romantic: she had been born in Dominica of Welsh and Scottish stock, though one of her great-grandmothers was said to have been Spanish and to have come from

Cuba. Rhys had worked as a chorus-girl in London. She had had a son who died at three weeks, and then a daughter she couldn't keep, and had left in a clinic. On 28 December 1924 Rhys's Dutch husband, Jean Lenglet, was arrested for embezzling money from the travel firm he had been working for. His story was that he had borrowed it in order to do a deal, but had lost money and so wasn't able to replace it before its absence was noticed. He was detained in the Santé prison for six weeks before his trial. She was poor, ill, and desperate. Bowen said that when they met her she was down to her last three francs, and 'possessed nothing but a cardboard suit-case and the astonishing manuscript' of 'an unpublishably sordid novel of great sensitiveness and persuasiveness'. Rhys recalled in the 1970s that the second time she met the Fords they asked her to go and live with them. She remembered that Bowen was particularly persuasive. It was as fateful a step as when Violet Hunt had asked first Brigit Patmore then Bowen herself down to Selsey, and had much the same consequences. Ford and Rhys fell in love. Their affair lasted for about a year and a half. And although Ford was still living with Bowen until 1928, it was decisive for all three. 'It cut the fundamental tie between himself and me', wrote Bowen. Rhys's despair after the end of the affair drove her further towards alcoholism; but it also produced her first powerful novel, *Postures*, later renamed *Quartet*, which despite being 'the least honest and the most self-excusing of Jean's novels', is virtually a *roman à clef* about the Fords and the Lenglets.[4]

The details of the affair are as difficult to ascertain as such things should be; though the difficulty of establishing hard facts is compounded by the wealth of fictional evidence. For besides Bowen's brief account in her memoirs (which don't mention Rhys by name), there are novels by each of the other three. Rhys's *Postures* (1928). Lenglet's duller (but probably historically more reliable) novel *Sous les verrous*, which he published in 1933 under the pseudonym 'Edouard de Nève', because he didn't want it known he'd been in prison. (Rhys herself had even translated and altered this work as *Barred* in 1932.) Finally, there is Ford's novel *When the Wicked Man*, written the year after *Quartet* appeared, but not published until 1931. Lola Porter in that novel, with her Creole origins, drunken violence, and 'vampire Carmen' demeanour, is at one level Ford's revenge for Rhys's portrait of him as H. J. Heidler in *Quartet*. Nevertheless, thanks to Carole Angier's marvellous speculative reconstruction, superimposing the various accounts, it is possible to sketch the main sequence of events.[5]

Paul Nash and his wife Margaret met Ford 'in the company of an attractive blonde'—Rhys—at the brasserie of the Gare de Lyons in December 1924. Ford had stayed with the Nashes at Dymchurch at the end of 1922 while Nash was illustrating *Mister Bosphorus and the Muses*. As the Nashes were getting into their train for the Riviera, Ford 'rushed along the platform and threw a bunch of keys at Paul, explaining that the little blond lady, to whom he had introduced us, had got into the train much higher up and had left the keys of her suitcase with him by mistake'. He told them he would write to Rhys and put her in touch with them. 'I bumped into that old rascal Ford', Nash told their mutual friend Tony Bertram: 'He was extricating or further involving himself—God knows which—by, with, or from some woman, some more or less new one, and looked a little distracted. I think she'd been making him a scene. He looked more like Silenus in tweeds than ever and was lamentably short of wind.'[6]

This could mean their affair had already begun (though before the discovery of this episode it was not thought to have started until she came to live with the Fords). Alternatively, her distress may have been more to do with Lenglet's arrest. It is odd that Rhys should have left Paris while her husband was in the Santé prison, but not impossible. In *Quartet* she compresses the six weeks between the arrest and the sentencing into about two weeks. The missing four could have included a brief stay on the Riviera, which she then cut lest they jeopardized readers' sympathy for Marya. As Carole Angier observes, in both *Quartet* and *Sous les verrous* the husband and wife are unable to contact each other for several days. This might have been because she had been too upset to stay in Paris. Nash detected her distress, and described her as 'The Ghost', because she never seemed to have 'any real existence', only a 'very pathetic and eventful history'.

Like the Nashes, she stayed at Cros de Cagnes, but claimed the only room she could find was in a bordello. When she turned up at their pension, 'The proprietress was aghast that Nash had the keys of such a woman in his keeping and assumed she was his mistress. She was flummoxed when Margaret calmly announced that she must have the woman's address in order to invite her to dinner. The proprietor [. . .] sighed: "Ah, les Anglais, what diplomats they are."' She doesn't appear to have stayed for long. She got 'frightened by her surroundings', and the Nashes paid her fare back to Paris: 'she then disappeared from our lives in the same ghost-like way in which she had appeared', said Margaret Nash.[7]

Rhys was certainly back by 25 January, when she was staying at the Fords' cottage in Guermantes while Lenglet was awaiting trial. William Bradley, whom Ford had befriended on the 1906 trip to America, was now living in Paris and acting as his agent, since Ford did not trust Pinker's son Eric after the row over the republishing of the Conrad collaborations. (He may have been right: both Pinker's sons Ralph and Eric went to prison for embezzlement.) Ford had to ask Bradley to cash a cheque, because: 'Stella is in bed with the flu, rather seriously, and I do not know when we shall get up to Paris or a bank and in the meantime the house is full of people, Miss Rhys being also sick and I have to do all the cooking and most of the house work, so I am too moider [American slang: murdered] to think of anything else but bothering you.'[8] On 10 February Lenglet was tried, and sentenced to eight months' imprisonment. He was taken to Fresnes, a southern suburb of Paris. It was probably at this point that Rhys agreed to live with the Fords. In *Quartet* the Heidlers insist that she should come. 'Now, look here', says Lois (Bowen), 'we want you to move into the spare room at the studio.' Marya Zelli (the Rhysean heroine) has initial qualms, but the Heidlers overwhelm her: ' "When can you move?" asked Heidler. "Tomorrow?"' Then her husband Stephan (Jean Lenglet) also urges her to accept: he can't see how else she can live. Lois intimates that her husband (she calls him by his initials 'H.J.'—for Henry James?) has had other affairs: ' "You know," Lois added, "H.J., I love him so terribly . . . and he isn't always awfully nice to me.' This confession of vulnerability makes Lois seem more sympathetic to Marya, and instead of alerting her to the danger of making a *menage à trois*, it inclines her to join them. Rhys's suggestion here—that Bowen was (like Leonora Ashburnham) prepared to countenance her man's affairs if she could manage them herself so as to keep him—rings false. It was Lenglet's view that Stella was complicit in the affair so as not to lose Ford. And it may be true that she was prepared to turn a blind eye once she realized what was happening, and perhaps realized that the affair couldn't last, and that it needn't destroy her life and Julie's home. But she said she was 'singularly slow in discovering' that Ford and Rhys were in love.[9]

Ford was finishing *No More Parades*, the second volume of the Tietjens series, and the book he had begun after he'd finished *Joseph Conrad*. He finished it on 25 March, in under five months. Tietjens's predicament, entangled in the familiar two passions, owes most to Ford's own wartime history, as he fell in love with Bowen and disentangled himself from Hunt. But now, as he was transforming those years into fiction, he had re-created, or helped to re-create, a similar scenario. There is no evidence that any of the tetralogy's characters are based on Rhys. But the sexually charged atmosphere of *No More Parades*, with Sylvia trying to seduce her husband, while others (his military superiors) burst into their bedroom, may have been influenced by the beginnings of Ford's affair with Rhys. He was certainly writing again with the force and anguish that new passions elicited from him. At first the atmosphere was probably restrained. In *Quartet* Marya serves Heidler his coffee in the mornings, and he disappears behind his newspaper: 'He had abruptly become the remote impersonal male of the establishment.' She tells her friend Cairn that the Heidlers have been 'wonderfully nice' to her. In *Sous les verrous* Stania tells Jan the Hübners are 'très gentil pour moi'. But then Ford became less impersonal. He would read out Rhys's prose in front of Stella, exclaiming 'Cliché! Cliché'. 'If he liked what he read, he put on a special solemn voice': 'He took her to the Cluny museum to see the tapestries, and took her to meet people: Hemingway, and Gertrude Stein (Jean talked with Alice), and once, going to a party, they shared the lift with James Joyce, who stood behind Jean and told her the back of her dress was undone, and he tried to hook it up.' In private Ford was making love to her. He was 'a romantic snob', she said later: 'his great ambition was to be like an Englishman, but a certain kind of Englishman, strong and silent, and sometimes he succeeded.' *Quartet* has Lois leaving the two of them alone in a bar after an evening at the *bal musette*. 'Do you know why Lois has gone off?', asked Heidler. And it is here that Rhys too suggests Bowen's complicity: 'She's gone away to leave us together—to give me a chance to talk to you, d'you see? She knows that I'm dying with love for you, burnt up with it, tortured with it.' Carole Angier says Heidler sounds just like Ashburnham, and Ford. And it's true that the scenario follows the Ashburnhams' pattern of taking in young women (Maisie Maidan, Nancy Rufford) and then taking them in. But Heidler sounds ridiculous in a way Ashburnham never does, precisely because Ford doesn't reproduce his passionate speeches. Heidler explains that he comes and opens Marya's door every night in order to look at her: 'One does meaningless things like that when one is tortured by desire. Don't you know that I wanted you the first time I saw you?' 'I love you, my dear, I love you. And I wish I were dead. For God's sake, be a little kind to me.' And so on. Sometimes he sounds more like Dowell: 'One knows that the whole damn thing's idiotic, futile, not even pleasant, but one goes on.' He explains that he and Lois have an 'arrangement': 'Lois and I each go our own way [. . .].' Marya makes an ineffectual effort to leave, but Lois dissuades her: 'It seems such a pity to smash up all our plans for you, just because H.J. imagines that he's in love with you—for the minute.' She goes on 'in a reflective voice': 'Of course, mind you, he wants things badly when he does want them. He's a whole hogger.' (Compare Bowen: 'when Ford wanted anything, he filled the sky with an immense ache that had the awful simplicity of a child's grief'; or her comment apropos Ford's infatuation with Rhys: 'He had got over it in due course.') When she tells Heidler she wants to go, he says 'in an impersonal voice': 'But that's not playing the game, is it?' The idea of its original title, 'Postures', is that 'Everybody pretends'. But whereas the Heidlers sound merely insincere, Marya's eventual succumbing to Heidler is presented as a pathetic-ally sincere failure to go on pretending: 'when she thought of an existence without Heidler her heart turned over in her side and she felt sick.'[10]

Lois wants to use Marya as a model, and while she is sitting for a portrait talks to her: 'Some of H.J.'s discoveries I wouldn't trust a yard', she says. 'Lois also discussed Love, Childbirth (especially childbirth, for the subject fascinated her), Complexes, Paris, Men, Prostitution, and Sensitiveness, which she thought an unmitigated nui-sance.' To Marya she gives 'a definite impression of being insensitive to the point of stupidity—or was it insensitive to the point of cruelty?' But Bowen was neither stupid nor cruel, and her memoir isn't insensitive. It was Ford's neurasthenic sensitivity, or the masochistic sensitivity of Rhys's victim role that irked her:

Life with Ford had always felt to me pretty insecure. Yet here I was cast for the role of the fortunate wife who held all the cards, and the girl for that of the poor, brave and desperate beggar who was doomed to be let down by the bourgeoisie. I learnt what a powerful weapon lies in weakness and pathos and how strong is the position of the person who has nothing to lose, and I simply hated my role![11]

This is exactly how Rhys cast the roles in *Quartet*, and to do so she had to make the Heidlers bourgeois (H.J. is a dealer in pictures rather than an artist), and married (as Ford and Bowen were not); and she makes Lois appear considerably older than Marya's 28 (whereas in fact Rhys was three years older than Bowen's 31). Ford too was struck by the life of destitution and recklessness that Rhys revealed to them. Sylvia Tietjens's insouciance may owe something to Rhys's self-destructiveness (for Violet Hunt cared too much about her reputation to publicize her infidelities as Sylvia does).[12]

In *Quartet* the Heidlers take Marya to their cottage at Brunoy, which is based on Guermantes. Ford probably spent most of the spring and summer there. 'I am going to resume turning my *Good Soldier* into French', a job that ought to have been finished by now', he told Jeanne Foster as soon as he had finished *No More Parades*. But we only have the thirty-seven page beginning, which was probably done two or three years earlier. He was writing uncharacteristically little that summer. He told Jeanne Foster in March that they were 'violently occupied' with the garden and with a second house ('said to be fourteenth century but not of course so old') that they had taken next to their cottage. Bowen called this 'a primitive kind of annexe with a beamed ceiling and an open fireplace, which made a good study for Ford'. He needed the room when they gave up their flat at 16 rue Denfert-Rochereau in the summer. He sounded buoyant when he told Foster: 'My young American friends say that [*No More Parades*] is one of the world's masterpieces, to be compared only with the Divine Comedy of

Dante. They probably exaggerate.' Mizener says Ford 'took things comparatively easy' for a while; but Rhys's and Lenglet's fictional versions suggest another story. In *Quartet* Marya begins to feel that Lois hates her. At Brunoy she confronts the Heidlers, accusing them of having made an 'arrangement'—'If he wants the woman let him have her'. There is a screaming row, in which Heidler is brutal to both women, then buries his face in his arms sobbing, then says 'in a calm and as it were explanatory way' that he's 'awfully drunk', adding: 'I'm going to bed. I shan't remember a thing about all this tomorrow morning.'[13]

When Lenglet was released from Fresnes on 18 June 1925 he probably stayed in Paris for a few days before being expelled. In *Quartet* and *Sous les verrous* Marya and Stania find hotel rooms for their husbands. Heidler has threatened to stop seeing Marya if she goes back to her husband. She does, but feels alienated from Stephan, who is broken and distracted by prison, and leaves for Amsterdam without her. Desperate, and still in love with Heidler, she summons him; but he rejects her. But the novel foreshortens the affair, placing its gruesome ending a year early. In *Sous les verrous*, when Jan leaves for Belgium (helped by Hübner's money), Hübner is with Stania at the station to see him off. Jan feels that if she cries at the farewell, it is only because her pity briefly overcomes her happiness at being Hübner's from now on. Yet the affair was engrossing and enervating Ford too. 'I have been going about in a state of deep depression', he told Bradley. He attributed this to thinking *No More Parades* seemed 'to be appalling in slip proofs'; but when he read the page proofs he thought 'it really seems to be something heavy and gloomy and big' (which is perhaps how he was feeling that June?): 'So I may yet knock spots off Mr Dostoevski, though that secret ambition of mine should be kept between ourselves.'[14]

The Heidlers didn't want Marya to leave at first in case a sudden departure caused a scandal. Lois doesn't want it known that her husband has affairs. Whether or not this was true of Ford and Bowen, they now wanted her to go—perhaps because Ford's infatuation had burnt itself out at Guermantes, or because they had been afraid of Rhys's violent outburst. What happened next, as Rhys remembered, was that 'A friend of an American lady came to Montparnasse searching for someone cheap to help her write a book [. . .] Ford and Stella both did their best to help me get this job':

I can still see Stella talking persuasively about how nice I was and how the American lady would be sure to like me. Ford wrote first an article on English 18th century furniture and next a Serbian Folk story saying I'd written both. I didn't mind this a bit as I quite agreed it was high time I got away from Montparnasse. So there I was on a very slow train which of course Ford had assured me was a very quick one, on my way to Juan Les Pins. It was the month of July and very hot.[15]

The American lady was Mrs Richard Hudnut, whose family had a large cosmetics firm, and whose daughter married Rudolph Valentino. Mrs Hudnut wanted Rhys to ghost a book 'on Reincarnation and Furniture' (Ford's use of the name in *Parade's End* for a furniture dealer is an appropriate joke). Her idea was that happiness could be reached by living in the same costumes and decors of your previous lives. The job was farcical: Rhys couldn't type or take shorthand, and was no historian. But the Hudnuts were kind to her, and she said she had 'an extremely happy time' at the luxurious

Château Juan-les-Pins. She was probably there for several months, and hoping to stay on the Riviera when this job was over, working for the Hudnuts' friends, when Mrs Hudnut had what she called 'a most extraordinary letter from Mr Ford'. The letter has disappeared, but apparently Rhys had written to tell him (or Bowen) that Mrs Hudnut wanted her to do a book of fairy stories as well, and Ford wrote back accusing her of exploiting Rhys 'disgracefully' by trying to get two books for the price of one. (He later explained that the letter had to be written because Mrs Hudnut was paying her a 'ridiculous' amount: 'He said that she was a very rich woman but that she was paying me less than she'd have to pay a competent housemaid in New York.' But she may have mentioned the advances Mr Hudnut had been making, and Ford may have written the letter in order to get her back, or because he thought she expected him to rescue her again.) The Hudnuts were furious, and told her that she'd obviously prefer not to be exploited, so she should telegraph the Fords to tell them she would be on the train to Paris the next day. She didn't go at once, but before she did the story came out that Mr Hudnut had been kissing her when he took her to the Casino at Monte Carlo 'Nearly every Sunday'. 'I didn't see any harm in it at all', said Rhys (thus casting doubt on the presumption that Marya's initial unwillingness with Heidler proves Rhys's with Ford); but the chauffeur had been watching in the mirror. In the event, Mrs Hudnut travelled to Paris with Rhys, and appeared to have 'thawed towards the end'. Ford met them at the Gare de Lyons, 'looking very pleased'; Mrs Hudnut 'gave him one look up and down then walked off with the porter and luggage'. He took her to a hotel where he had booked her a room. 'When I saw the room I thought of the Chateau Juan les Pins', she said, 'and very nearly burst into tears.'[16]

'It was after this that all the trouble started', wrote Rhys, meaning that it was now that she suffered the most. The 'Hotel de Rive' was near the Gare Montparnasse, as is Marya's Hôtel du Bosphore in *Quartet*. This was probably when Ford would visit her hotel room, as Heidler does Marya's:

He wasn't a good lover of course. He didn't really like women. She had known that as soon as he touched her. His hands were inexpert, clumsy at caresses; his mouth was hard when he kissed. No, not a lover of women, he could say what he like.

He despised love. He thought of it grossly, to amuse himself, and then with ferocious contempt. Not that that mattered [. . .] What mattered was that, despising, almost disliking, love, he was forcing her to be nothing but the little woman who lived in the Hôtel du Bosphore for the express purpose of being made love to. A *petite femme*. It was, of course, part of his mania for classification. But he did it with such conviction that she, miserable weakling that she was, found herself trying to live up to his idea of her.[17]

'He always hurried the end of his dressing, as if getting out of her bedroom would be an escape', wrote Rhys of Heidler; as he goes he leaves Marya some money. The rendering of Marya's squalor and misery is compellingly precise. Rhys's free indirect style is insinuating itself into Marya's thoughts, so perhaps we are supposed to wonder whether it is a true insight, or a blindness about her own masochistic listlessness. But is Heidler a good likeness of Ford? The two main things lacking from *Quartet* are the two essential facts of her relationship with Ford: the fact that they were both writers, and that he helped her writing; and the fact that she found him loveable. Rhys told Francis Wyndham that she regretted writing it with so much 'spite'. Later, she emphasized both the help and the passion: 'When it came to writing he was a very generous man and he encouraged me a great deal. I really don't think that he tried to impose his ideas on me or anyone else but his casual hints could be extremely helpful.' Generosity and encouragement don't figure in *Quartet*, where help is a trap, and endearments are barbed. Its bleak world seems not to comprehend men who do love women; it is a machine for their inexorable humiliation. If this is true to a cruel aspect of Rhys's relationship with Ford, it is quite unlike anything recorded of him by Elsie Hueffer, Violet Hunt, Stella Bowen, or Janice Biala, who said: 'unlike most men, Ford truly liked women—aside from being in love with them, etc.' Many readers of his novels would find the suggestion that he didn't really like women extraordinary. Rhys later told her editor and friend Diana Athill:

in real life the unhappiness was *much* more over having no money and my husband being in prison than it was about love. Ford wasn't in the least in love with me—God knows what he felt, he was a mystery to me, but I think he just hated being alone when Stella went into the country—and I wasn't in love with him. It's just that I was stuck and there was no-one else to help me.

But she told David Plante a very different story: 'Ford seemed her only friend. She fell for him. She thought she fell for him.' Francis Wyndham, who knew her well, suspects that she was very much in love with Ford—which is, anyway, clear from *Sous les verrous* and from *Quartet*'s anger.[18]

Duckworth published *No More Parades* in England in September. The novel's skill was widely acclaimed ('an astonishing method, and astonishingly effective'; 'an amazingly good, an heroic book'). Hugh Walpole found it 'the most remarkable picture of our Army in France that fiction has yet given us'. Edwin Muir said it was 'admirable [. . .] as a piece of technique; but it is also something more, for Mr. Ford has genuinely felt his theme' (though Muir found Tietjens's impassivity baffling, saying that Ford had imagined him in particular situations, but not 'in himself'). Some reviewers used 'that terrible word genius' that Ford wrote to earn. But the figure of Sylvia Tietjens provoked unease. Some, like the reviewer in *Times Literary Supplement*, praised the way that, 'with very great skill, Mr. Ford has packed an amazing impression of war', but went on to criticize his 'mixing up extremely unpleasant private affairs with his picture of war'. Ford, in other words, was still writing about things gentlemen were not supposed to discuss. Sylvia was perceived as 'one of the most thoroughly disgusting women in modern fiction' by someone who clearly didn't know Violet Hunt: 'there is no such woman outside a lunatic asylum or even [. . .] inside one.'[19]

When Albert and Charles Boni got the American edition out in November its reviews were less qualified. The Tietjens series was hailed as a 'Proustian Project'. Isabel Paterson, who later became a friend, and got *Last Post* dedicated to her, called *No More Parades* 'far and away the finest novel of the year'. Hemingway said that Louis Bromfield and Ford 'seem the most generally admired novelists in N.Y.'. Mary Colum (wife of Padraic, and later another friend) said it was 'probably the most highly praised novel of the year', and wrote a perceptive piece arguing that it was 'not a thoroughgoing English book', but 'as if it were the work of one of those aliens in the British Empire, Celt or Semite, who in their souls resent what England stands for'.

Ford's sympathies are more dual than this: he admires the England Tietjens stands for too. But Colum suggests why *Parade's End* is even now regarded more highly in America. She thought that, like the work of Eliot and cummings, it appealed to intellectuals (presumably because their sense of alienation was comparable). Yet whereas it sold only about 1,000 copies in England, in America the Boni edition went into at least five printings, selling over 9,000 copies by the end of 1926, and 12,601 copies before it went out of print in 1931; there was also a cheap reprint by Grosset and Dunlap in 1928. It must have been Ford's best-selling book so far. When he had told Scott-James that *Some Do Not . . .* had been well-received in America, he added: 'It was about time that I cut my notch in that country. Otherwise I am rapidly becoming a French writer.' He never lost his love of French stylists, but from now on he would speak more of becoming an American writer.[20]

In the autumn of 1925 Nina Hamnett found a studio for the Fords at 84 rue Notre-Dame des Champs, right in the heart of his beloved Montparnasse. There was plenty of space, but no kitchen, bathroom, or even living accommodation: just 'a water-tap, and electric light, and some heavy, moveable screens'. It has been part of Delecluse's Academy of Art. They decided to install an enclosed gallery with a bedroom and bathroom. 'Madame Annie and Julie, when in Paris, would have to be accommodated on two divans, behind the screens'. The view was, as usual, charming, overlooking the trees of a convent garden. Ford was working on *A Mirror to France*, his paean to French life and culture. Gertrude Stein told how one day while Hemingway was explaining to her why he wouldn't be able to review *The Making of Americans*, 'a heavy hand fell on his shoulder and Ford Madox Ford said, young man it is I who wish to speak to Gertrude Stein. Ford then said to her, I wish to ask your permission to dedicate my new book to you. May I.' She was 'awfully pleased'; even more so when she saw it: 'I am more pleased and touched than I can tell you with my book', she wrote. Later that year she dedicated to 'Miss Julia Ford' *A Book Concluding with As a Wife has a Cow*, illustrated by Juan Gris.[21]

They had little furniture for the new studio, and had to camp there while the builders were working on it. Nevertheless, they held a children's tea-party on Christmas Day, after lunch at the Nègre de Toulouse. 'Ford dressed up as le Père Noël', recalled Nina Hamnett: 'He looked magnificent as he was very tall.' He and Bowen then decided on a winter holiday in Toulon. The devaluation of the franc meant that they could just afford it. Their friends the Spanish painter Juan Gris and his wife Josette were there, and Josette found them rooms at the Hôtel Victoria. (Ford was to base the character of Marie Léonie Tietjens on her.) They took with them their Alsatian puppy, called Toulouse (because M. Lavigne, the owner of Le Nègre de Toulouse, had given him to them). Bowen said she 'fell in love with Toulon at first sight'. Its picturesque harbour, the quay lined with shabby but colourful old houses, its mountain backdrop, and bustling markets appealed to her painterly eye. It wasn't touristy. Josette Gris told them as they arrived: 'Il y a cinq cinémas et deux dancings. Ca fait juste la semaine!' The social life was geared to sailors. 'Why don't you come to Toulon', Ford suggested to Gerald Duckworth: 'It's delightful here now and wonderfully gay with the Navy—and cheap because the Navy has not got any money.' One day when British sailors began to overcrowd their favourite 'dancing' with a Russian balalaika band, a class-conscious Ford whispered to Bowen: 'Dance with a seaman if you like, but not with a petty officer.' It was a carefree break from Paris, Jean Rhys, house-moving, and the northern cold. Gris was impressed by Ford when they celebrated New Year's Eve together: 'He absorbs a terrifying quantity of alcohol. I never thought one could drink so much.' He found Ford 'middle-aged, rather drunken and quite witty'. Perhaps, like Rhys, he was drinking their affair into oblivion. Gris did a sketch of Ford for the *Saturday Review of Literature*. 'I rather like Ford in spite of all his eccentricities', he was to tell Gertrude Stein later in the year—the eccentricities being that he seemed to Gris to be 'always giving himself airs for some mysterious reason'.[22]

Their circle included Francis Carco (the author of *Perversité*); the critic Georges Duthuit (whose father-in-law, Matisse, was duly brought to dine with the Fords); and the painters Louis Latapie and Othon Friesz. The conversation was stimulating. Bowen was particularly glad to be hearing about painting; Friesz found her a studio below his in a quayside warehouse, 3 bis Quai du Parti, at £10 a year. Ford too found Toulon a delightful place to work. He began *A Man Could Stand Up*— and finished *A Mirror to France* in January, and was 'getting on pretty well with my novel' in the spring. Provence had always been his spiritual home; it was rapidly becoming hers too. They began looking for a house in the countryside to buy, and made an offer 'for an old five-roomed house on a hill with a shady *terrassed* garden. Luckily for our finances the offer was refused.' One day someone startled Bowen in the hotel restaurant by saying: 'Oh, you are Mrs. Ford, aren't you? I've just seen Ford and we are going to dine together.' It was H. G. Wells, motoring through Toulon with Odette Keun (his mistress after Rebecca West). Bowen recalled 'Wells and Ford sparring together as they had been in the habit of sparring on and off during the last thirty years'. Ford was sounding exhilarated by the success of *No More Parades*—though he hadn't yet been paid much for it. 'I really do seem to be booming', he told Duckworth: 'last Thursday a deputation of American citizens [. . .] came over from Nice to shake me by the hand and thank me for existence. I mean my existence, not theirs: yesterday by the same post I had two contracts from Lecture Agencies asking me to lecture—and so on. I suppose I probably shall next winter—and that will kill me.' They visited the Pounds, who had now settled in Rapallo, and Ford began trying to persuade Pound he too should visit America. He was to continue trying over the next fourteen years. They hired a carriage and drove to Portofino, where Bowen found the coast even more beautiful than Cap Brun. But she found it oppressive being glared at by 'Mussolini's heavy features stencilled all over the walls'. Pound evidently failed to persuade them that Fascism would nurture the arts.[23]

At Easter they began heading back to Paris, breaking the journey at Tarascon. Madame Annie stayed there in a hotel with Julie, while Ford and Bowen went on to Carcasonne, where they hired 'a ramshackle car' to take them into the Montaignes Noires and to Castelnaudary, where Ford wanted them to eat at the Hôtel de la Reine Jeanne, 'where the cassoulet has sat on the fire without a break for the last three hundred years':

The sun blazed outside the screened windows, the flies buzzed, and we partook of one of the most stupendous meals of our whole gastronomic experience. After finishing our second

Stella Bowen, Paris, 1920s

The small producer in Sussex, 1921

Ford (on the right) with fellow
officers of the Welch Regiment

Julie at St Agrève, 1923

Ford and Juan Gris, mid 1920s

Ford painted by Stella Bowen, 1924

Joyce, Pound, John Quinn, and Ford in 1923

Clockwise from top left: Jean Rhys in the 1920s; Jeanne Foster; Elizabeth Cheatham; Rene Wright in 1930

Ford and Pound at Rapallo, 1932

Right: Stella Bowen, Paris, mid 1920s

Ford with (from left to right) Caroline Gordon,
Janice Biala, and Allen Tate

bottle of admirable wine, and sampling the *fine maison*, Ford said that we really ought to send p.c.'s to all our friends to commemorate the menu. He was very unwilling, however, to stir from his chair, so I said I would go in search of picture post cards.[24]

She found an antique shop instead, and, remembering the empty studio, tracked down the owner in a nearby café, and announced that she wanted to buy 'the *armoire rustique*, the grandfather clock (it was a pot-bellied thing that did not work but looked nice), the walnut knee-hole writing table, and the antique flap-desk'. Ford was 'extremely sceptical about the whole transaction', and when he heard that she had no receipt for the 800 francs, almost persuaded her 'that (*a*) the purchase had never taken place, and (*b*) that the shopkeeper would pocket the money and keep the goods, or that (*c*) they would take six months to arrive and there would be hundreds of francs to pay for carriage'. But when they did arrive 'with almost nothing to pay and looking lovely in the studio', Ford 'generously admitted that I had good judgement', said Bowen, 'even in my cups!'

Ford had his desk and books in the little upper room they had built in the studio. Bowen at last had light and space to paint in Paris. They lived for more than a year 'plying backwards and forwards between the cottage at Guermantes', where Madame Annie looked after Julie because there wasn't enough space for them in the studio, and the rue Notre-Dame des Champs, where they now had Algerian rugs, 'a gramophone for dancing', and regular Thursday 'at home's, when 'Ford's American admirers would come early for a cup of tea, and [. . .] intimate friends would turn up later for a glass of vermouth before pushing off to a restaurant'. They ate at Lavigne's restaurant, or with the Bradleys in the Parc Montsouris or the Buttes Chaumont. Julie was now in her sixth year, 'well-grown, blonde and pink, laughing perpetually, and lavishing kisses and affection' upon her parents when they arrived on Friday evenings. She never had any nursery life, said Bowen: 'She travelled with us wherever we went, ate in our restaurants and was perfectly accustomed to mixing with all our grown-up friends.' Ford described her proudly as 'a regular little French woman'. Nina Hamnett said Julie didn't speak English at all; but she must have understood it. It was Ford's talk that Julie remembered most clearly from those years, his voice 'somewhat breathless and low', sounding 'more like Charles Laughton's than anyone else I can think of. I never heard it raised—though it could be, if the occasion called for it, quietly devastatingly cutting and even arrogant':

I first remember him when I was very small, telling me long stories after dinner, a serial that he had invented for me, of a brave sailor and a beautiful Alsatian girl, clockwork creations of an old watchmaker, which came alive at midnight and had the strangest adventures. These he would relate in the somber dining room of a hotel in Toulon, in his beloved Provence, while I sat on his lap and solemnly ate my way through the *corbeille de fruits* which was the inevitable dessert. Even as a small child, I was aware of his magic way with words and the quality of his talk . . .

And what a lot of talk there was. I remember sitting in cafés with Ford and my mother on the waterfront in Toulon or in the Closerie des Lilas in Paris, sedately sipping my grenadine, while for hours the wonderful talk went on, over my head. In Toulon there might be, among others, H. G. Wells or Juan Gris, in Paris Hemingway, Joyce, Ezra Pound—the Ezra of those days—Katherine Ann[e] Porter, and many other 'names,' and always the aspiring unknowns, hungry but vital—in those days the young men were hungry rather than angry—with whose work Ford was ever prepared to take endless trouble—an aspect of his character that has always made me specially proud of him. How many times have I heard him called 'Cher Maître.'[25]

They were seeing people with money. Bill Bullitt—later the first US Ambassador to the Soviet Union, as well as Ambassador to France—and his wife Louise Bryant would come to Paris with their handsome Turkish butler; one year they took Elinor Glyn's lavish house, 'all decorated in mauve taffeta and green brocade as a background for red hair'. Ford 'could never tolerate that anyone might be in a position to patronise him', said Bowen: 'At the least hint of patronage, his pride would flare up, and he would metaphorically double the stakes':

Ford, bitterly aware that his best suit was nothing but a poor old has-been, and that standing his share of the drinks meant that he could not have the shoes he needed, nevertheless talked the jargon of the rich as to the manner born. He presented a wonderful appearance of a bland, successful gentleman whose shabbiness was mere eccentricity and who regarded a preoccupation with the relative merits of Foyot and Larue, Vionnet and Poiret, the Ritz and the Hôtel George V, as very natural and necessary.[26]

Masculine vanity was particularly vulnerable for the artist, she thought, 'who exposes himself to the public in such peculiarly intimate fashion'; 'for this reason [Ford] often found it necessary to disguise himself as something very splendid and successful'. They went to 'afternoon parties of a more decorous and intellectual kind' given by Natalie Barney in the Rue Jacob, 'in a delightful old *pavillon* with tall trees and a little Greek temple in the garden'. There they heard recitals and poetry-readings, and met Gide, Valéry, and Edmond Jaloux. Bowen remembered Barney coming to their studio, and helping Ford to warm up the party: 'Ford, a tall mountain of a man whose dancing was never more than an amiable shuffle, took the floor with Miss Barney, short, plump, all in dripping white fringes, and the sight warmed the cockles of all hearts.' They gave many parties in the studio. Mary Bromfield found them 'very exciting': 'I remember [. . .] making conversation with Ford, who for some occult reason fancied himself as a lady-killer, but in spite of this was witty in the best manner of the English and really fun to talk to. Around about me was greatness and fame [. . .] the Hemingways, the F. Scott Fitzgeralds, the Archie MacLeishes [. . .] the Ludwig Lewisohns [. . .].'[27]

   When Herbert Gorman (American historical novelist, and biographer of Dumas and Joyce), came to a party in the rue Notre-Dame des Champs studio, he was surprised to find that 'the host was not visible'. Ford was 'up on the balcony putting the finishing touches to a novel while the gramophone squawked "Melancholy Baby"':

When he lumbered down the narrow stairs I saw a large torpedo-shaped man, blue-eyed, with blond hair turning gray and a miniature walrus mustache [. . .] he was pre-First World War in appearance. He spoke slowly, often almost tentatively, the words dying away in his throat as though swallowed and leaving his mouth open when he paused to listen. He seemed to suck in one's remarks. Later I discovered that the false teeth he was wearing at that time were a bad fit and sometimes dropped down. We exchanged a few fatuities while Ezra Pound entertained himself with a wild dance and then Ford's eyes suddenly brightened. He asked me if I were not the American friend of James Joyce. When I admitted it he reached for a large pale-gray Stetson-type hat hanging nearby, took my arm and led me from the noisy studio. We passed the rest of the evening and most of the night in a small café on the corner of the Rue d'Assas and the Rue Vavin.

Gorman found him 'a figure of transition', bridging 'two intellectual and creative eras'; 'the most receptive intellectual' he had ever known. They became good friends.[28] He described Ford drinking champagne at the zinc bar of the *bal musette*, and sighted 'what at first glance appears to be a behemoth in gray tweeds':

It is the Leviathan of the Quartier Montparnasse, the gentle Gargantua of Lavigne's, the sophisticated Doctor Johnson of Notre Dame des Champs, Ford Madox Ford. He plods happily and with a child-like complacency through the dance, his partner swaying like a watch-fob before him. After the music stops he will amble over breathing a trifle heavily in memory of the poisonous gas during the Great War and sit down and invite us to join his party. And then, at another table much nearer the dancing-floor, we see Stella and Olga [Rudge?—Pound's violinist friend, and later mother of his son Omar] and Jean [Rhys] and Ernest and Bill [Bird] and realize that this is Ford's Night at the *bal musette*.

The parties at the studio were more selective than those at the *bal musette*. The guests were mostly serious artists. 'All the same, there was a gramophone and people danced', said Goldring, 'but in a corner one could overhear Ford and Gertrude Stein discussing the case of Marcel Proust.' Ford too could be an 'indefatigable' dancer, recalled Sisley Huddleston: 'a trifle heavy, but enthusiastic'. Though it was Pound whose dancing captured his imagination: 'whoever has not seen Ezra Pound, ignoring all the rules of tango and of fox-trot, kicking up fantastic heels in a highly personal Charleston, closing his eyes as his toes nimbly scattered right and left, has missed one of the spectacles which reconcile us to life.'[29]

A Man Could Stand Up— was drafted by May. When it was nearly complete Ford asked Bradley to keep a copy of the manuscript in his safe: 'When I get towards the end of a book I always hate to have all the copies of a ms in one place for fear of fire.' It wasn't only the book that was almost finished: 'I am very nearly finished', he wrote, 'in both senses of the word.' There was trouble with Thomas Seltzer, the publisher of *Some Do Not . . ..* Doubting his solvency, Ford had persuaded Seltzer's nephew, Albert Boni, to buy the rights. But there was a difficulty about the copyright, and Seltzer continued selling copies of the book without paying Ford royalties. Ford was already furious with Seltzer over his failure to send money for the *transatlantic review* copies he had sold. 'I will undertake never to mention Selzer's [*sic*] name again—except in connection with brandy. I never even want to think of him again.'[30]

Besides the nervous exhaustion of finishing another of his most taut, intense novels, there was the tension of his affair with Rhys, which almost certainly continued that spring of 1926. She was again feeling dependent on Ford, and installed in another hotel room: 'depressing, in the rue Vavin', she said; 'A bedroom in hell might look rather like this one', thinks Marya. Carole Angier quotes Rhys's *Voyage in the Dark*, in which Anna imagines herself saying: 'You think I want more than I do. I only want to see you sometimes, but if I never see you again I'll die. I'm dying now really.' *Quartet* has Marya standing outside the Heidlers' studio, 'looking up at the lit windows', listening to one of the Thursday night parties. Angier says this was because Rhys was no longer invited. But this scene comes just after Heidler has insisted that she really 'must turn up occasionally' so as not to 'let Lois down'. Marya begins to lose control of herself, abusing Lois to Heidler. Later, she thinks to herself about Lois: 'One of these days just when she's thought of something clever to say about me for her friends to snigger at, just when she's opening her mouth to say it, I'll smash a wine-bottle in her face.' In another story drawing on Rhys's feelings about Ford, the heroine feels 'suspended over a dark and terrible abyss—the abyss of absolute loss of self-control'. Angier says that Rhys was drinking to deaden her pain, but it 'let out the rage inside her'. Marya tells Heidler: 'I'll walk into your studio and strangle your cad of a Lois'; and Heidler replies calmly: 'I know. As a matter of fact, I've thought several times that you might try some nonsense of that sort. So has she. So I'll simply give the concierge orders not to let you up in future if you do come.' That summer Ford wrote one of his fiercest expressions of feeling slighted and betrayed: the Villonesque poem 'Brantigorn', in which the narrator laments that the young protégé whose life he saved no longer visits him. The poem touches on Ford's feelings of betrayal by writers like Hemingway; but it also reflects the embittering of his relationship with Rhys.[31]

If Ford hadn't already been trying to extricate himself from the affair, he was now. Lenglet had returned illegally to France, and was living in the Parisian suburb of Clamart—where Jan lives in *Sous les verrous*. Jan and Stania visit each other once or twice. As Angier shows, it was probably at this point (August 1926) that Ford said something like Heidler's words in the *Quartet*'s August: ' "If you go back to your husband," he declared, "I can't see you again, you understand that?" ' After this 'He leaned back, looking impenetrable and alert, like a chess-player who has just made a good move'. Rhys said that Ford and Stella wanted to meet Lenglet, so she arranged a meeting at a café, La Taverne Panthéon. In *Quartet* Marya pleads with Stephan to take her with him to Amsterdam, but he abandons her. Rhys maximizes the pathos by making Heidler abandon her immediately afterwards. He gives a brutal explanation (which Rhys doesn't provide), and then says: 'I'm not being treacherous [. . .] I've never shared a woman in my life, not knowingly anyhow, and I'm not going to start now.' When Marya parries by saying that he forced her to share him—'for months. Openly and ridiculously'—he answers coldly: 'I don't know what you mean.' She pleads with him that she loves him. 'You haven't behaved as though you did', he replies, and talks on 'emphatically', building up to the *coup de grâce*: 'I have a horror of you. When I think of you I feel sick.' In *Sous les verrous* Jan doesn't leave voluntarily: Hübner reports him to the police, and he is sent back to the Santé. 'And in reality', says Angier, Lenglet 'was arrested on 4 August, 1926, for breaking his expulsion order, spent six days back in the Santé, and was expelled again.' Could Ford have reported him? It would be more explicable if he'd wanted Lenglet out of the way, so as not to have to share Rhys; whereas if (as *Quartet* suggests) it was Rhys he was trying to avoid, it would have been counter-productive to have had Lenglet arrested and expelled again. That would only have increased her dependence on Ford. (Heidler writes to Marya that he won't send her the large sum of money she wants: 'I certainly do not intend to help you to join your husband [. . .].' The suggestion is that his main motive is a notion of saving her from her desperate life with Stephan.) If Ford did report Lenglet, he is unlikely to have done so then, since on 29 July he told Jeanne Foster 'We are just starting out for Avignon on a holiday', where they stayed until early September. Angier says that the affair ended in 'August and September'; so it cannot have made much difference to Ford whether Lenglet was in Paris or not—unless he feared Rhys would encourage her husband to take revenge for what seemed to him a double betrayal. But again, Angier places Lenglet's talk of revenge after Ford returned from Provence, in September.[32]

'The Rhone could not be better', Ford told Stein: 'we row and paddle canoes & are copper-coloured'. It was probably this summer that Herbert Gorman glimpsed Ford:

swimming in the Rhone with the hot sun hovering over him [. . .] merged in the contentment of an impalpable atmosphere formed of historical memories and forgotten urges. And after he comes out of the glittering water he will make a nice hot cup of English tea for us while the gracious Stella will put us at ease and we will talk of Bertran de Born and the Courts of Love and the Fair of Beaucaire and—oh, yes! pure Thought and the Arts.[33]

Ford gave Rhys money to go to the Hôtel des Oliviers in Cros de Cagnes, next to Nice. (In *Quartet* Heidler sends Marya 300 francs for her hotel bill.) 'Perhaps Jean wanted to get away from John [Lenglet]; perhaps Ford wanted to get her away from him, or away from himself', writes Angier. Judging from her fictional heroines (Marya in the Hôtel des Palmiers, Cannes; Roseau also in a Riviera hotel in the story 'La Grosse Fifi') Rhys must have been in an alcoholic abyss of despair. Meanwhile Lenglet had once again returned illegally to Paris, and in the middle of September he was caught again, sent to the Santé, and expelled once more. Heidler had predicted as much, with a Fordian omniscience: 'And sooner or later he'll probably try to get back to Paris. That's what they all do, it seems. They come back to Paris and hide till they're arrested again. I mean, I'm not going to be mixed up with all that sort of thing.' Lenglet wrote to Rhys (either before arriving, or from prison) to summon her back to Paris. Both *Sous les verrous* and *Quartet* suggest that she returned, and stayed in Paris after he left. Both Marya and Stania break down after their lover writes to them offering money. Both the husbands threaten to go after him: Stephan even produces a revolver, and mutters: 'He thought I was well put away behind the bars. Wait a bit!' Lenglet wanted to kill Ford, and even told his next wife that he was arrested for trying to kill him (rather than for embezzlement). Marya and Stania each struggle with their husband to stop him, shout that they hate him but love the Fordian character, and end up unconscious on the floor. If this means that there was such a fight, and Lenglet ran out, possibly with a revolver, to find Ford, what happened? There's no hard evidence; but if he had confronted Ford, neither of them would have been eager to advertise their situation. But if Ford did report Lenglet to the police, it is most likely to have been now, when he was truly in danger. It is more likely that the moving force was not Ford, but Stella, who had a stronger motive for wanting to rid herself of Rhys and Lenglet. 'I remember hearing a French lawyer say to an American woman who was getting another woman cut off from her husband by threats of publicity and who uttered very vindictive things against her rival: "You should remember, madame, that it is you who hold the spoils!"', Ford said later. It is hard to see why Ford would have been present at such an interview unless he was personally involved, so the American woman is probably a protective disguise for an Australian woman, Stella Bowen. 'And on these grounds', continued Ford, the lawyer 'refused to take several steps that she wanted taken, such as getting the other woman expelled from France because of passport irregularities and the like.' A frustrated and angry Stella could have gone to the police as a last resort. In *Quartet* it's Marya who threatens to turn Stephan in, and it's her threat which makes him hurl her sideways so that she hits the table and collapses. As Stephan leaves the building, he runs rather implausibly into Mademoiselle Chardin, who wants to go away with him. If Lenglet had a scene with Ford, is it credible that it wouldn't have got into *Sous les verrous*? Whereas *When the Wicked Man* has Lola Porter urging Notterdam to denounce McKeown to the police. This might (if that novel is anything like the *roman à clef* the Rhys scholars have read it as) confirm that it was Rhys who wanted Lenglet deported, presumably in a bid to keep Ford.[34]

It was the eruption of drunken rage and menace and violence that most disturbed Bowen and Ford. She called Rhys 'a doomed soul, violent and demoralised', who 'showed us an underworld of darkness and disorder'. In *When the Wicked Man*, Lola Porter reveals an underworld to Notterdam—a rather caricatured gangland underworld, represented by the character McKeown, who tries to shoot Notterdam, as Ford would have known by then if he read *Quartet* that Lenglet had wanted to shoot him, even if he had not actually been able to get near enough to threaten him in the autumn of 1926. *When the Wicked Man* is one of Ford's weaker novels, and has been fiercely criticized for its lack of reality. Angier follows this approach, arguing that Ford split his feelings about Rhys between the two main female characters, painting 'a cruel, but not an inaccurate portrait' of her as the witch-seductress Lola Porter, and romanticizing her on the other hand as Henrietta Felise, 'that recurring ideal of his own imagination, the fragile, mournful, mysterious girl', which Jean Rhys had been to him in 1924. That ideal is certainly recognizable (in Rosamond Fogg Elliot and Brigit Patmore in life, or in Katharine Howard, Nancy Rufford, Valentine Wannop, in the novels). But there is, as we shall see, much more of a later love, Elizabeth Cheatham, in Henrietta Felise. *When the Wicked Man* becomes implausible the further its plot strays from his life: as Angier points out, what's missing is the actual affair between Lola and Notterdam that would account for her sexual rage (in the novel it is attributed to frustrated desire, like Sylvia Tietjens's cruelty, rather than to the jealousy of abandoned love). But *When the Wicked Man* doesn't even try to be 'plausible'. Though it draws on Ford's experience (collaborating with Conrad reimagined as Notterdam's partnership with Kratch; the women fusing elements of Elsie Hueffer, Bowen, Rhys, and Cheatham), it's not a *roman à clef*, but re-fuses biography into a plot and an atmosphere which is something quite other: a characteristically provocative Fordian blend of psychological impressionism, hallucination, fantasy, hysteria, and sardonic farce. It is a volatile mixture which is almost impossible to handle and survive, though Ford manages it superbly in *Parade's End* and the later pair of novels *The Rash Act* and *Henry for Hugh*. Its prime motive is not revenge, but another exploration of visionary experience and guilt. Notterdam is a Young Lovell transposed from medieval mysticism to Manhattan and macabre satire. The surprising fact to emerge from Angier's detective work is that however implausible the psychological motivations of the characters may seem, their actions are much more closely based on these actual events of the mid-1920s than anyone has believed. It may be that the book is too real to seem truthful. Certainly Lola makes Sylvia Tietjens seem tame. As Angier says: 'At the very least Jean *imagined* violent revenge on Ford at the end of their affair; and he felt it.' It is a harsh thing to have to say about Rhys, but it needs saying to counter the wild charges this wild book has provoked: Ford's characterization of Lola appears to be too true to be realistic. Even one of Rhys's staunchest champions in this respect concedes that Rhys when drunk behaved very much like Lola, and notes that Notterdam is struck by Lola's duality (when, as in Sylvia Tietjens, a violent sexuality emerges from an innocent-looking beauty). Which undermines her attack on Lola as an 'inconsistent' character, and as an 'implausible' portrait of Rhys.[35]

Ford was due to leave for New York on 20 October for a ten-week lecture tour to coincide with the publication of *A Man Could Stand Up*—. But first he took the family on a quick trip to England: 'we have been in London for the last ten days, looking after my mother who is getting very old', he explained to Jeanne Foster on 22 September— though it is possible he wanted to be out of Paris while Lenglet was still there. Lenglet was arrested on 16 September; sentenced to six days imprisonment; and released on the 22nd—by which time Ford had returned. Lenglet would have been told to leave the country at once, though in *Sous les verrous* Jan is given eight days notice to leave. Back in Paris, Ford and Bowen moved into an attic flat (with a bath!) at 32 rue de Vaugirard, a seventeenth-century building opposite the Palais du Luxembourg. They went to call on their friends Lewis and Nancy Galantière, but the concierge turned them away 'because we had our dog with us', Ford explained: '& I daresay because we looked like tramps', since they were splattered with paint from the moving. Ford 'replenished his wardrobe, he rehearsed his lectures. Everything was in readiness. His cabin had been booked, and his *visa* had been obtained.' But then, the night before the ship was to sail, he was told by the American Consulate that his visa had been withdrawn. Bowen rushed round in tears to Sisley Huddleston, in the hope that his 'semi-official status' could once again help Ford with the authorities. The next morning Huddleston went with him to the Consulate. At first the consul wouldn't give any reason for the abrupt decision, but eventually 'With great reluctance the consul intimated that somebody had comically alleged that Ford was going to America "for immoral purposes"'. Huddleston 'sat down then and there' to give the consul written assurances that the allegation was nonsensical. 'We had just time to rush, with a letter from the consul, to the proper official', wrote Huddleston, 'obtain a fresh *visa*, and put Ford in the train.' It isn't known who wrote that accusatory letter. It may have been a practical joke by one of *les jeunes* Ford had antagonized over the *transatlantic* (McAlmon?). But no one would have had better motives than Jean Rhys, bitter about Ford's 'immoral purposes', or Lenglet, who may have thought he was revenging himself on Ford for being denounced to the police. Ford may have been recalling the incident when he alluded to that US Immigration question about polygamy again in *It Was the Nightingale*, saying that 'the undesirable will always get in by means of forged papers, whereas the desirable are always inconvenienced, and are not infrequently excluded'. 'It is', he added, 'obviously better for a state to contain, say, truthful polygamists than lying ones' (p. 322). It is the comic version of the feeling at the end

of *The Good Soldier* that 'the passionate, the headstrong, and the too-truthful' polygamists like Ashburnham 'are condemned to suicide and to madness'; that society cannot
honestly desire desire.[36]

Rhys's rage was fed by her feeling that Ford had not only been insincere about his
feelings for her, but that 'all Ford had said about her writing, his concern for it, was
false. That was what hurt most.' But he continued trying to help her career. He
provided a preface for her first volume, *The Left Bank and Other Stories* (in which he
said that he 'wished to be connected' with Miss Rhys's work, 'so extraordinarily
distinguished by the rendering of passion, and so true'), encouraged Cape to publish
it, and tried to get Boni to take sheets of it for the American edition. He still felt
financially responsible for her: 'It appears that she will not get any money till May and
I do not quite know what to do about the allowance', he wrote to Bowen from New
York. Rhys herself always denied that Ford had paid her an allowance. But he did
make weekly payments to her while he was in America. Her next novel after *Quartet*,
After Leaving Mr Mackenzie, opens with Julia Martin being sent a weekly allowance of
300 francs (the same sum, as Angier notes, that Heidler gave to Marya) through
Mackenzie's lawyer, Maître Legros. (Rhys usually denied that Mackenzie was Ford,
though Angier says 'at least once she said he was'; and though the story reaches back
to the end of her first affair, with Lancelot Smith, who did pay her an allowance for
years, its Parisian setting and timing give it obvious parallels to the end of her affair
with Ford.) In *Sous les verrous* Stania is to be sent money through Hübner's lawyer,
Maître Petit. Ford knew John Quinn's lawyer, Maître Legrand, and Angier suggests
that Ford may have paid Rhys through him. However, Ford's correspondence with
Bowen during this American trip indicates that they were providing an allowance, but
through Rhys's friend and benefactor Germaine Richelot. In February 1927 Ford said
he had wired to stop the allowance. He had arranged for the Chicago publisher Pascal
Covici to pay Rhys $250 for her translation of *Perversity* (the title must have seemed
an ironic postscript to their affair) and said he would send Richelot the first $125 as
soon as Rhys agreed to the terms. 'If Jean does not there is no reason why we should
go on keeping her', he assured Bowen. He also sought further ways of letting Rhys
support herself by her writing: 'I have tried to get some of the magazines to publish
individual stories', he told Bowen. He tried to get an agent to 'make her a small
allowance while she is writing a novel'. 'It is difficult to know what to do. I wish I could
consult you', he said to Bowen: 'My inclination is to send Miss Richelot say $50 and
tell her to dole it out—but I do not know that that might not seem to be like weakness.'
By the end of the year they didn't know where she was: the letters she wrote Ford were
forwarded by Germaine Richelot to Bowen, who forwarded them anxiously to Ford.[37]

As with Hemingway and Coppard, Ford went on helping Rhys professionally all the
more after knowing that she wouldn't forgive him personally. With the money from
the stories and translation she was able to leave Paris to rejoin Lenglet in the spring of
1927. But there was probably one last encounter with Ford before she left. In *After
Leaving Mr Mackenzie* Julia follows Mackenzie into a restaurant six months after the
end of their affair, tells him she doesn't want his money, slaps him on the cheek with
her glove, and tells him she despises him. The Montparnasse gossip said Rhys did
much the same to Ford six months after their affair ended; though this may be

founded only on her novel, and be as untrue as the rumoured explanation—that she had had a child by him. Rhys worked her vengeance out in her fiction, first in the revenge stories 'Houdia' and 'The Spiritualist', then in *Postures*. It was, as Angier says, 'written in anger and revenge'. Ford had not only fostered her talent; he had—albeit inadvertently—given her her best subject: the misunderstanding and cruelty of human relations; the despair of the abandoned lover. Angier says that Ford was the turning-point in her life, 'because she had to give up her dream of being a happy woman', and had to wonder if what Ford had said to her about herself and her writing was true. 'In this way too it was Ford who made her into a writer.'[38]

16

1926–1927: USA

> . . . loving New York, next to Provence, better than any other place, [this author] lets himself go and writes of her as he would talk to his mother or his mistress, being very fond of them.
>
> (Ford, *New York is Not America*)

He had a noisy crossing on the *Savoie*, and slept badly. But he enjoyed it none the less. 'I am just going to rehearse my lecture before a ship's audience for the benefit of the widows & orphans' fund of the C[ompagnie]. G[enera]ˡᵉ· Transatlantique', he told Stella. When he arrived on 29 October 1926 he wrote to her: 'we passed thro' the tails of two hurricanes and I was as jolly as a sand boy, so if not a good soldier I can call myself a good sailor [. . .] The nicest people really were two cinema stars travelling incognito: Robert Montgomery & Vera Reynolds. They have invited me to stay on their ranch at Hollywood.' 'Lots of reporters' were waiting for him when he disembarked, he said. At least four papers reported his arrival, and his praise of American writers such as James, Crane, and Pound. Pre-publication sales of 4,000 promised success for *A Man Could Stand Up—*; he was commissioned to write weekly articles as visiting critic for the *New York Herald Tribune Books*; Bradley and his 'literary lawyer' Spingarn were confident that he could get a contract with the Boni brothers to give him a monthly $500 subsidy in return for all his novels. The optimism wasn't unjustified. His journalism and lecturing did give him publicity; *A Man Could Stand Up—* was reasonably successful (though not on the scale of *No More Parades*); and he did eventually get a contract with Boni (though for $400 per month, initially only for six months, but soon extended to three years). But there was devastating news too: his lecture agent had only managed to arrange one lecture. 'Pond is an absolute dud', he wrote to Bowen: 'It turns out that he knows *nothing* about the literary world—confining himself almost entirely to aviation & lion tamers & men of action.' But Ford didn't lose heart. He wasn't worried, he told Bowen: 'I shall sit down & do more writing.' She thought him 'a splendid & most courageous person'. The Bonis told him they wanted a new edition of his *Henry James*, a new Collected Poems, and two new novels: one 'about two old maids'—the Misses Hurlbird from Stamford, Connecticut, whom Ford had used for a cameo as Florence's aunts in *The Good Soldier*, and a 'Novel about Ney', which became *A Little Less Than Gods*. Bradley and Spingarn persuaded him it was essential for him to stay the full ten weeks: 'To go back wᵈ· be a confession of failure & fatal to my book sales [. . .].' Within a fortnight he'd managed to arrange another seven lectures—though most of them weren't, of course, for payment.[1]

He stayed with the Herbert Gormans at 47 West 12th Street for a couple of weeks.

'N.Y. is one long drag', he told Bowen—'but I don't say I don't like it. Yesterday [. . .] I was interviewed 16 times & that was very exhausting. To-morrow I am to sit to several photographers and two sketchers. To-morrow I am dining in state at the Bullitts & shall wear my tails for the first time.' He sat for a portrait by Georg Hartmann. 'I *do* miss you dreadfully—all the time & there is no one else', he reassured her.[2]

'I was astounded to hear that he had engaged to lecture', wrote Burton Rascoe: 'for he always speaks with such difficulty and with such a wheeze [. . .] that in private conversation with him it is very hard to understand what he says.' Confusion struck ominously at his first lecture. The Seamen's Church Institute had asked him to speak about Conrad. 'I do not think any man can have been more intimate than myself with Joseph Conrad', he told them, '—at any rate with Joseph Conrad as a writer and I think that this was the highest privilege of my life'—the qualification is crucial, and defines the focus of Ford's literary reminiscences: his subject is always his friends *as writers*. John Masefield had been speaking before him, so when Ford spoke about his collaboration on *Romance* he said Masefield had written the first review of it. The next day the *New York World* misreported Ford as having 'revealed a hitherto unknown literary secret when he told that the first part of "Romance", supposedly written by him and Conrad, was really the work of Masefield'. Ford wrote a witty reply, insisting that the speech 'was made before *not* after lunch too!'; and managed to turn the episode to advantage. Within a week the *World* published an interview with him, in which he not only defined his sense of 'Middle-westishness' in literature (anticipating Hemingway's assault on 'Abstract words') as a modern reaction to pre-war romantic notions of 'duty' and 'honour'—the very notions he had been anatomizing in *The Good Soldier* and *Parade's End*; but he also spoke about his conception of his audience: 'I write not for myself but for a sympathetic reader. I think it absurd that a man should pretend he's writing only for himself; he must imagine an audience for which he is doing whatever he is doing.'[3]

He had been nervous about speaking to the Seamen's Church Institute. But his next public appearance boosted his confidence, as he explained to Bowen—he was writing to her almost every day:

my speech at the Plaza—to 800 ladies—was a triumphant success & as it took place before all the Vanderbilts & Astors & Morgans of N.Y. it ought to do some good. I never imagined an audience could be so responsive: they took all my points before I could make them & I hardly finished a single sentence—for laughter or applause. It was to the American Woman's Association—so I spoke—without notes—just like that—about the Pankhursts & Votes for Women in England. They nearly went mad with enthusiasm when I paid—a really moving— tribute to M[rs.] Pankhurst.[4]

'I suppose an atmosphere of adulation stimulates me', he mused: 'And they all say that I *am* so modest.' He enjoyed an interview which said that meeting him dispelled all preconceptions about him:

You may have heard rumors that he was arrogant, conceited, and condescending; scathingly clever—at other people's expense, and a poseur [. . .] you may have rather leaned toward the mental image of a tall, loose-jointed individual: dark with a malicious eye, and a mouth that has tasted bitterness [. . .] So may Mr. Ford fool you utterly. He is the exact opposite of all this.

He was indeed the opposite of these things, but he wasn't innocent of them: he liked to give an impression of them in order to disavow it to his intimates. That dual impression is deeply characteristic—as it is with Ashburnham or Tietjens. Isabel Paterson described him in her review column: 'So at last we met Ford Madox Ford [. . .] large, very blond, unassertive and smiling; his voice is gentle and tentative, as if he thought every one had a right to a different opinion and it would take a great deal of explanation to get at the essential difference.' She wanted to know what happened to Tietjens after *A Man Could Stand Up*—, and found Ford 'pleasantly indulgent' to her demand: 'All will be revealed in two or three years, when the fourth volume appears.'[5]

He met Dreiser, Sherwood Anderson, Matisse's son, and 'crowds of local celebrities' at a party given by the Donald Friedes which had not been 'too wet', he told Bowen, 'as these parties are apt to be'—Prohibition was still in force, and the bootleg liquor could be ferocious. None the less 'M[r.] Horace Liveright regrettably slapped a girl's face in the middle of it & then collapsed into an armchair & cried with his hands over his face for the rest of the evening.' These were not 'usual N.Y. manners', Ford assured Stella, and discussed the possibility of her joining him:

I sh[d.] love that: we c[d.] have such a good time & the only *real* difficulties are money ones. The passport difficulties are really quite negligible. You could, that is to say, get y[r.] passport visaed in England to avoid notice in Paris & you could say you are an artist coming to arrange an exhibition [. . .] once you were here we c[d.] live together without the beginnings of a question asked. We c[d.] not travel legally together from State to State on account of the Mann Act—but that is never put in force except for blackmail or by impotent & avenging husbands—& anyhow I see no reason for going outside New York State.[6]

He took some rooms at 51 West 16th Street. They were quiet—'miraculously so for N.Y. . . . In revenge they are dark & buggy'. There was talk of a film contract for the Tietjens novels, though nothing came of it. *Harper's* and *Vanity Fair* wanted articles. Though he kept telling Bowen how much he liked New York ('better than Paris—tho' I w[d.] not care to live here'), she and Julie were rarely out of his thoughts: 'I seem to see you there, very clear & iridescent', he told her, 'like what you see thro' the small end of a telescope [. . .].' In the cold weather he had one of his 'old chest attacks'. 'Darling,' he wrote to Bowen:

I got a little alarmed about myself in the night—before last, all alone & with a pretty bad chest—& I thought I might die & never have put on record all you have been for me & done for me. So, as this is a quiet moment I'll seize it & say that if I've done anything during these last years & if I *am* anything it has been entirely due to you & never for a moment have I wished that we were not united & never at any time have I had anything against you. I do want to say this—& I'd want to have it published when I die—so I write it & keep it & publish it when I am dead. You have been the most splendid of human beings in the dreadful times we have been through together & all that I am I owe to you & to you alone.

She replied that this letter became her 'absolutely most treasured possession'. It was partly because Ford was telling her how he didn't want his involvement with Rhys to destroy their relationship. Bowen was still shaken by that episode. When Germaine Richelot gave her a letter from Rhys to send on to Ford, saying it was about her agent, Tilden Smith, Bowen expected it was 'about a good deal besides Tilden Smith'. 'You might let me know something of the affairs in that quarter', she wrote to Ford when she forwarded the letter: 'I worry when you say nothing.' (Six weeks later he was still saying nothing. 'I do wish you would not keep so silent on that subject', she said while sending on a second Rhys letter.) The tone of her letters to Ford—they wrote regularly during this trip—shows her unillusioned about his susceptibility to affairs, but understanding, forgiving, and loving. She told him: 'you are my own darling Great Man—And my Favourite Author'; 'you are really the only person in the world that I care to talk to!' And she begged: '*please* get finished with any too-exacting intimacies you may have formed & don't come back with any entanglements!' Ford was surprised to find the private lives of the Americans he knew matching up to his rendering of the Dowells in *The Good Soldier*. He told Stella about Jeanne Foster: 'It appears that her husband is impotent & always has been & so was Quinn—so she has had rough luck . . . but all American husbands appear to be like that. The way their wives talk about it w^d. amaze you!' Bowen could rise to meet his humour even on this potentially distressing topic. 'God bless her', she said of Foster, who had been working hard to make Ford's lectures a success. 'But *don't* have an affair with her because I can't bear any more Fair Hair! I hope you're not expected to demonstrate to all these ladies that English Husbands are Not Impotent?' 'I love you with all my heart & I want you back', she told him: 'And you know I would not exchange my life with you with anyone's life, & I'd do just the same all over again.'[7]

He had perhaps already begun to worry that she might hear gossip about him doing the same all over again, and provided her with amusing accounts of the women he was meeting:

Mrs Ballard is a perfect mystery. She asked me to dinner with her husband and another woman & then never turned up leaving me to entertain the other woman & whenever I phone her husband answers & rings off at once. I can only imagine that he is madly jealous—tho' why he sh^d. be jealous of me I can't see for I haven't yet had two words with the lady. On Sat. I saw her in a restaurant with her husband who said he was going to Philadelphia that night. She said that she *must* see me on Sunday so I asked her to lunch but she did not turn up to that either & I have not heard again. I fancy she must be having a terrible time—but it may be all imagination. Horwood with whom I dined last night thinks the husband is a homicidal maniac! He still has no teeth.[8]

'Darling: I do love you very much', the letter ends: 'How can you ask or doubt it?' But then, how could she *not*?

Gossip intensified when Violet Hunt's memoirs were published in America under the title *I Have This to Say*. 'The dirty cat!', said Bowen when she heard how much Hunt had written about Ford. 'Reporters keep ringing me up & wanting to interview me about it', he told Bowen. He was 'bothered and depressed' by the adverse publicity, and the possibility that it would jeopardize his sales and lecturing, not to mention his negotiations with Bonis, which were still in progress. In the meantime Rebecca West, who was in New York and meeting Ford regularly, 'sailed in & made matters excruciatingly more disagreeable':

She has told several people that V.H. is an admirable & martyred saint & that every word of the book is true. At the same time, if you please, she has rung up Fanny Hurst & Elinor Wylie—& heaven knows how many others, but both of these are very prominent N.Y. women—& said: 'Do come to lunch or dinner with Fordie & me!' . . . & there is actually a Miss West living in this house & her letters lie on the hall table. So as numbers of people call on me here half N.Y. thinks that Rebecca & I are living together. . . . Still I suppose one thing cancels out the other. I mean: if she lives with me her abuse can hardly be taken seriously: or, if she abuses me she can hardly be living with me.[9]

Luckily New York did not seem 'to care a damn'. The *New York Evening Post* asked him for poems. PEN invited him to be a guest of honour. Jeanne Foster, who was doing some publicity for him, suggested they should use photographs of Ford with Julie to present him as 'the good father'. The audiences didn't seem to hold his past against him: 'And—what for me is the greatest relief of all—', he told Bowen: 'I have just finished lecturing at the *Pen & Brush Club*—378 ladies, one table of 12 alone representing so the president told me sixty million dollars!—They gave me a perfect ovation—& I deserved it for I really spoke beautifully so that Elinor Wylie cried when I spoke of H.J. . . .' Worse than the effect on his reputation was the sheer embarrassment at having his private life made so sensationally public: 'I really had dreaded the occasion because it was disagreeable to think of talking to people who had read the S.[outh] L.[odge] book.' 'What really *has* harmed me here—oddly enough,' he wrote to Bowen, 'is Jessie's letter to the *Times*.' He sent Bowen his lecture notes for a talk at the 'Pen and Brush Club'. He had been invited to give a reading, but was then also asked to talk about his work: 'But to an Englishman—above all to such an atrociously English Englishman as the specimen you have before you—the mere thought of talking about his work is abhorrent. It isn't done.' Instead, he told some of the anecdotes from *No Enemy* about the books he read on active service—Conrad, Crane, James, Flaubert, Anatole France, Turgenev, Hudson: 'and that—if you care to listen—will tell you how—or rather why—some of my work came into existence.' 'What [. . .] really drives them mad!', he told Bowen, 'is talk about the war, so I am specialising more & more in that.' He lectured at Dartmouth College (in Hanover, New Hampshire) on 9 December, then stayed with friends in Boston, before leaving to lecture again at Williams College (in Williamstown, Massachusetts) on the 12th, and in New York on the 14th. The train back to Boston was restful, he told Stella, 'for I never seem to have stopped talking since I struck N.Y.': 'audiences fall in love with me on sight.' It wasn't just that adulation stimulated him. He depended on sympathetic listeners. 'I don't know why but I feel infinitely more homesick here in the country than in the towns—much more of a foreigner.' In New York he was with many of his Paris friends. Elsewhere, he began to feel alone.[10]

His social and literary engagements didn't leave him much time to write. Apart from Bradley, the Bullitts, Jeanne Foster, and the Gormans, whom he called on each morning 'after breakfasting at a coffee-bar on a high stool at the corner of 5th and 16th', he was seeing his American agents the Brandts, Sinclair Lewis, Edwin Arlington Robinson, Dreiser, Padraic Colum, Burton Rascoe, the poets Elinor Wylie and her husband William Rose Benét (who also co-founded the *New York Saturday Review of Literature*), e. e. cummings, Marcel Duchamp, Constantin Brancusi, and many others: 'The telephone goes continually', he told Bowen. An American on board the *Savoie* had told Ford: 'You English are incredible. For everything you prescribe a nice hot cup of tea'—whether for cold feet, diarrhoea, constipation, toothache or shingles. 'So one day he was drinking at Montmartre & a woman laid his head open with a bottle so that he was down & out for seven hours. When he came to he was in bed in the English Hospital and the nurse was saying to him: "What *you* want is a nice hot cuppertea!"' Ford had been telling this story 'with enormous effect to every one' he met in New York, he said to Bowen; but when he told it in front of Rebecca West, she came up afterwards and said: 'I don't see the point of *that* story. Because a nice hot cup of tea *would* be what w$^{d.}$ do him most good!'

So, last week I asked Rebecca to lunch at one & she arrived at 2.15. And then we were both asked—the same day!—to dinner at Lloyd Morris's at seven. At eight she phoned to say that she had started & had fainted in her taxi so she had gone back to her hotel. I *knew* that was a lie. So about ten I got [Lewis] Galantière to ring up her hotel & she was out, naturally. So I got Galantière to leave a message for her: 'A nice hot cup of tea is what *you* want!'

Next day at a dinner at the Whitelaw Reids'—the proprietors of the *Herald Tribune*—telephone again!—M$^{rs.}$ Ballard who wants Whistler's studio as reported (?) by me!—Rebecca naturally kept the whole party of N.Y.'s most distinguished—Mr Otto Kahn, the Archbishop (Prot.) of N.Y. & the rest—waiting 3/4 of an hour & when she came in she walked straight up—before all the guests waiting in a semicircle—straight up, not to the hostess but to me & exclaimed at the top of her voice: 'Fordie: you are the biggest liar in New York!' . . . Jean Gorman wants to found a society for not meeting Rebecca.[11]

West had provoked Ford's practical joke; but in Ford's telling of the story of his story, it becomes a classic example of Ford himself provoking an unjust denunciation.

On his birthday Ford wrote to Bowen that he had been 'speaking *triumphantly*' every day that week: 'I am really too tired [. . .] to remember where—except at Brooklyn XXth Century Club on Tuesday, at Columbia University Wednesday & at Princess Machiavelli's before Rockerfeller's & Roosevelt's [*sic*] & the like yesterday afternoon.' 'I don't mind—indeed I rather like—the speaking', he said: 'it is jolly to stand up & look in a leisurely way on 6 or 700 faces & think what you are going to do to them—but I get terribly exhausted afterwards & that is the trying time—the whole audience being led up one by one to be presented to you & to tell you how they admire y^r books—that is wearing! Still, flattery is nice!' After staying up all night to write 'a rather beautiful long article—about Trollope', he planned to spend the day in bed: 'Indeed that is what I enjoy most of all here [. . .] I shall lie & listen with vindictive pleasure to the telephone that I shall not answer.' The following day he signed his contract with Boni: 'I am quite satisfied myself and Bradley is chuckling like a rooster that has laid an egg', he wrote to Bowen. Bradley 'absolutely *dotes* on you', Bowen told Ford: he 'seems to believe in a beautiful mystical brotherly tie between you that I believe *you* don't recognize a bit!' What Ford did recognize was that Bradley's attitude was divided between admiration for his gifts, and envy of them. Bradley thought he should have a grander apartment—in Park Avenue—for entertaining. But Ford agreed with Jeanne Foster and Marjorie Reid Rodes (who had been the *transatlantic*'s secretary) that it was unnecessary: 'I had Miss Rockerfeller in to tea the other day & she was enchanted with the house. I tried to get her to get her father to buy up this old part of New York & preserve it as a kind of National Reserve & she seemed to think it was an idea. This part of N.Y. [still West 16th Street] is rather like Bloomsbury—wh. is a great rest to the eyes here.'[12]

Ford was a guest of honour at a PEN Club dinner at the Brevoort Hotel on 20 December, together with Hugh Walpole and Osbert Sitwell (who couldn't speak because he found 'the steam heat and climate of New York too much for him'). Henry Seidel Canby (editor of the *Saturday Review of Literature*) congratulated Ford on 'giving the literary world the best picture of a mature man in the World War' in *A Man Could Stand Up—*. But it was Walpole who spoke about him 'with such enthusiasm and such enviable generosity' that Ford said: 'I was covered with confusion and quite literally had the tears in my eyes. I was indeed so affected as to be totally unable to make any adequate reply and must have seemed curmudgeonly in the extreme to our audience.' Nevertheless he entertained the audience by telling them that what most impressed him about America was 'the extraordinary rapidity at which one is compelled to get about'. And he made up for what he felt was his lack of reciprocal generosity by dedicating *The English Novel* to Walpole in a letter recalling the occasion.[13]

Ford sent regular letters and postcards to Julie too, writing to her always in French, as 'Très, très chère petite princesse'. Bowen took her to England to visit the Coles for Christmas. Before they went, Bowen gave notice to Mme Annie, who refused to go with them; though she worried that Mme Annie, who had always been '*insupportably insolent and sulky*', would come back destitute and begin, 'as she did before, to ask for "loans"'; 'That woman's temperament has been a constant burden for 3 years & I've been a perfect slave to my own dread of upsetting her', she told Ford (who readily agreed). Bowen explained her worries to him on his birthday: 'So I am faced with the disagreeable prospect of her going to 6 Place du Maine (which naturally I can't forbid) & possibly digging up scandals about Jean who is very possibly still there.' Photographs of Julie arrived as a Christmas present. 'They are charming—and rather alarming', said Ford, 'so grown up and supercilious does the petit fruit de nos amours appear. I thank you ever and ever so much [for the pictures, or the daughter?]: you could not have sent me anything I liked more unless you would have added one of yourself. *Do* do this.' Three ladies had sent him ties for Christmas, he explained:

it is very awkward as I shall have to wear their ties when I go to see them and I cannot remember which sent which except that Mrs [Foster] sent a blue one. But it is impossible to reconcile everyone to my ties. In the lift going up to Boni's the other day Dorothy Galanti[è]re said: I wish you would let me choose your *ties* and coming down Mary Colum exclaimed, Oh, I just *despise* your *tie!*[14]

He evidently had better luck with Boni, who agreed to republish *The Good Soldier* as the first volume of the uniform edition that he had been hoping to arrange in America: 'then I shall dedicate the whole edition to you and there it shall be for a token *urbi et orbi*!'—his Christmas offering to Stella Bowen; but also, as she had probably begun to suspect from his defensive references to other women, a token that was to mark the ending of a relationship. 'On Heaven' had been addressed 'To V.H.' when he was in love with Brigit Patmore; and he had appeared at Hunt's parties as her partner while he was living with Bowen. The wry and generous 'Dedicatory Letter to Stella Bowen' he wrote for Boni's 'Avignon' edition of *The Good Soldier* was a comparable gesture, making public his affection for a woman he knew he was gradually leaving. Bowen had written to him when Hadley Hemingway had told her that Hemingway wanted a divorce. 'If only she were younger & had a better chance of remarriage it wouldn't be half so bad', perhaps wondering what her own situation would be were Ford to leave: 'What is shocking is to think of someone as miserable & as finished as that, with all the rage & bitterness there must be underneath, making these superhuman efforts to go down with a smile and with dignity, & to "behave well". Still, Thank God she can!' She already knew of these things from the Jean Rhys affair.[15]

'I have not any Xtmas feeling at all', he told Bowen. 'Naturally I shall not stop on Xtmas day in bed: I am to take the Gormans to dinner at the National Arts Club of which I have become a full member, go to the Bullitts' for tea and dinner and then to the van Doren's [*sic*] for a party.' But when he went to Mass the Xtmas feeling struck. He told Bowen how he would often 'pop in' to the church across the street 'from time to time for a minute or two':

But to-day with all the scarlet and green trappings and a beautiful choir singing the Adeste Fideles very purely and with immense fire it was almost more than my emotions could stand for thinking of Julie and you. I do hope Julie also went to Mass and that she goes on with her religious duties: there is so much happiness in the Church.

And I do want to tell you again, my darling, how good and brave and splendid I think you and how I thank God and you for all you have done for me.[16]

A letter written to Jeanne Foster the same morning tells a stranger version of the same story. In gratitude for her work on his behalf he had reinscribed to her the copy of *The Soul of London* he had originally given to Conrad. She was now much more than the 'Dear Mrs. Foster' of three months ago:

My Dear:
    I have just come in from Mass. N.Y. is very lonely without you: I wish we'd have gone to Mass together. I had quite—oh quite dreadfully!—a touch of nostalgia when they sang the adeste . . . not really for England or Paris—but I believe it was truly to live amongst Papists. I think they are, really, the only people one understands, *au fond*. They are one's real family as you and I are more kin than if we were related by blood. Perhaps what I really need is to be reconciled to the Church. I was looking at a plaster of paris statue of the Virgin and she said: 'This is the last Xtmas you will ever attend.' . . . just like that . . . [. . .]
    God bless you my dear: I think of you very much and write with true affection! And I prayed for you—like Hell—just now.
    Come back soon, soon to
        Yr
    F.[17]

Ford recalled this vision when he was back in New York eight years later, though he had reimagined the occasion as a wedding, and placed it on Christmas *Eve, ten* years before:

. . . Our Lady of the Seven Dolours is less pink than I thought She was and the Church of St. Philip Neri more grim in this Christmas Eve dusk. I last saw it some years ago, when I lived opposite. I had gone to see a wedding. Converted Jews, they were, the brilliant-cheeked bride, one of my publishers' secretaries [. . .] I was put behind a pillar so that I could not see the altar and the church had been terribly hot. So I sat looking at the statue at the end of the aisle.

Suddenly she turned Her eyes on me and said:

'You will never see Christmas here again.'

. . . That was ten years ago to the day, and as a matter of fact I have not celebrated Christmas in New York City since then. Perhaps She meant actually Christmas Day and actually the Church of St. Philip Neri. Or possibly, as my Toulon friends would interpret it for me, some deceased ancestor has interceded for me. . . .[18]

The lack of view makes the confusion understandable. There is little doubt about either the vision or the emotional intensity associated with it. At first it might seem like insincerity that he tells Bowen that what moved him was the thought of her and Julie, on the same day that he tells Foster that he feels closer to his metaphorical religious family than to his actual family. Yet he was emotionally so fraught precisely because the circumstances mobilized so many different strong feelings. It was probably Bowen's contempt for Catholic superstition that stopped him telling her the visionary details. But his comments about wanting Julie to continue as a Catholic suggest how concerned he was about her. He didn't want to lose touch with her as he had with Christina and Katharine (would he ever celebrate Christmas with her again, dressed as *Père Noel?*); and perhaps he hoped that the tie could be made stronger in religion than it was in blood. His letters show signs of anxiety that she might be forgetting him. As his third long-term relationship was crumbling, and as he pondered *The Good Soldier* once more, he was reminded again how ephemeral were his families built upon passion. When he had visited the Vatican in 1911, alienated from Elsie and their daughters, the Church had felt like his true and more lasting family. Now he feared the loss not only of his family life with Bowen and Julie; he also feared the loss of his mother, who was ill again. If Mary could stand for Stella (as the mother and child he feared not seeing again), she could also stand for his own mother, prophesying that she would not see him again. There is also some Fordian self-pity in the suggestion that it might be his own death he was imagining the Virgin to be prophesying; though it's also characteristic that his self-pity intensifies rather than excludes his pity for others. He had been overwhelmed by a wave of elegiac sentiment while writing about his Romney Marsh past: '[. . .] I quite suddenly realised for the first time that Crane and Conrad and James are all three dead together and I just could not go on with the article: that is I had to send away Miss Gordon and finish writing it myself [. . .].' (Miss Gordon was his new secretary, Caroline Gordon, of whom more later.) He also felt pity for his mother—'I wish she did not have to have pain', he wrote to Bowen; 'One ought to be able at that age to sink out of life'; for Stella, who would need her bravery (as Hadley Hemingway had needed hers); and for Jeanne Foster, who was burdened with the care of several invalid members of her 'blood kin'.[19]

'No. I am not in love with Mrs Foster', he reassured Bowen. Yet, although they were probably not actually lovers, his Christmas letter is very like a love-letter. Was he in the state described by I. A. Richards: 'Writers too, who find that they can imagine feelings and express them in words, may readily become fascinated by this occupation, as a kind of game, and lose sight of the real sanctions of the feelings in experience [. . .]

Seeing a chance to make a violent emotional effect, we forget whether this is the effect we desire.'[20] It is more likely that, as Janice Biala suggests, he was an intensely lonely man during this period. He loved women because they had been badly treated, but he also desired the effect of stirring a new love. He was a passion looking for a new object. He said he wrote of New York 'as he would talk to his mother or his mistress, being very fond of them'. Religion, too, was for him a form of intimacy rather than an ethical dogma. Characteristically, Ford could brace his self-pity against the fierce irony that let him joke about his flirtatiousness, as when he told Foster he had been praying for her 'like Hell' (like the devil or the damned? like mad? or 'like hell' he had?); or when he teased Bowen that he had seen his 'old flame Miss Kerr', who had played the hazardous part of his secretary during his 1924 trip to New York: 'She is now presiding genius over three boot factories and no longer stirs my emotions.'[21]

There was a 'riotous party' at the Gormans, where twenty-four bottles of Ford's punch were consumed. 'The drinking here is *really* rather deplorable', he told Bowen, giving a sketch of the hallucinatory alcoholic world that he was to reimagine in *When the Wicked Man*:

people, and quite nice people, really do make deplorable beasts of themselves deliberately and night after night, till it almost becomes a nightmare. I have not myself been inebriated for quite a month—the hangover next day, on account of the bad liquor is really too horrible to make it worth while. However it is not really difficult to avoid drinking; the most hospitable people are so eager to lap up the poison that they seldom press you to drink [. . .] Mrs [Kermit] Roosevelt told me that for the first four years of Prohibition she struck off her visiting list every one who got drunk at one of her parties, but latterly she has had to give it up or she would have no men friends left and precious few women.

This is not a very cheerful subject my dear one, but I really have been terribly impressed. . . . Poor old satan to reprove sin.[22]

'He is called don Juan at present and any number of women are mad about him', Foster wrote to Ezra Pound. 'I still haven't any flame here—not even M[rs] Roosevelt', he had assured Bowen. But one of the number of women particularly mattered: Rene Wright, whom Ford had met during his visit to America in 1906, and whom he fell in love with this winter. As with Elsie and Mary Martindale or Violet Hunt, the fact that they had known each other years before heightened the attraction. As with Mr Sorrell in *Ladies Whose Bright Eyes*, a present romance made him relive his remembered past. Wright was presumably at the 'wonderful New Years party'—dinner for twenty-four people in a speakeasy—that Foster described to Pound. Elinor Wylie and William Rose Benét invited the guests home afterwards for a second party. The bootleg liquor was flowing freely. 'About midway Ford got the idea that the party was too strong for his lady and snatched her home. The lady did not want to go and there were ructions. Both of them were sorry they did not stay.' 'I have never seen and hardly imagined such a scene as there was at Elinor's before I left', he wrote to Bowen, omitting any mention of his 'lady' for the moment: 'the floors of three rooms being entirely covered with reclining couples shoulder to shoulder so that stepping out was like leaving a battlefield. I got home about four, pretty sober—at any rate I walked—and by eleven I had begun my new book. . . . No, I am mixing my days: it was this morning that I began my book.'[23]

Rene Wright was a stylish, 'pleasant, full-bosomed' woman of 48 (only slightly older than Violet Hunt had been at the start of her affair with Ford). Ford wrote possibly his worst poem to her, calling her 'My dearest dear, my honey love; | my brown-eyed squirrel, my soft dove'. He told Bowen when he sent her a copy: 'I began to write it to Julie but it turned out too mature under my hands':

As a matter of fact it is really a paraphrase of the

> But when the night comes, with the first sleep
> I run, I run, I am gathered to your heart

of Mrs Meynell and of the Schubert *Du bist die Ruh* which I was singing at the van Dorens the other night. . . . But do not tell people that or they will call me a plagiarist. Anyhow it has set New York buzzing with admiration. Mrs Harrison Smith the wife of the Harcourt Brace partner said to me at tea today—you met her once outside the Dome—'How I wish I was Mrs Ford to have people write poems to me like that!' . . . The curious thing is that the New Yorkers love my singing voice and make me sing for hours and hours at their parties— particularly when Kerrigan is there. Then we sing alternately, he Irish folk songs and I English ones. I fancy my voice really has developed a little, probably owing to the lectures. But I know you will never believe that.

Harold Loeb said that Ford's younger friends found Rene Wright 'distinctly "middle aged"', and referred to her amongst themselves as 'the Brown Eyed Squirrel'. Judging by her studio photograph of this period, any squirrels that approached her were likely to end up as furs. She had married her second husband, Guy Wright, in Brooklyn in 1914, after the death of her first, and they settled in St Louis. Wright was the president of his father's investment company, and also a nephew of the founder of Czechoslovakia, Thomas Masaryk. By 1926 their marriage was foundering, which probably explains why she was alone in New York that winter. She was no bohemian, refusing to live with Ford until they could marry; which meant that Ford would have once again to try to divorce Elsie.[24]

   In the New Year the round of public appearances resumed. He was astonished that his 'first really big recognition' should be in the America he and Bowen had 'always rather despised'. 'I am buried under an average of four hundred ladies a night', Ford told Bowen, 'and some of them of extreme beauty, so it is hard to be swayed by one.' Hard, but not impossible.

Tomorrow I am speaking at a lady's [*sic*] club in Brooklyn—no, I see that is not till Thursday; but on Tuesday I am speaking to the Columbia University Writer's [*sic*] Club on Thursday in Brooklyn and on Saturday at a monster reception for me at Lady Speyer's. Last night I spoke at the Whitney Studio Club for Mrs Harry Payne Whitney, millionairess and member of the Four Hundred. It was *terribly* hot on the platform—so hot that I nearly fainted twice. However I went on talking. I believe that if you put me on a platform after I was dead I should talk. I don't mind the talking: what is trying is the subsequent reception, having to stand and have one's hand shaken for hours. However [i]t is supposed to give one publicity—and they appear to *love* me.

While he was writing this letter a young woman dashed into his room 'and fell panting into an armchair'. When she had caught her breath she blurted out: 'I am in love with a journalist.' It turned out that she was a schoolgirl whose journalist boyfriend Ford had turned away the day before, without realizing that the young Scotsman had been 'practically starving' ever since he arrived in New York, and that this had been his first assignment. The young woman tried to interview Ford herself, but broke down crying at the thought that her performance would make him think American girls were not 'well-bred': 'in the end I took this machine and wrote the interview for her', said Ford.[25]

He went to Dreiser's house-warming, and to tea with Muriel Draper, 'the wittiest woman in New York', though he managed to make her cry by showing her a letter from Julie: 'I did not know she had lost a daughter', he told Bowen. The following week he travelled to Chicago. Pond, the lecture agent, had only arranged two venues there at $200 a time—Jeanne Foster said he really didn't like Ford, and didn't believe he could lecture. But Harriet Monroe had invited him, and he gave a reminiscential talk to the Arts Club. At first he found Chicago depressing: 'I *hate* the aspect of the Middle West under dirty snow', he told Bowen. 'I don't wonder all the women in their stories go mad or to the bad.' This was partly because the expanses of the prairie state seen from the observation car on the train made him feel agoraphobic: 'I rather shudder at vast stretches of plain', he wrote, explaining that he 'did not feel safe' at the thought of the 'long uneventful days and communings with solitude' under the vast skies. He always needed an audience to feel secure. But his anxiety was also over money. He feared that the lecture tour was 'quite a dud'. He had hoped Carlos Drake's father would put him up, but instead he installed him in 'an extremely expensive room' at the Blackstone. (Ford later wrote that he had visited Chicago in order to persuade Drake 'to permit his son to take up literature as a profession, and to let him have a little money while he made his way'. The butchering 'magnate' replied that it would be a 'dreadful thing' if his son were 'to have on his gravestone the fact that he was a mere ink-slinger' rather than going into the family business. The attitude is that of Henry Martin's father in *The Rash Act*.) Samuel Putnam met Ford in the lobby of the Blackstone, and noted that he 'fidgeted constantly for something he never seemed able to find. And there was that ever recurring snort of his, which to me always suggested a cavalry charge.' It was perhaps this train of thought that caused Putnam to remind him that he had once written that 'the only two pursuits worthy of a gentleman are war and poetry'. 'I think', said Ford, 'we may leave out the war.' Putnam also recalled Ford saying: 'When George Moore dies, I believe I shall be the dean of English novelists.'[26]

Thanks to Jeanne Foster's tireless publicity campaign, Ford was constantly pestered by 'the most imbecile set of reviewers the *world* can ever have seen'. 'The Chicago Tribune photographers have just burst into this room without asking any leave and have fired off a magnesian [p]istol that has completely stifled me with the smoke of war', he complained, but consoled himself that at least he could give his protégés some publicity. He lectured at 'an immense convent school' at which some of the nuns knew his daughter Christina. Harriet Monroe was 'very affectionate and useful'; but when Ford visited the office of *Poetry*, she got him to write a 2,000-word article. George Dillon remembered: 'he astonished us all by dictating it, without hesitation, then and there. It was an extremely good article, in his wittiest style.' The impression of effortlessness was only an impression: the performance left him 'fairly dithering'. One of his most admiring reviewers, Fanny Butcher, came to interview him for the *Chicago Tribune*. The publicity had its effect, and invitations began to 'pour in'.

The British Ambassador was there for a dinner at the English Speaking Union, and Ford told Bowen he had specially asked him to attend. A 'confidante' of Hemingway's telephoned him to beg him not to call on Hemingway's parents, who lived in what Ford called 'a particularly Puritan and ridiculous suburb of Chicago called Oak Park', warning Bowen: 'Hemingway would never forgive you if you let people know that he was born there.' Dr Hemingway was thought (like Colonel Drake) to regard Ford as 'the devil, hoof, tails and all, who had led his son astray' because he had 'encouraged Ernest to become a writer'. But 'after all the interviews and fuss', said Ford, Dr Hemingway called him and begged him 'to go to lunch, dinner, tea, or stay in the house, or anything'. Hemingway's confidante had been exaggerating. Dr Hemingway wrote to tell Ernest of their 'delightful dinnerparty' with their 'very charming guest': 'He surely does appreciate you and your work. He gave us a wonderfull word picture of you and your boy'; and he added: 'Mother was so pleased with the Englishman. He seemed to enjoy his dinner and the Tea and all the other eats.' The hospitality and publicity raised his spirits. 'You see, these people love me w[h]en they see me. I have only got to appear in a room and smile with my shy modesty and whole cities fall for me', he told Bowen with sly mock-modesty, and continued with mock-heroism about having 'conquered' the Middle West, and wanting to assault Boston and Washington. That sense of 'stimulation and battle' he found attractive. After a fortnight in Chicago he spoke at the Women's Club at Rockford, Illinois. 'Don't worry about my successes with the ladies', he told Bowen. 'One never sees them twice and the once is always in bevies of 400 or so and I have latterly been so worried by the Pond affair that I can assure you that I have not been rendered complacent by any number of social successes':

You need not be fearful that N.Y. will become a necessity to me. Why should it? I like the place; it stimulates me and there are nice people in it, but it is just a means to an end. I have made a lot of useful business contacts and thought a lot of thoughts about modern civilisation which is almost more useful to me but, though I'd like well enough to return there from time to time, or even, if we could afford it, for us to have an apartment there for it *is* fun, I can perfectly well get on without it. You see, darling, *all* I think about is leaving you and E.J. comfortably off after my demise—and the best way to do that is to have a steady market for my books—preferably here, because the market is so large. I should come straight back from here only Mrs Foster is working tooth and nail to get me lecture appointments in Boston and Washington.

This was probably *almost* true of his feelings while in Chicago. He was being disin-genuous about Rene Wright, who must also have been on his mind (though he could hardly write to Bowen about her), but not insincere about wanting to return to France. He told Bowen he would be returning to New York via St Louis—presumably to see Wright. His feelings were dual about the Middle West. 'They say the M.W. will eventually secede from the East & have Chicago for its capital', he wrote to Stella from the train between Pittsburgh and Philadelphia: 'I hope it may.' 'I sh^d. like to come to N.Y. often—& I daresay even to Chicago.'[27]

In New York he returned to the defence of his version of Conrad. Jessie Conrad had resumed her denunciation of some of Ford's claims in her book, *Joseph Conrad as I Knew Him*. 'It's really quite good and not *very* offensive to me', Ford wrote magnanimously—and with relief—to Stella. But it was offensive enough to cause more damage, so Ford sent the *New York Times* an extract from *The Cinque Ports* to prove that he had supplied the story on which Conrad had based his story 'Amy Foster'. He then wrote to the *New York Herald Tribune Books* to state that he was not responsible for selling his letters from Conrad that were being advertised by T. J. Wise (Ford must have been furious that both Elsie and Violet were selling them). He used the occasion of correcting a mistake in the American edition of *The Nature of a Crime* to quote from Conrad's letters about their collaboration—'it would be delightful to catch again the echo of the desperate and funny quarrels that enlivened those old days'—and to emphasize that Conrad had been willing to collaborate once again at the end of his life: the Preface to *The Nature of a Crime* was 'the last piece of completed literary work that Conrad lived to execute; the correction of those proofs—of that preface and of the analysis of *Romance*—was his last completed literary action.'[28]

He now felt he had to defend himself against Hunt's book too, telling Bowen that 'everyone in New York—Bradley, Mrs Foster, the Bonis, the Gormans'—had advised him to stay long enough for it not to look as if he were being 'chased out of the field by it'. (It was also a convenient alibi to extend his stay.) He cancelled a dinner with T. R. Smith of Boni and Liveright (who had published Hunt's memoir). Mizener said that 'with success he had begun to treat publishers in an old-fashioned Edwardian style, as if they were not quite gentlemen. During these years he built up a reputation for being difficult that would complicate his relation with publishers for the rest of his life.' It is true that Charles Boni would not have been amused when he found out that Ford had been teasing him by telling him that Joyce's *Anna Livia Plurabelle* was part of what was to be 'a history of Ireland'. But it was Bradley and Foster who advised him to cancel the dinner with Smith; and Ford's ironic account to Bowen suggests that their stand had the desired effect: 'He really almost cried, he having, so it is said, an almost sentimental attachment to me. . . .' The episode had the kind of farcical ramifications that Ford exulted in being beset by:

Last night I was at a party at the Friedes when a *terrific* millionaire came up to me and expressed extravagant admiration—particularly, curiously enough, for the E.[nglish] R.[eview] to which he had been used to send manuscripts when he had been an undergraduate at Harvard of literary aspirations. I never published any and his father had forced him into business and he is now the Cedar Wood King of the world. The cedars of Lebanon belong to him. So he invited me to go home with him to a party of unparalleled debauchery that he was giving with all the vaudeville stars in New York in attendance—the sort of thing one reads about. So I went back with him. And his apartment was completely pannelled— twenty or thirty rooms—in tulip wood because he hates cedar. But there was not a soul there. And when he telephoned to all the people that were coming to his party—it was then past two—all their valets and servants replied that they were too drunk to stand. So the millionaire, weeping, confided to me all the sorrows of his life—which amounted to his not knowing what to spend his money on—and towards four announced that he was going to head a crusade to London to kill the tenant of S.[outh] L.[odge]. Then it turned out that he was financing Boni and Liveright who published S.L.'s book and the debauchery party had been arranged by Mr Tom Smith as compensation for that outrage. But as they had not been able to get hold of me—because I will not have anything to do with Horace [Liveright] or Tom Smith—they had arranged to send the Cedar King to Friede's party to trepan me to theirs.

But Mr Smith meanwhile had been giving the debauchery party supper at the Plaza to such purpose that they had all been carried home.[29]

As with Drake and Hemingway, this is (amongst other things) another story of a father opposed to a literary career for his son. Was Ford still exorcizing what he remembered as his father's last words to him: 'Fordie, whatever you do, never write a book'? It's also about Ford's omnipotence as an editor. Feeling Drake's and Hemingway's fathers resented his influence was an oblique way of asserting that influence. In this case his influence stopped the young man from becoming a writer. As with the story about Dr Hemingway's *volte face*, Ford plays up the melodramatic absurdity of the anecdote in order to keep his self-pity and self-importance in ironic check. 'It's funny how one sows the whirlwind and reaps. . . . I don't quite know how that metaphor works out', he wrote to Bowen, ostensibly about how he was still feeling the effects of his *English Review* days. Yet he knew that he was still provoking storms. He needed to be in their eyes.[30]

Back in New York, Ford decided to give a large tea-party in the 'rambling, old, gloomy' West 16th Street apartment that had been found for him by Ruth Kerr, who had acted as his secretary during his previous visit, and would later become his agent in America. Caroline Gordon, who was his current secretary, used to make tea on a gas ring in one of the two parlours; but this couldn't be done for fifty or sixty people, so he said he sent her to ask 'the janitrix' for something with which to boil water in another room. 'Why doesn't Mr. F—— use his kitchen?', was the reply. One of his doors led into a passage he had never explored. 'In the passage was a kitchen!' Both he and Gordon were amazed that the other one could have been there so long without realizing. He found it mysterious. 'This will seem incredible and I have not time to explain it', he wrote—as much could be said of most of his autobiography: 'it is nevertheless a true anecdote.' Whatever else it may signify about the spaciousness of old buildings, the story says much about his indifference to material comforts; and also about how he must have been eating out for most of his meals in New York.[31]

'I am all dated up till the last minute', he told Bowen as he was preparing to leave: 'lunching with the Roosevelts at one and sailing at four—and thankful I shall be when I am on the ship':

Yesterday was a day of disasters. Imprimis: I was caught by the customs house and made to pay $243.13 cts for income tax before they would give my visa. Secondly I got really impossibly intoxicated at Elinor Wylie's and have lost my false teeth—the newer set, so that now I am wearing the old ones with all the accompaniments of vomiting and the rest of it. What the Benet's had to drink [. . .] I cannot imagine. The company simply fell flat on the floor, I with them, as if we had been struck dead—and then revived after three quarters of an hour or so. It was probably therefore ether. So this morning I feel rather rotten: it is too bad to be made drunk for nothing, for I had really drunk nothing at all; I have been tremendously careful lately. But alcohol here is really the arrow that flieth by night [. . .].[32]

He visited Boston on 22 February—a Mrs Ames had arranged a literary luncheon for him. At Cambridge he spoke to undergraduates at the Harvard Union, 'recounting anecdotes about reading *The Red Badge of Courage* at the front', and telling them that 'Crane's imaginative powers had been so great that as he read the book he totally forgot he was within reach of the German artillery'. Then on the 24th he sailed for London on the SS *American Banker*. It was a merchant vessel with only five other passengers; $100 for a cabin and bathroom. 'Alas, I have decided that I cannot afford to cross the ocean with any jovial crew because I am so dreadfully behind hand with my work that I must positively write all the time I am on board ship', he told Ferris Greenslet: 'If I went with you who knows how many master pieces might not get written.' He couldn't afford the money either for a faster boat. It took eleven days—'a slow, dull passage', he told Greenslet: 'but I have managed to do a good deal of writing.' He met Bowen in London, and they travelled back to Paris for about a fortnight, and then south to revisit Toulon. Ford had after all managed to make a little money in America, and cheques began to arrive for the essays he had been writing about his visit. They were able to afford a room in the Grand Hotel Victoria, with a bath and felt impressed with their own affluence. Yet Bowen remembered this visit as less happy than the first, lacking 'the old café gatherings'. She said this was because Juan Gris had died—though in fact he didn't die until 11 May 1927. But Ford gave another account of their unhappiness to Jeanne Foster, when he wrote her a letter on the typewriter she had given him: 'I have been writing very hard at *New York is Not America* and, having naturally mislaid my spectacles have been suffering from all sorts of eyestrains and headaches and depressions.' 'America seems to have dropped out of the world', he told her, feeling disorientated at having dropped out of its world of admiring ladies: 'I keep on writing and writing about it with such intensity that I am quite dizzy when I look up and see from my window the plane trees and the sunlight.' In 'L'Envoi' to the book he again contrasts the Mediterranean's light and trees to the 'enchantment' of the Manhattan cityscape. New York represented 'hope' to him, and what it didn't have was the 'disillusion' he ascribed to the Mediterranean, and which was what he was feeling: because his hopes of success, and of love, lay 'so many thousand miles away'. The book explicitly sexualizes its social geography. Ford excused his ironies by saying of himself that he was 'apt between loving speeches to make fun of' the Americans he describes; and he adds: 'loving New York, next to Provence, better than any other place, he lets himself go and writes of her' as he would talk to someone he loved intimately. It was his characteristic writerly displacement, looking at one view with his mind somewhere quite other. He had Dowell's feeling that 'the world is full of places to which I want to return', and a desperate anxiety that he might not be able to return to New York—though he was planning to return in September, hoping to bring Ezra Pound with him. As his boat sailed past Nantucket, he had already been recording his feelings at leaving: 'One is never certain that one will return . . . not *certain*. / It is not decent to describe for an Anglo-Saxon audience the emotions that one feels at such thoughts as that it is not certain that one will ever return.'[33]

1927–1928: PROVENCE, NEW YORK, PARIS

Pound had been on his mind since the beginning of the year, when Ford had written an appreciative review of *Personae*. What most appealed to him in the poetry was what he was himself trying to do in his impressionistic travel books like *New York is Not America* as well as in his fiction: 'more and more he assumes the aspect of a poet who is the historian of the world.' He continued their affectionate sparring, teasing Pound for his 'singularly incomprehensible Philadelphian dialect' and his tennis style (like 'an inebriated kangaroo that has been rendered unduly vigorous by injection of some gland or other'). When *New York is Not America* was finished Ford probably visited Pound at Rapallo, and continued to write to him to try to arrange a lecture tour in the autumn. He wouldn't accept Pound's uninterest; Pound eventually had to tell him: 'All this endeavour is most noble of you. But I don't know how to make my intentions more plain than I already have done. I am not going to the U.S.A.' Ford took another tack, persuading him to let Irita van Doren publish Pound's 'How to Read, or Why'.[1]

Ford and Bowen were back in Paris in May. Natalie Barney sent out cards announcing that Ford was to give a talk about American Women of Letters, including Djuna Barnes, on 3 June. He was 'an amiable fellow and could talk about anything and had nice manners', said the composer Virgil Thomson, who met him at about this time. It isn't known if he gave the talk, but on that day his mother died in London, aged 76. He went to London for the funeral, staying for about a week. Although there is some confusion about the dates of composition for his next novel to be published, *Last Post*, Ford said that he had begun the writing in June or July, indicating that this most elegiac of his books was an oblique elegy for his mother. In the 'Dedicatory Letter' to Isabel Paterson (who had encouraged him to write the book by asking 'what became of Tietjens') he asked:

Do you not find [. . .] that, however it may be with the mass of humanity, in the case of certain dead people you cannot feel that they are indeed gone from this world? You can only know it, you can only believe it. That is, at any rate, the case with me—and in my case the world daily becomes more and more peopled with such *revenants* and less and less with those who still walk this earth.[2]

Jean Rhys had now finished her version of *Perversity* (by Francis Carco), for which Ford was to have written an introduction. 'As a translation I think it remarkably good', he told Covici, though he had himself 'been trying to make the translation itself look less brutal':

I certainly could not have done it as well myself for I do not know the French slang of the particular type that fills this book. The point is that French when translated into English appears so much more violent than when it is read in French that I really got a shock when reading the translation [. . .] it is due to the racial fact that English is not a language in which direct statements are ever made so that if you do make them, they stick unbearably out of the page [. . .]

Yet this attempt to help Rhys was as disastrous as the earlier ones. Covici had originally wanted Ford to translate the book; and even though Ford had made it quite clear that he hadn't the time to do it himself, and had therefore passed the work on to 'Mme Lenglet', Covici none the less published it under Ford's name. He probably thought it would sell better. Rhys felt that 'once again he had deliberately exploited and betrayed her'. It must have made her all the more determined to exact her revenge in *Quartet*, which she was then finishing. Ford wrote to Covici and the literary papers to correct the mistake, but when the translation was later reprinted it was again attributed to him.³

Samuel Putnam, who had talked to Ford in Chicago, came over to Paris. He and his wife were wheeling their baby down the rue de Vaugirard and 'literally' bumped into Ford, who was now based at number 32. He was as surprised as they were, but 'gallantly insisted upon pushing the baby's perambulator, discoursing all the while' about Rossetti and the Pre-Raphaelites. It was 'one of the most interesting expositions of the subject I had heard or read', thought Putnam. When he said he had decided to give up newspaper work for a while, Ford 'expressed his satisfaction, and then went on to explain: "The difference is that a journalist has to write *in* his environment, whereas the writer can only write *outside* of his".' Which is true of the writer's need to achieve a distance from the material; but particularly true of impressionist Ford, who wrote best of somewhere quite other. The next day he wrote Putnam a note saying he was 'pleased and not astonished' he had decided to settle in Paris, and made thoughtful suggestions about how he could add to his income.⁴

Ford and Bowen spent August in Provence. He had heard that Borys Conrad was in prison for a year, for defrauding a Mrs Bevan out of £1,100. Borys came back from the war seriously wounded and disturbed; after his father's death he 'seemed to have lost his head completely', and to have believed 'that his expectations would be enormous'. Ford wrote to Eric Pinker to invite Borys's wife and child to stay with them in Avignon: 'People like to get to France where as a rule nothing is known of their cases.' (Was he recalling his travels in Provence after the *Throne* case?) As Mizener says, the generous offer was not taken up. Instead, a friend of Jeanne Foster, the poet and dramatist Jane Dransfield, was with them, and recorded her 'tribute to a great writer, and to a friend for whom one could not do a favor without its being returned tenfold':

Ford, walking the August fields of Provence and naming for us each flower and herb—Ford, at seven every morning climbing narrow stairs to the hot attic of the little hotel at Villeneuve-les-Avignon, and there beneath a dormer window where M. Blanc, the proprietor, had cleared a space for a deal table and one straight chair, writing on his Corona (he was then finishing *The Last Post*) until ten, the hour for joining Stella, his wife, Julie his six-year-old daughter, and myself for bathing in the snow cold Rhone.—Ford, famous gourmet, eating without complaint the dreadful hotel meals—Ford, in spite of his weight, mounting the 160 steps of the Philip le Bel tower, eager with historical tales and the prospect of the best view in Avignon—getting up delightful excursions to Les Baux, or Nîmes, or leading us out on the bridge at Avignon to dance out in a round the old nursery song.—Ford, sitting for hours with his beer in the late afternoon on the terrasse above the river, sometimes with no word spoken, sometimes discoursing at great length on the beauty of the accurate and simple word, or on some phase of world civilization. At one such time he said (I quote my diary) 'George Washington was a traitor to civilization. It is the greatest pity there ever was a split between England and America. United they would be a power for good; divided, civilization is doomed'.[5]

He never lost his habit of teasing Americans—a habit which has exasperated some American critics of his novels. But his comment on Washington is more than mere wanton iconoclasm. His own transatlantic travels and travelogues—and indeed his *transatlantic review*—were a form of shuttle-diplomacy ('Let our ambassadors be our books') in the name of what he called 'the only sane Internationalism'. And his fears for European civilization proved prophetic about the results of the American political isolationism that so dismayed him.

That August his daughter Katharine married an Irish painter, Charles Lamb, who specialized in depicting peasant life. They lived in a caravan for a time, travelling about Ireland, but settled in Galway, when they built a house at Carraroe designed for them by Ford's old friend from his Limpsfield days, Harrison Cowlishaw. Mizener said that Ford 'gave her no sign'. Perhaps he did not know.[6]

The writing was harder than he made it seem. 'I have got on rather slowly, owing to bothers and depressions with my novel', he told Jeanne Foster. He had also been having 'a terrible time of anxiety with publishers'. He had made a contract with Friede for Boni and Liveright to take over the books he had published with Boni and Boni, and to publish all his work for the next five years, paying him a monthly advance of $300. But this depended on Friede being able to buy the plates of the books the Boni brothers had already published 'at a fair price'. But the Bonis refused to accept Ford's attempt to terminate the contract. 'There seems to be no solution except the very fantastic one of having Mr. Ford pay the difference between the fair price of $1200.00 that we offered and the $3100.00 that the Bonis insist on', said Friede. Ford was more successful with the Tietjens novels than he had ever been (or ever would be again). Friede was as eager to publish him as the Bonis were reluctant to release him. But he could not muster $1,900, and the result was simply to delay the American publication of *New York is Not America* until December, and to leave Ford bound to publishers he had alienated. The legal details were too specialized for him, and he was ill-advised by Bradley and Friede, who should have been more aware of the difficulties. In September Ford crossed the Atlantic once more, this time from Liverpool to Montreal on the Canadian Pacific liner, SS *Minnedosa*. He had another motive besides wanting to see Rene Wright; he had to go and try to disentangle the publishing muddle for himself. He finished *Last Post* on the day before the voyage ended, and celebrated at the ship's concert by offering 'to compose a limerick on any passenger's name for a dollar, with the return of the money guaranteed if he did not complete the verse within thirty seconds'. It was not an expedient to supplement his income: 'he certainly turned in a lot of dollars for the Seamen's Charities.'[7]

He arrived exhausted from overworking to finish the novel, and came down with a cold, 'almost as violent as at St. Agrève, with no sleep on account of suffocation'. He had to explain to Harriet Monroe why Pound hadn't come with him, which he did by distorting the facts to make it sound like a betrayal: 'Here I am back in New York, and, as is not unusual with me in a dilemma—naturally on account of Ezra. That poet undertook to come over with me and at the last moment did not.' Harrison Smith was 'mad to publish Last Post', but Ford wanted to persuade him to take on his other Boni publications as well. He met someone called Macy-Masins, who offered to put up $50,000 for a new transatlantic review, he told Bowen; Carl Brandt, who was now Ford's agent in America (working in conjunction with William Bradley) assured Ford he was 'very rich and honest'. Bowen was sceptical; she felt much more keenly than did Ford how the original review had impoverished them. She told him she regarded the idea 'with great fear':

Only I would like to ask you not to envisage using your bureau here in the studio in any way for the Review. Since I've been working here hard, regularly, I realise how much I count upon being quiet and alone in the studio. I think it is splendid that you have this as a sort of 'show' study, and for casual work, and I am sorry you have nothing better than the bedroom at 32 [rue de Vaugirard] for your regular writing. But one hopes to get something else some day at 32.[8]

It was still assumed that they would be living together when he returned. Ford had not yet told her about Rene Wright. But even before he did, she had begun to feel that, as she wrote: 'The desire for freedom was already beginning to work in me, and what he really needed was another mate [. . .] I wanted to belong to myself. I wanted to slip from under the weightiness of Ford's personality and regain my own shape.' In part, this meant a more serious engagement with her painting, in which she lacked confidence but which Ford encouraged fulsomely: 'It isn't any hypocrisy to say that I care more about the success of your art than about anything that could happen to mine', he told her. The admiration was mutual: 'I don't think you've ever in your life done anything better [. . .]', she wrote as soon as she had read Last Post:

Mark's death is a lovely poem. And poor Valentine! But all that is a bit too near the knuckle. Still I'm the only person who is going to feel that, and it doesn't make it less wonderful art [. . .] There is nothing better anywhere in Literature than Marie Leonie, Mark on Women, and the boy, and even Valentine's agonies even if she is so beastly normal! Anyway that is my opinion.

It was 'near the knuckle' not just because the novel drew on the way their love had ended Ford's relationship with Hunt—just when she felt his new loves would end their relationship; but also because Marie Leonie's house is modelled on Cooper's Cottage, Bedham, making the novel seem like an elegy for their union.[9]

Harrison Smith's interest persuaded the Bonis to agree to the terms Ford had asked for earlier; but the suspense had taken its toll on Ford. Bowen had become adept at stage-managing his life to shield him from financial worries. Whenever there was bad news, she said, 'the air would be so filled with pain that we could neither of us do any work at all'. He found coping with such anxieties in New York as enervating as it was exhilarating. His comment to Bowen when he inadvertently got her account overdrawn reveals how deeply financial anxiety weighed on him—as is evident from Tietjens's anxiety about his overdraft: 'I am horribly humiliated about the affair of the overdraft—more humiliated than I ever felt in my life.' 'I really had worked myself into such a stew over the delay [over the Boni contract] that yesterday with the relief I nearly went dotty with nerves and giddiness and the rest.' The spectre of agoraphobia still waited for him, when, as now, he felt lonely, staying in the National Arts Club to recuperate, and lying low until his contract had been settled. (He gave a dinner party for some literary friends—the Van Dorens, Isabel Patersons, Gormans, Van Loons, and Wylie and Benét—which he said 'restored my morale a good deal'.) He hadn't stopped working, of course. He wrote a brilliant review of Jean-Aubry's *Joseph Conrad: Life and Letters*, implicitly justifying the impressionist method of literary biography he had exemplified in his memoir of Conrad, as opposed to the embalmment of the 'official biography'. An impassioned article opposing militarism urged Americans to be more politically aware, and expressed his aesthetic internationalism: 'We died at Givenchy—I am speaking naturally of my own regiment, or you on the *Chemin des Dames*—in order that the ideal of the shining sword and the flashing helm might die forever as an active symbol of relationships between peoples [. . .] militarism is the antithesis of Thought and the Arts, and it is by Thought and the Arts alone that the world can be saved.' But his argument that 'jack-bootism' had had its day, and that 'Neither demagogue nor demi-god' would be able to rouse the masses with militarist rhetoric was all too soon to be proved an unfulfilled wish. E. M. Forster's *Aspects of the Novel* wrung a 'cry from the soul' in Ford's review. He admired Forster's novels; but Forster's comment that Gide was 'a little more solemn than an author should be about the whole caboodle' represented to Ford 'the whole attitude of the British don-critic towards our art': 'The novel, novel writing, form, language, construction, ancestry—all these things which are the object of serious study outside England in places from which come the first-class novels—all these things are "the whole caboodle" which, if you take seriously, you will never make fun of your children in the pages of *Punch*. You will be un-English.'[10] There was further suspense when *Collier's Weekly* expressed an interest in serializing his next novel, *A Little Less Than Gods*, which would have meant a good regular income (the magazine agreed to a price of $15,000 if they took the novel); 'castles in the air are agreeable building', Ford wrote to Bowen; this one never materialized. He had been planning to write this historical romance about Marshal Ney for many years. He heard the germ of it in Philadelphia in 1906, when a literary lady had told him that there used to live, in New Orleans, 'an old, mild gentleman who possessed a singular sword and was accustomed, gently and unemotionally to assert that he was . . . Michel Ney, soon to be a little dust'. Ney was executed in 1815 for high treason, after he switched sides: sent to oppose his old commander Napoleon's return from Elba he rejoined forces with him instead. In the story Ford invented to explain his survival, the machinations of the aloof, novelist-like plotter, the English *milor* Assheton Smith, cause Ney to be exchanged for his double, Baron de Frèjus. The double-motif was becoming increasingly fascinating to Ford, and was to exfoliate in his finest late novels, *The Rash Act* and *Henry for Hugh*. As in those books, one double's death is the other's survival; a plot which casts light back to *The Good Soldier*, where Ashburnham's death causes Dowell, his shadow, to realize that he was a kind of double ('I love him because he was just myself'; 'He seems to me like a large elder brother'); and to *Last Post*, in which Christopher's new life is glimpsed through the interstices of his large elder brother's death. Ford had probably discussed the idea of a Napoleonic novel with Conrad as early as 1902, and he thought of *A Little Less Than Gods* as a continuation of Conrad's unfinished *Suspense*, writing in the dedication that 'At one time it was to have become a collaboration with another writer [. . .] But a lamented death cut short his story and I considered myself at liberty to take it on again myself.' Ford often wrote of himself as Conrad's double; here, the elder double's death liberates the younger. The novel is touched by sibling anxieties of a different order, for it returns to the theme of incest used in *The Good Soldier* and *Parade's End*. George Feilding, the young English hero caught up in Napoleon's 'Hundred Days', falls in love with Hélène de Frèjus (wife of the Baron), only to discover that she is his illegitimate sister. In the autumn of 1927 Ford was approached by Burton Rascoe, the editor of the New York *Bookman*, who had been sent the manuscript of another unfinished Conrad manuscript, that of 'The Sisters'. Rascoe thought Ford knew nothing about the story, but thought: 'if I could implant into his mind the idea that *I believed* he did, he would say that of course he knew all about the story and would consent to finish it, or at least tell the *Bookman* readers how Conrad intended to develop it.' Mizener follows Rascoe in assuming that Ford was successfully beguiled at a lunch with e. e. cummings. But a letter from Ford shows that he didn't play into Rascoe's hands as Rascoe thought: 'I have read the Conrad story and reflected over it still more carefully and I don't think I can do what you want though it would amuse me to try it'; he then offered to describe what he knew of the plot, and instead of a 'formal continuation' to provide instead 'some comments on the writing which is extraordinarily interesting to me because it is so different from anything else that Conrad ever wrote'. Rascoe was not sure who was fooling whom: 'Ford turned in such an interesting and plausible article about Conrad's intentions that I have never been able to decide to this day whether what he wrote is true or imagined.' Plausible, because Ford said that he didn't remember seeing the manuscript, and that he didn't know every detail of Conrad's intention, but that they had discussed it when, around 1906, Conrad dug out the manuscript he had abandoned in 1896. Ford called it his 'forbidden story': 'what he, curiously, desired to write of was incest. I don't mean to say that he proposed to write of the consummation of forbidden desires, but he did want to render the emotions of a shared passion that by its nature must be most hopeless of all.'[11] Ford wasn't just (as Mizener suggests) reimagining Conrad in his own image—projecting the incest motif on to 'The Sisters' because he was about to elaborate it himself. He discusses it as a deeply personal story ('from time to time, as if guiltily, as if swiftly contemplating the obscene, he would take a peek into that locked drawer [. . .]'); and the 1917 reworking of the material into *The Arrow of Gold* has been described by his biographer Frederick Karl as Conrad's 'autobiographical' novel. Ford's synopsis—that 'The pensive Slav painter was to have married the older sister and then to have had an incestuous child by the other'—describes a theme which, as Karl says, Conrad did in fact use in the relationship between Nostromo and the Viola sisters. But it also describes what might have been the plot of Ford's own life at the time of his collaboration over *Romance*, when he married the younger sister and probably had an affair with the older. Ford was struck by the way 'The Sisters' seemed to suggest that he and Conrad were even more intimately double than he had realized: 'And, curiously enough *The Inheritors*, the first of our collaborations to be published, has a faint and fantastic suggestion of—unrequited—love between brother and sister. It was as much as anything, because of this that Conrad fiercely—almost fanatically—insisted on collaborating in this book [. . .].'[12]

Ford's original conception of the Ney novel was very different. Feilding is there for his relation to the Marwoodian Assheton Smith, who, like the equally contemptuous Mr Blood in the earlier novel *Mr. Fleight*, is stirred from his seigneurial lethargy to help his admiring younger protégé. The two synopses don't mention incest or exchanged identities. Ney was to have been shot, and the story was to have been Assheton Smith's tragedy as well, since he not only fails in his political intrigues, but in his love, eventually abandoned by the woman for whom he has been 'roused to a passion of the most ungovernable kind'. 'It is the tragedy of the strong silent man when he breaks down before emotion and he becomes at once ridiculous and tragic . . .', wrote Ford, perhaps thinking of himself with Jean Rhys or Rene Wright, though perhaps also recalling Marwood's behaviour towards Elsie. Thus, though he may not have originally thought of using the idea of Ney escaping, he eventually transformed the story into something quintessentially Fordian: the lost cause of hopeless passion; the narrowest escape from death, brought about through de Frèjus's suicidal sacrificing of himself in Ney's place; doubles; military action, followed by a new life across the Atlantic. (There is even a statue of Ney nearby one of Ford's favourite cafés, the Closerie des Lilas, where Ford told Sisley Huddleston about the projected novel. Huddleston thought Rude's statue 'induced him to take up the theme'.) But its dominant theme—which survived its transformations—is the hero-worship of the powerful—in particular Napoleon—by the young. At first he called it 'Demi-Gods'. This current too runs deep in Ford's fiction, through the insidiously powerful fourth-dimensionists in *The Inheritors*, Henry VIII, *Mr. Apollo*, Tietjens's or Campion's god-like presences. In *A Little Less Than Gods* Ford attempts a Flaubertian ambivalence about sentiment, re-creating George's awe in the presence of the great, while simultaneously suggesting an ironic view of such mystique. The novel draws on his feelings of awe for his father, and his circle of Victorian Great, or for Arthur Marwood. It also draws on his feelings of awe for the powers of other writers: Stendhal, James, and of course in particular Conrad. The eventual title alludes to Dryden's 'Song for St Cecilia', which uses the image of the speech of Gods to describe the power of music to control passion:

> Less than a God they thought there cou'd not dwell
> Within the hollow of that Shell
> That spoke so sweetly and so well.
> What passion cannot MUSICK raise and quell.[13]

The demi-god is not only the seemingly omnipotent soldier-politician, but also the artist, who can invoke immortal powers; though the novel is aware how both are susceptible to delusions of grandeur—the 'God-Complex'. Yet the novel rarely engages with its deepest feelings. It has haunting scenes (such as George's vision of

Hélène as an awesome Aphrodite-figure); but its fantasy and historical romance prevent it from being more than the *tour de force* Ford knew his historical fiction to be.

He also associated the book with Rene Wright, to whom he dedicated it, saying that he heard the story just after he had met her in New York. 'The penalties with which you then threatened me if I did not entertain you with diverting and mendacious inventions were many and singular.' He ran away to Philadelphia to escape them, where he was told the story, which he was then able to offer to her when they met and fell in love twenty years later. The dedication mentions fairy tale, and this story of the story had a logic which makes their own lives sound like fairy tale. But it is a fairy tale without a happy ending, perhaps because Ford feared that if he could not get a divorce from Elsie, his new passion would prove as hopeless as Feilding's for his sister.

Douglas Goldring saw Ford in New York that autumn, and found him more self-confident after the success of the Tietjens novels. Goldring felt nervous there, but Ford made 'gallant efforts' to make him feel at home, 'and discoursed learnedly on American food—the various kinds of oysters and their respective merits, the virtues of blue fish, avocado pears, American steaks and so forth. It was evident that he adored New York', the 'electric atmosphere' of which acted on him like 'an agreeable tonic'. After dinner they strolled towards Washington Square:

Indicating a small window at the back of one of the houses, in which a light happened to be shining, he said: 'And there, my dear Goldring, in that very room, where you see the light (whoof), the great Henry James was born. . . .' I made the necessary sounds to indicate the appropriate emotion. Not for a thousand dollars would I have suggested to Ford that the great Henry would have been inexpressibly shocked to have been born in a bathroom or toilet instead of in the front of the house, in the best bedroom. Ford's method was invariably to 'use precision in order to create an effect of authenticity' [. . .]

Whereabouts in New York Ford actually 'resided' I never discovered. I called for him once at an address he gave me and found him in a small and dingy apartment which he used as an office. The room into which he ushered me had no furniture at all except a small table, on which a typewriter reposed, and two hard chairs. Ford, who in those days had become rather stout, was dressed only in his under-garments. Like most New York apartments—and hotel bedrooms—the place was overheated, and he was sweating profusely. 'I just use this place to work in' he explained. I suppose it was the nearest approach to a garret that central New York afforded, and a garret was what he had always preferred. We had dinner together that night in a luxurious speak-easy where the food was excellent, the wine drinkable and the bill—to my European ideas—staggering.[14]

'The drink here is really terrible', Ford told Bowen: 'bad in itself and absolutely unavoidable if you go to people's houses. When I was not going out it was all right, but now I get slightly canned every night and I don't like that.' 'I wish I was not going to the van Loons where I suppose I shall have to drink too much.'[15]

He sat for another portrait by Hartmann. On 3 November he had what he called 'a most rapturous reception at Wanamaker's' when he spoke to 900 people. Then he had to speak at a farewell dinner for H. M. Tomlinson at the Players Club because Tomlinson was 'too shy'. Ford was invited to watch the football game between Yale and Brown by a young collector of his books who wanted an autograph. He asked if he could bring Rene Wright. 'As for recognition', he explained to his host, 'I am very big: wear light tweeds & carry a large bamboo cane: M^rs. Wright is small—but I don't know how she will be dressed.' He enjoyed the game 'well enough as a spectacle', he said: 'but it seemed to me rather monstrous as a game.' Afterwards he was introduced to Wilbur Cross, the editor of the *Yale Review*, who asked him for a short story. He had tried using a different lecture agent, Lee Keedick, for his trip, but Keedick had not told him of any bookings before he arrived, so he did not expect to lecture. But on 4 November he set off for Ohio, where he was due to speak the next day. 'My financial condition is still distracting', he told Bowen: 'I am just starting off for Springfield & have hardly a cent: but it can't be helped. Anyhow I haven't drawn on you.' He had managed to find enough money to send Julie a red-indian suit for her birthday. He made a speech about the war to the Springfield audience, which 'turned out to be almost entirely German', he said later, and made him feel hated—which was perhaps why he said Springfield was 'the city I most dislike in this country'.[16]

On his previous visit Ford had met Caroline Gordon and her husband the poet Allen Tate, who said Ford took him under his wing in 1927. His friendship with them was to become one of the most important of his last decade. 'I think he was the most generous man I have ever known', wrote Gordon:

Ford, at that time, had most of the New York publishers at his feet. I acted as his secretary and handled his mail. One morning I laid a manuscript of poems by Léonie Adams on top of the heap. He read the poems [. . .] and folded his hands on top of the heap and said, 'Tell her that I am completely at her service.' I gleefully relayed this message to Miss Adams and they became fast friends.

'He's awfully nice, and I love to see him take his sentences by the tail and uncurl them—in a perfectly elegant manner', she wrote to her friend Sally Wood. 'I don't believe there's anybody writing now who can do it so elegantly. At times he almost weeps over my lapses into Americanisms. "My deah child, *do* you spell 'honour' without a u?"' The Tates lived in a brownstone apartment house at 27 Bank Street, where they had free rooms in the basement and a small retainer in return for acting as janitors. They also had a room to let, and Gordon persuaded Ford to take it for $15 per week. When Ford told Bowen he was defensive: 'N.Y. is such a whispering Gallery that you might hear that I had taken a whole house and set up an establishment [. . .] Please, my dear, do not read any other motive into this but what I say.' But she may well have read another motive into his seizing on her comment that he should stay 'as long as possible', and trying to make it seem her choice that he should stay away. Which doesn't mean he wasn't sincere in telling her: 'I do not see any chance of my not *wanting* to return to my Julie and you for Xtmas, for I can't *bear* the thought of being away a second time at that season.' He said he would 'try to get in Bonsoir Julie' when he gave a radio talk on WEAF on 21 November, but the radio station tried to stop him: 'They say every one would want to if they let one person do it.' He went with Jeanne Foster to visit Ezra Pound's parents. 'They are delightful people', he wrote to Bowen: 'it was really like visiting Philemon and Baucis. We saw photos of Ezra as a baby and his first poems in an Idaho paper and no end of things that would make poor Ezra squirm.' He had hoped to see the Barnes Collection of modern art while near Philadelphia, and later said that he had got the secretary of an intimate friend—Jeanne

Foster—to cable Barnes to ask for permission: 'Dr. Barnes cabled back—from Geneva: "Would rather burn my collection than let Ford Madox Ford see it".' Ford doesn't explain the outburst, presenting it rather as another example of the farcically absurd persecution of his poor self by a violent world. But Barnes was notoriously cantankerous; and as a collector he was a rival of John Quinn's, and had recently discovered that Foster worked with Quinn.[17]

At the Tates' he had 'a beautifully bright room in a very old sort of Bloomsbury street', on the second floor, next to e. e. cummings's sister. 'I am rather buried amongst Southerners here', he told Bowen. Katherine Anne Porter, Robert Penn Warren, and Andrew Lytle were regular guests. His interest in his friends as people and as writers didn't preclude his wariness about their ideas. He was as sceptical about the Tates' brand of reactionary Agrarianism as he was about Pound's increasing admiration for Mussolini:

all the Tates' friends are from Kentucky or Tennessee or Virginia. It is rather queer: because of the Civil War you see American history quite reversed. Lincoln is the villainous bastard (He was *really* the son of a prostitute) who ruined the world & Stonewall Jackson the only hero. It is queer & rather ghostly & pathetic, being buried amongst the relics of a lost cause— in a Bloomsbury basement & hearing that if only Lee had not lost Gettysburg the world today w^d. be Elysium. . . . No industrial system: no Middle West: only kindly & courteous people of pure English blood! . . . of course it is rather like the French royalists—but really queerer and more passionate.[18]

Goldring was suddenly called back to Paris because of a family tragedy in which his 'sister-in-law and her husband had come to a sensational end'. He had to wait several days for the boat. 'Ford looked after me with a kindness and sympathy which I can never forget', he wrote:

He took me to parties to distract my thoughts and, on the day of my departure, even came to my hotel to help me pack. The ship sailed at midnight and, to fill up the time after dinner, Ford took me to call on some young friends of his, who were meditating masterpieces in what Londoners would call a slum [. . .] Ford—who at that time was one of the most prominent and respected men of letters in New York and much sought after by socialites—was perfectly happy. He was the Master, addressing a circle of attentive disciples. In this capacity, he discoursed for several hours on French and English prose, to an audience which hung on his words. As the beloved Professor, expounding his theme to a group of promising students, he was in his element.

Ford went down to the ship with him on 25 November, giving him a copy of the Avignon edition of *The Good Soldier*, inscribed 'to commemorate St. Katherine's Day in New York, MCMXXVII'. He probably needed some distracting himself, since he had heard only a few days before of the death of his old friend Charles Masterman, another of the *revenants* who were peopling his world.[19]

When Jeanne Foster paid in a cheque that she had cashed for Ford in February, he suddenly found himself overdrawn, and lived out Tietjensesque anxieties over having his rent cheque returned:

I was really agonised—you know my way [he wrote to Bowen, who did]—until it was elucidated, and of course it is disagreeable, for Miss Gordon who is also the concierge cashes all my cheques for me and the landlord is a literary gent, so I suppose it will be all over New

York. However it cannot be helped. I am such a duffer with that sort of thing that I suppose the only thing is for me to take my punishment and not grouse.

His financial outlook improved when Harold Guinzburg, 'who is the Viking Press and also Literary Guild and quite a charming person', took him up, inviting him to a reception in his honour. The Literary Guild took *The Last Post*, publishing their own large edition for their members slightly before the Bonis' edition. This assured him of a sale of around 30,000 to 40,000 copies—about ten times his average sales, and three times that of a success like *No More Parades*. They had kept him in suspense for so long that he became 'really ill' with relief, he told Bowen. He was perfectly aware of his need for a Madox Brownian neglect: 'I am rather appalled at the idea of success—as I always am.' Relations with the Bonis had deteriorated. Ford told Bowen that they had fixed their publication date for Friday 13 January, 'everyone says, out of spite'. He eventually disentangled himself from them, and was able to negotiate a contract with Viking for *A Little Less Than Gods*. Bowen was relieved to hear that Viking gave him a contract offering $7,000 a year. It would be 'absolute comfort & security for us', she wrote: 'I don't at all need or want anything different from what we've got now but I do feel a perfect *panic* at the thought of facing a precarious existence any more.' But the good news was tempered by *Collier's Magazine*'s refusal to take the novel as a serial without seeing a completed version.[20]

He wanted to keep trying to get *A Little Less Than Gods* serialized, and was pressed to stay on until *The Last Post* had been published. When it became clear he would not be back in Paris for Christmas, he wrote another New Year's tribute to Bowen, repeating his 'deep, deep admiration'. 'I sent you off to-day the first copy of the *Last Post*', he told her: '& that represents the end of a considerable labour that I could not even have begun without you & that I certainly could not have finished.' She was 'enormously pleased' with it. 'I don't believe you have any idea how much I admire your genius, & how proud it makes me of my association with you', she said: '*Your* admiration of *my* work I find very exaggerated!' But the tone of their letters was changing. 'I told you before you left that I very much wished to leave you free in every way, & I wanted to repeat it', she told him. Ford later wrote that he had made up his mind in 1928 to make New York his headquarters. She could no longer sustain the illusion that their former happiness could be restored:

But your letter, & the 'Last Post' together, seem to mark the end of our long intimacy, which did have a great deal of happiness in it for me, & which did involve us in a great deal of decent effort. I am not ashamed of any of it except the initial step of taking you away from an older woman. I wish with all my heart I had not done that.

I suppose you will come back from time to time, as you have told me to take the second apartment, & I believe we can build up a different & much more peaceful life.

Ford told her about Wright when he returned in February 1928; but she had already guessed as much when his return kept getting postponed. 'I am so sad that your birthday passed without a word from us', she wrote: 'I thought you would have already embarked. And equally that is why I didn't write for Xmas. It is all very dismal, tho' I am sure you don't lack for sympathy over there!' The second apartment was another small attic flat at 32 rue de Vaugirard. 'He thought that our Paris ménage could go on just the same in between the annual visits he proposed to make to America', said Bowen, 'but I did not [. . .] So, with Ford's consent, I went to see a lawyer.' Being alone in Paris had been 'dress-rehearsals' for the time when she would be 'permanently alone'. She later said that 'the exhilaration of falling out of love is not sufficiently extolled', and that the desire for freedom had begun to work in her.[21]

Before he left New York he spoke at the 'O. Henry Memorial Annual Prize-Story Dinner' at the Hotel Astor on 19 January, with Robert Bridges and Irita van Doren. He told Bowen the following day that he was depressed by the reviews of *Last Post*; but this was because most of them had not yet appeared. Eventually the book was reviewed widely in America and England, with enthusiasm and respect. There were some doubts: about how representative were the characters ('"The Last Post" at times is terribly like a psychopathic ward in some fabulous hospital for world-war wreckage'; though the characters were 'almost too real' for the *Boston Transcript*); about the book's being a sequel; and about Ford's major problem as a novelist, the relationship between his material and his technique—the technique in this case being widely hailed as 'flawless', 'ingenious', 'exceptional'. A dissenting voice was the fastidious Edwin Muir, who thought the book 'unnecessarily messy and chaotic. The author is neither a profound nor a subtle psychologist.' Whereas L. P. Hartley called Ford 'an ironist, a child of the present age': 'His world [. . .] has its own validity and moves in harmony with its own laws. Of all the "Tietjens" novels "Last Post" is surely the greatest *tour-de-force* [. . .] we are ready to forgive Mr. Ford all his faults of rhetoric and exaggeration and excess.' The scale of the complete series could now be recognized. The *Times Literary Supplement* said 'this tetralogy has an originality, a robustness and a tragic vigour which make it worthy of inclusion in the great line of English novels [. . .].' 'Mr. Ford Madox Ford is a great artist', wrote the *Birmingham Post*: 'he has completed what is not only his own finest work, but one of the outstanding books of our generation. He has brought his style to a control equally capable of a rarefied subtlety as of the most forceful intensity.'[22]

That summer Ford approached English editors, hoping that his success in America would make it easier to publish in English. It did not. The *Fortnightly Review* rejected two stories; the *Saturday Review* turned down his suggestion of a weekly article. And the *Sunday Express* even turned down his offer to write about the Dempsey–Tunney fight, despite his assurance that 'I know a good deal about boxing as I am a qualified Army Referee'. It was yet another sign that his literary future lay in America. Though the Tietjens books had been critical successes in England, Duckworth's sales were disappointing. Ford reckoned that he had sold a thousand copies of each volume of the tetralogy, and that half of these went to American collectors of first editions; figures which confirmed his conviction of English philistinism. He protested against what he called 'the miserable policy of the government in imposing an enormous super-tax on such unfortunate writers and artists as are doomed to live abroad because they can't afford to live at home', which seemed a product of 'the real hatred for the arts that exists in the British administrative classes'. As a gesture of defiance he even threatened to stop publishing in Britain—something which, thanks to his American success, he could afford to do. He told Gerald Duckworth: 'I have quite decided that I will give up publishing in England at all rather than submit to such a pettifogging injustice', and

saying that he proposed to write to Duckworth's firm asking them to end their
agreement. He did not want to offend Duckworth personally, with whom, as he told
Eric Pinker, he was 'so very intimate', so he took great care with the letter, drafting it
twice:

I write to you first to explain why I am doing this which I do with a great deal of grief—I
assure you with a great deal. We have always, as I have ventured to say over and over again,
worked together with all possible cordiality and if you have not contrived to sell me in any
large quantities I have always recognised at once the difficulties that stood in your way and
the fact that I am not built to be an English popular author [. . .]
   Do contrive to come back over to Paris and let us look upon the largest possible quantity
of wine when it is at its rosiest. I am being coerced into learning a number of new Charleston
steps, so Mrs. Duckworth will know what to expect. Stella asks me to convey her love to you
both and I'm
   Yours as always.

It was a gesture of self-destruction too. *Last Post* was the seventeenth book of his
published by Duckworth, who was keeping them all in print. It was not quite the
collected edition Ford wanted; but it was the nearest he was going to get to it. The
immediate effect was to get a better price from Duckworth for *A Little Less Than Gods*,
which may have been Ford's aim. 'I have made up my differences with Duckworth and
shall be going on with him at any rate for the next book or so', he told Eric Pinker: 'I
am glad for I hate changes and D. have always treated me very well.' 'Mr. Duckworth
was one of my oldest friends', he wrote in *It Was the Nightingale* (about Duckworth's
handling of the *transatlantic*), adding ruefully: 'he had been losing money over my
books for over thirty years, and I would have trusted him with my purse, my life and
almost with my reputation [. . .].' But *A Little Less Than Gods* was the last book he
published with the firm, and Ford's break with them is not explicable in business
terms.[23]
   The reason is perhaps that the period of his post-war association with
Duckworth's—1922–8—corresponds approximately to the period of his life with
Bowen—1919–29. It wasn't just a change of publishers that disturbed him, but the
upheaval of his family life that his affair with Wright had provoked. In both cases, he
wanted to end a long intimacy as amicably as possible. Perhaps his guilt at destroying
one relationship made him need to destroy the other. He also would have realized that
he would need more money for the life he planned with Rene Wright, who would not
be happy with the frugality of his life with Bowen; and he would need money to go on
supporting Bowen and Julie. Outwardly he and Bowen preserved the appearance of
family life for another two years. 'We could not be certain that Ford and Stella were
separated', wrote Allen Tate (who borrowed Ford's small flat along the hall from
Bowen's in the rue de Vaugirard in 1929), adding: 'This uncertainty was another step
forward in my European education.' They gave dances at the studio in the spring of
1928. 'Are we not always to be found in the studio on a Thursday giving tea to our
friends?', Ford asked Sisley Huddleston. It may have been at this time that he held the
party described by Morrill Cody in his fictional autobiography of James Charters,
a.k.a. 'Jimmie the Barman':

Ford was making considerable money at that time, and he spent much of it entertaining his Montparnasse friends with large quantities of the finest wines and liqueurs. He's a very generous man who loves to entertain. Once, after a trip to America, he brought back many bottles of bootleg gin and whisky to show Montparnasse the meaning of strong liquor. He arranged a long table with the bootleg liquor at one end and French liqueurs at the other. At first each guest tried the American synthetic products in order to turn up his nose at them. 'What terrible stuff!' But by two in the morning the bootleg gin and whisky was all gone, while the French brandies and liqueurs had only been nibbled at.[24]

Gertrude Stein—the dedicatee of *A Mirror to France*—reciprocated by giving a mirror to Ford: a gift which elicited high-spirited thanks:

My dear Confrère:
  What a perfect fairy godmother you are!
  My room is now complete: the only problem that remains is whether the glass should hang high—where it looks majestic—or low so that one sees oneself whilst writing at the table. At present it does the latter so that, when I look up for inspiration I see my own ugly face. On the other hand I am reminded of yr. kind thought—wh. shd. be inspiration enough!

The separation from Bowen was as civilized as such things can be. They quickly agreed that she should keep both the studio in the rue Notre-Dame des Champs and the larger flat in the rue de Vaugirard, and that Ford should keep the smaller flat, though he immediately told her to use it as she wished, adding that she might let his 'very poor friend called [William] Seabrook a writer and a very nice fellow' have it for a month. He formally acknowledged a debt to her of £2,704: they didn't want to repeat the arguments with Hunt about how much money Ford owed. 'Even when we were on the brink of separating', she wrote, 'we could still go out to dine together and have a grand argument about Lost Causes, or the Theory of the Infallibility of the Pope.' They were never bored. But the impression they tried to give of cheerful continuity was misleading. The scenes behind the scenes must have been ugly. Facing Bowen, and facing himself making her miserable took their toll on him: 'I have not been very well since getting back here and, till the last week have hardly gone out at all', he told Huddleston, adding: 'I am very behind with my novel and have been working very hard so that we have not met about at the usual places.' Bowen's memoir is slightly misleading, too, in implying that she left Paris after Ford left for America again. In fact she went to England and then to the south of France while Ford was still in Paris, and stayed away until he had gone. A letter she wrote to him after Easter hints at her initial bitterness at hearing about Wright, and at some of the discussions that Ford had had with both women. It also testifies to her magnanimity once she had come to terms with the idea of separation, and shows that her tone of gratitude to Ford in her memoirs was not an effect of sentimentality after his death (in contrast to Elsie Hueffer's eventual forgiveness): it was what she felt just when she realized their life together was over:

My dear.
  I feel I ought to write something definite to you just as soon as possible, so that you may make your own plans and be relieved of the strain of uncertainty.
  I am sure that there must be an absolute and public break between us. You yourself

dismissed the idea of a 'half and half' separation and indeed I have come to think that it would not be feasible [. . .]

I shall therefore tell people, when I get back to Paris, that my absence until after your departure was because we had mutually agreed to separate for good. I cannot make up any tale of having 'chucked you out', nor will I use the word 'divorce' except when driven to it as for instance with Julie and the servants and strangers. My reason for avoiding the word 'divorce' is not because I want to make difficulties for you and R., but because it seems to me undignified and ridiculous, when everyone knows the truth, and when Violet has so exhausted the topic of her marriage or non-marriage to you [. . .]

I want *not* to be the one to begin any scandal about you and R. and in any case I will not say ill of either of you. We have had too good a time together for me to want to malign you now. And I should like you to remember that you said I might always tell people that we remain good friends in spite of it all, and that we keep in touch and will meet from time to time. It will be *much* better for Julie that this should be so and will do much for my happiness if it may be a real fact. You said R. might object to your remaining friendly with me except for the sake of keeping up appearances to protect your reputation. That protection of course you will lose, but I think public opinion—for what it is worth—would be softened if we announce that our relations remain cordial, and if I might continue to know what you are writing etc., and be able to give people some news of your career. I think R. might be asked to be a sport about this. I am making everything else as easy as I can for her!

Don't let me become a 'bogie' for you both. I should so hate that!

If it ever becomes known that we separated on account of R. I should like it also to be known that you wanted not to break with me outwardly, and that it was I who wished to end it all.

Of course I quite realise that by asking for a definite separation I give up all right to dictate on your acts or movements. I only ask that you should consider the disagreeableness to me of your taking R. to the houses of our friends in Paris, or living with her very publicly near to me and Julie.

My dear, I really decided all this before leaving Paris, but I thought it would hurt us both so much to discuss it again. But ever since I *did* decide it, all my bitter feelings have gone and I feel so much more sympathetic towards you and so much more anxious that you should be happy. It was the revolt against a false position that made me feel savage. So do try to think nicely of me, I have been so proud of my connection with you, and I have got my darling Julie out of it, not to mention a wonderful education in life! Our separation will make me all the more devoted to Julie—and she will be so happy when you come back to your little flat, and she can be with you.

My dear, there is little enough I can do for you now, except to wish you luck, and hope that this decision will bring you as much peace of mind as it has brought me. Please don't ask to see me again to discuss it [. . .] Goodbye my dear. Do remember sometimes, as I always shall, that we were very happy together and do let us stay friends. God bless you always—

Stella[25]

Not wanting to see Ford again to discuss it is one sign of the fragility of her resolve, as that phrase about her being the one to want to end it all is perhaps a suggestion of how 'chilly and forlorn' she had felt when she discovered how Ford had been betraying and deceiving her. She must have felt 'all the rage & bitterness' underneath, as she thought Hadley Hemingway must have felt. The comment about wanting their continuing friendliness to be 'a real fact' hints at her disillusionment with Ford's genius for unreal facts. Her verdict in *Drawn from Life* on his freedom with fact is all the more surprisingly generous given how she had been hurt by it. It is also one of the few genuinely understanding comments on Ford's art, and the proximity between his impressionism in literature and his impressionism in life:

All his art was built on his temperamental sensitiveness to atmosphere, to the angle from which you looked, to relative, never absolute values. When he said, 'It is necessary to be precise,' I used to think that he meant—precisely truthful. Of course, what he really meant was that you must use precision in order to create an effect of authenticity, whatever the subject of your utterance, in the same way as the precision of a brushstroke gives authenticity to an image on canvas, and need have no relation to anything seen in fact. Words to Ford were simply the material of his art, and he never used them in any other way. This created confusion in his everyday life, for words are not like dabs of paint. They are less innocent, being the current coin in use in daily life.

It had been an education in art and life. Through Ford she had known many of the most important artists in Europe. She wrote after his death that to 'have the run of a mind of that calibre [. . .] was a privilege for which' she was still trying to say 'thank you'. She was away for Julie's baptism, for which Ford had miraculously persuaded Joyce to act as godfather. Jenny Bradley was the godmother. Joyce later explained that he was reciprocating Ford's act in christening *Finnegans Wake* as 'Work in Progress'. 'I don't see much use for a sponsor at all if the child (who is a nice little girl anyhow) can remove the devil etc on her own account', he wrote, 'but I accepted his invitation as an act of friendliness.' He was uneasy standing at the font. Ford wrote to Bowen to tell her that Julie was 'well and duly pickled this morning', and how, after demonstrating her knowledge of Latin, French, and English to the priest, and Italian to Joyce, she amazed Ford by the definiteness of her ideas about art when he took her to the Louvre.[26]

Lloyd Morris (who thought some of Ford's poems 'superb', and some of his fiction 'as profoundly conceived and finely executed as any produced in our time') told a curious story in which Joyce and Ford were again impersonating themselves as Catholics. He invited them to a large evening party, and they came. But Morris later noticed their absence, and found them 'irately pacing the garden path in the darkness. It developed that the presence of an unfrocked priest was an affront to their piety, and the venom of their indignation left Morris stupefied.' He hadn't imagined that Joyce, 'the acknowledged apostate', and Ford, 'who publicly flouted the sacrament of marriage', would mind. He had another surprise a few days later when he chanced upon them in a restaurant, this time 'peaceably enjoying luncheon' with the same unfrocked priest. Morris pontificates that the episode expressed Joyce's 'profound insecurity'; he doesn't comment on Ford's apparent inconsistency. But someone so profoundly secure in his earnestness and so immune to irony must have been an irresistible incitement to both men's parodic gifts. Their 'unusual' relations to Catholicism gave them something else in common, besides their devotion to literature and wine (though they had a comically protracted disagreement about whether red or white were better). Joyce referred to his friend as Father Ford.[27]

The Joyces left for Toulon, where they borrowed Ford's and Bowen's studio. Ford was working on *A Little Less Than Gods* when George Keating sent him the volume of Conrad's letters that Edward Garnett had published, having marked the one in which

Conrad makes sardonic fun of Ford's efforts over *The Inheritors*, saying that he thought of it as a 'skit', whereas Ford had been 'dead in earnest', and that Conrad had been ready to weep—'Yet not for him'. Ford was outraged that Garnett should publish this letter—which Conrad had told him to burn—just when the controversy over his book on Conrad appeared to have played itself out. Ford wrote a four-page letter to Garnett, bristling with the anger of betrayal, and headed reproachfully 'Private and not for publication in *perpetuity*'. He also told Garnett to burn it, which of course he didn't. Ford said: 'I have myself heard Conrad utter such bitter jeers against other people to whom he wrote in the same terms of adoration that he addressed to myself that I could quite well have invented the letter myself.' That is believable. His argument that by publishing such letters Garnett had discredited 'the memory of that unfortunate man' also had great force. But his claim that he was 'fairly indifferent' to Conrad's sarcasms against him is belied by his tone—and by the fact that he needed to repeat the old 'indifferentist' pose of his youth in order to convince himself he need not be hurt, saying he was 'absolutely indifferent' to anything that had been said about his relations with Conrad 'except in so far as they do anything to injure his memory'. He made the kind of fantastical claims that Garnett of all people censured in him: that Conrad had begged him to write the memoir of him; and a paranoid fantasy that Conrad 'was surrounded by people of whom he stood in dread', and tried to evade them by begging Ford to write to him via his secretary or at post-offices. 'Anyhow, I beg you not to take in bad part anything that I have writ[t]en', he said. 'It is written with a great deal of emotion':

My affection for Conrad was so great and remains so unchanged that I have never been able really to believe in his death, and at this moment it is as if he were sitting behind me waiting to read what I have tapped out. You see, we did live together, day in day out, for many years—ten, I daresay and even towards the end he could not really get on without me any more than I could or can get ob [*sic*] without him, and I do not shrink from saying that at this moment I cannot see for tears. Hang it all I worked for that man during years as hard as any other man ever worked for a man. And for what? You don't suppose I did it in order to go up to glory on his skirts. I can do it for myself thank you. Naturally he did the dirty on me from time to time. He had to and I never cared and don't care now.[28]

Who was Ford weeping for? For Conrad, for himself, for Stella, for Garnett; perhaps for all the friendshipwrecks Conrad had prophesied in 1909, and that the knowledge of Conrad's letters to Garnett probably brought back to him, at a time when his life was again becoming as desperately complicated as it had been in the fraught years with Violet Hunt. He quoted the remark in one of Conrad's last letters: 'Unlike the Serpent which is Wise, you are unchanging', saying to Garnett: 'And I think I am and you are too, and as we never did agree about anything in literature I see no possibility of our now doing so so there would be little use in our meeting even if you don't cherish the fell serpent's hatred that Conrad said you did for me.' It must have been particularly distressing to confront the evidence of Conrad's duplicitous changeability while writing *A Little Less Than Gods*, which was another act of symbolic rapprochement with Conrad: an attempt to revisit the ghost of their collaborative mutual dependency. Ford's distress was compounded by guilt about his own changeability. As in that phrase about Conrad's 'skirts', the letter to Garnett opposes friendships between men to relationships between a man and a woman, implying that the former are more lasting and profound than the latter. This is partly to reproach Garnett, by making his act of unfriendliness to Ford seem all the more serious. (Characteristically, Ford tells him that he is often asked about Garnett in America: 'And I can assure you that I never answer without the most eulogious inanities.') It is also to elevate his friendship with Conrad, suggesting that it transcended the petty exasperations of a highly charged creative spirit. Asking after Garnett's wife Constance, he adds: 'The two women I have always liked best all my life—I mean as one likes men—were—and are!—Connie and Jane Wells. And poor Jane is dead.' Even that parenthesis ('were—and are—') shows Ford worrying over his own changeability in his relations with women. His suggestion that he and Garnett should not meet when Ford gets to London the following week echoes Bowen's request that Ford should not ask to see her to discuss their break; as if he is transferring his feelings of guilt at betraying her on to Garnett, who had betrayed him.

1928–1929: ELIZABETH CHEATHAM

> Not till we can think that here and there one is thinking of us, one is loving us, does this waste earth become a peopled garden.
>
> (Carlyle to Emerson)

He had a new reason for feeling changeable. He was falling in love once more, this time with a 23-year-old American called Elizabeth Cheatham. She had been born in Arkansas, the only child of an episcopalian minister. When she was a young child the family moved to Pinehurst, North Carolina. She was a keen golfer, and had been taught to shoot by Annie Oakley, who had retired to Pinehurst. (After saying both Elsie and Violet had threatened him with guns, Ford might have been expected to be warier of a markswoman.) After going to college in New York and then Paris—she spoke fluent French—she designed book jackets, and is said to have designed two of Ford's. She was petite—5 feet $3\frac{1}{2}$ inches tall—and had dark hair. He sometimes called her 'Mouse', or—because of her complete self-confidence—'Pixie'.[1]

They met in Paris, probably in this spring of 1928. Ford's letters to her use as a talisman the initials 'R.V.A.D.', standing for 'rue Vavin at Dawn'. This was where and when he declared his love for her after a party given by or for Helen Ashbury, a young American sculptress friend of Ford's and Bowen's, in the studio at 84 rue Notre-Dame des Champs. Elizabeth's response—she said something about his being old—made him feel she couldn't love him. She could. Over the next year he wrote her a wonderful series of letters which give an intimate self-portrait of Ford as a literary lover during a period his previous biographers knew little about. They illuminate the end of his affair with Wright, and do much to account for his depressed state of mind while writing *When the Wicked Man*, as well as showing how much that novel draws upon his feelings for Cheatham.[2]

It wasn't just that he felt alone, with Rene Wright thousands of miles away. Stella Bowen's departure had left him involved with only one woman. But just as Wright was divorcing her husband Guy (on the grounds of 'general indignities') to free herself to marry Ford, Ford was repeating the pattern that had beset his life, entangling himself with a second woman. Was it his fear of betrayal that made him still unable to place all his trust in one lover, and that made loneliness so devastating for him? (Notterdam is described as having a 'spasm of loneliness'.) Was it the result of sibling rivalry—feeling that his mother had betrayed him by loving another brother, so that he could only defend himself by loving always another woman, and by imagining a telepathic rapport with his mother, and visions of goddesses, as consolation? One can only speculate; but the tenacity of the pattern is remarkable. He appeared to be as 'appalled' at the prospect of sexual success as at the prospect of literary success. Like his fictional protagonists, Ford himself could feel agoraphobic, enervated, and suicidal over his affairs. We have seen how infidelity to Elsie precipitated his 1904 breakdown; how his relationship with Hunt made him imagine his execution as Ritter Olaf; how he went to the war expecting to die and thinking of Brigit Patmore; and how he felt suicidal just as his new life with Stella Bowen was about to begin at Red Ford. Falling in love with Cheatham was bound to endanger his relationship with Wright; Cheatham's comment about his age, which meant so much to Ford, must have made his love for her seem what he found particularly seductive: a hopeless cause.[3]

Ford was due to leave for New York on 13 May 1928 for his second visit that year. His last few days in Paris were characteristically frenetic. Samuel Putnam's *New Review* held a dinner in Pound's honour, at which Ford was supposed to 'eulogize' Pound. But a drugged surrealist threatened Pound with a knife, whereupon the dinner broke up in confusion. Julie was ill, and Ford had to take her to see a specialist. He held a party at which, he said, all the glasses were broken. Just before leaving Paris Ford wrote a long letter to Bowen, agreeing that Julie should stay at the École Alsacienne, but asking that she should have regular religious instruction, 'either from a nun of the Ursuline order or from a Passionist priest of the Avenue Hoche who gave me what religious instruction that I had'. He explained: 'A clean Catholic will jump straight off when the time comes if it does. A child who has been all mucked up [by a compromise between religion and the 'free-thinking influence' Bowen didn't want Julie to lose] always ends by compromise after compromise and that is fatal for the intellect.' Odd, since his own education had combined free-thought and Catholicism, and his intellect had survived. 'If you regard Romanism in Julie from now on till eighteen or so as you now regard her belief in fairy tales', he told Bowen, 'it will go perfectly happily.' It mattered to him that the end of her parents' ménage marked Julie's beginnings as an artist: 'Just before I dispossessed her of this machine Julie produced the beginning of her first short story: Il était une fois une petite fille nommait Camille son papa etait monsieur Daddy. Il était bien pour elle, il lui donnait tout ce qu'elle pouvait désirer . . . And she has since told me that she has decided to become a writer.'[4] He explained how he had told just some very close friends that they were 'divorcing': Ann Drake, Bill Bird, and Gertrude Stein. 'Gertrude, I think, is of the opinion that you want to marry someone else, I being too old for you', he told her: 'At any rate she said that at *our* age we could not expect to retain affections.' (Stein was born in 1874, the year after Ford.) 'And as to my using the word "divorce"', he said, 'I solemnly aver to you that that is how I see it':

During all these years you have been just as much my wife in my private heart as any human being could have been. And, if we part, that is just as much divorcing me by you as if all the judges of the Divorce and Admiralty had sat on the case. I do not suppose that you will ever see it like that, but acknowledge at least that that is how I see it . . . And the question of real truth is what passes in one's private heart.

She told him how happy she was to 'get a last word' from him: 'I shall always be glad that you did not vanish without that!' She agreed about the undesirability of religious compromise, but objected to calling their separation a 'divorce' to anyone but Julie,

who thought they were 'divorcing' because Ford was always going to America. Julie
had asked to be taken to dinner at Carboni's on her last night with Ford. Afterwards,
Ford gave Bradley directions about the payments to be made to Bowen, and sat down
to finish his letter to her:

So you see, my dear, I have tried my best within my lights to fix things up well for you. I am
I suppose the muddler you have always called me but give me credit for having tried to do
my best. It is now 3.15 in the morning and I have still my letter to Bradley to write and a good
deal of my packing to do so I shall cut this short. After all there is no need for it to be my last.

But let me say that I esteem you and am attached to you as I have always done and been.
It is really the riding that has done it. We grew too tired before the settling down of peace.

Anyhow may God bless you at your rising up and at your lying down, at your setting out
and at your returning in from the same, which I suppose is a longer, but perhaps not more
noble way of saying: Here's to hoping.[5]

Elizabeth Cheatham was also on Ford's boat to New York, the *Suffren*, travelling with
a friend called Miriam Dodd. Every day of the ten-day voyage he wrote Elizabeth a
love-poem—except on the ninth day, when he wrote a poem for Miriam instead. One,
entitled 'Y.L.I. Quickstep: By which to remember Ripon', was written because she
told him she had been 'quite entranced by a young subaltern' of the Yorkshire Light
Infantry there. Others describe their kisses (in euphemisms); their love; the fact that
she and Miriam had a cabin on B deck, whereas Ford was below on C deck. One is 'A
Jingle', rhyming on her name. One, to the tune of 'Oh Rokehope is a pleasant place'—
the ballad Ford had quoted at Bowen's suggestion for the epigraph to *Last Post*—
anticipates the difficulty of their seeing each other in New York, where Rene Wright
was to meet Ford:

> Oh Gotham is a pleasant place
> If it were not that you and I
> Within a barren stony space
> Shut in from sea and sky
> At noon must say goodbye.[6]

An eerie poem (recalling Goethe's 'Der Fischer' and Burne-Jones's 'The Depths of
the Sea') imagines death at the hands of 'Cruel mermaids':

> The deep sea and kindness can never together abide
> If you went over here by the ship's steep side
> Swift, swift would the mermaids glide
> And would grasp you
> And, engulphing, enclasp you
> Bearing you down, down,
> Down, down, down to where the weeds wave brown
> And there with their slanting eyes in ecstasy glancing aside
> They would lie at your side
> Drinking the last of your breath
> Whilst on cometh Death!
>
> It is perhaps better to live on the land,
> Beside meres or red-fringed pools,
> It is perhaps better there when the evening cools

The parching furrows, to lie in a secret glade
And watch the pixies, or to have a pixy
Delicate and tricksy,
Or a wicked small angel from the hand of Botticelli,
Brown eyed and wanton-tressed
Glide near and tell 'ee
Enticingly and tauntingly, what are the delights of the Blessed,
A little wanton angel to evade your hand
And to smile mockingly and glide a foot further and stand
That little away and to say
'No, not for you, monsieur, no, not, not, never for you!'

Yet I would not be on the land;
I would not walk on the grass of the fields in dew,
I can mock at the mermaids in the foam,
I can pity the mermen who have none but mermaids
For their mates.
The poor sea-kings, wearily, yearning and yearning,
I can pity.
For here in this comic, floating city,
Lights ablazing, red wine flowing, and the great shaft, turning, turning
Turning, turning the screw,
Amidst the harsh, desolate and bitter wastes of the tides,
Within the ship's steep sides[,]
Oh, pixie, pixie, pixie . . . there is you![7]

'He said my funny face framed by short curly hair looked just like one of Botticelli's cherubs', Cheatham noted at the bottom of the page. The languorousness of the sexual fantasy is old-fashionedly pre-Raphaelite, making Ford sound less controlledly ironic about his vision of mermaids than was T. S. Eliot about J. Alfred Prufrock, who had only 'heard the mermaids singing, each to each', but not for him. Yet a note is beginning to be heard in Ford's verse that found its best expression in his last poems to Janice Biala, the *Buckshee* sequence. The relaxed but muscular style; the casual crescendo leading up to wonder at the young woman's love for him; the thanks to God for the unexpected gift of her: all these anticipate the later poems. The last poem, celebrating their extra time together when the ship was delayed, even uses the same term, thanking God for 'The Buckshee Day'.

On that voyage 'developed the realest, most wonderful love affair of my life!', wrote Cheatham in her journal of the trip. 'Ford Madox Ford, the noted English novelist, had pleased me by being nice to me in Paris, and not long before we sailed (on the same boat, perchance!) had startled me by asking me to marry him' (this was probably the declaration in the rue Vavin):

He is 30 years older than I, and somewhat lionized in Paris, so I didn't take him seriously. But on board the Suffren, where we were together constantly, he at length proved his devotion beyond a doubt, and inspired in me a like devotion. We had such fun together, and such hectic discussions (because this affair of ours has many complications, & I had to say no whenever he begged me to marry him, yet show him that it wasn't that I didn't care for him but just that outside circumstances would *have* to work themselves out before we could marry) about ourselves and lots of other things, and he was so *sweet* to me (made love so entrancingly, did all sorts of little things to make me happy, wrote me a poem every day!— in short he spoiled me dreadfully) that we spent a blissful nine days together.[8]

Ford also figures in the amatory memorandum book she kept: a publication called *My Him Book*, with illustrated headings like 'High School Hims', 'Matinee Hims', 'National Hims', and so on. Ford is mentioned—with considerable accuracy—under 'Jazz Hims', 'Sad Hims', 'Steamer Hims', 'Paris Hims', 'Dinner Hims', 'Popular Hims'; and he is one of only four 'Love Hims'.

In New York he stayed at the Hotel Carteret on West 23rd Street, she with friends on Park Avenue. They must have had about a fortnight of each other's company in New York. When Elizabeth's parents arrived, Ford was invited to meet them on 2 June. Then she went to a wedding in Pennsylvania, leaving Ford alone. Mizener, who didn't know of Cheatham, said Ford was 'glad to get back to New York and Mrs. Wright'; he wasn't. 'I *have* been a poor old crock', he wrote to Cheatham: 'all of 66 & more . . . 72 perhaps! Oh rue Vavin at dawn!' He complained of a sprained foot which 'collapsed & swelled to the size of my waist' and kept him confined to his room. He quoted lines of Christina Rossetti to her: 'she was a great poet & my aunt by marriage & I am supposed to have got such poetic gifts as I have from her. . . . I mean from her example & society. But I suppose I shan't write any more poems—except the one I must not send you for your wedding day—& I am tired, tired.'[9]

A week later she was still in Pennsylvania. 'I do nothing but write & write & write', he wrote. 'I have got half of my book done & have Napoleon & Ney & all on the brain. I have just introduced a little American girl into the middle of Lyons with Napoleon coming in at one end of the town & Monsieur [the King's heir] & the duc d'Orleans bolting out at the other.' The little American girl in *A Little Less Than Gods* is Bessie Coleman, from North Carolina, who is introduced in the second chapter of Part II. George Fielding saves her from a mob, whereupon she 'had been woefully in love' with him. She has an American father and an English uncle, 'bright little eyes', and 'a queer, clear enunciation, as if she took pains to keep all her words spaced apart'. She is only a cameo character: the design of the novel was already too definite for Ford to want to reimagine it, and he would go on to create a major character based on her in *When the Wicked Man*. Bessie is also a compound character, being partly based on his cousin 'Hattina', who died young. (His family hoped he would marry her, he said; which gives another personal angle to this story of incest.) But he needed to imagine Cheatham reading his work, and being moved by the allusions to her. She had become his sympathetic silent listener. He even worked references to her into his journalism, including an allusion to their declaration, commenting on 'the very young American— to whom in the neighbourhood of the rue Vavin toward dawn I present the aspect of being a hundred and two, but still going and still admiring!—'; and then he told her in a letter to make sure she would see it. He wrote that, 'when I read a book I always seem to see the writer's face looking up at me through the pages'. He hoped his own face would smile out of his pages at his intimate silent readers. He was gratified by what she thought of what she read: '*Didn't* you know I c^d. write like the *Last Post*— well: wait till you read the *Good Soldier*. Or the book after next!'[10]

He was enervated to the pitch of visionariness. 'My dear: the other night I woke just at dawn & I could have *sworn* you were just going out of the room', he told her. 'I was so certain of it that I called out your name. It was the morning of Wednesday—June 13. I wonder if you were thinking of me specially.' He wondered if it might have been what he called 'the other thing [. . .] a farewell visit! It was dreadful. Dreadful! Just catching sight of you in the grayness.' And he asked her to make him see her: 'Tell me about the house you are in—& the room you are in: I want to see you, and the room in Pinehurst, particularly.' She had gone back with her parents, to act as a secretary for her mother. He was getting up at six to write, and became so tired that one day he fell asleep over the typewriter. It is a tribute to his professionalism how little this exhaustion shows in the novel. His letters elaborated on how thoroughly she was possessing him. The 'wicked little American girl creeps into my novel every day', he told her. When she suggested it might be better for him to try to forget her, he said: 'Dear: I am very unhappy—but I w$^{d.}$ not have it otherwise.' Truer than he knew? He had a genius for making himself unhappy by forming impossibly complicated liaisons, and not having it otherwise. He appeared, like Edward Ashburnham, to desire only that 'the girl being [. . .] miles away, would continue to love him': 'I got as much pleasure when you write, "I love you" as I have ever had out of any one thing in the world', he told her.[11]

They wrote regularly. When she told him she felt more confident about her painting, Ford cast himself as the past master: 'That is the real great thing in life when you feel a sudden shove forward taking place within you with regard to one or other of the arts . . . Alas, it is long since I had occasion to feel one'—though he added: 'However, I find my Ney novel rather interesting because it is a return to an old manner.' He travestied his decrepitude for her. 'Oh yes, my dear, I am getting older every minute now: you only just prophesied in the rue Vavin that dawn! I still limp; I wear black spectacles—I only need a dog on a string!'[12]

He was candid with her about the perplexity of his relations with Rene Wright. It had become clear that they really had little in common. But she had divorced for Ford's sake, and he felt honour-bound to hold himself 'at her disposal'. They began arguing about money, and Wright, who was unwell, found herself cast in Hunt's role:

I can't make the settlements that R. wants and I still do not know what will happen. R. you see has been used to circumstances of splendour that would kill me and that I can't—and don't pretend to try—to maintain. [. . .] I daresay she might set up a separate establishment of her own [. . .] So you see it is all very vague—as all my life has really been. And my tastes are so very simple [. . .] I must stick to R if she wants me, which I often think is not the case— or I should not allow myself to write this. But if you are still free in January and R. finds she cannot support the idea of the Rive Gauche . . [.] well, you know to whom I shall come right away.[13]

Cheatham's parents became anxious about her involvement with so much older a man, and her father wrote a tactful letter to her about what he called 'your affair with Mr Ford'. 'The discrepancy in your ages is very wide and even if *everything else* was right, this would be a serious question', he counselled: 'and you will, of course, not think of rushing into an arrangement that is so serious to your future life without taking time to thoroughly test out your heart.' Ford became disconsolate as the parental pressure made itself felt, and as he began to despair of freeing himself from Wright. 'Exactly half the year was finished at midnight last night—the half of the year that saw us know each other,' he wrote to Cheatham: 'I suppose that this half year will see us parted.' But then he added: 'I shall never give up the idea of you'; and his letters urge that they should counter the resistance by will-power. 'One of us has to keep all on willing', he told her, adapting Meary Walker's stoic phrase about keeping all on going.

Dear: don't say 'loved & *lost*': not ever. Never: never, whilst grass grows and water runs. As long as you *know*—and you *do* know—that the feeling continues unchanged, unchanging & unchangeable there is no loss. One has just gone into the next room: though all the mountains of the Himalayas lie between [—Ashburnham again]. . . . and then it is merely a question of will. If you say: 'We will go to Europe every year when we are together'—we shall. . . .[14]

His response when she told him about the bird-bath outside her window suggests his state of mind: 'there is nothing so restful for the spirit as [bird-watching]. Even English nerve doctors know that & send you to the Zoo to watch them if you have a nervous breakdown.' His next sentence explains why: 'I have finished my novel—at least the writing of it [. . .].' Wright left for Boston, and Ford planned to leave at the end of July '& then go to Europe via the Azores & Lisbon in a long trip so as to get a rest', but to return as early as possible in the New Year, when he hoped 'things will then be settled for good'. Cheatham thought about taking a job in Pittsburgh. Yet the amatory banter continued. Ford sent her Mauriac's *Thérèse Desqueyroux* and a French translation of *War and Peace*: 'The first isn't a bad modern book, the second is an interminable classic: I do not imagine anyone ever read it straight through. I know I never could, but if you are in a mood for keeping up your French it is not bad to dip into from time to time.' He asked again for a description of her surroundings:

You have not yet described your room to me: do, it makes such a difference to me to know the sort of frame into which I have to put my image of you. Otherwise it is rather a numb affair. Perhaps you will think that is too materialistic a way to look at it. It is not really so, but I love to such an extent in mental pictures that if I have not got one I get numbed—as if there were a blind spot in the vision.[15]

He loved, as he lived and as he wrote, 'in mental pictures'.

As his departure approached he developed 'another touch of foot-trouble', and told her, 'yesterday with the heat & vexations I was almost at the last gasp'. He wrote blurbs for publishers, and an article on Conrad's language for Rascoe's *Bookman*. When George Keating showed him the manuscript of the section of *Nostromo* he had written, he experienced a vertiginous time-shift: 'It really gave me quite a turn—those old memories.' In the same letter we hear the first mention of his next book: 'On the boat I shall write a short history of the English Novel & revise an old novel of mine—all this being dull & tiresome stuff, but necessary to keep the pot a boiling.' *The English Novel from the Earliest Days to the Death of Joseph Conrad* is a highly civilized pot-boiler, and its full title suggests how Ford's recent returns to the earliest days of his collaboration with Conrad shaped his conception both of 'the English Novel', and of the friend he was always elegizing. The novel was the post-war manuscript 'Mr Croyd', which he was to revise for Viking. Neither work shows Ford at his highest creative pitch; but they do show how at his most disturbed, or most exhausted, he could still write engaging, vivid prose. The same day he sat down to write an essay on his collaboration with Conrad, putting into perspective Conrad's comments about him.[16]

Ford explained to Cheatham that he didn't come down to visit her at Pinehurst because: 'if I have to carry through this job I want to do it in style. I mean that, if there is to be a breach I don't want it to be of my making & don't want to have occasioned it.' He wanted Wright to make the decision for him; but she wasn't ready to make the decision he wanted her to make, which left all three of them in an impasse for another year. On the eve of his departure he wanted to telephone Cheatham: 'it will be torturing to hear y^r voice without seeing or touching you—but better than nothing'; but the new moon seemed 'a sort of bond' between them. 'Very, very dear Elizabeth: my dear one', he wrote just after they had spoken: 'I *must* write just a note while your voice is still in my ears—& it seemed such a sad voice.'[17]

He sailed for Marseilles on the SS *Patria* on 27 July. While the boat was 'Off Nantucket' he wrote the dedication of *A Little Less Than Gods* 'To: Rene Katherine Clarissa'. It was another of his public declarations to a woman from whom he was becoming estranged in private. There is a bitter irony beneath the affectionate mockery with which he signs him off:

And I have the consolation of thinking that if your hypercritical taste turns from these pages that are laid at your feet you, at least, can take refuge in the writings of authors more attractive.

I, on the other hand, am condemned to remain for ever

Humbly and obediently your servant,
F. M. F.[18]

During the voyage he took refuge in visualizing his previous one, with the woman he found more attractive. He wrote to Cheatham: 'This is a very dreadful landscape of sea things & the boat going slow thro' the fog & the siren hooting incessantly. / The cabin isn't like the other cabin—but all cabins suggest all other ones & it seems as if every minute you must be pushing the door a little open & peeping in.' He repeated his itinerary, only to add: 'I don't care where I go or what I do.' 'I am really very tired mentally but I shall have to write, write, write all the time on this boat. I expect to write & finish a short book—a treatise on the English Novel, before I get to Marseilles. That is a good thing because it keeps me from thinking—but it is wearing too. I lost 21 lbs in weight in N.Y.' He was torn between asking her to wait for him—which, when he was depressed enough to doubt that they would ever be able to be together, seemed unreasonable to ask—and sacrificing himself by freeing her for the fate he dreaded: 'Oh pixie, pixie, keep yourself for me if you can—but if the right beau jeune homme comes along be happy [. . .] if he did come I sh^d go down the wind like a puff of dust [. . .] But go on willing, dear heart, if you still care & believe that I do always & always.' He tried to tease his way out of the anxiety of betrayal, telling her he had written a poem to a 'young woman' on the boat one night. 'She has scarlet hair . . . So there! / But she [is] the daughter of a Baptist missionary going to convert the Portuguese and she is aged only eleven.' He was getting on with his 'monograph on THE NOVEL, which is a stupid thing to do but I have not much heart for anything else'. He became accident-prone. After Palermo he wrote to her:

fully ten days ago I slipped on the deck which was wet and came down with all my weight on my right wrist which appeared at frist [*sic*] to be broken but wasn't and has yielded pretty well to Absorbine Junior. Then three days ago, my hand being still weak I tried to open a brass-framed window—a regular guillotine and it descended suddenly smashing the third and fourth finger tips of my right hand and my left thumb.[19]

It took him two hours, he said, to type even a short letter. At Naples, he saw Vesuvius erupting. It was probably on this voyage—'as smooth as a millpond from start to finish'—that he later recalled getting, at Gibraltar, 'infinite joy watching for hours, in the completely lucid water that was lit up by the reflection of the sunshine from the white sand of the bottom . . . watching the innumerable dolphins that drifted in shoals round and round the ship, hanging in space [. . .] It was because the rays darted upwards and gilded the forms of those graceful, fishlike beasts, a spectacle so engrossing that I completely forgot Rock, Peninsula, and Continent, and spent the greater part of my stay hanging over the side of the vessel—forgetting not only my own troubles, of which I had a peck, but also those of a world that had more than sufficient.'[20] He was irritated by the deference shown to a 'fat fool' of an American banker on board 'just because he was called banker'. 'This is wrong', Ford recalled thinking: 'I am the only person on this boat who, for what it is worth, am of any distinction [. . .] Never did I obtain money from my fellows in order to speculate in dubious undertakings and so get myself the air of a prince whilst being the meanest kind of chevalier of industry.' (One of the attractions for him of the Rive Gauche was that 'It contains no financiers'.) When he got to Marseilles on 13 August, he 'wanted to go to a hotel where Alexandre Dumas, Chopin, George Sand, Gounod, Flaubert, Mistral, Gambetta, Sarah Bernhardt, Wagner and Anatole France had all stopped together or apart and that remained much in the same state as it had been in the days of the Count of Monte Cristo'. But the American friends he had made on the voyage thought the rooms too dark and too cheap. He stayed in the expensive Hotel Bristol for a week, during which he was 'absolutely penniless', because Brandt's cable sending him $200 had been delivered to the wrong bank. He wrote to Bradley that he was 'really sick with rage at the methods of payment obtaining in New York', and asking him to telegraph 1,000 frs.

I can't get away without paying the bill and can't pay the bill without money [. . .] I really think these continual annoyances will drive me to suicide in the end—that is to say I wish they would, but I probably lack that kind of courage. I have written over 100,000 words since I left for New York and have not had a day's holiday and several thousand dollars are owing to me and I am perpetually penniless.

The numbers of words and dollars are no exaggerations. Brandt collected $9,615 for him in 1928. He was also depressed at not hearing from Julie. His state of mind was almost that of Henry Martin (in *The Rash Act*, the novel he was to write four years later): feeling driven to attempt suicide by drowning, thanks to poverty and unrequited passion. The dolphins didn't only distract him from his troubles; they represented a fantasy of escape from all trouble.[21]

He spent a month in Carqueiranne, near Toulon, finishing *The English Novel*, revising 'Mr Croyd', and correcting the page proofs of *A Little Less Than Gods*, which

read better than in the slip proofs, when he had 'hated' the book. He sent Cheatham
a card of the open-air restaurant of the Hostellerie du Beau-Rivage where he was
staying, looking out over the coastline: 'This is where I eat!/ O RVAD always.' 'I bathe
a great deal,' he told Gertrude Stein, 'and treasonable as it may sound to the Rhone,
the sea does make swimming an easier affair.' He became 'extraordinarily pink'.
'Duckworth clamours that I should come to London to attend on the birth of my next
book and, since I do not know when that feat of the accoucheur is to take place—or
indeed whether I can afford to go—I remain suspended.' He had told Bowen he would
keep away from Paris until Julie's birthday at the end of November. His plans kept
changing. He felt ill. He wrote an exasperated letter to Pound, whose articles on 'How
to Read, or Why' he was still persuading Irita Van Doren to take for the *New York
Herald Tribune*: 'I don't see how she could publish them because they are really
incomprehensible: I offered to annotate them so that the ordinary reader might
understand something of what they treated. But it was beyond me. There is too much
politics on this planet!' At the end of September he went to Monte Carlo, to take the
boat from Nice to Corsica, where he had a fortnight's holiday, and visited Napoleon's
house.[22]

He headed north; partly because, as he told Stein: 'Poor Bradley [. . .] seems to be
going to lose his child and I may run up to Paris to see if I can do him any good'; partly
because Rene Wright was coming over. From Arles he sent Cheatham a postcard of 'a
very beautiful avenue of Roman Tombs' at Les Alyscamps, where he said he had spent
a long time as a boy. 'Getting towards Paris & nearer you now / always', he wrote.
When he got to Paris in November he cabled her to tell her he'd 'Arrived safely':
'thanks dear letters have written unchanging always Ford.' Unfortunately his relations
with Wright hadn't changed either: 'I don't see how I can go on with R. much longer,
our tastes are so mutually *hostile*, so that a break might come at any moment', he told
Cheatham; but it didn't. 'R. is in a hotel in the rue de l'Université but except going up
and down the Avenue de l'Opera & looking in at the windows of American shops we
have done very little.' She disapproved of the Quartier Latin that meant so much to
Ford. Bradley's daughter died. Bradley got knocked down by a taxi. 'Paris is very
dreadful', Ford told Cheatham. (The publication of Jean Rhys's *Postures* in late
September can't have helped.) He could no longer bear to go down the rue Vavin
'because of the poignancy of its memories'. But a bus he took down the Boulevard
Raspail made a detour because of road-works. It went: 'right past the spot where you
said what you said—Oh, R.V. a D.—it was almost unbearably . . . I could almost say,
sweet. And, late that night I went back there and delayed for ever so long on that very
spot, just thinking.' 'Alas', he continued: 'I can only write in terms of the emotions
because material things are just now screwing themselves up to a pitch that makes them
too complicated to think about.' He quoted a sentence from 'the Anglican Prayerbook'
ending: 'and learn the truth of this gracious promise: "As thy days so shall thy strength
be!" And, oh I swear to you that I could not get through another minute of it if it were
not for that—and you!' He was to use the phrase 'As Thy Day' as a working title for
the novel *Henry for Hugh*, in which Henry Martin's belief in an ironic providence—
and the love of two women—keeps him living. It made Ford feel worse that he didn't
feel he should write love-letters to her while he was ostensibly with Wright:

This is Thanksgiving Day—and [. . .] I choose it to write to you. For if I have any cause for thanksgiving it is because you are in the world. I daresay, my dear, you will have understood that I do not write you regular love-letters because as things for the moment are it would seem too much of a duplicity: but I think too you will understand how absolutely you have wound yourself round me and that it will be like that till the end—of me at any rate.

She gave him hope that she still had hope. 'My dear', he replied to one of her letters, 'I think the quaintest, the loveliest thing you have ever written to me was to the effect that you might have been voting for the last time as an American citizen. Please God, from whom all blessings flow, that it will be so. . . .'[23]

Rene Wright was haranguing him about money. As he explained to Cheatham, he had settled more than he could afford on Bowen and Julie, but Wright resented this, despite her own wealth:

She [. . .] took the view that I was victimizing her for the sake of pouring money into Stella's lap [. . .] and that I was a European fortune-hunter out after her horded gold [. . .] American women of that class are so hypnotised by their own money that they think the whole of the rest of the world has its eyes fixed on and ought to run its life to the tune of their dollars [. . .] our relations are really most extraordinary: she won't go back on what she has said and I won't make any advances and the most violent rows—always about what I allow Mrs Ford or spend on E.J.—break out at any moment. She lives in an hotel on the other side and makes me [grubstake] her all day long at fabulously expensive places—for naturally she does not believe that I am practically stoneybroke, but that it is merely meanness [. . .] But the worst of it is that in both England and America I have had the worst year I have had for very long—largely because whilst I was changing publishers the old publishers soft-pedalled [m]y last book—which was the LAST POST [. . .] I'd like you to burn this if you don't mind. What I have written about R. may seem rather mean—but I want you to know where I . . . you and I . . . stand. That R & I should ever marry isn't I think possible, our tastes are so extravagantly different. She has only once been to this apartment and then she disliked it so much for its bareness and want of ribbons and things that she said I must get rid of it at once and take an apartment in the Etoile Quarter—where I hope you can imagine me!
    But indeed it isn't written in a mean spirit—rather in a comic one. It is such a case of international misunderstanding.
    [. . .] she has been dreadfully ill [. . .] So that I think it a duty to hold myself at her disposal as long as she can stand it because she did put herself through the divorce which was very unpleasant for my sake. Of course too we have three times parted for good, but each time next morning she has rung me up & told me to come & take her out for lunch and has been particularly goodhumoured. But one day I suppose she won't and that will finish it [. . .] it would be lovely for you and me to run about Paris like a pair of ragamuffins and I should not care a bit. But what you said in the rue Vavin at dawn has this much truth about it that I haven't perhaps got life enough left to lump together enough to leave you properly provided for—and of course the bottom *may* have fallen altogether out of my markets [. . .].[24]

Bowen had said that though she wanted to preserve Julie from 'anything which would puzzle her'—such as seeing Ford with another partner—she didn't mind her meeting Rene Wright 'casually'. But by now she and Ford were not meeting or speaking (perhaps because she thought he had wanted to bring Wright to Paris), which cannot have been easy while sharing the same block of flats, and had its own comic potential. 'Stella was giving a large party in the studio,' he wrote, 'and a number of people kept on coming in here by mistake and as I did not know about the party I was puzzled and very much bothered, for I had not a leaf of tea nor a drop of liquor in the house.' Allen Tate had been awarded a Guggenheim Fellowship on Ford's recommendation, and in late November he, Caroline Gordon, their daughter Nancy, and friend Léonie Adams, arrived in Paris. They were soon faithful attenders of Ford's 'Saturday evenings four flights up at 32 rue de Vaugirard'. The other regulars were Ralph Cheever Dunning (the formalist poet Ford had published in the *transatlantic*), 'a survivor of the pre-war period', and Lincoln Gillespie, an avant-garde poet with a hole in his head covered by a silver plate (' "You don't believe me?" he would say; and he always said it, forgetting that he had told us before. He would lean forward, push back a strand of hair, and ask me to tap the plate'). Gordon remembered them playing a game in which they would assign their acquaintances 'to the appropriate circle of Dante's Inferno'. Ford 'talked little but rather nodded agreement or disagreement'—a marked change from his volubility at New York soirées. Tate recalled his occasional glances back to the past: 'My great-great-grandfather in Poland repudiated his titles and moved to Alsace.'[25]

He sent Cheatham a copy of his rare volume *Women & Men* for Christmas; and he began his next novel, provisionally 'Notterdam' (and eventually *When the Wicked Man*), which would express his despair at the disintegration of his life as he separated from Bowen, his despair over his affair with Cheatham, and his frustration with publishers. He also sent her a telegram of dazzling ambiguity: 'A lovely lovely New Year to you and all yours which means me too please stop affairs a little improved self unchanging.' ('Me too please' or 'please stop affairs'? 'Unchanging' because not 'a little improved', or unchanging love?) His own New Year's Eve was far from 'lovely': it was probably this year that he was 'actually set on by racketeers [. . .] but got off rather successfully with a little damage to my teeth and throat'. The tone of his correspondence with Cheatham did change in 1929. She had begun to suspect that Ford was perpetuating the ambiguity of his affairs, and she berated him for being 'noncommittal'. He replied that if he sounded so it was because he hated 'saying things against R.'. He then committed himself 'to the very deepest':

I promise you my dearest love, that I will never marry anyone but you. I don't promise that there will not be delay but I promise you that. I don't need to promise you that I won't—I suppose one must use the words—make any attempts on your virtue or ask you to carry on any intrigues with me. You know already that I never shall. And I also assure you solemnly that I cannot live without your love and support.[26]

The point about not making attempts on her virtue was also partly for her parents' benefit; but *When the Wicked Man* confirms the impression given by his letters to her that their affair was never consummated. He told her he couldn't leave before 20 January 'because the divorce will not be made absolute before then'. This makes the divorce seem a certainty, whereas in fact it was not until three days later that he wrote to 'Elsie Hueffer's solicitors, in a final attempt to free himself from her. 'I should be obliged', he told them with devastating understatement, 'if you would suggest to her that the present would be an appropriate time for completing [the divorce] proceedings':

For I was recently told—very much to my surprise, for I do not receive newspaper cuttings—that Mrs Elsie Hueffer had stated in Court that her reason for not completing these proceedings was that she was a Roman Catholic—this being the only reason that I ever heard. And I heard it only New Years Eve last. I at once consulted a priest here and he gave it as his opinion that there would be no difficulty whatever in having the marriage dissolved by Rome.

It is true that Elsie's counsel in her 1924 attempt to stop Hunt calling herself Hueffer in print had misunderstood the case, and had claimed in court that Elsie would not divorce because she was a Roman Catholic. (He probably wasn't used to cases of Catholics trying to divorce Anglicans.) It is just possible that Ford had only just heard this, and believed it. Elsie had feared that a divorce might compromise her Catholic daughters, and Ford may have imagined that she had converted for their sake. He may even have thought that Christina, having become a nun, might have persuaded Elsie to convert. Mizener disbelieved Ford entirely here, claiming that he had known about Elsie's alleged Catholicism since 1924 (though he only produces evidence that Ford knew of the case *before* it happened, which does not prove he knew the report of it); and that the anonymous priest was a disguise for his own opinion. Yet Ford's letters to Cheatham are very explicit in saying that he had gone to confession on New Year's Day; that 'the priest said that, to satisfy Rome, I must have my marriage dissolved there, though it was only a civil marriage'; and that he was to see 'the doyen of Saint Sulpice' to discuss getting the marriage dissolved. 'I don't myself care much about it', he told her, 'though it is disagreeable to be excommunicated as one would I suppose be—but it would take time and money.' Thus he apparently thought Elsie would require a dissolution before agreeing to a civil divorce. Alternatively, he may have been trying to give her an opportunity to relent, by saying that of course she wasn't a Catholic, and no longer objected to divorce. He implied that if she consented, he would pay her alimony when he could afford it. Elsie was unrelenting. Her solicitors told him: 'she wishes the matrimonial position to be left as it is', and that her decision had been made 'for the sake of the children'. It was the last communication of any kind from her. Ford may not have expected much more; his confidence about the divorce being made absolute comes in a letter he expected Cheatham to show to her parents. He probably wanted to convince them that his *intentions* were honourable, even if his private life did not seem so. He was also living out one of his fictions again, since it is in *Last Post* that Sylvia Tietjens announces her intention to divorce Christopher and get Rome to dissolve their marriage; a solution which Ford said had been suggested to him by an actual case, the 'Marlborough marriage'.[27]

Mizener thought this was the end of Ford's hope of marrying Wright. But his depressed tone in the New Year comes from the threat to his hopes of marrying Cheatham, and from her doubts about him. (Of course if Elsie had divorced him, he was capable of feeling obliged to marry Wright while loving Cheatham.) 'I think it absolutely certain that she will not ever want really to marry me,' he told Cheatham of Wright, 'for she has always been used to the circumstances of the very rich which I can't provide and would not if I could for, although I am a hard-shelled Tory, I hate, hate, hate any manifestations of wealth.' He assured her that they never met 'except in restaurants and hotel vestibules and the like', and that 'no sort of gilty [*sic*] relationships—as they are called—exist or have existed between me and *any* human soul' since he had met her. But Wright was 'still very ill', and he was determined that the break between them should not be of his making.[28]

He wrote what may be his bitterest letter to Elsie's solicitors. Its ostensible purpose was to persuade her to think again, but he couldn't help revealing his rage against her—a self-destructive act which can only have hardened her resolve:

surely it must be obvious to the most limited intelligence that it cannot be to the advantage of children to have a father covered with the volcanoes of mud that Mrs Hueffer has from time to time thrown over me. And if I am at this late moment anxious that the matter should be compounded it is precisely in the interests of Mrs Hueffer's children who happen to be my own and for whom I retain a deep affection.

I am aware that as a writer or as a personality I am completely ignored in Great Britain— or so completely as makes no difference. But in the United States and in this country that is far from being the case and I do not see how after my death discussions of this case can be avoided which must be extraordinarily disadvantageous and painful to my children and possibly even to Mrs Hueffer herself. I assure you that I am making no threats. I have never commented on Mrs Hueffer's proceedings either in public or in private and I have no intention of ever either doing that or of ever stating my case.

[. . .] the temper of the times in [America and France] is very hostile to the idea of one human being's crippling the life of another human being for a matter of over a quarter of a century. For a quarter of a century is a long time in a human life and a quarter of a century of revenge or a quarter of a century of suffering are things that appeal to the imagination of simple people.

For myself I am completely indifferent to the esteem in which I may be held—but if such a position is set up what one may well ask oneself will be the feelings of those unfortunate children? They will find themselves with a father of considerable notoriety over half the globe but blackened to an equally considerable pitch and at the same time their mother will be represented to that same half-globe as a person of extremely unenviable character and actions. I am not myself commenting on Mrs Hueffer[;] I am merely stating what will inevitably happen after my death—not because of any merits of my work but because I have a number of ardent champions in the United States and here whom I shall be unable to restrain after my death. And of course people in the United States and here are extremely anxious to read of mysterious scandals.

And mysterious the affair must remain, the only explanation to the normal man being one of implacable revengefulness [. . .]

It is at least reasonable—if not highly scrupulous—to attempt by legal subterfuges to keep one's children from a father whom one supposes to be a person of infamous life. But that only obtains to their tender years and it is beyond the power of the law to prevent my access to them should they be so disposed. That being the case it is obviously untrue to say that the only way to benefit my children is to continue to ruin my life.[29]

He only made that claim to be indifferent to what people thought when he cared too much. 'He was absurdly and disastrously sensitive to possible criticisms of himself', said Bowen. It might be thought not strictly true that he had never stated his case against Elsie. He *had* left indications, such as the legal deposition of 1913, novels like *The New Humpty-Dumpty* and *The Good Soldier*, or even this letter. And he had, of course, given both Hunt and Bowen glimpses of what he felt about her. Bowen wrote of 'the bitterness with which Ford used to speak of' Elsie. Yet he never published any comments about her; nor did he try to influence their children or her friends against her. His desperation and his desire to persuade made him distort his own feelings—though, as with his art, to distort in order to express them, since the pose of not commenting or resenting enables him to show exactly how much he can repress what he feels strongly. But this didn't stop him being a sure judge of character: he knew Elsie had not forgiven him, and the argument about the children was hypocrisy. She never got over his leaving her, and doubtless guessed that he wanted to remarry. He was not only right about her vengefulness, but also in his prophecy about how she would be viewed by posterity.

Ford carried on defending himself in 'categorical replies' to what he called Cheatham's 'catechistic letter':

Your next few paragraphs are about Rene. I don't think you can quite understand the position or be just to her—indeed I don't believe anyone could quite understand it, least of all myself. You see, we have known each other and been attached to each other for nearly twenty years and that makes a great difference in approach between two persons. But I could not at this moment say whether she cares for me in the least. I daresay she does not and only finds me a convenient sort of Cook's guide to Paris. I *think* that when she divorced her husband she really meant to marry me but I think that when she discovered [. . .] how hard up I was she made up her mind not to. I have asked her constantly what her intentions were but she has always turned it off. At the same time one is cowardly and hates to give pain so I have never said that marriage is impossible between us, though I really think it would be even if there were no you. So I rather drift. You see she has been very ill and I sometimes think she is not quite sane.

I do quite agree that, as you say I 'can't go on indefinitely being engaged to her and telling you that I love you' and I quite know that before very long I must take my courage in my hands and tell her that I cannot go on with her.[30]

Elizabeth had written: 'I want to know whether you still love her at all or whether you love me enough to face what we'd have to face.' Ford assured her again that there was nothing between him and Wright 'of an amatory nature': 'I have not said that I loved her since we met in New York nor has she said as much once to me. I hate giving these details because it seems so indelicate but I know that they are what you want to know.' She had also told him that the only thing that would endanger her love for him would be to discover he had not been telling her the truth. 'I do not think, my dear one,' he replied, 'that I ever told you a material untruth—though I may from time to time have represented myself as more of a hero or more of a martyr than other people would consider me. But I remember warning you at the beginning of our acquaintance that I was a bad man with whom most people would say you had better have nothing to do.' He had been 'absolutely true' to her since they met, he said: 'and, if you like to put it that way, for a number of years before. You may say that that is what an American woman's honour deman[d]s from her man.' He wasn't even seeing Wright very often now: 'she is all the time over the other side buying clothes and we only meet for dinner and the play or something—mostly concerts.' But he wanted to 'get on without mortifying her' if he possibly could; by which he meant he didn't want to jilt her if he could not be with Cheatham. Elizabeth's doubts about him compounded his anxiety that they would never be united—an anxiety which centred on money: his doubt that he would ever have enough to provide for her now and after his death—an outcome which his depression drew him to imagine even more often than usual. 'The real obstacle at the moment is purely financial', he told her. Viking's monthly payments of $700 for *When the Wicked Man* had ended in November. But the way Ford explained the situation shows it to have been more equivocal: 'If I were perfectly sure of a period in which we could live in peace and without financial worries I would say goodbye to R. tomorrow. But I don't want to hurt her feelings before it is necessary. I think she is really enjoying herself as things go and her health is enormously improving. If there *were* any passion at all about our relations I would break with her at once.' That is the Dowell in Ford speaking, casting himself as the nurse to his cold partner, while his dual personality all the time wishes he could marry the girl. In Ford's version it is Cheatham who has been non-committal too:

You see, my dear, ours has been such an extraordinary—if rather beautiful—association. You had such an astonishing effect on me, so suddenly, that before I knew where I was there was my declaration of the R.V.A.D—which if reckless was perfectly sincere. It was your answer to it that coloured the rest of my actions. I mean I simply could not, after that, believe that you could really come to love me or to care dreadfully. Indeed I do not think I really believed that till a month or so ago when one of your letters forced me to the conviction that you do. And I did not think that to receive the deferential attention of an elderly person of a sort of professorial eminence could do any young girl any harm. And you must remember that, even at our parting in New York you did not give any pledges to me so that I really thought then that, after a season of parties in your native country, you would be writing to me that the real Prince Charming had come along.[31]

It was a double-bind: the more despondent he became, the less energy he could put into what he called his 'business affairs'; as they suffered, the more he despaired of ever being able to afford happiness. He complained of a 'fit of mental weariness' due to his 'paralysing' financial worry. 'And, my dear, dear one I do have to remember your declaration of R.V.A.D. It was the first time anyone ever called me old. But it is true enough.' At first he had joked about it. But from now on he began to feel his age, and to feel it as an insuperable barrier between them. When he heard about the delay—and cost—of getting his marriage dissolved, he told her: 'it depressed me because it seemed as if not only the earthly, but the heavenly powers were manifesting against us.'[32]

He sailed at the end of January, handing over his flat to the Tates rent-free until May in exchange for Caroline Gordon's retyping of a 500-page manuscript. 'He is really one of the best men I have ever known', wrote Tate to Andrew Lytle: 'Not for that alone, but because he has a simple heart', he added obtusely, 'and hates the English'; 'He is the best company we have here'. Ford didn't know until the last moment whether Wright would travel with him. But the *de Grasse* was a cabin-class ship, and she could not 'stand anything but the comfort of a first-class liner'. Ford wired Cheatham while the boat was still at Le Havre: 'Sailing all alone all love.' Wright stayed in Paris. 'It will be lovely if you met me at N.Y.', Ford wrote to Cheatham; though there was a possibility that Wright's sister might do the same: 'if she did we would preserve a certain coolness of demeanour.' Elizabeth did come to see him in New York, where Ford was staying at the Hotel Carteret again, but there was a certain cooling of their demeanour after they had talked out their position: 'To sum up all our discussions', he wrote to her:

it w^{d.} seem that what stands between us is—on your part—your, or your parents', religious scruples and, for me, the hard details of business. I hope—I think we both hope—that these are not insurmountable.

But, as you seem to wish it, there is nothing for me to do but to give you up—at any rate for the time. And that does not mean that I ask you to wait—though Heaven knows how I hope that you will!—it means that I ask you to consider yourself absolutely free of any sort of smallest pledges you have ever given to me.

But when the time arrives—& I pray it may arrive soon—I propose to present[?] myself to you again and ask you to marry me according to the rites of Rome & the laws of this country—& naturally of my own. I do not imagine that your parents could then—in human-ity—wish to stand between us supposing you still to care for me. That is all I can say.[33]

Presumably she (and her parents too) had 'religious scruples' because they now knew that he had neither been able to divorce Elsie Hueffer nor disentangle himself from Rene Wright. Later that year he said he had been considering whether to apply for US citizenship 'out of sentiment'. Did he hope to do in America what he had failed to do in Germany, assuming another nationality in order to divorce Elsie abroad? If so, the Cheathams must have disliked the idea of him still being thought to have a wife in England. 'I am rather a sick man today,' he told Cheatham, who had now gone back to Pinehurst, 'but I must just thank you for y^{r.} dear letter and then hop back to bed. I just collapsed after you went.' P.S.: 'I *won't* live without you.' But then, so as not to let her worry, he cabled her: 'Much better writing unchanging.' As he explained in the letter, he knew that such collapses tended to be psychosomatic: 'Of course it is mostly nerves with me and I suppose I do not really deserve sympathy—but, oh, I want it.' He explained that Wright was due to arrive on the *Berengaria* on 5 March, and that he would be glad to 'get it over'. He found it difficult writing to Cheatham under what he called 'the new reservation' since he had told her to consider herself free: 'I mean that I cannot very honourably write you love-letters after the one meant for your father to see [. . .] it is almost impossible to write about the weather and the crops as the saying is—and love will come creeping in.' He had been to a wedding reception of Dorothy Galantière, who had divorced in order to marry the sculptor Roy Sheldon. 'The great feature of it was that Galantière was there, doing the honours. It was very impressive to hear him say to the bride: "I think I *must* be going now", and to hear her answer: "See you tomorrow!". It seemed rather cynical but who is one to judge.' The implica-tion was that his own apparently cynical conduct oughtn't to be judged: that it might even be seen as impressive in its civilized self-suppression. He felt lonely eating in restaurants without Elizabeth. One night he got drunk: 'Claire Smith, the wife of my English publisher, said that I insulted her. However, that was only a joke.' The waiter tried to cheat him out of $25, and the proprietor was afraid to make him give it back lest he denounced the restaurant for breaking the Prohibition law. 'However, I got it all right', Ford assured Cheatham. 'Well, there are the weather and the crops for you', he said. Then he even described the weather itself, which consisted of snow and ice: 'But, oh, mouse, mouse, mouse what a help you could be to your poor old lion in all slippery places.'[34]

When he felt better he renewed his literary contacts, seeing the Gormans, Van Dorens, Dorothy Parker, Heywood Broune, Isa Glenn, Isabel Paterson, Jonathan Cape (his 'English publisher' now), and Harrison Smith. He suggested he might be able to find Cheatham some advertising work in New York, for a man who owed him a favour, and whom he described—with mock-self-promotion—as 'a major in H.M. Army like myself'. She was now his 'poor caged mouse': 'Dearest, you are quite wrong as to the rules of this rather bitter game', he wrote, sounding more like Jean Rhys's Heidler than Dowell or Ashburnham. 'Because I let you tell your parents that I wanted you to consider yourself free it would not be honourable of me to write you love letters so as to entice you back into your cage.' Yet he wanted to remain passive and let her decide his fate, as he said she had in the rue Vavin, by telling him what to do about Wright—though he also knew it was an unreasonable thing to ask of her:

It makes such a difficult situation. I mean that, if I ask you to decide whether or no to break with her at once, that is putting rather a tie on you [. . .] On the other hand there [is] no particular sense in making her unhappy if you decide that you do not care enough for me. I should in that case do my best to make her happy. So perhaps you had better not write on that subject at all, unless you feel that you simply can't bear my seeing her at all . . . At any rate be sure there will not be any marriage.

He took an apartment at 30 West 9th Street, just off 5th Avenue: 'A nice sitting and a small bed room and bath but no kitchinette and a tiny garden to walk in and think of you.' And he told her not to put her address on the letters she sent there, and to sign them 'just M for MOUSE' in case Wright were to find them.[35]

She did, or she guessed, a week later. 'I was last night so overwhelmed, not only with reproaches but threats . . . of revelations & the rest', he told Cheatham: 'I will absolutely keep off your course from now on' and 'get back to Europe as quickly as I can.' Harold Loeb found him 'looking ponderous and helpless' when Ford introduced him to Wright. They gave him the impression that they 'seemed very fond of each other', which was true, though Ford was characteristically keeping his private life opaque, while evidently using the presence of an unsuspecting third person to reduce the risk of upsetting 'scenes' (as the Ashburnhams use Dowell, and as Hunt had complained Ford used his secretary). 'Several times he asked me to call for them at her hotel', recalled Loeb, 'and I would find them sitting close together downstairs in the lobby. Apparently he was not permitted to go up to her room. She told me, some weeks later when I was taking her in a taxi to meet Ford at a cocktail party given for AE [the Irish poet George Russell] by his publishers, that Ford could not marry her because he had never obtained a divorce from his wife, and that she could not live with him unmarried. All the way uptown she was on the verge of tears.'[36] Wright may have told Ford she wouldn't live with him unless he could divorce Elsie. But this may have been a face-saving story they invented to conceal the other reason they were breaking with each other: Elizabeth Cheatham. The break with Wright took its toll on him. As when he had left Elsie or Violet, Ford's guilt at being the cause of suffering made him feel the victim of suffering. He had lost hope. His 'business affairs' went 'from bad to worse'. Despite largely favourable reviews, the sales figures for *A Little Less Than Gods* were 'absolutely shocking'. Other plans fell through. 'Of course that is only the normal fate of the writer and except for you I should not complain', he wrote to Cheatham: 'but as it is the position is near-suicidal':

You see, my dear, I am convinced that I can't make the grade—for the first, or almost the first time in my life, and that it is [no] good your waiting even if you wanted to wait and that there is no good my hoping to put back the hands of time. And anyhow it was such a forlorn, poor hope!

[. . .] And indeed I am really frightened to keep you any more, ever so remotely involved in this desperate affair [. . .]

It was a farewell letter, though each line cried out to be gainsaid. 'I don't suppose, my dearest dear, that you will mind much', he said, and echoed her father's phrase: 'for you don't even yet know your own heart [. . .].' He closed with the same blessing with which he had said good-bye to Bowen:

All through the war I carried a talisman given me by Dr Wallis Budge of the British Museum—the valedictory psalm in Hebrew: The Lord guide thee, the Lord guard thee, the Lord watch over thee at thy goings out and at thy comings in from the same . . . So I pray that for you.

    Goodbye my darling. I have never loved anyone but you—and that's too late.
    Your Ford Madox Ford
    Write to me, dear, or not, as you think best: but do, if you do, in view of last night, not put any address.[37]

As that postscript shows, he couldn't leave it there. When they wrote to each other at Easter, he tried again to say good-bye:

Dear heart, I have been thinking—& indeed I have been mentally too ill to write—too proud, if you like, to fight! And I think we ought not to write at all. You see, my only beloved, if you care it seems to me that the quicker you forget the better & if you don't care—why you just don't care! And my job is to give someone else (as you put it) as good a time as I can & it does not seem very honourable to go on writing to you. So we had better go on without [words?] of each other: it would madden me to know that you had found a someone else—tho' I suppose you have already. And news of me won't matter to you.

    I didn't sleep at all on Easter night there was a mouse in my cupboard: so I wrote the enclosed.

    God always bless you my darling: I am quite unchanging & always shall be: always: always.
    Y^r FMF
    I can't bear it, you know.[38]

The enclosed was a poem entitled 'Mouse! Mouse!', which recalls 'To Christina at Nightfall' ('He wanted, he supposed, really to regard her as a daughter', wrote Ford of Notterdam thinking about his love in *When the Wicked Man*):

> It was the little mouse
> That ate my heart away!
> The little peeping, creeping mouse
> That cheeps at dawn of day:
> She ate my heart away
> And for it left instead,

Within the heavy, sigh-filled place
A heavy lump of lead.

I have no heart for play,
I have no heart to sleep
Awaiting in the silent house
Dawn and the mouse's cheep:
But silent all the day
I creep the streets along
Remembering the dawn of day
And the mouse[?] cheeping song.

He even included the opening lines in the novel he was then writing, *When the Wicked Man*, so that Cheatham would know that the character Henrietta Felise was based on her. Notterdam even thinks of Henrietta Felise as 'a pixie':

She was very small. Exceedingly small and fragile-boned: if she had not appeared so healthy you would have had to call her miniature. Her hair was mouse-coloured and extremely fine. If he had to give her a nickname he might have called her: 'Mouse.'

'It was the little Mouse,
That ate my heart away,
The little peeping, creeping Mouse
That creeps at dawn of day. . . .'

Something like that. An old rhyme.
Her lips were very full and pouted; her eyes, extremely large-pupilled, appeared above all to be puzzled. Puzzled about you, about life, about her own self. Their glance ran over your brows, your cheeks, your mouth, to return to your eyes. She sat up, holding her note-book as if it had been gathered reins, her elbows close to her sides, her chin singularly tucked into her neck. She might have been reining in an elegant horse, to music, in a *haute école* act.
[. . .] When she entered, it was unadulterated joy. She would come in, little, startled, her eyes large with pleasure, moving delicately her delicately boned limbs—raising her hand to her hat, placing a magazine on a little table.
Merely to look at her was entire happiness. When he took her in his arms she pressed her lips on his. It was mental health, peace, chastity, sobriety.
There was only one shadow on the situation—he did not know whether or not Elspeth intended to divorce him. She had said in her fury that she would not but he imagined that eventually reason would come to her aid.[39]

The discovery of Ford's letters to Cheatham overturns all previous biographical readings of *When the Wicked Man*, and illuminates one danger of reading fiction biographically: we can never be sure all the relevant biographical material is available, and therefore can never completely disentangle transcription from invention.

Ford was writing so lovingly about his affair with Cheatham because he feared it was now truly finished. Notterdam's celebration of 'mental health, peace, chastity, sobriety' was Ford's elegy for a love of which he had not felt the like since the war. He had good reason to fear that Cheatham had already found 'someone else'. Her grandson remembers her telling a story of how she had a dinner with Ford and another man called Hugh Carter, during which both men asked, while the other was out of the room, what she was doing with *him*? Carter was the fourth and final 'Love Him', and she married him on 21 April 1929, duly inscribing him in the single space for the 'Wedding Him' on the last page of the 'Him Book'. She took Ford at his words and didn't tell him. But he was not one not to notice her interest in his rival. On the page for 'Sad Hims', she marked Ford's name with a cross, meaning 'my fault'.

1929: THAT SAME POOR MAN

> We are all so afraid, we are all so alone, we all so need from the outside the
> assurance of our own worthiness to exist.
>
> (Ford, *The Good Soldier*)

When Stella Bowen wrote to ascertain Ford's plans—she probably wanted to avoid
being in Paris if he was going to be back with Wright—he replied bitterly: 'I do not
know what my movements will be. As your letter practically precludes my seeing Julie
I see no reason to return to France which I suppose will suit you. On the other hand
I may—but I simply don't know, being past caring.' He told Bradley he was 'really too
tired at this moment to think about anything'. At the beginning of the year he had told
Cheatham he was 'in a sort of apathy, with nothing in the world to care for'—which
is one reason why he called the protagonist of *When the Wicked Man* Notterdam. When
he finished the book in May his familiar post-novel depression made him feel even
worse. L. P. Hartley had said that 'Self-justification and self-pity are at the root' of the
characters in *A Little Less Than Gods*. This is even more true of the novel through
which he had been pondering his complicated tangle of feelings about Cheatham,
Wright, Bowen, and Elsie Hueffer. His guilt at deceiving Wright, and involving
Cheatham in that deception—not being able to stop writing her love-letters even as he
felt he ought to give her up—was offset by his feeling that he was fundamentally
honourable: that he had been forced into an invidious position by Elsie's continued
vengefulness. After all, he had changed his name and his country now, so her dread of
being shamed by another woman claiming to be 'Mrs Hueffer' no longer applied.
When the Wicked Man returns to other periods when he felt as much betrayed as
betraying. Notterdam's old friend and partner Kratch has Ford's old friend and
collaborator Conrad's hypochondria; he has also had an affair with Notterdam's wife
Elspeth (who combines aspects of Elsie and Bowen, whose given name was Esther), as
Ford felt he had been betrayed by Marwood and Elsie. Lola Porter's vindictiveness
when spurned by Notterdam owes much, as we have seen, to Jean Rhys's anger at
being cast off by Ford. It probably also draws on Rene Wright's outbursts, and
demands that Ford should pay for her. Notterdam's renunciation of Henrietta Felise
is very close to Ford's conduct with Cheatham:

You can't . . . *détourner*, the French again call it, the daughter of anyone called Henrietta
Villiers Faukner. Plenty of words for that sort of thing the French have. But it can't be done.
He would have to put her back.
    And then . . .
    What could he do? It would not be possible to live without looking at the small, quivering

wrists? It would not be possible to live without ever—without ever—*ever*, you understand!—hearing the queer accent of her o's. For what else had he traversed again and unendingly the immense panorama of this vast continent? . . . Sleep after toil, port after stormy seas. . . .

But the novel is more interesting than 'a shamefaced piece of poetised autobio-graphy'—Ford's verdict on Conrad's *Arrow of Gold*, paraphrasing Renan, 'who said that as soon as one begins to write about oneself *on poetise un peu*'. The story could be said to 'poetise' Ford's own life, and romanticize the outcome of his relationship with Cheatham, by allowing Notterdam to regain Henrietta Felise in the happy end. (Notterdam escapes death at the hands of the gangster McKeown, shooting him in a hallucinatory state in which he mistakes him for his lecherous *alter ego*.) The plot implies that he saves his soul, and his love, because he has turned aside from his wickedness—as Ford must have felt he had done, in renouncing Cheatham, rather as Ashburnham renounces Nancy Rufford. 'Is villainy then constituted by a frame of mind or by a train of actions?', thinks Notterdam. Was Ford remembering how he had told Bowen that what people *were* mattered more than what they had *done*? It is another of his reimaginings of the 'Bingel and Bengel' theme: Notterdam (like Ford) is a composite of both: he feels his heart is in the right place (like Bingel), but feels unjustly maligned for his actions (like Bengel). He feels Henrietta Felise is 'pure' despite having lost her virginity to another man, whereas he is 'a lousy villain' for desiring her. It is central to Ford's concept of 'passion' that men suffer for their desire. But he had not attempted to seduce Cheatham, and felt he was—like Notterdam—'more of a hero or a martyr than other people would consider' him.[1]

The novel is equivocal about guilt. It obliquely protests Ford's innocence in 1928 and 1929: 'He was guiltless—but Henrietta Felise was to suffer, because in conse-quence he, Notterdam, was not to be a free man. He had not been able again to discuss the matter with Elspeth, and he had not had the courage to give news of that disaster to the girl who looked out like a bird over the tree-tops in Gramercy Park.' Ford had not felt able to discuss Cheatham with Rene Wright; he had also been trying to protect Cheatham from the disastrous news that he would not be a free man. But the novel is also disarmingly candid about Notterdam's inability to feel shame and guilt (as Ford found it impossible to believe he had been betrayed by Marwood and Conrad, or that he was morally bound to remain married to Elsie). There is a moral truth here—that people don't always *feel* responsible for their own actions—though it's not a view to make moralists feel comfortable. It is an impressionist's ethics, whereby a person's sense of responsibility can be profoundly indifferent to facts, or uncannily alienated from them. 'Even now he could not *believe* that this sick monkey [Kratch] had taken his woman. Not *believe*. Only his intellect said it', writes Ford of Notterdam, with the impressionist's perpetual fascination with what people can get themselves to believe. 'It was only by arriving at the date of Kratch's operation and by picking up traces as a sleuth picks up footprints that he had arrived at the conviction of his own guilt.'[2] Yet Ford was not writing autobiography, of course, and Notterdam is not simply equatable with his author. His wickedness is in part Ford's satire on the iniquities of commercial publishing. He is certainly one of Ford's *alter egos* in this novel about doubles. But his predicaments reflect not only the problems of Ford's life but the preoccupations of his art. This quintessentially Fordian tale of a man on the edge of breakdown becoming a time-visionary, seeing the past superimposed on the present like a reflection seen in a window, allegorizes his tendency to cast his mind back at moments of crisis, and his need to arrive at convictions by living in mental pictures.

While the Viking Press was reading the novel, Ford turned back to one of his unpublished post-war manuscripts, 'English Country', revising it for publication as *No Enemy*. It was his 'reminiscences of active service under a thinly disguised veil of fiction'—'poetised autobiography' indeed—written 'partly in the line and partly just after the Armistice'. He described it to Hugh Walpole as 'a perfect paean to the English countryside in the middle of war reminiscences'. Most of the best writing about the war invokes that contrast; part of the uniqueness of *No Enemy* lies in the way Ford inverts the expected emphases. Instead of foregrounding the horror of trench war, he makes its psychological effects real by showing how much the destruction of actual landscape caused the mind to return to mental pictures of remembered landscape. The book deserves to be recognized as a classic book about the war. Ford added to Walpole: 'it is the best prose I ever wrote.' As with *The Marsden Case* and *Parade's End*, *No Enemy* is concerned not so much with the war as with its after-effects. In a draft for a foreword he said: 'the book is not a War book: it is, rather, an after-war book.' Introducing his semi-fictional *alter ego* Gringoire, the also semi-fictional 'Compiler' writes: 'This book, then, is the story of Gringoire just after . . . Armageddon.' It was subtitled, 'A Tale of Reconstruction'. Formally, it is a tessellation of hallucinatory impressions. The technique is continuous with those of the early piece 'Nice People'; of the vertiginous vignettes of *The Good Soldier*, of the post-war fragment 'True Love & a G.C.M.'; and even a later novel like *When the Wicked Man*: to juxtapose haunting impressions, and then wonder what they might mean. As with Woolf's 'moments of vision', or Joyce's 'epiphanies', the effect is to pose 'meaning' and 'coherence' as both a problem and a necessity. *No Enemy* explores how different forms of duality can cohere: the wartime past and the post-war present; outside and inside (the book's two parts are titled 'Four Landscapes' and 'Certain Interiors'); landscape and humanity; Gringoire and the Compiler; artist and critic; imagination and matter; fact and fiction. The relating of fragmentary memories enacts Gringoire's painful process of self-reintegration. As Sondra Stang said, it is 'a very personal—and at the same time objective—account of the process of regaining sanity'. It is also Ford's answer to Pound's criticism of impressionism's ocular fetish, since questions of his mind and his history were also for him inevitably questions of his art. Gringoire says 'before August, 1914, I lived more through my eyes than through any other sense, and in consequence certain corners of the earth had, singularly, the power to stir me'. Once the war started, 'aspects of the earth no longer existed' for him. *No Enemy* shows how the war turned Ford into a much more explicitly psychological novelist. It accounts for the shift in narrative modes during *Parade's End*, from the Edwardian meticulousness of surface at the opening of *Some Do Not. . .* , to the streams of consciousness in *Last Post*. It also accounts for the increasing attention he gives to the body, and the relationship between the mind and body, from *The Marsden Case* onwards. The pre-war Ford could never have written, as the post-war one did, thinking about Elizabeth Cheatham while Notterdam thinks of Henrietta Felise: 'His whole being was bound up in that naked imp under her stuff of brilliant chrysanthemum.' *No Enemy*'s elusive ironic play with its fictionalized identities makes it Ford's 'most original and introspective book' as autobiography (Stang again). When Ford reread it after a decade, its duality took on yet another aspect: 'I really believe it is rather a beautiful book and can almost afford to say so since it was written so long ago [. . .] and in such different circumstances that it really seems to be the work of another man.' An artist's works will always seem 'other': this is one sense in which Eliot's judgement holds that 'the more perfect the artist, the more completely separate in him will be the man who suffers and the mind which creates'. Ford's doubling of himself in his fictional personae ensured that *No Enemy* had *already* seemed to be the work of another man, or even of other men. His art, deriving from impressionist and expressionist traditions that Eliot mistrusted, shows up the limitations of Eliot's dictum, which cannot explain why *The Good Soldier* is so much better a novel than *When the Wicked Man*, even though Ford's mental suffering informs both. In the case of *When the Wicked Man*, it is, rather, the failure to integrate technical creativity and personal suffering, that damages the novel. Eliot's theory of 'impersonality' is based on classical and Renaissance writers (about whom, as with Shakespeare, we simply happen to know little); it has scant toleration for romantic or post-romantic forms which foreground the expression of personality, or autobiography. Ford's explorations of the artist's dual being is the more necessary position for the modern critic.[3] Like all Ford's most compelling writing, *No Enemy* engages with his feelings about death, and his own near-death in the war. Its remembered landscapes and interiors become oblique elegies for his dead comrades (Ford called the book 'a tribute to the country and my comrades in arms'). But, as he suggested in the dedication he composed on Midsummer Day 1929, it had also drawn strength from his post-war feeling (it must have seemed another man's feeling now) of survival and new life; not only his own rebirth, but the birth of his daughter Julie, to whom he dedicated it in a gesture of hope that he wouldn't become estranged from her too:

Très, très, chère petite Princesse,
    When you shall come to read English—which I hope will not be too soon—you shall find here adumbrated what the world seemed like to me just when you were preparing to enter it. . . . a confused old world which your coming rendered so much clearer and dearer. And as these pages were written in the expectation of you—and for you!—I have thought better to leave them exactly as they were, bearing as they obviously do the traces of sufferings that, thank God, you never knew. And so, when you come to read them, give a tender thought to him to whom you have so often written—quitoubliejamé et qui t'aime de tou son coeur et encore beaucoupluss!

                                                                                    F.M.F.

He wanted Julie to read herself into the book (though she doesn't figure explicitly in it), just as he wanted Bowen to see herself in Valentine Wannop, or Cheatham to read herself into *A Little Less Than Gods* and *When the Wicked Man*. Writing, for him, always involved this combination of intimacy and impersonality: a paradoxical duality of self-revelation and self-concealment; an imagined sympathetic silent listener in the faceless public audience.

It was perhaps during this stay in America that Ford visited Robber Rocks, in the woods near the New York–Connecticut border, 'the country headquarters for Allen

Tate, Hart Crane, and others'. Malcolm Cowley met him there, and noted his 'roving eye for younger women, whom he especially liked to fascinate'. 'They would be fondled by Ford, and then escape him up the stairs', he said. 'Ford, heavy and wheezing by that time, would follow them to the head of the narrow stairs, and the door would close in his face. He would wheeze back down, and a little while later he'd follow another young woman until she took refuge behind a locked door.'[4] If he seemed the comic lecher to Cowley, it may have been because he kept his deeper needs so private: the need to forget Cheatham; to find consolation.

Ford saw a lot of Richard Hughes in New York—'really a fine writer and a keen intelligence'—and he began another project that summer: *A History of Our Own Times*. It was to be the history of *his* own time, from about 1870 to the time of writing. Feeling his age had made him want to render his age. As with the genesis of *Parade's End*, one impulse to write it was an anxiety of amnesia. He explained that, despite his good memory, 'I have been astonished at my own forgetfulness [. . .] So I have here attempted to re-memorize those times', for himself and for others. He planned three or four volumes and completed the first—1870–95—within a year. But it was not published in his lifetime, which meant that he could not afford the time to write the others. Mizener argues that Ford's turning back to two ten-year-old manuscripts ('Mr Croyd' and *No Enemy*), his return to historical romance in *A Little Less Than Gods*, and now his decision to write history, all indicate that he was 'having trouble finding subjects for novels'. It is true that he told George Keating in 1930 he was 'too tired to undertake more fiction', and that he didn't begin his next novel, *The Rash Act*, until December 1931. But this is not to say, as Caroline Gordon did, that 'In his late fifties his powers failed him; he was no longer able to write fiction and kept himself going by writing over and over a sort of fictionalized autobiography'. *The Rash Act*, together with the *variety* of his late fictionalized autobiographies testify to the unfairness of that charge. Nor is it to say that he was having trouble finding subjects. Soon after finishing the first volume of the *History* (in July 1930) he worked on *Return to Yesterday*, incorporating into it the more reminiscential passages he had cut from the *History* when trying to condense it for publishers. After *Return to Yesterday* he began *The Rash Act*. Rather, it shows that he was entering a new phase of his career, in which his historical, cultural, and autobiographical writings overshadow his novels. The publication of *No Enemy* and the beginning of the *History* initiated this phase. Both began in autobiography, and heralded a new burst of autobiographical creativity that was to produce some of his best writing. Though he never stopped reimagining his own experiences and observations as fiction, he would increasingly reimagine himself and his memories. He had never been only a novelist. His history-writing goes back as far as *The Cinque Ports* (1900), and includes his wartime propaganda books. He had read widely in history books to research his historical romances of each century since the fourteenth: *Ladies Whose Bright Eyes*, *The Young Lovell*, *The Fifth Queen*, *The 'Half Moon'*, *The Portrait*, *A Little Less Than Gods*, *Romance*—the vignettes in *Zeppelin Nights* cover an even greater range, from Greek and Roman battles, through early Christianity, to the coronation of George V. His conception of what he called 'creative history' was always novelistic, of course. In *Great Trade Route* he relates a Mediterranean legend about the Virgin Mary helping gypsies, adding: 'It is a good legend. Just as impressionist art tells things more truly than photographs, so its story reveals the true history of the earth far more truly than it can ever be revealed by the scientific historian.' That is the justification for all Ford's writing, whether of fiction, autobiography, or history: what reveals 'true history' is 'story'.[5]

There was also the pressing need for money, of course. He now had two as-yet unpublished novels on his hands, and was wary of the danger of glutting the demand for his fiction. He needed to find new projects for which publishers would pay his advances. He may have still had the—forlorn—hope that if he could improve his financial position, he could return to Cheatham. But if he did, the second half of 1929 saw it come crashing down. In July Viking, who had already angered Ford by rejecting 'Mr Croyd', rejected *When the Wicked Man*, thus confirming the exasperation with publishers that had invigorated the book. At the same time Jonathan Cape told Ford he should revise it to make it appear less as if written by an American. Once again Ford's hopes of finding a publisher who would believe in his work and publish his collected edition were shaken. 'I do not like the idea of a novel of mine being hawked about from publisher to publisher', he wrote to Bernice Baumgarten (of Brandt and Brandt) in a furious letter that demanded the respect he was not being paid: 'It never happened to me before in my life and I am too old to bear the experience with equanimity now.' He retorted to Baumgarten's 'strictures' on the novel:

That is hardly a matter that I can discuss. I was trying in the book a technical experiment which seems to me to have been successful and you are, I suppose, aware that I have been a good deal praised for the technique of my fiction and that I have had a good deal of influence on the technique of the more modern novelists of today. It seems therefore more likely that I am right in the matter than a group of tradesmen who have no literary experience, whatever their skill or want of skill in marketing the literary products of others. But that is an agelong struggle and when you have lived as long as I have you will see that in such affairs the publisher is invariably wrong. They are not unnaturally afraid of innovations and the innovations almost invariably win out.[6]

He wrote a spirited preface to Richard Aldington's *Imagist Anthology*, revisiting the heady days of pre-war literary hostilities. But the tone was predominantly elegiac, like the title: 'Those were the Days.' In part it is mock-elegiac. Pound (as Aldington was later to say) was too 'sulky' to send in poems, so Ford took the opportunity to tease him. He had written of him a decade earlier that 'There can have been few men whose deaths have so often been announced', and proceeded to supply long and mostly fictitious page references in the index under 'Pound, E.', to 'his decease', 'his revisitation', and 'his further decease'. Now he announced Pound's death again, referring to him as 'the late Mr Pound'. He recalled imagining himself dead, and as Pound's companion in death—'at that date I died: I determined to become as dead and silent as Mr Pound.' A postscript explains the joke with an elegantly turned compliment: 'I hear at the last moment that the author of CATHAY is not actually—however spiritually—with Homer, Plato, Sophocles, the Swan of Avon, Rimbaud, Bertran de Born and all those just men. It is therefore only because of his dilatoriness in sending in his contribution that he can be styled "the late".' But the tone of mock-elegy for himself is made sombre by his reimagining of his own death: 'today, being the same age as Flaubert when he was half way through BOUVARD ET PECUCHET [. . .].' Ford was 56. Flaubert died when he was 58, leaving his last novel unfinished.[7]

Ford complained of feeling unwell, and said that his doctor had told him it was imperative to get away from New York. Mizener thought that this meant he needed to get away from the 'demoralizing objections' to *When the Wicked Man*. Certainly his pride was wounded enough for him to get Baumgarten to arrange for his release from the Viking contract, and to tell her he would no longer use Brandt and Brandt as his agents. Perhaps he felt they were more in sympathy with the publishers than with their authors. But Mizener didn't know of Elizabeth Cheatham, because of whom Ford was already profoundly demoralized. It was this despair that made him act so self-destructively in his professional affairs. He wrote his last goodbye letter to her, heartbreaking and heartbroken, before he sailed:

Very dear Elizabeth,
    It cannot be friendship. You can be sure of that from what you saw of my emotion. So it must be goodbye—unless you can [a pencil addition says 'I meant to write "wait" but I couldn't'.] But no, of course you can't.
    I would like to ask you one thing—and that is not to shew my letters to anyone. It is not that there is anything to be ashamed of in them; but let that little bit of secrecy remain warm and quiet between us—and also I *beg* you not to let me know when you marry. Oh, and do not show anyone the inscription in the Conrad book, please.
    And remember that there is in the world someone who cares for you more tenderly than you can conceive of—And that for ever. Et quand vous serez bien, bien vielle, Le soir à la chandelle Assise au coin du feu devisant et filant. . . .
    I sail almost for certain on the Berengaria, on Wednesday next. But please, please do not send any farewell, for you might think of it. It w^d. kill me[.] I have been so miserable here.[8]

There is no record of whether they met before he left. His comment about what she had seen of his emotions might refer to their last meeting in February, or to the emotion he had shown in his letters. Even this last letter wasn't his last word. He sent a pathetic telegram from the *Berengaria*: 'Viens voir la lune nouvelle du pont me portera jamais plus bonheur.' It is probably just as well she hadn't told him she was married to Hugh Carter. She took him at his word, respecting his wishes about not making his letters public, maintaining their shared secrecy until her death, when she left them to her grandson. The adaptation of Ronsard (which he had also written to Bowen), shows how much Ford wanted his love remembered. Hemingway said Ford told him 'that a man should always write a letter thinking of how it would read to posterity'.[9]
    Correcting a typescript (it was probably *When the Wicked Man*) on board the *Berengaria* seemed 'a horrible experience' when Ford recounted it in *It Was the Nightingale*. The point of the reminiscence is to dramatize the moment when he decided to stop composing at the typewriter and to use a pen. Besides signifying his feeling that his work was deteriorating and in need of new methods, the story evokes his unhappiness and frustration at the time (though it makes it sound more purely a matter of literary technique than it can have been, and argues that the longeurs in the typescript were passages he had put in for the sakes of his various secretaries): 'I slashed at that horrible prose [. . .] Time after time I threw that typescript from end to end of the smoking-room at six in the morning. Then one's head is at its clearest and

there is no one to mark your despair. . . . Even nowadays I almost cry when I see the back of that book [. . .].'[10]

In London Ford visited the Golfers' Club in Whitehall Court ('Telegrams, "Niblicks"'). His frustration with his American publishers made him reconsider his English market. Bradley had been acting as his agent with British publishers, but Ford now arranged for Ralph Pinker to take over (J.B.'s son, now managing the London office, while his brother Eric ran the one in New York). Ford's business affairs were no simpler than his love affairs, and Bradley seems to have been something of a saint, writing to him: 'you can always count on me as before, agent or no agent'. Ford hoped that a London-based professional would be able to persuade a publisher to take on the collected edition, and he gave Pinker an interesting list of the proposed volumes:

1.   *The Good Soldier*
2.   *Some Do Not . . .*
3.   *No More Parades*
4.   *A Man Could Stand Up—*
5.   *Last Post*
6.   *Joseph Conrad* and *Henry James*
7.   *Ladies Whose Bright Eyes*
8.   *Romance*
9.   *A Mirror to France*
10. New *Collected Poems*, including *Mr. Bosphorus*
11. *Ancient Lights*
12. *The Inheritors* and *The Nature of a Crime*

Of his thirty books published before 1911, only the poems and the Conrad collaborations were to be included. The most striking exclusion is the *Fifth Queen* trilogy. He told Pinker he wanted to give Cape *No Enemy* instead of *When the Wicked Man* (because the latter was 'rather a lurid affair' which would 'give English critics a great chance to jeer at New York, which I should hate'); and also that he would not let Cape have any more books unless he agreed to take over all his future work as well as the collected edition. Mizener thought this plan was based on 'a serious overestimation of his bargaining position'. Ford disliked Cape, and had mistrusted him since he heard that Cape had said he only wanted to lure Ford away from Duckworth 'in order to wipe Gerald's eye'. He hoped Pinker would find another publisher, so he was not going to make terms easy for Cape. Yet he was not being as unreasonable as Mizener suggested in saying that Ford was threatening to refuse Cape *No Enemy*: in fact he was recommending it, but leaving Cape to make the choice between it and the novel. The Wall Street Crash and the Depression meant that Ford never got his collected edition, and only got the kind of contract he wanted in the late 1930s. But in the summer of 1929 he was only asking for what Duckworth and the Bonis had almost been doing for him since the mid-1920s.[11]

Even Ford's close friends didn't know about his feelings for Cheatham. When the Tates saw him again in Paris in September 1929 they thought his despondency and loneliness were due to his having broken with Wright, which he had also now done. Tate said he was 'back from New York and an unsuccessful courtship of a lady from St. Louis, for which he had spent almost the last farthing of the large sums he had made'.

Morley Callaghan, the Canadian novelist, who had met him in New York, recalled that this summer he would pass Ford 'taking the night air all by himself, his hands linked behind his back'. Ford was too literary for Callaghan's Hemingwayesque tastes. 'Ford of many models', he called him. But he conceded: 'I knew no man loved good contemporary writing more than he did.' 'And one night at dinner I heard him make a remark I have never forgotten: "No writer can go on living in a vacuum".' It was the same advice he had given Bowen a decade before. But now Ford felt he was living in an emotional vacuum, which must have made him feel it was hard to 'go on living'. Caroline Gordon said 'a fool doctor had told him he was likely to kick off any minute', and she remembered Ford demanding that the Tates should spend all their evenings with him 'at a period when he was undergoing all sorts of terrific troubles'. He played dominoes or Russian Bank 'two or three evenings a week' at the Deux Magots or the Closerie des Lilas with Tate, who said Ford needed four cognacs a night 'to prevent insomnia', and remembered him behaving with an odd, distressed abruptness. One fine autumn evening they were walking by the Petit Luxembourg when Ford said suddenly: 'One might be a peer of the realm or a member of the Académie Française. There is nothing else.' There was no 'context' to the statement: Ford was projecting himself into a frame of mind; provoking the neophyte with a paradox. He both did mean it (those were the true guarantors of charisma in the respective countries) and he didn't (one might also be an artist). But when one knows of his feelings for Cheatham, that sense that 'There is nothing else' takes on a devastating personal significance too.[12]

Ford resumed his Saturday evening soirées, though they now became 'much more literary and tyrannously competitive', as he revived the *bouts-rimés* game, copying out the rhyme-words from sonnets by Shakespeare or 'my aunt Christina Rossetti, a beautiful poet', with which the guests had to compose their own poems. 'Ford himself usually won,' said Tate, 'and gave as a second prize a melancholy-looking round cake which was sliced at once and eaten with moderate zest by the company.' New additions to the company were the poet Howard Baker, a protégé of Yvor Winters from California, studying at the Sorbonne, and his wife Dorothy, who later wrote *Young Man with a Horn*; Morley Callaghan; the translator Willard Trask, and his wife, Mary, who danced in the Fokine ballet as Joan McIntosh; Walter and Lillian Lowenfels; Lee and Virginia Hirsch; Mae Mathieu, a correspondent for the *New Yorker*, and a Dr McCarthy, 'a small, mincing fellow, always dressed in sombre black suits and stiff high collars', who was later thought to have been the original for the transvestite doctor in Djuna Barnes's *Nightwood*. Occasional attenders included John Peale Bishop (who remembered Ford's pride that he could usually compose two sonnets to everyone else's one: 'He was wonderfully vain and easily hurt'); Robert Penn Warren, poet and friend of the Tates, who came over from Oxford for his Christmas vacation; and Ford's friends who were visiting Paris, such as Richard Aldington. William T. Bandy, in Paris to study Baudelaire, was a more regular attender, together with his fiancée Alice Burghardt. They invited Ford and his circle to their wedding. At the Saturday meeting two days before the wedding Ford chose rhyme-words appropriate to marriage. The prize, thanks to 'Ford's Machiavellian hand', was awarded to Bandy, and the runner-up's wooden spoon to Burghardt. They decided to eat the prize that evening, as a 'pre-wedding' cake, but it was too stale to yield to the knife. Ford brought in 'a heavy wooden mallet, the kind used to tenderize steaks. After several whacks, it finally was possible to penetrate the icing. Strangely enough, the interior of the cake was moist and delicious.' Another of the Saturday nucleus was Polly Boyden, 'restless and delightful Polly, who was a poet from Chicago and who was then living in Paris with her three children and their German nurse'. When Mary McIntosh asked him later how he had found the time to give her and Boyden a course in French literature, he replied 'in his low, thoughtful way: "Well, you see—I was very fond of you"'. Edward Dahlberg described Boyden as 'a fine, buxom, and rather demented wench', and said that he knew Ford had asked her to marry him, but she refused. When I asked Janice Biala about this, she said it didn't mean very much: Ford used to propose to lots of women. He was 'neither over-sexed nor a town bull', she told Arthur Mizener: 'but he was *always* a very lonely man, and had to live with someone.' In the same letter she says Ford once counted up eighteen ladies he had been involved with. Only eleven can even now be identified with any degree of certainty: Elsie, Mary, Hunt, Patmore, Miss Ross, Bowen, Rhys, Wright, Cheatham, Boyden, and Biala. The other seven might include the young woman Ford said he was courting in Hampstead before his engagement to Elsie; Miss Thomas (the *English Review* secretary); Rosamond Fogg Elliott; Gertrud Schablowsky; Jeanne Foster; Caroline Gordon; or even the 'Blanche' to whom *When the Wicked Man* was dedicated. But we are unlikely ever to know the complete story; and without knowing it, must be wary of attaching too much importance to what facts we have (as Mizener did with Rene Wright).[13]

He was particularly lonely that year. 'Especially at night', remembered Samuel Putnam:

He never came near the Dôme, but would stroll down to the Deux-Magots and sit at a table waiting for an audience of one or two. Most often it was Arabella Yorke [. . .] and her mother, Mrs. Selina Yorke, now in her seventies but earning her living still as fashion editor of the Paris *New York Herald*. With them Ford would sit for hours and reminisce. Others might come and be invited to drop down, it made little difference; all that was needed was a pair of listening ears, and Ford the fictionist was at his best. Unquestionably a born story-teller, he carried his fictionizing over into real life; or perhaps one should say that for him the demarcating wall between fiction and what ordinary mortals know as the truth simply melted away.

This is acute on Ford's need for a sympathetic listener, and his provocative fictionalizing, though his examples show exactly how hard it is to establish the facts of the fictions. Leon Edel, then 22 and only beginning his life's researches into Henry James, was taken by Léonie Adams and Caroline Gordon to interview Ford about James's plays. Ford sat by the piano in the rue de Vaugirard flat, reminiscing in his 'wheezy manner, that seemed like a walrus snorting'. He described James as 'insincere'—he evidently had no illusions about the master's flattering description of him as '*le jeune homme modeste*'. The townspeople of Rye, he said, considered James 'a sort of magician and one man confided in him that he had committed a murder'. Edel decided he was 'listening to a mythomaniac, who told his fantasies rather badly'; though he liked Ford's 'geniality and amenability', and now feels inclined to soften the strictures on Ford in his biography of James. 'Why did the people around him belittle him and seem just to tolerate him even as they hovered around him?' Mary McIntosh answered her own question by describing Ford's 'way of talking and acting superiorly (and even though one is superior it is a peculiarly irritating trait)'. His dual role as 'both peer and father' to *les jeunes* was still making the young Americans as uneasy as it had made the young English Imagists and Vorticists.[14]

Mizener is probably right to connect Putnam's description of Ford and the Yorkes with the passage in *The Rash Act* describing Henry Martin's solitary, slightly paranoid life—though he equates it with Ford's life of 1928 instead of 1929:

He went out for most of his meals. Sometimes he found an acquaintance to talk to him. As often as not he did not. He imagined that some people still avoided him—but he might have been mistaken [. . .] he sat, most evenings, at the table of Miss Cameron in a café! She had a rather noticeable moustache and occasionally she drank far too many *petits verres* [. . .] They sat huddled together for hours in a corner of a rather noisy café.[15]

One evening around this time, Ford was alone with George Seldes, the foreign correspondent for the *Chicago Tribune*, whom he knew well. Seldes witnessed his feeling of failure and self-pity when Ford broke down and cried:

He told me, 'I started Joseph Conrad when he was a sea captain and couldn't even write English.' [. . .] Then he said, 'I gave Hemingway his first literary job when I made him editor of the *Transatlantic*, when I went away for a trip. Now every one of them is famous and famous and famous—and I'm forgotten, and nobody cares about my work.' He brought out half a bottle of Napoleon brandy with a label on it from the 1840s or 50s. It was like lightning with honey mixed. Eventually we drank the half bottle and he told me the story of the misery he'd had, and the crowning misery was 'And now the Conrad set has come out with Joseph Conrad's name on it, and my name is no longer on the back of each of the novels.' And he cried, he really cried.

Though Ford felt lonely, he lived sociably. He gave teas in his little flat on Thursday afternoons. Putnam said the gatherings became 'quite famous in the Quarter', and were attended mostly by young women writers—Ford's 'Ladies Whose Bright Eyes', he called them:

I believe they were attracted, for one thing, by his paternal air, and this was a role that he loved to play. As the ladies sat on the divan and smiled up worshipfully, he would mince up and down the floor with a gait that slightly resembled that of an overgrown duckling, would show his teeth through his mustache in a restrained fatherly smile or would give an equally restrained chuckle, and would thereupon proceed to drop bright little bits of elderly, reminiscent wisdom.[16]

F. S. Flint, who was usually 'riotous', breezed in one afternoon, having had something to drink before he arrived, seemed 'vastly amused with everybody and everything', and insisted on speaking French—which he did much more fluently than the other expatriates. Ford got uncharacteristically angry, and after much 'pacing up and down, chewing his mustache, sniffing, and all but choking', suddenly burst out: 'For God's sake, Flint, remember that you are an Englishman and a gentleman!' Flint took his 'mocking departure' soon afterwards, whereupon Ford sighed: ' "I'm sure I don't know why it is that Flint always insists on speaking French when he's—er—" sniff— "When he's—er—" For there were some things that simply were not mentioned.'

He was playing the role that was himself: the Englishman as seen from the outside—in this case, through American eyes. (In *When the Wicked Man*, which Ford had tried to write like an American, the protagonist Notterdam is an Englishman who assumes Americanness.) It was a performance that enabled him to see himself, and so to be himself. 'I like New York', wrote this Englishman and gentleman, 'better than any other place in the world—hardly excepting Paris. I am more at home there, I feel more myself and I have far friendlier human contacts.' It was the 'intellectual curiosity' of his American friends he particularly valued. 'I don't want your money, I loathe your mass production. But I do want contact—as much contact as possible—with the American mind. . . .'[17]

Not only the *mind*, of course. He 'proposed' to Caroline Gordon 'in a Parisian church, of all places'. She told him he was 'crazy', and later said 'he should have been ashamed of himself'. She had the maturity to take his art more seriously than his amorousness; though, as with his love for Jean Rhys, his feelings for the woman were inseparable from his feel for her writing. 'Ford took me by the scruff of the neck', said Gordon metaphorically, about three weeks before she and Tate left Paris to return to America. Suddenly, the secretarial role was reversed:

[. . .] Ford heaved a sigh and asked me if I had done any writing. I told him that I had started a novel but that I was going to have to throw it away. He heaved another sigh and said, 'You had better let me see it.' I brought him the manuscript a few days later. He read the manuscript through, then said: 'Why has nobody told me about this? What were you going to say next?' I recited the sentence. He said, 'That is a beautiful sentence. I will write it down.' This procedure was repeated several times. It ended with Ford taking my dictation for three weeks. The result was a novel called *Penhally*.[18]

If I complained that it was hard to work with everything so hurried and Christmas presents to buy he observed 'You have no passion for your art. It is unfortunate' in such a sinister way that I would reel forth sentences in a sort of panic. Never did I see such a passion for the novel as that man has.

She remained a devoted admirer, saying 'I really like being in his vicinity', despite what she called his 'mild tyrannies'. 'To have even one person sort of planning things so that you can get your work done helps a lot.'[19]

Mary McIntosh met Hemingway at one of Ford's teas in 1929—charming, 'having a very pleasant time that day'. This was several years after the period Hemingway later recorded in *A Moveable Feast*: 'He didn't act as if his sense of smell was being offended by the presence of Ford in that small, warm room.' Behind Ford's back Hemingway was as stabbingly contemptuous as ever. In September Allen Tate met him, and was asked: 'You're a friend of Ford, aren't you?'. Tate 'admitted' that he was, and that Ford had lent them his flat. 'Well', said Hemingway: 'you know he's impotent.' Tate was taken aback, but managed a decorous reply about how it must be sad for Ford, but that he wasn't interested in Ford's sexual powers, not being a woman. He was simply grateful for Ford's kindness. Hemingway's comment was the kind of lie—contemptuous and spiteful—that Ford never told. (What he did say was the kind of joke he made to Edward Dahlberg in 1930, when he remarked—as he had previously to Bowen—that all American men were impotent. Perhaps Hemingway took it upon himself to exact the national revenge.) Even Jean Rhys doesn't portray the Fordian Heidler as impotent. Ford was rightly wary of Hemingway, often portraying him as physically threatening. Yet he continued to champion Hemingway's writing. John Peale Bishop remembered him as 'a generous gentleman', telling him how he first read *A Farewell to Arms*: 'And I wept with admiration and envy', said Ford.[20]

Most evenings he dined with the Tates and the Trasks, often joined by Léonie Adams and Polly Boyden: usually at Michaud, the Cochon de Lait (renowned for its suckling pigs), or Lipp's, with its famous sauerkraut. Sometimes he would dine alone. In the mornings he worked on the *History*, and even planned to write a cookery book. He had found an American publisher for *No Enemy*, the Macaulay Company. But the book was published less than three weeks after the Wall Street Crash of 28 October 1929. There were few reviews (though Herbert Gorman wrote a perceptive one, calling it 'the book of himself'); and Ford blamed the publisher as much as the economy, calling their advertisement 'well meant but absolutely useless'. He felt that Macaulay should have described the book as 'the actual stuff out of which my immortal War Saga was built', rather than 'throw his money down the drain by talking about my brilliant brains because every one in the world hates brilliant brains as they do the devil'. The ensuing worldwide depression was disastrous for an author in Ford's position: only rarely a best-seller; looking for a publisher to invest heavily in him; and desperately hard up. In 1928 he had received $9,615 from Brandt & Brandt; in 1929, only $5,055. The Crash had not only wiped out his chances of adequate royalties on one of his most interesting books. It also devastated the small amount of money he had been able to invest in America as a security for future years. The poverty of the 1930s would be the worst he had had to face.[21]

Ford became ill again, suffering from 'a troublesome form of blood-poisoning', and requiring a series of minor operations. He had to dictate letters lying on his back. But he was recovered enough to hold a Thanksgiving dinner with the Tates at the Maison Paul on the Île St Louis. Gertrude Stein was invited, as she was to the birthday party Ford held for Julie in Bowen's studio. In December he gave thanks to Hugh Walpole, who had published a tribute saying: 'There is no greater literary neglect of our time in England than the novels and poems of Ford.' 'I don't however *feel* a blighted man', Ford assured him, 'for I do quite as well as I want to in America which is all one man ought to want—and indeed I have almost forgotten that I am an English writer at all and have not even published my last three books in England.' It is just that the public *will* not read me', he explained: 'Someone told me years ago that the Americans would never read me because they could not tell whether I was in earnest or not, whereas the English knew I was too damn in earnest to want to read me.' Is he in earnest here? If the English felt he was too damn in earnest about the seriousness of the novel, they also mistrusted his earnestly delivered ironic fantasies—such as when, to make the point, he told Walpole that his 'last French book' (*what* last French book: *Entre St Dennis et St Georges?*) 'sold a quarter of a million copies'. Typically, he mixed his pique and provocation with praise of the young writers, both English and American, that he thought the English shouldn't neglect: Hemingway, Elizabeth Madox Roberts, Richard Hughes. Walpole even tried to interest English publishers in Ford's collected edition. His failure confirmed Ford's chagrin at the English book world.[22]

One evening towards the end of 1929 Hemingway asked Tate to meet him at a café. 'Gertrude has taken me back into favour', he explained. He was to take his wife Pauline for an audience that evening, and wanted the moral support of the Tates, the Bishops, and Scott and Zelda Fitzgerald. Alice Toklas escorted the ladies to the rear of the Grand Salon, to entertain them while Stein 'engaged the men'. Tate was astonished to see Ford already there, wheezing in a low chair that was too small for him. He couldn't believe that Hemingway would be capable of asking Ford too, at the same time that he was slandering him privately. The programme was a lecture by Stein on American literature, 'of which she was the climax'. The true genius of America was for abstraction, she argued. Emerson had been going in the right direction; James was partly abstract, in his design, but had 'sold out to European experience'. Suddenly she turned to Ford. 'Ford', she said, 'simply won't do.' 'Fordie is hopeless—*all* European, *all* experience.' (Ford had been the first to say as much: 'I daresay I am too European', he told Pound nine years earlier.) She paused. Nobody laughed. Ford 'stared from his fish-like eyes, his mouth open not for speech but for air'. The well-bred Tate felt someone had to say something, so he mumbled 'How interesting, Miss Stein', which she misheard, and answered sternly: 'Nonsense, my dear Tate, nonsense'. He thought she was reading his mind.[23]

One of the stories about Ford that Putnam said happened to be true, was that, at a literary banquet, he had challenged Andé Gide to a duel because Gide had said 'something uncomplimentary' about Conrad. This may have been at the PEN dinner in December 1929, hosted by Joyce and Paul Morand, at which Ford was a guest of honour together with Aldous Huxley. Unfortunately Putnam didn't give any more details, though he said: 'All Paris laughed over it for a number of days.'[24]

It was Bowen's last Christmas in the studio in the rue Notre-Dame des Champs, which was due to be demolished. She recalled the excitement with which they would decorate an enormous Christmas tree, directing a beam of light from a hole in the room onto the crèche of modelled wax figures. Her friend the Russian neo-romantic painter Pavel Tchelitchew painted a blue night sky on a 'paper cyclorama', and helped with the decorations ('Il faut un peu plus de mystère à gauche'). The *père noel* would come in via the roof and the balcony. He always wore the same red costume, and was usually Ford, gazing benevolently down, holding a sackful of presents. This year he played the role for the last time. George Keating had sent over some home movies which included the only known sequences of Ford on film, walking in a park—probably the Luxembourg Gardens—and playing tag with some children. The film gave Julie 'a great deal of pleasure', he said. 'I would write longer but Julie insists on my doing her homework for her and I have to find out what a pair of tro[u]sers will cost if you procure 1m30 of cloth at frs 45 the metre 0m70 of lining at 3frs 30 the metre and fifteen francs for the making. And I[']m sure I don't know what it comes to.' For Christmas he inscribed her a copy of *No Enemy*: 'à Esther Julia Madox Ford / de son père Ford Madox Ford / qui t'aime de tout son coeur et encore beaucouplus / Paris / Noël MCMXXIX.'[25]

1930–1931: JANICE BIALA

In February Ford accompanied the Trasks on a trip to London. Over sherry at the Café Royal he unfolded a plan that, once back in Paris, they should come and live with him, and Willard could be his secretary. They agreed, and when they returned, the three of them moved into the larger apartment at 32 rue de Vaugirard, which Bowen had given up when she and Julie moved from the studio in the rue Notre-Dame des Champs to a studio flat in the rue Boissonade. 'Ford used to call it, jokingly, our "ménage à trois"', recalled McIntosh. They had two bedrooms, a living-room, a small dining-room, and small kitchen between them:

Ford got up very early every morning, started writing at five o'clock, and worked through until noon. This was his day's work and he never did otherwise no matter how late he had stayed up the night before. In the afternoon and the evening until all hours he led a very full social life. We used to wonder how he could possibly keep up such an arduous schedule.

When he gave 'a dinner party of any pretensions', he wouldn't sit at the table himself, but 'devoted all of his attention to the cooking and serving'. Every afternoon they would walk in the Jardin du Luxembourg, just across the street. Julie, who was still living with Bowen, would visit regularly to spend the afternoon; sometimes Ford would take her to Mass on Sunday mornings. McIntosh remembered him as 'probably the most generous person I have ever known, with the greatest of all generosities, the giving of himself'.[1]

The frenzied social life was perhaps his way of escaping the loneliness that echoes through hopelessly passionate letters he sent Caroline Gordon once she was back in America. 'Dear, Dear Caroline', he wrote to her in February: 'you may be quite certain that whenever I do strike the United States I shall come quite straight to you, even if it were only to be turned down when I got to you. But you seem to want me to come and I can't say what life that gives me.' 'I have practically nothing to bring me back here', he told her: 'I live for nothing but the time when I shall see you next.' The following month he told her he planned to emigrate to the USA 'for good': 'but if I can't get near you, what is the good?' It must have become clear by now that she was reciprocating his passion only with friendship. 'It is very late & I am very tired', he wrote in a wave of pathos: 'this is like the letters I write you every night & don't mail. One day you will see them all! Oh my dear: it gets worse & worse. I can't go on.' By the beginning of April he had become still more morbid, partly because the work he was going on with, the *History*, made him imagine himself as history:

My dear, I don't suppose we shall ever meet again [. . .] But I go on making plans—to take a French boat to New Orleans and then go up the river, say as far as Cairo, and then strike across in your direction and settle down near you . . . till death us do part. But I daresay that is the last thing you might wish and I see no chance of my being able to do it for years—and I shan't last for years. My 'circumstances' are very bad and grow steadily worse [. . .]

Otherwise I am steeped to the heart in the eighties and nineties and the world of today hardly exists for me—except for you, shadowy and so extraordinarily real, walking about ruined choirs amongst daffodils that are by now as dead as the eighties. It is a queer muddle or it would be if there were any Purpose. One is so used to think of the miracles of Scientific thought that have conquered space and time and all the rest of it that it seems to be only a bad joke on the part of Provvi that I can't just walk out into the Luxemburg and see you beside the statue of Verlaine that is in Kentucky. And one has only minutes to live and all this time is being wasted. I seem to be gradually dying from the feet upwards, at any rate I go out so little that when I do go out I can hardly walk and I have aged so visibly in the last three months that I could not bear to have you see me. So it's just as well that we shan't meet again. In any case, in a very short time all that will remain of me will be just in your memory and I'd just as lief you did not remember me as half moribund. I suppose though, it does not matter much as long as it's one brain that dies last.[2]

But suddenly, on May Day, 1930, one of the most important days in Ford's life, he found a future again. Willard Trask's friend, Eileen Lake, had come from America, bringing her best friend, Janice Biala. He asked the two women to Ford's Thursday afternoon, and Biala had come in the hope that she might meet Ezra Pound. Soon afterwards, the Trasks asked Ford and the two women back to supper, for what turned out to be 'the liveliest our little salle à manger had ever contained':

Ford was at his best, appreciative in listening and joining in enthusiastically. In the living room after supper he sat between the girls on the sofa and I sat facing them in my big chair. Ford did most of the talking then—leading it, anyway—and I felt that they all had quickly become friends; they laughed and talked easily, delighted with each other. Then it was that I had one of the strangest experiences of my life: I saw, literally *saw*, the transformation of Ford, as though he were a monarch moth shedding his cocoon. We had always thought of him as an old man [. . .] But here he was, become a young man. Ford, of course, always liked women and I knew that he was especially fond of one of the women [Polly Boyden?] in our group that year; but never had I seen him like this. He was ardent, he was charming, he was a man in love!

Later that evening Ford took Eileen and Janice out to see some boîtes and to do some dancing, and the girls told us later that he danced with them all night long. I heard him come in after dawn; nevertheless, he met Willard and me for our noon dinner. Our conversation that day was entirely about the night before and the two girls from New York. Eileen was really the showpiece of the pair. She was a poet, tall, blonde, and fascinating, born and raised in Antigua, which fact always seemed to increase her interest for everyone, and we thought that naturally she would be the one that Ford would be taken with. So we started talking about her—wasn't Eileen charming, wasn't she attractive, and so on? Ford listened and agreed with all we said, and then paused and said very quietly, 'And the little dark-haired one is nice.' And, just from the way he said it, I knew instantly that he was in love with Janice, that it was for her that he had been transfigured the night before.

His poem 'Fleuve Profond' describes another party of a few days later, at which Eileen ('Elaine' in the poem) harangues Ford about the female characters in *Parade's End* until dawn. Underneath the cacophony of the conversations and the strains of music from the Paris night, Ford quietly addresses the poem to Biala, quietly watching. As

Eileen says 'I JUST LOATHE | MISS WANNOP', and 'I LOVE YOUR SYLVIA', Ford suggests
that his own fate is auspiciously re-enacting Tietjens's, as, immune to the seductive
glamour of the Sylvia-like Eileen, he falls in love with her opposite, the woman with
Valentine's quiet integrity.[3]

Biala was less than half Ford's age, a fact which disconcerted their Paris friends. All
of the women he lived with wrote or painted. But Biala was his first thoroughly
bohemian partner, caring little for money, social status, and domestic comforts. Her
devotion to the arts matches Ford's. A dedicated and distinguished painter, her
recognition came late, and in New York—like Ford's. Mary McIntosh said Biala told
her: 'I have looked all my life for a man with a mind as old as my own and what
difference does it make if, when I find the man, he has a pot belly?' Sixty years later
she thought she hadn't said it. What she told Mizener gives a better impression of what
they thought about their compatibility: 'The difference in age didn't make any difference—it made us more chivalrous to each other and we knew we didn't have any time
to waste.' She was born in 1903, into a Jewish family called Tworkovski living in Biala,
about thirty miles west of Brest Litovsk, in Russian Poland, but emigrated to America
in 1913. She studied at the Art Students' League. Her brother, Jack Tworkov, took up
painting too in order to show her that 'he could do better'. To avoid being confused
with him, she took the name of her birthplace. As Mizener says, 'she was a fighter,
ready to fly at anyone who was not ready to give Ford his due, in a way that Ford
himself was never able to'. Her dry humour matched his. In some exhibition notes she
wrote about her 'personal tastes in art':

Thinks Cézanne the greatest painter in the world—(whenever she manages to forget the
others)—hopes to form a company some day to steal El Greco's view of Toledo which comes
back always as the most beautiful picture in the world—nothing done about this project as
yet because cannot figure out how to steal it from the company of stealers when it's stolen.
Greatest influence—believe it or not—Mozart. Would like to have been the conductor of an
orchestra or a matador. But alas—didn't even achieve being a ballet dancer.[4]

They were together for the rest of Ford's life, living out Ford's ideal of a relationship:
'The years I spent with him were a long passionate dialogue', recalled Biala: 'Starting
from opposite points of view, opposite backgrounds, each convinced the other, converted the other.' She was one of *les jeunes* that Ford had always courted. He told
Pound proudly that she was 'rather modern'. His views shifted towards the political
Left during his last decade. Neither of them were communist. Ford thought both
communism and fascism were 'mass-manias'. But under Biala's influence he became
particularly concerned about the fate of the Jews in Europe, and active in writing to
newspapers supporting Jewish refugees from fascism. He spoke out forcibly against
Franco, Mussolini, and 'the atrocious Mr Hitler'—in marked contrast to his friends
Pound and Lewis.[5]

Edward Davison, who met Ford and Biala later, said their friends 'liked and
admired her for her candor and blazing honesty as well as for her unmeasured devotion
to Ford'.[6] When Biala was, as she put it, 'raising hell about something', he would say:
'Marwood told me once that I would always pick women of low vitality.' None of his
women *had* been of low vitality, of course, which was perhaps Marwood's sardonic

point. But part of Ford's point was that he felt himself to be more vital, surer of himself than in the days when he had felt unable to cope with Elsie's or Violet's emotional demands. 'Perhaps after the war he needed propping up. He had been shot to pieces', said Biala, when Sondra Stang asked her about Bowen's description of him as 'a great user-up of other people's nervous energy': 'But he didn't need any propping up in my time', continued Biala:

It is true that Ford was terribly demanding, but of no one more than of himself. And he lived at the top of his bent. He was very demanding, both of himself and of me. This took the form of our doing things together—housework, cooking, gardening, typing. There was no one else to do these things. And besides, he wanted us always to be together, side by side in everything, before the world.[7]

Ford described his feeling of extraordinary luck in his *Buckshee* sequence of 'Poems for 'Haïtchka in France'—Haïtchka is the diminutive of Biala's Hebrew name, Schenehaia, meaning 'pretty creature', as Ford explains in 'Fleuve Profond'. '*Buckshee*, derived from the universal Oriental *bakschisch*', he also explains, is 'a British Army word and signifies something unexpected, undeserved and gratifying'. It expresses the burst of creativity that the new affair unleashed: 'if you have given up the practice of writing verse and suddenly find yourself writing it—those verses will be buckshee'; but of course it also signifies the entry of Biala into his life:

> I think God must have been a stupid man,
> To have sent a spirit, chivalrous and loyal,
> Cruel and tender, arrogant and so meek,
> Gallant and timorous, halting and as swift
> As a hawk descending—to have sent such a spirit,
> Certain in all its attributes, into this Age
> Of our banal world.
> [. . .]
> 'Haïtchka, the undaunted, loyal spirit of you!
>
> Came to our world of cozening and pimping,
> Our globe compact of virtues all half virtue,
> Of vices scarce half-vices, made up of truth
> Blurred in the edges and of lies so limping
> They will not spur the pulse in the utterance;
> [. . .]
> A coin of gold dropped into leaden palm,
> Manna and frankincense and myrrh and balm
> And bitter herbs and spices of the South
> Are you and honey for the parching mouth . . .
>
> Because God was a stupid man and threw
> Into our outstretched palms, 'Haïtchka, you![8]

In *Return to Yesterday*, which he was finishing a year later, Ford says about superstitions:

The longest and most disastrous runs of ill-luck in my life have followed the one on the presentation of an immense opal to a member of my household; the other on a lady who was driving with me and others in a closed automobile exclaiming in an open space in Harlem: 'Look at that immense crescent!' She was indicating the new moon which in consequence I saw through the front glass.

From that day for a long time—indeed until about a year ago—I experienced nothing but disaster: in finances, in health, in peace of mind, in ability to work.

It was the meeting with Biala that he felt signalled his change of luck, and the consequent renewal of his power to work. He told her he was a changed man with her. They celebrated the anniversary of their union for the rest of their lives together. Six years later he wrote the poem 'Coda' 'for an anniversary between the feasts of SS. James & Paul (Otherwise May Day) & That of Saint Joan of Arc', a superb, confident, conversational meditation on time, love, and art, which recognizes, as he wonders at the time he has been spending with Biala, that his life had found its new, last rhythm.[9]

The work of his last decade also changed. Though he had always been powerfully reminiscential, it was only in the 1930s that he wrote his memoirs: the two magnificent volumes, *Return to Yesterday* (1931) and *It Was the Nightingale* (1934). His *Portraits from Life* (1937; published in England as *Mightier Than the Sword*, 1938) blends criticism and reminiscence, more in the manner of *Joseph Conrad*, but none the less contains some of his best, most personal, prose. The two unclassifiably energetic and entertaining books of travel and cultural meditation, *Provence* and *Great Trade Route*, also strike this new, personal note. Biala is a character in both, and illustrated both. Julie, too, appears as 'the Little English Girl' in the latter, and as 'Julia Madox Ford' in the index. Ford had mentioned Violet Hunt in print (writing a Literary Portrait about her, or a preface to one of her books; or in combative footnotes running through *The Desirable Alien*); but he always wrote impersonally, as her critic, not her companion. Otherwise, he had kept all mention of his women out of his memoirs, believing that people shouldn't 'kiss and tell'. (Elsie is only mentioned once in *Return to Yesterday*, as the 'member of my household'. Violet doesn't appear in *Ancient Lights*; Stella isn't in *It Was the Nightingale*. None are mentioned in *Thus to Revisit*. The novels tell a different story, fictively.) He didn't relax that principle in *Great Trade Route*; but it was the first time he wanted to write, in his own person, about intimacy and companionship in his private life. *Provence*, which compounds history, cultural comparison, reminiscence, and intimate guidebook, was 'more personal than most of my other books', he told its publisher, adding: 'it's one's personality that the public seems to want . . .'[10]

Ford sent Biala to call on Julie and her mother in the rue Boissonnade: 'the nicest home we ever had', said Bowen. They both liked Biala very much: 'we were pleased when Ford asked for our blessing on his approaching union with her', wrote Bowen, adding that Biala 'made him happy until the day of his death, and she developed a strong affection for Julie'. When Biala got back, Ford wanted to know what she thought of Bowen. As Biala told her later: 'I said that I had more respect for him, because he'd had a woman like you.' Ford made a characteristic gesture of sexual Quixotism, offering to get a Mexican divorce from Elsie Hueffer in order to marry Bowen now that he had left her.[11]

They were terribly broke. In February Ford had to ask Bowen to lend him 50 francs because he was 'at the moment penniless'. *No Enemy* had crashed in America with

Wall Street, and Ford had been unable to find an English publisher for it. It is a scandal that one of the most significant pieces of prose about the experience of the First World War has still not been published in England. In the spring of 1930 he wrote a preface to a limited edition of *Robinson Crusoe*. But his book-reviewing had lapsed—there is only one review (for the *New York Herald Tribune Books*) listed for 1930. George Keating 'overwhelmed' Ford by offering to pay his fare to New York. He didn't feel he could accept, but he suggested that Keating could buy the rights to the *History* if he advanced Ford £400, and then tried to negotiate with a publisher. Nothing came of the idea. Yet he could still be very optimistic, said Biala:

if we had $10 in the bank, Ford felt very carefree & we celebrated the occasion generally by going to the Cochon de Lait for a good dinner. We also celebrated the signing of a contract, we celebrated again the day we finally received the money etc. etc. But every cent he could spare from our very spartan needs went to Stella. Which is not to say it was much.

It was, she said, typical of their life together, which was 'dominated by constant money troubles & Ford's not too good health. Aside from that he was pretty happy.' Indeed, it was probably the happiest phase of his life. They had let the flat in the rue de Vaugirard, and, were 'living on credit in a small country pub' at Ballancourt at the end of June and throughout July. It was a sort of honeymoon. He had to write to H. G. Wells saying that he was 'completely destitute', and asking for Wells's help in applying to the Royal Literary Fund. Wells sent him a personal cheque for 2,000 francs instead. Julie stayed with them for a while. Biala tried to teach her to swim, but Julie wouldn't follow her into the icy water. Ford was revising the *History of Our Own Times*, which had been rejected by four English publishers. 'If I am fifty-six and you twenty-eight we have twenty-eight years in common', he wrote in a passage near the beginning: 'and the differences of our unknown pasts, if the course of man back to the beginning be considered, will be almost infinitesimal.' Biala was near enough to 28 for him effectively to be imagining her as his sympathetic listener. (Presumably the significance of 'twenty-eight' is its being half of his 56; Biala was then 26.) 'You are making momentarily all things new—but not, relatively, so new as all that.' It wasn't just that Biala was one of the young artists making literature and painting new, though in relatively classical ways; she was also making him new, in a way that made the tangles and guilts of the past seem much less significant than the future they had in common. It is a paradoxical line to take at the beginning of a history book, of course; and the fact that it comes there shows that his feeling of new life was anything but an irresponsible escape from the past. Rather as *No Enemy* had been for Bowen, the *History* had become Ford's attempt to explain his past life to his new partner. The original text includes a wealth of autobiographical information, which, while it animates the international events with his personality for the general reader, for the intimate reader it builds up a picture of the world he had lived through and been informed by.[12]

Back in Paris in early September, Wambly Bald reported in the *Chicago Tribune* that Ford had told a group at Lipp's he had married Biala. (Bald suspected it might be a joke.) Soon afterwards, Ford sailed alone to New York for what he thought would be a brief visit, though he had to stay for three months. It was a hard separation; but it was proving impossible for him to make a living outside America. Susan Jenkins of

Macaulay (who had published *No Enemy*) had expressed interest in the *History*, but the company kept delaying a decision. They had kept the manuscript of *When the Wicked Man* for over four months, waiting to see how *No Enemy* sold before committing themselves. Ford couldn't wait—he needed the money—so he got his agent, Ruth Kerr, to ask for it back so that he could revise it; and then he sold it instead to Liveright, whom Dreiser had recommended to him. This probably made Macaulay even less eager to take the *History*. In June he had tried it on Morrow, who said they wanted it finished before they would make an offer. Ford proposed a compromise: he'd finish it all except Chapter VII before the book was commissioned; 'VII is simply about the Arts and no-one will want to read it—so that if I dropped dead or took to drink—which I suppose is what Morrow is afraid of, he would have a perfectly complete book.'[13]

He revised *When the Wicked Man* on the boat. 'I got up very early and started working over NOTTERDAM', he wrote to Biala. 'The book has some merits and I think I can see my way to make it hold water', he continued nautically, 'after I have cut out a good deal of heavy matter and excised a number of c[oa]rsenesses. When I wrote them they seemed rather finely real—but I guess the *genre* is not for me.' The main problem with the genre of *When the Wicked Man* is the difficulty of saying what its genre *is*. Is it a novel of crime? Of the underworld? Of fantasy? Of America? Of business life? Of romance? Its mixture of all these is one of Ford's most ambitious attempts at con-fusion, and its success is only intermittent, even though, as he told Biala, 'I have put an enormous amount of work into it'. Harold Loeb offered to take Ford and Susan Jenkins with him and his girlfriend Marjorie to visit the Tates in Tennessee:

We had just got out of Virginia through the beautiful Shenandoah Valley onto the Tennessee upland road. We were doing seventy-eight, a dauntless lady driving Mr. Loeb's large open Buick. The car had occasion to lunge into the left-hand ditch, to swerve on its two left wheels across the road, inclining at a very acute angle, taking, I should say, eight hours to cross, and to crash into the right-hand ditch.

That ambushment of Destiny had been caused by a negro's flivver, doing forty and swerving right across our seventy-eight. And that reaching out of the finger of annihilation did have its after-effects. I shiver now, thinking of it, I suppose because, instead of applying to St. Christopher whilst it happened, I was thinking of my home in the rue Vaugirard and said to myself:

'Well, I've had a good life . . .' imagining with complete composure that, as they used to say, my last hour had struck. . . . Being indeed sure of it! So that it was rather a bump, after the car had settled in the ditch, to have to return to the problems of life, the most immediate of which was to get a lorryful of men that was passing to haul us out of the ditch. . . .

Loeb remembered Ford, 'ponderous, relaxed and smiling faintly', saying to the others, with equal composure, 'Let's stick to the high road'. It is a classic piece of Fordian impressionism (like the collision between Tietjens's and Valentine's dog cart and General Campion's car in the silver fog in *Some Do Not . . .*): the sensations described before they, or their cause, are understood; an occasion which has a powerful impression upon its perceiver, and makes him imagine his own death, and feel momentarily like his own ghost.[14]

After the accident they asked at a filling station about the way to Clarksville, and were told of a short-cut, 'an unpaved road but more direct', said Loeb:

It was dark by then but we decided to risk it. The road led through deep woods part of the time and was somewhat eerie [. . .] Every now and then we saw a sign along the side of the road with one word on it, 'FORD'. Nobody made any comment. Silence was the mood of the night. I was driving. It was very dark beneath the trees and my Buick's lights were not what lights have since become. Suddenly [. . .] a tremendous splash! Water rose on all sides, the road disappeared and no one knew quite what had happened. The car had stopped though, and, as the waters subsided, we finally made out that we were in the middle of a smoothly flowing river. No one was hurt. Even the engine had not stopped running. Ford remarked after a pause, 'Those signs! And I thought they were welcoming me!'[15]

'He lectured in Nashville', wrote Caroline Gordon, 'and we all went up to support him during the terrible tea at the woman's [sic] club and an even more terrible dinner at the Hermitage which should have been nice as the guests were hand picked.' 'Here I am back in Clarksville after a dreadfully exhausting time in Nashville', Ford told Biala:

I lectured at Vanderbilt University on Henry James yesterday morning, spoke at a lunch for John [Crowe] Ransome, also at the opening of a bookstore and went to a cocktail party of an uproarious type before motoring back here, all the while going about in crowds of shouting or squealing Southerners—all males south of the Mason & Dixon line shout and all females squeal. Loeb and company left from Nashville and I might have motored back with them but the tension between Susie and Marjorie was very trying at sixty miles an hour and I want to lecture here tomorrow evening.[16]

Ford showed the Tates photographs of Biala. Caroline Gordon said 'I liked her face and thought she looked like a gal who could do without fine clothes if it should be necessary, which ought to mean something in a man's life even if it rarely does'. He also took them her portrait of Julie, which Gordon thought 'captured a quality of Julie's which is the thing I always remember her by, so I liked it'. 'We had a grand time', said Gordon: 'going in swimming—we had several balmy days when it was enjoyable—drinking corn liquor and talking. Only Ford made me go over every inch of my manuscript with him which kept me pretty tired all the time.' The novel was the one she dictated parts of to him in New York in 1927, *Penhally*. She said she had always meant to dedicate it to him. He told her not to, but it must have been out of the pride which apes humility, since he was hurt when she didn't. 'You *are* vain', she wrote to him while apologizing; 'I ought to have seen that the gesture might please you. But really I think of you as being vain about more frivolous things—cooking?—I *knew* all along that you would be disappointed in the book—it seemed silly to dedicate it to you.'[17]

When he got back to New York he heard that *Cosmopolitan* had offered $1,000 for 'Notterdam', but that his agent Ruth Kerr had turned it down. 'I am rather sorry that she did, but when her commission was taken off and half paid to the Viking Press there would have been only about $450 left of which half would have gone to Stella, leaving very little more than enough to pay my fare home', Ford wrote to Biala. In New York he stayed with Eileen and her husband, Dr Michael Lake, in their tall studio at 50 West Twelfth Street. His gout was bad, and Micky Lake bandaged his foot for him. It was while looking up at the 'criss-cross of beams in the roof' of their studio that he thought out the intricately tangled form of his volume of reminiscences, *Return to Yesterday*, he said in the letter dedicating it to the Lakes. Both 'Notterdam' and the *History* were being looked at by Longmans, who said they wanted the *History*. He wasn't surprised that they didn't want to pay anything like his starting price of $2,500, and indicated that he would take less; but they also wanted to wait until the economy improved. It was while he was waiting for their decision on 'Notterdam' that he decided he 'must write something new so as to make enough to keep us just going', so that he could make the right publishing arrangements for 'those books that are written taking so long', like the *History*. The 'something new' was *Return to Yesterday*. His feeling that this change of tactics was necessary proved well founded when Longmans wouldn't agree to his terms.[18]

He landed on his gouty feet, as ever. 'Yesterday we lunched—or dined, I don't know which—at the Kohns at four in the afternoon and stayed there playing Rummy till ten—at which I won $10.60', he told Biala:

Afterwards we most of us we[n]t to Chaffards and s[a]t till near one drinking beer and eating oysters. As a result I have a touch of gout today and shall have to go to the Roosevelt hotel in one slipper and one shoe. (I have at last desperately bought myself some black shoes! Also some underpants and two wing-collars!) I had to because the WORLD trepanned me into going to lunch with their representative and Mary Borden and debate about English v. American women. Mary Borden is one of my oldest friends and also a best seller here. She is married to an English Major General. (She is Borden's Milk of Chicago) and has written the most frightful things about the manners of American women. So the WORLD asked me to defend the A.W. It was rather a bum show really, because when Mary got there she refused flatly to attack her compatriotes. It was of course one thing to be bitchy from the safe distance of Westminster but another to do it here in the middle of her family. So it was rather a funeral— for the WORLD's reporteress. Then Mary and I were flashlighted, lunching all alone together, and that upset her because [she] thought the General would be upset.

Then I went on [to] see Tom Smith of Liveright's. He was full of geniality and flattery, says he wants to become my publisher and has done so for years—which is of course true. I tried to get him to make an offer without having seen anything, but he wanted to see NOTTERDAM, so I told him he could have till Friday to read it. He is a rogue and a bad man but he has long had an affection for me—Liveright was the real obstacle to my going to them, but Liveright is now out of the firm—and knows all or nearly all my books. That would be a great advantage if it ever came to printing a collected edition. So I had decided to take the matter altogether out of Ruth Kerr's hands and attend to it myself. There at any rate it rests till Friday. If he likes NOTTERDAM he proposes to give me a small settled income against royalties for the rest of my life. That would suit me as well as anything; of course the firm may go broke, but anybody may, here at any moment. In the [me]antime Scribner's are considering my REMINISCENCES for the Magazine and if Smith does not come through they may . . . It is an anxious world, you see.

The rogue and bad man did come through, taking both *When the Wicked Man* and *Return to Yesterday* for Liveright, and agreeing to take a second novel, and also a 'volume of Descriptive Travel Prose'; though yet again Ford had to settle for less than he thought the books were worth. He didn't even get an advance for the novel; and his difficulties in getting paid didn't do much to reduce the anxiousness.[19]

Ford took the *Mauretania* back to Europe, completing *When the Wicked Man* 'off the Scillies, 1st December, 1930'. Harold Loeb remembered crossing to Europe with him, partly because Ford had promised to help him with an unsatisfactory manuscript. Biala thought that if he did travel with Ford, he would have travelled in 1st class, and Ford in 3rd. 'He never talked over the manuscript', Loeb said. Instead, he gave a virtuoso performance of his creative generosity and transformative genius:

every now and then—while we were in Paris [. . .] Ford would come up with a few pages written in large long hand barely revised covering some section of my story. His chief contributions were good portraits of an old fanatic, effective Zionist, and of my heroine whom he made into a Jewish housefrau type, solicitous and over health conscious in respect to her man. I accepted the Zionist and there he is still frozen into my unpublished, though quite the best of my four novels, manuscript [. . .] he quite easily entered the frame of my novel which he read only once, to become part of it, slightly altered, but a creation that seemed to live.[20]

Again he felt that his last hour had struck. He had a heart attack. It wasn't until the end of March that he could write (to Hugh Walpole): 'I have recovered a good deal of the vitality that I thought had gone for ever with my heart attack last December.' Nevertheless, his vitality impressed Joyce when he was introduced to Biala early in 1931. Joyce thought she was his 'eighth or eighteenth' wife (and later said that Ford's six wives were one less than H. C. Earwicker's: again the number is an invention: was he fusing Ford with his Henry VIII?). He wrote two verses about Ford to the tune of 'Father O'Flynn':

> O Father O'Ford, you've a masterful way with you,
> Maid, wife and widow are wild to make hay with you,
> Blonde and brunette turn-about run away with you,
> You've such a way with you, Father O'Ford.
>
> That instant they see the sun shine from your eye
> Their hearts flitter flutter, they think and they sigh:
> We kiss ground before thee, we madly adore thee,
> And crave and implore thee to take us, O Lord.[21]

Ford and Biala went south in January, to stay in Stella's old attic studio at 3 quai du Parti in Toulon. Joyce had intended to ask him to write a preface for *Tales Told of Shem and Shaun* if C. K. Ogden refused. Ogden accepted. Now Joyce had been asked to write an introduction for a translation of Italo Svevo's *Senilità*, but he suggested Ford instead. Ford agreed willingly, taking the opportunity to try to correct Joyce's predilection for white wine:

I hope you have given up white wine and prosper, though naturally I do hope you prosper whether or no. Still le premier devoir du vin est d'être rouge. I am sure the wine of Cana must have been. But alas! all the really drinkable wines about here—and there are one or two really lovely ones—are white. There is one in particular—Domaine de Cavalière—that is one of the best I have ever imagined.[22]

Then they found the Villa Paul on Cap Brun, with 'one of the most beautiful views in the world'. You could see as far as Corsica. It was to be their sanctuary for the next five years, and Ford was to use it as the model for the Villa Niké in *The Rash Act* and *Henry for Hugh*.

The Villa Paul stood high above the sea, towards which there sloped a long garden with fig trees and oranges and a water cistern [. . .] The shutters of its upper windows were always closed. They concealed the domestic life of M. le Commandant and Madame, who lived a dim but passionate existence on the upper floor, sub-letting the *rez de chaussée* and the garden to Ford and Janice.

The ground-floor shutters were always open. They had once been painted palest grey, and were folded back against the pinkish stucco walls whose flaking surface discovered patches of a previous periwinkle blue. Through the windows you stepped into two small rooms with rough grey walls and red tile floors. Behind these, on one side was the kitchen, dark and primitive, and on the other a sleeping alcove and *cabinet de toilette*. The parlour walls were painted with crude but charming bouquets of flowers, which Ford had discovered under a peeling modern wallpaper [. . .] Before the house was a wide *terasse* whose comfortable balustrade served as a sideboard for outdoor meals. There was a shady tree and a fountain with goldfish and a great view right across the harbour to Saint Mandrier.[23]

This is Stella Bowen's painterly description, though the first thing she says about the Villa bespeaks the difference between her and Biala: 'Ford had, of course, acquired a home that was picturesque but entirely without amenities.'

They settled in during March, and Ford recuperated quickly in the Toulon sun—his constitution was remarkably strong, considering what he had suffered during the war. But one can see his renewed preoccupation with death in a remarkable letter to T. R. Smith:

What has happened to WHEN THE WICKED MAN? I am so mazed by the various cables that I don[']t know when to expect its publication. In the meantime I've had no letter from you so you may, for all I know, be expecting me to leave for New York today.

I am getting on like a house a-fire with the Reminiscences [*Return to Yesterday*] now and have reached the point when if I suddenly drop dead, you could just clap 'Thus to Revisit' on to what is written and with a little editing have a very good book. So you may consider yourself safe. However, though you precious near did lose me in December my health is immensely improved by staying down here and I hope to finish the book, as I've said, in July and that it will be one of my best books. The only real trouble is that I have such an immense lot of matter to write about that I don[']t know what to select and what to leave out.

[. . .] The more I think of WHEN THE WICKED MAN the more I feel that it is one of the considerable *moral* books of the world. If you can get your advertising people to take that line it might have an enormous sale as a problem book. If it is advertised merely as a phony or funny it will just go down with the ruck of novels until God in his good time sees to it that laurel wreaths are put around the marble brows of my statue in the Hall of Fame. But you and I will be dead by that time and others will enjoy the fruits. In the meantime you occupy the place of the Deity.

I am taking a villa down here and in all probability giving up my Paris apartment so when in search of youth and beauty—I mean of course the restoration of your own, little necessary as that may be, you come sailing to these shores, you will be able to find a bed and the goodly fruits of the earth such as my hands shall cause to grow, each in their due season [. . .][24]

The imagination of his own death here leads to thoughts of creativity: first the reminiscences, in which he is trying to preserve the 'matter' of his life; then the novel that Liveright was about to publish: a study of wickedness, guilt, and a character whose imagination of his own death takes the form of shooting his *Doppelgänger*. Thinking of this book makes him think of the Deity, not only as a judge of men, but as the ultimate literary critic—though this thought causes Ford yet again to imagine himself being dead before he becomes famous. (Nearer death, he told Stanley Unwin: 'I have always, myself, staked my all on the plan that my books should sell, if largely at all, after my death. In that way there will be something for my descendants. One has, I think, to take one's sales either before or after one's decease. One can't expect both.') Again, the fear of death gives new life to his vision of himself as the creator, causing (in his biblical cadences) the fruits of the earth to grow, each in their due season. *Return to Yesterday*, which can be read as another mode of accounting for his past to Biala, expresses this quintessentially Fordian duality. It is one of his most morbid books, giving a harrowing account of his 1904 breakdown, elegizing his dead friends James, Crane, Conrad, Meary Walker, and Marwood, and leading up to the outbreak of Armageddon. But it is also one of his most humorous and liveliest, returning to yesterday's books, reworking and incorporating passages from *Thus to Revisit* and *Women & Men* to express a sense of having lived through, and survived, the anxiety, depression, and grief of his pre-war self. He wrote that 'the real pleasure of travel lies in returning', and felt similarly about travelling back in time, redeeming suffering through reminiscence. The book was also another version of the history of his own times, telling not only of his own experiences, but of the literary and political movements with which he had come into contact: impressionists, modernists, anarchists, Fabians, Tories, Liberals. 'I have tried to give a picture of the times rather than a biography of myself', he told Victor Gollancz: 'but egotism will come creeping in.'[25]

He devoted a lot of care to causing the fruits of the earth to grow. They decided to stay in Toulon for the summer after Bowen sent Julie down to stay with them. He told Hugh Walpole, who had encouraged Gollancz to publish *Return to Yesterday* in England: 'we live a life of a frugality which would astonish and for all I know appal you', consisting of 'almost complete vegetarianism, a prohibition such as Gotham never knew, an immense view of the Mediterranean and agricultural labours that begin at dawn and end after sunset'. The vegetarianism was out of poverty rather than principle. They kept rabbits, and also chickens so that Julie could have chicken to eat. 'Ford insisted on letting them wander all over the garden, though it was hell to get them into the chicken coop at night', said Biala, 'because, he said, if you raise animals for the table, you should give them the best life possible while they are alive.' Julie 'refused to eat a chicken she had known personally'. And Biala said she and Ford tried one, 'but couldn't swallow it for the same reason'. The poem 'L'Oubli—, Temps de Sécheresse' tells of the drought that August, and (like all the *Buckshee* poems) gives a beautifully natural impression of their life at Villa Paul, as well as an intimation of Ford's sense that his getting back in touch with the earth, Antaeus-like, was giving him new strength. His perennial themes of time and memory are reinvigorated by a sense of having survived:

> Well then . . . we have outlived a winter season and a season of Spring
> And more than one harvesting

In this land where the harvests come by twos and by threes
One on another's heels.——

Do you remember what stood where the peppers and egg-plants now stand?
Or the opium poppies with heads like feathery wheels?
Do you remember
When the lemons were little, the oranges smaller than peas?
We have outlived sweetcorn and haricots,
The short season of plentiful water and the rose
That covered the cistern in the day of showers.
And do you remember the thin bamboo-canes?
We have outlived innumerable flowers,
The two great hurricanes
And the unnumbered battlings back and forth
Of the mistral from the Alps in the North [. . .][26]

It is, as Mizener says, 'astonishing how Ford conveys the tone of their life—difficult, often anxious, sometimes illuminated, and always something he would have no other way' (p. 402). The 'battlings back and forth' evoke life's other battles, which the pleasure in the landscape is able to overcome. These poems achieve his ideal of quiet talking to a lover as his earlier verse had never done.

His relations with publishers had been deteriorating. Despite the successes of *Parade's End*, the Depression had made publishing *When the Wicked Man* hard, and the *History* impossible. He had a particular 'genius for creating confusion and a nervous horror of having to deal with the results' where publishers were concerned. As he wrote to Victor Gollancz, 'I find that either I have not the gift of writing clear letters or that publishers do not read what I write. At any rate the result is always muddles.' His letters were clear (though often confusingly complicated), and the publishers did read them. In part, the muddles came about because of Ford's desire to use the Madox Brown Grand Manner when he felt publishers were trying to beat him down; but also because he was under such financial strain that he kept changing publishers too quickly, and trying to change the terms of his contracts. The result was that he sometimes confused himself about which agreement was in force. He knew changing publishers was not a good idea in the long term, not least because it jeopardized his long-term plan for a collected edition. After Viking published *A Little Less Than Gods* he had told them:

I am writing to Brandt [his agent] by this mail or the next about my collected edition. As I suppose you know Bonis had begun this, but it stopped when our agreement—mine with them, I mean—stopped. I quite thought you had been spoken to about taking it over but was surprised to find when I left N.Y. that no one in the office had heard anything about it—but I suppose you know that it is quite in *my* mind to give you all my books for good, for I hate changing publishers; and indeed nothing is more unprofitable.[27]

But it is hard to think of the long term when there are bills to pay and mouths to feed. (It is hard, too, for people with the security of a salary to imagine the insecurities artists face when desperate to sell their work.) When Viking rejected *When the Wicked Man*, it became clear that it wasn't in *their* mind to publish Ford's collected edition. It is not surprising that he now got into one of his muddles with Viking and Liveright, and had to get his old friend and collector George Keating to disentangle the business when Liveright weren't paying Ford as much as he had expected. Viking had paid him $3,500 in 1927 as an advance for *A Little Less Than Gods*; and then, in the summer of 1928, another $3,500 for *When the Wicked Man* (plus an unspecified sum for 'Mr Croyd'). When Viking rejected *When the Wicked Man*, in order to get the book released, instead of repaying the advance, Ford agreed to reimburse them 'from one half of the total sales and royalties' of *When the Wicked Man* and 'Mr Croyd', up to the sum of $3,500. Mizener says that this was 'a costly arrangement' for Viking. *When the Wicked Man* had sold only 3,233 copies by the end of 1931, and 'Mr Croyd' was never published. Certainly the sales figures had collapsed since the 1920s. But a sale of over 3,000 books was not contemptible during the Depression. Viking had recouped their advance on *A Little Less Than Gods*, which sold all of its first printing of 5,000 copies, and went into a second impression of 1,000. They would have lost much less money if they had accepted *When the Wicked Man* when Ford had offered it to them in the summer of 1929, and published it before the Wall Street Crash. When they heard Liveright were to publish it, they threatened legal proceedings to get their half of the royalties.[28]

Smith didn't mollify Ford by saying, when he had read the manuscript of *Return to Yesterday*: 'You have written so much on the subject already that your public, English and American, are looking forward to the reminiscences up to 1931.' Ford took this as a criticism of his careful crafting of the book to end it on 4 August 1914. His hope that the reminiscences could be written quickly to earn the leisure to finish the *History* proved delusory. It had been a demanding and dangerous book to write. Summoning back the spectres of despair and breakdown, lost friends and lost causes, had taken its toll. 'No doubt you are not interested in whether a book is an artistic whole or not, but I am', he wrote back: 'I have put everything I know in the way of literary skill into this book and have worked so hard at it that my health has completely broken down again and I do not wish to see the results of all this labour frittered away. The world before the war is one thing and must be written about in one manner; the after-war world is quite another and calls for quite different treatment.'[29] Which is exactly what he gave it, in both his novels and reminiscences dealing with post-war experience. After this difference had been settled, and Smith had reassured him that the material was of the 'utmost importance', and that it was 'admirably done', he then rejected the jacket design Ford had sent them, done by Biala under the pseudonym 'Novgorodsky'. He said he was enclosing their alternative, 'which certainly has more advertising value if not as much artistic value', but he didn't. His cynical distinction between the values of art and advertisement betrayed exactly the attitude that *When the Wicked Man* excoriates. If Ford was still living in the paranoid world of that novel months after it had been published, it was because the values he stood for *were* under attack from commercialism—as they had been since the rise of the novel. When Liveright then delayed payment of the money they owed him for the novel, Ford felt no need to revise his opinion of Smith's character—except perhaps in so far as thinking about that 'rogue and a bad man' in relation to his novel of publishing iniquity, *When the Wicked Man*, may have suggested the idea of naming his next protagonist 'Smith'. T. R. Smith urged him to find manuscripts by other writers for him, as they had agreed, telling him 'there is no man alive today whose opinion I judge of more importance about any manuscript than your own'; but Ford's craving for praise didn't blind him to 'geniality and flattery'.[30]

When the Wicked Man was published in America on 20 May 1931, and dedicated 'To Blanche'—whoever she might be (Biala said she must have been 'one of Ford's women'). The reviews were mixed, but it was widely discussed, and sold well enough to be reprinted on 23 May. In a buoyant mood, Ford wrote a farcical letter to Pound, exorcising some of his frustrations with publishers and their unreadable contracts:

Dear Ezra,

This is to authorise and empower you without let, hindrance, fee, honorarium, deodand, infangtheff, utfangtheff freely to translate or cause to be betrayed any work of mine save only my commentary on the Book of Genesis into any tongue or language save only the dialects of the Isle of Man and of the City of Philadelphia, Pa in its pre-1909 variety or sameness.

We may shortly be passing through Genoa and would like you to lunch with us at any there hostelry designated by you.

I had yesterday the agreeable news that my latest novel is a best seller in New York. As however the largest sale of any book in that city has not yet exceeded four hundred copies this year and since no publisher has more than $11 in his bank I do not—though they need it—propose to have the seats of my pants reinforced.

May God and your country pass you by in their judgments is the prayer of
FMF[31]

On 21 June 1931, a month after the publication of *When the Wicked Man,* Oliver Hueffer sat back after 'an exceptionally good dinner', and said: 'I've never felt better in my life.' He had a seizure and died. Ford, who wrote: 'My brother's character and temperament must much have resembled my own', wrote about the moment when he realized his brother was dead:

I was sitting on the terrace [of the Villa Paul], reading the English paper. I noticed that a piece had been cut out. Below the excision I read: '—imer Street, etc.' Then I knew my brother was dead. I was at the time just finishing a book and at such times I am always depressed and nervous. A finished book is something alive and, in its measure, permanent. But until you have written the last word it is no more than a heap of soiled paper. I fear preposterous things—that one of the aeroplanes that are for ever soaring overhead here might drop a spanner on my head. . . . Anything. . . . So a member of my household had cut out from the paper the necrological announcement, hoping to hold back the news till I should have finished the book. But I knew that there had been the words: 'He was the author of a number of works which achieved great popularity, amongst the best known being: *A Book of Witches; A Tramp in New York; The Lord of Latimer Street,* etc.' And these were the exact words.[32]

The book Ford was finishing was *Return to Yesterday*, one of the volumes of reminiscence in which he sought to preserve his mortal memories as permanent memoirs. The near coincidence of Marwood's death and his own near-death in 1916 had led Ford to imagine what it would be like to have been Tietjens, a Marwood-like character who shared many of Ford's own experiences. Now the death of his brother, coexisting with fears of his own death (whether by heart attack or by preposterous accident), enabled him to turn again to the subject that always elicited his most effective work: the imagining of his own death. His letters in the 1930s show how sustained was this preoccupation. He had often thought of Oliver as his double. His next novel (the first book of a double-novel) would be about a man who survives attempted suicide (like Heimann in *The Marsden Case*); a man who is able to live by assuming the identity of his double (as Maréchal Ney escapes in *A Little Less Than Gods*).[33]

21

DOUBLES

Rhetorical man is an actor; his reality public, dramatic. His sense of identity, his self, depends on the reassurance of daily histrionic reenactment. He is thus centred in time and concrete local event. The lowest common denominator of his life is a social situation. And his motivations must be characteristically ludic, agonistic [. . .] He assumes a natural agility in changing orientations [. . .] From birth, almost, he has dwelt not in a single value-structure but in several. He is thus committed to no single construction of the world; much rather, to prevailing in the game at hand [. . .] He accepts the present paradigm and explores its resources. Rhetorical man is trained not to discover reality but to manipulate it. Reality is what is accepted as reality, what is useful.

(Richard Lanham, *The Motives of Eloquence*)

> so wide appears
> The vacancy between me and those days
> Which yet have such self-presence in my mind,
> That, sometimes, when I think of it, I seem
> Two consciousnesses, conscious of myself
> And of some other Being

(Wordsworth, *The Prelude*, 1805–6)

Introductory

No single work of Ford's remaining years has the pitch and power of his two great fictions. But there is a case to be made for the later work as a whole. Although the individual performances are not diffuse, their author has diffused himself throughout a range of forms: and taken up a variety of proses. This is one reason why no single work from this period concentrates his full creative energies. To do justice to them one must consider all the forms together, making as it were a composite portrait from the novels, memoirs, criticism, and the generically protean discourses of *Provence* and *Great Trade Route*. Only thus can one bring out the strengths and the enduring significance of Ford's final phase.

So although this chapter seeks to establish the coherence and subtlety of the last novels, and a later one considers the reminiscential and critical works, the argument is continuous. For the major emphasis in all these books is on the question of personality: what it is; how it is formed and developed; how it is experienced (whether by its own self, or by another; and whether in society, or in art); whether it can be changed, or exchanged—escaped from; and how it can be expressed. Furthermore, Ford's late phase is his most sustained and most intricate exploration of his most personal theme, the duality of personality: of how one's personality seems both self and other.

The best of Ford's novels after *Parade's End*—*When the Wicked Man*, *The Rash Act*, and *Henry for Hugh*—deserve attention for four main reasons. First, they are much more interesting works than has been recognized, but their often striking differences from his best-known fiction have obscured their interest.[1] Too frequently they have been written off for not being *The Good Soldier* or *Parade's End*, or for being their pallid doubles. But lesser work need not be failed or unachieved work. These books have also suffered because the most valuable qualities in the prose are often precisely those which get overlooked in the necessarily reductive activity of critical 'placing'. Ford's literary polymorphousness still perplexes and eludes such critical manœuvres, which is why too much of the criticism is still bogged down in preliminaries. Secondly, although these novels are of interest in themselves, they are also fascinating for the ways Ford uses their experimental forms and plots to reflect upon his life, his mind, and his writing—not least because the light they do shed on these things is not always what it has been taken to be. Here too, Fordian self-reflectiveness is not only a matter of autobiographical material getting reflected in fiction. For (thirdly) these books frame some of his most suggestive and profound reflections on arts and the mind in more general terms, and on literature in particular: on how and why people write and read books, and on what those experiences are like. They are not (as they have been taken to be) symptomatic of psychological problems; though they may originate in (or at least draw upon) anxieties and reveries, they make them into powerful metaphors. They are allegories of writing and reading, as well as allegories of sustaining a 'personality'. In particular, they can be read as Ford's most intimate fables about the nature of the writer's life; of *literary* personality. The final reason to study the late novels is for the sense they make of Ford's entire *œuvre*. They embody and elaborate principles that can be seen to inform most of his work, developing and exemplifying his ideas about literature in an oblique mode, in subtler and more penetrating ways than was always possible in his more direct critical formulations. These neglected books can reveal lesser-known qualities of the better-known works, and suggest how some of the long-standing critical debates about them might be reinterpreted.

Doubles and Detectives

The settings, subjects, and plots of the last novels are extremely diverse. But there is a pair of crucial continuities. First, their preoccupation with the double, or *doppelgänger*. We have seen the centrality of dual personalities and doubled protagonists in Ford's writing. The figure of the double becomes progressively more explicit and more important in the five last novels. In *A Little Less Than Gods* the relationship between George and Hélène is itself double—half-siblings and lovers: it is haunted by their shared identity—the way in which a blood-relation is in an inescapable way something akin to your double. The sub-plot doubles the theme of duality, as Baron de Frèjus gives himself up to soldiers who have mistaken him for his look-alike, Ney. In *When the Wicked Man* Joseph Notterdam, a distant descendant of Nostradamus, is haunted by the apparition of his *doppelgänger*. Although the theme of the 'double' is again something of a sub-plot, it is more closely integrated to the main plot: partly because it is to the protagonist that he appears, but also because when Notterdam is driven to the point of shooting at his double—which appears when he is drunk—the person he actually shoots is the notorious gangster, McKeown. He has mistaken the identity of his own double. In *The Rash Act* and *Henry for Hugh*, Henry Martin is able to exchange identities with Hugh Monckton because they are physically almost doubles. This exchange is the main plot of both books. Similarly, the plot of *Vive Le Roy* stems from the royalist Chamberlain de la Penthièvre's realization that he can use Walter Leroy to impersonate his double, the assassinated king, in order to stabilize the regime. Critics have been properly wary of such patently para-realistic devices. Caroline Gordon claimed that mistaken identity is 'almost irresistibly attractive to novelists'. Certainly Ford became more and more captivated by the possibilities represented by the 'double'. But some temptations are fortunate, and issue in knowledge. Once again the critics have been too quick to assume that it is a temptation to which Ford could only succumb, rather than one which he might have recognized, mastered, and exploited for technical ends. There is no adequate account of what he gains through such symbolism.[2]

The second continuity through these five novels is that they are all Ford's homage to the detective story, which he had come to feel exemplified a high point in narrative technique: in the total subordination of the subject-matter to the manner of revelation, and the heightening of the reader's suspense:

No one rebukes or suspects [note the detective term] the writer of detective stories for attending to his technique; yet his sole essential device is, precisely, the 'time-shift'. He knows that if he began one of his romances with the earlier years of his characters no one would read him. So he begins with a murder, harks back, returns to the present, harks back again [. . .] These works when they are good are often miracles of conscientious and conscious workmanship. They are read by the million—and very properly—simply because the device of the poor old time-shift gives to their pages an illusion of reality that no other device can convey. The breathless reader thus obtains vicarious experience. He has lived those scenes.[3]

This is not to say that these *are* detective novels in any conventional sense. They are distinctly not; though this hasn't stopped critics from dismissing them as bad impersonations of the genre. They are informed by the detective novel; by its preoccupations and techniques. But their relation to that form is more oblique. Ford said that *Henry for Hugh* showed the workings out of Henry Martin's destinies 'in what is in effect an inverted detective story'.[4] Obviously an *inverted* detective story is not going to work towards last-page revelations about the mechanism of the entire plot. Instead, this plot is its *donnée*, which empowers other forms of interest: psychological and imaginative freedoms and sophistications not otherwise readily attainable; sustained insights into characters slowly beginning to understand (or failing to understand) what the reader has been prompted to guess much earlier (such as Walter Leroy's substitution for the assassinated king in *Vive Le Roy*), or what had never been kept secret from the reader (such as Henry Martin's assumption of another identity).

However, their detective fascinations have caused these books to be wrongly suspected. They have been seen as pot-boiling attempts to break into the lucrative market of crime and suspense, and even less forgivably, as failed pot-boilers. But they are much riskier speculations than that: more innovative and above all more intelligent. Ford jokes about the lure of the lucrative readership when in *Vive Le Roy* the money Walter and Cassie are smuggling to the French communists is built into a copy of a Simenon novel. (In New York Ford had tried to find an American publisher for Simenon.)[5] The mystery for the writer is how to get money out of a book. Rather than cashing in on the detective market, Ford is the 'old man mad about writing', searching, as ever, for 'the new form'.

In his 'Autocriticism' of *The Rash Act* he indicates how the novelist must become a detective of sorts:

The more modern novelists—or, at any rate, those of the school to which Mr. Ford Madox Ford belongs—write with two purposes. They try to produce work according to the canons that they have derived from the light vouchsafed them. Within those limits they try to render—not to write about—their times without *parti pris*. For them the conception and preliminary working out of a novel become an investigation. They say: Given such and such characters, public events of the day being so and so and the set of circumstances being so and so, what will eventuate?[6]

A novel can 'become an investigation' into what will happen, as a detective investigation asks: Given such characters and circumstances, what did eventuate? Ford's pun is more than an ingenious conceit. It bears witness to his art-long fascination with detection, prediction, investigation, and with how the detective is the conscious novelist's and reader's double—keeping characters under surveillance (in one of the dominant figures of *Vive Le Roy*) to catch revealing clues, significant suppressions, and striving for an omniscient comprehension of human motive. And in this respect the novelist has the edge over the detective. As Walter Leroy's girlfriend Cassie Mathers thinks, 'sleuths cannot tell you what goes on inside a man's mind'. The novelist can. The double novels investigate how an investigation into the double is itself an act of detection about one's personality: how knowing your double becomes knowing you're double.[7] In calling *The Rash Act* and *Henry for Hugh* an inverted detective story, Ford implies they move from act to consequences rather than from clues to agent. The detection is of who the protagonist really is. Primarily this means that Henry's entourage eventually discover that he has been impersonating Hugh since his suicide. But it also means that through impersonating Hugh's identity, Henry is able to discover what his own identity really is. Through Hugh's eyes he can see himself from outside, reappraise his past life, and reimagine his future in such a way as to give him the happiness he could not find previously. The psychological and suspenseful elements enhance each other, managing to make the detection psychologically interesting, and the introspection suspenseful.

Style

The foremost impediment to criticism of the late books is that they are so little read that they require paraphrase; but, founded upon plots which are implausible by the canons of realism, they paraphrase badly. However, a reader can experience what a paraphrase might not extract: when you read them they are neither conventionally 'realistic' nor floundering under absurdity, but are attempting something quite other:

Nevertheless Notterdam continued to regard his ancestor as a stage figure in a long furred cloak, one hand extended in a motion of calling on spirits to appear . . . And this fellow who haunted him, Notterdam, after moments of extreme depression, fatigue or alcoholic indulgence might well be a sort of devil, called up involuntarily by him, Notterdam . . . People who drank too much got delirium tremens . . . The horrors! . . . He said to himself fiercely that he certainly did not drink enough to have delirium tremens . . . But how could you know? How much did you have to drink to get the horrors? Could you measure it by pints . . . or by hangovers? . . . So many hangovers per snake, so many per pink toad . . . [So] many per *doppelgaenger*!

He remembered to have read as a boy a story by a German author with a name like Lippschuetz . . . Of a man who had been haunted by a double of himself called a '*doppelgaenger*.' The appearance of the double had always presaged disaster of a hideous nature. Finally he had fired a pistol through the double's heart—to see that he had fractured a mirror and to fall dead . . . The story had been called, he thought, the *Student of Prague*—or it might have been Vienna. At any rate it had immensely impressed him as a boy, so that traces of the *doppelgaenger* legend had fixed themselves on his memory whenever he had come across them. There was a picture by an Italian painter called—he did not remember the name . . . The picture was called 'How They Met Themselves!' . . . It represented a pair of guilty lovers—though there was nothing to shew their guilt—walking in a thin wood . . . A spinney like Goldencroft Shaw where he had gone wrong with Lottie . . . The doubles of those two had appeared to them. The man was represented as grasping at the hilt of his sword under his cloak, the woman sinking back with arms outstretched.

He had not been able to understand why the arms were outstretched . . . Their doubles should have appeared to himself and Lottie whilst they sinned. Or perhaps afterwards whilst they walked in Priory Wood . . . Lottie, he remembered, had said with a laugh 'Well, that's over!' He himself had been rather awed: as if in church. . . .

But would they meet their doubles, he and Henrietta Felise, if they walked together after . . . ? In Europe, for the *doppelgaenger* could perhaps not cross water? In Italy? Probably in Germany, in the Hartz Mountains . . . That was the sort of place . . . But would they be guilty lovers? Where would be the guilt of it? . . . None for her. For himself perhaps . . . 'Some beguiling virgins with the broken seals of perjury!'

That was it . . . They would both have to be guilty. And of some dreadful sin. The man would have murdered the woman's husband . . . Why! By God, if he and Lola Porter walked in a wood after having slept together . . . In the Hartz Mountains . . . He *had* murdered her husband. They say the *doppelgaenger* of the Hartz is produced by refractions of shadows on mists. A wooded misty country.

On the fourth—or it may have been the fifth—day after Porter's death, Notterdam who had been revolving these thoughts slowly in his mind and had been silent for a long time, said suddenly to Henrietta Felise who was standing, buttoning a glove on the other side of his table:

'I suppose it is true that I murdered Porter.'

Her face was infinitely sad.

'You are bound to think that,' she said, 'I suppose that it is true that *we* did, if you insist on it.'

He exclaimed:

'No, no! That isn't so. The responsibility is mine.'[8]

This is not Ford's best prose. It is over-written where it strains for a Conradian suggestiveness ('The horrors!'; 'guilty. And of some dreadful sin') which it never quite delivers—perhaps because it doesn't take them quite earnestly. But it is representative—and not just of the later novels—in its texture and focus. That is, a novel which contains writing like this is not going to be one which exists for the sake of improbable plot contrivances and wishful supernaturalisms. On the contrary, the paraphernalia of doubles and mistaken identities exist in order to heighten the type of awareness rendered here: the grappling of an unexceptional and not particularly disciplined mentality (an *homme sensuel moyen*) with baffling and perplexing matters of psychology and morality: of guilt and responsibility; of sexuality, the moral imagination, and art. For a critic to write (as Arthur Mizener does about *Vive Le Roy*) that 'This shifts the reader's attention away from the events themselves to the interior dialogue of a mystified observer just when the interest depends most on what is happening' is merely to berate the book for not being the kind of novel he is generally arguing it shouldn't try to be in the first place. For, in the novel of Fordian 'impressionism' it is axiomatic that the interiority of the baffled participant ought to take priority over external plotting, chronology, factuality, or authorial commentary. His friend Burton Rascoe found much to praise in the handling of 'a psychological situation superbly portrayed by an artist who has no living equal in imaginative work of this kind'; but he was sceptical of the kind, feeling that Ford had 'abandoned, toward the end, the high art of which he is capable and sallied into a species of melodrama out of gangster fiction', making the book a 'failure'.[9]

The conscious artist had no illusions about the kind of illusion he was purveying. The blurb for the later novel, *The Rash Act*, argues for the late novels as offering a sequential history of Ford's post-war times. It must have been written with Ford's advice if not his typewriter: 'Mr. Ford continues in *The Rash Act* the contemporary history that he began with the *Tietjens Saga* which was the story of the war and continued with *When the Wicked Man* which covered the after-war boom years.' But being the historian of his own times was only half his dual novelistic purpose. His synopsis of *When the Wicked Man* calls it 'an incredible story about New York and modern life in New York'.[10] The complementary emphasis on the 'incredible'—on all the elements of fantasy and visionariness that make for the artist's exploration of identity and expression of personality—distances his work from the documentary realisms of writers such as Galsworthy, Dreiser (to whose *Sister Carrie* Ford alludes by giving Henry Martin a sister Carrie), or even Dos Passos. The double novels are not aiming for the credibility of conventional verisimilitude. They are psychological investigations, and in their 'species of melodrama', 'the framework of melodrama is turned to the uses of psychology'.[11] The synopsis recognizes that it is psychological extremity which gives the book its order: Notterdam's recurrent visions, his 'hallucination is the theme that holds the story together': 'the facing of the young man as he was progressively through the years by the seasoned older man that he is now to point the gradual disintegration of his character'. This says much about how a time-shift can reveal transformations. It also hints at Ford's own feelings of moral, mental, and physical disintegration after his affair with Elizabeth Cheatham. In the novel, Henrietta Felise allows Notterdam to reintegrate his character, as his new loves perhaps made Ford feel recombined.

One strength of the writing—exactly the kind of effect that cannot survive para-phrase—comes from the deft use of pronouns to convey the confusion and reflection of identities that the passage ponders. 'The picture was called "How They Met Themselves!" . . . It represented a pair of guilty lovers—though there was nothing to shew their guilt—walking in a thin wood . . . A spinney like Goldencroft Shaw where he had gone wrong with Lottie . . . The doubles of those two had appeared to them.' The doubles of which two appeared to whom? Did Notterdam and Lottie see their own doubles? Or did they see the images of the figures in the Rossetti painting? If these possibilities flit across the reading consciousness, they are soon displaced by the next sentence, which has moved back from Notterdam 'going wrong' with Lottie, to the description of the painting: 'The man was represented as grasping at the hilt of his sword under his cloak, the woman sinking back with arms outstretched.' We know where we are again: back with Rossetti's 'guilty lovers' meeting their own doubles. But the momentary disorientation is of the essence, creating an uncertain rapport between self and other; and between self and art, as the mind matches its experience of sexual guilt against representations of such guilt, and sees them anew. Our experience of art is not only a matter of testing representations against our own lives. But it is true that our appreciation of a novel or a picture changes after we have undergone similar experiences.

If the uncertainty of pronoun-reference here is resolved, it is replaced by another kind of doubleness in the language: *double entendre*. The latent sexuality in the descrip-tion of the painting has the same duality of innocence and knowingness caught by the euphemism 'gone wrong'. The words connote different realms of experience before and after the wrong-going: before, it is a conventional warning, perhaps frighteningly enigmatic, but quite unspecific; afterwards, it suggests a specific but suppressed despair. As in *The Good Soldier*, perplexity comes from sexuality being thus both pressed and repressed. 'It represented a pair of guilty lovers—though there was nothing to shew their guilt.' How then do we know that they are guilty? It presents an enigma to the innocent, but is not itself innocent to the reader who recognizes the sexual innuendo in the image of 'The man [. . .] grasping at the hilt of his sword under his cloak, the woman sinking back with arms outstretched'.

The device of dual reference is refracted through a spectrum of examples. Does 'this fellow who haunted him, Notterdam' name the fellow doing the haunting or the fellow being haunted? The answer is of course both, but the momentary halt as we read recognizes the momentary jolt as Notterdam recognizes that he is being haunted not by any ordinary ghost, but more disconcertingly, by himself. (This turn is redoubled later in the same sentence: 'a sort of devil, called up involuntarily by him, Notterdam': is Notterdam the devil or his involuntary invoker?) Similarly, the clause 'But would they meet their doubles' follows on from the paragraph recalling up Notterdam's going wrong with Lottie. So we assume it too refers to *their* doubles. But it is qualified by 'he and Henrietta Felise', as a past relationship is diffracted through a present one. (There is a vital continuity here with Ford's optics of the time-shift in his autobiographic prose, where past selves are repeatedly refracted through a misty impressionist present.) Or in the next paragraph, we probably assume that the sen-tence 'They would both have to be guilty' refers to himself and Henrietta Felise (whom he has just been thinking about). But as we continue the focus is pulled back

to the Rossetti painting: 'And of some dreadful sin. The man would have murdered
the woman's husband . . .'—which of course calls Notterdam back to his obsessive
guilt for the death of Lola Porter's husband, for which he feels responsible because he
repudiated a contract with him, precipitating the writer's suicide. So we see in retrospect that the sentence could apply to Notterdam and Lola Porter as well.

Self-Reflection

These are not just pieces of psychological 'justification' or motivation: the painting, or
an earlier love, occurring to Notterdam simply because (his mind has recognized) they
have a bearing on his own predicament. It's a characteristically Fordian turn outwards,
to larger questions of art and psychology too. He explores the *doppelgänger* motif as an
embodiment of self-recognition: someone meeting and recognizing their self in the
other. Ford had included an illustration of his grandfather Ford Madox Brown's
painting of William Tell's son in *Ancient Lights*. He himself was the model for the
picture, displaying with innocent expressionlessness the halves of the split apple.
Underneath the photograph is the caption: 'I seem to be looking at myself from
outside.' In the Dedication Ford writes about his earliest memories, to record them
(before he forgets them) for his children. By juxtaposing the painting of himself as a
child, with the dedication to his own children, he is able to look at himself in another—
whether an artistic or a genetic reproduction. Furthermore, the outward gaze of the
painting suggests another sense. Not only does the 1911 Ford look at the painting of
the 1877 Ford, but the portrait reflects and returns that look. The painting sees the
spectator; or rather, the spectator sees himself as seen by (himself in) the painting. The
'facing of the young man as he was [. . .] by the seasoned older man that he is now' is
a feature shared by Ford's novels and his autobiographies.

Ford remained fascinated by the transparencies and reflectivenesses of a medium,
whether painting, or writing; glass or mist. When he revised *Ladies Whose Bright Eyes*
in 1934 for a new American edition he had wondered (*through* Mr Sorrell):

Was it then possible that the ages superimposed themselves the one over the other? That they
co-existed [. . .]

Yes, they co-existed. It was perhaps only the human perception that could not appreciate
co-existing scenes. Though you can of course. You can look at thin mist and see the mist or
you can equally look through the mist and see the sun.[12]

The optical duality is a variation upon the image of the window used in the essay 'On
Impressionism'. In *Henry for Hugh* he combines the two, suggesting that looking
through a window can take you back to an earlier phase. Henry Martin remembers
some lines from Herbert:

He couldn't think of the name of the fellow who had written that. He had also written:

　　　　'A man that looks on glass on it may rest the eye
　　　　Or if he pleases through it pass and so the heavens espy! . . .'

That meant that you looked through the surface to find the real truth. . . . If you looked at
Jeanne Becquerel, for instance, you saw a glad figure from a Greek frieze moving lightly
before the sea of Ulysses under Hellenic skies.

And later in that novel, when Henry looks into a mirror, he gets entangled by the chronology of his past, and his mind takes him back, showing him not the reflection of his present surroundings, but those of four months before.[13]

Thus although Notterdam cannot remember who painted 'How They Met Themselves', Ford certainly would have remembered (though presumably he wanted not to make Notterdam implausibly cultured, or too evidently autobiographical). And he uses this other work of art to reflect upon his own past self of nearly thirty years before. He had included the painting (with an illustration) in his 1902 monograph on *Rossetti*, where he says that it:

shows Rossetti's strong liking for subjects connected with the supernatural—his strong liking, because so very much of Rossetti's most fervent individuality is thrown into, and expressed in, this drawing of two lovers, who, walking in a wood, meet their *doppel-gaengers* and are lamentably stricken by the presage of approaching disaster. It is one of Rossetti's best designs. (p. 108)

Rossetti's 'fervent individuality' is thrown into his depiction of duality: his melodramatic confrontation of the doubled couples. If Rossetti could thus be said to meet himself in his painting, how much of Ford's individuality is expressed by his fervour for it? The enthusiasm of the prose suggests that it isn't only Rossetti who has a strong liking for the supernatural. Think of Ford's visions, fairy stories, novels about the fourth dimension, divine apparitions, witchcraft, fate, and providence.

Art

It was suggested that Ford's 'double' novels can adumbrate a central aesthetic; and it is implicit here too. An art of duality reduplicates the personality of the artist: you can look at yourself in your creations. And this can be extended to the audience: the viewer—or reader—can meet themselves in the work of art, and thus also in the personality of the artist. The danger with this kind of critical mapping is that it tends to make everything sound undifferentiated, or solipsistic, and to neglect one vital attraction of art: the encounter of otherness; the recognition of other individualities, other values, other experiences. So it needs to be stressed that Ford's preoccupation with doubleness does not leave him a Narcissus in a hall of mirrors. Instead, the encounter with the *doppelgänger* is necessarily also an encounter with the other, the strange. In part the uncanniness stems from the change in view: the double is *unheimlich* because we see ourselves in an *un*familiar way: from outside. And of course it also stems from other supernatural aspects: the disembodied, ghostly visitation; the ancestral or the prophetic (both incarnated in the figure of Nostradamus). Doubles do not just reduplicate and confirm what is known. They can stand for new realizations, more profound self-recognitions—such as Notterdam's gradual and inescapable recognition of his own responsibility for a human death. For a writer ritually catechized as irresponsible, this seems to me a passage which plays a humane intelligence on the question of responsibility and evasion, showing how the supernatural, the improbable and the fantastical can be used to help us to recognize the real, and to face up to ourselves and our actions. *When the Wicked Man* draws on Ford's seeing himself as 'a bad man with whom most people would say' Cheatham should 'have nothing to do'. Bad or wicked, but not evil, not unredeemable. If Ford had really been the unscrupulous liar he was sometimes travestied as being, would he have scrupled about trying again to get divorced from Elsie, rather than simply claiming to be unmarried or divorced?[14]

The cultural density of the prose is striking too. Within two pages Notterdam's mind touches on Nostradamus; a (possibly fictitious) work of fiction; Rossetti; German folk-lore; Shakespeare; and interpretation of the folk-lore ('refractions of shadows on mists'). Goethe is not mentioned, but it is the highest peak of the Harz mountains, the Brocken, with its famous spectre, that is the setting for the Walpurgisnacht in *Faust*. This chapter of *When the Wicked Man* (the first in Part III) condenses four or five days of the thoughts of a reasonably knowledgeable man. It is not then implausible that Notterdam's mind should be drawn to think about works of imagination, especially since it is these works which investigate most sensitively just the states of mind he is passing through: 'a nightmare of unreality' (p. 167), haunted by guilty remembrance. But Ford's intent goes further. He places art at the centre of the moral and psychological imagination, intimating that it is in the otherness of art that we come to recognize ourselves: just as Notterdam meets his own meeting with his *doppelgänger* in Rossetti's painting of the lovers meeting their doubles; or meets the succession of his lovers and his respective guilts (Lottie, Lola, Henrietta Felise) in Rossetti's guilty lovers. It is a double process. Because Notterdam has been 'impressed' from an early age by the idea of the *doppelgänger*, he has been particularly alert to its various manifestations. So it is again plausible that the thought of his own ancestral double should lead on to thoughts of literary doubles. But these thoughts in turn refract the thoughts that called them up: as his thoughts move in and out of the German story (which is as he thinks of it suggesting his ultimate attempt to shoot his own double, and is thus almost a double of the novel's plot), or the Rossetti painting, the works of art allow his (and our) perceptions of his circumstances to crystallize. In the phrase which Conrad made Ford hear, art can 'make you *see*'.

It is further characteristic of Ford to provide us, just where the fluidity of the prose makes it most suggestively ominous, with a visual image which can be taken as a figure for what the writing is doing. 'They say the *doppelgänger* of the Hartz is produced by refractions of shadows on mists.' A novel such as this one indeed produces an apparition—the illusion of a character—by processes of refraction: as here, where the experiences of character, reader, author, and earlier characters, readers and authors are all refracted through and reflected in each other, to create a virtuoso impression of the hallucinatory discourse of the not-quite-conscious; the sense of moral perceptions shaping themselves out of the numbed blur of baffled conscience. Ford's style of interior monologue is far from Joyce's experiment with Molly Bloom, say (though he is often reprehended for palely imitating that too). His 'nightmare of unreality' is achieved not with the Joycean slapstick of unpunctuation and vibrantly hectic free-association. Nor is it done with the formal dazzle of the diabolical illusionist found in Nabokovian prose. Instead Ford aims at a very real correlative for states of 'unreality': nightmare, delirium, reverie; one of his greatest achievements is to perfect a language to convey the not-quite-verbal: a sublime of the subliminal. The aim is to 'defamiliarize' our sense of 'reality': to make us see how the truth of our subjective experience is actually much stranger, more 'other' than our conventional modes of representing it will allow.[15]

The argument has so far touched on two autobiographical aspects of art: how artists can hide themselves in a work of art, and how readers or viewers (like Notterdam recalling Rossetti) can find them, and themselves, there. The autobiographic is implicit in the aesthetic being adumbrated. Art, for Ford, is neither merely propagandist nor merely ludic. Its mode of teaching *by* delighting is one which involves its beholder in a process of self-transformation through (self)-recognition. Notterdam's thoughts touch on this too: 'The story [. . .] had immensely impressed him as a boy, so that traces of the *doppelgaenger* legend had fixed themselves on his memory whenever he had come across them.' An 'impressionist' autobiography is compressed into that word 'impressed', which doubles the casual sense of 'aroused his wonder' with the fateful possibility that the story 'impressed itself upon him': was a formative experience, making him its double. But the duality of the language properly refuses the reductivism of saying either that the story is responsible for Notterdam's obsession with his *doppelgänger*, or that his propensity for being thus obsessed is what makes him so impressed by instances of doubles. Art, that is, only transforms a self which is susceptible of artistic transformation.

The rest of the sentence about Notterdam's impressionability is also eerily attentive to the psychology of his curious obsession. To say that 'traces of the *doppelgaenger* legend had fixed themselves on his memory' is to conjure up a glimpse of the phantom attaching itself to its victim. Notterdam is dually passive and active. Traces of the legend 'had fixed themselves on his memory', but only when he had actively 'come across them'. The idea of *doppelgängers* having 'fixed themselves on his memory' suggests, partly through its reflexiveness and partly through the disturbing proximity of 'themselves' and 'his memory', the accumulative mechanism whereby Notterdam's susceptibility to doubleness issues in visions of his own double. Furthermore, the phrase 'come across' hovers between the sense of Notterdam encountering a work of art (coming across it casually, in a book or a picture), and the sense of the lovers in the painting coming across their doubles. The ambiguity here serves to suggest that for someone as sensitized as Notterdam (or Ford) to the idea of the double, each reminder of it strikes him as slightly uncanny.

This passage is representative of Ford's unique manner of bringing his expansive and tireless intelligence to bear on the writing of each sentence. The case made for his eminence as a stylist needs to rest here, rather than constricting 'style' trivially to mean something purely lexicographic, or auditory, musical, transcendental (which is always the dangerous lure of his own favourite term, 'cadence'). Although he often elaborated the musical implications, he also retained a more personal sense: the quality of a voice, its timbre and its familiar rhythms and turns; and the way these things are deeply expressive of a personality (*persona*, the mask that the voice sounds *through*: *personare*).

What particularly matters in these books is the process of imagining: the experience of reading a style accumulatively nuanced with uncanny effects. Paraphrasing a novel is inevitably reductive and provisional. But this prose is so elusively gestural, a suggestive mental shorthand, that it is peculiarly resistant. How *could* you paraphrase

Notterdam's introspective reflexions? Rather than inviting précis, it tends to expand as the reader is incited imaginatively to fill in the ellipses and account for the abrupt transitions, to detect what has been suppressed. Notterdam's mind rambles, but Ford's style is anything but slack. C. H. Sisson, commenting on the superiority of Ford's prose to his poetry, has written: 'It takes more words, of course, and Ford always needed, for his effects, the slow build-up of prose. No paragraph or page can adequately illustrate the peculiar confluence of conscious effect and involuntary motivation which characterizes Ford's best work.'[16]

Doubles and Biography

When the Wicked Man in particular presents something closer to the rarefied symmetries of a Jamesian plot, poised on the edge of gothic melodrama (like that 'stage figure in a long furred cloak') while experimenting with fictional possibilities, than a naturalistic transcription of material detail. The Fordian hero is the man of vision, not *The Man of Property*. Thus a paraphrase of how Notterdam shoots the gangster McKeown by mistake for his own double makes the book sound idiotic. Ford himself said that 'the plot of every work worth consideration should be capable of standing up against unsympathetic statement'. *When the Wicked Man* does stand up in the reading: the plot is justified subtly enough never to seem as idiotic as its paraphrase, which fails to capture the crucial shock of disorientation as someone whom Notterdam thought was his double (as Ford's autobiographies often consider others as his doubles) is suddenly recognized as someone irredeemably other. Robert Alter has distinguished between split doubles—the Jekyll-and-Hyde types in which the *alter ego* is disturbingly different from the familiar self—and mirror-image doubles—in which the self is reduplicated rather than divided. Dowell claims to be Ashburnham's *alter ego*, but feels inadequate in not being his double. Tietjens has both a double (his brother Mark) and an *alter ego*—his own, which appears stranger as he sees his past life from the distance of France. In both stories such ideas of the double are handled realistically. In the late novels feelings of mental duality are projected into the 'incredible' theme of the physical double, enabling Ford to foreground the psychology of duality more than would be possible with a conventionally realistic plot. (Dostoevsky was once again his as-yet unacknowledged master.) Though here too we must distinguish between *When the Wicked Man*, which justifies the fantasy as a psychologically realistic rendering of Notterdam's hallucinatory disintegration, and *The Rash Act*, *Henry for Hugh*, and *Vive Le Roy*, which treat realistically their fairy-tale plot of actual doubles and actual and sustained exchanges of identity. This variety testifies to Ford's inventiveness, even when using the same motif in a group of novels.[17] By confronting Notterdam with time-shifts of himself, *When the Wicked Man* interestingly brings both types together. Seeing the other as his self (as Jekyll is forced to do), Notterdam sees himself, as if from outside, as something quite other (as Dorian Gray does in contemplating his portrait).

The double novels explore that sense of the precariousness of identity which haunts the earlier fiction. With almost the same name, or almost the same appearance, very little stands between the identities of a man and his double. Ford's novelistic fascination with imagining the experience of others gives him a sense of his own identity as something arbitrary—why am I thus, and not like another?—but also as something plural, protean, and fragile. The apparition of a double simultaneously disturbs and makes visible one's identity.

One central question—at once critical and biographical—that this book is intended to address, is what Ford's imaginative preoccupation with doubleness can be said to express about his personality. The line taken by the two biographers who have attempted the most psychological penetration is that his writing about doubleness is *symptomatic* of a tragically doubled psychology. Mizener's biography is founded upon the notion of a 'fundamental division' in Ford's nature: 'The pain of living with his own divided nature was unendurable to Ford, and he spent much of his life and his imaginative energy inventing an alternative and more flattering image of himself that he could endure; the major source of the romancing Ford did all his life lies here.'[18] Because the Freudian premises here (art is a day-dream, an evasion of the reality principle) are ones our culture now inhabits, this is an argument that is difficult to dislodge. We might notice a curious circularity about it, however. The writing is seen as the 'flattering image of himself' replacing the 'divided nature' he could not endure; but it is the writing which has provided the evidence of the divided nature. The division is thus not something that is escaped from in the fiction, but something for which the fiction discovers the most compelling images and articulations. Thomas Moser's 'psychobiography' goes further along the same pathological route, arguing that the art originates from a need to escape from an unendurable self into other selfhoods. He argues about *The Rash Act* and *Henry for Hugh* that: 'Henry standing for Hugh shows Ford recognizing that he tried to be Marwood'. Admittedly many of Ford's and Marwood's traits are recognizable in Henry and Hugh. The novels certainly reflect, and reflect on, Ford's sense of Marwood's influence, and his imagining of what being Marwood might be like. But the partial truth in Moser's psychobiographic argument becomes distorting when it neglects the aesthetic implications.[19]

Fordian doubleness is an exploration of psychological dualities rather than an expression of self-division: that is, the concern is with multiplicity of a not necessarily pathological nature. It was attention to this 'tenuous complexity of life' that Ford so admired in *Ulysses*, with its pair of wanderers, Dedalus and Bloom: 'The mind of every man is made up of several—three or four—currents all working side by side, all making their impress or getting their expression from separate and individual areas of the brain. It is not enough to say that every man is homo duplex; every man is homo x-plex. And this complexity pursues every man into the minutest transactions of his daily life.'[20] This is the manifesto of Fordian impressionism, whether that of *Parade's End* ('In every man there are two minds that work side by side [. . .]') or of the double-novels ('But under these two there had been a third Henry Martin'). Though Ford was committed to the method, he appears to have felt that an extreme version of it, a fascination with split personalities, was particularly prevalent after the war (perhaps a symptom of war-induced neuroses): 'the duplex personality motive is being worked to death in England', he said. In his late novels he could be said to work it to death and beyond: to the ghostly apparition in *When the Wicked Man*, or the assumption of dead Hugh's identity by Henry in *The Rash Act*.[21]

However, Ford's interest in duality or multiplicity does not simply reflect mental complexity. It also reflects upon his interest in the arts: in how art can spring from and answer to a sense of duality; how a novelist can disperse himself amongst a cloud of his characters, apparently disintegrating his own personality, but then reintegrating it in the form of the whole; how writing about doubles becomes (doubly) writing about the doubleness of writing and reading.

Changing Identity

The Rash Act and *Henry for Hugh* are the best of the late novels. Few readers are likely to go as far in their enthusiasm as did Ford when he wrote to George Keating: 'I consider these two novels are my best books—at any rate they fill exactly my ideas of what a novel should be.'[22] None the less, like the other double novels, they sustain a compelling, animated narrative; unlike them, they also develop a depth and subtlety otherwise only found in the autobiographic prose of this phase. Their plot, which combines Ford's major theme of the 'dual personality' with the story of an exchange of identities (sounded tentatively in 'True Love & a G.C.M.' and 'The Colonel's Shoes'), is hardly less fantastical than the hallucinatory paraphernalia of *When the Wicked Man*. Though many reviewers acknowledged their ingenuity, the double novels also met with the critical outrage they consciously risked. One found *The Rash Act* 'sophisticated rather than profound'; another dismissed it as 'nonsense': 'a very silly and unimportant fantasy.'[23]

The synopsis Ford wrote as a blurb for *Henry for Hugh* concedes contrivance, though he divides the responsibility for it between novelist and character: 'There can be few men who have not wished at one time or another to change identities with some more fortunate being and this Henry Martin has contrived to do, aided by tempest, suicide, the exigencies of the stock-markets and the enthusiasms of Southern natures.'[24] Henry Martin has 'contrived' to change his identity, but he has also been aided by his author's concatenation of the propitious circumstances. Ford plays down the rashness of acting another's role—the difficulty of fooling all Hugh's acquaintances even some of the time; the gap between a commonplace wish and the uncommonness of its being fulfilled. He reiterates the story's basis in fact: it 'was suggested by an incident of the great storm' in Toulon of August 1930.[25] To the end he seeks the dual response of belief and incredulity. He tells a sensational tall story, while insisting that it represents a universal wish, and anyway might well have happened ('The affair was never further cleared up').

The comment about the widespread desire to change identities suggests one answer to a central critical question of this chapter: if we reject Moser's interpretation ('Henry standing for Hugh shows Ford recognizing that he tried to be Marwood'), then how should we understand this story of impersonation? In what other ways does it answer to Ford's imaginative needs and experiences? The answer would be that, instead of being an expression of the fantasy world in which Moser (and to a lesser extent Mizener) have tried to imprison Ford, it is a book *about* fantasy. A novel like *Vive Le Roy* takes seriously the widespread omnipotence fantasy of the 'If I were king' variety. Ford is perfectly explicit about how Henry's intention 'to adopt the personality of Hugh Monckton' was a decision of his 'subconscious mind': 'His conscious mind had had no idea of his motive [. . .] But the motive must have been there.' He is also explicit about how Henry comes consciously to recognize his unconscious motive of trying to be Hugh. This could be taken as evidence confirming Moser's argument. But there are three essential aspects that argument ignores. First, the universality of imaginative role-playing. When Ford wrote of Tietjens 'electing to be peculiarly English in habits and in as much of his temperament as he could control' he recognized how his own persona had involved such choices, conscious and unconscious. It is also as true of the Tory-squire/Marwood side of Tietjens as much as of the Ford side. Anyway, as we have seen, it is true of Ford long before he knew Marwood. It should rather be traced to his desire to be like his 'peculiarly English' grandfather than his German father. He wrote about the wish to exchange identities at least as early as 1904, while trying—unsuccessfully—to recover at Winterbourne Stoke (when he told H. G. Wells: 'I wd. change with you and sympathise, if only I cd. be $1/10^{th}$ of a live man once more!') and later that year when imagining transfusing his soul with the Bâle chimney sweep. But it would be a mistake to confuse all his role-playing with these anguished wishes. The Ford who posed as a baron (von Aschendorf, or of the Cinque Ports), or who told Goldring he was a German courtier, had not really tried to become these things, nor did he believe he had. Secondly, the terms with which Ford frames such impersonations reveal the continuities between everybody's wondering about being someone quite other, and the artist's impersonation of other subjectivities. The impressionist adopts the personalities of his characters in order to express 'as much of his temperament as he could control'. The double novels, then, need to be read as on one level allegories of the artist's *metempsychoses*. Thirdly, the way Ford writes of Marwood shows how he saw his identification with Marwood was a special case of this aesthetic 'sympathetic identification': 'by a grim stroke of destiny', wrote Ford, 'a tormenting disease made it impossible for him to be anything more than a looker on at that life of careers and movement in which he took so keen an interest and for which he was so marvellously equipped.' One of the things Ford most identified with in Marwood was thus what made him most like an impressionist artist: his aloof, specular detachment; the play of sceptical intelligence (Marwood's 'generous enthusiasms and contempts') over the life from which he felt alienated. It is a tormenting unease that marks out the post-romantic artist from society. Henry standing for Hugh thus shows not so much Ford's fixation on a particular friend, but art's engagement with fantasy, and the engagement of Ford's fantasy with art. The increasingly hallucinatory quality of his writing after the war is the culmination of Ford's experiments in fantasy, which began his literary career with his fairy tales, and continued through works as varied as *Mr. Apollo: A Just Possible Story* (1908), *Ladies Whose Bright Eyes* (1911), *The Young Lovell* (1913), and *Mister Bosphorus and the Muses* (1923). One salutary effect of reading the double novels is that they reveal how much the other fictions—and not only the overtly fantastical stories, but even the apparently 'realist' novels—draw on fantasy and romance.[26] So the tragicomic resolution of *Last Post* appears less as a reneging on the achievements of *Parade's End*, and more as representative of the generic balance Ford sought throughout his writing. What matters most in his double-novels is the process of imagining: the *experience* of fantasy, and the ways in which (as Freud recognized) art can invoke or exploit fantasy. Occasionally wishing to be someone else, or imagining what it would be like to be them, is far saner than actually trying to be them. *Writing* about characters fantasizing about being someone other is—in Ford's hands—responsible novelistic psychology.

Moser's argument that Ford tried to become Marwood after Marwood's death unconvincingly exaggerates Ford's frank discussion of how he modelled Tietjens on Marwood. However, the foregrounding in the double novels of the desire to exchange identities reveals in retrospect how important the theme had been all through Ford's *œuvre*. Dowell's identification with Ashburnham ('I love him because he was just myself') now appears as something much more central than his last-moment assertion might at first make it seem, since the story only exists for us at all because of Dowell's desire to present Ashburnham to us: his patient following of every exploit; his continual imagination of what it would have been like to be Edward, constantly frustrated by the impossibility of transfusing himself—by his awareness of the inescapable otherness and enigma (or is it emptiness?) of his friend.[27]

Biographical impulse shades off here into broader questions of the nature of identity; of sexuality, friendship, sympathy, and art. The remainder of this chapter will discuss how *The Rash Act* and *Henry for Hugh* focus and investigate the major concerns of Ford's art: the various dualities of imagination, writing, and reading; and the insight these concerns give him into the nature of personality.

Sympathetic Imagination

Desiring to exchange identities is an extreme case of Ford's most important aesthetic doctrine, 'sympathetic imagination'. He is not a philosophically precise or consistent theorist of the notion of sympathy, which has a long and controversial history. His novelistic exercise of the same sympathy renders him too curious and tolerant of its varieties and inconsistencies to permit of analytic rigour. But all his criticism rests on a broad sense of how art effects a 'contact' between individuals; how 'feeling with' or 'feeling like' someone quite other militates against human isolation; how it enables knowledge, understanding, self-understanding, and—in another recurrently important term—'vicarious experience'.[28] Ford had enough sympathetic comprehension to understand the opposite need for remorseless analysis. He knew how excess of sympathy can lead to sentimentality and incapacity; and he construed one aspect of the novelist's challenge as the squaring of pity and pitilessness. When in an important early letter to Galsworthy (who always represented for Ford a 'temperament of infinite pity and charity') in which he is exploring the ethical implications of authorship, he says 'there is more to be said for your sympathy than for my disdain', his deference to Galsworthy's position enacts the sympathy that his exaggeration attributes exclusively to the other. It is characteristic of many of Ford's pronouncements about the arts characteristically to pair into contradictory injunctions: while exemplifying 'sympathetic imagination', none the less 'the novelist must be pitiless at least when he is at work'.[29] (We shall find a similar opposition in his discussions of 'personality' in the chapter on autobiography.) It is partly this version of logical instability that has most infuriated his critics, who have seen it as inconsistency, irresponsibility. But Ford's grasp of novelistic organization is too strong for us to believe that he could not control a critical argument. He cares too much about the issues not to care about how he discusses them. So why does he invite outrage with his insouciance, and contradiction with his contradictorinesses? It is another aspect of his quest for a dual response, of course. However, this example does shed light on the why of the technique. What needs stressing is that Ford's oscillations enact the true sympathy they advocate, in ways that a mere compromise (one part sympathy to one part remorselessness) could never do. Rather than appreciating both points of view from an objective, external standpoint, he enters entirely into each one separately. It is a novelist's mode of argument: his ideas become characters; he sets up a dramatic situation and watches the conflict. He isn't interested in rational compromise. (What would a compromise between Christopher and Sylvia Tietjens be like? It is unimaginable. No such entity exists.) So he dramatizes the long argument between pitying Galsworthy and the remorselessly critical Edward Garnett over whether Bosinney should commit suicide or not at the end of *The Man of Property*, 'so as to show the effects of the cruelty of the middle classes'.[30] Ford's oscillations between the opposing sides bring out the drama of the conflict; they are the pulse of a more profound sympathy than comes from a dispassionate synthesizing.

Sympathetic imagination is what, for Ford, enables art. But artists do not have a monopoly on it. In his conception art ministers to, and heightens, what is a universal capacity. Henry standing for Hugh is Ford's most sustained fable for the universal desire for experience of the other: wishing to exchange identities; to be buoyed up in the stream of another's consciousness; to see with someone else's eyes (and thus to see your own self from outside). Like all his good fiction, the double novels exemplify Ford's 'critical attitude' in the way they thus fuse the narrative imagination with his critical as much as his autobiographical concerns. Rather than reading them as symptomatic of a neurotic attempt to evade or falsify selfhood, they should be read as explorations of the aesthetic as well as the psychological. He devoted his life to art, and to pondering what he called 'the function of the arts in the Republic'. *The Rash Act* and *Henry for Hugh* are his best fictional elaborations of why we need art; what it does for us; and how it works.

The double novels also demonstrate the *coherence* of Ford's aesthetic: the interlocking of his key terms. He writes in the dedication to *A Little Less Than Gods* that 'the novelist is there to give you a sense of vicarious experience. What, without him, would you know?' Vicarious experience—a notion which Ford continually invokes and investigates—is only approached through sympathetic imagination of another's experience.[31] This activity is of course a form of mental division, splitting the mind between two consciousnesses. But it is simultaneously a mental doubling. Identification with the other makes it the self's double (and *vice versa*).

Writing

These doublings and divisions are true of characters like Dowell and Henry Martin; but they are equally true of the writer and the reader. *The Rash Act* and *Henry for Hugh* investigate both these aspects. In arguing for the novels as fables of art, I need to show that the allegory is conscious, inscribed in the story, and not forged by the critic. This is easily done once one moves from plot-paraphrase to the presentation and texture of the novels. For they are entirely characteristic of Ford in their intense literariness. The events are mediated through a palimpsest of texts: epitaphs, legal documents (wills, codicils, contracts), quotations, allusions, passports, cables, letters, newspapers, bank notes, a calendar, and poetry (photographs, sculpture, paintings, museum treasures, film, and music also figure). Ford is constantly alert to how selfhood is negotiated through art and writing: how writing both informs and expresses a personality. When Henry is staging his death, and worrying about the impression he will make, Ford writes: 'Why should he desire to leave impressions? It was nevertheless a strong urge and no doubt there is something vital in all strong urges. Something going to the root of life. An intimation perhaps of immortality.'[32] One can hear through Henry's thoughts Ford's own questioning of his 'impressionism'. Why should *he* desire to leave his literary impressions? To allay the fear of death? To write his own elegy after his own heart attack and the death of his brother and double, Oliver? Ford's use of the double is his final form of imagining his own death. Killing your double, as Notterdam tries to, has been seen as an expression of a suicidal wish. Similarly, according to an East Prussian superstition, if you look into the mirror and see the reflection of another (in other words, if the double becomes the other), it is an omen of your death.[33] But as in *Parade's End*, Ford's late novels redeem the suicide into a new life through the death of another (McKeown in *When the Wicked Man*; Hugh Monckton; the French king in *Vive Le Roy*). Apollo could redeem a life if another would die instead (which is one reason Ford was drawn to the *Alcestis*, in which Admetus tries to find another to die for him; it may also be why he found the human sacrifice that is Christianity so congenial). At this level, too, his work can be read as offering fables for why writers write: suggesting that the ordeals of their characters can exorcize their own depressions and morbidities.

As so often, Ford's writing can be read in this dual way, taking the narrative as in part an allegory about narrative. But there is also an abundance of far less speculative evidence in the double novels. Henry and Hugh are both themselves writers. Besides his history of gossip, *Be Thou Chaste*, Henry has also attempted a novel. In *The Rash Act* he himself connects the writing of novels with sympathetic imagination: 'he began to think that he knew nothing in the world about anything—or at least about life. People's lives. How did they live? . . . Even where! He was pretty sure he had given up the novel he had once begun because of that. He could imagine characters but not how they lived' (p. 71). His identification with Hugh is his saving as a writer, in the sense that *Henry for Hugh* ends with Henry and Eudoxie writing vicariously as Hugh:

Eustace had brought along a whole valise of Hugh Monckton's writings on gold. . . . He had written reams on gold that no one would publish because of their unorthodoxy. . . . In a couple of days, Eustace said, Henry Martin with his talent and Eudoxie with her real genius, would be able to knock together a real preface by Hugh Monckton that would at last give poor dear Hughie a chance to express himself. . . . They could not refuse to the poor fellow the opportunity to make his voice heard. . . . From beyond the cold grave. . . .[34]

This may not make Henry a novelist, but he does possess the impressionist's talent for giving an impression of someone else, expressing a personality. He is able to do this, and to convey the life of Hugh's mind because of what he has learned about how Hugh lives—what being him is like. He resembles the novelist imagining his way into the life of his character, and inventing plausible actions and words. And in this respect he is conversely the character standing for the novelist: expressing the temperament of the novelist as a specialist in sympathetic identification. The double novels show Ford playfully aware of how his characters might reflect upon him; or how they can all too easily harden into *personae* through which the author tries to express his own personality. These ideas take an intriguing turn when the persona of Hugh Monckton that Henry has assumed to screen his own identity begins to become eerily expressive of Hugh's personality: 'He thought bitterly that he had lost all touch with his own remembrances. For ages! He had been forced to live in the memories of that other man. . . . That afternoon he had thought for a minute that Hugh Monckton had been speaking through him.'[35] The novelist Ford speaks through his character Henry's remembrances here, intimating the feeling of alienation from his own selfhood caused by forcing himself to live imaginatively in the minds of his characters, as if he were to lose all touch with his own identity. One must remember that Henry has received a devastating blow on the head from the boom of the sailing boat during the great storm. His disorientating blow duplicates Hugh's wartime sabre-wound (without which he would not pass for Hugh). And both wounds stand for Marwood's 'tormenting disease', which, as Ford says of Hugh, made him 'unable to enjoy most human pleasures'; for Ford's breakdowns, which made him too unable to enjoy most human pleasures; and also for Ford's own mentally unhousing shell-concussion, which caused him literally to lose touch with his own memory, and which, curiously, itself doubled his earlier fictional account in *Ladies Whose Bright Eyes*, of the man concussed out of his own time and person. The theme of the double is doubled by Ford's familiar theme of the man involved with two women. And here too, the idea of sexual reluctance (as with Dowell's prudishness, or Tietjens's principle that 'some do not') and suffering for sexuality (as Ashburnham and Tietjens suffer) is associated with this dual involvement: Henry's inability to enjoy human pleasures takes the form of being overcome with a pain in the head whenever sexual involvement threatens. These particular convolutions of doublenesses are expressions of Ford's feelings about what had caused his mental suffering in his personal life. But it is also an expression of his sense of what the writer's life is like: what, in Violet Hunt's telling phrase, it meant for Ford to be 'an author unfortunately doubled with a man'. She said Ford 'refused absolutely with his intellect to face' the problems that beset such a doubled person, by which she meant 'writs and duns, bores and viragos'. But her fine phrase brings out how, in his fiction Ford not only faces these things, but the fundamental fact of being, as an artist, a dual personality: someone who, as Ford said of Dürer, 'must have been a man who saw beside all visible objects their poetic significance, their mystical doubles'.[36]

By calling his protagonists 'Smith' Ford indicates that they are already inevitably duplicated (or x-plicated)—perhaps as his given Christian name 'Ford' duplicated his grandfather's. He also insists that—as with the two Ford Madoxes—there is a family tradition of artistry. The great great grandfather shared by Henry Martin Aluin Smith and Hugh Monckton Allard Smith was 'Xavier Alcyone Faber, born Ploegsteert, 1789, died Nieppe 1860'.[37] Francis Hueffer's middle name was Xavier; Ford felt he had nearly died himself at Nieppe in 1916. But the crucial detail is 'Faber'—smith, perhaps; more generally 'maker', including both the maker of art and the forger of duplicates. Ford makes the name suggest how, though not artists to the same degree that he was, Henry/Hugh stands for the artist, the writer. In part he may stand for a particular writer, since Ford said he had in mind Hart Crane, who did indeed commit suicide, jumping from a steamship on 26 April 1932, while Ford was completing the first draft of *The Rash Act*. Ford explained to the American publisher of *The Rash Act*, Ray Long (of Long and *Smith*): 'Henry Martin's prototype—the man of whose life I was thinking—did actually commit suicide last month. But he was a great poet, an audacious pervert and a hopeless dipsomaniac. Henry Martin was none of these. He was just a sympathetic nonentity—the world as it is today, amiable but without purpose or faith.'[38] Henry Martin is not a great poet; but the words Ford uses to describe him could also capture one aspect of great poetry: 'sympathetic nonentity' is poised between saying Henry is insignificant, and saying that he represents something akin to the Keatsian 'Negative Capability'—the ability to lose one's own identity in sympathetic imagination of the other. (Though it's also importantly characteristic of Ford's sceptical genius to air a doubt about fictional identification: is there a danger to the self if the sympathizing agent becomes a 'nonentity'; how far should we want to become this, even while writing or reading?) Henry's sympathy for Hugh is what transforms his 'entity' into a new identity. He is double in this sense too. He is an artist doubled with a man, as well as a *homo duplex* compounded from Ford and his character. Henry's family motto is '*Sine Fabro Nihil*: that translated: By Hammer and Hand all Art doth stand.' The blacksmith's motto was a touchstone for Ford of conscious craftsmanship. The Monckton version of the motto makes the connection between the two senses of *faber* as artist or smith: '*Sine Fabro Ars Nulla*. . . . There is no art without a Smith.'[39] The saturation of these works in the literary establishes the truth of the motto. The characters are not aesthetes, not particularly bookish. But even so their entire world gets its texture from texts. Their every words bear the imprint of the already written. Without art what would they be, and what could they know?

It is critically fashionable now to claim that subjectivity is only a prescribed text: that you are already written and spoken by language. By contrast, Ford subtly implies that our belief in people, and in ourselves, is oddly sustained by the textual. When Eudoxie tells Henry 'You will have to document yourself', Ford suggests more than the narrative import—that Henry must master the circumstances of Hugh's life if he is to sustain conviction in himself as Hugh. There is a glance at how the novelist documents his characters to make them credible. (The moment when Henry reads Hugh's suicide note, and a drop of his own blood falls on Hugh's signature, suggests not only the blood-brotherhood of the two men, but also the way the artist must inform his creations with his own life-blood.)[40] There is perhaps also a glance at how the artist (whether in a novel, or a novelistic autobiography) is, precisely, documenting himself. But behind these nuances is the idea that the self is formed and transformed by art.

Ford's prose is everywhere concerned with art in these direct and oblique ways; and especially with the dualities not just of authors, but of the modes and medium of their art: with the way plots must double the events they reconstruct; with the way 'English words have double effects'.[41] But it is not self-regardingly preoccupied with 'the problems of the artist'. The central way he investigates what art can do for everyone is by thinking about reading. In particular, he investigates the *experience* and the interiority of reading (which is why the texture of the prose is so crucial), and the way reading can give the impression of shifts in time, place, and identity.

Reading

The Rash Act and *Henry for Hugh* are intelligible as fables for the psychology of reading as well. As in so much of Ford's work, reading in these books is as omnipresent as writing and textuality, and it is of course inseparable from them. The characters read, or have read, everything from tombstones to candy wrappers; and from Turgenev to telegrams.[42] The crucial instances of reading come in *The Rash Act* when Henry reads and later rereads Hugh's codicil and the long accompanying letter. The first reading, while Henry is still suffering from the effects of concussion, is presented in a curious double vision. It is not just that there are two texts (codicil and letter), framing Henry's disoriented reinterpretation of his relationship with Hugh. For there is also the doubleness that is inherent in the act of reading. Henry/Hugh is the *homo duplex* that is man reading. For while he is reading Hugh's words, he is also experiencing his own thoughts (partly about how like Hugh he is becoming). Reading Hugh's letter lets him vicariously experience Hugh's personality with hallucinatory vividness:

The phraseology of Hugh Monckton's letter was not as insular as his language last night. It was, nevertheless, extraordinarily redolent of his personality. It seemed to fill the whole, dim room. And Henry Martin was continually looking up from the letter. As if to see whether Hugh Monckton was not standing over his grip with the full light on his face. . . . And suffering. (p. 232)

When he rereads the letter at the end of the first novel, he understands more clearly that Hugh not only wanted Henry to conceal Hugh's suicide (to protect the Monckton shareholders), but also wanted Henry 'to prolong for Hugh Monckton, here on earth' the life of pleasure that Hugh's war-wound denied him (p. 348). That is, it is by reading that Henry effects the identification with another. In doing so he stands for all readers imagining other identities as they read; and at the same time realizing more about their own identities and predicaments. For Ford writes brilliantly about how reading is an autobiographic act: how it summons up scenes of our own past lives that a book may double; how the reading mind is constantly reassessing itself in relation to the minds about which and into which it is reading. In short, he uses the plot of sympathetic identification—of the switch of identities—to explore the idea of sympathetic identification in art, and particularly in reading.

Cornelia Cook has written well of how Ford's comedy of Henry's self-transformation brings together the fictional and the autobiographic:

The creation of fictions itself becomes central in the novel with the change of identity. A fictional character is compelled to invent a new fictional self. Needless to say, it can't be done. Henry Martin must await the information his author will—and entertainingly does—provide, through the other 'characters' who conspire with their creator to sustain the fiction, and through memories and observations which remain inaccessible to Henry Martin until verbalized for him. We are not allowed to forget that, however, [*sic*] 'sympathetic', Henry Martin is a 'nonentity'—a blank until words that are involuntarily his cohere to form a past for him; an object who takes his identity from description by others (by Hugh Monkton [*sic*], a policeman, a hotel-waiter, an estate agent, a would-be mistress, and scheming lover), who is defined by a series of likenesses or possibilities (including his relationships with Hugh Smith, with his father, with the chance-met red-nosed Smith who predicts his financial nemesis, and with his own proliferating selves, Pisto-Brittle Smith, White Man Smith of Magdalen, and the conflicting subjects he labels Henry Martin I, II and III). The frantic and sustained making of the 'maker' (Smith, once Faber) is but one aspect of the comedy of self-consciousness in this work.[43]

One need only add that, in his dependence on other people's verbalizations to provide him with Hugh's character, Henry stands for the reader awaiting the creation of fictional identities. His attempt in *Henry for Hugh* to discover from Jeanne Becquerel what his relationship with her is supposed to be is a fine example of this comic readerliness:

'You were of course very agitated,' she answered. 'But it is not very flattering to me that you should not remember what happened. . . .'
He said that he remembered what happened as far as he was concerned. . . . What interested him was to know what went on on her side of the door, as it were. . . . He meant what went on behind the forehead she had just tapped. He begged her to continue her story. . . .
She looked at herself in the mirror again for a long time. . . .
He felt impatience. . . . He might be on the verge of actually knowing what had been her relationship with Hugh Monckton. (p. 179)

Knowing what went on in her head—what goes on in another consciousness—will enable him to know his own putative past. The long look in the mirror reflects that relationship between her story and their respective selves. Her story is his mirror of himself. He is like the reader, plunged into an affair without the requisite orientation, and awaiting the continuation of the story to fill in the picture of Hugh. As 'Hueffer' Ford is bound to have heard how some Americans drop initial 'H's. So for Henry Martin, 'Hugh' might sound like 'You' (the switching of name to pronoun gets doubled when Eudoxie's name is diminished to 'Yu-Yu'): the picture of Hugh is the picture of himself. Before the exchange of identities, 'Henry Martin had never had any but a vague idea of what he himself would look like to an outsider'.[44] Through attending to the stories about Hugh, he sees himself from outside, reflected in Hugh. So the reader discovers and rediscovers an identity in reading. This becomes an increasingly important motif in Ford's own autobiographies, which are negotiated largely through his memories of his literary experiences.

So far the discussion has concentrated on the sympathetic imagining which doubles author with character (or characters, or book), or reader with character. E. M. Forster, in a 1925 essay which chimes with many Fordian sentiments about literature, discusses the remaining form of sympathetic doubling: that between writer and reader. Forster's argument is directed against the cult of self-expression and an over-insistence on personality. His wariness of these things produces a classic delimitation of what literary biography can achieve, since, in his less austere version of T. S. Eliot's doctrine of the impersonality of great art, Forster argues: 'that all literature tends towards a condition of anonymity, and that, so far as words are creative, a signature merely distracts us from their true significance.'[45] Ford's admiration for the self-effacing craftsmanship of Hudson and Turgenev, which make readers forget they are reading, is germane here. Forster continues with an outline—equally Fordian—of the dual personality:

Just as words have two functions—information and creation—so each human mind has two personalities, one on the surface, one deeper down. The upper personality has a name. It is called S. T. Coleridge, or William Shakespeare, or Mrs. Humphry Ward. It is conscious and alert, it does things like dining out, answering letters, etc., and it differs vividly and amusingly from other personalities. The lower personality is a very queer affair. In many ways it is a perfect fool, but without it there is no literature [. . .] It has something in common with all other deeper personalities, and the mystic will assert that the common quality is God, and that here, in the obscure recesses of our being, we near the gates of the Divine [. . .] What is so wonderful about great literature is that it transforms the man who reads it towards the condition of the man who wrote, and brings to birth in us also the creative impulse. (p. 93)

The—temporary—fusing of identities in Ford's novels stands, finally, for this way reading temporarily transforms the reader towards the writer. The double novels are instances of (as well as metaphors for) how the writing and reading of psychological novels approaches the fusion of identities, rather than the expressions of authorial self-division that they have been taken to be. The same could be said even in biographical terms, since the characters of Christopher Tietjens or Hugh Monckton are themselves not just Marwood-figures, but *fusions* of Ford and Marwood (and traits of others). Of course, the very act of expressing the self in such a way constitutes a kind of self-division too, since the work of art then stands, reified and alienated, outside the self, but doubling it (which is one reason why an artist might feel 'doubled with a man').

   This is how, for Ford, art effects 'contact' between individuals. In showing Dowell discovering that Ashburnham is 'just myself', Ford wants us to recognize the Ashburnham and the Dowell in ourselves; and at the same time he is saying '*The Good Soldier*, c'est moi!'; in reading his book, we make contact with his personality. This is why it is important that so many of his double-figures stand as doubles for writer and reader. One vital way his prose creates its community of the imagination is through imagining writing and reading; through imagining being his own reader, and reciprocally imagining that reader imagining in turn being the novelist. Reading Hugh's suicide note, Henry 'felt that it was himself writing!'[46] Most of all, his creative tact is shown in the way these things are not shown off in the prose. Although visible to the alerted eye, they are not obtrusively insisted on (it is the peril of criticism to overemphasize them). He has a scrupulous sense of how novelists must beware of using fiction to aggrandize themselves, by saying things of their characters that they would like to say of themselves—as when Henry Martin thinks: 'It was confusing. He could not collect whether he was speaking well of Hugh Monckton or of himself.'[47] Nor are Ford's fictions exclusively or narrow-mindedly allegorical. They do not just *stand for* the dualities of art and the mind, but exemplify them. As in the excerpt from *When the Wicked Man*, the texture of the prose intimates the experience of duality.

The Self and the Other

The double-novels are, finally, realized fables of a more universal self-transformation: the creation of a self. But it must be stressed that what saves the Henry/Hugh novels from being the irresponsibly wishful escapist fantasy their paraphrases usually make of them is that Henry does not actually become Hugh. (Another indication that Ford didn't fool himself or expect seriously to deceive others with his playful fabrications.) At times Henry is transformed *towards* the condition of Hugh. 'He wasn't sure that he hadn't become Hugh Monckton for good and all', writes Ford; but Henry is soon once again sure that he hasn't. Eudoxie has seen through the impersonation from the start, and Aunt Elizabeth just before her death reveals that she too recognizes the imposture. At the end of the second book he answers once again to the name 'Henry Martin', when he is recognized by his ex-wife's ex-lover Mrs Perceval. But although he goes back to being Henry, he doesn't stop being Hugh. In the interview in the penultimate chapter Hugh's cousin Eustace 'wanted to put off applying for leave to presume the death of Hugh Monckton. . . . Indefinitely!'[48] By writing Hugh's preface, and keeping him fictively alive, Henry is still—though to a lesser extent—acting as Hugh. The exchange of identities cannot be sustained. But Henry only becomes fully himself by accepting himself as truly double. The double novels, that is, are psychological fables about the inevitable *dédoublement* of personality, and especially *literary* personality. Ford's biography has concentrated too much on the residue of his 'upper personality'—the often amusing accounts of his dinings-out; his querulous letters to publishers; in Forster's grandly impatient shorthand, his 'etc.'. What has been neglected is what his creative work can tell us about that more significant personality.

The encounter with his double lets Henry see himself (as Ford shared the universal desire to see *himself*) from outside. Seeing the other as your self entails the mirror image: seeing yourself as the other. We have seen how Henry had only a vague idea of what he himself would look like to an outsider'; and the novels about him allow him that knowledge through trying to become that outsider. 'In any case, it had frequently in the old days occurred to him that if he met himself in the street he might well not recognize himself. On the other hand, if he met that other fellow he might very well imagine it was himself he was meeting.'[49]

Ford's last books are the culmination of his progressive discovery of the otherness of the self. He was writing in the era of the discovery of the unconscious, the id. But although it is often unconscious instinctual drives that surprise Fordian man—sexuality, terror, self-preservation, or the death-wish—he is also perpetually surprised by self: by the conscious or subliminally conscious mind that suddenly appears in a new light, seen through new eyes. Conrad, whose tale 'The Secret Sharer' presents his fable of the self as *doppelgänger*, diagnosed such self-alienation in a letter to his aunt, Marguerite Poradowska:

But you are afraid of yourself; of the inseparable being always at your side—master and slave, victim and tormentor—who suffers and causes suffering. That's how it is! Man must drag the ball and chain of his individuality to the end. It is the [price] one pays for the infernal and divine privilege of thought; consequently, it is only the elect who are convicts in this life— the glorious company of those who understand and who lament, but who tread the earth amid a multitude of ghosts with maniacal gestures, with idiotic grimaces. Which do you prefer—idiot or convict?[50]

It is not necessary to have been shell-shocked in order to find the self alien, mysterious, fascinating, or even (for Conrad) macabre. Ford always advocated 'surprise' in art. One reason he felt that 'all real projections of life are astonishing' was that, for him, all real projections of himself were astonishing.[51] Conversely (and perversely) he was also astonished that his readers were astonished, or more often, outraged, to find themselves (as they thought) portrayed in his books. *The Rash Act* jokes revealingly about the dangers of (un)sympathetic identification. Everyone thinks Henry's book on gossip, with the suggestively reproving title *Be Thou Chaste*, is about them: 'Almost everyone would manage to recognise him or herself in almost any character' (p. 177). Ford is also a master of the surprise that comes from recognizing oneself in one's own character: suddenly seeing the self as a defamiliarized stranger—'that inseparable being forever at your side'.

From the alien fourth-dimensionist girl in *The Inheritors* (1901), who 'was familiar till it occurred to you that she was strange', through Dowell not being able to conceal from himself that he loves Ashburnham, and Tietjens surprising himself by speaking, to the series of memorable surprises around which Ford constructs his reminiscences, Fordian man is perpetually surprised by selves, rendered in a style of sustained mild surprises, exaggerations, makings strange.[52]

A writer's feeling of alienation from him or herself can be exacerbated by the infernal and divine privilege of language. In so far as a work of literature expresses the self, it then stands in the relation of *doppelgänger* to the self (as had *No Enemy* when Ford reread it after a decade). But the moment of defamiliarization is equally a re-familiarization. For it is the comprehension of the self's otherness that enables self-knowledge, whether for writers, readers, or anyone else.

The novelist and the reader both have a double relation to the world. They are both in it, and observing it from outside. But this is true of everybody. We are all both agents and observers. The Fordian feeling of being 'on the edge'—of life, disaster, suicide . . .—also stands for feeling on the edge of one's own selfhood, puzzling to find out who or what you are.[53] H. G. Wells described Ford with affectionate malice: 'Ford is a long blond with a drawling manner, the very spit of his brother Oliver, and oddly resembling George Moore the novelist in pose and person. What he is really or if he is really, nobody knows now and he least of all; he has become a great system of assumed personas and dramatized selves.'[54] It is resourceful of Wells to be able to find two doubles for Ford (one of whom must not be confused (unless in a Stoppard play) with his other double, George Moore the philosopher). But he is himself too self-assured to recognize how Ford's writing magnificently transforms his self-doubt into artistic certainty. His prose is a massive and intricate investigation into the self: a public enquiry into what he is really.

Theatricality and Fabrication

Wells's not-unsympathetic insight is valuable in its juxtaposition of Ford's self-doubt and his self-dramatizations. His sentence suggests (without recognizing it) how Ford explores the theatricality of personality itself. The double novels are amongst Ford's most searching accounts of theatricality. The autobiographies jostle with finely ob-served details of how a personality can be transformed by imitating, quoting, acting. But *The Rash Act* in particular is much more explicitly concerned with the self as a performance. The Roman dancer's epitaph—He danced. He gave pleasure. He died.—resounds through the novel not only as the motto of art as a monument chastened by, but outfacing, death; but also as an exemplary answer to the question of how to live.[55]

The phrase 'the rash act' refers primarily to suicide. But the coincidence of Henry's failed and Hugh's successful suicides enables Henry to act out the part of Hugh. The pun intimates that much of our action is acting. This insight is implicit in Tietjens's stiff self-consciousness, and his continual gauging of his actions in terms of conven-tional roles. Tietjens even wonders, before his decisive action in battle: 'what the Hell was he? A sort of Hamlet of the trenches?' Henry Martin also compares himself to Shakespeare's most histrionic (as well as most morbid, suicidal, and divided) hero: he 'did not think he had shown himself wanting in resolution [. . .] Then why did he seem like Hamlet to himself?'[56] Whereas in *When the Wicked Man* it was the double who seemed to have stepped out of a melodrama, Henry constantly sees himself acting performances when he wants to perform acts:

On the stage when an actor lights a candle the whole large stage will be flooded as if with sunlight. It was so with this dawn of the fifteenth of August [. . .]

You cannot spoil dark night and immense, wheeling stars by any parody. In such a place when the air is just flesh-heat you are conscious only of being at one with immensity. You are no separate being and even to you your weightiest preoccupations are without importance. You say: 'If I had *acted* then in another way my situation would now be less unfortunate. . . .' But your regrets have little poignancy.

But that dawn flickered suddenly into existence [. . . as Henry is about—as he hopes—to flicker out?] The stage was suddenly set. You could no longer commune with infinity. These were the great boards on which to enact tragedy.

(p. 181: italics added)

He suddenly realizes that he has got the date wrong. He wanted to stage his death on the feast of the Assumption, but instead he ends up with St Roch: 'who was Saint Roch!' His unspectacular hagiography consists of curing and feeding plague victims, then being saved by a dog when he had himself succumbed. 'Was that the sort of story you wanted to have attending on your extinction?' asks Henry, who feels it is 'another grin of Destiny'. There is a curious sense in having a story attending on your extinc-tion, instead of an audience, of how the stories that are told about you themselves define your audience. Even in his despair, Henry thinks of his identity in terms of drama and narrative: staging his end, leaving impressions.

The *dramatis personae* includes other actors, notably Henry's ex-lover, Wanda, who 'had given to his nights raptures that could only be *read* into the ends of fairy tales', and her glamorous 'double', Hugh's film-star companion Gloria Sorenson. The effect of the accumulated dramatic details is not to imply insincerity on the part of characters who are always acting. Rather, as in *Hamlet*, it is to show how integral is role-playing to their identities. The novels show—and the insight is crucial to the autobiographies as well—the subtle and often confusing ways in which the role becomes the character. When Henry, in the role of Hugh, argues with the communist Macdonald, he finds himself believing in himself as Hugh. The fact that—out of courtesy to the others present—he has been speaking in French performs a double displacement. Speaking in a foreign language, impersonating another self, he re-creates himself in the image of another Shakespearean hero: 'French is easier to talk in that way than English and, delivered in a slow drawl, the speech had been not without its effect—even on himself. As if he had been playing Macbeth and had worked himself up to feeling himself to be that King.'[57] Like Ashburnham, whose words create his passion for him, and thus irrevocably transform his role, and his life, Henry's acting affects himself in proportion as it affects his audience. His conviction gains infinitely the moment another soul will believe in it. Ford's fiction—like Conrad's—is an attempt to convince himself of the reality of his impressions by trying to convince his readers. He said of Conrad: 'he was never convinced that he had convinced the reader.'[58] Both writers are at their best when they dramatize and foreground this doubt, and at their worst when it makes them assert what they don't quite believe. Ford's comment could stand as an analysis of the theatrical personality, which, lacking conviction in itself, needs to convince an audience in order to believe in its own existence. It intimates Ford's awareness that his attention to the reader springs from his need for readers to give him their attention. It also suggests how the doubling of the self might be an internalizing of one's desired audience: turning yourself into the soul who can share your conviction in your own identity.

As so often, Ford combines these delicate soundings of personality with his scruples about the dangers inherent in such self-sustaining theatrics. In *Vive Le Roy* the place of the theatrical in the personality is investigated through an argument between Cassie Mathers and M. de la Penthièvre about the Russian communist ex-dictator:

'You are unjust,' Cassie said hotly. 'You will not tell me that that man is made up of nothing but histrionics. He has a great heart and splendid nature . . . And courage!'

M. de la Penthièvre made a sign of assent with his hand.

'Yes,' he said, 'it is when you have a great heart, a splendid and generous nature and the courage, as that man has, of the lion, and when you can add to them an unrivalled gift of histrionics that you win all suffrages.' (p. 184)

The unobtrusively observed gesture makes de la Penthièvre's (and Ford's) point: an entirely untheatrical self, one bereft of expressive gesture, is unimaginable. Histrionics may obscure or deceive the self, or they may express the heart; and it is as rash to deny their effects as it is to confuse them with the real personality.

In *The Rash Act* it is the two Mariuses—'Marius Guiol and Marius of the Reserve'—who provide the grotesque parodic counterpoint to Henry's histrionics of the self. They are another set of doubles, who as it were duplicate Daudet's *Tartarin of Tarascon*, the Provençal fabulator *par excellence*. They are Ford's fascinated travesty of himself as irrepressible improver of stories:

He imagined that the two Mariuses even believed their story. They might even have *seen* a revolver when he [Henry] had sprung out of the boat. One of them would have invented that fire-arm. The other would have contagiously believed it. Then he would have communicated the contagion to the first and the two of them would have infected the third. . . . They would say they had run up the path after him. He had seen them creep. They were the fat Mariuses of the Marseilles district. Incredible boasters and liars. To the extent that they were capable of believing themselves. With truthful asseverations. . . .

Henry is capable of believing himself as Hugh. But the qualification Ford makes not only distinguishes him from the absurdity of the self-deluded Mariuses, but has an important bearing on the question of Ford's own veracity:

To keep himself from making slips he had had to act to himself the part of Hugh Monckton. And it had proved easy. It had been like when you valorously set out on a course of lying. You come to believe yourself in the end.
    And he had lied very little.[59]

The distinction between self-dramatization which is *like* valorous lying, and actual lying, suggests how Ford thought of his own fabulations: he concedes that they do involve lying, but only very little. But the persuading himself to believe in his own roles is ultimately justified by the effect of the performance. He gave pleasure.

    Ford's dramatic rewriting of the self raises other questions besides those of sincerity or veracity. The suspense in the novels about how long (and how convincingly) Henry can sustain his exchange of identities stands for a broader question about the extent to which the self can be changed. The characters keep revolving the alternatives between which they perform: destiny or escape; reduplication or transformation? What control do they have over their lives? What possibilities of making a new start?

Fate, Sexuality, Death

From the first sentence—'The morning seemed to herald a glorious day.'—we are plunged into a world of omens and prophecies. The sunrise *seems* to augur well for Henry's glorious death and transfiguration. He plans at least figuratively an Assumption for himself: a rising out of obscure penury into posthumous glory, thanks to a heroically performed suicide. (Should this be read as a fable for how fame can transfigure the death of an artist?) But of course Henry has got the wrong day; he has misread the omen. Part of his sense of vacillation comes from not being able to sustain a conviction that he is the victim of a tragic fate. Immediately after the passage about how 'You cannot spoil dark night and immense, wheeling stars by any parody' (p. 181), and about how the dawn sets the stage for his tragic act, Henry's *day* is spoilt by just such a parody—a grotesque parody of an omen from a Greek tragedy:

A grotesque—an almost abhorrent—message from Destiny opened the ball. An immense, skeleton-grey bird was flying slumberously along the edge of the sea. At little more than the height of a man [. . .] With the slow beating of its vast spread of wings it had all by itself the air of a portent [. . .] Towering and screaming it let fall a small fish. The fish struck smartly on Henry Martin's left shoulder. . . . An omen! [. . .] The fish was silver . . . a fortune must be coming to him. It was a grim and atrocious pleasantry on the part of Destiny [. . .] He had been doomed in his mother's womb. (p. 182)

Henry is not enough of a classicist to know that such omens are profoundly equivocal; how, as he learns later, Destiny 'hands you bouquets with its right hand; but its left, not knowing that you are a favoured individual, socks you one that damn near leaves you down for the count' (p. 334). Getting socked with the silver fish does indeed pre-figure Hugh's fortune; but it also prefigures the blow to the head that Henry will receive when the (pre-destined?) storm intervenes in his suicide. That blow almost 'leaves him down for the count'; but it is also his salvation, enabling his impersonation of Hugh. Saying that Henry's destiny is double is another way of saying that he is destined to be double. His 'hybrid origin'—'He was a product of a wild boar of the Ardennes and a First Family of Fall River', has left him morally as well as psycholo-gically dual: a mixture of animal impulse and 'New England Conscience', both wild and fallen. Ford's own 'hybrid origin' was, in his terms, a doubling of equally 'Nordic' elements. But the events of his life so often contrived to make his national predicament seem divided, as he was the Desirable Alien in Germany, and the undesirable alien Hueffer in wartime England, that it is unsurprising he felt fated to doubleness by 'the two strains inside' himself.[60]

One way the books image Henry's preoccupation with fate is by recurrent reference to stars. Do the 'immense, wheeling stars' preceding the dawn govern the events (or rather the non-event) of the day? Henry is presented as pre-eminently a creature of the stars: 'He certainly wished no ill to his father but he could not imagine anything happening to him that should make him, Henry Martin, worry about him from the interstellar spaces where he drifted. . . .' His father mockingly styles Henry's life as a drifting towards stars. He responds to Henry's wish to become a writer instead of taking over the family business by saying: 'if you want to hitch your wagon to a star you can. But not on my money!'; and he repeats the phrase when disapproving of Henry's (adulterous) liaison with Wanda: 'No, sonny. It isn't this star that you're going to hitch your wagon to. Not this star! You go find another. . . .'[61] The astrologi-cal notion of 'influences' affecting human fates corresponds to Henry's feelings about his father: 'all his life, he had felt against him a tremendous obstinacy. Willing him to do something.' The effect of the paternal will is to make Henry feel 'will-less, numbed'.[62] For the first time Ford was able to sustain the investigation, begun in 'True Love & a G.C.M.', into his relationship with his father, which he presumably had begun to feel was responsible for his suicidal desires, as Henry's relationship with his father precipitates his suicide attempt. And that word 'will-less', which he had used of his impressionism, suggests that he was also explaining the kind of artist he had become—the passive, visionary kind—in terms of that sense of the father as con-science and censor.

If Henry's fate is 'figured in the drift of stars', stars also represent the elusive ideals he consciously follows: literature and women. (The connection is made more explicit in the figure of Gloria Sorenson: a *film* star, whose 'glory' is physical.)[63] Sexuality too comes within fate's orbit in the late novels. Whereas in *When the Wicked Man* Notterdam's visions of his erotic past conjured up the vision of his double (with the haunting and overwhelming force of the Young Lovell's vision of the White Lady), *Henry for Hugh* finds its image for remorseless sexual guilt in Hugh's head-wound, duplicated by Henry's concussion. In either case, sexual thoughts precipitate intense pain. When Eudoxie sees Henry struggling in the storm, she waves her neckerchief to attract him towards a sheltered spot. After she recounts this, M.

Lamoricière (the financial adviser) likens her to a siren, luring mariners ashore (and to their death):

She exclaimed:
  'Like Circe, then. Not just any old siren. . . . La première venue des syrènes.'
  M. Lamoricière laid his hand over his heart and bowed.
  'You at least, Madame,' he said, 'never turned man into a beast.'

With Eudoxie Henry finds the relationship he desires, of sexuality without guilt: love that does not turn man into beast. Ford also uses Henry's sexual predicament to explore the relationship between creativity and sexuality—particularly frustrated sexuality. Henry ponders: 'sexual irritation had made him do the only work he had ever accomplished'; and later:

It is a bad knock for your virility when a woman shews that you have no sex attraction for her. Most men—or many—took it out in writing, diaries, verse, or even novels, preferably with happy endings. Others took it out in suicide, profuse gifts, the quoting of lots of verse. And even in trying to create a living novel with a happy ending that should go on after their deaths! That seemed natural.[64]

Henry is another in Ford's series of heroes, beginning with George Heimann and Christopher Tietjens, who do what they want and take what they get for it, but find happiness rather than despair. Walter Leroy, too, suffers in order to expiate his guilt for the sexual: his fear that he will become insane if he sleeps with a woman. However, fairy-tale happiness such as Henry's is only possible after a long pondering on his equivocal situation—one which mobilizes two of Ford's most intimately charging themes: the polygamous relationship, curiously combined with the idea of sexual reluctance and impotence.[65] In becoming Hugh, the books keep asking, how much has he actually changed?

wasn't it a refutation of the Catholic's denial of perfectibility? Or even of progress?
    There he was, rather ludicrously, in something of the same situation as had been his a year or so ago. . . . In apparent possession of a woman who in no way interested him [Alice/ Jeanne] whilst another woman [Mrs Perceval/Eudoxie]—who might, he had thought, have been the making of him was not his! But he had progressed.

He has had 'a second start'; but how much progress is actually possible? Ford's letter to *The Rash Act*'s American publisher is unequivocal in its contradicting that Henry has progressed. Ford had by this time completed the first volume: '*His* tragedy is that whatever he does—whatever feeble action he commits himself to—he always finds himself in exactly the same situation [. . .] So it will go all his life.'[66] At this date Ford conceived Henry's fate as like Dowell's, who feels he has ended up 'very much where I started thirteen years ago'. Ford wrote that the moral was to be: 'if you change your identity without changing your nature you will find yourself very soon in no better hole than you occupied before.' His involvement with Rene Wright and Elizabeth Cheatham may have made him fear he was 'unchanging' in a troubling way: that in changing his identity from city gentleman Hueffer to rural recluse Ford, and starting a new family with Bowen, he may not have changed as much of his nature as he had hoped. He planned the sequel of Henry Martin's story to conclude similarly in this unequivocally unprogressing way: 'In the end he will finish in Springfield, Ohio, living on $5,000 a year [the sum with which he began] that his father leaves him on condition that he inhabits that city for eight months out of the year.'[67] In the writing he changed his mind. But although the actual ending of *Henry for Hugh* does allow Henry the progress of attaining the union with Eudoxie that might be the re-making of him, the rest of the diptych offers something more richly equivocal.

New Life

The Rash Act was originally going to be titled 'New Life'.[68] One reason why the book so urgently questions how new is Henry's new life has to do with Ford's questioning of how new were his own new lives. After ambiguously expecting a suicidal end in the war, he surprised himself with his own re-assumption as a new persona, 'Ford'. So George Heimann and Henry Martin are both driven to attempt suicide, but through that act are initiated into their true identities (Heimann as Earl Marsden; Henry as *homo duplex*, himself). Ford had had another reprieve from death after his heart attack in 1930; and Oliver's death must have left him feeling that there but for the grace of God went Ford. Now, with Janice Biala, he had entered a new phase of his life. Once again the question is how much the renewals are fated, and how much self-willed re-inventions of the self. 'New Life' also stands for the author's re-invention of other selves, whether of real or imaginary people. Henry's desire to write Hugh's book is expressed in precisely these terms: 'In it he would put clearly and concisely the views that Hugh Monckton had expressed—and by attributing that part of the book to Hugh Monckton he could make that poor fellow, at least to that extent, live again.'[69] Reciprocally, the writer's creation of new life for his characters gives him new life—not merely by giving him (and his readers) vicarious experience of other lives, but by enshrining his personality in a monument that will endure beyond his death. In so far as Arthur Marwood is one of the people both Tietjens and Hugh resemble, then one can accept Moser's view of the novels as expressions of Ford's grief, and wishful attempts to let Marwood live again (as Ford indeed said he wished to). But it can only be one motive amongst many shaping such complex works. Henry's plan to write for Hugh could equally stand for Ford's memorializations: of Conrad in *Joseph Conrad*; of Marwood in *Parade's End*; or in *A Little Less Than Gods*, the 'historical novel in which Ney should live again'.[70] What most attracts Ford to such subjects is their possibilities of lively fabulation: of creating the illusion of reanimation.

Despite the romance ending of *Henry for Hugh*, Ford sustains much of the ambiguity about 'progress'. A happy ending is both a termination and a prophecy for future happiness. But Eudoxie's euphoria as the couple reach the Italian frontier—'We're free!'—is held in check by a sinister omen: the sight of the Fascist guard, absurd but threatening: 'rifles, bayonets, machine guns, Sancho Panzas, Falstaffs and peak-hatted Gog-Magogs, silhouetted against the clear sky' (p. 327). After the war, and the Depression, the signs heralding a new war made a belief in human progress and perfectibility harder than ever to sustain. Although the novels side with Monckton Toryism rather than Martin *laissez-faire*, they remain sceptical about the public efficacy of adopting a public identity, especially given the power of a Crash to erase people's social standing. Personal happiness, they suggest, involves maintaining a certain amount of fictiveness in one's relation to the world: in being able to see the fairy-tale hero and heroine ('Eudoxie had become a princess with still streaming cheeks'; p. 329) double the citizens of the Republic.

The political double-take of the ending re-frames the ethical question of escape in national terms. Henry and Eudoxie escape from the French police, but exchange them for the Italian guards. How far can a new life escape from the oppressions of the old one? Ford's art has been misrepresented as itself escapist, notably by Moser's fable that Ford tried 'to escape—into his own imagination, or into oblivion, or into another's consciousness'. Moser identifies the drive, but not its results. His argument misses how, rather than valuing 'art as escape', Ford's art has a morally intelligent dual attitude to escape. His writing, above all in the double novels, expresses the human *desire* for escape, but equally, the ultimate impossibility of that escape being complete. In his 1928 Preface to Marc Chadourne's *Vasco*, he describes the protagonist of that book in a way which suggests that he may already have been thinking out the frenetically static story of Henry Martin:

the Frenchman is a raging spirit fleeing from the damnation of the daily round, the daily face of his own in the glass. He is driven before the wind like a poor wretch blasphemously fleeing before the Erinyes, his motive being 'To go: to go no matter where, so it be but to go,' his end and aim: 'To be re-born, free, the shackles off, naked like Adam on the shingles of the world's end.'

So he goes—to Tahiti, to the Marquesas, to a leper colony—who knows where? but always to find in the end his own mentality, his own problems, his own self, despairing.[71]

What interests Ford here, and was to become the centre of his late novels, is the way the attempt to escape from the self (captured in that characteristic mirror image) can end with a return to the self, an autobiographic act of self-identification. Ford's plot adroitly compacts almost all these elements (even being 'driven before the wind', in the storm scene). Perhaps he saw a double of his own cherished rebirth-plot in the work of someone quite other. Henry's exchange of identities with his double expresses at once his desire to escape from himself, and how the attempt lands him in a reduplication of his former circumstances, allowing him to reinterpret his own past. The main difference is that Henry does escape from his despair. Ford tunes a fine comedy from the repetitions and coincidences of his fate.

It is Hugh who makes the connection between literature and escapism. Pondering 'Means of escape' from his unbearable headaches and despair of the heart (he has been jilted by Gloria), he says with an edge of bitterness: 'They say there are books called literature of escape. . . . I have not found any . . .' This is partly because any escape offered by literature can only ever be illusory and temporary. But it is also because, for Ford, that element in literature which does minister to the desire to forget, alter, or transcend the self, is always ultimately in the service of an ethical realism. Literature takes us out of ourselves not just to give us a rest (though it may at one level do that too), but to show us 'where we stand'. Ford said that 'if you are at all worried your Literature of Escape must be such as will come out of its covers and grip you with the insistence of life itself'. That is, if the fiction is to efface the reality, it must have an even more powerful effect. But the only way it can do this is by gripping you 'with the insistence of life itself'—by returning you to feel the 'life' from which you thought you were escaping. The examples Ford gives in the same articles are stories which were later published in *No Enemy*. They tell of the books he was reading when his worries were at their most intense: during the battle of the Somme. In particular he dwells on reading *What Maisie Knew*, saying that 'The doubling of vision that resulted is one of the most bewildering of my memories'. The 'queer doubling of effects' was due to 'that singular way Life came over into the mood of the book read'; precisely, that is, due to the reciprocal ways the literature and the war Ford wanted to efface transfused into each other. Just after rereading *Maisie* he fell, 'by an extraordinary coincidence', 'right bang, bewildered weariness and all, into the midst of an Affair that must almost exactly have duplicated the affair of Maisie and her parents', with a young girl caught in the crossfire of parental adultery:

What happened was that whilst I lay extended in a lounge in the hotel hall in a state of utter exhaustion I at some point found upon my knee a small, fluffily clothed, dark, preternaturally intelligent child who said very clearly with a strong French-American accent: 'They *say* Mummie's gone to Heaven. But I can't find any tram-car that takes you *au ciel*', whilst at the same time a man that I didn't in the least know, with an accent of the most extreme nervousness, was muttering in my ear: 'What else could I do? I had to knock the fellow down. And take the child!'[72]

Literature can alter our perceptions of the world, making it at once stranger and more familiar. But its double effects are not escapist.

In *The Rash Act* Henry 'tried to lose himself in imagining what it would be like if he became actually' Hugh. But by assuming Hugh's identity, although he is able to lose his financial and romantic anxieties, he does not lose his own. Henry discovers: 'Changing your identity was more difficult than had at first appeared'. This is partly because in his new incarnation he is forced to confront those anxieties in his double that he had tried to evade as himself: 'He would have to face it! [. . .] He had avoided thinking out his case. For months [. . .] He set his mind the job of telling his story in the barest possible way [. . .] He had to go back. There was no escape. He must reconstitute the whole scene.'[73] The irony of Henry's attempted escape from himself is that it doubles rather than solves his difficulties. It makes his life formidably complicated, fraught with dangers of discovery and prosecution. Even if the technical feat of impersonation were not so demanding, the new role carries with it the more complex responsibilities of Hugh's business, money, and art treasures. Henry finds himself not only assuming greater responsibilities for himself, but also for others. Most importantly, Henry's concern is for his *alter ego*, Hugh. The title of the sequel substitutes 'Henry for Hugh', but it also indicates how much Henry does '*for* Hugh'. He maintains the fiction long enough to protect Hugh's reputation and the shares of the family business; and also to spare Aunt Elizabeth's grief. But when Macdonald denounces Henry to a newspaper as an impostor, and the newspaper informs the police, Henry is in danger of jeopardizing the Monckton name. At one point his impasse appears inescapable: rumours are starting to say that either Monckton feigned suicide to engineer a temporary slump in Monckton shares, enabling him to buy them up before their prices rose again; or, if the suicide had been Henry Martin's and not Hugh's, there would be a scandal that Hugh had let his relative die 'for the want of a few cents'. At the close he is transformed into the familiar Fordian altruist (Ford establishes the contrast with the obnoxious cousin Eustace, who insinuates to Henry: 'There's nothing of the altruist about me'): he returns to being Henry for Hugh. Throughout the complex turns of his predicament Henry rises to meet the multifarious challenges, fulfilling the prophecy Ford had thought of taking the title from: 'As thy day[s], *so shall* thy strength *be*.'[74] In this sense, though Henry may not improve his situation, he progresses morally, discovering the resilience his times require. He is in the line of Fordian post-war survivors.

The double novels are concerned with understanding the pattern of a life, by getting a second chance at living, or managing a particular situation. One of the problems with the Henry Martin diptych is that Henry is no more effective in escaping his perplexing circumstances in his Hugh avatar than he was before. M. Lamoricière embezzles his profits, absolving 'Hugh' from any putative guilt for putative insider trading on his own shares. And the communist secretary, Macdonald, absconds with Jeanne Becquerel, resolving the sexual entanglement of the *menage à trois*.[75] However, neither event is inherently implausible; and both are more plausible than it would have been for Ford to have transformed Henry into a Hugh-type man of action. The wish to have one's life over again, or to be able to relive and improve a particular episode, is a universal one; and it is certainly an escapist *wish*. But Ford's novels do not fulfil the wishes they articulate. Rather, they set wishfulness against responsible confrontation of one's self and one's time, showing in patient detail how escape is impossible.

When the Wicked Man was a form of ethical stocktaking. Guilt, such as that Notterdam was finally able to absolve (if the plot never quite resolves the extent of his responsibility) does not loom so large in *The Rash Act* and *Henry for Hugh*. One recent critic has noted that Henry Martin doesn't find a *doppelgänger*, but a public identity. In the decade in which Ford was working intensively on *A History of Our Own Time*, he was turning from the nightmare of personal responsibility to the arena of public action: to what in 1935 he called 'the serious problem of how to live'.[76] Joe Notterdam was meant to represent the irresponsibility of American business methods which had resulted in the Wall Street Crash. Ford also wanted the private life of Henry Martin to illustrate 'a phase of universal desire whilst all around him civilisation quakes'. The phrase is ambiguous: is the universal desire for suicide, or for exchanging identities (which the 'Autocriticism' had argued was also a universal wish)? Either way, there is a curious suggestion that the death-wish following the Crisis may suggest that the Crisis is itself the manifestation of a death-wish. Ford plays on the word 'crisis' as a turning-point: *The Rash Act* and *Henry for Hugh* not only record the effects of the cataclysm, but the life-saving transformation Ford thought necessary: a turning away from the cutthroat capitalism of the publishers in *When the Wicked Man*, or the Pisto-Brittle business in *The Rash Act*, to the more paternalistic business methods of the Monckton family, somehow combined with the Mediterranean smallholder economics by which Henry lives with his entourage at the Villa Niké.[77]

'As thy day' is the motto for how we must face and meet our circumstances. It is also the motto for the novelist of history, who aims to render 'our own times'. Escape is

Ford in the 1920s

Ford *c*.1930

Ford in the 1930s

Chicago, 1927. 'I like this best of any of the photos of me, it's more how I seem to myself!'

Ford and Biala

At Les Sablettes, near Toulon, 1935

With Biala at the
Villa Paul, *c.*1934

Ford painted by Biala, 1932

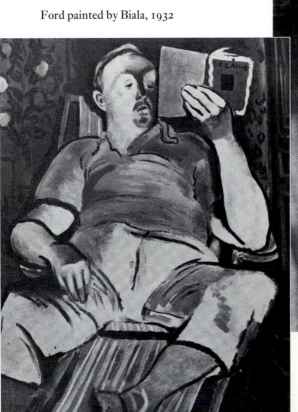

Dr Ford at Olivet
College

Ford with the
novelist Dorothy
Speare, 1937

Ford in North Carolina, 1939

In the garden of the Villa Paul, *c*.1932

part of Ford's subject, but it is not his technique. The terms of Henry's self-confrontation are also the terms of a novelist dedicated to exploring the full significance of an
'affair'; a novelist aiming at what Ford called the 'exhaustion of aspects'. The novel-
plus-sequel form (the formal expression of the doubleness it treats) is committed to
elaboration and investigation.[78] He too must tell his story in the barest possible way,
but without evading what is important. 'He must reconstitute the whole scene.'
Henry's exchange of identity cannot be sustained. The fairly tale of complete self-
transformation can only be imagined; the impersonation can only last as long as it does
through his rigorously sustained sympathetic imagination of what Hugh would do at
each step. From the demands of art Ford sought no escape. He wrote that before he
started *Parade's End*: 'I still dreaded the weakness in myself that I knew I should find
if I now made my prolonged effort.' Here too the novelist's terms double the characters': all Ford's post-war heroes dread their own weaknesses, their inabilities to
extricate themselves, their proximity to madness; yet all of them make their prolonged
efforts, understanding themselves as they transform themselves. Ford's works such as
these, which are most animated by the longing to escape are, in Christopher Ricks's
words about Tennyson—another writer preoccupied with suicide and escape—those
which 'most scrupulously imagine the implications of what it would be to escape'—or
to try.[79]

Tonal Duality

The double novels are characteristically dual renderings, at once idealizing characters
and exposing them to a corrosive scepticism. But whereas before the war the moral
double-bind led to the tragic outcome of *The Good Soldier*, afterwards Ford's primary
mode is tragicomedy.[80] He is everywhere the comedian of despair. His protagonists are
driven to their psychological edge. Some, like Ashburnham and Hugh Monckton, are
driven over into the abyss, as Ford had felt he was about to be from 1913 to 1917. In
all the post-war fiction, they are saved and transfigured as Ford felt he had been in
1918/19. The aesthetic problem he poses himself is to combine the tragic sufferings
and comic reprieves so as to heighten the effect of each. The danger is that the two
modes will cancel each other out: tragicomedy risks facetiousness about anguish (the
weakness of *When the Wicked Man*) or portentousness about the commonplace
(the flaw of *The Marsden Case*). Eudoxie is amused by 'all these failures to suicide'
in *The Rash Act* (p. 246). But Hugh's suicide has been successful, and the exuberance
of the ending is tempered by the elegiac regard for Hugh's memory, and his writings.

The Rash Act has been described as 'a subtle variation on the theme of the drowning
man who sees his life flash before him'.[81] Ford seizes upon this primal doubleness: the
momentary conjuncture of dying life and incipient death. His invocation of the
commonplace stresses how it is the death which gives 'new life' to the life, making
visionaries of us all: 'They say that men about to drown see their whole lives with
extraordinary vividness' (p. 17). And he saw how a novel based around a death by
water would give his reminiscential-autobiographic mode free rein, subordinating the
whole life to the tragicomic moment of failed suicide—or rather the doubly tragicomic
moment of the absurd coincidence of a failed and a successful suicide. The double

novels are particularly valuable for their insight into death as Ford's primary impulse to create, or re-create. Ford's art attempts to reconcile him to death, while also militating against it. Every dancer has his epitaph, but the art of elegy performs its own dance in answer to the dancer's death.

The Rash Act is Ford's *Tempest*. Hugh alludes unconsciously to the 'sea-change' which prefigures his exchange with Henry (p. 92). And, without wishing to press the analogy to absurdity, the double novels, following the tragic phase consummated by *The Good Soldier*, not only stand in a similar relation to the *œuvre* as Shakespeare's late romances, but are also suffused with a comparable magnanimity, and are celebratory of the art which celebrates.

The tonal unease in *When the Wicked Man* points up the success of the tragicomic poise of *The Rash Act* and *Henry for Hugh*. Ford wants Notterdam to appear both truly wicked and yet sympathetic. The book, like Ezekiel's God, is both critical and forgiving: 'Again, when the wicked *man* turneth away from his wickedness that he hath committed, and doeth that which is lawful and right, he shall save his soul alive.' (The next verse in the Authorized Version ends: 'he shall not die.')[82]

Ford originally wanted to subtitle *When the Wicked Man* 'A Morality', but Liveright, the American publisher, objected. Ford's reply indicated the novel's generic doubleness: 'If you don't like Morality as a subtitle—and I'm not sure myself that it is advisable—call it A ROMANCE.'[83] But this fudges rather than fuses its categories: 'A Morality' implies the form of ethical intransigence that it is usually the province of 'Romance' to dissolve. More dubious is the question of whether Notterdam's being driven to shoot at what he thinks is his own double in fact constitutes a turning away from his wickedness (rather than an inability to confront his past, his self). The plot simply cuts through any doubts with the *coup de canon* with which he shoots McKeown and inadvertently becomes a popular hero. Whereas Henry's salvation involves a true integration of guilt and love, remorse and self-acceptance, Notterdam's involves a mere erasure of his past. Ford's more responsible fictions know that such escape will not last. Psychologically the resolution lacks conviction, since the haunting guilt that has produced the visions would scarcely be so facilely exorcized. The ending in effect gives Notterdam *two* doubles—McKeown as well as Nostradamus—but it only really engages with the more superficial one: the public enemy, the wickedness of Crash-doomed capitalism. The ethics of commerce and of sexuality are not integrated until *The Rash Act* and *Henry for Hugh*.

The late novels represent a modulation of Ford's fiction, not the decline they have too often been diagnosed to be. However, their myths of art place them less with conventional novels and rather with the idiosyncratic discourses *Provence* and *Great Trade Route* in which Ford investigates the origins and qualities of his artistry. They are also continuous with his autobiographic series, charting his pre-war despairs (in *Return to Yesterday*) and post-war regeneration (in *It Was the Nightingale*). But finally, the tonal poises of *The Good Soldier* and *Parade's End* become more intelligible and impressive. Not only do *The Rash Act* and *Henry for Hugh* enable us to reread those earlier masterpieces with renewed attention to the aesthetics of doubleness, sympathetic imagination, elegy, and so on; but once Ford's development towards tragicomedy becomes apparent, two critical issues concerning the earlier books become more tractable. First, the unaccustomed tonal complexity of *The Good Soldier* becomes more intelligible: the suggestion to call *The Good Soldier* 'The Roaring Joke' appears as a rich and illuminative irony (and not sarcasm at the publisher's expense). And secondly, the intention of *Last Post* is clearer. This is not to say that no critical doubts about it remain, but an understanding of the tragicomic resolution makes it unreasonable to object that the note of mental torment is not sustained.

When Ford wrote to Pound that *The Rash Act* was 'more like what I wanted to write than anything I have done for years' he was recalling Henry James's revelation to him about the private import of particular stories: 'You understand. . . . I *wanted* to write the *Great Good Place* and the *Altar of the Dead*. . . . There are things one wants to write all one's life, but one's artist's conscience prevents one. . . . And then . . . perhaps one allows oneself. . . .'[84] Ford interprets James's confessional obliqueness to mean that artists who allow their personal desires to overrule their artistic consciences are in danger of betraying their art: 'That is the first—or the final, bitter—lesson that the Artist has to learn: that he is not a man to be swayed by the hopes, fears, consummations or despairs of a man. He is a sensitised instrument, recording to the measure of the light vouchsafed to him what is—what *may* be—the Truth.' Ford's letter to Pound suggests that *The Rash Act* is particularly self-revealing; expressive of his intimate, literary life. Ford's life as an author may have seemed 'unfortunate' to Violet Hunt, who had shared in the anguish of his Edwardian and wartime affairs. But the late novels show that being an author doubled with a man was not necessarily a sad story.

1931–1933: WEATHERING THE DEPRESSION

> You may yourself be amazingly poor compared to what you were, yet [. . .] you may spend days churning the sea along the warm sands into that white strip of foam that from above the aviators see stretching from Carqueiranne, next to Toulon, to Rapallo where Mr. Pound sits brooding violent communications to the Anglo-Saxon Press under the shadow of the monument to Columbus. . . .
>
> (Ford, *Provence*)

Liveright's delaying of his payments cut off Ford and Biala's only source of income that summer of 1931. 'Of course things are very bad in New York and they pay practically no-one who is abroad and unable to sue them', said Ford, starving stoically. He had to ask Pound for a loan of $100, since, as he explained, 'we are now approaching literal starvation having been without enough to eat for many weeks'; 'for a long time we have been living practically out of garden but now the drought has brought even that nearly to an end'. 'Herez the hors d'oeuvres', said Pound, who was struggling himself, loyally sending what he could by return, and making up the rest the following day. When Ford thanked him he said he 'really slept well last night for the first time for a long time'.[1]

Julie stayed for ten weeks, until 22 September. Ford and Biala returned to their Paris flat as soon as Padraic and Mary Colum (who had rented it from them) had found somewhere else. Bowen had been planning to winter in Toulon in her old attic studio, but Ford persuaded her to stay with Julie in the Villa Paul. She 'found it difficult to enter again into Ford's life', but agreed that the villa and garden would be better for Julie than a 'noise-some quay-side slum'. She and Julie arrived at noon, and Ford and Biala left in the evening. When they got back to 32 rue de Vaugirard they found it was due to be demolished.[2]

Biala told a story exemplifying Ford's generosity even when poor himself:

One day one of those innumerable Georgian Princes turned up. He introduced himself as a friend of some American girl that Ford knew and liked. He came to ask Ford for money because he couldn't pay his hotel bill, etc., etc. Ford asked me to make out a check for a small sum. I looked protestingly at him—but Ford paid no attention. The prince was outraged and insulted by the smallness of the sum. We didn't tell him that it was exactly one-half of the Ford account, and he left, another enemy. Ford used to boast that every member of his family died poorer than he'd been when he was born. He was very proud of that.[3]

They got back to Paris to find that the publication of *Return to Yesterday* had provoked a scandal in London. 'MONSTROUS STORY ABOUT THE KING', ran the headline in the

Daily Herald on the day of publication. The story, which Ford said he had from Masterman, was that King George had 'asked all the leaders of all the Irish parties to meet in a Round Table conference at Buckingham Palace under his own Presidency' in order to settle the question of Irish Home Rule 'to the satisfaction of all his Irish subjects'. But the Liberal Cabinet was unanimously against the idea: 'They wanted to do nothing that could enhance Royal prestige.' According to Ford, the king had said: 'Very well, gentlemen. I am the richest commoner in England. If you wish me to abdicate I will abdicate, supposing that to be the wish of the country. But before that we will have a general election and I have not much doubt as to the results as between you and me.' So, adds Ford, 'he had his conference'. There was an 'Indignant Denial of Any Pre-war Threat to Abdicate' from a Palace Official, and even Lloyd George, who had been Chancellor of the Exchequer at the time and went with Asquith to represent the government, said he 'had never heard of such a thing'. It was exactly the sort of publicity Ford didn't need, resurrecting the old spectres of unreliability and untruthfulness. Whether that was how Masterman told the story or not, it wasn't quite factually true. The prime minister, Asquith, advised the king to intervene by calling the conference. The king agreed, and suggested that it should be the Speaker who presided. It was after the king's opening speech that the Liberals became angry, thinking he favoured the Unionist cause. The conference tried to break up on its second day, but the 'forceful tact' of the Speaker kept it going for two more days. It is not impossible that the king made the threat then, to hold the conference together, though if he did it is not otherwise recorded. When the *Herald* rang up Victor Gollancz (who had published the book), he told them: 'I hope the statement is true because it seems to me a magnificent example of genuine kingship'; but his comments weren't printed. This was clearly Ford's view of the story too. He told Gollancz he could 'delete that paragraph in subsequent editions'—'I am quite literally and naively a subject of H.M. and entertain the greatest admiration for him as Head of the State [. . .] After all it is doing a sovereign no disservice to emphasise the fact that he was sincerely and actively concerned to put an end to assassination, mutiny and chaos in a part of his dominions.' His version presents the king as the altruistic superior to the Liberal politicians. He felt it was 'the lamest piece of denial I have ever seen', and, as Mizener says, 'it did not deny Ford's essential point'.[4]

Having taken stock of his old life, he now turned to express his sense of his new life in fiction, beginning *The Rash Act* in December. In March 1932 he signed a contract with a new publishing firm, Long and Smith. Ray Long had been the editor of *Cosmopolitan*, and Richard R. Smith an editor for Macmillan. Long had come to Paris, and word got around that the firm had plenty of money to spend. When Bradley introduced them, Long offered Ford $200 a month as an advance against royalties, provided that he wrote a book every twenty months; the contract covered the next three novels, plus the *History*. As Mizener says, 'Here, in the Depression, was $2,400 a year assured to Ford for at least two and a half years; it seemed too good to be true and, as things turned out, it was.' Keating had warned Ford not to get involved with dubious publishers. But this offer was too good to turn down, and there weren't for the moment any alternatives. Some of the payments were slightly delayed, and Ford began to worry Bradley, who was still looking after his interests in an informal way, about the

reliability of Long and Smith. When he finished *The Rash Act* in May Biala wired
Bradley: 'Book finished has remittance come if not Ford proposes not deliver manuscript wire at once Janice Ford.' By the time Bradley got the cable Ford had got the
money, so a potential row was avoided. But Bradley reassured Ford sternly: 'It never
occurred to me that the delay of a few hours would disturb your peace of mind or that
you could be so distrustful of your new publishers. I really think it is only fair to
them—and to me who brought them to you—to assume that they are honest and
solvent till they have given definite proof to the contrary.' Ford sent off the manuscript, and Ray Long wrote a long letter to say that they were 'highly enthusiastic', it
was 'an extraordinary piece of work', but to explain that they were disappointed that
the protagonist didn't commit suicide at the end (as he tries to at the beginning).
Despite his anxieties about the firm's credibility, and despite the arguments with
Liveright the previous year, Ford was able to write a tolerant and tactful reply—
perhaps because Long had written as a reader and critic, who cared about the art of the
book, rather than as merely its merchandiser:

My dear Long,
   I am flattered indeed that you and your friends should have taken Henry Martin so
seriously [. . .] You see the RASH ACT is the beginning of a trilogy that is meant to do for the
post-war world and the Crisis what the TIETJENS tetralogy did for the war. It is to give the
years of crisis from the point of view of a central character, as SOME DO NOT and NO MORE
PARADES gave the war from the point of view of Tietjens. Now the chief characteristic of these
years is want of courage—physical and moral. We are in the miserable pickle that we are in
simply because *no one* has the courage either to spend money, commit suicide or anything
else. Henry Martin is the typical man of this period [. . .] *His* tragedy is that whatever he
does—whatever feeble action he commits himself to—he always finds himself in exactly the
same situation.[5]

The contract with Long and Smith gave him the security to write *The Rash Act*, his
best novel of the 1930s. When he was asked by *Harper's* magazine for a series of articles
he was able to tell Bradley he would only accept if he were paid in advance, and could
write on whatever he wanted. What he really wanted to work on was his new novels
and the *History*. He told Bradley, crossly: 'You do not seem to realize that as soon as
I had finished the novel I began working on the History [. . .] Still I suppose people
can't get used to the fact that I am rather industrious.' He no longer felt he had the
time to spend on ephemera, good though his journalistic pieces could be. Nevertheless, he did suggest a compromise to Bradley: 'I have long wanted to write a sort of
book of travel going over again the not very extensive but quite interesting territory
round which I have *patauged* [splashed] for the greater part of my life, getting their
atmosphere all over again as the phrase use[d] to be':

This would make a book rather than a series of articles but if [Hartman of *Harper's*] would
like to use the separate chapters as articles I shouldn't mind. They would probably turn out
to be something that he liked because my method being anecdotal and, as far as I can see, my
stock of anecdotes being inexhaustible he would be getting something like separate units in
another book of reminiscences centered round places rather than chronologically and in any
case containing a good deal about cookery. What I should propose to treat of starting from the
East, would be Rome and Naples in one chapter, the Italian and French Rivieras in another,

Provence around Tarascon and Avignon in a third, Paris a fourth, Strasbourg and the Moselle Country in a fifth, the Rhineland in a sixth, London and the South of England in a seventh, New York in the eighth and the country from Philadelphia to Clarksville, Tennessee in the ninth.[6]

He continued propagandizing to help *les jeunes*. He was gathering promising new manuscripts to show to Long and Smith. In January he had written an introduction to a new edition of Hemingway's *A Farewell to Arms*, praising the 'discipline' that let Hemingway be 'remorselessly economical' in the use of words:

The curse of English prose is that English words have double effects. They have their literal meanings and then associations they attain from the writers that have used them. These associations as often as not come from the Authorised Version or the Book of Common Prayer. You use a combination of words once used by Archbishop Cranmer or Archbishop Warham or the Translators in the XVI & XVII centuries. You expect to get from them an overtone of awfulness, or erudition or romance or pomposity. So your prose dies.[7]

The whole essay is one of Ford's most detailed investigations into the effects of reading; and as here is suggestive not only about what Hemingway excludes to give his prose its ahistorical freshness, but also about Ford's more difficult challenge: his attempt to use language *with* its manifold historical associations, and stay alive.

He followed up these ideas in an essay on Pound's *How to Read*, arguing that Pound was the major poet of the age, because he could sustain interest over long poems. But he complained that it was this very question of *architectonics* that Pound's treatise glossed over. 'HOW TO READ is thus an induction into frames of mind rather than a literary text book.' As much should be said for all Ford's critical writing, including this review, which includes some of his most suggestive remarks about both the texture and structure of prose, while humouring Pound by explaining his obscurities and rectifying his omissions. He commended Pound's commendation of Flaubert, saying that 'in his precepts almost as much as in his work, practically all that is known of the texture of writing is embodied'. Ford's own formulation of what matters in the texture of writing is a classic modernist analysis, which, while it uses a new image from painting, is alive with how verbal style involves so much more than the purely pictorial:

Writing as it today is practised is—consciously or unconsciously—a sort of *pointillisme*. You put point beside point, each point crepitating against all that surrounds it. That is what Ezra means by 'charged' words. They are such as find electricity by f[r]iction with their neighbours. That was the Flaubertian device [. . .] he perceived that words following slumberously—obviously—the one the other let the reader's attention wander.

It is thus that Ford's style renders the ideas, attitudes, and mannerisms of his own time. Which is what Pound's reiterated objections that Fordian impressionism was 'of the eye' kept missing. It is thus, too, that Ford tactfully rebuffs Pound's criticism of his *idées reçues* by showing how, in the miniature plots of syntax, word against word, the ideas he marshals are critically 'rendered': *held* in such a way as to be *seen*. It's what Pound meant by 'logopoeia': 'the dance of the intellect among words.'[8]

Ford continues his review by moving to the more complex questions of structure. 'It is when you come to the larger aspect of the conjunction of phrase with phrase, sentence with sentence, paragraph with paragraph that the matter becomes more obscure':

That is finally the tyranny of the subject—of the idea. In that too Flaubert codified—clarified—matters for us. The whole of BOUVARD ET PECUCHET, as of MADAME BOVARY and EDUCATION SENTIMENTALE, is one long protest against ideas following one on the other slumberously. He evolved the doctrine of surprise. The whole province of art is to interest, and interest is made to exist by a continual crepitation of surprise, minute or overwhelming.[9]

The matter becomes obscure because in a work as long as a novel, the relationships between words, phrases, sentences, paragraphs, and chapters become too complex—too numerous—to attend to. And yet it is our subliminal, intuitive, response to these things that gives us a sense of a work's tones and effects. And it is precisely in this matter of what Pound called 'preparing effects' (and which he found tiresome in impressionist prose) that Ford excelled. Ford's 'ideas' (Tory feudalism, the 'great trade route', Catholicism, Englishness) need to be understood in this fundamentally Symbolist way, as elements composed into surprising sequences, rather than as propaganda for intellectual positions.[10]

Stella Bowen had been hit hard by the fall of the franc against the pound: the little capital of hers that the *transatlantic* hadn't swallowed was no longer producing enough interest for her to keep out of debt. Ford and Biala let her stay at the Villa Paul with Julie, so she could sublet her London studio and live on the proceeds. This meant Ford and Biala had to live in Paris at 32 rue de Vaugirard. But Paris was more expensive, and he told Caroline Gordon that T. R. Smith (of Liveright) was not paying him what his books were earning. So, before the payments from Long and Smith started arriving, they were 'short of food, sometimes for longish periods'. When Bowen's American friends Ramon Guthrie and Carl van Doren wrote that they had got her portrait commissions in America—enough to pay for her voyage and more—she decided to leave. She sailed at Easter 1932, leaving Julie with their 'aristocratic French neighbours' at the Villa Paul until Ford and Biala could return to look after her. They set off after they had let their Paris flat to Katherine Anne Porter and her husband Eugene Pressly. Porter had met Ford through the Tates in New York, and though she disliked his 'pompous English manner' she said she enjoyed spending time with him; and, her biographer suggests, she realized Ford might be useful to her. In Paris he was, suggesting that she should translate some French songs for Harrison of Paris—a small firm run by Barbara Harrison and Monroe Wheeler. But Ford annoyed her by involving her in the problems of trying to sublet their Paris flat. 'She told Pressly that Ford had been her *bête noire* since she arrived and that she had been interviewed five times about the apartment. Each time the Fords reduced the rent until finally they offered to let her have it free.' When she objected, he irritated her even more by telling her 'very irritably' that it was 'notorious that she did not know how to manage her life and should be taken care of'. While that explains his motive for interfering, it also shows how his patronage of the young could provoke their animosity. But Porter dissembled her resentment to Ford and took the flat anyway, to be further outraged when he told her that the Tates were arriving in July, and that without consulting any of them he expected them to share the flat. It was an understandable idea, since she was living in the same block as the Tates when they met; but it 'foreshadowed the kinds of disagreements which caused Porter's final break with Ford and Biala'. Meanwhile, they lent her money. Porter gave the Tates a marvellous impression of Biala:

Janice is a little creature, thin, young and too much acquainted with hardship and trouble for her years, abrupt, courageous and baffled. Very mature in her feelings, uniformed, full of Jewish melancholy. She gave me a lovely painting of a tawny cat, and I bought a golden portrait of Julie in a straw hat for three hundred francs. She is nearly always good and when she is at her best is a really serious good painter . . . She hasn't an atom of frivolity in her, but a very caustic and clever humor. She does the most amusing sketches of Ford I ever saw . . .[11]

In the spring of 1932 Ford and Biala headed for Toulon. The payments from Long and Smith meant that for the first time in their life together they didn't have to worry about money. Ford said it was to provide him with 'a long, long holiday and afterwards a long, long rest. So it was rather precious beyond most moneys.' But his American friends (the Bradleys?) had advised him not to pay it into his American bank. He turned it into francs, and entrusted it to Biala, saying of himself: 'I am constitutionally incapable of not losing money.' When they got as far as Tarascon, Ford had himself 'shaved and perfumed with orange-flower water', and they set out 'through the roaring arcades of the market', getting blown down to the castle by the Mistral ('It is not a wind. It is force that overwhelms a whole country, pushing, dragging, thundering, panting—towards the Sahara. It will overset stone carts and carry uprooted oak trees half across a country'):

And leaning back on the wind as if on an up-ended couch I clutched my béret and roared with laughter. . . . We were just under the great wall that keeps out the intolerably swift Rhone. . . . Our treasurer's cap was flying in the air. . . . Over, into the Rhone. . . . What glorious fun. . . . The mistral sure is the wine of life. . . . Our treasurer's wallet was flying from under an armpit beyond reach of a clutching hand. . . . Incredible humour; unparalleled buffoonery of a wind. . . . The air was full of little, capricious squares, floating black against the light over the river. . . . Like a swarm of bees: thick. . . . Good fellows, bees. . . .
    And then began a delirious, panicked search. . . . For notes, for passports, for first citizenship papers that were halfway to Marseilles before it ended. . . . An endless search. . . . With still the feeling that one was rich. . . . Very rich.[12]

'I hadn't been going to do any writing for a year', mused Ford, recognizing what an unlikely prospect it was: 'But perhaps the remorseless Destiny of Provence desires thus to afflict the world with my books. . . .' Nevertheless, the wry cynicism of this afterthought (which is the closing flourish of this hilarious finale of his beautiful book on *Provence*) didn't detract from the carnivalesque enjoyment of the scene of his catastrophe. 'Ford was amused for months at the thought that some astonished housewife cleaning fish might have found a thousand-franc note in its belly.'[13]

It may have been that summer at Toulon that Ford had another of the near escapes that seemed his fate and his forte. Julie recalled how on an expedition to buy her espadrilles 'Ford slipped and fell' between the front and back wheels of a big lorry: 'in the endless second, while the truckdriver slammed on his brakes, from somewhere beneath the vehicle, came this perfectly calm British voice remarking conversationally,

"Now, Saint Christopher, here's your chance!"' His sleeve was pinned down by one of the rear wheels, but his arm was unhurt.[14]

At the Villa Paul Ford was 'working at—or rather working up' the *History*, which he assured Ray Long was getting 'considerably shorter and crisper'. He had a new secretary to help him: Richard Murphy, 'a young Greenwich Village novelist as yet unpublished', who, said Ford, 'never learned how to write and has hacked both my machine and his own'. Murphy often went to visit Samuel Putnam, who was staying in Willie Seabrook's and Marjorie Worthington's villa on the other side of Sanary. But he had to be back by dusk to feed the chickens, 'for that was a sizable part of his secretarial function'. Murphy told Putnam he 'had undertaken to explain to Mr. Ford the phenomenon of Oscar Wilde'. But Ford gave an answer worthy of Queen Victoria: 'I don't care to hear about it', brushing the idea aside: 'I know that such things are rumored, but I am sure that they do not exist!' This was somewhat histrionic, since he knew many homosexuals through Bowen, who, said Biala, 'patronized a number of them'. Ford 'couldn't bear them—though he did his best when they were good writers, like Glenway Westcott'. But Murphy and his homosexuality had become a burden. 'I'm frightfully sorry you have this situation on your neck', sympathized Katherine Anne Porter, demonstrating a prejudice that puts Ford's unease in perspective, and also shows that even her dead friends were not safe from epistolary back-stabbing:

I used to have no prejudice against perverts, or furnish your own word if that's too harsh, but I do have now, if any conviction founded on experience should be called prejudice [. . .] Hart Crane finished the last of my sympathies in that direction: I suppose you heard he jumped overboard the Orizaba between Cuba and New York. . . . I think it was well done. . . . The only suicide I have ever known that I approved of most thoroughly.

Murphy next attempted 'an initiation into Ronald Firbank, but this likewise failed to take'. His days were numbered. One day Ford asked his secretary to climb a tree to see if the figs were ripe. 'In the first place', said Murphy, 'I can't climb trees; and in the second place, I shouldn't know a ripe fig if I saw one.' 'You wouldn't know a ripe fig!', blustered Ford: 'Well, I—er—I—simply can't have a secretary who doesn't know ripe figs!'[15]

Bowen's three-month stay in America stretched into six months. Julie went to Normandy to stay with the Marcoussis, whose daughter Madeleine was her best friend. Ford and Biala got a new cat, black with green eyes, that summer. Biala, always a cat-lover, told Julie they called him Shalamis, 'parce que je crois qu'il est juif'. At the end of July Ford and Biala left for a trip that he wrote up for one of the *Harper's* articles, 'I Revisit the Riviera', in which his present impressions of the Italian Riviera and the French Côte d'Azur return him to the yesterday of his previous visits. They saw Pound at Rapallo early in August; not only could they afford to travel, but they paid back his loans. Ford and Pound had their photograph taken standing beneath the statue to Columbus. Ford told Ray Long:

Columbus landed in Rapallo after committing his indiscretion. Your publicity people might be able to make something allegorical out of that—I don't quite see what. Ezra, at any rate, is the greatest poet the new world has ever sent to the old. Columbus was presumably the greatest explorer the old world ever sent to the new. I don't know quite where I come in but you might get one of your people to work it out.[16]

Pound wrote up a slapstick discussion with Ford as an interview for the Rapallo paper *Il Mare* (the style of which anticipates Beckett's 'Three Dialogues with Georges Duthuit'). It describes Ford as the 'grandfather of contemporary English literature', and says 'We were present when his friend Pound attacked him, verbally':

Pound: What are the most important qualities in a prose writer?
Ford: What does 'prose writer' mean? The Napoleonic Code or the Canticle of Canticles?
Pound: Let us say a novelist.
Ford: (In Agony) Oh Hell! Say philosophical grounding, a knowledge of words' roots, of the meaning of words.
Pound: What should a young prose writer do first?
Ford: (More and more annoyed at the inquisition) Brush his teeth.
Pound: (Ironically calm, with serene magniloquence) In the vast critical output of the illustrious critic now being interviewed (changing tone) . . . You have praised writer after writer with no apparent distinction (stressing the word 'apparent' nearly with rage). Is there any?
Ford: There are authentic writers and imitation writers; there is no difference among the authentic ones.[17]

Pound added an editor's note: 'Pestered the next day as to what a young writer ought to read, Ford groaned: "Let him get a DICTIONARY and learn the meaning of words."' Pound was to recall this in his Canto XCVIII: 'And as Ford said: get a dictionary | and learn the meaning of words.' One reason Ford deserved an honourable mention there was that throughout the summer of 1932 he worked hard trying to publicize *A Draft of XXX Cantos*. He persuaded Hemingway, Eliot, Joyce, Hugh Walpole, Archibald MacLeish, Edmund Wilson, William Carlos Williams, Allen Tate, Basil Bunting, H.D., John Peale Bishop, and others to contribute 'testimonials' to Pound's poetry. Ford added one himself, together with an editorial note signed 'D.C.'—presumably 'Daniel Chaucer'—in which, perhaps returning the ironic compliment of Pound's Rapallo interview, he said that for a quarter of a century Pound had been 'not merely a Pride's Purge but an undeviatingly guiding light and an unparalleledly stimulating irritant'. *The Cantos of Ezra Pound: Some Testimonials* was published by Farrar and Rinehart in 1933, and sent out with their American edition of the poems. 'Thanks for the abundant wreathes', said Pound.[18]

Ford and Biala were back in Toulon in early August 1932. In the middle of the month the Tates arrived with Sally Wood. Ford 'behaved badly' according to Tate, by wanting them all to stay at the Villa Paul, but they found it 'impossible to sleep or work', so Tate at last 'won the battle, and got away' to the Villa Les Hortensias they rented nearby. 'Now, you're not likely to fall in love with Ford', Gordon had reassured Wood: 'and I for one will be rather pleased if he falls in love with you.' They met every night, either at each other's villa, or at a restaurant. 'The talk was constantly about novel writing', recalled Wood. 'Referring to Galsworthy as "poor Jack," Ford said he was only interested in country weekends where the host gave all his guests candles to go up to bed.' Wood says that 'Ford was highly regarded by the French because he considered the balanced sentence, the sound of words and phrases, important'. Under

Ford's influence, Allen Tate began writing a novel, 'Ancestors in Exile', which he never finished, but parts of which went into his Fordian only novel, *The Fathers* (1938). When they went swimming, Ford warned them that it was a *plage populaire*, and that they would catch germs from the people who went there. It was an uncharacteristic piece of social fastidiousness: perhaps he was teasing the patrician Southerners? Wood's reminiscence of one outing shows how ancestry and exile was on all their minds:

Ford received an invitation from someone he called 'the hope of British painting,' Sir Francis Rose, to visit him in a village above Cagnes. He naturally wished to take Janice and the Tates, and Caroline decided that we should all go [. . .] Not being used to England, I did not realize at first that Rose's Lime Juice played a part; the connection became clearer when we realized we were also staying with a Guinness, married to a South American painter, and then met Miss Hennessey. It became a special milieu. The Spanish painter, Picabia, arrived the following day, very talkative. But the special guest that evening, besides Ford, was a Bourbon, who had some rather distant hope of the French throne, and his much older wife. When she turned out to be a Hapsburg, Ford simply withdrew. Caroline said, 'Look at him. He thinks you mustn't talk to a Hapsburg.' This ancestral scruple left the old lady alone, for the younger people were amusing themselves elsewhere, but Caroline and Allen, whose southern manners made them take quite the opposite view, leapt into the breach.[19]

Before the war Ford had told Alice Toklas the story of being followed in France for his resemblance to the Bourbon claimant. That story was already the germ for his novel of 1936, *Vive Le Roy*, in which an American replaces his double the king. But the appearance of an actual Bourbon claimant doubtless reminded him of the subject, and may have prompted the writing of the novel.

The Fords also took their visitors on a memorable expedition to one of the *calanques*, or narrow creeks on the coast near Cassis, for a rehearsal of a *pastorale*. Ford was impressed by these popular romances, specimens of 'a living art' rather than 'a mere survival'. The most famous is the story of Aucassin and Nicolette, but 'the peasantry and labourers and small tradesmen of the villages of Provence continue to make up these pieces or to modify old ones'. He said he was invited not as *poète* but because of his 'local reputation as a chef who can dispute as to the correct preparation of *bouillabaisse* through a whole afternoon and far into the evening'. A party of about twenty people went in small fishing boats. The rehearsal was indeed accompanied by what he called 'a Homeric banquet', cooked 'in immense caldrons on the beach over leaping fires of dead wood from trees and driftwood from the water':

The place was unimaginable unless you had seen it. Try then to figure for yourself blood-red cliffs into which a blue, shining mirror should have introduced itself for miles—a fjord of the Mediterranean, a beach only to be approached in boats, with the dark green, red-trunked stone- and umbrella-pines, the multi-coloured boats grouped at the landing, the incredible blue of the sky, the incredible whiteness of the light, the ten-foot flames beneath the cauldrons but pale beneath the sun. And beneath the surface of the mirror the shoals of vermilion, of ultramarine, of amethyst fishes—and octopuses darting, like closed parasols, through the waving groves of the algae. . . .[20]

The point of his recollection is not only to 'make us see' the scene in this virtuoso piece of scintillating impressionism (though his description deserves to be read in full). As he explains in *Provence*, 'What brings it into the story here' is that Tate, 'being at that banquet on the shore of the sea of Virgil, went home and wrote his noble poem ['The Mediterranean'] having for its inspiration how the Trojans, landing on those shores, feasted beside the sea'. What this modestly doesn't mention, but Tate's pedestrian account does, is that the inspiration came from Ford, saying to him during the seven-or-eight-hour dinner: 'In a cove like this the refugees from Troy must have stopped many times to eat and rest, and in such a place the Harpies must have descended upon Aeneas and his followers.' Tate was remembering the conversation after nearly thirty years; but those 'must have's sound authentically Fordian. They reveal his affinity with Classical writers like Virgil, who becomes an impressionist historian of culture (as Ford was), incorporating mythological fictions such as the Harpies into his legendary narrative of the founding of a real city, Rome. It's not just that Ford's books like *Provence* proceed by comparable fusions of history and fantasy. It's what he was also doing even during the feast itself, wanting to people the landscape from the literary past. MacShane says the expedition provides insight into 'Ford's sense of pleasure at simple things', and 'more importantly, the sense of tradition and history he attached to ordinary events in Provence'. Both points are true (though the things like *bouilla-baisse* or Provençal history are not simple), but they need to be combined. As in the memorial inscription to the Roman dancer in *The Rash Act*—'SALTAVIT. PLACUIT. MORTUUS EST.'—Ford's 'sense of pleasure' is inextricable from art and culture, 'tradition and history'. He was a cultural hedonist, for whom an exceptional meal was given significance by a critical attitude to the techniques of *bouillabaisse*, and an imagining of the literary associations of the scene. Art gives pleasure, and pleasure has its aesthetic aspect.[21]

They were back at the Villa Paul early in August. After William and Jenny Bradley came to stay, Bradley told Ford: 'It was nice to see you in your own garden', adding: 'and I think you have never seemed to me quite so much at home anywhere else—not even in New York!' While asking Carl Van Doren for a testimonial about Pound, Ford told him: 'I hope you prosper. I do, for a change. I am just publishing a novel which I think is my best because I have had ample leisure and propitious circumstances in which to write it and I am just finishing the first volume of my HISTORY OF OUR OWN TIMES which ought to be out next spring.' But the idyll was shattered that August by 'an extraordinary piece of news' from Bradley: 'Ray Long, who had gone to California to rest, was so upset there by the death of one of his oldest and best friends, that he decided he had need of a complete change of air and scene and set sail at once for the South Seas! He said he would be back in about two months, but Smith is still without an exact date for his return. There is a publisher for you!' By the following January the story had changed: Ford had told Caroline Gordon that Long had 'eloped to the South Seas with his stenographer and fifty thousand dollars of the firm's money'. It was a disastrous development for Ford, leaving him at the mercy of Smith, who disapproved of the contract Long had given him. The publication of *The Rash Act* was delayed until 24 February 1933, which meant that it came out ten days before Roosevelt closed the banks. Ford told Pound it had 'naturally been absolutely submerged'. Worse still, once more he was having a book published by a firm that had lost confidence in him, and which was trying to wriggle out of any further obligations. If Smith could have done anything to sell the book despite the worsening Depression, he wasn't inclined to. The novel wasn't as widely reviewed as Ford's recent books, and few of the reviews were enthusiastic, several complaining once again at lapses in Ford's grasp of American language and life. Smith had rejected the *History* in December, when Long was still away, having effectively gone into retirement; and he explained to Bradley that he presumed Ford would try to find another publisher, adding: 'frankly, there are very few novelists, even among those best established, who can expect such advances these days.' The monthly advances of $200 from Long and Smith stopped in March 1933. He now had Stella's 'complete penniless' to worry about, and had again to turn to Pound for a loan.[22]

Soon after Ray Long's disappearance, Ford and Biala set off for Germany. Ford wrote another essay for *Harper's* about revisiting the Rhineland that he had come to know so well in 1904 and 1910–11. Biala has told how one of the 'Extravagant things' that happened to him happened when they reached Paris:

The house we lived in on the rue Vaugirard was to be torn down. Everybody was asked to pay their taxes by a certain date—months before they would normally be due—and move out. This was very inconvenient. We were about to leave for Germany. There was no time and no money to do both. A choice had to be made. Germany won. The apartment—with literally everything it contained—was left to the tax collector. Not a saucepan, not a dish, absolutely nothing was taken out, just a four-dollar easel. I might add that the furniture—all Louis XIII or Louis XV—in that apartment would bring fabulous prices today; like Tietjens, Ford knew furniture.[23]

They visited Cologne, Boppard, Coblenz, Worms, Mainz, Strasbourg; and spent two days with Katherine Anne Porter, who was staying (at the Krafft Hotel) in Basel, where Pressly had been posted. Allen Tate, like many of Porter's friends, noticed a change in her this year. 'She has become a great personage', encouraged by Westcott and Wheeler, who 'were not in the least self-conscious about seeming affected or precious'. Her new hauteur is evident in the notes she made about the Fords' visit:

they were both in better spirits and were so pleasant my rage and fury and uncharitableness towards them vanished. I had hoped never to see them again, but now I feel rather friendly towards them; mostly towards Ford, who is after all just what he is: but Janice is a 'little soul' no doubt about it [. . .] petty and small grained and incapable of growth. But something touching, too, in that dryness and thirstiness and little sharp-edged nervousness. She has the kind of eye that can pick out every smallest fleck on the surface, but sees nothing of the whole design, nor of anything underneath. During the two days they were here, literally I never heard her speak one decently perceptive or friendly thing about one living being. . . . It would end by annoying me if I had to stay around her but blessedly I do not.[24]

Biala was dumbfounded when she later discovered the hypocrisy of Porter's friendliness. Porter's warm, friendly, gossipy letters to them gave the very different impression that on paper she was one of their closest friends of the early 1930s. However, the portrait Biala was painting of her the following year suggested that she had seen the flecks in Porter's surface, betraying the hardness under the aristocratic pose. Caroline Gordon said she and Tate called it—privately: 'Battling Porter. A stout, washerwomanish woman sitting in a corner, her mitts poised almost as if for action. If there were only another figure with a sponge and a towel it would be perfect.' Ford told Hugh Walpole about their German trip: 'the weather was cold and the state of things depressing'—Nazi rallies were becoming more widespread—'so we did not get much out of it'.[25]

In the first week of November he cut off the top of his left thumb with a sickle. The shock of the accident, the collapse of his contract with Long and Smith, and their delay in publishing *The Rash Act* (which meant Ford had no book out that year), and then news that Julie had been ill, left him feeling morbid. When he wrote to Stella before Christmas, he discussed his will, saying: 'I have not been well for quite a time and having entered one's sixtieth year makes me think of the future. I got a good deal of shock when I cut the end off my thumb and do not seem to make much recovery.'[26]

Ford told Stella he was looking forward 'rather with dread' to the Christmas festivities at Toulon in 1932: 'we know too many people here by now, though some of them are nice.' He sent Stella 100 francs (there were then 124 francs to the pound) as Julie's Christmas present: 'The money will serve for pocket money but do ask her to spend a little of it on someone else or on charity. I think it really desirable to inculcate in her a little thoughtfulness for others. Tell her I will write to her when she writes to me. Perhaps she could find some poor French person and give them a little. I will of course make it up to her.' His dread was increased by the prospect of Richard Smith suspending his firm's payments, and telling Ford he could sue Long if he cared to. 'Ford, faced with privation, has got very hoity-toity—poor devil', said Caroline Gordon: 'Janice told K[atherine]. A[nne] Porter]. He walks the floor at night and pictures Julie starving. It is at times like these that it is very difficult for his friends to rally round him.' A remark of Biala's suggests that part of his anxiety may have been to do with wanting to have another child, but feeling they couldn't afford it: 'People rush around having children', she told Gordon, 'and then their friends have to support them. I would not feel that I could afford a child.' No matter how poor Ford was, he was always contriving charity for others. Soon after getting back to Paris, he was trying to arrange support for Caroline Gordon and Allen Tate. He and Biala arranged a wedding reception for Porter and Eugene Pressly, who had come back to Paris, where Pressly had been given a permanent post in November, and who were to be married on 18 March, with Ford as the best man, as well as a witness together with Biala. Biala sang 'Safe in the Harbor of Marriage' all morning ('No Safe Harbor' was to become the working title for Porter's *Ship of Fools*); Julie was a bridesmaid, and brought along a bouquet of heather. After the ceremony they went to a café and drank champagne on the terrace in the midday sun. Roosevelt closed the banks on 6 March, but the party had to go ahead: the invitations had been sent out. Ford was exhausted from working on *It Was the Nightingale*: 'having worked too hard and too long I was in Paris and in desperate need of a long holiday. . . . Well, no one in Paris had any money. . . . We had to give a wedding reception [. . .] on frs 60 *pour tout potage*. And the whole, largish number of Americans who came could not muster frs 75 between them. It was amusing . . . but also a little tiring. . . . Or maybe I was too tired already.'[27]

About twenty-five people came to the party at the Fords' studio that evening, and danced until three, 'sometimes in the courtyard under a full white moon'. This new studio was at 37 rue Denfert-Rochereau, in the 5th Arrondissement, opposite the Bal

Bullier. 'Ground floor with Soupente [loft] f 450—but no comfort', as Ford explained to Pound: 'Gas but no water and outside W.C.' He used it as the model for Cassie's studio in *Vive Le Roy*. The Tates had stayed with them before returning to America in January. Ford signed a contract with Lippincott for *It Was the Nightingale*, but had to borrow money from Pound again until their first payment arrived. 'GORR dem it!!!', replied Pound, who wasn't much better off himself; but he obliged, adding: 'aint life just wonnerful.' Ford had said: 'I *ought* to have plenty of money for there is plenty of demand for my writing in your country—but it does not work out that way.' 'We all OUGHT to have plenty of money', snapped Pound: 'I have thought so for twenty years.' Though they could agree this far on the economics of art, as they could about its economy, Ford was not impressed by Pound's ventures into economic thought—his infatuation with Mussolini's dictatorship and with Major C. H. Douglas's theory of Social Credit. When Faber sent him a copy of Pound's *ABC of Economics* he replied: 'I am obliged to you for sending me Mr. Pound's ABC but I am afraid I cannot write about them [*sic*]. I do not think I could write about economics even if you gave me a £1,000, though after that I might be able to write a short note about extravagance. If you were publishing Mr. Pound's Cantos it would be different. I would write volumes for you for nothing.'[28] Hitler became Chancellor of Germany on 30 January 1933. When Dreiser asked Ford for a piece for the *American Spectator*, he was unenthusiastic: 'I simply can't write anything short, try as I may'; but in a postscript he asked: 'Do you suppose you would like a little [article] about the state of Jewry, which in Europe has become pretty parlous with the arrival of Hitler and the closing of Palestine? I was a little responsible for the Balfour Declaration and have for a long time wanted to write something about Zionism.'[29] At the end of March the money finally came through from Lippincott. He repaid Pound; and on 1 April they returned to Toulon, handing over the flat to an American painter called Peter Blume. Back at the Villa Paul, Ford continued campaigning on Pound's behalf, trying to find an English publisher for the *Cantos*, and putting him in touch with a publisher who wanted Pound to translate *The Odyssey*.[30]

Bowen could no longer afford to live in Paris. On 16 May she sailed reluctantly to England, having installed Julie—now 12—in a *pension de famille* so that she could finish the school year at the École Alsacienne. At midnight, feeling desolate in the third-class women's cabin, 'listening to the creaking timbers of the vessel', Bowen remembered that it was her fortieth birthday. Ford was sad, not only because he would see Julie less often, but because, as he explained to Caroline Gordon: 'I should have preferred Julie never to learn English and certainly not to go to an English school and become the usual English hobbledehoy.' She rarely wrote to him, and he couldn't keep his bitterness out of his letters to her from this time, in which his love is inflected with the kind of sardonic hauteur Francis Hueffer might have used when he called Ford the patient but extremely stupid donkey:

Dearest Julie;
    This time I am going to write t[o] you in English because it seems rather ridiculous that you should have a father who is an English author and yet expect him to write to you in another language.
    I was very glad to get your letter. It was high time you wrote. Do you know that I have only

had one letter from you since we left Paris? That is not right because you must know that I should be anxious about you considering that you are living with strangers.

I am glad you are doing better at school this term. It is certainly astonishing that you should be first in orthography at school. Your companions must be amazingly bad for I never saw so many faults in French as there were in your last letter [. . .]

I finished my book [*It Was the Nightingale*] yesterday and now I am going to take a rest. This is how I take my rest. I got up this morning at five. Then I washed up till seven. Then I watered the garden till ten. Then I made the breakfast. Then I breakfasted. Then I worked in the garden till twelve. Then I put the lunch on to cook. Then I took a bath—and so did Janice. Then we had lunch. After that I lay down on my bed and tried to improve my mind, reading articles about the political situation in the Pacific Ocean—but it was rather difficult because Janice insisted on reading aloud passages from the life and letters of Gaugin, the artist [. . .]

Good bye little—or rather large—monster. I send you many kisses too and am always the ageing—not to say aged—father who loves you.[31]

He wrote parts of this letter in French, telling her that it was because he wanted her to understand them. When he wrote later for her birthday he used French again, in order to tell her he regretted *horriblement* that she was in London, and urging her not to forget her French education—not least because if, as he hoped, she were to develop any literary ambitions, she would have the possibility of becoming a French poet.[32]

Ford asked Stella to place *It Was the Nightingale* in England. This may have been because he was still angry with Bradley over the débâcle with Long and Smith: when he heard that the firm had filed a petition for bankruptcy, he must have thought that his original doubts about them (which Bradley had reproved him for) had been vindicated. None the less, he had used Bradley to deal with Lippincott; he may just have felt that Stella, who was to get the English royalties of the book, would be able to get better terms. He got angrier with Bradley throughout the year, partly because Bradley tended to patronize when trying to reassure Ford or remind him what he had agreed with publishers. When Ford wrote that he feared they had been 'spoofed' by Smith, Bradley replied: 'The fact remains, whether we were "spoofed" or not by these people, we got from them an advance of nearly $2,000 for a book which has sold little more than 1,000 copies.' Mizener calls this an 'unfortunately jaunty remark', but it is not surprising that Ford was infuriated by the implications that the book wasn't *worth* $2,000; that if it had only sold 1,000 copies it was Ford's fault, not his publishers; and that therefore Ford could consider himself to have tricked *them*. He wrote a haughty reply, patronizing back in his grandest manner, complaining that Bradley wrote like 'a person openly hostile' to Ford's interests, and reminding him that the $2,000 was supposed to cover the *History* as well:

That I did not try to enforce legally the specific performance of [the contract to publish *A History of Our Own Times*] was due to your confirmation of Mr Smith's untrue statement [of 20 January] that his firm was on the point of bankruptcy [. . .] Yet not only are you paid, but it is your moral duty to assure yourself as to the financial soundness of the houses into contact with whom you bring your clients. Long & Smith's non-publication of the HISTORY has been ruinous to me. You must be aware of that yet no one could read into your letters and your handling of the matter anything but that your sympathies are with the defaulting publishers as against your client.[33]

Their relationship never recovered. The following year he told Bowen (via Biala) that he would not let Bradley handle any of his future work.[34]

It was a frustrating time. When Ford and Biala got back after ten days in Juan les Pins, they found that 'The drought destroyed everything in the garden except for the semi-tropical things like melons and pimento'. Another American publisher, Bobbs-Merrill, had rejected the *History* in August, having expressed interest in June. When Horace Shipp wrote to ask if he could dedicate *The Second English Review Book of Short Stories* to Ford, he replied that he didn't feel well-enough known in England to do the book any good: 'A dedication should radiate lustre on a book, not the book on the dedicatee.' Publishing in England, he said, 'is like dropping things down wells so deep that even after years of waiting no reverberation comes to the listener at the well-head'. As Bowen was deciding to leave France, Ford was writing in *It Was the Nightingale* about his realizations that he had to leave England after the war.[35]

It is a book of 'real power', though what Mizener acknowledged with this clause he took away in the next, attributing the power to 'Ford's eloquent, inaccurate vision of the England he believed had mistreated and humiliated him because he had fought in the front lines'. It's true the book draws on his feeling of England's indifference to its artists and veterans; and that, like all his post-war work, it engages with the question of what the effects of the war had been on the mind—the European mind, but also his own (which involves reimagining the paranoia, anxiety, and pathos that saturated 'True Love & a G.C.M.' and 'Mr Croyd'. Primarily, however, it's the book of a survivor, not a victim. It describes 'the staging of a literary come-back', he said. The elegiac impulse is as active as ever, stirring reminiscences of his dead friends Galsworthy and Marwood. And the decade it covers is framed by the cataclysms that dominated Ford's sense of modern history: the war and the Depression, or 'Crisis', as he called it—the known outcome that looms over the reminiscences of literary Paris in the 1920s. But the main story is of a series of rebirths: his own at Red Ford; Marwood's as Tietjens; the *English Review*'s as the *transatlantic*; the renaissance of the literary Middle West of America (including America in Paris). Its power comes rather from its celebrations; from the note of gaiety that was new in his reminiscences, but which became central to his later work.[36]

FORD'S AUTOBIOGRAPHY

[. . .] a novelist lives in his work. He stands there, the only reality in an invented world, among imaginary things, happenings, and people. Writing about them, he is only writing about himself. But the disclosure is not complete. He remains, to a certain extent, a figure behind the veil; a suspected rather than a seen presence—a movement and a voice behind the draperies of fiction.

(Joseph Conrad, 'A Familiar Preface' to A Personal Record)

There are times when I look over the various parts of my character with perplexity. I recognise that I am made up of several persons and that the person which at the moment has the upper hand will inevitably give place to another. But which is the real me? All of them or none?

(W. Somerset Maugham, A Writer's Notebook)

The real unity of an artist is his personality.

(Ford, Preface to Nathan Asch, Love in Chartres)

Novel Autobiography

The dual form of *It Was the Nightingale*, fictionalized reminiscence, is both familiar and new. *Joseph Conrad* and *Return to Yesterday* were called novels, but not autobiographies. As Ford explained in *It Was the Nightingale*, he had previously 'written reminiscences of which the main features were found in the lives of other people and in which, as well as I could, I obscured myself'. *No Enemy* had, like his novels, dealt more directly with his own experiences, but refracted through the fictional persona 'Gringoire'. The main features of *It Was the Nightingale* were also found in his own life. But here too he doesn't present the book as straightforward 'autobiography', but as a paradoxical combination of autobiography and novel. He had doubts about exactly *how* this duality should be construed. 'I am a little afraid of "autobiographical *novel*" as the subtitle', he told the publishers: 'Will it not tend to make the serious reader regard it as not a serious book?' This was itself a paradoxical joke, since he had always defined his kind of writing against the 'serious book'. *It Was the Nightingale* was published without any subtitle. But the paradox of the novelistic autobiography was given a new turn in the dedicatory letter to Eugene Pressly (who typed it out from what Ford called—with some justice!—his 'minute and indecipherable script'):

They say every man has it in him to write one good book. This then may be my one good book that you get dedicated to you. For the man's one good book will be his autobiography. This is a form I have never tried [. . .]

I have tried then to write a novel, drawing my material from my own literary age [. . .] I
have employed every wile known to me as novelist—the timeshift, the *progression d'effet*, the
adaptation of rhythms to the pace of the action.[1]

The phrase 'my own literary age' is revealingly dual. Does it refer to the age in which
he lived, or the age he has reached? The literary milieu in which he lived, or his own
literary autobiography? The uncertainty intimates how all Fordian autobiography is
exactly that: '*literary* autobiography'; the expression (as we shall see later in this
chapter) of what he called 'literary personality'. It took an honest writer, William Rose
Benét (whose wife, Eleanor Wylie, 'the beautiful poetess', told Ford they had become
engaged while reading 'On Heaven' in Central Park), to see what *It Was the Nightingale* was about: 'it is an honest book about a writer.' It doesn't only tell the story of why
he left England, how he edited the *transatlantic*, and how he visited America; it is also
the story of how he became 'Ford Madox Ford'; how he came to be the person who
wrote *Parade's End*.[2]

In saying this might be his best book because it is his autobiography, and that he has
tried to make it a novel, he contemplates the idea that it is his best *novels* that are his
truest autobiography—*The Good Soldier* and *Parade's End*. The duality is a challenge
to the tendency to forget that autobiographies are *written*, always to a degree
fictionalized; and to the unthinking assumption, upon which so much thinking about
literature is constructed, that autobiography and fiction can be kept separate. It was a
duality that had always been important to Ford's prose, but which was to become more
so during the 1930s. Perhaps 'autobiographical novel' would after all be the best
description for books like *Provence, Great Trade Route*, and *Mightier Than the Sword*.

Ford had always been aware of the autobiographical component of his fiction: '*I
never have written a book that has not by someone or other been called autobiography*', he told H. G. Wells, who had been outraged by the *Glasgow Herald*'s review
of *Tono-Bungay* as 'substantially autobiographical'. 'Please trace the *Fool* who started
this to his lair & cut his obscene throat', demanded Wells. Ford tried to mollify him
with his own autobiography: 'A Southend Paper even said that what it considered the
improper parts of my "Fifth Queen" must have been lived through by the author, as
the descriptions were so vivid. What does it matter? Why I have even been accused of
being my own grandfather [. . .].'[3]

The inaccuracy of a provincial review may not have mattered to Ford, but the
relationship between fiction and autobiography mattered much. For all its animated
persuasiveness the letter leaves open the question of *why* this case does not matter: is
it because the review is wrong, and the novel only insubstantially autobiographic; or
because it is irrelevant whether it is autobiographic or not? Ford's example of himself
is also curiously open: ostensibly he is ridiculing the reviewer who could not distinguish an improper author from his rendering of impropriety (if it is that). But he does
not actually say that, saying instead 'What does it matter?' The presumed dismissal
only serves to raise the prurient possibility that the reviewer might have been right.
Similarly, he does not deny that all his own books are autobiographical. This is partly
because he is setting himself up as an example to Wells: I don't mind, or write denials
to the papers, so neither should you. But it is also because he is aware of the degree to
which all literature is inescapably autobiographical.

What is at stake here, of course, is the definition of autobiography, and Ford's own approaches to the definition are revealing about all his work. We have seen him repeatedly reversing or intermingling the terms which are conventionally opposed: novel on the one hand, and autobiography or reminiscence on the other. When writers write about themselves they tend to *poetiser un peu*. The paradox of memory and romance was at the heart of *Romance*: the idea that memory does not simply recover the experience of the past, but actively transforms it, making seem romantic in retrospect what was frightening or painful at the time. This makes autobiography approach fiction. Ford never wrote a book—even a book of history, or biography, or reminiscence—that has not by someone or other been called fiction. Harold Loeb wrote categorically of Ford's 'inability to separate fact from fiction', which assumes both that Ford couldn't tell the difference and that others always can. Our senses of certainty, of knowledge, of literature, are founded on that opposition between fact and fiction, and the assumption of a clear demarcation between them. But where can we find the two so unequivocally demarcated? In religion? In political campaigning or the persuasive oratory of lawyers? In the histories families retell to each other? In the post-Freudian self?[4]

Many have testified to Ford's 'imaginative memory'. Most agree that his reminiscences aren't quite like anyone else's. He 'treated himself and his friends alike as literary subjects', said Lloyd Morris, 'creating an effect of authenticity'. 'He fabricated and elaborated his life as assiduously as he fabricated and elaborated his books', Herbert Gorman recalled: 'One listened to him with mouth agape and wished that if it were not all true at least fifty per cent of it might be based upon fact.' Gorman recorded some such elaborations: Liszt playing for him; Ford helping Marconi 'flash the first wireless message across the Atlantic'; James, 'tears in his eyes', running to him 'with a novelistic problem to be solved'; or the great chef Escoffier declaring: 'I could learn cooking from you, Ford.' 'They were so magnificent, these stories', said Gorman. 'One accepted the fact that Ford was a walking novel, a romance, as well as a man and that was a rather good thing to be [. . .] there are moments when the lie becomes a creation and contains a subliminal truth in itself.' Even Arthur Mizener, in 1963, had praised 'Ford's several volumes of half-fictionalized reminiscences that are often imprecise in fact but always magnificently true to the quality of the time and place they deal with'. After seven years of trying to sort the fact from the half-fiction he fell out of sympathy with his subject, and became less sanguine about the origins of Ford's drive to fictionalize. By 1971 he was calling the reminiscences 'a novel, perhaps questionable genre that is nevertheless, in Ford's hands, wonderfully entertaining'. Unfortunately this note of appreciation is largely absent from Mizener's biography, in which his own longing to believe himself properly critical often serves as an alibi for unwarranted denigration; and in which the reminiscences are treated as 'questionable' because seen as pathological. Ford himself was well aware of his imagination's restlessly transformative power; and of how it treated even his own memory as the material for fiction: 'That is how it comes back to me', he could note, as if with surprise, at his own reminiscence: 'but no doubt my memory is doing a little imagining for itself.' Allen Tate best understood the implications for the biographer of such a walking novel: 'Ford himself must be approached as a character in a novel, and that novel a novel by Ford.' Which means asking less whether what Ford said is *true*, and more what it *means*; what it expresses; how it is constructed.[5]

What words mean is inextricable from *how* they mean. What matters for Ford in autobiography is not its truth as a factual record, but its efficacy as writing: does it grip the reader through an accumulative *progression d'effet*, expressive cadences, *mots justes*? In calling his reminiscences novels he was not only emphasizing their fictionality, but their narrative discipline. 'Ford's memoirs are not mere chat', wrote Marshall McLuhan: 'The chat is a series of epiphanies of carefully considered social and literary structures and their inter penetration.' Their expressiveness as forms has generally been ignored. However, a strong version of the impressionist argument has been turned against Fordian impressionism, to say that when writing has a contempt for fact it becomes *only* autobiography: that is, Ford's reminiscences, even his critical judgements, are held by some to be of value only for what they tell us about him, rather than for what they tell of the people remembered or criticized.[6] Yet his memoirs and studies are never as egotistical or solipsistic as this implies. As this chapter will attempt to show, he is always too attentive to what his subjects are saying to force other individualities into merely reduplicating his own. It is a fundamental principle of his art that artists should not impose their own views upon, and thus distort their subjects and reduce their work to the status of propaganda. There is, however, an affinity between his interest in his reminiscences and his interest in doubles. 'I venture to obtrude this small piece of personality', he explains apropos a passage about how little he felt he had changed since his childhood, 'because it is a subject that has always interested me'—at which point he interrupts himself lest we should find him self-absorbed, explaining: 'the subject, not so much of myself, as in how far the rest of humanity seem to *themselves* to resemble me.'[7] Another kind of egotism is intimated here, in the idea that the 'rest of humanity' are concerned with whether or not they resemble him. But it is the egotism a writer needs: not just because artistic communication is founded upon a sense of human community; but also because, acutely conscious of their *difference*, artists generally crave recognition of their humanity, and acceptance of their personalities.

Impressionist poetics commit him to the view that what matters is the perceiving subject's impression rather than the factuality of the objects perceived. Fordian biography and autobiography is thus as impressionist as fiction. Impressionism is an expressive theory, since it sees the work of art as expressive of the quality of mind of the artist—in Ford's term, of the artist's 'personality'. 'The "memoir" of today', Ford had lamented in 1909, 'is a loosely strung necklace of anecdotes without, as a rule, any attempt to give a view of the subject's personality or to render the atmosphere of the world in which he lived.' He soon set about doing both when beginning his first volume of memoirs, *Ancient Lights*, the following year, whether 'the subject' were himself or his Pre-Raphaelite predecessors. Writing *A History of Our Own Times* was for him 'merely a continuation' of his 'lifelong ambition': 'to record my own time in my own terms [. . .].' 'I must therefore face with equanimity such charges of egoism as may be laid against me, impersonality being beyond my powers.' It was, by his definitions, beyond any novelist's powers, since 'If you want to be a novelist you must first be a poet and it is impossible to be a poet and lack human sympathies or generosity of outlook'; and since 'imaginative prose or literature is that writing which most reveals the personality of the author'. Such dicta might seem flatly to contradict his advocacy of the Flaubertian 'novel of Aloofness'. But he conceded that even Flaubert hadn't achieved aloofness—he was too 'fascinated' by his Emma Bovary. The point is that aiming at aloofness can check the impulses to moralism and sentimentality. There is a second sense in which it isn't a contradiction, but a paradox of aesthetics, whereby the effort to efface one's personality can be more effective, more tantalizing, more expressive, than undesired self-revelation.[8]

Literary Personality and Tone

Because a novel invents or recombines facts, and a reminiscence may transform them, the fictionality of such works prevents them from being factually autobiographic. Nevertheless, although they do not express all or only the circumstantial facts of a life, they express a living personality. It is in this sense, I think, that Ford says it does not matter whether a reader thinks a book is literally autobiographical. What does matter is the quality of mind that gets conveyed, and if the book is well written this will happen whether or not the reader thinks some of (say) *Tono-Bungay* is based on Wells's youth. It is also in this sense that Ford can say that the 'true truth' of Conrad's fiction is more important than the day-to-day factual chronicle of his anguished life; or, with astounding tautologic (and in unobtrusive blank verse): 'Conrad was Conrad because he was his books.' More explicitly, Conrad: 'was an unrivalled autobiographer—not only in his records and reminiscences but in all his writings for publication.'[9] This is characteristic of the way Ford is himself doing what he has observed someone else doing. It is a book review, one of an author's 'writings for publication' that are not novels or records or reminiscences. And what Ford says of Conrad is equally true of himself: he too is a compulsive autobiographer, even in this review, which he conducts by contrasting Jean-Aubry's belletristic portrait of Conrad with his own experience: 'Which was Conrad? The bothered, battered person who wrote innumerable, woeful, tactful, timid letters that are here, connected by a string of properly noncommittal prose, or the amazing being that I remember. With a spoken word or two he could create a whole world [. . .].' As Ford must have feared for himself (this review is driven by a fear of what literary biographers can make of *any* writer's life), his own biography has been excessively concerned with the bothered, battered person of letters—what E. M. Forster called the 'upper personality'—and not attentive enough to the deeper or 'lower' personality of the artist as expressed in his prose. Ford's critics might say of this that he is remaking Conrad in his own image. In *Joseph Conrad* he certainly presents his collaborator as something more than just like-minded—something more like his double. It would be a valid objection if all he did were to project his own personality onto his ostensible subject, effacing the personality of the other instead of himself. But that is not how his reminiscences work. As here, the fact that his comments on Conrad are also true of himself does not make them any less true of Conrad. The writing becomes an exploration of profound affinities between two very different individuals. It is a tribute to Ford's tact that even where his own touch is evident in the handling, the individuality of his subjects is preserved. It is for this reason that critics keep returning to his magnificent study of Conrad, trusting its presentation of a fellow-writer's personality even while distrusting its factual reliability (a combination which only serves to make it a more Conradian book). It gives one of the best pictures of what it is like to live a life dedicated to the novel.

What *is* this 'personality' expressed by Fordian prose? It is clearly not the man you would have met at a party. Nor, for all Forster's subtle, guarded hints of sexuality, is what he called the 'lower personality' equatable with the unconscious mind. It is not exactly the person behind the social roles and works of literature, since personality is not intelligible independently from its roles, and a writer's personality is not definable independently from the literature it produced. It is, rather, what Ford calls 'literary personality'. This phrase conveys the way a writer's personality as a writer is influenced by literature (as he was so strongly influenced—as a man as well as an artist—by Madox Brown, Conrad, and James). It also conveys how it is the personality which produces the literature; and that it is this 'literary personality' that the literature truly expresses. Since literary works are the main *events* in a writer's life, his autobiography and biography should attend to this 'literary personality'.[10]

The literary personality that has been emerging from this study is a consistently dual one: engaged participant and detached observer; at once sympathetic and ironic, private and public, subjective and objective. The books of reminiscence present Ford himself in a similar way: as both an interior self and a realized other. The formal method he develops—and which makes his reminiscences so individual and appealing, as well as so controversial—is to write books which are generically dual: at once reminiscence and novel. In the dedication of *It Was the Nightingale* he said he hadn't attempted autobiography before. 'But I have reached an age', he said—he was now in his sixtieth year—:

when the charge of vanity has no terrors as against the chance of writing one good book. It is the great woe of literature that no man can tell whether what he writes is good or not. In his vain moments he may, like Thackeray, slap his forehead and cry: 'This is genius' . . . But in the dark days when that supporter abandons him he will sink his head over his page and cry: 'What a vanity is all this!' . . . And it is the little devil in human personality that no man can tell whether he is vain or not [. . .]

I have tried then to write a novel [. . .]. (p. vi)

Characteristically, Ford's discussion of vanity and judgement becomes an example of what it discusses. Is it vain to call your autobiography a novel? Or to suggest that this will only be your true autobiography to the extent that it *is* a novel? One could see it as a ploy to evade responsibility towards factual truth, while at the same time claiming a superiority over fact: anyone can write an autobiography, but only an artist can turn an autobiography into a novel. On the other hand, it seems to me to be an exceptionally candid, intelligent consideration of the problems inherent in the genre. By making the idea that 'no man can tell whether he is vain or not' double the idea that 'no man can tell whether what he writes is good or not', Ford suggests how, for the autobiographer, whoever writes badly writes vainly; but also how if you think you are writing well, you are probably at least as vain. (Ford also knew that Thackeray's cry was doubled by Conrad's praise of 'Excellency, a few goats': so does Ford obscure his own life in the lives of others.) The disclaimer about his literary canons, too, might be a rhetorical set-piece—an excuse to mention his technical accomplishments under the guise of deprecating them. But Stella Bowen was probably right to think otherwise, giving full weight to Ford's claim that no man knows whether what he writes is good: 'he never even felt sure of his gift!'[11]

Uncertainties such as this are the chief feature of Ford's literary personality; though 'uncertainties' gives too one-sided an impression: rather, it is the play of certainty—psychological and artistic sureness—and uncertainty—about himself, his writing, the meaning of his life's events—which characterizes his writings about himself. As in his novels about imaginary people, he makes uncertainty into a positive value. 'Nobody ever wrote more about himself than Ford', said Graham Greene, 'but the figure he presented was just as dubious as his anecdotes.' The scale of his reminiscence makes it easy to mistake the risky distinctiveness of his self-presentation for undisciplined 'garrulous self-esteem'.[12] His rendering of himself is so exact that it has provoked many to character assassination—rather as his novels have incited assassination attempts upon their main characters. What has been generally overlooked is the art with which Ford has made this possible. Rather than a vain man who cannot help writing about himself, he is a writer who presents character—Ashburnham's, Tietjens's, his own—in its full contradictoriness, complexity, and uncertainty; someone about whose vanity we can never be quite sure, any more than we can ever be quite sure about Ashburnham's motives, Tietjens's paranoia, or the motives of altruists.

These uncertainties of attitude resist turning into a pose, an 'attitude' of uncertainty, through Ford's mastery of tone. For this kind of literary uncertainty is primarily a matter of tone: it is impossible to form definitive judgements of an Ashburnham, because we cannot be sure what attitude his narrator takes towards him, or expects us to take towards him; nor do we know what attitude Ford takes towards either the narrator or the character, or expects us to take towards them. In his reminiscences Ford goes back and multiplies himself. The dual figures of author and man, present remembrancer and remembered selves, are doubled within the books by Ford as both narrator and character: the narrating self and the selves narrated. How can the biography of such a person be 'definitive'? Absurdity!

If we cannot always be sure whether *The Good Soldier* is 'The Saddest Story' or 'The Roaring Joke', how in his *propriae personae* can we tell if he is in earnest? This is one of the jokes his memoirs earnestly repeat: 'Years ago, as I have elsewhere related, S. S. McClure had told me that my books would never sell in America because Americans could not tell whether I was or was not in earnest, whilst they would not sell in England because the English knew that I was too damn in earnest.'[13] The question of earnestness trips throughout *It Was the Nightingale*, which treats serious matters like recovering from the war, feeling alienated from England, writing novels, in tones oscillating between the elegiac and the slapstick. For example, Ford's decision to leave England for good is presented, with dense time-shifting and psychological depth, in terms of his literally stepping off the edge, or rather, teetering 'on the edge', of a Campden Hill kerb. After writing with mock self-reference: 'It was the passion of Germany in those days [1898] to be able to explain that every great man and especially every great artist was of Teutonic descent', he continues, sounding earnest: 'I am writing much more than half seriously' (p. 61). But how much more than half? And how much less than wholly seriously?

It is Graham Greene who most accurately defined Ford's tonal duality, writing in a review of *Provence*: 'He is an author who, like his old friend Henry James, has a personality which calls both for respect and mockery. A fine writer with traces of a most engaging charlatan [. . .] As in his fiction he writes out of a kind of hilarious depression.'[14] Ford's best critics are those who, like Greene, have recognized that his ideas and opinions, as well as his 'personality', are offered in just this dual manner. For example, his notion of a 'Great Trade Route', is one which it is rash to take too literally. It bears some relation to historical trade routes, but as the books progress, taking in all the places Ford was visiting, it becomes clear that it is the route of a personal odyssey rather than of an academic history of civilization. It is Ford's 'impression' of this history, rather than the history itself. Arguing that 'Provence is not a country nor the home of a race, but a frame of mind', he makes it clear that the significant geography of these books is the frame of his mind. It is in this sense that these books, generally thought of as travel writing, deserve to be considered as further facets of Ford's autobiography; a mapping of his mental and literary odyssey. *Great Trade Route* begins with an explicitly autobiographical casting back to the origins of his habit of cultural fantasy, and finding it at one with the mental duality which engendered his fiction:

Even as a little boy I knew that I had the trick of imagining things and that those things would be more real to me than the things that surrounded me [. . .]

With me these visions are extraordinarily vivid and persistent. There are times when I see beneath me more than a whole hemisphere stretch out from Cathay to Tennessee, shimmering in a gentle sunlight. . . . I sit thinking of nothing in particular in my New York Room. . . .

This vision of the route initiates the book, as his vision of the line materialized into *Parade's End*. (*A History of Our Own Times* begins from a similar god-like perspective: 'Let us imagine ourselves high in the air [. . .].') The limits of the route are Cathay and Memphis, Tennessee—'But not the Memphis, Tennessee, that you mean. Ah, no, it is the Memphis, Tennessee, of my childhood's imagination.'[15] The place-name caught his imagination when he saw it in an atlas, and remained suggestively confused with its Egyptian namesake. The 'Great Trade Route' is thus a literary construct, something based as much on Ford's reading as on his travelling. Its other limit may have been suggested by childhood reading too; but it is also Ezra Pound's 'Cathay': Ford's 'Cathay with the mandarins in flowered silks and jewelled stairs and gilded junks' is the world of Pound's 'Poem by the Bridge of Ten-Shin' and 'The Jewel Stairs' Grievance'.

Mizener argued that 'Ford valued highly the personal opinions he set forth in [*Provence* and *Great Trade Route*] and meant them to be taken seriously' (p. 425). But rather than taking them seriously as impressions, Mizener tried to take them seriously as opinions, claiming that 'The value of both these books frankly depends on the value of Ford's views: even their historical information is selected and arranged—and surrounded with personal anecdotes—in such a way as to make it meaningful only as an illustration of Ford's opinions' (p. 424). While he is right that the books 'are not meant to be merely entertaining', his argument that they are vitiated by idiosyncrasy comes from a refusal to grant Ford his *donnée*, the distinction between fact and impression. One should take the idea of a 'Great Trade Route' as one reviewer took the stories in *Mightier Than the Sword*: as 'humorous fantasy'; as a fiction which remains entertaining despite our suspicions about its factuality—or which becomes all the more entertaining precisely because it flouts and teases our understanding of the factual.[16] 'His opinions are not the result of a careful contemplation of the world', said Mizener; 'they are simply the play of an ingenious fancy around the places Ford liked and the activities he was interested in' (p. 425). The description is reasonably accurate (except that they are not 'simply' anything). But the implication that the books are misconceived because they are plays of fancy rather than 'a careful contemplation of the world' is simply Mizener's misconception of what Ford has attempted and achieved. The ingenious play of fancy performs a careful contemplation of himself, in his full dual combination of splendour and absurdity. One could even say that it is a fiction—one fully plotted out in *Great Trade Route*—that these books are really about Provence or the Great Trade Route. They are about Ford's mind playing upon these ideas, as one of the quotations picked out by Mizener frankly announces: 'You see, Biala addressed the New Yorker, that's how his mind works. You'd think he couldn't connect his uncle's hauling tobacco in sleds [at Lexington, Virginia], and Nîmes and Thomas Jefferson and Madeira and indigo and Charles I, all in one sentence. But he will and cite them as instances of the Route being all one civilization.' There *is* a serious aspect to the idea of the Great Trade Route, but it is characteristically oblique. The preaching—about culture, about food, about travel—to which Mizener objected is a form of pseudo-preaching: a smoke-screen of parodic sermonizing which allows the smuggling in of a subliminal import. 'What I—and civilization—most need is a place where, Truth having no divine right to glamour, experiments in thought abound.'[17] Ford's books on culture exemplify 'the frame of mind that is Provence'. They are the culmination of his conviction that literature should provoke thought rather than instruct with fact ('the province of the imaginative writer is by exaggeration due to his particular character—by characteristic exaggeration, in fact—precisely to awaken thought': exaggeration in fact?).[18] The dual attitude to preaching is at once symptom of and solution to the technical problem of how to express his views without simply succumbing to the malaise they diagnosed. For it is the babble of competing prescriptions that characterizes the 1930s—fascism, communism, Keynesianism, social credit, technocracy, agrarianism, and so on, Ford had his convictions about the menace of fascism, of industrialism, of militarism. But expressing his personality as a writer meant something other than writing ephemeral polemical tracts. How should someone who sees civilization foundering, but who mistrusts preaching, preach? As with sentimentality and romance in his novels, Ford's answer is to exaggerate the manner of preaching to the point where an extreme case is indistinguishable from parody or critique. His manner of preaching arouses scepticism. His critics say he has failed because his sociology and history are inexact, or his views unsystematic. But to engage and sustain scepticism is a significant success in a dogmatic age.

His writing doesn't advance a rigorous philosophical position or consistent social programme. But it does represent a literary ideal. The late books on culture and literature are all continuations of his long championing of the 'Republic of Letters'—a notion of human solidarity which should militate against local antagonisms of nation and race. His idea of a 'Great Trade Route' is, above all, an image for the trans-nationalism of literature; for the community of artistic intelligence which he always felt was mankind's only hope in a world of aggressive militarism.

Egotism?

When Pound pestered T. S. Eliot to publish Ford in the *Criterion*, Eliot, who had recently read *Thus to Revisit*, answered: 'the difficulty, if I asked him, would be to get some of his really best work but not simply his egotistical meanderings about his own services to English literature.'[19] The analysis is characteristically sharp. To Eliot, the advocate of 'impersonality', Ford's meanderings around his literary self were anathema. But rather than being, as Eliot implies, a failure to deny the self, they are an attempt to do something quite other: to put egotism, and its relation to writing, decidedly in the foreground. As Eliot knew, a chastening Olympian severity brought its own temptations to vanity. In William Empson's fine phrase imagining Shakespeare puzzling over how to present Hamlet's uncertainties: 'The only way to shut this hole is to make it big.'[20] That is, rather than trying to prevent vanity creeping in altogether, Ford opens out the question of vanity into something all-encompassing. Thomas Mann wrote that: 'Love for oneself is always the beginning of a novelistic life [. . .] for only when one's ego has become a task to be assumed, does writing have any meaning.' Ford's reminiscences become explorations of this intimate link between writing and the ego, as his ego becomes a task he assumes: a task of rendering, of self-understanding. (This is one way in which not knowing whether or not you are vain relates to not knowing whether or not you are a good writer. It would be vanity to think you knew.) 'He is not so much an egotist,' wrote Arthur Waugh, 'as a universal interpreter of alien egotism.'[21]

One way in which the reminiscential books reflect this concern with vanity is through their play of mirrors. The author of *A Mirror to France* often advocated impressionism as a 'mirror'. I have suggested how Ford sees something new in the cliché, realising that once the impressionist starts mirroring himself, the critical problem is to differentiate insight from narcissism. In *Return to Yesterday* Ford introduces his remembrance of Meary Walker and his other Bonnington peasant friends with a brief sketch of his own life between 1894 and 1903, adding: 'I give so much of autobiography though these are reminiscences. In that form the narrator should be a mirror, not any sort of actor, but the reader may like so much of chronology' (p. 139). It is a slightly unsettling moment, as the author steps in to tell us that he is not really 'in'—merely a chronological convenience. The dedicatory letter has introduced us to this idea of the narrator as mirror. Ford writes to Michael and Eileen Hall Lake: 'I subscribe myself your mirror to my times' (p. ix). The visual metaphor is as difficult to get one's mind around as it is deceptively simple. Ford is their mirror, but looking into this mirror, they see not themselves but *his* times. Of course, the Lakes are 'in' the dedication, which explains how the book was thought out while Ford was staying with them (in New York in September 1930). So they will see themselves in his book too.

But the impressionist scruple audible in Ford's phrasing is: how far can a reflection of 'my time' manage to efface 'me'?

The ambiguities of the mirror image are central to Ford's art. In the essay 'On Impressionism' we saw how the artist is presented as someone looking out through a window, but also seeing in the glass a reflection of the face of 'a person behind you'. This person could be a sympathetic soul. By implication it is someone sharing your room. The implied intimacy makes it possible to take this reflected face as an image of the reader. On the other hand, if the 'you' whom Ford is addressing is the reader, then the face reflected in the glass is that of the author, whose personality can be glimpsed on the printed page as the reader looks beyond the print into the envisioned world of the book. There is also a possibility of menace in the 'person behind you': it could also stand as a less sympathetic reader—a censor figure, father, literary mentor, critic, persecutor. But for the autobiographer, the person behind you is the person that you were—your past self, the subject of your book (There is a hint of unease here too: an uncanny feeling that the other might be your double; or an image of depersonalization.) At the same time, while rendering this past self, you will be expressing your 'personality', the important 'person' behind the 'you' that is caught up in the social trammels of egotism and self-dramatization. The implication here is that it is by writing and by reading that you find out who the person behind you really is; and thus you can find out who it is that you have become. Autobiography is Ford's mirror to himself. Throughout his writing it is manifest that he felt it both necessary and difficult to regard himself. 'He is not a proper man who will not look in the face his day and his time', he wrote; and he also felt that 'nothing is more difficult, nothing is more terrible than to look things in the face'.[22] The language here is fraught with the sense of anxiety coming from trying to assume responsibility for the figure you cut in the world. But there is also an undertone of disturbance at looking at your own face. Ford's autobiographies suggest a personal motive behind his critical desire for 'self-effacement': a desire to express his personality (his smile) in art, while concealing his person: his physical appearance. He was found to be both attractive and repulsive by those who knew him, and he was aware of the dual quality of his person. Much of his behaviour with women, and with words, is attributable to a desire to persuade us that he is really something quite other than he might seem—'not so dreadfully ugly, really', as Valentine tells Tietjens. Ford can be heard regarding himself as Dowell says: 'I couldn't regard myself as personally repulsive. No man can.'[23] When Ford reimagines himself as the 'fabulous monster' Tietjens, he poses his difference as the stuff of fable: what makes people talk, makes them wonder. In so far as this redeems monstrosity into marvel, it is because Ford is himself a 'fabulous monster' in another sense: someone with a strange gift for fable.[24]

His autobiographies turn himself into his voice, which entrances us, makes us see. What it makes us see is his effaced face, just as the visuality of the writing erases the language's vocality: in order to 'see', you have to forget that you are reading, listening. And yet, behind this double disavowal of his literary personality—a face you don't see, a voice you don't hear—is the supreme impressionist art, and therefore the 'personality' of the artist. Ford's own voice was expressive in this dual way, the incantatory falling drone at once impersonal and idiosyncratic. The very act of effacement testifies to the skill of the self-effacing self. Thus even at its ostensibly least autobiographic—in *The Good Soldier*, say—Ford's impressionism seeks to establish the self at the centre of its purported effacement. 'You can't see me', says the impressionist, 'but here I am.' So speaks the child's voice within the mature artist's language. Which is not to say that writing, or Ford's writing, is nothing more than a child's cry for the attentions of a dead father, of superior writers (Conrad, James) who just would not recognize his talents, or of a largely apathetic reading public. It is much more than these things, but it is one of the strengths of Fordian autobiography that he candidly confronts the origins of his creativity. 'Like most other creative artists, his personal atmosphere was always charged with a highly emotional egotism', said Stella Bowen. Ford recognized as much through the eyes of Dowell, though his words about Florence go further, suggesting both that it is not only creative artists who are prone to vanity and egotism, and that vanity need not have only negative effects: 'You see, the mainspring of her nature must have been vanity. There is no reason why it shouldn't have been; I guess it is vanity that makes most of us keep straight, if we do keep straight, in this world.'[25]

The candour is evident in the way the autobiographies reduplicate the dual effects which have helped to incite them, inviting both mockery and respect. For Flaubertian or Hudsonian self-effacement is not what Ford's writing ultimately achieves (which is where so much formalist criticism of his novels has gone awry). The very modes in which Ford makes us see—his exaggerations, implausibilities, evident fabulations, tonal complexities—all problematize not only the things seen, but the modes of seeing. Even when at his most fluent and compelling, he sows seeds of doubt, allowing us room to disbelieve our inner eyes. It is at this point that what to some critics has sounded like buttonholing charlatanry becomes difficult to distinguish from a form of tact—a respecting, even encouraging of dissentient views. His writing says 'Look at me!' less with arrogance or childlike pride, and more with surprise at what he has discovered himself to be. It creates a dual sense of authority and wondering uncertainty. 'It's really all I can do to understand myself', says Major Edward Brent Foster in Ford's lively farce of 1912, *The Panel*—a work which none the less touches on subjects that he took seriously: marriage, deception, getting enmeshed by conflicting sexual commitments, and literature (p. 128). Even Henry James is subjected to the Fordian uncertainty of attitude. Ford uses the novel's comedy to come to terms with features of his own life—his telling of white lies and the ensuing confusions; his tendency to assume James's manner. He closes scenes with Foster saying: 'So that there, in a manner of speaking, we all are'. In Mizener's excellent words, Foster: 'has, he feels, become the youngest major in the British army by reading the novels of Henry James, in which one has to work very hard to find out where the characters who are always saying, "there we all are," in fact are.'[26] The notion that literature can have this kind of effect in itself is a serious joke, but it is compounded by the fact that the very books which 'made him *see*' intellectually, have also ruined his eyesight.

'It's really all I can do to understand myself' is the exclamation of the compulsive autobiographer too, and is itself at once earnest and jokey. Is it all he can do because it is so compelling? Because it is what he most wants to do? Because it is the only thing he is fitted for? Or because it is such an endless and difficult task it does not allow time for anything else?

Working to find out 'where we all are' is another form of Ford's continual concern with what he called 'that question which has tormented me all my life—as to where we really stand'.[27] He understands with marvellous revelatory humour that 'where we stand' is inextricable from *how* we stand—alienated from England, one foot on the kerb, one out over the abyss. As embodied persons, our mental attitudes are influenced and expressed by our physical ones. Ford is a great writer about the body, and the ways we are conscious and subliminally conscious of it. His handling of this fundamental duality gives a particular character to much of his writings: an acute sensitivity to the gaps and lags between body and mind, and between conscious and subconscious minds. His baffled, often neurasthenic characters are always realizing what they have just been doing—or even thinking. As Mizener writes of Valentine Wannop, unconsciously she has 'decided to seek Christopher out at Grays Inn and to commit herself to him for life. But consciously she does not find out about that decision till some time later' (p. 498). There is often a hallucinatory sense of disjunction, blurring, being 'out of synch.' with oneself. At the risk of making himself sound unusually muddled or confused, he is unusually candid about the mental muddles and confusions and minute surprises of everyday life. In his first-person prose the same is true. He is constantly being surprised by himself, or what others tell him of himself, whether it is McClure complaining of his tones, or E. V. Lucas telling him he is not 'really' English: 'That hit me in the face like a discharge from a fireman's hose', writes Ford, not to say that the former Mr Hueffer had never considered himself to be not entirely English, but to say that it had never struck him in quite the same way, or with the same force.[28] In an autobiographical sketch written in 1936 he wrote: 'My mental autobiography could be disposed of in about twenty words': '*In my hot youth*—which wasn't really so torrid— *I yearned to be*—like Horace, Cervantes, Bunyan, and others—*both poet and soldier; having been them, I find myself to have become pacifist and prosateur* . . .'[29] 'which makes twenty-two words', adds Ford, subtracting the extra ones—the self-parodic running commentary between the italics. It is a graphic example of how he was always finding himself to have become something—in this case making the discoveries or self-redefinitions in the course of writing. It also illuminates why Fordian autobiography is interminable: it is not merely that the life continues after the books have been finished (and vice-versa), but that someone who keeps being surprised by reimagining what they have been all along is not going to reach a static sense of what they *are*: they are always finding themselves to have become someone quite other—themselves. One way in which he perpetually becomes someone quite other is through re-telling and re-inventing his reminiscences, so that his stories of the past continually transform into something quite other.

Vicarious Experience

It is Ford's 'literary personality' that his impressions express: the dual personality of a man who is also a man of letters. It is a *literary* personality in a more penetrating sense too. The point is not just that Ford writes *literary* autobiography because most of his reminiscences concern writers. It is that, for him, literature itself is a vital means of human contact. '[F]or experience of our fellow men we have to go almost entirely to books', he wrote, because it is only in 'naturalistic novels that we can hope nowadays to get any experience of modern life, save that individual and personal experience [. . .] which comes always too late.' 'The Province of Art', therefore, 'is the bringing of humanity into contact, person with person.'[30] This happens within art, as a Dowell is brought into contact with an Ashburnham, or a Christopher Tietjens with a Valentine Wannop. But it also happens in the experience of art, as the reader comes into contact with the mind and personality of the author. Ford's reminiscences are as much concerned with the books he has known as with their authors. Thus *Great Trade Route* begins with recollections of his childhood reading; or *Return to Yesterday* with his 'oldest literary recollection'—reading Kipling while on a train; or *Ancient Lights* with Thackeray's description of Colonel Newcome's house.[31]

Just as his childhood imaginings became a reality for him (and part of the delight of *Great Trade Route* is that they *do*: he does get to Memphis, Tennessee—as we shall see), so his reading becomes a part of his experience. While looking into the mirrors which are other writers, Ford also reflects upon himself, investigating how he became the person and also the writer that he finds himself to have become. A memory of reading W. H. Hudson gives the extreme form of Ford's claim for literature:

Twenty-five years ago—really twenty-five years ago—I lay on my back on the top of the great shoulder of the downs above Lewes—looking into the crystalline blue of the sky. There drifted above me frail, innumerable, translucent, to an immense height, one shining above the other, like an innumerable company of soap bubbles—the globelike seeds of dandelions, moving hardly perceptibly at all in the still sunlight. It was an unforgettable experience. . . . And yet it wasn't my experience at all. I have never been on that particular down above Lewes, though I know the downs very well. And yet I am not lying! In the 'nineties of the last century, I read that passage in *Nature in Downland*—and it has become part of my life. It is as much part of my life as my first sight of the German lines from a down behind Albert in 1916 . . . which is about the most unforgettable of my own experiences in the flesh. . . . So Mr. Hudson has given me a part of my life. . . . Indeed, I have a whole Hudson-life alongside my own . . . and such great pleasure with it. That is what you mean when you say a man is a creator . . . a creative artist. He gives to the world vicarious experience.[32]

What can one say in the face of such a claim? Ford pre-empts the charge he expects to provoke, by saying he's not lying, and that the experience wasn't factually his. Is it a form of self-delusion, then? Or is it, as I shall be arguing, a more subtle exploration of how literature creates its mental impressions? Such reminiscences about reading and self-reverie are crucial to an understanding of Fordian autobiography. He writes beautifully about how this vicarious experience provided by literature can re-create one's life: 'The word "author" means "someone who adds to your consciousness".'[33] Successful impressionism thus not only gives the writer's impression of an experience, but it also gives readers an experience, which in some cases approaches the impression that it was identical with the author's experience. It is another form of Ford's refusal to distinguish fact from impression, and one that makes the notion of biography doubly tenuous: not only does his writing resist a distinction between what actually happened and Ford's impression of it; it also resists a distinction between what actually happened to him, and what happened in his reading. Ford's biography is thus inescapably literary and critical: the story of his contact with literature and how it impressed itself upon him. He was not the first to discuss literature as 'vicarious experience'. Dickens, for example, wrote that '*Adam Bede* has taken its place among the actual experiences and endurances of my life'. What is striking about Ford's presentation of the idea is that he generally doesn't simply erase the difference between read and lived experiences. Even his account of visiting Lawrence in Eastwood (if the visit didn't actually happen) is more than merely a confusion of categories: the explicit point of the story is the influence on Lawrence of his intellectual milieu; the implicit points are that good writing like Lawrence's expresses its author's literary personality, and that it influences its readers, becoming a part of their literary milieu. As with his memory of reading Hudson, or reading *The Red Badge of Courage* in the Salient, he was a greater reader than liar. Generally, Ford gives the dual sense of wonder at the power of literature to seem like other experiences, together with the knowledge or suspicion that it only seems so. The impression that 'that is I, not Hudson, looking up into the heavens', is not cancelled by the concession that 'it wasn't my experience at all'.[34]

The claim that 'it is I, not Hudson', is an exaggeration, as is the whole notion of vicarious experience—however vivid our imagination, we do not actually confuse ourselves with the consciousnesses about which we read.[35] But as so often, Ford's are 'illuminative exaggerations'. In his essay 'On Impressionism', he gave an example of impressionist method, offering a false statement, then amending it, explaining that 'for a moment the false statement crystallised quite clearly what I was aiming at'. It is a good description of the procedures of *The Good Soldier*, which he was then writing, in which Dowell's impressions are succeeded by further impressions which drastically revise the picture. The false statement was that 'Art, in fact, should be addressed to those who are not preoccupied'. Ford then returns to restate:

When I used just now the instances of a man mad for love, or distracted by the prospect of personal ruin, I was purposely misleading. For a man mad as a hatter for love of a worthless creature, or a man maddened by the tortures of bankruptcy, by dishonour or by failure, may yet have, by the sheer necessity of his nature, a mind more receptive than most other minds. The mere craving for relief from his personal thoughts may make him take quite unusual interest in a work of art.[36]

Part of this critical passage's purposeful misleading is its pretence that it is not autobiographic; or rather, its dual effect, which makes us wonder whether it is not Ford himself who is 'mad for love, or distracted by the prospect of personal ruin', even as it casually presents these cases as if they were merely possibilities of human predicament—things he had noticed, perhaps, amongst casual acquaintances, or by reading about them. They have something of the status of his impressions garnered from reading, though here the process is working in reverse. For he was in fact 'mad for love' in his infatuation with Brigit Patmore, which had begun six months before the essay was published; he was in the bankruptcy courts; he was becoming increasingly indebted to Violet Hunt, an arrangement which was a perpetual reminder of social dishonour and commercial failure. Knowing these things, we see that what we have here are Ford's actual feelings and memories being presented as if they were his observations. The essay argues that the English social preoccupation with 'good form' is fatal to art. It would be 'bad form' for him to write explicitly about his emotional and financial perplexity, so the essay has to negotiate the social preoccupation by appearing not to be autobiographic. And yet, by the very fact of its 'critical attitude', the essay marks out Ford as someone with a 'quite unusual interest in a work of art'. And, characteristically, he uses the form of a critical essay to reflect, obliquely, on his own motives for his aesthetic preoccupations and predilections. His own 'mere craving for relief from his personal thoughts' must have been overwhelming at the time. One of the things he is trying to explain to himself here is how it was his most profound distresses which called forth his most searching writing.

In its extremity, Ford's refusal to distinguish between impressions of things experienced and things read approaches to a doctrine of literary impersonality: if the impression is well rendered, what matter if it is Hudson, or Hueffer doing the lying (on the Downs)? His reminiscences freely alter not only the details of an episode, but sometimes even the characters involved.[37] While most people are prepared to acknowledge that they might change details in their memories and anecdotes without meaning to, or to make a better story, few would want to go as far as Ford, and disavow the distinctions between fact and impression, and between a writer's memory and a reader's. We would like to think that such blurring of subjectivities is something that only happens by mistake, when we forget whether someone told us a fact, or whether we read it; or in insanity, in states of delusion, or depersonalization, or multiple personality. Nevertheless, Ford's impressionism is not the kind of premature senility implied in V. S. Pritchett's description of Ford's later reminiscences as his 'anecdotage'.[38] The provocative exaggeration of his position serves to illuminate a paradox of fiction and memory that we do not often stop to notice. We resist Ford's merging of imagination and memory, living and reading, knowing that our own individuality depends on the sureness of our own memory. We know that our subjectivity is constituted by memory, as some of the greatest writers of our century have repeatedly demonstrated—Proust, Joyce, Woolf, even Beckett, in his *reductio ad absurdam*, imagining the death of memory, an amnesiac near-selflessness. Yet what is so unobtrusively strange about the modern works which explore memory is that they make us feel its centrality for ourselves, by showing us how it constitutes the self of someone other: Marcel, Stephen Dedalus, Mrs Dalloway, or John Dowell. The forms of their books give us their pasts to remember. It is at this level of sympathetic identification with fiction that Ford is right. His books of reminiscence reconstitute this sense of alienation with regard to himself. They convey what one of Nabokov's deranged reminiscers calls 'the logical impossibility to relate the dubious reality of the present to the unquestionable one of remembrance'.[39] Ford's form of literary autobiography seeks to reconstruct his literary experience, but the result is to create an uncertainty about whether it *is* his autobiography, his experience. Conversely, this generates a dual sense of his life—which is why the books express him so well: we have the life the books render, plus the suggestion of another life that they don't capture. Most people are familiar with that feeling that what they read or hear about themselves doesn't express them. But few autobiographers have been so candid about foregrounding the impossibility of their task. The dual structure so characteristic of

Fordian reminiscence (this is exactly my impression, though it isn't a fact) captures a truth about the strangeness of memory—the way it makes us all dual beings, existing between two times—making his literary memories more mysterious, odd, alive. His war-amnesia made him seem his own double. He wrote of how his 'collapsed' memory divided present from past, 'so that to read my own books is for me a singular experience'.[40] But given the way Ford courted the charge of egotism, the point that needs making about his autobiographic writing is that it doesn't exist simply to express himself, in however fictionalized a form. His accounts of reading other writers go beyond egotism to achieve a surprising form of humility. His fictions about reading are facts about literature: testimonies to the genius of writers like Conrad, Crane, Lawrence, and Hudson. His autobiography, like his personality, is literary in this sense too.

Writing about yourself poses a particular kind of problem for a Fordian writer, since the writers he admires are characterized by an effacement of self, a 'selflessness'. 'Flaubert, then, evolved the maxim that the creative artist as Creator must be indifferently impartial between all his characters', wrote Ford. 'That Turgenev was by nature . . . because of his own very selflessness':

To noble natures like those of Flaubert and Turgenev the mankind that surround them is insupportable . . . if only for its want of intelligence. That is why the great poet is invariably an expatriate, if not invariably in climate, then at least in the regions of the mind. If he cannot get away from his fellows he must shut himself up from them. But if he is to be great he must also be continually making his visits to his own particular Spasskoye [Turgenev's estate]. He must live always both in and out of his time, his ancestral home, and the hearts of his countrymen.[41]

It is a classic modernist statement of the artist as exile, none the less true for being true to the letter about Ford. What follows from it, and is at the heart of his autobiographic prose, is that if the artist exists both in and out of his time, home, and the hearts of his countrymen, then to a great extent he is half-alienated from his own self.

Ford expressed the duality of literary experience by writing of the reader's 'being stirred to the perception of analogies or to the discovery of the sources of pleasure within himself'. Without the first part of this double principle the second part would be an aesthete's aesthetics. Ford sounds unusually like Proust here, who, in his own great autobiographical fiction, described the writer's work as 'a kind of optical instrument which he offers to the reader to enable him to discern what, without this book, he would perhaps never have perceived in himself'. ('In reality every reader is, while he is reading, the reader of his own self.') Or like Conrad's Marlow, who speaks of 'the chance to find yourself. Your own reality—for yourself'. Literature can offer that chance through reading—or writing—the fictional reality of someone quite other. But Ford is more radical: reading—the reading that matters—is, for him, a process of self-transformation as much as of self-discovery. 'For there is reading and reading', he explains: 'the reading that one pursues in order to make, possibly the subject matter, but more usually the personality of the writer, an intimate part of oneself; and the reading that one does for several other reasons—to pass the time, to know what the fuss is all about, to excite certain emotions, or merely to escape from oneself!'[42] This is the valuable truth bound up with the provocative claim that Ford has actually had (say) Hudson's experiences: one may occasionally feel something like this about the subject matter, but more usually one reads in order to 'make [. . .] the personality of the writer, an intimate part of oneself'.

This comment comes in explanation of Ford's antipathy to biography; of why he has 'never *really* read a Life of a Poet'. If your 'experience' is not what actually happened to you, then how should your life be written? Clearly we won't encounter the significant personality of a poet in a conventional biography: for it is a literary personality rather than a historical one. He wrote that Rossetti's work 'is almost always a matter of re-reflected personal influences'. Much of his own criticism is a reflecting on his own personal and literary influences, which are re-reflected in his art. 'To get at the value of [. . .] any original spirit', he said: 'You have to ask yourself what you would be, what your mental development would have been, how your intimate self would have grown, if that man had never existed.' What gives coherence to a book like *Mightier Than the Sword*—ostensibly a random gathering of portraits of eleven different writers—is that it is asking this question about Ford's growth as a writer; investigating 'his literary fathers and sponsors'. It proceeds by a form of what Freud called 'family romances' (fantasies in which real parents are replaced with ideal substitutes), doubling his absent father with James, 'the Master', and constructing an alternative family tree of literary impressionists.[43]

Literary Personality

Ford's most detailed account of what he means by 'personality' comes in another appreciation of Hudson. It is one of his finest critical essays (and one of the lesser-known):

We may regard 'Green Mansions' as revealing the secret of Mr. Hudson's personality. It is the story of a man who goes into a forest, in beneath the huge boughs that are the mansions for so many beings. And here, in the green twilight, going often and steadfastly, he is aware of a voice, a bird-voice, that, invisible in its origin, dogs his footsteps, in the secret places of Ecuador [. . .] at last, shyly and capriciously, the being of the bird-voice reveals herself to him. She is a woman with the spirit of a bird, with the elusive charm, with the tender and fluttering mind, with the coloured and tenuous form, with the fluting and thrilling voice. In the soul of the man there arises an immense, an overpowering passion for this bird-creature, for this protectress of all living things of the forest, for this spirit-woman who is at one with all perching, fluttering and creeping things. And when—since union between man and spirit is in the nature of things impossible—the man loses the wood-being he is filled for ever with a pervading, an endless regret.

That is Mr. Hudson. He reveals himself: he shows us in the book the nature of the dream that he has dreamed. He is—in his being as an author—a man, silent, hungry-eyed, filled with a regret and with an ideal. The ideal is to find a Being with whom he may be at one, a Being who, in return, will be at one with all the creatures of all the Green Mansions of the world. The regret is that he is born a man, since to man this union cannot ever be granted.

So we may picture him, silent, devoured by a passion, standing by a hedgerow, gazing in between the leaves, into the deep and glamorous interior, watching hungrily the little creatures who flutter about the hem of invisible garments.

This, of course, is a picture of the being who seems to look out at us from the pages of the books, not of the Mr. Hudson who walks the streets of London Town, or sits watching the gulls from a rock on the Lizard. A writer reveals himself in his books as distinct from the writer in his person [. . .] Nor yet is this picture [. . .] any more than a partial portrait of a phase. (pp. 158–9)[44]

Each book gives a 'partial portrait' (the pun is James's) of a different phase. Ford then quotes the opening of *Nature in Downland*, which moves from remembering the thistledown in Sussex, to an earlier memory of South America. Ford comments:

in this passage there is shadowed the whole of the writer—of the writer who, having galloped with young gallantry through the thistledown of early life on the pampas, comes with the fresh eyes of a stranger and the keen love of an exile into green and ancient lands, there to spend long hours in the delight of lying still, of gazing at common things, of giving himself up utterly to the spirit of the place. These are, as it were, the biographical details—and there are biographical details enough cropping up, as reminiscences, as comparisons, or as the framework of romances, throughout Mr. Hudson's long tale of works. (pp. 160–1)

Hudson's time-shift from present Sussex to past Argentina appeals to Ford, for it makes the writing a (partial) composite portrait of the successive phases of his experience, rather as the long tale of his works, his entire *œuvre*, composes the tale of his long life, his essential and literary autobiography.

As he writes on Hudson, Ford too leaves enough autobiographical traces of his own, shadowed behind the 'impartial' tone of the establishment press. There is something strange about saying of that opening passage from *Nature in Downland*: 'this is the first passage of Mr. Hudson's work that we ever read.' The first-person plural of the authoritative journal may sometimes persuade us that 'we' share the author's reasonable and responsible public opinions. But can it convince us that we had the same history of private reading? The oddness introduces a personal voice, which enables the reader to perceive a central analogy: that between Hudson's life-story expressed in his writing, and Ford's expressed in his writing about reading. Rereading Hudson makes him remember his first reading, as gazing at thistledown made Hudson remember his first such observations. Thus when Ford says 'in this passage there is shadowed the whole of the writer', we glimpse Ford himself shadowed in the phrase with which he often indicated himself: 'the writer'. His own story has become shadowed in Hudson's.

The description of *Green Mansions* is equally alive with analogy; this time, between the strangely dual object of the man's passion—'bird-voice', 'spirit-woman', 'wood-being'—and the dual subjectivity of Hudson himself—as author and character (such is Ford's tact that it does not feel like an impertinence for him to talk as if the man in the story were Hudson); as the personality 'who seems to look out at us from the pages of the books', and the man about town. The crucial word here is 'Being': 'He is—in his being as an author—a man, silent, hungry-eyed, filled with a regret and with an ideal. The ideal is to find a Being with whom he may be at one, a Being who, in return, will be at one with all the creatures [. . .].' For Ford, Hudson is this Being: himself a mysterious, spiritualized 'being' who seems to smile from his pages, and one who was for Ford always an example of the artist's 'being at one' with the world, the observer who effaces himself to become the unobtrusive recorder of a life his presence does not disturb or distort.

The union between man and spirit is impossible in the nature of things; but Ford's language of criticism makes it possible in the nature of literature. (One can see why this fable appealed to the author of *The Young Lovell*.) For the author's personality becomes precisely that dual being: at once an actual human being, Hudson the man who wrote the books—and a spiritual presence inhabiting their forms. Gazing between the leaves of Hudson's books, Ford observes 'into the deep and glamorous interior'; the 'dark forest' that for him is the heart of another.

Ford reads *Green Mansions* as an oblique allegory for the life of a writer, driven by a passion for an unattainable ideal of union and rest. What is important for Ford's biography is this mode of reading. The prose is read as an oblique autobiography of Hudson's being as a writer. The analogy with Ford's own autobiography suggests that not only is the method one which can be applied generally, but that this is a particular instance. That is, in addition to the hints of Ford's own biography audible in details of his experience (including the experience of reading), the whole essay should be read as an oblique autobiography, indicating that this is the mode in which he expects his own books to be read. It is entirely characteristic that it should itself be an instance of the mode of oblique autobiography it adumbrates. His own books work in this dual way, as partial portraits of the phases of his life, and also as expressions of his artistic ideal.[45] Hudson's personality lets itself appear in the mansions of his pages rather as the woman makes herself mysteriously visible in the forest. Translating his picture of Hudson, seeking union with the spirit-woman, into his own terms conveying the intimacy of reading, Ford expresses the nature of the passion that inspires his art: like Hudson's, it sounds both sexual and religious, but is something simpler and more fundamental: a craving for communion with a sympathetic being, a desire for understanding and for love: 'after all, it is the power to render convincingly circumstances observed with zest that most surely makes us know a writer, and, if he be lovable, makes us love him' (p. 159). What makes Ford knowable and admirable as a critic as well as a novelist is his power to do just that. His criticism renders convincingly the literary effects he observed with zest—as he does in discussing Hudson's prose. He does not make the claims of a Johnson or a Leavis to be defining absolute standards of value. Impersonality was beyond his powers as a critic too, as it is beyond the powers of every critic. Which is perhaps what he meant when he said (apropos *Mightier Than the Sword*): 'I am not really a critic but an appreciator [. . .].' Rebecca West thought Ford's 'transforming memory' incapacitated him as a critic: 'A man can hardly say anything valuable about the great works of literature if he cannot remember a single one of them as they were written.' Many writers (Pound, Sinclair Lewis, Greene, Lowell) were excited enough by his general precepts to be unperturbed by idiosyncrasies of particular judgement. But Ford's particular judgements have their champions too. Compton Mackenzie, for example, said: 'When I consider the critical minds with which I have come into contact I find that I have no hesitation in declaring that of the many judgements I have listened to on literature, the least fallible of all were Ford Madox Ford's.'[46]

At his critical best he has an astonishing ability to make himself at one with the author he is observing. He is under no illusions about the differences between himself and Hudson. Most of his reminiscences about the older man involve their differences, such as when Hudson insists that he is not the 'stylist' Ford tries to call him. But beneath the differences of person, there is none the less a profound affinity between their literary personalities. It is not just that Hudson was one of Ford's favourite authors, however; nor that while writing about him Ford could make himself at one with a very different temperament. His criticism is also revealing as it shadows forth the way in which he made his authors a part of himself.

The most immediate way he did that was to become a writer like them. It was reading Hudson, or James, or Conrad, that made him want to write; reading Crane during the war that made him want to write again. The passage from *Nature in Downland* is significant in this way too. The sight of the thistledown in August 1899 reminds Hudson of his 'old days on horseback on the open pampa'. And it is this transport of reminiscence that sows the seed of writing—that gives him the germ for the book on the Downs. It is a turn from reminiscence to creativity that Ford was to make his own. His literary autobiography expresses his literary personality in this specific sense: it tells the story of how he became a writer, what made him want to write, and why he wrote the way he did; the story of why he began the project of understanding and expressing himself. Thus *Ancient Lights* tells of his Pre-Raphaelite youth, and how it shaped his literary aspirations. His two major autobiographies, *Return to Yesterday* and *It Was the Nightingale*, divide his life into the pre-war and the post-war (the declaration of war ends the first volume, and Ford's demobilization begins the second; the abyss between demanded more intense fictionalizing, in *No Enemy*, and *Parade's End*.) 'The world before the war is one thing and must be written about in one manner', he insisted: 'the after-war world is quite another and calls for quite different treatment.' So with the Hueffer before the war, and the after-war Ford (and so with the pre-war and post-war passages of *Parade's End*). *Return to Yesterday* treats the period of his young adulthood, and though it scarcely discusses his works, its subtext is the story of the mind that produced *England and the English*, *The Fifth Queen* trilogy, and *The Good Soldier*. *It Was the Nightingale* 'is really the story of the writing of two works', says one critic: '*Parade's End* and itself.' Dealing with the period between the First World War and the Depression, it also gives the psychological background to his novels of what he called the 'Crisis': *When the Wicked Man*, *The Rash Act*, and *Henry for Hugh*.[47] The cultural stories told in *Provence* and *Great Trade Route* also sketch Ford's life and travels in France and America. We are also made to realize how the views in these books are projections of a distinctive mind.

The conception of literary personality that emerges from Ford's criticism is something very different from the conventional account of his impressionism. For example, Mizener's not-unsympathetic discussion relies on crudely fixed notions of 'experience' and 'feelings':

The impressionist's subject, then, is always himself, *his* personality, usually—in Ford's case, in any event—as the writer imagines himself to have felt during some important experience of his own. The nominal subject is an objective correlative, a set of circumstances which, though different from the actual circumstances of his own experience, allows him to express

his feelings about these actual circumstances in exactly the pattern they have taken for him.
(p. 256)

But 'expression', for Ford (in the criticism of Hudson, for example) is not a question
of wrapping up his feelings about actual circumstances in the veils of art. What
circumstances? Whose actuality? 'Invented stories contain a kernal of mystery', writes
John Bayley, 'because no one—probably not even the author—knows in what relation
they stand to a possible fact.' Ford's critical imagery pictures something transcendent,
a disembodied vision of the quintessential self: something like a soul; an expression of
ideals, desires, inspirations. Even in his reminiscences Ford is more concerned with
self-expression at this more metaphysical, allegorical level, than with rendering his
feelings about actual circumstances. Just as asking which actual woman Hudson may
have had in mind for his 'spirit-woman' is not going to tell us anything important
about his being as a writer, so criticism of Ford—especially of his reminiscences—will
be frustrated where it tries to explain the writing, or the 'feelings', in terms of the
'actual circumstances'. Michael Levenson, in one of the best discussions of Fordian
impressionism, calls it 'a *subjectivity in which the subject has disappeared*'.[48]

  Two figures Ford uses to express expression beautifully capture this paradox. First,
the envisioning of the author's self-expression as a facial expression. With Turgenev,
or Shakespeare, or Hudson, it is as a smile. His memory of meeting Turgenev, for
example, was of 'a singular, compassionate smile that still seems to me to look up out
of the pages of his books'. We know so little about Shakespeare's biography that he is
'personally nothing but a wise smile and a couple of anecdotes'. George Moore's
literary expression is more severe: 'The face of Mr Moore that seems to look up at us
from his pages has cold eyes.' It is a ghostly effect, the personality of the dead
animating their work. But in so far as it images literary immortality, Ford may hope for
the same disembodied survival. In terms of literary autobiography, it also suggests
how a writer might think of his work as purging from his personality the accidents of
the physical and the unattractive. This is perhaps the subtext of his recalling the
newspaper interview saying: 'Mr. F—— is one of the most ill-favoured men I have
ever seen. But he has a kind smile.' Presumably he preferred to be remembered, as he
remembered Turgenev, by the smile.[49]

  The danger of thinking in terms of an author's 'personality' is that it tends towards
hypostasis, displacing the accidents, the lived variety, the developments and instabil-
ities of a life by a specious abstraction claiming quintessence. Ford's own life testifies
to the futility of the attempt. The image of the smile is wise here too, partly through
its suggestion of the Cheshire Cat in *Alice in Wonderland*, which 'vanished quite
slowly, beginning with the end of the tail, and ending with the grin, which remained
some time after the rest of it had gone': ' "Well! I've often seen a cat without a grin,"
thought Alice, "but a grin without a cat! It's the most curious thing I ever saw in all my
life".'[50] Literary personality is as recognizable as a face or a smile; but as elusive as the
disembodied grin of the Cheshire Cat, only visible in its moment of evanescence.

  Secondly, Ford uses the idea of 'rhythm'. Again, what is significant is that it is a
purely literary quality—something that cannot be decoded as referring to 'actual
circumstances'. It is the imprint of the personality upon whatever subject matter is

treated. But the personality does not pre-exist. It is brought into being by its expression, which enables you to hear the person you have become.

And that brings us to Vers Libre. You will find in all life; you will find in all your thoughts; in all careers and all human vicissitudes one certain thing—rhythm. The rhythm of your thoughts will seem to change from day to day, upon occasions, for periods. But it won't change much. You will always think in words and sentences averaging out at about the same number of syllables. You will think only in long and involved sentences, or in short sentences alone—or in one or two or three long sentences brought up sharply by a sentence of only three or four words [like the clause at the end of this paragraph?]. But however you do phrase your thoughts to yourself, the rhythm of your thought phrases will be your personality. It will be your literary personality . . . your true one.[51]

Here Ford's discussion is far subtler than, say, E. M. Forster's. All his formulations about artistic expression have this duality of speaker and listener, even when, as here, the speaker is imagined as being his or her own listener. Literature is not, for him, a matter of expressing ourselves to others, as if we all know what we are, and the only problem is how to transport unproblematic meanings from A to B. Rather, it is the search for how to 'express ourselves to ourselves'.[52] Ford expresses himself to himself by expressing himself to others. 'It is certain my conviction will gain immensely as soon as another soul can be found to share it.' His reminiscences, as well as his fictions, depend on this aesthetics of persuasive performance. Fordian autobiography discovers a self in the act of convincing his readers (and therefore himself) of the reality of that self. It thus becomes an exorcism of self-doubt; a forging of conviction in himself.

Ford's argument that the true personality is a quality of style, of verbal manifestations, rather than an essence, makes him a predecessor of deconstructive criticism (as does his relentless destabilizing of the notion of an objective reality). The personality in the text speaks an elegy for the death of the author. And yet there is an important difference. His aim is not so much to discredit any notion of personality, as to champion the truth of 'literary personality'. It is a dual attitude to selfhood, which can recognize the truth of an individual's feelings and identity, while also recognizing that these things are everywhere mediated by language, even by literature.

Philippe Lejeune argues that when authors say, as Ford does about Hudson, that their fiction is their true autobiography, something paradoxical is happening. Although apparently deprecating autobiography, the comment simultaneously uses 'autobiography' as the criterion for judging the novels: it makes the novels important in so far as they are the true autobiography, express the true personality. But while it is true that the same word, 'autobiography', is being used both as one term in the comparison, and also as the ground of the comparison, it means very different things in each position. For what this trope does is radically to change what one means by autobiography, from the conventional sense of narrating your life history, to the sense in which Ford uses it, of expressing your literary personality. Goldring wrote well about why it is necessary to include this literary personality in a consideration of a writer's character:

Like all great artists, he put the best of himself into his work, and the residuum that was left over when the gold had been extracted laboriously from the quartz did not always conform to approved, conventional standards. As a human personality he was, no doubt, a mass of contradictions, but his prevailing characteristics were his essential kindness, his boundless generosity, a quality frequently imposed upon by the selfish and unscrupulous, his breadth of mind and freedom from petty jealousy.[53]

Fordian autobiography is a dual mode, combining intimacy with reticence, self-expression with self-concealment. What he writes of Stephen Crane (or the similar insights into Ford Madox Brown and Conrad) can be read as an oblique allegory for his own autobiographical fabulation: 'Crane would assert that he had been in all sorts of improbable spots and done all sorts of things, not vain-gloriously lying, but in order to spin around his identity a veil behind which he might have some privacy. A writer needs privacy.'[54] In Ford's own writing, and in the kind of literature that most appealed to him, the literary personality is best expressed by the fictions which are evolved to spin veils around the self. It is an argument which dissolves the boundaries between autobiography, fiction, and criticism. Conventionally, biographical subjects are seen as the external causes of their writing. Ford places the writer within literature; sees his personality as literary.

Role Play

Telling expressively self-protective stories about yourself is a form of role-playing. Ford recognized this connection in Crane as well as in himself. 'Everybody who knew Ford attested to his inveterate role-playing—H. G. Wells, Edward and David Garnett, Douglas Goldring, Violet Hunt, Ezra Pound, Richard Aldington, D. H. Lawrence, Stella Bowen, Ernest Hemingway, Robert McAlmon, and Robert Lowell, to mention the better-known ones.'[55] He is not only one of the great role-players, but also one of the great writers about self-dramatization: both about the ways his characters (such as Christopher and Sylvia Tietjens) set their own scenes to achieve their effects; and about how he did much the same, both in his life and in his autobiographical writing. A revealing cross-light is shed on the notion of role-playing by an anecdote which for Ford exemplified Marwood's unconventionally incisive political judgement:

I do not believe that Marwood had much sense of humour, but his dry statements of essential facts were so strange to the greater part of English humanity of his day that he could keep a roomful of men laughing as long as he was in it. He said one afternoon at Rye Golf Club to the Conservative member for that borough:

'You know',—he was speaking as a Tory—'we ought to have had Lloyd George to do our dirty work. We have always had to have someone to do our dirty jobs. We had Disraeli and we had Chamberlain. We ought to have had Lloyd George.' The Conservative member laughed as if he thought Marwood an amiable lunatic. His mind was incapable of making the jump of seeing Mr. George as anything but a Radical devil with hoofs and tail.[56]

Marwood's mental jump of seeing Lloyd George as something other—a Conservative—is taken up into the technique of the writing. The parenthetic phrase '—he was speaking as a Tory—' asks us to concur that our conversational poses are themselves mental leaps. We can 'speak as' many different persons, some of them inconsistent. Our personalities are constructed by the multiple overlaying of roles: child, friend, adversary, lover, voter, worker, player, resident, traveller, parent, writer . . . When Roland Barthes writes that the 'deceptive plenitude' of subjectivity 'is merely the wake of the codes that constitute me', his onslaught on our sense of our individuality as an inviolable essence is unmistakable.[57] This is an uncompromising denial of any residual 'self' which can transcend historical and linguistic specificities. 'You' are an echo-chamber of the discourses you have encountered—nothing more. One can doubt this—and inquiring scepticism is preferable to benign acquiescence or malign deroga-tion—but still recognize how much of the personality, of one's sense of individuality, *is* constituted by factors outside the self. Showing how something has been con-structed need not devastate it: deconstruction is not necessarily destruction.

The sheer diversity of Ford's roles is as astounding as the zest with which he observed himself playing them. There is the young radical Bohemian, wearing Rossetti's Inverness cape and consorting with Russian anarchists. Or there is the Rural Recluse, buried in a country cottage, living a life of Pre-Raphaelite pseudo-feudalism. But then this alternates with the landed-gentry act. Conrad's double, the earnest Collaborator, pacing up and down the Pent and waking up Jessie Conrad and the children as he thumped the oak beams of the ceiling, was himself doubled with the *jeune homme modeste* that he became walking with James on the road from Winchelsea to Rye. There is even a theatricality about the Suicidal Depressive; for that too requires its audience, whether it was Elsie, or the nerve specialists of Germany (or, later, Violet Hunt, taking away Ford's bottle of poison). The role of Edwardian Man About Town was played with great panache, and coloured his actions as Editor of the *English Review*. The society Great Figure then turned Soldier, in which role the stoic Victim of shell-shock alternated with the Military Expert and patriotic Propagandist. The Unsung War Hero returned to become the Small Producer, jokily trying to sell Pinker his pigs as well as his manuscripts. Becoming the transatlantic Cosmopolite, he returned to the role of 'Only Uncle of the Gifted Young', casting a new circle of neophytes. He was as good at finding others to play the roles he had assigned them as he was at playing his own. Towards the end of his life, lecturing at Olivet College, he became the Dean of English Letters, an unacademic academic.

His literary roles were as multifarious. He was the Poet, the Historian (first of the English past, then of the English and European present), the Novelist, the Art Critic, the Topographical and Nature Writer, the Literary Critic, the Travel Writer, the Cultural Commentator, the Autobiographer—often most of these in the same book.

In a brilliant essay on 'Joyce's Anti-Selves', Hugh Kenner writes: 'Joyce spent his life playing parts, and his works swarm with shadow-selves.' 'Parody was the medium of his art,' continues Kenner, 'and he played these parts that he might better write them. To make Bloom an authentic parody of himself, Joyce turned himself for long periods into a parody of Bloom.' Though Ford is not primarily a parodist, his exag-gerations and elisions give a caricaturist's edge to his portrayals. This is as true of his presentation of himself as of his presentation of his characters. One could say that to make Ashburnham, or Tietjens, or Ford Madox Ford, a parody of himself, he turned himself for long periods into a parody of the English country gentleman, or Arthur Marwood, or himself. This suggests the danger of trying to explain the books, as Mizener does, as projections of his 'England' of the mind. This approach assumes that he lived a fantasy-life (as a psychological evasion of an unbearable reality), and that his fiction is simply an expression of the same fantasy. Instead, we should try to explain the life by the fiction, looking at how he lived his way into his roles often as technical experiments rather than psychic needs. Wyndham Lewis, who described Ford as possessing 'a vivid and theatrical imagination', commented with his usual malign relish: 'This ex-collaborator with Joseph Conrad was himself, it always occurred to me, a typical figure out of a Conrad book—a caterer, or corn-factor, coming on board—blowing like a porpoise with the exertion—at some Eastern port.'[58] Lewis himself had a knack of suggestive travesty, and beyond his immediate purpose of ridiculing Ford, he none the less suggests the extent to which Ford was enmeshed in literature. He acted the Conrad character because he needed to be able to write the Conradian character, whether collaboratively or on his own (in Conrad's books as well as his own). He also resembles a Conrad character because many of Conrad's characters resemble him: Lord Jim, Martin Decoud, Razumov, Peter Ivanovitch, de Barrall, or the mysterious double who appears in 'The Secret Sharer'.

The psycho-biographic case against Ford's role-playing rests on the assumption that he managed to convince himself that his fantasies were true. Although there is an important half-truth here—that any sort of self-presentation involves convincing others and yourself of the authenticity of the role you are playing—his own writing is finely aware of the ways in which it is possible not to be deluded by the roles you are playing (as we have seen in *The Rash Act* and *Henry for Hugh*). 'One of the most poignant sayings of our time', he wrote, 'is that of M. Cocteau about Victor Hugo. He exclaimed, "That man's mad. He thinks he's Victor Hugo"': 'Victor Hugo appears mad because he believed—he finally kidded himself into really believing—that he was as inspired by the great moral purpose as the *Victor Hugo* that he set before the public. Mr. Ruskin went really mad in the effort to be as moral as the *John Ruskin* of the *Stones of Venice*.'[59] Certainly the man who wrote this knew about what he called 'the self-engrossment of humanity'. His attention as a novelist to how people's self-engrossment stops them attending to each other let him frame his astute advice to novelists not to have their characters answer each other too fully and directly: people are usually too engrossed in their roles, and composing their next speeches for that. He knew, too, about the dangers of believing in his own roles. But it is a deeply sane observation about a mode of insanity. He did not believe he was the 'Ford Madox Ford' set before the public in his journalism and his reminiscences. But he *was* the Ford Madox Ford who (like his grandfather) knew 'the absolute madness of work': the old man mad about writing. He stage-manages a fine comedy from the exchanges between the literary personality expressed, and the theatrical personality displayed. Nor, one should add, did he confuse his *Henry James* with the real Henry James, or his *Joseph Conrad* with the real Joseph Conrad, as an attentive reading of either book will keep demonstrating. Novelists have a vested interest in character. A novelist of the stream-of-consciousness, like Joyce of Ford, needs to imagine himself inside his characters. An analyst of social posing and posturing, like Waugh or Ford, must act himself into the gestures and routines of his subjects. Mizener thought Ford's 'worst faults' were 'his weakness for dramatic extravagance and for talking about himself'. In his autobiographies they became his best subjects and techniques.[60] Writing of the extent to which an author can appear in his own person in his fictions, Ford makes a distinction uncommon for the time, between the author himself and the 'author-character' who appears inside the book. 'It is obvious', he says, 'that the author, being the creator of his characters, may, if he will, create himself.'[61] The phrasing precisely encompasses the dual aspect of Ford's unusual literary self-consciousness. The author creates himself—as a theatrical social person, as a character within his books, and as a literary personality expressed by them. But he nevertheless remains aware of his duality: of the separation between the man who suffers and the mind which creates, the being of the man and the being of the author, the role-playing self and the written roles.

Feeling himself 'incapable of self-assertion', he asserted fictional selves. He 'was nearly all his characters', said Biala. Robert Lynd thought 'the most interesting character Ford ever invented was Ford Madox Ford'. Goldring, who saw him in England, France, and America, said that 'In spite of his impersonations as a "quick-change" artist [. . .] it is remarkable how in certain basic and essential qualities he remained, throughout his life, himself'. But it would be better to recognize how essential to his self his theatricality was. Writing about a comparable 'protean quality' of Crane's, Ford recalled: 'I have known him change his apparent personality half a dozen times in the course of an afternoon.' What Ford said of Conrad was equally true of himself: 'really to know' him 'you had to realize that he was always acting a part'. He makes two exceptions: Conrad's solicitudes for his family, and his passion for the novel. And the latter at least is itself dramatic, Ford argues, since Conrad '*was*' his characters. The literary personality is a self-dramatizing one; the roles are literature. In an early essay Ford wrote of Burne-Jones what was again equally self-reflexive: that he 'was singularly open to the influence of reminiscences, and they seem to have acted upon him with all the force that actual surroundings produce upon other men'. The essay ends with a complex act of reminiscence, recalling Oliver Madox Brown's poem about his pet chameleon to find an image for the way the Pre-Raphaelite colourists Ford is remembering recorded their memories and impressions: 'For, even as the "weird chameleon of the past world" reflects colours that are or have been in his surroundings, so do these men of a past age reflect the colours of a past race or a time that seem good to them. Yet the chameleon remains the chameleon—and the artist himself.'[62] It is the Fordian kind of impressionist artist's very susceptibility to inhabit other roles and other times that characterizes his self.

Published writers are public people, and 'every public man has a dual personality', wrote Ford; 'is, that is to say, *homo duplex*'. His use of pseudonyms—Hermann Ritter, Fenil Haig, L. C. Pash, Daniel Chaucer, Didymus, E. Roterodamus, Francis M. Hurd, Baron Ignatz von Aschendrof, Faugh an-Ballagh Faugh, even 'Ford Madox Ford'—testifies to a need to multiply and dramatize personae. Not only are authors particularly subject to what he called 'the agonies of the duplex personality', but it makes them particularly sensitive to all human contradictions. Ford especially prizes in others the virtue he pre-eminently possessed: the ability, which he diagnoses in Conrad, to 'see vividly the opposing sides of human characters' (itself dually a tribute to James's tribute to Turgenev: 'He felt and understood the opposite sides of life').[63] Ford is often accused of being inconsistent (as a critic, a theorist, a thinker). 'Of course it is given to no man to be consistent', he wrote. This was not just special pleading. He believed it 'characteristic of a confused world [. . .]' that 'Truth should have developed the bewildering faculty of the chameleon and have taken on like Janus, two faces. . . .' What has seemed like childishness or irresponsibility to sterner critics can seem like responsibility towards this view of moral and intellectual incoherence. (Compare Keats: 'What shocks the virtuous philosop[h]er, delights the camelion Poet.') He had the courage of his own lack of convictions, or the courage of his conviction about the lack of univocal truth; about the superiority of the research of an 'artistic revolutionist' (as he called his grandfather) over what Madox Brown himself dismissed as a 'facile completeness'. What systems and principles Ford does proffer are frankly self-contradictory: his Toryism, revolutionariness, medievalism, feminism, anarchism. But that is his way of rendering his self-contradictory times in their own terms. Even when he is playing the role of critic, or social commentator, or cultural analyst, his imagination is thoroughly dialogic, novelistic. He wants his ideas to stand forth like his characters, in the bewildering cloud of their complexity and inconsistency. The dual responses his writing provokes ('It is all one whether he convince his reader or cause to arise a violent opposition. For the artist's views are of no importance whatever') are modes of engaging the reader, fostering emotion and amazement. He is modernist here, manifesting what Marshall McLuhan called 'the Symbolist and Imagist doctrine that the place of ideas in poetry is not that of logical enunciation but of immediate sensation or experience'. This is entirely consistent with his aesthetic principles, since the presentation of perplexity, the atomization of the moral and philosophical viewpoint, becomes a strategy for his self-effacement. Sisley Huddleston rightly thought Ford's passivity was an expression of his literary technique; his mode of 'hypnotizing himself' into a state of visionary 'inspiration, receptivity'. But it also expresses the emotional tumultuousness it suppresses, as Harold Loeb noticed, and as Ford himself portrayed in his characters like Tietjens as well as in his memoirs. That is, his emphasis on 'technique' is, like Conrad's, sincere; but it is also a smoke-screen for his engagement with his material; a mode of distancing himself from his emotions in order to realize them.[64]

He is scrupulous to portray the opposing sides of the authors he discusses, finding that they contain multitudes. He found 'two Jameses'. In Galsworthy he saw 'two distinct psychologies working side by side in the same being'; whereas 'two beings may have looked out of Lawrence's eyes'. Dreiser he presents as a man of volatile, inconsistent gusto. But the portrait conveys a subtle perception of both men's existing between two worlds, that of imagination and that of fact:

When I converse with Mr. Dreiser, he converts me, according to the temporary set of the tide of his passions, into a simulacrum of something that for the moment he abhors. I become for him a Nazi Jew-baiter; a perfidious Briton; an American financier; the proprietor of brothels in Paris; an unpractical poet [. . .] At all these simulacra of myself for hours and hours Mr. Dreiser hurls gigantic trains of polyphonic, linked insults. . . .[65]

But whereas, in the hands of a Wyndham Lewis, say, this would become mere ridicule of Dreiser's obsessiveness, Ford turns to consider himself, and shows himself to be a simulacrum of Dreiser, his double, in his ability to imagine himself as all kinds of other beings—other simulacra of himself: 'whatever simulacrum of myself he may be in the mood to rid the earth of, it is certain not to be the *persona* of the mood I am in for the moment.' Part of the elaborate joke is Ford's awareness that in catching Dreiser in his inconsistency Ford is presenting him as a simulacrum of Ford. The tact of the portrait comes from its warm sense of affinity between the two writers—an affinity which at first sight seems impossible, since Dreiser is turning Ford into his pariahs, while Ford is showing Dreiser as one of his: the novelist as propagandist, who wants to 'rid the earth' of whatever he takes Ford to be. Yet it is precisely in this imaginative extravagance that the affinity lies. Ford's prose often induces an awareness of multiplicity in his readers too (as that image of the face reflected in the glass might intimate). What Charles Williams said incisively about *Parade's End*—'The reader was split; it was part of the nightmare'—could be said, differently, about the reminiscences: the reader is multiplied; it is part of the excitement.[66]

The personae of Ford's moods are nowhere so apparent as in his attitudes to nationality. His Anglo-German origin framed his conception of his own being as something dual. But throughout his work nationality becomes a focus for the multiplicity of ways in which someone can be *homo duplex* or *homo x-plex*. Henry Martin's transfusion into Hugh Monckton, for example, transposes Ford's feeling that he had become an American writer. In 1934 he wrote about how America had become 'a vast hive of buzzing literary life', and continued: 'So I regard myself, and am generally regarded, as an American writer.' Douglas Goldring said that 'Ford could, when he wished to do so, make himself feel like a Frenchman, like a German, or like an American'. *It Was the Nightingale*, which tells of Ford's own decision to leave England, follows a double change as the Gallophile becomes an honorary American. In the typescript of his 'Autocriticism' of *The Rash Act* Ford cast himself as an example of 'The modern Franco-American writer'.[67] His sympathetic imagination of alien nationalities operated both inside and outside his novels. When he wrote that he had spent the greater part of his life since the war 'in literary America', it is clear that the country of the literary mind doubles the geographical country. He had indeed spent much time in the United States, but 'literary America' could also mean 'the society of American writers', which could be found anywhere (one suspects) along the 'Great Trade Route', and particularly in Paris and the South of France.[68]

'In electing to be peculiarly English in habits and in as much of his temperament as he could control—for, though no man can choose the land of his birth or his ancestry, he can, if he have industry and determination, so watch over himself as materially to modify his automatic habits—', Ford himself 'had quite advisedly and of set purpose adopted a habit of behaviour that he considered to be the best in the world for the normal life.' The strange thing here is that he is writing not (ostensibly) about himself, or even about Conrad, but about Tietjens, a man English enough not to need to 'elect' to be so. But the prose is precise. Tietjens has elected to be '*peculiarly* English in habits and in as much of his temperament as he could control'—something which even a born Englishman can do, and which Ford sometimes did. Rather than simply using his personal experience of uncertain nationality as copy for his fiction, he uses it to observe how all nationality has an element of uncertainty, role-playing, self-creation and self-determination. It is a characteristic example of how something that at first sight looks like a weakness of Ford's writing—undigested autobiography padding the fiction—is a strength: a turning of a personal peculiarity into a tool of insight. In T. S. Eliot's fine sentence on Baudelaire: 'his weaknesses can be composed into a larger whole of strength.'[69]

In his autobiography as well as his fiction, it is the dualities of particular individuals more than of generalized nationalities that most interests Ford. The moments of his reminiscences that are the most searching (because the most self-searching) come when he perceives the personalities of other writers as simulacra of his own: when he imagines Dreiser, or Conrad, or Hudson, as his double. Returning to the remark from *It Was the Nightingale*—'I have written reminiscences of which the main features were found in the lives of other people and in which, as well as I could, I obscured myself' (p. vi)—we can see how well it describes his autobiographical method, which is to build up a 'composite portrait' of himself by juxtaposing a series of portraits of his doubles. The portrait thus composed is of his being as a writer—'the writer'. In his reminiscences Ford finds his own features in the lives of others, in which he 'obscures' himself. As he says of Hudson, one gets a clear impression of his personality, even of many of his past experiences and backgrounds, from what he writes about something quite other.

Conrad becomes his double when Ford describes his liking for coincidences: 'He liked to amuse himself with resemblances between himself and other great men.' He resembled Ford in this, who was amused by the resemblance of his name and Henry Ford's; or the idea of the Jacobean 'Ford with his melancholy hat' in the Mermaid Tavern.[70] Thus Ford's autobiography progresses by composing narratives of how humanity seemed to itself to resemble him. When a writer so skilled at vivid physiognomic description, and one who habitually thinks of an author's personality as a metaphysical 'smile' talks of 'features', the word glances at how encountering a double is an immediate, physical, disconcerting experience; and one which is archetypally autobiographic, as it lets you see yourself as the other. Ford's autobiography is also a matter of physical self-knowledge: of finding his physical features in the faces of others, as well as finding the features of his own life in theirs. Physical as much as psychological or temperamental resemblance intrigued him too. His physical doubles—those either he or his acquaintances thought he resembled—included his brother Oliver, Edmund Gosse, George Moore, Oscar Wilde, and Arthur Marwood.[71] In finding, and portraying, himself as the double of other writers whom he reveals as dual personalities, Ford's reminiscences embody him as himself pre-eminently a dual personality. Dowell's uncertainty about whether Leonora, as she begins to crack up, is 'no longer herself', or is 'being, for the first time, her own natural self', is Ford's uncertainty about his own true self. When Dowell talks of his 'dual personality', it is in relation to his discovery about Florence: 'I suppose that my inner soul—my dual personality—had realized long before that Florence was a personality of paper.' Doubling Dowell's scorn for Florence's vacuity is Ford's autobiographical sense that a writer's 'inner soul' is, in the end, a personality of paper; that 'Man is explicable by his imaginative literature alone'. He advocated 'the study of technique' as a means of 'the writer's finding himself'. It is in this sense that he could say that 'Ezra is first and foremost his CANTO'S'; or that 'Conrad was Conrad because he was his books'; or that Jung could say 'It is not Goethe that creates *Faust*, but *Faust* that creates Goethe'. And it is in this sense that Ford's own books—all his books—make up his own autobiography.[72]

1933–1935: ON THE GREAT TRADE ROUTE

It is the original curse of Anglo-Saxondom that her civilization forever wavers between the Teutonic and the Latin that are the opposed currents of her two-fold soul.

(Ford, 'The Real France, That Goes to Bed at Nine')

It Was the Nightingale was reviewed more widely and favourably than any of his books since the Tietjens novels, apart from *Return to Yesterday*. Ford the reminiscer had been reborn out of Ford the novelist. He would finish one more novel after *Henry for Hugh*: the Simenonesque story of mistaken identity, abduction, and political machinations in France, *Vive Le Roy*; and he was to leave another novel, provisionally called 'Professor's Progress', unfinished at his death. But the rest of his writing would mostly follow the discursive, reminiscential mode Ford had been developing in these books of hallucinatory, carnivalesque, reminiscence. One reviewer noticed the significance of the way Ford 'introduces the stream of consciousness method into reminiscence'. (That could have been said of Proust too, of course: but the tonal difference is decisive. Rather than striving for Proust's consolatory, recuperative aestheticism, Ford captures the chaos and oscillation of the mental life.) *It Was the Nightingale* is a protean performance rather than a poetic transfiguration of the past. Comparing it to Roy Campbell's *Broken Record*, V. S. Pritchett said that Ford was 'much more the showman, a heavier and more festive fellow [. . .], brilliant and laborious'. He wasn't entirely convinced, finding him 'too brilliant for his own story'; but the point is a crucial one: that Ford had transformed himself, as a writer, into something more like the verbal pyrotechnician Wyndham Lewis had blasted him for not being back in 1914. In a later book Ford was to recognize this change, comparing the writer to the ringmaster:

When you are a conscious writer you watch your subjects, your characters, your words, in particular, as you put them down . . . as if they were lions, wolves, or plaguy little cats performing on the sawdust of the ring. And 'Crack!' goes your long whip and they skip into their places and Columbine goes slick through the paper hoop and lands beyond on the white horse's back like a gull on the wave-crest. . . . And at the end of fifty years or so—if you are any good—you can make the beastly little things called words do what you want even when your back is turned or your eyes closed. . . .

Caroline Gordon felt that reading *It Was the Nightingale* was like entering the vortex: 'The thing that particularly impressed me about the book was the ease with which you reached out and dragged anything you wanted into your own private whirlpool [. . .].'[1]

It was not only in the 'Autocriticism' of *The Rash Act*, but also in writing about Pound that Ford had been clarifying what he was attempting himself. In his own testimonial to Pound he said: 'Mr. Pound's cursory pronouncements in prose may seem to you mostly nonsense, but even his nonsenses give one to think [. . .] To keep the thought of the world sane extravagances too are necessary.' Ford's own prose knows thought-provoking extravagance, though, as here, what might *seem* nonsense stimulates a recognition of a sane truth: that imagination and fiction are actually *necessary*: they guarantee sanity, by reminding us that the world is not always as the leader-writers, political economists, and other purveyors of reading-matter that passes for 'serious' tell us. (It is characteristic of Ford's imaginative tolerance that even while making a case for extravagance, the 'too' recognizes the simultaneous need for economy; and that the perfect cadence of the sentence exemplifies this economy, the sane monosyllables accommodating—and needing—the well-matched expansive polysyllables 'extravagances' and 'necessary'.) He pursued the idea in a review of the *Cantos* written in October, and entitled 'Mediterranean Reverie'. Again, the style of 'reverie' is a necessary extravagance, one which can do justice to the extravagant energies and achievements Ford admired in Pound. 'Mr. Pound's words are singularly alive', but their singular life comes from Pound's 'Boisterousness—which is also vitality'; and this in turn comes from the fact that Pound's life, like Ford's, is anything but singular. His 'erudition in fantastic human instances and invention' is not merely a matter of book-learning. Pound has lived these other lives in imagination. Discussing Pound as 'professor of the Romance languages, cattle hand in liners, Cook's guide to Spain, founder of movements in London', tennis player, and 'professional sculptor, duellist, bassoonist and composer of operas', he says: 'He has acquired his fantastic erudition by really being in turn all these things.' 'Fantastic erudition' equivocates finely between the senses of impressive actual learning and—perhaps equally impressive—imaginary information (a fantasy-erudition). Having been himself an Englishman, a German, now a Franco-American too, a poet, composer, soldier, cook, small producer, traveller, critic, Ford knew what this meant. *It Was the Nightingale* is about 'really being in turn all these things', and thus becoming himself, in words which are, themselves, 'singularly alive'.[2]

Ford and Biala stayed in Toulon through the autumn of 1933 while Ford wrote the sequel to *The Rash Act*, *Henry for Hugh*. Porter and Pressly were due to visit, but did not. Caroline Gordon congratulated Ford on what he had written for Pound's *Cantos*, saying: 'in what you write there is "beauty and emotion and excitement," even in a simple occasional piece like that one.' It was probably in reply to this that he wrote a curiously confessional letter:

I really believe I write, hardened though I may seem, with as much difficulty as any schoolboy who follows his pen round his mouth with his tongue—I don't mean merely letters, I mean everything—and the condition grows. I used to write French with greater fluency than English but lately I have been writing articles and letters in French and found them as difficult as English. I don't suppose it means that I am losing fluency: merely that, as my time on earth may be presumed to be shortening, I am more and more determined to express exactly what I mean. Still I manage to turn out pretty regularly my thousand words a day at the story of Henry Martin who is now really getting it in the neck.[3]

He was perhaps anxious that the freedom of his late style of reminiscential reverie might seem too casual: that he might appear to have abandoned his commitment to the technical rigours of *le mot juste* and the *progression d'effet*. He had not.

When Lippincott seemed pleased with *It Was the Nightingale*, Ford told Gordon: 'So perhaps I have found my earthly home. As H[enry] J[ames] used to say—it would be nice to find one's final publisher but it would be rather like going into an almshouse!' He tried to interest them in the idea of a collected edition, but they estimated that it would cost about $5,000 to buy up the electroplates and stock of *Return to Yesterday* and the eight books on the list Ford had drawn up for Bonis in 1927, and that they would be unlikely to recoup this amount during the Depression. They expressed an interest in reissuing the novels of *Parade's End* as the *Tietjens Saga*; and they published Ford's next four books. Mizener says rightly that 'A collected edition, Ford thought, made evident a man's acceptance as a writer, as one of those "Deans of English Letters" that he so longed to be'. But he is wrong to imply that there was something delusory or anachronistic in such a belief, when he says: 'The persistence with which he carried this Edwardian idea into the 1930s is revealing.' But it doesn't reveal anything about Ford that the other collected editions Mizener mentions don't reveal about their authors: Conrad's Dent uniform edition (1923–8); Galsworthy's Manaton edition (1923); Wells's Atlantic edition (1924). It is the idea of the collected edition which is persistent. It survived the Depression—there are uniform editions of novels by Philip Gibbs and Rafael Sabatini listed at the end of *The Bulpington of Blup* in 1932. And the idea persists into the later twentieth century, with collected editions of Hardy, Lawrence, Forster, Greene, Compton-Burnett, Gerhardie, Pym. If they signal 'acceptance' they do so by helping to create it: they make the books freely available; they construct an *œuvre*; and they do confer prestige. Ford ought to have one.[4]

His publishing ambitions never compromised his principles, however. When Jenny Bradley told Ford that a German publisher, under Nazi control, wanted to look at *It Was the Nightingale*, probably with a view to translating it, Ford replied: 'I gathered from your letter that you know I should not want to be published by a Nazi publisher. I certainly do not. Please tell the gentleman so.'[5]

Ford and Biala came to Paris at the end of the year, staying in the flat at 37 rue Denfert-Rochereau again, and spending Christmas with the Porter-Presslys. The previous year Porter had wondered about the way Ford got neglected even by those he had helped, saying that she had never seen 'an essay or article about him signed by one of these discoveries of his'. But now, and despite what her biographer calls a 'temporary truce' with Ford and Biala, she chose not to reciprocate Ford's dedication, and published the French song-book he had got her to work on without any dedication. She had written to Biala that 'most human beings—and I suppose artists are that, after all—suffer some blow to their self-esteem in being helped, and develop the canker of ingratitude'. Porter, who liked being the grand-dame, and living with younger men, appears particularly to have resented Ford's patronage. Ford and Biala planned to 'return to Toulon which is our home' at the end of March. Ford sent the manuscript of *Henry for Hugh* to Lippincott on New Year's Day, 1934. Twelve days later, after a short rest, he was trying to get Lippincott to take the *History*, and also suggesting a new idea: the book on *Provence*.[6]

Julie came to stay. She had not only reached the 'awkward age' of adolescence, but had become overweight—she had high blood-pressure and 'something maladjusted in her metabolism'—and Ford, his own terrors of childhood shyness brought back, wrote Bowen a demoralized and devastating letter saying that she had:

been bullied into the idea that she is clumsy and ugly—which there is not the least necessity—or indeed warrant—for her thinking so that to see her slouching along the streets with her back hunched up, her hands in her pockets and her coat tails flying is really a lamentable spectacle if you consider that only a short time ago she had a beautiful figure and a certain grace of carriage.[7]

Biala got her to pose in the nude. And as soon as Lippincott paid for the manuscript, Ford sent her money for some dancing lessons. When he heard that some of the other children at King Alfred School had been arguing against Catholicism, he became anxious that Julie was being 'brutally coerced into apostatising'. The touch of melodrama suggests that he was as worried about her faith in him, just as his bitterness about 'the whole pumblechookishness of English middle class life' was intensified by the fear that Julie would no longer follow the French education that he had wanted for her, and that she had been getting at the École Alsacienne. He may also have feared that she would be turned against him not just by English values in general, but by particular English people like Bowen's friends the Sitwells (who hated Ford, according to Biala), or her friends in the Labour movement. Bowen had brought her to England because Ford couldn't give them the support needed to stay. She deeply resented his implications that she was being neglectful, and that Julie would only experience 'a month or two of realities' at Toulon. She became uncharacteristically angry, and hit back with a defence of middle-class values that was an implied criticism of Ford: 'I am succeeding, after a period of harrowing insecurity & anxiety in building up a new life & background for Julie. She is becoming acquainted with family life & with people who have honourable standards of conduct. In Paris we knew scarcely one happily married couple with children, & I had no where to turn for help & cooperation in matters of health & education.' Bowen herself felt more confident in England. She also felt that it was Ford who had exacerbated Julie's awkwardness, making her feel ashamed of her school clothes to the point where she hid her cap under her mattress, and her jacket under Ford's overcoat; and that his anti-English influence was making it hard for her to adapt to England and learn English. She rejected Ford's assumption that Julie would spend all of the summer at Toulon, saying: 'I am not prepared to give her up during all her free time.' Her letter ends in frustration and despair at having to explain herself all over again, stopping coldly with: 'I do not think it is any use, any more. S.' They managed to reach a practical compromise before long. Julie continued to visit, and Bowen continued acting as Ford's agent in London, succeeding in placing *It Was the Nightingale* with Heinemann. Yet Ford and Stella remained angry with each other, and from now on communicated mainly through Biala—though Ford actually wrote half of the letters to Bowen that Biala signed.[8]

In March 1934 Ford took Biala on her first visit to London, for three months. Perhaps he wanted to show her the city of his birth; he probably also wanted to re-establish contact with the literary life of England, and try to find an English publisher for the *History* and *Henry for Hugh*. On Good Friday he was working at *Provence* in 'the garret of a gloomy, fog-filled, undignifiedly old, London house'—Cheltenham House, at 31 Southampton Street (now Conway Street), Fitzroy Square, and went to look again at the urn over the doorway of Madox Brown's house at 37 Fitzroy Square—the 'funeral urn' that he had felt might fall and crush him as a boy, and that he had included a photograph of in *Ancient Lights*. What struck him most was that 'London does not change very much'. He was impressed by the barber at Charing Cross Station: 'The tonsorial artist put his sheet round my neck without any visible emotion, flourished his scissors, made a few passes, and then with a fine casualness remarked: "Forty years ago it was that I first cut your 'air, sir [. . .]."' At least he had not been completely forgotten in England. It is the fine casualness of Ford's temporal artistry, in which the present impression of the city is at once story and autobiography, all blended with his-own fine casualness of illuminative exaggeration: 'you would say that the same rabbits, ducks and puppies decorate to-day the naturalist's shop at which at the age of eleven you bought your first jackdaw.'[9] In *Provence* Ford writes about taking Biala to see what he considered 'the only Great View in London or the British Empire':

It is to be seen from the third step of the left-hand entrance staircase of the National Gallery. You look from there across Trafalgar Square, down Whitehall, that wide, historic street that has seen the fall of our kings and the making of the histories of worlds, to the dreaming spires of the Abbey in which Nelson expected to be buried and was not and the other, taller-mounting spires of that Mother of Parliaments who too has played her not always inglorious part in the story of our planet. In certain weathers and most usually at dusk these things are lifted up; Whitehall becomes a majestic canyon, the spires tower and tower, filling the skies, and if the Londoner ever wants to be inspired with the thought of his Imperial destinies there is the place where he may be proud. That View cannot show you the Parthenon, or the Forum of Rome, or the Place de la Concorde or even the Maison Carrée at Nîmes. But in its way it is enough!

It is, as Mizener says, an 'outburst of ironic patriotism', which conjures back Ford's memories of being that proud Londoner, while remaining aware that he is turning a View into a 'story'—the story of our planet; history. Impressionistic history, of course, just as this story of a view is a reminiscential impression, ironized by the fact that it is no longer like that: 'the only thing that Biala could see were the pink, shuddering, illuminated letters of publicity' on the electric signs that made London seem like New York. As ever, Ford is the technically conscious impressionist, curious whether a particular composition of forms will produce the *effect* of imperial emotions; equally characteristically, he is sceptical about them once they are conjured (if only in memory). Later in the book such patriotism is disavowed immediately it is expressed: 'Patriotism is the meanest of all the virtues and an alcoholism to which one succumbs at one's peril.' Yet *Provence* also has a moving description of Ford's feeling for Provence. It is 'a loving equanimity': 'Having once seen it you may, like a lover who is convinced that his young woman still desires him beyond the mountains and across the seas, draw strength from the knowledge that that land exists and is unchanging. There will be no actual need to visit it again.' Like Ashburnham's hope that Nancy 'should go five thousand miles away and love him steadfastly as people do in sentimental novels'? It is a revealing comment about the significance of travel to Ford, and his investment of passion in views and places, securing them against the displacements and impermanencies of love.[10]

Juliet Soskice asked them to dinner. Biala remembers her telling them she never ate garlic (Ford had probably been advocating it), without realizing that her—good—cook had used plenty of it for the lamb they were eating. She was evidently fond of Ford, said Biala, and was coolly affectionate towards him. They looked up Douglas Goldring, who was writing art reviews for the *Studio*, and who they hoped would be able to help arrange a London exhibition for Biala. But, said Goldring, 'The London art world had forgotten him', and they got nowhere. Goldring felt that Ford was disappointed in him for not having the necessary influence; and that Biala was disappointed when she showed him her paintings and, though he admired them, he was tongue-tied. Nevertheless, they dined together several times. Goldring was shocked to see Ford in such 'reduced circumstances' at his age. He told Ford that Violet Hunt wanted to see him again, but Ford refused. He and Biala visited the British Museum, which brought back Ford's memories of the Garnetts, and of his researches in the Reading Room on Henry VIII, interrupted by his need to rush out for a cigarette, when he would be waylaid by someone like Edward Garnett, and taken off to the Vienna Café. Now Ford was struck with the feeling, which he said he had had all his life, but had never before put into words, that the British Museum was one of the world's 'two earthly paradises'—the other being Provence. 'I have spoken with some contempt of scholars and scholarship', says Ford. But now he felt it was 'absurd to decry scholarship': 'Accuracy of mind and a certain erudition are as necessary to the imaginative writer as is native genius. But I was born in the days of the full desert breath of the terrible commercial scholarship of Victorian times'—the days when, he jokes, preparing a pamphlet on 'Shakespeare's Insomnia, Its Cause and Cure' gave someone the right to emend and annotate into extinction the works of great writers. The British Museum was a reminder of how his own career as a novelist had been founded on the erudition acquired while studying Henry VIII. Ford's view of erudition had changed: he was less interested in historical reconstruction, and more in historical fabulation (though that shift was already visible when he decided to turn the true story of Aaron Smith into 'Seraphina', and to recast his novelistic biography of Henry into the trilogy of historical novels). *Provence* and *Great Trade Route* are, amongst other things, paeans to the erudition which enlivens travel: 'the eruditions necessary for pleasure'—the store of human instances, coincidences, illuminative exaggerations, that can bring a place to life, by turning it into a narrative impression. They spent a sunny weekend at Bignor, in Sussex, with a friend from his Bedham days, Anthony Bertram. *Provence* describes Ford's musings on the familiar Pulborough train, and their visit to the Roman Villa at Bignor. From there they saw Roman Chichester, another stop on what Ford was already describing as the 'Great Trade Route'. He was not only mapping out his books about the flux of Latin civilization, but also gauging the changes in himself since he had been buried in the

Sussex countryside after the war. Now he found that the moment he left London, he felt a sudden claustrophobia about being on an island, and that: 'The dreadful greennesses of the countrysides frighten me.' He was also taking stock of how much he had changed as a writer. When Janet Adam Smith asked him to write something on James for the *Listener*, he told her: 'I have written so much about Henry James and the subject is so vieux jeu—and in a sense, dangerous, that I cannot bring myself to write about him any more. Besides, as the years have gone on I have grown more and more antipathetic to the Master of Rye. Why not ask Mr. [T. S.] Eliot himself to do it: he has been reversing my mental processes.'[11] Ford saw Eliot, Walpole, Richard Hughes, and the Compton Mackenzies in London this spring. He met an intelligent young admirer, Edward Crankshaw, a reader for Allen & Unwin, who was to become one of his most supportive friends for the rest of his life. Crankshaw remembered:

This heavy, rather lumpy figure in shapeless, battered tweeds, panting, often gasping like a fish, would sit upright, legs apart, on a hard chair in a bare attic room like a king on his throne—and talk like an angel about everything under the sun—without the faintest suggestion that he had no idea where next week's rent was coming from—showering on his listeners pure gold.[12]

Heinemann published *It Was the Nightingale* on 28 May, soon after Ford had left England. Crankshaw wrote to Ford about it at the end of the year: 'Apart from the familiar pleasure of contact with your mind—much more familiar than you know— which is one of the intensest pleasures known to me and one of the most stimulating, I was simply bowled over by the technical brilliance of the whole thing.' It was exactly the kind of reaction any writer needs; but the fact that Crankshaw went on to make some tactful technical criticisms of the book would only have made Ford more interested. Crankshaw kept up his admiration, telling Ford that *Joseph Conrad* was 'one of the most beautiful books written on any subject in any age in any language in the world', and that 'the most amazing feat in the literature of this century' was the second part of *A Man Could Stand Up*—. Was he wrong to think that Ford was 'someone who, with all his faults, was a great man'? Crankshaw began, as Mizener said, to act as 'an unofficial and very skillful literary agent for Ford', introducing him to his firm. Trying to help Ford, or get him to help himself was 'like trying to drag a horse out of a burning stable', said Crankshaw. Stanley Unwin had great respect for Ford's writing, and took him on, publishing his last five books in England. At last he had found another 'sympathetic and imaginative' publisher with the confidence in his talent to persist with his books, and with tact in his dealings with authors. As a result, their relationship was the warmest Ford had with a publisher since Duckworth; and his fame experienced a 'mild revival' in England.[13]

The night before they returned to France, Goldring saw them again—it was to be his last meeting with Ford—at 'a sort of bottle-party, got up at short notice by Lett Haines and Cedric Morris [painters they had known in Montparnasse], though our nominal hostess was Lady Ankaret Jackson. Ford, at nearly sixty—now a stout and rather stertorous figure—revolved slowly but majestically round the room, with Biala in his arms.' On 15 May Ford and Biala sailed to Dieppe, and travelling via Paris, Dijon, and Orange, reached Tarascon by Pentecost Sunday. (Ford was still fond of dating events by festivals and saints' days—perhaps as much because it turned calendar-numbers into characters and stories, as out of piety.) They were told there was a bullfight at Nîmes that afternoon, and they could just get there in time if they took the bus. They did. Biala drew the *mise à mort in situ*, and Ford wrote a spellbinding account, bristling with vivid disavowals, in *Provence* which rivals Hemingway in its understanding of the *effects* of the spectacle:

when, at the arrival of the time for the *véronique*, with a matchless bull and a Lalanda to go through it, that amazing and prolonged dance of butterflies was performed, impenetrably grave Lalanda with his back to his charging adversary, swinging the scarlet cape to right and left in his rear, with the rhythm of a flashing crinoline when a woman runs . . . why, that so passed out of the realm of human and animal possibilities that I felt that if Lalanda should slip and fall the bull would stand to attention, waving his *fleuret* and inviting his adversary to recover his feet. . . . And the knowledge that the bull wouldn't only added to my breathlessness. . . . But that is the impression, that of two courteous and engrossed duellists functioning in a fairy tale.

It is the fantastic and the unthinkable [. . .] it was as if he were walking, a marine deity, to his wedding, through scarlet foam with a black attendant dolphin gambolling around him. . . . And the countless thousands, the whole parti-coloured lining of that immense Roman bowl, thinking as I thought, feeling as I felt—to give me the infection of all their minds and the infinite satisfaction of being at one with one's fellows over a supreme work of an incomparable art! [. . .] It is to have that feeling of unity in admiration that I go now and then to see a *mise à mort*—I, a man who cannot bring himself to kill a snail, and who when I have won out in an argument have a feeling of shame.

Typically of Ford's delicately interconnected prose, the argument doesn't stop here. Lest the appreciation of the fight seem callously aesthetic, Ford works in later an ominous human *mise à mort* which struck them later that day, just after they had admired the Maison Carrée at Nîmes—'the most beautiful building that was ever built'. The 'singular Destiny of Provence gave one of her enigmatic smiles': 'An automobile coming from behind our backs knocked down—before the very portals of that house—just under our faces and so that he actually touched one of our unfortunate American ladies, a poor old peasant. And there he lay dead. . . .'[14] Ford stayed at the Villa Paul over the summer to finish *Provence*. When there was discussion of his nephew, Peter Soskice, coming to stay, Ford described their daily routine at the Villa Paul in a letter to his sister Juliet. Peter, who was 15, had begun to write. Ford thought he had 'really a gift for verse', and felt that 'probably it would do him good to talk about these things with me'; though his encouragement is balanced by a warning about the sparseness of their life in Toulon:

Janice orders that contrary to all habit, precedent, family practice, the laws of war and the dictates of humanity, I should take up my pen and write to you . . . Et voila!

It is mostly about Peter's coming here. We should like to have him very much and I should think it might be good for him to lead the frugal life of the Provençal peasant—which is what we very emphatically do, though whether he would like it so much I am not so certain. We live almost completely in the open air. I get up at five or five thirty, most days; water the garden; work; breakfast about eight, when Janice graces the scene. Then we both work till lunch; take a siesta till half past three or four; work in the garden till dinner and go to bed between half past nine or ten. People of course come to lunch or dinner or tea fairly often and that hospitality is returned; but I personally often do not go off the estate—two acres—for two or three weeks. On the other hand Peter could diversify this programme by bathing—the Mediterranean is just below the garden—boating, if he liked to hire a boat, fishing, going to the Movies of which there are seven in Toulon and several hundred in the surrounding villages, making motor trips or running about with the local boys and girls—or he could work in the garden when those gaieties pall. There is no necessity for him to bring a tent if that prospect alarms you; he can have a room correctly furnished in Louis Philippe mahogany with frescoed walls, but we sleep in the open air under a light roof and I should think it would be good for him to do the same. We live very frugally indeed, mostly on things out of the garden, our conversation is mostly about painting, writing and gardening, with intervals devoted to Mr Hitler who is here unpopular; the society we see consists of Americans and French people in about equal proportions and those mostly writers or painters. The sun shines all day; it never rains; the nights are cool; the dawns exquisite but it is usually too hot to do anything between one and four or so.

There were other diversions. On 17 July Ford and Biala crossed the border at Menton for the day, as they often did, having breakfast in France, lunch at Monte Carlo, tea in Italy, and dinner back in France. She drew a vibrant pair of illustrations: 'The Great View into Italy from Provence', showing the 'minatory array of fixed bayonets, machine-guns, uniforms and arresting fists' of the fascist border-guards, contrasted with 'The Great View from Italy into Provence', showing the single guard 'lolling in a deck-chair, a Stetson hat well down over his closed eyes, waving to the passing traveller a negligent hand that tells him to put back his extended passport'. Their point was that 'as an international gesture the dozing guardian is more satisfactory. . . . Manners after all makyth Nations'.[15] There was a 'tropical spell' in September, and enough water for a bumper crop of tomatoes, aubergines, and pimenti. Towards the end of September he was replying to praise from a young writer called Graham Greene:

My dear Sir: Thank you very much: yr. letter being undated I can't tell how long I have left it unanswered—but at any rate during the interval, the occasional remembering of it has given me little touches of pleasure and the feeling that all is not lost!

My only complaint is that you shd. say: 'I am a novelist' & then not send me one of yr. novels! It makes correspondence rather like duelling in the mist with an opponent armed with one doesn't know what weapon!

Send me something—& then we can go on![16]

When Greene sent his latest novel, *It's a Battlefield*, Ford told him it was 'a truly admirable work [. . .] construction impeccable; writing very good indeed & atmosphere extraordinarily impressive', and added: 'I would not have believed that such writing cd. come out of England.' His animus against England couldn't stop him from being one of the best recognizers this century of literary talent. Greene's gratitude for his encouragement while he was struggling to begin never left him. Even at the end of his life he was still rereading *The Good Soldier*, and still thought it 'one of the best in the language this century'. *The End of the Affair* wouldn't have been possible without it. 'I can't tell you the pleasure your letter gave me', he wrote back: 'I have for so long admired you as so incomparably the finest living novelist that your praise goes to my head.'[17]

Ford had also been encouraging Anthony Bertram, who wrote to him:

Looking up your old letters the other day I realise again what an enormous amount I owe you. There is one of several pages giving me the most detailed & valuable criticism. I wonder, now that you have approved of my later products, whether you would let me dedicate my next book in some such words as To Ford Madox Ford, one of the greatest writers of English prose, who encouraged me to write when I was very young & is therefore partly responsible for my continuing to write, I dedicate the first experimental novel that I have felt sufficiently advanced in technique to attempt.

Ford said he'd accept the dedication 'with the greatest pleasure', but was wise enough to advise against such mawkish wording, 'or all the panjandrums—or is it panjandra since they are certainly neuters?—of the United Kingdoms [sic] will throw their bed-pots over you and the book'. Instead he suggested: 'To F.M.F. who went down the drain Anno MCMXIV & since that date abandoned all hope of a glorious resurrection', saying it would 'probably best redound to your reputation'. It was tributes like these from Greene and Bertram that made Ford think of himself as a Dean of English Letters, a role he needed to play to bolster his self-confidence in the face of poor sales. If the tributes didn't exist, the role-playing would be arrogant self-advertisement. But it was Ford's generous nature to deserve such hyperbolic praise, and his fate that the hyperbole tended to make people feel it was his exaggeration.[18]

On 19 October, just after *Henry for Hugh* was published by Lippincott, Ford and Biala sailed on the *Koenigstein* to New York from Antwerp, with their Paris neighbours, the poet Walter Lowenfels, his wife, and their baby twins. Apart from Ford they were 'Jews of assorted sizes', he said. He was photographed on the boat holding the babies. They had booked a passage on a German line, after being assured in Paris that it was not run by Nazis. It was. A Nazi professor of philosophy got drunk, and started boasting that 'all Jews, all Catholics, all Communists' would be put up against a wall and shot. There was a nostalgic moment as the boat passed the Kent coast: 'Eventually a grey hillside with clumps of coppices on the shoulder. I used to own that spot once. Slowly it glides by too. *Tempi passati; tempi passati*, Conrad used to groan after he had left that place and mood.' It was snowing when they landed in the brown mud at Weehawken dock. Ford and Biala took the only pre-1840 apartment they could find on Lower 5th Avenue: number 61. It was 'incredibly mouldy; the radiator in the studio does not function at all; that in the living-room broils you. The refrigerator in the night makes sounds like the Yeth hounds passing overhead on Exmoor; the bath water appears to come through the refrigerator.' Ford was warned not to use the gas-stove 'for fear of explosions'. He suffered from gout. A destitute violinist called—he had read Ford's address from a newspaper interview—hoping that he could introduce him to friends who would hire him to play after their dinners.[19]

On Christmas Eve Ford went to the Church of St Philip Neri. He remembered his feeling when last there in 1926 that the statue of 'Our Lady of the Seven Dolours' had looked at him and told him: 'You will never see Christmas here again.' He wondered how it was that the prophecy appeared wrong; yet that night, over the telephone, they were invited by Theodore Dreiser to spend Christmas Day at the house he had built overlooking Croton Lake near Mount Kisco. Much of *Great Trade Route* is concerned with questions of Providence: the bad luck that the violinist should come to him while Biala was out shopping and Ford had no money; or the coincidence of hearing what

sounded like a shoot-out on the street while Biala was reading an account of remembered courtly combat in Malory. Once again, Providence seemed to him to be working
itself out: the prophecy had meant he wouldn't be in that church on Christmas Day.
Dreiser was very friendly towards Ford, telling him: 'Dear Ford: There is no one I
would rather see than you', and later praising *Provence* by saying: 'You are a Poet as
well as a master observer [. . .]'—though Ford was to take this as ironic name calling
from a fellow novelist, writing that 'when Mr. Dreiser wishes finally to indicate that I
am a sort of fusionless village imbecile he says: / "You're a poet. . . . That's what you
are. A regular poet."' Dreiser had become interested in the Technocracy movement,
founded by the engineer Howard Scott, a socialistic attempt to overcome the Depression by using more machines. The notion was anathema to Ford, who felt that what he
called 'The Small Producer' 'must again inherit the earth', and enjoyed quoting Lenin
to support him. Rather than Scott's Machine Master, he advocated an ideal type who
'can set his hand to most kinds of work that go to the maintenance of humble
existences'. Scott was also at Mount Kisco that Christmas, advocating totalitarian and
anti-Semitic solutions, and sounding to Ford like another version of the Nazi professor. It's not surprising that Biala got into an argument with him. Ford noted wryly that
'Next morning the engine of the Technocrat's Ford stalls on the little Ferry', and had
to be pushed off by two small boys. Back in their freezing flat he began the year as he
meant to go on, opening the window, and trowelling soil from the window-boxes into
a cracked soup-tureen, in which he planted mustard and cress seed. He was 'a Small
Holder again'.[20]

Walter Lowenfels drove Ford in his Ford—a two-seater—to Flemington, New
Jersey, at the end of January 1935. Ford went to attend the trial of Bruno Hauptmann
for the kidnapping in 1932 and murder of the son of Charles Lindbergh, the first man
to fly solo across the Atlantic. Ford had been commissioned by the Associated Press to
cover the trial. Like the jury, he was convinced of Hauptmann's guilt; but the death
sentence disturbed him, partly because it turned the legal process into a ritual sacrifice,
like a bullfight, and 'exhibitional murder by the body politic' seemed a condemnation
of a civilization; but also because Hauptmann had fought in the trenches as a teenager,
which Ford felt mitigated his responsibility: he was of the 'Lost Generation'. The trial
became 'a long-running carnival circus'. On the first Sunday of the trial the court-
house was opened to sightseers: about 60,000 visitors flocked to the rural town of less
than 3,000. 'I found those Flemington days almost more than I could stand', wrote
Ford. A young reporter from the New York *Post*, David Davidson, met Ford there. To
the journalists, celebrities like Ford brought in by the papers were known as 'trained
seals'. Alexander Woollcott, 'the sage of the *New Yorker*', was also there, as were the
novelists Fannie Hurst and Kathleen Norris. But Ford was 'the most distinguished
trained seal of the lot', and Davidson, himself an aspiring novelist, was 'flattered to do
service' for him. He said Ford was 'well described at the time as resembling a beached
whale and very near destitution because of the meager sales of his novels in the
Depression'. He showed Ford around the town so that he could 'stock up on overnight
supplies'. At the drugstore Ford asked, 'wistfully', for 'the very smallest quantity of
toothpaste that you sell', and elsewhere for 'the cheapest spirits you stock, and the very
smallest quantity'. Biala joined him, drawing the scene in the court-house as the

crowds were waiting for the verdict to be delivered on the following day, 14 February. Hauptmann was found guilty, and electrocuted two years later.[21]

Provence, dedicated 'To Caroline Gordon who chronicles another South and to Allen Tate who came to Provence and there wrote to "that sweet land" the poem called "The Mediterranean" [. . .]', was published in March 1935 by Lippincott (who had also published *It Was the Nightingale* and *Henry for Hugh*). Ford had revised *Ladies Whose Bright Eyes*, which Ruth Kerr's Gotham House wanted to publish, but relinquished so that he could offer it to Lippincott, to keep as many of his books as possible together. When he was offered only $250, Ford replied: 'I have unfortunately to live', and said: 'I remain mindful of the fate of the philosopher's horse. The philosopher, you know, thought that if he reduced his horse's ration one grain a day, the horse would not notice the reduction and would be gradually induced to live on nothing. But the horse died.' Jefferson Jones, the managing editor, came up with $500, having already advanced him $1,250 for *Provence*, and $375 for his next novel, *Vive Le Roy*. This was less than he had been getting from Long and Smith, but more than Lippincott was prepared to go on paying. When Ford suggested a contract for future work, Jones said that they had already lost over $3,000 on the first two books, and that unless one of the next two proved successful 'we feel it would not be sound business judgement to commit ourselves to any new arrangement'. Telling him to feel free to approach other publishers, they were effectively saying they didn't think he would ever prove successful: 'so long as the public will not buy your books, we are helpless.' Once again he was being told he was bad business, and once again the collected edition seemed a mirage. If the Mizener view of Ford as unreasonably touchy were right, there should have been an eruption in the grandest of crushing manners. Instead, he replied: 'I'm much obliged to you for your letter and glad you see your way to publishing LADIES WHOSE BRIGHT EYES on those terms':

I am sorry those books have not done better. I can't really understand it for the ovations I receive in this country and the crowds of people and letter-writers from Hugh Walpole to Park Lane ladies who assure me that I'm the very greatest writer in the world are such that you would think I was the biggest of all big sellers. I spoke at a meeting last Friday and I might have been a Hollywood star.[22]

He knew that 'Of course all that is to be very much discounted', and that he would never be the biggest seller. (The next year Margaret Mitchell's *Gone with the Wind* sold 1,500,000 copies.) But the disparity between praise and sales must have been perplexing. Perhaps he was restraining disappointment and anger because he had had bitter experience of alienating publishers *before* they published a book. Or perhaps he hoped the sales of *Provence* would change Jones's mind. They didn't. Only 2,547 copies were sold out of the 3,350 Lippincott printed. Or perhaps he could be truly stoical, realizing that in the long term what mattered was the quality of the work. *Provence* is a charming, captivating book; an essential expression of Ford's love of the Mediterranean and of French culture—essential for readers of *The Good Soldier* and *Parade's End* as well as for travellers. It is, as the reviewers said: 'gay, discursive, satiric, brilliant: it is before all else readable'; 'a new and exciting interpretation [. . .] not only a magnificent revelation of "the frame of mind that is Provence," but an autobiography, a history and a philosophy as well [. . .] in no sense the usual superficial travel book'; 'Written in the exact and beautiful English of a great stylist'. Even the *Catholic World* liked the book. The reviewer regretted his fondness for the Albigensian heretics, of course, but thought: 'Mr. Madox Ford would probably be the last to deny his frivolity and general unreliability as a theologian.' Ford told Caroline Gordon that the book was part of his project to 'raise the "serious" book to the level of the novel by writing it with as much passion and similar technique'.[23]

In New York Ford gave an interview to advertise the publication. He concocted a delightful ancestral romance to account for his culinary expertise: 'Ford Madox Ford, he breaks in to explain, rather runs to uncles. One of the tribe, who was a forty-niner in California, later married an Italian duchess. At their home in Italy, Ford put in his time learning to cook. The chef who taught him later became affiliated with the King of Italy. Ford feels that he acquired at this time the finest possible grounding in culinary technique.' He made some serious prophecies about politics too. The central one, that there would not be another European war for many years, was what he had wanted to believe, and what he had been saying for a long time. Though he was wrong, his reasons were mostly proved right. 'Hitler, encouraged by his recent success in the Saar, would probably like to acquire Memel and the Polish Corridor, or even Alsace-Lorraine, if he didn't believe he'd get all Europe after him for it.' He thought Hitler would not attack France because 'Germany would undoubtedly find herself opposed by Russia, whose army is the strongest and most efficient of them all'. 'The next war, in the opinion of Ford, will undoubtedly be fought between Japan and the United States or Japan and Russia.'[24]

He began writing for the *American Mercury*. 'Hands Off the Arts' appeared there in April 1935—an eloquent case for the educative role of art, as distinguished from propaganda and factual instruction. It is the counter-argument to what he calls the 'sadist objurgations of a technocrat leader' he had heard recently. Howard Scott seemed the heir of the Prussian *Kultur* he had opposed twenty years before; a champion of technological 'instruction'. 'But whereas instruction is a pumping in of records of facts', wrote Ford, 'education consists in the opening of men's minds to the perception of fitnesses'. The arts 'do not instruct; they sensitize'. He gives a subtle account of how, through engrossing yourself in a work of art 'that most permanently has impressed itself on your personality', 'You will ensure in yourself a certain change': 'You will ensure for yourself a moment of silence and in that your perceptions of human values will become more clear in your subconsciousness. For the immediate effect of the contemplation of matchless things is a marking time of the spirit, a deep oblivion of the material passions of the world surrounding you.'[25] This belief that oblivion was both the source and sign of art had always been at the core of his aesthetics. He once defined 'rendering' as 'that subtle trickery of the beholder into an oblivion of himself that is art' (—which? the trickery or the oblivion?) It is a fine essay, which reveals not only the way Ford's thinking about art was adapting to face the new challenges from technology and totalitarianism, but also its essential continuity with his pre-war aesthetics. The 'marking time of the spirit' recalls the 'pause in the beat of the clock' experienced by the spectator in *The Soul of London*, or Ford's rapt responses to Holbein. It is, also, still an essentially Jamesian stance. Though the essay doesn't mention James, this passage is an excellent analysis of those crucial moments in James's novels—Isabel Archer alone with the sculpture in Rome; Milly Theale confronting the Bronzino at Matcham—when contemplation of a work of art offers a clarification of human values—a moment of spiritual significance. Paul Palmer, the editor of the *American Mercury*, liked the second article, on Conrad, so much that he invited Ford to continue with a 'series of portraits of well-known English authors whom you have known personally'. It was a godsend, since Curtis Brown (who was now acting as Ford's agent in London) had written to say that there was no market for the *History*, the first volume of which Ford had just finished revising. The portrait project changed as Ford wrote these essays over the next two years, eventually including un-English writers like James, Turgenev, and Dreiser. When collected, they formed one of Ford's best books of critical reminiscences: *Portraits from Life*, published in England as *Mightier Than the Sword*.[26]

Ford set off to Tennessee to visit the Tates. He took a train to Philadelphia, and a bus to Washington, where he stopped for a day or two. Parts II and III of *Great Trade Route* describe his journey through New Jersey, Delaware, Maryland, and Virginia. This may have been when he visited Gunston Hall, Mount Vernon, and other Virginia mansions, on his way. The Tates had 'quite a pleasant bungalow jus[t] on the edge of a wood in a suburb [a]bout five miles from the centre of Memphis', he wrote to Biala on 6 April. She was staying in New York to prepare an exhibition of her paintings of Provence, including her drawings for Ford's book, at the Gallery Passedoit: 'Here I am in the sunny South and there is a blizzard blowing and it's infinitely colder than New York and I'm writing just a note to say good night to you, in my frozen bedroom after an exhausting day—three interviews, the lecture at the ladies' club, a dinner of six here and a party of about fifty that [. . .] has just broken up at about one in the morning. . . .' The next morning he went into more detail, showing how he was beginning to explain to himself his difficulty in selling books:

The Lady's Club lecture was like any other Ladies' Club lecture. You need not have worried about my untruth in telling Lippincott's that I was lecturing: I knew I should have to and I did—just as I knew that Lippincotts would not have books there and they didn't. The Ladies had ordered ten copies by wire and did not get them—and there is not a copy for sale in the t[ow]n—partly owing to the bookseller having sold the five she had ordered and to her not having received the copies she had re-ordered. Don't be too enraged about this: it is always the same.

He had told Lippincott he thought the booksellers were an obstacle too: he suspected they disliked him. His publishers always claimed there was little demand for his work. But his public appearances convinced him that the demand exceeded the supply.[27]

The blizzard must have abated, since *Great Trade Route* also describes how he watched humming-birds from the Tates' balcony, and visited the zoo with Caroline Gordon. Robert Penn Warren had invited Ford to speak on 'What is a provincial literature' at the Writers' Conference organized by the *Southern Review* at Baton Rouge, Louisiana, on 10 and 11 April, as part of the celebration of the seventy-fifth anniversary of Louisiana State University. Writers like Randall Jarrell, John Peale Bishop, and Hodding Carter attended. Faulkner was expected, but is not mentioned in the transcript. The Tates drove Ford to Baton Rouge with John Gould Fletcher, who arrived 'armed to the teeth', according to Caroline Gordon. He had rowed with the Tates, then wrote to ask them to take him with them to Louisiana. When he heard Ford was going too he said that an Englishman had no right to be there, and threatened to fight both Ford and Gordon 'to the death'. 'When he got there he was as mild as milk and was particularly nice to Ford', Gordon told Sally Wood: 'I really think the man is mad.' Ford heard two speeches by Huey Long there: the first, to a gathering of farmers, in a dialect Ford couldn't understand; the second, at lunch at the University, 'in exactly the dialect, with the vapidity, with the images—and even some of the accent—of a Cambridge—England—Head of a College addressing his staff on a not very important occasion'.[28]

Ford makes his first appearance in the transcript of the proceedings on the second day, giving the audience 'whatever benefit my considerable experience with magazines may provide':

The periodicals with which I have been associated have been noncommercial. Some capitalist gives the money, and it runs out [. . .] The commercial editor has to take the business manager's opinion. If you want to have a Southern magazine, let it not be necessarily Southern but simply good (and noncommercial) as *a result of the editor's instinct or knowledge of the community in which he works*. The problem is very clear. I talk of imaginative literature [. . .] The only permanent matter is imagination [. . .] The imaginative magazine is precluded from commercial success.[29]

In the closing session he offered definitions which were also self-definitions:

1) Provincial literature is native and of the folk, as in the mummers and troubadours.
2) Provincial literature is based on vast knowledge of your region. ('My glass is small but I drink out of my own glass.') You can't write successfully without accumulating a vast store of human instances. This gives you tranquillity.
3) But you must write with your eye on the world, which is your public. I have stood all my life for complete cosmopolitanism [. . .] There is only one republic that has ever lasted—the republic of the arts, and in the long run there is no nationality in the arts. But to write successfully, you must broaden your knowledge of your home [. . .] I've almost given up the novel because I don't have enough knowledge of New York.[30]

With his penchant for playing the poor lion in a den of savage Daniels, Ford pursued his advocacy of cosmopolitanism by telling the Southerners 'You do not grow up as a writer until you discover you have to write for someone else, that writing is a communication with an ideal reader or class, not necessarily a large public'; and by defending 'New York against the flower of the Intelligentsia of the Deep South'—the very writers who had been forging the doctrine of regionalism and Agrarianism throughout the 1930s—saying that New York 'overcomes the writer's loneliness' (it overcame his) and that it was encouraging Southern writers. Ford felt Fletcher 'prowling at the back of the audience asking them why they do not lynch me' (he had been arguing with Fletcher in the car to the university about the merits of George Washington), and Caroline Gordon 'starting with indignation at my every second word'. The transcript indeed has both Fletcher and Gordon shouting 'Oh, not at all!' in unison, to his argument that New York was a good distributing centre for writers. In his closing remarks, however, Ford told them what they wanted to hear. 'You in the South now have the world at your feet', he said: 'The North and the East are exhausted. The industrialism of the Midwest is even worse than eastern industrialism.' He even mischievously claimed to have argued out the question of industrialism and propaganda with Lenin and Trotsky, and that they had agreed with him. The Conference proved that the South was once again becoming prosperous, he said. He expressed surprise that none of the women writers he admired, like Gordon or Elizabeth Madox Roberts, had been asked to address the meeting. And he ended with an eloquent defence of agrarianism, suggesting that the history of the Civil War could be transcended: 'You were conquered in a war; now, at peace, you are conquering the conqueror of your former conquerors. That is *revanche noble!*' His economic arguments made sense in the Depression, and anticipated the radical and ecological movements of the second half of the century. 'Seventy years ago you stood for the fruits of the earth and the treasures of the craftsman, means of wealth that alone can be coterminous with the life of this earth.' The industrial system, which had triumphed since the Civil War, now seemed 'crumbling into its final decay', whereas the South kept faith with its tradition of agriculture: 'measured by human lives, the pursuits and earnings of the husbandman constitute the only wealth that is and must be as durable as humanity itself'. After he had finished his tribute to the Agrarians as the hope for 'the future of civilization', Penn Warren asked him to talk for another half-an-hour, 'to fill in the schedule before the next meeting'. In *Great Trade Route* he renders himself hearing his voice going on talking: 'What the devil is it saying? . . . I must pull myself together.' He did so, in typical Fordian style, by telling them a story: a delightful little vignette, told in a probably fictional English dialect which must have been incomprehensible to them. 'It can be made a long story', he explains:

In short, it is the tale of a cook in her kitchen who said to a stable-boy who came in dripping with wet out of the rain:

'You are wet now. You cannot be anything but wet. Fetch me a bucket of water.' The stable-boy fetched the water. He poured it over the cook and remarked: '[. . .] *You're* wet now. You can't be anything but wet. Fetch it yourself. . . .'[31]

The story was about a tiny hamlet on the borders of Yorkshire and Lancashire. Ford tells how forty-one of the sixty inhabitants died during the American Civil War, 'Of the results of deprivation during the Cotton Famine'. He could almost be talking about the American South here, and when he closes with the hamlet's 'old tradition' of heaving a brick at any oncoming stranger, the story's relevance to the Agrarian regionalists becomes clear. Ford's ideal of cosmopolitan literary culture can include writers from the most diverse of regions. But regionalism itself needs to beware of the parochialism and prejudice that leads to violence and civil war. It's characteristic of the way he can get himself—in life or in writing—out of a tight corner with an inventive story, told so that, only gradually, 'your perceptions of human values will become more clear in your subconsciousness'. 'They have not lynched me', he notes with relief: 'Mr. Tate even laughed a little. . . .' Ford didn't believe in 'provincial literature', only literature. The Memphis paper that had interviewed him when he arrived wrote a follow-up piece saying he had 'created quite a stir in literary circles'. He wrote an important essay on 'Techniques' for the first issue of the *Southern Review*, which had been started as a result of the Baton Rouge Conference.[32]

Ford took the train back to Tennessee with Tate (Gordon drove on to New Orleans with Polly Lytle for four or five days). Biala sent a telegram calling him back to New York to sign a contract with Oxford University Press for a new volume of *Collected Poems* and for *Great Trade Route*. He was back in time for the opening of her exhibition. At the end of May William Carlos Williams became involved in Ford's gathering of impressions about American (agri)culture for *Great Trade Route*, taking the Fords to a New Jersey truck farm. Williams recalled the sight of Ford, who gave him 'the impression of having been poured into his clothes or any chair that was fortunate enough to contain him', 'Incongruous to the last degree' as he 'whisked himself about the New Jersey farm landscape'. Pursuing him across a field he saw a snipe racing before them. 'He never saw it to my knowledge', said Williams, thinking Ford too deep in conversation with their host. But Ford had seen it, and more of it. He saw it fly up into the air in front of them, then fall to the ground 'with a smash that one would have thought would have broken every bone in its little body. And fluttered, broken, along the ground towards us [. . .] sending out its heart-rending wails just not inches outside our grasp.' It was an example of the maternal στοργή (affection) that he knew about from Gilbert White, when a parent jeopardizes its own life for the sake of its offspring. And, as one can detect from the passion of the description, it becomes an emblem for human versions of altruism, including that sacrifices made by the artist while sending out his heart-rending renderings.[33]

Ford had lunch with Paul Palmer at the Plaza to discuss the series of *Portraits from Life*. He wrote to Orrick Johns, the secretary of the left-wing Organisation Committee of the American Writers' Congress, saying that he felt 'a certain delicacy' about an invitation from the Congress: 'though I might almost be called an American writer I am not a citizen of this country so that I consider that I ought not to meddle in the internal politics of the U.S.A.' There was another visit to the Tates now at Benfolly, Clarksville, Tennessee, in the middle of June, during which Ford told Howard Lowry of Oxford University Press that it was very humid, and that he was 'managing, if languorously, to get together lots of re-impressions for the G.R.'. He also explained that he had made over the American rights of these two new books and others to Biala. At the end of June he arranged the Oxford contract with Dr Lowry. And on the 29th Ford and Biala boarded the *Roma* bound for Naples. They had to travel third class. The crossing took nearly a fortnight, and Ford described it as 'simply Purgatory': it was an 'immense, heaving, roaring, hysterically screaming, pushing, shoving, stinking ship'; it was too noisy to sleep; Ford took refuge in the 'dim Jewish quarter', full of orthodox Jews bound for Palestine. The food was 'fantastically barbarous; the purser who invented it must have had an imaginative genius'. The menus promised a different meal each day, but the food was always the same. The first-class passengers paraded above, 'gorgeous cinema stars [. . .] hair blowing back in the dawn wind [. . .] as far above my head as Pallas Athene when she rescued Athenians from battlefields'. They stopped at Gibraltar; then at Malaga, where there was time to see the cathedral, and an exhibition of modern Spanish art. Ford thought the 'literal renderings of sores, bleeding wounds, torments, tortures' were not sadistic, but 'the manifestations of tradition, of education . . . of religion, perhaps'. When thanking Anthony Bertram for *Men Adrift*, the novel Bertram had dedicated to him, Ford argued that 'Christ-ism'—modelling yourself, as Tietjens does, on 'the English ideal of the Redeemer' and expecting to have 'a good time'—needs to be distinguished from Christianity: 'Christianity isn't you know a Sunday supper with the maids given the evening off; it is eating flesh and drinking blood.' (Need one add that this was another passage that Graham Greene marked in his copy of Ford's letters?) They had wanted to take a coastal steamer from Pompei up the Italian coast to get back to Toulon, but Mussolini had invited a large group of boys to sing *Giovinezza* for him, and the noise of the incessant practising was so unbearable they got off at Monte Carlo on 11 July, and reached the Villa Paul two days later.[34]

1935–1936: THE CAUSE OF GOOD
LETTERS

I am the kind of person whose truths eventually swim up to the surface.

(Ford to Julie Ford, 11 September 1935)

Julie came to stay at the Villa Paul in the summer of 1935. She recalled helping Ford with the 'early morning irrigation of his vegetable patch' as he thought out his day's writing—his alternative to playing patience:

Ford was always a devoted gardener, with a real green thumb—and at the Villa Paul in Cap Brun he would stand at the top end of a furrow and lay the hose there, and I would watch the water trickle down to my end, past the lettuces, cucumbers, and beans, while he did some more thinking and cogitating. Then I would call, he would move the hose, and the process would be repeated again and again. But woe betide me if I started to chatter! The social amenities were for later in the day, when the writing was done—that terrible, all-consuming writing that had to be completed whatever the cost, if the deadline were to be met, the advance earned. We would sit on the terrace under the stars, looking down the hill toward the Mediterranean and watching the twinkling lights of the boats in the water. Then he and I would discuss—oh, philosophy, art, justice—all the things that a teenager grows earnest about. From tolerance of all things but cruelty and dictatorship, to the right amount of garlic and herbs to put in a particular casserole. . . . And what a teacher he was! My rapid improvement in Latin, under his tutelage, positively got me into trouble with my teacher, who could not understand this sudden improvement—and how could I explain to her that it was not that my father did my homework *for* me, but merely that when he taught I could learn—which was more than I could say for her?[1]

They took trips to nearby Les Sablettes, and along the Côte d'Azure to Nice and Ventimiglia. Julie went to stay with the Marcoussis for the second half of August. There had been tension with both Julie and Stella when Louis Marcoussis had told Ford in front of others that Julie, who rarely wrote to Ford, had written to him. It was exacerbated by the fact that a trip to Italy that Ford had promised Julie had to be put off until 15 August because the heat was too great for Ford's heart; at which point Bowen was piqued that the plans she made had been changed. Biala wrote to Bowen: 'I am of course ready to have Julie in my house at any time or all the time, but I must at all costs protect Ford from unpleasantnesses.' That Fordian plural suggests that Ford had actually dictated the letter for Biala to sign, as he often did at this time. It was about now that Julie told him she would leave the Catholic Church, which Biala said made him very unhappy. She later remembered having many rows with Ford during her teens. In September Ford wrote Julie a massive letter. He was hurt by what she had been saying about him (or what he had been told she had been saying), and felt he needed to explain himself to her, and assure her that his objections to her English traits didn't mean that he didn't love her:

I think I am going to write a serious letter to you because I am in the mood and because it is possible that we may never meet again—though that will not be my fault. You suffer under various difficulties as regards myself. You don't I think doubt my deep affection for you any longer [she evidently *had* doubted it earlier] but there are other queernesses about me that no doubt puzzle you. Politics no doubt have a great deal to do with it. You live apparently amongst the middle-class Left in England and I live about the world with no politics at all except the belief—which I share with Lenin—that the only thing that can save the world is the abolition of all national feelings and the prevailing of the Small Producer—and the Latin Tradition of clear-sightedness as to what one means oneself.

Why I lay great stress on the French and Latin languages for you is this: Anglo-Saxondom is a hybrid collection of human beings all of whose refineménts and practical sense comes from the Latin Tradition and all of whose vaguenesses and self-deceptions and worship of the Second Class in trains, arts, cuisines, vintages and personal habits comes from the Teutonic strain [. . .]

England is admirable on account of its legal system—which is why I wanted you to be trained as an international lawyer in Paris. You would thus have got the best of both mental worlds—which could only have helped you in whatever subsequent artistic career you might espouse—because only clear thought can help you when you approach artistic problems. The logic of painting or writing or music is just as clear and is provided by the same mental processes as that of the Law whether of England or the Code Napoléon.

[. . .] But use what clarity of mind you have to prevent your taking sides until you are sure what side your essential temperament will force you to take. You made, for instance, the violent pronouncement the other day: 'I de*test* the pre-Raffaelites,' a sentiment no doubt put ready made into your mouth [. . .] You cannot really know very much about these direct and collateral ancestors of your own whilst you were speaking to one who passes for the greatest living expert in that particular matter. I am indeed usually called the last of the pre-Raffaelites and you, if you practise any of the arts—as I hope you will—will inevitably in time inherit that sobriquet [. . .]

I recall these instances of your table-talk more in order to explain what I mean when I say that you live among people who de*test* all that I stand for than to criticise yourself. In the natural course of things you will eventually react so violently against your present phase that your present phase, if I find it rather trying, is nevertheless a thing to welcome.

I may of course be only enhancing the feeling of abhorrence that you were represented as feeling for me by writing all this. But I think that, by now, you have achieved a better understanding of how I feel towards you. If I don't cover you with the flattery that you are accustomed to and consider your due it is because I do immensely want to be able one day to be proud of you for yourself and not merely to say that I am enraptured at your on dits [i.e. *on dits*] in the style of someone else. You inherit certain duties from people who for generations have ended their lives in indigent circumstances. So that, not only should you not be so abhorrent of indigence—which nowadays is a thing rather to be proud of: but to carry out those duties you should eschew all easy triumphs. . . . That first of all. And then eschew all triumphs at all. The victor is always contemptible and to hurt people's feelings by words is the most contemptible of all human employments. My grandfather who—as time goes on you will discover to have been not a person to de*test* whatever your friends may tell you—

used to give as a rule of life: Believe nothing: hurt nobody. It is a very good rule. Try to follow it now and then.

There was a time when you used to say je tème de tou mon queur é encor beaucou plussss [je t'aime de tout mon coeur et encore beaucoup plus] and then I was proud of you because it was an expression of yourself [. . .] You are old enough now to understand what all this is about and when you are a real grande personne you will realise the truth of it.

You see, if you will think of it, I am the kind of person whose truths eventually swim up to the surface. They seem silly to you now as they seem to the press and public of your country. But if you think of the persons whose truths, historically, have eventually swum up to the surface of public consciousness and have prevailed you will see that it is the lonely buffaloes, ploughing solitary furrows who have generally produced those truths. So with what used to be called your thoughtless playmates go on jeering at me and what I stand for but nevertheless consider that, in the bottom of your purse, you have a ticket for a lottery which may eventually draw one of the gros lots.

I should not pay much attention to M. Marcoussis. I daresay you may one day write something good—you probably will if you can come across anyone who knows what English is for and how it should be handled [. . .]

And as for me if you put it that jer thème de tou mon qhueur é enchor boocou plusss é ke je toubli jamé you would not be so far from the truth.[2]

It's an extraordinary piece of writing. No one but Ford could, or would, have written it. Its hybrid of hauteur and intimacy, aloofness and pathos, is quintessentially Fordian: at once self-dramatizing and honest. Mizener says that 'however well it expresses his feelings', the letter 'was not calculated to persuade a fourteen-year-old to understand and love him'. Not calculated, assuredly, but not as inappropriate to her age as he implies. She would be a 15-year-old in six weeks, and was mature enough to enjoy Ford's serious conversation at the Villa Paul. Rather than being condescending, he was paying her the compliment of treating her as an adult. When he explains that the reason he is sad she no longer writes to him in French is that her 'English is full of redundancies and unnecessary phrases and that gives me pain', he is showing affection for her in the way he knew best: by giving her technical advice on how to write. In fact Ford could see perfectly well that it was too harsh, and decided not to send the letter. Instead, in a characteristic gesture of expression and suppression, he told her that he had written it, and that it had cost him two days of hard work, but that he had put it to one side as being too 'grande personne' for her, and that she should have it one day. (She must have done, since she kept it with his other letters to her.) Meanwhile, Ford's truth was indeed eventually swimming up to the surface: Julie began at this time to show symptoms of that 'dogged sincerity in the Arts' that he had predicted. Indeed, the force of his predictions must have been hard to resist. He wants to be proud of her for herself, but in order to become herself she has to come into her pre-Raphaelite inheritance; as Ford had become most truly himself by following the precepts of his pre-Raphaelite grandfather. (This wasn't blind loyalty to family traditions: Ford knew that his own art was growing further than ever from that of the Pre-Raphaelites; and his writings on them had become more critical of them. But he didn't want Julie simply to deny that legacy.) Part of the family inheritance is the duty to be an artist. Ford is training her to be a genius, just as he had been trained in the hothouse atmosphere of his Pre-Raphaelite ancestors. Julie 'began agitating to be allowed to leave school at fifteen to study stage design'. Bowen at first resisted, feeling she should matriculate first; but though she was a prodigious reader, her education was still so patchy that it would be a difficult task. Bowen let her go to the recently opened London Theatre Studio, where she felt 'she was in her element at last'. What Ford modestly called her 'inheritance from the pre-Raffaelites'—it was more her inheritance from him—had indeed given her her 'share of dogged sincerity in the Arts'.[3]

Ford worked hard at the *Portraits from Life* through the summer. On 10 October he and Biala made a quick trip to Geneva. They had watched the Italian troops 'entraining for Africa'—Ford told Palmer: 'I can't say that the populace were particularly enthusiastic; we seemed to be the only people who cheered the troops—and that of course only because they are probably going to very nasty deaths, poor devils.' There was 'nothing but war and rumours of war' around Toulon, and they found the noise of aeroplanes and howitzers disturbing. Italy had invaded Abyssinia on 2 October, and Ford and Biala wanted to see the League of Nations delivering its verdict. Returning to Switzerland brought back memories of the last of his dismal nerve-cures of 1904. In *Great Trade Route* he describes being 'visited by one of those fits of absence' that came upon him anywhere, and made him seem somewhere quite other. Here he has a vision of the entire Great Trade Route, stretching from (Ezra Pound's?) Cathay to (the Tates') Memphis, Tennessee. The point is not just to marvel at the impressionist's hallucinatory 'vision', but to contrast Ford's vision of the essential unity of civilization, with the sight of the League of Nations dithering while that civilization trembles on the brink of war. His contempt for politicians was rarely so explicit:

Our leaders of thought are despised and our leaders in material quests are as degenerate, physically and mentally, as any body of men the world has ever seen. Physically almost more than mentally, since they are at least capable of a sufficiency of mental activity to plunge a world into war. But if you took all the Cabinets of the Western world and set them, provided with enough tools, in any rural solitude, they would starve and freeze and soak to death without the physical or mental imagination to plant a brussel sprout or to gather reeds for the thatching of a primitive shelter. . . . And those men govern . . . Us![4]

Having watched the 'representatives' at their lunch, he continues, with a scathing indictment of democratic capitalism that still has powerful relevance, at a time when governments of East and West are intoxicated with the values of a triumphal consumerism that is threatening the life of the entire planet:

How could it be otherwise? We do not choose them for their intellect, their artistic intelligence, their altruism, the mellifluousness of their voices, their physical beauty, their abstract wisdom, their seasoned knowledge of the values of Life. We choose beings who hypnotically suggest that they and they only can fill our individual purses, our maws, our stores, our banking accounts with property that at the moment of their appeal for our suffrages belongs to the heathen stranger . . . or our fellow-countrymen. (p. 104)

The *Mercury* essays proved frustrating during the rest of the year. Palmer had admired the one on James, telling Ford: 'A half dozen people have spoken to me in words of extraordinary praise about the Henry James piece—I am sure it is the best essay ever written about him.' But he was disappointed with the one on W. H. Hudson, feeling that his readers would not know enough about the group of intellectuals Ford had described (those of the Mont Blanc lunches: Garnett, Belloc, the Fabians). Again, if Mizener were right about Ford's touchiness, he should have exploded with rage when Palmer sent the piece back. But he reacted courteously: 'I daresay you are right about the *Hudson*.' He said he thought every educated American *would* know about the Fabians 'because of the big part they have played in Left Developments in both branches of anglo-saxondom'; and where he might be expected to be least concession-ary—in the matter of technique—he said modestly: 'As for the presentation I daresay you are right: at any rate Janice agrees with you and I know I do exaggerate my method now and then. I'll look it over again and turn it round a bit.' Then Palmer objected that the Wells essay had 'a good deal too much about yourself in the portrait and not enough of Wells'. This did exasperate Ford. 'This is of course an impasse', he wrote. 'You are practically asking me to submit articles for your approval.' Nevertheless, he proposed a compromise—one which was necessary to his financial survival as much as to his peace of mind, and one to which Palmer readily agreed: that Palmer should pay him on receipt of the twelve articles he had asked for, and then Ford would amend them for no extra charge if he agreed with the suggestions. He agreed to rethink the Wells piece, though in this case he didn't agree with the criticism. 'You object to the personal tone', he replied, 'but you asked me to write personal articles. Indeed the James article was the most personal thing I ever wrote.' Yet he ends with a character-istic disavowal: 'in order to oblige you I will make the Wells one more impersonal. I should do so in any case when the articles appear in book form because I disapprove of personal writing myself.' Such power-struggles are scarcely uncommon between author and editor, though Ford's indignation was partly stoked by his feeling that he had not tried to exercise control over what his contributors wrote when he was editing the *English Review* or the *transatlantic review*: 'When I was an editor I would not have behaved in such a way to the meanest worm amongst the people who wrote for me.' The wrangling went on until September 1936. Yet even the bitterest moment is founded on a bedrock of friendship and sympathy. When Palmer balked at the prospect of essays on Pound and Dreiser (because the authors had insulted him), Ford wrote: 'You are, you know, treating me very badly', but then said very reasonably that he wouldn't demand that Palmer accept them, but would send the Dreiser piece anyway since he had already written it. He ended by imagining the end to which Palmer's editing would reduce him: 'Thanks for your invitation which sounds good. We'd accept with enthusiasm except that these vexations and uncertainties will prob-ably prevent my coming. . . . I mean you wouldn't probably like to have a coffin delivered on your person.' Melodramatic, certainly: but Ford did worry about his work, and the difficulty of making a living from it, to the point of illness. Palmer didn't think he was being unreasonable, and answered by cabling at once that he would guarantee Ford $450 for 'Dreiser, Swinburne, and the recapitulation [presumably the essay, 'There were Strong Men', published in the book but not in the *Mercury*]'. He followed up the cable by writing: 'Your letter is irresistible—I hereby desist from any argument about orders for articles.' 'I congratulate you on your cable', wrote Ford as soon as he got it: 'Now you shall not go down to posterity along with the gentlemen who killed Keats and refused to publish Chatterton so that he took his own life. Anyhow I'm much obliged for it.' 'Just to let you see the labour these things cost me,' he added, 'I send you what is the third re-writing of this article without having it re-typed. I know you think that I sit down and airily dash off these things whilst playing Chopin on the piano and whipping eggs for a soufflé-maraschino. But it is not so.' He also found it 'difficult to re-read' Lawrence for the essay on him, because he was 'not a hell of a lot in sympathy with him'. As a gesture to show how his friendship had not been dimmed by the wrangling, he dedicated the book version to Palmer, who was overwhelmed: 'Little did I ever think—when I first opened *The Good Soldier* and *Some Do Not* or whatever it was—that one day its distinguished author would address me in a letter, in person, or least of all in print': 'If there have been written finer biographical essays in the language, I do not know of them. And if there is someone writing today who employs prose to his benefit as beautifully and as masterfully as you do I do not know his name [. . .] I shall remember with a very real feeling of pride and pleasure that I was privileged to publish these essays.'[5]

'Once the wolf nearly got us', recalled Biala. For three months the money the *American Mercury* had been cabling to Toulon didn't appear. 'So many firms were failing that Ford was afraid to confirm his fears that this one too had gone bust [. . .]'. On Christmas Day, 1935, he had to write to Julie from Toulon to explain: 'I can't send you any Christmas present because we have literally no money at all.' Their arguments about indigence during the summer perhaps still rankled. He advised her to 'try market-gardening or carpentry. They are both good for exactness of thought and movement and will be useful when, the middle classes having been finally extinguished in a year or so, you have to adapt yourself to proletariate conditions. I don't know where we should be now if I hadn't known how to market-garden.' Bowen was equally desperate. She had been writing the 'Art Notes' for the *News Chronicle* for a year, but feared the job would end. The anxiety became unbearable. Finally, said Biala, 'the situation got so bad that Ford blew in the last five dollars on a cable to New York:

The answer came back that the money had been paid regularly each month. Restored to life, with the telegram in my hand, I went back to the bank and this time refused to take the usual no. After much running around and looking up of books, it was discovered that the money was there all right. I asked to see the director, to tell him what I thought of his bank, but I was so enraged that I could only open my mouth, but not a word came out. I took the tram home to Cap Brun. It was winter and quite dark by then. There was an accident. Part of the platform I was standing on got ripped off. I didn't even notice it. When I finally got to my stop, I found Ford waiting for me with the announcement that there was to be a total eclipse of the moon in about ten minutes. So we walked up the road, until we got to a comfortable-looking bush. We sat down in the damp grass in front of it and waited for the eclipse of the moon.[6]

Early in February he and Biala moved up to Paris so that he could get hold of the books by the authors he was writing about for the *Mercury*. When Ford invited Edward Crankshaw to visit them and meet some French painters, Crankshaw bicycled to Dover to take the ferry. Ford devoted a lot of his time to taking him around to introduce him to 'a remarkable number of painters, all of whom, Crankshaw was astonished to discover, he was on intimate terms with'.[7]

Great Trade Route, the large book ruminating on their travels over the previous two years, was finished on 18 March 1936. It had been a particularly hard book to write a synopsis for in advance: 'It is always very difficult for me to write synopses of books however clear they may be in my mind', he wrote to Lowry, 'because even in my mind I always entangle the subject as much as possible'. This one is studiedly entangled, making it even harder than usual to summarize in retrospect. The 'idea' of the title is comprehensible enough, though necessarily impressionistic. It 'completes the circular promenade of the Great Trade Routes' begun in *Provence*:

The 'main theme' of the GREATER ROUTE will be the gradual transference from the Mediter-ranean to the N. Atlantic of (at any rate the economic and to some extent the cultural) centre of civilisation [. . .] You might call it a book of mental travel. Just as the author of PROVENCE sat down, as you might say, in London and thought about Provence and sat down in Provence and thought of London, Paris and other stretches of the world from China to the Scilly Islands, so he proposes to sit down in N.Y. City, New Orleans, Havana, the Azores, G[i]braltar, looking over Africa, Naples, Genoa, Rapallo, Ajaccio or Ventimiglia and think about the other portions of the Route—about Columbus, and kitchen-gardening and Colum-bia and other Universities and the culture of tobacco and cotton and humanity [. . .] The 'purpose' of the GREATER ROUTE is to be not so much a guide as a companion to the traveller [. . .][8]

The stretching, entangling syntax prefigures the book. The image of the Route—'the only territory in the world where the tides of civilization flow for ever backwards and forwards. . . . Along the Great Trade Route that has been the main civilizing factor of the world since the days when the merchant was sacred'—entangles his sense of the history of culture with the geography of his own travelling, physical and mental. But what matters in it is less its polemics against nationalism, industrialism, and war, honourable and eloquent though they are, but more the quality of the personality expressed: the imaginative complexity and gusto which can only be experienced when the book is read. The fusing of the mental and physical journeys make it impossible to follow in the way a guide-book can be followed. But few other books give the impres-sion of companionship with the author. It has the feel of *impressions de voyage*, and occasionally the form of diary entries—though the apparent spontaneity is carefully crafted to make the thesis seem to arise naturally from the material. It is Ford's most Sternean book, which is why he originally subtitled it 'A Sentimental Journey'. It is not conventional autobiography, though much of its material comes from Ford's life. But, with *Provence*, it gives the best impression of what it must have been like to think like him, or talk to him.[9]

Though *Provence* and *Great Trade Route* are not quite like anything else in Ford's *œuvre*, their project is continuous with some of his earliest books, such as *The Cinque Ports*, and the trilogy about *England and the English*. He saw them as contributing to:

a group of books that I have been engaged upon for some years dealing with the soil, the history and the political and social problems of a wide tract of the earth running from Marseilles to New York via Paris and London and returning by way of Madeira Gibraltar and Malaga towards Greece and the northern Mediterranean back to Marseilles—an oval peregrination that I call the *Great Trade Route*.

He was writing about the importance to him of the distinction between Nordic and Mediterranean civilizations as early as 1923, when he said the idea came to him while playing cricket with his battalion just after they had come out from 'a very nasty place' in the line.[10]

Vive Le Roy was published in early April 1936 in America. It was Ford's last completed novel. He suggested that Lippincott could bring it out under a pseudonym, because it was quite unlike his former novels. He hoped to break into the market for detective fiction, and was perhaps worried that a detective novel by Ford Madox Ford would sound like a pot-boiler. The difficulty he had been having getting his work published since the Depression, and of starting his collected edition, must have made him feel that his name was no longer an asset. It was also an oblique grouse against Lippincott for not having sold *Henry for Hugh* and *Ladies Whose Bright Eyes* hard enough. *Vive Le Roy* was published under his own name, however, and the modest edition (just over 2,500 copies) sold out.[11]

The novel is a lively compendium of Fordian preoccupations: doubles, concealed kinship, a feared connection between sexuality and insanity, a fear of war, the need for society to rediscover a form of feudal agrarianism, and, above all, detection. Both Ford and Biala enjoyed reading detective stories, and 'Ford thought that some of the best constructed books of that time were, precisely, written by detective story writers', said Biala. She remembered him toying with two ideas for novels during their life together: 'a detective story in which the murderer was the reader' (the ultimate Fordian betrayal?); and 'a book about a happy marriage—the point being how could you make such a book interesting?'[12] Neither plan was realized. But in *Vive Le Roy* he tries to raise the detective story to a serious form, and much of the energy of the book comes from its agile interplay between popular conventions and Ford's highly developed literary sensibility. The hero, Walter Leroy, is first seen clutching a detective novel. It turns out to be by Simenon, a writer Ford admired for his technical mastery; but it also turns out that it is 'precious' to Walter because it contains, concealed within, $20,000 that American communists had collected for, and Walter had agreed to deliver to, the Leftist radicals, who are engaged in a civil war with the royalists. It's a compelling symbol for a writer who got so little money out of his books: at once a sly hint of the wish that Ford's own detective novel should make money, an acknowledgement of the mercenary motive of most detective writers, but also the conscious artist's faith that it is art that is the true source of value.

Despite, or perhaps because of, this sustained playful intelligence, *Vive Le Roy* eluded attempts to classify it. Some reviewers complained that the solution to its ostensible mystery—that Walter has been kidnapped, and used to impersonate his double, the assassinated king—became obvious too early. Some felt that because it wasn't taking its conventions conventionally enough it might be a spoof. The *Times Literary Supplement* said readers would have to make up their own mind whether Ford's intention were 'straightforward or satirical'—as if readers had no right to enjoy the ambiguity impartially detected by an anonymous reviewer—and thought the story 'undoubtedly makes an excellent, if most unusual, thriller'. It was not published in England until 20 July 1937. The British reviewers generally felt Ford had succeeded in giving pleasure: 'The book is brilliantly entertaining, admirably written and by no means superficial. Devotees of the stereotypical adventure-story may be a little bothered by the ending, but all devotees of the stereotyped should be bothered now and then.' (Instead of the disappeared hero being returned to the heroine, Ford's story ends with Cassie waiting with Penkethman's mother until another clandestine meeting can be arranged with Walter, who is left acting the role of king, having seen the necessity of sustaining the illusion if peace is to be restored, and having become resigned to the part within which he's imprisoned.) As with the improbably coincidence of names in *The Rash Act*, the central punning here on 'Leroy' and *le roi* sets the scene in the world of romance, however psychologically subtle or solidly specified. Forrest Reid grasped Ford's characteristic mix of plot-fantasy and psychological finesse. He rightly said that it was 'an extravaganza': 'an altogether lighter and slighter thing than the Tietjens novels'; it was 'improbable, fantastic, yet thanks to the reality of the characters, as we read, credible'. Frank Swinnerton called Ford 'the most wantonly versatile novelist alive'. And Graham Greene, who was generally becoming another of his passionate advocates, observed that *Vive Le Roy* was not meant to be one of Ford's 'vintage growths': 'It is amusing, romantic, exciting, full of ridiculous and irrelevant inventions', as well as 'one of Mr. Ford's most delightful heroines'. (She uses a wonderfully inventive euphemistic slang, saying 'Beautify it all' instead of 'Damn it all', and so on.) Ford, he said, 'has the Victorian gift of being able to draw adorable women, but he can do what James and Hardy could not, convey immense sexual appeal'. It carried 'Mr. Ford's unmistakable stamp—an outrageous fancy and a kind of pessimistic high spirits'. *The Times* found Penkethman 'a most engaging addition to the portrait gallery of distinguished sleuths'.[13]

Mizener suggests that Walter and his lover Cassandra Mathers are based upon Eugene Pressly and Katherine Anne Porter (who had been struggling with a book on Cotton Mather). Yet Ford makes Cassie a painter like Biala rather than a writer. Biala enjoyed detective stories. *Vive Le Roy* was the one Ford had promised to write for her if she stayed faithful to him.[14] The detective, Penkethman, is a recognizably Fordian dual personality: 'a great, fat, enormous, clumsy, active, obtuse, sympathetic, stupid, diabolically penetrating lump of flesh and intellect', whose paternal interest in the young couple is explained when it turns out that he is in fact Walter's father. Mizener calls the story a '*Prisoner of Zenda* in modern political dress', arguing that Ford is endorsing the ideal of an absolute monarchy: that he is indeed crying 'vive le roi' through the novel. But the book is of course much more complex than this. Walter is reported as dead after being kidnapped; the title also expresses Cassie's conviction that he is still alive. Mizener quotes the intelligent grand chamberlain, de la Penthièvre, commenting on Lenin as 'a very admirable tyrant, his machine lopping off heads, arms, feet, where they would not conform or could not conform to the perfect sphere of his governmental theories'. But though de la Penthièvre makes Fordian pronouncements, so does his *alter ego* Penkethman, who discovers the chamberlain's plot. The point of Ford's plot is not to champion absolute monarchy and denounce communism; it is to suggest peace can only be achieved if the warring factions (within society, within ourselves) are fused: if communist Leroy can also become *le roi*—as Ford the prehistoric Tory was increasingly sympathizing with the Left. It was violent faction that most alarmed him in the 1930s, and the last thing he would have wanted was simply to espouse any one faction himself. It was too important to him as a novelist to be able imaginatively to enter into the different sides of the question. What he had said in 1911 about having had 'three sets of political opinions' in his youth was still true of his attitude to politics in the 1930s. The roles that he had combined in London society at the turn of the century he now combined in the impressionist prose of *Great Trade Route*, with its hybrid of socialist and anarchist philosophy expressed from a Tory attitude and challenging bourgeois assumptions about luxury, status, and patriotism. He was surprised to find that his views were crystallizing into pacifism in the late 1930s. He said of *Great Trade Route*: 'I have just finished a book which to my astonishment has turned out to be an impassioned plea for peace'; though he was wary of confessing publicly to such a degree of *parti pris*. The dedication (signed jointly with Biala) says that they 'regard all—but ALL!—Politicians with ABHORRENCE'; and that the book adumbrates 'if it adumbrates anything at all—a faint belief in the desirability of Quietist Anarchism'. *Vive Le Roy* adumbrates the need to acknowledge the complexity and contradictoriness of oneself and others. Ford, like Cassie, 'did not see that his inclination towards a humanitarian form of communism need interfere except theoretically with his noble absolutism'. Fiction offers another mode of integration, since it allows the life of fantasy to be fused with the actual history of one's own times. The book ends on this note, when Penkethman's mother offers Cassie a glass of schnapps, saying that it will help her to 'sleep like a queen and have such charming dreams'. The novel's hallucinatory actuality is just such a charming dream, which encourages the integration of the fantastic and the real.[15]

As with Ford's Edwardian satiric romances, his presentation of the history and politics of the time is sometimes too true to be believable. The idea of a royalist coup in France might now seem like a fictional cliché. But there were riots in Paris during the first week of February 1934, after which Paul Doumerge formed a National Union ministry of all the parties except the royalists, socialists, and communists, to avert a civil war. Biala recalled the rue Denfert-Rochereau being cordoned off with machine-guns, and that Daladier had ordered the troops to fire on demonstrators. 'At the time, there was a strong movement in France to replace the Republic with the Comte de Paris, as King of France', she said. Their friend the architect and decorator Marcel Le Son (to whose son *Great Trade Route* is dedicated) was a royalist. He hinted to them that a *coup d'état* was imminent. 'We were to have dinner with him & his wife on a certain date,' wrote Biala, '& he said: "if I don't keep the appointment, it will be because I'm in prison".' Ford's choice of the book's subject came from his 'speculating how a revolution of that kind might come about'. He had told Julie that the riots had made a strong impression, describing how the royalists and communists made a common cause, and how the communists had fought the police all along the street.[16]

The biographical summary written for Lippincott's dust-jackets of *Ladies Whose Bright Eyes* and of *Vive Le Roy* is a comparable mix of fantasy and history. Ford called it 'a fairly satisfactory biographical notice of the author', and suggested that it should be used in England too (except that the statement that he had 'left England for good' in 1922 was toned down to make it sound like the effects of patriotism rather than its opposite, saying that he lived in the South of France after his 'health had been severely affected by the War'). Among the old familiar facts are some new features: 'His grandfather having been born in France and retaining the habit of speaking French, Mr. Ford babbled in French before he knew English and has always had the conviction that French is the best language in which to write prose.' T. S. Eliot has been added to the list of writers discovered for the *English Review*: a claim likely to provoke an immediate denial. (Less than three years before, Ford had written to a reviewer: 'Did I, by the bye, publish Mr. T. S. Eliot in the ENGLISH REVIEW? I don't believe I did. . . . More trouble you will have made for me!') Italian has been added to English and French as another language in which he wrote war propaganda. There is also a romance that he wrote 'poems in French that were recited to the *poilus* in the trenches by the actors and actresses of the Odeon Company'. These are almost certainly untrue, apart from his conviction about the French language. But they give the true impression that he is qualified to speak about western culture.[17]

Julie had been due to stay in Paris at Easter. When she cancelled the trip at short notice Biala wrote to Bowen that Julie ought to keep the arrangements she made: 'Ford's heart is in a pretty bad state and if we have stayed in Paris it was partly with the expectation of having her here for Easter and he frets a good deal about her health. That is of course my funeral but we have distresses enough without adding to them.' Julie then wrote to say she would come soon. She later remembered visiting them frequently in the new flat they had found that spring, at 31 rue de Seine:

There were always people and parties—some of the people well known, some not—and still again the young unknowns, *les jeunes* with holes in their socks, who knew that they could always count on him for advice and encouragement. Some of them later achieved fame, some did not. There was good food, too—in particular a running rivalry with some friends of his, the Le Sons, which took the form of alternating dinners, one week at their apartment, the next week at Ford's, where each side would try to outdo the previous week's efforts. Not very good for the figure, perhaps, but what a marvelous chef Ford was! That was at the rue de Seine, a peacock blue and yellow building owned by Raymond Duncan, brother of Isadora, a gentleman who wore at all times a Roman toga and sandals, his long silver hair bound by a fillet about the brow. The apartment was attractive enough . . . but the building was cold and drafty and not very comfortable, and Ford was getting old . . . and ill.[18]

As they 'got over moving', Ford finished his best long poem. 'Coda', which he sent as 'a free offering' to Harriet Monroe, to atone for the mix-up with the other 'Buckshee' poems (which she had published without being told they had already appeared in England). She didn't print it; but it appears as the masterly close of his 1936 *Collected Poems*, where it is the coda both to the group of ' "Buckshee": Last Poems', and to the book. There is something odd about a lifelong poet writing his 'Last Poems' while still very much alive. But Ford evidently felt they were his farewell to verse. He told Monroe that he wrote so little (poetry) now, so 'this may be the last verse I ever put together'. It was. 'Coda' is thus his own coda as a poet, a powerful meditation on the passing of time, and the strength of art to withstand its passing, to redeem decay into 'patina'. Robert Lowell said of these 'Last Poems': 'In these reveries, he has at last managed to work his speaking voice, and something more than his speaking voice, into poems—the inner voice of the tireless old man, the old master still in harness, confiding, tolerant, Bohemian, newly married, and in France.' They also, as Frank MacShane saw, get his novelistic techniques into his verse in a more successful way than ever before: techniques of visual and auditory impression, time-shift, and psychological monologue.[19]

Early in the summer Ford had written a review of Edward Crankshaw's book *Joseph Conrad: Some Aspects of the Art of the Novel*, praising the light Crankshaw shed on 'the Difficult Art of conveying vicarious experience', and his imaginative sympathy with his subject: 'The resemblance of mental attack is at times startling', he wrote. So startling that it gave Ford a kind of vicarious experience that was his own experience: 'Reading the book I seem to be a third of a century back.' Thanks to Crankshaw he was soon physically back in the Kent he had known with Conrad, when he and Biala sailed from Dieppe on 4 July 1936 to stay with the Crankshaws at Penshurst for a month. He needed a rest; as he explained only half-jokingly to Palmer: 'I am overburdened with an enterprise that is slowly driving me to the grave. Can you imagine what it is to try for six weeks to read SWINBURNE? to try and try and TRY, like Bruce's spider . . . and to fail.' Clare Crankshaw remembers him working at a bureau in one corner of the room while in another corner Biala worked on a painting of the Battle of Gettysburg. In the evenings he read from the proofs of his poems. Mrs Crankshaw described his 'shabby grandeur', and his 'chameleon quality' which manifested itself when they went walking in the woods:

Ford was wearing his usual good quality but threadbare jacket and well-made worn-out trousers and seemed completely and unconsciously bohemian, until they came upon a woodman. Then his manner changed; he acquired a gentlemanly authority and a hazel twig, which he tapped against his calf while he addressed the woodman as 'my man'. He had normally an air of what Mrs Crankshaw called 'asinine nobility', an immediate and indiscriminate helpfulness, perhaps a touch of Don Quixote. It should not be assumed from this, however, that he was unknowing; there was nearly always an element of self-consciousness, parody and humour, often missed.[20]

There was also an element of experiment: of testing how his impressions of England had stood up over the fourteen years he had lived abroad. When he wrote about revisiting London soon after this trip, he noted how manners between classes had been changing: 'You know they don't say Sir every fifth word and more.' As he would test young Americans at South Lodge with his incomprehensible whispers, so he was seeing whether the woodman would respond to the posture of the ruling class. What such impersonations concealed was his feeling that his intellectual alienation from Britain was now complete. Two years later he said of his returns to London: 'I didn't find it very exciting. There did not seem to be anybody there to talk to and those one could talk to didn't much understand what one said.' Biala thought he made his criticisms of England out of love, not hostility. Despite the efforts of Unwin, Crankshaw, and Greene leading to a revival of interest in his work, he was 'a disappointed lover'.[21]

Ford got Crankshaw to invite Graham Greene to lunch, after which Ford and Greene walked through the fields for the rest of the afternoon, having 'one of those conversations which seemed to include everything while focusing mainly on writing', but of which Greene could later remember not a word. He found Ford a comforting presence; Ford inscribed his copy of *The Good Soldier*: 'For the / Writer of It's a Battlefield / the writer of This, with / admiration & good wishes. / Ford Madox Ford / 21 July MCMX[X]XVI.' On 5 August he and Biala returned via Boulogne. Back in Toulon, Ford was crippled with his gout, which had been bothering him for some time but now got worse, causing insomnia. He blamed it on the muddle he had got into with Oxford University Press. Six months before he had told his agent: 'I suspect every publisher without exception these days.' He didn't see any reason to except Oxford. They had, as Ford put it to their New York editor, Lowry, made him 'skip about like a flea on a hot plate to get the ms together' for his poems, but then seemed to him inordinately slow while they were trying to establish the rights to republish from the various (and in some cases defunct) publishers. The English side of the Press delayed for a further three years; were about to publish the poems when Ford died and the Second World War broke out; shelved the project; and later forgot about it; so the volume did not appear in England. When they objected to Biala's illustrations for *Great Trade Route*, Ford refused to let the book be published without them, and even suggested trying to find another publisher. He can't have been much consoled by their assurance that they wanted to publish the *Poems* 'as an item of esteem', even though they had been assured they would lose money on them. None the less, on the same day that he wrote a resolute letter to the New York branch of the Press hinting at legal action, he wrote an equable letter to Lowry himself telling him that he was sure Lowry personally had acted 'with the best of goodwill' towards him, and suggesting they 'regard these differences with good humour'. It shows once more how reasonable Ford could be with his publishers. As Lowry told one of his colleagues: 'you will find Mr. Ford most pleasant to deal with; he is concerned apparently more with ideas than with his fees!' In this case Ford found an ingenious means of preserving good humour. 'The old sunfish I fear is worried about the domestic happiness', wrote Lowry: 'And I dare say all Provence trembled when Fordie told the lady the bad news.' True that Biala's letters to the Press were fiercer than Ford's; but Lowry didn't realize that Ford either wrote them himself, or at least collaborated on them. As with his paired letters, it was a dual response which enabled him at once to provoke and placate them. Crankshaw acted as intermediary between Ford and the publisher he worked for, Stanley Unwin, who wanted not only to take on Ford's new work (even the *History*), but also to publish the collected edition. Ford told Paul Palmer: 'it's the consecration of one's long and weary life.' Though, as he said to Allen Tate, 'what little money there is in it goes to Stella and Julie so that it does nothing for us'. When he wrote to Unwin to settle details about rights, the idea of the collected edition again encouraged him to imagine his own death; though his letter was alive with (or haunted by) the difference between the death of the author and the life of the book:

My English rights are settled, through trustees, on my daughter, and as she has not any urgent need for money I don't want large advances because I think—rightly or wrongly— that the less my books sell before my death the more chance they will have selling after that event . . . at any rate in England. On the other hand in the United States the life of a book, according to my by now sufficiently long experience, is so very short whether the author be dead or alive, that I may as well get what I can out of my work. Besides, as going to America is very expensive, I as a rule need the money.[22]

It was agreed that Allen and Unwin would bring out *Great Trade Route* in England, whereas Oxford would continue publishing it in America, and said they would be prepared to publish all the illustrations. But dealing with three different publishers meant that Ford got contradictory instructions about where to send what—and all this soon after the proofs and the manuscript were lost when Oxford posted them back but they were impounded by the post in Paris because of a misunderstanding about whether duty should be paid on them. (When he heard that a mysterious parcel had been impounded, Ford said he assumed someone had been sending him 'snow'—cocaine.) 'You know, this is like being mad', an exasperated Ford told Lowry; though, as he said to Allen Tate when the confusion was finally sorted out, the madness wasn't necessarily of his own, or all of his own making: 'I have at last adjusted my lunatic strife with the Oxford University Press—you know, either I must be mad or they. They are really unimaginable people. No wonder Roger Bacon invented gunpowder to blow them up when they contracted to publish his works.'[23]

There was disappointing news from America too. Ruth Aley, Ford's New York agent since 1935, had raised his hopes that *Vive Le Roy* could be sold to the movies. But she couldn't sell it. She also told him that a John Day & Co. wanted to publish the Tietjens books in one volume in New York; but this too was premature: Day had not even made an offer. *Parade's End* wasn't to appear until 1950, when it was published by Knopf. She wasn't making any progress with the collected edition either. Besides these frustrations, and the agonizing gout, which was only now letting him 'hobble around' again, the worst blow was that they could no longer afford to stay in Toulon. He wrote to Pound for the first time for over two years (he half-facetiously said that the break was because of Pound's 'want of generosity' in not helping him 'log-roll' René Béhaine when he had solicited Pound's help back in 1933: 'I swore on the bones of St Gengulphus, some of which are handy in the Cathedral here, that I would never write to you again. I herewith break my vow'). 'We are having to give up this place and go and live in one room in Paris', he explained. 'It's impossible to make a living outside New York, one's agents are always so incompetent and we'd both die if we had to live in the U.S.A. for good.' He told Allen Tate that the date for the moving was fixed for 1 October. It was 'the end, alas, of a phase!' Another remark in this letter foretold his last phase. Tate had been 'professoring' at Memphis, which made Ford wonder: 'We most of us have so much to overwrite ourselves to get the little thin oatmeal. I don't believe I should mind a similar job very much; at least I am tired of writing for the pot . . . though I suppose I shall have to go on.' In 1937 Ford would begin his own professoring.[24]

Ford told Tate, while he was thanking him for sending *The Mediterranean and Other Poems*, that Biala had said that morning: 'It's odd, you know, the Tates seem to be the only friends or family we have in the world.' Ford agreed, and came straight in to write to them, adding: 'It's true that we haven't any more got any real friends—in the sense of people one can talk to without having to explain every second word and both Janice and I are pretty good at making enemies.' That impression that their friendship was particularly precious is a sincere one. But it's typical of how his striving to give the right impression about one aspect could give the wrong impression about another. By dramatizing his affection for the Tates, he makes himself sound isolated, pitiable. (Which—together with their left-wing interests, so uncongenial to the Agrarian Tates—was perhaps why Caroline Gordon was later to make the absurd claim that Ford and Biala 'seemed to inhabit a closed world, a sphere which rolled here or there, from France to New York and back again, but never changed inside'. Ford's political and social ideas changed more in the 1930s than in any other decade. It was a change which placed him unequivocally outside the more impermeable sphere of the Tates' reactionary nostalgia.) Yet only the day before he had written a charming letter to his old London friend R. A. Scott-James, now the editor of the *London Mercury*, introducing him to Katherine Anne Porter and Eugene Pressly, who were moving to London because Pressly expected to be attached to the American Embassy there:

If my friends the Porter-Presslys (Katherine Anne Porter, author of FLOWERING JUDAS and generally regarded, I should say with justice, as the finest prose writer bar none in U.S.A. and one of the most amusing women; plus Eugene Pressly, Embassy attaché at Paris and great—but incredibly silent and discreet—authority on international finance, husband of said K.A.P.) ring you up in the next few days you might be a little nice to them . . . socially I mean [. . .] They are very intimate friends of ours.

Even when advocating the countryside as a retreat Ford lived an intensely social life. He had guests staying even while he was writing to Tate: they were probably the Crankshaws, who visited the Villa Paul in the late summer. They may have been too much younger, and perhaps a little too servile, for Ford to think of them as friends rather than admirers; and he hadn't known them as long as he had known the Tates. Yet their relationship shows how able he still was to make new friends. 'Crankshaw is a good boy', he confided to Tate. He told Ford to look on him as his secretary (rather than as his publisher's reader: but the tone of abasement is typical of his letters to Ford). Clare Crankshaw remembered one particular way he made himself useful:

Both Ford and Janice were at that time rolling their own cigarettes, Ford rather painstakingly and with more paper than tobacco. He so often ran out of matches that Edward secretly bought a packet of twelve boxes and handed one over each time Ford ran out, pretending he just happened to have one on him. Ford accepted each new box with extravagant, unsuspecting gratitude and innocent joy, never querying their provenance.[25]

Mrs Crankshaw remembers that the Villa Paul seemed stark to them, even compared to their own simple Penshurst cottage. The charcoal stove needed to be unclogged with hair-pins, and there was no bathroom. But 'the furniture was good and there were plenty of books'. Yet despite, and also partly because of, its frugality, Ford was desperately sorry to have to leave. As he wrote in a letter to Ruth Aley, he felt his health entirely depended on staying there; and although he had a knack of writing almost anywhere, from the lids of bathtubs to the cabins of boats, he found his study at the Villa Paul particularly congenial. It was, paradoxically, its lack of possessions that made him feel proprietorial about the place. He had constructed his writing-desk as a carpenter's parody of bourgeois solidity and domesticity:

I usually write in my home in Provence at an extraordinarily knocked-together table with flanking shelves of walnut bed-panels, supported by sawn-off chair legs and above me an immense deal shelf supported in turn by sawn-off broom handles and nobody is more contented than I or prouder of his atelier. And when neighbours come in and I show them my contrivance they say: *Tiens, mais vous avez du goût!* as if it surprised them.[26]

Pound wrote to Ford that it was 'at any rate a feat for any madOX to be printed by the asses of Oxon'. Ford's dealings with Oxford continued to madden him during that autumn of heat and Mistral. When the head of the American house suggested that Ford's agent may have added to the confusion, Ford told him a story:

You may be right about the Literary Agent . . . but I'm inclined myself more to the opinion that it's a poltergeist that is the main cause of these confusions, if not Old Nick himself. I ought perhaps to have told you at the beginning that my earliest known—apart from legendary—ancestor was fined ten crowns and ordered to stand in the pillory for printing, in the XV century, insults to the Sorbonne, and ever since my forbears have been occupied in making themselves disagreeable to and in being persecuted by Universities—the most egregious of them being the Famous Dr. John Brown, inventor of the Brunonian system of Medicine. Him Frederick the Great invited to be his body surgeon but the invitation being sent to the University of Edinburgh, that body preferred to send out a John Brown of their own whom that sovereign, on discovering the imposture, threw into gaol and kept there till his death.

I am moved to these historic reminders by the fact that the agreement you have sent me is quite different from the one that I last signed and sent out to you—which may be the work of the aforesaid Literary Agent. But how do you account for the fact that the copy of the POEMS that you have kindly sent me has neither title page, h.[alf] t.[itle] p.[age] nor roman signatures but begins at p. 49 and after p. 63 returns to p. 3 and so continues? That I think must be the work of the poltergeist [. . .].[27]

It is a good example of how he could fictionalize his genealogy or autobiography to turn frustration into humour. Despite the confusion, he was able to write again on the following day to offer Oxford his *History*. His contract obliged him to offer them the next book after *Great Trade Route*; he explained that even though Oxford had turned down *Portraits from Life* he ought to offer another—though he was beginning to despair of ever finding a publisher for the book he had been working at since 1929. He described how although he still planned 'in some indefinite future' to write 'three heavily documented volumes of the history, roughly speaking, of the nations which surround the North Atlantic—their political, international, social and aesthetic developments', he was proposing to write a one-volume condensation:

As for the temper of the book I imagine it will be as impartial as is humanly possible, because—except when hostilities were taking place—I was never able to take sides exclusively with any one party to any quarrel indeed I have been mostly too prone to take both or three or four sides at once. Thus, during the Boer War I aspired to see both Mr Chamberlain and President Kruger hung on the same tree though I was as relieved as anyone else at the relief of Mafeking. Or again, during the late war I did my best with enthusiasm—and both pen and sword as it is called—to serve the Allied cause and have never felt any regret for having done so. But that does not obscure for me the fact that Bismarck was one of the greatest of world statesmen . . . And so with all the other sides of life.[28]

But Oxford wouldn't make a commitment before seeing the complete condensation, which he needed the advance to write. The following month he sent Oxford some notes to help them with their publicity. They explain both his view of his own dual life as writer and man of action, and the persona of what he called his 'mental travel' writing—a persona which combines 'advice' on the one hand (about 'cooking, reading, farming, fighting, the Fine Arts, the Stage . . . how they all—and particularly politicians—should be handled if the civilisation which we know and which is founded on the civilisation of the Mediterranean is to have any chance of continuing') and 'enthusiasm' on the other (for 'the Greek Anthology, the Maison Carrée as for the sea food of New Orleans or Marseilles, the painting of Clouet, the military genius of Stonewall Jackson'). 'It is in short', he said, 'what in the old days would have been called humane literature':

The point to be made about the GREAT TRADE ROUTE is that it is not the book of a meditative gentleman who stands before ruined temples and pours mournful soliloquies on old unhappy things, but as it were the testament of a man usually of action who has spent a long life not only on writing and study but on digging, editing, carpentry, cooking, small holding, fighting both literally and metaphorically and in every kind of intrigue that could advance what he considers to be the cause of good letters . . . and particularly on running round the part of the world here treated and observing with disillusioned eyes politicians and public men of every type and shade.[29]

The running round continued: on 11 November Ford and Biala sailed for New York on the *Lafayette*. They found a new apartment—in 5th Avenue again, this time number 10, above a French restaurant. Edward Dahlberg went to their Thursday afternoon teas there. 'It was the only literary salon I know that was not a carrion sty and humbug', he wrote: 'there was, surely, that "caitiff choir" of fops, panders, lady poetasters, literary agents [. . .] that inevitably surround a man of letters. But you could see about him also a gifted face, the poet William Carlos Williams, the rare painter, Marsden Hartley, the original puritan artist, Elizabeth Sparhawk-Jones, or capture the flittering image of the gentle Brancusi.' The flat had: 'three or four secondhand Quatorze chairs, a poor spindly table, the scantest number of books, a jetty sphynxed cat, several of his wife's, Biala's paintings of Paris rains, or murmurously lighted artichoke-coloured buildings along quays or the Seine, all of which was served to you with tea and Sutter's cakes.' Ford seemed 'an obese, porcine Falstaff' to Dahlberg: 'He spoke and breathed with much labor so that his words were hardly audible'—that was being increasingly remarked. Ford got himself a new agent—George Bye—and tried to get his old friend Ferris Greenslet, of Houghton Mifflin, who had given him a contract for the book of *Portraits from Life*, to do in America what Allen and Unwin were to do in England: publish his new books—including the *History*!—while gradually republishing the old ones, to produce the collected edition. (In fact they had only published his last three new books by his death, when the war came and the project was abandoned.)[30]

The newspapers were full of Edward VIII's affair with Mrs Simpson that December. Ford wrote a wistful piece about the king, and read it for NBC on 7 December. Three days later Edward abdicated. Ford's elegiac tone had been curiously prophetic. He had begun by recalling Edward at his father's Coronation (which Ford had witnessed in 1911), standing 'lonely, embarrassed and aloof'; a vignette which seemed to foreshadow Edward's plight as once again he stood alone, this time against cabinet and country. Ford asked Paul Palmer: '*Did* you hear my broadcast [. . .] I hear there were few dry eyes amongst those who heard it—but I can't find anyone who did. The NBC were so overwhelmed by it that they have rung me up every half hour since to tell me so'; then he added: 'The NBC have just rung up to say that they are cabling my broadcast to the King!' WABC also asked him to do a broadcast. Ford spoke for half an hour on 19 December supporting Roosevelt's Works Progress Administration and its investment in the Arts.[31]

It may have been this winter that Ford and Biala went to see 'a Soviet film of the fabulous Red General who played havoc with the Whites'. Ford found it exhilarating to see the rendering of machine-gun-fire on film; but on the way back, without the protective screen of the cinema, the drama became life: 'A taxi emerged from East Thirteenth Street, followed by a small crammed car. There was a too familiar unmistakable crack; something, much too familiarly, brushed the rim of my hat . . . from Clarksville, Tenn. I grabbed by the arm the New Yorker, who had not finished Mallory [sic], and dived under a stationary taxi at the sidewalk edge.'[32]

1937: OLIVET AND THE TATES

Ford could pick up talent from the flyspeck,
and had Goethe's gift for picking a bright girl.

(Robert Lowell, 'Ford Madox Ford and Others')

Ford and Biala spent a pleasant Christmas in Paoli, Pennsylvania, with the wood-carver and furniture designer Wharton Esherick (whose studio is described in *Great Trade Route*), and returned to New York for the New Year. The most important meeting of that season was with Joseph Brewer, a publisher who had become president in 1934 of Olivet College, a small liberal arts college of about 300 students in Michigan, managed by Congregationalists. Brewer had gone to Oxford after Dartmouth College, and had joined the *Spectator* as private secretary to the editor, St Loe Strachey (whose son he had befriended at Oxford). He had met Ford in London in the early 1920s and had been so impressed by his enthusiastic knowledge about American literature that, he later felt, this meeting had strongly influenced him. Brewer wrote that 'few had yet begun to look to America as a land of literary or artistic promise'. But he found in Ford and the Tates artists who shared his sense of the vitality and significance of the writing that was appearing in America: from writers like Sinclair Lewis and Sherwood Anderson in the Middle West, and the *Fugitive* group associated with Vanderbilt University, including Tate, John Crowe Ransom, and Robert Penn Warren. At Olivet he introduced an innovative combination of creative work, directed by artists-in-residence, and Oxford-style tutorials. He had the cosmopolitan modernist tastes that would have appealed to Ford. His personal art collection (which he loaned to the college) included work by William Roberts and de Chirico; and he got Le Corbusier to design a presidential residence, though he couldn't get funds to build what would have been the first Corbusier building in America. Instead, he got both Le Corbusier and Frank Lloyd Wright to visit the college. The well-known writers he attracted included Sinclair Lewis and W. H. Auden. He also pioneered the idea of the Writers' Conference. The Tates, who had taken part in the first annual Conference at Olivet in the summer of 1936, encouraged his plan to get Ford there. Caroline Gordon wrote that Brewer's 'brightest idea [. . .] is to create a chair of letters or whatever you'd call it and get you to fill it'. When they met at Christmas it was agreed that Ford would become writer and critic in residence at a salary of $1,500, giving a lecture-course in comparative literature until December, and would come to the 1937 Writers' Conference for an additional fee of $150. Robie Macauley, who was a student at Olivet, writes that:

for one brief period under the presidency of Joseph Brewer, Olivet College had an extraordinary life as a center of education in the arts [. . .] people such as Ford and Sherwood

Anderson taught writing there. Allen Tate, Caroline Gordon, Katherine Anne Porter, William Troy and others taught in the summer sessions. Count Korzybski, the semanticist, gave a series of lectures one year. Among the occasional speakers were Gertrude Stein, Carl Sandburg and Carl Van Vechten. The work in music and art was likewise good. The trouble, as usual, was lack of money [. . .].[1]

Ford's connection with Olivet changed his life, and lasted until his death. The other main project of his last years was also planned that Christmas: his last, longest, and most erudite book, *The March of Literature*, which was commissioned by the Dial Press.[2]

Great Trade Route was published on 12 January 1937 in England and 18 February in America. The American reviewers enjoyed 'the delight of Mr. Ford's reminiscences, which is never-failing', and took the book in the impressionist spirit in which it was offered: 'All this may not be literally accurate as history, but it is good as a theory of life.' The British were hyperbolic in their enthusiasm, perhaps because his raconteur persona was more congenial to them than the austere technician of formalism he had presented himself as before the war. Humbert Wolfe thought it 'the best effort in Mr. Ford's long and distinguished literary career', an 'inexhaustible cornucopia', 'in part an autobiography, in part a consideration of world-movements, and in part sheer high spirits'. Edward Crankshaw wrote a paean to Ford as one of Britain's 'greatest and most timely artists', saying that pessimistic readers who felt such good counsel only ever comes too late would read it as 'one of the most beautiful pieces of prose artistry the century has produced, delighting in the progressive digressions on everything under the sun'; whereas optimists could have all these enjoyments 'together with a sudden, surprising, strengthening access of hope'—a good analysis of Ford's dual tone, which appears to be offering radical political solutions while knowing quite well that they are a lost cause: a fiction of political economy. Crankshaw also caught Ford's cast of mind sharply: 'Possessed (as his readers all know) of one of the fullest and most vital minds to be found, a mind which is yet neither strictly speaking analytical nor logical, Mr. Ford's unique value is as a fertilizing agent. Here, from everything his fingers touch, spring suggestions for rebirth.' And he concluded by stating the terms in which all Ford's discursive books need to be judged: 'Most people with a message try to compose a work of art into which they may pump their propaganda. Mr. Ford has woven his ideas to make a work of art which could not exist without them.' Graham Greene had already discussed Ford in print in a fine essay about the 'eternal time-question' in narrative technique, in which he had called him 'the most able living novelist, devising a technique more complicated than Conrad's to disguise the same time problem'. His review of *Great Trade Route* reaffirmed the judgement, and brought out the interconnection of ethics, aesthetics, religion, and politics in Ford's writing.

Mr. Ford's genius has always been aristocratic. His flirtation with the Fabians was of the briefest; his real heroes were Tories and landowners, Tietjens and the Good Soldier. Perhaps that is why Mr. Ford, so incontestably our finest living novelist and perhaps the only novelist since Henry James to contribute much technically to his art, is not very widely read. The world, absorbed in the Communist–Fascist dog-fight, is ill prepared to listen to this Tory philosopher who finds the Conservative politician as little to his taste as any other. And yet men of Mr. Ford's character have much to offer: there is something disagreeably easy in the notion that only two political philosophies can exist and that we must choose between them. Mr. Ford is a Catholic, though he has seldom been in sympathy with his Church, and it is no coincidence that the subject of *Great Trade Route* is similar to that of the recent Pastoral Letter issued by the Catholic Bishops in this country [. . .] He would have every man a part-time agriculturalist, because such a man is free in a sense unrecognized by either Fascist or Communist, free from the State ideal.

The compacted doctrines here say as much about Greene as about Ford, of course; but the implication is powerful. Ford's fineness as a novelist has to do with his ability not to settle for reductive, dehumanizing 'choices': able to invent a 'Toryism' which is free from party; a Catholicism that has more to do with Romance than with Rome; a political philosophy which is free from a totalitarian (and, for Greene, idolatrous) view of the State. His genius is aristocratic not merely because most excited by aristocratic types, but because it is above the common enslavements to faction. Its spirit is, instead, that of fiction: a creative independence from the received categories. As when he redefines the word 'gentleman', from the class-fetish he has been accused of making out of it, to 'a person living in harmony with the cosmos'. It was this freedom with, as much as freedom from, fact that irritated the scholarly historians (as it still does). D. W. Brogan, for example, complained about the book's 'deep indifference to what the pedantic world calls fact', which damaged it 'as a philosophy of life or history'; though he credited it with 'real attractions' as a 'sentimental journey'. There were none of the dismissive reviews that beset most of the earlier books; instead, *Great Trade Route* was hailed as 'a most extraordinary and brilliant book', 'far more than a record of travel', 'a terrific sociological and philosophical onslaught'. Ford was receiving the kind of critical acclaim any writer dreams of; 'selling' reviews, some of them in papers with large circulations. But the book only sold about 1,100 copies in America, and about 1,400 in England.[3]

Ford made one of his rare replies to a reviewer when he was accused of vilifying Abraham Lincoln in *Great Trade Route*. He wrote an eloquent letter defending himself, pointing out: 'Throughout the book I use the term legalised murderers for soldiers of whatever Army—Lee's, Stonewall Jackson's, Napoleon's, my own comrades in the late war—and by implication of myself [. . .]'; and he contrasts Lincoln with Grant: 'a cunning and capable strategist', but 'as a tactician [. . .] the greatest villain.' The argument is illuminating about *Parade's End* as well as about the American Civil War: 'The great General is not the one who gains the most victories. He is the one who accomplishes his victories or retreats with the smallest loss of life.' It is characteristic of Ford's ethical subtlety that he can combine a sweeping dictum about war in general with a sensitive consideration of particular soldiers and battles.[4]

While Biala was preparing her second exhibition at the Gallery Passedoit in New York, which opened on 23 February, Ford was writing blurbs and notices to help his latest discoveries, and arranging to write for *Vogue*.[5] As usual, his altruistic activities left him broke, and at the end of February he was having to ask his agent Bye to advance him money against his next instalment from the Dial Press, rather as Pinker had done at the beginning of the century. He had to boil pots, sending Bye an 'article on spices' to place. He had tried to interest Greenslet in 'Mr Croyd', telling him it struck him as 'a remarkably spirited performance—like the Tietjens books but more bitterly humorous'; Greenslet said he recognized 'old friends and feelings' in it, but that his other readers were probably right in finding it 'too definitely dated to sell'. Ford hoped to find an American publisher who would give him a similar contract to Unwin's; but Greenslet wasn't even interested in the Tietjens novels; he thought they too had dated after the publication of Remarque's *All Quiet on the Western Front* and Zweig's *Sergeant Grischa*. Ford explained to Bye what he wanted: 'a publisher with whom I can remain for good, who will assure me of a modest income and who will arrange for a collected edition.' This wasn't unreasonable. By 'a modest income' he meant a salary of $150 a month paid as an advance against royalties; by 'collected edition' he meant the kind of subscription edition Unwin was prepared to undertake. Bye continued negotiating with other publishers—Doubleday, Harpers, Bobbs-Merrill—but none would accept Ford's terms.[6]

He was in demand as a speaker. He was scheduled to speak on the radio on 28 February (in a programme called 'the Court of Literary Justice'). On 9 March he talked at a 'Round Table luncheon' at the Town Hall Club, outlining the ideas of *Great Trade Route*, and then making a new and un-Tory suggestion: 'We should be able to vote for measures, not for men [. . .] Real democracy needs a national system of voting devices—some speedy electrical arrangement so that the people could register their will directly and immediately.' A worried listener asked a 'dismayed question': 'But wouldn't that abolish Congress?' 'Mr. Ford appeared surprised that any one should be concerned about that', the *Herald Tribune* reporter noted, but he reassured the woman Congress could still discuss the proposed measures. Then, on 15 March, he was broadcast in another NBC programme, 'Dinner at Nine'. He lectured in Boston when he and Biala went there for Houghton Mifflin's publication of *Portraits from Life* on 23 March. They were back in New York by the 27th, when Ford replied to a letter from a member of the New York Typographical Union who had written to urge him to make his publishers use printers who were unionized. 'I am, of course, completely favourable to organized labor, in every department', wrote Ford, scarcely conforming to the 'Tory' stereotype. Though he was in favour of improving the lot of the printers, he could see that one group's solidarity could be another's alienation, and explained tactfully that 'the copyright laws which are passed in the interest of your unions' were 'in two ways exceedingly oppressive to authors—and like all other protective measures do no good to yourselves': refusing copyright to foreign books not printed in America reduces the sales of foreign authors; and since, 'in revenge all other foreign countries have taken similar steps against American Writers', American authors also suffer. So he suggested that though he would do what he could to support the printers' union, they should consider making a concession over copyright before appealing to what Ford called—in the union spirit—his 'brothers of the pen'.[7]

Soon he and Biala were off on the Great Trade Route once more, en route to the Tates, who had generously invited them to spend the summer at Benfolly until the Olivet conference. On 10 May they passed through New York, heading for Washington by Greyhound bus, accompanied by Biala's sister-in-law, Wally Tworkov, who was acting as Ford's secretary. (She was 'forever in awe at the ease with which he could turn out one graceful phrase after another'.) Ford wrote to Bye that he wanted to meet

Roosevelt, who had just signed the US Neutrality Pact (in which Ford must have been interested) on 1 May, and that he had been told he could on 11 or 12 May. The meeting didn't happen. Biala said she thought this might have been a joke of Ford's. But he had known the president's distant cousins, the Kermit Roosevelts, a decade before; and he told Julie he'd sent the president a copy of his talk on the WPA, and that Roosevelt had written twice to thank him. As soon as they arrived in Clarksville, Tennessee, in the middle of May, Morton Zabel invited Ford to be the guest speaker at a fund-raising dinner to mark the twenty-fifth anniversary of the magazine *Poetry*, and to talk to the Renaissance Society at the University of Chicago. He went. At the dinner he gave a moving elegy for Harriet Monroe, the founder and editor of *Poetry*, who had died suddenly the previous year. At the university he reminisced, in the manner of *Portraits from Life*, about his literary past. To soothe himself on his travels he read 'fifteen works of Aristotle in the original and eleven detective stories—the Aristotle being really the more entertaining of the two. He actually knew more about things like the breeding habits of the cuckoo than all the ornithological societies of the British Empire put together until a year or two ago.' When he got back to Clarksville, exhausted, he wrote to tell Unwin: 'I have just got back here after the ferocious but relatively triumphant course of lectures and interviews and all the usual ballyhoo at Chicago. Before then I had an even more ferocious course of the same thing at Boston, where I was offered an LLD. and, incidentally, two professorships, one of which I may take.'[8]

Biala's abrasiveness, Ford's indigestion, and Wally Tworkov's politics were a challenge to the Tates' Southern courtesy. 'The Fords brought with them Janice's sister-in-law', Gordon told Sally Wood:

—no I don't think he's making any passes at her. She is a pretty, modest child (one of those half-dozen typical Jewish faces you see so often in New York). A rabid Communist[,] she asked me shyly the other day 'How wise would it be to have the Daily Worker sent to me here? I can't live without it?' I think she thought she might be ridden off of Benfolly on a rail if caught with a copy of the Worker. It would be too impossible if she were at all like Janice but she is really a sweet child and very agreeable. Wife of Janice's brother, Jack, whom I can live a long time without meeting.[9]

She told Wood about 'the strangest visitation' they had ever had. A young man got out of a car by their gate, urinated by their post-box, came up to the Tates who were on the point of shouting 'defense d'uriner', regarded Allen Tate 'fixedly and muttered something about Ford'. It was the 20-year-old Robert Lowell. When Merrill Moore had introduced him to Ford that spring, Ford had announced that he was 'the most intelligent person he had met in Boston'. He was not too old to be still discovering geniuses. Lowell later quoted this as an example of Ford's quality of combining generosity and contempt, saying: 'Now I think that was more his low opinion of Boston than his high opinion of me'—'he saw through Boston. Its English pretensions and its Puritanism were very distasteful, and no man was less puritanical than Ford.' At the time Lowell was understandably flattered. He said he was going through a difficult period in his life. 'Ford really rescued him from a bad situation', Gordon told Wood. 'His family decided he was crazy because he wants to be a poet and had him in a psychopathic sanitarium [sic].' Tate joked that the family had only given their consent for him to come to Tennessee because 'doubtless in the Lowell mind' it was 'not unlike a madhouse'. Lowell's conduct that summer certainly contributed to the madhouse atmosphere of Benfolly. With 'keen, idealistic, adolescent heedlessness' he offered himself as a guest. 'The Tates' way of refusing was to say that there was no room for me unless I pitched a tent on the lawn', he said, but, undeterred, he returned a few days later having bought a tent in Nashville. He stayed three months. 'Indoors', he felt, 'life was Olympian and somehow crackling.' The weather blew hot and cold; so did the creative tempers: 'It's awful here', wrote Biala. 'In every room in the house there's a typewriter and at every typewriter there sits a genius. Each genius is wilted and says that he or she can do no more but the typewritten sheets keep on mounting. I too am not idle. I sit in the parlor where I paint on three pictures at once in intervals of killing flies.' Tate described the hothouse:

My wife Caroline Gordon, with one idiotic servant, ran the precariously balanced *ménage*. Ford could eat French food only, but Ida, with the occasional assistance of her mother Electra, the washerwoman, could not even cook Tennessee, much less French. Ford was unhappy in the 95°F. but every morning he paced the columned gallery—which had nothing but the earth to support it—and dictated to Mrs. Tworkov several pages of *The March of Literature*. There was a persistent tide that seldom ebbed of visitors from Nashville, from Louisville, from New York, from Europe. It was a situation perversely planned by fate to expose human weakness. There were no scenes.[10]

Ford had a way of coping with the tensions of what Mizener called 'the Tates' fiercely uncompromising intellectual warfare', by saying about matters he didn't want to discuss: 'I am too old and too distinguished to think about it.' Lowell, intoning 'the Miltonic blank verse that he wrote every morning' inside his tent, made Ford nervous. Gordon said that Ford was so 'enraged at being taken literally' when he had told Lowell to 'go south young man and write' that he wouldn't speak to him at all at the table—'the explanation given', said Lowell, 'being that he is afraid I will write memoirs 30 or 40 years from now in which I will describe him as an over-stout, gouty old gentleman deluded by the poetry of Christina Rossetti and potentialities of the ideogram.' He was right. Lowell's poem on Ford from *Life Studies* emphasizes his breathlessness and gout, and the 'lies that made the great your equals'—though Lowell also remained one of his most influential admirers. After Gordon had 'given Ford hell' about not speaking to him he began addressing him as 'Young man'. Lowell recalled him humorously advising him to give up eating sweet corn lest he inherit 'the narrow fierceness of the Red Indian'. When the cistern at Benfolly ran dry, Ford tried to help by building a dewpond, sinking an old wash-tub into the ground and filling it with 'a tangle of barked twigs', 'almost igniting with the heat'; it didn't work. 'As for our activities, Heaven knows what they will or won't be', he wrote to Dale Warren of Houghton Mifflin, 'because consorting with the Tates is like living with intellectual desperados in the Sargoza Sea.' One exploit was 'an attack en masse upon the University of Vanderbilt, Nashville, ending in a glorious victory for the forces of intellect'. This was because John Crowe Ransom had been offered the post of head of the English Department at Kenyon College in Gambier, Ohio. Ford thought Ransom's departure had 'been forced by a very base University intrigue & he shd. be supported', so he joined Tate in campaigning for Vanderbilt to match Kenyon's offer, and not let someone of Ransom's stature leave. A dinner was organized for 10 June to mark the twenty-fifth anniversary of Ransom's teaching at Vanderbilt, and his departure. It was held at a suburban road-house. About forty people attended. Ford, 'as an international figure', was the main speaker, dressed in new white duck trousers, 'a beat-up dinner jacket', and espadrilles. '[B]etween wheezes' he introduced the telegrams which Tate read out, from fifty or so supporters, including T. S. Eliot, Edmund Wilson, Mark and Carl Van Doren, Archibald MacLeish, and Katherine Anne Porter. Tate said it was 'a huge success'; but it was a Pyrrhic victory. Ransom told Frank MacShane that Ford's speech made it clear he should leave, 'if only to teach Tennessee a lesson, so that in future that state might give proper recognition to her writers'; after this, he said, 'he simply had to go to Ohio'. He founded the *Kenyon Review* when he got there, and asked Ford to contribute to the first issue, as he had to the first issue of the *Southern Review*.[11]

'This is one of the noisiest spots in the world', wrote Ford from Benfolly, 'what with children and chickens and birds and cows and steamboats and Tennessean voices and doors slamming in the wind.' Biala, who came to think the Tates as poisonous as they could be hospitable, said that the doors were open because Caroline Gordon insisted on opening them, including the door to Ford and Biala's bedroom; she suspected the Tates of trying to break up their relationship (as Biala heard that Penn Warren thought Gordon tried to break up his marriage). But despite the interruptions, the noise, and the fraught nerves, Ford was getting his daily thousand words written with the 'regularity of a grandfather's clock', and had sent a third of *The March of Literature* to the publisher by 11 June.[12]

In July 1937 the Tates, Ford, Biala, and Lowell squeezed into the Tates' Ford V8 to drive to Michigan. They reached Urbana, in Illinois, by the first night; but Ford was so exhausted by the cramped car that he and Biala took the train from there: they needed some time away from the others. The Olivet conference began on 18 July. There were three hour-long lectures in the mornings, Round Table discussions in the afternoon until four, followed by personal interviews for writers to discuss their work with members of the staff. There was another lecture or a reading each evening, this time open to Olivet students. Besides Ford, the Tates, and Katherine Anne Porter, the staff included Jean Starr Untermeyer, Paul Engle, and Carl Sandburg. Ford lectured on 'Beginnings of Fiction', 'Developments of Fiction', 'Picaresque Fiction', and 'The Consciously Designed Novel'. Both staff and students found it exciting to 'get to know these people as human beings, with all their little eccentricities'. It was perhaps at this conference that Ford displayed an unusual one for him: rivalry. 'There was no love lost' between Ford and Sandburg, remembered Glenn Gosling, a professor of English at Olivet. 'Fordie and Carl were always very funny about each other [. . .] Fordie would affect not to know who Carl was. Carl, for his side, would say, "Ford? Yeah I know him. He's the kind of a guy, you ask him what does he think of Shakespeare and by God he tells you!"' One of the students, Laura Verplank, recalled a reception at which Ford sat in the dining-room talking to one group, while Sandburg held forth in the sitting-room. Ford was 'really the lion of the evening', but even so, Caroline Gordon thought she should try to shoo people into the dining-room to make sure his audience didn't dwindle.[13]

'While the writer's conferences were on, people came from all over the state and Chicago to visit the exhibitors, bring their manuscripts, and get the advice of Ford and other writers', wrote Biala; 'The finest and best known writers of the time came to Olivet. Everyone was interested and excited.' They had 'no sense of being cut off from the world', she said, 'because the world was constantly dropping in to see us'. As soon as the Olivet conference ended—on 31 July—Ford and Biala took the train to Boulder, Colorado. He had been invited by Edward Davison, who ran the 'Writers' Conference of the Rocky Mountains', and wanted Ford to be there for the last two weeks of it. She had two exhibitions booked, one at Boulder, the other at the Denver Museum. Ford found Boulder 'enervating on account of the altitude and the want of oxygen in the air'. Davison noted that he was 'over-weight, out of condition, breathless and in considerable pain'. Amongst the other writers present were Ransom, John Peale Bishop, Sherwood Anderson, Howard Mumford Jones, and Whit Burnett (of *Story* magazine). For the first four days he gave informal lectures to a group of twenty or thirty people, based on what he had written of *The March of Literature*. Lowell was still pursuing him. He met his future wife Jean Stafford at Boulder. When, on 3 August, Ford gave a formal lecture on 'The Literary Life', recounting his relations with Conrad and James, Lowell was in the auditorium, which held 650 people. 'I watched an audience of three thousand walk out on him', he exaggerated, 'as he exquisitely, ludicrously, and inaudibly imitated the elaborate periphrastic style of Henry James. They could neither hear nor sympathize.' Davison said he spoke on Conrad, but referred to him solely by his Polish name, which the audience didn't recognize. Ford lectured sitting down, and ignored the microphone that Davison had provided: 'at one point a young woman jumped onto the platform and moved it closer to him, but he soon managed to get away from it again.' Even those close to him could hear little, so people slipped out quietly after about half of the lecture. He retained his *sang-froid* during the lecture, but he spent a day or two in bed afterwards.[14]

They left their stifling apartment to stay with the Davisons. Ford was genial once more, sitting 'at the piano singing the Irish famine "taty" song'. He said he would cook *Chevreuil des Prés Salés* for the farewell dinner. Davison fell in with the joke, and got a neighbour 'to burst in and announce himself as the game warden come to arrest Ford for killing a deer out of season'. Nearly a quarter of a century later, Lowell said he thought it was still the best dinner he had ever had: 'The wines were balanced, and every course came as it should, and the venison came, and we ended with syllabub, and you felt in Paradise at the end. You never realised that the venison was mutton that Ford had cooked.'[15]

Denver was 'disillusioningly quiet' when they got there in the third week of August 1937. Ford wrote one of his new series of 'Portraits of Cities' about it, describing it as a 'Ghost City', failing to live up to its history of gold-rushes, and their 'hysterias, crowd-madnesses, pestilences'. It was partly to do with Ford's discomfort at mountain altitude: 'if you try to raise your voice, you fall to panting like a carp on a pond bank [. . .] Perhaps everything here has died for want of oxygen [. . .].' 'We tried for three weeks there and in the neighbourhood to raise a game of Poker—and it could not be done. We were perhaps alarming in aspect!' 'God, what a State!', Ford wrote to Pound about Colorado once he was back at Olivet on 23 August. He tried to interest Paul

Palmer in the 'Portraits of Cities', telling him they were 'on the whole s[p]iteful', adding that he explains in them that he doesn't know why cities like Denver should exist at all:

Indeed I am in rather a spiteful as well as a muddled mood. Contact, for instance, with the (rather wealthy, middle class) students of this institution where I am due to take a chair of Comparative Literature as well as with students from half a dozen other State Universities where I have been pottering about or lecturing, has given me such an appalled view of the secondary education of this country, that I feel that nothing can save it but something like a revolution in the whole country's educational methods. . . . And crisscrossing the eastern states from say Baltimore to the Rocky Mountains has given me a good many other causes for appalment so that I don't really see what is to become of this—let alone European—civilisations [sic].[16]

He vented similar frustrations in an essay on 'The Sad State of Publishing' that summer, explaining how the publishers' obsession with the 'best seller' had made the business purely speculative; and he followed it up with a puff for Carlos Williams, Dahlberg, and e. e. cummings—experimental writers who were having difficulty getting published in such a market. If he was dispirited, however, he was not despairing. He immediately tried to effect that revolution of America's education by trying to persuade Pound to take up a similar job as a writer in residence. If Pound responded his answer hasn't survived; Ford suggested they should meet, either in Paris or Rapallo that winter to discuss it.[17]

Back at Olivet Ford and Biala moved into a small white clapboard bungalow, 329½ East Cottage Street, which is still known as 'the Ford Madox Ford cottage'. Robie Macaulay says it was 'not much bigger than a hen coop':

He was a large stout man and I was always surprised to see that he actually fitted inside. My impression was that the place was in complete chaos and that Ford was the center of disorder. Some operation was always ponderously, with many interruptions, under way, whether it was cooking *coq au vin* (Ford was a magnificent chef) or marking the proofs of a book. In the midst of all this mobilization, Janice Biala, Ford's wife, was always per[f]ectly composed and efficient. Quite different in temperament, she was a good balance. She was (and is) an excellent painter, witty in conversation, attractive, and as direct and informal as Ford sometimes was overawing and roundabout.[18]

Lowell had come with them to Olivet, to serve 'as a sort of conscripted secretary [. . .] taking dictation in the mornings, and typing it out in the afternoons'. For all Ford's unease with him, it must have been gratifying that such an evidently gifted young writer was acting towards him as he had towards Conrad. 'As he is a very great master of English prose the training is very valuable,' wrote Lowell, 'and I would not want to miss the opportunity.' His reminiscence about his work on *The March of Literature* is a homage to Ford's reminiscences and criticisms:

> Taking Ford's dictation on Samuel Butler
> in longhand: 'A novelist has one novel, his own.'
> He swallowed his words, I garbled each seventh word—
> 'You have no ear,' he said, 'for civilized prose,
> Shakespeare's best writing: *No king, be his cause never so spotless,*
> *will try it out with all unspotted soldiers.*'

> I brought him my loaded and overloaded lines.
> He said: 'You live a butterfly's existence,
> flitting, flying, botching inspiration.
> Conrad spent a day finding the *mot juste*; then killed it.'
> Ford doubted I could live and be an artist.
> 'Most of them are born to fill the graveyards.'
> Ford wrote my father, 'If he fails as a writer, at least
> he'll be head of Harvard or your English Ambassador.'[19]

When Natalie Davison heard from Jean Stafford that Lowell was secretly planning to accompany the Fords back to Europe, she warned them: 'if I were in your boots and he succeeded in his little plan, I am sure I would push him off the rail before we reached Cherbourg.'[20]

'Ford never actually taught writing', Macauley thought, '(though he discussed manuscripts).' What he best communicated was 'what *being* a writer means'. Literature appeared to him 'as a kind of family tree. One writer "descended" from another in that the accumulated knowledge of the older passed on to the younger'. 'By this figure', Macauley shrewdly observes, 'he would have most likely chosen James as his father and Flaubert as his grandfather and traced himself back to Horace at least'. Well, not Horace; but he did imagine tracing himself back—in an eye-twinkling note in *Great Trade Route*—to an equally illustrious English literary ancestor (or two): 'After all, why shouldn't I be descended from Shakespeare as well as from John Ford, who wrote *'Tis Pity She's a Whore*? Someone must be . . .' 'Ford's method of teaching was narrative and anecdotal', said Macauley:

Usually his stories were not simple illustrations of the point; they contained a great many relative and tangential things. Thus, a student asking about drama, might get as an answer a quite involved and probably half-imaginary story about Goethe that seemed to end up a considerable distance from the original question. If he thought about it, however, he would realize that along the way Ford had introduced a dozen relevant ideas and, though he had never given a direct answer, he had given an extraordinarily complete one. After listening to Ford, I always found other teachers something like a human true-and-false test.

He was giving lectures based on *The March of Literature*—an impressionist textbook, in that it creates the illusion of orderly literary history in order to subvert and detemporalize it. 'Ford had none of that sense of time and death that turns books into mere middens or archaeological finds for critics and scholars. He was the least academic man who ever taught and for him all books, in themselves, were contemporaneous.' As Macauley says, 'Ford always spoke to writers and readers', not to critics and professors. His memory was the most extraordinary Macauley had ever encountered. Ford would lecture on Tuesday mornings, sitting in a big easy chair in the Klock Commons (a large room in Dole Hall), one of his students, Bill Selden, remembered:

He was an immense sort of balloon-like man—looked like a cartoon out of *Punch*. He would say, smoking Turkish cigarettes all the time:
'And of course, the modern novel began with the Spanish writer (harrumphphph).' The students would say:

'Who—What—Who?' They'd say to each other, 'How do you *spell* that?' We didn't really dare ask Ford how to spell it. Then he would go on to some other momentous revelation, and do the same thing. It was a very entertaining and interesting experience.[21]

The students would sit on the floor around him. Brewer and Glen Gosling (another professor and former Rhodes scholar to Oxford) would also come to hear him. On Fridays he would have tea served to a small group of students in his office, 'a small shadowy room in the basement of the library', the shelves crammed inappropriately with theological tracts. The groups discussed Hitler, Mussolini, Roosevelt, the Spanish Civil War. They also listened to Ford's anecdotes of Kipling, Wells, and James. One student, Charles Fiske, thought his story-telling had an 'intense vibrant immediacy, making such a person as Henry James as real as tea on an English afternoon'. There was also a group 'invited to drop over in the evenings to read *Madame Bovary* with the Fords', but it fizzled out because the students' French was not good enough. Sometimes he would work, with his characteristic generosity towards younger writers, with individual students on their own manuscripts. When Fiske took him Spenserian verses 'beyond the worst excesses of Elizabeth's age', Ford commented kindly, but suggested that he should attempt American subjects. Two years later, he was mentioning Fiske in print as one of the students whose work 'would adorn the pages of any magazine, literary or profane, in the world'. When Macauley showed him a story he had set in China, even though he knew nothing about it, Ford told him it was a bad story, but said: 'The good thing is that you're trying to write about something you don't know. Writing about what you know is a mistake.' This is not only the opposite of his advice to Fiske, but is also paradoxical, to say the least, coming from an author who wrote so much better on what he knew well (Edwardian society, the war, his life) than on what he knew less well (America, business). But he was responding to the autobiographical fixes of his fledgling authors; 'he must have been bored by the ineptitude of Olivet student, would-be writers', thought Macauley—though if he was he didn't show it. Except, possibly, when Macauley asked him what Ford thought he should do after leaving college, and was told: 'Join the Marines.' 'He always told us to read a new author named Eudora Welty, who was about the best young American writer he'd come across.' His presence had 'the greatest impact on Olivet's students', whether he was promoting the classics or the avant-garde, lecturing or socializing. But Macauley thought that the students were not reading him, but Auden, Kafka, or Waugh.[22]

He would entertain at home, too, sitting with his gouty, bandaged foot up, and being waited on by Biala and the students, or cooking dinner for a select few. They had a wild cat that would perch on top of a tallboy and pounce on the guests. 'Fordie would say, "Oh, that's all right. Don't worry". But it never did that to him!' 'Life at Olivet was really very gay', said Biala:

The dean, of the *ancien régime*, gave a lecture entitled 'Do Gentlemen Drink Wine?' knowing perfectly well that Brewer had a very good wine cellar, and anyone could see the empty bottles outside our back door [. . .] Brewer [. . .] had a collection of modern art, the first seen in those *parages*, and he was a terrific tap dancer. Ford and I did a lot of good to that place in another way. Socially the sexes were rigorously separated. There were constantly parties either for men only or for women only. We put a stop to that. The first time Ford was invited to one of those men-only parties he replied politely, 'Sorry, I don't go to parties where there are no women.' And the first time I was invited to one of those only-women parties, I replied, 'Sorry, I don't go to parties where there are no men.' So then the younger crowd decided to follow suit and pretty soon all the parties were mixed.

Not to be outdone by Brewer's tap-dancing, Ford learned to tango from the college's South American composer.[23]

When they left Olivet at the beginning of December 1937 Ford gave a flamboyantly fictive interview to a local paper. It was titled 'Ford Madox Ford, Cook, Baron, Novelist, Brings Zest to Faculty', and described him as 'Olivet's lone Famous Name'. He explained his privileges as 'Baron of the Cinque Ports', saying that he had held a canopy over the king's head during the Coronation. 'Olivet students find Mr. Ford amazingly like William Rose Benét's description of him, "An old sea-lion of the ledges," find his lectures intimate, anecdotal, and alive [. . .] Bohemian Ford is literally a storehouse of stories', concluded the reporter, whose language suggests he or she wasn't one of his students: 'odd bits of knowledge, provocative theories (abolish copyrights, learn only enough German to read Heine, the last war destroyed Christianity, there are no good translations, the only literature is that which serves only to entertain.)'[24]

After they left Olivet they stayed with their friend Professor Cox at 130 Morningside Drive in New York from 1 December 1937 until their ship, the *Lafayette*, sailed on the 4th. They got to Paris by the 14th, and Ford worked at *The March of Literature*: 'It is written from the aesthetico-critical rather than the annalist's point of view', he wrote to Allen & Unwin's publicity department, 'and forms a sort of comparative history of creative writing from, as you might say, Confucius to Conrad'; and he went on to describe his astonishment at how much more 'readable' the classics now seemed to him: 'I found myself for instance reading the *Book of Job*, *Orlando Furioso*, or Chaucer's *Palamon and Arcite* [*The Knight's Tale*] as if they were say Mrs. Agatha Christie and, trying to rest my mind with light literature, I found myself turning to Dante's *Paolo and Francesca* as being more restful company. . . .' But progress was slow. They had wanted to avoid a severe Mid-Western winter, but Ford caught a cold and developed complications. He wrote to Brewer: 'Unfortunately, I have been really seriously ill with a severe heart attack complicated with lung trouble ever since we got here.' Julie came to visit at Christmas, but the tension between them persisted. He still wanted to arrange that meeting with Pound, having come to feel that it was important for Pound to teach in America. 'The Olivet experiment is extremely meritorious', he told Pound, adding that 'in other ways the moment is crucial, if only because I shan't last for ever.' He also wanted to see Pound before he died: 'the arrow that flies nocturnally has had two or three shots at me lately.' He sent New Year greetings, and suggested they should meet half-way between Paris and Rapallo—'say at Marseilles'—partly because the rue de Seine flat, though in a handsome five-storey stucco block, was sparsely furnished and 'troglodytic': they lived there 'like the poorer sort of peasants in old and mouldering rooms without water laid on or *central Heizung*'. (He later joked to Pound: 'We have now added to the palatialness of this apartment, kitchens, baths, eau, gaz, électricité, open wood fires and most of the things demanded by the Victorians.') 'My deah ole Freiherr von Bluggerwitzkoff, late baron of the Sunk

Ports etc/', replied Pound—Ford had perhaps sent him a clipping of his Olivet interview—to say that he couldn't leave Rapallo, since he was organizing a series of Purcell concerts. 'Dear Bertran de Struwwelpeter y Bergerac', Ford replied in the middle of February, 'I was taken seriously ill with heart trouble shortly after getting your last and am not much better now, but just able to write.' He had always teased Pound about the pain his incomprehensible letters caused him, but this was serious. He told Unwin: 'I have been extremely ill for a long time and am still very weak', and was unsure whether Unwin had written to him or whether he had 'only dreamed the letter'. He had written half of *The March of Literature* before they left America, but had 'only managed to crawl through about half a chapter since then', he said, adding: 'heaven only knows when I shall get it all done.' Nevertheless, the fact that he could write long, tactful, often amusing letters shows that he was gradually recovering during February and March. His illness prevented them from travelling south, and he always felt the south of France restorative. It wasn't until they returned to America in the spring that he really began to feel better.[25]

1938: 'AN OLD MAN MAD
ABOUT WRITING'[1]

He was the last great European man of letters.
(Allen Tate, 'Random Thoughts on the 1920's')

When Biala had an exhibition at the Gallery Zak in Paris in March 1938 Ford was exuberant about her success. He told Crankshaw: 'it turned out rather a triumph. Not only did she sell some pictures—one to the State for the Jeu de Paume!—but the gallery proprietor Mme Zak has taken on her fortunes.' He was 'still insufferably feeble—unable to walk even a few yards' ('I can only crawl about', he told Gertrude Stein), and he was wondering how he would get through his work in America: New York University had invited him to lecture in April, and now there was talk that he would be asked 'to re-organise its literary department'; then there was the spring's teaching at Olivet. Yet he was phenomenally active for such a sick man. He finished an article on food for the *Forum* magazine, and proposed to write others on the 'international situation'—not about what he called its 'newsy' aspects; but the topics he suggested are oddly, though perhaps characteristically, contradictory. One idea was to discuss the moral effect of the First World War: he felt that enthusiasm for war had been lessened by that war's destruction of 'Fine Illusions'—the 'big words' of Faith, Loyalty, Courage, Patriotism: he reckoned without the coarse illusions of racism and national destiny. Yet the second idea was one which anticipated precisely the threat of another war; this was that, as in 1914–18, 'Both England and the United States have *got* to provide insurance for France: the world has to'; once again French civilization must be preserved, since it is all that keeps Anglo-Saxondom from lapsing into barbarism: this line was more prescient. He offered to write a preface for Crankshaw's translation of René Béhaine. Ford told Crankshaw: 'I am getting Picasso to write something about Spain', and asked him if he could translate it and place it in England. Not least, he continued trying to get Pound to Olivet. Pound had said he wanted to communicate directly with Brewer, to ask questions such as whether Olivet used his book, and whether Brewer would get a printing press 'for the DISTRIBUTION of knowledge and ideas'. Ford suggested that he should intercede ('Dear God, Father Divine', he wrote: 'I know that Your awful face must be veiled to the lesser mackerel nuzzling between Your toes in the ooze'), probably fearing that once Pound got Brewer's ear he would bite it off. But Ford rephrased the terms into an altruistic gesture of self-sacrifice that Pound could only refuse:

Dear Ezra,
    Do exercise a little imagination and try to understand the situation. I am an *extremely* sick

man and your incomprehensible scrawls are a torture to me [. . .] Get the waiter at your hotel to write your letters for you; he will at least write comprehensible dog-English. Your 1892 O Henry stuff is wearisomely incomprehensible by now.

The situation is this: I am offering to give up my job at Olivet to you because you have been making noises about Universities for a long time and it would give you a chance really to do something [. . .] I teach what I want to—i.e. comparative literature from the beginning of time to the moment of speaking. No one interferes with me in the slightest degree. Nor would they with you. I don't know just what they would do if you tried to introduce your politics into your teaching—nothing at all probably unless you were too loudly communist in which case the local farmers would shoot you.

Please understand: I am not a confidence trickster trying to induce you into some disastrous folly. *I am not trying to persuade you to take the job.* You would probably turn that pleasant place into a disastrous sort of hell. But it is my duty to say that there the place is for you & the College authorities want you because they admire you as a poet and a teacher. Nor is it part of a sinister conspiracy on my part to rob you of your claim to be the greatest discoverer of literary talent the world has ever seen. I don't care a damn: I wish to God I had never 'discovered' anyone. . . . The only conspiracy I am in is to get you the Charles Eliot Norton professorship at Harvard to which Olivet would be a stepping stone.[2]

'I do NOT want your job', Pound replied. Ford told him: 'It is not a case of your getting me out of a job—or not any longer for I am so weak that it is unlikely that I shall be able to get through this half year there, though I am going to have a try.' 'ONCE you git an idea in yr/ head it is difficult to deracinate it', wrote Pound: 'Let me put it in another form. I do not want YOUR job. I do not want the JOB you have got/ whether you keep it or not. I will not go [to] Olivet and teach'; though he remained interested in Ford's other suggestion of a possible post at New York University.[3]

Mightier Than the Sword was probably published in England on 22 February 1938. Ford had originally wanted to call the book 'Mightier Than Swordsmen', but Houghton Mifflin preferred *Portraits from Life* for the American edition. 'I always bow to the Rhadamanthine decrees of sales and publicity departments', Ford grudged, 'but on this occasion with more regret than usual:

Because it is time that people should be reminded that we are mightier than the swordsmen . . . as witness the Rt Hon David Ll. George whose foul pen is murdering the reputations of the poor fool swordsmen now dead whom he allowed to be murdered in life to bolster up his brief authority . . . which miserable things these eyes witnessed![4]

What makes *Mightier Than the Sword* so much more than a gallery of vivid, entertaining portraits is precisely this sense of the *power* of literature: its ability to transform realities; to bring the dead back to imagination; to impress itself upon the personality, and transform its readers in the act of reading; to make you *see*. Ford wrote another provocative preface disputing the boundary between fact and impression, biography and novel, death and life:

I determined [. . .] to erect to my—nearly all dead—friends not so much a monument more sounding than brass, but an, as it were, intimately vignetted representation that should force the public to see that circle of strong personalities as I want them to be seen. I am, that is to say, a novelist, and I want them to be seen pretty much as you see the characters in a novel . . . as if one should see the frequenters of the Mermaid Tavern in an historical romance. . . . Ford with his melancholy hat, Jonson with his learned sock, and the Shake-speare who had once bitten off the heads of chickens prior to roasting them outside the Globe Theatre for the clients whose horses he held. . . .[5]

What is 'mightier than the sword?'; 'the pen is'. The creative potency of artists is inscribed by their sexuality, and Ford's prose is subconsciously fertile here, with its language of erecting, intimacy, forcing, and that violent image (suggesting castration?) of decapitating the chickens. The concluding chapter 'There Were Strong Men' confronts the fact that all his subjects are male. He was perfectly prepared to concede 'that women have done better work than men in the last hundred years'; but says 'there are certain social difficulties in knowing very intimately a writer of a sex different from one's own'. But Moser is surely right to suggest that the difficulties were temperamental as much as social: that for all the power of his imagining of female characters and advocacy of women writers, his 'deepest intellectual and emotional responses are to men'. Creative fertility is associated with the *duplex* or *x-plex* personalities of the writers that so intrigued him. He is not merely concerned with their 'multiple person-alities' as men; rather, with how their forms of mental complexity are characteristic of them as artists. Turgenev's apparition with his 'singular and fantastic double', the translator Ralston, is a symbol of the singular and fantastic doubleness of literature, which can let the writer or reader imagine being someone quite other. In one extraor-dinary passage Ford imagines Alexander II reading Turgenev's *Sportsman's Sketches* with such sympathetic imagination that 'suddenly the Tsar himself was Yermolaï', the serf; and that the experience was instrumental in prompting the Tsar to emancipate the serfs. The vignette is an illustration of the pen's might. It is also an example of what it illustrates. The Tsar's act of imagination is doubled by Ford's act of imagining being the Tsar, reading his own favourite book. Finally, the episode is an example of another Fordian premiss: that the way to know and to understand writers is to read their books rather than their biographies. It is partly the lack of biographical informa-tion about Turgenev's private life that makes him such a sympathetic character to Ford. 'He moves surrounded by the cloud of his characters as a monarch by his courtiers; and, once more like a monarch, surrounded by crowds of admirers and detractors who all viewed him in the light of their own images, preconceptions, and desires.' Ford has been accused of reimagining his writer-friends in his own image. This passage shows how aware he was of that danger; but how he avoided it by attending to the writers' works as well as their *milieux*. It also suggests how he felt his own personality should be understood, as expressed by the fictions which effaced and clouded it. At this level he might be accused of self-aggrandizement: of saying that he too as a writer was like a monarch (since in the Republic of Letters the pen is mightier than the sceptre too); that he was again identifying with the autocrat. But this would be to forget that he was writing about the Turgenev he found so noble, before whom he was so humble, and whose art he found so moving. It is these qualities that save Fordian reminiscence from the name-dropping kind of self-aggrandizement that is the peril of the form. They leave one with the sense, not of a specious intimacy with the famous, but of the mysterious *un*familiarity of what we thought we knew, whether it be the personalities of writers whose work we know, or our sense of the stability of our own personalities.[6]

Mightier Than the Sword is not a book of academic literary criticism. But its insights into the complex relations between privacy and publication are ignored by critics at their peril. It is, above all, well written. Its profoundly Fordian dual form, again doubling biography with autobiography, was praised by reviewers. 'Mr. Ford Madox Ford is one of the masters of modern prose and a critic who can criticise himself', said the *Daily Telegraph*: 'This book of candid yet kindly criticism is an excellent entertainment.' 'Somehow Mr. Ford escaped the peculiar seriousness of his seniors in the period,' observed V. S. Pritchett, 'and I imagine this is why his own mark has not been as strong as his talents warranted. It is always exciting to read Mr. Ford.' He went on shrewdly: 'Before everything else a personality, he excels at recreating an impression of the personality of people like Turgenev, Hardy or James, by gathering together the least expected fragments. Bizarre as they may be, they are kept in place by an unusual common sense.'[7]

When William Carlos Williams wrote to offer Ford his thanks for the book—he particularly admired the Crane and the Hudson—he wrote well of its strange dual quality: 'I don't know what it is that you are offering in your books—something extremely old and very new. I think the portraits gather up a good deal of your best to say and present it to us in a manner to make us ashamed [. . .] you are conscious of a living phrase.' Readers of the book are conscious of a living phrase too: the lifelike phrases his subjects speak (and which feel all the more familiar if we know their own phrases, or Ford's previous words about them); and also the life in Ford's own language as he renders them—an energy which makes new the old forms of memoir. Like many who knew Ford, Carl Van Doren praised his ability to make us see the literary past: 'The literary history of those years became a living record when he talked.' *Mightier Than the Sword* is essential Ford because its reimaginings of the past are among his best; and because it shows him alive to his present too. Van Doren said he was unlike most 'veterans', who 'seem too often to have stopped growing themselves [. . .] and to have lost the savor of the growing world. Ford had not done that.'[8]

This was true even as the political situation grew bleaker. Just before they sailed for America, Ford wrote Julie a 'farewell letter'. Although it is alive with plans to meet her again, whether at Olivet or in Europe, his mildly desperate cadences suggest that he feared he might not—either because of his own health, or because, after Hitler's annexation of Austria the week before, war seemed increasingly probable:

Dearest Julie,
This is by way of being a farewell letter, for we expect to be sailing by the NORMANDIE on Wednesday. I am sorry not to have seen more of you. It is a pity you could not have been here whilst Janice's exhibition was on, because she had to be at the exhibition most of the day and I had to sit here alone and should have been glad of your ministrations for I am still pretty feeble, practically unable to walk and so on. Still, it was not to be. I shall hope to see more of you when we come back—whenever that will be. But I have got back to work again, which is a good thing, though I cannot do much—which is not so good because lots of money won't flow in unless I work hard and we shall not be able to realise the project of your coming to Olivet unless lots of money does flow in. [. . .]

I hope you are shouting A bas Chamberlain good and strong at any demonstrations that are going. It makes us ashamed to be leaving Paris now that Mr. C. has brought his friends the Huns so near. But I guess I should not be much good when the city is bombed. . . . Think of the rue de Seine in ruins, like Barcelona, and me in a gas mask pouring water on the ashes of my manuscripts and Janice trying to save the cat—which is the first thing she would think of.

I hope you have got a good hide hole in a lonely place in the country for when they bomb London. It does not make me very comfortable to think of you there, I can tell you, and us across the sea!

Goodbye, my dear MONSTER. I am too tired to write more . . . By the bye if you would get two or three more razor blades and put them into an envelope and mail them here right away—or perhaps better still to the NORMANDIE at Havre I should be obliged. They are a great luxury for me.

Your quite old

F.M.F.[9]

They arrived on 29 March, and stayed with Professor Cox again in New York until 5 April. Ford gave a university lecture. It was a 'complete disaster', according to Biala. They needed the $100, but Ford was still feeling so ill she was trembling with fear lest he should faint, especially when 'some jackass' asked her 'Was Ford married to Violet Hunt? She says he was.' They arrived back at Olivet during a blizzard. In the spring he was 'getting a little strength together' after his illness, he told Palmer. But for all the fuss made of him at Olivet, he didn't feel at home outside France. The food upset him: 'If we can ever find something decent to eat I might once more resume my Gargantuan activities', he said: 'As it is, I can't do much more than crawl about.' The travelling had reinvigorated his imagination, and he had characteristically expressed and mastered his regret at having to leave France by writing an essay about the necessity of being there. In 'A Paris Letter' he imagines standing on the Pont des Arts, between the Louvre and the Institut de France, facing the Île de la Cité to the east; the bridge becomes a symbol of the centrality of Art to Paris, and of France's centrality: 'One has first to find out if this city stands where, sempiternally, she has always done, at the center of our Mediterranean civilization [. . .].' The moral he draws from his meditation on the vitality of the city's cultural life is the fictional–impressionist one that 'if you may not go to Paris on the Seine, you must invent a Paris of your own'— which is approximately what he was doing at Olivet. The essay is obliquely autobiographic in another way. He is talking of how the Paris skyline is populated with memories of the great writers who have lived there: 'that garret window there was once Lamartine's; beside it, the famous one of Béranger. And next to that is the garret window of Heine; and the next that of Ronsard. Then that of Dante, and then Villon's when he had a garret. And here, on high, lodged Thackeray, and here Goethe. . . .' Which is why he never minded living in garrets himself. It is another example of how Ford's erudition can transform a scene into embodied literary history, illuminated by a felt autobiographic involvement. Simply walking down Paris streets elicits thoughts about art, poverty, and greatness. These questions cannot be weighed solely in the abstract: they weigh upon him, as they must upon anyone with artistic ambitions:

And you do, don't you?, at that point square your shoulders and declare that, though it may be your destiny to be second rate, from now onwards your prose shall have a spine and your verse some significance and your thought some exactitude.

Because you will never be any good until you realize that you are second rate . . . *Atque ego . . . atque ego* . . . Till then you will envy, and try to race with, the first-rate and your lungs will be a pain and there will be no help for you. The blessed state will come when you resign yourself to leave the palms and parsley crowns to Villon and Ronsard; then, in your ears shall be the plaudits that crowds and judges reserve for good seconds.[10]

The 'you' is disconcertingly insistent, and hovers disconcertingly between direct address and impersonal generality (between 'you the reader' and 'one'). But whether advice to the neophyte or the wisdom of Ford's own age (or, of course, both), one can't but wonder how we are to take that clause about being second rate. Is it Ford's Villonesque testament; an acknowledgement of his own limitations? There's a touch of 'the pride that apes humility' about it, perhaps. Being second rate compared to Carl Sandburg or Georges Simenon would be one kind of destiny—a particularly damning one for someone of Ford's high aspirations for the Arts. Being second rate compared to Dante, Villon, Goethe, or Heine would be quite another—one that wouldn't preclude a destiny of being first-rate amongst your contemporaries. I don't think Ford doubted he had done first-rate work; but there is perhaps another kind of autobiographical recognition in this passage: a sense that, after thinking of his life in terms of his contacts with the 'strong men', the 'authentic immortals' of *Portraits from Life*, he was aware of a distance from them. 'I cannot hope for immortality', he wrote, adding: 'I have aimed at it.' In planning his collected edition, and trying to provide for Julie, he was becoming more than ever concerned with what would happen to his books, his name, his child, after his death.[11]

He was still very weak, though 'beginning to return to something like health' in the spring. The 'cussedly damp climate' at Olivet left him 'so crippled with rheumatism' that, as he told George Keating, 'I can't even dress myself or brush my own hair'. When Alvin Hamer tried to enlist Ford's support for Hemingway's *To Have and Have Not*, banned by the Detroit Wayne County Prosecutor from all commercial distribution, Ford uncharacteristically declined. He didn't want to enter a controversy about public affairs in America, and suggested that the response in Detroit if he did would be xenophobic, along the lines of: 'All foreigners are not only lecherous but aim at corruption of the morals of American youth. That is too well known to need contradiction.' He added, wisely, that 'all censorships invariably defeat themselves and the only effect of this one will be to increase Hemingway's sales'; and that in a court case he would 'make a horrible muddle of things under cross-examination' and would get accused of publicity-seeking. Even so, it was the kind of opportunity for embattled championship of good writing that a stronger, less overworked, Ford would have found it hard to resist.[12]

He did have the strength to work furiously. Besides his teaching—which he was surprised to find that he rather enjoyed—he was racing to finish *The March of Literature*. He had set himself the deadline of 14 July—Bastille Day—as the date he would be free of his most massive single book (the four novels of *Parade's End* add up to about the same length). He had been 'doing nothing else but write from five in the morning till seven in the evening in order to get it finished', he told Unwin. One of his neighbours, Sam Robinson, heard the typewriter going 'night after night' as well as 'day after day'. On 12 July Robinson heard, through the badly insulated walls, 'a great ROAR from Ford'. After a 'tremendous rush' the book was finished with two days to spare. They went out to celebrate with champagne, and he and Biala took the type-script to Battle Creek the next day to express it to the Dial Press. A week later he told Paul Palmer he was 'still fairly dizzy' from finishing it.[13]

Brewer had persuaded the trustees to give Ford an honorary doctorate at the Olivet commencement ceremony on 19 June. The college Orator, Dr Akeley, presented him for the degree with an amazingly playful, fictionalized biographical sketch, for which Ford must have provided the outlines:

He is a Dr. of Agriculture of the University of Sorbonne. He has proved his right to the degree and its relevance to culture by his garden at Toulon and by his demonstration to the Society of Gourmets in a New York restaurant that garlic, properly cooked, does NOT smell but does most delectably flavor meat.

He is a communicating member of the French Institute.

He is an incomparable lecturer on military tactics. He has known war as a colonel in charge of two regiments in action, as a casualty blown up at Becourt-Becordel [*sic*], as a reflective exponent of better ways towards peace.

[. . .] Reared amongst the tumultuously-bearded great of the mid-Victorian era, bludg-eoned by the enormity of their self-righteous indignations, enlightened by the meanness of their dispositions, he gave himself to a passionless reconstitution of his day, passionate only to engender a creative record for his time, a carefully architectured imaginative literature. Writing with a due vision for the inner truths of his ambience he left the world to draw its own morals and so came nearer the truth than the ax [*sic*] of the moralist or the index of the commentator ever can.

[. . .] First to praise Dreiser in England; first to credit Joyce and Stein; first to publish the works of writers like D. H. Lawrence, H. M. Tomlinson, Wyndham Lewis; first to publish a short story by Arnold Bennett and by Galsworthy; guarantor of Conrad's first novel, Almayer's Folly. What he has done for Englishmen and expatriates he has done in equal measure for Robert Frost, H.D., Ezra Pound; for Ernest Hemin[g]way, Caroline Gordon, Glenway Westcott. And his latest pupil, Maureen Whipple, a girl from Utah, has this summer attested the keenness of his scent for talent by winning the Houghton Mifflin prize for novels submitted in competition.

[. . .] As the monks of the early monastic orders stood by the culture of remembered antiquity amidst the undignified barbarities of medieval Anglo-Saxon leisure, so has this genuinely Catholic spirit stood incorruptibly by art for the refinement of human feeling, of human intercourse, of human expression while his race was thinking with its blood, the circulating medium of its barbarous economic system.[14]

Ford might have made an improbable monk, but the gowns did make him think of the church (perhaps reminding him of the Investiture of the American cardinals). 'I can tell you I looked swell in my robes', he told Keating: 'I have always wanted to be a cardinal because just think what a fine expanse of scarlet that would make!' As the joking suggests, he was predictably ambivalent about academic formality. 'However if you ever address me as doctor again', he warned Keating, 'I shall return the letter unopened and marked "addressee unknown."' He told Julie that his 'proper style is now F.M.F., D. Lit.; Professor Emeritus of Comparative Literature &c. &c. So the laugh is on me.' He asked Unwin not to address him as 'Dr. Ford', and went on to consider, like the prose technician he was, the expressive effects of various forms of address. 'Dr. Ford Madox Ford' was 'altogether too preposterous as an appellation and although "Dr. F. M. Ford" would be preferable it rather extinguishes one's personality'—one's personality that was represented by the names one shared with one's grandfather, perhaps. Besides, he added, 'I feel as I always feel, so extremely undoctorial. I have one literary honour of which I am rather proud—that of an author whose works have been communicated to the French Institute—which is, I believe, expressed by the letters E.C. de l'I. de F.'. At this point he heard himself beginning to sound uncharacteristically doctorial, and shifted into gently self-mocking fictionalized autobiography: 'but that seems to be too complicated for common use as is also my other singular qualification—Chevalier of the Order of Peter Karagerogevitch—or I think it's that, if it isn't St. Nicholas of Serbia.' The title-page of Allen and Unwin's edition of *Provence*, published on 1 November 1938, styles the author 'Ford Madox Ford / LL.D.'. He was proud to be an academic at Olivet because it was so un-academic an academy, where he could feel so undoctorial while teaching and lecturing.[15]

He had needed to finish *The March of Literature* by 14 July to be ready for the next Writers' Conference, which, besides Ford and Sandburg, included Katherine Anne Porter, Léonie Adams, and William Troy. Afterwards, Ford went to Detroit to give a radio broadcast as advance publicity for the book. The Dial Press thought that a lecture tour would also help their sales. 'Some fellow wants me to do a lecturing tour which is a thing I despise', Ford grumbled to Keating, 'but if he offers me a sufficiently attractive program I shall have to accept it, though I expect the winter travelling will finish me off. Verily, peace hath her perils greater than in war.' Nevertheless he agreed, offering to help however he could. As Mizener says: 'He had worked harder gathering material for it than he had for any book he ever wrote: the amount of rereading he had done was staggering, and the strain of writing its nearly 900 pages had cost him much more than he could afford.' His relations with the Dial Press were cordial. When he told Grenville Vernon that Stanley Unwin 'expresses himself as being in ecstasies over the work', and was saying that it was 'a privilege to be permitted to publish it', Vernon replied 'to that we say amen for us!', and his colleague Burton Hoffman also wrote on the same day to tell Ford: 'We are proud to have the book on our list and consider it one of the finest pieces of creative non-fiction which it has been our privilege to see.' But then the Dial objected to calling the book a 'History of Literature', because, as Ford explained to Unwin: 'that would imply a history of all literature whereas practically I treat of those literatures that have had an influence on the European and American literatures of today. I mean that I have only just touched on Persian, Arabic, Japanese, Polish literatures, etc.' But he didn't like their suggestion of 'The *March* of Literature', which sounded too modishly like *The March of Time*. The Dial Press wanted to publish as early as possible. But when Ford got the first batch of proofs in the middle of the Writers' Conference he was appalled: the text had been savaged, and much of the quotation that he felt essential had been cut out without his being consulted. He had quoted a lot of Pound's *Cathay* poems, but the Dial had hoped to use translations from Chinese by Arthur Waley instead, whom the Dial also published. Ford explained to Pound that 'there would appear to be no legal means here of forcing a publisher to print books as their writers write them'. He felt it spoiled the book, arguing: 'I meant it to show without saying it in so many words that for the last twenty-five years or so, you and I have supported in our different ways almost the entire burden of the aesthetics of literature in this world'. 'To say so has its invidious sides', he added, recognizing the exaggeration which could overlook innovators like Lawrence, Joyce, Lewis, Eliot, Hemingway, Stein, or Carlos Williams (to name only some of the most prominent figures in English). But the comment reveals his hope that *The March of Literature* would finally reveal to the world his influence and his range: 'to prove it by quotation is convincing.'[16]

Already exhausted by the writing, Ford became depressed and ill over the cutting, and wired to Vernon: 'Do what you like to book. I have lost all interest in it.' He had to return the proofs of the English edition of *Provence* to Unwin, explaining: 'I simply do not feel well enough actually to correct the book.' Hoffman tried to flatter Ford back into co-operation, assuring him that he and his colleagues were 'all convinced that not in a long time has a book of such brilliance and magnificence been written'; that *The March of Literature* was a work of 'real greatness', and could be as successful as books like Van Wyck Brooks's *The Flowering of New England* (which had won the Pulitzer Prize in 1936) or George Santayana's novel *The Last Puritan* (an unexpected best-seller of the same year). He also offered to hire a professional indexer for the book. They even used Ford's suggestions for promotion, designing posters in the form of giant books. Ford recognized that Hoffman was working hard on his behalf, and he offered him his next proposed book: a collection of 'historical vignettes', provisionally titled 'Old Year's Gifts', some reprinted from *Zeppelin Nights* (which he had discovered was never published in America), some still to be written. Hoffman expressed interest, so Ford sent in a typescript, though the book was never published. There was a temporary rapprochement with Hoffman. But his way of explaining to Ford why he thought the cuts were necessary must have rankled. He said the book was being 'only indifferently received by the booksellers'; and while arguing that it should be cut to stop it looking like 'just another book on literature', he couldn't help blaming Ford, telling him that his 'selling reputation' was not a good one.[17]

Ford hoped to get Julie over for a visit during her summer holidays. But when she wrote saying she couldn't leave her mother, he reproached her once more for neglecting him:

Yes, to write to an aged and infirm parent whom one leaves apparently destined for an early demise is usually considered good form but you are perhaps above these merely social considerations. In any case I am still carrying on, though still practically crippled and unable to walk more than a yard or two. But after innumerable tests the doctors—eight of them— decided that my heart is not diseased, only weak so that if I am careful I may carry on yet for a time more.[18]

He told her he was glad they were getting money from his books: 'I wish we did! Last season was the worst I have ever had and but for this professorship I don't know what would have become of us.'

He and Biala left Olivet on 9 September, and a week later were visiting the Eshericks again, in Paoli, Pennsylvania. This was probably the visit recalled by Paul Metcalf, then the boyfriend of Esherick's daughter. No sooner had Ford manœuvred himself with difficulty out of the car, than Esherick's young son of twelve or so, Peter, proposed a game of softball—'a ludicrous notion, on the face of it'. To everyone's surprise Ford agreed. 'He stood on the plate, bat in hand', while Metcalf lobbed a pitch in to him. 'He hit it weakly to the ground, pointed to Peter, and said, "Peter, run that out for me." That was the game of soft ball.' Metcalf's memories of Ford reveal him as reading and cooking with the myriadmindedness that characterizes his prose (only with place-shifts instead of time-shifts):

I remember Ford reading in the living room. There were books scattered around the room, on tables and shelves. Ford would sit in a chair, take up a book, light a cigarette, read for a while, smoking and reading. Then he would set the book down, leaving it open, put the cigarette, still lit, in an ash tray, move to another chair, and repeat the process. Until the room was eventually ringed with open books and half-spent cigarettes.

He cooked dinner one night, following a similar process. He would start something, a sauce perhaps, get it half done, and put it on a shelf. He then went to something else, and after that, something else; until, as meal time approached, he was encircled with the ingredients of dinner (and countless ash trays). Miraculously, it all came together in the end.[19]

When Chamberlain visited Berchtesgaden on 15 September, and Hitler said he would annex the Sudetenland, war looked ever more likely. Six days before the Munich Conference, when Chamberlain, Daladier, and Mussolini agreed to transfer the Sudetenland to Germany, Ford cabled to Bowen: 'In case war would you wish send Julie here theatre job possible.'[20]

Ford and Biala headed back to New York for the publication of *The March of Literature* early in October. After several discussions with Hoffman about becoming the Dial Press's 'fiction editor and literary advisor', Ford told Unwin: 'I must say I find them very agreeable people to work with.' Yet a week later he was breaking with them irrevocably, writing to Hoffman: 'I think it must be evident to you by now that the Dial is not the publishing house for me nor I the writer for the Dial [. . .] Will you please regard this as final?' Why the sudden change? Mizener speculates that their offer of $100 per month was tactlessly low. Yet since he was already virtually doing for nothing the job of recommending promising authors (and had been asked to do it for Unwin for nothing, without being offended), that is unlikely—especially since the Dial's offer of 'the sole and exclusive power of selection and recommendation of manuscripts for publication' was precisely what he had long realized was essential if his discoveries were to get into print. Ford's letter suggests the more likely explanation—the Dial could not sell Fordian prose: 'there would be no purpose in my trying to edit your fiction', he told Hoffman, 'since what you think you could sell I should not like and you would not think you could sell what I should like.' What they seemed not to be able to sell at the time was *The March of Literature*. The early reviews of Ford's most important critical book were unfavourable.[21]

He put a brave face on the book's fate when he told Unwin that it was 'marching very well' in America. Even odder, he lamented that it was meeting with 'practically no opposition in press', saying that it was 'disappointing because the book contains a good many attacks on the professorial school and one would expect that the professorial school would hit back but they haven't'. Though he realized that not being savaged by the reviewers was 'not a thing really to grumble at', he had invested too much in that Wilde image of a poor lion in a den of savage Daniels not to provoke an attack. 'I don't wonder whether it would not be a good thing if you got somebody professorially minded to look through the book before its English publication and formulate objections', he told Unwin. Those negatives show him knowing that it would not be a good thing, but that he wanted it anyway: 'perhaps that would be asking for trouble', he noted, having all but asked for it. The first known review of *The March of Literature* was by Ernest Boyd in the *Saturday Review of Literature*, and had appeared on 8 October five days before Ford's letter to Unwin. It's unlikely that Ford hadn't read it by then; he certainly had in time to make another of his rare replies to criticism. In effect Boyd had done just what Ford told Unwin he wanted (of course he may have been preparing Unwin for the review, trying to persuade him that such attacks would be good publicity, that they needn't give Unwin second thoughts about publishing it in England). It enabled him to write a coruscating letter, reciting what he had called his 'long and strenuous anti-academic career', complete with another version of his genealogy—his family's Four-Hundred-Years-War against academicism:

It is an eternal fight which in the case of this present writer has been going on now for nearly half a century and in the case of this writer's family has persisted for something like four hundred years. His earliest noteworthy ancestor was an apprentice of Gutenberg and, setting up for himself as a printer in Paris, he wrote and printed a pamphlet declaring that the University of Sorbonne [*sic*] did not know how to teach Latin and so was fined five hundred crowns in the year 1490. His great-great-grandfather [Dr John Brown] was expelled from the University of Edinburgh for telling that University that it did not know how to teach medicine and his father was expelled from the University of Berlin for telling that University that it did not know how to teach Romance Literature, whilst his grandfather cut this writer out of his will, at any rate temporarily, because he proposed to go to the University of Oxford. Today this writer has written a long book to prove that none of the universities of the world know how to teach literature. Mr. Boyd naturally resents this.[22]

Ford concluded that there was 'no pleasing the academic critic with any type of creative esthetic work'. Yet the image he uses to characterize his 'eternal fight' intimates more complex motives than a desire to please. His picture of his massive work, setting out 'modestly if in proportions elephantine', suggests a strong degree of identification between the book and its author, whose weight passed the 240 pound mark in November (when he was under doctor's orders to record it weekly). Ford casts *The March of Literature* as Goliath against Boyd as David, provoking a contest implying the death of the book—and thus figuratively his own death, since the book had become as closely bound up with his life—and its *raison d'être*, literature, as its writing had become associated in his mind with his death. Herbert Read called it 'the literary testament of a man who had more absolute aesthetic zest for the art of writing than anyone else in his generation, and as such it will give endless enjoyment to all who are in any degree touched by the same madness'—Ford himself describes it in the Dedication as 'the book of an old man mad about writing—in the sense that Hokusai called himself an old man mad about painting'. Just as that phrase 'mad about' hesitates between popular passion and isolated affliction, so Ford's stated purpose hovers between optimism and despair. He wants to restore 'a lost art—that of reading': a noble cause, but one which may well be already lost. The book defines his literary genealogy, taking it further back than those imaginative ancestors he had known, and remembered in *Mightier Than the Sword*, to the Classical Greek and Latin authors he had studied as a child. He shares his enthusiasm for all the great works, mostly European, that shaped his imagination. It is—like all his books—the book of himself in a more significant sense: as an expression of his literary personality:

the quality that is necessary for the production of the Art of Literature is simply that of a personality of wide appeal. An art is the highest form of communication between person and person. It is nothing more and nothing less. The more attractive the personality making the communication, the wider in extent, the deeper in penetration and the more lasting, will be the appeal.[23]

Joking seriously, Ford construed this 'appeal' sexually, as (in the slang of the day) 'sex appeal'. He didn't want Georges Schreiber's sketch of him used in the publicity for *The March of Literature* because: 'A portrait to affect favourably the sale of the book should have at least some S.A. and that portrait looks like a representation of a man who has been third degreed by half a dozen psychiatrists for a hundred hours on end.' Herbert Read admirably captured the attractiveness of the book:

it is an immensely entertaining book, inciting you to read what you have not read, to re-consider what you have read, and to agree or disagree with a critic for whom literature is a kind of vital food, upon which the very breath of life depends. Ford carries his impudent swagger and his nonchalant voice through the literature of Egypt and China, Greece and Rome, the Middle Ages and all the more recent and more familiar periods. He is always present in person, whatever he discusses. When he writes about Tibullus, for example, it is the very Ford who used to breed pigs on a twelve-acre holding in Sussex. And like all his critical and biographical books, this is liberally besprinkled with anecdotes and asides derived from his own experience. Its defects are, of course, the defects of such an omnipresent personality. It is a bundle of prejudices. Certain authors, like Fielding and Thackeray, make Ford foam at the mouth; and that it is not merely their moralisings which disgust him is shown by his discriminating appreciation of a poet so moral as Wordsworth. His prejudices do not seem to proceed from any definite standpoint—that is perhaps why they do not irritate one.

Besides his passion for writing, what had impressed Read most was Ford's 'modesty of the true artist'—which is, surely, the standpoint from which his critical judgements proceed. Ford knew how 'Omnipresent personality' was a perilous quantity for a writer, liable to egotism and histrionics. What he can't tolerate in Thackeray is a levity about narratorial convention: 'Thackeray at times projected his scenes so wonderfully that now and then he trembles dreadfully excitingly on the point of passing from the stage of purveyor of the nuvvle to that of the real novelist.' But, says Ford, what keeps him back is a class-bound fear of being thought immoral: 'the dread spectre of the Athenaeum Club was for ever in his background.' Thus Ford explains what he imagines as 'the greatest literary crime ever committed', the 'sudden, apologetic incursion of himself into his matchless account of the manœuvres of Becky Sharp on Waterloo day in Brussels'. Sterne and Fielding, too, interpose their narrators into their narratives in ways which parody and invert the techniques of illusion. Ford's own persona—in narrative and in life—is so imbued with its own versions of Sternean time-shifting and Fieldingesque gentlemanliness that one might expect to find him more appreciative. But the obstacle is a double one. First, by writing mock-heroic or mock-autobiography, Fielding and Sterne appear disrespectful of the novelist's vocation—something that was sacred to Ford. It's a limitation of his criticism, certainly, that this blinds him to the subtleties of psychology and representation—and comedy—that such choices enable.[24]

Ford's other objection is equally paradoxical. 'It is obviously not our province here to be moralists', he writes, having objected precisely to the morality of Fielding and Sterne. At first he appears to be denying his impressionist's convictions: 'But the high mission of the novelist and the high function of the novel in the republic is so to draw life that from their pages the public may learn at least that life is first of all governed by cause and effect—that if you are lousy, and I use the word on purpose, you will live like a louse and, if there is a hell, go to hell.' But the argument becomes more complex when it becomes clear Ford's objection to *Tom Jones* is that the story reads like a reproach to himself (or like the gossip Ford knew had circulated about him): 'And what other word could describe Tom Jones—the miserable parasite who was forever wreathed, whining about his benefactor's knees, whose one idea of supporting himself was to borrow money simultaneously from his heart's adored and two mistresses, and who was such a miserable hero of romance that in a dueling age he could not even handle a rapier?' As he explains later, when we read good books they can read us. 'So the interest of this type of work is both personal and impersonal. In reading it we make better acquaintance not merely with life but with ourselves.'[25]

It is the authors who sound most like Ford—in technique, in manner, even in material—that are the ones he deplores! Fordian impressionism can countenance a first-person narrator, as in the bravura example of *The Good Soldier*. Yet Ford cannot forgive Sterne and Thackeray for self-display.[26] This seems like another set of Fordian paradoxes; but few artists practise precisely as they preach. He preaches that one should avoid what he's trying to avoid, because he knows he has difficulties avoiding it. And in his practice he doesn't simply avoid, but problematizes the issues of personality as opposed to impersonality; vanity as opposed to modest self-effacement; sentimentality as opposed to indifference. So Dowell is both narrator and participant; *The Good Soldier* both romance and satire; the autobiographies both factual and fictional . . .

The *March of Literature* was an extraordinary literary history for its time: neither nationalist nor Marxist-historicist; not exactly formalist either, though a celebration of the history of forms, and especially the novel. Its postures and opinions are less the indulgence of tastes than a captivating demonstration of what it means to read, and of reading's civilizing effects. When, soon after Ford's death, Margaret Cole read his last published book, she wrote at once to Bowen: 'I must tell somebody—since I cannot tell Ford—what a tremendous justification it is for being *homme de lettres*.' She cavilled at his prejudices and omissions. 'But I have not for years read anything that so really *breathed* the spirit of literature as a thing that lived & went on through every sort of language & through every sort of age [. . .].' She thought 'the perversities which aggravated one so in Ford's contemporary judgements are burnt away in the fire of a real love for literature [. . .] I do not think that Ford could have closed his career better.' She added a postscript to reassure Stella she wasn't drunk, and ended: 'Tell Julie her father *was* a great writer, who cared for other writers.'[27]

28

1938–1939: THE ABYSS

For an ill man he had a busy autumn and winter in New York. There were two radio broadcasts arranged to coincide with the launch of the book; on WHN on 7 October; and on NBC on the 14th. The second, on 'The Commercial Value of Literature', was recorded, and the recording has survived, leaving us one of the rare traces of Ford's speaking voice—faint, occasional words inaudibly mumbled in the hypnotic dying falls of his sentences, a compelling paradox of pathos and quasi-liturgical aloofness. He describes his teaching and lecturing in the Midwest, first lamenting how many of his students asked him whether literature would make them money, then arguing (as he had been exemplifying in his novels throughout the 1930s) that a knowledge of the arts was *essential* for success and sanity even in business; that 'that time will not be ill spent that you have passed in adventuring your soul amongst the masterpieces'. (If these words could stand as Ford's epitaph, they could dually stand for Conrad's, since they echo Conrad's words from the *English Review* on Anatole France.) He gave an interview with the *New York Post* on the 19th, musing on how the Great War's violence not only destroyed one generation of Englishmen, but left the next as 'spiritually stunted neurotics'. Chamberlain's cabinet seemed representative of English decline. Ford said they had been 'taken in by Hitler's bluff' at Munich. The interviewer called Ford 'A brooding mountain of a man', and felt he was hearing 'an epoch rather than a man' talking.[1]

He was going to see the pick of the new plays, he told the *Post*, adding that he was particularly interested in a biographical drama about Oscar Wilde by Leslie and Sewell Stokes, starring Robert Morley. George Keating got him tickets for the Cornell–Columbia football game on 29 October. Meanwhile, his doctor was telling him to slow down, but, as Mizener says, Ford's 'pleasure in society and his habit of hard work made it impossible'. Ford had to write to tell Brewer that he wouldn't be able to get back to Olivet, because: 'the doctor says I certainly mustn't travel in order to lecture during the winter, so I shan't be coming either to Evanston or Kalamazoo. I am very sorry but I keep on being rather ill.' Neither he nor Brewer wanted to sever the connection with Olivet, so Brewer had him made 'Professor of Comparative Literature on Leave'. He was able to lecture nearer to New York, however. His pocket diary shows him talking to the Women's City Club in Boston on 18 November (he was also there for a Book Fair), and visiting Bennington, Vermont, on the 21st, probably to speak at the women's college there.[2]

Jack Lindsay sent Ford a questionnaire from the Moscow journal *International Literature*, asking 'what in your opinion are the prospects of the struggle for peace and culture against Fascist aggression, and the role of the USSR in this struggle?' Ford had spent the previous two decades trying to persuade himself that there wouldn't be another war. But his answer now made it clear that, after the Munich Conference, he thought the prospects for peace were bleak:

I wish to say as personal opinion that universal European fascism is now, outside the U.S.S.R., actually in operation. It seems to me quite obvious that the late arrangements at Bechtersgarten [sic] and Godesberg were in the nature of a pact between allied and similar capitalist interests in England, France, Germany and Italy. In my view, international, vertical divisions between the European great powers, always with the exception of the U.S.S.R., have practically disappeared being replaced by a stratified division separating the employing administrative class from the employed and the administered. And we are arriving at a stage similar to that which characterized Europe in 1848–9 when to put it at its shortest, practically all the thrones in Europe were menaced and were only restored by the armed forces of Prussia. As far as I am concerned I do not believe that we shall ever see another international war on a large scale but we might well if the left forces of the world could compass any unity, see before very long universal civil war but the left is at present disunited all the world over and the right is—or I, at least, am firmly convinced of it—is already united, at any rate in Europe and the East.

It is obviously not for me to prescribe what should be the action of the U.S.S.R. in these circumstances. What is most urgently needed at this moment is effective universal propaganda with the aim of awakening the democratically inclined but sluggishly minded to the extreme danger in which democracy finds itself at this moment. This, it seems to me could only be effected by the founding of a great press and a great radio system and I do not see where either the funds or the energies sufficient to promote such activities are to be found.[3]

The idea that nationalism was a thing of the past by 1938 seems—with hindsight—as naïve as the belief that there wouldn't be another world war. And the argument that vertical divisions between states were being replaced by horizontal divisions between classes is oddly undermined by his own comparison with the class-conflict of 1848–9. What the letter does show is that nationalist conflicts were being replaced by class-antagonisms in his own mind; that his political views had been shifting from a Tory idealization of the nation to a more left-wing understanding of political power (here his political pronouncements lagged behind his novelist's insights: this shift is implicit in *Parade's End*). It also shows his correspondingly increasing preoccupation with public events. He had drafted a searching essay, gloomily entitled 'Death with Dishonour', during September, as Chamberlain was visiting Hitler at Berchtesgaden and Godesberg, which tried to square his pacifism with his dismay at the attempt to appease German aggression. His sense of the danger Hitler represented was exemplary; and though his letter was imperfectly prophetic, it makes perfect sense as a reaction to its time.[4]

Ford was a guest at a PEN dinner at the Algonquin together with Pearl Buck (who had won the Nobel Prize that year) and Sinclair Lewis (who had won it in 1930). When Lewis spoke, his praise was so fulsome that Ford was flummoxed: He told Crankshaw:

Mr. Sinclair Lewis in announcing me as a guest for the evening declared that I was not only the greatest novelist writing in English that there had ever been but one of the outstanding literary figures of all time. And he was dead sober too. It astonished me so much because I thought he was talking about Mr. Thomas Mann, that when he finally mentioned my name

I was so astounded that I completely forgot the speech I had made up to congratulate Pearl Buck on her reception of the Nobel Prize and had to content myself with talking about my grand-aunt Eliza—the famous lady who said: 'Sooner than be idle, I'd take a book and read,' which was the only thing that came into my head at that moment [. . .].

He wrote to Lewis to apologize for having omitted 'any thanks to yourself or expression of admiration for your work—for which the merest decency would have called!' and assured him of his 'real appreciation' of Lewis' work. Lewis replied magnanimously:

Any tribute that I have paid to you was merely the most plain statement of fact, and if there are people who do not recognise your dukedom in English letters, the joke is on them and not on those of us who have so admired and profited from your books. I have often thought that your story of collaboration with Conrad was the one great book on the technique of writing a novel that I have ever read.[5]

The break with the Dial Press had left Ford once again without an American publisher. His own work, he told Unwin early in 1939, was 'quite at a standstill'; but even though he was finding it difficult getting up enough momentum to attack the new novel, he and Biala needed an advance to live on. He had lunch with Quincy Howe of Simon and Schuster, and suggested a contract for four books: the third volume of the 'Great Trade Route' project, now provisionally called *Forty(?) Years of Travel in America*; the new novel, *Professor's Progress*; the *History*; and an anthology, 'presumably of his own work', Mizener says, but Ford's comment to his agent George Bye that he had got 'a very good assistant who will do most of the work' suggests it would be a more demanding project, perhaps intended as a companion volume to *The March of Literature*. Howe was interested enough to negotiate with Bye, but balked at Ford's reasonable but unorthodox terms: he wanted an advance equal to the amount actually earned by his last book of the same type (novel or discursive book). Not having a publisher meant that he also had to hang fire on what he called his 'editorial projects'—his attempts to get new writers published. When he told Crankshaw: 'I want to give as much chance as possible to writers who have no chance at all', the scheme sounds like one of his most decisively lost causes. Yet many of the writers he was discovering at the time were good causes: Jean Stafford, Edward Dahlberg, Crankshaw (who had just sent him a novel), and now Eudora Welty, whom Katherine Anne Porter had recommended to him. He told her she had 'a very remarkable gift', and recommended her in turn to Unwin, Stokes, and Knopf.[6]

Richard Hughes's second novel also elicited his admiration, if it was expressed in a curiously double-edged tone. There is an undertow of disapproval, which is almost envy, perhaps because Hughes seemed so closely to have assimilated the world of his adored Conrad:

My dear Hughes:
I have had *In Hazard* some six weeks now and having read it with enthusiasm in the first two days, I have been wondering what to write to you about it. Because, the book being a masterpiece, it demands some sort of at least coherent comment. And my brain has been so limp since finishing my last enormous book that coherence is the last thing to be expected of it. However, my wife has for the last thirty-six hours been doing nothing but saying that *In*

Hazard is the greatest and most amazing novel ever written and that seems to be the best thing to say about it. And I really don't know what to add. Your gift is so individual and it is profitless to attempt to form judgments of individualities when they express themselves in writing. One can write about *Typhoon* because it has literary skill and poetry and obviousnesses; but if *In Hazard* has literary skill—and possibly even obviousnesses, though I haven't observed any, both are completely obscured to the reader by the extraordinary overtones of your temperament [. . .] I have seen one or two notices that quite miss all its points and resolve themselves into saying that it is or isn't better than *Typhoon*. It isn't, of course, better than *Typhoon*. *Typhoon* was written by a great writer who was a man. *In Hazard* is written by someone inhuman—and consummate in the expression of inhumanities.[7]

This might be taken to reveal a contradiction in Ford's critical thought. He had all his critical life advocated passionless detachment in a writer; whereas, when he finds it, he reacts ambivalently. This letter suggests that he might have been admiring in others (and in theory) a quality that it wasn't in his own temperament to sustain. Knowing his work hazarded being swamped by sentimentality, he strove to offset sentiment with mercilessness. His own work oscillates between pity and aloofness, pathos and irony. But when he confronts a writer with a greater degree of aloofness, he shudders instinctively, as in the poem 'Immortality'; or when he said he felt 'even mentally distressed at merely remembering the writings of George Moore—as if you were making acquaintance with what goes on in the mind behind the glacial gaze of the serpent that is the Enemy of Man'. It is another instance of a writer's critical pronouncements not quite squaring with his creative performances: a smokescreen-fiction necessary to the production of greater fictions.[8]

The letter to Hughes might seem to renege on Ford's principles in a stranger way. His reluctance to criticize is striking coming from such an advocate of technical self-consciousness and the critical attitude. But there are two reasons why it is not a lapse— not entirely explicable by cerebral limpness. First, the letter is itself a small masterpiece of expressive equivocation. He says he can't write about *In Hazard* in such a way as to give a very clear idea of what the book is like and how it strikes him. In the course of which it becomes clear that the more he admires the writing, the more he is appalled by its matter and meaning. The 'inhumanities' of the book are (presumably) its portrayal of the world's indifference to human fates. The chief engineer survives the storm, but falls asleep against the rail with exhaustion, falls overboard and drowns. Ford was susceptible to this view of cosmic indifference, but he also needed an opposing view, whether of divine providence, or simply the love of the artist for his creations. He could only accept *Madame Bovary*'s styptic drawing of bourgeois provincial life by emphasizing that Flaubert had fallen in love with his heroine. Even the (intermittent) sense of an actively malign destiny in Conrad was preferable to him than that feeling of moral void. The second reason for Ford's reluctance to criticize Hughes lies at the heart of his view of the relation between creation and criticism. He had always opposed the productions of conscious artistry with works written with an inscrutable naturalness. *Thus to Revisit* has Conrad saying of Hudson: 'You can't tell how this fellow gets his effects! [. . .] He writes as the grass grows. The Good God makes it be there. And that is all there is to it!' Ford felt that with writers like Hudson, Shakespeare, or James, neither their genius nor their techniques could be explained. And, despite his advocacy of criticism, his critical writing is often frustrating to modern academic critics because (as with the letter to Hughes) its seems to shy away from the task of analysing techniques and evaluating results. Yet what is at issue here is not a failure of Ford's, but the novelist's predicament. As John Fowles (another technically highly self-conscious writer) has written (apropos William Golding, another admirer of *In Hazard*), working novelists normally have 'only a very approximate *Gestalt*-like picture' of their contemporaries, 'the very opposite of the serious student's precise and detailed one'; and that 'One's relation to them is particularly difficult to put in words, not least because language here is so dominated by the vocabulary of professional study and criticism. We cannot judge family; we have too much an interest, either for or against, in their cases.' This is precisely what bothers academic critics (but not novelists like Sinclair Lewis) about books like *Henry James*, *Joseph Conrad*, or *The March of Literature*. Ford doesn't have the concern of an Eliot or a Leavis to establish hierarchies, and divide the saved from the damned. Rather than Fowles's metaphor of kinship, Ford uses the idea of passion. It is a passion for literature that he wants to express, and to foster in others. As he explains in the mockingly serious dedication to *The March of Literature*, a depressingly small proportion even of the educated buy and read many books. 'So it occurred to us three', he tells Joseph Brewer and Robert Ramsay (Olivet's Dean), 'that there must be something wrong with the way in which the attractions of literature and the other arts are presented to our teeming populations':

The solution of the problem seemed to us to be that that presentation must be in the wrong hands—that, in fact, such tuition, whether by word of mouth or in books, should be, not in the hands of the learned, but in those of artist-practitioners of the several arts—in the hands, that is to say, of men and women who love each their arts as they practice them. For it is your hot love for your art, not your dry delvings in the dry bones of ana and philologies that will enable you to convey to others your strong passion.[9]

The compelling ambiguity of that last sentence conveys several ideas: that a love for your art will be what helps you to make others understand the importance of art; that it will enable others to become artists (if you convey your passion to them, they won't be able to resist its force either); and that it is your love for an art that makes that art do what only art can: convey your passions (not just your passion for the arts, but all human feelings). But most teachers of literature must hope that there is a missing middle here—that one can teach without losing a love for the arts. Ford's contentious dichotomy is very much of his time. As he was writing, the teaching of literature was changing, and his experiments at Olivet were in the vanguard of that change. The idea that contemporary literature should be on the syllabus was what energized the Cambridge criticism of I. A. Richards, William Empson, and F. R. Leavis, and the New Criticism of Ford's friends Ransom, Tate, and Penn Warren. The most influential literary criticism of the first half of this century was mostly written by artist-practitioners: James, Shaw, Pound, Eliot, Lawrence, Woolf, Brecht. The reinvention of the literature syllabus, and the institutions of writers-in-residence and the writing workshop have meant that our university teaching of literature resembles what Ford was fighting for rather than what he was fighting.

Suddenly, at the end of 1938, came a letter from Elizabeth Cheatham, still Mrs Hugh William Carter, still living in her parents' town, Pinehurst, with 'children & problems and work'. The problems centred on her husband, who was alcoholic and was being dried out in a hospital—'a situation made to arouse Ford's sympathy', said Biala. She thought Ford had 'a real tenderness' for Elizabeth. 'It was such a pleasure to have your letter', he replied: 'I think of you very often, wondering what has become of you—& then suddenly, there you were [. . .].' 'I do not think you were ever made for commercial work,' he told her, '& perhaps in real painting you may find yourself—& the consolation & pleasure that there is in work.' He told her about 'Janice—M$^{rs.}$ Ford, professional name Biala'; and then sketched himself: 'As for me, Mouse dear, I do not imagine you would find me mentally much changed—but I contracted rheumatism all over me and a "heart" in Michigan so I have to be rather inactive.' It made him work all the harder, he said, and taste 'a good deal of what is called "success"'. 'I am told on every hand that I am the Most Eminent Living English Man of Letters as well as the Dean of American Literature whatever that may mean', he told her: 'But it does not mean much money [. . .].' Hearing from her again was a potent summons to the past. But it says much about his new serenity with Biala that in reminiscing about Paris in the late 1920s he could also imagine a future meeting: 'They were nice, innocent, frail, youthful days! (Youthful! I hear you say, oh R. V. a. D! But they were youth, by comparison, for me!) and wouldn't it be fun—& lovely—if suddenly, you from the R. V. & I from the rue N. D. des Champs, met: And Hullo!, from you & Hullo! from me, and "Let's go & have a coffee at the Rotonde!" '[10] When she wrote the long letter he had asked for, he told her 'Y$^{r.}$ letter just tore my heart strings: I am such a large lump it seems reasonable that Fate should bang me about but I had always hoped that little you w$^{d.}$ scrape through unnoticed—& one can do nothing for you—except sympathise—& what good is that?'[11]

The correspondence took his mind off his illness, said Biala. He left Elizabeth's letters and his replies on his desk for her to read. The last one she remembered was what she called a 'real love' letter: 'Ford the novelist had taken over completely. I was surprised at the tone of the letter—& saw by his embarrassment that he had completely forgotten why he was even writing the letter.' He didn't send it but tore it up, she said. Was he really embarrassed by what usually never embarrassed him: the dissolving of the boundary between real life and fiction? Or was it embarrassment at the danger of his provocative game, as he caught himself beginning yet again to set up a scenario of two passions? His displaying of the letters, and tearing up the passionate one, suggests his determination not to let himself damage his precious rapport with Biala.[12]

'I have grown so monstrous & inactive since my illness that I sh$^{d.}$ almost be afraid to let you see me', he told Elizabeth. Ill health dogged him into the new year. He was having difficulty getting started with his new novel, *Professor's Progress*—the opening paragraph exists in four different drafts, a number unprecedented in his surviving manuscripts. He experimented with the short story once again, perhaps because he was too short of breath for the novel; but also because he couldn't find a publisher who would give him an advance for the novel, so he told Unwin he would have to 'by hook or by crook make a living by writing for the really atrocious journals of this city'. 'Here is the story', he wrote to a prospective publisher: 'I've been trying in it to find a new form for the short story as in the old days, Conrad and I tried to find a new form for the novel. It seems to me that if one could bring the short story nearer to a real reminiscence without melodramatic working up of scenes, one ought to be able to achieve something more real than the usual machined short story.' Reminiscential form produces a reminiscence about his collaborative formal experiments. It's not known which story he meant: the manuscripts of seven unpublished stories have survived from the 1930s, showing that he was a more persistent experimenter with the form than his self-deprecatory comments about his inability to write short make him sound.[13]

Soon after having dinner with William Carlos Williams on 6 January Ford was encouraging Unwin to publish his *White Mule*. Williams was, he said, 'the best prose writer and one of the acutest minds alive'. Ford soon found another way to promote Williams. He, Williams, and Edward Dahlberg were sitting in Ford's apartment one day, Dahlberg recalled, 'talking about Pound's Fascism and Jew-Baiting', about which they were 'very distressed'. Suddenly Ford turned to Dahlberg and said: 'Why don't we start a group, meet, say once a month, in order to get Bill Williams' books published?' Dahlberg was exuberant. Ford thought about a name: 'What do you think of calling the group the Friends of William Carlos Williams?' The Society of the Friends of William Carlos Williams it—portentously—was, and came to include Pound, Archibald MacLeish, Sherwood Anderson, Padraic and Mary Colum, Alfred Stieglitz, Katherine Anne Porter, Charles Olson, Kenneth Burke, e. e. cummings, Allen Tate, Henry Miller, Auden and Isherwood, George Keating, James Laughlin, Marianne Moore, Waldo Frank, Paul Rosenfeld, Marsden Hartley, Elizabeth Sparhawk Jones, Brewer, Dahlberg, and of course Biala, Ford, and Williams himself. Ford was the president, Gorham Munson the treasurer, and Paul Leake the secretary. They met for a Dutch Treat dinner on the first Tuesday of each month at the Downtown Gallery on West Thirteenth Street. Ford wanted the society to help others besides Williams. Its purpose was 'the encouragement of the more serious creative Literature in America'. As Ford explained to Brewer, he was 'really trying to get a kind of Academie Goncourt in this country'. By May he had also instituted an annual prize of $500 for 'a piece of creative writing of conspicuous merit', preferably in manuscript, by 'a writer of talent who shall have already published imaginative work without sufficient recognition'. There was a dinner in honour of Dahlberg (the first guest) on 4 April, at which he read from his manuscript of *Can These Bones Live*—a book for which Ford promised to write the introduction, though he didn't live long enough to do it. (Instead, Dahlberg wrote some 'tender words' as a dedication to him.) The next, on 2 May was for e. e. cummings, who discourteously refused to attend. Nevertheless, it went ahead, with forty-seven people to dinner, and with cummings's poems 'read at great length and brilliantly by Williams himself'. 'Ford presided at all these meetings', wrote Dahlberg, 'and I must say a wonderful galaxy of genuine people in the arts attended these affairs.' Ford opened the proceedings once the meal was begun. 'Someone would recite an original poem', recalled Williams. 'Someone would read another. Then there would be an essay or an article critical in nature on some subject pertinent to the time.'[14]

Williams said the Society 'horribly embarrassed' him: 'I couldn't see it, didn't want it, other than as a courtesy to him, but so it went.' He thought it should have been called *Les Amis de Ford Madox Ford* instead, since 'few of the members and practically none of my countrymen knew anything about me'. But he 'felt obliged to behave according to the role' he had been assigned: 'so I did my best, but I was not comfortable in it.' He said Ford understood perfectly well how he felt about it, and he told Robert McAlmon: 'It all means very little to me except as it relates to Ford.' In 1932 Williams agreed with Pound: 'Yes, I have wanted to kick myself (as you suggest) for not realizing more about Ford Madox's verse. If he were not so unapproachable, so gone nowadays.' Ford was too much like Williams's father. Yet by 1939 they had become closer: 'I've gotten to like the man', Williams wrote to McAlmon: 'If I can be of any use to him toward the finish of his life, and let me tell you it is toward the finish of his life unless I'm much mistaken, I'm willing to let him go ahead.' His affection comes through in a strange tribute written soon after Ford's death: 'To Ford Madox Ford in Heaven':

> A heavenly man you seem to me now, never
>   having been for me a saintly one.
> It lived about you, a certain grossness that
>   was not like the world.
> [. . .]
> I laugh to think of you wheezing in Heaven.
>   Where is Heaven? But why
> do I ask that, since you showed the way?
>   I don't care a damn for it
> other than for that better part lives beside
>   me here so long as I
> live and remember you. Thank God you
>   were not delicate, you let the world in
> and lied! damn it you lied grossly
>   sometimes. But it was all, I
> see now, a carelessness, the part of a man
>   that is homeless here on earth.

Ford had written of his 'always migratory life' in *Provence*—a book which, like its sequel, celebrates the circulation of culture along the Great Trade Route as it celebrates the movement of music as the type of a dynamic art. '[N]o place outside Provence has ever seemed really a home to me', he said. Now he no longer had a home in the South. 'We are desperately trying to save up enough to buy a cottage by Lyons where they are cheap and not too far from Paris, and yet still in the Midi', he wrote to Julie in one of his last letters to her: 'We are tired of wandering forever without a home.'[15]

Dr Williams was right about Ford's health. In January Ford was telling Unwin he had been 'so poorly so long'. He had got 'pretty well' around New Year's, 'then began to work again and went about and lectured and dined and went to receptions and then had another collapse'—a 'bad relapse' this time. Anxiety over money didn't help, but he managed to get a loan of £250 from Unwin by mortgaging 'Mr Croyd'—offering him the manuscript 'in what they call escrow here', until Ford either repaid the money or decided that the time was right to publish the novel (he felt it should wait until after his death—'or rather until after the deaths of several people who might possibly recognize themselves in one or other of the characters'). It was an embarrassing request to have to make. He felt it was 'indecent', and apologized for the pain he felt his letter would cause Unwin; but he had no one else to turn to: 'for the people I live with here are all writers or painters and extremely poverty stricken.' As Frank MacShane says, 'It is to Sir Stanley Unwin's credit that he agreed to this loan at a time when he probably realized it could never be repaid'. True, but Unwin also made Bowen (who had had only £10 to live on in the previous month, and whose telephone had now been cut off) cede two-thirds of her royalties on *The March of Literature*. But either because Ford was too ashamed of having to beg back some of what little he had been able to give her; or because he was too ill; or because he felt he could say things that he couldn't in his own person, he composed another letter to Bowen which was signed by Biala but obviously written by himself:

Ford has been forced by our very severe necessities to try to mortgage his Mr. Croyd novel [. . .] you will not really lose by this because Ford will be able to go on writing a new novel which he's begun instead of having to keep us going by writing articles which he's really not fit to write. The Mr. Croyd book in any case will not be published until after Ford's death. Owing to Ford's very long and serious illness from which, umberufen, he's just beginning to emerge, we are almost penniless and have absolutely no other resort than that of appealing to Unwin, otherwise I should not ask you to agree to this.

Ford would have written to Julie long ago except that he could not have written cheerfully and he does not want her to guess how bad things are with us.

He slowly improved during February. A doctor decided to raise his diaphragm. As he explained to Brewer:

I am glad your stomachic trouble is clearing up and that you can squirm inside your clothes. It is certainly a relief and I could do it myself if I didn't have to be strapped up so tightly all the time that I can't begin to squirm anyhow. I have really had a miserable experience with my health and doctors for a long time until at last, more or less by accident, we hit upon a really miraculous doctor who found out after eight others had given wrong diagnosis that I had something internal displaced and since then I have made—umb[e]rüfen—remarkable strides towards physical and mental recovery. Indeed, if the weather would only let me take a little exercise, I might be something like my own self before very long. I have even begun a novel and got two chapters nearly finished, so although we have plenty of other worries like everybody else, I am personally fairly cheerful.[16]

The loan from Unwin was better medicine: 'I think I may say that I am restored to rather more than my usual state of health and activity', Ford thanked him, 'and as that is largely due to the relative tranquillity of mind induced by having some money in the bank I am proportionately grateful.' The tone is typical of his relations with Unwin, showing how reasonable he could be with an understanding publisher. Unwin, thinking of other ways to help, offered to pay him 'a commission on any GONE WITH THE WIND' Ford might discover for him. Ford explained why, even in his present straits, he 'could not possibly think of accepting it': 'I have made it a strict rule never to profit in any way from author[s'] works that I have recommended for publication.' But, he added, if Unwin could arrange a salary 'for the rather considerable labours I shall be undertaking on your behalf and if once more you would let that imaginary sum let you increase Mrs Bowen's share of those royalties I should take it as a favour'.[17]

His renewed vigour let him continue his campaign against the increasing atrocities taking place against Jews. He wrote a long, impassioned letter to the Colonial Secretary, Malcolm MacDonald, urging the creation of a Jewish Republic in Palestine: 'I am aware, sir, that in your official capacity it is no part of your function to ameliorate the world condition of the Jews but that desire must exist in the heart of every civilized man and it must be of benefit to our country should she conduce disinterestedly to that end.' At the same time he pointed out the damage that would be done to Britain's reputation by Chamberlain's announcement (on 27 February 1939) that his government would recognize Franco's regime—without, as Ford said, 'sufficient guarantee for the protection of the Republican population'. Americans, he said, saw in Chamberlain 'a dictator with no one to control him, who, at the bidding of the totalitarian dictators, has delivered infinite thousands of innocent humanity to a certain butchery'. He also sent copies of the letter to *The Times* and the *Manchester Guardian*, but they didn't print it, perhaps feeling that his rhetoric was exaggerated. But history proved him right about both the Jewish and Spanish cases, though not about the Americans, who recognized Franco on 1 April. Ford continued writing political letters to newspapers that spring and summer. In one of them he made, with calm omniscience, his most appalling prophecy—the one which proves how clearly he understood the history of his own times—that 'if the Jews cannot be granted a real national home with— as was the intention of those of us who first advocated this project—a national flag with the power to make diplomatic representations to governments oppressing Jews, this race must end in being exterminated'. These preoccupations are evident in the manuscript of his last, uncompleted novel, 'Professor's Progress', which mentions the Nazis entering Vienna, and anticipates 'The abyss into which their civilization was about to be plunged'.[18]

The Tates invited him to stand in for Stark Young at an alumnae seminar on southern writers at the Woman's College in Greensboro, North Carolina, where they were now teaching. Ford gave his last lectures to Caroline Gordon's students at the beginning of March. He spoke to an audience of several hundred on the evening of the 3rd, on how the writer was 'a particularly solitary and uncertain person in his mind': 'The great writer is probably a great writer because he knows his own defects and tries to cure them.' Gordon later wrote that she had been worried about his health, and that they 'debated as to whether it would be safe to let the old man make the talk he was bent on making'. But according to Biala, Ford was angry with Gordon for having arranged a big reception for him, after he had specifically asked her not to because he wasn't well enough: after they left, Biala remembers him saying he never wanted to see 'that woman' again. They would have had another reason to be angry if they had realized that Gordon felt (as she was later to tell Biala) that Ford had lost his powers in the 1930s because he was happy. When they reached the classroom the next morning Gordon saw that 'his veined, rubicund face had gone ashen from the effort of climbing the stairs'. As he sat down, 'legs spread wide to support his great weight', she was reminded of 'a big white whale [. . .] forcing the breaths through his wide open mouth'. Yet, as Allen Tate later remembered, he was in good form. He was billed to speak on 'The Southern Novel'. While waiting for the students to arrive, he picked up a copy of the *Saturday Evening Post* and glanced at the serial in it. He looked up suddenly. 'The fishlike gaze had brightened. He said, with a chuckle: "I see that our method has reached the *Post*"', then 'charmed and stimulated' his audience with comments on the 'form, character, and technique of the short story and the novel', interlaced with remiscences of James, Kipling, and others. Gerard Tetley, the nephew of Oliver Hueffer's first wife, had taken dictation from him in London thirty years before. He had been 'shipped' to America at the age of 20 because of some 'irregularity' in the way Oliver had handled his in-laws' trust funds. He was now living in Virginia, and when he heard Ford was coming he drove the sixty miles to Greensboro. They spent two or three hours together, and Tetley was moved to see him again—though surprised to see him looking more like Oliver. But he felt Ford was distant and not glad to see him (he simply knew too many people, Biala says); and he was 'less interested in the past than he was in the immediate future of literature in America'. He felt Ford would have preferred not being reminded of Hampstead, Airlie Gardens, Winchelsea, Oliver's misdemeanours, and—in particular—Elsie: the only woman he felt bitter about, according to Biala. Ford had allowed his name to be used for a beer advertisement. Biala was angry that Tetley wrote to Goldring that Ford was now selling his name.[19]

Ford *was* interested in the past he shared with Elizabeth (Cheatham) Carter. When she had written to him that winter he had suggested they meet in New York. But then he had written to tell her about his visit to Greensboro, about eighty miles from Pinehurst. She had come to meet him and Biala there before he lectured. It was exactly a decade since their forlorn parting. After Greensboro he and Biala went to visit her at Pinehurst, 'met her children & heard about her troubles'. They were back in New York by 7 March. 'I was sad parting from you—& remain sad—but so busy', he wrote to Elizabeth: 'And perhaps seeing you brought me luck: for (A.) My rheumatics went just as I started out & (B.) yesterday I sold a book for a price that will keep us from financial jitters for quite a time. Janice sends her love.' This was 'Professor's Progress', which he had finally managed to sell to Frederick Stokes. (Stokes had published *The Brown Owl* in America; so, as with Unwin in England, his last publishers were also his first.) 'Oh Mouse dear! So hurried', he signs off.[20]

By the middle of March he was as furiously active as ever: 'I am really kept in such a continuous whirl,' he told Crankshaw, 'making up for the time lost during my illness [. . .].' He heard Auden speak on 'Effective Democracy' at the Foreign Correspondents' Dinner Forum on 16 March, and, impressed by his earnestness and eloquence, invited him to join the Williams Society. 'I have every reason to be satisfied with my own publishers' in England, he told him, but felt they would agree on 'the necessity to drive a powerful wedge into the solid wall of obscurantism, that is the commercial publishing of today' in America. He had been getting frustrated at what seemed an increasing commercialism: an unwillingness amongst publishers to take risks with authors who weren't best-sellers; and an unwillingness amongst readers to buy anything but best-sellers. He didn't only have his own books in mind. In one of his last essays on the literary scene he quoted a letter rejecting Eudora Welty: 'These highly developed, sensitive, elusive, tense and extremely beautiful stories will certainly appeal to discriminating readers but we haven't the hope that it would be possible to sell even the modest first edition of the book.' 'Could the wildest imagination of any one unknowing what goes on in our markets have produced, as an extravaganza, such a letter?', asks Ford. Auden took a more down-to-earth view, writing in a comically schoolboyesque postscript to his reply to Ford: 'P.S. All Publishers are crooks who loathe art.'[21]

This difficulty of getting good writing published started Ford thinking about turning editor again. It may have seemed like a way to arrange for a small salary for himself. It may also have been that the Williams Society, founded for the same reason, had exhilarated him once more with being at the hub of literary revolutions. It would be a reincarnation of the *transatlantic review*, an organ of the 'Seven Arts and the Three Democracies', to be distributed in America, France, and Britain. 'Roughly speaking', Ford told William Bird (printer of the old *transatlantic*), 'our chief job would be to keep democracy alive in the world'. In the middle of March he launched an epistolary blitz upon potential contributors, national editors, and sponsors, with the help once again of Wally Tworkov as secretary. Bird was asked to be the editor for foreign affairs, and to book for a suitable office. George Keating was enlisted to investigate the possibility of taking over an existing magazine like the *Dial*. Paul Morand, William Bullitt (at the American Embassy in Paris), and Ford himself were to write political articles. Maxim Litvinov, the Commissar for Foreign Affairs in Moscow, was asked for an 'official pronouncement of the European foreign policy of the Soviet Union'. Crankshaw was asked to 'look after the London affairs' of the review, as well as to write for it. Tate, H. G. Wells, Hemingway, and Katherine Anne Porter were all asked for contributions. Ford would presumably have made space for the writers he had been encouraging: Williams, Dahlberg, cummings, Welty, Paul Bartlett, and doubtless some of his more talented Olivet students. He had met a young business man named Charles Fenn at one of the musical evenings given by the furniture-maker Walter Charak. Fenn was working for an American textile firm, but had been trying to write stories, and recalls showing Ford his third attempt one day when Ford visited his flat. Ford crossed out the first four pages, saying: 'Of course I'm diffuse myself, in a different way'; it mattered less in novels than short stories. Like many of the young writers Ford advised tirelessly, Fenn found his practical advice invaluable when he later became a playwright and a novelist. He advised reading Simenon for style: Fenn was struck by how much more interested he was in style than in content. Ford told him he admired Shaw's style, but wasn't interested in his didacticism. Fenn would take Ford to lunch at the Brevoort, a rendezvous for left-wing writers; in return, Ford would provide delicious potato-salads and cheeses, with a bottle of California claret, in his two box-rooms at 10 Fifth Avenue, where, Fenn says, he 'never lamented living in what most New Yorkers would have called near-poverty'. They met about six or eight times. Biala painted his portrait (she recalled him as a 'handsome young man'). Fenn became one of Ford's few friends in business, and was soon involved in the plans for the review. One of *les jeunes*, he would call Ford 'Mr Ford'; Ford would call him 'Fenn'. He recalled Ford telephoning him one day and asking him to come round:

I found him coatless, pacing the floor, gasping because of the damp weather (in the war his lungs had been ravished by gas). He came straight to the point. 'I'm going to start up the *Transatlantic*.' The top buttons of his trousers gaped, and the garment would have fallen to the ground if he had not sat down just in time. 'What I propose,' he went on between gasps, 'is to do the whole thing in Paris. It's cheaper there; besides, I want to live in France, still the most civilized country—against all the odds. And I'd like you to handle things here in New York where most of the copies will be sold. Would you do it?' His musical voice was broken by the gasps so that it wasn't easy to understand him. We talked for an hour and he explained his plan in detail before falling back exhausted.

A week later he showed me a letter he was sending to his publishers setting forth his plans and asking their help in distribution: a beautiful exposition put together with both clarity and brevity. But when we went to discuss the matter they were obviously doubtful about a magazine whose staff would consist of this 'old man mad about writing' and his young man who seemed to have no qualifications at all. Evasively, politely, they asked Ford if he really felt up to taking on such a task. Ford shamed them with his eager talk and confidence. So they promised their help, and notes were recorded for our joint co-operation. But the interview had left Ford exhausted. Then he became dispirited about the war threat.[22]

After a second meeting the publishers, Stokes, rejected the *transatlantic* scheme, and Ford had not found the financial backing before he sailed for France. He was terribly disappointed. Fenn, who later had the curious distinction of having recruited Ho Chi Minh into the American Secret Service, was right about Ford's feelings about the war. An unpublished essay Ford wrote at this time exhorts Americans to 'carry civilization one stage further forward' (roughly what he hoped his new magazine would enable), and urges them not to applaud totalitarian regimes. In the autumn of 1938 he had thought of writing a book on the international situation, from his 'rather aloof— nowadays distinctly left—point of view'. Unwin had been interested, but the Dial Press had rejected it, so Ford thought of using some of the material in the third book on the Great Trade Route, in a section on Washington, DC. But that problem of squaring novelistic aloofness with growing left-wing sympathies became engrossing: it was a reformulation of his old preoccupation with trying to square humane pity with artistic remorselessness; and it had been demanding a novel—'Professor's Progress'— in which he could work through his mental transformations of the past decade.[23]

He wrote a provisional synopsis for Stokes of how he thought the novel would go. It would be 'the attempt to trace and account for the growth of mind of a reasonably cultured and civilised man from complete indifference to public affairs to an extreme interest in them—a development which has taken place in nearly all cultured men the world over in the last ten years or so'. The hero, Godfrey Bullen, is a university professor of modern history, 'kindly, goodhumoured, humourous', 'blond, cheerful, forty-five and vigorous, chastely resplendent in his new autumn tweeds'. Mizener read the novel (as he did all Ford's fiction) as 'essentially Ford's improved version of his own life during his last years'. There are similarities. Bullen had been 'revising the

Essex University curriculum in the nationally significant way Ford believed he had been changing Olivet's'; and he has Ford's rapport with *les jeunes*. 'Time and again', writes Ford, students 'would be ready to accept him as counsellor, guide, guardian, inspiration, Dutch uncle!' 'Here', says Mizener, 'is Ford's longing to believe that, even at sixty-six, he could be the affable, influential "Dutch uncle" to young intellectuals.' Apart from the slip over Ford's age (he was 65), the worst thing here is the insidious implication that because Ford wanted to believe something it couldn't be true. Ford *was* a 'counsellor, guide, guardian, inspiration' to many younger writers. He took about 200 of their manuscripts with him to France that summer. Writers like Pound, Rhys, Gordon, Dahlberg, Auden, e. e. cummings, and many who are less famous, all expressed their devotion and gratitude. His Olivet students did recall him as an affecting, stimulating presence. Auden wrote that he and Isherwood wanted to meet Ford, whose work they had admired for so long, and added: 'I think Some Do Not is one of the best novels I have ever read.' (Biala recalls that the four of them met for lunch in New York.) Ford was not deluded about his effect on the young. Does modesty require that a writer should not use such insights in creating fictions about other people?[24]

Bullen shares Ford's physique, his new political self-definition. Formerly 'he has regarded all politics and political movements with contempt as leading to historical inaccuracies'. Then he is 'awakened to the existence of social problems in the world'. Yet in another sense he is moving in the opposite direction to Ford's. Mizener insinuates that Ford made Bullen a historian because he had himself written a work of modern history. But Bullen has been precisely the kind of historian Ford never wanted to be, 'drawing deductions from the observations of life by annalists and statisticians'. Now he resigns his professorship, and 'sets out with the idea rather of observing life'. Ford is turning from aloof renderer to the kind of engaged propagandist he had berated Wells or Lawrence for being. Bullen is turning from understanding life academically to understanding it aesthetically in the broadest sense—not as an aesthete, but with imaginative sympathy. His wife 'makes him see the Abyssinian conquest, the Spanish civil war, Nazists [*sic*] excesses, the German pogroms of Jews and finally the American reactionary classes'; she doesn't just make him see them *as* illustrations of a Marxist analysis, or make him see their *ideology*; she makes him see them—as a Fordian novelist would try to do, and as Biala had done for Ford. Bullen's ideal is 'The most complete, the most enlightened individualism'; his vision of utopia reads like an impressionist manifesto, advocating 'absolute freedom for every human being to express or to colour his communications with his fellows along the lines of his individuality'. One of the best characters in the fragment is the composer Poggio, a follower of Garibaldi's (owing something to Viola in Conrad's *Nostromo*). Mizener said 'Ford invented a marvelously subtle variation on the lonely old buffalo figure in Commendatore Raymondo Poggio', and that he felt 'tender' towards the character, who is 'reduced to making a living by playing patriotic songs from Garibaldi's time to bored New York Italians in a restaurant whose proprietor employs him out of pity'. This is well put, though the character was not all invention, owing much to 'the queer, tragic Borschitzky' who Ford said gave him violin lessons, told 'the most extraordinary stories', and who cut his throat because the British Museum would only accept the manuscripts of the dead'. Ford's involvement with this character reveals something much more complex than self-improvement in Ford's fictionalizing. If Bullen represents Ford's insights and enthusiasms about his educational experiments, Poggio represents his self-doubts: his perfectly realistic self-knowledge that he was still finding it hard to get his books published in America, to get his books sold in England, and to avoid having to write journalism for his living when he needed time for the work he hoped would endure. (Before he left for France he agreed to write a set of six articles for the *Saturday Review of Literature*.) The dual identification with Bullen *and* Poggio is deeply characteristic, as is the fact that each identification is itself dual: a combination of identifications with, and distances from, Ford's own experiences. Poggio hears that the Metropolitan Museum will only accept the manuscripts of dead writers, so he posts the manuscripts of his 'unsupportably dull violin sonatas' to the Museum and commits suicide. Ford was not only making us see his own death here. He wants to make us see that the novel's way of making us see can make us see more than the novel or the novelist. The news turns Bullen momentarily into death's double: 'The death of that old man had reduced Godfrey's mind to absolute motionlessness.' But thinking nothing, he begins to see everything. The individual case makes real for him the statistical cases of fascist murders he has been reading about. 'But this old man was coloured and vivid. You seemed to see into him.' The episode allegorizes Ford's visionary individualism, which is not the *laissez faire* hallowing of one person's right to exploit another in the name of the free market; it is the belief that people can only be 'seen', comprehended, in their individuality. The typescript ends with the death of Poggio, and Janice Biala wrote on its last page that it was the last page Ford ever wrote. He planned to continue the book, of course; but Poggio's death reads as Ford's epitaph for himself, fictionalizing his (accurate) prediction that his works would be valued more after his death.[25]

As the Bunyanesque title ironically hints, the remainder of Bullen's progress was not to have been an easy one. The synopsis shows him the much-victimized gentleman Ford often wrote about and often was. He is betrayed by his communist wife (with his communist assistant, the Swede Frenssen); and shunned by his wealthy friends, who fear he too has succumbed to communism when he shows moral scruples about not wanting to invest his money in firms which exploit their workers—a scruple he attributes to 'old fashioned Tory patriotism'. He takes a lover himself, an actress called Carol Handy (or Meredith in the fragment of the novel), despite her passionate right-wing sympathies, but she too betrays him, leaving him for a Russian prince-playwright. In May 1939 Ford was imagining that Bullen would end rather as he had done, taking a professorship in a small Michigan college. Though again, unlike Ford, Bullen withdraws (as Tietjens had) into self-reliant isolation. He is now shunned by the Left (for his association with Carol), but is not really unhappy—'not even politically', since he can settle down to writing the life of the French statesman Freycinet (who 'had raised France from among the ashes of desolation' after the Franco-Prussian War), and become the kind of 'Quietist Anarchist' that he discovers—being 'One of the few people who ever read DAS KAPITAL to [the] end'—was Marx's ideal.[26]

In the middle of April Ford and Biala went to spend a fortnight at Olivet, 'in perpetual snow' which exacerbated Ford's ill health. His doctor suggested a sea voyage, which they couldn't afford; as an alternative he asked Allen Tate to recommend somewhere to stay on the sea-coast of the Carolinas or Virginia. Ford was gratified by the progress his Olivet students had made 'both in the matter of knowledge of literature and manners in the last three years'. When he wrote up this visit later for the *Saturday Review of Literature* (as the first of a set of articles that paid for their passage to France) he described not only the snows, but 'the luxuriant trees that shade all the streets' of Michigan's villages. Most important to him, however, was the extraordinary 'hunger for expression' amongst the people of the Midwest, the flow of 'really readable' manuscripts arriving in his office. 'It is really a folk literature flourishing in circumstances that you would say were the most unlikely', he wrote. 'I have been very busy here lecturing', he told George Shively, of Stokes: 'I am making some progress with the Professor book, and rather like what I am doing at the moment, which means, I suppose, that I shall react violently against it before I get the book finished. At any rate that is my usual fate.'[27]

When they got back to New York Ford heard that Pound was visiting America. Carlos Williams met him 'by accident in Washington', Ford told Tate, and said that 'the author of the Cantos seems very mild and depressed and fearful'. He was hurt that Pound had 'made no sign' that he was coming. Pound had other things on his mind, having come with his own plan of saving civilization by interesting American politicians in Social Credit, and influencing them against waging war on Italy and Germany. He was depressed, says his biographer Noel Stock, 'because he was not having the success in Washington that he thought he might have, either with regard to monetary reform or in finding an advisory position through which he might place his knowledge of Europe, history, and economics at the service of his country'. When Pound came to New York early in May he did look up Ford. It was a reunion Ford had wanted for a long time; but the political abyss between them was wider than ever. Pound had travelled in a first-class suite on an Italian liner. He said he had made a second-class booking, but had been given the suite because the ship was empty. 'He seemed irritated at the thought that Ford might think he was in Mussolini's pay', recalled Biala, 'because he came over in the royal suite on an Italian boat. (I don't think Ford thought it).' But neither he nor Carlos Williams were convinced by Pound's protestations that he was not now a fascist. Williams said that Ford and Biala had 'been arguing with him in favor of lechery—or anything at all—to keep him amused or distracted between poems'. Williams was with Ford on 25 May, when Pound was supposed to come and say goodbye to Ford and Biala before they left for France. He didn't turn up.[28]

They thought of crossing the Atlantic on a Norwegian tramp steamer: it would have been cheaper than one of the large passenger lines, but also would have furnished copy for the next of the *Saturday Review* articles, which, said Ford, would be on 'literary subjects as they arise in the course of my next month's travels'. There were to be others on Normandy and London. But they decided against the Norwegian boat: 'my doctor is afraid of the cooking', Ford told George Stevens (of the *Saturday Review*). So they booked a passage on the *Normandie*, to sail on 30 May. He wrote a tactful, passionate letter to the editor of the *Saturday Review* to 'protest against the tepidity' of a review of Joyce's *Finnegans Wake* by Ford's friend (and fellow 'Friend of William

Carlos Williams') Paul Rosenfeld. Ford celebrated the 'peculiar, hieratic qualities of Mr. Joyce's mind', and his 'unparalleled investigation into the uses to which words and their associations can be put', his audacity in taking the opposite course from the impressionist ideal for 'simpler and always more simple words and constructions' (an ideal which Ford's French-sounding construction there curiously and characteristic-ally transgresses), and seizing, instead, on 'the polysignificance of English as the philosophic basis of his labors'. *Finnegans Wake* was 'almost the one event of amazing importance sufficient to withdraw our attention from public events'. Ford signed the letter 'Faugh an-Ballagh Faugh'. Joyce rightly said this letter was 'possibly the last public act' of Ford's life. There was just time to begin one last argument with publishers before leaving America. Not only had Stokes asked for a synopsis of *Professor's Progress*; after turning down the plan for the new review, they then consist-ently rejected the young authors Ford was recommending to them: Dahlberg, Bartlett, and then Welty. Ford told Bye he was 'so fed up with Stokes from every possible point of view' that he suggested Bye should try to transfer his work to Harrison Smith, who had set up a new firm, the Harrison Hilton Co., and was also running the *Saturday Review*. Stokes were 'completely out of sympathy with my views of what writing should be', he said; though he didn't want 'any unpleasantness' with the firm (such, perhaps, as he had had when Viking had threatened to litigate against Liveright over *When the Wicked Man*). He didn't want to aggravate Shively, who seemed to him 'a just man struggling with adversity'.[29]

He wrote to Elizabeth Carter the week before they left. They were 'naturally anxious' about her, he said, and hoped her 'young tyrants flourish and are just naughty enough but not too naughty'. A priest wrote to ask him about appearing in a *Catholic Who's Who*, but Ford replied: 'I'm really not a very good Catholic and genuinely dislike personal publicity.' 'My health is now definitely or very nearly restored', Ford told Unwin just before they left: 'but my doctor here has come to the conclusion that I shall never be ten years younger until I shall have consumed nothing but French cooking for at least four months.' They planned to stay near Le Havre 'so as to be able to make a quick getaway in case of war' (he told Carter), with 'an interlude in London or somewhere in Kent'—probably Sandhurst, where the Crankshaws were now living. Ford had written to Crankshaw: 'either you must come to the mountain or the mountain must transport itself into Kent.' He needed some seclusion to finish the novel, which he was supposed to finish by September, before returning to Olivet for a fortnight in October, when he was to 'deliver a series of lectures covering the whole of the modern literary technique'. 'My activities here have become so multifarious', he wrote to Unwin, 'and the telephone rings so continuously that, although normally I write better in New York than anywhere else, the practice has become nearly impos-sible so I hope to find tranquillity in Normandy.' He died there within a month. Allen Tate thought he went to France knowing he would die. Dahlberg said: 'He detested Nazism, and I believe he wanted to die before another world war took place, before France was destroyed.'[30]

On his last day in New York he wrote his last known letters. One was to George Bye, giving him a free hand about transferring him from Stokes to Harrison Smith. When the young poet Charles Olson heard Ford was sailing for France, he 'felt a loss', and had written telling him: 'I shall miss you. It has meant very much to me to have known you this winter. I seek always a man with eyes as sweet as yours, and of such gentle essence. Forgive me, but I have wanted to say this for a long time.' 'Thank you', Ford replied: 'For [m]e also it was a great pleasure to have made your acquaintance and I hope that our pleasant relationship may continue for many years'; and he encouraged him to submit work for the Williams Society prize. What may be his last letter was a handwritten note to Jean Stafford returning some of her manuscripts: 'These are swell! / I will write about them from the Normandie: this—packing—house is full of all the devils in hell. So can no more.'[31]

They set sail that evening. Ford fell ill on the voyage. They reached Le Havre on 4 June, and moved across the Seine to the picturesque port of Honfleur. They stayed at the hotel *Le Cheval Blanc*, then Biala found an apartment. He was in considerable pain from uraemia, but the French doctor would not give him pain-killers because of his heart. After a week Biala sent for Julie; Bowen brought her; they stayed in a nearby hotel and Julie visited Ford each day for a week. As usual, she remembered, he was in 'beautiful but inconvenient rooms'. Most of the time he was too delirious to know her, though when he did she thought he was glad of her presence. He was outwardly composed, despite the pain. Julie remembered him as working on his *History* at Honfleur, but Biala said later that he was too ill. Biala asked him if he wanted to see Bowen, but 'He was too sick to care about such matters and said no'. Julie had to go back to London: her course at the Theatre Studio was coming to an end. He got a letter from Elizabeth Carter, saying that her husband was out of the hospital and that they were living together again: 'In short all is gas and gingerbread' was his comment. After Julie left Ford became desperately ill. 'He complained piteously all the time of being so cold and unable to bear his sickness and weariness any longer', wrote Biala to Julie. On 24 June he sank into a slumber, and when he woke he was 'rarely in his real mind'. In his delirium he thought he was back in the trenches, and once he said: 'They can't do this to us. We are British officers.' He asked Biala where Julie was, having forgotten that she had left. He only forgot once who Biala was, asking her 'kindly and jocularly': 'when you speak of us, who do you mean?' When she answered 'you and me', he asked: 'And who are you?' On 25 June Biala moved him to the Clinique St. François at Deauville, 'the most pleasant hospital I have ever seen', Crankshaw told Unwin. He was tended by 'the most charming and devoted nuns'. Biala called in a local doctor, 'a little, mean-looking man', she said: 'after the first visit, Ford having been not a very good patient, he said: "It is obvious that Monsieur has always done whatever he wanted in his life." He said it spitefully and I could see *he'd* never done anything he wanted to do in his life. But how right he was.' Ford improved for a day, but then grew worse. He had diarrhoea. On Monday 26 June 1939 they waited all day for the clinic doctor to come and relieve his nausea, but he never came. Ford got very cold. While he was asleep Biala went out to get him clean pyjamas and a dressing-gown. When she returned he was awake, and told her 'he had died a thousand deaths waiting' for her. He suddenly said he was hungry at about a quarter to five, so she called the sister. 'After she left', wrote Biala to Julie, 'he made some movement and fell forward into my arms. I don't believe he was at all conscious of what was happening. He died almost immediately.' 'His life was a battlefield and he died a lonely and terrible death', she said later. The pain, the prolongation, the delirium, the imagined sufferings, make it more terrible than many deaths, though Stella Bowen thought that Biala 'did everything that it is possible for one human soul to do for another, to comfort his last days'. She wrote to Julie the following day to describe his last hours. 'I cut off in the most sentimental fashion, a little of his beautiful hair', she said: 'I hope it doesn't spoil his looks. He looks so calm and noble. I am sure you love him too.'[32]

He had not asked for a priest, and had no last rites. But Biala thought he would have wanted to be buried by the Church. Ford was not 'croyant', she wrote to Julie, but would have thought a proper funeral 'convenable'. She asked Lucie Le Son to tell their friends that the funeral would be on 1 July. There was a requiem mass, and Ford was buried in the cemetery on the cliffs at Deauville. Biala dropped a *bouquet garni* into the grave. Only Lucie Le Son came from Paris. Edward Crankshaw heard the news on the radio, and came over from Kent. There were nineteen telegrams, mostly from America. 'I wish I could believe in another world in which he is now sitting relaxed on a rock with sweet smelling herbs', Biala told Julie, 'looking at the Mediterranean and smiling with amusement at my efforts to be convenable. He is such a darling and I love him so much.' 'His last home had the great view he had always loved', wrote Mizener, though his death almost proved as unsettled as his 'always migratory life'. Biala was told after the war, when she moved back to France in 1947, that a drunken gravedigger had buried him by mistake in unhallowed ground reserved for temporary graves.[33]

ABBREVIATIONS

Editions of Ford's books used

Published in London unless otherwise indicated. {Abbreviations used in notes given in curly brackets}

This list is arranged chronologically by date of first publication. An alphabetical list can be found on pp. 495–7 of volume I.

The Brown Owl (T. Fisher Unwin, 1891)
The Feather (T. Fisher Unwin, 1892)
The Shifting of the Fire (T. Fisher Unwin, 1892)
The Questions at the Well, pseud. 'Fenil Haig' (Digby, Long, 1893)
The Queen Who Flew (Bliss, Sands & Foster, 1894)
Ford Madox Brown (Longmans, Green, 1896)
Poems for Pictures (John MacQueen, 1900)
The Cinque Ports (Edinburgh and London: William Blackwood and Sons, 1900)
The Inheritors (William Heinemann, 1901)
Rossetti (Duckworth, 1902)
Romance, with Joseph Conrad (Smith Elder, 1903)
The Face of the Night (John Macqueen, 1904)
The Soul of London (Alston Rivers, 1905)
The Benefactor (Brown, Langham, 1905)
Hans Holbein (Duckworth, 1905)
The Fifth Queen (Alston Rivers, 1906)
The Heart of the Country (Alston Rivers, 1906)
Christina's Fairy Book (Alston Rivers, 1906)
Privy Seal (Alston Rivers, 1907)
England and the English (collecting Ford's trilogy on Englishness—*The Soul of London*, *The Heart of the Country*, and *The Spirit of the People*—into one volume; New York: McClure, Phillips, 1907)
From Inland and Other Poems (Alston Rivers, 1907)
An English Girl (Methuen, 1907)
The Pre-Raphaelite Brotherhood (Duckworth, 1907)
The Spirit of the People (Alston Rivers, 1907)
The Fifth Queen Crowned (Eveleigh Nash, 1908)
Mr. Apollo (Methuen, 1908)
The 'Half Moon' (Eveleigh Nash, 1909)
A Call (Chatto & Windus, 1910)
Songs from London (Elkin Mathews, 1910)
The Portrait (Methuen, 1910)
The Simple Life Limited, pseud. 'Daniel Chaucer' (John Lane, 1911)
Ancient Lights and Certain New Reflections (Chapman and Hall, 1911)
Ladies Whose Bright Eyes (Constable, 1911)
The Critical Attitude (Duckworth, 1911)
High Germany (Duckworth, 1912)

The Panel (Constable, 1912; published in USA as *Ring for Nancy* (Indianapolis: Bobbs-
Merrill, 1913))

The New Humpty-Dumpty, pseud. 'Daniel Chaucer' (John Lane, 1912)

This Monstrous Regiment of Women (Women's Freedom League, [1913])

Mr. Fleight (Howard Latimer, 1913)

The Young Lovell (Chatto & Windus, 1913)

Collected Poems (Max Goschen, [1913, though dated '1914'])

Henry James (Martin Secker, [1914, though dated '1913'])

Antwerp (The Poetry Bookshop, 1915)

The Good Soldier (John Lane, 1915)

When Blood is Their Argument: An Analysis of Prussian Culture (Hodder and Stoughton, 1915)

Between St. Dennis and St. George: A Sketch of Three Civilisations (Hodder and Stoughton,
1915)

Zeppelin Nights, with Violet Hunt (John Lane, 1915)

The Trail of the Barbarians, translation of war pamphlet by Pierre Loti, *L'Outrage des barbares*
(London: Longmans, Green, 1917 [actually published 1918])

On Heaven and Poems Written on Active Service (John Lane, 1918)

A House (The Poetry Bookshop, 1921)

Thus to Revisit (Chapman & Hall, 1921)

The Marsden Case (Duckworth, 1923)

Women & Men (Paris: Three Mountains Press, 1923)

Mister Bosphorus and the Muses (Duckworth, 1923)

Some Do Not . . . (Duckworth, 1924)

The Nature of a Crime, with Joseph Conrad (Duckworth, 1924)

Joseph Conrad: A Personal Remembrance (Duckworth, 1924)

No More Parades (Duckworth, 1925)

A Mirror to France (Duckworth, 1926)

A Man Could Stand Up— (Duckworth, 1926)

New Poems (New York: William Edwin Rudge, 1927)

New York is Not America (Duckworth, 1927)

New York Essays (New York: William Edwin Rudge, 1927)

Last Post (Duckworth, 1928)

A Little Less Than Gods (Duckworth, 1928)

The English Novel: From the Earliest Days to the Death of Joseph Conrad (Constable, 1930 [first
published Philadelphia: Lippincott, 1929])

No Enemy (New York: Macaulay, 1929)

Return to Yesterday (Victor Gollancz, 1931)

When the Wicked Man (Jonathan Cape, 1932)

The Rash Act (Jonathan Cape, 1933)

It Was the Nightingale (William Heinemann, 1934)

Henry for Hugh (Philadelphia: J. B. Lippincott, 1934)

Provence (George Allen & Unwin, 1938 [first published Philadelphia: Lippincott, 1935])

Vive Le Roy (George Allen & Unwin, 1937 [first published Philadelphia: Lippincott,
1936])

Collected Poems (New York: Oxford University Press, 1936)

Great Trade Route (George Allen & Unwin, 1937)

Mightier Than the Sword (George Allen & Unwin, 1938 [first published as *Portraits from Life*
(Boston: Houghton Mifflin, 1937)])

The March of Literature (George Allen & Unwin, 1939)

Parade's End (one-volume edition of all the Tietjens novels: *Some Do Not . . .* , *No More Parades, A Man Could Stand Up*—, and *Last Post*) (New York: Alfred A. Knopf, 1950)
{*Letters*} *Letters of Ford Madox Ford*, ed. Richard M. Ludwig (Princeton, NJ: Princeton University Press, 1965)
{*Reader*} *The Ford Madox Ford Reader*, ed. Sondra J. Stang (Manchester: Carcanet, 1986)
{*History*} *A History of Our Own Times*, ed. Solon Beinfeld and Sondra J. Stang (Manchester: Carcanet Press; Bloomington and Indianapolis: Indiana University Press, 1988)

Abbreviations used of others' works

Angier, *Jean Rhys*	Carole Angier, *Jean Rhys: Life and Work* (London: André Deutsch, 1990).
Belford, *Violet*	Barbara Belford, *Violet: The Story of the Irrepressible Violet Hunt and Her Circle of Lovers and Friends—Ford Madox Ford, H. G. Wells, Somerset Maugham, and Henry James* (New York: Simon and Schuster, 1990).
Bennett, *Journals*	*The Journals of Arnold Bennett*, ed. Newman Flower, 3 vols. (London: Cassell and Company, 1932).
Bowen, *Drawn from Life*	Stella Bowen, *Drawn from Life* (London: Collins, 1941).
Goldring, *The Last Pre-Raphaelite*	Douglas Goldring, *The Last Pre-Raphaelite: A Record of the Life and Writings of Ford Madox Ford* (London: Macdonald, 1948).
Goldring, *South Lodge*	Douglas Goldring, *South Lodge: Reminiscences of Violet Hunt, Ford Madox Ford and the English Review Circle* (London: Constable, 1943).
Green, *Ford Madox Ford: Prose and Politics*	Robert Green, *Ford Madox Ford: Prose and Politics* (Cambridge: Cambridge University Press, 1981).
Harvey	David Dow Harvey, *Ford Madox Ford: 1873–1939: A Bibliography of Works and Criticism* (Princeton, NJ: Princeton University Press, 1962).
Hemingway, *Selected Letters*	Carlos Baker (ed.), *Ernest Hemingway: Selected Letters* (London: Granada, 1981).
Huddleston, *Bohemian Literary and Social Life in Paris*	Sisley Huddleston, *Bohemian Literary and Social Life in Paris* (London: Geo. G. Harrap & Co., 1928).
Hunt, *The Flurried Years*	Violet Hunt, *The Flurried Years* (London: Hurst & Blackett, [1926]).
Imagist Anthology	[Richard Aldington (ed.)] *Imagist Anthology* (London: Chatto and Windus, 1930).
Judd, *Ford Madox Ford*	Alan Judd, *Ford Madox Ford* (London: Collins, 1990).
Karl, *Joseph Conrad*	Karl, *Joseph Conrad: The Three Lives* (London: Faber & Faber, 1979).
Londraville	Janis and Richard Londraville (eds.), 'A Portrait of Ford Madox Ford: Unpublished Letters from the Ford–Foster Friendship', *English Literature in Transition*, 33/2 (Feb. 1990), [180]–207.

MacShane	Frank MacShane, *The Life and Work of Ford Madox Ford* (London: Routledge & Kegan Paul, 1965).
Mizener	Arthur Mizener, *The Saddest Story: A Biography of Ford Madox Ford* (London: The Bodley Head, 1972).
Moser	Thomas C. Moser, *The Life in the Fiction of Ford Madox Ford* (Princeton, NJ: Princeton University Press, 1980).
Najder, *Joseph Conrad*	Zdzisław Najder, *Joseph Conrad: A Chronicle* (Cambridge: Cambridge University Press, 1983).
Poli	Bernard Poli, *Ford Madox Ford and the Transatlantic Review* (Syracuse, New York: Syracuse University Press, 1967).
Pound/Ford	*Pound/Ford: The Story of a Literary Friendship*, ed. Brita Lindberg-Seyersted (London: Faber & Faber [1983]).
The Presence of Ford Madox Ford	*The Presence of Ford Madox Ford*, ed. Sondra J. Stang (Philadelphia: University of Pennsylvania Press, 1981).
Putnam, *Paris Was Our Mistress*	Samuel Putnam, *Paris Was Our Mistress* (New York: Viking, 1947).
Saunders	Max Saunders, *Ford Madox Ford: A Dual Life*, vol. 1 (Oxford: Oxford University Press, 1996).
Secor and Secor, *The Return of the Good Soldier*	Robert Secor and Marie Secor, *The Return of the Good Soldier*, English Literary Studies Monograph no. 30 (University of Victoria, BC, 1983).
Snitow	Ann Barr Snitow, *Ford Madox Ford and the Voice of Uncertainty* (Baton Rouge: Louisiana State University Press, 1984).
Stang and Cochran	Sondra Stang and Karen Cochran (eds.), *The Correspondence of Ford Madox Ford and Stella Bowen* (Bloomington and Indianapolis: Indiana University Press, 1994).
Tate, *Memories and Essays*	Allen Tate, *Memories and Essays: Old and New: 1926–1974* (Manchester: Carcanet Press Ltd., 1976).
Wells, *Experiment in Autobiography*	H. G. Wells, *Experiment in Autobiography: Discoveries and Conclusions of a Very Ordinary Brain (Since 1866)*, 2 vols. (London: Victor Gollancz and the Cresset Press, 1934).
Wood, *The Southern Mandarins*	*The Southern Mandarins: Letters of Caroline Gordon to Sally Wood, 1924–1937*, ed. Sally Wood (Baton Rouge: Louisiana State University Press, 1984).

NOTES

To avoid cluttering the text with index numbers, I have normally gathered together the references to form one or two footnotes per paragraph. Letters and manuscript material by Ford or Violet Hunt (and letters to them) are at Cornell University (Division of Rare Books and Manuscript Collection) unless otherwise indicated. Items preceded by an asterisk in the notes were missing from David Dow Harvey's bibliography, or from the supplementary bibliographies in the Ford issue of *Antaeus*, 56 (Spring 1986).

Chapter 1

1 Ford's ranks are recorded in his Army Book at Cornell. *'Pon . . . ti . . . pri . . . ith', *La Revue des Idées* (Nov. 1918), 233–8. This article, written in French, says Ford left England from Southampton. Ford to Lucy Masterman, 18 July 1916: *Letters*, 66. Judd, *Ford Madox Ford*, 279, says Ford was sent to Albert on the 16th; but he has misunderstood Mizener, 285, who says Ford was attached to the 9th Battalion on the 16th. He was still in Rouen on the 18th. Ford to the Misses Hueffer, 18 July 1916: transcribed in Katharine Lamb to Mizener, 1 Dec. 1969. Katharine to Mizener, 23 Apr. 1964. In 'English Country', *New Statesman*, 13 (6 Sept. 1919), 565, he recalled hearing the 'thrushes of Rebimont-Méricourt', and the corresponding passages from *No Enemy*, 43, 47, make it clearer that this refers to his de-training on his way to the Front, and suddenly becoming aware of birdsong over the noises of the train and the men. This was presumably at Méricourt-Ribemont, some 8 km SW of Albert. In 'English Country' he gives the date as 'the 17-7-16', though on the evidence above it was probably the 18th.

2 Sugrue to Mizener, 19 Apr. 1966. Mizener alters Sugrue's first name to 'Thomas'.

3 Martin Middlebrook, *The First Day on the Somme* (London: Allen Lane, The Penguin Press, 1971), 262–5, 295. *Letters*, 66–7. Judd, *Ford Madox Ford*, 282 n., says that the 9th Welch War Diary for July shows approximately 20 killed, 31 missing, and 354 wounded. Ford to Lucy Masterman, 28 (not 11, as Mizener has it, 570, n. 18) July 1916: *Letters*, 66–7 (omissions in square brackets are my own).

4 Judd, *Ford Madox Ford*, 280–1. *A Man Could Stand Up—*, 104. *Return to Yesterday*, 429. See p. 586, n. 21.

5 *It Was the Nightingale*, 175. Ford to Masterman, 7 Sept. 1916: copy in Ford's ration book at Cornell (see Mizener, 289–90, though he mistranscribes the letter). Ford's memory of being lost is corroborated by the detail that when his Colonel wanted him to resign his commission, he sent a copy of his letter to South Lodge: see Mizener, 289, 571–2, n. 25. Ford to F. S. Flint, 23 June 1920: *Letters*, 106. *'Supper Reminiscences', *New York Herald Tribune Magazine* (18 Aug. 1929), 20–1, 23, recalls his batman staying with him for the 'ten days or so' he spent at Corbie.

6 *Mightier Than the Sword*, 264–5. Mizener, 287. Ford to Conrad, 6 Sept. 1916; transcribed in *The Presence of Ford Madox Ford*, 172–3, 176.

7 *Mightier Than the Sword*, 245.

8 'Great Writers', 39: from the second (unpublished) part of the typescript 'Towards a History of Literature'.

9 Manuscript p. 18 of III:i, corresponding to p. 131 of the published text. This deletion is not mentioned in Charles G. Hoffmann, 'Ford's Manuscript Revisions of *The Good Soldier*', *English Literature in Transition*, 9/3 (1966), 145–52.

10 Moser, 212.

11 Ford told Martin Secker, 18 Aug. 1918, that he would write a new novel called 'G.C.M.': *Letters*, 88–9 (Ludwig did not know of the manuscript of 'True Love & a G.C.M.' See 'True Love & a G.C.M.', 34. *No Enemy*, 64.

12 See Mizener, 371; though in his comparison with a reworked section in *A Man Could Stand Up*— his selections make 'True Love' sound less interesting than it is.

13 'Ford Madox Ford a Visitor Here; Tells of His Work', *Chicago Tribune* (22 Jan. 1927), 8; an interview with Fanny Butcher. Mizener, 573, argues that he is describing 'True Love & a G.C.M.'; Harvey, 371, suggests 'That Same Poor Man', also known as 'Mr Croyd'. 'True Love & a G.C.M.', 64. Where the manuscript pages have two numbers, references are to the pencil ones usually at the foot of the pages—not the irregular typed numbers at the top. I have silently corrected typographical errors.

14 *No Enemy*, 62 (misquoted by Judd, *Ford Madox Ford*, 278). *The Collected Poems of Wilfred Owen*, ed. C. Day Lewis (London: Chatto & Windus, 1963), 48–9. *A Man Could Stand Up*—, 105. 'True Love & a G.C.M.', 64.

15 *No Enemy*, 44. The sight of Martinpuich on p. 43 locates the episode during Ford's ten days in Sausage Valley.

16 *No Enemy*, 45 (which also mentions Gilbert White). *A Man Could Stand Up*—, 205.

17 Putnam, *Paris Was Our Mistress* (New York: Viking, 1947), 125–6.

18 See Judd, *Ford Madox Ford*, 279, on Ford's probable military duties. 'True Love & a G.C.M.', 57–8. The episode was reworked into *A Man Could Stand Up*—, 66–7.

19 'The Miracle', *Yale Review*, 18 (Winter, 1928), 325.

20 *Mightier Than the Sword*, 251. 'On Impressionism', *Poetry and Drama*, 2 (June, Dec. 1914), 174.

21 'True Love & a G.C.M.', 32 (cf. 26), 59. In 'Young America Abroad', *Saturday Review of Literature*, 1 (20 Sept. 1924) 121–2, Ford argued that the imagination of elsewhere was what distinguished the imaginative writer from the journalist: 'The journalist will write best about Chartres when he is in Chartres; the imaginative writer will not get his views of Chartres into perspective until he has left Chartres for many months. That is a profound truth. I have lived about half my life in the country; about half my life in towns. I have written a good deal about the country and a good deal about towns, but I have always written about towns when I have been in the country and always about the country when I have been in towns. A certain touch of nostalgia is an almost essential element for the imaginative writer; he will usually write better about the woman before the last with whom he has been in love than about the lady for whom at the moment his sonnets are ostensibly written. But perhaps one ought not to let out that secret. . . .' Cf. *No Enemy*, 247–8.

22 Ford to C. F. G. Masterman, 5 Jan. 1917: *Letters*, 81–3.

23 Max Webb, 'Ford Madox Ford's Nonfiction', unpublished Ph.D. thesis (Princeton University, 1972), 219.

24 'On the Edge', *Bystander*, 11 (11 July 1906), 81–2, 84. *The Good Soldier*, 144. *The Marsden Case*, 324–6.

25 *Men of the Time: A Dictionary of Contemporaries*, 12th edn. (London: George Routledge and Sons, 1887).

26 Ford called his series of literary revaluations in the *transatlantic review* 'Stocktaking'. See *It Was the Nightingale*, 186: 'I stood there for a long time, taking stock. Like Robinson Crusoe.' 'True Love & a G.C.M.', 104–5.

27 'On Impressionism', 323, 174.

28 *Mightier Than the Sword*, 70–1. This trope (and another version of this reminiscence) is discussed in ch. 23 below (in the section on 'Vicarious Experience', pp. 449–54).

29 *Women & Men* (Paris, 1923), 60–1.
30 Pound to Quinn, 15 Aug. 1916; quoted by B. L. Reid, *The Man from New York* (New York: Oxford University Press, 1968), 256.

Chapter 2

1 Kemmel is about 5 miles SSW of Ypres. 'Mr Croyd', ch. 1: see Mizener, 289. Otherwise, quotations from this work are taken from the revised third typescript at Cornell, titled 'That Same Poor Man'. Rejoining the battalion is described in *It Was the Nightingale*, 175; though the date given (17 Sept.) must be wrong: his letter to Lucy Masterman of 23 Aug. (quoted on p. 16) shows him back by at least that date. Review of *New York is Not America*, *Time*, 10/25 (19 Dec. 1927), 32.

2 23 and 25 Aug. 1916: *Letters*, 68–70. The story about the prince and the piano is in 'Last Words about Edward VIII', the transcript of a radio talk broadcast on WJZ (7 Dec. 1936), 4–5. Tietjens too makes successful experiments in draining the land: *A Man Could Stand Up—*, 215. Judd, *Ford Madox Ford*, 279.

3 Cooke's report on Ford is at Cornell; quoted by Mizener, 571–2, n. 25. It was dated 6 Aug., and the adjutant, Captain R. R. Whitty, sent a copy to South Lodge because Battalion HQ didn't know where Ford was. Ford to C. F. G. Masterman [7 Sept. 1916], from the copy in his ration book at Cornell: Mizener, 289–90.

4 Ford to Masterman [7 Sept. 1916]. Ford to Cathy Hueffer, 6 Sept. 1916: House of Lords Record Office.

5 Conrad to Ford, 15 and 16 Aug. 1916 [in Hunt's transcriptions]. Hunt, *The Flurried Years*, 261, confusingly implies that the first of these letters was sent in response to Ford getting his commission in 1915. See F[anny] B[utcher], 'Ford Madox Ford a Visitor Here; Tells of His Work', *Chicago Tribune* (22 Jan. 1927), where he says Conrad sent him 'a fiver' while he was returning to the Front after being gassed. (Mizener, 507, n. 16, says he placed the episode in Feb. 1917, but that is to assume Ford meant returning to the Front from Menton in 1917, rather than returning after his shell-shock of July 1916, or collapse after his visit to Paris in Sept. 1916—after he had probably experienced a gas attack in the Salient.) *Return to Yesterday*, 134, says Conrad sent a 'money order telegram'. Though Conrad's communication hasn't survived, the story is quite possible. Ford had indeed predicted the book's success, telling Pinker in 1905: 'I spent a couple of days with Conrad & read *Chance*. I think it's really like to do [. . .] the trick of popularity—this time' [n. d., but *c*.Oct. 1905: Princeton (quoted by Mizener, 110, 543, n. 15). On 23 Feb. 1914 Conrad wrote to Hunt: 'Ford by that sort of inspiration which nobody possesses but he, has been all along prophesying success for that book. I confess I didn't believe him' [in Hunt's transcription]. (Karl, *Joseph Conrad*, 747, erroneously assumes Conrad was writing to Elsie.) Mizener, 570, n. 16, offers a paraphrase of this letter as if it were a quotation. He takes it to show that Ford had been proved right long before the Somme. But *Chance* was published in Jan. 1914, and though successful enough to deserve congratulation in Feb., took two years to sell 13,000 copies: Najder, 390. Thus if Ford is right about having bet on a sale of 14,000, it is perfectly possible this figure was reached while he was in France.

6 F[anny] B[utcher], 'Ford Madox Ford a Visitor Here; Tells of His Work'. Ford to Stella Bowen, 20 Jan. [1927], identifies 'F.B.'. Ford to Conrad [first week of Sept.], 6 and 7 Sept. 1916: *Letters*, 71–6. There are more-accurate transcriptions of these letters in *The Presence of Ford Madox Ford*, 170–7.

7 *A Man Could Stand Up—*, 88. Aldington, *Death of a Hero* (London: Chatto & Windus, 1929), also compares the bombardment to a symphony: see 373, 435.

8 I am grateful to Nick Dennys of the Gloucester Road Bookshop for letting me consult Greene's library while it was being catalogued. *Letters*, 75–6. Conrad died on 3 Aug. 1924; *Joseph Conrad* was probably published that Nov.; *No More Parades* dates the beginning of composition as 31 Oct.: 9.

9 Hunt, *Their Lives* (London: Stanley Paul, 1916) [3–4]. *No More Parades*, 308–10. *No Enemy*, 81–6 (which also mentions reading proofs). He had begun reading the proofs in July: Ford to Lucy Masterman, 11 July 1916: *Letters*, 65–6. See ch. 14 on *Parade's End* for a further discussion of *'A Day of Battle'.

10 Ford to Masterman, 28 July 1916: *Letters*, 66–7. Aldington, *Death of a Hero*, 253.

11 'Literary Causeries: IV: Escape. . . .', *Chicago Tribune Sunday Magazine* (Paris) (9 Mar. 1934), 3, 11. This essay mentions Anatole France's *Sur la pierre blanche*, the *Crainquebille* volume of stories, and a work he calls *Histoire Comique* (presumably *Histoire contemporain*). Ford to Conrad [first week of Sept. 1916], mentions reading another work of France's, *Pierre Nozière: The Presence of Ford Madox Ford*, 172. Ford's important recollections of rereading *What Maisie Knew* are discussed on p. 417. The different versions of the reminiscence about rereading Crane are not unanimous as to date and place: 'Literary Causeries: IV: Escape. . . .', places the episode 'whilst we were in support, somewhere between Kemmel Hill and the small town of Locre'; 'Stevie', *New York Evening Post Literary Review* (12 July 1924), 881–2, agrees about Kemmel Hill, but gives the date as autumn 1917 (when Ford was in England); Mizener, 288, quotes from the typescript of *Mightier Than the Sword*: 'lying awake in a tent in the moonlight towards four of a September morning in 1916, on the slopes behind Kemmel . . . I was reading the *Red Badge of Courage*' (the corresponding passage is on p. 163 of the book). *Thus to Revisit*, 108, places it in the Somme, 'in Bécourt Wood'; 'Stevie & Co.', *New York Essays*, 30, just says 1916; *The English Novel*, 55–6, places it in the Salient in Sept. 1916; and *Return to Yesterday*, 49, says Kemmel Hill, 1916 (though p. 63 appears to argue for 1917!). The first explanation seems the most probable, and would support the date of Sept. 1916; it is also clear from this article that Ford was reading both in the Somme and the Salient, so the confusion is understandable.

12 Ford to the Adjutant, 9/Welch BEF, 7 Sept. 1916: *Reader*, 478. Ford to Medical Orderly, 8 Sept. 1916; copy in the ration book at Cornell. Mizener, 290.

13 'Trois Jours de Permission', *Nation*, 19 (30 Sept. 1916), 817–18; a more elaborate account is in *No Enemy*, 153–63 and 261–2. Both works also describe attending a performance of Delibes's *Lakmé* at the Comédie Française: *No Enemy*, 165–6 and 194–221. The ferrets are also mentioned in *Joseph Conrad*, 192, and *Provence*, 292.

14 Ford to C. F. G. Masterman, 13 Sept. 1916; *Letters*, 76. Mizener, 291, follows Harvey, 49, in doubting Ford's claim to have altered the book and written a French epilogue for it. However, the anonymous new 'avant-propos' which Harvey quotes is almost certainly Ford's.

15 Rhyl is now in Clwyd. Ford was at Kinmel Park by 12 Oct. 1916: Ford to Masterman: *Letters*, 76–7 (the British Library's copy of the original is headed Kinmel Park, which Ludwig omits). Mizener, 291. *It Was the Nightingale*, 249.

16 Pound told Wyndham Lewis that 'Ford's brother Oliver is in the trenches' in the same letter reporting that a shell had burst near Ford 'and that he has had a nervous breakdown and was for the present safe in a field hospital': *Pound/Lewis*, ed. Timothy Materer (London: Faber & Faber, 1985), 52–3. Materer dates the letter [July 1916]; but it is unlikely David Soskice (Pound's informant) would have heard about Ford's shell-shock within two or three days of the explosion. Ford told

Katharine: 'Y^{r.} uncle Oliver was badly wounded about a fortnight after I was evacuated':
10 Dec. 1916. Frank Soskice [later Lord Stow Hill] to Arthur Mizener, 20 Sept.
1967.

17 Ford to Masterman, 12 and 25 Oct. 1916; *Letters*, 76–7. The manuscript at Cornell, 'Un
jeu de cricket', is dedicated 'à C.F.G.'. It became 'Une partie de cricket', *Bibliothèque
universelle et revue suisse*, 85 (Jan. 1917), 117–26, and was reprinted as the envoi to *No
Enemy*, 293–302, where it appears with a fictional dedication 'TO CAPITAINE UN TEL AT
PARIS'. This is probably 'that article for Randall' that Ford mentioned to Masterman in
his letter of 12 Oct. (*Letters*, 77). Randall worked for Masterman at Wellington House.

18 Ford to Lucy Masterman, 27 Oct. 1916; *Letters*, 77–8.

19 Ford to Lucy Masterman, 27 Oct. 1916. Ford to C. F. G. Masterman, 25 Oct. and 29
Nov. 1916: *Letters*, 77–8 (emended).

20 Ford to Masterman, 5 Jan. 1917: *Letters*, 81–3. Ford to Conrad, 19 Dec. 1916: *The
Presence of Ford Madox Ford*, 177–8. He also told the story of the young herdsman in
Return to Yesterday, 118–19. Ford to Cathy Hueffer, 15 Dec. 1916: House of Lords
Record Office. Ford to Katharine, 10 Dec. 1916. Katharine to Mizener, 18 Jan. 1966.
Olive Garnett's diary, 13 Sept. 1916. Christina entered the Convent of the Holy Child
at Mayfield as a postulant on 16 Sept. 1916: Sister Winifred Wickins to Max Saunders,
25 July 1992.

21 'I Revisit the Riviera', *Harper's*, 166 (Dec. 1932), 65–76 (66). Ford to Masterman, 5 Jan.
1917: *Letters*, 81–2.

22 Mizener, 285. Sugrue to Mizener, 19 Apr. 1966. There are no surviving mentions by
Ford of Sugrue. But Ford rarely mentioned his fellow soldiers, so this need not cast
doubt on Sugrue's closeness.

23 Edgar Jepson, *Memories of an Edwardian* (London: Martin Secker, 1938), 212–13. See
also Robie Macauley, 'A Moveable Myth', *Encounter*, 23/3 (Sept. 1964), 56–8.

24 Ford to Cathy Hueffer, 15 Dec. 1916: House of Lords Record Office. Cf. Goldring, *The
Last Pre-Raphaelite*, 197. Ford to Masterman, 5 Jan. 1917: *Letters*, 82. Nieppe is on the
border between Belgium and France, about 5 miles SSW of Kemmel, and 'near
Plugstreet' (Ploegsteert), as Ford had it when he wrote the poem 'Clair de Lune' there,
and dated it 17 Sept. 1916: *On Heaven*, 42–5. Violet Hunt at first had her doubts about
Ford's claim to have been gassed. But on 12 Mar. 1917 she noted: 'He is very ill I think.
I begin to believe in the "gassing" [. . .]': Secor and Secor, *The Return of the Good
Soldier*, 50–1.

25 'I Revisit the Riviera', 66. Ford to C. F. G. Masterman, 5 Jan. 1917: *Letters*, 81–3. (The
VAD was the Voluntary Aid Detachment, an organization of first-aid workers and
nurses.)

26 Ford to Catherine Hueffer, 5 Jan. 1917: House of Lords Record Office. Ford to Lucy
Masterman, 6 Sept. 1916 and 8 Sept. 1917: *Letters*, 74–5, 84. Even as late as 1929, in a
response to a questionnaire in the *Little Review*, 12 (May 1929), 91–3, Ford was still
figuring himself as having died, saying that Pound had sent him the serialization of
'Women and Men', and that: 'One had seemed, for those aspects of life, to be for so long
dead that watching one's progress through your polychromatically enclosed and speck-
led pages afforded one some of the pleasure and curiosity of gazing down on one's
posthumous literary self. Oh yes, pleasure! For it was as if one discovered that after
three years of death one's work had for so long survived.' He places this episode 'during
heaviest days of the war, in France'. But Pound only got the manuscript from him in the
summer of 1917, after Ford was back in England for the duration: *Pound/The Little
Review: The Letters of Ezra Pound to Margaret Anderson: The* Little Review *Correspond-*

ence, ed. Thomas L. Scott and Melvin J. Friedman, with the assistance of Jackson R. Bryer (London: Faber and Faber, 1989), 96.

27 *On Heaven*, 46–52 (51); the poem is dated 7 Jan. 1917. *'A Day of Battle', *Reader*, 461. Ford to Katharine, 12 Dec. 1916: slightly misquoted by Goldring, *The Last Pre-Raphaelite*, 197.

28 *'War & the Mind: 2. The Enemy', ed. Sondra Stang, *Yale Review*, 78/4 (Summer 1989), 503–10 (507–8). Published together with *'A Day of Battle' ([497]–503), to which, as the prefatory note explains, it is a companion piece. I have made slight changes in transcription, based on the autograph manuscript at Cornell. The essay was written in the summer of 1917.

29 David Nokes, 'Death Masks', *TLS* (7 Aug. 1987), 848. See Carlos Baker, *Ernest Hemingway: A Life Story* (London: Collins, 1969), 68.

30 Aldington, *Death of a Hero*, 224.

Chapter 3

1 Ford left Rouen on 8 Jan. 1917. *Provence*, 272. In *Return to Yesterday*, 402, Ford said he 'used to meet' Arnold Bennett on the Lower Corniche at Menton: 'He would be walking slowly along with a magnificent carriage and pair following him.' But Bennett's journals show him in England throughout Jan. 1917, so Ford's reminiscence appears a 'magnificent' invention; the point of it is to contrast Bennett's determination to make a fortune by his writing with Ford's unbusinesslike and self-sacrificial attitude. Bennett's *Journals*, iii. 119–21, do, however, have him on the Riviera in 1926, when Ford was at Toulon: could Ford have conflated 1917 and 1926?

2 *'Supper Reminiscences', *New York Herald Tribune Magazine* (18 Aug. 1929), 20–1, 23 (20). *The Marsden Case*, 301–4 (302). Ford also referred to the journey in 'Stocktaking [. . .]: VIII. The "Serious" Book', *transatlantic review*, 2/3 (Sept. 1924), 274.

3 Mizener, 295. 'Stocktaking [. . .]: VII. Post Tot . . .', *transatlantic review*, 2/1 (July 1924), 65. Ford to Flint, 19 Feb. 1917; *Letters*, 83–4 (though a spurious extra 'more' slips into Ludwig's text).

4 Judd, *Ford Madox Ford*, 306. *A Man Could Stand Up—*, 186–7. Other accounts of German prisoners are in *Letters*, 79–80,* 'War & the Mind', and *Return to Yesterday*, 118–19, 329.

5 Flint to Richard Aldington, 9 Mar. 1917: Texas. Ford to Flint, 19 Feb. 1917: *Letters*, 83. Flint told Aldington (in the letter of 9 Mar.) that he had refused Ford's request in a letter written 'in beautiful French'—this letter, of 26 Feb. 1917, is also at Texas (in both autograph and carbon typescript)—and then sent another letter which repented and accepted the job; but that Ford never received either letter. This is a pity, since the first contains a touching tribute to Ford's style: 'j'ai pour cette plume littéraire une très grande estime. C'est une des plumes anglaises le plus distinctive que je connaisse.'

6 Mizener, 573, n. 2, follows Ford's service record in placing him at Abbeville from 25 Feb. to 15 Mar. But this is inaccurate. Hunt's diary has him back in London on 7 Mar. (Flint met him in London on the 8th: see p. 28), and there until at least 5 Apr. She had heard he had been 'discharged to duty' on 7 Feb., and misunderstood this to mean he had returned without telling her (entry for 24 Feb.); but Ford's letter to Flint shows him still in France on 19 Feb.: Secor and Secor, *The Return of the Good Soldier*, 48–55, 43. Ford to Hunt, 6 Jan. 1917: Princeton.

7 Ford to Cathy Hueffer, 23 Mar. 1917: House of Lords Record Office. Ford to Hunt, 8 Jan. 1917: Princeton.

8 Hunt, diary entries for 22, 2, and 4 Mar. 1917: Secor and Secor, *The Return of the Good Soldier*, 51–3, 46–7. See Saunders, 491–2. Miss Ross was almost certainly the Miss Gladys Ross who lived with Mr and Mrs W. H. Brain, of The Croft, Dinas Powis and Crwt-e-ala, Michaelson-le-Pit (both near Cardiff, on the Penarth side). She was governess to their children. I am grateful to their nephew, Christopher Braine, for this information (telephone conversation, 1 Nov. 1995). Ford to Lucy Masterman, 13 May 1916: *Letters*, 64–5. Diary entry for 27 Apr. She almost certainly does mean Patmore as the first of Ford's infidelities, since she says he was 'not blamed, but *choyé*' [pampered] the first time.

9 8 and 9 Mar.: Secor and Secor, *The Return of the Good Soldier*, 48–9.

10 22 Mar.: Secor and Secor, *The Return of the Good Soldier*, 52.

11 Secor and Secor, *The Return of the Good Soldier*, 52: entry for 22 Mar. 1917. See e.g. *Mr. Fleight*, 243: 'But I'm a man, damn you, with the passion of a man and the heart of a man [. . .] But no [. . .] I'm not a man. I'm not even a dirty little antelope [. . .]'; and 'Literary Portraits—LII.: "Cedant togae . . ."', *Outlook*, 34 (5 Sept. 1914), 303–4: 'When I get up in the morning, full, as the saying is, of beans, or when amongst my fellow-men I find it necessary boastfully to claim pre-eminence, I say loudly: "It is I that am the stout fellow [. . .]" But when I am alone and with God I get gradually less and less certain. I imagine myself to be ageing, intellectually petering out, and unable to stand the racket of my own day. The truth is probably somewhere between the two . . .'

12 Jepson, *Memories of an Edwardian* (London: Martin Secker, 1938), 210, 212. Barry, 'The Ezra Pound Period'. *Bookman*, New York, 74 (Oct. 1931), 159–71 (165). Hunt's diary for 26 Mar. says 'Dined Bellottis with the Ezra Pound crowd'. Secor and Secor, *The Return of the Good Soldier*, 68, n. 91, 53, n. 49.

13 Greenslet (an editor for Houghton Mifflin, who later published Ford's *Portraits from Life*), *Under the Bridge* (Boston: Houghton Mifflin, 1943), 161–2. *Return to Yesterday*, 329. Hunt saw Ford off from Euston, and was there when he met Greenslet: Secor and Secor, *The Return of the Good Soldier*, 54, confirms the meeting, and provides the date. Her presence isn't mentioned by the two men, which shows that both Ford and Greenslet elaborated the reminiscence. (It's possible that Greenslet's 1943 version was influenced by Ford's of 1931.) However, it's characteristic of Ford, who was often accused of egotism in writing his memoirs, to play down his private life, and in particular to say little about his partners. Mizener, 296.

14 Mizener, 564, n. 15. On 571, n. 19, for example, he unfairly described as 'clearly imaginary' Ford's story (in *Great Trade Route*, 339–40), of feeling a strong emotion as his 'battalion was marching into the line' in the Somme, and the men began singing. But 'the story of how he marched "my battalion" into the line' is Mizener's imaginary story. Ford in fact wrote: 'My battalion was marching [. . .]', which any member of it would have been able to say, and does not imply he was commanding it. Judd unfortunately reiterates Mizener's slur: *Ford Madox Ford*, 280.

Wells, *Experiment in Autobiography*, ii. 622. Mizener, 574, n. 18. Wells to Goldring, 30 May 1945: quoted in Goldring, *The Last Pre-Raphaelite*, 89–90. Mizener, 293. *Wells, letter to the editor, *Manchester Guardian* (27 Nov. 1924), 5: 'Sir,—I see you quote a story from some new book by Mr. Ford Madox Hueffer (Captain Ford) about my bicycling seven miles to ask him not to collaborate with Conrad. This story is a pure invention.' (See Saunders, i. 115, 524). In *Joseph Conrad*, 39, 51–2, Ford is still replying to Wells's response to *Thus to Revisit*. He reasserted his reminiscence in *Return to Yesterday*, 224. Wells, *The Bulpington of Blup* (London: Hutchinson & Co., [1932]), 321. Mizener, 294. Ford to C. F. G. Masterman, 5 Jan. 1917: *Letters*, 82.

15 *The Marsden Case*, 144. Wells cites *It Was the Nightingale* as evidence of Ford's post-war self-dramatizing in *Experiment in Autobiography*, 622. *The Bulpington of Blup*, 307–8.

16 Bowen, *Drawn from Life*, 62. 'True Love & a G.C.M.', 52, 80. In Aldington's *Death of a Hero*, Winterbourne is also persecuted by his colonel: see 428.

17 *Reynolds's Newspaper* (London: 11 Jan. 1920), 2.

18 Ford to Lucy Masterman, 28 July 1916: *Letters*, 66–7. Ford to C. F. G. Masterman, 7 Sept. 1916; Mizener, 289–90. *Some Do Not . . .* , 255; cf. 292, in which Tietjens feels his department has 'all sorts of bad marks against' him.

19 Quoted by Mizener, 572, n. 25.

20 See Paul Fussell, *The Great War and Modern Memory* (New York and London: Oxford University Press, 1975), ch. 4: 'Myth, Ritual and Romance'. See e.g. Kipling's 'A Madonna of the Trenches', *Debits and Credits* (London: Macmillan, 1926). Ford had written a comparable story about a war 'vision' before his experiences in the Somme and Flanders: 'Fun!—It's Heaven', *Bystander*, 48 (24 Nov. 1915), 327–30.

21 The medical board met on 4 or 5 Apr. 1917: Secor and Secor, *The Return of the Good Soldier*, 55. Mizener, 295–6. Judd, *Ford Madox Ford*, 306. *It Was the Nightingale*, 7, reimagines Powell's commendation as: 'Possesses great powers of organisation and has solved many knotty problems. A lecturer of the first water on military subjects. Has managed with great ability the musketry training of this unit.'

22 She visited Redcar from 29 May to 8 June, and 1 Aug. to 2 Sept. Mizener, 296, asserts that Ford was moved to Redcar 'Around the first of the Year'—i.e. 1918. But Hunt's diary shows he was there by at least the end of May 1917. When, on 8 Sept., she heard confirmation of a rumour that Ford had failed to settle a betting debt, she sent him a cheque to the creditor, noting with satisfaction: 'A showerbath string pulled.' Cf. *Last Post*, 106: 'Sylvia delighted most in doing what she called pulling the strings of shower-baths. She did extravagant things, mostly of a cruel kind, for the fun of seeing what would happen.' See Secor and Secor, *The Return of the Good Soldier*, 11–12. The relation of the diary to *Parade's End* was first discussed by Moser, 323–4, n. 11.

23 Diary for 13 Apr. Ford's anxieties that Hunt was blackening his reputation were well founded. Her diary records conversations about Ford living on her money with W. L. George (6–7 Apr.), Eleanor Jackson (21 Apr.), and Iris Barry (12 July); on 28 Feb. she says she has heard that Nora Haselden and Jane Wells have been avoiding her company because of her talk about Ford. Secor and Secor, *The Return of the Good Soldier*, 56–7, 55, 57–8, 68, 45–6. (Also see 50, n. 44, where the Secors note other examples of Hunt using her friends to gather information about Ford.) She records his requests for money on 3 and 14 May. They had a big row about it on 24 Oct., when Ford rebuked her: 'when one lent one didn't insult too', and she notes: 'It was true, & I was ashamed, but when he told me not to "whine in a voice like a creaking door," I lost all control & pinched & buffeted him. He lies like a jelly fish instead of taking me by the wrists & stopping me.' Ford to Catherine Hueffer, 19 Apr. 1917: House of Lords Record Office. Hunt's diary entry for 1 Apr. 1917 says that Sextus Masterman told her that a letter ordering Ford to relinquish his commission was awaiting him in Wales; but she suspected it might have been an April Fool's joke. On 23 Apr. Hunt recorded that she had a letter from Ford saying 'he has applied to be allowed to relinquish his commission! He cannot "stand the merciless financial strain." No one could, he believes.'

24 Hunt, *The Flurried Years*, 25. Hunt to Ethel Colburn Mayne, *c*.1925: Princeton; quoted Secor and Secor, *The Return of the Good Soldier*, 23. This probably refers to 1918, when he left her for Stella Bowen; but it is also probably typical of their arguments during 1917.

25 Diary entry for 29 April. Watts is mentioned in the diary *passim*; see esp. the entries for 22, 23, 30 June, 19–21 July, 1 Oct., and 8 Nov. Entries for 9 May and 13 Nov.: Secor and Secor, *The Return of the Good Soldier*, 61, 83.

26 There is another jealous mention of Haselden in the entry for 19 Apr. The verdict on Mrs Powell is in the entry for 24 Aug. Ford to Flint, 19 Feb. 1917: *Letters*, 83–4. Hunt to Harold Monro, n.d. [but late 1918]: Texas. Ford also flirtatiously inscribed a copy of *The Good Soldier* for another of Hunt's friends, Mary Crawley, with the quotation from p. 135: 'The real fierceness of desire, the real heat of a passion long continued and withering up the soul of a man is the craving for identity with the woman that he loves. He desires to see with the same eyes, to touch with the same sense of touch, to hear with the same ears, to lose his identity, to be enveloped, to be supported': copy inspected at Ulysses Bookshop, 7 Jan. 1992. Hunt mentions Mrs Crawley in her 1917 diary: see Secor and Secor, *The Return of the Good Soldier*, 49, 51.

27 Diary entry for 13 July: Secor and Secor, *The Return of the Good Soldier*, 68. The identification is confirmed by a letter from Dr Henry Head to Hunt (as 'Mrs Hueffer'), 7 Nov. 1922. Sir Russell Brain, 'Henry Head: The Man and his Ideas', in *Henry Head Centenary*, by Kenneth Cross and others (London: Macmillan, 1961), 33–8. Roger Poole, *The Unknown Virginia Woolf* (Cambridge: Cambridge University Press, 1978), ch. 9. Though Head retired in 1919, the letter to Hunt shows he was still seeing her socially in 1922. So when Ford told Scott-James he had seen her 'analyst' in 1920, it might have been Head (17 Apr. 1921: Texas). Ford to Hunt's solicitors, Richardson, Sadlers & Callard, 24 May 1920, also says that she asked him to see her doctor. Presumably George Heimann's experiences with Dr Robins in *The Marsden Case* draw upon Ford's in 1917 or 1920 (though they may also draw upon his earlier experiences with Dr Tebb).

28 Entries for 1, 21, and 26 Aug., and 2 Sept.

29 Entries for 5 Sept., 20 and 29 July, 10 Sept., 3 Oct., 30 Sept., 23 and 22 Oct. The bleeding was a symptom of Hunt's syphilis. On 6 Nov. she wrote: 'The lump of mucous in my nose came away'; and on the following day she was given an 'Electric exam' by her new doctor: 'proves that I have no septum. To a certain extent I am like old Edward Fairfield with half his nose eaten away. I will not tell Ford. It seems as if the author of all my *maux* was O.[swald] C[rawfurd].' This disproves Mizener's suggestion that she may not have known how she got the disease: 149.

Mizener, 297, was misled by Bowen's memoirs into saying that Pound introduced her to Ford in the spring of 1918. Judd reproduces the error: *Ford Madox Ford*, 313. Bowen, *Drawn from Life*, 61, is vague about the circumstances of the meeting—understandably so, since she was too generous to want to appear as if she were attacking Hunt in print; and anyway she may have been embarrassed by the fact that she had become involved with Ford after having made friends with Hunt, and suppresses Ford's relationship with Hunt in *Drawn from Life*. A letter from Ford to Bowen, 19 Aug. 1919, confirms that they first met at Selsey, and not (as Mizener says) in London. Hunt's diary shows her meeting Bowen on 20 July 1917.

30 Ford to Bowen, 26 Oct. 1917. Hunt, diary for 12 July and 4 Dec. (and see the Secors' helpful notes on Undine and her uncle on 68 and 84).

31 Ford dates this 17 Dec. 1917 in *On Heaven*; Hunt's diary confirms the date. On 'Poor Ford's birthday' she wrote: 'I sent him a box of preserved fruits & some vests & plants & tablecloths. He sends lovely poems one last prayer but disclaims them saying they are written to *bouts rimés*.' None of the poems in *On Heaven* are dated early Dec. (the 'Regimental Records' are assigned to 18–21 Dec.), so the lyric he sent Hunt on 4 Dec.

(which she later thought was 'To Stella') appears not to have survived. (There are no known manuscripts of unpublished poems written in 1917.)

32 Hunt showed her 'ultimatum' to Byles on 30 Oct. If it was sent, there's no evidence of any reply before the letter she notes on 19 Jan. (quoted below), in which Ford supposes that their 'relations are at an end'. However, he did send her the poems during Dec. It is possible he simply didn't reply to the ultimatum before then. Certainly, on 14 Nov. she was still waiting for his next move: 'If he asks to come I shall say Come if you care to stay with me under the new régime. But no. I *can't* force myself to swallow the long long affront his behaviour to me is. Can I?'

33 Ford to Lucy Masterman, 13 Jan. 1918: *Letters*, 86–7.

34 Hunt's diary: entries for 19–22 Jan. 1918. *Grace Lovat Fraser (née Crawford), *In the Days of My Youth* (London: Cassell, 1970), 240. Hunt says in her diary entry for 2 Oct. that 'there will be a paragraph in the *Weekly Dispatch*—about my wearing Ford's tin helmet', but I have not been able to find it. The Secors assume that this is the occasion recalled by Fraser, which she places in the autumn or winter of 1917. Yet Ford was not on leave in Sept. or Oct.: there is no record of him in London between 19 June and the last week of Jan. 1918, apart from one day he spent there on 25 Oct.—but he went from Selsey with Bowen, while Hunt stayed behind. It seems more probable that there were (at least) two raid parties at which Violet wore a tin hat, and that the one mentioned by Fraser (with Ford and Hunt together in London) actually happened in Jan. 1918.

35 Secor and Secor, *The Return of the Good Soldier*, 85, n. 136.

Chapter 4

1 Epigraph from Bowen, *Drawn from Life*, 62. Hunt's Diary, entries for 30 Dec., Christmas and New Year's Eve. Ford to Lucy Masterman, 31 Jan. 1918: *Letters*, 86–7. 'Footsloggers' *mentions* Britannia, but only to say 'I do not think | We ever took much stock in that Britannia | On the long French roads, or even on parades': *On Heaven*, 65–6. Ford also told Pinker he expected to be going out to fight again in Feb.: 6 Jan. 1918: *Letters*, 85–6. Ford to Katharine Hueffer, 13 Mar. 1918, in which he also told her he had instructed his bank to send her £2 each month, and to put some money into war loans for her. Ford to Bowen, 7 Nov. 1918.

2 Ford's army book gives the dates for his substantive promotion to captain, the acting promotion to brevet major, and for his attachment to the HQ of N[orthern] C[ommand] at York as lecturer from 13 Mar. 1918 to 14 July 1918. But his letters to Bowen (i.e. 28 Aug. and 6 Sept.) show he lectured for a longer period—at least till 6 Sept. Mizener, 574, n. 18. Ford managed to give the artist William Roberts the impression he was a colonel that spring. They met at a luncheon party at the Eiffel Tower restaurant, with Hunt, Lewis, and Iris Barry, and talked about war artists. 'Hueffer said that Duncan Grant should be made a War Artist and invited to paint a war subject.' Roberts remarked that as a conscientious objector Grant would hardly wish to paint the war. 'The colonel turned to me and snapped sharply: "Well, what does that matter?" Intimidated by his rank and manner, I remained silent, inwardly thankful that I had joined the Artillery and not the Welch Regiment as Lewis had advised me to do': Roberts, *Five Posthumous Essays and Other Writings* (Valencia: privately published, 1990), 45.

Mizener, 302 n., says Ford found it 'very suspicious' he wasn't asked to stay on in the army permanently as Education Advisor; but he was asked: Ford to Bowen, 7 Nov. 1918. His letter to her on 10 Nov. 1918 explains why he could not accept: 'it w^{d.} be a bore'; he was 'only flattered by the Commander in Chief thinking of me for it'. Ford to

Bowen, 24 Aug. and 6 Sept. 1918 mention the first six lecture topics; the letter of 6 Sept. included lecture notes on Censorship, Musketry and Cyphers; Ford's notes for the last three have also survived. *No Enemy*, 30–1. *Great Trade Route*, 46: he illustrates the point with just such a digression, about how the same principle applies to physical tasks—a sudden change of direction while drilling, or unexpected order while marching, can restore concentration. *A Mirror to France*, 279–80. Ford's notes for a 'Lecture on France' (which is the one about French Civilization) bears out the story, including the headings: 'If you had lashings of leave'/'Vie Parisienne'.

3 Ford described some fellow-officers referring to him as 'old Hoof' in a letter to Bowen, 22 Nov. 1918.

4 Ford to Hunt, 12 May 1918. He was also obliged to deny that he owned the 'large entailed estates in Prussia' he had claimed he was heir to. Ford to Bowen, 26 June 1918. Ford to Iris Barry, 4 July 1918: *Letters*, 87–8. Ford to Bowen, dated '4/1/18' [but must be later (since none of his other letters address her as 'Darling' before Oct. 1918). Sondra Stang and Karen Cochran, eds., *The Correspondence of Ford Madox Ford and Stella Bowen* (Bloomington and Indianapolis: Indiana University Press, 1994), 53, argue for 4 Jan. 1919; but as it seems to develop points from his letters to her of 1 and 3 Nov. 1918 (and as the reference to the Huns coming makes little sense after the Armistice), it is more likely he wrote '1' for '11' for the month; thus 4 Nov.? 1918] says: 'No: I don't suppose I'm really, *really*, an extinct volcano as a writer [. . .]' My quotations from the Ford/Bowen correspondence are taken directly from the original letters at Cornell. Unfortunately the published volume arrived too late for me to include page references, but the dates given in my notes enable the published versions to be easily found.

5 Serendipity Books, Catalogue 45 (Berkeley, 1989), item 178. *'Rambling Remarks', *British Weekly*, 64 (29 Aug. 1918), 345. Ford to Bowen, 6 Sept. 1918. *Outlook*, 41 (27 Apr. 1918), 408–10. *TLS* (18 Apr. 1918), 187.

6 The 1984 Virago reprint of Bowen's *Drawn from Life* gives her date of birth as 1895. But Bowen to Ford, 29 Apr. 1919 says she'll be 26 on 16 May 1919. This is correct: her birth certificate gives the year of her birth as 1893, and her given names as Esther Gwendolyn. Serendipity Books, Catalogue 45, item 174 (though 'Stillis' is glossed incorrectly as Bowen alone). *Drawn from Life*, 11, 29, 61–2.

7 Ford to Bowen, 1 and 28 Aug. 1918. Bowen, *Drawn from Life*, 64.

8 Bowen, *Drawn from Life*, 61–3. Ford had *looked*—novelistically—at Phyllis, whose talents for dancing and poetry-reading are recognizable in *The Marsden Case*'s Clarice Honeywill.

9 Ford to Bowen, [n.d. but before 28 Aug.], 22 Aug.; 18 Sept. 1918. Mizener, 300–1, has an inaccurate transcription of the letter of 22 Aug. Cf. *Great Trade Route*, 204 on the court martial. Ford to Iris Barry, 4 July 1918: *Letters*, 87–8. Ford to Secker, 18 Aug. 1918: *Letters*, 88–9.

10 Ford to Bowen, 24 and 28 Aug. 1918. Constance Garnett's 1895 translation gives the name of the Prairie as 'Byezhin'. Bowen, *Drawn from Life*, 62. Ford to Bowen, 28 Aug. 1918.

11 *No Enemy*, 66–7, 70.

12 Mizener, 299–300 (quoting *No Enemy*, 10). Bowen, *Drawn from Life*, 165.

13 Ford to Bowen, 18 Sept. 1918.

14 Ford to Bowen [n.d., but 1 Sept. 1918]. Conrad, epigraph to *Lord Jim*: see Saunders, i. 244–5, 550. *A Man Could Stand Up—*, 203. *The Good Soldier*, 135. Ford to Bowen, 6 Oct. 1918.

15 Judd, *Ford Madox Ford*, 320. Ford to Bowen, 2, 6, 8, 10, and 11 Oct. 1918. Bowen to

Hunt, 12 Oct. 1918. Mizener, 574, n. 15. Ford to Bowen, dated '4/1/18', but [4 Nov.? 1918: see n. 4 above for the re-dating].

16 There is a picture of Busby Hall among the illustrations to Richard Gill, *Happy Rural Seat* (New Haven, Conn.: Yale University Press, 1972), following p. 170. Gill describes the house, rebuilt in 1764, and the 'large horse-chestnut tree' in the garden, on which Ford modelled Groby Great Tree, on 275. He thinks it 'doubtful that Ford ever visited the estate, since the family was not in residence from 1905 "to approximately 1925" ' (276): doubtful he was invited, but not impossible he went to look. Ford to Bowen, 17 Nov. 1918. Ford to Read, 25 June 1921: *Letters*, 133. Read, *Annals of Innocence and Experience* (London: Faber and Faber, 1940), 194; *'War Diary', in *The Contrary Experience* (London: Faber and Faber, 1963), 134–5 (entries for 1 and 14 Sept. 1918); and *'Views and Reviews: An Old Man Mad About Writing', *New English Weekly*, 16 (9 Nov. 1939), 57–8. Ford mentioned having 'an awful High Brow day' with a staff captain, presumably Read, in an undated letter to Bowen [1 Sept. 1918]. James King, *The Last Modern: A Life of Herbert Read* (London: Weidenfeld and Nicolson, 1990), 57, 67. Wells, *Experiment in Autobiography*, 359, says that when Frank Harris took over the *Saturday Review* in 1894 he wrote to Wells (who had already written for him in the *Fortnightly*) to ask him to contribute. Ford, who was six years younger than Wells, would have been just 20 at the time, and wouldn't then have had the editorial influence he claimed. It's not impossible Ford met Wells then (or there), but their earliest surviving correspondence dates from about five years later. Ford to Bowen, 22 Nov., 13 Dec., and 28 Aug. 1918.

Chapter 5

1 Ford to Bowen, 7, 1, and 11 Nov. 1918. The copy of the *'Salvage' notice with Ford's inscription is at Cornell. Bowen, *Drawn from Life*, 60. Pound to Quinn, quoted in Noel Stock, *The Life of Ezra Pound* (Harmondsworth: Penguin, 1974), 273, 'Preparedness', *New York Herald Tribune Magazine* (6 Nov. 1927), 7, 18. Ford sent the poem with a covering note (saying 'I daresay you will understand it') on 10 Dec. 1918. It was published (with some revisions) in *Art & Letters*, 2/1, NS (Winter 1918–19), 7. Mizener, 301–2, where he mistakenly says Ford wrote to Bowen from 'Easton' (Eston) on Armistice Day; the letter of the 11th is headed 'Redcar'.

2 Ford to Herbert Read, 9 Dec. 1918: University of Victoria, BC. Ford to Bowen, 13 and 17 Nov. 1918. Judd wonders 'whether there wasn't also some inwardness over his taking the Q.M.'s daughter to the dance. The colonel's lady, Mrs. Pope, might have felt put out because he had previously been attentive to her—in the matter of his poems, for instance' (*Ford Madox Ford*, 318): but it may have been Mrs Powell who helped him choose the poems for *On Heaven*. Powell was his CO when Hunt visited him at Redcar in Aug. 1917, and thought he was *amouraché* of Mrs Powell (see diary entry for 24 Aug.: the Secors say in a note that it was Mrs Powell who helped him select the poems). It was certainly around this time that he began getting the volume together: see Ford to Lucy Masterman, 8 Sept. 1917: *Letters*, 84. Cf. *It Was the Nightingale*, 199, on the social equality of officers within the mess. A deleted passage from 'The Colonel's Shoes' about 'very nasty things' being said about Gotch 'and women and the Colonel' *might* draw on the possible scandal caused by Ford's attentions to either woman: see Mizener, 572, n. 25.

3 Ford to Bowen, 10 Nov. 1918; 6 and 7 Jan. 1919 (for the peace-time job); 24 Nov. and 13 Dec. 1918. As Alan Judd explains, the PRI is the President of the Regimental Institute ('concerned with finance and administration'); ACIs are Army Council In-

structions. The QM was the father of the Miss Hill Ford had taken to the dance: *Ford Madox Ford*, 318–19.

4 Ford to Bowen, 17 Nov. 1918. Cf. *Return to Yesterday*, 75–6: 'I never took any stock in politics. But political movements have always interested me'; elaborated on 87: 'I repeat—I must have said it a thousand times already—that I have never taken any part in party politics. I have always doubted my ability to interfere in the lot of my fellow beings [. . .] But I have always taken a passionate interest in politics everywhere and have never missed a chance of witnessing political activities.'

5 *Ford Madox Brown*, 393.

6 *It Was the Nightingale*, 4–6, 9–10. The other versions are in *Return to Yesterday*, 404–5; 'Editorial', *transatlantic review*, 1/2 (Feb. 1924), 70–1; and *No Enemy*, 119 (the version in which the journal refuses the article). Bennett, *Journals*, ii. 227, 229, 236–9. Bennett to Pinker, 29 Sept. 1918: *Letters of Arnold Bennett*, ed. James Hepburn (London: Oxford University Press, 1966), i. 266. Mizener, 301. Kinley Roby, *A Writer at War: Arnold Bennett: 1914–1918* (Baton Rouge: Louisiana State University Press, 1972), 291–3. Bennett to Beaverbrook, 4 Nov. 1918: *Letters of Arnold Bennett* (London: Oxford University Press, 1970), iii. 76–7. Wells, *Experiment in Autobiography*, ii. 703–4. Peter Buitenhuis, *The Great War of Words: Literature as Propaganda 1914–18 and After* (London: B.T. Batsford, 1989), 134, 138–40. Buitenhuis's otherwise fair reading of the version in *It Was the Nightingale* is marred by his misunderstanding Ford's comment about writing his article while on 'active service' as being a claim that he was at the Front in 1918. Ford to Bowen, 10, 11, 27, and 31 Oct. 1918. *'Pon . . . ti . . . pri . . . ith', *La Revue des Idées* (Nov. 1918), 233–8.

7 Ford to Bowen, 24 Nov., 6 Dec., and 22 Nov. 1918 (the original of which is torn).

8 Ford to Bowen, [Sunday] 24 Nov. 1918.

9 Ford to Bowen, '9' [though postmarked '8'], 12, 13, and 22 Dec.; and 24 Nov. 1918. 'Thus to Revisit . . . : III.—The Serious Books', *Piccadilly Review* (6 Nov. 1919), 6 *It Was the Nightingale*, 8. Mizener, 302, 574, n. 17.

10 Ford to Bowen, 2 Dec. 1918. *Pound, 'Editorial on Solicitous Doubt', *Little Review*, 4/6 (Oct. 1917), 20–1. *Israel Solon also praised the serial in 'The Reader Critic', *Little Review*, 5/1 (May 1918), 62–4. Ford to Read, 9, Dec. 1918: University of Victoria. The review was *Arts & Letters*, which Read edited with Osbert Sitwell, and to which Ford contributed his poem 'Peace'. Cobden-Sanderson also wrote to ask if he could publish Ford. See Ford's reply, 1 May 1919: original in possession of Mr Herbert Eaton; photocopy at Cornell.

11 'Literary Causeries: III—And The French', *Chicago Tribune Sunday Magazine* (2 Mar. 1924), 3, 11. Cf. *It Was the Nightingale*, 243–4. Mizener, 302, gives the date as the 1st; but Ford to Bowen, 7 Jan. 1919, supports Goldring's date of the 7th, based on War Office records which say 'Relinquished commission on account of ill-health' on that date: Goldring, *The Last Pre-Raphaelite*, 185. *The Times* (7 Jan. 1919), 12, says: 'Lt. F. M. Hueffer relinquishes his commn., on account of ill health (Jan. 7).' *The Last Pre-Raphaelite*, 206–7. Ford to Bowen, 14 Jan. 1919, says he is leaving for London on the 15th. Bowen to Ford, 'Friday' [May 1919?].

12 Ford warned Stella about his mail being opened in a letter of 21 Mar. 1919 (not 31 Mar. 1929, as Mizener says on 574, n. 20). Alec Waugh to Douglas Goldring, quoted in Goldring, *The Last Pre-Raphaelite*, 208. He also recalled them giving a *bouts rimés* party, probably at Clifford Bax's studio, that January. Scott-James, 'Ford Madox Ford When He Was Hueffer', *South Atlantic Quarterly*, 57 (Spring, 1958), 250. Ford to Bowen [n.d.; 15 Mar.? 1919]. Mizener, 303, 574, n. 19. 'Mr Croyd', 238. Joan Hardwick, *An*

Immodest Violet: The Life of Violet Hunt (London: Andre Deutsch, 1990), 151, claims that his appearance (which she exaggerates, saying he 'dressed in old rags and looked little better than a tramp') was provocative, and meant to dramatize the idea that Violet had abandoned him to destitution, and thus win the sympathy of their mutual friends. Yet since Hunt presumably held possession of most of Ford's civilian clothes, and he had little money, it is hard to see what else he could have done. Pound to William Carlos Williams, 28 Jan. 1919: *The Selected Letters of Ezra Pound*, ed. D. D. Paige (New York: New Directions, 1971), 145. Harold Monro's notes for the Poetry Bookshop reading indicate that Ford read for 35 minutes to an audience of 64 people: British Library (I am grateful to Joy Grant for this information). The lecture may have been the one Marjorie Watts, *P.E.N.: The Early Years* (London: The Archive Press, 1971), 6, says that Ford gave to the Tomorrow Club in Long Acre, founded by Amy Dawson Scott, and a precursor of her PEN organization. Mizener, 303. Ford to Bowen [15 Mar.?], 17, 19, and 20 Mar. 1919. Olive Garnett's diary, 12 Feb. 1918, notes that Elsie was moving to Burnt House Farm, Charing, to set up a joint household with a Mrs Griffiths and her daughter. But on 22 Sept. 1918 she reports Elsie writing about the breakup with the Griffithses, whom she accused of extravagance.

Chapter 6

1 Hunt to Scott-James [n.d., but Mar.–Apr. 1919]: Texas. Goldring, *The Last Pre-Raphaelite*, 207, quotes an undated letter from Hunt to Jepson giving the dates of her 'marriage' as from 5 Sept. 1911 to 29 Mar. 1919. Bowen, *Drawn from Life*, 65, 59. *It Was the Nightingale*, 3, 92. *No Enemy*, 148. There is a third version in *'Rough Cookery', New York Herald Tribune Magazine* (29 July 1928), 18–19, 23. *It Was the Nightingale*, 89–96, 101, 103. For a discussion of this passage in relation to the form of *It Was the Nightingale*, see Saunders, 'A Life in Writing: Ford Madox Ford's Dispersed Autobiographies', *Antaeus*, 56 (Spring 1986), 47–69. The Beatrice oil-stove is also mentioned in 'Rough Cookery'; in Ford to Scott-James, 6 Apr. 1921 (Texas); and in Ford to Bowen, 4–5 Apr. 1919. Ford to Bowen, 'Thursd. Night' (and written into Friday), misdated '6' (which is followed by Mizener, 304, who thus misdates Ford's arrival in Red Ford) but in fact 3–4 Apr. 1919. *It Was the Nightingale*, 96–7, 101.

2 *No Enemy*, 148. Judd, *Ford Madox Ford*, 323. Ford to Cathy Hueffer, 9 June 1919: House of Lords Record Office. See *['Autobiographical Information']. Mizener, 304, 547, n. 23. Ford had of course invoked fairy tale from his first book onwards. For post-war examples, besides the idea of the Gingerbread Cottage in *No Enemy*, see 'Mr Croyd', 61, 63, 158, 188; also Timothy Weiss, *Fairy Tale and Romance in Works of Ford Madox Ford* (Lanham and London: University Press of America, 1984). Ford to Bowen, 4–5 Apr. 1919. *'Rough Cookery' places the episode in Feb. (to give an impression of the cold).

3 The Easter visit is established by Ford to Bowen 'Wed. Aftn.' [23 Apr. 1919], saying 'You have been gone 21 hours now!' (This dating is fixed by a letter (dated 'Sunday' [4 May 1919]) in which Bowen says he has been there a month, and that she had visited 'a fortnight ago'.) There are no letters surviving between 8–12 May (when Ford expected her for the second visit) and 17 May. On Phyllis, see Bowen to Ford, 'Thursday Morning' [3 Apr.? 1919]; [23 and 24 Apr. 1919]; and 'Thursday—later' [1 or 8 May 1919]; and Ford to Bowen, 25 Apr. 1919. On Kitty, see Bowen to Ford [5 and 24 Apr. 1919]; and Ford to Bowen [7? and 28 Apr. 1919]. Ford to Bowen [28–9; 23; 8–9 Apr. 1919]; 18 May 1919.

4 Bowen to Ford, Thursday [24 Apr. 1919] and Wednesday [23 Apr. 1919].

5 Bowen to Ford, Thursday [24 Apr.? 1919]. Ford to Bowen, 25[–26] Apr. 1919.

6 Ford to Bowen, [19 Mar.]; 25 Apr.; and 5 May; Bowen to Ford, Sunday [4 May 1919]; Ford to Bowen, 27 Apr. 1919. Bowen's brother was used as a model for Valentine Wannop's brother Edward, whose presence delays Valentine's and Christopher's affair in the penultimate chapter of *Some Do Not . . .*. Ford to Bowen, 22 Dec. 1918, comments on a drunken officer Tom had invited back to sleep on Bowen's sofa. Ford may have conflated the two men into Valentine's drunken brother. In *It Was the Nightingale* Ford transposed cat and dog, saying he had 'a dog and a man-servant' by his second night at Red Ford: 104. Ford to Bowen [7? Apr. 1919] and 11 Apr. 1919 show he bought the mongrel, Beau, between those two dates.

7 Ford to Bowen, 5 May; Bowen to Ford, Thursday [24 Apr.? 1919]. Bowen, *Drawn from Life*, 66–7.

8 Ford to Bowen, Sunday Night [4 May 1919].

9 Ford to Bowen, 21–2, 18–19, and 24–5 May 1919. 'Pure Literature', *Agenda*, 27/4–28/1 (Winter 1989–Spring 1990), 5–22 (7–8). 'From the Soil: (Two Monologues)', *Collected Poems* [1913], 118–21.

10 Christopher Driver, 'The Agamemnon and Other Family Feuds', *Guardian* (2 Apr. 1991), 29: a memoir of Raymond Postgate. John Saville's entry on Margaret Cole (1893–1980) for the *DNB* identifies her as an original for Valentine, but erroneously places that character in *The Fifth Queen* trilogy. Bowen, *Drawn from Life*, 223. Margaret Cole is one of the few important 'originals' missed by Moser (219). See Betty Vernon, *Margaret Cole: 1893–1980* (London: Fabian Tract 482, 1986). Secor and Secor, *The Return of the Good Soldier*, 70, n. 102.

11 Tate, *Memories and Essays* (Manchester: Carcanet, 1976), 29. Mizener, 305. Freud, 'Psycho-Analytic Notes on an Autobiographical Account of a Case of Paranoia (Dementia Paranoides)' (1911), *Standard Edition*, vol. 12 (London: The Hogarth Press and the Institute of Psycho-Analysis, 1958), 71. Anthony Storr, *Jung* (London: Fontana, 1973), 31. Ford to Bowen, 21–2 May 1919. *It Was the Nightingale*, 104–5, 205, 106, 108, 111–13. Later they found a rook with a broken wing on Ford's birthday, and named it 'O Sapientia' after the collect for 17 Dec. (112). Bowen to Ford, Sunday [4 May 1919]. 'True Love & a G.C.M.', 88.

12 Ford to Bowen, 30 and 23 May 1919; 'Monday Aft[n.]' [28 Apr. 1919]. Bowen to Ford, 30 May 1919, and 'Saturday' [26 Apr. 1919].

13 Ford to Bowen, 2–3 May 1919. Hunt to Ford, Sunday [4 May? 1919]; and Mar. 1919. Bowen to Ford, 'Thursday—later' [22 May 1919].

14 Hunt to Scott-James, [Mar.–Apr.? 1919]: Texas. Hunt's diary entry for 28 May 1919 bears this out, though it also suggests she knew Ford was writing to Stella too: 'I had seen Stella in the Street opposite Clifford Baxes studio where she was going to get F's letters. I had it out with her.' She also heard that Stella had told someone else that Ford had been 'trying for years to get rid of' her. Ford gave the address to Pinker (5 June 1919: *Letters*, [93]), and to younger friends like Herbert Read and Harold Monro; but not to those close to Hunt, like his mother, or Masterman (Ford to Cathy Hueffer, 9 June 1919: House of Lords Record Office. Ford to Masterman, 28 June 1919: *Letters*, 94–6. Juliet to Hunt, 30 June [1927]; Bowen to Hunt, 30 May 1919. Hunt to Cathy Hueffer, 'Thursday' [n.d.]: House of Lords Record Office. Belford, *Violet*, 246.

15 Bowen to Ford, 'Tuesday' [3 June? 1919]. See n. 23 below for the dating of Ford's name-change; also Saunders, i. 1–4. Ford to Bowen, 23, 17–18, 20–1 May 1919. Mizener, 304–5. Hunt to Wells, n.d. [1920?]: University of Illinois at Urbana; quoted by Belford, *Violet*, 246. In a scrap of reminiscence (filed in box 13/18 of the Wallis papers

of Cornell's Ford and Hunt collection) Hunt claims Ford forged her name on two cheques. But her diary for 30 June 1919 admits signing his name to withdraw £15.

16 Ford to Cathy Hueffer, 9 June; 3 July 1919: House of Lords Record Office. Barry Hollingsworth, 'David Soskice in Russia in 1917', *European Studies*, 6 (1976), 73–97. Mizener, 306, says the first of the three gentlemen was probably Edward Heron Allen (whom he gives 'a drawling voice', mistranscribing the words 'a drawing room'). But Allen is more likely to have been the second, who denounced Ford to the police as a spy. But the Secors make a persuasive case that the three were perhaps the men Ford made what Hunt calls a 'scene' about on 11 Mar. 1917: Byles, her solicitor Kenneth Dolleymore (who had sent Ford the letter in 1916 withdrawing Hunt's financial guarantee), and Ernest Sims, a fellow member of the Welch Regiment whom she had got to spy on Ford: Secor and Secor, *The Return of the Good Soldier*, 50 and n. 44, 43, n. 2.

17 Joan Hardwick, *An Immodest Violet*, 152, says 'It was characteristic of him that he should write to such close friends as the Mastermans announcing his new name and his new address at the same time as putting the blame for the break upon Violet and failing to mention that his new love was already established at his new address.' See also Belford, *Violet*, 246, 241. Secor and Secor, *The Return of the Good Soldier*, 50. Hunt, diary for 30 June 1919. Her 1919 diary also mentions meeting with Ford as late as 13 Oct., and 13 and 20 Nov., but notes for 4 Dec.: 'F. did not come.' Waugh to Goldring, quoted in Goldring, *The Last Pre-Raphaelite*, 208–9.

18 Phillis Shanks to Hunt, 23 June 1919. Ford to Read, 2 Sept. 1919: *Letters*, 97–9.

19 Ford to Masterman, 28 June 1919: *Letters*, 94–6.

20 Bowen to Ford, 'Sunday' [4 May 1919]; Ford to Bowen, 5–6 May 1919.

21 Ford to Bowen, 2–3 May 1919.

22 For 'Bingel and Bengel', see Saunders, 330–1, 378. Ford to C. F. G. Masterman, 28 June 1919: *Letters*, 94–6. A. J. P. Taylor, *English History: 1914–1945* (Oxford: Clarendon Press, 1965), 125–8. See Saunders, i. 394, 589.

23 Ford's change of name is discussed in Saunders, i. 1–4. The petition is dated 4 June, the date Ford gives for his visit to Pinker: *It Was the Nightingale*, 129. The film was made as *The Road to Romance*, starring Ramon Novarro, and shown in 1927. It was reviewed by the *New York Times* on 10 Oct. 1927. It must have been in this year (not 1923 or 1924) that Ford was horrified to see 'the photographs of what Hollywood had made of my forgotten work' outside the cinema that was showing the film. He ran to the nearest speakeasy, 'asked the clerk for a dose of the strongest alcohol he had, mixed with sal volatile, which encourages the heart. . . . And, in those fumes as, gradually I grew calmer, I saw poor Mr. Pinker and his sanguine spectacles in his office and the garden of Red Ford when that day I got back to it.' He never saw the film. *It Was the Nightingale*, 116–29 (128). See Harvey, 17, and Mizener, 575–6, n. 1. Ford was less lucky with an offer of $500 for the film rights of *Ring for Nancy* (the American title of *The Panel*) made by Bobbs Merrill in Feb. By the time Pinker had heard from Ford and replied in July, the offer no longer stood: Bobbs Merrill to Pinker, 22 Feb. 1919 (telegram) and 11 Aug. 1919: Northwestern. Bowen, *Drawn from Life*, 69.

24 *It Was the Nightingale*, 117, 132–4. *A Man Could Stand Up—*, 270. 'The "Alcestis" of Euripides, freely adapted', 13. *The March of Literature*, 118–19. Harvey, 120, casts doubt on Ford's story about this translation, on the grounds that Ford's claim that the play was never produced because the only copy was lost is disproved by the existence of two versions (now both at Cornell). However, one is a radio script, dated 'London, 1950', and thus obviously prepared after Ford's death. The other may either be the lost

copy, which may have eventually been found and returned; or it could be a new version. Neither possibility would disprove Ford's account. That he had undertaken the work for Playfair is confirmed by a letter from G. Calthrop ('For Mr Nigel Playfair'), from the Lyric Opera House, Hammersmith, to Ford, 9 Jan. 1919, saying: 'Mr Playfair wants to know how you are getting on with "Alcestes" [sic].' Ford says Playfair told him the play was to go into rehearsal at Drinkwater's Birmingham Repertory Theatre; but the theatre's newscutting file contains no mention of Ford's *Alcestis*.

25 Juliet Soskice to Hunt [*c*.19 June 1919]. Cf. Ford to Bowen, 20–1 May 1919: 'if I do owe her money I sh^d. like to try & pay it slowly—& if I don't I want the fact stated, by a lawyer if possible [. . .].' Goldring, *South Lodge*, 197. Hunt to Ford [n.d., but later than 20 Nov. 1920—when Ford and Bowen's daughter was born, whom the letter mentions—and probably *c*.1929]: Princeton. A manuscript scrap at Cornell (filed in box 13/18 of the Wallis papers) claims Ford said he owed her £2,000, but she said the figure was only £1,500.

Chapter 7

1 Ford to Read, 11 June 1920; to Flint, 23 June 1920: *Letters*, 102–8. Bowen, *Drawn from Life*, 67–8. Ford to Pinker, 22 Jan. 1920: *Reader*, 478–9. (Cf. Ford to Pinker, 24 July 1919: *Letters*, 96–7.) The 'Northern Newspapers' money was from the Northern Newspaper Syndicate, presumably for *'The Colonel's Shoes', *Reynolds's Newspaper* (11 Jan. 1920), 2. Mizener, 314 and 577 n., says this story was being turned down by the syndicate in Aug. 1921. But he didn't know it had already been published, so the letter he cites must refer to a second story—possibly 'Enigma'.

2 'Thus to Revisit . . . : III.—The Serious Book', *Piccadilly Review* (6 Nov. 1919), 6. 'Stocktaking [. . .]: VIII.: The "Serious" Book', *transatlantic review*, 2/3 (Sept. 1924), 277. *A Man Could Stand Up—*, 34. *No More Parades*, 185.

3 Hunt to Scott-James, n.d. [Mar.–Apr.? 1921]; Ford to Scott-James, 17 Apr. 1921: Texas. Ford to Hunt, 22 Mar. 1920. Telegrams from Ford to Hunt, 20 and 24 Apr. 1920. Rosamond died on 3 Apr. 1920: Belford, *Violet*, 247. K. Dolleymore (of Richardson, Sadlers & Callard) to Ford, 18 May 1920; Ford to Richardson, Sadlers & Callard [n.d., but a reply to theirs of 18 May] and 24 May 1920.

4 Ford to Monro, 30 May 1920: *Letters*, 99–100. *Chapbook*, 3 (July 1920), 20–4. Mizener, 311.

5 Ford to Hunt [n.d., but 9–14 Aug. 1920]. Byles died on Sunday 8 Aug. 1920.

6 Excerpt from Walpole's diary for 19 July 1920, in Rupert Hart-Davis, *Hugh Walpole* (London: Macmillan, 1952), 195; quoted by Harvey, 513.

7 23 June 1920: *Letters*, 107–8.

8 Ford to Read, 11 June 1920; to Monro, 9 June 1920: *Letters*, 102–4, 101–2. Part of the joke is that both Kipling and Newbolt were still alive in 1920.

9 Ford to Read, 11 June 1920: *Letters*, 102–4. Flint visited between 23 June (Ford to Flint: *Letters*, 105–8) and 5 July (Ford to Monro: *Letters*, 113). Letter to the Editor, *Anthenæum* (16 July 1920), 93–4: repr. in *Letters*, 110–12. Ford to Flint, 2 June 1914: *Reader*, 476. Flint, *Otherworld: Cadences* (London: The Poetry Bookshop, 1920), 17–18. I am grateful to the late Sondra Stang for this suggestion. Mizener, 311, says they moved to Scammells Farm 'At the end of July'; but Ford to Pound [2 Aug. 1920] (*Pound/Ford*, 37–8, gives the date as 'Tomorrow 3/8/20'; this letter was misdated by Ludwig as '[September, 1920]': *Letters*, 123–4. Pound to Ford, 30 July 1920: *Pound/Ford*, 34–7.

10 Ford to Monro, 9 June and 30 May 1920: *Letters*, 101–2, 99–100. The manuscript of

'Serenada' (now at Cornell) is in Harvey, 123, but he doesn't mention the relationship to *A House*.

11 Ford to Read, 24 July 1920: *Letters*, 115. *Antwerp* was first published anonymously as *'In October 1914', *Outlook*, 34 (24 Oct. 1914), 523–4.

12 Ford to Harold Monro, 9 June 1920; *Letters*, 101–2. *Poetry*, 17 (Mar. 1921), 291–310. Harvey, 53, 222–3.

13 Bowen, *Drawn from Life*, 78.

Chapter 8

1 30 June 1920: *Letters*, 109–10.

2 Ford to Read, 11 June and 24 July 1920: *Letters*, 102–4, 113–5.

3 Ford to Harold Monro, 9 June 1920: *Letters*, 101–2. Ford to Pound, 19 Sept. 1920: *Letters*, 124–5. Ford to Pound, 26 July 1920: *Pound/Ford*, 33; and 29 July 1920: *Letters*, 118–19. Ludwig wrongly annotates this—and other letters on pp. 114 and 130—as referring to *The Marsden Case*; whereas 'Mr Croyd' is much more probable. *The Marsden Case*'s dates of composition (given on the same page as the dedication to Edgar Jepson) are probably accurate: Sept. 1921 to Jan. 1923. Ford to Pinker, 21 Oct. 1920: Berg Collection, New York Public Library. Like many of Ford's books, 'Mr Croyd' went through a change of names. In its earlier stages it was either known as 'Mr Croyd', after the central character, or 'The Wheels of the Plough', after Jethro Croyd's pre-war best-seller. When Ford revised the manuscript in 1928 for Viking, he changed the title to a phrase from Ecclesiastes: 'That Same Poor Man'. However, after the publication of *When the Wicked Man* (1931) it would have been confusing to publish another book with as similar a title, so it is not surprising that his last thoughts returned to his first. In one of his last letters it has become 'Mr Croyd' again, so I have used this title throughout (Ford to Stanley Unwin, 25 May 1939: *Letters*, 324–5). Stanley Unwin was considering publication in 1939.

4 The quotations are from the 1928 revised typescript at Cornell entitled 'That Same Poor Man', 87, 375, 58, 8–10, 99, 394, 128, 365, 361–2, 500, 378, 87, 192, 44, 57, 308, 223, 485, 304, 46.

5 Ford to Flint, 3 Aug. 1920: Texas. Pound, *'Hudson: Poet Strayed into Science', *Little Review*, 7/1 (May–June 1920), 13–17; repr. in *Selected Prose*, ed. William Cookson (London: Faber, 1973), 402. Wells and Mayne, Letters to the Editor, *English Review*, 31 (Aug. 1920), 178–9. Ford to Pound [2 Aug. 1920]: *Pound/Ford*, 37–8. George Engleheart did indeed write challenging Ford's claim that *vers libre* was a 'form' rather than the avoidance of form. Mrs E. Peter also joined the correspondence, stressing the entrancing power of a rhythmical beat, but she made no direct mention of Ford or jazz: *'Rhyme and Metre or Vers Libre', *Athenaeum*, 4709 (30 July 1920), 155. Ford to Wells, 1 Aug. 1920: *Letters*, 119–22. Ford drafted a reply: 'Appendix: An Eminent Novelist & the Present Writer', but it was (wisely) not published. He incorporated Wells's letter into the book of *Thus to Revisit*, 29–30 n. He repeated the story in 'Literary Causeries: XI. "Huddie"', *Chicago Tribune* (Paris) (27 Apr. 1924), 3, 11; and in *Return to Yesterday*, 248–50 (where Wells is camouflaged as 'an eminent politician', and *Mightier Than the Sword*, 159–60.

6 'Mr Croyd' (quoted from 'That Same Poor Man' version), 322. Ann Thwaite, *Edmund Gosse* (London: Secker and Warburg, 1984), 453. 'Dedicatory Letter to Stella Ford', *The Good Soldier*, 2.

7 Ford to Pinker, 8 and 13 July 1920: *Reader*, 479–80. Ford to Pinker, 1 June 1916 and [n.d., but Sept. 1920–May 1921]: Princeton. Lane to Pinker, 12 and 26 July 1920:

Northwestern. Ford to Pinker, 17 May 1921: *Letters*, 131–2. Ford to Monro, 9 June 1920: *Letters*, 101–2. Alec Waugh to Pinker, 27 July 1920: Northwestern. Ford to Waugh, 26 July 1920: *Letters*, 16–17. *TLS* (12 May 1921), 310. Dorothea Mann, *Boston Transcript* (27 July 1921), 6. See Ford to Flint, 17 Mar. 1921, asking him to make sure the Poetry Bookshop doesn't send *A House* to the *TLS*: 'There is a gent on that paper who goes out of his way to abuse me personally [. . .].' *Thus to Revisit*, 19, 25. Mizener, 315.

8 *It Was the Nightingale*, 138. Ford to Isidor Schneider, 14 Sept. 1929: *Letters*, 188–90. Pound to Ford [7 Sept. 1920]: *Pound/Ford*, 41–3. Mizener, 389 n. Hunt to Elsie Hueffer, 10 Aug. 1920.

9 Olive Garnett, diary for 21 Aug. 1920 and New Year's Day 1921, quoting the two letters. Wells to Hunt [9 Mar. 1923]. Hunt, 'Read, Mark . . .', *Saturday Review*, 134 (5 Aug. 1922), 222–3. Hunt to Scott-James [Mar.–Apr. 1921]: Texas. Hunt told Scott-James she visited on the 20th, but Ford told him it was the 28th. Ford to Scott-James, 6 Apr. 1921: Texas. Ford to Pound, 30 Aug. 1920: *Letters*, 122. Mizener, 312, 576, nn. 8–9. Goldring, *The Last Pre-Raphaelite*, 206. Bowen, *Drawn from Life*, 72. Ford to Pound, 19 Sept. 1920: *Letters*, 124–5. The only evidence for a later meeting is discussed on p. 578, n. 16.

10 Bowen, *Drawn from Life*, 69, 72, 77, 78, 75. Ford to Harold Monro, 30 May 1920: *Letters*, 99–100.

11 In *The Pisan Cantos* Pound recalled 'Fordie that wrote of giants'; not only the folk-tale giants of the story 'Riesenberg', but the literary giants he memorialized: Canto LXXIV, *The Cantos of Ezra Pound* (London: Faber and Faber, 1975), 432.

12 Ford to Pound, 30 Aug. and 19 Sept. 1920: *Letters*, 122, 124–5. In *It Was the Nightingale*, 179, Ford wrote of Proust: 'I had not read a word he had written', but explains that he had 'heard with avidity all that was to be heard of him'.

13 Ford to Read, 19 Sept. 1920: *Letters*, 126–8. Bashkirtseff was a painter and diarist. Mathilde Blind had translated and introduced her *Journal* (London: Cassell & Company, 1890).

14 Read, *Annals of Innocence and Experience* (London: Faber and Faber, 1940), 199.

15 Ford to Bowen, 22 Oct. 1927. Hunt to Scott-James [Mar.–Apr.? 1921]. Ford to Scott-James, 6 Apr. 1921: Texas (saying that on 3 Nov. he had seen two of Violet's letters to Mrs Hunt); Hunt to Scott-James [Mar.–Apr.? 1921]: Texas (saying that he had seen one). Ford to Scott-James, 17 Apr. 1921: Texas. Hunt to Scott-James [Mar.–Apr.? 1921]: Texas. Ford to Messrs Richardson, Sadler and Callard, 19 Sept. 1920 (including a transcript of Hunt to Ford, 16 Sept. 1920); Ford to Hunt, 22 Sept. 1920. Belford, *Violet*, 247–8, gives a misleading impression by omitting Ford's offer to read the novel, and only saying that he preferred not to.

16 Ford to Harold Monro, 15 Nov. 1920: Texas. Mizener, 313. Cole, *Growing up into Revolution* (London: Longmans, Green, 1949), 82–3. Ford was at the Coles' until the second or third week of December: Ford to Clifford Bax [date unclear, but either 10, 16, or 18] Dec. 1920: Texas.

17 Goldring, *South Lodge*, 124–6, says the manifesto 'was duly printed in a variety of Left-Wing periodicals'. However, I have been unable to trace publication. Ford wrote to Hardy on 17 Dec. 1920, enclosing the appeal and a covering note (signed by G. D. H. Cole, J. L. Hammond, and himself, explaining that it would be printed in the *Manchester Guardian* on 29 Dec. However, it did not appear then. Hardy replied on 19 Dec., declining to sign: Dorset County Museum. Goldring, *Odd Man Out: The Autobiography of a 'Propaganda Novelist'* (London: Chapman and Hall, 1935), 209. Ford to Monro,

26 Jan. 1921 (Texas). This letter mentions meetings at the Mont Blanc and at Devonshire Street, and names [Goldsworthy] Lowes Dickinson, [Douglas] Cole, and J. L. Hammond as other interested people. A footnote (possibly by Monro) at the end of Ford's letter to the manager of the Poetry Bookshop, 8 Feb. 1921 (Texas) says 'Letter to Ford 16/2/21 explaining the Irish Manifesto (Woolf etc) [. . .]'.

18 Bowen, *Drawn from Life*, 74. Ford to Katharine, 20 Jan. 1921.

19 Mizener, 313. Bowen, *Drawn from Life*, 84, describes the isolation, cold, damp, burst pipes, and mud of a Bedham winter. Ford to Scott-James, 6 April 1921: Texas. Hunt to Scott-James [Mar.–Apr.? 1921]: Texas. Sinclair's story was 'Lena Wrace', printed in the *English Review*, 32 (Feb. 1921), 103–15, immediately before the sixth instalment of 'Thus to Revisit'. Lena is thirteen years older than her new lover Norman Hippisley, who is 34 (Ford's age when getting to know Hunt in 1907–8). She has money. She dreads 'the moment when he'd "take" to writing again, for then he'd have to have a secretary'. The story ends with the unsurprising revelation that he has been having an affair with his secretary, Ethel Reeves, for three years. There is also a Rosamond or Brigit figure in the story, Barbara Vining. What Lena says about her may reflect what Hunt was saying about Brigit (it certainly echoes Leonora Ashburnham's attitude to her husband's mistresses): 'I tell you, I'd rather have Norry there with Barbara than not have him at all' (108, 111).

20 Ford to Scott-James, 6 and 17 Apr. 1921: Texas.

21 Bowen, *Drawn from Life*, 78–9, 82. Catalogue 45 from Serendipity Books (Berkeley, 1989) confirms the attribution (Item 180), and lists jackets by Bowen for the Duckworth editions of *The Marsden Case*, *Some Do Not . . .* , and *New York is Not America* (Items 183, 185, and 188). Ford to Jepson, 8 May 1923, says *The Marsden Case*'s jacket is by her: *Letters*, 149–50. The jacket illustration for *A Mirror to France*, also reproduced as the frontispiece, is hers too. Ford to Monro, 30 Mar. 1921: Texas. Tauchnitz was a German publisher who produced paperback editions for sale primarily on the Continent of British and American works.

22 Ford to Harriet Monroe, 10 Feb. 1921: *Reader*, 481. Ford to Flint, 12 May 1921: *Letters*, 131. *It Was the Nightingale*, 164–5. Price, 'Ford Madox Ford', *University of California Chronicle*, 27 (Oct. 1925), 346–65 (352, 348, 349). In 'Literary Causeries: XII: On Causeries as Such', *Chicago Tribune Sunday Magazine* (Paris: 4 May 1924), 3, Ford expressed his ambivalence about an earlier article Price had written on him, 'Ford Madox Hueffer', *Poet Lore*, 31 (Autumn 1920), 432–53: 'He knew more about my writings than any soul in the created world: certainly he knew a great deal more about them than I know myself, my memory having collapsed at a certain period in the late war, so that to read my own books is for me a singular experience. He provided me with a Philosophy, which, heaven knows, is a thing I leave to the poor b . . . y Huns; he provided me with views of the Cosmos—whatever that is! with a religion of my own. . . . Well, he provided me with so much that it was like waking up and discovering that one was really the Prince of Wales.' Ford to Coppard, 26 Mar. 1923: Texas. Ford again asked him not to write to him as 'Capt.' on 15 Dec. 1923: *Letters*, 155. 'The Great View' had been on Ford's mind in *Thus to Revisit*: he quotes from it as an example of his youthful 'rhymed *vers libre* on p. 206. Pound, 'On Criticism in General', *Criterion*, 1 (Jan. 1923), 143–56 (145); *Pound/Ford*, 190, n. 36 notes the connection with the poem. Price was at Coopers until the middle of June: see Ford to Harold Monro, 16 June 1921: *Letters*, 133.

23 Samuel Putnam, *Paris Was Our Mistress* (New York: Viking, 1947), 119–20. Bowen, *Drawn from Life*, 79–80. Ford to Monroe, 7 Nov. 1921: *Letters*, 136–7.

24 *The Good Soldier*, 136. 'Joseph Conrad', *John O'London's Weekly*, 6 (Dec. 1921), 323; see
    Harvey, 62, 223. Ford to Jepson, 9 July 1921: *Letters*, 134. Mizener, 315, thought Ford
    'began to believe' what is surely ironic boasting to Pinker (suggesting the line he thought
    Pinker should take with publishers) that he was 'setting the Hudson on fire with various
    articles and poems': 25 July 1921: Huntington. He counters this, and Ford's claim that
    'articles about me have been appearing in the heavy monthlies', by pointing out that
    'Ford's total publication in American magazines during 1921 consisted of one chapter of
    Thus to Revisit and "A House"', and saying that 'Nothing but reviews of *Thus to Revisit*
    was written about him': 315 n. True, 1921 was one of his more fallow years. But Ford
    had won the *Poetry* prize; and Mizener relegates to an endnote the other crucial point,
    that Ford was not just thinking of 1921. Price's first article on him had appeared in the
    autumn of 1920. He may also have been recalling Pound's remarks on him in the *Little
    Review* in May–June. The *Yale Review* had asked him for an essay on Conrad in 1920,
    but didn't publish it when they found out it had already appeared in America as part of
    Thus to Revisit; instead they waited for 'A Haughty and Proud Generation', *Yale
    Review*, 11 (July 1922), 703–17; but Ford was negotiating with them during 1921. See
    Ford to Wilbur Cross, 1 Sept. 1920 and 7 Nov. 1921: Yale. The latter has an amusing
    detail about a letter from the *New York Evening Post* (who had published ch. 11 of *Thus
    to Revisit* in March) addressing a letter to Ford at 'Bedlam'; Ford said that when it
    eventually reached him, it was superscribed: 'Not known in Bethlehem Hospital'.

25 Ford to Pinker, 17 May 1921: *Letters*, 131–2.

26 Serendipity Books, Catalogue 45, Item 181. *Thus to Revisit*, 45. Pound to Ford, 22 and
    26 May 1921 and [June–July? 1921]; Liveright to Pound [n.d.]: *Pound/Ford*, 57–60,
    189, n. 18. *It Was the Nightingale*, 199. Ford to Read, 25 June 1921: *Letters*, 133. Pound
    to Isabel Pound, 22 Oct. 1921: quoted in *Pound/Ford*, 61; see also 62.

27 Latham to Ford, 22 June 1921: Huntington. Ford to Latham, 14 Aug. 1921: *Reader*,
    482–4.

28 Latham to Ford, 6 Sept. 1921; Ford to Latham, 27 Sept. 1921: Huntington. Ford to
    Read, 5 Oct. 1921: *Letters*, 135–6. *'Just People' was probably begun at Red Ford (p. 1
    gives his name as 'Hueffer', which is deleted and replaced with 'Ford'), though the
    address on the cover sheet is Bedham. The 22-leaf typescript at Cornell appears
    unpublished, but it contains versions of anecdotes published elsewhere. ('The Waiter'
    retells the story published in 'What Happened at Eleven Forty-Five', *Throne*, 5 (25 Oct.
    1911), 142–3, and rewritten for *Return to Yesterday*, 301–3. The violinist in 'The
    Violinist and the Hotel Keeper' also appears in *Return to Yesterday*, 300. One of the
    'Two Very Worried Gentlemen' is the American friend on whose farm Ford recalled
    working in *Return to Yesterday*, 159–61.) The title-page of *The Marsden Case* gives the
    composition dates as 'Sussex, September, 1921. / St. Jean-Cap-Ferrat, January, 1923'.

29 Ford to Latham, 27 Sept. 1921 (Huntington), says he has asked Pinker to send the
    contract 'by the next mail'. Ford to Read, 5 Oct. 1921: *Letters*, 135–6. Latham to Ford,
    11 Jan. 1922: Huntington. Ford told Jepson: 'I have just finished my novel for
    Macmillans [. . .]' on 12 Feb. 1922: *Letters*, 137–9 (138). He sent it to Eric Pinker with
    a letter misdated 29 Feb. 1922 (1922 wasn't a leap year): Princeton. He told Eric Pinker
    on 6 July that Macmillan had rejected it: Huntington. Mizener, 578, n. 27.

30 Ford to Jepson, 8 May 1923: *Letters*, 149; cf. 138 (12 Feb. 1922), where Ford says much
    the same to Jepson. For example, see Ann Barr Snitow, *Ford Madox Ford and the Voice
    of Uncertainty* (Baton Rouge: Louisiana State University Press, 1984), 203. The bio-
    graphical significance of the novel is discussed by Mizener, 322–33, 489–94; Moser,
    209–13.

31 *TLS* (10 May 1923), 320. Gerald Gould, *Saturday Review*, 135 (26 May 1923), 704. *Punch*, 165 (18 July 1923), 71–2. For these, and the other reviews discussed below, see Harvey, 339–40.

32 Snitow, 201. Forster, 'T. S. Eliot', *Abinger Harvest* (London: Edward Arnold, 1936), 88.

33 Bowen, *Drawn from Life*, 61.

34 For example, Jessop recalls being preoccupied by 'the deadness in the voice of George Heimann' during the trial scene: a phrase which suggests—misleadingly—that George is himself about to die, or that his voice somehow stands for the war's deaths (284). Robert Green, *Ford Madox Ford: Prose and Politics* (Cambridge: Cambridge University Press, 1981), 127.

35 Peter Renny, *Golden Hind*, 1 (July 1923), 38.

36 *Nation and Athenaeum*, 33 (23 June 1923), 397–8.

37 Paul Wiley, for example, is content to attribute George's suicide-attempt to his fear of publicity: *Novelist of Three Worlds: Ford Madox Ford* (Syracuse, NY, 1962), 209.

38 *Mightier Than the Sword*, 191–2. *DNB*. Barbara McCrimmon, 'W. R. S. Ralston (1828–89): scholarship and scandal in the British Museum', *British Library Journal*, 14/2 (Autumn 1988), 178–98.

39 In *Henry James*, too, Ford writes of Ralston's 'suicidal tendencies': 75. McCrimmon, 195, says Ralston was 'found dead in his bed', and that 'It was suspected that he had committed suicide'—though the only evidence she cites is Ford's reminiscence. Moser, 210, notes that the bringing together of the central names Heimann and Marsden brings together Hueffer and Marwood. But 'Marsden' (a name Ford would have known from the feminist Dora Marsden, and from the middle name of Lawrence Marsden Price) also echoes '*Mar*tindale'—and Charles 'Masterman': George was called 'Charles' in the manuscript, which is at Cornell. Like the name Tietjens, the name Heimann is derived (via Hijmann) from Dutch Protestant ancestry. It is suggestive of more than other names, of course: Hymen? High-Man? Heim-man (the man, like Ford, in search of *heim*—home, or rest)? Jessop's vision of the fine figure of a man under the shadow of imminent disgrace is central to much of Ford's work. Besides the presentations of Ashburnham and Tietjens, cf. *Henry James*, 153–5, and *Joseph Conrad*, 129–30 (discussed in Saunders, i. 388–9 and 406 respectively). John Meixner, *Ford Madox Ford's Novels* (University of Minnesota Press: Minneapolis, and Oxford University Press: London, 1962), 196, argues that the waiter scene undercuts the romance ending. Admittedly it introduces disturbing feudalist implications, but it seems to me to re-inforce romance's redemptive fortuity.

40 Ford to Hunt, 12 June 1909; see Saunders, i. 288.

41 Mizener, 23, 30. Ford to Elsie Martindale [3 Mar. 1894]. Ford had also alluded to the passage at the end of *The Fifth Queen Crowned*, when Katharine makes her great idealistic stoical final speech while thinking of her youth 'away in Lincolnshire, where there was an orchard with green boughs, and below it a pig-pound where the hogs grunted': 313.

42 For examples see the manuscript *'Letters in England' (pseud. L. C. Pash), 10; *'A Literary Causerie: On Some Tendencies in Modern Verse', *Academy*, 69 (23 Sept. 1905), 982–4; *Ancient Lights*, 264, 289; 'A Declaration of Faith', *English Review*, 4 (Feb. 1910), 543–51; 'Literary Portraits—XXXI.: Lord Dunsany and "Five Plays"', *Outlook*, 33 (11 Apr. 1914), 494–5; 'On Impressionism', 328; 'Literary Portraits—XLVIII.: M. Charles-Louis Philippe and "Le Père Perdrix"', *Outlook*, 34 (8 Aug. 1914), 174–5; *Henry James*, 13, 62, 141; *Thus to Revisit*, 203; *Some Do Not . . .*, 284; 'Not Idle', *New*

York Herald Tribune Books (1 July 1928), 1, 6; *No Enemy*, 272–3; *It Was the Nightingale*, 59, 69. On Mr Tietjens's death, see *Some Do Not . . .* , 261, 269; *Last Post*, 90, 284–5.

Chapter 9

1 Mizener, 314, wrongly says Pinker died in January. See Najder, *Joseph Conrad*, 465. *Return to Yesterday*, 59–60. Ford also wrote about Pinker's death in *It Was the Nightingale*, 116.

2 Pound to Ford [13 Jan. 1922]; Ford to Pound, 21 Mar. 1922; Pound to Ford, [between 21 and 27 Mar. 1922]: *Pound/Ford*, 63–7, 190, n. 26 (p. 64). Pound, 'On Criticism in General', *Criterion*, 1 (January 1923), 144–5. For Llona, see *Pound/Ford*, 65, 66–7, 189, n. 25. Nothing came of the project to get Ford translated into French until he signed a contract with Simon Kra for six novels in 1924: see pp. 585–6. For Roth, see Mizener, 320, 578, n. 27; and Pound to Joyce, 19 Nov. 1926: *The Selected Letters of Ezra Pound*, ed. D. D. Paige (New York: New Directions, 1971), 203–4. Ford to Coppard, 26 Mar. 1923: Texas. *Women & Men* was published by the Three Mountains Press in Paris in April 1923.

3 Ford to Monro [n.d., but *c*. Apr. 1922]: Texas. Monro's notes on the Poetry Bookshop Readings (information kindly supplied by Joy Grant to Max Saunders, 1 Mar. 1988). Ford to Forman, 10 May 1922; Bowen to Mrs Forman, 16 May [1922]: UCLA. *It Was the Nightingale*, 160, 166–71; Ford placed the dinner in Sept., but Lewis was in London between 9 and 13 May 1922, but not in Sept. (See Mark Schorer, *Sinclair Lewis* (New York, Toronto, London: McGraw-Hill, 1961), 331–2.) There is a seating plan for the dinner on the verso of an undated letter from Ford to Forman (UCLA); this collection has correspondence from Ford and Bowen about the May meeting, but no indications of one in Sept. There is a barely legible name on the seating plan that might read 'West' and might be the 'celebrity'—perhaps Edward Sackville West? An anonymous reviewer for the *TLS* (12 May 1921), 310, had said that 'the fact that he has become [. . .] "one of the literary figures of the day" seems to have obsessed his mind and dulled his powers'. Ford to Jepson, 10 May 1922; quoted by Goldring, *The Last Pre-Raphaelite*, 214.

4 Bowen, *Drawn from Life*, 76, 82. Ford to Jepson, 1 July 1922: *Letters*, 140–1. Ford to Cathy Hueffer [n.d., but *c*.1 July 1922]: House of Lords Record Office.

5 *Pound/Ford*, 60. Ford to Liveright, 6 July 1922: Huntington. Ford to Bertram, 14 Aug. 1922: *Letters*, 141–2. Mizener, 578, n. 29. 'Towards a History [. . .]' was finished by at least 26 Dec. 1922, when Brandt and Kirkpatrick (who were now acting as Ford's American agents) sent it (retitled as 'Stock Taking Towards a Revaluation of English Literature') to the *Yale Review* (Yale). Eliot to Ford, 4 Oct. 1923. Eliot said he had got many suggestions from the work, and courteously threatened to plunder Ford's ideas if he didn't publish it quickly. (Privately, however, he was less polite, telling John Quinn he regretted Pound's tendency in his articles to imitate Ford, 'who writes vilely and who never omits to mention that he is an Officer (British) and a Gentleman': quoted in Donald Gallup, *T. S. Eliot & Ezra Pound: Collaborators in Letters* (New Haven, Conn.: Henry W. Wenning/C. A. Stonehill, Inc., 1970), 30; and *Pound/Ford*, 74. Eliot told Sydney Schiff, 31 Aug. 1920, that Ford was 'very readable, but after a time one comes to feel that he is an unpleasant parasite of letters'; and he explained to Pound on 22 Oct. 1922 that he didn't want Ford in the *Criterion* for several numbers yet 'because there are a great many other people beside myself who do not like him'; though he did add: 'If you happen to hear however of his having done anything praiseworthy you might let me know': *The Letters of T. S. Eliot*, ed. Valerie Eliot (London: Faber and Faber, 1988), i. 404–5, 585–7.) Harvey, 121, 227–9, misses the connection between typescript and serial,

thinking (as did Mizener, 315) that the former was unpublished. Ford had complained to Anthony Bertram, 22 Aug. 1922, that Mrs Williams-Ellis's study, *An Anatomy of Poetry* (Oxford: Basil Blackwell, [1922]', 'suffers from a lack of standards and indignations. People think that you can write criticisms without these, but you can't really—or only English Criticism, which blows hot-and-cold, or rather tepid-and-lukewarm, all the time': *Letters*, 145. Ford to Clifford Bax, 10 Dec. 1920 (about *Thus to Revisit*): Texas. 'Stocktaking [. . .] II', *transatlantic review*, 1/2 (Feb. 1924), 56; 'IV', 1/4 (Apr. 1924), 169; 'V', 1/5 (May 1924), 323-5; 'VI', 1/6 (June 1924), 450. The last instalment of the serial was in Nov., the penultimate number before the review folded. 'Pure Literature' has been published subsequently in *Agenda*, 27/4–28/1 (Winter 1989/Spring 1990), 5–22. 'X', 2/5 (Nov. 1924), 504. Ford also cites (under its variant title) the *Life of a Scotch Naturalist* in the previous instalment: *transatlantic review*, 2/4 (Oct. 1924), 397. In *Return to Yesterday*, 48, he said: 'the writer whose cadences have most intimately influenced me were those of Thomas Edwardes [. . .].'

6 Bowen, *Drawn from Life*, 82. Ford to Monro [n.d., but after 14 Aug. 1922 (*Letters*, 141–3), when Ford asked Bertram for an introduction; and before the middle of Nov., when Ford left for France]: Texas. Goldring, *The Last Pre-Raphaelite*, 218. Ford to Bertram, 14 Aug. 1922. Ford to Jepson, 15 Aug. 1922: *Letters*, 143–4. [Cathy Hueffer, signed 'Dadala'] to Frank [Soskice], 15 July [1921 or 1922]: House of Lords Record Office. *Drawn from Life*, 79.

7 Answer to 'Three Questions': 'Ford Madox Hueffer', *Chapbook*, 27 (July 1922), 14–15. *Yale Review* to Cornelia Landon (of Brandt and Kirkpatrick), 9 Jan. 1923: Yale. 'Third Rate Poet', *Golden Hind*, 1 (Oct. 1922), 15–20. Eliot to Ford, 2 Feb. 1923.

8 'A Haughty and Proud Generation', *Yale Review*, 11 (July 1922), 703, 716–17. Pound's 'Paris Letter' on it in the *Dial*, 72/6 (June 1922), [623]–39, appeared a month earlier; but it is dated 'May', a month after Ford had finished his. The *Yale Review* to Ford, 13 Apr. 1922: Yale. Eliot's essay on it appeared the following year. Ford also wrote a longer appreciation of the book for the English press: '"Ulysses" and the Handling of Indecencies', *English Review*, 35 (Dec. 1922), 538–48.

9 Ford to Jepson, 15 Aug. 1922: *Letters*, 143.

10 Bowen, *Drawn from Life*, 83–4. Monro to Ford, 14 July 1922: UCLA (Monro didn't *lend* them the villa, as Mizener said: 321). *It Was the Nightingale*, 241–2. Their plans to leave had however already been formed over the summer. They originally hoped to leave in Nov., but the previous tenant wanted to stay on: Bowen to Monro, 24 Sept. [1922]: UCLA. It was an indication of how engrossed in her own obsessions, and out of touch with Ford's life Elsie now was, that she thought Ford was leaving England to escape from Mary Martindale: Mizener, 578, n. 30. Pound to Ford, 22 May [1921]: *Pound/ Ford*, 57–8. Ford to Jepson, 15 Aug. 1922: *Letters*, 145–6. Bowen to Jepson, 8 Oct. 1922 (Princeton), mentions Ford struggling with a great poem: Mizener, 578, n. 30. Ford to Bertram, 24 Oct. 1922, says he is still writing at it; Ford to Jepson, 25 Nov. 1922, says he has just finished it: *Letters*, 145–7. The composition dates are given on p. 126 as 'Sussex: *October* 1922–Tarascon *June* 1923'.

11 Ford to Conrad, still trying to renew their friendship by saying he is having a copy of his latest book sent, 8 Nov. 1923: *Letters*, 156–7.

12 James King, *Interior Landscapes: A Life of Paul Nash* (London: Weidenfeld and Nicolson, 1987), 118. King says Ford stayed with Nash at Dymchurch in 1922 or 1923: it was almost certainly 1923, since Ford left for France in Nov. 1922. Mizener, 321. *Mister Bosphorus*, 103.

13 The phrase comes from Ford's *'Note by the Author' to the publication of the first scene in the *Chapbook*, 37 (May 1923), 19–23 (23). The collapse of the magazine meant

that no more was serialized. Ford to Jepson, 25 Nov. 1922 and 8 May 1923; Ford to Wells, 14 Oct. 1923: *Letters*, 146–7, 149–50, 154.

14 See n. 10 above on the composition dates for the poem. Eliot, *The Waste Land: A Facsimile and Transcript of the Original Drafts Including the Annotations of Ezra Pound*, ed. Valerie Eliot (London: Faber and Faber, 1971), pp. xxii, xxiv. Joseph Wiesenfarth, 'Fargobawlers: James Joyce and Ford Madox Ford', *Biography*, 14/2 (Spring 1991), 110. Conrad to Ford, 20 Nov. 1923.

15 Mizener, 578, n. 29. Bowen, *Drawn from Life*, 85–6.

16 Bowen, *Drawn from Life*, 86–7. Hemingway (in Paris) to Harriet Monroe, 16 Nov. 1922, says Ford is 'coming to town tomorrow': *Ernest Hemingway: Selected Letters*, ed. Carlos Baker (London: Granada, 1981), 72. Ford to Hunt, 21 Nov. 1992. Judd, *Ford Madox Ford*, 443, says Hunt and Ford later had no direct contact. However, Mrs Joseph Pennell wrote to Hunt on 15 June 1930 about Ford: 'I think you were more than kind to dine with him.' Ford was in London in 1927 and 1929, so it may have been on one of these occasions that they dined. Bishop, *New Directions: Number Seven*, 462. Ford to Jepson, 25 Nov. 1922: *Letters*, 146–7. Wiesenfarth, 'Fargobawlers', 96. Joyce to Ford, 10 Jan. 1923: *Letters*, ed. Richard Ellmann (London: Faber and Faber, 1966), iii. 70. George Painter, *Marcel Proust*, 2 vols. (Harmondsworth: Penguin, 1977), ii. 354–6. *It Was the Nightingale*, 177–80, 270. *Drawn from Life*, 90.

17 *It Was the Nightingale*, 174–7, 206; Ford dates the meeting around 25 Nov.—but then immediately disavows the date! Ford wrote again about the Notre Dame plaque, discussing its moving understatement in a probably unpublished typescript of 1929, 'Years After'.

18 Ford to Jepson, 25 Nov. 1922: *Letters*, 146–7. Mizener, 320. See Harvey for details of editions. Goldring, *The Last Pre-Raphaelite*, 215.

19 Bowen, *Drawn from Life*, 92–4. Bowen to Monro, 31 Dec. 1922 and 23 Feb. 1923: UCLA. Ford to Monro, 1 Jan. 1923: Texas. Monro to 'Mrs. Ford', 23 Apr. 1923: UCLA. *Drawn from Life*, 109, says the cottage in Bedham was let for a year 'Soon after coming to France [. . .]'. Ford to Bertram, 20 Jan. 1923: *Letters*, 147–8. The second Duke of Westminster's first marriage was dissolved in 1919, and he married his second wife (of four) in 1920. In 1921 Consuelo Vanderbilt remarried, after a notorious divorce from Charles Richard, the ninth Duke of Marlborough. *It Was the Nightingale*, 209–10, describes a comical conversation with 'His majesty's Uncle'—the Duke of Connaught.

20 Ford to Jepson, 28 Jan. 1923: quoted in Goldring, *The Last Pre-Raphaelite*, 223. Renard's remark translates as: 'Yes. Man of Letters! I shall be that until my death. . . . And if by chance I should be eternal, I shall produce literature throughout eternity. And never tire of producing it, and always produce it, and say to hell with rest, like the wine-grower who stamps his foot in my story 'The Wine-Grower'. *A Mirror to France* gives the composition dates on 290. Bowen to Monro, 31 Dec. 1922 (UCLA) mentions the sovereign; when Ford retold the story in *It Was the Nightingale* (186) it had become 'a number of golden guineas'. Ford to Monro [March 1923]: *Letters*, 148–9, mentions the sovereign. *It Was the Nightingale*, 203, 207. Ford to Monro, 20 Feb. 1923: Texas. Ford to Wells, 14 Oct. 1923: *Letters*, 154. He also wrote to Conrad: 'I think I'm doing better work as the strain of the war wears off': 7 Oct. 1923: Yale.

Chapter 10

1 Humphrey Carpenter, *A Serious Character: The Life of Ezra Pound* (London: Faber and Faber, 1988), 429. Bowen, *Drawn from Life*, 96. Bowen to Ford, 11 Mar. 1923; Ford to Bowen, 'Feast of St. Cyriax' 16 Mar. 1923, and [9 Mar. 1923] 'Feast of Sainte

Francoise'. Ford mentions the play in several other letters written while he was working on it: ([8 Mar.]; [13 Mar.] 'Feast of St. Euphrasius'; 14 [Mar.]; [20 Mar.] 'Feast of St. Joachim'; Wednesday 9 [May 1923]; 10 May). On 5 May he told her he had written 'two or three words of *Lady R.*': given the day-by-day accounts of the play, this could refer to it. Which would make it likely that it is what Ford calls 'my Recamier play' in a later letter to Bowen: 21 [Nov. 1927]. Katharine Hueffer to Ford [Mar. 1923]; Ford to Bowen, Monday 'Real Feast of St. Joseph' [19 Mar. 1923].

2 Bowen, *Drawn from Life*, 100–1, 103, 105. *It Was the Nightingale*, 225, 228–9. Ford to Bowen, [8] May 1923 [Ford says 'Tuesday Evg./7/5/23'; but Tuesday was the 8th]. Ford to Jepson, 8 May 1923: *Letters*, 149–50.

3 Ford to Bowen, 11 and 10 May 1923. Stang and Cochran, 200 n., gloss the bullfighting terms with a reference to the glossary of Hemingway, *Death in the Afternoon* (New York: Scribner's, 1960), 393. '*Mañadas*: herds; *cap[e]a*: "informal bullfights or bull baitings in village squares in which amateurs and aspirant bullfighters take part. Also a parody of the formal bullfight given in parts of France or where the killing of the bull is prohibited".'

4 Bowen, *Drawn from Life*, 105–8. Ford to Jepson, 14 June 1923: quoted in Goldring, *The Last Pre-Raphaelite*, 224–5. *It Was the Nightingale*, 227–32. Ford to Bertram, 4 July 1923: *Letters*, 150–2. Ford sent Harold Monro a postcard ([Saturday] 9 June 1923: Texas) saying they would be at St Agrève from 'Tuesday next', i.e. 12 June. Bowen to Monro, 14 July [1923]: UCLA. *It Was the Nightingale*, 237–8. They probably got back to Paris on 3 Sept. Pound told his mother on [Thursday] 30 Aug. 1923 (Yale) that Ford was expected back on 'Monday'. See Bernard Poli, *Ford Madox Ford and the Transatlantic Review* (Syracuse, New York: Syracuse University Press, 1967), 18. *It Was the Nightingale*, 237–45 (on waiting for Joyce). McAlmon, *Being Geniuses Together*, revised, with supplementary chapters by Kay Boyle (London: The Hogarth Press, 1984), 221–2. *Drawn from Life*, 113.

5 *It Was the Nightingale*, 248–9, 255. Bowen, *Drawn from Life*, 110–11, says 'in the Place Médicis', but Bowen probably meant the Place Edmond Rostand, at the intersection of the Boulevard St Michel and the rue des Médicis.

6 Cadiou, 'Homicide par impudence: vie et mort des cités et ateliers de Montparnasse', *Connaissances de Paris et de la France*, 8–9 (Nov.–Jan. 1971–2), 91–3. Bowen, *Drawn from Life*, 111. Ford to Cathy Hueffer, 18 Sept. 1923: House of Lords Record Office. Pound to Homer Pound, 12 Sept. 1923: *Pound/Ford*, 71. Goldring, *South Lodge*, 139–42.

7 Bowen, *Drawn from Life*, 111–12; 114 supports Ford's story that Oliver proposed the review. *It Was the Nightingale*, 255–6.

8 *It Was the Nightingale*, 256–9. *Pound/Ford*, 71–3. *It Was the Nightingale*, 262–4, 282. Ford to Jepson and to Wells, both 14 Oct. 1923; to Coppard, 28 Sept. 1923: *Letters*, 153–4; 152–3. Poli, 23, 40, 19–20. Bowen, *Drawn from Life*, 114–15. Joyce to Harriet Shaw Weaver, 9 Oct. 1923: *Letters of James Joyce*, ed. Stuart Gilbert (London: Faber and Faber, 1957), 203–4.

9 Poli, 20. Joseph Wiesenfarth, 'Fargobawlers: James Joyce and Ford Madox Ford', *Biography*, 14/2 (Spring 1991), 97. Noel Riley Fitch, *Sylvia Beach and the Lost Generation* (New York: Norton, 1983), 153. *It Was the Nightingale*, 266, 271, 276, 266–7, 274 (one of the photographs taken at this meeting with Quinn shows Ford slung in the chair: see Judd, *Ford Madox Ford*, facing p. 296—though his caption about a review conference is misleading: the occasion was a reception for Quinn, and the *transatlantic* had not yet been founded), 283–95. 'A Portrait of Ford Madox Ford: Unpublished Letters from the Ford–Foster Friendship', ed. Janis and Richard Londraville, *English Literature in*

Transition, 33/2 (Feb. 1990), [180]–207—henceforth 'Londraville'. (Poli, 21, shows that the fear about Harris was probably justified.)

10 Ford to Wells, 14 Oct. 1923: *Letters*, 154. *It Was the Nightingale*, 295–6, 263. Stein, *The Autobiography of Alice B. Toklas* (London: John Lane: The Bodley Head, 1933), [268]. Bowen, *Drawn from Life*, 115, 110. Mizener, 328, 579, n. 10. Poli, 21–2. Ford told Gertrude Stein on 18 Sept. 1924 he had lost over 100,000 frs.: *Letters*, 162–3. Since the review was still losing money at that date, the figure is consistent with the 120,000 frs he mentioned to Jeanne Foster (and which, according to his calculations, would have been equivalent to about $6,000 or £1,200), 26 Mar. 1925: Londraville, 189. Foster later told Poli (21–2) she thought Quinn had given Ford $2,000 in 1923 and then a later sum. But this does not square with B. L. Reid's account, in *The Man from New York* (New York: Oxford University Press, 1968), 615. The exchange rates at the time were: £1 = 74 frs; £1 = $4.55; therefore $1 = 16.26 frs: *The Times* (1 Oct. 1923), 21. Ford said Quinn had stipulated that 'the *Review* should be turned into a limited company according to French law. It was this that really proved the undoing of the *Review*. The charges for founding and registering that company exhausted nearly half our original capital, and the exasperation and minute formalities insisted on by M^c L—— [the lawyer] caused me more labours and loss of time than all the rest of the *Review* together': *It Was the Nightingale*, 297. Poli, 21–2, says no legal documents concerning either the review or the company can be found, and that the company 'probably never had any legal existence'.

11 Poli, 25, 43 (quoting Bird to Poli, 10 Nov. 1961).

12 Ford to Coppard, 28 Sept. 1923: *Letters*, 152–3. Eliot to Ford, 14 Aug. and 4 Oct. 1923. See *The Waste Land: A Facsimile and Transcript of the Original Drafts Including the Annotations of Ezra Pound*, edited by Valerie Eliot (London: Faber and Faber, 1971), 129. (There are three other letters from Eliot to Ford at Cornell: 2 and 4 Feb., and 11 May 1923.) Eliot published Ford's essay 'From the Grey Stone' in the *Criterion*, 2 (Oct. 1923), 57–76 (it became the last chapter of *A Mirror to France*). Ford to Jepson, 14 Oct. 1923: *Letters*, 153. Ford to Flint, 15 Oct. 1923: *Reader*, 485. Ford to Wells, 14 Oct. and 15 Nov. 1923: *Letters*, 154, 157–8. Ford to Bertram, 16 Oct. 1923: cited by Poli, 30. (Bertram contributed a London art column to the review.) Ford to Goldring, 15 Oct. 1923: Goldring, *South Lodge*, 142–3, implies that Goldring is to send a contribution. Pound to Lewis, 7 Oct. [1923]: *Pound/Lewis*, ed. Timothy Materer (London: Faber and Faber, 1985), 137–8. Lewis to Eliot, n.d. [but Oct.–Nov. 1923]: *The Letters of Wyndham Lewis*, ed. W. K. Rose (London: Methuen, 1963), 137–8.

13 Ford to Jepson, 15 Sept. 1921. 'Joseph Conrad', *John O'London's Weekly*, 6 (10 Dec. 1921), 323. *'Mr. Conrad's Writing', *Spectator Literary Supplement*, 123 (Supplement to 17 Nov. 1923), 744, 746; this is the essay Ford refers to in a letter to Martin Armstrong (associate literary editor of the *Spectator*), (29 Nov. 1923: *Letters*, 158–60) in which he says he 'wrote the article to oblige Mrs. [Amabel, wife of Clough] Williams Ellis because I promised her a long time ago that I would review something for the Spectator'. Ford to Conrad, 7 Oct. 1923: Yale. Conrad to Ford, 13 Oct./18 Nov. 1923. This letter has been the source of considerable confusion. Conrad wrote the first version to Ford on 13 Oct. (original now at Yale). Ford printed the original, which was then in his possession, in *Return to Yesterday*, 196–7 (from which my quotations of the first paragraph are taken). When he asked if he could quote a paragraph in the review, Conrad typed him an expanded text on 18 Nov., adding a holograph note before and after it. (This is the version that Ford reproduced in *Joseph Conrad*, facing p. 11.) Jean-Aubry (*Joseph Conrad: Life and Letters*, 2 vols. (London: Heinemann, 1927), ii. 323) evidently combined the two, and confused matters further by adding the date 23 Oct.

1923. John H. Morey, 'Joseph Conrad and Ford Madox Ford: A Study in Collaboration', unpublished dissertation (Cornell University: 1960), 222, wonders whether Conrad wrote the revised version on 23 Oct. instead of 18 Nov. But there is no evidence that he did: it is more likely that Jean-Aubry mis-transcribed the 13th Oct. as the 23rd. See Harvey, 63; and Mizener, 329, 580, n. 12. The quotation in the indented paragraph is taken from Ford's transcription of the original version sent to Conrad for approval in the undated letter quoted below.

14 *Return to Yesterday*, 204–5. Ford to Conrad [n.d., but between 7 and 13 Oct. 1923]: Yale.

15 Ford to Hardy, 21 Oct. 1923: Dorset County Museum. Hardy to Ford, 18 Oct. 1923: Poli, 32. Prospectus, Nov. 1923, reproduced by Goldring, *South Lodge*, 143–6. An almost identical version dated Dec. 1923 is reproduced by Poli, 37–41, who also reproduces the title-page [38].

16 Eliot's letter was printed in 'Communications', *transatlantic review*, 1/1 (Jan. 1924), 95–6.

17 Steffens, to Laura Suggett, 4 Oct. 1923: Poli, 36. Carlos Drake, *Mr. Aladdin* (New York: Putnam's, 1947), 32: Poli, 37. Ford did publish Drake's stories in the *transatlantic*.

18 Ford to Jepson, 14 Oct. 1923: *Letters*, 153. Ford to Eliot, 8 Oct. 1923: *Reader*, 484–5. Bowen, *Drawn from Life*, 117. Ford to Goldring, 15 Oct. 1923: Goldring, *South Lodge*, 142–3; 'you infernal scoundrel' because Goldring had revealed in *Reputations* (London: Chapman and Hall, 1920), 217–19, how 'at least the first five or six numbers of *The English Review* were edited from the Shepherd's Bush Empire'. Reid became Mrs Robert Rodes in 1924. She helped find contributors and advertisers, and dealt with business when Ford wasn't available. 'One occasion when he was not available', she remembered, 'was when he learned that he must comply with a system of detailed records and accounts with books open for inspection and audit': letter to Poli, 15 Apr. 1964, quoted 28–9.

19 *'The Editor in France', *Poetry*, 23/2 (Nov. 1923), 91–2.

20 Ford to Conrad, 8 Nov. 1923: *Letters*, 156–7. Ford misremembered the title as 'Story of a Crime', and thought it had appeared in the first number of the *English Review* (in fact it came out in vol. 2, from Apr. to May 1909. Conrad to Ford, 10 Nov. 1923; 18 Feb. 1924; Ford to Conrad, 14 and 22 Feb. 1924; Conrad to Eric Pinker, 17 Feb. 1924: Yale.

21 Ford to Katharine Hueffer, 23 Nov. 1923: Poli, 35. She didn't write for the review, but suggested Geoffrey Coulter, who provided Dublin letters. On 31 Dec. 1923 Elsie Hueffer and Katharine moved from Charing to Helen'slea, in Appledore: they couldn't get the tenant out of Kitcat.

Chapter 11

1 Bowen, *Drawn from Life*, 116. The Russian firm, 'Imprimerie Cosmos', only printed the first number: Poli, 26. 'Editorial', *transatlantic review*, 1/2 (Feb. 1924), 66. Steffens, 'N.E.P.', *transatlantic review*, 1/2, 53–5. *It Was the Nightingale*, 300–4, 310. Bunting, in 'The Only Uncle of the Gifted Young' (Radio Transcript), 9. Poli, 26, 64. Ford to Coppard, 1 Dec. 1923: *Letters*, 160–1. 'Communications', *transatlantic review*, 1/1 (Jan. 1924), 94–6: see Poli, 54–5. A dummy 'Preliminary Number' was prepared, which includes interesting variant passages from *Some Do Not . . .*: Princeton. See Poli, 42; Frank MacShane, 'A Conscious Craftsman: Ford Madox Ford's Manuscript Revisions', *Boston University Studies in English*, 5 (Autumn 1961), 178–84; and *The Presence of Ford Madox Ford*, pp. xvi, 180–2. Goldring, *The Nineteen Twenties* (London: Nicholson & Watson, 1945), 195.

2 'Communications', *transatlantic review*, 1/1 (Jan. 1924), 93. See Poli, 147–62 (exp. 147). Mizener, 331–2.

3 Poli, 45. *It Was the Nightingale*, 298, 276. Ford compresses the time-scheme, saying that Bird offered the office on the day of the meeting with Quinn (12 October). Poli, 25, suggests Ford and his staff moved to the quai d'Anjou in December. But Ford to Conrad, 18 Jan. 1924 (Yale), says he only noticed the copy of *The Rover* Conrad had sent him 'just this minute when we were moving the office'. Ford's editorial for the second number gives the date of the move as 1 Jan. 1924 (74). Bowen, *Drawn from Life*, 117. Ford, Introduction to Hemingway, *A Farewell to Arms* (New York: The Modern Library, 1932), pp. ix–xx (pp. x–xi). *It Was the Nightingale*, 305–6.

4 Bowen, *Drawn from Life*, 119–20. She says they left Oliver's cottage 'After about three months' (i.e. Dec.); a dating accepted by Mizener, 579, n. 8. But *The Autobiography of William Carlos Williams* (New York: Random House, 1951), 185, 200, says he went to a party there in Jan. 1924. And Ford to Mrs Huddleston, 16 Jan. 1924 (Texas) has Bowen 'away house hunting' in the new year.

5 Ford to Mrs Huddleston, 16 Jan. 1924: Texas. Goldring, *South Lodge*, 147–64, has a chapter on 'Mary and Cecil' (147). Bowen, *Drawn from Life*, 121–2. Loeb, *The Way it Was* (New York: Criterion 1959), 207–8. As Mizener, 579, n. 6, notes, there is another version of the story (though also based on Bowen's testimony, spoken to Jean Rhys) in Rhys's *Quartet* (Harmondsworth: Penguin, 1973), 40–1. Huddleston, *Bohemian Literary and Social Life in Paris* (London: Harrap, 1928), 143, implies that drunken fights were regular occurrences at the Fords' Boulevard Arago parties. Ford, letter to the editor of the *American Mercury* [Nov. 1936]: *Letters*, 265. Williams, *Autobiography*, 194–5. Loeb, *The Way it Was*, 202. McAlmon and Boyle, *Being Geniuses Together* (London: The Hogarth Press, 1984), 167. Mizener, 332.

6 Mizener, 333. Juliet Soskice to Frank Soskice, 28 Jan. 1924 (House of Lords Record Office), says she has written to Ford. Ford to Katharine, 29 Jan. 1924. If Ford was still in contact with Christina at this date he was probably not subsequently. According to Hugh Kenner she told a scholar 'that her father had been dead to her since 1924': 'The Tradition of Intelligence', *National Review*, 23 (1971), 539–40. The significance of the date is unclear, though it may be due to the fact that Elsie Hueffer brought another suit against Violet Hunt after Hunt wrote to the *Weekly Westminster* (19 Jan. 1924), 388, correcting an error in their list of Prize Poems: 'My husband never published a book called "From Ireland and other Poems".' Hunt, who had signed herself 'Violet Hunt Hueffer', had to pay costs, and the judge made a perpetual injunction restraining her from calling herself Mrs Hueffer (see Goldring, *South Lodge*, 128–9, though he misdates the *Times* report, which was published on 10 Feb. 1925). Hunt tried to persuade Ford (through Ethel Colburn Mayne) to publish a statement in the newspapers saying they were married. Ford said he would be willing to write saying that Hunt had 'every moral right to consider herself Mrs Hueffer'; but he was not to be fooled into asserting her legal right, nor to say that she *was* Mrs Hueffer: 5 May 1924. Ford to Cathy Hueffer, 30 Jan. 1924: House of Lords Record Office. Conrad to Eric Pinker, 4 and 12 Feb. 1924: Jocelyn Baines, *Joseph Conrad* (London: Weidenfeld & Nicolson, 1960), 432–3. Ford to Katharine, 15 Mar. 1924. Cathy Hueffer to Frank Soskice, 4 Feb. 1924: House of Lords Record Office. The portrait is in the possession of Oliver Soskice, and is illustrated following p. 288. Joyce to Quinn, 5 Feb. 1924: *Letters of James Joyce*, ed. Gilbert (London: Faber & Faber, 1957), 209–10.

7 *It Was the Nightingale*, 300. Poli, 63–4. [Ford], 'Chroniques: I', *transatlantic review*, 1/4 (Apr. 1924), 200–1. 'Literary Causeries: II. Vill Loomyare', *Chicago Tribune Sunday*

Magazine (Paris) (24 Feb. 1924), 3. Joyce told McAlmon: 'Ford has come so often to the well and talked about support given me in the past that I have consented to give him the four masters bit (which is only a sidepiece) for his next number. The review is very shabby in my opinion': [n.d. but early 1924]: *Letters of James Joyce*, 208–9. Was Joyce wary of being flattered by Ford? 'You've soft a say with ye, Flatter O'Ford', he writes in *Finnegans Wake* (London: Faber & Faber, 1964), 512. Huddleston, *Bohemian Literary and Social Life in Paris*, 139, 264. Huddleston was a representative official Englishman in another sense. His resemblance to Shakespeare's 'portraits', and his frequenting of Shakespeare & Company, got him 'facetiously known as "Mr Shakespeare"'. He recorded how Ford kept up the joke when Pound's mother-in-law, Olivia Shakespear, visited Paris, by introducing them: 'You cannot have met for centuries. Mrs Shakespeare [*sic*]—Mr Shakespeare', 252–3. Poli, 73–4. Joyce to Harriet Shaw Weaver, 8 Feb. and 24 Mar. 1924: *Letters of James Joyce*, 210–13.

8 Hemingway knew of Ford by 1922, when he told Harriet Monroe (on 16 Nov.) that Ford was about to arrive in Paris; twelve days later he was in Lausanne, writing to ask his wife if she had written to the Ford Madox Fords yet; he had met Ford by 10 Feb. 1924, when he told Pound he had 'discounted Ford's report that you were expecting us to occupy [Pound's flat] until your return': *Selected Letters*, 72–4, 110–11. Hemingway to Stein and Toklas, 9 Nov. 1923: *Selected Letters*, 100–3 (103). *It Was the Nightingale*, 267, 272–3. Ford also described Hemingway's shadow-boxing, 'balancing on the point of his toes, feinting at my head with hands as large as hams and relating sinister stories of Paris landlords', in his introduction to *A Farewell to Arms* (New York: The Modern Library, 1932), pp. ix–xx (p. xiv). Mizener, 580–1, n. 22.

9 Hemingway to Pound, 17 Mar. 1924: *Selected Letters*, 113. 'Literary Causeries: VIII: So She Went into The Garden', *Chicago Tribune Sunday Magazine* (Paris) (6 Apr. 1924), 3, 11. Gertrude Stein, *The Autobiography of Alice B. Toklas* (New York: Harcourt, Brace and Co., 1933), 271. The tea was on 10 Apr.: Carlos Baker, *Ernest Hemingway: A Life Story* (London: Collins, 1969), 161.

10 *Autobiography of Alice B. Toklas*, 263–6. *It Was the Nightingale*, 161–2. Poli, 71. Stein and Toklas were in England from 5 July to 15 Oct. 1914: see John Malcolm Brinnin, *The Third Rose: Gertrude Stein and Her World* (London: Weidenfeld and Nicolson, 1960), 208, 215. Hemingway to Stein, 17 Feb. 1924: *Selected Letters*, 111–12. Ford to Stein, 18 Sept. 1924: *Letters*, 162–3. Stein to Carl Van Vechten, 17 Mar. 1924: quoted by Donald Gallup, 'The Making of *The Making of Americans*', *The New Colophon*, iii (New York: Crawford, 1950), 54, 58–63, 66 (59, 61). As Poli, 72, argues, Ford's comment in 'Chroniques', 'Editorial', *transatlantic review*, 1/5 (May 1924), 350: '[. . .] Miss Stein's work will better bear division than the story of Mr. Coppard and, fortunately, Miss Stein kindly allows us to divide her up [. . .]' proves that Ford thought it *might* have been possible to publish the whole work in one issue.

11 Ford to Foster, 22 Feb 1924: Londraville, 186–7. *It Was the Nightingale*, 329. 'Literary Causeries: XII: On Causeries as Such', *Chicago Tribune Sunday Magazine* (Paris) (4 May 1924), 3. 'Literary Causeries: I: The Younger American Writers', *Chicago Tribune Sunday Magazine* (Paris) (17 Feb 1924), 3. 'Literary Causeries: X: Mystifications', *Chicago Tribune Sunday Magazine* (Paris) (20 Apr. 1924), 3; 'Did Wells Read [Edouard] Rod', *Chicago Tribune Sunday Magazine* (Paris) (4 May 1924), 7. *Literary Causeries: XIII: The Play's the Thing . . .', *Chicago Tribune Sunday Magazine* (Paris) (11 May 1924), 3, 10. 'Literary Causeries: II: Vill Loomyare', *Chicago Tribune Sunday Magazine* (Paris) (24 Feb. 1924), 3. 'Literary Causeries: IV: Escape . . .', *Chicago Tribune Sunday Magazine* (Paris) (9 Mar. 1924), 3, 11.

12 'Literary Causeries: IX: Zoe Mou, Sas Agapo' and 'XII: On Causeries as Such', *Chicago Tribune Magazine* (Paris) (13 Apr. and 4 May 1924), 3, 11; Ford to Conrad, 21 May 1924: Yale. Mizener, 337. *The March of Literature*, 714–15.

13 'Literary Causeries: VII: Pullus ad Margaritam . . .', *Chicago Tribune Sunday Magazine* (Paris) (30 Mar. 1924), 3, 11. 'Communications', *transatlantic review*, 1/1 (Jan. 1924), 97.

14 'Preface' to *Transatlantic Stories* (London: Duckworth [1926]), pp. vii–xxxi (p. xxv). Ford to Conrad [n.d., but written on the verso of a letter from Victor Llona to Ford, 16 Apr. 1924].

15 Ford to W. H. Thompson, 5 Feb. 1926: *Letters*, 166–8. Jessie Conrad to Eric Pinker, 30 Apr. 1924: quoted by Najder, *Joseph Conrad*, 487–8, 607, n. 262. 'Stocktaking [. . .] X.: The Reader', *transatlantic review*, 2/5 (Nov. 1924), 502–3. Ford doesn't name the family: he says he was 'the casual adult in the house, say a not very esteemed uncle'. But Oliver Soskice has confirmed that his grandfather had this argument with Ford. Ford says it was 'last Spring'; as he was in the South of France in the spring of 1923, he must mean 1924. *Daily Mail* (25 Apr. 1924), 14; 'C.M.', *Manchester Guardian* (25 Apr. 1924), 7; Ralph Strauss, *Bystander*, 82 (7 May 1924), 409; *English Review*, 39 (July 1924), 148–9; *TLS* (24 Apr. 1924), 252. The *Daily Express* (3 May 1924) (on inconclusiveness and lack of moral); Gerald Gould, *Saturday Review*, 137 (17 May 1924), 512 ('I have had a nightmare. I have been lost in a strange country, full of fantastic emotion and desperate incident [. . .] I have conversed with people whose conversation seemed incoherent as their motives seemed incredible [. . .] His gifts are amazing: but he insists upon wasting them'); *Punch*, 147 (2 July 1924), 26 ('no definite conclusion [. . .] some of the characters are also extremely unpleasant'). These (and other) reviews can all be found in Harvey's bibliography. *L. P. Hartley wrote a perceptive, ambivalent review in the *Spectator*, 132 (3 May 1924), 720: 'a bewildering book [. . .] no writer was ever more self-conscious [. . .] fascinates while it baffles [. . .] It is a triumph of Mr. Ford's method to have made his portrayal of Tietjens moving and organic [. . .] We find it hard to believe that the War and the years before the War produced the colours and patterns Mr. Ford's kaleidoscope gives them; that they were as wicked or as witty or as wrong-headed. But we are sorry when the pageant comes to an end.' The book was less widely reviewed when it was published in America in Oct. *It Was the Nightingale*, 326, says the American edition sold 'relatively little'. The sales figures for the Seltzer first American edition aren't known. But the A. & C. Boni royalty statements (at Cornell) show that after they took it over, they sold 926 copies by 30 June 1928; whereas the Grosset and Dunlap cheap reprint had sold 6,000 copies by then.

16 'Chroniques: I: Thus to Re-Visit', *transatlantic review*, 1/6 (June 1924), 468–73. 'Literary Causeries: I. The Younger American Writers', *Chicago Tribune Sunday Magazine* (Paris) (17 Feb. 1924), 3. 'Preface', *Transatlantic Stories*, pp. vii–xxxi (pp. xxx–xxxi). See Poli, 61. Pound to Ford, 26 May [1921]: *Pound/Ford*, 59.

17 'Chroniques: I: Editorial', *transatlantic review*, 1/2 (Feb. 1924), 69. A. J. P. Taylor, *English History 1914–1945* (Oxford: Clarendon Press, 1965), 214–16. 'Chroniques: I: Thus to Re-Visit', *transatlantic review*, 1/6 (June 1924), 468. *'The Passing of Toryism', *McNaughts's Monthly*, 5/6 (June 1926), 174–6. Gorman, 'Ford Madox Ford: A Portrait in Impressions', *Bookman* (New York), 67 (Mar. 1928), 59. 'Those Were the Days', *Imagist Anthology*, p. xv. *A Mirror to France*, 71–2. Cole, *Growing Up Into Revolution* (London: Longmans, Green and Co, 1949), 127–8.

18 Poli, 59. *It Was the Nightingale*, 311. Preface to *Transatlantic Stories*, p. xxiv.

19 Hemingway, *The Sun Also Rises* (New York: Scribner's, 1926), Bk. I, ch. 3. *Pound/Ford*,

75. Hemingway to Pound, n.d.: *Selected Letters*, 114–16; Baker dates it *c*.2 May, but it was probably written later, since Ford was in London in May: 2 May is the earliest possible date; if Ford's recollection of seeing Pinker and Conrad on the 9th and 10th is correct, then Hemingway's letter must date from 10 May at the earliest. Hemingway's suspicion about pseudonyms presumably refers to the piece by 'R. Edison Page' on 'Recent English Novels', *transatlantic review*, 1/5 (May 1924), 365–6, which seemed to be replying to what Poli calls Hemingway's 'childishly vulgar attack on critics—described as "eunuchs of literature" [which] would be almost pointless if it were not directed at Ford himself'. (Hemingway, letter 'And to the United States', 1/5 (May 1924), 355–7.) 'Page' mentions 'four novelists of real importance' writing for the English of the time: Conrad, Ford, Douglas, and Wells. And he says: 'The only recent novel of vigour and charm and truth to English life is . . .'. Mizener, 335, rightly says this would have been understood as an allusion to *Some Do Not . . .* , then being serialized in the review. But the wrongly asserts what Poli, 78–9, and Hemingway wrongly suspected in thinking the pseudonym was Ford's. It was Edgar Jepson's, for whose name it is an almost perfect anagram. (Jepson's *Memories of an Edwardian* (London: Martin Secker, 1938), cites other work published under this pseudonym: 308, 311.) However, Hemingway's suspicion may have had other foundations: in the Preface to *Transatlantic Stories*, pp. xxiii, xxvi, Ford confessed to submitting one of his own pieces to the review anonymously. Preface to *Transatlantic Stories*, p. xvi. 'Chroniques: I', *transatlantic review*, 1/4 (Apr. 1924), 200; the poem is 'At the Fairing'; there are typescripts at Cornell and the House to Lords Record Office. Pound to Ford, 7 May 1924: Texas. Lindberg-Seyersted and Henderson, '*Pound/Ford*: Addenda and Corrections', *Paideuma*, 14/1 (Spring 1985), 121–2. The published text is reprinted in *Pound/Ford*, 77, and varies in many details from the original.

20 Ford to Conrad, 22 Feb. 1924: Yale. See Londraville, 185–7. Pound to Ford, 7 May 1924. Poli, 95–6, prints a copy of a letter, presumably drafted by Ford and sent to all the subscribers, but in this case signed by Bowen (probably confirming that Ford was in London on that date), to Gertrude Stein, 9 May 1924. Ford to Stein, 18 Sept. 1924, mentions her shares (*Letters*, 162–3). A later letter to Stein, 24 Nov. 1924 (Yale), lists the shareholders (which disproves Poli's idea, 126, n. 39, that Pound and Bird were not shareholders but only on the editorial board). *It Was the Nightingale*, 331, mentions the Duchesse de Clermont-Tonnerre, but she is not listed in the letter; Poli, 97 n., suggests Ford had confused her with Mrs Romaine Brooks—both women were friends of Natalie Barney. Ford to Jeanne Foster, 26 Mar. 1925, says that Friend and his wife put in just under 40,000 frs (about $2,100 or £490)—about the same amount as Quinn's contribution: Londraville, 189–90. The exchange rate on 1 July 1924 was 1 fr = 5.28 cents; and £1 = $4.32. Ford wrote to Foster (22 Feb. 1924) about the possibility of Jean Starr Untermeyer buying shares; but again, Ford doesn't list her as a shareholder in Nov.: Londraville, 186–7. Ford to Conrad, 21 May 1924: Yale. *It Was the Nightingale*, 336–7. Mizener, 336. Ford to Joyce, 29 July 1924; to Monroe Wheeler, 24 Nov. 1924: *Letters*, 161–3. Bird to Poli, 10 Nov. 1961, quoted by Poli, 99. Pound to Homer Pound [June 1924]: *Pound/Ford*, 78.

21 Conrad to Ford, 22 May 1924; Ford to Conrad, 31 May 1924; Yale. *Return to Yesterday*, 207; he calls the boat the *France*, but the letter to Conrad is written 'à bord' the 'Paquebot "Paris"' ', a ship in the Transatlantique line. Ford arranged for *Romance* to be translated by Marc Chadourne for the Paris publisher Simon Kra; it was published as *L'Aventure* in 1926. Ford told Conrad: 'I have just signed a contract with Kra for the translation of six of my novels [. . .] I am making the translation of the three modern

novels myself and those of the historical ones in collaboration with Soupault' (3 Apr. 1924: Yale); see Harvey, 16, for a variant version. None of these translations were published. Kra's records were destroyed in the war, so the contract cannot be verified. However, a manuscript (but no proofs) of Ford's own translation of about a quarter of *The Good Soldier* has survived; the fact that the first two (of 37) pages are typed on *transatlantic review* stationery shows that Ford was doing some work on the translation in 1924, though he later said that he had begun it in Bécourt-Bécordel Wood in July 1916: *Return to Yesterday*, 429. See Sondra Stang and Maryann De Julio, 'The Art of Translation: Ford's "Le Bon Soldat"', *Contemporary Literature*, 30/2 (Summer 1989), [263]–79. However, Ford to Jeanne Foster, 26 Mar. 1925, proves he hadn't finished the translation by that date, let alone received proofs: Londraville, 190. The second edition of *The Good Soldier* wasn't published until the spring of 1927, so 1924 is too early for those proofs. Could he have meant the proofs of the American edition of *Some Do Not . . .* , the story of his other good soldier? Ford to Sylvia Beach, 12 and 20 Jan. 1923 (Princeton), show Ford trying to get copies of *The Good Soldier* from Lane, presumably for translation purposes. Ford told William Bradley that *Some Do Not . . .* was to go to Kra; 25 Jan. 1925: *Reader*, 487–8. Ford suggested to Jean Rhys that she might do one of the translations: Carole Angier, *Jean Rhys* (London: André Deutsch, 1990), 135. Conrad was still keeping his distance in his last letter to Ford (24 May 1924: Yale). He wouldn't sign the agreement with Kra that Ford sent, but said 'I have nothing to do with it'; this was ostensibly because he had already said he was happy to give Ford all the rights for translations of their collaborations; but it also suggests (as indeed does his ceding of the translation rights) that he wanted to have nothing to do with anything Fordian.

22 'Chroniques: I: Editorial', *transatlantic review*, 2/1 (July 1924), 94–8. 'Chroniques: III: And from the United States', *transatlantic review*, 2/2 (Aug. 1924), 209–13, *It Was the Nightingale*, 328, 333.

23 *It Was the Nightingale*, 332–4. Rascoe, *A Bookman's Day Book* (New York: Liveright, 1929), 257–9: the lunch was on 13 June; the tea on the 24th. Ford told Rascoe of an 'unusual experience': 'Some one had given him a card to a certain club, and by mistake he had gone into another club, across the street. Ford did not learn until that afternoon and quite by accident, that he was putting up at the wrong club'. Markham Harris, 'A Memory of Ford Madox Ford', *Prairie Schooner*, 29 (Winter 1955), 252–4.

24 Hemingway to Pound, 19 July 1924: *Selected Letters*, 118–19. Poli, 105. *It Was the Nightingale*, 309–10 (implying that Bunting was the first poet of his acquaintance to be expelled). Besides the Baroness, the August issue contained 'Three Poems' by Bryher; more of Gertrude Stein's serial; a story, 'In the Garden', by Dorothy Richardson; William Carlos Williams on McAlmon's prose; a letter from Erik Satie, 'Cahiers d'un Mammifère'; and Dos Passos' story 'July'. 'I greatly admired Ford Madox Ford', wrote Dos Passos: 'so when he asked me for a story to publish [. . .] I went to considerable trouble to fish out *July* and to rewrite it': Poli, 105.

25 '[Chroniques:] III: And from the United States', *transatlantic review*, 2/2 (Aug. 1924), 209–13. Ford was also annoyed at Hemingway's failure to follow (or to notice) his instructions. In the editorial for the July number, which he had left for Hemingway to finish, he had ended a paragraph on the essays to be included with the words 'Mr. etc . . . Hemingway continue . . .', so that Hemingway could describe the issue once the contents had been finalized. Instead, Ford's note was printed as it stood: see 'Chroniques: I', 2/1 (July 1924), 98; and '[Chroniques:] Editorial', 2/3 (Sept. 1924), 298. The Paris *Chicago Tribune* thought this pan-American number one of the best-

edited (10 Aug. 1924): Harvey, 345. Poli says the effect was to try to turn the *transatlantic* into an American little magazine (108).

26 Ford to Powys [n.d., but added to Powys to Ford, 26 May 1924: UCLA]. Ford to Geoffrey Wells, 24 July 1924: Texas.

27 Bowen, *Drawn from Life*, 127–9, 132–3. 'A Memory of Ford Madox Ford', 254: Mrs Murphy may have been the beautiful Katherine Murphy mentioned in *Being Geniuses Together*, 92. Ford to Pound, 14 July 1924: published by Brita Lindberg-Seyersted and Archie Henderson, '*Pound/Ford*: Addenda and Corrections', *Paideuma*, 14/1 (Spring 1985), 123. Hemingway to Stein and Toklas, 9 Aug. 1924: *Selected Letters*, 120–1; see 112n. for the death of Quinn. Reid, *The Man from New York* (New York: Oxford University Press, 1968), 630. Asch, transcribed from a radio broadcast on KPFA, Berkeley, 21 Nov. 1961: Poli, 116–17.

28 Hemingway to Stein and Toklas, 9 Aug. 1924: *Selected Letters*, 120–1.

29 Ford to Stein, 18 Sept. 1924: *Letters*, 162–3. Marjorie Rodes to Poli, 15 Apr. 1964: quoted by Poli, 115n. Hemingway to Stein and Toklas, 15 Aug., 14 Sept., and 10 Oct. 1924: *Selected Letters*, 122–3, 125–8. *It Was the Nightingale*, 342. Preface to *Transatlantic Stories* (dated 'June, 1925'), pp. xxvi, xx.

Chapter 12

1 Bowen, *Drawn from Life*, 122–4. Ford to Scott-James, 3 Feb. 1925: *Letters*, 165–6. *Joseph Conrad*, 31–4; p. 6 says the book was started at 'GUERMANTES, SEINE ET MARNE, *August*'; p. 254 identifies the paper as the *Daily Mail*, and identifies the station as in the Parisian suburbs. Conrad died on 3 Aug. The *Daily Mail* report appeared the following day, on 9–10.

2 '[Chroniques:] Editorial', *transatlantic review*, 2/3 (Sept. 1924), 297.

3 [Wilbur Cross, editor of the *Yale Review*] to Ford, 23 Nov. 1920 and 17 May 1921, expressly asked for a discussion of Conrad's 'personality'. The essay Ford wrote for him was published as the Conrad chapter in *Thus to Revisit*, so the *Yale* asked for another essay, which they got: 'A Haughty and Proud Generation.' Ford to the Editor, *Yale Review*, n.d. [but *c*. early Nov. 1920]: Yale.

4 Ford to Jepson, 15 Sept. 1921: Harvey, 62. Putnam, *Paris Was Our Mistress*, 119, 121. Ford to the editor of *The American Mercury* [Nov. 1936]: *Letters*, 266. 'Stevie and Co.', *New York Essays*, 24–5.

5 Ford to [Henry] Forman, 27 Aug. 1924: UCLA.

6 *Joseph Conrad*, 251–6; he says he was writing the essay on a Sunday (which must be 10 Aug.), and that he saw the newspaper on Monday: which was 4 Aug.; can he not have noticed the Fordian coincidence of dates? He said he'd written it at 'fever-heat' in a Dec. 1926 inscription in a copy now at Princeton: Harvey, 62. He repeated the device of having a French appendix to an English book in *No Enemy*, but the dual effect is different there, since one of the chapters is a translation of the epilogue; whereas the effect in *Joseph Conrad* is of the French being too poignant to be bearable in translation. Keating's copy of *Joseph Conrad* is now at Yale. See *A Conrad Memorial Library: The Collection of George T. Keating* (New York: Doubleday, Doran, 1929), 422–3.

7 *Joseph Conrad*, 156–7, 13, 29, 147, 171. 'Great Writers' [unpublished third chapter of 'Towards a History of English Literature' Part II; 48. 'And on Earth Peace . . .', *New York Herald Tribune Books* (26 Dec. 1926), 1, 6.

8 Markham Harris, 'A Memory of Ford Madox Ford', *Prairie Schooner*, 29 (Winter 1955), 256–7. Mizener, 582, n. 5. Raymond Brebach, 'Conrad, Ford and the *Romance Poem*', *Modern Philology*, 81/2 (Nov. 1983), 169–72.

9 McAlmon and Boyle, *Being Geniuses Together* (London: The Hogarth Press, 1984), 164, 116. Ford objected to McAlmon's lack of selection: 'From a Paris Quay (II)', *New York Evening Post Literary Review* (3 Jan. 1925), 1–2; in the same piece, despite Hemingway's spite, Ford was still saying that: 'The best writer in America at this moment (though for the moment he happens to be in Paris) the most conscientious, the most master of his craft, the most consummate, is my young friend, Ernest Hemingway.' 'Conrad Supplement', *transatlantic review*, 2/3 (Sept. 1924) [325]–50. The other contributors were H-R Lenormand, Ethel Colburn Mayne, and Antoni Potocki. Poli, 114. Mizener, 340–1.

10 Hemingway, 'Pamplona Letter', *transatlantic review*, 2/3 (Sept. 1924), 300–2. Poli, 110–11. Mizener, 340. '[Chroniques] II: Paris Letter: Editorial', *transatlantic review*, 2/5 (Nov. 1924), 550. Rascoe, *We Were Interrupted* (Garden City, New York: Doubleday, 1947), 184–6 (185).

11 Goldring, *South Lodge*, 156. Baker, *Ernest Hemingway* (London: Collins, 1969), 183. Bowen, *Drawn from Life*, 129–30. The Bal du Printemps was the model for Braddocks' *bal musette* in ch. 3 of *The Sun Also Rises*. *Drawn from Life*, 129–30. Rhys, *Quartet* (Harmondsworth: Penguin, 1973), 54–5. Ford to Harold Loeb, 23 Oct. 1923 (Princeton), invites him to a meeting at Huddleston's flat to discuss starting an Anglo-American Club, since premises have become available (which might suggest that Ford was trying to preserve the *bal musette* from being clubbed). Nathan Asch said Ford started these dances 'to ingratiate himself' with the Friends (Poli, 117); but he had been giving large parties long before he met them.

12 Gorman, 'Ford Madox Ford: A Portrait in Impressions', *Bookman* (New York), 67 (Mar. 1928), 56–7. *Quartet*, 55. Rhys's use of the *bal musette*, and her portrait of Ford as Heidler in this novel are well-known (and discussed on pp. 282–99); but it hasn't been noticed that Ford doubles as Rolls. See Mizener, 344.

13 *Pound/Ford*, 74, 81. *Joseph Conrad*, 6. Poli, 120. *The Nature of a Crime* (London: Duckworth, 1924), 11. In *Return to Yesterday*, 192, Ford reiterated the point, observing that Conrad (who read Ford's preface and wrote one of his own to accompany it) had passed it for the press. Huddleston, *Bohemian Literary and Social Life in Paris*, 138; Huddleston, *In and About Paris* (London: Methuen, 1927), from the dedication of the book to Ford, pp. vii–ix.

14 '[Chroniques:] IV: Editorial', *transatlantic review*, 2/6 (Dec. 1924), 682. The episode does not figure in *It Was the Nightingale*'s account of the review, which one would expect it to if it had been significant. Ford could have been extrapolating from Hemingway's menacing language; or he may have taken it as the joke it sounds as if it may well have been. Hemingway to McAlman, c.15 Nov. 1924: *Selected Letters*, 133–4.

15 Poli, 127. Ford to Stein, 24 Nov. 1924 (Yale); Mizener, 343, says mid-Nov., but this letter shows it could not have been before the 25th. Ford to Wheeler, 24 Nov. 1924: *Letters*, 163–4.

16 See Poli, 51; Mizener, 331–2. Free-copies offer: 'Chroniques', 1/5 (May 1924), 351; Book Service, 2/1 (July 1924), 134; *Some Do Not . . .* offer: 'Paris Letter', 2/5 (Nov. 1924), 551. Noel Riley Fitch, *Sylvia Beach and the Lost Generation* (New York: W. W. Norton, 1983), 179–80. Preface to Rhys, *The Left Bank & Other Stories* (New York and London: Harper, 1927), 7–27 (24).

17 *It Was the Nightingale*, 314–15, 342–4. Poli, 129; 132, based on an interview with Asch, 17 Feb. 1963.

18 Ford to Coppard, 17 Feb. and 8[?] Mar. 1927: Texas (the first says 'Jonathan Capes', but Jonathan Cape was Coppard's publisher). Poli, 132. *It Was the Nightingale*, 156–7, gives Ford's account of Coppard's poverty and politics. Coppard's *It's Me, O Lord!*

(London: Methuen, 1957) confirms the gist. Ford, 'Half Pixie and Half Bird', *New York Herald Tribune Books* (27 Feb. 1927), 4. The one letter of Conrad's that Ford sold—the one published as frontispiece to *Joseph Conrad*—he said he had sold 'for the benefit of contributors to Transatlantic Tales [*sic*]': written on a folder at Princeton, quoted by Harvey, 63. Mizener, 581–2, n. 32. Some of this money might thus have gone to Coppard, which might be the basis of the 'dollar bills' in the story. Ford offered the letter for sale in a letter to James F. Drake, 24 Oct. 1927: *Reader*, 493.

19 Coppard to Ford, 9 Mar. 1927. Hemingway to Arnold Gingrich, 3 Apr. 1933: *Selected Letters*, 384–6. Biala to Max Saunders, 30 Jan. 1990.

20 'An Interview with Janice Biala', *The Presence of Ford Madox Ford*, 221.

21 *Coleridge's Poetical Works*, ed. Ernest Hartley Coleridge (Oxford: Oxford University Press, 1969), 319–23 (321). Southey later expanded the poem into 'The Devil's Walk': see *Poems of Robert Southey*, ed. Maurice Fitzgerald (London: Oxford University Press, 1909), 420–5 (421).

22 *TLS* (13 Nov. 1924), 727; Hugh l'A Fausset, *Manchester Guardian* (19 Nov. 1924), 7; Christopher Morley, *Saturday Review of Literature* (*SRL*), 1 (27 Dec. 1924), 415; *Dial*, 78 (Apr. 1925), 338; Louis Weitzenkorn, *New York World* (7 Dec. 1924), 8. The anonymous reviewer for the *New Statesman*, 24 (6 Dec. 1924), p. xvi, said: 'At first his method strikes the reader as rather tiresome and egotistic, but he soon finds he is getting a clearer conception of Conrad the man than any other book or essay has given him.' Mark Van Doren, 'First Glance', *Nation* (New York), 120 (14 Jan. 1925), 45, thought it 'surely one of the most conceited books ever published', but recognized shrewdly: 'Mr. Ford has developed his vanity as a vehicle for wit, or something like wit, so that it must be judged on literary, not personal, grounds.' Though he thought it failed here where *Thus to Revisit* had succeeded. For the full range of the reviews, see Harvey, 348–57.

23 Garnett, *Nation and Athenaeum*, 36 (6 Dec. 1924), 366, 368; *Weekly Westminster* (14 Feb. 1925), 473. Garnett's publication of Conrad's letter is discussed on pp. 332–3.

24 Edwin F. Edgett, *Boston Transcript* (13 Dec. 1924), 4. *Joseph Conrad*, 73, 19, 20. 'On Impressionism', *Poetry and Drama*, 2 (June 1914), 167. Carol Jacobs gives a provocative discussion of Ford's impressionism in 'Poor Timing', *Agenda*, 27/4–28/1 (Winter 1989–Spring 1990), 67–76.

25 *TLS* (4 Dec. 1924), 826. *Joseph Conrad*, 90–1. The story may have an element of truth. Ford says Conrad had been in 'the same hydrotherapie as that in which Maupassant died'. Conrad revisited the hydrotherapy spa at Champel-les-Bains outside Geneva in 1894. Maupassant had died in an asylum in Paris; but Conrad had been reading him avidly at Champel. See Owen Knowles, *A Conrad Chronology* (London, Macmillan, 1989), 18–19. Mizener, 342. See 534, n. 18, on the unreliability of Jessie Conrad's testimony. H. L. Mencken said Ford's 'footnote in the literature books' would depend on his collaboration with Conrad: *American Mercury*, 4 (Apr. 1925), 505–6. Burton Rascoe rebutted his argument the following year, saying that Ford was 'one of the best' living stylists if not the best, and that 'Conrad never came within miles of Ford's competence and ease in manipulating the resources of the English lauguage [. . .] it is open to question whether Conrad ever wrote a finer novel than [*No More Parades*]': 'Contemporary Reminiscences', *Arts and Decoration*, 24 (Feb. 1926), 57. In 'The Literary Life', *Contemporary Literature*, 30/2 (Summer 1989), 179, Ford urged young aspirants to find their Master, and 'live yourselves attendants upon their immortality'. Ford [to the editor of the *TLS*, n.d.].

26 *Joseph Conrad*, 188.

27 *The Flurried Years*, 204–5; Hunt's account corroborates Ford's account of the conversation and Conrad's anger as, 'his eyes darting fire', he asserted: 'I believe in the Divine Right of Kings.' *Joseph Conrad*, 20.

28 *Some Do not . . .*, 43; discussed further on pp. 262–3 below.

Chapter 13

1 Epigraph: Nietzsche, translation from J. P. Stern, *Nietzsche* (London: Fontana/Collins, 1978), 78; Lewis Gannett, *New York Herald Tribune*, 9 Apr. 1936. Lunn, **Switchback* (London: Eyre & Spottiswoode, 1948), 221–2.

2 Biala in conversation with Max Saunders, 9 Apr. 1994. Rexroth, introduction to **Buckshee* (Cambridge, Mass.: Pym-Randall Press, 1966), pp. xvii–xxii (p. xvii); the volume also includes a fine introduction by Robert Lowell, pp. xi–xiv. *The Rash Act*, 35.

3 Swinnerton, *The Georgian Literary Scene* (London: Dent; Everyman Library edition, 1938), 178. **Mackenzie, *My Life and Times*, 10 vols. (Chatto & Windus, 1963–71): iii. 16; iv. 199, 201; and viii. 159. 'Towards a History [. . .]', 2: the words italicized here were deleted.

4 *The Presence of Ford Madox Ford*, 218–19; Madox Brown's second wife was Emma Hill. Cannell, 'Portrait of a Kind Eccentric', *Providence Sunday Journal* (20 Sept. 1964), W-20. Max Webb, 'Ford Madox Ford's Nonfiction', unpublished dissertation (Princeton, 1972), 281.

5 Woolf to Hugh Walpole [8 Nov. 1931]: *A Reflection of the Other Person: The Letters of Virginia Woolf*, vol. iv, ed. Nigel Nicolson with the assistance of Joanne Trautmann (London: Chatto & Windus, 1978), 401–2. An editorial note cites *Thus to Revisit*; but Woolf's question about Ford's name-change makes *Return to Yesterday*, published on 2 Nov., almost certainly the book she was reading. Brigit Patmore, *My Friends When Young: The Memoirs of Brigit Patmore*, ed. Derek Patmore (London: Heinemann, 1968), 56. Anderson, 'Legacies of Ford Madox Ford', *Coronet*, 8 (Aug. 1940), 135–6. Dahlberg and Bishop, in *New Directions: Number Seven*, 467 and 462. Goldring, *The Last Pre-Raphaelite*, 251. Biala to Mizener, 25 June 1970.

6 *Return to Yesterday*, 418. *Mightier Than the Sword*, 282–3. The other versions are in 'On Impressionism', *Poetry and Drama*, 2 (Dec. 1914), 324; 'Thus to Revisit: IV. New Forms for the Old', *Piccadilly Review* (13 Nov. 1919), 6; *Thus to Revisit*, 139–40; *Return to Yesterday*, 417–19; *The March of Literature*, 583.

7 Kenner, 'Joyce's Anti-Selves', *Shenandoah*, 4/1 (Spring 1953), 33.

8 Williams, 'Mightier than Most Pens', *Time and Tide*, 19 (12 Mar. 1938), 350.

9 'Tradition and the Individual Talent': *Selected Essays*, third enlarged edn. (London: Faber, 1951), 21.

10 There is an unpublished story at Cornell which turns on a hypnotic sleight of hand, called 'Podmore's Brother'. The name 'Podmore' appears, sandwiched mysteriously between the names of Cicero and Napoleon, in a speech of Stephen's in *Ulysses* beginning 'Sounds are impostures': (Oxford: Oxford University Press, 1993), 578.

11 *Contacts* (London: Cassell, 1935), 11. Ford tells a similar story in **'The Game and Play of Golf', *Bystander*, 33 (7 Feb. 1912), 290–1, about doing 'the Buster in two', 'just before Christmas' 1911.

12 Snitow, 203. Lloyd Morris, 'A Remarkable Literary Figure of Our Era: Ford Madox Ford, Novelist, Poet; a Guide and Friend of Writers', *New York Herald Tribune Weekly Book Review* (22 May 1949), 1, 18. Ford was fond of citing Renan's remark that 'as soon as one begins to write about oneself one begins to "poetise"—ever so little, possibly, but still to poetise!': *Thus to Revisit*, 85. Markham Harris, 'A Memory of Ford Madox

Ford', 261, gives a good example of what he calls a characteristic 'nostalgic and semiapocryphal anecdote' about the kind of debate about literary technique that Wells dramatized in *Boon*. *Harold Loeb, 'Ford Madox Ford's *The Good Soldier*. A Critical Reminiscence', *London Magazine*, 3/9, NS (Dec. 1963), 65–73, writes well on Ford's poker-faced humour.

13 See e.g. Julian Maclaren-Ross, *London Magazine*, 4 (Aug. 1964), 88–95; repr. in *Hemingway: The Critical Heritage*, ed. Jeffrey Meyers (London: Routledge & Kegan Paul, 1982), 486. Bunting, 'Preface' to Ford's *Selected Poems* (Cambridge, Massachusetts: Pym-Randall Press, 1971), p. ix. *The Torrents of Spring* (London: Jonathan Cape, 1933), 102–3, 17. Carlos Baker, *Ernest Hemingway* (London: Collins, 1969), 199.

14 *A Moveable Feast (London: Jonathan Cape, 1964), 78–9.

15 Stella Bowen told Ford about Hemingway's treatment of them in *Fiesta*: 'He has touched me off rather nastily—rather on Jean's lines—So I feel very discouraged! Even you don't quite escape': 8 Feb. [1927]. Patmore, *Private History* (London: Cape, 1960), 99, 101.

16 Hemingway to Charles Fenton, 29 July 1952: *Selected Letters*, 776. Walter Lowenfels, 'The End Was Ugly', *American Dialog*, 3/2 (1966), 34–5. Mary McIntosh, in *The Presence of Ford Madox Ford*, 207. Bunting (Preface to *Selected Poems*, p. ix) said he wouldn't have recognized Hemingway's caricature if he hadn't named it. *A Moveable Feast*, p. 75.

17 Cannell, 'Portrait of a Kind Eccentric'. Mizener, 208.

18 27 Dec. 1931: *Pound/Ford*, 99–100.

19 See Robert Green's excellent discussion of Tietjens's theatricality: *Ford Madox Ford: Prose and Politics*, 138–9. The quotation is from p. 43 of the typescript of *Return to Yesterday* at Cornell.

Chapter 14

1 Epigraph: Hermann Hesse, *The Journey to the East*, tr. Hilda Rosner (London: Peter Owen, 1964), 44–5. 'Ford Madox Ford, Cook, Baron, Novelist, Brings Zest to Faculty': unidentified Michigan paper from late 1937; clipping from Olivet College Library. *'Epilogue', probably to *Women & Men*, though not published there; written while Ford was in the army, between Feb. 1917 and Jan. 1919: p. 13 of the manuscript at Princeton: see James Longenbach, 'Ford Madox Ford: The Novelist as Historian', *Princeton University Library Chronicle*. 45 (Winter 1984), 150–66.

2 'Literary Portraits—LIII.: The Muse of War', *Outlook*, 34 (12 Sept. 1914), 334–5. The manuscript of *'A Day of Battle' is dated 15 Sept. 1916; but it was not published until 1980, in a version edited by Sondra Stang in *Esquire*, 94 (Dec. 1980), 78–80; page references are to the revised version included in the *Reader*, 456–61.

3 *It Was the Nightingale*, 197; cf. *Joseph Conrad*, 192. *No More Parades*, 6. *A Man Could Stand Up*—, [pp. vi–vii]. Cf. *Great Trade Route*, 96. Aldington, *Death of a Hero* (London: Chatto & Windus, 1929), 256, also stressed the effect of 'worry'.

4 *The Marsden Case*, 305. *A Man Could Stand Up*—, [63]. Cf. Aldington, *Death of a Hero*, 395, 429.

5 'Epilogue', 13. Ford didn't fight in the Apr. 1917 battle when the Canadians took Vimy Ridge. But he may have been in the area with his Canadian Casual battalion in Feb. 1917; he was certainly quite near, when stationed at Abbeville in charge of German prisoners.

6 Jones, *In Parenthesis* (London: Faber and Faber, 1963), 164. In *The Good Soldier* Protestantism is traced back to the 'piece of paper' signed by Luther: 53. *It Was the*

Nightingale, 53, refers to the 'Scrap of Paper speech', Britain's answer to which was to declare war. Ford says the memorial tablet to the British dead in Notre Dame is 'the fitting tailpiece' to the answer to that speech—as if the war began and ended with a text. *No Enemy*, 162–3. This episode is discussed further on p. 417 above.

7 *A Mirror to France*, 183.

8 *It Was the Nightingale*, 14. See e.g. *Some Do Not* . . . , 111: 'In every man there are two minds that work side by side, the one checking the other.' *Reader*, 457. Cf. Ford's essay *'In Defence of the Looker-On', *Bystander*, 33 (14 Feb. 1912), 345–6.

9 *Return to Yesterday*, 375. As Moser observes, 212, Marwood did not die before the war but in May 1916—not long before the idea of using him occurs to Ford in the Salient. Was Ford thinking of how their friendship had died again around 1912? Or is it an impressionistic way of saying Marwood died before Ford went to the war? Either way, the comment suggests Ford had heard of Marwood's death before leaving for France.

10 *It Was the Nightingale*, 189–90.

11 *Some Do Not* . . . , 251. *Return To Yesterday*, 375: italics added.

12 See Moser's discussion of the tetralogy, 214–54, and esp. 217, on its engagement with 'highly charged memories' from Ford's youth onwards.

13 *Reader*, 459.

14 See Longenbach, 'Ford Madox Ford: The Novelist as Historian', 162.

15 Van Doren, quoted in 'Ford Madox Ford, *Parade's End*: The Story of an Old Book Newly Made, ed. Harold Strauss (New York: Knopf, 1950), 12. (There is a copy of this publisher's prospectus at Cornell.) *Ford Madox Brown*, 342. See e.g. E. V. Walter, 'The Political Sense of Ford Madox Ford', *New Republic*, 134 (26 Mar. 1956), 17–19; Mizener, 515; and Gene Moore, 'The Tory in a Time of Change: Social Aspects of Ford Madox Ford's *Parade's End*', *Twentieth Century Literature*, 28/1 (Spring 1982), 49–68.

16 *Return to Yesterday*, 81–2.

17 'Stocktaking [. . .] V', *transatlantic review*, 1/5 (May 1924), 323 n.

18 See 'Literary Portraits—XXXVIII.: Mr. W. H. Mallock and "Social Reform"', *Outlook*, 33 (30 May 1914), 751–2; 'Literary Portraits—XLVIII.: M, Charles-Louis Philippe and "Le Père Perdrix"', *Outlook*, 34 (8 Aug. 1914), 174–5; *When Blood is Their Argument*, 301.

19 *Return to Yesterday*, 76. Cf. Madox Brown to Shields, 16 Apr. [1886]: 'I believe the manufacturers look upon a good broad margin of starving workmen as the necessary accompaniment of cheap labour' (quoted in *Ford Madox Brown*, 376). Ford's Tory view also recalls Marwood's 'Actuarial Scheme' Ford published in the *English Review*. See Saunders, i. 251.

20 Green, *Ford Madox Ford: Prose and Politics*, 14. *The Soul of London*, 152. Conrad, Preface to *The Nigger of the 'Narcissus'*. 'Literary Portraits—XVIII.: Mr. A. G. Gardiner and "Pillars of Society"', *Outlook*, 33 (10 Jan. 1914), 46–7.

21 *Return to Yesterday*, 76. 'A Declaration of Faith' [signed 'Didymus'], *English Review*, 4 (Feb. 1910), 543–51.

22 *A Man Could Stand Up—*, 266. Snitow, 231, reads *Last Post* differently, arguing that 'The feudal system is not dead at all but only sleeping'.

23 *Return to Yesterday*, 75–6; cf. 87, and Ford to Bowen, 17 Nov. 1918 (on p. 56 above).

24 'Literary Portraits—XXXVIII.: Mr W. H. Mallock and "Social Reform"': 'the Tory party has always been the stupid party and now it is purely imbecile [. . .].'

25 'Literary Portraits—XLVIII.: M. Charles-Louis Philippe and "Le Père Perdrix"', *Outlook*, 34 (8 Aug. 1914), 174–5.

26 See Donald Davie, *Ezra Pound: Poet as Sculptor* (London: Routledge & Kegan Paul, 1965).

27 Bradbury, 'Introduction' to *Parade's End* (London: Everyman's Library, 1992), p. xx.

28 Compare 'Chroniques: I', *transatlantic review*, 2/1 (July 1924), 96–7, on how officers must know everything about their men. 'Literary Portraits—XI.: Mr. R. A. Scott-James and "The Influence of the Press"', *Outlook*, 32 (22 Nov. 1913), 718–19.

29 See Benjamin, 'The Work of Art in the Age of Mechanical Reproduction', in *Illuminations*, trans. Harry Zohn, ed. Hannah Arendt (London: Fontana, 1970), 242.

30 *Ford Madox Brown*, 331. *History*, 15.

31 See Saunders, i. 156, on *'progression d'effet'*. See *Provence*, 239–40, on the emotiveness of music's motion. See Walter Allen, 'Books in General', *New Statesman and Nation*, 31 (20 Apr. 1946), 285: 'Whether such a ruling class ever existed is not the question. What matters is that Ford imposes his own belief in it upon the reader; and he is helped by the very boldness of his conception [. . .]'; and Mizener, 371. Preface to *Collected Poems* [1913], 15–16. Camilla Haase, 'Serious Artists: The Relationship Between Ford Madox Ford and Ezra Pound', unpublished dissertation (Harvard University, 1984), 206, asks which came first: the experience Pound retailed in *Gaudier-Brzeska* (New York: New Directions, 1974), 86–7, of coming out of a metro train in Paris—which was to go into his haiku 'In A Station of the Metro'; or his reading of Ford's impression of the Shepherds Bush exhibition. Certainly Pound was impressed by Ford's impression, and referred to it in 'Mr Hueffer and the Prose Tradition in Verse': *Pound/Ford*, 19–20. The two renderings indeed have much in common. But with two such close literary friends, questions of influence and priority are not always clear-cut. Yet Pound's Paris experience presumably came first, since he dates it 'Three years ago', and the essay reprinted *in Gaudier-Brzeska* first appeared as 'Vorticism', *Fortnightly Review*, NS 96 (1 Sept. 1914), [461]–71. This would place it in 1911. Anyway, the poem was first published in 'Contemporania', *Poetry*, 2/1 (Apr. 1913), 1–12; whereas Ford's essays 'Impressionism—Some Speculations' (that were reworked into the Preface) didn't appear until the Aug. and Sept. issues of the same magazine. However, Pound might have known Ford's earlier essay on what he called 'the poetry of the normal', about the emotions aroused by seeing a crowd from the top of a bus outside a tube station: 'Literary Portraits.: XXIII.—The Year 1907', *Tribune* (28 Dec. 1907), 2.

32 *Great Trade Route*, 339–40, tells how he was moved by the singing of the men as his 'battalion was marching into the line' in the Somme. It was a situation that brought together two ideas that for Ford were already under the shadow of death: those of the crowd and art. He wrote of: 'we 678 men—who were soon to be not more than 215'. See Chapter 3, n. 14.

33 Rita Kashner, 'Tietjens' Education: Ford Madox Ford's Tetralogy', *Critical Quarterly*, 8 (1966), 150–63. W. H. Auden, 'Il Faut Payer', *Mid-Century*, 22 (Feb. 1961), 3–10; Ambrose Gordon, *The Invisible Tent: The War Novels of Ford Madox Ford* (Austin, Texas: University of Texas Press, 1964); Robert Andreach, *The Slain and Resurrected God: Conrad, Ford and the Christian Myth* (New York University Press, 1970); and Moser, 241–54 respectively.

34 Bradbury, 'Introduction', *Parade's End* (London: Everyman's Library, 1992), pp. xv, xii.

35 Tzvetan Todorov, *Mikhail Bakhtin: The Dialogical Principle* (Manchester University Press, 1986).

36 Bradbury, 'Introduction', *Parade's End* (London: Everyman's Library, 1992), pp. xxi, xix.

37 See *Some Do Not . . .* , 310; *No More Parades*, 115; *A Man Could Stand Up—*, 264; and *Last Post*, 131.

38 *No More Parades*, 256.

39 *No More Parades*, 250–2. Ford to Cathy Hueffer, 6 Sept. 1916: House of Lords Record Office. The inseparability of optimism and pessimism was a Fordian view too: 'idealist and cynic are one flesh', he wrote in *The Spirit of the People*, 171.

40 See *Some Do Not . . .* , 205, for example, on Valentine's pacifism.

41 See Stuart Sherman, 'Vanity Fair in 1924', *New York Herald Tribune Books* (16 Nov. 1924), 1–2; and John Colmer, *Coleridge to Catch-22: Images of Society* (London: Macmillan, 1978), 147.

42 *A Man Could Stand Up—*, 265. *Joseph Conrad*, 204–8.

43 Gordon, *The Invisible Tent*, 119. Lloyd Morris, 'Mr. Ford's Saga', *Saturday Review of Literature*, 3 (4 Dec. 1926), 365, praised Ford's 'superb sense of structure' in *A Man Could Stand Up—*: 'The war experiences of Tietjens form the central episode of the book. Mr Ford, with that extremely assured craftsmanship which one has come to take for granted in his work, has set them in frame [. . .] There are those of us, and I am one, who believe that he has carried the traditional English novel to its greatest formal achievement' (passages not quoted by Harvey).

44 *Thus to Revisit*, 29. Cf. *Mightier Than the Sword*, 150; *Provence*, 69; and *Great Trade Route*, [13].

45 *No More Parades*, 251. Ford queried Masterman on 5 Jan. 1917: 'I wonder where you stand in all these earthquakes?': *Letters*, 82.

46 On Tietjens as a good man see *Some Do Not . . .* , 173, and *Last Post*, 220. *Some Do Not . . .* , 290: note the technical pun, since time-shifted novels don't go 'straightforward' either. *No More Parades*, 250. See also Walter Allen, 'Books in General', *New Statesman and Nation*, 31 (20 Apr. 1946), 285.

47 'Thus to Revisit . . . : I.—The Novel', *Piccadilly Review* (23 Oct. 1919), 6. Showalter, *The Female Malady* (London: Virago, 1987), 173.

48 *No More Parades*, 185. Compare *Some Do Not . . .* , 215: ' "If," Sylvia went on with her denunciation, "you had once in our lives said to me: 'You whore! You bitch! You killed my mother. May you rot in hell for it . . .' [. . .] you might have done something to bring us together. . . ." '; and *A Man Could Stand Up—*, 34.

49 Walter Yust, 'Ford's Major Tietjens in the Trenches', *New York Evening Post Literary Review* (6 Nov. 1926), 3. Seiden, 'The Living Dead—VI: Ford Madox Ford and his Tetralogy', *London Magazine*, 6 (Aug. 1959), 50.

50 Seiden, 'The Living Dead—VI: Ford Madox Ford and his Tetralogy', 49. The influence of James's stories of threatened innocence—especially *What Maisie Knew*—must also be remembered. See Joseph Wiesenfarth, 'The Art of Fiction and the Art of War: Henry James, H. G. Wells, and Ford Madox Ford', *Connotations*, 1/1 (Mar. 1991), 68–9.

51 Seiden, 'The Living Dead . . .', 49–50 (where he argues that *The Idiot* fails because despite his perceptive praise of *Don Quixote*, Dostoevsky won't let us laugh at Myshkin). 'Literary Portraits—XXIII.: Fydor Dostoievsky and "The Idiot." ', *Outlook*, 33 (14 Feb. 1914), 206–7. Ford was replying to criticisms of his remarks on Dostoevsky in *Henry James* and in the *Outlook*: see Harvey, 183–4. *The March of Literature*, 850.

52 *'Fordie', The Working Novelist (London, 1965), 1. *No More Parades*, 52.

53 *No More Parades*, 306.

54 *Britain in the Century of Total War* (London: The Bodley Head, 1968), 125.

55 Walter Allen was prophetic, in 'Books in General', *New Statesman and Nation*, 31 (20

Apr. 1946), 285: 'It is the moral attitude that makes the work impressive; and it is, one thinks, as a study of a certain type of Englishman, the type Ford called the Tory but which might more truly be considered the Christian Gentleman in an age no longer propitious for his survival, that it will be read in the future.'

56 *No More Parades*, 141, 189. Though Ford may have found significance in the name Tietjens, like most of the names he uses it was found rather than invented. He would have known of the soprano Therese Tietjens who died in London in 1877. And the poet Eunice Tietjens was on the Advisory Committee of *Poetry*—so Ford would have seen her name listed in the same issue as 'A House'.

57 *Provence*, 304: a passage marked by Graham Greene in his copy. Edward Shanks, 'Ford Madox Ford: The Man and his Work', *World Review* (June 1948), 61.

58 *Some Do Not . . .* , 212 (faith); *No More Parades*, 196, 209 (hope); 188–9, 214–15, 234 and *A Man Could Stand Up—*, 38 (charity).

59 **'Epilogue'*, 14. Hicks, quoted in 'Ford Madox Ford, *Parade's End*: The Story of an Old Book Newly Made', 12. *Mightier Than the Sword*, 221. This passage has been thought (i.e. by Mizener, 568–9, n. 3) derivative from Hemingway's *A Farewell to Arms* (New York: Scribner's, 1929): 'I was always embarrassed by the words sacred, glorious and sacrifice and the expression in vain [. . .] Abstract words such as glory, honour, courage, or hallow were obscene beside the concrete names of villages, the numbers of roads, the names of rivers, the numbers of regiments and the dates': 196. But what derivativeness there is the other way around; though Hemingway was to make into something arrestingly different the idea that he would have read in *The Good Soldier*. 'For all good soldiers are sentimentalists—all good soldiers of that type. Their profession, for one thing is full of the big words, courage, loyalty, honour, constancy': 33. Both owe something to Conrad's 'A Familiar Preface' to *A Personal Record*, on 'the power of mere words; such words as Glory, for instance, or Pity': p. xi. *No Enemy*, 93. *Some Do Not . . .* , 106, 202, 106. There is a somewhat fuller discussion of 'values' in *Parade's End* in Saunders, 'Ford Madox Ford and the Reading of Prose'.

60 'Preparedness', *New York Herald Tribune Magazine* (6 Nov. 1927), 7, 18.

61 *Some Do Not . . .* , 44.

62 Phonetic Cockney for 'Bank Holiday'.

63 Bennett, *Journals*, ii. 241–2: entries for 12 and 14 Nov. 1918.

64 Woolf, 'The War from the Street' (1919), *The Essays of Virginia Woolf*, ed. Andrew McNeillie (London: The Hogarth Press, 1988), iii, 3–4. In Exodus 32–4 Moses breaks the first decalogue, and God has to produce a second edition.

65 McCarthy, *New York Review of Books* (14 Feb. 1985), 27. **'Epilogue'*, 13; the passage is quoted at the start of this chapter.

66 He uses the phrase 'Lost Generation' in his preface to Marc Chadourne's *Vasco* (London: Jonathan Cape, 1928), 9–15; and in *Provence*, 223. Ford to Percival Hinton, 27 Nov. 1931: *Letters*, 203–4.

67 It could be compared with Herbert Read's 'The Coward', the first section of 'The Raid', *Ambush*, Criterion Miscellany, 16 (London: Faber & Faber, 1930); A. P. Herbert's *The Secret Battle* (London: Methuen, 1919); Aldington, *Death of a Hero*, 332 (a particularly relevant passage, relating fear to neurosis and repression). 343, 376, 394; and Jones's *In Parenthesis*, esp. 121, 144, 156, 162. See also Lord Moran, *The Anatomy of Courage* (London: Constable, 1945).

68 *The Marsden Case*, 221. No Enemy, 64. 'Mr Croyd', quoted by Mizener, 289: 'He had, for too long, been too much afraid, himself, of going mad.' Also see *A Man Could Stand Up—*, 74, on different kinds of fear. 'An Interview with Janice Biala (1979)', in *The*

Presence of Ford Madox Ford, 225. Shanks, 'Ford Madox Ford: The Man and His Work', *World Review* (June 1948), 62.

69 *No More Parades*, 118. Ackroyd, *T. S. Eliot* (London: Hamish Hamilton 1984), 180.

70 *Reader*, 461. One should note that Ford had already imaged the war as a cloud, and had written about the war dead, in articles written before his army service: 'Literary Portraits—LIII.: The Muse of War', *Outlook*, 34 (12 Sept. 1914), 334-5; and 'Literary Portraits—LXIX.: Annus Mirabilis', *Outlook*, 35 (2 Jan. 1915), 14-15.

71 Mizener, 589, n. 12. *It Was the Nightingale*, 173. *No More Parades*, 106, 140. The third vision is similar. Tietjens imagines a map of the battlefield 'with the blood of O Nine Morgan blurring luminously over it' (308).

72 *It Was the Nightingale*, 205-6.

73 Mizener, 506. *A Man Could Stand Up—*, 85 (the phrase 'solid noise' is also used in the second paragraph of *No More Parades*: 'solid noise showered about the universe'). *No More Parades*, 194.

74 *It Was the Nightingale*, 176-7.

75 *Joseph Conrad*, 208. Seiden, 'Persecution and Paranoia in *Parade's End*', *Criticism*, 8/3 (Summer 1966), 246-62; repr. in R. Cassell (ed.), *Ford Madox Ford: Modern Judgements* (London: Macmillan, 1972), 166-7.

76 Freud, 'Psychoanalytic Notes upon an Autobiographical Account of a Case of Paranoia (Dementia Paranoides)', *Standard Edition* (London: The Hogarth Press and the Institute of Psycho-Analysis, 1958), xii. 1-82.

77 See 297, 393-6, 407, 414.

78 *The Good Soldier*, 291. Shanks, 'Ford Madox Ford: The Man and His Work', 60. *The Flurried Years*, 225 ff. *Ancient Lights*, p. xii. *Ford Madox Brown*, 249.

79 **Epilogue', 14; see n. 1 above. 'Literary Portraits—LXXI.: Enemies', *Outlook*, 35 (16 Jan. 1915), 79-80, on Ford's persecutory feeling of being hated, and on the ambiguous idea of the 'hatred of women'. *John Batchelor, *The Edwardian Novelists* (London: Duckworth, 1982), 93 and 115, remarks how *The 'Half Moon'*, *A Call*, and *The Simple Life Limited* also deal in paranoia. *No More Parades*, 19.

80 **Michel Mok, 'Ford Madox Ford Sadly Adds "S" to British Nerve', *New York Post* (24 Oct. 1938), 9.

81 The quotations are from J. Laplanche and J.-B. Pontalis, *The Language of Psycho-Analysis* (London: The Hogarth Press and the Institute of Psycho-Analysis, 1973), 296.

82 Lawrence, quoted by Aldous Huxley, *The Letters of D. H. Lawrence* (London: Heinemann, 1932), p. ix.

83 Aldington, *Death of a Hero*, 18.

84 Fussell, *The Great War and Modern Memory* (New York and London: Oxford University Press, 1975), 76.

85 'From a Paris Quay', *New York Evening Post Literary Review* (13 Dec. 1924), 1-2.

86 Rose Macauley, 'The Good Ford', Kenyon Review, 11 (Spring, 1949), 283. Charles G. Hoffmann, *Ford Madox Ford* (New York: Twayne Publishers, 1967), 106.

87 *Death of a Hero*, 256-7, 376.

88 Mizener, p. xv. Hoffmann, *Ford Madox Ford*, 54, notes 'a definite suggestion of latent homosexuality in Grimshaw's relationship with Leicester'. Also see Moser, 80. *The Good Soldier*, 291. See Susanne Kappeler, *Writing and Reading in Henry James* (London: Macmillan, 1980), 58, who makes a similar point about *The Aspern Papers*.

89 *Return to Yesterday*, 51, 46, 47. Biala in conversation with Max Saunders, Paris, 23 Apr. 1987.

90 *Saturday Review of Literature*, 20/5 (27 May 1939), 3-4, 15-16; repr. in *Reader*, 138-45.

91 *Reader*, 138. Rossetti was senior assistant secretary in the Excise Office (which later became the Inland Revenue) from 1869 to his retirement in 1894: *DNB*.

92 Flaubert to Amélie Bosquet, reported by René Descharmes, in *Flaubert, sa vie, son caractère et ses idées avant 1857* (Paris: Ferroud, 1909), 103, n. 3.

93 *The March of Literature*, 812. See also 'Emma', *New York Herald Tribune Books* (10 June 1928), 1, 6: 'With all his boasted aloofness of the Creator, Flaubert was in love with his Emma.' Richard Lid has argued—with more respect for literary influence than for gender—that *The Good Soldier* 'is a *Madame Bovary* told from the viewpoint of Charles Bovary': 'Return to Yesterday', *Jubilee*, 9 (Mar. 1962), 37–40. There is a good comparison by James T. Cox: 'The Finest French Novel in the English Language', *Modern Fiction Studies*, 9/1 (Spring 1963), 79–93 (including a discussion of 'a number of suggestions that Dowell is homosexual').

94 290. Here too Dowell sounds very like Ford: Ford saying that Olive Garnett and the Cowlishaws were his only friends; or later telling Edward Garnett of his fondness for Constance Garnett and Jane Wells.

95 Ed. Joseph Wiesenfarth, *Contemporary Literature*, 30/2 (Summer 1989), 177.

96 For example, the first chapter of *Mightier Than the Sword* is called: 'Henry James: The Master.'

97 Van Wyck Brooks, *Opinions of Oliver Allston* (New York: Dutton, 1941), 240 n., doubted that Ford 'was a good mental diet for the young Western boys'; 'the fatherly Ford appealed to their filial instincts [. . .]'. *Mightier Than the Sword*, 54. Saunders, i. 118.

98 *Henry for Hugh*, 169. Henry is thinking of how his father knew he was about to commit suicide but did nothing to prevent it: a possible transposition of Ford's feelings about his father dying without him being able to prevent it.

99 *Introductory Lectures on Psychoanalysis*, *Standard Edition*, vols. xv (1961) and xvi (1963): xvi. 400.

100 Freud, 'On the Grounds for Detaching a Particular Syndrome from Neurasthenia under the Description "Anxiety Neurosis"' (1895), *Standard Edition*, vol. iii (1962), 92–9.

101 In *Return to Yesterday*, 298, he writes that 'A sense of persecution is bad for a child's mental development as a rule'. He is discussing religious education, so here too the persecutory anxiety is related both to parents and to God.

102 Freud, *Standard Edition*, xii. 51. Bayley, 'Cutting it short', *London Review of Books*, 5/20 (3–16 Nov. 1983), 9. *The Heart of the Country*, 98–9; cf. 205. *No More Parades*, 173.

103 'True Love & a G.C.M.', 92. *Reader*, 460.

104 The phrase occurs in '4692 Padd'; there is a variation in *Great Trade Route*, 201. Nancy's madness also invokes the thought of divine justice (in her reiterated credo, and in the novel's epigraph).

105 *Mr. Fleight*, 189. Ford wrote to Bowen on 21 May 1919 that he had been 'walking in the garden in the cool of the evening—like God!' *No More Parades*, 107–8. *A Man Could Stand Up—*, 153.

106 See *The English Novel*, 123; and 'Techniques', *Southern Review*, 1 (July 1935), 23, 33. Both works explicitly invoke the Flaubertian idea of the aloof, godlike author.

107 'Ulysses, Order, and Myth' (1923): *Selected Prose of T. S. Eliot*, 177.

108 Jones, *Essays in Applied Psycho-Analysis* (London: The International Psychoanalytical Press, 1923), 204–26. *'Mr. Conrad's Writing', *Spectator Literary Supplement* to the issue of the *Spectator*, 131 (17 Nov. 1923), 744, 746. E. J. D. Radclyffe, 'A Freudian Synthesis', Literary Supplement to the issue of the *Spectator*, 131 (17 Nov. 1923), 746.

109 *No More Parades*, 189.

110 See e.g. *The Fifth Queen*, 28: 'He would be perpetually beside the throne [. . .] he would be able to give all his mind to the directing of this world that he despised for its baseness, its jealousies, its insane brawls, its aimless selfishness, and its blind furies.'

111 'Literary Portraits—VIII.: Professor Saintsbury and the English "Nuvvle"', *Outlook*, 32 (1 Nov. 1913), 605–6.

112 *The Shadow-Line* (London: Dent, 1923), 131–2. Jeffrey Meyers, *Joseph Conrad*, 403, n. 15, points out the allusion.

113 On *Parade's End* and the *Aeneid* see Theoharis C. Theoharis, 'No More Virgil', *Antaeus*, 56, (Spring 1986), 93–106. 'War and the Mind' was the collective title Ford gave to the two essays *'A Day of Battle' and *'The Enemy': see *Yale Review*, 78/4 (Summer 1989), [497]–510, where they were first published together, edited by Sondra Stang. *A Man Could Stand Up—*, 102. *The Heart of the Country*, 31–2.

114 *'Epilogue', 16.

115 See Moser, ch. 4: 'Impressionism, Agoraphobia, and *The Good Soldier* (1913–1914)'. He notes the significance of Ford's setting much of *Ladies Whose Bright Eyes* on Salisbury Plain (84), and argues (on 169) that Ford's agoraphobia there contributed to Dowell's vision of judgement (*The Good Soldier*, 82). But he misses the link with *Parade's End*.

116 *A Man Could Stand Up—*, 72–3.

117 *Reader*, 461. Ford to Conrad, 19 Dec. 1916: *The Presence of Ford Madox Ford*, 177–8. *'Just People', [1].

118 Freud, *Standard Edition*, xii. 54. *The Cinque Ports*, 167–8. Freud. 'Introduction to *Psycho-Analysis and the War Neuroses*', *Standard Edition*, vol. xvii (1955), 206–10.

119 *Standard Edition*, xii. 68–9.

120 See James Hurt, 'The Primal Scene as Narrative Model in Ford's *The Good Soldier*', *Journal in Narrative Technique*, 8/3 (Fall 1978), 200–10.

121 When Ford wrote an introduction to an edition of *Robinson Crusoe* (San Francisco: Grabhorn Press, 1930), he argued that the novel best expressed the isolation of an author like Defoe who could 'never show his real self', and whom Ford imagined writing in 'a passion of loneliness' (pp. x, xii). Ford to Garnett [Nov.? 1900]: Northwestern.

122 Ford to Bowen, 22 Oct. 1927. Mizener, 366–7. Hoffmann, *Ford Madox Ford*, 98.

123 *Some Do Not . . .* , 41, 36, 49, 55. There is a fine discussion of Sylvia's anarchic pagan energies of sexuality and evil by Sondra Stang, *Ford Madox Ford* (New York: Frederick Ungar Publishing Co., 1977), 109–16.

124 Richard Gill, **Happy Rural Seat* (New Haven, Conn.: Yale University Press, 1972), 275–6, notes that there is a large horse-chestnut tree in the garden of the Marwoods' seat, Busby Hall.

125 See *Jonathan Bate, 'Arcadia and Armageddon: Three English Novelists and the First World War', *Etudes Anglaises*, 39/2 (Apr.–June 1986), 156–9. William Marwood's death in 1934 was curiously similar to the death Ford had imagined for Mark Tietjens in 1927: see Kenneth Young, *Ford Madox Ford*, Writers and Their Work (Longmans, Green & Co, 1956), 33.

126 See Robie Macauley, 'The Good Ford', *Kenyon Review*, 11 (Spring 1949), 269–88; esp. 284–5 on Tietjens as *Last Post*'s 'unseen center'.

127 Greene, 'Introduction', *The Bodley Head Ford Madox Ford*, vol. 3 (London: The Bodley Head, 1963), 6. Malcolm Bradbury, 'Introduction', pp. xix, xxvi.

128 Aldington, too, was struck by the paradoxical pathos of the music: 'The bugler was an artist and produced the most wonderful effect of melancholy as he blew the call—which in the Army serves for sleep and death—over the immense, silent camp. Forty thousand

men lying down to sleep—and in six months how many would be alive?': *Death of a Hero*, 302.

129 See James Heldman, 'The Last Victorian Novel: Technique and Theme in *Parade's End*', *Twentieth Century Literature*, 18 (1972), 271–84. Ford's 'ability to describe the quality of life, the bristling, tangled, harassed stream of consciousness' was praised by Cyril Conolly, *New Statesman*, 30 (4 Feb. 1928), 533. L. P. Hartley thought *Last Post* the 'greatest *tour-de-force*' of *Parade's End*: *Saturday Review*, 145 (18 Feb. 1928), 199. *[Parker, under pseudonym 'The Constant Reader'], 'A Good Novel and a Great Story', *New Yorker* (4 Feb. 1928), 74–7; repr. in *The Dorothy Parker Reader* (New York: The Viking Press, 1973), 487–91.

130 Ford's radio talk about the Abdication, *'Last Words about Edward VIII', 5, suggests that Campion's visit of inspection to the cook-house, 'as when a godhead descends', was based on a visit by the Prince of Wales to the 'camp kitchens' of the Welch Regiment. *It Was the Nightingale*, 19–20. Ford stages a similar funeral in *Mister Bosphorus*, 117.

131 *It Was the Nightingale*, 233–4. On 121, Ford tells an anecdote of his father's about injured survivors of the war of 1870 which provided the germ for the Armistice party.

132 Ford to Eric Pinker, 17 Aug. 1930: *Letters*, 196–7. Ford to Ralph Pinker, 17 Aug. 1929: Princeton; see Mizener, 590n. Ford to Ray Long, 2 July 1932: *Letters*, 208. Ford to Jefferson Jones (of Lippincott) 1 Jan. 193[4]. The blurb appeared on the jacket of Lippincott's *Vive Le Roy*. Ford to Cumberlege, 27 Oct. 1936, calls it 'fairly satisfactory': *Letters*, 263–4. Ford to George Keating, 23 Jan. 1937, asks him to send copies of the first three books to Ferris Greenslet, as Houghton-Mifflin were considering publishing them in one volume. Ford to George Bye, 8 Mar. 1937, says he wants 'to begin the collected edition with the three Tietjens books in one volume': *Reader*, 504–5. Erskine-Hill, 'Ford's Novel Sequence': *Agenda*, 27/4–28/1 (Winter 1989–Spring 1990), 53. See Mizener, 399, 508–9. Also see p. 302 above.

133 Meixner, *Ford Madox Ford's Novels*, 217–21 (220). Mizener, 508. The arguments of Erskine-Hill, and of Cornelia Cook ('Last Post', *Agenda*, 27/4–28/1 (Winter 1989–Spring 1990), 23–30) for *Parade's End*'s coherence as a tetralogy seem to me more cogent. *History*, p. xx.

134 *It Was the Nightingale*, 203.

135 See Robert J. Andreach, *The Slain and Resurrected God: Conrad, Ford and the Christian Myth* (New York: New York University Press, 1970). Joseph Wiesenfarth, *Gothic Manners and the Classic English Novel* (Madison: The University of Wisconsin Press, 1988), 179, argues that Valentine too undergoes a symbolic death and rebirth. In *A Man Could Stand Up*— she says to the headmistress interviewing her: 'It *is*, you know, rather more my funeral than yours [. . .] Still, it's I that's the corpse. You're conducting the inquest': 58.

136 'Preparedness', *New York Herald Tribune Books* (6 Nov. 1927), 7, 18. 'Emma', *New York Herald Tribune Books* (10 June 1928), 1, 6.

137 According to this typology, *Some Do Not* . . . presents an Agony—Tietjens's mental suffering from shell-shock and Sylvia's torments. *No More Parades* evokes the Crucifixion—with Tietjens imagining O Nine Morgan, and Sylvia imagining Father Consett, as the sacrificial victims. *A Man Could Stand Up*— shows Tietjens's Resurrection; and *Last Post* either the Ascension, or what happens after the Last Trump.

138 Snitow's chapter on *Parade's End*, one of the best recent readings, brings out its romance aspect well. 'Thus to Revisit: II. The Realistic Novel', *Piccadilly Review* (30 Oct. 1919), 6.

139 *'Pink Flannel', *Land and Water* (8 May 1919), 14–15. Ford to Bowen [21–2 May

1919]. 'The Miracle', *Yale Review*, 18 (Winter 1928), 320–31. Another unpublished story at Cornell, 'Enigma', deals with a couple's mysterious disappearance that is associated with war-warped psychologies.

140 *The Last Pre-Raphaelite*, 201. *It Was the Nightingale*, 100. He places this episode during the battle of the Somme, but the date he gives it of 13 July is at least five days before he reached the line.

141 **'Pure Literature'* (originally written as pt. II, ch. 2 of 'Towards a History of English Literature': published in *Agenda*, 27/4–28/1 (Winter 1989–Spring 1990), 5–22 (7). 'Just People', 8, 1. By contrast with Tietjens's exploits, General Campion finds that talking to Tietjens, who proves him wrong, undermines his belief in himself—showing how words can disturb as well as convince: *No More Parades*, 102.

142 *A Man Could Stand Up—* [63].

143 Conrad to Ford, 4 Dec. 1916.

144 The classic statement is Viktor Shklovsky's 'L'Art comme procédé', in *Théorie de la littérature*, ed. Tzvetan Todorov (Paris: Éditions du Seuil, 1966), 76–97 (see 83). Shklovsky's *On the Theory of Prose* (1929) is included in a reading list appended to Ford's *The March of Literature*, 861; but *O teorii prozy* (Moscow, 1925) was not then available in translation.

145 See Bradbury, 'The Denuded Place: War and Ford in *Parade's End* and *U.S.A.*', in Holger Klein (ed.), *The First World War in Fiction*, rev. edn. (London and Basingstoke: Macmillan, 1978), 193–209, on dematerialization. Bradbury, 'Introduction', *Parade's End* (London: Everyman's Library, 1992), p. xvi.

146 *No More Parades*, 35. **'Epilogue'*, 15.

147 'From a Paris Quay (II)', *New York Evening Post Literary Review* (3 Jan. 1925), 1–2.

148 Freud, 'A Disturbance of Memory on the Acropolis' (1936), *Standard Edition*, vol. 22 (1964), 245–6.

149 *Romance*, 25.

150 Preface to *Transatlantic Stories* (London: Duckworth and Co., [1926]) xxix–xxx. See Mizener, 347.

151 David Lodge, for example, argues that modernist writing is characteristically 'metaphoric', as opposed to the 'metonymic' material realism of Galsworthy and Bennett: *The Modes of Modern Writing: Metaphor, Metonymy, and the Typology of Modern Literature* (London: Routledge, 1977).

152 Schorer, 'An Interpretation' prefaced to the Vintage reissue of 1951, pp. xiii–xiv.

153 Jones, *In Parenthesis*, 179.

154 John McCormick, *Catastrophe and Imagination* (London: Longmans, Green, 1957), 219.

155 e.g. Green, *Ford Madox Ford: Prose and Politics*, 152. See p. 182 above.

156 *Some Do Not . . .* , 107–8.

157 Bradbury, 'Introduction', pp. xxvii, xiv.

158 *Some Do Not . . .* , 196. He does spell it out in *The Marsden Case*, via Ernest Jessop, who writes of 'the great war that goes on forever between the two sexes. The oldest war of all, and the most engrossing of all, since in that there is never peace—an armistice now and then, perhaps!': 184.

159 *Some Do Not . . .* , 160.

160 In *The Marsden Case* George crashes his car (into a dung-heap) while on his way to see Clarice (258); and soon after Jessop sees her on a train in France, it is bombed (303–4).

161 *A Call*, 128. See *The Marsden Case*, 96; *No More Parades*, 98; *A Man Could Stand Up—*, 213; *Last Post*, 98, 106, 154; also *New York is Not America*, 188. Moser, 308, n.

44. See Moser on the association of sexuality and insanity or violence: 84 on Sorrell; and 267 on Henry Martin.

162 Gordon. *A Good Soldier: A Key to the Novels of Ford Madox Ford* (University of California Library: Davis, 1963), Chapbook No. 1. The bewitching Burne-Jones lady in 'True Love & a G.C.M.' and the mention of Circe in *Vive Le Roy*, 149, should be added to her list. See also Lionel Stevenson, *Yesterday and After* (New York: Barnes & Noble, 1967), 84. *A Little Less Than Gods*, 198.

163 Greene, quoted in Strauss, *Ford Madox Ford, Parade's End*, inside front cover; Kenneth Young, *Ford Madox Ford*, 30.

164 *It Was the Nightingale*, 191, 160. Ford says he also saw Minto in Galsworthy's *The Silver Box*. But J. P. Wearing's *The London Stage* lists her as appearing in *Joy*, but no other Galsworthy plays from 1906 to 1929 (Metuchen, NJ, and London: Scarecrow, 1981–4). Since *It Was the Nightingale*, 37, also mentions *Joy*, this is probably the play Ford was recalling.

165 *The Flurried Years*, 213, discussed in Saunders, i. 368. Cf. Proust, *Time Regained*, trans. by Andreas Mayor (London: Chatto & Windus, 1970), 268: 'The man of letters envies the painter, he would like to take notes and make sketches, but it is disastrous for him to do so. Yet when he writes, there is not a single gesture of his characters, not a trick of behaviour, not a tone of voice which has not been supplied to his inspiration by his memory; beneath the name of every character of his invention he can put sixty names of characters that he has seen, one of whom has posed for the grimaces, another for the monocle, another for the fits of temper, another for the swaggering movement of the arm, etc.' *It Was the Nightingale*, 192. Ford may have been recalling his grandfather's comment on having used well-known figures such as Carlyle and F. D. Maurice as models for *Work*: 'As my object [. . .] is to delineate types and not individuals, and as, moreover, I never contemplated employing their renown to benefit my own reputation, I refrain from publishing their names': *Ford Madox Brown*, 195.

166 *It Was the Nightingale*, 187. Peter Buitenhuis, *The Great War of Words* (London: Batsford, 1989), 13 (on Masterman and Tietjens). I am grateful to Dr O. Flint for information about his father, whom, however, he doesn't think contributed to Tietjens's character. *Ford Madox Brown*, 126. T. S. Eliot, *Collected Poems, 1909–1962* (London: Faber & Faber, 1974), 217.

167 Moser, pp. 5, xi. Coleridge, *Biographia Literaria*, ed. George Watson, corrected ed. (London: Dent, 1965), ch. 13, p. 167.

168 Mizener, 368.

169 John Batchelor claims: 'A perpetual social and emotional adolescence may be taken to characterise Frod the man and the novelist.' Yet only three pages before he has shown why Ford the novelist shouldn't be thus characterized, since the portrait of Tietjens diagnosing his own moral adolescence 'displays sustained and delicate self-knowledge' on Ford's part: *The Edwardian Novelists*, 117, 114.

170 Isherwood, *Tomorrow*, 10 (Nov. 1950), 53–5. Moser 215, finds 'one fundamental weakness' in 'the incredible perfection of the hero'. Cf. Mizener, 206–8. For examples of criticisms and corrections of Tietjens see *Some Do Not . . .* , 44, 141, 145, 168, 267, 291; *No More Parades*, 136, 259. For Sylvia's charge see *No More Parades*, 141, 178, 189. *A Man Could Stand Up—*, 216. See Snitow, 217.

171 Milan Kundera, *The Unbearable Lightness of Being*, trans. Michael Henry Heim (London: Faber & Faber, 1985), 221. *The March of Literature*, 438. See Mizener, 403–4, who relates this argument interestingly to Ford's later verse.

172 *It Was the Nightingale*, 190, 200.

173 In a seminar on Narrative at the University of Cambridge, 1981.

174 *Some Do Not . . .* , 32. The closest lines from *Mister Bosphorus* are the following—all explicitly sexual enough to make one wonder how sexually to understand Macmaster's version: 'The Gods to each ascribe their various fates: | Some entering in; some baffled at the gates!' (56); 'The Gods to each ascribe a differing lot! | Some rest on snowy bosoms! Some do not!' (57); 'Do you suppose she really *is* his wife? | The Gods to each ascribe a differing life' (58).

175 M. D. Waterhouse, 'Experiments in English Fiction, 1915–1930, with Special Reference to Ford Madox Ford and Henry Green', unpublished dissertation (Oxford University, 1981), 196–7, gives as examples Tietjens and Valentine both thinking of the 'stuff to fill graveyards' and the 'Pink! Pink!' chaffinch song; and notes the coincidence that their names both get mistaken ('Wanstead' and 'Tea-tray'). A further example occurs in *A Man Could Stand Up—*, when both think how strange it is that he has never even sent her 'a picture-postcard'; 204, 237. Green, *Ford Madox Ford: Prose and Politics*, 149.

176 Freud, 'The Uncanny' (1919), *Standard Edition*, vol. xvii (1955), 244. 'The Younger Madox Browns', *Artist*, 19 (Feb. 1897), 50.

177 *No More Parades*, 194; Tietjens and Sylvia both visualize the front in the image of a moving serpent: 19 and 228. On 192 Sylvia thinks: 'It was undeniably like something moving. . . . All these things going in one direction'; a sentiment echoing Tietjens's preoccupation with the way his bloody vision of Morgan is 'Moving!'

178 'Thus to Revisit: IV.—New Forms for Old', *Piccadilly Review* (13 Nov. 1919), 6. *Ancient Lights*, 215–17, argues that the Pre-Raphaelites disturbed their viewers in ways that were 'all important in the development of modern thought'.

179 *Ladies Whose Bright Eyes*, 349, 359. The novel is discussed more fully in Saunders, i. 307–11.

180 Snitow, 190.

181 'Stocktaking: VIII. The "Serious" Book', *transatlantic review*, 2/3 (Sept. 1924), 281.

182 See p. 21 for a discussion of this story.

183 Stocktaking: IV. Intelligentsia', *transatlantic review*, 1/4 (Apr 1924), 169.

184 *A Man Could Stand Up—*, 124–5; my italics.

185 'Stocktaking: I', 75–6. Cf. *'A Day of Battle', 456.

186 'A Miracle' was probably begun after Jan. 1928, and was finished by April. See Bill Breck (of Brandt & Brandt) to Helen McAfee (of the *Yale Review*), 2 Feb. 1928; and the *Yale Review* to Breck, 14 Apr. 1928: Yale. Williams, *Sewanee Review*, 59 (Jan.–Mar. 1951), 154–61; repr. in *Selected Essays* (New York: Random House, 1951), 315–23 (316). Malcolm Bradbury agrees, calling the sequence 'the greatest modern war novel from a British writer': 'Introduction', *Parade's End*, p. xiii. John Colmer's praise is equally high, finding the rendering of Tietjens's thoughts on the death of O Nine Morgan as a greater example of the stream-of-consciousness technique than can be found in Joyce or Woolf: *Coleridge to Catch-22: Images of Society* (London: Macmillan, 1970), 148.

Chapter 15

1 Ford to Huddleston, 24 Dec. 1924: Texas. *'Supper Reminiscences', *New York Herald Tribune Magazine* (18 Aug. 1929), 20–1, 23.

2 Martien Kappers-den Hollander, 'Measure for Measure: *Quartet* and *When the Wicked Man*', *Jean Rhys Review*, 2/2 (Spring 1988), 7, notes that *When the Wicked Man* mentions *Triple Sec* as one of the least successful works Notterdam's firm has published.

Angier, *Jean Rhys*, 123, 138, 662. The quotation is from a draft of Rhys's autobiography *Smile Please*, quoted by Angier, 135. See *Jean Rhys: Letters 1931-66*, ed. Francis Wyndham and Diana Melly (London: André Deutsch, 1984), 65 n.

3 Rhys, quoted by Diana Athill to Arthur Mizener, 28 Mar. 1966. Angier, 134. Compare Ford's advocacy of brevity in 'From a Paris Quay (II)', *New York Evening Post Literary Review* (3 Jan. 1925), 1-2: 'the great need of our time being the saving of time, any soul that can give us very quick, irrefutable and consummate pictures confers a great boon on humanity.'

4 Angier, *Jean Rhys*, 6-7, 113, 121-2, 138, 153. Bowen, *Drawn from Life*, 166-7. Rhys wrote an unpublished response to Mizener's biography in 1972-3; it is titled *L'Affaire Ford', and exists at the McFarlin Library, University of Tulsa, in one of her exercise books; and also in a typed transcription (to which my references are given). *L'Affaire Ford', 3, 219. Rhys to Mizener, 7 Dec. 1965 ('I do think that this affair was quite important perhaps to Ford—certainly to Stella').

5 Paul Delaney, 'Jean Rhys and Ford Madox Ford: What "Really" Happened', *Mosaic*, 16/4 (Fall, 1983), [15]-24, suggests interestingly that *The Good Soldier* is relevant here too, as a 'prospective' text: one whose plot about an adulterous 'four-square coterie' the quartet were acting out a decade later. Angier, *Jean Rhys*, 154-6. *When the Wicked Man*, 55. Angier's 1990 biography supersedes her early volume (also called *Jean Rhys*) in the Penguin 'Lives of Modern Women' series, 1985. Some of the ground-work for her account of the affair was done by Martien Kappers-den Hollander in 'A Gloomy Child and its Devoted Godmother', *Autobiographical and Biographical Writings in the Commonwealth* (1984), and 'Measure for Measure: *Quartet* and *When the Wicked Man*'.

6 The episode is recounted by *James King, *Interior Landscapes: A Life of Paul Nash* (London: Weidenfeld and Nicolson, 1987), 118-19; though he misquotes both Margaret Nash's typescript, 'Memoirs of Paul Nash: 1913-1946' (p. 35), and Nash's letter to Anthony Bertram, 2 Mar. 1925 (both at the Victoria and Albert Museum Library, the latter in Bertram's transcription). King says Ford stayed with the Nashes 'in 1922 or 1923', but since Ford was in France from Nov. 1922, it's unlikely to have been 1923. Nash's letter to Gordon Bottomley, 31 Dec. 1922, mentions that Ford had told him what he thought of the prose parts of a book of Nash's, which sounds as if he had been staying by that date (Victoria and Albert Museum Library).

7 'Memoirs of Paul Nash: 1913-1946', 36. Angier, *Jean Rhys*, 138. The meeting with the Nashes in Paris, and this stay at Cros de Cagnes, don't figure in her biography. She says Rhys met Nash in 1926—during a visit to Cros de Cagnes in that year—but cites no evidence: 158. Yet Nash's dates appear incontrovertible. He told Gordon Bottomley on [20 Dec. 1924] they were leaving for Paris the following day; and both his letter to Bertram and his wife's memoir are unequivocal about the meeting happening in 1924. The most likely date would be after Lenglet's arrest on the 28th. *Sous les verrous* has Stania's friends helping her immediately after Jan's arrest. *Interior Landscapes*, 118-19. King says the Nashes paid her fare to England, but 'Memoirs of Paul Nash: 1913-1946' says Paris (37).

8 Ford to Bradley, 25 Jan. 1925: *Reader*, 487-8. See Ford to W. H. Thompson, 5 Feb. 1926: *Letters*, 166-8. Karl, *Joseph Conrad*, 867. Ford's comment that 'Miss Rhys is here but has been too ill to do anything about that ms' suggests that she had been staying for some time. This is one place where Angier guessed wrongly, suggesting that the Fords might have wintered in Toulon, and that Rhys was staying with Germaine Richelot; 140. On 3 Feb. Ford was still writing of 'grippe and a houseful of people' (to Scott-James: *Letters*, 165-6) which might suggest that Rhys was still there.

9 *Quartet* (Harmondsworth: Penguin, 1973), 36, 39, 45–6, 43. In *Sous les verrous* (see n. 10 below) Stania (Rhys) tells Jan (Jean Lenglet) before he is sent to Fresnes that Hübner (Ford) has raised some money for her, and says: 'Alors, je vais habiter chez lui.' In *When the Wicked Man* Notterdam (the quasi-Fordian publisher hero) has caused Lola Porter's author-husband to commit suicide by withdrawing his publishing contract. Lola begs him for help, and kisses his hand 'as if she had been a slave'. He thinks: 'The idea that this beautiful, flashing, little creature was actually starving remained almost his strongest and most shuddering impression of the night. He had actually promised to take her home and have his wife look after her' (162). Angier, *Jean Rhys*, 139–41. This scene might have the same source as the one towards the end of the affair in *Quartet*, in which Marya begs Heidler: 'Oh, please be nice to me. Oh, please say something nice to me. I love you.' 'She was quivering and abject in his arms, like some unfortunate dog abashing itself before its master' (102).

10 Mizener, 345–7, follows the dates of composition given in the book, and says *No More Parades* was finished in May at Guermantes. But Ford to Jeanne Foster, 26 Mar. 1925, written from 16 rue Denfert-Rochereau, says he corrected the last draft and sent it to the publishers 'yesterday' (so the May date must refer to the date he wrote the dedicatory letter to Bill Bird): Londraville, 189–90. Ford to Bradley, 21 June 1925 (*Reader*, 488–9), reports delivering the page proofs. Angier, *Jean Rhys*, 141–3. *Quartet*, 59, 56–7, 53, 60, 63–4, 70, 9, 71; *Sous les verrous*, by 'Edouard de Nève' (Paris: Librairie Stock, 1933), 84–6. Cairn has been identified with Hemingway, but as Angier persuasively argues (136 n.), he owes much more to Ford's other assistant on the *transatlantic*, Ivan Beede (though she spells his name 'Bede'). David Plante, 'Jean Rhys: A Remembrance', *Paris Review*, 76 (Fall 1979), 238–84—hereafter 'Plante'—(260–1). Bowen, *Drawn from Life*, 63, 166.

11 Rhys, *Quartet*, 47–9. Bowen, *Drawn from Life*, 167.

12 Rhys, *Quartet*, 29.

13 Rhys, *Quartet*, 77, 80–2. There are letters from Ford at Guermantes on 3 Feb. (to Scott-James: *Letters*, 165–6); 26 Mar. (to Jeanne Foster); 25 Apr. (to Robert Gibbings: Texas); and *No More Parades* says he was there on 25 May. But they had still kept on the Denfert-Rochereau flat, and Ford was obviously in Paris occasionally that spring and summer. (The rue Denfert-Rochereau is now part of the rue Henri Barbusse.) See e.g. Ford to Bradley, 21 June 1925: *Reader*, 488–9. There has been much confusion about the sequence of Ford's addresses in 1924–5, largely due to Bowen misdating their move into the studio in the rue Notre-Dame des Champs as 'Towards the end of 1924' instead of 1925. She says (133) they gave up 'the nasty little flat in the Rue Denfert-Rochereau and had spent the summer at Guermantes'; but this must have been in 1925 too (see Mizener, 583–4, n. 19; though he is misled on 341 into saying they gave up the Denfert-Rochereau flat in 1924). *Quartet* has the Heidlers living in a studio, but Ford and Bowen were not living in one between the time they left the Boulevard Arago studio and the time they moved into the Notre-Dame des Champs studio in late 1925. Mizener, 333, says the Arago tenancy expired 'Early that spring'; but the only source he cites, Bowen, *Drawn from Life*, 124, has them still there in the summer of 1924. It's impossible to date the move from Arago to Denfert-Rochereau precisely, but it must have been after 14 July 1924, when Ford wrote to Pound from Arago ('*Pound/Ford*: Addenda and Corrections', *Paideuma*, 14/1 (Spring 1985), 123), and before 24 Nov., when Ford told Stein he was in a flat too small for a meeting of the review's twelve 'shareholders' (Yale). Angier, *Jean Rhys*, 137, assumes that when Rhys moved in with them it must have been into Lett Haines's studio, which Bowen was using to work in. But Bowen is clear that

that studio offered the peace and privacy she needed, and which the Arago studio didn't afford. She says when the tenancy at the Boulevard Arago expired, they moved into the 'poky little apartment in the Rue Denfert-Rochereau' (125). My guess is that they were still living in the Arago studio when Rhys met them in the autumn; that they had moved to the Denfert-Rochereau flat by the time they asked her to come and live; but that she simplified their existence for the book, preferring the grander setting. In *Quartet*, 40–1, Lois describes a party in the same studio they are living in with Marya. It appears to be the same party Bowen describes and situates in the Arago studio (120–1): discussed above, p. 146. Alternatively, this could mean that Rhys met Ford before October . . .

Bowen, *Drawn from Life*, 124. Ford to Foster, 26 Mar. 1925: Londraville, 190. Mizener, 347. Angier, 143–5. *Quartet*, 80–2, 99, 115.

14 Lenglet was in Brussels that July, not Holland, as Angier guesses: see Ford to Sylvia Beach, 22 July 1925 (Princeton), asking Beach to send Lenglet a copy of *Ulysses* to write about. In *Quartet* Marya leaves for a hotel after the row at Brunoy several months before Stephan is released. I follow Angier (145) in thinking that *Sous les verrous* is closer to the actual events: there, Stania stays with the Hübners after Jan has been deported. Angier, *Jean Rhys*, 146–7. Ford to Bradley, 21 June 1925: *Reader*, 488–9: written from 16 rue Denfert-Rochereau, and saying 'We are stopping in Town for this week'; so he may well have been at the station when Lenglet left.

15 Rhys, *Quartet*, 89–90. Rhys, **'L'Affaire Ford'*, 4. The essay on Furniture has been lost, though this mention of it confirms the extent to which Tietjens's connoisseurship in *Last Post* was based on Ford's. 'The Tale of Dushan: A Serbian Folk Story . . .' is in Jean Rhys's Executor's Archive.

16 *Last Post*, 291. Angier, *Jean Rhys*, 147–50. Rhys cut the Hudnut episode out of *Quartet*, but used it in *Good Morning Midnight*. As Angier argues, the omission shows how Rhys transformed events in order to make Marya seem a fated outcast, and to make her fate seem unmitigatedly cruel. Rhys, **'L'Affaire Ford'*, 4–6. Plante, 262.

17 Plante, 262. Rhys to Tony Gould, quoted in a radio programme, 'The Only Uncle of the Gifted Young', broadcast on 15 Feb. 1974: transcript at Washington University Libraries, St Louis; 3. Angier, 150. In *Quartet* the visits occur before Marya is sent to Cannes, whereas in **'L'Affaire Ford'* they take place after her return to Paris, which would be towards the end of 1925. *Quartet*, 92.

18 See Judd, *Ford Madox Ford*, 361. 'The Only Uncle of the Gifted Young' (radio transcript), 3. Biala, in *The Presence of Ford Madox Ford*, 222; also see Mary Gordon, 'A Man Who Loved Women, a Womanly Man', *Antæus*, no. 56 (Spring 1986), 206–14. Rhys, quoted by Athill to Francis Pagan (who owned Cooper's Cottage in Bedham from 1926–84: quoted by Judd, *Ford Madox Ford*, 363. Plante, 263.

19 Gerald Gould, *Daily News* (28 Sept. 1925), 4; 'P.J.M.', *Manchester Guardian* (9 Oct. 1925), 9. *Walpole, 'The Novels of 1925', *John O'London's Weekly* (5 Dec. 1925), 373–4. Muir, *Nation and Athenaeum*, 38 (31 Oct. 1925), 186. On Ford's 'genius' see H. C. Harwood, *Outlook* (London), 56 (3 Oct. 1925), 230; P. C. Kennedy, *New Statesman*, 25 (10 Oct. 1925), 727; *Observer*, (11 Oct. 1925), 4. Ralph Strauss, *Bystander*, 87 (14 Oct. 1925), 168, called the book 'vivid and brilliant, and startlingly outspoken'.

20 John W. Crawford, *New York Times* (8 Nov. 1925), 9; Paterson, *New York Herald Tribune Books* (22 Nov. 1925), 3–4. Hemingway to Louis and Mary Bromfield, *c*.8 Mar. 1926: *Selected Letters*, 196. Colum, *SRL*, 2 (30 Jan. 1926), 523. Mizener, 586, n. 8, gives some of the sales figures, based on the Boni royalty statements at Cornell. One of these mentions that the Grosset and Dunlap reprint had sold 1,103 copies by 31 Dec. 1929, giving a total figure of nearly 14,000, for the American sales, but showing how quickly

the sales peaked. Bradley to Ford, 29 Mar. 1926 (saying the novel had sold 'close on 10,000'). Ford later told Stanley Unwin it had sold 43,000 copies: 23 Mar. 1939. But he was confusing the figures with those for *Last Post*, his only novel to sell more. Ford to Scott-James, 3 Feb. 1925: *Letters*, 165–6.

21 Bowen, *Drawn from Life*, 130–1. Ford was writing from the new studio by at least 19 Oct. 1925 (letter to Huddleston: Texas). On 11 Nov. he thanked Huddleston for his book *France and the French*, but said he wouldn't read it until he had finished his own book on that subject (letter at Texas). The book incorporates material written during the war and published in *When Blood is Their Argument*, but the composition dates are from 1 Mar. 1923 (when he was writing the chapter 'From the Grey Stone' at Harold Monro's Cap Ferrat villa) to 18 Jan. 1926. Stein, *The Autobiography of Alice B. Toklas* (London: John Lane, The Bodley Head, 1933), 235. Stein to Ford [n.d., but *c*.May 1926]. Harvey, 529. Stein, *A Book Concluding with As a Wife has a Cow* (Paris: Galerie Simon, 1926).

22 Hamnett, *Laughing Torso* (London: Constable, 1932), 188–9. Goldring, *South Lodge*, 175, dates the party tentatively in 1926. But Ford was in America that Christmas. Goldring, *The Last Pre-Raphaelite*, 248, evidently describes the same occasion, saying Hamnett was also there. Hamnett remembers Ford giving her an inscribed copy of *Some Do Not . . .* on Christmas Day 1925. *Drawn from Life*, 132–7. Judd, *Ford Madox Ford*, 61. Ford to Duckworth, 9 Mar. 1926: *Letters*, 168–9. Gris to D.-H. Kahnweiler, 4 Jan. 1926; Gris to Pedro Penzol, 10 Jan. 1926; to Stein, 15 Sept. 1926; to Kahnweiler, 18 Mar. 1926: *Letters of Juan Gris*, collected by D.-H. Kahnweiler; trans. and ed. Douglas Cooper (London: privately printed, 1956), 176–7, 195, 189. The sketch appeared in *SRL*, 3 (11 Dec. 1926), 419; see Harvey, 370, 529; it is reproduced in *The Presence of Ford Madox Ford*, 1, 195.

23 Bowen, *Drawn from Life*, 138–9, 147, 142–6. Later, when she couldn't afford to keep on the studio, she handed it over to the travel writer and journalist William Seabrook, who wrote *Jungle Ways* there. According to the composition dates in the books, *A Man Could Stand Up—* was begun on 9 Jan. (p. 275), and *A Mirror to France* was finished on 18 Jan. (p. 290). Ford to Duckworth, 9 Mar. 1926: *Letters*, 168–9. *It Was the Nightingale*, 213–15, also describes the deputation of Americans. See *A Mirror to France*, 114, on Ford's inclination towards Provence. Ford to Bradley, 8 Mar. 1926 (*Reader*, 490) says they will be 'very hard up in a fortnight', and that it is 'quite certain' he will accept James Pond's offer for a lecture tour. The 'Emmerich' mentioned in the same letter is the second of the two lecture agents. See Ford to Bowen, 'Sunday 13th' [Nov. 1927].

24 Bowen, *Drawn from Life*, 148–9.

25 Bowen, *Drawn from Life*, 150–1. Ford to Jeanne Foster, 29 July 1926: Londraville, 191–2. Nina Hamnett, *Laughing Torso*, 188–9. Mizener, 349. Julia M. Loewe, in *The Presence of Ford Madox Ford*, 201–2.

26 Bowen, *Drawn from Life*, 152–6.

27 Bowen, *Drawn from Life*, 153–6. Bromfield, 'A la Recherche du Temps Perdu', *Town and Country* (Jan. 1943), 28.

28 Gorman, 'Ford Madox Ford: The Personal Side': *Princeton University Library Chronicle*, 9 (Apr. 1948), 119–22.

29 Gorman, 'Ford Madox Ford: A Portrait in Impressions', *Bookman* (NY), 67 (Mar. 1928), 56–7. Goldring, *The Last Pre-Raphaelite*, 249. Huddleston, *Bohemian Literary and Social Life in Paris*, 144.

30 Ford to Bradley [Apr.–May 1926]: *Reader*, 489–90. The composition dates say *A Man Could Stand Up—* was finished on 21 July (p. 275); but the Dedication to Gerald Duckworth is dated 'Paris, May 18th, 1926'. The later date is thus probably when Ford

finished with the proofs. The novel was probably published in Oct. Mizener, 352, says the confusion over *Some Do Not . . .* was only cleared up in 1927, when it 'became Boni's exclusive property and Ford sold him the rest of the tetralogy'.

31 Angier, *Jean Rhys*, 151–4: she speculates that Rhys left for London while Ford was in Toulon, but returned to Paris in the spring. *Quartet*, 93, 96, 93–4, 97, 101–2. Plante, 263. 'La Grosse Fifi', in *The Left Bank and Other Stories* (London: Jonathan Cape, 1927), 185. 'Two Poems in an Old Manner: I: Brantigorn', *New Poems*, 29–30. Ford sent a draft called 'Look to Your Ends' to Harriet Monroe with a letter of 6 July 1926, calling it 'a ballad I amused myself by writing last night': Chicago.

32 Angier, *Jean Rhys*, 156–60. Rhys, *Quartet*, 99, 115, 127. Plante, 263. Ford to Foster, Londraville, 191–2. Juan Gris wrote to Gertrude Stein from Boulogne sur Seine, 24 July 1926: 'Yesterday we went to the Fords, they are coming to dine here next Wednesday [28 July] before they go to Avignon' (*Letters of Juan Gris*, 193). Both these letters suggest the Fords were leaving on or very soon after the 29th. Ford sent Stein the card (of a restaurant by the Pont-d'Avignon), dated 'Thursday' [26 Aug. 1926; postmarked 27 Aug. 1926] (Yale), saying they would be in Provence until 'early September'. Both *Quartet* and *Sous les verrous* show the Lenglet characters furious for revenge on the Ford characters, so it is possible that Lenglet believed Ford had reported him. See p. 297.

33 Ford, p.c. to Stein [26 Aug. 1926]: Yale. Gorman, 'Ford Madox Ford: A Portrait in Impressions', *Bookman* (New York), 67 (Mar. 1928), 56–60.

34 Rhys, *Quartet*, 127. Lenglet's fourth wife, Henriëtte van Eyk, wrote in her autobiography that a friend confirmed hearing the story that Lenglet had tried to shoot a man he suspected of being Rhys's lover: *Dierbare Wereld* (Amsterdam: De Bezige Bij, 1973), 139. In an interview with Robert Henk Zuidinga in the Dutch magazine *De Haagsche Post* (19 Mar. 1977), 7, she said Lenglet had told her he was arrested not for embezzlement, but because he tried to kill Ford. Jan van Leeuwen in *Sous les verrous* shares Stephan's murderous impulses towards the Ford character. I am very grateful to Martien Kappers for these references: letter to Max Saunders, 12 Aug. 1991. Angier, 158–60: she dates this 'probably late August by now, even early September'; Ford's card to Stein (see previous note) has him still in Provence at the end of Aug., and not planning to return to Paris until early Sept.; it seems most likely that Ford gave her the money after he returned to Paris in early Sept. There is no evidence (in fact or in fiction) to suggest that Ford and Rhys met in Provence that summer. Rhys said of herself: 'because she didn't know what else to do, didn't want to stay in Paris, hated Ford, she accepted her husband's offer to go to Amsterdam, though he was angry about what had happened between his wife and Ford, whom he hated, too. He never forgave Jean for Ford. They went almost immediately': Plante, 263–4. But Angier is surely right to doubt this, saying that both Stephan and Jan leave their wives in Paris, 'And John too almost certainly left Paris alone'. *Quartet*, 100, 142–3. Mizener, who assumed that the affair with Rhys was much briefer, glosses over these months from Aug. to Oct. In one sentence: 352. An episode in Rhys's story 'In the Rue de l'Arrivée' might refer to an encounter in Paris that autumn: 'that afternoon she had passed a gentleman whom she knew intimately—very intimately indeed—and behold the gentleman had turned his head aside, and coughing nervously, pretended not to see her': *The Left Bank and Other Stories*, 117; quoted by Angier, *Jean Rhys*, 162. Ford to Elizabeth Cheatham, 14 Jan. [1929; but misdated 1928]. *When the Wicked Man*, 284.

35 Bowen, *Drawn from Life*, 166. *When the Wicked Man*, 312. Angier, 154–6, 142, 163. Martien Kappers, 'Measure for Measure: *Quartet* and *When the Wicked Man*', *Jean Rhys Review*, 2/2 (Spring 1988), 8–10.

36 Ford to Foster, 29 July and 22 Sept. 1926: Londraville, 191–3. Carole Angier to Max
    Saunders, 2 Mar. 1992. Mizener, 358, implies that they didn't acquire the flat in the rue
    de Vaugirard until 1927. But Ford and Bowen to Nancy Galantière, 14 Oct. 1926, says
    they've just moved into a new apartment. Ford to Bowen [30 Oct. 1926] is addressed
    there, which confirms that this was the new flat. Bowen, *Drawn from Life*, 159.
    Huddleston, *Bohemian Literary and Social Life in Paris*, 140–2. The date can be fixed by
    a letter (at Texas) from Robert P. Skinner (of the US Consulate, Paris) to Huddleston,
    21 Oct. 1926, about the 'Ford Madox Ford incident'; and by Bowen to Ford, 9 Nov.
    [1926], expressing concern about the passport, and mentioning Mr Skinner. One might
    have suspected Hemingway, except that he evidently helped Ford out of this scrape:
    Ford to Bowen [30 Oct. 1926] tells her to thank Huddleston and Hemingway. It's also
    possible that Lenglet wanted to keep Ford in France in order to exact either money or
    revenge. *The Good Soldier*, 291. Bowen to Ford, 11–13 Dec. [1926], wonders (surpris-
    ingly) whether it had been Violet Hunt who 'made the trouble over your visa'. However,
    she goes on, 'If only we may be spared any Lenglet scandals'.

37 Plante, 263. Rhys, *The Left Bank and Other Stories*, 26–7. Ford's preface, 'Rive Gauche',
    was revised into ch. 2 of *A Mirror to France*. Since that book was completed by Jan. 1926
    (p. 290), all but the last five pages of the preface were probably written in 1925. Ford to
    Bowen, 'Monday' [3 Jan. 1927]. Angier, *Jean Rhys*, 160–2, 61–4. She says Legrand was
    the lawyer for the *Transatlantic*; but Poli, 23, says that Legrand, 'who indeed knew Ford
    and Quinn very well, claims that he never transacted any business with Ford concerning
    a review'; which is not quite true: Quinn paid Ford the $2,000 he contributed via
    Legrand: Reid, *The Man from New York* (New York: Oxford University Press, 1968),
    615. Legrand's disclaimer might mean that he transacted Ford's *personal* business,
    which he may have remembered more accurately. Bowen to Ford, 29 Oct. 1926, says: 'I
    have seen Legrand about the taxes, & did not forget the Richelot cheques.' This might
    mean that they got Legrand to send Richelot the cheques. See Mizener, 583, n. 15. Ford
    to Bowen, 4 Feb. [1927]; 'Sunday 13th' [Feb. 1927]. Ford may have paid via a lawyer,
    but then changed to Richelot to conceal his altruism from Rhys (which might be why
    she denied the allowance). Mr Mackenzie pays Julia for six months after their affair has
    ended—from Oct. to Apr. The Rhys–Ford affair ended around Sept. 1926. So it's
    possible that Ford paid while he was in America, but stopped the payments in the spring
    of 1927 when he was back in Paris. In *Quartet* (p. 127) Heidler writes to Marya in
    Cannes saying he won't pay her the large sum she has asked for (in order to rejoin her
    husband): this would correspond to Aug. or Sept. 1926. Julia writes to Mr Mackenzie:
    'Why didn't you give me enough to go away when I first asked you?' (p. 16). Then she
    remembers that the last time she had seen him (Oct.), he was going away 'for an
    indefinite time': this might correspond to Ford's going away to America in Oct. 1926—
    for, as it turned out, four months. Bowen to Ford, 11 Jan. [1927]: 'I have just forwarded
    another letter from Miss Richelot [. . .] Meanwhile I go on with the weekly payments';
    and 17 Dec. [1926].

38 Angier, *Jean Rhys*, 164–5, 173, 175. Rhys, *After Leaving Mr Mackenzie*
    (Harmondsworth: Penguin, 1971), 26. Mizener, 583, n. 15; though he doesn't cite the
    source for the gossip. See *Quartet*, 114: 'Towards the end of his explanation he became
    definite, even brutal, though not to excess.'

Chapter 16

1 In *New York is Not America*, 13, he misremembered the ship as the *Paris*. (This was
   followed by Frank MacShane, *The Life and Work of Ford Madox Ford* (London:

Routledge & Kegan Paul, 1965), 196.) But the Boni press release at Cornell gives the ship and date. There are clippings at Cornell from the *New York Evening Post* and the *New York Herald Tribune* (both 30 Oct. 1926) and two unidentified papers. *It Was the Nightingale*, 343. Ford to 'Messrs J. B. Pinker & son' [*sic*], 10 June 1927: Princeton. Ford to Bowen, [28–9 Oct. 1926]; 'Saturday' [30 Oct. 1926]; 'Monday Morning: 15th [Nov. 1926] (listing six appearances he had been arranging; his Plaza speech on 10 Nov. makes the seventh); 'Friday 19th' [Nov. 1926] (in which the Bonis have agreed to a six-month contract at $400 per month); 27 [Nov. 1926] (which says the Boni contract is now to be for three years). (In the meantime, Bowen to Ford, 11–13 Dec. [1926], explains that she has heard from Jenny Bradley that the six-month contract had been replaced with a twelve-month one.) There were also negotiations with Harper's. Ford to Bowen [6 Nov. 1926] says Bradley is asking them for $650 per month, and is confident of $500. Bowen to Ford, quoted in Ford to Bowen, 9, 18 Nov. [1926]. Mizener, 352–3, 584, n. 28, 586, n. 8. Boni's royalty statements show 4,613 of their copies of the novel sold (there is no evidence for how well the 1928 Grosset and Dunlap cheap reprint sold). But in 1960 Albert Boni told Harvey (p. 59) that each of the first three Tietjens novels was 'successful commercially', selling over 10,000 copies each. Ford to Bowen, 'Tuesday 2ᵈ·' [Nov. 1926], mentions the synopses, and Ford told her on the 16th he had been working on them. These might be the 'Synopses of Novels' at Cornell. These outline four projects. 1) 'Bond', a story of an impotent husband who runs off with Miss Bond; his wife asks their best friend to persuade him to return. He does, but the wife has now fallen in love with the best friend, who has fallen in love with Miss Bond; 'my speciality is unhappy love', writes Ford: 'there would be lots of it here.' 2) 'Hallows End'; the story of the two spinsters. 3) An 'immensely agonising story': 'Mʳˢ· Fall's husband is a brute—a *bad* brute. He leaves her. She falls passionately in love with another woman. Achingly. Mʳ· Fall returns . . . & carries off the other woman.' 4) 'After Waterloo: Ney.'

The reviews of *A Man Could Stand Up*—found by Harvey, 366–72, give a misleading impression of disappointment. *Delbert Clark, 'The Third Volume of Ford Madox Ford's War Study', *Sun* (Baltimore, Maryland) (18 Dec. 1926: clipping at Cornell), found the novel fascinating but irritating. But all the others I have found were favourable: 'Does anyone manipulate the English language better than Ford does?', asked *'Touchstone', *New Yorker* (13 Nov. 1926), 98, 100; *'With Pen of Magic', *News* (Buffalo, New York) (27 Nov. 1926: clipping at Cornell); *'The Bookman's Guide to fiction' thought it 'in all ways worthy of its fine predecessors': *Bookman* (New York), 64/5 (Jan. 1927), 622–4 (623); *Punch*, 172 (12 Jan. 1927), 55 (in doggerel); *I. A. Richards said 'Mr. Ford has crowned a distinguished career' with the war-chapters of Part II—he particularly admired the way the book fought the 'morbid effect' by which the passage of time was making people believe the war was enjoyable: 'In the Wake of the Novel', *Forum and Century*, 77/3 (Mar. 1927), 479–80. Ford drew Bowen's attention to the *New York World*'s review (31 Oct. 1926), 11, entitled 'Ford's Tremendous Revelation': see Bowen to Ford, 'Tuesday Dec 1st, [30 Nov. 1926].

2 Ford to Bowen [30 Oct. 1926]; 'Tuesday 2d.' [Nov. 1926]; and 7 Nov. 1926. MacShane, 197; he reproduces both of Hartmann's portraits of Ford (this of 1926, and another of 1927) facing 205.

3 Rascoe, 'Contemporary Reminiscences', *Arts and Decorations*, 26 (Dec. 1926), 55, 92: quoted by Mizener, 354. Ford inscribed an excerpt from his speech to the Seamen's Church Institute into George Keating's copy of *Joseph Conrad* (Yale): see *A Conrad Memorial Library: The Collection of George T. Keating* (Garden City, New York: Doubleday Doran, 1929), 422–3. 'Masefield Spins Sea Yarns', *New York World* (4 Nov.

1926), 17. Ford, Letter to the Editor, *New York World* (8 Nov. 1926), 12: in *Letters*, 169–70. *Harry Salpeter, 'Ford M. Ford Discusses Letters', *New York World* (14 Nov. 1926), 11M. See pp. 224 and 595, n. 59, on the 'big words'.

4 11 Nov. [1926]. Jeanne Foster was less impressed: she wrote to Pound about this Plaza engagement: 'Ford did not realize just how to key his voice and was not heard. Now, at two engagements that I made for him, he spoke exceedingly well, movingly, seriously and made a hit with the audience [. . .]': 7 Jan. 1927: Londraville, 197.

5 Ford to Bowen, 'New Year's Day' [1927]. *Joseph Moncure March, 'Can This Be Ford Madox Ford?', *New York Evening Post Literary Review* (13 Nov. 1926), 4. Bowen to Ford, 'Tuesday Dec 1st' [30 Nov. 1926]. Paterson, 'Turns with a Bookworm', *New York Herald Tribune Books* (21 Nov. 1926), 27.

6 Ford to Bowen, 'Saturday 27th.' [Nov. 1926]. In January 1927 Stella was told that she would not be able to visit America with Ford before Elsie Hueffer died. 'How I wish she would', she told him: 17 Jan. [1927].

7 Ford to Bowen, 7 Nov. [1926]; 8 [Nov. 1926]; 15 [Nov. 1926]; 'Friday 19th.' [Nov. 1926]; and 'Saturday 20th.' [Nov. 1926]. Bowen to Ford [30 Nov. 1926]; 11 Jan. [1927]; 21 Dec. [1926]; 2 Jan. [1927]; 11–13 Dec. [1926]; 27 Dec. [1926]; and 4 Dec. [1926]. Ford to Bowen [26 Nov. 1926].

8 Ford to Bowen, 'Tuesday 16th Nov.' [1926]. From Ford to Bowen, 12 Nov. [1926], it's clear that it's Horwood who has no teeth. Ford to Bowen, 19 [Nov. 1926], explains that he thinks Mr Ballard drank, and beat his wife.

9 Bowen to Ford, 11–13 Dec. [1926]. Ford to Bowen, 'Saturday 20th' [Nov. 1926]; [23 Nov. 1926]; and 'Thursday' [2 Dec. 1926].

10 Ford to Bowen, 'Thursday' [2 Dec. 1926]; 17 [–20] Dec. 1926; the '*Pen & Brush Club*' is perhaps an error for the 'Book and Play Club'. Ford to Bowen, 'Monday Morning: 15th' [Nov. 1926], mentions the following engagements: 'I am speaking at Mrs. Reid's—proprietress of the N.Y. Herald on the 30th Nov: at the *Book and Play Club* 2nd Dec: *Pen and Brush Club* 5th Dec.: *Pen Club* (Galsworthy's show) 8th Dec: N.[ew] H.[ampshire] [the one engagement Pond had secured, at Dartmouth] 9th.'. He gave a speech and poetry reading at the Women's University Club on 3 Dec. ('I made quite half the audience wipe its eyes—talking about Henry James!': Ford to Bowen, 'Saturday' [4 Dec. 1926]). Ford to Bowen, 'Sunday 5th' [Dec. 1926]. Ford to Bowen [10 Dec. 1926] describes the trip to New Hampshire. Ford's itinerary is at Cornell. Mizener, 585, n. 34, erroneously placed these lectures during Ford's 1927–8 tour (and misdates the Dartmouth lecture as the 9th).

11 Ford to Bowen, '15th' [Nov. 1926]; [22 Nov. 1926]; 'Saturday' [4 Dec. 1926]; 'Thursday' [2 Dec.? 1926]. Otto Kahn was the most prominent art patron in New York.

12 Ford to Bowen, Friday 17[–20] Dec. 1926; 'Tuesday' [21 Dec. 1926]. Bowen to Ford, 17 Jan. [1927]. He also spoke to 'an immense crowd at a tea at the house of a Mrs Ten Eyck Wendell' on 19 Dec.; on 30 Dec. he read his own and Pound's poems to the 'U. S. A. Poetry ass[ociatio]n'. At one of the readings the audience cheered when they thought the poems were all Ford's; 'but several people groaned when I said that no's 2, 4 & 6 were Ezra's': Ford to Bowen, 27 and 31 Dec. 1926.

13 'F. M. Ford, Hugh Walpole Guest of P.E.N. Club', *New York Herald Tribune* (21 Dec. 1926): Harvey, 370. 'Author's Apology', *English Novel* (London: Constable & Company Limited, 1930), p. vii.

14 Bowen to Ford, 11 and 17 Dec. [1926]; Ford to Bowen, 'Xtmas Eve' and 'Jour de Noel' [1926]. Ford has typed 'Mrs Forster', presumably in error for Jeanne Foster.

15 Ford to Bowen, 'Xtmas Eve' and 'Jour de Noel' [1926]. Mizener, 584, n. 30, corrects

Harvey's doubts about Boni's 'Avignon' edition of *The Good Soldier* really forming part of a planned 'Collected Edition': the idea was to build up a 'uniform, rather than a collected edition' by republishing old works when possible alongside the new books— a similar arrangement to the one he had with Duckworth. Ford to Duckworth & Co., 12 Jan. 1927, says the proposed Boni edition would include *The Good Soldier*, *Ladies Whose Bright Eyes*, *Collected Poems*, *Henry James* (with additions), *Joseph Conrad*, and *Some Do Not* . . . and its successors. 'I might add possibly some of my historical novels, and I should think you might reprint my *Soul of London*, which I believe is out of print. In that case I would add a chapter or two to it.' They also planned to issue a uniform volume containing all three Conrad collaborations. Bowen to Ford, 9 Nov. [1926].

16 Ford to Bowen, 'Xtmas Eve [1926]' and 'Jour de Noel' (a single diary-like letter).

17 Londraville, 182. 'Xtmas Day in the morning': Londraville, 193 (though their transcription confuses the Gormans with 'Germans'.

18 *Great Trade Route*, 79.

19 Ford to Bowen, 22–3 [Dec. 1926]; and 31 Dec. [1926]. The article was 'Stevie & Co.', *New York Herald Tribune Books* (2 Jan. 1927), 1. Londraville, 205, n. 30.

20 Ford to Bowen, 'Sunday 9th' [Jan. 1927]. Richards, *Practical Criticism* (London: Routledge & Kegan Paul, 1929), 262–3.

21 Biala, in conversation with Max Saunders, 22 Sept. 1990. *New York is Not America*, 7. Ford to Bowen, 'Sunday 9th' [Jan. 1927]. *It Was the Nightingale*, 332–3 describe Ruth Kerr, who later acted as his agent in America.

22 Ford to Bowen, 'New Years Day' [1927]. Kermit Roosevelt was the son of President Theodore Roosevelt.

23 Foster to Pound, 7 Jan. 1927: Londraville, 197–8. Ford to Bowen, 'Tuesday' [21 Dec. 1926]; 'New Years Day' [1927]; and 'Monday' [3 Jan. 1927]. Mizener, 362. Ford was presumably referring to Wright when he said 'I have met one born New Yorker who used to be here in 1906 . . . but that one—such a nice person too!—was only on a visit here and has gone back home—to somewhere in Missouri': *New York is Not America*, 34; 64 describes telephoning to St Louis. The dedication to *A Little Less Than Gods* recalls Rene in Central Park. Ford told Harold Loeb he had met her on a visit to his uncle's tobacco plantation (i.e. in Virginia): *Loeb, 'Ford Madox Ford's "The Good Soldier": a Critical Reminiscence', *London Magazine*, new series, 3/9 (Dec. 1963), 67. But *Great Trade Route*, 340, says he never got there. The book was presumably *New York is Not America*, the volume of essays written during this visit. Ford recalled 'stealing away as if over corpses' from the drunken party, like an artist saying farewell to the stuff to fill graveyards: *Great Trade Route*, 85.

24 Mizener, 361–2, 586, n. 12. 'Winter Night-Song', published in *New York Herald Tribune Books* (23 Jan. 1927), 4; and in *New Poems*, the volume that was also published in Jan. 1927. Ford to Bowen, 'Friday Feb 4th' [1927]. He probably also wrote the much better poem 'To Petronella at Sea' during this period in New York (or on the boat there). It is not known to have been published before it appeared in *New Poems* (probably published in Jan. 1927). Ford told Elinor Wylie that only two poems in that volume had been written in New York; and all the others except 'Winter-Night Song', 'Auprès de ma Blonde', and this poem are known or likely to have been written before. See Harvey, 68. Its theme of restless travel, with love offering a hope (or mirage?) of peace, is thoroughly Fordian, reminiscent of his earlier version of 'Du bist die Ruh'. It may also have been written for Rene; though 'Petronella' was the middle name of Lenglet's mother, and Rhys later used the name in the story 'Till September Petronella'. See Angier, *Jean Rhys*, 103.

25 Ford to Bowen, 'Monday [3 Jan. 1927]'; 'Sunday 9th' [Jan. 1927] and 'Monday' [10 Jan. 1927].

26 Ford to Bowen, 'Friday 7th' [Jan. 1927]. Muriel Draper is mentioned in *Provence*, 203–4. Foster to Ezra Pound, 7 Jan. 1927: Londraville, 197. Ford to Bowen, '19th Jan '26' [for 1927]. *New York is Not America*, 236–7; 225–40 describes some of his impressions of Chicago. *It Was the Nightingale*, 311–12. Putnam, *Paris Was Our Mistress*, 119–20.

27 Ford to Bowen, '19th Jan '26' [for 1927], 'Thursday 20th Jan' [1927], and 'Saturday 22 Jan' [1927]. George Dillon, in *New Directions: Number Seven*, 469–70. The article was 'Poeta Nascitur . . .', *Poetry*, 29 (Mar. 1927), 326–33. Ford also told the story about Hemingway's father in *It Was the Nightingale*, 313. (Poli, 100, n. 3, cites Biala saying that Ford visited Hemingway's parents in 1926; but this is a mistake: as he implies, the correct date is Jan. 1927, between Ford's letters to Bowen of the 22nd and 27th.) F[anny] B[utcher], 'Ford Madox Ford a Visitor Here; Tells of His Work', *Chicago Daily Tribune* (22 Jan. 1927), 8 (but with no photograph). Clarence Hemingway to Ernest Hemingway, 27 Jan. 1927: Mizener, 355–6, 585, n. 37. Ford to Bowen, 27 Jan. [1927], says he is due to speak on the radio on the 28th. Ford to Bowen, 29 [Jan. 1927], says he is to speak at the 'University here' on Monday [31 Jan. 1927]; and to leave for New York (via St Louis) on Wednesday [2 Feb.]. If he went to St Louis it can only have been for a day, since he was on the train in Pennsylvania on 3 Feb. Ford to Bowen, 29 [Jan. 1927] and 3 Feb. 1927.

28 He was 'Between Pittsburgh and Philadelphia' on 3 Feb. (Ford to Bowen). Ford to Bowen, 17 Dec. 1926 and 'Xtmas Eve' [1926]. Jessie Conrad, *Joseph Conrad as I Knew Him* (London: Heinemann, 1926; Garden City, New York: Doubleday Page, 1926). Her later book, *Joseph Conrad and His Circle* (London: Jarrolds Publishers London, 1935), gave her fullest account of Conrad and Ford: see Harvey, 502. Ford to Harriet Monroe, 7 Feb. 1927, thanking her for having 'made things so nice' for him in Chicago, and asking her to copy out the passage from a copy of *The Cinque Ports* he had heard of in Chicago: *Reader*, 491–2. Ford to the Editor, *New York Times*, 19 Feb. 1927: Princeton. Mizener, 355, 537, n. 19, 581–2, n. 32. Ford to Editor of *New York Herald Tribune Books*, 15 February 1927: *Letters*, 170–2.

29 Ford to Bowen, 'Saturday 22 Jan' [1927]; 'Thursday' [2 Dec.? 1926]; and 'Sunday 13th' [Feb. 1927]. T. R. Smith to Ford, 1 Dec. 1926. Foster to Pound, 7 Jan. 1927: Londraville, 198. Mizener, 355. Ford told Bowen that Donald Friede was 'the millionaire who finances Boni and Liveright': 'Monday' [3 Jan. 1927].

30 *Ancient Lights*, 156. Ford to Bowen, 'Sunday 13th' [Feb. 1927].

31 *It Was the Nightingale*, 333–4. *New York is Not America*, 53. Ford to Bowen, 'Friday 18th Feb' [1927], says he gave tea to 66 persons.

32 Ford to Bowen, 'Friday 18th Feb' [1927].

33 MacShane, 196. Ford to Greenslet, 20 Feb. 1927: *Reader*, 492; and 7 Mar. 1927: Harvard. Bowen, *Drawn from Life*, 146–7. Bowen to Ford, 25 Nov. [1926], says Gris was not going to Toulon due to illness. Ford to Foster, 24 Mar. [1927]: Londraville, 193–5. He lost his glasses in Chicago: see Ford to Bowen, 'Saturday 22 Jan.' [1927]. *New York is Not America*, 241, 11–12. Ford to Pound, 28 Mar. 1927: *Pound/Ford*, 88; also see Foster to Pound, 7 Jan. 1927 (Londraville, 197), which shows that Ford had the idea at least several months earlier. *The Good Soldier*, 19.

Chapter 17

1 'Ezra', *New York Herald Tribune Books* (9 Jan. 1927), 1, 6: repr. in *Pound/Ford*, 82–7; see 88–90 for the trip to Rapallo (Ford probably left Paris on 22 April: he wrote to

Duckworth & Co. on 84 rue Notre-Dame des Champs paper that day) and the correspondence about lecturing. The dates of composition of *New York is Not America* are given as 15 Oct.–9 Apr. in the English edition, and 1 Dec.–9 Apr. for the American. The subtitle on the manuscript at Cornell (which does not appear in the book) is 'Being a Mirror to the States', implying that it should be read as a companion volume to *A Mirror to France*. It is one of Ford's slighter books, but was received favourably as 'amusing', 'charming', and 'witty' (see Harvey, 373–8). Pound to Ford, 23 June [1927]: *Pound/Ford*, 90. See 89–91 on 'How to Read, or Why'.

2 Ford wrote to Pound from Toulon on 9 May 1927 (*Pound/Ford*, 88–9), saying 'We leave for Paris the day after tomorrow'. This is supported by his letter to Elinor Wylie, 2 June 1927 (Yale), saying 'We [. . .] arrived on the 12 May'. (But see ch. 18, n. 2, below for some conflicting evidence.) Mizener, 357, 585, n. 1. *George Wickes, *The Amazon of Letters: The Life and Loves of Natalie Barney* (London: W. H. Allen, 1977), 166, 249. Cathy Hueffer did not die in 1924, as Alan Judd says: *Ford Madox Ford*, 278. Ford told Pound he had had to pay for his mother's illness and funeral: 15 June 1927: *Pound/Ford*, 89–90. Later in June Violet Hunt began pestering Juliet Soskice, saying that Cathy Hueffer had promised to leave her some furniture: Juliet to Hunt, 22, 24, and 30 June [1927]. *Last Post* dates the composition in the English edition as beginning on 7 June, and in the American, 7 July. Both agree that it was begun in Paris; but, as Mizener says (585, n. 1), Ford was in the Hotel Belgravia, Grosvenor Square, on 7 June. And he had begun it by 25 June, when he told Donald Friede he was making 'quite satisfactory progress with the novel [. . .]': Liveright Files. Mizener follows MacShane, 200, in saying that Ford had begun dictating the novel to Caroline Gordon before he left New York in Feb. 1927; neither cite any evidence for this claim. If the source was Caroline Gordon's memory, she may well have been recalling work on the ending of the book when Ford returned to New York in the autumn. *Last Post*, pp. v, vii. The death of Jane Wells on 6 Oct. 1927 probably prompted this elegiac passage, which continues: 'It is only yesterday that I read of the death of another human being who for the rest of time will have for me that effect. That person died thousands of miles away, and yesterday it would have astonished me if she had walked into my room here in New York. To-day it would no longer.' See Ford to Edward Garnett, 5 May 1928; and G. P. Wells (ed.), *H. G. Wells in Love* (London: Faber & Faber, 1984), 16, 40–1. Elinor Wylie was also terminally ill: see Ford to Bowen, 22 Oct. 1927.

3 Ford to 'Mr Kovici' [*sic*], 5 Jan. 1927: Jean Rhys Archive. Ford to Messrs Covici, 17 June 1927. The quotations are taken from a first draft which also includes comments (also cut from the second version of the letter) doubting the publishability of the book. Harvey, 97. Angier, *Jean Rhys*, 164. Ford to L. Tilden Smith (Rhys's agent), 17 Mar. 1929: Jean Rhys Archive, says he sent a copy of his introduction to Covici but it got lost together with the top copy of the translation. Ford then sent the carbon. It is thus possible that without Ford's introduction and original covering letter, Covici may have forgotten Ford was not the translator, and genuinely thought the work was his; or he may have suppressed the introduction because it made it clear Rhys and not Ford had translated the book, and he was determined to use Ford's name. Ford to the editor, *Publisher's Weekly* [n.d. but *c*.Mar. 1928]. Ford to Isabel Paterson, 5 Mar. 1928: *Letters*, 176–7.

4 Putnam, *Paris Was Our Mistress*, 121. Ford's stationery at this period bore both the rue de Vaugirard and rue Notre-Dame des Champs addresses. The letter to Putnam is dated 28 July 1927: Princeton. So the meeting must have been on 27 July.

5 Mizener, 357. Ford to Eric Pinker (18 July 1927: Princeton), inviting the Conrads, says

they are going on 1 Aug.; *Last Post*, 292, says 'Avignon, 1st August'. Ford told Samuel
Putnam (28 July 1927: Princeton) that he was leaving Paris 'this evening'. Dransfield, in
New Directions: Number Seven, 470–1. Mizener notes the parallel with Tietjens walking
Valentine through the countryside and thinking of the names of flowers. Cf. *It Was the
Nightingale*, 114–15, and *Last Post*, 169. Ford didn't finish *Last Post* until 22 Sept.: Ford
to Bowen, 'Thursday night' [22 Sept. 1927]; see Mizener, 585, n. 4.

6 *New York is Not America*, 11, 10. Mizener, 358, 389 n.

7 Ford to Foster, undated [but first week of Sept. 1927]: Londraville, 190–1, where it is
misdated '1925'. The intimacy of the salutation 'My dear Jeanne' shows that it must
come later than the letter of 29 July 1926 to 'Dear Mrs. Foster': 191–2; Ford made no
trip to the USA in 1925; but the Liverpool–Montreal boat he is planning to take 'next
Thursday week', and which is to arrive on the 24th, must be the one recorded in *Last
Post*, 292: 'St. Lawrence River, 24th September' 1927. (The American edition, which
gives different composition dates to the English, omits this: see Harvey, 71. But the St
Lawrence date is confirmed by Ford to Bowen, 24 Sept. 1927, from Montreal.) Ford to
Friede, 25 June 1927: Liveright files; Friede to Arthur B. Spingarn (Ford's lawyer), 25
July 1927. Albert Boni told Harvey (59)—in 1960—that the rupture had come about
because 'Ford was by that time producing essays and reminiscences, not the novels for
which he had been paid'. C. F. Crandall, 'When Sinclair Lewis Wrote a Sonnet in
Three Minutes, Fifty Seconds', *New York Herald Tribune Book Review* (2 Sep. 1951),
4.

8 Ford to Bowen, 1 Oct. [1927]. Ford to Monroe, 4 Oct. 1927: Chicago (quoted in *Pound/
Ford*, 91–2). Bowen to Ford, 14 Oct. [1927].

9 Bowen, *Drawn from Life*, 168–9. Ford to Bowen, 21 Dec. 1927; 1 Oct. [1927]; Bowen to
Ford, 14 Oct. [1927]; and 8 Nov. [1927].

10 Mizener, 358. Bowen, *Drawn from Life*, 162–3. Ford to Bowen [17–19 Oct. 1927]; and
22 Oct. 1927. 'The Other House', *New York Herald Tribune Books* (2 Oct. 1927), 2;
discussed in Saunders, i. 123. 'Preparedness', *New York Herald Tribune Magazine* (6
Nov. 1927), 7, 18; illustrated with a photograph, of Bowen's portrait of Ford playing
patience. 'Cambridge on the Caboodle', *Saturday Review of Literature*, 4 (17 Dec. 1927),
449–50.

11 W. L. Chenery [of *Collier's*] to Carl Brandt, 26 Oct. 1927. Ford to Bowen, 22 Oct. 1927.
A Little Less Than Gods, pp. v, vi. *The Good Soldier*, 291. Jessie Conrad denied that the
novel was a continuation of *Suspense: Joseph Conrad and his Circle* (London: Jarrolds
Publishers London, 1935), 221. See Saunders, i. 493, for Ford's claim to have discussed
this project in 1915. Ford knew that when Conrad died he wouldn't have wanted Ford
to finish the book for him, and that isn't what he did. But there was some justification
for Ford's thinking of it as a continuation. Ford had evidently told him of his plan for
a Ney novel in 1921, perhaps fearing they might both try to write the story independently, since Conrad replied: 'The novel I am writing (very slowly) now has ['nothing' is
probably omitted] to do with the Restoration—or anything so reasonable as that. The
date is Jan. Febr. 1815, but all the action takes place in Genoa, and thereabouts, and
does not touch upon affairs in France except in the most distant way. It ends with Nap's
departure from Elba. / We can't possibly clash': 15 Dec. 1921: Yale; quoted by Harvey,
61. Chronologically this is where Ford's novel begins. Karl, *Joseph Conrad*, 534–5, 537,
562, 364–6. Rascoe, *We Were Interrupted* (Garden City, NY: Doubleday, 1947), 227–30.
Ford to Rascoe, 9 Nov. 1927: *Letters*, 173–4. Conrad returned to the fragment during
the war, reworking it into *The Arrow of Gold*: see Najder, *Joseph Conrad*, 507, n. 2. See
Ford's letter to the editor, *Bookman*, 68 (Oct. 1928), 217–18, denying that 'The Sisters'

should be assumed to be an early study for *The Arrow*, but is 'the beginning of a quite different story'. Rascoe tells another story about Ford's opacity. After the lunch with cummings, 'As we were walking down Fifth Avenue to my office . . . he excused himself and asked us to wait while he went into the Guaranty Trust Company Bank, at Forty-fourth Street. Cummings expressed astonishment to me that Ford should have business with the bank. He asked Ford, when he came out, if he had an account there. Ford said, no, he didn't but that he had once gone there with John Quinn and had discovered that the bank had an *urinoir*, since then he had often used it, because, he said, "American cities are not so solicitous of a man's comfort as Paris is." Cummings said, "It *would* take Ford to find an *urinoir* in a bank on Fifth Avenue and have the courage to use it without having an account there"'; op. cit., 230. In fact Ford had an account with the Guaranty Trust in Paris by at least the following Aug. (see Ford to Bradley, 13 Aug. 1928: *Letters*, 178–9); so it is not at all impossible that he had dealings with the New York office in late 1927. Mizener, 361. 'Tiger, Tiger; Being a Commentary on Conrad's *The Sisters*' appeared in *Bookman*, 66 (Jan. 1928), 495–8, together with Conrad's fragment. It was combined with another article, 'On Conrad's Vocabulary', *Bookman*, 57 (June 1928), 405–8, to make the introduction to the volume *The Sisters* (New York: Crosby Gaige, 1928), 1–16 (quotation on 6). See also Saunders, i. 420–7.

12 Karl, *Joseph Conrad*, 365–6. 'Introduction' to *The Sisters*, 7.

13 'Synopses of Novels' includes a brief 1½ page autograph titled 'After Waterloo: Ney' (number 4). There is also a six-page typescript at Cornell, titled 'Demigods'. Huddleston, *Bohemian Literary and Social Life in Paris*, 138; and the dedication to his *In and About Paris* (London: Methuen, 1927), pp. vii–ix. Ford mentioned the statue in his 'Paris Letter: Editorial', *transatlantic review*, 2/5 (Nov. 1924), 549: 'his sword raised, his side-whiskers rigid, his shaven mouth open.' The composition dates given in the British edition of the novel are: 'NEW YORK, 9th Jan./PARIS–NEW YORK–CARQUEIRANNE, 27 August, 1928' (p. 310). But in fact Ford told Bowen on 13 [Nov. 1927; not 3 Nov., as Mizener says, 589, n. 8] that he had written the first page 'last night—or rather this morning'. On 'Monday 21st' [Nov. 1927] he said: 'I have begun DEMI-GODS which is the provisional title of the Ney book and what with reading up for it and worrying over it I am fair moidert'; by 25 Nov. [1927] he told Bowen he had finished the first chapter. There is also a 302-page manuscript at Washington University, St Louis, which bears the earlier titles 'Demi-Gods' and 'Less than Gods'. *The Poems and Fables of John Dryden*, ed. James Kinsley (Oxford University Press, 1970), 422–3. Ford had been long familiar with these lines, quoting them in 'Literary Portraits—XLVI.: Professor Cowl and "The Theory of Poetry in England"', *Outlook*, 34 (25 July 1914), 109–10, but saying there that he cannot explain why he finds them so moving. In an obituary essay Ford wrote on Hardy, he called him 'one of the greatest of poets and an incomparable fingerer of the heart strings of men': 'Thomas Hardy, O.M. Obiit 11 January, 1928', *New York Herald Tribune Books* (22 Jan. 1928), 1–3.

14 Goldring, *South Lodge*, 179–81; *The Last Pre-Raphaelite*, 259. The quotation about using precision is from Bowen, *Drawn from Life*, 164. As Mizener says, 359, this garret was in West 13th Street.

15 Ford to Bowen, 'Sunday 13th' [Nov. 1927].

16 Ford to Bowen [30 Oct. 1927]; 6 Nov. [1927]; and 10 Nov. 1927 [the date of the Tomlinson dinner]. He also spoke at the National Arts Club on 16 Nov.: Ford to Bowen, 16 [Nov. 1927]. Mizener, 360–1. Ford to James T. Babb, 8 and 11 Oct. 1927: Yale. Ford visited New Haven on 15 Oct. Ford to Cross, 22 Oct. 1927 and 5 May 1929: Yale. 'The Romantic Detective', *Yale Review*, 17 (Apr. 1928), 517–37; the story had

earlier appeared in the *London Mercury*, 18 (Dec. 1927), 133–46, as 'A Mascot'. Ford to
Foster [first week of Sept.]: Londraville, 191. Ford to Bowen, 'Sunday 13th' [Nov.
1927]; 30 Oct. 1927; 'Halloween' and 4 Nov.; Bowen to Ford, 4 Dec. [1927]. *Return to
Yesterday*, 35. Untitled typescript at Cornell beginning 'When that I was a little, little
boy [. . .]'.

17 Gordon was working for him by at least Dec.: see Ford to Bowen, 22–3 [Dec. 1926].
Gordon, in *The Presence of Ford Madox Ford*, 200. Gordon to Sally Wood, fall 1927: in
The Southern Mandarins: Letters of Caroline Gordon to Sally Wood, 1924–1937, ed. Sally
Wood (Baton Rouge: Louisiana State University Press, 1984), 31. Tate, *Memories and
Essays: Old and New: 1926–1974* (Manchester: Carcanet Press, 1976), 47. Ford to
Bowen, 29 Nov. 1927. Ford was at Bank St by at least 16 [Nov. 1927]: Ford to Bowen.
It Was the Nightingale, 333. Ford to Bowen, 'Sunday 13th' and 'Monday 21st' [Nov.
1927]. WEAF later became NBC. *Great Trade Route*, 228. Foster to Pound, 7 Jan. 1927:
Londraville, 197. John Richardson, 'The Loves and Hates of Doctor Barnes', *Vanity
Fair*, 54/8 (Aug. 1991), [70]–3, 112–13.

18 Mizener, 359. Ford to Bowen, 30 Nov. 1927. Ford's reaction to Allen Tate's 1928 book
Stonewall Jackson: The Good Soldier is not recorded.

19 Goldring, *South Lodge*, 181–3. Ford's cable to Lucy Masterman, 20 Nov. 1927, reads:
'My Dear Lucy so Much Regret All My Sympathies.'

20 Ford to Bowen, 29 Nov. 1927; 13 Jan. [1928; misdated 1927]; 10 [Nov., but misdated
Dec. 1927]; and 'Friday' [9 or 16? Dec. 1927]. Harvey's supposition that the Literary
Guild edition preceded the Bonis' is supported by an inscribed copy Ford gave to Ruth
Kerr for Christmas: Bertram Rota Catalogue 200, Winter 1975–6. Ford told Bradley the
novel was 'to appear early in January': 28 Nov. 1927: *Letters*, 174–5. Mizener, 360, says
that the Guild 'was supposed to be good for about 25,000 copies', and he disputes
Ford's claim that he sold 50,000, saying the more likely figure was 30,000–35,000 (see
Goldring, *The Last Pre-Raphaelite*, 244–5, for Ford's figure). Yet on 586, n. 8, he shows
that the Guild estimated their membership at 30,000–40,000 at the time, which confirms what Ford told Bowen on 6 Jan. [1928, but misdated 1927]: '35,000 of Last Post
is pretty good!' The Boni edition sold 3,417 copies by 30 June 1928. Ford told Bowen
the terms of Viking's contract on 25 Nov. [1927], and cabled on 4 Dec. to say he had
signed. Bowen to Ford, 4–6 Dec. [1927]. Viking also expressed an interest in his idea for
a new *transatlantic review*. See Ford's telegram to Bowen, 11 Dec. 1927: Viking Press
anxious publish but taking absolutely no personal risk'. Ford to Bowen, 21 Dec. 1927,
explains that Huebsch of Viking had blocked the plan.

21 Ford to Bowen, 21 Dec. 1927; and 30 Dec. 1927 [cable saying 'yes take apartment']. On
13 [Nov. 1927] he had told her he wished to avoid Paris when he returned—presumably
so that any scenes would not be too public. Bowen to Ford, 3 Jan. [1928]; 25 Nov.
[1927]; and 20 Dec. [1927]. *Return to Yesterday*, 429. Mizener, 362. He was in Paris by
13 Feb., when he wrote to Gerald Duckworth: *Letters*, 175–6. Another letter of the same
date, to Percival Hinton, says that he returned 'on Saturday'—11 Feb.: Goldring, *The
Last Pre-Raphaelite*, 244. It's possible he was back earlier: the composition dates at the
end of the American edition of *A Little Less Than Gods* include 'Paris, February 4'. He
was probably still in New York when he wrote to Bernice Baumgarten on 25 Jan. 1928.
Ludwig says the letter to Isabel Paterson of 5 Mar. 1928 was written in New York; but
the letter is explicit about Ford having left: *Letters*, 176–7. Bowen, *Drawn from Life*,
168–9.

22 Ford to Bowen, 20 Jan. [1928, misdated 1927]. *Harry Hansen, 'The First Reader: The
Ford Saga', New York *World* (10 Jan. 1928), 5—five days earlier than the first review

found by Harvey—William McFee's in the *New York Herald Tribune Books* (15 Jan. 1928), 3. These are the only two known reviews to come out before the 20th; there were eventually at least 25. See Harvey, 375–9. The reviews quoted or paraphrased are: T. S. Matthews, *New Republic*, 53 (25 Jan. 1928), 279; *TLS* (26 Jan. 1928), 60; Cyril Connolly, *New Statesman*, 30 (4 Feb. 1928), 533; Gerald Gould, *Observer* (5 Feb. 1928), 8; *Boston Transcript* (8 Feb. 1928), 4; Hartley, *Saturday Review*, 145 (18 Feb. 1928), 199; Edward Shanks, *London Mercury*, 17 (Mar. 1928), 592–3; *Manchester Guardian* (2 Mar. 1928); *English Review*, 46 (May 1928), 614. *Percival Hinton, *Birmingham Post* (3 Jan. 1928). Other significant reviews omitted by Harvey are: *Fanny Butcher, *Chicago Daily Tribune* (21 Jan. 1928: final edition), 11; *Dorothy Parker, *New Yorker* (4 Feb. 1928), 74–7; *Daily Telegraph* (10 Feb. 1928), 15.

23 Mizener, 357, 585, n. 1. Ford to J. B. Manson, 11 Jan. 1929: *Reader*, 493–4. He gave a comparable estimate of the disparity between his American and English sales to Percival Hinton, 13 Feb. 1928—the same day he wrote to Duckworth: Goldring, *The Last Pre-Raphaelite*, 244–5. Mizener, 383, couldn't resist casting doubt on Ford's figures: 'he was selling—as he told himself—in the tens of thousands in the United States and only in the hundreds in England'; all the evidence in Harvey's bibliography indicates he was. Ford to Duckworth, 13 Feb. 1928: *Letters*, 175–6; there are two typescript versions of this letter at Cornell. Ford to Pinker, 19 Mar. 1928. The sixteen other titles are listed opposite the title-page of *Last Post*. *It Was the Nightingale*, 296–7. Mizener, 589, n. 3, cites a letter from Ford to 'Gerald Duckworth'; but in fact this was addressed to 'Messrs Duckworth', and was a friendly letter saying though he had 'always appreciated' their association, the last of the Tietjens novels seemed an appropriate moment at which to break. Jonathan Cape to F. Wicken (of J. B. Pinker and Co.), 15 Mar. 1928 (Northwestern) expresses an interest in publishing the first three Tietjens novels, but is wary of treading on Duckworth's heels.

24 Tate, *Memories and Essays*, 49. Ford to Huddleston, 28 Mar. 1928: Texas. 'Charters', *Thus Must Be the Place: Memoirs of Montparnasse* (London: Herbert Joseph Ltd, 1934), 100–1. Cody worked for the US Embassy. Hemingway wrote an introduction. See W. T. Bandy, 'Memories of Montparnasse', *Cumberland Poetry Review*, 3/2 (Spring 1984), 37–41, who warns that most of the book's events took place, 'though not always in the manner in which they are presented' (p. 37).

25 Ford to Stein, 'Wed 4th April' [1928]: Yale. Ford to Huddleston, 28 Mar. 1928: Texas. Mizener, 364–5, 586, n. 18, 569, n. 10. The debt included Bowen's share of the price of Cooper's Cottage at Bedham, and her investment in the *transatlantic review*. When she heard of Ford's contract with Viking she told him: 'I regard the results of this trip of yours as beyond all expectations & as far more than justifying you as a "speculation" on my part!': 4–6 Dec. [1927]. Ford also agreed to make over to her all his British earnings until the debt plus 5% interest had been repaid, after which she was to get £200 a year 'destinée a constituer une dot [dowry] pour Esther Julia Madox'; in addition he was to pay her half of what he earned in America, 'up to a maximum of $4,800', for her and Julie's maintenance. The figures reasonably reflected Ford's financial position in 1928—he earned $7,000 in 1926, he told Bowen (12 Nov. [1926]), and they thought his Viking contract would give him about the same sum (Bowen to Ford, 4 Dec. 1927)—though, as Mizener says, the 'arrangement turned out to be largely theoretical, thanks to the Depression and the drastic decline in Ford's earnings'. By 1932 he still owed her £2,500. Ford to Bowen, 12 May 1928. Bowen, *Drawn from Life*, 165, 169. Mizener, 363. Bowen to Ford, 18 Apr. 1928; 30 Apr., and 1 June [1928]. Bowen later wrote to Biala: 'I feel all right in my conscience about the rôle I played in Ford's life even if it didn't

succeed [. . .] But I am tired of looking backwards, & tired of remembering how much things hurt [. . .] I shall always be grateful to you for relieving me of the habit of worrying about Ford which I went on doing even after we parted, & it didn't do any good' (n.d.; quoted by Mizener, 364). She can be heard still worrying about Ford in her letter of 18 April.

26 Bowen, *Drawn from Life*, 164, 169, and 221. See Goldring, *The Last Pre-Raphaelite*, 251. Joyce to Harriet Shaw Weaver, 8 and 16 Apr. 1928: *Letters*, iii. 175–6, cited by Richard Ellmann, *James Joyce*, new edn. (Oxford University Press, 1983), 563. The baptism took place on 18 Apr. at the church of St Louis en L'Île. Ford to Joyce, 17 Apr. 1928: State University of New York at Buffalo. Ford to Bowen, 'Tuesday' [but presumably 18 Apr. 1928, which was a Wednesday].

27 Morris, *A Threshold in the Sun* (New York and London: Harper & Brothers Publishers, 1943), 216–18, 244. Wiesenfarth, 'Fargobawlers: James Joyce and Ford Madox Ford', *Biography*, 14/2 (Spring 1991), 101.

28 Ellmann, *James Joyce*, 602. Joyce to Harriet Weaver, 16 and 26 Apr. 1928: *Letters of James Joyce*, iii. 176. *Letters from Joseph Conrad*, ed. Edward Garnett (Indianapolis: Bobbs-Merrill, 1928), 168–9. Conrad to Garnett, 26 Mar. 1900: *Collected Letters*, ed. Frederick Karl and Laurence Davies (Cambridge: Cambridge University Press, 1986), ii. 256–7. Ford to Garnett, 5 May 1928.

Chapter 18

1 Epigraph: Carlyle to Emerson, quoted by John Ruskin, *Praeterita* (London: Rupert Hart-Davis, 1949), 155. Ford to Cheatham, 15 July 1928. Cheatham was completely unknown to Ford's biographers until, after her death on 6 Aug. 1990, her grandson Tom Carter wrote to Alan Judd. Judd saw Ford's letters and poems to her, and added a brief postscript to the English paperback and American editions of his biography. I am grateful to him for his generosity in passing on the information to me immediately. I am also extremely indebted to Mr Carter: for his kindness in sending me copies of the *58 letters, notes, cards, and telegrams from Ford to Cheatham, as well as some of her papers; for showing me the *ten poems he wrote for her; and for discussing his grandmother with me in Mar. 1991. The originals of Ford's letters and poems to Cheatham are all now at Cornell.

2 Judd (p. 452 of the 1991 Flamingo paperback edn.) says that they appear to have met in 1927; but the main evidence for this is one of the first two letters from Ford, which bears the date '9 May 1927'. But this is almost certainly a misdating (which Ford managed regularly). There are several reasons for believing that it must have been written in 1928. First, because two other letters prove Ford was still in Toulon on 9 May 1927, whereas this letter is written from Paris, and says 'I don't go to the studio every day & only just got y^r note just now', rather than excusing himself by saying he had been away. (The other letters are Ford to Elinor Wylie, 2 June 1927 (Yale), and Ford to Pound, 2 May 1927 (*Pound/Ford*, 88–9), which have him leaving Toulon on the 11th and reaching Paris on the 12th.) Secondly, because the black border of the writing paper places the letter after 3 June 1927, the date of his mother's death. Ford was still using this paper in May 1928: his long letter of the 5th to Garnett is written on it. Whereas Ford to Elinor Wylie, 2 June 1927 (Yale) is not. Thirdly, the next (correctly) dated communication between them is a poem dated 17 May 1928, after which Ford is writing to her regularly. It seems unlikely that there would be a break of more than a year in such an intense correspondence. Cheatham sailed with him in the middle of May 1928; and the

poems he wrote her then show they were already intimate; so a dinner rendezvous a few days before the sailing is highly probable. Cheatham's notebook titled 'My Trips' lists fifty-five people she met in Paris. Ford is the fifty-third, which supports the view that they met soon before the voyage. Finally, Ford writes that he has to take Julie to a consultation with a specialist that day. Ford to Bowen, 'Friday May 12 1928' [*sic*: presumably 11–12 May], talks of her having seen a specialist 'yesterday', who 'would not think of operating till the end of the month'. While Bowen was away from Paris in May 1928 Ford had consulted two doctors about Julie.

The other evidence for Judd's belief that they had met in 1927 and that 'by January, 1928 the affair had clearly begun' concerns two letters dated '14 Jan. '28 ' and 'Tuesday 29th Jan 1928'. But in both cases Ford has made the common mistake of using the old year's date in the new. Both refer to his imminent voyage to New York by the *De Grasse*, on which he left Paris on 30 Jan. 1929; 29 Jan. was a Sunday in 1928, but a Tuesday in 1929. Finally, and most decisively, on 28 July 1928 Ford wrote to her that the first half of the year 'saw us know each other'.

Ford sent an undated copy of the photograph (illustrated following p. 416) that he said he liked best, saying 'This is for a birthday greeting really, for it sh^d. reach you just about—Oh RVAD—the anniversary of Helen Ashbury's party'.

Ford to Cheatham, 16 June 1928; 14 Jan. [1929; misdated 1928].

3 The Wrights were divorced on 11 May 1928: clippings from St Louis newspapers at Cornell. *When the Wicked Man*, 125. *It Was the Nightingale*, 255.

4 Mizener, 383. Putnam, *Paris Was Our Mistress*, 89–90. Ford to Bowen, 'Friday May 12 1928' [*sic*: presumably 11–12 May, since the 11th was Friday, and the letter was continued into the following morning]. This letter implies he was to leave the following day, though he told Bowen he had a reservation on the *Suffren* for the 14th: 'Tuesday' [though probably Wednesday 18 Apr. 1928]. 'Saint Christopher', *New York Herald Tribune Books* (3 June 1928), 1, 6. For similar comments about a Catholic upbringing, see *Return to Yesterday*, 298; and *The Presence of Ford Madox Ford*, 225.

5 Bowen to Ford, 1 June [1928]. Ford to Bowen, 'Friday May 12 1928' [*sic*: presumably 11–12 May]. A postscript outlines elaborate travel-plans to return to Paris via Vancouver, Shanghai, and Marseilles. But it was not to be: he sailed back from New York to Marseilles in August.

6 Cheatham numbered the poems, and added brief glosses to some. The stanza is quoted from 'What the Shaft Said', dated 17 May 1928 and inscribed 'For Elizabeth Cheatham'; the poem was later published, as the first of 'Two Songs', in the *Imagist Anthology* (London: Chatto and Windus, 1930). The second, 'To the tune of *Nicolette au Clair Visage*', was the eighth poem to Cheatham, a haunting song-dialogue about how long they will wait, be true, and be sad in their love. By the time they were published the affair had ended, and Ford removed the dedication.

7 'For May 18th 1928'.

8 From a diary entitled 'My Trips'.

9 The American edition of *A Little Less Than Gods* has Ford in New York on 21 May 1928: 361. But he may not have disembarked until the 22nd, which would be the day the last of the shipboard poems was written (if one was written per day, and they have been numbered in the right order). Ford's first letter to Cheatham is dated 23 May: he is still unpacking, having been 'apartment-hunting' (he didn't find one on this trip). Ford to Mrs Anna F. Cheatham, 31 May 1928. Ford to Elizabeth Cheatham, 'Saturday' [9 June 1928].

10 Ford to Cheatham, 16 June 1928. Mizener, 589, n. 8. *A little Less Than Gods*, 155; 181–
2, 187, 196–7, 213–14, 287–8, 304–5 etc. *'Auto-Plagiarism', unpublished typescript, 4.
'Not Idle!', *New York Herald Tribune Books* (1 July 1928), 1, 6. (Ford was still incorporating covert messages to Cheatham as late as 8 Dec. 1929, in a review in the *New York
Herald Tribune Books*, 4.) *'Salute to Adventure' (review of Herbert Gorman's *Dumas,
The Incredible Marquis*), *Forum*, 82/5 (Nov. 1929), p. vi. Ford to Cheatham, 23 June
1928.

11 Ford to Cheatham, 16, 23 June 1928. Mr Cheatham to Elizabeth, 3 July 1928. *The Good
Soldier*, 276–7.

12 Unfortunately none of Cheatham's letters to Ford appear to have survived. Ford to
Cheatham, 25 June; 1 July 1928.

13 Ford to Cheatham, 1 July 1928. Ford to Jeanne Foster, 27 July 1928, says 'Renee' is
'very much recovered by now': Londraville, 195.

14 Mr Cheatham to Elizabeth, 3 July 1928. Ford to Cheatham, 1 July; 15 July; 23 June
1928.

15 Ford to Cheatham, 6 July 1928. The completion date in the book is 27 Aug. 1928, but
that would refer to correcting the proofs. Ford told Cheatham about his work revising
the typescript: 'I finished my book yesterday at noon after working two days and one
whole night without stopping'. Ford to Cheatham, 12 July 1928. 'I love' could almost be
a typographical error for 'I live'; but the phrase 'numb affair' prepares for it so delicately
that it's possible that a man who lived and wrote 'in mental pictures' and visions should
love in them too. George Feilding and Hélène de Frèjus do.

16 Ford to Cheatham, 21 July 1928. One of the blurbs was for Josephine Herbst, whose
novel *Nothing is Sacred* he reviewed in the *Bookman*, 68 (Sept. 1928), 87–8. An incisive
sentence from that review indicates how his thinking about the history of the novel had
illuminated the flaws of *A Little Less Than Gods*: 'That really is the problem that is
before the modern novelist. If the novel in the future as in the past can only exist with
the unusual, the hero, the type, or the demi-god for its sole pabulum it must in a more
and more standardizing world end by losing all contact with life—and by dying as a
form of art.' 'On Conrad's Vocabulary', *Bookman*, 67 (June 1928), 405–8 (which became
the second half of Ford's preface to *The Sisters*).

   Mizener, 388, said 'He did a hurried revision of *That Same Poor Man* ['Mr Croyd']
before leaving New York, and was unhappy when Viking turned it down'. But not only
does this letter to Cheatham make it clear he was revising the novel after leaving New
York; but also a letter from B[ernice] B[aumgarten] of Brandt and Brandt to Ford, 17
Dec. 1928, proves that Viking were then still intending to publish the novel. The essay
on Conrad was the typescript 'Oh Two such silver currents', which was revised as
'Working with Conrad', *Yale Review*, 18 (June 1929), 699–715; and became the third
chapter of *Return to Yesterday*.

17 Ford to Cheatham, 21; 26 July 1928.

18 Mizener, 385. The dedication reads 'To: Rene Katherine Clarissa David' in the Viking
edition. *A Little Less Than Gods*, p. ix.

19 Ford to Cheatham, 28 July; 3 Aug.; 10 Aug. 1928.

20 Ford to Bradley, 13 Aug. 1928: *Letters*, 178–9. *Great Trade Route*, 394. He doesn't date
this episode, but gives the name of the ship as 'the enjoyable, vanished, white *Providence*
of the Fabre line': probably a slip for the *Patria*, which was a Fabre line boat.

21 *It Was the Nightingale*, 125–6. *A Mirror to France*, 73. *'Seeing Europe—at Its Worst',
New York Herald Tribune Magazine (16 June 1929), 1–3. His recollections of his
journey are mostly to do with being overcharged because he was travelling with Ameri-

cans. Ford to Bradley, 13 Aug. 1928: *Letters*, 178–9. Ford to Cheatham, 22 Sept. 1928. The account of 'Commissions Received from Brandt 1928' is at Cornell.

22 Ford misdated the composition of *The English Novel* a year early when he wrote in the English edition in 1930: 'This book was written in New York, on board the S.S. *Patria*, and in the port and neighbourhood of Marseilles during July and August, 1927.' He told Cheatham on 22 Sept. 1928: 'I duly finished my book yesterday and sent if off', and that he was 'going to take a week or so in Corsica and shall then come back here to correct up the typescript and get the last swimming of the season.' This probably refers to *The English Novel*; though his comment to Bradley on the same day—'Now I have got that novel off my hands'—might mean that he had finished the revision of 'Mr Croyd' (though of course this reference might be to the proofs of *A Little Less Than Gods*): *Letters*, 180–1. Mizener, 389, says erroneously that Ford worked on *The English Novel* during the spring of 1929. Ford to Bernice Baumgarten, 28 Aug. 1928. Ford to Cheatham, 25 Aug.; 22 Sept. 1928. Ford to Stein, 8 Sept. [1928]: *Letters*, 179–80. Ford to Pound, 10 Sept. 1928: *Pound/Ford*, 91. Pound's articles were published in the *New York Herald Tribune Books* the following January. Mizener, 385, says Ford travelled back to Paris via the Jura and Strasbourg; but his evidence is Ford's letter to Stein (8 Sept.) saying 'I rather meditate' taking that route. In the event he spent longer in Corsica than he had originally planned; and there is no evidence he actually reached the Jura or Strasbourg this year. Ford to Bradley, 22 Sept., says he'll be staying at the Savoy Hotel, Monte Carlo, on 24 Sept. Ford, cable to Cheatham (misspelt as 'Miss Cheavsam'), 16 Sept. 1928. His letter to Cheatham of 22 Sept. implies that he is leaving for Corsica at once. A postcard on 13 Oct. tells her he planned to leave for the mainland that night. He cabled her from Toulon on 15 Oct. to say he'd written from Corsica (where there was a postal strike). Ford to Julie, 15 Oct. 1928 (from Toulon), says he returned from Corsica on the 14th, 'très enrhumé'.

23 Ford to Stein, 8 Sept. [1928]: Yale; Ludwig omitted this sentence in the *Letters*, 179–80. Ford to Cheatham, 25? Oct. [1928]; cable and letter, 11 Nov. 1928. Angier, 145. Mizener, 386. Ford to George Oppenheimer, *Letters*, 181–2, shows he was back in Paris by at least 9 Nov., though he probably arrived earlier: he had promised Julie (15 Oct. 1928) he would be there by 1 Nov. Ford to Cheatham, 29 Nov. 1928.

24 Ford to Cheatham, 8 [Dec. 1928; misdated 8 Nov., but the envelope says 'Par S.S. Paris / 9th Dec 1928'. The New York postmark of 19 Dec. supports the Dec. date]. Given Ford's wish the letter should be burnt, I quote it with trepidation. But the tone of his exact words seems crucial given his comment about writing it in a comic rather than a mean spirit (the comedy wouldn't survive paraphrase). Cheatham chose not to burn it, and a biographer can only be grateful to her for preserving the best picture we have of Ford's relationship with Rene Wright.

25 Bowen to Ford, 12 Aug. [1928]. Ford to Cheatham, 7 Jan. 1929; 13 Dec. 1928. Mizener, 360. Tate, *Memories and Essays*, 47–9, 53–4; 'Allen Tate', in *The Presence of Ford Madox Ford*, 13. Tate's reminiscences need to be treated with caution. His claim in the former that he was met in Paris by a summons from Gertrude Stein is disproved by Ford's letter to Stein a month later, 25 Dec. 1928 (Yale), asking if the Tates could call on her. In the latter he misremembered his own address in New York as Perry Street (rather than Bank Street). Veronica Makowsky, *Caroline Gordon: A Biography* (New York and Oxford: Oxford University Press, 1989), 87.

26 Ford to Cheatham, 13; 31 Dec. 1928. Ford to Ruth Kerr, 4 Feb. 1929, describes being attacked. Mizener, 386, mistakenly places the assault in New York. It is possible the episode happened the following year, and Ford misdated the letter; but he was in Paris

on 4 Feb. 1930 too. He told Cheatham he began the novel on 11 Dec. In the book he changed the starting date to his birthday, 17 Dec. (p. 320). Cable to Cheatham, 30 Dec. 1928.

27 Ford to Cheatham, 31 Dec. 1928; 14 Jan. [1929; misdated '1928'; but it picks up the discussion of the letters of 31 Dec. 1928 and 7 Jan. 1929, and refers to his plan to sail by the *de Grasse* at the end of the month, which he did]. Ford to Darley & Cumberland [and not to Robert Garnett, as Mizener says on p. 388], 3 Jan. [1929, misdated 1928]. Goldring, *South Lodge*, 128. Mizener, 388, 590, n. 16. Darley & Cumberland to Ford, 22 [Jan. 1929]: quoted in Ford to Darley & Cumberland [between 24 and 28 Jan. 1929]. *Last Post*, 290. Ford to Bowen, 22 Oct. 1927. Elsie had moved back to Kitcat with Katharine on 7 Oct. 1924: Katharine to Mizener, 11 Dec. 1966. After her divorce from the Duke of Marlborough, Consuelo Vanderbilt had married a Frenchman, Jacques Balsan, in 1921. But in France the marriage of a Catholic to a divorcée could not be recognized unless her marriage could be annulled by the Roman Catholic Church. She had to appear before an English tribunal of Catholic priests, and argue that her mother had forced her to marry the duke against her wishes (which was true). The annulment was granted in Feb. 1927, and caused 'a storm' in New York. See David Green, *The Churchills of Blenheim* (London: Constable, 1984), 144–5.

28 Mizener, 389. Ford to Cheatham, 31 Dec. 1928.

29 Ford to Darley & Cumberland [between 24 and 28 Jan. 1929].

30 Ford, cable to Cheatham [undated, but late Jan. 1929]. Cheatham's 'catechistic letter' was dated 22 Dec., but Ford didn't receive it until 7 Jan., after he had got her letters of 23 and 25 Dec. Ford to Cheatham, 14 Jan. [1929]; 7 Jan. 1929.

31 Ford to Cheatham, 14 Jan. [1929, but misdated 1928]. Ford's account with Brandt and Brandt for 1928 shows that Viking made five payments totalling $3,500.

32 Ford to Cheatham, 14 Jan. [1929]; 31 Dec. 1928.

33 Mizener's account of this period is seriously inaccurate. He has Ford going to New York with Wright at the end of 1928 (p. 386). MacShane, 204, is even further out, saying Ford returned to New York in May 1929. Mizener also thought that Ford had vacated his flat to move into Bowen's, when she moved out to a new apartment in the rue Boissonade (386). But as Bowen, *Drawn from Life* makes clear (180, 183; though it doesn't give a date), this was after Ford returned to Paris in the summer of 1929. Tate to Lytle, 21 Dec. 1928: Thomas Daniel Young and Elizabeth Sarcone (eds.), *The Lytle–Tate Letters: The Correspondence of Andrew Lytle and Allen Tate* (Jackson and London: University Press of Mississipi, 1987), 14–15. Tate, *Memories and Essays*, 48–9. Veronica Makowsky, *Caroline Gordon*, 80. Ford to George Oppenheimer (of Viking), 9 Nov. 1928, indicates that the manuscript was probably 'That Same Poor Man' ('Mr Croyd'): *Letters*, 181–2. Ford to Cheatham, 'Tuesday 29th Jan' [1929, though misdated 1928]; 16 Feb. 1929 (addressed to 320 West 80th Street, New York, where she was staying).

34 *'I Won't Become a Citizen!', *New York Herald Tribune Magazine* (27 Oct. 1929), 1–2, 28 (p. 2). Ford to Cheatham, 20 Feb. 1929; 23 Feb. 1929 (cable and letter). Being cheated by the waiter made enough of an impression for Ford to describe the episode in *'Seeing Europe—at its Worst', *New York Herald Tribune Magazine* (16 June 1929), 1–3.

35 Ford to Cheatham, 28 Feb. 1929.

36 Loeb, 'Ford Madox Ford's "The Good Soldier": A Critical Reminiscence', *London Magazine*, NS, 3/9 (Dec. 1963), 66–7. Here he places his meetings with Ford and Wright in 1929. Mizener, 384, 589, n. 6, appears not to have noticed this dating, but

points out that the 1930 dating Loeb uses in *The Way it Was* (New York: Criterion Books, 1959), 189–90, is impossible. He places the meetings in the summer of 1928, which is possible, though Wright's unhappiness suggests it was nearer the end of their affair. Ford to Cheatham, 9 Mar. 1929.

37 See Harvey, 380–3, for reviews of the novel. Ford to Cheatham, 9 Mar. 1929. Valentine Wannop gives Tietjens a similar talisman in *Some Do Not . . .* , 347–8; he had been thinking again about the idea of divine protection when he wrote the story 'A Miracle', discussed on p. 258.

38 Ford to Cheatham, 2 Apr. 1929.

39 *When the Wicked Man*, 212, 301, 79, 256.

Chapter 19

1 Ford to Bowen, 16 May 1929. Ford to Cheatham, 14 Jan. [1929]. Ford to Harrison Smith, 5 May 1929 (saying he expects to finish the novel the following week). Ford to Bradley, 16 May 1929. Mizener, 389 and 590, n. 18, is probably right to guess that the 'New York, 15th May, 1929' at the end of the novel refers to the date the first version was completed, since Viking had seen it by 10 July: see Ford to Bernice Baumgarten, *Letters*, 185–6. Hartley, *Saturday Review*, 146 (24 Nov. 1928), 692, 694. *When the Wicked Man*, 287, 224–5, 313. See Ch. 21 for a further discussion of *When the Wicked Man*. *'Auto-Plagiarism', 3. Hunt, thinking of Ford's attitude to Brigit Patmore, wrote of 'the peace of Renunciation that he was so good at': Hunt, *The Flurried Years*, 95. *When the Wicked Man*, 200, is revealingly candid here too about Notterdam's comparable doubts about whether he actually wants to consummate his passion for Henrietta— doubts Ford presumably had about his own feelings for Cheatham.

2 *When the Wicked Man*, 254–5, 288–9.

3 Ford to Victor Gollancz, 1 Mar. 1932; to Walpole, 2. Dec. 1929 and 28 May 1930: *Letters*, 204–5, 190–2, 195–6. 'Gringoire' appears in Hugo's *Notre-Dame de Paris*, in which he is an anachronistic version of the Norman poet Pierre Gringore (*c*.1475–1636, according to the *Oxford Companion to French Literature*). The poetized version of an actual poet may have caught Ford's imagination; or he may have been remembering the one act comedy *Gringoire*, by Theodore de Banville, that Violet Hunt and her mother saw in 1887 (see Violet Hunt and Margaret Hunt, Diary for 1887, entry for 4 Nov.), and which was staged in London throughout the 1890s, and in 1914 and 1922. *No Enemy*, 9, 21. Stang, *Ford Madox Ford* (New York: Frederick Ungar, 1977), 49. Also see Samuel Hynes, 'The Genre of *No Enemy*', *Antaeus*, 56 (Spring 1986), 125–42; and Paul Skinner, 'Just Ford—An Appreciation of *No Enemy: A Tale of Reconstruction*', *Agenda*, 27/4– 28/1 (Winter 1989–Spring 1990), 103–9. It was perhaps because *No Enemy* isn't like any other book that Ford found it harder than usual to settle on a title: the manuscript at Cornell lists twenty-six alternatives. *When the Wicked Man*, 222. T. S. Eliot, 'Tradition and the Individual Talent' (1919), *Selected Essays*, third enlarged edn. (London: Faber, 1951), 13–22 (18).

4 *Conversations with Malcolm Cowley*, ed. Thomas Daniel Young (Jackson and London: University Press of Mississippi, 1986), 7–8.

5 Ford to Hugh Walpole, 2 Dec. 1929: *Letters*, 190–2. He dated the composition of the *History* as beginning on 1 July 1929. After a long struggle Ford eventually got Stanley Unwin to agree to publish it, but then substituted *The March of Literature* in the contract. See Ford to Ruth Aley (misspelt 'Ailey'), 12 Aug. 1936, and ch. 25, n. 30 below. It was eventually published in a fine edition by Sondra Stang and Solon Beinfeld: see 225 for the composition dates; p. 13 for quotation. Stang said (p. xv) that Ford set

about writing the book 'Around 1928–29, at the height of his powers as a novelist [. . .]'. I have found no evidence he was working on it before the summer of 1929. This edition includes two proposals in which he outlines three volumes (pp. 226, 228). See Ch. 20, n. 12 on the relation between the *History* and the memoirs. In a letter to H. G. Wells, 28 July 1930, he says he has just finished the first of four. Mizener, 390. Ford to Keating, 26 May 1930. Gordon, 'The Story of Ford Madox Ford', *New York Times Book Review* (17 Sept. 1950), 1, 22. *Great Trade Route*, 112.

6 Ford told George Oppenheimer (of Viking) on 9 Nov. 1928 that he had finished revising 'Mr Croyd' and was getting it typed: *Letters*, 181–2. Bradley's misfortunes delayed the delivery of the typescript to Viking until 17 Dec. 1928: Bernice Baumgarten (of Brandt & Brandt) to Bradley, 17 and 19[?] Dec. 1928. Viking told Baumgarten they planned to get the book typeset at once; but they were appalled by the state of the typescript— missing pages, defective spelling and punctuation; said that Ford had not revised a love scene as he had promised; and wanted an improved copy. This bears out Mizener's comment that Ford's revision was 'hurried' (p. 388); and perhaps also Ford's comment to Cheatham (14 Jan. [1929]) that his lassitude was damaging his career. Viking had rejected it by 31 Dec. 1928, when Ford told Baumgarten he had 'always disliked' the book. The undated cable to Brandt & Brandt quoted by Mizener, 388, in which Ford protested 'I rewrote Poor Man at urgent request of Oppenheimer and also Carl Brandt against my own judgement and wishes' was sent from France, and indicates that he heard the news while in Paris in Jan. 1929—which would help account for his despondency in his letters to Cheatham at the time. Ford to Baumgarten, 10 July 1929: *Letters*, 185–6.

7 Aldington isn't named as editor for the *Imagist Anthology* (London: Chatto and Windus, 1930); but his autobiography, *Life for Life's Sake* (London: Cassell, 1968), 130–1, reveals him as having been the prime mover. *Thus to Revisit*, 168, 229. *Imagist Anthology*, pp. xi, xiii, xvi.

8 Ford to Baumgarten, 7 July 1929 (quoted by Mizener, 390); 10 July 1929: *Letters*, 185–6; and Baumgarten to Ford, 2 Aug. 1929. Ford to Cheatham [n.d., but late July 1929]. Ford's *Imagist Anthology* introduction is dated 'New York: August 1, 1929' (which makes it hard to see why Mizener said he helped Aldington during the spring of 1929: 393). *It Was the Nightingale*, 339–42, has Ford lunching with William and Louise Bullitt on 1 Aug., and investing money on the 4th. A telegram to Cheatham from the SS *Berengaria* confirms he took that boat: the date-stamp is faint but appears to read '1929 Aug 9'. So if the boat sailed as advertised, Ford would have left New York on 7 Aug. He was in London when he wrote to Harold Monro on 16 Aug. 1929: UCLA. He had quoted Ronsard's lines (slightly rewritten, as here), which promise the beloved that when she is old she will regret both the famous poet's love and her proud scorn, in a previous letter to Cheatham (9 Mar. 1929), adding: 'it isn't you know just vanity that, for I have given you love enough, my dearest, to celebrate you a little.'

9 Ford to Bowen, 28 Aug. 1918. Hemingway to Mizener, 12 May 1950: *Selected Letters*, 694–5. Hemingway said Ford's remark made 'such a bad impression' on him he 'burned every letter in the flat includeing [*sic*] Ford's'.

10 *It Was the Nightingale*, 221–2. He says there the *Berengaria* 'rolled towards Paris over the winter seas', but there is no record of his having been on that boat other than for this summer crossing. He only wrote five holograph chapters in his next book, *Return to Yesterday*; but there are complete holograph versions for the next two, *The Rash Act* and *It Was the Nightingale* itself. After that, Ford returned to the typewriter.

11 Ford to Harold Monro, 16 Aug. 1929 (UCLA), is on Golfers' Club stationery, though the name of the club has been deleted, and replaced with 'Apt 7/22'. Ford to Ralph Pinker, 17 Aug. 1929 ('Golfers' Club' undeleted). Bradley to Ford, 16 Aug. 1929. Mizener, 392–3. Ford to Pinker, 11 Sept. 1929: *Letters*, 186–8 (Ludwig says this is to Eric Pinker, but it is more likely to be to Ralph: the letter itself is addressed simply to 'Dear Pinker'.

12 *Callaghan, *That Summer in Paris* (New York: Coward-McCann, 1963), 117–18. Gordon to Sally Wood, early Spring 1932: Wood, *The Southern Mandarins*, 100. Tate, *Memories and Essays*, 57–8; also *The Presence of Ford Madox Ford*, 13. The last-known communication with Wright is indicated by Ralph Pinker's letter to Ford, 7 Jan. 1930, saying that he has cabled her $280 as instructed. This was presumably Ford's repayment of a loan, signifying the formal ending of their affair. She remarried her ex-husband Guy in 1933, after he had divorced his third wife that March. This time they stayed married until his death in 1946. She lived on until 1957. See Mizener, 589, n. 6.

13 Tate, *Memories and Essays*, 54–5, 57–8, 60. Mary McIntosh, in *The Presence of Ford Madox Ford*, 207–9, 212. She places the *bout rimés* parties on Thursdays; but Bandy recorded dates that fix them on Saturdays: *W. T. Bandy, 'Memories of Montparnasse: Ford Madox Ford's Sonnet Parties', *Cumberland Poetry Review*, 3/2 (Spring 1984), 37–41, remembers Ford sometimes composing three sonnets. John Peale Bishop, in *New Directions: Number Seven*, 460–2. Dahlberg, *Epitaphs of Our Times* (New York: G. Braziller, 1967), 271. Biala, in conversation with Max Saunders, 22 Sept. 1990. Biala to Mizener, 3 Oct. 1968.

14 Putnam, *Paris Was Our Mistress*, 125–6. One story, about Ford being startled by birdsong in No Man's Land, is discussed above on pp. 7–8. Another story Putnam relates is that the small flat at 32 rue de Vaugirard 'had formerly belonged to a favorite professor of his at the Sorbonne and that he had taken it for old sake's sake'. Putnam says he later learned that Ford had never been at the Sorbonne. While he is not known to have studied formally there, Ford did often talk of having attended lectures at the Sorbonne, which he may well have done while in Paris in 1892. See Saunders, i. 512, n. 19. Ford told Goldring that the flat had belonged to 'An old professor to whom I was greatly attached'. It is possible that Ford, living in the Quartier Latin, knew professors from the Sorbonne; but Ford told Goldring he went to the Sorbonne '*after I left Eton* (whoof)'—where he had *not* been at school. Goldring explains that Ford 'used the terms "Eton" and "the Guards" in a symbolic sense', in order to convey an impression of having been to 'one of our historic public schools' and having 'served in a famous regiment' to American listeners who were not familiar with University College School and the Welch Regiment. Something comparable is probably true of Ford's story of the Sorbonne professor. Alternatively, the joke may have been on Goldring, and his ability to retain his public school hauteur along with his socialist principles. Goldring, *South Lodge*, 178–9. Leon Edel to Saunders, [13 Feb. 1996] and 19 Jan. 1996. *The Presence of Ford Madox Ford*, 206.

15 Mizener, 382, 589, n. 1. *The Rash Act*, 170–1.

16 Seldes, in *Denis Brian, *The Faces of Hemingway* (London: Grafton Books, 1988), 49–50. Seldes dates the evening 'the late twenties or early thirties'. The mention of the Conrad edition might suggest an earlier date (see Ford to W. H. Thompson, 5 Feb. 1926: *Letters*, 166–8). But it's unlikely he would have thought his work forgotten while *Parade's End* was doing well between 1926 and 1928. Whereas the dropping of his name from the collaborations might still have been rankling in 1929. Putnam, *Paris Was Our Mistress*, 122–4.

17 *'I Won't Become a Citizen!', *New York Herald Tribune Magazine* (27 Oct. 1929), 1–2, 28; excerpted as 'America's Chief Attraction', *The 1930 European Scrapbook* (New York: Forum, 1930), 175–6.

18 Gordon, in *The Presence of Ford Madox Ford*, 200. Here she implies the dictation was done in New York in 1927. But the following, contemporaneous, quotation makes it clear it was in Paris at the end of 1929.

19 Gordon to Wood, 21 Jan. 1930, and early Spring 1932: Wood, *The Southern Mandarins*, 51; 100. Makowsky, *Caroline Gordon*, 87. Malcolm Cowley recalled someone saying Gordon 'once had an affair with Ford Madox Ford', but he found it hard to believe, saying 'Ford had an attractive mind, but it stopped there': *Conversations with Malcolm Cowley*, ed. Thomas Daniel Young (Jackson and London: University Press of Mississippi, 1986), 195.

20 *The Presence of Ford Madox Ford*, 207. Tate, *Memories and Essays*, 60. *Dahlberg, *Alms for Oblivion* (Minneapolis: University of Minnesota Press, 1964), 9–10. *New Directions: Number Seven*, 461. In his 'Introduction' to a later edition of Hemingway's novel (New York: The Modern Library, 1932), Ford wrote: 'I experienced a singular sensation on reading the first sentence of A FAREWELL TO ARMS. There are sensations you cannot describe.'

21 *The Presence of Ford Madox Ford*, 209. Leon Edel to Saunders [13 Feb. 1996]. Ford told Ralph Pinker on 26 Sept. 1929 that he was sending the first two chapters of the *History*; but Pinker wrote on 1 Nov. to acknowledge receipt of the second. Ford to Ruth Kerr, 10 Sept. 1929. Gorman, *New York Herald Tribune Books* (29 Dec. 1929), 5. Harvey, 384–5, lists only seven: I have found only three others: a brief, mixed notice in *'Recent Books', *New Yorker* (23 Nov. 1929), 117–22 (120–1): 'A book by Ford Madox Ford is always a book about Ford Madox Ford, and if you like Ford Madox Ford, you will like "No Enemy"'. *Herschel Brickell, *North American Review*, 229/1 (Jan. 1930), in the un-numbered 'Literary Landscape' pages bound into the front [p. xii]: 'an excellent piece of writing, as anything from Ford's pen is likely to be'; and *Basil Davenport, 'Without Rancor', *Saturday Review of Literature*, 6 (1 Feb. 1930), 92: 'It must be read by any one who is trying to piece together any complete impression of the war. There is nothing like its full and sane acceptance of reality without rancor in any other book of this generation—no, nor anywhere else since the earliest piece of realism in literature, the soldier's speech in the "Agamemnon" [. . .].' Ford to Ruth Kerr, 12 Nov. 1929. Mizener, 591, n. 13, speculates that, like Henry Martin in *The Rash Act*, Ford may have bought shares in Anaconda Copper. Brandt & Brandt to Ford, 27 Jan. 1930.

22 Ford to Hugh Walpole, 2 Dec. 1929, 28 May and 16 Dec. 1930: *Letters*, 190–6. Ford to Stein, 24 Nov. 1929: Yale. Ford to Keating [n.d., but Dec. 1929] also mentions 'a series of minor operations'. The three books not then published in England were *The English Novel, No Enemy, and When the Wicked Man* (though *New York Essays* and *New Poems* had also been published solely in New York).

23 Tate, *Memories and Essays*, 63–5. In the book he dates this evening as 'One bright Sunday morning in December'. But in two letters to Mizener, 3 and 26 Aug. 1969 (Vanderbilt), he gives slightly different accounts, placing it in late Oct. or early Nov. Makowsky, *Caroline Gordon*, 86–7, tells a different version, which accounts for Tate's tartness towards Stein, who presents herself as outranking all the men, including him: 'She informed him that, "being a Southerner, he could not be expected to know any history!"' Ford to Pound, 19 Sept. 1920: *Letters*, 124–5.

24 Putnam, *Paris Was Our Mistress*, 126. Ellmann, *James Joyce*, 622 n.

25 Bowen, *Drawn from Life*, 181–2. Bowen turned towards Tchelitchew as a mentor,

telling Ford: 'He is really very intelligent on the subject [of painting] and may really turn out to be the person I need to make me "see" much in Modern Painting': Bowen to Ford, 4–6 Dec. [1927]. Mizener, 393. Ford to Keating [n.d., but Dec. 1929]. The film is discussed by Biala, *The Presence of Ford Madox Ford*, 224; though it is misdated as having been made in 1930; whereas Ford's letter thanking Keating is written the Christmas before he changed apartments at 32 rue de Vaugirard in the spring of 1930. Serendipity Books, Catalogue 45: item 191.

Mizener, 393, says that in the autumn of 1929 Ford 'made a quick trip to New York to try to straighten out his New York publishing arrangements'; but he cites no evidence. I think the assertion must be based on three letters to Ralph Pinker, of which Ford's carbon copies at Cornell have been catalogued as having been written in New York: 30 Sept., 23 Oct., and 4 Nov. However, the originals of all three (at Princeton) are written on 32 rue de Vaugirard paper. Besides, Ford gave his cable address as Paris in another letter to Pinker of 26 Sept., in which he is still waiting for the proofs of *No Enemy* to reach him from America. If he was in Paris on 26 Sept. he would not have been in New York by the 30th. Bandy is definite about Ford being in Paris for his *bouts-rimés* parties on 26 Oct. and 2 Nov.; so by the same logic of slow transatlantic crossings, neither of the other two letters can have been written in New York. Now can he have made the trip between 1 and 23 Oct., or 4 and 20 Nov. (when he signed a typescript he sent to Keating: see Harvey, 92), since letters to Ruth Kerr of 15 Oct. and 12 Nov. were also written from France. He told Walpole on 2 Dec. 1929 he would visit New York as soon as the holidays finished: *Letters*, 192. He was still in Paris on 13 Dec., when he signed Constable's contract for *The English Novel*: Constable's files. His next known transatlantic crossing was in the autumn of 1930.

Chapter 20

1 Mary McIntosh, contribution to *The Presence of Ford Madox Ford*, 206–13 (209, 210, 207). Bowen, *Drawn from Life*, 180.
2 He also wrote her a poem, *'The Sailor's Wife: (Tout Doux)', inscribed 'Ford did this for Caroline' and dated 21 Dec. 1929. The manuscript, apparently unpublished, is at Princeton. Ford to Gordon, 24 Feb., 25 Mar., and 2 Apr. 1930: Princeton.
3 *The Presence of Ford Madox Ford*, 211. Biala, in conversation with Max Saunders, 22 Sept. 1990, said she didn't think Pound was at the party, so that she didn't meet him until she went to Rapallo with Ford in 1932. But 'Fleuve Profond' mentions 'Ezra' as at late-night Paris party. The Pounds were in Paris in June 1930, when they had dinner with Ford and the Trasks: *Pound/Ford*, 92. Charles Norman, *Ezra Pound* (New York: Macmillan, 1960), 303–4. Ford was excited, and kept repeating 'Pound is coming'. 'Fleuve Profond' was first published in *New English Poems*, ed. Lascelles Abercrombie (London: Victor Gollancz, [Oct.] 1931), 176–8. It also appears in the 1936 *Collected Poems*.
4 *The Presence of Ford Madox Ford*, 211–12. Biala in conversation with Max Saunders, 10 Apr. 1994. 'Biala (Janice Ford)'; notes for an exhibition of her work at Olivet College: Olivet College Library. Her portrait of Ford reading a book on Cézanne is reproduced following p. 416.
5 Biala to Mizener, 3 Oct. 1968. Ford to Pound, 8 Mar. 1933: *Pound/Ford*, 119–20. The novel Ford left unfinished at his death, 'Professor's Progress', also had a working title 'Left Turn': Ford to Unwin, 25 May 1939: *Letters*, 324–5. Ford took his stand in the section 'FOR the Government' in *Authors Take Sides on the Spanish War* (London: Left Review [1937]), 11: 'I am unhesitatingly for the existing Spanish Government and

against Franco's attempt—on every ground of feeling and reason. In addition, as the merest commonsense, the Government of the Spanish, as of any other nation, should be settled and defined by the inhabitants of that nation. Mr. Franco seeks to establish a government resting on the arms of Moors, Germans, Italians. Its success *must* be contrary to world conscience' (p. 11). Hitler and Mussolini are discussed in *Great Trade Route*: see 434–5 on 'mass-manias'. *Provence* also mentions Hitler several times: on p. 332 Ford hopes 'that the end of Mr. Hitler—and soon—may be a long stay in a cage in the Thiergarten of some small South German town'. *It Was the Nightingale*, p. ix.

The letters to newspapers on Jewish questions were not published (or if they were, the publications have not yet been traced). Ford told Bradley on 8 June 1932 he was planning a series of articles on Zionism, which he had 'for long been interested in'; and he claimed to have been 'the first person to propose what afterwards became the Balfour declaration' (*Letters*, 207. In *Provence*, 63, he says he tried to impress on Masterman 'the desirability of making the return to Zion of the Jews one of the items of our return to peace [. . .]'). He asked Dreiser if he would take an article for *The American Spectator* 'about the state of Jewry, which in Europe has become pretty parlous with the arrival of Hitler and the closing of Palestine': *Letters*, 216–17.

He wrote to the editor of the *Daily Mail* just before 6 Mar. 1933 (Mizener, 593, n. 5, wrongly dates this 13 Mar.) asking if he could write a centre-page article on 'the case of the Jews in Europe'; and he made a similar request to the editor of the *Daily Telegraph* on 13 Mar. On 18 June 1933 he asked Maxwell Perkins (of *Scribner's*) if he could write him an article on Zionism (Mizener, 593, n. 5). He told Jenny Bradley he didn't want to be published by a Nazi publisher: 18 Dec. 1933. He approached the editor of the *British Journal* on 2 Feb. 1934 suggesting a piece on Jewish refugees; and he repeated the idea to the editor of the *New York Times*. A letter from Ford to W. P. Crozier of the *Guardian* says that Crozier had asked (on 10 Mar.) for his views on Palestine. In 1937 Ford asked Paul Palmer if he could write on Zionism for the *American Mercury*: 29 July; *Letters*, 280. He offered to sign a manifesto against Nazism (Ford to Albert H. Gross, 7 Dec. 1938; see *Pound/Ford*, 198, n. 38). He wrote a letter to the *New York Times* about anti-Semitism on 31 Mar. 1939.

6 *The Presence of Ford Madox Ford*, 212, 222. They met Davison at the 1937 Writers' Conference at Boulder, Colorado. Mizener, 394.

7 'An Interview with Janice Biala (1979)', *The Presence of Ford Madox Ford*, 222–3. Bowen, *Drawn from Life*, 83.

8 *Collected Poems* (New York: Oxford University Press, 1936), 293–4. The subtitle 'Poems for' Haïtchka in France appears where the sequence (minus the 'Coda') was first published, in *New English Poems*, edited by Lascelles Abercrombie (London: Victor Gollancz, 1931), 172–92. The idea of God as a 'stupid man' rewrites that of God as a 'kind man' in 'On Heaven'. God is perhaps 'stupid' in the sense that the Tory party is stupid; though the poem also replies obliquely to Francis Hueffer: Ford's patience has been rewarded; sexuality can be joyful, proving the father 'stupid'.

9 Mizener, 393; see also 402–4 for an excellent discussion of 'Coda'. *Collected Poems* (1936), 319. Biala told Mizener the poem was written 'for the anniversary of the beginning of our life together': 3 Oct. 1968. *Return to Yesterday*, 300. The composition dates give the book as finished on 8 Aug. 1931. Biala in conversation with Max Saunders, 20 Sept. 1990. She denied that he had said he was a new man with each woman; and she even doubted that he was really changed with her.

10 Ford also used the strange device of inventing a male character, 'the Patient New Yorker', and dividing Biala's role in both *Provence* and *Great Trade Route* between her

propria persona and this fictionalized *alter ego*. Biala to Max Saunders, 15 Feb. 1990. *Return to Yesterday*, 300. Ford to J. Jefferson Jones (of Lippincott), 4 Sept. 1934.

11 Biala told Mizener, 14 Oct. 1968, that Ford *took* her to see Bowen. Mizener, 394. But her memory played her false here. Biala to Bowen, 17 Mar. 1947, mentions: 'the very first time I saw you—when Ford sent me to you for your approval.' This version is borne out by Bowen, *Drawn from Life*, 183–7; 190.

12 Ford to Bowen [n.d., but on verso of Sue Jenkins to Ford, 10 Feb. 1930]. Ford to Keating, 26 May 1930. Biala to Mizener, 14 Oct. 1968. Biala to Saunders, 4 July 1989. Ford to Wells, 28 July 1930: Illinois. He asked Wells for another loan on 3 Sept. 1930 (Illinois). Ford to [Ralph] Pinker, 18 June 1930, says 'I am in the country for the rest of the summer'. Ford wrote to his agent, Ruth Kerr, from Ballancourt on 2 July 1930. The *History* has Ford there on 14 July (p. 225) and 27 July (p. 12). Biala in conversation with Max Saunders, 22 Sept. 1990. Ralph Pinker to Ford, 7 Feb. 1930, says the *History* is with Dent after having been turned down by Benn, Gollancz, Chatto and Windus, and Macmillan. *History*, 16–17. Most of the autobiographical passages were later cut. Beinfeld and Stang's fine edition restores them; but what they don't say is that they were cut because they were used in *Return to Yesterday*—presumably because Ford couldn't find a publisher for the *History*; though the cutting also served his purpose of trying to make the *History* more 'readable' (see Ford to Ray Long, 2 July 1932: *Letters*, 210). For example, 83–4 and 166–8 of the *History* became 133–4 and 104–7 of the memoirs. The autobiography also recycled sections of *Thus to Revisit* and *Women & Men*: see Harvey, 54, 75–6.

13 *Wambly Bald, *Chicago Tribune* (Paris) (9 Sept. 1930), 4. Ford to Stein, 30 Aug. 1930 (Yale), says he is leaving on the 6th; Ford to Wells, 3 Sept. 1930 (Illinois), says the 7th. Jenkins to Ford, 10 Feb. 1930. Ford to Jenkins, 27 Feb. 1930: *Letters*, 192–3. Ford to Ruth Kerr, 2 July 1930. Ford to Dreiser, 18 Apr. 1931: *Letters*, 201. Mizener, 395, makes Ford's behaviour to Macaulay and Viking sound unreasonable; but it wasn't unreasonable to get frustrated at the difficulty of publishing books as interesting as *No Enemy*, *When the Wicked Man*, and the *History*, nor to be disappointed at the small sales of those that were published.

14 Ford to Biala, 'Wednesday morning—10th' [Sept.?; dated 1930 by Biala]: original in possession of Biala. Wood, *The Southern Mandarins*, 61–3; the letter of 20 Oct. 1930 saying 'This last week has been hectic' implies that Ford was at the Tates' around 15–20 Oct. *Great Trade Route*, 32. *Loeb, 'Ford Madox Ford's *The Good Soldier*', *London Magazine*, 3/9 (Dec. 1963), 67–8. Mizener, 399–400. Ford didn't drive: Biala in conversation with Max Saunders, 22 Sept. 1990.

15 Loeb to Mizener, 13 Sept. 1964.

16 Gordon to Sally Wood, 20 Oct. 1930: Wood, *The Southern Mandarins*, 62. Ford to Biala, 17 Oct. 1930: Biala.

17 Gordon to Wood, 20 Oct. 1930: Wood, *The Southern Mandarins*, 61–3. Gordon to Ford [n.d. but 1931].

18 Ford to Biala, 27 Oct. 1903: Biala. The composition dates of *Return to Yesterday* say it was begun at 50 West 12th Street on 4 Nov. 1930. Viking had paid him $3,500 for *A Little Less Than Gods* and advanced him the same sum for *Notterdam* (see p. 382); so again Ford's willingness to accept less than $2,500 for the *History* was not unreasonable.

19 Ford to Biala, Monday 10 Nov. [1930]: Biala. *Gladys Oaks, 'Ford Madox Ford and Mary Borden Weigh Manners', *New York World* (16 Nov. 1930), Women's Section, 1, 4. The second chapter of *Return to Yesterday* was published in *Scribner's*, 90 (Oct. 1931), 379–86. The contract with Liveright, signed on 21 Nov. 1930, says that Liveright were

to pay Ford, within thirty days of publication, 'a sum equal to the royalty earned on advance sales of this work', and that this sum would be regarded as an advance against all royalties the book earned. In other words, no sales, no payment. The terms for the 'volume of Descriptive Travel Prose' were the same. For the 'volume of Literary and Social Reminiscences' [*Return to Yesterday*] the contract specifies an advance of $1,000 on signing, and a further $500 on publication.

20 *When the Wicked Man*, 320. Loeb to Mizener, 13 Sept. 1964. Loeb dates the crossing 1931, but Ford didn't cross from America to Europe again until 1935.

21 Ford to Walpole, 30 March [1931]: misdated 1930 in *Letters*, 193–4. Biala, in conversation with Max Saunders, 21 Sept. 1990, said she doubted the seriousness of this attack; that it may just have been a chest pain. Joyce to Harriet Shaw Weaver, 16 Feb. 1931: quoted by Richard Ellmann, *James Joyce* (Oxford: Oxford University Press, 1983), 635–6 n.

22 Mizener, 395. Ford to T. R. Smith, 2 Mar. 1931, says that wires will still reach him at 3, quai du Parti, Toulon, for 'a fortnight or so'. Bowen, *Drawn from Life*, 191. Mizener, 400, 592, n. 21, rightly notes Ford's admiration for Joyce, but calls him 'extraordinarily untouchy with Joyce in literary matters', as if he were not equally magnanimous in his relationships with Conrad, James, Pound, or Hemingway—just to name those he worked with most closely. He was always 'extraordinarily untouchy' with fellow artists, only occasionally becoming touchy with publishers. Unfortunately, when the publishing did not go well, he had to write letters. The records from Ford's own and from publishers' files left Mizener with a very unrepresentative impression of his temperament. Ford to Joyce, 9 Mar. 1931: *Letters*, 199. Svevo's publishers, Putnam's, rejected the idea.

23 Ford to Hugh Walpole, 30 Mar. 193[1]: *Letters*, 193–4, where it is misdated 1930. Bowen, *Drawn from Life*, 191–2. See *The Rash Act*, 287, and *Henry for Hugh*, 101–2.

24 Ford to Caroline Gordon, 25 Sept. 1931: Princeton. Ford to Smith, 14 Mar. 1931: *Letters*, 199–200 (quoted with slight emendations).

25 Ford to Unwin, 15 Mar. 1938. See Harvey, 54, 76. 'I Revisit the Riviera', *Harper's*, 166 (Dec. 1932), 65. Ford to Gollancz, 4 July 1931.

26 Bowen, *Drawn from Life*, 190. Ford to Walpole, 30 Mar. 193[1]: *Letters*, 193–4. Walpole sent some chapters of the book to Gollancz with a covering letter: Walpole to Ford, 18 Dec. 1930 and 7 Jan. 1931. Biala in conversation with Max Saunders, 22 Sept. 1990. *The Presence of Ford Madox Ford*, 224. *Collected Poems* (1936), 306–10 (308). Mizener says the poem describes Aug. 1933, which shows a high opinion of Ford as a weather prophet, since the poem was first published (as 'Vers L'Oubli', in *New English Poems*, 188–92) in Oct. 1931. One of the 'two great hurricanes' was presumably 'the great storm of three Augusts ago' at Toulon that Ford mentioned in his Sept. 1933 'Autocriticism' of *The Rash Act*, and which gave him the idea for that book: *Reader*, 267.

27 Bowen, *Drawn from Life*, 162. Ford to Gollancz, 28 Dec. 1931. Ford to George Oppenheimer (of the Viking Press), 9 Nov. 1928: *Letters*, 181–2.

28 Ford to T. R. Smith, 17 Apr. 1931. Keating to Ford, 21 May 1931. He explained that when Viking told Liveright they 'had a lien on the book' (*When the Wicked Man*) they were probably within their rights; but that nevertheless Ford was indeed due for a payment: $500 was to be paid on 21 May, $250 to go to Viking, and $250 to be cabled to Ford. However, Ford was apparently wrong to expect $500 from Liveright upon receipt of the manuscript of *Return to Yesterday*. Keating explained that the first payment, of $500, was due upon publication, but he promised to help get Liveright pay

him this sum on receipt of the manuscript instead—which they did, sending him four monthly instalments of $125 from 14 Sept. (Smith to Ford, 11 Sept. 1931). Mizener, 386, 388, 395. His comment that *When the Wicked Man* 'sold only 3,233 copies during its first year' is slightly misleading, since the figure comes from Liveright's royalty statement to the end of 1931, when the book had been out for just over seven months. See Harvey, 72, for the figures for *A Little Less Than Gods*. Smith to Ford, 25 Mar. 1931.

29 Smith to Ford, 16 July 1931; Ford to Smith, 27 July 1931.

30 Smith to Ford, 6 Aug. and 11 Sept. 1931. Biala told me (22 Sept. 1990) she thought Ford never forgave Smith for publishing Hunt's memoir.

31 Biala in conversation with Max Saunders, 22 Sept. 1990. Ford to Victor Gollancz, 6 June 1931: 'I have just heard from New York that my novel which was published on May 20 was reprinted on May 23': quoted Harvey, 77. Ford to Pound, 6 June 1931: *Pound/Ford*, 92 (a better transcription than Ludwig's, *Letters*, 202. Mizener quotes two reviews of the novel: Burton Rascoe saying it seemed like 'the collaboration of a genius and a pulp-paper hack . . . bristling with gaffes in documentation'; and a more negative one from the *Saturday Review*. It is true that Ford's mastery of American idioms and institutions was not complete (though one should note that Notterdam is an Englishman who has emigrated; and what gaffes there are weren't noticed by Liveright's editor). Mizener says it 'is not a good novel' (p. 390), so he tries to make Ford sound unreasonable in getting angry with Viking for rejecting it. Although several reviews had doubts about the supernatural element in the book, and found its *handling*—its mix of psychological realism and caricature—problematic, the *subject*—Ford's use of a businessman as protagonist—was recognized as an achievement. In general, the book was seen as a skilful work by an author who could write more convincingly. Mizener may also have been misled about the reviews because many of them were not included in Harvey's bibliography. The main omissions were:

*William Soskin, 'Ford Madox Ford Enthrones the Business Man in Fiction', *New York Evening Post* (20 May 1931), 13.

*Isabel Paterson, 'Books and Other Things', *New York Herald Tribune* (20 May 1931).

*Gustav Davidson, 'Looks at Books', *Mirror* (23 May 1931). Brief note: 'Ford Madox Ford scores once more with *When the Wicked Man* [. . .], a novel that throbs with the fever, the cross-currents, the hopes, ambitions, the treacheries, disasters and self-revealments of modern life. To make the friendship of Joe Notterdam, publisher-hero of the book, and the three women who mould and break him, is to walk the via dolorosa of our age, one with him in his tragedy, his awareness, and his defeat before the forces of society and existence'. [Clipping at Cornell.]

*Starr Lawrence, 'Austere Tensity In Ford's Novel Of Tangled Love: Tragic Turmoils Carry Terrific Mental Shock by Irony and Subtlety', *Public Ledger—Philadelphia* (23 May 1931), 8.

*Muriel Fuller, 'Ford's English New York' (May? 1931). Source unidentified. [Clipping at Cornell.] Mixed: the time-shifts are 'confusing yet no other style could bring the nervous pulsating life of New York to the reader'. But complains: 'one is always conscious that the author is an Englishman writing about America'.

*'New York's Dizzy Life', *Shanghai Times* (26 July 1931). Mixed. The 'sometimes exceedingly painful indirection' is ultimately justified; 'Mr. Ford, it is obvious, has courage, the courage to tackle great contemporary themes. He does not succeed in

suggesting depth below depth of moral conflict, as does Dostoyefsky, but he is at least contemporary.' Reproves the inconsistency of Ford's Americanisms. [Clipping at Cornell.]

32 Judd, *Ford Madox Ford*, 427. *It Was the Nightingale*, 253-4. If they were the exact words, the newspaper had garbled the title of one of Oliver's books, which should read *A Vagabond in New York*.

33 The composition dates at the end of *Return to Yesterday* say it was finished on 8 Aug. 1931. But the dedication is dated 14 July. The coincidence with Bastille Day may be impressionism; but taken together with the reminiscence about Oliver's death the probable sequence is that Ford finished the book in late June or early July, and that the Aug. date refers to the date the proofs were corrected. *Letters*, 193, 200, 251, 295.

Chapter 21

1 The more perceptive recent criticism includes James E. Simmons. 'The Late Novels of Ford Madox Ford', unpublished Ph.D dissertation (University of Wisconsin, 1967); Cynthia Fuller, 'The Divided Self: A Study of Modern Identity in the Novels of Ford Madox Ford', unpublished Ph.D dissertation (University of Massachusetts, 1970); and Cornelia Cook, 'Going Beyond Modernism', *English*, 33 (Summer 1984), 159-67.

2 Moser, 75, describes how the earlier characters Alfred Milne and Mr Apollo 'figure in Ford's imagination as doubles'; and he notes Ford's reference in *Mr. Apollo* to the 'double ganger'. Gordon, quoted by MacShane, 221 n. Paul L. Wiley's fine study, *Novelist of Three Worlds: Ford Madox Ford* (Syracuse, NY: Syracuse University Press, 1962), has an illuminating chapter on 'Mythical Landscapes in the Late Novels'.

3 'Autocriticism: *The Rash Act*': *Reader*, 267. On detective stories see also *It Was the Nightingale*, 193-4, and *The March of Literature*, 832-3.

4 *Reader*, 269.

5 Biala in conversation with Max Saunders, 10 Apr. 1994.

6 'Autocriticisms: I. Ford Madox Ford', *Week-End Review*, 8 (9 Sept. 1933), 249.

7 Ford's interest in detectives goes back at least as far as *A Call*, and the story 'Fathead and the Great Gadsby Fraud', *Tramp* 1 (Apr.–July 1910), 107–15, 216–23, 315–24. It can also be seen in 'A Mascot', *London Mercury*, 17 (Dec. 1927), 133–46. In this story, a French official has, as a mascot, a tooth. He worries at it as if it were loose in his mouth (suggesting how a novelist writes out of a kind of subliminal disturbance, an inability to leave a subject alone). The official is a bit of a tall-story teller: like an impressionist novelist, he fabricates plots to try to account for strange facts and impressions. *Vive Le Roy*, 148. V. S. Pritchett's review of this novel brings out admirably how Ford's writing makes the reader a detective of language, of style: 'there comes a time, after a chapter or two, when one gets the hang of that impossibly allusive style and its incurably oblique dialogue, and there is a certain excitement in finding what the book is about': *New Statesman*, 14 (24 July 1937), 151.

8 *When the Wicked Man*, 168–70. I have not been able to trace 'a German author with a name like Lippschuetz'. But the plot is that of the film *Der Student von Prag* (directed by Stellan Rye in 1913; remade in 1926 and in 1935). The screenplay by Hanns Heinz Ewers draws on E. T. A. Hoffmann's 'Story of the Lost Reflection'. The film is discussed in detail by Otto Rank, in *The Double: A Psychoanalytic Study*, trans. and ed. Harry Tucker Jr (Chapel Hill: University of North Carolina Press, 1971): see 4–7 for a summary. I am grateful to Dr Peter Hutchinson for drawing my attention to Rank's work. A later essay, 'The Double as Immortal Self', in *Beyond Psychology* (New York:

Dover, 1958), 62–101, is equally suggestive about how the double-motif can mobilize feelings about the past and the future, death and immortality, identity and art.

In a review of Herbert Gorman's *The Place Called Dagon*, *New York Herald Tribune Books* (30 Oct. 1927), 5, Ford mentions the brothers Grimm and the Hartz Mountains, and writes of 'the type of book that creates enduring legends'.

9 Mizener, 523. Rascoe, *New York Herald Tribune Books* (31 May 1931), 7.

10 The quotation was transcribed from the dust jacket on a copy in Ulysses Bookshop, Museum Street, in 1992. 'When the Wicked Man. . .'. The name 'Notterdam' is characteristic of the story's attempt to seem both incredible and real, combining the jokey pun (Not a damn) with the modernized form of 'Nostradamus', purveyor of incredible but persistently compelling prophecies. It may have sounded less strange to American ears, approximating to the American pronunciation of 'Notre-Dame'. It is also a surprisingly realistic name, as Paul Noterdaeme, the Belgian president of the UN Security Council in 1991, might attest.

11 Isabel Paterson, review of *The Rash Act*, *New York Herald Tribune Book Review* (26 Feb. 1933), 4. The anonymous *New York Times Book Reviewer* (12 March 1933), 16–17, thought the reverse: 'the symbolism gets in the way of the psychology'; though the review explains this as meaning that Ford has confused a representative figure with an extraordinary one—which is true enough, but also true of most good novels.

12 *Ladies Whose Bright Eyes* (Philadelphia: J. B. Lippincott, 1935), 302–3 (258 of the British reissue (Manchester, Carcanet, 1988)). The passage is a revision of p. 303 of the Constable 1911 edition. Ford added the date 'Dec. 1934' at the end of the revised version, indicating that the revision was completed by then.

13 *Henry for Hugh*, 156, 278, 284.

14 See e.g. Mizener, 98, arguing that Ford could be 'wholly irresponsible in the most convincing way'. Ford to Cheatham, 14 Jan. [1929, misdated 1928].

15 *Isabel Paterson (to whom Ford had dedicated *Last Post*) commented on this combination of realism and the fantastic in her review: 'Things that simply couldn't happen are insisted upon [. . .] But they happen with a curious nightmare effect, to real people. Joe Notterdam and Bill Kratch are real': *New York Herald Tribune* (20 May 1931).

16 *English Poetry, 1900–1950: An Assessment* (Manchester: Carcanet, 1981 [2nd edn.], 52. Isabel Paterson noted Ford's resistance to paraphrase, because he 'has already compressed his material to the limit, and conveyed his meaning by innumerable allusions, suggestions and implications', in her review of *It Was the Nightingale*, *New York Herald Tribune Book Review* (22 Oct. 1933), 7.

17 Ford, 'A Haughty and Proud Generation', *Yale Review*, 11 (July 1922), 709. Alter, 'Playing Host to the *Doppelgänger*', *TLS* (24 Oct. 1986), 1190.

18 This interpretation possibly began with Richard Aldington's comment about a Mr Hyde Ford and a Dr Jekyll Ford in his autobiography, *Life for Life's Sake* (New York: Viking, 1941), 149–50. Among more recent critics, John Meixner's study, *Ford Madox Ford's Novels* (Minneapolis: University of Minnesota Press, 1962), was probably the first to emphasize the role of the double in Ford's novels, and to interpret it as evidence of 'a serious division in the psyche of their author': 263–4. Mizener, p. xv.

19 See 'Creative Writers and Day-Dreaming' (1908), *Standard Edition of the Complete Psychological Works of Sigmund Freud*, vol. 9 (London: The Hogarth Press and the Institute of Psycho-Analysis, 1959), 141–53. Moser, 268. A similar distortion occurs in his reading of *Mr. Fleight*, which he says 'can be read, then, as Ford's pledge of allegiance to Marwood, as his longing, even, to *be* Marwood': 113. Certainly Ford

mostly admires the Marwoodian Mr Blood, and certainly Mr Fleight longs to be like him. But the novel tells the story of how it is impossible that Fleight should become like Blood (the names imply the intractability of the class strata: you can't attain blood by social climbing). Moser's argument won't allow that a novelist can use fiction to ponder resemblances and fantasies while bringing them into critical focus.

20 Wiley, *Novelist of Three Worlds*, 275, identifies a theme of the 'healing of the divided self' central to the late novels. Ford, 'A Haughty and Proud Generation', 716.

21 *Some Do Not . . .*, 111. *The Rash Act*, 295. Ford to Geoffrey Harry Wells, 24 July 1924: Texas.

22 1 June 1938: *Letters*, 294–5. Ford told Stanley Unwin on 29 Mar. 1939 that he thought *Henry for Hugh* 'by far the best written and the best constructed' of all his books: *Letters*, 317–18; though it should be added that he was trying to persuade Unwin to publish it in Britain.

23 *Nation* (New York), 137 (2 August 1933), 138; Herbert Agar, *English Review*, 57 (Oct. 1933), 434–5.

24 'As Thy Day', *Reader*, 268–9.

25 The phrase is in both the 'Autocriticism' and the later synopsis: *Reader*, 267, 269. Ford was in Paris, and 25 miles south at Ballancourt, during the summer of 1930. The claim that the story was a true story might be a fiction, of course. *The Rash Act*'s epigraph cites a *Times* Law Report of 14 July 1931. The Bastille Day dating might indicate a fictional game. Certainly, no such report appears in *The Times* for 14 or 15 July 1931.

26 *The Rash Act*, 220. 'Communications', *transatlantic review*, 1/1 (Jan. 1924), 93–4. *Some Do Not . . .*, 222. Ford to Wells: n.d. (Illinois; quoted by Mizener, 93). *Return to Yesterday*, 267; discussed in Saunders, i. 182–4. Timothy Weiss, *Fairy Tale and Romance in Works of Ford Madox Ford* (Lanham, Maryland, New York and London: University Press of America, 1984) gives a sound survey of this topic. Also see E. M. Forster, *Aspects of the Novel*, ch. 6. See *Vive Le Roy*, 11, 239, 243–4, for examples of Walter and Cassie wondering what being a monarch would involve. Arnold Bennett called *A Call* a fairy tale: [pseud. 'Jacob Tonson'], 'Books and Persons', *New Age*, 6 (17 Mar. 1910), 471.

27 *The Good Soldier*, 291.

28 A selection of his significant discussions of sympathetic imagination should include: *Rossetti*, 186, 189 on sympathetic identification; *The Spirit of the People*, 170, on the Englishman's 'want of sympathetic imagination'; 'Literary Portraits: XVIII. Major Martin Hume', *Tribune* (23 Nov. 1907), 2, praising: 'the gift of sympathetic insight into the hearts of his opposites'; *The Critical Attitude*, 89: poets 'must be in some sympathy with their fellow men'; *When Blood is Their Argument*, p. vii, on Ford's love for 'that form of imagination which implies a sympathetic comprehension of the hopes, fears and ideals of one's fellow-men', and 65: 'the public function of the arts is the discovery of sympathetic relations between man and men'; *Women & Men*, 21: 'the instinctive gift of the imagination which is sympathy'; 'Thus to Revisit: III. The Serious Books', *Piccadilly Review* (6 Nov. 1919), 6: 'That a serious book should possess form, imaginative insight, or interest for anyone not a specialist, would, generally speaking, be considered a very unsound proposition'; *Thus to Revisit*, 186; 'An Answer to "Three Questions"', *Chapbook*, No. 27 (July 1922), 14–15: 'The function of poetry in the Republic is still, always has been, and always will be to instil imagination—that is, sympathetic insight!—into the Human Brute that man is'; *Great Trade Route*, 424: 'I am a novelist and it's part of my job to work myself into the minds of all sorts of people. . . . And then one has glimpses. . . .'

29 Ford to Galsworthy, [October 1900]: *Letters*, 10–14 (12). *It Was the Nightingale*, 35. *Mightier Than the Sword*, 168.

30 *Mightier Than the Sword*, 184–5.

31 (London: Duckworth, 1928), p. viii. For a fuller discussion of these topics of 'sympathy' and 'vicarious experience' in Ford's work, see Saunders, 'Ford Madox Ford and the Reading of Prose', unpublished dissertation (University of Cambridge, 1986), 37–48. For mentions of 'vicarious experience' not discussed there, see 'Literary Portraits—X.: Mr. Clement Shorter and "Borrow and His Circle"', *Outlook*, 32 (15 Nov. 1913), 677–8; and 'Stocktaking [. . .] I', *transatlantic review*, 1/1 (Jan. 1924), [76].

32 *The Rash Act*, 185.

33 Rank, *Beyond Psychology*, 92; *The Double*, 63.

34 p. 320. Hugh's financial unorthodoxy recalls Marwood's Actuarial Scheme in the *English Review*. See Saunders, i. 251.

35 *Henry for Hugh*, 64.

36 Synopsis of *The Rash Act*. Hunt, *The Flurried Years*, 122–3. Holbein, 8.

37 *Henry for Hugh*, 279.

38 Ford mentions [Jean-]Henri Fabre of Avignon in *Provence*, 60, 69; he may have intended the 'Fabers' of *The Rash Act* as homage to this literary naturalist. Or could he have heard Jean Rhys talk of her lover Lancelot Grey Hugh Smith, one of 'the Hugh Smiths' who had cousins called 'the Martin Smiths'?: Angier, 61–2, 65. Lancelot Smith's wealthy connections make him a plausible source for Hugh Monckton Smith. In having Henry Martin assume the name of the car magnate, Ford was probably also transforming his own substitution of 'Hueffer' for the name that doubles his grandfather's with that of the great car 'maker', Ford: an allusion which suggests both the 'Hugh' (as in 'Hueffer') and the 'Henry'.

Ford to Long, 2 July 1932; *Letters*, 208–11. Katherine Anne Porter had written to Biala, 22 May 1932, telling them about Crane's death. Ford had begun *The Rash Act* at the end of 1931. He told his agent Ruth Kerr in a letter of 8 Dec. 1931 that he was 'just starting a novel which will probably work out to be in three parts' (quoted in Mizener, 405). And the first ending in the Cornell manuscript is dated 15 May 1932.

39 The motto also appears in 'Literary Portraits—VII.: Mr. Percival Gibbon and "The Second-Class Passenger"', *Outlook*, 32 (25 Oct. 1913), 571–72; *The Good Soldier*, 57; *Last Post*, 286; *It Was the Nightingale*, 59; 'London Re-Visited', *London Mercury*, 35 (Dec. 1936), 183; and *Great Trade Route*, 223. *The Rash Act*, 206.

40 *Henry for Hugh*, 60. *The Rash Act*, 208.

41 Terence Cave discusses the 'doubling' of plot, especially in detective fiction, in 'The Prime and Precious Thing', *TLS* (4 Jan. 1985), 14. Ford, 'Introduction' to Hemingway, *A Farewell to Arms* (New York: The Modern Library, 1932), pp. ix–xx (p. xv).

42 See *The Rash Act*, 35 (the tombstone of the Roman dancer: '*SALTAVIT. PLACUIT. MORTUUS EST.*'); 11 ('His father had achieved the name Aluin-Smith with some difficulty on his candy-wrappers'); 138 ('He had been reading Turgenev'); 156 (Henry's father's cryptic cable refusing to send money, which makes Henry all the more determined to attempt suicide).

43 'Going Beyond Modernism', *English*, 33 (Summer 1984), 164.

44 *The Rash Act*, 255, 42.

45 'Anonymity: An Inquiry', in *Two Cheers for Democracy* (London: Edward Arnold, 1951), 93.

46 *The Rash Act*, 208. Replying to Ray Long's comments on the novel, Ford wrote: 'You

seem to have entered into his problems as closely as I have myself': 2 July 1932: *Letters*, 208.

47 *The Rash Act*, 255.

48 *Henry for Hugh*, 271, 323.

49 *The Rash Act*, 42, 43.

50 Conrad to Poradowska [20 July? 1894]: *The Collected Letters of Joseph Conrad*, ed. Frederick R. Karl and Laurence Davies (Cambridge: Cambridge University Press, 1983), i. 161–2.

51 See e.g. *Joseph Conrad*, 189–90. Review of Marjorie Worthington's *Manhattan Solo*, *New York Herald Tribune Books* (14 Feb. 1937), 4.

52 See e.g. *A Man Could Stand Up—*, 196: 'Tietjens surprised himself by saying: [. . .]'; *The Marsden Case*, 152: 'now his face was all white triangles.'

53 For examples of people being (or feeling) on the margins of life, see *A Call*, 222 (on the Orthodox priest Grimshaw talks to); *The Good Soldier*, 144; *Thus to Revisit*, 135; *The Marsden Case*, 326. As we shall see in the section on 'Vicarious Experience', pp. 449–54, Ford sees the role of art as the salving of this alienation.

54 Wells, *Experiment in Autobiography*, ii. 617.

55 Ford pays another tribute to the Northern Boy of Antibes in *Provence*, 51–2. See Wiley, *Novelist of Three Worlds*, 269–71.

56 *A Man Could Stand Up—*, 203. *The Rash Act*, 29. See also 230: 'He was through with this damn Hamlet mood'; and 228, where Henry sees Hugh as another Hamlet.

57 *The Rash Act*, 54: italics added. *Henry for Hugh*, 114.

58 *Joseph Conrad*, 206.

59 *The Rash Act*, 249, 296.

60 Ibid. 343.

61 Ibid. 158, 34, 57.

62 Ibid. 116, 95.

63 In *The Rash Act* she appears as 'Wanda' as well as 'Gloria' Sorenson (see 228, 144). In *Henry for Hugh* she has become Gloria Malmström, perhaps suggesting the maelstrom of suffering that sexual glory brings in its wake in a Fordian plot. See e.g. 56.

64 *The Rash Act*, 267, 165. *Henry for Hugh*, 96–7.

65 See Carol Ohmann, *Ford Madox Ford: From Apprentice to Craftsman* (Middletown: Wesleyan University Press, 1964), 41–5, and Snitow, 89, on the theme of sexual reluctance.

66 *The Rash Act*, 263, 264. See *Provence*, 126, on the 'heresy of perfectibilism'. Ford to Ray Long, 2 July 1932; *Letters*, 208–11.

67 *The Good Soldier*, 272. Synopsis of *The Rash Act*, 5. *Letters*, 209.

68 See the bound manuscript at Cornell.

69 *Henry for Hugh*, 220. Ford was also giving new life to an idea he had come across in his friend Marc Chadourne's novel *Vasco* (London: Jonathan Cape, 1928), for which he wrote a preface, explaining how Vasco 'comes upon a being—an American—who seems to have been re-born and to have attained to some of the qualities that Vasco had wished for himself' (p. 13). Henry Martin Smith, an American, comes across an Englishman who seems to embody qualities he wished for himself; by impersonating him, he is able to assume those qualities while allowing his friend to be reborn.

70 Huddleston, *In and About Paris* (London: Methuen, 1927), pp. vii–ix.

71 Moser, 142–3, 132. Preface to *Vasco*, 12–13.

72 *The Rash Act*, 88. 'Literary Causeries. IV: Escape . . .', *Chicago Tribune Sunday Magazine* (9 Mar. 1924), 3, 11 (the dates Ford gives here for his readings are problematic. He

can't have read Conrad in Bécourt Wood on 15 July because he hadn't left Rouen by that date; he's unlikely to have reread *Maisie* on 2 and 5 Aug., since he was in the Casualty Clearing Station at Corbie then, suffering from amnesia). Cf. *No Enemy*, 161–4.

73 *The Rash Act*, 41, 324. *Henry for Hugh*, 85, 88–9.

74 *Henry for Hugh*, 52, 220, 322, 299. Deuteronomy 33: 25.

75 James E. Simmons. 'The Late Novels of Ford Madox Ford', unpublished Ph.D dissertation (University of Wisconsin, 1967), 154.

76 Cynthia Fuller, 'The Divided Self: A Study of Modern Identity in the Novels of Ford Madox Ford', unpublished Ph.D dissertation (University of Massachusetts, 1970), 165. Ford, 'The Real France, That Goes to Bed at Nine', *New York Herald Tribune Books* (31 Mar. 1925), 4. Fuller argues that the late novels represent an ideological *volte face* from *Parade's End*, in which the public official opts after the war for rural isolation.

77 *Reader*, 268. See Green's fine study, *Ford Madox Ford: Prose and Politics*, 120–5, on the sociological paradoxes of Ford's agrarian utopia.

78 *Thus to Revisit*, 44. Cornelia Cook, 'Going Beyond Modernism', 160. Ford originally proposed a trilogy of novels: see Mizener, 405.

79 *It Was the Nightingale*, 179–80. Ricks, *Tennyson*, Masters of World Literature Series (London: Macmillan, 1972), 92.

80 See *Vive Le Roy*, 145, for example: 'She seemed to be surrounded by scepticisms'. Ford wrote to a 'Mr Mack' on 19 Aug. 1933 (*Letters*, 219–21): 'it is only by piling one damn commonplace complication on another that you arrive at the tragi-comedy or the comic tragedy that life is. . . .'

81 Anthony Fothergill, *TLS* (30 Sept. 1983), 1059.

82 18: 27. Ford had known this text as a child. In *Ancient Lights*, 87, he recalled sending it as part of a long telegram intended to keep the telegraph office open until his father had finished writing a review of the *Messiah*.

83 Ford to T. R. Smith, 2 Feb. 1931.

84 Ford to Pound, 8 Mar. 1933: *Letters*, 218–19. *Thus to Revisit*, 49. The anecdote about James is reshaped in *Mightier Than the Sword*, 25.

Chapter 22

1 Ford to Pound, 18 and 23 Aug. 1931; Pound to Ford, 20 and 21 Aug. [1931]: *Pound/Ford*, 92–4. Ford to [Harry I.] Kohn, 17 Oct. 1931, indicates that he did indeed have to put a lawyer on to Liveright.

2 Ford to Caroline Gordon, 25 Sept. 1931: Princeton. Ford to Padraic Colum, 21 Sept. 1931; to William Bradley, 23 Sept. 1931. Mizener, 592, n. 27. Bowen, *Drawn from Life*, 191. Ford to Harriet Monroe, 2 Nov. 1931: *Reader*, 494–5, says they have just returned to their old apartment for the winter. Mizener, 404, is right to say they were back by 2 Nov.; but wrong to say (on p. 406) that they got back at Christmas.

3 *The Presence of Ford Madox Ford*, 224–5.

4 *Daily Herald* (2 Nov. 1931), 1 (MacShane, 229–30). *Return to Yesterday*, 434–5. Gollancz to Ford, 10 Nov. 1931. Ford to Gollancz, 8 Nov. 1931: *Letters*, 202–3. Mizener, 592–3, n. 28 (who misdates this letter as 9 Nov.), notes that there was no second English edition of the book; the first (of 1,250 copies) sold 1,121 copies at list price, and 87 were remaindered. Mizener, 404. George Dangerfield, *The Strange Death of Liberal England* (London: Constable, 1936), 396–9.

5 Mizener, 405–6. Ford to Ray Long, 2 July 1932: *Letters*, 208–11. Bradley to Ford, 14 May 1932. Mizener, 408–9, 593, n. 6, says Ford confused Long and Smith by sending

two alternative endings, neither of which he says have survived. He cites letters from Richard Smith to Bradley, 22 Dec. 1931, and Bradley to Ford, 3 Jan. 1932. But these dates are impossible. Ford can't have sent alternative endings less than a month after Mizener says he began the book, and four months before he sent Long and Smith the manuscript. In fact, Bradley's letter must have been misdated for 3 Jan. 1933, as the letter it quotes from Smith of 22 Dec. (Mizener's source for the other letter) must be 22 Dec. 1932: Smith's cable to Ford of 13 Jan. 1933 saying 'I have also received a cablegram from Bradley, reporting that you wish the last chapter of THE RASH ACT omitted [. . .]' confirms this dating. Thus what actually happened was that Ford sent his original ending (dated 15 May 1932 in the bound manuscript at Cornell). Long objected, so in July 1932 Ford offered to send him a slightly revised alternative (*Letters*, 210). In an undated letter to Long he said: 'Here is that addition to chapter the last. I think it makes the position clear.' (Presumably he sent a typescript, which has not survived, but which corresponds to the ending of the Cornell manuscript, which is dated 7 Sept. 1931 to 10 July 1932. In other words, Ford wrote the additional matter, headed 'Part IV Chapter III', only parts of which were used in the published text, the week after he had written to Long on 2 July.) But it didn't make the position clear. When Smith sent the proofs in Dec. [1932], after Long's disappearance in Aug., he said to Bradley: 'We had considerable difficulty in interpreting his ideas as to the use of the alternative ending, and I finally decided on more or less of a combination use of both endings.' Ray Long's letter to Ford, 20 June 1932, describing his and his colleagues' first reactions, makes no mention of such alternatives: he suggests that Ford *should* write a different ending. In the event, it only took one sequel, *Henry for Hugh*, to complete the work.

6 Ford to Bradley, 8 June 1932: *Letters*, 205–8. Ford to Long, 2 July 1932, says he is 'getting on pretty fast' with the *History*. Mizener, 408, thinks Ford was unreasonable in saying he was 'in demand in New York', and in expecting *Harper's* to agree to his terms. But there had been more arguments with Liveright, who had delayed the American publication of *Return to Yesterday*, and had produced 'obviously incomplete' royalty statements (Ford to Liveright, Inc., 26 Mar. 1931). And the contract with Long and Smith did mean that his work was paid for in advance by a New York firm; and it enabled Ford—for a while—not to have to rely on uncongenial journalism for his living. As he explained to Bradley: 'There are other reasons why I don't want to write these things. In the first place I don't write articles well and do not add to my reputation when I write them. In addition writing them spoils my style so that it takes me a long time to get back to book writing.' He wrote two of the articles for Harper's: 'I Revisit the Riviera', 166 (Dec. 1932) [65]–76; and 'For Poorer Travellers', 166 (Apr. 1933) [620]–31. Ludwig, 206 n., calls this letter to Bradley Ford's first mention of the 'Great Trade Route' idea. But he had sketched the idea at least four years earlier, in *The English Novel*, 23. And the plan outlined to Bradley corresponds more closely to the uncompleted project 'Portraits of Cities', discussed on pp. 659–60.

7 'Introduction', *A Farewell to Arms* (New York: The Modern Library, 1932), pp. ix–xx (pp. xv–xvi); repr. in the *Reader*, 246–54.

8 'Pound and How to Read', *New Review*, 2 (Apr. 1932), 39–45; repr. (with omissions) in *Pound/Ford*, 105–6. Pound, 'How to Read', *Literary Essays of Ezra Pound*, ed. T. S. Eliot, rev. edn. (London: Faber & Faber, 1960), 25.

9 *Pound/Ford*, 101, quotes Pound's defence in the *Active Anthology* against Ford's 'serious charge', saying 'you can't get everything into 45 pages'. He said the same thing in the *ABC of Reading*, 2nd edn. (London: Faber & Faber, 1961), 89; Ford isn't named

there, but what Pound calls 'the only intelligent adverse criticism' of his book is clearly Ford's.

10 See H. M. McLuhan, 'Tennyson and Picturesque Poetry', *Essays in Criticism*, I/3 (July 1951), 263: discussed below, ch. 23.

11 Bowen, *Drawn from Life*, 190, 195–7. Ford to Gordon [n.d., but *c.*12 Mar. 1932]: Princeton. Easter fell on 27 Mar. Ford and Biala reached the Villa Paul some time between 29 Mar. and 10 Apr. 1932: letters to Horace Shipp. Porter to Pressly, 8 and 10 Mar. 1932: paraphrased by Joan Givner, *Katherine Anne Porter: A Life* (London: Jonathan Cape, 1983), 272–3. Porter's *French Song-Book* was published in 1933. Porter to Biala, 22 May 1932, explains that she wasn't able to send 'your three hundred francs' because she had had to spend them on hospital bills. Pressly to Biala and Ford, 12 June [1933], says 'Next month we plan to send a thousand francs back to you'. Porter to the Tates, 6–13 Mar. 1932: *Letters of Katherine Anne Porter*, edited by Isabel Bayley (New York: The Atlantic Monthly Press, 1990), 75.

12 *Provence*, 367–8. Biala in conversation with Max Saunders, 20 Sept. 1990. Wood, *The Southern Mandarins*, 111, establishes the year. Gordon to Sally Wood, 'end of May, 1932', says she 'had a long letter from Ford the other day' describing the episode; this is a letter dated only 'St George's Day alias Shakespeare's Birthday' [23 Apr. 1932]: Princeton. Makowsky, *Caroline Gordon* (New York and Oxford: Oxford University Press, 1989), 113, also places the episode in 1932. Mizener, 412, misplaced it, and the Tates' visit to Toulon, in 1933. Goldring records a very slightly different version of the story, placing the incident halfway along the suspension bridge between Tarascon and Beaucaire: *South Lodge*, 193.

13 *Provence*, 359. Biala, in *The Presence of Ford Madox Ford*, 198.

14 *The Presence of Ford Madox Ford*, 202. Julie places this episode before she and Bowen moved to London in 1933. Ford to Bowen, 2 Nov. 1933. His version in *Great Trade Route*, 27–9, agrees in all the essentials except the date. It doesn't mention Biala, whom Julie says was present. He says the episode happened 'The other day', and mentions that he was also going to look for a book about transatlantic trade that would help with *Great Trade Route*. The manuscript was not complete until 18 Mar. 1936 (Ford to H. F. Lowry: Oxford University Press (New York)). There's no hard evidence for when the beginning was written. But *Provence* was finished on 3 Sept. 1934 (Ford to Bertram, 14 Sept. 1934: *Letters*, 233–5), and *Great Trade Route* was one of his next projects (together with *Vive Le Roy* and his essays for the *American Mercury*). It was certainly underway by 4 June 1935 (Ford to Ruth Aley); but was quite probably begun earlier in the year. So the phrase 'The other day' could refer to any time between 1932 and early 1936. Ford associates his luck in escaping injury with his luck in finding a relevant book; so he may have altered the chronology to make both seem more immediate to *Great Trade Route*. Biala in conversation with Max Saunders, 20 Sept. 1990, said she thought Julie was 12 or 13 at the time (which would thus have been 1931 or 1932).

15 Ford to Long, 8 Aug. 1932: *Letters*, 211–12. Ford to Pound [July? 1932]: *Pound/Ford*, 108 Ford to Harriet Monroe, 7 June 1932 (University of Chicago), also mentions a young poet called [Richard] Angers who was helping him. Putnam, *Paris Was Our Mistress*, 126–7. Biala to Mizener, 14 Oct. 1968. Porter to Biala, 22 May 1932.

16 Bowen, *Drawn from Life*, 218–19. Biala, postscript on Ford's letter to Julie, 'Dimanche', 14 [Aug., but misdated '14/7/32'] 1932. Ford to Pound, [July? 1932]: *Pound/Ford*, 108. 'I Revisit the Riviera', *Harper's*, 166 (Dec. 1932), 65–76 (*revised as *Provence*, 265–84). Mizener, 594, n. 11, says Ford's letters to Bradley of 19 July and 11 Aug. 1932 date the trip as from 21 June to 4 July. But this is a month early: the letter of [Tuesday]

19 July says 'We expect to start along the coast on Thursday morning'—21 July; that of
11 Aug. says 'We had quite a pleasant trip and have been back exactly a week'. Ford to
Julie, 20 July 1932, says they are leaving the next day for Cannes, Antibes, and Monte-
Carlo. Biala in conversation with Max Saunders, 22 Sept. 1990. *Pound/Ford* dates the
meeting 'late July–early August' (p. 108), which is supported by the interview with
Pound in *Il Mare* (see below), which says he was there in the beginning of Aug.: *Pound/
Ford*, 108. Ford to Long, 8 Aug. 1932: *Letters*, 211.

17 Quoted from Olga Rudge's translation, 'Madox Ford at Rapallo', in Pound's *Pavannes
and Divagations* (Norfolk, Conn.: New Directions, 1958), 153–5. Also in *Pound/Ford*,
108–11, though the original Italian version is there misattributed to Rudge (see Brita
Lindberg-Seyersted and Archie Henderson, '*Pound/Ford*: Addenda and Corrections',
Paideuma, 14/1 (Spring 1985), 124). The Italian interview appeared in *Il Mare* on 20
Aug. 1932.

18 Pound, *The Cantos* (London: Faber, 1975), 689. The phrase is echoed in Canto C (p.
719). See *Pound/Ford*, 178–9, for these and other mentions of Ford in the *Cantos*.
Pound to Ford, 27 Feb. [1933]: *Pound/Ford*, 118. Ogden Nash (of Farrar & Rinehart)
to Ford, 26 Aug. 1932, makes it clear that the initiative was Ford's.

19 Mizener, 412, places the Tates' visit in 1933; but Wood's recollection that Ford was
working on *It Was the Nightingale* confirms her dating of 1932. Gordon to Wood, early
spring, 1932: Wood, *The Southern Mandarins*, 99. See also 120–1. Ford dated that book
as finished in Toulon on 11 June 1933; whereas Gordon told Wood she planned that
they should sail for France on 21 July 1932 (*The Southern Mandarins*, 110, 111).
Makowsky, *Caroline Gordon*, 113, dates their visit Sept. and Oct. 1932. But Tate to
Lytle, 22 Aug. 1932, *Thomas Daniel Young and Elizabeth Sarcone (eds.), *The Lytle–
Tate Letters: The Correspondence of Andrew Lytle and Allen Tate* (Jackson and London:
University Press of Mississipi, 1987), 62–4, shows they arrived around 15 Aug.; and
*The Republic of Letters in America: The Correspondence of John Peale Bishop and Allen
Tate*, ed. Thomas Daniel Young and John J. Hindle (Lexington: University Press of
Kentucky, 1981), 75 (which also confirms the 1932 dating), has Tate still at Toulon on
12 Nov. Francis Rose was a student of Picabia's (who arrived the next day), and was
promoted by Gertrude Stein, whom he met in 1931. See England and Co.'s *Sir Francis
Rose: 1909–1979: A Retrospective* (London, 1988).

20 Mizener, 412, places the feast in the summer of 1933. But Ford's recollection in
Provence, 171, that it was 'not two years' since he heard the *pastorale*, dates it correctly
as 1932 (since he had sent the first six chapters to Lippincott by 29 June 1934 (letter to
Jefferson Jones), and thus would have been writing the chapter on 'Church and Stage'
in the latter half of the year). This dating is supported by Tate's recollection, quoted
from MacShane, 215. Makowsky, *Caroline Gordon*, 113, dates the feast Oct. 1932. But
Tate to Lytle, 22 Aug. 1932 (which corroborates Ford's account of the feast), describes
it as happening 'last week': *The Lytle–Tate Letters*, 62–4. *Provence*, 291–3.

21 Tate to MacShane, 24 July 1961: MacShane, 215. *Provence*, 293; also see p. 51 for
another mention (and an illustration) of the Antibes tablet. *The Rash Act*, 35.

22 Bradley to Ford, 4 Sept. 1932. Ford to Van Doren, 29 Aug. 1932: Princeton. Bradley to
Biala, 31 August 1932. Gordon to Wood, late Jan. 1933: Wood, *The Southern Mandarins*, 135. Smith told Bradley of his disapproval of Long's contract: 20 Jan. 1933. Ford
to Pound, 8 Mar. 1933: *Letters*, 217–18. Mizener, 409, 411. *The Rash Act* sold 'little
more than 1,000 copies' in America: Bradley to Ford, 2 Sept. 1933; Mizener, 410.
Whereas the English edition sold 1,156 copies: Harvey, 77. See Harvey, 397–9, for
reviews of *The Rash Act*. There was a more enthusiastic one by *C. E. Bechhofer

Roberts, in 'Some New Novels', *New English Weekly*, 3/25 (5 Oct. 1933), 595–6. Bradley to Ford, 24 Jan. 1933, includes an excerpt from Smith's letter of 27 Dec. rejecting the *History*. Ford to Pound, 8 Mar. 1933: *Letters*, 217–18. Ford repaid Pound when he got Lippincott's advance for *It Was the Nightingale*: Mizener, 411.

23 'For Poorer Travellers', *Harper's*, 146 (Apr. 1933), 620–30. Mizener, 411, says that they went to Germany from Rapallo. But they were back from Rapallo by at least 6 Aug. (Ford to Victor Gollancz, 6 Aug. 1932: *Reader*, 496–7), and Ford wrote to Joyce from the Villa Paul on 29 Aug. to persuade him to write a testimonial for Pound (*Reader*, 497–8). Whereas the *Harper's* essay describes the grape harvest in the autumn (p. 626). Ford to Ruth Kerr, 7 Sept. 1932, says 'We were in Italy lately and are going to Germany in a day or two but shall be back in Paris before you will have time to answer this and then very shortly back here [presumably the Villa Paul], probably for the winter'. On 25 Oct. Ford wrote to Hugh Walpole: 'We were in Germany for some time just now' (*Reader*, 498). Biala, in conversation with Max Saunders, 22 Sept. 1990, confirmed that there were separate trips to Italy and Germany. I have found no more precise evidence of their whereabouts between 7 Sept. (Ford to A. R. Orage, probably written from Toulon: *Letters*, 215–16) and 25 Oct. On 11 Sept. 1933 Ford wrote to Caroline Gordon: 'It is just about a year since we came back from Germany with the Strasbourg paté': *Letters*, 229. Bradley to Biala, dated '11. 9. 32', says her description of the Rhineland sounded dismal. Though an American, he usually used the English form of dating. If he did here, then she must have reached the Rhineland between 8 and 10 Sept.' Biala, memoir in *The Presence of Ford Madox Ford*, 197–8.

24 Quoted by Joan Givner, *Katherine Anne Porter*, 277–8.

25 Gordon to Wood, later Jan. 1933: Wood, *The Southern Mandarins*, 134. Ford to Walpole, 25 Oct. 1932: *Reader*, 498.

26 Ford to Hemingway, 6 Nov. 1932: *Letters*, 216. The accident must have happened before this date: Ford to Pound, n.d. (*Pound/Ford*, 112–13), also mentions it, and is typed similarly using only lower-case letters as a result. This letter dates from several days before 6 Nov., the date of Ford's next letter to Pound. Ford to Bowen, 22 Dec. 1932.

27 Ford to Bowen, 22 Dec. 1932. *The Times* (23 Dec. 1932), 16, for exchange rates. Gordon to Sally Wood, late Jan. 1933, and 1 Dec. 1932: Wood, *The Southern Mandarins*, 135, 127. Ford told Gordon they expected to return to Paris on 15 Jan.: *The Southern Mandarins*, 127. Ford to Otto Kahn, 9 Feb. 1933, asks for $1,000 for the Tates. *Provence*, 366. Enrique Hank Lopez, *Conversations with Katherine Anne Porter: Refugee from Indian Creek* (Boston: Little, Brown & Co., 1981), 196. Mizener, 416. Pressly was secretary to the first secretary at the US Embassy. Givner, *Katherine Anne Porter*, 282 (identifying the café as the Deux Magots, though Biala in conversation with Max Saunders, 10 Apr. 1994, said it was another café next to the Mairie), 323. *It Was the Nightingale* gives the dates of composition as: 'PARIS, Jan. 12th–/TOULON, June 11th, 1933' (p. 344).

28 Biala in conversation with Max Saunders, 9 and 10 Apr. 1994. Tate to Mizener, 3 Aug. 1969: Vanderbilt. Mizener, 411. *Pound/Ford*, 119–21. Robert Green, *Ford Madox Ford: Prose and Politics*, 123–4, has the best discussion of parallels between Ford's and Douglas's ideas, including the rejection of both capitalism and socialism, and 'a belief in the potential of creative anomaly'. Ford to Faber & Faber, 1 May 1933.

29 Ford to Dreiser, 27 Feb. 1933: *Letters*, 216–17. Ford would have discussed the Balfour Declaration with Masterman.

30 Ford to Pound, [Monday] 27 Mar. 1933 (*Pound/Ford*, 121), says they return to Toulon

on Saturday, which would be 1 April. Ford to Pound, [? April 1933], and [15 Apr. 1933]: *Pound/Ford*, 123, 121–2. See 122–3 for Pound's exasperated reply of 17 April.

31 Bowen, *Drawn from Life*, 222–3. Ford to Julie, 1[0?] June 1933. Ford to Gordon, 11 Sept. 1933: *Letters*, 228.

32 Ford to Julie, 25 Nov. 1933.

33 Bradley to Ford, 7 July 1933, gives some idea of their misunderstandings (as well as of Bradley's fundamentally good intentions). He responds to Ford's anxiety that the fall of the dollar will devalue the outstanding portion of his Lippincott advance, and asking if Lippincott has bought francs to pay him with, by quoting back Ford's letter in which he raises the question but doesn't give specific instructions. Bradley then replies to Ford's question about whether Cape had wanted *It Was the Nightingale* by reminding Ford that Gollancz had rejected it. They were still trying to get money from the Bonis for the Tietjens novels, but Ford had told Bradley: 'I hope you will not let Spingarn [Ford's lawyer] run up an account against *me*.' Bradley quoted this back to Ford, saying: 'Although it is not, I believe, customary for an agent to assume the legal expenses of his client, I accept all responsibility for what has been done thus far.' Bradley to Ford, dated '2. 10. 33.'. Mizener, 593, n. 8, cites this letter as 2 Sept. He may have been right. Ford's reply, quoting Bradley's letter back to him, is dated '10. 9. 33'. Ford didn't use the American style of dating, so one of them must have mistaken the month.

34 Biala to Bowen, 4 Aug. 1934.

35 Robert Center (of Bobbs-Merrill) to Ford, 3 June and 15 Aug. 1933. Ford to Shipp, 25 Aug. 1933: *Letters*, 223–4 (he makes a similar complaint about his English reception in a letter to Gerald Bullet, 24 Aug. 1933: *Letters*, 222). Ford had provided an excellent foreword to the first collection: *The English Review Book of Short Stories*, compiled by Horace Shipp (London: Sampson Low, Marston, [1932]), pp. vii–xi. Shipp's *The Second English Review Book of Short Stories* (London: Sampson Low, Marston & Co. [1933]), appeared with the dedication 'To | Ford Madox Ford | First Editor of | The English Review'.

36 Mizener, 413–14. ['Autobiographical Information'] written for Lippincott.

Chapter 23

1 *Return to Yesterday*, pp. vii–viii. *It Was the Nightingale*, pp. vi, xi. Ford to J. Jefferson Jones (of Lippincott), 26 July 1933.

2 *Return to Yesterday*, 420. *It Was the Nightingale*, p. x. Benét, 'Uncle Ford', *SRL*, 10 (21 Oct. 1933), 199. *Return to Yesterday*, 420.

3 Mizener, 463–4, says Ford 'wrote or collaborated on thirty-two novels', but goes on to list 31, including the fragment *The Nature of a Crime* and the fictionalized reminiscence *No Enemy*. Ford to Wells, 20 Nov. 1908: *Letters*, 28–9. Wells [to Ford], written on the press-clipping from the *Glasgow Herald* of 14 Nov. 1908. *Privy Seal* was actually banned by the Southend Library Committee. There was a cartoon in the *Southend and Westcliff Graphic* (23 Oct. 1908), 11, with a caption commenting on the 'novel of an alleged objectionable character'. The *Essex Weekly News* (30 Oct. 1908) reported the banning, which it felt unjustified.

4 *Thus to Revisit*, 85. See Samuel Hynes, 'Ford and the Spirit of Romance', *Edwardian Occasions* (London: Routledge & Kegan Paul, 1972), 71–9 (esp. 76): 'Time inevitably simplifies and orders experience, turning Reality into Romance; and once an event has occurred, it exists only in memory, and is subject therefore to a romanticizing process which Ford seems to regard as an inevitable, and not undesirable condition of exist-

ence.' Loeb, *The Way it Was* (New York: Criterion Books, 1959), 202–4. Putnam, *Paris Was Our Mistress*, 125.

5 The *New English Weekly*, 10 (25 Feb. 1937), 397–8, praised the 'rare and distinctive gift of imaginative memory' displayed in *Great Trade Route*. Morris, 'A Remarkable Literary Figure of Our Era: Ford Madox Ford, Novelist, Poet; a Guide and Friend of Writers', *New York Herald Tribune Books* (22 May 1949), 1, 18. Gorman, 'Ford Madox Ford: The Personal Side', *Princeton University Library Chronicle*, 9/3 (Apr. 1948), 121–2. Mizener, *'His Great Achievement Was Helping Literature Leap Into This Century', *New York Times Book Review* (17 Nov. 1963), 5–6; *'The Gowld Standard', review of *Your Mirror to My Times*, *New Republic*, 164/24 (12 June 1971), 33–4; the review continues: 'It is a sort of fictionalized autobiography in which scarcely a single fact is true, though nearly every alleged fact bears some distant relation to an actual one, in which every actual event is "improved" in order to bring out what Ford feels to be the distinguishing characteristics of the man or the occasion under discussion.' That 'scarcely' is representative of his exaggerations which refuse Ford the benefit of the doubt. The introduction to Mizener's *The Saddest Story*, p. xxi, concedes that Ford 'practically invented a form of fictional reminiscence; it may be a dubious genre, but in it he wrote two fascinating books'. 'Literary Portraits—XXIV.: Mr. William de Morgan and "When Ghost Meets Ghost"', *Outlook*, 33 (21 Feb. 1914), 238–9. Tate, in *The Presence of Ford Madox Ford*, 13.

6 McLuhan to Felix Giovanelli [Sept. 1948]: *Letters of Marshall McLuhan*, ed. Matie Molinaro, Corinne McLuhan, and William Toye (Toronto: Oxford University Press, 1987), 204. See e.g. John Batchelor's claim that Ford's comment that 'a writer has in England no social position' only reflects his own lack of success: *The Edwardian Novelists* (London: Duckworth, 1982), 93. Batchelor counters that the commercial successes of writers such as Wells, Shaw, and Bennett prove the contrary. But in fact Ford is talking not of money but of class and philistinism.

7 *Ancient Lights*, 253.

8 'The Critical Attitude: English Literature of To-day', *English Review*, 3 (Oct. 1909), 484; repr. in *The Critical Attitude*: see p. 60. Also see p. 32 on how the imaginative writer's 'actual and first desire must be always the expression of himself [. . .]'; and 'On Impressionism'. *History*, 12. *The English Novel*, 129, 123. *The March of Literature*, 520.

9 Ford, 'The Other House', *New York Herald Tribune Books* (2 Oct. 1927), 2; *Joseph Conrad*, 25.

10 'Notes for a Lecture on Vers Libre', *Critical Writings of Ford Madox Ford*, ed. Frank MacShane (Lincoln: University of Nebraska Press, 1964), 155–62 (160). Also see 'Techniques', *Southern Review*, 1 (July 1935), 25; and *The March of Literature*, 715. Ford used the phrase earlier in a letter (probably to Charles Sarolea), 5 Nov. 1912: Edinburgh University Library, in which he explains that his series of 'Literary Portraits' aimed to discuss the literary personality of each writer.

11 Bowen, *Drawn from Life*, 80. Ford himself says as much in his French tribute to Conrad, discussed on p. 167.

12 Greene, 'Ford Madox Ford', *Spectator*, 143 (7 July 1939), 11. Morton D. Zabel, review of *Return to Yesterday*, *Nation* (New York), 134 (6 Apr. 1932), 403–4.

13 *It Was the Nightingale*, 151. The 'elsewhere' to which he here returns is *Return to Yesterday*, 347.

14 'The Good Life', *London Mercury*, 39 (Dec. 1938), 217–18.

15 *Great Trade Route*, 19, 25. Peter Monro Jack recognized the significance for the book,

and all Ford's work, of this childhood game with which it begins: 'The World and Ford Madox Ford', *New York Times Book Review* (21 Feb. 1937), 2. *History*, 3.

16 *TLS* (26 Feb. 1938), 136. Max Webb, 'Ford Madox Ford's Nonfiction' (Princeton dissertation, 1972), 295, writes well of how the idea of the trade route 'is *both* a little ridiculous and serious at the same time'.

17 *Great Trade Route*, 142. Mizener, 424. *Provence*, 67–8.

18 *The Critical Attitude*, 32.

19 Eliot to Pound, 22 Oct. 1922: *The Letters of T. S. Eliot*, ed. Valerie Eliot, vol. 1 (London: Faber & Faber, 1988), 586.

20 Empson, *Essays on Shakespeare*, ed. David Pirie (Cambridge: Cambridge University Press, 1986), 84.

21 Cited by Otto Rank, *The Double* (Chapel Hill: University of North Carolina Press, 1971), 34. Waugh, review of *Return to Yesterday*, *Fortnightly Review*, 130 (Dec. 1931), 800–2. Ford offers an interesting discussion of the 'Egotistic Document' of writers such as McAlmon in 'From a Paris Quay (II)', *New York Evening Post* (3 Jan. 1925), 1–2.

22 *The Critical Attitude*, 187, 8. Cf. 'Literary Portraits—XIX.: Gerhart Hauptmann and "Atlantis"', *Outlook*, 33 (17 Jan. 1914), 77–9: 'Prose [. . .] is a matter of looking things in the face.'

23 *Some Do Not . . .* , 172. *The Good Soldier*, 143–4.

24 *Some Do Not . . .* , 209.

25 Bowen, *Drawn from Life*, 162. *The Good Soldier*, 138.

26 Mizener, 221. *Mightier Than the Sword* has a fine parody of James's dictation, in which James elaborates 'So that here we all are' into: 'So that here, not so much locally, though to be sure we're here, but at least temperamentally in a manner of speaking, we all are' (p. 35). Ford probably had the last sentence of *The Ambassadors* in mind.

27 'Thus to Revisit: I. The Novel', *Piccadilly Review* (23 Oct. 1919), 6.

28 *It Was the Nightingale*, 57.

29 *Portraits and Self-Portraits*, collected and illustrated by Georges Schreiber (Boston: Houghton Mifflin Company, 1936), 39–40. MacShane notes that there are in fact 24 words in this 'half-facetious' sketch: *The Life and Work of Ford Madox Ford*, 238, 287, n. 25. This may be because Ford might not have counted the two 'and's, which he generally wrote as simplified ampersands; however, the typescript at Cornell is written as printed here.

30 *The Critical Attitude*, 150, 28, 64.

31 Max Webb, 'Ford Madox Ford's Nonfiction', 44, explains well how, at the start of *Ancient Lights*, 'The juxtaposition of his remark and the passage from a novel places the reader at once in a world half real and half fictional, a fitting introduction for what is to come'.

32 *Thus to Revisit*, 77–8. Cf. *Return to Yesterday*, 34. *No Enemy*, 59–60, draws upon this memory when picturing something he had actually seen: aeroplanes and shell-bursts over the lines. A later version, in *Mightier Than the Sword*, 70–1, is discussed on p. 14 above. Ford must have read the book not in the Nineties but after it was published in 1900!

33 Ford, Introduction to Hemingway's *A Farewell to Arms* (New York: The Modern Library, 1932), p. xvii.

34 Dickens, cited by Stephen Gill, 'Introduction', *Adam Bede* (Harmondsworth: Penguin Books, 1908), 13. *Mightier Than the Sword*, 71.

35 See pp. 400–1 on vicarious experience and sympathetic imagination.

36 'On Impressionism', *Poetry and Drama*, 2 (Dec. 1914), 330; 331 (though the text there reads 'a man made for love').

37 In one example Ford describes an argument between Hudson and one of a group of writers, saying 'it might have been myself' (*Thus to Revisit*, 73). In a later version the same argument takes place between Hudson and Belloc (*Mightier Than the Sword*, 61–3). Yet to the experienced reader of Ford, that 'might have been' shows Ford incorporating an uncertainty into the reminiscence.

38 *'Fordie', *New Statesman and Nation*, 63 (22 June 1962), 906–7. Mizener is more explicitly reproving, talking of Ford *falling* into reminiscence, finding it 'irresistible'; 438.

39 Nabokov, *Ada* (Harmondsworth: Penguin Books, 1971), 198.

40 'Literary Causeries: XII. On Causeries as Such', *Chicago Tribune* (Paris) (4 May 1924), 3.

41 *Mightier Than the Sword*, 209. The last four sentences were marked by Graham Greene in his copy of *Memories and Impressions* (the fifth volume of the Bodley Head Ford), 132.

42 'Thus to Revisit: III. The Serious Books', *Piccadilly Review* (6 Nov. 1919), 6. Proust, *Time Regained*, trans. Andreas Mayor (London: Chatto & Windus, 1970), 283. *Heart of Darkness* (Edinburgh: John Grant, 1925), 85. 'Great Writers': an unpublished typescript chapter from *Towards a History of Literature*, Part II, p. 44.

43 *Rossetti*, 2–4. 'D.G.R.', *Bookman* (London), 40 (June 1911), 116. *'A Literary Causerie: On Some Tendencies of Modern Verse', *Academy*, 69 (23 Sept. 1905), 982–4 (983).

44 'The Work of W. H. Hudson', *English Review*, 2 (Apr. 1909), 157–64 (signed 'E.R.').

45 The better criticism recognizes Ford's particular fusion of criticism and autobiography. See e.g. E. Buxton Shanks's review of *Collected Poems*, *Poetry and Drama*, 1 (Dec. 1913), 492–3, on the 'critical and autobiographical introduction which is more important than any other pronouncement on poetry made in our time'.

46 Ford to Paul Palmer, 11 Feb. [1936; misdated '1935']. West and Mackenzie are quoted in Frank MacShane's fine introduction to *Critical Writings of Ford Madox Ford* (Lincoln: University of Nebraska Press, 1964), pp. ix–xiv (pp. xii–xiii).

47 Hudson, *Nature in Downland* (London: Longmans, Green & Co., 1900), 3, 5, 6. Ford to T. R. Smith, 27 July 1931. Elaine Lees, 'Novels of Impressions: Ford Madox Ford's Autobiographies' (University of Pittsburgh dissertation, 1976), 127.

48 Bayley, 'Other Selves', *London Review of Books* (27 Oct. 1987), 19–20. Levenson, *A Genealogy of Modernism* (Cambridge: Cambridge University Press, 1984), 119.

49 *Mightier Than the Sword*, 191, 70–1. Things get more complicated in *It Was the Nightingale*, 33, when Ford pictures Turgenev smiling through Galsworthy's pages. *Henry James*, 10. *The Critical Attitude*, 94. *It Was the Nightingale*, 334. See also 'Literary Portraits: XIV. Miss Marie Corelli', *Daily Mail* (Books Supplement) (20 July 1907), 3; 'Literary Portraits: XX. Authors' Likenesses and a Caricaturist', *Tribune* (7 Dec. 1907), 2; 'Literary Portraits—IX.: Mr. Thomas Hardy and "A Changed Man"', *Outlook*, 32 (8 Nov. 1913), 641–2; 'Thus to Revisit: V. Biographical Criticism', *Piccadilly Review* (20 Nov. 1919), 6; and 'Immortality', *Chapbook*, 3 (July 1920), 20–4 (quoted above, pp. 83–4).

50 'Lewis Carroll', *Alice's Adventures in Wonderland* (London, 1865), ch. 6.

51 See ch. 8 of Forster's *Aspects of the Novel*: 'Pattern and Rhythm'. 'Notes for a Lecture on Vers Libre', *Critical Writings of Ford Madox Ford*, 160.

52 'The Work of W. H. Hudson', 162. In a radio talk, 'The Commercial Value of Literature', he argues that art makes a person 'capable of expressing himself to himself without violence': *Contemporary Literature*, 30/2 (Summer 1989) [321]–7.

53 Lejeune, 'The Autobiographical Contract', in *French Literary Theory Today*, ed. Tzvetan Todorov (Cambridge: Cambridge University Press, 1982), 192–222 (217). Goldring, *The Last Pre-Raphaelite*, 253.

54 *Mightier Than the Sword*, 53–4. Note again the expressive pattern of syntax. See Max Saunders, 'A Life in Writing: Ford Madox Ford's Dispersed Autobiographies', *Antaeus*, 56 (Spring 1986), 47–69, for further examples of writerly self-protection.

55 Edward Krickel, 'Lord Plushbottom in the Service of the Kingdom: Ford as Editor', in *The Presence of Ford Madox Ford*, 98.

56 See *No More Parades*, 180: 'Tietjens had staged his meeting with herself remarkably well.' *Return to Yesterday*, p. 376.

57 *S/Z*, trans. Richard Miller (New York: Hill and Wang, 1974), 10.

58 Kenner, *Shenandoah*, 4/1 (Spring 1953), 24–5. Lewis, *Rude Assignment* (London: Hutchinson, 1951), 121–2.

59 *Mightier Than the Sword*, 251, 267. This remark is also discussed on p. 9 above.

60 *Joseph Conrad*, 190, 188. Ford to Palmer, 29 July 1937: *Letters*, 280. Frances Donaldson has written of Waugh: 'He was a tremendous actor. His whole life was an act and you never knew what was true and what wasn't.' Quoted in *Radio Times* (18–24 Apr. 1987), 99. Mizener, 426.

61 *The Critical Attitude*, 34. Cf. Green, *Ford Madox Ford: Prose and Politics*, 181; 'Ford had to invent his own life'.

62 *Ancient Lights*, p. viii. Biala, in *The Presence of Ford Madox Ford*, 219. Lynd, *Observer* (7 Mar. 1948), 3. Goldring, *The Last Pre-Raphaelite*, 259. 'Stevie', *New York Evening Post Literary Review* (12 July 1924), 881–2. *'Men and Books', *Time and Tide*, 17/21 (23 May 1936), 761. 'Sir Edward Burne-Jones', *Contemporary Review*, 74 (Aug. 1898) [181]–95 (189, 195). Cf. *Ford Madox Brown*, 254.

63 *Between St. Dennis and St. George*, 24. Some of the pseudonyms can be found in Harvey's index. But for 'E. Roterodamus', see Harvey, 162: D107; for 'von Aschendrof', see Harvey, 163: D110; for 'Faugh an-Ballagh Faugh' see Harvey, 269: D413; for Francis M. Hurd, see Saunders, i. 424–5. 'Hermann Ritter' and 'L. C. Pash' were used for the apparently unpublished manuscripts *'Wagner educationally considered' (see Sondra J. Stang and Carl Smith, '"Music for a While": Ford's Compositions for Voice and Piano', *Contemporary Literature*, 30/2 (Summer 1989), 186–7), and *'Letters in England' [1904–5]. Neither are listed by Harvey, though the piece he mentions on p. 110, 'On Letters in England', appears to be a revised introduction to the latter, a 27-page letter which fictionalizes Ford's retreat to the New Forest during his 1904 breakdown. 'Literary Portraits—XLV.: Mme. Yo. Pawlowska and "A Child Went Forth"', *Outlook*, 34 (18 July 1914), 79–80. *Mightier Than the Sword*, 93. James, *Partial Portraits* (London: Macmillan, 1888), 296.

64 *Mightier Than the Sword*, 235. Keats to Richard Woodhouse, 27 Oct. 1818: *Letters of John Keats*, ed. Robert Gittings, corrected ed. (London: Oxford University Press, 1975), 157–8. For example see Levenson, *A Genealogy of Modernism*, 57; and C. H. Sisson, 'An Afterword' to *The English Novel* (Manchester: Carcanet, 1983), 43. *Ford Madox Brown*, 409–10. *The Spirit of the People*, p. xv. Cf. Ford to Wells [May 1905]: *Letters*, 21–2: 'one reads to disagree': a statement that begs one both to agree and disagree! McLuhan, 'Tennyson and Picturesque Poetry', *Essays in Criticism*, 1/3 (July 1951), 263. Huddleston, *Bohemian Literary and Social Life in Paris*, 139.

65 *Mightier Than the Sword*, 32, 183, 114, 215.

66 Williams, 'Mightier than Most Pens', review of *Mightier Than the Sword*, *Time and Tide*,

19 (12 Mar. 1938), 350: repr. in *Ford Madox Ford: The Critical Heritage*, ed. Frank MacShane (London: Routledge and Kegan Paul, 1972), 166–8.

67 *'Writers of America—VIII: An Author Both Sides of the Atlantic', *Listener*, 12 (19 Sept. 1934), 500–1. The typescript of this article at Cornell, entitled 'The American Scene', was previously thought to be unpublished. Goldring, *The Last Pre-Raphaelite*, 257. The phrase 'Franco-American' appears twice in the Cornell typescript, but was deleted for the published version of the 'Autocriticism'.

68 Ford to Janet Adam Smith (the assistant editor of the *Listener*, for whom he had written his transatlantic article), 3 June 1934; *Letters*, 232–3.

69 *Some Do Not . . .* , 222. Eliot, 'Baudelaire', *Selected Essays*, third enlarged ed. (London: Faber, 1951), 422.

70 *Joseph Conrad*, 88. On Henry Ford see 'Not Idle', *New York Herald Tribune Books* (1 July 1928), 1, 6; and *Great Trade Route*, 182 ('my distinguished namesake'). *Mightier Than the Sword*, 5.

71 Wells, *Experiment in Autobiography*, ii. 617. For Moore, Gosse, and Wilde see *It Was the Nightingale*, 27.

72 *The Good Soldier*, 234, 142. 'Stocktaking [. . .] IX.: The Serious Book', *transatlantic review*, 2/4 (Oct. 1924), 399. 'Techniques', *Southern Review*, 1 (July 1935), 28. 'Pound and *How to Read*': *Pound/Ford*, 102. *Joseph Conrad*, 25. Jung, 'Psychology and Literature', in *The Spirit in Man, Art and Literature*, trans. R. F. C. Hull (London: Routledge & Kegan Paul, 1971), 84–105 (103).

Chapter 24

1 Epigraph from 'The Real France, That Goes to Bed at Nine', *New York Herald Tribune Books* (31 Mar. 1935). Mizener, 413–14. *Return to Yesterday*, 420. (Ford repeats the story in *It Was the Nightingale*, x.) Benét, *SRL*, 10 (21 Oct. 1933), 199. *Boston Evening Transcript* (2 Dec. 1933), 1, 3. Pritchett, *Fortnightly Review*, 136 (July 1934), 122. *Mightier Than the Sword*, 224–5. Ford's best formulation of the paradox whereby the writer must impress without intruding is in 'Techniques', *Southern Review*, 1 (July 1935), 20–35: 'The reader wants to be filled with the feeling that you are a clever magician; he never wants to have you intruding and remarking what a good man you are' (p. 32). Gordon to Ford [n.d., but 1934].

2 The 'Autocriticism' is discussed above, pp. 387–8. *Pound/Ford*, 117. Ford to Pound, 8 and 28 Oct. 1933: *Pound/Ford*, 129, 130. *'Mediterranean Reverie', *Week-End Review*, 8 (11 Nov. 1933), 495–6: *Pound/Ford*, 131–3.

3 Porter to Ford and Biala, 26 Nov. 1933. Gordon to Ford [n.d., but probably 1933 rather than Cornell's attribution of '[1934?]': the Pound testimonials came out in March 1933. Ford to Gordon, 11 Sept. 1933: *Letters*, 227. Ford's reply to the question 'Que pensez-vous de la France?' was published in the *Intransigeant* (5 Jan. 1934), 1. Harvey, 401.

4 Ford to Gordon, 11 Sept. 1933: *Letters*, 228. Ford to Duckworth & Co., 12 Jan. 1927. Lippincott to Bradley, quoted by Jenny Bradley to Ford, 6 Dec. 1933. Mizener, 415. It is also clear that publishers like T. R. Smith encouraged the idea, as did Ruth Kerr. In her letter to Ford, 18 Aug. 1932, she expressed a wish to publish 'a definitive edition of the works of F.M.F.' by the publishing firm she had joined.

5 Ford to Jenny Bradley, 18 Jan. 193[4: misdated 1933].

6 Mizener, 417, 594, n. 23, was wrong to say they had given up the flat in the autumn of 1933, and that they returned to Paris early in 1934. See Ford to Jenny Bradley, 13 and 18 Dec. 1933 (both from 37 rue Denfert-Rochereau). Ford was still writing from there on 14 Jan. to Gerald Bullett: *Letters*, 231–2; and on 3 Feb., to Julie. Givner, *Katherine*

Anne Porter (London: Jonathan Cape, 1983), 285. Porter to Biala [*c*.6 May 1932]. Ford to J. Jefferson Jones (of Lippincott), 1 Jan. [1934, misdated 1933]. Ford to Jefferson Jones (of Lippincott), 12 Jan. 1934: *Letters*, 230–1.

7 Bowen to Ford, 16 Apr. [1934?]; Ford to Bowen, 19–23 Jan. 1934.

8 Biala in conversation with Max Saunders, 22 Sept. 1990. The records of King Alfred School show Julie attending from Autumn 1933 to the summer term 1936, under the name 'Esther Julia Madox Ford'. Bowen to Ford, 1 Feb. [1934]. Bowen, *Drawn from Life*, pp. ix, 223, 230, and 239–44 describe their life in London. Ford to Bowen, 19–23 Jan. 1934. Ford to Julie, 3 Feb. 1934. Judd, *Ford Madox Ford*, 418, says Biala told Bowen 'Some years' after Ford's death that she had been signing his letters to her. In fact it was some days afterwards: Biala to Bowen, 10 July 1939.

9 Goldring gives the date of the London visit as 1932, basing it on two letters of Ford's which he transcribes, but the originals of which have disappeared: *South Lodge*, 192–4 (Goldring, *The Last Pre-Raphaelite*, 268–9, has a sketchier account based on the same information). He says the first was written from 32 rue de Vaugirard, which supports the date he gives for it of 2 Feb. 1932. He says Ford wrote the second letter on 15 Feb. (implying 1932, but not giving Ford's address). Ford says 'I still want to come to London', and asks Goldring to enquire about rooms. Goldring says Ford and Biala duly appeared, 'but not until May or June'. They were in London in May 1934, whereas all Ford's surviving letters from May–June 1932 place him in Toulon. There is no other evidence that they were in England in 1932, and Biala (in conversation, 22 Sept. 1990) confirms that her first visit to London was in 1934. It is possible that the first letter was written in 1932 and the second 1934; or that, if both are from 1932, that Ford considered making the trip in 1932 but they didn't in fact get to London until 1934. MacShane, 228, says they arrived in April. But Ford to Jenny Bradley, 9 and 19 Mar. 1934, were written from London. Ford to Caroline Gordon, 12 Oct. 1934 (Princeton), says they were in London for 3 months. They returned to Paris between 9 and 12 May: letters to the Trustees of British Museum and Mr Looker (of Constable) respectively. *Provence*, 79, 89, 40. Ford to Carl Laemmle, 11 Apr. 1934: draft at Cornell. Laemmle was president of Universal City. Ford was sending him copies of *The Panel*, *Ladies Whose Bright Eyes*, *When the Wicked Man*, and *Mr. Apollo* as bases for films; he also mentions *The Rash Act* and *Henry for Hugh*; but none were ever filmed. *'London Does Not Change Very Much', *Harper's Bazaar*, 10/5 (Aug. 1934), 32, 86–8; revised and incorporated into *Provence*, 192–205. The phrase, with which Ford ends the article, appears on p. 205 in the book.

10 *Provence*, 25, 257, 91–2. Mizener, 417. In a letter to Jacques Chambrun, 19 Nov. 1934, Ford suggests an article on 'PATRIOTISM as a form of Inferiority Complex'. *The Good Soldier*, 280.

11 Biala to Saunders in conversation, 20 Sept. 1990 and 9 Apr. 1994. Goldring, *South Lodge*, 192–3. *Provence*, 221–2, 249, 280, 286, 295. Ford to Bertram, 14 Sept. 1934: *Letters*, 233–5. Ford to Bertram, 27 Sept. 1935 (*Letters*, 243), identifies Bertram as the 'kind host' of *Provence*, 299. Ford to Janet Adam Smith, 3 June 1934: *Letters*, 232–3. Mizener, 594, n. 15, says Ford 'even began to believe he no longer admired James', the phrasing implying some sort of delusion. But Ford did write the piece: *'An Author Both Sides of the Atlantic', *Listener*, 12 (19 Sept. 1934), 500–1. It is mainly about the superiority of New York to London as a literary centre, but ends with a tribute to James that leaves no doubt that Ford's admiration was unabated, and clarifies what Ford meant by saying that the subject was dangerous: 'He was the greatest novelist—perhaps after Turgenev—that the world has ever seen, the most consummate artist, the most

contagious figure. But that alone made him dangerous—infinitely dangerous. For if a figure is so great that you have no hopes of surpassing him you are in terrible peril of imitating his tricks [. . .].' Bowen had told Ford that his 'present hatred of everything English' made him view her and Julie's new life 'with fantastic suspicion' (1 Feb. [1934]). It was James's assimilation of Englishness that Ford found antipathetic, not his art. Eliot was reversing Ford's mental processes because he too was becoming Anglicized, whereas Ford told Scott-James: 'I have practically become an American writer [. . .]': 2 Apr. 1935: Texas.

12 MacShane, 228. Crankshaw, 'Afterword', *The Presence of Ford Madox Ford*, 238.

13 Harvey, 78. Crankshaw to Ford, 20 Dec. 1934; 20 June, 19 Dec. 1935; and Crankshaw to Unwin, 2 July 1939. Mizener, 417–18. *The Presence of Ford Madox Ford*, 238, 239. Biala told me (22 Sept. 1990, in conversation) she wasn't sure Ford had ever met Unwin.

14 Goldring, *South Lodge*, 194; *The Last Pre-Raphaelite*, 234. Goldring explains how Violet Hunt had quizzed him about Ford's visit when she heard about it, and asking why he didn't come to see her. Ford's passport gives the date for their arrival at Dieppe. *Provence*, 286–7, 287–8, 353–4, 364. Ford's postcard to Anthony Bertram, 20 May 1924, says 'Janice has just come through her first bull-fight'. Ford also described the bullfighting (and Biala's 'startling' drawings) in a letter to Bertram, 14 Sept. 1934: *Letters*, 233–5. There he describes the odd effect of the crowd's unanimous detestation of another fighter, Chicuelo; the corresponding account in *Provence* is on 338–41, where Ford mentions Hemingway's book (*Death in the Afternoon*). MacShane, 230, makes the interesting suggestion that Ford sensed a parallel between Chicuelo's career and his own: the artist compelling respect from an unappreciative audience; though it is balanced by the picture of Lalanda as the supernatural genius, uniting his audience in awe.

15 Ford to Juliet Soskice, 9 July 1934: Oliver Soskice. Ford told Bertram (14 Sept 1934: *Letters*, 233–5) that he had sent *Provence* to Lippincott 'a week ago last Monday'—that is, on 3 Sept. (The first six chapters had been sent at the end of June: Ford to Jefferson Jones, 29 June 1934.) Biala in conversation with Max Saunders, 22 Sept 1990. Ford's passport bears stamps indicating that he entered and left Italy on 17 July. *Provence*, 333–5.

16 Ford to Bertram, 14 Sept. 1934: *Letters*, 233–5. Ford to Greene, 24 Sept. 1934: *Reader*, 499–500.

17 4 Dec. 1934: Reader, 500. Judd, *Ford Madox Ford*, 420. Greene to Ford, 18 Dec. [1934].

18 Bertram to Ford [n.d., but between 14 Sept. (the date of Ford's letter praising his novels: *Letters*, 233–5) and 27 Sept. 1934—the date of Ford's reply: *Letters*, 235–6]. *Men Adrift* (London: Chapman and Hall, 1935) appeared dedicated to Ford as 'A master of the writer's craft [. . .]'. Alan Judd, 'In the Second-Hand Bookshops', *Sunday Telegraph* (2 Sept. 1990), writes that the character Gillespie in Anthony Bertram's novel appears to be inspired by Ford. It wasn't only novelists and publishers who sent Ford such tributes. Ruth Kerr had written to him on 9 Nov. 1933 to make what she called 'my declaration of personal faith in you as a great writer'.

19 Harvey, 79, says *Henry for Hugh* was probably published in Oct.; the first known review is 13 Oct. Mizener, 421, says they came up to Paris in late Nov., but this is impossible. Ford's passport shows he arrived in New York on 1 Nov.; he wrote to Dreiser on 14 Nov. from New York, saying he got there some days ago: University of Pennsylvania. Mizener, 425, says they made the crossing in Oct. Ford was still in Toulon on 13 Oct., when he wrote to Jefferson Jones of Lippincott suggesting topics he could lecture on: 'Modern Travel or Cooking and Wine or the International Situation or the making

of novels with references to H. James, Conrad, Wells, Bennett, France, Proust, Hemingway and the young Americans and their methods—and my own'; they probably left for Paris soon after this date. Ford to Caroline Gordon, 12 Oct. 1934 (Princeton), says they were booked to sail from Antwerp on 19 Oct. *Great Trade Route*, 48–57, describes the crossing. Lowenfels is described as the 'leader' or 'Fuehrer' of their party (pp. 48, 65). Lowenfels, 'The End was Ugly', *American Dialog*, 3/2 (1966), 34–5. *Great Trade Route*, 64, 65, 67–8. MacShane, 230–2, implies that Ford left for America after Christmas in Dec. 1933; but there is no record of a trip then, and the details he takes from *Great Trade Route* about the 5th Avenue apartment refer to the visit at the end of 1934. Ford's letters show him in Paris until he left for London in March 1934. Mizener, 422 and 595, n. 4, citing Jefferson Jones to Ford, 5 Dec. 1934.

20 *Great Trade Route*, 79, 81, 188–9, 83, 89. Ford says he was last in the church ten years before: it was ten years before the date he was finishing the book, but it was eight years between his visits of 1926 and 1934. Dreiser to Ford, 4 Mar. and 1 June 1935. *Mightier Than the Sword*, 217. 'The Small Producer', *American Mercury*, 35 (Aug. 1935), 445–50. See W. A. Swanberg, *Dreiser* (New York: Charles Scribner's, 1965), 401, on Dreiser and Scott. Mizener, 422, says Ford rowed with Scott; but Biala (in conversation, 22 Sept. 1990) confirms that it was her, described as the 'patient New Yorker': *Great Trade Route*, 82–3.

21 Lowenfels, 'The End was Ugly', 34. *Great Trade Route*, 198. A drawing of the court by Biala is reproduced on p. 208. *Great Trade Route*, 178–9, has Ford and Biala travelling through New Jersey together by train; and p. 219 says they arrived at Flemington together by train. Though Biala confirms Ford's comment that he spent 'those long weeks' at Flemington, his letter of 28 Jan. to Max Perkins is on his 5th Avenue stationery. He may have taken his writing-paper with him, of course; but he probably returned to New York briefly at the end of the month, then went back to Flemington with Biala. Mizener, 426, who doesn't mention that Ford attended the trial, says he wrote a pair of articles. In fact there were at least three. He wrote a piece on 24 Jan. 1935, which appeared in the *New York World Telegram* that day (pp. 1, 4) as 'Koehler in Destiny's Role, Ford Madox Ford Declares', and in the *New York Times* on 25 Jan. (p. 18) as 'Tribute to Judge Paid by Novelist'. *'Hauptmann from Lost Generation: British Novelist Says Horror of War at 17 Separated Him from Normal Mankind', another piece for the Associated Press, appeared in the *Philadelphia Bulletin* (Evening) (26 Jan. 1935), 12. Then Ford wrote a piece for the *New York Times* on the day of the verdict (14 Feb. 1935), 11: 'Trial is Likened to a Bull Fight.' Ford elaborated his impressions of the trial to include an account of his stay at Flemington, and his thoughts about justice and punishment, in 'Fiat Justitia', *Great Trade Route*, 197–220. *Great Trade Route*, 202. Davidson, 'The Story of the Century', *American Heritage*, 27/2 (Feb. 1976), 22–9, 93. I am most grateful to Carla Davidson for sending me a copy of her father's article.

22 Ruth Kerr to Ford, 18 Aug. 1932. J. Jefferson Jones to Ford, 11, 21 Jan. and 20 Feb. 1935; Ford to Jones, 12 Jan. and 22 Feb. 1935.

23 Harvey, 80. 'Katherine Woods, *New York Herald Tribune Books* (24 Mar. 1935), 1. Noel Sauvage, *New York Times Book Review* (24 Mar. 1935), 9. *'Check List of New Books', *American Mercury*, 35 (June 1935), 244–9 (247). *Catholic World*, 141 (Aug. 1935), 636. *Provence* was not published in England until 1 Nov. 1938, where it was also reviewed enthusiastically. See Harvey, 421–3. Ford to Gordon, 12 Oct. 1934: Princeton.

24 Ford told Robert Penn Warren on 25 Mar. 1935 he had lectured at New York Univer-

sity 'lately'. *Marion Cook, 'Europe Faces Years of Peace', *Rockefeller Center Weekly*, 2/11 (14 Mar. 1935), 10. For an earlier statement of political optimism, see 'Preparedness', *New York Herald Tribune Magazine* (6 Nov. 1927), 7, 18.

25 *American Mercury*, 34 (Apr. 1935), 402, 406–7.

26 *The Pre-Raphaelite Brotherhood*, 31. 'Conrad and the Sea', *American Mercury*, 35 (June 1935), 169–76, later became ch. 4 of *Mightier Than the Sword*. Palmer to Ford, 5 Apr. 1935. Curtis Brown to Ford, 11 Mar. 1935. Mizener, 595–6, n. 13.

27 Mizener, 426–7, says that 'they' started out in 'late March'. Ford's letter to Biala proves she was not with him on this visit, as does Gordon's letter to Wood, Spring 1935: Wood, *The Southern Mandarins*, 185. The catalogue at Cornell gives the exhibition dates as 25 Apr. to 9 May. Both Ford and Biala signed a copy of *Provence* inscribed to Julie, dated 'New York 1 April MCMXXXV' (Serendipity Books, Catalogue 45, item 198). Ford wrote to Paul Palmer on 1 Apr. and to his friend the novelist Isa Glenn (2 Apr.) from New York before he left. He probably visited Glenn in Washington on this trip; though in *Great Trade Route*, 287, he concedes he is 'mixing in yet another journey', and includes Biala. He had reviewed Glenn's *A Short History of Julia* in the *Bookman* (New York), 72 (Jan. 1931), 530–1. The other journey may have been one Ford evidently made (probably this time with Biala) to the Tates at Nashville in June: see p. 484. Ford to Biala, 6–7 Apr. [1935]: Biala. *Great Trade Route*, [172]–261 of Part II describe the train journey. The bus trip is described in Part III. MacShane, 233. Biala's curriculum vitae: Olivet. Ford to J. Jefferson Jones, 22 Feb. 1935.

28 Max Webb, 'Ford Madox Ford and the Baton Rouge Writers' Conference', *Southern Review*, NS, 10/4 (Oct. 1974), 894, 895, 900–1. *Great Trade Route*, 376–7; 26–7, 382. Penn Warren to Ford, 2 Apr. 1935. Gordon to Wood, Spring 1935: Wood, *The Southern Mandarins*, 187. Mizener, 427, erroneously gives the dates at 11–12 April.

29 B. A. Botkin's transcript is published in 'Conference on Literature and Reading in the South and Southwest, 1935', with an introduction by Thomas W. Cutrer, in *The 'Southern Review' and Modern Literature: 1935–1985*, ed. Lewis P. Simpson, James Olney, and Jo Gulledge (Baton Rouge and London: Louisiana State University Press, c.1988), 38–78 (esp. 66–7 and 74–8 on Ford). Also see MacShane, 234; and Cutrer, *Parnassus on the Mississippi: The Southern Review and the Baton Rouge Literary Community, 1935–1942* (Baton Rouge and London: Louisiana State University Press, 1984), 58–9.

30 'Conference on Literature and Reading [. . .]', 75.

31 Ibid. 75, 77–8. The New Orleans *Item* corroborates Ford's account of Fletcher's outbursts, saying that after another of his tirades against New York, Ford said 'Oh, come', and that 'settled that': quoted by Webb, 901. *Great Trade Route*, 379–84, 362–3. Fletcher, in *New Directions: Number Seven*, 474, confirms Ford's story about his dialect story—though he thought Ford was reading a poem.

32 *Memphis *Commercial Appeal* (7 and 12 Apr. 1935); there was also an interview in the *Baton Rouge Times* (10 Apr. 1935), 8: 'Southern Rise in Literary World is Forecast by Ford Maddox [*sic*] Ford': clippings at Cornell. 'Techniques', *Southern Review*, 1/1 (July 1935), 20–35. Cutrer, *Parnassus on the Mississippi*, 59.

33 Wood, *The Southern Mandarins*, 185. *Great Trade Route*, 405. He was back in New York by 18 Apr.: Ford to Arnold Gingrich. Mizener, 436, includes the truck-farm visit in his account of later 1936. But Williams to Ford, 27 May 1935, saying he will present himself the following day to take Ford on a tour of inspection of one or two truck farms in the neighbourhood. Williams, 'Les Amis de For Maddox Forde! [*sic*]'; reproduced as a

frontispiece to *Antaeus*, 56 (Spring 1986). Sondra Stang's introduction to that Ford issue, 7–8, compares Williams's account with Ford's, which is in *Great Trade Route*, 184. See *A Man Could Stand Up—*, 252–3.

34 Ford was in New York on 4 June: letter to Ruth Aley. He was back by the 27th: Ford to Lewis Gannett: *Reader*, 500–1. Ford to Lowry, 18 June 1935: Oxford University Press (New York) files. Mizener, 427. Biala's curriculum vitae: Olivet. Ford to Orrick Johns, 24 Apr. 1935. See MacShane, 263. Ford to Palmer, 5 June 1936: *Letters*, 250–1. Mizener, 428, says typically that 'Ford came away from this luncheon with a different conception of what had been agreed on than Palmer'. But the letter of Ford's he cites ('It was also quite definitely settled that you would take the Pound and Dreiser at our conversation at the Plaza') was written a year later (5 June 1936: *Letters*, 250–1). Palmer had written: 'as I intimated when you were here, I have my doubts about Dreiser and Pound' (27 May 1936). Indeed, when Ford had written to him on 6 May 1935 (*Letters*, 236–7) to suggest a list of names, he had replied that all the names were agreeable except Dreiser, Christina Rossetti, and Pound (14 May 1935). Ford claims (in his letter of 5 June 1936) that he persuaded Palmer to accept the essays despite having been insulted personally by Dreiser and Pound. This is quite probable, since in his letter of 27 May 1936 Palmer does the same thing: voices his doubts about Dreiser and Pound, but then adds: 'I am entirely open to persuasion—the final decision will be made after I have read the MSS.' It was this that irritated Ford—not any misunderstanding about the subjects of the essays. He did not like (and could not afford) to write pieces on approval, and felt, quite reasonably, that he was well-enough established for editors to commission his work in advance. Other writers he thought of including (but didn't) are Bennett, Meredith, Christina Rossetti (Ford to Palmer, 6 May 1935: *Letters*, 236–7), Yeats (Ford to Palmer, 10 Oct. [1935]), and George Moore (Ford to Ruth Aley, 25 Dec. 1935). Ford to Lewis Gannett, [Thursday] 27 June 1935 (*Reader*, 500–1), is written c/o the Lakes, and says 'We shall leave on Saturday for Naples'. See *Great Trade Route*, 387–421; 438, for the voyage (407, 402, 408–9, 391–2, 395–8, 414–15, 438). Ford to Bertram, 15 Oct. 1936: *Letters*, 246. Ford's passport. *Great Trade Route*, 421. Biala in conversation with Max Saunders, 22 Sept. 1990. Ford to Palmer, 11 Sept. 1935, says they've been back 'two months today': *Letters*, 242–3.

Chapter 25

1 Julie was at Toulon by at least 30 July, when Bowen sent her a card from London. Julia M. Loewe, memoir in *The Presence of Ford Madox Ford*, 201–3 (202).

2 Biala in conversation, 20 and 22 Sept. 1990. 'Biala' to Bowen, 6 June and 31 Aug. 1935; Bowen to Biala, 2 July [1935] (saying that Julie had only written once to M. Marcoussis, in the previous year, and that perhaps Madeleine had forwarded one of Julie's letters to her); and 20 Aug. [1935?]. Julie, postcard to Bowen, 16 Aug. 1935 (from Nice, having been to Ventimiglia the previous day, and planning to go back to Italy the next). See Mizener, 432. Julia Loewe, 'Introduction' to Bowen, *Drawn from Life*, p. x; she adds: 'it is a comfort to me that by the time he died, when I was eighteen, I had made my peace with him.' Ford to Julie, 11 Sept. 1935: *Letters*, 237–42. I have restored some of Ludwig's ellipses from the Cornell original.

3 Mizener, 429. Ford to Julie, 23 Sept. 1935. It was probably at the end of this year, and in response to this toned-down and abridged version, that Bowen wrote to Biala: 'What Julie's attitude to her father is, really depends upon Ford himself. I have been reminding her for a long time that she owes him a letter, & made other efforts to keep her up to her filial duties; but his attitude in general & towards me in particular has made these

efforts rather futile, & it is only Ford himself who can remedy the position he has created [. . .] it is an unkind & unsuitable letter to have written to a child of her age': 8 Dec. [1935?—written from 26a Belsize Square, NW3, where Ford told Scott James (28 or 29 Sept. 1935) Bowen was then living]. See e.g. 'Pre-Raphaelite Epitaph', *Saturday Review of Literature*, 10 (20 Jan. 1934), 417–19. Bowen, *Drawn from Life*, 239.

4 Ford to Palmer, 10 Oct. 1935 [the digits '35' are unclear, having been typed over what were probably the upper-case symbols above those numbers. But the dating can be confirmed because Ford is sending Palmer his essay on Hudson, which Palmer comments on in his letter of 5 Nov.]. Ford says they are going to Geneva 'tonight' for a day or two. Ford to Palmer, 11 Sept. 1935: *Letters*, 242–3. Ford's passport records his crossing into Switzerland on 11 Oct. *Great Trade Route*, 91–107, describes this visit to Geneva (98, 100, 102). They were back by the 15th, when Ford wrote to Bertram that they had 'just been for the last few days' in Geneva: *Letters*, 245–6.

5 Palmer to Ford, 5 Nov. 1935. Ford to Palmer, 17 Nov. 1935: *Letters*, 247–48. Palmer to Ford, 6 Dec. 1935. Ford to Palmer, 19 Dec. 1935: *Letters*, 249–50. Ford to Palmer, 5 June 1936: *Letters*, 250–1. See above, Ch. 24, n. 34, for details of Palmer's unhappiness about the Dreiser and Pound pieces. Palmer repeats the terms of his cable in the letter to Ford, 22 June 1936. Ford to Palmer, 16 June 1936; and 17 Nov. 1935: *Letters*, 247–8. Palmer to Ford, 21 Sept. 1936. Ford became further exasperated when, on 27 Aug. 1935, Palmer sent the proofs of the Dreiser essay (which Ford had sent with his letter of 16 June 1936, but which was not published in the *American Mercury* until Apr. 1937 (after the book had come out), making it the last in the series, and) which had been cut because the magazine was to be given a smaller format (as Palmer had explained to Ford on 31 July 1935). Ford replied: 'Curse you! Curse you! (bis). | It is only yesterday that I was boasting to the editor of the LONDON MERCURY when he was entreating me to write for him, what a splendid fellow you were and how you gave me endless space and paid mornamillion for everything. | However, it was bound to come and I weep for you. I do!': 2 Sept. 1936.

6 Biala, in *The Presence of Ford Madox Ford*, 198. Ford to Julie, 25 Dec. 1935; quoted by Mizener, 431. Biala to Mizener, 3 Oct. 1968. Biala in conversation with Max Saunders, 22 Sept. 1990. Bowen to Biala, 27 Jan. [1936?]. The eclipse was on 8 Jan. 1936. Ford to Ruth Aley (his new agent in America), '8 Jan 35' [amended to 1936].

7 Ford to Palmer, 11 Feb. 193[6: though dated '1935']. Mizener, 432, says they moved north in March. But Ford to J. Jefferson Jones, 17 Feb. 1936, speaks of having thrown away a typescript 'down at Toulon', implying they had already left by then. Mizener, 432, says that 'Only Picasso seemed to be too much for him', and that Crankshaw thought Ford was glad not to find him in. This is unlikely. Ford had reproduced some of Stein's Picassos in the *transatlantic* (Poli, 85), and Biala said they got on well with Picasso: Judd, *Ford Madox Ford*, 425.

8 Ford to Lowry, 18 Mar. 1936; 4 June 1935: Oxford University Press (New York) files.

9 *Provence*, 232. The subtitle appeared only on the dust-jacket of the English edition.

10 Ford to Stanley Unwin, 8 June 1938. He says *Provence* (published *after Great Trade Route* in England) is 'another (not the second)' of this group of books. So if *Great Trade Route* is not the first, he must have been thinking back at least to books like *A Mirror to France* and *New York is Not America*. *A Mirror to France*, 276. This chapter was originally published in the *Criterion*, 2 (Oct. 1923), 57–76. The cricket match was probably the one written up as 'Une Partie de Cricket' in the 'Envoi' to *No Enemy*: see ch. 2, n. 17.

11 Ford to J. Jefferson Jones, 20 May 1935. He repeated the suggestion in another letter to

Jones of 11 Dec. 1935, saying: 'I still think you have been so uniformly unsuccessful with my books that my name can not be any good to you and you might just as well try the effect of a new writer on the public'—which may have been part of his motive for changing his own name after the war. (Harvey, 80, notes that 2,547 copies were printed for the American first edition, and that 2,498 were sold. The others were probably the review and complimentary copies. The English edition, not published until 20 July 1937 by Allen and Unwin, sold 1,160 copies out of 1,510; 225 were destroyed by bombing.

12 Biala to Mizener, 29 June 1966; 14 Oct. 1968.

13 Lippincott's editors felt the book dragged, because they expected Walter's disappearance to be briefer than it is. They suggested the title 'The Disappearance of Walter Leroy' would better signal the kind of mystery concerned: Bradley to Ford, 30 Sept. 1935. Ford suggested some alternative titles: 'Long Live the King . . .'; 'Lost Leroy'; 'When the King Enjoys his Own Again' ('from the Jacobite ballad'); or 'The King is Dead': Ford to Jones, 11 Dec. 1935 and 17 Feb. 1936. Lewis Gannett, *New York Herald Tribune* (9 Apr. 1936), 21: 'I began to suspect the solution on page 11'; Fanny Butcher, *Chicago Daily Tribune* (11 Apr. 1936), 12: 'spoofing of the most delicate kind'. *TLS* (24 July 1937), 543. *Punch, 193 (4 Aug. 1937), 139–40. *Reid, 'Fiction', *Spectator*, 159 (6 Aug. 1937), 253. Swinnerton, *Observer* (25 July 1937), 6. Greene, review of *Great Trade Route*, *London Mercury*, 35 (Feb. 1937), 422–4, and of *Vive Le Roy*, *London Mercury*, 36 (Aug. 1937), 389–90. *Times* (10 Aug. 1937), 15.

14 Joan Givner, *Katherine Anne Porter* (London: Jonathan Cape, 1983), 215–16, 288. Biala told Mizener, 29 June 1966, that Ford promised the story if she stayed faithful for one year. She told me 'five years': in conversation, 20 Sept. 1990.

15 Mizener, 432–4, 522–3. *Ancient Lights*, 120–1. *Vive Le Roy*, 149, 67, 245, 321. Ford used Penkethman again in an apparently unpublished story, 'Pearls', of which there is a fragmentary draft at Cornell. *Great Trade Route*, [9].

16 Neville Williams, *Chronology of the Modern World: 1763–1965*, revised edn. (Harmondsworth: Penguin, 1975). The dedication of *Great Trade Route* says to Nickie Le Son that because 'it occurred to you to throw your steam locomotive with energy and accurately at one of our knees', they took him for a particularly small producer, scrapping his machine at an early age. Biala in conversation with Max Saunders, 20 Sept. 1990. Biala to Mizener, 29 June 1966. Ford to Julie, 3 Feb. 1934.

17 Ford to G. F. J. Cumberlege, 27 Oct. 1936: *Letters*, 263–4 (though Cumberlege's initials are given wrongly as 'E. C.' here and in the preceding letter. Ford to John Chamberlain, 21 Nov. 1933: *Letters*, 229–30. Ford may himself have initiated the confusion over Eliot. In 'Declined With Thanks', *New York Herald Tribune Books* (24 June 1928), he had written that he *thought* he had published Eliot in the *English Review*.

18 Biala to Bowen, Easter Saturday [10 Apr.] 1936. The copy of *Vive Le Roy* inscribed to Julie by Ford in Paris, dated 24 Apr. 1936, suggests she came soon after Easter (which was on 12 Apr.): Serendipity Books, Catalogue 45, item 200. The first letter I have found bearing the new address is Ford to Lowry, 24 Mar. 1936: Oxford University Press (New York) files. Julia M. Loewe, in *The Presence of Ford Madox Ford*, 203.

19 Ford to Palmer, 2 July 1936: *Letters*, 252–4 (253). Ford to Monroe [n.d., but pre-11 July 1936]: Chicago. Lowell, 'Foreword to *Buckshee*', reprinted in *Ford Madox Ford: The Critical Heritage*, ed. Frank MacShane (London: Routledge and Kegan Paul, 1972), 267. MacShane, *The Life and Work of Ford Madox Ford*, 236.

20 *'Men and Books', *Time and Tide*, 17/21 (23 May 1936), 761–2. There are further quotations from this important essay in Saunders, i. 11. Ford to Palmer, 2 July 1936:

Letters, 253. Ford's comments about the effort of reading Swinburne are a continuation of his sparring with Palmer over the subjects of these essays. He told Palmer: '[. . .] you put me to a great deal of trouble by suddenly asking me to substitute for George Moore, about whom I could have written with ease and enthusiasm, the antique figure of my godfather [Swinburne] who presents for me about as much interest as the once celebrated John Brown, Queen Victoria's ghillie': 5 June 1936: *Letters*, 250–1. But in fact it was Ford who made the suggestion, suggesting on 10 Oct. [1935]: 'How would you like Swinburne or W. B. [Y]eats in place of Moore?' Presumably Ford was still piqued that Palmer wouldn't let him write on Pound. Mizener, 434. Ford's passport shows that they embarked in Dieppe on 4 July 1936, and returned to Boulogne on 5 Aug. (not 4 Aug., as Mizener says). Ford wrote a letter to Paul Palmer from Penshurst which he dated 20 June 1936; but this is almost certainly a mistake (for 20 July?), since he encloses the essay on Swinburne, saying 'I shall do the concluding article right away and that will finish the job'—meaning that this letter must have been written after he wrote Palmer the letter of 2 July about still reading Swinburne that morning. Ford's letter to Palmer dated 2 July is headed with Crankshaw's address (The Nunnery Cottage, Penshurst): 'We have just got over moving from one apartment to another prior to leaving for the Nunnery.' Mizener evidently misread the dating as 24 July 1936 (p. 596, n. 6), despite the fact that Ford explains that, struggling with a new typewriter, he mistyped 'July 2 436' instead of 'July 2 '36'. Mizener says Ford wrote 'Coda' 'after their return to Paris'; but Ford sent it to Harriet Monroe, saying he had finished it 'two hours ago', in an undated letter which she has stamped 'ANS'D H.M.' with the dates 11 and 30 July 1936: Chicago. If she received the letter in Chicago by 11 July, it must have been posted before Ford left France on 4 July. (The letter of 11 July is not at Cornell; but that of the 30th says 'I believe I thanked you for sending us the *Buckshee* poems', which presumably refers to the 11 July letter. But even if she didn't receive 'Coda' until 30 July, it must have been written before Ford returned to Paris.) Anyway, it was finished before 5 June 1936, when Lowry told Ford that Oxford University Press had sent Monroe a copy (Ford may either have forgotten, or decided to send her another copy personally). Ford's note says the poem was 'Written in the rue de Seine for an anniversary between feasts of SS. James & Paul (Otherwise May Day) & That of Saint Joan of Arc. MCMXXXVI'—i.e. between 1 and 30 May 1936. Judd, *Ford Madox Ford*, 426.

21 'London Revisited', *London Mercury*, 35 (Dec. 1936), 180. Ford to E. S. P. Haynes, 24 Jan. 1939; *Letters*, 309–10. Biala in conversation with Max Saunders, 22 Sept. 1990.

22 Judd, *Ford Madox Ford*, 421. Ford told Ruth Aley on 12 Aug. 1936: 'I am leaving for Toulon in half an hour.' Ford to Aley, 25 Dec. 1935. Ford to Lowry, 23 Sept. 1935. Mizener, 435, 596, n. 8. Lowry to Ford, 24 June 1936. Ford to Oxford University Press and to Lowry, 14 July 1936; Lowry to [H. V.] Clulow, 24 June 1935; and memo to Clulow and Miss Nicholson, 24 June 1936: Oxford University Press (New York) files. Biala to Oxford University Press, 13 June and 12 Aug. 1936 were both written on the same days as letters from Ford, and their grand manner sounds like his: Oxford University Press (New York) files. Ford to Palmer [July 1936, misdated '20 June 1936']. Ford to Stanley Unwin, 16 Sept. 1936. Ford to Tate, 6 Sept. 1936: *Letters*, 257.

23 G. F. J. Cumberlege (the head of OUP in New York, even though he was based at the London Office) to Ford, 2 Sept. 1936. Ford to Lowry, 4 Sept. 1936. Ford to Tate, 6 Sept. 1936: *Letters*, 259.

24 Ford to Aley, 7 Sept. 1936. Ford to Pound, 6 Sept. 1936: *Letters*, 260–2. Ford to Tate, 6 Sept. 1936: *Letters*, 258. Mizener, 434, says they stayed at Toulon until late Oct., but

cites no evidence. They had moved by at least 20 Oct. 1936, when Biala wrote to Bowen from 31 rue de Seine.

25 Ford to Tate, 6 Sept. 1936: *Letters*, 257–8. In 1990 she could still remember saying it, though added ironically that she only found out after years of practice what double-dealers they were; especially Gordon, whom she thought filled with bitterness and hatred (conversation with Max Saunders, 22 Sept. 1990). Gordon to Bowen, n.d.: quoted by Mizener, 425. Ford to Scott-James, 5 Sept. 1936: *Reader*, 502. Crankshaw to Ford, 16 Nov. and 16 Dec. 1936. Judd, *Ford Madox Ford*, 426. Ford to Julie, 'jeudi' [between 16 Aug. and 1 Sept. 1936, though misdated 1934 at Cornell] says the Crankshaws are staying.

26 Judd, *Ford Madox Ford*, 426. Mizener, 434, quotes Ford's letter to Ruth Aley, 7 Sept. 1936, saying: 'I may tell you that we are having to give up this villa—on which my health entirely depends—and go to live in one room in Paris simply because of this uncertainty [about contracts].' But he doesn't indicate that the Cornell carbon copy from which he takes it has this paragraph (and the next, from which he also quotes) deleted; so it is not clear whether Aley actually received the letter in this form. *Great Trade Route*, 227.

27 Pound to Ford, 11 Sept. [1936]: *Pound/Ford*, 141–2. Ford to Tate, 6 Sept. 1936: *Letters*, 259. Ford to [G. F. J.] Cumberlege, 19 Sept. 1936: *Letters*, 262–3. In 'Declined with Thanks', *New York Herald Tribune Books* (24 June 1928), 1, 6, Ford wrote: 'I come of a long line of ancestors nearly all of whom—*absit omen!*—died in reduced circumstances owing to the fact that they supported, in periodicals or with printing presses advanced, iconoclastic or highbrow literature. The earliest discoverable of them was a fifteenth century printer who was fined and imprisoned for printing a pamphlet full of disrespect for the Sorbonne—the University of Paris: the last, my father, started with distinguished ill success one journal in Paris in support of Wagner; another in Rome in support of Schopenhauer and two in London, "The New Quarterly," to spread the fame of Schopenhauer, and "The Musical World," to champion Wagner. For myself, I have spent the greater part of my life in such pursuits.' He gave another humorous version of his anti-academic ancestry in his reply to Ernest Boyd's criticisms of *The March of Literature*, *Saturday Review of Literature*, 18 (22 Oct. 1938), 9 (also in *Letters*, 300–3). Ford inscribed the misbound copy to Julie as a curio for New Year's Day 1938: Serendipity Books, Catalogue 45, item 199.

28 Sondra Stang, 'Introduction', *History* [p. xv]. Ford to Cumberlege (whose initials he gives erroneously as 'C.F.G.', like Masterman's), 20 Sept. 1936. Ford had proposed the one-volume condensation in a letter to Ruth Aley, 9 Sept. 1935.

29 G. F. J. Cumberlege to Ford, 6 Oct. 1936. Ford to H. F. Lowry, 4 June 1935: Oxford University Press (New York) files. Ford to Cumberlege, 27 Oct. 1936: *Letters*, 263–4.

30 Mizener, 435. Ford's letter to Paul Palmer, 2 July 1936 (*Letters*, 252–4), suggests that one motive for the trip was to observe politicians: 'We propose arriving in N.Y. two or three days after what is going to happen to your President happens . . . say on the 11/11/36'. Roosevelt was re-elected on 3 Nov. with a landslide victory. Ford told Crankshaw on 10 Nov. 1936 that they were packing to board the *Lafayette* that night. Though he told Scott-James (also on 10 Nov.) that the boat would sail on the 11th: Texas. Dahlberg, in *New Directions: Number Seven*, 466–9. Ford to Greenslet, 28 Dec. 1936, mentions 'my—new—agent'. Greenslet sent the contract for *Portraits from Life* just before they sailed for New York: see Ford to Greenslet, n.d. [catalogued as 'Oct 1936?' at Cornell, but probably Nov.: Ford expects to be in Greenwich Village 'in a week or two']. Stanley Unwin to Ford, 6 Nov. 1936, agrees to publish the *History*. But, as Unwin explained to Bowen, 6 Oct. 1938, Ford decided to substitute *The March of Literature* for the *History*.

31 A. J. P. Taylor, *English History: 1914–1945* (London: Oxford University Press, 1965), 402–3. 'Last Words About Edward VIII', unpublished manuscript. Mizener, 435, says it was broadcast over WJZ; but the Museum of Broadcasting, New York, which holds a recording of the broadcast, lists it as aired on NBC. Ford to Palmer, 9 Dec. 1936: Yale; quoted by Mizener, 435–6. The typescript at Cornell, 'Talk Delivered over WABC', was revised for publication as 'W.P.A. and American Civilization', *Talks*, 2 (Jan. 1937), 29–34. Harvey, 266, says this talk was given over CBS radio.

32 *Great Trade Route*, 76–7.

Chapter 26

1 Ford to Palmer, [9] Dec. 1936: Yale; and 7 Jan. 1937. Mizener, 438–9. Brewer, in *New Directions: Number Seven*, 462–6. He said he met Ford in '1923 (or thereabouts)' in a mutual friend's flat in Lincoln's Inn. Ford was staying in Dyneley Hussey's flat there in May 1924. But Brewer's recollection that Ford was still living in England makes a date before his move to France at the end of 1922 more likely. Bill Selden to Max Saunders, 2 Dec. 1989. Ford told Palmer, 16 Mar. 1938, that the college had 305 students and 45 teachers: *Letters*, 290–2. Maurice Hungiville, '"The Last Happy Time": Ford Madox Ford in America', *Journal of Modern Literature*, 6/2 (Apr. 1977), 214–16, 220. Goldring, *The Last Pre-Raphaelite*, 261–2. MacShane, 252. Transcript of 'Brewer—Ford Madox Ford Symposium' held at Olivet, 3 Apr. 1974 (Olivet College Library): 5, 27; p. 28 says Padraic and Mary Colum also visited (perhaps on Ford's recommendation: see Ford to Brewer, 19 Feb. 1938). Tate to Mizener, 29 Jan. 1969: Vanderbilt. Gordon to Ford, n.d. [but Fall 1936, says Mizener, 597, n. 16]. Macauley, 'The Dean in Exile: Notes on Ford Madox Ford as Teacher', *Shenandoah*, 4/1 (Spring 1953), [43]–8.

2 Ford to George Bye, 28 Dec. 1936 (Columbia), says that Grenville Vernon (of the Dial Press) wants him to write a 'HISTORY OF WORLD LITERATURE'. Mizener, 439, says that *The March of Literature* was 'the history of literature he had wanted to write for many years'. Yet to support this he cites (on p. 597, n. 18) a letter to Pinker of 3 June 1921, which is about 'Towards a History of English Literature' (see Harvey, 121).

3 Harvey, 83, gives the American publication date as 12 Jan., but Oxford University Press's files say 18 Feb. Peter Jack, *New York Times Book Review* (21 Feb. 1937), 2. John Patton, *New York Herald Tribune Books* (21 Feb. 1937), 5. *Wolfe, 'Ford Madox Ford Writes his Best Book', *Sunday Referee* (17 Jan. 1937), 6. *Crankshaw, 'Philosophic Travel', *Time and Tide*, 18 (6 Feb. 1937), 171. Greene, 'The Dark Backward: A Footnote', *London Mercury*, 32 (Oct. 1935), 562, 564–5; 'The Landowner in Revolt', *London Mercury*, 35 (Feb. 1937), 422–4. *Great Trade Route*, 228. Brogan, *Spectator*, 158 (22 Jan. 1937), 134. Lowry told Ford (30 July 1936: Oxford University Press (New York) files) 'We definitely want to drop the subtitle, "A Sentimental Journey" [. . .]'. It didn't appear on the title page of either edition, but was retained on the Allen and Unwin jacket. Ford disliked Sterne's bawdiness as well as his sentimentality, but he knew the digressive mode of his reminiscences owed much to *Tristram Shandy*. A. G. Macdonnell, *Observer* (17 Jan. 1937), 4. See Harvey, 83–4, for the sales figures; there was no second edition in either country; 405 copies of the New York edition were jobbed in 1939. See MacShane, 241, and Mizener, 423, for interesting discussions of the book.

4 John Patton, *New York Herald Tribune Books* (21 Feb. 1937), 5. Ford's reply appeared in the issue of 14 Mar. (p. 28): *Letters*, 273–5.

5 Biala's curriculum vitae at Olivet mentions that she had two shows with Georgette Passedoit, in 1935 and 1937. Both Dreiser and Zadkine wrote appreciations for the catalogue, which were quoted in the notes for her November exhibition at Olivet (Olivet

College Library Archives). Ford to William Carlos Williams, 28 Jan. 1937 (*Reader*, 503–4), gives the day of the opening, which is confirmed by the catalogue in Oxford University Press's (New York) files. Ford wrote to Alfred Knopf on 23 Jan. 1937: 'This blurb writing is becoming almost insupportable. Half my table is covered with books asking for them [. . .]'; none the less, he provides a letter full of quotable material on Marjorie Worthington's *Manhattan Solo*—a novel he also reviewed in the *New York Herald Tribune Books* (14 Feb. 1937), 4, where he admired how 'she can make the most tremendously exciting tragic dénouments out of the most inconspicuous materials and surroundings'. The letter to Knopf classes Worthington with what Ford calls 'Quietist authors' (Gaskell, Trollope, Gissing), with 'the quality of, once it has been presented to your attention or taken hold of you of holding you quietly breathless. . . . Because you will see in it your own daily problems solved or left unresolved, your own daily life going on around you—and if you are a woman you will see yourself triumphing where your success is indifferent to you and worsted in departments of life where to triumph would leave you a little ashamed.' Ford also wrote a review of Caroline Gordon's *None Shall Look Back* for Scribner's in-house magazine *Bookbuyer, 3/2, NS (Apr. 1937), 5–6. A typescript on John Peale Bishop's *Act of Darkness* (1935) is not known to have been published as a review, but may have been used as a basis for a blurb. Ford met 'the editress' of *Vogue*, on 26 Jan. 1937: see Ford to Bye, [Monday] 25 Jan. [1937: misdated 1936]: Columbia. Ford told Bye on 26 Jan. 1937 (Columbia) that *Vogue* wanted two articles; but only one was published: *'Take Me Back to Tennessee', *Vogue* (New York: 1 Oct. 1937), 104–5, 134, 138, 140. This was the only part of the *Portraits of Cities* book that is known to have been published. See n. 10 below.

6 Ford to Bye, 25 Feb. 1937 (Columbia) and 22 Mar. 1937. The 'article on spices' might be *'In Praise of Garlic', one of two pieces Ford wrote on food for *Harper's Bazaar*, and which discusses herbs and spices: (Aug. 1937), 104, 126, 129. The other is *'Four in the Morning Cookery' (Oct. 1938), 107, 134–6. Ford to Greenslet, 30 Jan. 1937. Ford had renamed the book *That Same Poor Man*. Mizener, 436, says that in 1927 Ford had called the book '"unreadable," the work of a madman'; he neglects to say here that Ford had revised the book in 1928 (see Mizener, 388). See above, p. 6, for the possibility that Ford was referring not to 'Mr Croyd' but to 'True Love & a G.C.M.'. He also asks Greenslet for extra copies of Houghton Mifflin's catalogue with a note about him: 'I want to send one to my daughter with the hope that it may make her more respectful to her ancestor.' Greenslet to Ford, 15 Feb. 1937. Ford to Bye, 8 Mar. 1937: *Reader*, 504–5. Bye to Ford, 17 Mar. 1937 (Columbia), mentions Harpers and Bobbs-Merrill.

7 A memo in the Oxford University Press (New York) files dated 26 Feb. 1937 announces Ford's broadcast on station WINS. 'Novelist Offers Utopia Born of Electric Voting', *New York Herald Tribune* (10 Mar. 1937), 21. A recording of the 'Dinner at Nine' broadcast was not kept: Library of Congress to Max Saunders, 26 Feb. 1987. But it may not have been a live broadcast, since Ford told H. G. Leach on 1 Mar. 1937 that he would have dinner with them on the 15th. Ford to Winnie Winson, 27 Mar. 1937 (Washington University, St Louis), shows him back in New York by that date. Ford to Ralph Wright, 27 Mar. 1937: *Letters*, 276–7.

8 Mizener, 439, says they set off for Tennessee on 30 Apr, but he cites no evidence. They can't have left New York then, because they inscribed a copy of *Great Trade Route* to the Lakes in New York on 1 May (copy inspected at Ulysses Bookshop, London, on 3 Aug. 1992); and Ford also inscribed a copy of *Portraits from Life* to Julie there on the same day (Serendipity Books, Catalogue 45, item 201). They must have left on the 1st or soon after, but they headed north rather than south, to Boston. Ford wrote to Bye (6 May

1937: Columbia) from Boston, saying they would be passing through New York on their
way to Washington and Clarksville. Rachel Wolodofsky ('Wally' for short) met Ford and
Biala in 1934, the year before she married Jack Tworkov. See her memoir in *The Presence
of Ford Madox Ford*, 215–17. Ford's friend who took them to dinner in Washington was
probably Isa Glenn. Ford wrote to Bye from the Hotel St James in Knoxville, Tennessee: the letter is dated 'Friday 14' [May 1937], and says they are heading for Clarksville
'this morning' (Columbia). Ford to Julie, 30 Aug. 1938. Zabel to Ford, 9 May 1937.
Ford to Zabel, 18 May 1937: *Reader*, 506. A publicity announcement in the Oxford
University Press (New York) files has Ford lecturing at the University of Chicago on the
26th and to the Poetry Society on the 27th. Zabel had asked Ford to review Edgar Lee
Masters's book on Whitman for *Poetry*, and Ford apparently told him a review was 'in
progress'; but Ford eventually decided against it: 'I have tried very hard to do this but
I can't think of anything profitable to say about that good, grey poet and I find I can't
say anything at all sincere that wouldn't hurt the feelings of my great friend, Mr
Masters' (Ford to Zabel, 18 May 1937). It's a rare blank spot in such an inventive and
tolerant critic. Mizener, 440, 598, n. 20. There is a typescript of Ford's talk at the *Poetry*
dinner, catalogued by Cornell as 'Speech given at a fund-raising dinner [. . .]'; it is a
touching elegy for Harriet Monroe, the founder and editor of *Poetry*, who had died the
previous year. MacShane, 251–2. Ford to Unwin, 29 May 1937: *Letters*, 277–8.

9 Gordon to Wood, May 1937: Wood, *The Southern Mandarins*, 209–10.

10 Gordon to Wood, May 1937, and 10 July 1937: Wood, *The Southern Mandarins*, 209,
210–13. Tate to Andrew Lytle, 19 May 1937 (dating the Fords' arrival as 14 May):
Thomas Daniel Young and Elizabeth Sarcone (eds.), *The Lytle–Tate Letters* (Jackson
and London: University Press of Mississippi, 1987), 108–9. Ian Hamilton, *Robert Lowell*
(London: Faber & Faber, 1983), 42, has an amusing story about the party that Moore
arranged for Ford to meet Lowell. When one guest was introduced, he was told that
Ford only spoke French. Lowell, memoir in *The Presence of Ford Madox Ford*, 204–5;
'Visiting the Tates', *Sewanee Review*, 67 (Autumn 1959), 558–9. Lowell's remark about
Ford's low opinion of Boston is borne out by the unpublished essay, 'Boston'. What he
disliked was what made him uneasy about himself: what he calls the city's 'dimidiated'
(or divided) personality, and the puritanical New England conscience.

The essay was written for what was to have been the third volume of the trilogy
including *Provence* and *Great Trade Route*. The synopsis is provisionally titled 'A Little
Tour at Home', and suggests writing about the voyage from Naples (considering
civilizations from Periclean Athens onwards), and then Boston, Detroit, 'Bullensville,
Michigan', Chicago, Denver, Kansas, Pittsburgh, Richmond (Virginia), Washington,
Charleston, Baltimore, and New York, with a final chapter ('How to be happy though
human') on the boat returning to the Mediterranean. The working title became 'Portraits of Cities'. Mizener, 440, mentions the project dismissively, as if it were only a way
of getting publishers to finance Ford's ambitions to travel, and says the idea was
dropped. But the idea was a reasonable one given the good reception of the other two
books; and in fact Ford wrote at least four of the chapters: *'Boston'; *'From Boston to
Denver'; *'Denver' and *'The Athens of the South' (on Nashville). Only the last of
these was published, as *'Take Me Back to Tennessee', *Vogue* (New York) (1 Oct.
1937), 104–5, 134, 138, 140. The book was to be illustrated by Biala. Ford to Greenslet,
12 June 1937 (*Letters*, 279), gives a more international list of cities: 'Boston, New York,
Washington, Natchez, New Orleans, Chicago, Detroit, Denver, Salt Lake City, Los
Angeles, San Francisco, Panama (?), Havana (?), Marseilles, Dijon, Paris, Strasbourg,
London.' (Indeed, the third volume of the trilogy had originally been conceived not in

terms of cities, but of the 'Great Trade Route', 'taking in the parts of it which I have not hitherto treated', Ford told Unwin (3 Nov. 1936): 'the English South Coast, the U.S. Deep SOUTH and back by way of the Azores, Tangiers, Jaffa and the Mediterranean shores.') Ford never abandoned the project altogether. On 19 Apr. 1938 he told Palmer he found he had 'not got either the material or the frame of mind to write them'. But on 29 Nov. he was suggesting another version of it to George Bye (*Reader*, 506–8), called 'Forty (?) Years of Travel in America', and now including St Louis, Lexington (Virginia), and Grand Rapids (Michigan). See Mizener, 453.

Biala to George Davis (of *Harper's Bazaar*), 21 June 1937. Tate, 'FMF', *New York Review of Books*, 1/2, special issue (Spring/Summer 1963), 5; repr. in *The Presence of Ford Madox Ford*, 12–15.

11 Tate, in *The Presence of Ford Madox Ford*, 15. Mizener, 439, 597–8, n. 18. Wood, *The Southern Mandarins*, 211. Lowell to Richard Eberhart [n.d.]: Dartmouth College Library: quoted in Hamilton, *Robert Lowell*, 50. 'Ford Madox Ford', *Life Studies*, 2nd edn. (London: Faber & Faber, 1968), 63–4. Tate to Mizener, 29 Jan. 1969 (Vanderbilt), confirmed Ford's fear that Lowell would write about him '*en pantouffles*', and said he did in his poem on Ford. *The Presence of Ford Madox Ford*, 12. Lowell, 'Visiting the Tates'. Lowell, Foreword to *Buckshee*, repr. in *Ford Madox Ford: The Critical Heritage*, ed. Frank MacShane (London: Routledge and Kegan Paul, 1972), 267. Ford to Warren, 11 June 1937: *Letters*, 278–9. MacShane, *The Life and Work of Ford Madox Ford*, 251. Ford to Pound, 30 May 1937: *Pound/Ford*, 145–6. *Thomas Daniel Young, 'In His Own Country', *Southern Review*, 8/3 (July 1972), 572–93. Ford, 'A Paris Letter', *Kenyon Review*, 1 (Winter 1939), 18–31.

12 Ford to Bye, 11 June 1937: Columbia. Judd, *Ford Madox Ford*, 430, Biala also told me in conversation, 22 Sept. 1990, that she thought Allen Tate was anti-Semitic. Ford to Dale Warren, 11 June 1937: *Letters*, 278–9.

13 Mizener, 440, says the Conference was to begin on 15 July; but the programme (in the Olivet College Library Archives) gives the dates: 'Olivet Writers' Conference, 18 July– 31 July 1931'. Biala in conversation with Max Saunders, 20 Sept. 1990. 'Brewer—Ford Madox Ford Symposium': transcript of a discussion held at Olivet College, 3 Apr. 1974 (Olivet); 11, 5, 7–8.

14 *William Dunn, 'Genius-in-residence', *Detroit News Magazine* (29 Apr. 1979), 15, 35– 6, 38–9. Mizener, 441. Ford to Bye, 29 July 1937: Columbia. Ford to Grenville Vernon (of the Dial Press), 18 Aug. 1937. There's no address indicating where this letter was written; but it says: 'We found Colo. rather enervating', and that they are 'back here where we expect to stay for some little time'; 'here' was presumably Olivet where Ford certainly was by 23 Aug. (Ford to Pound: *Pound/Ford*, 148–9) until the end of Nov. Davison to Mizener, 8 Apr. 1969: quoted by Mizener, 441. Mizener, 443; MacShane, 257. Lowell, 'Foreword' to *Buckshee* (Cambridge, Mass.: Pym-Randall Press, [1966]), pp. xi–xiv; repr. in *Ford Madox Ford: The Critical Heritage*, 265. Mizener, 441, says the audience behaved with sympathy and respect, but Lowell told MacShane, 257, a different story: there was no public address system; the audience became restless and began to shout 'Louder', then began to leave noisily. Mizener, 598, n. 23. Hamilton, *Robert Lowell*, 51.

15 Mizener, 441–3. Davison to Mizener, 8 Apr. 1969. Lowell, in *The Presence of Ford Madox Ford*, 205.

16 Biala to Allene Talmey (of *Vogue*), 29 July 1937, says they plan to be at Boulder till about 18 or 20 Aug. But on the same day Ford wrote to Bye they would be there till about the 15th (Columbia). *'Denver', 5, 1, 3, 5. See n. 10 above on the 'Portraits of Cities'. Ford

to Pound, 23 August 1937: *Pound/Ford*, 148–9. Ford to Palmer [Sept.? 1937]: *Letters*, 280–2.

17 'The Sad State of Publishing', *Forum*, 98 (Aug. 1937), 83–6. 'The Fate of the Semiclassic', *Forum*, 98 (Sept. 1937), 126–8. Ford to Pound, 23 Aug. and 13 Nov. 1937: *Pound/Ford*, 148–50.

18 Bill Selden to Max Saunders, 2 Dec. 1989. Macauley left after a year to follow Ransom to Kenyon. Macauley, 'The Dean in Exile', 46–7.

19 Lowell to Charlotte Lowell, 24 Aug. 1937: quoted by Hamilton, *Robert Lowell*, 52. *'Ford Madox Ford', *History* (London: Faber & Faber, 1973), 118. The Shakespeare is (slightly garbled) from Ford's favourite speech in *Henry V*: IV. i. Ford dictated letters to Lowell too. One to J. B. Orrick, 3 Sept. 1937, is signed 'R. T. S. Lowell, secretary to F. M. Ford': Oxford University Press (New York) files.

20 Natalie Davison to Biala, 27 Oct. 1937.

21 Macauley, 'The Dean in Exile', [43]–6. Selden to Saunders, 2 Dec. 1989. 'Brewer—Ford Madox Ford Symposium', 2. Macauley says the cigarettes were French, and that Ford would call them 'Dust and dung'. He also said that he was able to understand about 80–90% of Ford's speech, but thought others would have found his English accent confusing. *Great Trade Route*, 35 n. He says his grandmother Emma Madox Brown's mother's maiden name was 'Judith Hall'. One of Shakespeare's daughters was called Judith; another, Susanna, married John Hall (*William Shakespeare: The Complete Works*, ed. Stanley Wells and Gary Taylor (Oxford: Oxford University Press, 1986), pp. xv, xvii). But in fact Emma Hill's mother was Catherine Stone: Teresa Newman and Ray Watkinson, *Ford Madox Brown* (London: Chatto & Windus, 1991), 46. Ford may have been misremembering another connection, however. In his *Ford Madox Brown*, 59, he says Brown met Emma Hill while visiting Stratford-upon-Avon 'in connection with the portrait of Shakespeare'.

22 Selden to Saunders, 2 Dec. 1989. Macauley, 'The Dean in Exile', [43]. Maurice Hungiville, '"The Last Happy Time": Ford Madox Ford in America', *Journal of Modern Literature*, 6/2 (Apr. 1977) (subsequently 'Hungiville'), 219. Macauley to Saunders, 2 Feb. 1990. Macauley, 'Introduction' to *Parade's End* (New York: Knopf, 1951), pp. v–xxii (p. v).

23 'Brewer—Ford Madox Ford Symposium', 9, 4. Macauley and Laura Verplank were amongst those invited to dinner. *The Presence of Ford Madox Ford*, 221–2. Hungiville, 217.

24 Unidentified clipping from Olivet College Library Archives. Ford explained his notion of abolishing copyrights in 'The Sad State of Publishing'. He wrote to Henry Goddard Leach (the editor of *Forum*) that: 'The War [. . .] got rid of Faith, Loyalty, Courage and all the other big words as motives for human action': 18 Feb. 1938: *Letters*, 287.

25 Mizener, 444, says they left in Nov.; but Ford says several times he will stay at Olivet until Dec. (see for example Ford to Palmer [Sept.? 1937] and to Stanley Unwin, 5 Sept. 1937: *Letters*, 280–3). The interview in the local paper also says he's leaving on 1 Dec. Ford to Christopher Morley, 27 Nov. 1937 (Texas), says they will stay with Cox from 1–3 Dec.; so perhaps they made the entire journey on 1 Dec. Ford and Biala to the Tates, 4 Dec. 1937, 'a bord le Lafayette': Princeton. *Great Trade Route*, 63–4, describes Professor Cox. 'Food', *Forum*, 99 (Apr. 1938), 241–7, describes how they complained about the insipid cooking on the boat, whereupon the chef produced the best cassoulet de Castelnaudary they had ever had (p. 247). Ford to S. Bagnall (of Allen & Unwin), 16 Dec. 1937: *Letters*, 286–7. Ford to Brewer, 19 Feb. 1938. Bowen, *Drawn from Life*, 244. This was Julie's last visit before she was summoned to see him when he was dying.

Biala, in conversation with Max Saunders, 22 Sept. 1990, said there was always tension when Julie visited them in the rue de Seine. In her introduction to the 1984 Virago reprint of her mother's book, she said they had 'many rows', but that she had made her peace with Ford by the time he died. Biala was sceptical of this. Biala painted her portrait at the rue de Seine (when Julie was about 15, she thought); and on one visit she had a dress made for her out of silver cloth. Ford to Pound, 1 Jan. 1938: *Pound/Ford*, 150–1. Pound to Ford, [?7 Jan. 1938]: *Pound/Ford*, 151–2. Ford to Pound, 17 Feb. [1938]: *Pound/Ford*, 152–4. This letter was misdated '37' by Ford: Ludwig follows the error: *Letters*, 270–2. Ford to Unwin, 24 Feb. 1938. Ford to Bye, 16 Apr. 1938: Columbia.

Chapter 27

1 *The March of Literature*, p. vi. See *Collected Poems* [1913], 13. In *Ancient Lights*, 296, Ford wrote: 'Hokusai in his later years was accustomed to subscribe himself: *The old man mad about Painting*. So I may humbly write myself down a man getting on for forty, a little mad about good letters.' Cf. *It Was the Nightingale*, 124, 126. The epigraph is from an article by Tate in the *Minnesota Review* (Fall 1960).

2 Ford to Crankshaw, n.d. [but *c*.17–21 Mar. 1938]. The painting bought for the Jeu de Paume was the Battle of Chancellorsville (Biala's curriculum vitae: Olivet). Ford described the exhibition in similar terms to Julie ([20 Mar. 1938]: *Letters*, 292–3; though here he says she sold only 'a couple of others'); and Unwin (15 Mar. 1938). Ford to Stein, 1 Mar. 1938: Yale. 'Food', *Forum*, 99 (Apr. 1938), 241–7; Ford to Henry Goddard Leach, 18 Feb. 1938 (*Letters*, 287–9), says he's glad Goddard likes the article; it was written after their crossing from New York on the *Lafayette*, which it describes. Biala (in conversation with Max Saunders, 22 Sept. 1990) said Ford didn't get the piece from Picasso. Ford to Pound, 16 Mar. 1938: *Letters*, 290–2 (slightly emended according to the text in *Pound/Ford*, 156–7).

3 Pound to Ford, 18 Mar. [1938]; Ford to Pound, n.d. [*c*.20 Mar. 1938]; Pound to Ford, 22 Mar. [1938]; *Pound/Ford*, 157–60.

4 Harvey, 85. Ford to Ferris Greenslet [n.d. but early Nov. 1936] and [n.d., but Nov.? 1936]. Lloyd George, whom Ford had always mistrusted, had published his *War Memoirs* between 1933 and 1936 (6 vols.: London: Ivor Nicholson & Watson).

5 *Mightier Than the Sword*, p. [5]. Ford had written exactly such a historical romance about Shakespeare biting the head off a chicken in *Zeppelin Nights*, 128–36.

6 *Mightier Than the Sword*, 292, 195, 210–12, and 205. Moser, 290, 291.

7 E. B. Osborn, *Daily Telegraph* (22 Feb. 1938), 6. Pritchett, *London Mercury*, 37 (Mar. 1938), 550–1. See also *Ralph Thompson, 'Books of the Times', *New York Times* (23 Mar. 1937), on *Portraits from Life*. 'The book is as much autobiography as anything else and as satisfying a blend of autobiography, biography and criticism as we have had for a long time.' See Mizener, 438 and 597, n. 15, for more negative responses to the criticism in the book.

8 Williams to Ford, 1 May 1937. Van Doren, in *New Directions: Number Seven*, 470.

9 [20 Mar. 1938]: *Letters*, 292–3.

10 Ford's passport. Biala in conversation with Max Saunders, 10 Apr. 1994. Ford to Unwin, 15 Mar. 1938. Ford to Pound, [*c*.20 Mar. 1938]: *Pound/Ford*, 158–9. Mizener, 446. 'A Paris Letter', *Kenyon Review*, 1/1 (Winter 1939), [18]–31. Harvey, 270, suggests that this was perhaps 'the last article he wrote for publication before his death', and that it 'possibly deals with the Paris he found in mid-June, 1939'. But Ford didn't see Paris in 1939 before he died. Ford had sent the essay to John Crowe Ransom by at least Oct. 1938: see Ransom to Ford, 13 Oct. [1938], thanking Ford for letting him see this

'most exhilarating piece'. Ransom's suggestion that Ford might bring the essay 'completely down to date' might indicate that the version Ford sent him was already several months old. Ford referred to 'my *Paris Letter*' when he wrote to Henry Goddard Leach, the editor of *Forum*, on 19 Apr. 1938. And the suggestion that Leach might want to use Biala's design of the Île de la Cité indicates that this is the same essay. 'I am sending you at last that article', he begins: 'it is meant to be challenging and not soothing to your and my compatriots.' This refers to the taunts to Anglo-Saxons in 'A Paris Letter'. On 11 May 1938 Ford asked Leach: 'Did you get my article on the *Pont des Arts?*', which confirms the essay sent on 19 Apr. as this one. However, it was probably written in France or on board the *Normandie* (Biala, in conversation with Max Saunders, 22 Sept. 1990, said she thought Ford had been well enough to work during the voyage. Edward Dahlberg, *Epitaphs of Our Times* (New York: G. Braziller, 1967), 267–8, said he asked Ford to write a 'Paris Letter' for a magazine he had co-founded with Dorothy Norman, *Twice a Year*. He commissioned the article at a party held in Ford's honour before his departure for France (thus Nov. or early Dec. 1937). Ford sent it, but Dahlberg and Norman rejected it. It was presumably after this he sent the piece to Leach—who also rejected it (Leach to Ford, 17 May 1938). His last piece written for publication was probably either his letter defending *Finnegans Wake* (see pp. 546–7), or the essay on 'Dinner with Turbot', published in *Vogue* (New York), 15 Sept. 1939), 104, 130–1. 'A Paris Letter', 27, 26.

11 *Mightier Than the Sword*, [5]–6. Ford to Unwin, 15 Mar. 1938.

12 Ford to John O'Hara Cosgrave, 29 Apr. 1938: Case Reserve Western University. Ford to Keating, 1 June 1938: *Letters*, 294–5. Ford to Hamer, 11 May 1938: *Letters*, 293–4. But he did speak at a dinner in Chicago on 24 May establishing a poetry prize in memory of Harriet Monroe: *'University Accepts $5,000 to Establish Poetry Prize Fund', *Chicago Maroon*, 38/115 (27 May 1938), 1.

13 Ford to Robert Penn Warren, 3 June 1938. Ford to Unwin, 15 July 1938. Olivet symposium, 8–9. Mizener, 447. Ford's dedicatory letter in *The March of Literature*, to Brewer and the Dean of Olivet, gives the symbolic date of 14 July. Ford to Palmer, 21 July 1938: Yale; quoted by Mizener, 449.

14 Mizener, 447. A copy of the citation is at Cornell. The Sorbonne degree and the 'colonel in charge of two regiments in action' sound like Fordian fictions. The other statements are mostly exaggerations based on truth. His review of Dreiser's *The Titan* found the book appalling, though he later became an admirer of Dreiser and his work ('A Literary Portrait: Chicago', *Outlook*, 35 (6 Mar. 1915), 302–3). Although he wasn't the first to publish stories by Bennett and Galsworthy, he was an early admirer and publisher of both, and may have said so just after listing his discoveries. Conrad had published *Almayer's Folly* in 1895, before he met Ford; but Ford was supporting him while he wrote *Heart of Darkness*, *Lord Jim*, and *Nostromo*. Mizener gets Akeley's name wrong, and garbles the spelling of Almayer, which Akeley got right. Ford mentions Maureen Whipple in a letter to Unwin, 4 Aug. 1938: *Letters*, 298–9: her novel was published as *The Giant Joshua* (Boston: Houghton Mifflin Company, 1941).

15 Ford to Keating, 28 June 1938: *Letters*, 296. Ford to Julie, 30 Aug. 1938. Mizener, 599, n. 8, says that though Ford wanted to be a professor emeritus, he was actually appointed as professor on leave. Ford to Unwin, 14 Nov. 1938. Biala, in conversation with Max Saunders, 22 Sept. 1990, said Ford didn't have mixed feelings about becoming a professor because Olivet was 'special'.

16 He had some help with the book: the tables at the end were compiled by Olive Carol Young, who had been acting as his secretary at Olivet: see Ford's letter to the Editor, *Saturday Review of Literature*, 18 (22 Oct. 1938), 9. Hungiville, 216. Ford to Burton

Hoffman, 16 June 1938, says that the conference begins on 17 July. It also mentions that [Lee] Keedick will be sending Ford the itinerary for his lectures soon. (Hoffman had been trying to arrange the lectures since May: Hoffman to Ford, 19 May 1938. Mizener, 442, confusingly discusses these plans during his account of 1937. Ford to Hoffman, 31 July 1938, says he will be broadcasting from Detroit 'tomorrow'; but Ford to Unwin, 4 Aug. 1938 (*Letters*, 298–9), says 'Yesterday I had to go into Detroit to world broadcast over short wave an account of the History of Literature that I've just finished'. Ford to Keating, 1 June 1938: *Letters*, 294–5. Mizener, 449. Ford to Grenville Vernon, 13 June 1938; Vernon to Ford, 21 June 1938; Hoffman to Ford, 21 June 1938. Ford to Vernon, 25 June 1938: in a letter to Ford of 13 Oct. 1937, Vernon corrected a slip he had made in actually referring to the book as 'The March of Time'; he says here that he meant 'The March of Literature', but Ford's illness had possibly made him forget that this was the title they wanted. Ford to Unwin, 13 Oct. 1938: *Letters*, 299–300. Ford to Hoffman, 31 July 1938. Ford to Pound, 21 June 1938 and 10 Nov. 1938: *Pound/Ford*, 160–2.

17 Ford to Vernon, 1 Aug. 1938. Ford to Unwin, 4 Aug. 1938: *Letters*, 298–9. Hoffman to Ford, 1 and 17 Aug. 1938. Ford to Hoffman, 23 Aug. 1938 and 7 Sept. 1938. Ford to Keating, 20 June 1938 (Yale), asks him to send a copy of *Zeppelin Nights*; thanking him when it arrived, he said he thought the vignettes were some of his 'best writing' (28 June 1938: *Letters*, 296). He also proposed a series of them to Palmer, 21 July 1938: Yale. Some of Ford's vignettes were reprinted in the *Minnesota Review*, 2 (Summer 1962), 467–511: see Harvey, 270–1, for details.

18 Ford to Julie, 30 Aug. 1938.

19 Ford to Paul Palmer (from Paoli), 16 Sept. 1938: Yale. Metcalf to Saunders [n.d., but Oct. 1990] and 6 Nov. 1990.

20 Ford, telegram to Bowen, 23 Sept. 1938.

21 Mizener, 449. Ford's diary. Biala to Saunders in conversation, 22 Sept. 1990. Ford to Unwin, 12 Oct. 1938. Ford to Hoffman, 19 Oct. 1938. Unwin to Ford, 31 Oct. 1938, quotes from an earlier letter of 18 Aug. encouraging him to steer promising manuscripts towards them. Mizener, 452–3, makes Ford sound fickle by juxtaposing the remark about 'agreeable people' with a much later one (Ford to Unwin, 16 Feb. 1939: *Reader*, 508–10) saying he 'found them unsupportable as individuals'. By this time he had accused them of acting in bad faith over a manuscript (which he had probably recommended to them) by Wendell Wilcox: see Hoffman to Ford, 13 Mar. 1939.

22 Ford to Unwin, 13 Oct. 1938: *Letters*, 299–300. Boyd, 'Confucius to Hemingway', *Saturday Review of Literature*, 18 (8 Oct. 1938), 12. Ford, Letter to the Editor, *Saturday Review of Literature*, 18 (22 Oct. 1938), 9. Ford also wrote a personal note to Irita Van Doren to complain about her having published George Whicher's review of *The March of Literature* in the *New York Herald Tribune Books* (23 Oct. 1938), 7: 25 Oct. 1938: *Letters*, 300–3. Whicher's description of it as 'a book of taste, not to be confused with a book of instruction, which it superficially resembles' is a good one, though it would have discouraged Ford, who hoped the book would sell widely as a textbook. He may have also objected to the objection that he slights American writers in the book.

23 Ford's diary, 22 and 29 Nov. 1938. *Read, 'An Old Man Mad About Writing', *New English Weekly*, 16 (9 Nov. 1939), 57–8. *The March of Literature* (London: George Allen and Unwin, 1939), pp. vi, v, 4–5. The scope of the book is so vast that at one point Ford suggested two volumes, so that 'Milton, Molière, Racine, Pope, Goethe, Thackeray and Tolstoy etc.' should not be treated 'much more cursorily than Virgil or Dante or Chaucer'. Ford to Grenville Vernon, 6 Nov. 1937.

24 The sketch appeared in *Portraits and Self Portraits*, collected and illustrated by Georges Schreiber (Boston: Houghton Mifflin, 1936), 39–40. Ford to Hoffman, 16 June 1938. *The English Novel*, 78–9.

25 *The March of Literature*, 572, 807–8.

26 See *The English Novel*, 78–9 and 93; and cf. *The March of Literature*, 572.

27 See the discussions of the book by Cassell, *Ford Madox Ford*, 290–1; MacShane, 260; and Mizener, 450–1. Cole to Bowen [n.d.]. She also discussed the book in '"Inside the Whale"—and Outside it', *Tribune* (15 Mar. 1940), 20–1.

Chapter 28

1 Ford's pocket diary gives the dates for the broadcasts: Mizener, 599, n. 14. The recording is held by the Museum of Broadcasting, New York. 'The Commercial Value of Literature: A Radio Talk Given by Ford Madox Ford', *Contemporary Literature*, 30/2 (Summer 1989), 327. Conrad's review of France's *L'Île des pingouins*, *English Review*, 1/1 (Dec. 1908), 188, alludes to his *La Vie littéraire* as describing 'the adventures of a choice soul amongst masterpieces'. Ford's diary gives the date for the interview, which was published the following week: *Michel Mok, 'Ford Madox Ford Sadly Adds "S" to British Nerve', *New York Post* (24 Oct. 1938), 9.

2 Mizener, 452, 599, n. 19. Ford to Brewer, 24 Oct. 1938. Mizener, 598, n. 26, says Lee Keedick (who was handling the tour) only got firm bookings from The Friends of American Writers (in Chicago), Northwestern University, and the Western State Teachers College in Kalamazoo. Ford to [William] Troy, 17 Nov. 1938, says they will come to Bennington on Monday [21st]: Yale. Brewer to Ford, 1 Nov. 1938. Mizener, 452, also mentions Briarcliff, and says Ford gave half-a-dozen lectures during Nov. and Dec. The diary has the entry 'Speech Carnegie Hall' for 18 Dec., but Janice Biala has no recollection of Ford speaking there, and I have come across no other evidence that he did.

3 Ford to T. Rokotov (the editor of *International Literature*), 29 Oct. 1938. The magazine did not publish the responses to its questionnaire.

4 There are two incomplete drafts of this unpublished essay at Cornell: a three-page holograph, and nine-page typescript. Oddly, the holograph is dated 30 Sept. and the typescript 9 Sept.

5 *PEN News* (Feb. 1939), 7–8, doesn't mention Ford, but says that the guests included Lewis, Buck, and Christina Stead. Ford to Crankshaw, 26 Nov. 1938: *Letters*, 304–5. Ford to Lewis, 25 Nov. 1938: *Letters*, 303–4. Ford had expressed his admiration for Lewis in a review of *Dodsworth*, *Bookman* (New York), 69 (Apr. 1929), 191–2. Lewis to Ford, 30 Nov. 1938, quoted by Mark Schorer, *Sinclair Lewis* (McGraw-Hill: New York, London, Toronto, 1961), 642; and dated by MacShane, 263 and 288, n. 51.

6 Ford to Unwin, 18 Jan. 1939: *Letters*, 307–8. Ford to Bye, 29 Nov. 1938: *Reader*, 506–8. Mizener, 453. Howe to Bye, 30 Nov. 1938. Ford to Crankshaw, 26 Nov. 1938: *Letters*, 304–5. Ford to Welty, 3 Nov. 1938, 7 Jan. 1939, 19 Jan. 1939, 25 May 1939: *Reader*, 510–12.

7 Ford to Hughes, 26 Nov. 1938: *Letters*, 306–7. Cf. the poem 'Immortality', discussed on pp. 82–4.

8 *It Was the Nightingale*, 26.

9 *Thus to Revisit*, 69–70. John Fowles, 'Golding and "Golding"', in *William Golding: The Man and his Books*, ed. John Carey (London and Boston: Faber & Faber, 1986), 156. *The March of Literature*, pp. v–vi.

10 Ford to Elizabeth (Cheatham) Carter, 7 Dec. 1938. Biala to Saunders, 11 Oct. 1990.

11 Ford to (Cheatham) Carter, 18 Jan. 1939.

12 Biala to Saunders, 11 Oct. and 11 Nov. 1990.

13 Frank MacShane prints all four in 'A Conscious Craftsman: Ford Madox Ford's Manuscript, Revisions', *Boston University Studies in English*, 4 (1961), 178–84. Mizener, 600, n. 24 (though he only mentions three versions). Ford to Unwin, 16 Feb. 1939: *Reader*, 508–10. Ford to George Davis, 5 Dec. 1938. If he was writing stories as potboilers, they weren't boiling pots. A similar letter to Lee Hartman (of Harper and Brothers: 8 Feb. 1939) indicates that Davis turned it down; *Harper's* didn't publish it either. The story was probably **'Mus*ee*um: A Reminiscence . . .', which Bye told Ford had returned to his office after four trips out to prospective publishers: 28 Apr. 1939: Columbia. The other more reminiscential of the unpublished stories are **'Nightmare' and **'Last Nickels'. Another manuscript, 'The Narrowest Escape from Death', was published as **'The Khitmutgar of Ootacamund', *Your Life*, 3/2 (Aug. 1938), 96–8. The plot is that of Jessop's shadow-play in *The Marsden Case*; Ford's working title for the story had been 'Near Death': Ford to Bye, 1 Apr. 1938. On 2 Apr. 1935, for example, Ford had told Scott-James: 'I'm the very worst short story writer in the whole world and practically never write them': Texas.

14 Ford's pocket diary. Ford to Unwin, 18 Jan. 1939: *Letters*, 307–8. Ford also tried to interest Unwin in *Forward, Children*, a novel about tank fighting in the Great War by Paul Alexander Bartlett. (He describes the book in 'Travel Notes: I. Return to Olivet', *Saturday Review*, 20 (10 June 1939), 13–14.) Dahlberg, *Epitaphs of Our Times* (New York: G. Braziller, 1967), 268–9. Press release for the Society, 8 Mar. 1939, referring to a dinner the previous evening. There is a revised version, dated 'Monday, March 13' at Princeton, which has been wrongly assigned to 1938. '[Membership listing of the] Society of the Friends of Carlos Williams'. The details about the prize (which Ford thought of as 'like the Prix Goncourt': Ford to Brewer, 17 Feb. 1939) are from a circular letter asking for nominations for judges. The copy sent to John Herrmann (another of the Society's members), dated '5.11.39' (American style for 11 May 1939) is at Texas. Dahlberg was told 'Ford had persuaded a woman to give fifteen hundred dollars as a prize', and that he was to receive it. Williams to Robert McAlmon, 25 May 1939, says he thinks a woman friend of Ford's has donated $1,000 for the prize: *The Selected Letters of William Carlos Williams*, ed. John Thirlwall (New York: McDowell, Oblensky, 1957), 179. Ford to Tate, 19 May 1939 (Princeton) and 3 May 1939: *Letters*, 318–19. Press release. 'The attendance included Sherwood Anderson, John Herrmann, Louis Zukovsky, Higgins, [Alfred] Mendes and lots of other young poets and prosateurs.' Cummings's poem on Ford, the ninth from Χαῖρε (New York: Oxford University Press, 1950), 9, is quoted by Harvey, 510, and reprinted by MacShane [191]. Williams to MacShane, 7 Feb. 1955; quoted by MacShane, 264–5.

15 *The Autobiography of William Carlos Williams* (New York: Random House, 1951), 299–300. Williams to Pound, June 1932; Williams to McAlmon, 25 May 1939: *Selected Letters* (New York: McDowell, Obolensky, 1957), 125–7, 179. 'To Ford Madox Ford in Heaven', *Selected Poems*, ed. Randall Jarrell (Norfolk, Conn.: New Directions, 1949), 116–17 (the poem was first published in 1940). **Williams, *I Wanted to Write a Poem* (Boston: Beacon Press, 1958), 96. *Provence*, 20, 239–40 (where he argues that in painting it is 'ocular progress' over a composition that 'causes aesthetic pleasure and emotion'. Ford to Julie, quoted in *The Presence of Ford Madox Ford*, 203.

16 Ford to Unwin, 18 Jan., 3 Feb. 1939 (*Letters*, 307–8, 310–11); 23 Mar. 1939. Ford to Crankshaw, 14 Mar. 1939: *Letters*, 315–16. Ford to Unwin, 16 Feb. 1939: *Reader*, 508–10. MacShane, 267. 'Biala' to Bowen, 16 Feb. [1939; dated 1938, but Ford to Unwin, 23

Mar. 1939, thanking Unwin for the loan, fixes the year]. Bowen to Biala, 9 Mar. [1939].
Ford to Brewer, 17 Feb. 1939. Brewer to Ford, 17 Mar. 1939: 'It is wonderful that
raising your diaphragm has done so many fine things for you.' On 19 Jan. 1939 Ford had
told Scott-James he had written the first chapter of a novel: *Letters*, 308-9.

17 Ford to Unwin, 23 Mar. 1939.

18 Ford to MacDonald, 27 Feb. 1939: *Letters*, 311-14. On 31 Mar. 1939, the day Britain
and France pledged to support Poland, Ford wrote to the *New York Times* urging
Americans not to add their support 'unless a categoric undertaking is given by all three
powers that all anti-Semitic enactments or manifestations by Poland shall now and
forever be suppressed'. The letter was not published. Ford to W. P. Crozier of the
Manchester Guardian, who had solicited his views on Palestine, on 11 May 1939 (also
unpublished). 'Professor's Progress', 106-7, 71.

19 Mizener, 460, 601, n. 1, mis-dates the visit as April. Ford's letters to (Cheatham)
Carter, 27 Feb., 1 Mar., and [8 Mar.] 1939 pinpoint Ford as in Greensboro on Friday
3rd and Saturday 4th March. *Greensboro *Daily News* (4 Mar. 1939); **Record* (4 Mar.
1939); **The Carolinian* (3 Mar. 1939), 5. *Julie Montgomery Street, 'Impressions of the
Seminar', Woman's College *Alumnae News*, 1939. Gordon, 'The Story of Ford Madox
Ford', in *Highlights of Modern Literature*, ed. Francis Brown (New York: Mentor,
1954), 113-18. Tate to Mizener, 29 Jan. 1969: Vanderbilt. As Mizener says, both the
Tates erroneously place the visit in 1938. Biala to Saunders, 11 Nov. 1990; and in
conversation, 22 Sept. 1990 and 10 Apr. 1994. Tate thought Ford seemed in *better*
health at Greensboro, but Biala insists that he can't have been very observant, since
Ford was dying. Ford apparently bore Allen Tate no grudge: back in New York he
wrote him a friendly letter: 3 May 1939: *Letters*, 318-19. Gerard Tetley, 'The Frailties
of Ford Madox Ford', *Footnote*, 1 (June 1949), 9-13, says Ford lectured on 'the
romantic age of literature'. (Also see his letter to Goldring, *The Last Pre-Raphaelite*,
274-6.) Gordon's class was on 'the novel', and Ford's opening gambit sounds more like
an introduction to an account of impressionism. Tetley's letter to Elsie Hueffer, 24 Oct.
1945, says the lecture was on 'contemporary English literature'. Ford wrote to Tetley a
week or two later to ask him to find a farm house somewhere in the Piedmont tobacco
country, where he could write throughout the summer. Tetley found him a very old
house in the mountain town of Patrick; but by then Ford had settled on going instead
to France. Tetley to Elsie Hueffer, 14 Mar. 1948 and Good Friday [1948?].

20 Ford to (Cheatham) Carter, Wednesday [8 Mar. 1939].

21 Ford to Auden, 23 Mar. 1939: *Letters*, 316-17. Charles Osborne, *W. H. Auden: The Life
of a Poet* (London: Eyre Methuen, 1980), 190. 'Travel Notes: I. Return to Olivet',
Saturday Review, 20 (10 June 1939), 13-14. Auden to Ford, n.d. [but between 23 Mar.
and 4 Apr. 1939]. Ford complained to William Bird, 14 Mar. 1939, that in America
'there is absolutely nothing doing either for me or anybody else except for best sellers
whose work gets more and more absolutely childish'.

22 Ford to Bird, 14 Mar. 1939. See e.g. Rachel Wolodofsky (Wally Tworkov) to Bowen, 3
Apr. 1939. Ford to Bullitt, 10 Mar. 1939. Ford to Keating, 13 Mar. 1939 (*Letters*, 315)
and n.d., Ford to Litvinov, 14 Mar. 1939. Ford to Crankshaw, 14 Mar. 1939: *Letters*,
315-16. Ford to Tate, 13 Mar.; to Wells, and Hemingway, 14 Mar.; to Porter, 15 Mar.
1939. Fenn, interview with Max Saunders, 3 July 1990; also 'Ford Madox Ford', an
unpublished obituary tribute, dated 'December 1939', and kindly supplied by Mr Fenn.

23 Ford to Brett Stokes, 16 Mar. 1939 (filed at Cornell together with the proposal Fenn
describes). MacShane, 265, says Ford hoped Harpers might publish the magazine.
Mizener, 456, 600, n. 28. Ford to (Cheatham) Carter, 8 Mar. 1939 ('yesterday I sold a

book'). George Shively (of Stokes) to Ford, 22 Mar. 1939, proves they had a contract for his novel (though they are offering to release him if their refusal to publish the review in America would make him want to extricate himself. They *say* they don't want to lose him). Mizener, 455. Fenn also wrote a study of Ho Chi Minh: *Ho Chi Minh: A Biographical Introduction* (London: Studio Vista, 1973). Ford, 'Thinking Aloud', unpublished typescript. Bye to Ford, 28 Apr. 1939 (Columbia), says it has been returned to his office after four trips out. Ford to Unwin, 23 Sept. 1938; quoted by Mizener, 456. Unwin to Ford, 6 Oct. 1938. Ford to Bye, 29 Nov. 1938: *Reader*, 506-8.

24 Synopsis of 'Professor's Progress'. 'Professor's Progress', fourth version of first paragraph, quoted by MacShane, 'A Conscious Craftsman', 181. Mizener, 456-7. MacShane, *The Life in the Fiction of Ford Madox Ford*, 269. Auden to Ford [n.d., but between 23 Mar. and 4 Apr. 1939]. Biala in conversation with Saunders, 22 Sept. 1990.

25 A deleted passage on pp. 7-8 (of the second typed draft) runs: 'And he had achieved a thought really new for him—that of the Nation as being really ruled by its financial interests.' 'Professor's Progress', 76, 108. Mizener, 597, n. 13, 459, 600, n. 28. Ford to Bye, 30 May 1939: Columbia. The *Saturday Review*, 20/5 (27 May 1939), 3-4, 15-16, had already published his intriguing reminiscence of Wilde. Only the first of the further six was written: 'Travel Notes: I. Return to Olivet', 20 (10 June 1939), 13-14. *Return to Yesterday*, 79-81.

26 Synopsis. 'Professor's Progress', 18 (quoted by Mizener, 456), 70a, 68.

27 Ford to Tate, 3 May 1939: *Letters*, 318-19. Ford was at Olivet by 14 Apr., when he wrote to Bye: 'Here we are in the midst of daily snow storms, trying to carry on the good work of civilizing this country': Columbia. 'Travel Notes: I. Return to Olivet'. Ford to Shively, [Sunday] 21 Apr. 1939: he says they will leave [Olivet] on Sunday [the 23rd], and hope to be back in New York by Tuesday [the 25th]. Ford wrote to Alfred Mendes (another young writer whose work he was promoting) on the 26th from 10 Fifth Avenue, saying he had just got back from Olivet, and offering to write a preface for Mendes's book *Black Fauns*: Washington University, St Louis.

28 Ford to Tate, 3 May 1939: *Letters*, 318-19. Stock, *The Life of Ezra Pound* (Harmondsworth: Penguin Books, 1974), 462. *Pound/Ford*, 169. Biala, quoted by Charles Norman, *Ezra Pound* (New York: Macmillan, 1960), 363. Williams to Robert McAlmon, 25 May 1939: *Selected Letters*, 177.

29 Ford to Harrison Smith (of the *Saturday Review of Literature*), 10 May 1939: *Letters*, 319-20. Ford to Stevens, 17 [May] 1939: *Letters*, 320-1. Ford wrote to Bye, 8 May 1939 (Columbia), sending the synopsis as saying he wanted to get the matter settled before he left. Ford to Welty, 25 May 1939: *Reader*, 511-12. *Saturday Review of Literature*, 20 (3 June 1939), 9: repr. in *Reader*, 288-90. Joyce to Frank Budgen, end of July 1939: *Letters of James Joyce*, ed. Stuart Gilbert (London: Faber & Faber, 1957), 405-6. See Wiesenfarth, 'Fargobawlers: James Joyce and Ford Madox Ford', *Biography*, 14/2 (Spring 1991), 106-11, on the significance of the pseudonym. Ford to Bye, 30 May 1939: Columbia. Ford to Crankshaw, 23 May 1939: *Letters*, 323-4.

30 Ford to (Cheatham) Carter, 23 May 1939; to Revd Matthew Hoehn, 23 May 1939. Ford to Unwin, 25 May 1939: *Letters*, 324-5. Ford to Crankshaw, 23 May 1939: *Letters*, 323-4. Ford to Brewer, 8 May 1939. Tate, in *New Directions: Number Seven*, 487. Dahlberg, *Epitaphs of Our Times*, 271.

31 Ford to Bye, 30 May 1939. Olson to Ford, 26 May [1939]; Ford to Olson, 30 May 1939. Ford to [Jean Stafford], 30 May 1939.

32 Mizener, 461-2. Judd, *Ford Madox Ford*, 440-1. Biala to Saunders, 11 Oct. 1990 and 11 Nov. 1990. Biala to Elizabeth Carter [26 Nov. 1939]. Julia M. Loewe, in *The Presence*

of Ford Madox Ford, 203. *History*, p. xvi. Crankshaw to Unwin, 2 July 1939. 'An Interview with Janice Biala', *The Presence of Ford Madox Ford*, 225, 218. Biala to Julie, 'Tuesday' [27 June] 1939 (quoted by Mizener, 462, though he mis-dates it as 30 June; he also says Ford was moved to the Clinique on the 24th, but Biala says 'Sunday', which was the 25th). Biala, *The Presence of Ford Madox Ford*, 197.

33 Judd, *Ford Madox Ford*, 441, 444. Biala to Julie, 'Tuesday' [27 June] 1939. MacShane, 267. Biala to Saunders, 11 Nov. 1990, says she *paid* for a permanent grave. There is nothing temporary about the simple pink granite gravestone she provided, which simply reads: 'FORD MADOX FORD/1873 1939'. But she was not sure whether the body was moved.